10/10/00

SEVENTH EDITION

STRATEGIC MANAGEMENT

AND BUSINESS POLICY

Entering 21st Century Global Society

Thomas L. Wheelen

Visiting Professor, Trinity College,
Dublin, Ireland

J. David Hunger

Iowa State University

Prentice Hall
Upper Saddle River, New Jersey 07458

Senior Acquisitions Editor: David A. Shafer
Editor in Chief: Natalie E. Anderson
Executive Marketing Manager: Michael D. Campbell
Managing Editor (Editorial): Jennifer Glennon
Assistant Editor: Michele Foresta
Editorial Assistant: Kim Marsden
Production Supervisor: Nancy Fenton
Managing Editor: James Rigney
Manufacturing Supervisor: Tim McDonald
Text Design: Carol Rose
Production Services: Books By Design, Inc.
Cover Design: Regina Hagen
Illustrator (Interior): Network Graphics; Books By Design, Inc.
Cover Art: © John Still/Photonica
Composition: G & S Typesetters, Inc.

Library of Congress Cataloging-in-Publication Data

Wheelen, Thomas L.
    Strategic management and business policy : entering 21st century
global society / Thomas L. Wheelen, J. David Hunger. — 7th ed.
      p.   cm.
    Includes bibliographical references and index.
    ISBN 0-201-61543-6 (hc.)
    1. Strategic planning.   I. Hunger, J. David.
II. Title.
HD30.28.W43   1999
658.4'012—DC21   99-34101
                                         CIP

Prentice-Hall International (UK) Limited, London
Prentice-Hall of Australia Pty. Limited, Sydney
Prentice-Hall Canada, Inc., Toronto
Prentice-Hall Hispanoamericana, S.A., Mexico
Prentice-Hall of India Private Limited, New Delhi
Prentice-Hall of Japan, Inc., Tokyo
Pearson Education Asia Pte. Ltd., Singapore
Editora Prentice-Hall do Brasil, Ltda., Rio de Janeiro

Printed in the United States of America

10 9 8 7 6 5 4 3 2

Preface

For this, the 7th edition of our book, we have chosen to keep the text portion (the 14 chapters) unchanged from the 6th edition, but to replace or update the cases. These 32 cases emphasize the key issues facing corporations in the globally oriented 21st century: a rapidly changing environment and a more complex set of international variables to be managed. Since strategic management is a field of inquiry that focuses on the organization as a whole and its interactions with its environment, our set of cases emphasizes competitive advantage in a global society. **Twenty-four cases are either new or updated revisions of popular cases.** Nineteen cases contain international strategic issues. The cases range from small entrepreneurial ventures to global multinational corporations in nine industries. Seven cases come from different regions of the globe:

- *The Body Shop* (Britain)
- *A Joint Venture in China* (China)
- *Airbus Industrie* (European Union)
- *Whirlpool—The First Venture into India* (India)
- *Seven-Eleven Japan* (Japan)
- *Carnival Corporation* (Panama)
- *Mikromashina of Moscow* (Russia)

This textbook, *Strategic Management and Business Policy*, received the prestigious McGuffey Award for Excellence and Longevity in 1999 from the Text and Academic Authors Association.

Objectives

This book focuses on the following objectives, typically found in most strategic management and business policy courses:

- To develop an understanding of strategic management concepts, research, and theories.

- To develop a framework of analysis to enable a student to identify central issues and problems in complex, comprehensive cases; to suggest alternative courses of action; and to present well-supported recommendations for future action.

- To develop conceptual skills so that a student is able to integrate previously learned aspects of corporations.

- To develop an understanding of the emerging global economy and its potential impact on business activities in any location.

- To develop an understanding of the role of corporate governance in strategic management.

- To develop the ability to analyze and evaluate, both quantitatively and qualitatively, the performance of the people responsible for strategic decisions.

- To bridge the gap between theory and practice by developing an understanding of when and how to apply concepts and techniques learned in earlier courses on marketing, accounting, finance, management, production, and information systems.

- To improve research capabilities necessary to gather and interpret key environmental data.

- To develop a better understanding of the present and future environments in which corporations must function.

- To develop analytical and decision-making skills for dealing with complex conceptual problems in an ethical manner.

This book achieves these objectives by presenting and explaining concepts and theories useful in understanding the strategic management process. It critically analyzes studies in the field of strategy to acquaint the student with the literature of this area and to help develop the student's research capabilities. It also suggests a model of strategic management. It recommends the strategic audit as one approach to the systematic analysis of complex organization-wide issues. Through a series of special issue and comprehensive cases, it provides the student with an opportunity to apply concepts, skills, and techniques to real-world corporate problems. The book focuses on the business corporation because of its crucial position in the economic system of the world and in the material development of any society.

Features New to This 7th Edition

- This edition includes 32 cases—24 new or revised and updated.

  - **Seven global cases** (*Body Shop, Joint Venture in China, Airbus, Whirlpool in India, Seven-Eleven Japan, Carnival,* and *Mikromashina of Moscow*) have been added to reflect integration of international issues throughout the chapters.

  - **Four classic special-issue cases** (*Recalcitrant Director, Wallace Group, Audit,* and *Brookstone Hospice*) and **three** appliance industry cases (*Appliance Industry Note, Maytag,* and *Whirlpool*) have been carried forward from the 6th edition. **One** timeless classic small entrepreneurship case has been brought forward from an earlier edition (*Inner-City Paint*).

  - **Fourteen popular cases have been revised and updated** from the 6th edition (*Arm & Hammer, Tasty Baking, Microsoft, Apple, Walt Disney, Carnival, Harley-Davidson, Reebok, Kmart, Wal-Mart, Nordstrom, Home Depot, Body Shop,* and *Vermont Teddy Bear*).

  - **Ten cases are brand new** (*Cisco, Sun, Circus Circus, ACIS, Whirlpool-India, Seven-Eleven Japan, Sunbeam, Mikromashina of Moscow, Joint Venture in China,* and *Airbus.*)

- **Eleven cases have been written exclusively for this book.**

- **The 28 cases dealing with issues in strategic management are comprehensive** (deal with the entire strategic management process). These cases are excellent to use in team analyses and presentations. These cases are grouped into nine industries:

  - Food (2 cases)

  - Computer/Internet/Software (4 cases)

  - Entertainment/Travel (4 cases)

  - Recreation Equipment (2 cases)

  - Major Home Appliances (1 industry note and 3 cases)

  - Mass Merchandising/Department Stores (3 cases)

  - Specialty Retailers (3 cases)

  - Small/Medium Entrepreneurial Ventures (2 cases)

  - Manufacturing (4 cases)

- **This edition includes 19 cases containing international issues.**

  - Six cases are of companies operating primarily outside North American (*Body Shop, Joint Venture in China, Whirlpool-India, Seven-Eleven Japan, Mikromashina of Moscow,* and *Airbus*).

  - Thirteen cases are of North American–based companies with significant international operations and issues (*Microsoft, Apple, Cisco, Sun, Walt Disney, Carnival, ACIS, Harley-Davidson, Reebok, Major Home Appliance Industry, Maytag, Whirlpool,* and *Wal-Mart*).

- **This edition includes cases of companies at all stages of corporate development.**

  - Small / medium entrepreneurial companies (with founder as CEO) (*Inner-City Paint, Vermont Teddy Bear, Brookstone Hospice, Recalcitrant Director at Byte,* and *Wallace Company**).

  - Large / very large entrepreneurial companies (*Apple Computer, Cisco Systems, Sun Microsystems, Microsoft, Reebok, Home Depot,* and *Body Shop*).

  - Established companies (*Tasty Baking, Circus Circus, Carnival, Harley-Davidson, Major Home Appliance Industry, Whirlpool, Kmart, Wal-Mart, Nordstrom, Seven-Eleven, Maytag,* Walt Disney,* Arm & Hammer* [*Church & Dwight*],* and *Sunbeam**).

  - Business units / joint ventures (*ACIS, Whirlpool-India, Joint Venture in China, Airbus,* and *Mikromashina of Moscow**).

- **This edition includes cases that can be used to illustrate specific aspects of the strategic management process.**

  - **Corporate Governance**

    Recalcitrant Director at Byte (also social responsibility)

    The Wallace Group

---

*Note: Diversified into multiple industries.

- **Social Responsibility and Ethics**

  The Audit

  Brookstone Hospice

  Recalcitrant Director at Byte (also governance)

- **Environmental Scanning**

  U.S. Major Home Appliance Industry (industry analysis)

  Whirlpool-India (societal factors)

  Mikromashina of Moscow (societal factors)

  Seven-Eleven Japan (societal factors)

  Joint Venture in China (societal factors)

  Airbus (industry analysis)

  Circus Circus (societal and industry factors)

  The Wallace Group (organizational analysis)

  Vermont Teddy Bear (organizational analysis)

- **Strategy Formulation**

  Maytag (objectives and strategy)

  Arm & Hammer (strategy)

  Tasty Baking (strategy)

  Microsoft (strategy)

  Apple Computer (strategy)

  Cisco Systems (strategy)

  Sun Microsystems (strategy)

  Carnival (strategy)

  Reebok (strategy)

  Whirlpool (strategy)

  Mikromashina of Moscow (strategy)

  Airbus (strategy)

  Kmart (strategy)

  Wal-Mart (strategy)

  Sunbeam (strategy)

  Nordstrom (strategy and policies)

  Body Shop (strategy and policies)

- **Strategy Implementation**

  Walt Disney (business unit synergy)

  ACIS (structure/organizational design)

  Harley-Davidson (productivity)

  Seven-Eleven Japan (structure/organizational design)

  Home Depot (culture)

  Vermont Teddy Bear (programs and procedures)

Joint Venture in China (programs and procedures)

Sunbeam (executive succession)

- **Evaluation and Control**

Nordstrom (culture and policies)

Brookstone Hospice (policies)

The Audit (accounting methods)

Inner-City Paint (financial controls)

Sunbeam (performance evaluation)

Features Common to the 6th and 7th Editions

The 14 chapters of text are continued unchanged from the 6th edition. Key features are:

- **Core and distinctive competencies** are examined within the framework of the resource-based view of the firm (Chapter 4).

- The firm is conceptualized as a **learning organization** that can learn from its own experience (Chapter 1).

- **Cooperative strategy** (strategic alliances, joint ventures, etc.) is added to competitive strategy and tactics in a separate business strategy chapter (Chapter 5).

- **Hypercompetition** is discussed in terms of its impact on industry analysis and competitive strategy (Chapters 3 and 5).

- **Activity-based costing and value-chain analysis** (both industry and firm value chains) are used to identify those activities and functions that can be outsourced or developed to gain competitive advantage (Chapters 3 and 10).

- **International issues** (a separate chapter in previous editions) are now integrated throughout the text chapters where appropriate.

- **Corporate governance** is coupled with **social responsibility and ethics** (Chapter 2).

- **Corporate strategy** is reconceptualized and presented not only in the traditional sense as portfolio analysis and as directional strategy for the firm as a whole, but also as "parenting" of business units to transfer core competencies (Chapter 6).

- The top-down **orientation** toward strategic management has been softened by showing how people at all organizational levels are becoming increasingly involved in strategic management as members of a learning organization (Chapter 1).

- The **resource-based view of the firm** has been expanded to include an examination of core and distinctive competencies (Chapters 4 and 7).

- An **industry matrix** adds to industry analysis by providing a means to summarize strategic factors facing a particular industry (Chapter 3).

- Two specially boxed features—**21st Century Global Society** and **Strategy in a Changing World**—illustrate not only how the global environment is affecting strategic decisions, but also how strategic concepts are being applied in actual organizations.

- A section on **Global Issues for the 21st Century** highlights how international issues will be affecting strategic management in the future.

- **Projections for the 21st Century** end each chapter by forecasting what the world will be like in 2010.

- A **short case or experiential exercise** focusing on the material covered in each chapter helps the reader to apply strategic concepts to an actual situation.

- A list of **key terms** and the pages on which they are discussed enable the reader to keep track of important concepts as they are introduced in each chapter.

Time-Tested Features

This edition contains many of the same features and content that helped make previous editions successful, including the following:

- A **strategic management model** runs throughout the first ten chapters as a unifying concept.

- Special chapters deal with strategic issues in **managing technology and innovation**, **entrepreneurial ventures and small businesses**, and **not-for-profit organizations** (Chapters 11, 12, and 13, respectively).

- Internal and external strategic factors are emphasized through the use of specially designed **EFAS**, **IFAS**, and **SFAS tables** (Chapters 3, 4, and 5).

- **Corporate governance** is examined in terms of the roles, responsibilities, and interactions of top management and the board of directors (Chapter 2).

- **Social responsibility and managerial ethics** are examined in detail in terms of how they affect strategic decision making (Chapter 2).

- Equal emphasis is placed on **environmental scanning** of the societal environment as well as on the task environment. Topics include forecasting and Miles and Snow's typology in addition to Porter's industry analysis (Chapter 3).

- Two chapters deal with issues in **strategy implementation**, such as organizational and job design plus strategy-manager fit, action planning, and corporate culture (Chapters 8 and 9).

- A separate chapter on **evaluation and control** explains the importance of measurement and incentives to organizational performance (Chapter 10).

- **Company Spotlight on Maytag Corporation** features illustrate the issues in each chapter and serve to integrate the material (Chapters 1–13).

- **Suggestions for in-depth case analysis** provide a complete listing of financial ratios, recommendations for oral and written analysis, and ideas for further research (Chapter 14).

- The **strategic audit**, a way to operationalize the strategic decision-making process, serves as a checklist in case analysis (Chapter 10).

- The **Strategic Audit Worksheet** is based on the time-tested strategic audit and is designed to help students organize and structure daily case preparation in a brief period of time. The worksheet works exceedingly well for checking the level of daily student case preparation—especially for open class discussions of cases (Chapter 14).

- **Timely, well-researched, and class-tested cases** deal with interesting companies and industries. Many of the cases are about well-known, publicly held corporations —ideal subjects for further research by students wishing to "update" the cases.

- **An Industry Note for use in industry analysis** of the major home appliance industry is included for use by itself or with the Maytag and Whirlpool cases.

- **Key Theory** capsules explain key theories underlying strategic management. This feature adds emphasis to the theories, but does not interrupt the flow of the text material.

Supplements

Supplemental materials are available to the instructor from the publisher. These include Instructor's Manuals, Win/PH Test Manager, video clips, a Web site, and overhead transparencies.

Instructor's Manuals

Two comprehensive Instructor's Manuals have been carefully constructed to accompany this book. The first one accompanies the text chapters; the second one accompanies the cases.

TEXT Instructor's Manual

To aid in discussing the 14 chapters dealing with strategic management concepts, the TEXT Instructor's Manual includes:

1. *Suggestions for Teaching Strategic Management:* Discusses various teaching methods and includes suggested course syllabi.

2. *Video Guide:* Presents summaries of free videos and suggestions for classroom use.

3. *Chapter Notes:* Includes summaries of each chapter, suggested answers to discussion questions, suggestions for using end-of-chapter cases/exercises, plus additional discussion questions (with answers) and lecture modules.

4. *Multiple-Choice Test Questions:* Contains approximately 50 questions for each of the 14 chapters totaling over 700 questions from which to choose.

5. *Transparency Masters:* Includes over 170 transparency masters of figures and tables in the text plus other exhibits.

CASE Instructor's Manual

To aid in case method teaching, the CASE Instructor's Manual includes detailed suggestions for use, teaching objectives, and examples of student analyses for each of the 32 cases. This is the most comprehensive Instructor's Manual available in strategic management. A standardized format is provided for each case:

1. *Case Abstract*

2. *Case Issues and Subjects*

3. *Steps Covered in the Strategic Decision-Making Process*

4. *Case Objectives*

5. *Suggested Classroom Approaches*

6. *Discussion Questions*

7. *Case Author's Teaching Note*

8. *Student-Written Strategic Audit or Paper*

9. *EFAS, IFAS, SFAS Exhibits*

10. *Financial Analysis:* **Ratios and common-size income statements**

Instructor's Resource CD-ROM

The Instructor's Resource CD-ROM contains tools to facilitate instructors' lectures and examinations. These include PowerPoint™ Electronic Transparency Masters, a collection of over 170 figures and tables from the text. The instructor may customize these presentations and can present individual slides for student handouts. The Instructor's Manuals have also been added to the Instructor's Resource CD-ROM.

Win/PH Test Manager

Containing all of the questions in the printed Test Item File, Test Manager is a comprehensive suite of tools for testing and assessment. Test Manager allows educators to easily create and distribute tests for their courses, either by printing and distributing through traditional methods, or by on-line delivery via a Local Area Network (LAN) server.

Videos

Video clips featuring cases in this book plus company and industry vignettes for use with various chapters are available free to adopters of this textbook. These video clips can be used to accompany various chapters in the text to provide examples of strategic management issues and concepts.

PHLIP/CW

Strategic Management and Business Policy, 7/e, is supported by PHLIP (Prentice Hall Learning on the Internet Partnership), the book's companion Web site. An invaluable resource for both instructors and students, PHLIP features a wealth of up-to-date, on-line resources at the touch of a button! A research center, current event articles, interactive study guide, exercises, and additional resources are combined to offer the most advanced text-specific Web site available.

Visit **www.prenhall.com/wheelen**

An alternate Web site you can access is:

http://www.bus.iastate.edu/jdhunger/strategy

Transparencies

NEW! One hundred and thirty professionally prepared overhead transparencies are now available for instructors' use.

Acknowledgments

We are grateful to the people who reviewed this edition for their constructive comments and suggestions. Their thought and effort has resulted in a book far superior to our original manuscript. This was one of the best set of reviewers ever to work on this book.

Kimberly Boal, Texas Tech University
Robert DeFillippi, Suffolk University
Helen Deresky, SUNY at Plattsburgh
Patricia Feltes, Southwest Missouri State University
Calvin Fields, Western Illinois University
Steven Floyd, University of Connecticut
Charles R. Gowen, III, Northern Illinois University
Marilyn Helms, University of Tennessee at Chattanooga
Alan Hoffman, Bentley College
Douglas Micklich, Illinois State University
Ann Morinoni, Lake Superior State University
Rebecca Morris, University of Nebraska at Omaha
George Puia, Indiana State University
Mike Raphael, Central Connecticut State University
Barbara Ribbens, St. Cloud State University
Margaret White, Oklahoma State University

Our thanks go to Patricia Mahtani, Project Manager at Addison Wesley Longman, for her coordination of the work going into this 7th edition. We also thank the many other people at Addison Wesley and Prentice Hall who worked to supervise and market this book. Some of these people are Joyce Cosentino, Marketing Coordinator, and David A. Shafer, Senior Editor. We are especially grateful to Nancy Benjamin at Books By Design, Inc., for her patience, expertise, and even disposition during the copyediting and production process.

We thank Betty Hunger for her preparation of the subject and name indexes. We are also very grateful to Kathy Wheelen for her first-rate administrative support and to Anne Marie Summit for her typing of the CASE Instructor's Manual. Thanks also to Dr. Patricia Ryan of Colorado State University for calculating ratios and common-size statements for each case. We are especially thankful to the many students who tried out the cases we chose to include in this book. Their comments helped us find any flaws in the cases before the book went to the printer.

In addition, we express our appreciation to Dr. Ben Allen, Dean, and Dr. Brad Shrader, Management Department Chair, of Iowa State University's College of Business, for their support and provision of the resources so necessary to produce a textbook. Both of us acknowledge our debt to Dr. William Shenkir and Dr. Frank S. Kaulback, former Deans of the McIntire School of Commerce of the University of Virginia for the provision of a work climate most supportive to the original development of this book.

Lastly, to the many strategy/policy instructors and students who have moaned to us about their problems with the strategy/policy course: we have tried to respond to your problems and concerns as best we could by providing a comprehensive yet usable text coupled with recent and complex cases. To you, the people who work hard in the strategy/policy trenches, we acknowledge our debt. This book is yours.

Tampa, Florida   T. L. W.
Ames, Iowa   J. D. H.

Dedicated to

Kathy, Tom, and Richard

Betty, Kari and Jeff, Suzi, Lori, Merry, and Smokey: Those for whom this book was written; and to Elizabeth Carey and Jackson S. Hunger: without whom there would be no book; and to Jane Hunger Randal and Jim Hunger: two siblings who actually read this book!!

Special Dedication by Tom Wheelen

In the year 2000, to my family in America, who trace their roots and heritage from Ireland:

- Great Grandparents
    1. David Whelan (1806–1858) and Mary Killan (1822–18xx) of Cork, Ireland
    2. William Layhon and Margaret Shae of Ireland

- Grandparents
    1. Thomas Wheelen (1849–1911) of Cork, Ireland, and Hannah I. Laylon (1863–1934) of Burke, New York
    2. William E. McGrath (1865–1939) of Tipperary, Ireland, and Catherine McCarthy (1867–1932) of Clare, Ireland

- Parents
    Thomas L. Wheelen (1892–1938) of Gardner, Massachusetts, and Kathryn E. McGrath (1895–1972) of Fitchburg, Massachusetts

- Me
    Thomas L. Wheelen (1935–) of Gardner, Massachusetts

- Children
    Kathryn E. Wheelen (1967–) of Fairfax, Virginia
    Thomas L. Wheelen II (1968–) of Fairfax, Virginia
    Richard D. Wheelen (1970–) of Charlottesville, Virginia

Contents

Part Six   ***INTRODUCTION TO CASE ANALYSIS***

Part Seven   ***CASES IN STRATEGIC MANAGEMENT***

About the Contributors

Moustafa H. Abdelsamad, D.B.A. (George Washington University), is Dean of the College of Business at Texas A&M University–Corpus Christi. He previously served as Dean of the College of Business and Industry at Southeastern Massachusetts University and as Professor of Finance and Associate Dean of Graduate Studies in Business at Virginia Commonwealth University. He is Editor-in-Chief of *SAM Advanced Management Journal* and International President of the Society for the Advancement of Management. He is the author of *A Guide to Capital Expenditure Analysis* and two chapters in the *Dow Jones–Irwin Capital Budgeting Handbook.* He is the author or co-author of numerous articles in various publications.

Stephen E. Barndt, Ph.D. (Ohio State University), is Professor of Management at the School of Business, Pacific Lutheran University. Formerly, he was head of a department in the Graduate Education Division of the Air Force Institute of Technology's School of Systems and Logistics and taught at Central Michigan University. He has over 15 years of line and staff experience in operations and research and development. He has co-authored two fundamentals texts, *Managing by Project Management* and *Operations Management Concepts and Practices,* as well as numerous papers, articles, chapters, and cases addressing such subjects as organizational communication, project management, and strategic management. He is Director of Pacific Lutheran University's Small Business Institute and serves on the Editorial Review Board of the *Business Case Journal.*

Ben M. Bensaou, Ph.D. (MIT Sloan School of Management), M.A. (Hitotsubashi University, Tokyo), M.S. in Civil Engineering and D.E.A. in Mechanical Engineering from, respectively, École National des TPE, Lyon and Institute National Polytechnique de Grenoble, two Grandes Écoles in France. Dr. Bensaou is an Associate Professor of Technology Management and Asian Business at INSEAD, Fontainebleau, France, and 1998–1999 Visiting Professor at Harvard Business School. In 1994 and 1997 he was a Visiting Professor at Aoyama Gakuin University in Tokyo. His publications include papers in *Management Science, Information Systems Research, Strategic Management Journal, Harvard Business Review,* the *European Journal of Information Systems,* book chapters, and conference proceedings. He has been consulting for Asian, European, and U.S. corporations since 1993. Professor Bensaou grew up in France, and was educated in Japan. He and his wife, Masako, live in Belmont, Massachusetts, with their three sons.

James W. Camerius, M.S. (University of North Dakota), is Professor of Marketing at Northern Michigan University. He is Vice-President of the Society for Case Research, Marketing Track Chair of the North American Case Research Association, and Workshop and Colloquium Director of the World Association for Case Method Research. He is a research grant recipient of the Walker L. Cisler College of Business at Northern Michigan University and also a 1995 recipient of the Distinguished Faculty Award of the Michigan Association of Governing Boards of State Universities. His cases appear in over 90 management, marketing, and retailing textbooks in addition to *Annual Advances in Business Cases,* a publication of the Society for Case Research. His studies of corporate situations include Kmart Corporation; Tanner Companies, Inc.; Mary Kay Cosmetics, Inc.; Sasco Products, Inc.; The Fuller Brush Company; Wal-Mart Stores, Inc; Longaberger Marketing, Inc.; Encyclopaedia Britannica International; RWC, Inc.; and several others. His writings include several studies of the case method of instruction. He is an award and grant recipient of the Direct Selling Education Foundation, Washington, D.C., and is listed in *Who's Who in the World, America, Midwest, American Education,* and *Finance and Industry.*

Roy A. Cook, D.B.A. (Mississippi State University), is Assistant Dean of the School of Business Administration and Professor of Management, Fort Lewis College, Durango, Colorado. He has written and published a textbook, numerous articles, cases, and papers based on his extensive experience in the hospitality industry and research interests in the areas of strategy, small business management, human relations, and communications. He serves on the editorial boards of the *Business Case Journal,* the *Journal of Business Strategies,* and the *Journal of Teaching in Travel and Tourism.* He is a member of the Academy of Management, Society for Case Research (past president), and the International Society of Travel and Tourism Educators. Dr. Cook teaches courses in Strategic Management, Small Business Management, Tourism and Resort Management, and Human Resource Management.

Richard A. Cosier, Ph.D. (University of Iowa), is Dean and Fred B. Brown Chair at the University of Oklahoma. He formerly was Associate Dean for Academics and Professor of Business Administration at Indiana University. He served as Chairperson of the Department of Management at Indiana for seven years prior to assuming his current position. He was formerly a Planning Engineer with The Western Electric Company and Instructor of Management and Quantitative Methods at the University of Notre Dame. Dr. Cosier is interested in researching the managerial decision-making process, organization responses to external forces, and participative management. He has published in *Behavior Science, Academy of Management Journal, Academy of Management Review, Organizational Behavior and Human Performance, Management Science, Strategic Management Journal, Business Horizons, Decisions Sciences, Personnel Psychology, Journal of Creative Behavior, International Journal of Management, The Business Quarterly, Public Administration Quarterly, Human Relations,* and other journals. In addition, Professor Cosier has presented numerous papers at professional meetings, has co-authored a management textbook, and has a chapter on conflict that is included in a popular management text. He has been active in many executive development programs and has acted as a management-education consultant for several organizations. Dr. Cosier is the recipient of Teaching Excellence Awards in the M.B.A. Program at Indiana and a Richard D. Irwin Fellowship. He belongs to the Institute of Management Consults, Inc., Beta Gamma Sigma, the Academy of Management, Sigma Iota Epsilon, and the Decision Sciences Institute.

Andrew James Croll, B.A. (Appalachian State University), is currently teaching 4th grade in Boone, North Carolina. He previously resided in Charlottesville, Virginia.

David B. Croll, Ph.D. (Pennsylvania State University), is Professor of Accounting at the McIntire School of Commerce, the University of Virginia. He was Visiting Associate Professor at the Graduate Business School, the University of Michigan. He is on the editorial board of *SAM Advanced Management Journal.* He has published in the *Accounting Review* and the *Case Research Journal.* His cases appear in 12 accounting and management textbooks.

Gordon Paul Croll, B.A. (University of Alabama), is currently the executive Vice President of Cavalier Reporting and the President of Cavalier Videography. He resides in Charlottesville, Virginia.

Dan R. Dalton, Ph.D. (University of California, Irvine), is the Dean of the Graduate School of Business, Indiana University, and Harold A. Polipl Chair of Strategic Management He was formerly with General Telephone & Electronics for 13 years. Widely published in business and psychology periodicals, his articles have appeared in the *Academy of Management Journal, Journal of Applied Psychology, Personnel Psychology, Academy of Management Review,* and *Strategic Management Journal.*

Michael I. Eizenberg, B.A. (Clark University), M.A. (Tufts University), Honorary Doctorate (Richmond College), currently serves as president and CEO of Educational Travel Alliance (ETRAV), an organization he founded in 1999. ETRAV is the developer of

WorldLINK, the Internet solution that provides support for educational travel programs worldwide and a broad range of other "value-added" travel services. From 1997–1999 Mr. Eizenberg served as "Entrepreneur in Residence" at Bentley College in Waltham, Massachusetts, where he divided his time between teaching, mentoring aspiring entrepreneurs, researching, and writing. Mr. Eizenberg co-founded American Council for International Studies (ACIS), an educational travel organization in 1978. He guided ACIS' growth from a tiny start-up with seven employees to a leading international organization with offices in Boston, Atlanta, Chicago, Los Angeles, London, and Paris and 100 employees worldwide. In 1987, ACIS was acquired by AIFS, Inc., then a publicly held company, with diversified holdings in the field of international education. Mr. Eizenberg stayed on as President of ACIS until 1997. During this time he also served as a member of the board of directors of AIFS, Inc., and of the board of trustees of Richmond College.

Cathy A. Enz, Ph.D. (Ohio State University), is the Lewis G. Schaeneman Jr. Professor of Innovation and Dynamic Management at Cornell University's School of Hotel Administration. Her doctoral degree is in organization theory and behavior. Professor Enz has written numerous articles, cases, and a book on corporate culture, value sharing, change management, and strategic human resource management effects on performance. Professor Enz consults extensively in the service sector and serves on the board of directors for two hospitality related organizations.

Ellie A. Fogarty, M.L.S. (University of Pittsburgh), M.B.A. (Temple University), is the Business and Economics Librarian at the College of New Jersey. She is active in the American Library Association, where she serves on the Business Reference Committee; the Special Libraries Association, where she is President of the Princeton-Trenton chapter; and the New Jersey Library Association.

Donna M. Gallo, M.B.A. (Boston College), is a Ph.D. candidate at the University of Massachusetts, Amherst Isenberg School of Management, and is a Visiting Assistant Professor of Management at Bentley College in Waltham, Massachusetts. Her cases appear in several strategy textbooks. She is the co-author of the following strategic management cases: "The Boston YWCA: 1991," "Chipcom," and "Cisco Systems."

Gamewell D. Gantt, JD, C.P.A, is Professor of Accounting and Management in the College of Business at Idaho State University in Pocatello, Idaho, where he teaches a variety of Legal Studies courses, including the Legal Environment of Accounting and the Legal Environment of Technology Management. He is a past President of the Rocky Mountain Academy of Legal Studies in Business. His published articles and papers have appeared in journals including *Midwest Law Review, Business Law Review, Copyright World,* and *Intellectual Property World.* His published cases have appeared in several textbooks and in *Annual Advances in Business Cases.*

Norman J. Gierlasinski, D.B.A., C.P.A., D.F.E., C.I.A., is Professor of Accounting at Central Washington University. He served as Chairman of the Small Business Division of the Midwest Business Administration Association. He has authored and co-authored cases for professional associations and the Harvard Case Study Series. He has authored various articles in professional journals as well as serving as a contributing author for textbooks and as a consultant to many organizations. He has also served as a reviewer for various publications.

Irene Hagenbuch, B.S. (Bentley College), is currently working as an Operations Specialist for Warburg Dillon Read in Stamford, Connecticut. Among her various roles at Warburg Dillon Read, Irene has spent time with the Precious Metals, Domestic Equities, and Fixed Income Groups. Some of her responsibilities have included the reduction of settlement risk through operational controls, new product development, design and testing, and general project management. Irene is an avid skier and runner. In her spare time, she enjoys foreign travel.

Paul P. Harasimowicz Jr., D.D.S., B.S., 1957, University of Vermont, D.D.S., 1961, McGill University. Graduated from Gardner High School and Elm Street School in 1953 and 1949, respectively. Self-employed dentist in Gardner, Massachusetts, since 1963.

Alan N. Hoffman, D.B.A. (Indiana University), is Associate Professor of Management, Bentley College, Waltham, Massachusetts, and was formerly Assistant Professor of Business Environment and Policy at the University of Connecticut. He is co-author of *The Strategic Management Casebook and Skill Builder,* with Hugh O'Neill. Recent publications have appeared in the *Academy of Management Journal, Human Relations,* the *Journal of Business Research, Business Horizons,* and the *Journal of Business Ethics.* His cases appear in more than 20 strategy textbooks. He is co-author of the following strategic management cases: "Harley-Davidson: The Eagle Soars Alone, "The Boston YWCA: 1991," "Ryka Inc.: The Athletic Shoe with a 'Soul,'" "Liz Claiborne: Troubled Times for the Women's Retail Giant," "Snapple Beverage," "NTN Communications: The Future Is Now!," "Ben & Jerry's Homemade, Yo! I'm Your CEO," and "Chipcom, Inc."

J. David Hunger, Ph.D. (Ohio State University), is Professor of Strategic Management at Iowa State University. He previously taught at George Mason University, the University of Virginia, and Baldwin-Wallace College. His research interests lie in strategic management, corporate governance, leadership, conflict management, and entrepreneurship. He is currently serving as Academic Director of the Pappajohn Center for Entrepreneurship at Iowa State University. He has worked in management positions for Procter & Gamble, Lazarus Department Store, and the U.S. Army. He has been active as consultant and trainer to business corporations, as well as to state and federal government agencies. He has written numerous articles and cases that have appeared in the *Academy of Management Journal, International Journal of Management, Human Resource Management, Journal of Business Strategies, Case Research Journal, Business Case Journal, Handbook of Business Strategy, Journal of Management Case Studies, Annual Advances in Business Cases, Journal of Retail Banking, SAM Advanced Management Journal,* and *Journal of Management,* among others. Dr. Hunger is a member of the Academy of Management, North American Case Research Association (NACRA), Society for Case Research (SCR), North American Management Society, World Association for Case Method Research and Application (WACRA), and the Strategic Management Society. He is past President of the Society for Case Research and the Iowa State University Press Board of Directors. He is currently serving as NACRA's Web Master (nacra.net). He is currently serving on the editorial review boards of *SAM Advanced Management Journal, Journal of Business Strategies,* and *Journal of Business Research.* He is also a member of the board of directors of the North American Case Research Association (Midwest representative), and the North American Management Society. He is co-author with Thomas L. Wheelen of *Strategic Management, Essentials of Strategic Management, Strategic Management and Business Policy,* as well as *Strategic Management Cases (PIC: Preferred Individualized Cases),* and a monograph assessing undergraduate business education in the United States. His textbook *Strategic Management and Business Policy* received the McGuffey Award for Excellence and Longevity in 1999 from the Text and Academic Authors Association. Dr. Hunger received the *Best Case Award* given by the McGraw-Hill Publishing Company and the Society for Case Research in 1991 for outstanding case development. He is listed in various versions of Who's Who, including *Who's Who in the World.* He was also recognized in 1999 by the Iowa State University College of Business with its Innovation in Teaching Award.

George A. Johnson, Ph.D., is Professor of Management and Director of the Idaho State University M.B.A. program. He has published in the fields of management education, ethics, project management, and simulation. He is also active in developing and publishing case material for educational purposes. His industry experience includes several years as a project manager in the development and procurement of aircraft systems.

Michael J. Keeffe, Ph.D. (University of Arkansas), is Associate Professor of Management and Chairman of the Department of Management and Marketing at Southwest Texas State University. He is the author of numerous cases in the field of strategic management, has published in several journals, and is an associate with the consulting firm of Hezel & Associates in San Antonio, Texas. He currently teaches and conducts research in the fields of strategic management and human resource management.

John A. Kilpatrick, Ph.D. (University of Iowa), is professor of Management and International Business, Idaho State University. He has taught in the areas of business policy and strategy, international business, and business ethics for over 20 years. He is on the editorial board of the Sage Series in Business Ethics. He has served as co-chair of the management track of the Institute for Behavioral and Applied Management since its inception. He is author of *The Labor Content of American Foreign Trade,* and co-author of *Issues in International Business.* His cases have appeared in a number of organizational behavior and strategy texts and casebooks, and in *Annual Advances in Business Cases.*

Jay Knippen, D.B.A. (Florida State University), is a Professor of Management, University of South Florida. He is co-author of *Breaking the Barrier to Upward Communication* and the author of over 80 articles, primarily in the field of Management Skills. He has served as President, Vice-President, Treasurer, and Program Chairman of the Southern Management Association; and Vice-President of Finance of Decision Sciences. He has received numerous outstanding Teaching Awards and 11 listings in *Outstanding Educators of America.*

Donald F. Kuratko is the Stoops Distinguished Professor of Business and Founding Director of the Entrepreneurship Program, College of Business, Ball State University. He has published over 140 articles on aspects of entrepreneurship, new venture development, and corporate intrapreneurship as well as seven books, including the leading entrepreneurship book in American universities today, *Entrepreneurship: A Contemporary Approach* (The Dryden Press, 1998). In addition, Dr. Kuratko has been a consultant on Corporate Intrapreneurship and Entrepreneurial Strategies to a number of major corporations such as Blue Cross/Blue Shield, AT&T, United Technologies, Ameritech, The Associated Group (Acordia), Union Carbide Corporation, ServiceMaster, and TruServ. The Entrepreneurship program that Dr. Kuratko developed at Ball State has received national acclaim with such honors as The George Washington Medal of Honor (1987); The Leavey Foundation Award for Excellence in Private Enterprise (1988); National Model Entrepreneurship Program Award (1990); The NFIB Excellence Award (1993); and the National Model Graduate Entrepreneurship Program Award (1998). The Ball State program is continually ranked as one of the top 265 business programs in the nation, including *Business Week* and *Success* magazines' national rankings. It has also been ranked one of the top ten business schools for entrepreneurship research. Dr. Kuratko's honors include: Professor of the Year for five consecutive years at the College of Business, Ball State University, Outstanding Young Faculty for Ball State University in 1987; recipient of Ball State University's Outstanding Teaching Award in 1990; and named Ball State University's Outstanding Professor in 1996. Dr. Kuratko was also honored as The Entrepreneur of the Year for the State of Indiana in 1990 (sponsored by Ernst & Young, *Inc* magazine, and Merrill Lynch), and he was inducted into the Institute of American Entrepreneurs Hall of Fame in 1990. In addition, Dr. Kuratko was named the National Outstanding Entrepreneurship Educator for 1993 by the U.S. Association for Small Business and Entrepreneurship.

Sharon Ungar Lane, B.S.L.M.E. (University of Massachusetts at Amherst), M.B.A. (Bentley College), worked at General Electric for ten years in Manufacturing Management until she chose to take a leave to care for her two daughters. Sharon has previously published two strategic management case studies ("Tootsie Roll, Inc." and "Liz Claiborne, 1993: Troubled Times for the Woman's Retail Giant").

Daniel J. McCarthy, D.B.A. (Harvard University), is a Professor of Strategic Management, Northeastern University, and has held the McDonald and Walsh Professorships in the College of Business. He teaches and conducts research in the areas of strategic management, high technology businesses, and international business, emphasizing Russia. He is a Fellow at the Davis Center for Russian Studies at Harvard University, and has been Associate Dean as well as Director of the Graduate School of Business at Northeastern. He is a member of the editorial board of *The Academy of Management Executive* and reviews for numerous management journals. Dr. McCarthy is the co-author of four editions of *Business Policy and Strategy: Concepts and Readings,* and two editions of *The Business Policy Game.* He has published over 30 articles in such journals as *California Management Review, Journal of World Business, Research Policy, IEEE Transactions on Engineering Management, The Academy of Management Executive, Business Horizons,* and *Thunderbird International Business Review.* He has consulted extensively in the United States and Europe for more than 40 companies, and serves as a Corporate Director of Clean Harbors Inc., Managed Comp Inc., and Tufts Associated Health Maintenance Organization.

Bill J. Middlebrook, Ph.D. (University of North Texas), is Professor of Management at Southwest Texas State University. He has served as Acting Chair of the Department of Management and Marketing, published in numerous journals, served as a consultant in industry, and is currently teaching and researching in the fields of Strategic Management and Human Resources.

Edward S. Mortellaro Jr., D.M.D., M.S., B.S. (University of Florida, Florida State University and University of South Florida), is in practice as periodontics dentist in Brandon, Florida. He is an expert shopper at Home Depot.

Martin J. Nicholson, B.S. (Civil Engineering, University of Notre Dame), U.S. Army (two years Polar Research in Greenland). Retired in 1996 with 38 years as Civil Engineer with State of California (Caltrans). Married: Wife, Elizabeth, 4 children, 5 grandchildren. He graduated from Gardner High School (MA) and Sacred Heart School in 1953 and 1949, respectively.

Shirley F. Olson, D.B.A. (Mississippi State University), is Vice-President of J.J. Ferguson Companies in Greenwood, Mississippi. She was formerly associated with Millsaps College–Jackson, Mississippi, as Professor with concentrations in strategic management and behavioral management. She has authored over 150 articles and numerous cases. She also has an active consulting practice focusing primarily on strategic planning.

Thomas M. Patrick, Ph.D. (University of Kentucky), is Professor of Finance at The College of New Jersey. He has also taught at Rider University and the University of Notre Dame. He has published widely in the areas of Commercial Banking and Small Business Finance. His research appears in such journals as *Journal of Consumer Finance, Journal of International Business Studies, Journal of Small Business Management,* and *Banker's Monthly.* He also serves on the editorial review boards of a number of academic journals.

Sheila M. Puffer, Ph.D. (University of California, Berkeley), is a Professor of International Business and Human Resources Management at Northeastern University. She has also been a faculty member at the State University of New York at Buffalo, and a visiting scholar at the Plekhanov Institute of the National Economy in Moscow where she received a diploma from the executive management program. She is a Fellow at the Davis Center for Russian Studies at Harvard University. She is the editor of *Academy of Management Executive,* and is an editorial board member of three additional journals. Dr. Puffer's publications include the co-authored and co-edited books *Behind the Factory Walls: Decision Making in Soviet and U.S. Enterprises, The Russian Management Revolution, Managerial Insights from Literature, Management International: Cases, Exercises, and Readings, Management Across Cultures: Insights from Fiction and Practice,* and *Business and Management in Russia.* She has published more than 50 articles in journals including *Journal* *of World Business, Thunderbird International Business Review, European Management Journal, Academy of Management Executive, California Management Review,* and *Administrative Science Quarterly.*

John K. Ross III, Ph.D. (University of North Texas), is Associate Professor of Management, Southwest Texas State University. He has served as SBI Director, Associate Dean, Chair of the Department of Management and Marketing, published in numerous journals, and is currently teaching and researching in the fields of strategic management and human resources.

Patricia A. Ryan, Ph.D. (University of South Florida), is an Assistant Professor of Finance at Colorado State University. She has published in numerous journals including the *Business Case Journal, International Journal of Case Studies, Journal of Accounting and Finance Research, Journal of Finance and Strategic Decisions, Advances in Business Cases and the Midwest Review of Finance and Insurance.* Her work has also appeared in *Strategic Management and Business Policy, 6th Edition,* and *Research and Cases in Strategic Management.* She has served on multiple review boards and is currently the Editor of *Advances in Business Cases,* a publication of the Society for Case Research.

Richard C. Scamehorn, M.B.A. (Indiana University), B.S. in Aeronautical and Aerospace Engineering (University of Michigan), is Executive in Residence at Ohio University's College of Business. Prior to Ohio University he was with Diamond Power Specialty Company, where he served as President, Vice-President of Marketing, and Vice-President of Manufacturing. He has conducted business and traveled in 49 countries and served on boards of directors of companies in Australia, Canada, China, Finland, Korea, Mexico, South Africa, Sweden, the United Kingdom, and is listed in *Who's Who in Finance and Industry in America* and the *International Businessmen's Who's Who.*

Stanley R. Sitnik, D.B.A. (George Washington University), M.B.A. (Seton Hall University), B.S.S.S. (Georgetown University), is currently teaching Advanced Business Financial Management to M.B.A. students. He was previously Assistant Professor of Finance, Securities Broker-Dealer, Founder and CEO of several companies engaged in the acquisition, development, and operation of natural gas and coal producing properties. He is presently an associate of MLC S.A., an international consulting firm based in Geneva, Switzerland.

John Stanbury (Halifax, Nova Scotia, Canada), M.B.A. (Concordia University, Montreal, PQ Canada) M.A., Ph.D. (Ohio State University), is Adjunct Associate Professor of International Management at University of Maryland, University College. He previously taught at Concordia University and the University of Ottawa in Canada, and Ohio State University, Towson University, IUPUI and Indiana University in Kokomo. His research focuses largely upon his own work experiences with engineering consultancy firms in developing countries and includes books, articles, and cases on Management in P.R.C., Singapore, Nigeria, Philippines, Venezuela, Soviet Union, Korea, and the United Kingdom.

Laurence J. Stybel, Ed.D. (Harvard University), is co-founder of Stybel Peabody Lincolnshire, a Boston-based management consulting firm devoted to enhancing career effectiveness of executives who report to boards of directors. Services include search, outplacement, outplacement avoidance, and valued executive career consulting. Stybel Peabody Lincolnshire was voted "Best Outplacement Firm" by the readers of *Massachusetts Lawyers Weekly.* Its programs are the only ones officially endorsed by the Massachusetts Hospital Association and the Financial Executives Institute. He serves on the board of directors of the New England Chapter of the National Association of Corporate Directors and of the Boston Human Resources Association. His home page can be found at **www.stybelpeabody.com**. The "Your Career" Department of the Home Page contains downloadable back issues of his monthly *Boston Business Journal* column, "Your Career."

Paul M. Swiercz, M.S., Ph.D. (Virginia Polytechnic Institute and State University),

M.P.H. (University of Michigan), served on the faculty at Saginaw Valley State University from 1982–1984, where he was elected to the position of Chairman of the Department of Management/Marketing. From 1984–1986 he was a Visiting Professor at the graduate School of Labor and Industrial Relations at Michigan State University. In 1986 he joined the faculty at Georgia State University, where he was a member of the Department of Management and a Senior Research Associate in the W.T. Beebe Institute of Personnel and Employment Relations. In 1992 he joined the faculty at George Washington University as an Associate Professor of Human Systems and Employment Relations Policy. Dr. Swiercz is the founder and principal in the firm Executive Development Services International l (EDSI). In his capacity as a consultant and trainer he has directed workshops for AT&T, General Motors, Management Science Associates, the State of Georgia, the Pentagon, and others. He has been a principal investigator on a number of research projects, including those sponsored by the State of Georgia, the Hewlett Foundation, and the Society for Human Resource Planning. Dr. Swiercz has published more than 30 refereed research articles; his cases studies on *Home Depot* and *Delta Airlines* have appeared in the six best-selling strategy textbooks; and he has been interviewed by numerous news organizations, including CNN. He currently serves as editor of the journal *Human Resource Planning* and is director of the Strategic HRM Partnership Project at George Washington University.

John F. Talbot, B.S.E. (Fitchburg State College), retired mathematics teacher from Lunenburg High School in Lunenburg, Massachusetts, graduated from Gardner High School (MA) and Sacred Heart School in 1953 and 1949, respectively.

John J. Tarpey (1936–1996), M.A., M.Ed., and B.S. (Assumption College, Fitchburg State College, and University of Massachusetts), was a retired teacher and coach from Gardner High School in Gardner, Massachusetts. He was a true lifetime friend of Thomas Wheelen. He will be greatly missed by his family—his wife, Gloria, and his children, John, Maureen, Carolyn, and Emily—and his many friends.

Arieh A. Ullmann, Ph.D. (St. Gall University, Switzerland), is Associate Professor of Strategic Management, Binghamton University, State University of New York. He was a Research Fellow at the Science Center Berlin (Germany) and held visiting positions at the Free University of Berlin (Germany) and Haifa University (Israel). Professor Ullmann has authored and edited several books, among them the first comprehensive management casebook in Romania. He is the author of cases and articles that have appeared in the *Case Research Journal, Journal of General Management, California Management Review, Academy of Management Review, Policy Studies Journal, Journal for Environmental Policy,* and several German journals.

Joyce P. Vincelette, D.B.A. (Indiana University), is Professor of Management at the College of New Jersey. She was previously a faculty member at the University of South Florida. She has published articles, professional papers, chapters, and cases in management journals and strategic management textbooks. She has also been active as a consultant and trainer for a number of local and national business organizations as well as for a variety of non-profit and government agencies.

Kathryn E. Wheelen, B.A. (University of Tampa), has worked as an administrative assistant for case and textbook development with the Thomas Wheelen Company (circa 1879). She is currently employed by CarMax.

Richard D. Wheelen, B.S. (University of South Florida), has worked as a case research assistant. He is currently a buyer at Microserv, Inc., in Seattle.

Thomas L. Wheelen II, B.A. (Boston College), is a graduate student at the University of Colorado in Telecommunications. He has worked as a case research assistant.

Thomas L. Wheelen, D.B.A., M.B.A., B.S. Cum Laude (George Washington University, Babson College, and Boston College, respectively), is Professor of Strategic Management, University of South Florida, and was formerly the Ralph A. Beeton Professor of Free Enterprise at the McIntire School of Commerce, University of Virginia. He was awarded Fulbright Scholar. He was Visiting Professor at both the University of Arizona and Northeastern University. In 1999, the International Board of Directors of the Society for Advancement of Management (SAM) awarded Dr. Wheelen the Phil Carroll Advancement of Management Award in Strategic Management. He is a graduate of Gardner High School (MA) and Sacred Heart School in 1953 and 1949, respectively. He has worked in management positions for General Electric and the U.S. Navy and has been active as a consultant and trainer to business corporations, as well as to federal and state government agencies. He currently serves on the board of directors of Adhice Fund and the Society for the Advancement of Management, and on the Editorial Board of *SAM Advanced Management Journal.* He is the Associate Editor of *SAM Advanced Management Journal.* He served on the board of directors of Lazer Surgical Software, Inc., and on the *Journal of Management* and *Journal of Management Case Studies.* He is co-author of *Essentials of Strategic Management, Strategic Management and Business Policy, Strategic Management and Business Policy—World Version,* and *Strategic Management Cases (PIC: Preferred Individualized Cases),* as well as the *Public Sector* and co-developer of *Financial Analyzer (FAN)* and *Strategic Financial Analyzer (ST. FAN)* software. His textbook *Strategic Management and Business Policy* received the McGuffey Award for Excellence and Longevity in 1999 from the Text and Academic Authors Association. He has authored over 40 articles that have appeared in such journals as the *Journal of Management, Business Quarterly, Personnel Journal, SAM Advanced Management Journal, Journal of Retailing, International Journal of Management,* and the *Handbook of Business Strategy.* He has over 130 cases appearing in over 55 text and case books, as well as the *Journal of Management Case Research.* He has served on the board of directors of the Southern Management Association and the Society for the Advancement of Management, as Vice-President-at-Large and Vice President of Strategic Management for the Society for the Advancement of Management, and as President of the North American Case Research Association. He is a member of the Academy of Management, Beta Gamma Sigma, Southern Management Association, North American Case Research Association, Society for Advancement of Management, Society for Case Research, Strategic Management Association, and World Association for Case Method Research and Application. He is listed in *Who's Who in Finance and Industry, Who's Who in the South and Southwest,* and *Who's Who in American Education.*

Other Contributing Authors:
Phillippe Lasserre
Sharon Meadows
Jocelyn Probert

Chapter 1

Basic Concepts of Strategic Management

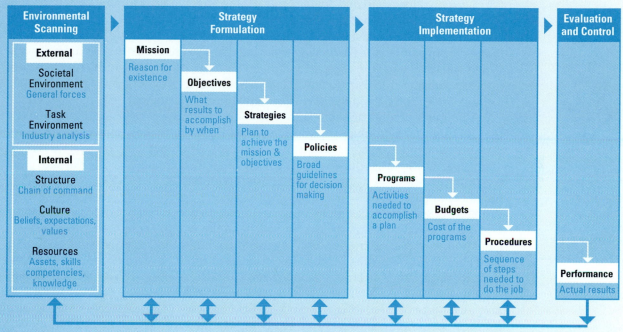

Steven Borsse was fed up. Borsse, who owned his own underwater search business in Sebastian, Florida, had paid $358 in November 1996 for a two-year, prepaid membership with America Online, Inc. (AOL). This package had offered Borsse a real savings compared to the usual monthly cost of $9.95 for the first five hours of use plus $2.95 for each hour thereafter. Unfortunately, in December 1996, AOL began offering a new plan charging $19.95 a month for *unlimited* online time. The attractiveness of the new flat rate plan was such that subscribers flooded AOL's circuits, preventing Borsse and thousands of other AOL customers from getting online. After unsuccessfully trying 20 times in one night to get through to AOL's jammed customer service center, Borsse complained. "It's literally impossible to get on AOL at night. I do business on the Internet, and this has really hurt me."

Founded in 1985 by Steve Case, America Online bragged in its 1996 annual report that it was "the world's first billion-dollar new media company." (See *aol.com* on the World Wide Web.) From its inception, the Dulles, Virginia, company had worked to dominate the developing Internet provider industry through an extremely aggressive growth strategy. Management emphasized saturation marketing by distributing free computer diskettes to almost every person in North America—some people actually received as many as 20 AOL disks in one year! These disks offered a month's free America Online service. Distribution was so intense and so thorough that it became an object of jokes. One cartoon showed an archeologist unearthing an Egyptian mummy only to find an America Online disk inside the coffin!

America Online's fast growth strategy was very successful. AOL's total revenues jumped from a little over $38 million from 182,000 subscribers in 1992 to more than $1 billion with over 6 million subscribers in 1996. By 1996, AOL had become the dominant Internet provider in North America, leaving behind its slower growing competitors, CompuServe, Prodigy, and the Microsoft Network, among others.

AOL introduced its unlimited usage plan on December 1, 1996. Admitting publicly that it would have trouble meeting the added demand, management was eager for market share and decided to go ahead—regardless. Four days later, the system was already overwhelmed. About 75% of the subscribers had changed to the flat rate plan. Customer usage soared from 1.6 million hours online in October to over 4 million hours in January.

Steven Borsse was not alone in being unable to access his AOL Internet connection. AOL became the busy signal heard around the world. Those subscribers lucky to get through stayed online for hours to avoid having to redial. Frustrated customers filed class action law suits for breach of contract against AOL in California and New York. To placate state attorneys general from 36 states, AOL offered to give subscribers refunds and free usage. Unfortunately customers still couldn't get access to AOL to take advantage of these offers. Because subscribers were unable to access AOL to cancel their subscriptions, they continued being charged for the service, or, rather, lack thereof.

AOL founder and Chairman, Steve Case, finally admitted that management had made a big mistake. "I would acknowledge it is a failure. We thought we had a pretty good grasp when we were making projections, but we were wrong." Realizing that the company had to do something to keep from losing its customers to the competition, Case went on to say, "We have made a commitment to our customers. . . . We'll deliver on this commitment, but it will take time." The company was in the process of spending $250 million to expand capacity by June 1997. Until capacity was expanded, management actually resorted to asking subscribers *not* to use the service! Meanwhile, the Microsoft Network, which had begun offering a flat rate in November 1996, was already expanding capacity by 25% to avoid the same problem.[1]

What went wrong? How could such a promising company as America Online make such a critical error? One reason was a lack of strategic management. Decisions were made piecemeal to the disadvantage of the company as a whole. To achieve fast growth, marketing was emphasized over all other business functions. Excellent advertising and promotional programs were implemented without considering how they would affect day-to-day operations. Hungry for market share, management pushed sales far beyond the ability of the company to support both current and new customers. The company had a good strategy for growth, but it failed to properly manage that strategy.

1.1   *The Study of Strategic Management*

Strategic management is that set of managerial decisions and actions that determines the long-run performance of a corporation. It includes *environmental scanning* (both external and internal), *strategy formulation* (strategic or long-range planning), *strategy implementation,* and *evaluation and control.* The study of strategic management, therefore, emphasizes the monitoring and evaluating of external opportunities and threats in light of a corporation's strengths and weaknesses. Originally called business policy, strategic management incorporates such topics as long-range planning and strategy. **Business policy,** in contrast, has a general management orientation and tends primarily to look inward with its concern for properly integrating the corporation's many functional activities. *Strategic management, as a field of study, incorporates the integrative concerns of business policy with a heavier environmental and strategic emphasis.* Therefore, *strategic management* has tended to replace *business policy* as the preferred name of the field.

Phases of Strategic Management

Many of the concepts and techniques dealing with strategic management have been developed and used successfully by business corporations such as General Electric and the Boston Consulting Group. Over time, business practitioners and academic researchers have expanded and refined these concepts. Initially strategic management was of most use to large corporations operating in multiple industries. Increasing risks of error, costly mistakes, and even economic ruin are causing today's professional managers in all organizations to take strategic management seriously in order to keep their company competitive in an increasingly volatile environment.

As managers attempt to better deal with their changing world, a firm generally evolves through the following four **phases of strategic management**:[2]

Phase 1. *Basic financial planning:* Managers initiate serious planning when they are requested to propose next year's budget. Projects are proposed on the basis of very little analysis, with most information coming from within the firm. The sales force usually provides the small amount of environmental information. Such simplistic operational planning only pretends to be strategic management, yet it is quite time consuming. Normal company activities are often suspended for weeks while managers try to cram ideas into the proposed budget. The time horizon is usually one year.

Phase 2. *Forecast-based planning:* As annual budgets become less useful at stimulating long-term planning, managers attempt to propose five-year plans. They now consider projects that may take more than one year. In addition to internal information, managers gather any available environmental data—usually on an ad hoc basis—and extrapolate current trends five years into the future. This phase is also time consuming, often involving a full month of managerial activity to make sure all the proposed budgets fit together. The process gets very political as managers compete for larger shares of funds. Endless meetings take place to evaluate proposals and justify assumptions. The time horizon is usually three to five years.

Phase 3. *Externally oriented planning (strategic planning):* Frustrated with highly political, yet ineffectual five-year plans, top management takes control of the planning process by initiating strategic planning. The company seeks to increase its responsiveness to changing markets and competition by thinking strategically. Planning is taken out of the hands of lower level managers and concentrated in a planning staff whose task is to develop strategic plans for the corporation. Consultants often provide the sophisticated and innovative techniques that the planning staff uses to gather information and forecast future trends. Ex-military experts develop competitive intelligence units. Upper level managers meet once a year at a resort "retreat" led by key members of the planning staff to evaluate and update the current strategic plan. Such top-down planning emphasizes formal strategy formulation and leaves the implementation issues to lower management levels. Top management typically develops five-year plans with help from consultants but minimal input from lower levels.

Phase 4. *Strategic management:* Realizing that even the best strategic plans are worthless without the input and commitment of lower level managers, top management forms planning groups of managers and key employees at many levels from various departments and workgroups. They develop and integrate a series of strategic plans aimed at achieving the company's primary objectives. Strategic plans now detail the implementation, evaluation, and control issues. Rather than attempting to perfectly forecast the future, the plans emphasize probable scenarios and contingency strategies. The sophisticated annual five-year strategic plan is replaced with strategic thinking at all levels of the organization throughout the year. Strategic information, previously available only centrally to top management, is available via local area networks to people throughout the organization. Instead of a large centralized planning staff, internal and external planning consultants are available to help guide group strategy discussions. Although top management may still initiate the strategic planning process, the resulting strategies may come from anywhere in the organization. Planning is typically interactive across levels and is no longer top down. People at all levels are now involved.

General Electric, one of the pioneers of strategic planning, led the transition from strategic planning to strategic management during the 1980s. By the 1990s, most corporations around the world had also begun the conversion to strategic management.

Until 1978, Maytag Company, the major home appliance manufacturer, could be characterized as being in Phase 1 of strategic management. See the **Company Spotlight on Maytag Corporation** feature to see how this company began making the transition from its budget-oriented planning approach to strategic management. We will follow Maytag throughout much of this text to illustrate concepts and techniques from each chapter.

Benefits of Strategic Management

Research has revealed that organizations that engage in strategic management generally outperform those that do not.[3] The attainment of an appropriate match or "fit" between an organization's environment and its strategy, structure, and processes has positive effects on the organization's performance. For example, a study of the impact of deregulation on U.S. railroads found that those railroads that changed their strategy as their environment changed outperformed those railroads that did not change their strategies.[4]

A survey of nearly 50 corporations in a variety of countries and industries found the three most highly rated benefits of strategic management to be:

- Clearer sense of strategic vision for the firm.

- Sharper focus on what is strategically important.

- Improved understanding of a rapidly changing environment.[5]

COMPANY SPOTLIGHT

Initiation of Strategic Management at Maytag

Maytag Corporation is a successful full-line manufacturer of major home appliances. Beginning with its very successful high-quality washers and dryers, it branched out through acquisitions into cooking appliances (Magic Chef, Hardwick, and Jenn-Air), refrigerators (Admiral), and vacuum cleaners (Hoover). Until 1978, however, the corporation (then known simply as Maytag Company) was strictly a laundry appliances manufacturer. Its only experience with any sort of strategic planning was in preparing the next year's budget!

In 1978, Daniel Krumm, Maytag's CEO, asked Leonard Hadley (at that time the company's Assistant Controller in charge of preparing the annual budget) and two others from manufacturing and marketing to serve as a strategic planning task force. Krumm posed to these three people the question: *"If we keep doing what we're now doing, what will the Maytag Company look like in five years?"* The question was a challenge to answer, especially considering that the company had never done financial modeling and none of the three knew much about strategic planning. Hadley, trained in accounting, worked with a programmer in his MIS section to develop "what if" scenarios. The task force presented its conclusion to the board of directors: A large part of Maytag's profits (the company at that time had the best profit margin in the industry) was coming from products and services with no future. These were repair parts, portable washers and dryers, and wringer washing machines.

This report triggered Maytag's interest in strategic change. After engaging in a series of acquisitions, including Magic Chef, to broaden its product line within the United States and Canada, management became interested in becoming a player in the European major home appliance industry. The trend toward the unification of Europe plus the rapid economic development of the Far East suggested to management that Maytag could no longer survive simply as a specialty appliance manufacturer serving only North America. It subsequently purchased Hoover in 1988 to not only acquire its worldwide strength in floor-care appliances, but also Hoover's strong laundry, cooking, and refrigeration appliance business in the United Kingdom and Australia. Although the strategy appeared to be sound at the time, the corporation later found that it had paid far too much for Hoover's European operations—its plants were outdated and inefficient.

MAYTAG CORPORATION

To be effective, however, strategic management need not always be a formal process. As occurred at Maytag, it can begin with a few simple questions:

1. **Where is the organization now? (Not where do we hope it is!)**

2. **If no changes are made, where will the organization be in one year? two years? five years? ten years? Are the answers acceptable?**

3. **If the answers are not acceptable, what specific actions should management undertake? What are the risks and payoffs involved?**

Studies of the planning practices of actual organizations suggest that the real value of strategic planning may be more in the future orientation of the planning process itself than in any written strategic plan. Small companies, in particular, may plan informally and irregularly. Nevertheless, a recent study of small businesses revealed that even though the degree of formality in strategic planning had no significant impact on a firm's profitability, formal planners had twice the growth rate in sales.[6]

Planning the strategy of large, multidivisional corporations can become complex and time consuming. It often takes slightly more than a year for a large company to move from situation assessment to a final decision agreement. Because of the relatively large number of people affected by a strategic decision in such a firm, a formalized, more sophisticated system is needed to ensure that strategic planning leads to successful performance. Otherwise, top management becomes isolated from developments in the business units, and lower level managers lose sight of the corporate mission and objectives.

1.2 *Globalization: A Challenge to Strategic Management*

Not too long ago, a business corporation could be successful by focusing only on making and selling goods and services within its national boundaries. International considerations were minimal. Profits earned from exporting products to foreign lands were considered frosting on the cake, but not really essential to corporate success. During the 1960s, for example, most U.S. companies organized themselves around a number of product divisions that made and sold goods *only* in the United States. All manufacturing and sales outside the United States were typically managed through one international division. An international assignment was usually considered a message that the person was no longer promotable and should be looking for another job.

Today, everything has changed. **Globalization,** the internationalization of markets and corporations, has changed the way modern corporations do business. To reach the economies of scale necessary to achieve the low costs, and thus the low prices, needed to be competitive, companies are now thinking of a global (worldwide) market instead of a national market. Nike and Reebok, for example, manufacture their athletic shoes in various countries throughout Asia for sale in every continent. Instead of using one international division to manage everything outside the home country, large corporations are now using matrix structures in which product units are interwoven with country or regional units. International assignments are now considered key for anyone interested in reaching top management. To emphasize the importance of globalization to strategic management, we end each chapter with a special section, 🌐*Global Issues for the 21st Century*.

As more industries become global, strategic management is becoming an increasingly important way to keep track of international developments and position the company for long-term competitive advantage. For example, Maytag Corporation purchased Hoover not so much for its vacuum cleaner business, but for its European laundry, cooking, and refrigeration business. Maytag's management realized that a company without a manufacturing presence in the European Union (EU) would be at a competitive disadvantage in the changing major home appliance industry. See the 🌐**21st Century Global Society** feature to see how regional trade associations are changing world trade.

Globalization presents a real challenge to the strategic management of business corporations. How can any one group of people in any one company keep track of all the changing technological, economic, political-legal, and sociocultural trends around the world? This is clearly impossible. More and more companies are realizing that they must shift from a vertically organized, top-down type of organization to a more horizontally managed, interactive organization. They are attempting to adapt more quickly to changing conditions by becoming learning organizations.

21ST CENTURY GLOBAL SOCIETY

REGIONAL TRADE ASSOCIATIONS REPLACE NATIONAL TRADE BARRIERS

Previously known as the Common Market and the European Community, the **European Union (EU)** is the most significant trade association in the world. The goal of the EU is the complete economic integration of its 15 member countries— *Austria, Belgium, Denmark, Finland, France, Germany, Greece, Ireland, Italy, Luxembourg, The Netherlands, Portugal, Spain, Sweden,* and the *United Kingdom*—so that goods made in one part of Western Europe can move freely without ever stopping for a customs inspection. One currency, the euro, is eventually to be used throughout the region as members integrate their monetary systems. The steady elimination of barriers to free trade is providing the impetus for a series of mergers, acquisitions, and joint ventures among business corporations. The requirement of at least 60% local content to avoid tariffs is forcing many American and Asian companies to abandon exporting in favor of a strong local presence in Europe. The EU is committed to open membership negotiations with Eastern European countries before the end of the century.

Canada, the *United States,* and *Mexico* are affiliated economically under the **North American Free Trade Agreement (NAFTA)**. The goal of NAFTA is improved trade among the three member countries rather than complete economic integration. Launched in 1994, the agreement requires all three members to remove all tariffs among themselves over 15 years, but they are allowed to have their own tariff arrangements with nonmember countries. Cars and trucks must have 62.5% North American content to qualify for duty-free status. Transportation restrictions and other regulations are being significantly reduced. Some Asian and European corporations are locating operations in one of the countries to obtain access to the entire North American region. Discussions are underway to extend NAFTA farther south to include Chile.

South American countries are also working to harmonize their trading relationships with each other and to form trade associations. The establishment of the **Mercosur** (Mercosul in Portuguese) free-trade area among *Argentina, Brazil, Uruguay,* and *Paraguay* means that a manufacturing presence within these countries is becoming essential to avoid tariffs for nonmember countries. Claiming to be NAFTA's southern counterpart, Mercosur is extending free-trade agreements to Bolivia and Venezuela.

Asia has no comparable regional trade association to match the potential economic power of either NAFTA or the EU. Japan, South Korea, China, and India generally operate as independent economic powers. Nevertheless, the **Association of South East Asian Nations (ASEAN)**—composed of *Brunei, Indonesia, Malaysia, the Philippines, Singapore, Thailand,* and *Vietnam*—is attempting to link its members into a borderless economic zone. With the EU extending eastward and NAFTA extending southward to connect with Mercosur, pressure will build on the independent Asian nations to soon form an expanded version of ASEAN.

Source: D. Fishburn, ed., *The World in 1997* (London: The Economist Group, 1996).

1.3 Creating a Learning Organization

Strategic management has now evolved to the point that its primary value is in helping the organization operate successfully in a dynamic, complex environment. Inland Steel Company, for example, uses strategic planning as a tool to drive organizational change. Managers at all levels are expected to continually analyze the changing steel industry in order to create or modify strategic plans throughout the year.[7] To be competitive in dynamic environments, corporations are having to become less bureaucratic and more flexible. In stable environments such as have existed in years past, a competitive strategy simply involved defining a competitive position and then defending it. As it takes less and less time for one product or technology to replace another, companies are finding that there is no such thing as a permanent competitive advantage. Many agree with Richard D'Aveni (in his book *HyperCompetition*) that any sustainable competitive advantage lies not in doggedly following a centrally managed five-year plan, but in stringing together a series of strategic short-term thrusts (as Intel does by cutting into the sales of its own offerings with periodic introductions of new products).[8] This means that corporations must develop *strategic flexibility*—the ability to shift from one dominant strategy to another.[9]

Strategic flexibility demands a long-term commitment to the development and nurturing of critical resources. It also demands that the company become a **learning organization**—an organization skilled at creating, acquiring, and transferring knowledge, and at modifying its behavior to reflect new knowledge and insights. Learning organizations are skilled at four main activities:

- Solving problems systematically

- Experimenting with new approaches

- Learning from their own experiences and past history as well as from the experiences of others

- Transferring knowledge quickly and efficiently throughout the organization.[10]

Learning organizations avoid stability through continuous self-examination and experimentation. People at all levels, not just top management, need to be involved in strategic management—helping to scan the environment for critical information, suggesting changes to strategies and programs to take advantage of environmental shifts, and working with others to continuously improve work methods, procedures, and evaluation techniques. At Xerox, for example, all employees have been trained in small-group activities and problem-solving techniques. They are expected to use the techniques at all meetings and at all levels, with no topic being off-limits. Research indicates that organizations that are willing to experiment and able to learn from their experiences are more successful than those that do not. For example, in a study of U.S. manufacturers of diagnostic imaging equipment, the most successful firms were those that improved products sold in the United States by incorporating some of what they had learned from their manufacturing and sales experiences in other nations. The less successful firms used the foreign operations primarily as sales outlets, not as important sources of technical knowledge.[11]

1.4 *Basic Model of Strategic Management*

Strategic management consists of four basic elements:

- **environmental scanning**
- **strategy formulation**
- **strategy implementation**
- **evaluation and control**

Figure 1.1 shows simply how these elements interact; Figure 1.2 expands each of these elements and serves as the model for this book. The terms used in Figure 1.2 are explained in the following pages.

Figure 1.1
Basic Elements of the Strategic Management Process

Environmental Scanning

Environmental scanning is the monitoring, evaluating, and disseminating of information from the external and internal environments to key people within the corporation. Its purpose is to identify **strategic factors**—those external and internal elements that will determine the future of the corporation. The simplest way to conduct environmental scanning is through **SWOT Analysis**. SWOT is an acronym used to describe those particular **S**trengths, **W**eaknesses, **O**pportunities, and **T**hreats that are strategic factors for a specific company. The **external environment** consists of variables (**O**pportunities and **T**hreats) that are outside the organization and not typically within the short-run control of top management. These variables form the context within which the corporation exists. Figure 1.3 depicts key environmental variables. They may be general forces and trends within the overall *societal* environment or specific factors that operate within an organization's specific *task* environment—often called its industry. **(These external variables are defined and discussed in more detail in Chapter 3.)**

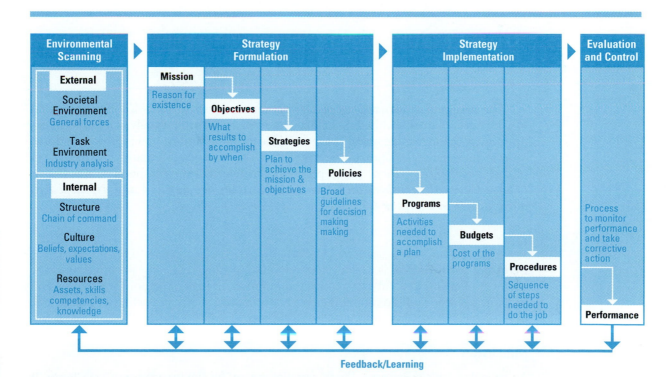

Figure 1.2
Strategic Management Model

Figure 1.3
Environmental
Variables

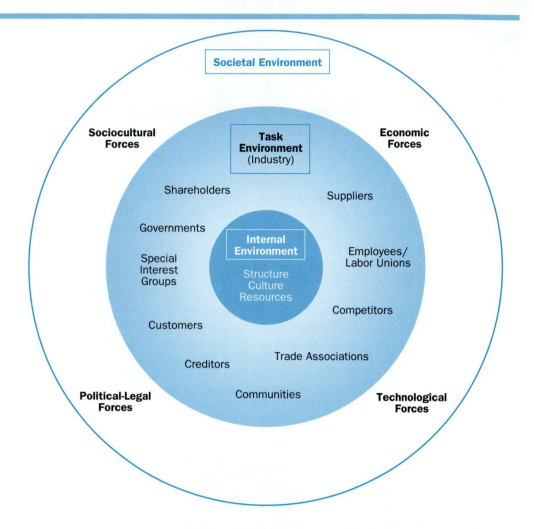

The **internal environment** of a corporation consists of variables (**S**trengths and **W**eaknesses) that are within the organization itself and are not usually within the short-run control of top management. These variables form the context in which work is done. They include the corporation's *structure, culture,* and *resources.* Key strengths form a set of *core competencies* which the corporation can use to gain competitive advantage. *(**These internal variables and core competencies are defined and discussed in more detail in Chapter 4.**)*

Strategy Formulation

Strategy formulation is the development of long-range plans for the effective management of environmental opportunities and threats, in light of corporate strengths and weaknesses. It includes defining the corporate *mission,* specifying achievable *objectives,* developing *strategies,* and setting *policy* guidelines.

Mission

An organization's **mission** is the purpose or reason for the organization's existence. It tells what the company is providing to society—either a service like housecleaning or a product like automobiles. A well-conceived mission statement defines the fundamental, unique purpose that sets a company apart from other firms of its type and identifies the scope of the company's operations in terms of products (including services) offered and markets served. It may also include the firm's philosophy about how it does business and treats its employees. It puts into words not only what the company is now, but what it wants to become—management's strategic vision of the firm's future. (Some people like to consider *vision* and *mission* as two different concepts: a mission statement describes what the organization is now; a vision statement describes what the organization would like to become. We prefer to combine these ideas into a single mission statement.)[12] The mission statement promotes a sense of shared expectations in employees and communicates a public image to important stakeholder groups in the company's task environment. *It tells who we are and what we do as well as what we'd like to become.*

One example of a mission statement is that of Maytag Corporation:

> To improve the quality of home life by designing, building, marketing, and servicing the best appliances in the world.

Another classic example is that etched in bronze at Newport News Shipbuilding, unchanged since its founding in 1886:

> We shall build good ships here—at a profit if we can—at a loss if we must—but always good ships.[13]

A mission may be defined narrowly or broadly in scope. An example of a *broad* mission statement is that used by many corporations: *Serve the best interests of shareowners, customers, and employees.* A broadly defined mission statement such as this keeps the company from restricting itself to one field or product line, but it fails to clearly identify either what it makes or which product/markets it plans to emphasize. Because this broad statement is so general, a *narrow* mission statement, such as the preceding one by Maytag emphasizing appliances, is more useful. A narrow mission very clearly states the organization's primary business, but it may limit the scope of the firm's activities in terms of product or service offered, the technology used, and the market served.

Objectives

Objectives are the end results of planned activity. They state *what* is to be accomplished by *when* and should be *quantified* if possible. The achievement of corporate objectives should result in the fulfillment of a corporation's mission. Minnesota Mining & Manufacturing (3M), for example, has set very specific financial objectives for itself:

1. To achieve 10% annual growth in earnings per share.

2. To achieve 20%–25% return on equity.

3. To achieve 27% return on capital employed.

The term "goal" is often used interchangeably with the term "objective." In this book, we prefer to differentiate the two terms. In contrast to an objective, we consider a **goal** as an open-ended statement of what one wants to accomplish with no quantification of what is to be achieved and no time criteria for completion. For example, a simple statement of "increased profitability" is thus a goal, not an objective, because it does not state how much profit the firm wants to make the next year.

Some of the areas in which a corporation might establish its goals and objectives are:

- Profitability (net profits)
- Efficiency (low costs, etc.)
- Growth (increase in total assets, sales, etc.)
- Shareholder wealth (dividends plus stock price appreciation)
- Utilization of resources (ROE or ROI)
- Reputation (being considered a "top" firm)
- Contributions to employees (employment security, wages, diversity)
- Contributions to society (taxes paid, participation in charities, providing a needed product or service)
- Market leadership (market share)
- Technological leadership (innovations, creativity)
- Survival (avoiding bankruptcy)
- Personal needs of top management (using the firm for personal purposes, such as providing jobs for relatives)

Strategies

A **strategy** of a corporation forms a comprehensive master plan stating how the corporation will achieve its mission and objectives. It maximizes competitive advantage and minimizes competitive disadvantage. For example, after Rockwell International Corporation realized that it could no longer achieve its objectives by continuing with its strategy of diversification into multiple lines of businesses, it sold its aerospace and defense units to Boeing. Rockwell instead chose to concentrate on commercial electronics, an area that management felt had greater opportunities for growth.

The typical business firm usually considers three types of strategy: corporate, business, and functional.

1. **Corporate strategy** describes a company's overall direction in terms of its general attitude toward growth and the management of its various businesses and product lines. Corporate strategies typically fit within the three main categories of *stability*, *growth*, and *retrenchment*. For example, Maytag Corporation followed a corporate growth strategy by acquiring other appliance companies in order to have a full line of major home appliances.

2. **Business strategy** usually occurs at the business unit or product level, and it emphasizes improvement of the competitive position of a corporation's products or services in the specific industry or market segment served by that business unit. Business strategies may fit within the two overall categories of *competitive* or *cooperative* strategies. For example, Maytag Corporation uses a differentiation competitive strategy that emphasizes quality for its Maytag brand appliances, but it uses a low-cost competitive strategy for its Magic Chef brand appliances so that it can sell these appliances to cost-conscious home builders.

3. **Functional strategy** is the approach taken by a functional area to achieve corporate and business unit objectives and strategies by maximizing resource productivity. It is concerned with developing and nurturing a *distinctive competence* to provide a company or business unit with a competitive advantage. Examples of functional

Figure 1.4
Hierarchy of Strategy

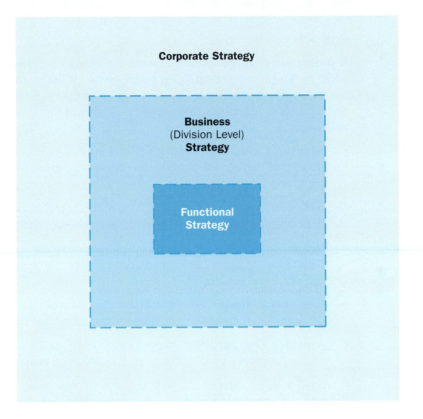

strategies within an R&D department are *technological followership* (imitate the products of other companies) and *technological leadership* (pioneer an innovation). To become more efficient throughout the corporation, Maytag Corporation is converting from a manufacturing strategy of making different types of home appliances under the same brand name in one plant to a more cost-effective strategy of making only one type of appliance (for example, dishwashers) for many brands in a very large plant. Another example of a functional strategy is America Online's marketing strategy of saturating the entire market with a low-priced product (as contrasted with selling a higher priced product to a particular market segment).

Business firms use all three types of strategy simultaneously. A **hierarchy of strategy** is the grouping of strategy types by level in the organization. This hierarchy of strategy is a nesting of one strategy within another so that they complement and support one another. (See Figure 1.4.) Functional strategies support business strategies, which, in turn, support the corporate strategy(ies).

Just as many firms often have no formally stated objectives, many firms have unstated, incremental, or intuitive strategies that have never been articulated or analyzed. Often the only way to spot a corporation's implicit strategies is to look not at what management says, but at what it does. Implicit strategies can be derived from corporate policies, programs approved (and disapproved), and authorized budgets. Programs and divisions favored by budget increases and staffed by managers who are considered to be on the fast promotion track reveal where the corporation is putting its money and its energy.

Policies

A **policy** is a *broad guideline* for decision making that links the formulation of strategy with its implementation. Companies use policies to make sure that employees throughout the firm make decisions and take actions that support the corporation's mission, objectives, and strategies. For example, consider the following company policies:

- **Maytag Company:** Maytag will not approve any cost reduction proposal if it reduces product quality in any way. (This policy supports Maytag's strategy for Maytag brands to compete on quality rather than on price.)

- **3M:** Researchers should spend 15% of their time working on something other than their primary project. (This supports 3M's strong product development strategy.)

- **Intel:** Cannibalize your product line (undercut the sales of your current products) with better products before a competitor does it to you. (This supports Intel's objective of market leadership.)

- **General Electric:** GE must be number one or two wherever it competes. (This supports GE's objective to be number one in market capitalization.)

- **America Online:** The company could have used a policy stating that a new marketing program would not be implemented until proper support was in place.

Policies like these provide clear guidance to managers throughout the organization. ***(Strategy formulation is discussed in greater detail in Chapters 5, 6, and 7.)***

Strategy Implementation

Strategy implementation is the process by which strategies and policies are put into action through the development of *programs*, *budgets*, and *procedures*. This process might involve changes within the overall culture, structure, and/or management system of the entire organization. Except when such drastic corporatewide changes are needed, however, the implementation of strategy is typically conducted by middle and lower level managers with review by top management. Sometimes referred to as operational planning, strategy implementation often involves day-to-day decisions in resource allocation.

Programs

A **program** is a statement of the activities or steps needed to accomplish a single-use plan. It makes the strategy action-oriented. It may involve restructuring the corporation, changing the company's internal culture, or beginning a new research effort. For example, consider Intel Corporation, the microprocessor manufacturer. Realizing that Intel would not be able to continue its corporate growth strategy without the continuous development of new generations of microprocessors, management decided to implement a series of programs:

- They formed an alliance with Hewlett-Packard to develop the successor to the Pentium Pro chip.

- They assembled an elite team of engineers and scientists to do long-term, original research into computer chip design.

Another example is AMR's SABRE Group (the computer reservations unit developed by American Airlines), which forged alliances with Microsoft and Time Warner to start selling airline tickets directly to customers on the Internet.

Keep in mind, however, America Online's experience. Be careful of introducing a new program without ensuring its fit with the organization's overall strategies and objectives as well as its impact on the rest of the firm.

Budgets

A **budget** is a statement of a corporation's programs in terms of dollars. Used in planning and control, a budget lists the detailed cost of each program. Many corporations demand a certain percentage return on investment, often called a "hurdle rate," before management will approve a new program. This ensures that the new program will significantly add to the corporation's profit performance and thus build shareholder value. The budget thus not only serves as a detailed plan of the new strategy in action, it also specifies through pro forma financial statements the expected impact on the firm's financial future.

For example, to become a significant global competitor in cars and trucks, the Daewoo Group of Korea budgeted $11 billion over the four-year period from 1996 to 2000 to quadruple its annual production of automobiles to two million vehicles (more than Chrysler Corporation produced). In addition to spending on its new plants in the Czech Republic and Romania, Daewoo budgeted $300 million and $650 million, respectively, to build new plants in Poland and Uzbekistan as part of its European expansion program.[14]

Procedures

Procedures, sometimes termed Standard Operating Procedures (SOP), are a system of sequential steps or techniques that describe in detail how a particular task or job is to be done. They typically detail the various activities that must be carried out in order to complete the corporation's program. For example, Delta Airlines used various procedures to cut costs. To reduce the number of employees, Delta asked technical experts in hydraulics, metal working, avionics, and other trades to design cross-functional work teams. To cut marketing expenses, Delta instituted a cap on travel agent commissions and emphasized sales to bigger accounts. Delta also changed its purchasing and food service procedures. See the **Strategy in a Changing World** feature to see how these procedures supported Delta's objectives and strategy. *(Strategy implementation is discussed in more detail in Chapters 8 and 9.)*

Evaluation and Control

Evaluation and control is the process in which corporate activities and performance results are monitored so that actual performance can be compared with desired performance. Managers at all levels use the resulting information to take corrective action and resolve problems. Although evaluation and control is the final major element of strategic management, it also can pinpoint weaknesses in previously implemented strategic plans and thus stimulate the entire process to begin again.

For evaluation and control to be effective, managers must obtain clear, prompt, and unbiased information from the people below them in the corporation's hierarchy. Using this information, managers compare what is actually happening with what was

STRATEGY IN A CHANGING WORLD

STRATEGIC MANAGEMENT AT DELTA AIRLINES

Delta Airlines initiated an aggressive cost-cutting program in April 1994 called "Leadership 7.5" in order to become profitable in a highly competitive industry. Because of deregulation, new competitors, like Southwest Airlines, were able to introduce low-cost strategies to offer extremely cheap fares (and minimal service) to gain market share—resulting in half-filled flights for full-service companies like Delta Airlines. Delta had not turned a profit since 1990 and chose to institute a turnaround strategy (a type of retrenchment corporate strategy) to achieve an objective of reducing annual expenses by $2.1 billion by June 1997 (and make a profit). To fulfill this strategy, management had to change many of the policies for which the company had long prided itself: lifetime employment, high pay, lush in-flight services, and routes to every destination. The "Leadership 7.5" program attempted to reduce the amount of money it spent on each airplane seat from 9.76¢ in 1994 to 7.5¢ in 1997 per flight mile.

The company budgeted $400 million in savings from marketing, $300 million from layoffs, and $310 million from onboard services. To reduce the number of employees, technical experts in hydraulics, metal-working, avionics, and other trades were asked to design cross-functional work teams. Marketing expenses were cut by instituting a cap on travel agent commissions and emphasizing sales to bigger accounts. In addition to layoffs, purchasing and food service procedures were changed.

The success of Delta Airlines's turnaround strategy can be evaluated by measuring the amount the firm was spending on each airplane seat per flight mile. Before the "Leadership 7.5" program was instituted in April 1994, the cost per seat was 9.76¢. By the end of 1995, it was down to 8.4¢. The program seemed to be working, but Delta needed to reach 7.5¢ by June 1997 to achieve the corporate objectives of reducing annual expenses by $2.1 billion and make a profit.

Source: D. Greising, "It Hurts So Good at Delta," *Business Week* (December 11, 1995), pp. 106–107.

originally planned in the formulation stage. For example, the success of Delta Airlines's turnaround strategy was evaluated in terms of the amount spent on each airplane seat per mile of flight. Before the "Leadership 7.5" program was instituted in April 1994, the cost per seat was 9.76¢. By the end of 1995, it was down to 8.4¢. The program seemed to be working, but it needed to reach 7.5¢ by June 1997 to achieve the company's objective of reducing annual expenses by $2.1 billion.

The evaluation and control of performance completes the strategic management model. Based on performance results, management may need to make adjustments in its strategy formulation, in implementation, or in both. **(Evaluation and control is discussed in more detail in Chapter 10.)**

Feedback/Learning Process

Note that the strategic management model depicted in Figure 1.2 includes a feedback/learning process. Arrows are drawn coming out of each part of the model and taking information to each of the previous parts of the model. As a firm or business unit develops strategies, programs, and the like, it often must go back to revise or correct decisions made earlier in the model. For example, poor performance (as measured in evaluation and control) usually indicates that something has gone wrong with either strategy formulation or implementation. It could also mean that a key variable, such as a new competitor, was ignored during environmental scanning and assessment.

1.5 *Initiation of Strategy: Triggering Events*

After much research, Henry Mintzberg discovered that strategy formulation is typically not a regular, continuous process: "It is most often an irregular, discontinuous process, proceeding in fits and starts. There are periods of stability in strategy development, but also there are periods of flux, of groping, of piecemeal change, and of global change."[15] This view of strategy formulation as an irregular process can be explained by the very human tendency to continue on a particular course of action until something goes wrong or a person is forced to question his or her actions. This period of "strategic drift" may simply result from inertia on the part of the organization or may simply reflect management's belief that the current strategy is still appropriate and needs only some "fine-tuning."

Most large organizations tend to follow a particular strategic orientation for about 15 to 20 years before making a significant change in direction.[16] After this rather long period of fine-tuning an existing strategy, some sort of shock to the system is needed to motivate management to seriously reassess the corporation's situation.

A **triggering event** is something that acts as a stimulus for a change in strategy. Some possible triggering events are:

- **New CEO.** By asking a series of embarrassing questions, the new CEO cuts through the veil of complacency and forces people to question the very reason for the corporation's existence.

- **External intervention.** The firm's bank suddenly refuses to approve a new loan or suddenly demands payment in full on an old one.

- **Threat of a change in ownership.** Another firm may initiate a takeover by buying the company's common stock.

- **Performance gap.** A performance gap exists when performance does not meet expectations. Sales and profits either are no longer increasing or may even be falling.

Iomega Corporation is an example of one company in which a triggering event forced its management to radically rethink what it was doing. See the **Strategy in a Changing World** feature to show how one simple question from the new CEO stimulated a change in strategy at Iomega.

1.6 *Strategic Decision Making*

The distinguishing characteristic of strategic management is its emphasis on strategic decision making. As organizations grow larger and more complex with more uncertain environments, decisions become increasingly complicated and difficult to make. This book proposes a strategic decision-making framework that can help people make these decisions regardless of their level and function in the corporation.

TRIGGERING EVENT AT IOMEGA CORPORATION

Iomega Corporation is a successful manufacturer of computer storage devices. Its most popular line of products is the Zip drive, a book-sized, portable storage device that uses a new kind of floppy disk with a capacity of 100 megabytes—equal to about 70 standard floppy disks. Earning $8.5 million on $326.2 million of sales in 1995, the company's stock price escalated from $5 per share in 1995 to $112 (after adjustment for a stock split) in April 1996.

Until Kim Edwards took over as Iomega's CEO in 1993, the company had been an unglamorous provider of niche computer storage products. Soon after he joined the company, Edwards asked his team to name some potential new markets for the company's products. After a long pause, one person said, "The Air Force really likes our Bernoulli Box." Thought Edwards, "Geez, this isn't good." The Bernoulli Box was a powerful storage device, but it was so expensive and specialized that only a few buyers, such as the military, had any use for it. "I realized the company had no clue that there was a mass market out there, waiting for a fun product," commented Edwards. Soon Iomega's engineers developed a series of products to appeal to this mass market: the Zip drive, the Ditto tape backup system, and the Jaz removable hard drive, which holds one gigabyte of data—ten times as much as the Zip.

Source: L. Gomes, "Iomega Adds Zip to Ho-Hum Business of Floppy Disks," *Wall Street Journal* (June 17, 1996), p. B6.

What Makes a Decision Strategic

Unlike many other decisions, **strategic decisions** deal with the long-run future of the entire organization and have three characteristics:

1. **Rare:** Strategic decisions are unusual and typically have no precedent to follow.

2. **Consequential:** Strategic decisions commit substantial resources and demand a great deal of commitment from people at all levels.

3. **Directive:** Strategic decisions set precedents for lesser decisions and future actions throughout the organization.[17]

Mintzberg's Modes of Strategic Decision Making

Some strategic decisions are made in a flash by one person (often an entrepreneur or a powerful chief executive officer) who has a brilliant insight and is quickly able to convince others to adopt his or her idea. Other strategic decisions seem to develop out of a series of small incremental choices that over time push the organization more in one direction than another. According to Henry Mintzberg, the most typical approaches, or modes, of strategic decision making are:[18]

- **Entrepreneurial mode.** Strategy is made by one powerful individual. The focus is on opportunities; problems are secondary. Strategy is guided by the founder's own vision of direction and is exemplified by large, bold decisions. The dominant goal is growth of the corporation. America Online, founded by Steve Case, is an example of this mode of strategic decision making. The company reflects his vision of the Internet provider industry. Although AOL's clear growth strategy is certainly an advantage of the entrepreneurial mode, its tendency to market its products before the company is able to support them is a significant disadvantage.

- **Adaptive mode.** Sometimes referred to as "muddling through," this decision-making mode is characterized by reactive solutions to existing problems, rather than a proactive search for new opportunities. Much bargaining goes on concerning priorities of objectives. Strategy is fragmented and is developed to move the corporation forward incrementally. This mode is typical of most universities, many large hospitals, a large number of governmental agencies, and a surprising number of large corporations. Encyclopaedia Britannica, Inc., operated successfully for many years in this mode, but continued to rely on the door-to-door selling of its prestigious books long after dual career couples made this marketing approach obsolete. Only after it was acquired in 1996 did the company change its marketing strategy to television advertising and Internet marketing. *(See http:// www.eb.com.)* It now offers CD-ROMs in addition to the printed volumes.

- **Planning mode.** This decision-making mode involves the systematic gathering of appropriate information for situation analysis, the generation of feasible alternative strategies, and the rational selection of the most appropriate strategy. It includes both the proactive search for new opportunities and the reactive solution of existing problems. The J. C. Penney Company is an example of the planning mode. After a careful study of shopping trends in the 1980s, the retailing company discontinued its sales of paint, hardware, major appliances, automotive items, and electronics to concentrate on apparel and home furnishings. Declining personal incomes and greater uncertainty in the 1990s led Penney's to emphasize private brands. This new merchandising strategy allowed the company to offer the high quality of goods often found in better department stores at a competitively lower price.[19]

In some instances, a corporation might follow a fourth approach called **logical incrementalism,** which is a synthesis of the planning, adaptive, and, to a lesser extent, the entrepreneurial modes of strategic decision making. As described by Quinn, top management might have a reasonably clear idea of the corporation's mission and objectives, but, in its development of strategies, it chooses to use "an interactive process in which the organization probes the future, experiments and learns from a series of partial (incremental) commitments rather than through global formulations of total strategies."[20] This approach appears to be useful when the environment is changing rapidly and when it is important to build consensus and develop needed resources before committing the entire corporation to a specific strategy.

Strategic Decision-Making Process: Aid to Better Decisions

Good arguments can be made for using either the entrepreneurial or adaptive modes (or logical incrementalism) in certain situations. This book proposes, however, that in most situations the planning mode, which includes the basic elements of the strategic management process, is a more rational and thus better way of making strategic decisions. The planning mode is not only more analytical and less political than are the other modes, but it is also more appropriate for dealing with complex, changing environments.[21] We therefore propose the following eight-step **strategic decision-making process** to improve the making of strategic decisions (see Figure 1.5):

Figure 1.5
Strategic Decision-Making Process

Source: T. L. Wheelen and J. D. Hunger, "Strategic Decision-Making Process," Copyright © 1994 and 1997 by Wheelen and Hunger Associates. Reprinted by permission.

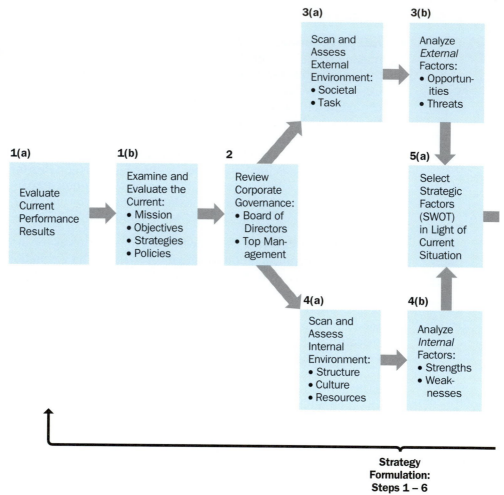

1. **Evaluate current performance results** in terms of (a) return on investment, profitability, and so forth, and (b) the current mission, objectives, strategies, and policies.

2. **Review corporate governance,** that is, the performance of the firm's board of directors and top management.

3. **Scan and assess the external environment** to determine the strategic factors that pose **O**pportunities and **T**hreats.

4. **Scan and assess the internal corporate environment** to determine the strategic factors that are **S**trengths (especially core competencies) and **W**eaknesses.

5. **Analyze strategic (SWOT) factors** to (a) pinpoint problem areas, and (b) review and revise the corporate mission and objectives as necessary.

6. **Generate, evaluate, and select the best alternative strategy** in light of the analysis conducted in *Step 5.*

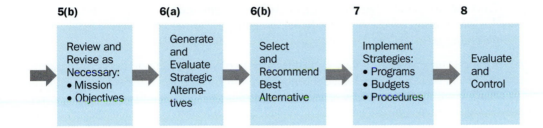

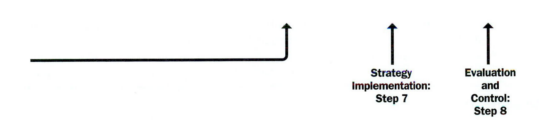

7. **Implement selected strategies** via programs, budgets, and procedures.

8. **Evaluate implemented strategies** via feedback systems, and the control of activities to ensure their minimum deviation from plans.

This rational approach to strategic decision making has been used successfully by corporations like Warner-Lambert; Dayton Hudson; Avon Products; Bechtel Group, Inc.; and Taisei Corporation.

1.7 Global Issues for the 21st Century

- The **21st Century Global Society** feature in this chapter described how nations are forming regional trading associations. These associations act to increase trade among member nations, but make it increasingly difficult to trade between regional blocs. This has significant implications for corporations operating within these regions. Firms need to decide if they will do better as a regional or as a global competitor.

- It is likely that the world will eventually be composed of three dominant trading blocs: one each in Europe, Asia, and the Americas. Because of local content regulations, multinational corporations will need to have meaningful manufacturing and marketing activities in every trading bloc, or else be relegated to just one part of the world.

- Globalization creates opportunities, but it also poses threats to companies that are not able to adapt quickly enough to a more complex and changing environment. As a result, firms are attempting to adopt the characteristics of a learning organization. Thus employees at all levels of the organization will need to have greater access to the information necessary to evaluate company performance and to suggest strategic changes.

- As more people at all levels and units are involved in strategic decision making, there will be a greater need for more access to information, but greater difficulty in dealing with it. Too much information could cause chaos. Coordination may become increasingly difficult.

- Increasing pressure on organizations for a quick response to changing conditions may make it difficult for corporations to engage in the planning mode of strategic management. Even with its faults, the entrepreneurial mode is exceptionally agile.

Projections for the 21st Century

- From 1994 to 2010, the world economy will grow from $26 trillion to $48 trillion.

- From 1994 to 2010, world trade will increase from $4 trillion to $16.6 trillion.[22]

Discussion Questions

1. Why has strategic management become so important to today's corporations?

2. How does strategic management typically evolve in a corporation?

3. What is a learning organization? Is this approach to strategic management better than the more traditional top-down approach?

4. Why are strategic decisions different from other kinds of decisions?

5. When is the planning mode of strategic decision making superior to the entrepreneurial and adaptive modes?

Key Terms

adaptive mode (p. 19)
budget (p. 15)
business policy (p. 3)

business strategy (p. 12)
corporate strategy (p. 12)
entrepreneurial mode (p. 18)

environmental scanning (p. 9)
evaluation and control (p. 15)
external environment (p. 9)

functional strategy (p. 12)
globalization (p. 6)
goals (p. 11)
hierarchy of strategy (p. 13)
internal environment (p. 10)
learning organization (p. 8)
logical incrementalism (p. 19)
mission (p. 10)
objectives (p. 11)

performance gap (p. 17)
phases of strategic management
    (p. 3)
planning mode (p. 19)
policy (p. 14)
procedures (p. 15)
program (p. 14)
strategic decision-making process
    (p. 19)

strategic decisions (p. 18)
strategic factors (p. 9)
strategic management (p. 3)
strategy (p. 12)
strategy formulation (p. 10)
strategy implementation (p. 8)
SWOT Analysis (p. 9)
triggering event (p. 17)

Strategic Practice Exercise

Mission statements vary widely from one company to another. Why is one mission statement better than another? Develop some criteria for evaluating a mission statement. Then, do one or both of the following exercises:

1. Evaluate the mission statement of Celestial Seasonings:

   Our mission is to grow and dominate the U.S. specialty tea market by exceeding consumer expectations with the best tasting, 100% natural hot and iced teas, packaged with Celestial art and philosophy, creating the most valued tea experience. Through leadership, innovation, focus, and teamwork, we are dedicated to continuously improving value to our consumers, customers, employees, and stakeholders with a quality-first organization.[23]

2. Find the mission statements of three different organizations, which can be business or not-for-profit. (*Hint:* Check annual reports. They may be in the library or on a company's web page.) Which mission statement is best? Why?

Notes

1. A. Barrett, P. Eng, and K. Rebello, "For $19.95 a Month, Unlimited Headaches for AOL," *Business Week* (January 27, 1997), p. 35; T. Petzinger, Jr., "'Gunning for Growth,' AOL's Steve Case Shot Himself in the Foot," *Wall Street Journal* (January 24, 1997), p. B1; L. Zuckerman, "America Online Moves to Placate Angry Users," (Ames, Iowa) *Daily Tribune* (January 18, 1997), p. B4.

2. F. W. Gluck, S. P. Kaufman, and A. S. Walleck, "The Four Phases of Strategic Management," *Journal of Business Strategy* (Winter 1982), pp. 9–21.

3. C. C. Miller, and L. B. Cardinal, "Strategic Planning and Firm Performance: A Synthesis of More Than Two Decades of Research," *Academy of Management Journal* (December 1994), pp. 1649–1665; P. Pekar, Jr., and S. Abraham, "Is Strategic Management Living Up To Its Promise?" *Long Range Planning* (October 1995), pp. 32–44.

4. K. G. Smith, and C. M. Grimm, "Environmental Variation, Strategic Change and Firm Performance: A Study of Railroad Deregulation," *Strategic Management Journal* (July-August 1987), pp. 363–376.

5. I. Wilson, "Strategic Planning Isn't Dead—It Changed," *Long Range Planning* (August 1994), p. 20.

6. M. A. Lyles, I. S. Baird, J. B. Orris, and D. F. Kuratko, "Formalized Planning in Small Business: Increasing Strategic Choices," *Journal of Small Business Management* (April 1993), pp. 38–50.

7. C. Gebelein, "Strategic Planning: the Engine of Change," *Planning Review* (September/October 1993), pp. 17–19.

8. R. A. D'Aveni, *HyperCompetition* (New York: Free Press, 1994). HyperCompetition is discussed in more detail in Chapter 3.

9. R. S. M. Lau, "Strategic Flexibility: A New Reality for World-Class Manufacturing," *SAM Advanced Management Journal* (Spring 1996), pp. 11–15.

10. D. A. Garvin, "Building a Learning Organization," *Harvard Business Review* (July/August 1993), p. 80. See also P. M. Senge, *The Fifth Discipline: The Art and Practice of the Learning Organization* (New York: Doubleday, 1990).

11. W. Mitchell, J. M. Shaver, and B. Yeung, "Getting There in a Global Industry: Impacts on Performance of Changing International Presence," *Strategic Management Journal* (September 1992), pp. 419–432.

12. See A. Campbell, and S. Yeung, "Brief Case: Mission, Vision, and Strategic Intent," *Long Range Planning* (August

1991), pp. 145-147; S. Cummings and J. Davies, "Mission, Vision, Fusion," *Long Range Planning* (December 1994), pp. 147–150.

13. J. Cosco, "Down To the Sea in Ships," *Journal of Business Strategy* (November/December 1995), p. 48.

14. L. Kraar, "Daewoo's Daring Drive Into Europe," *Fortune* (May 13, 1996), pp. 145–152.

15. H. Mintzberg, "Planning on the Left Side and Managing on the Right," *Harvard Business Review* (July-August 1976), p. 56.

16. This phenomenon of "punctuated equilibrium" describes corporations as evolving through relatively long periods of stability (equilibrium periods) punctuated by relatively short bursts of fundamental change (revolutionary periods). See E. Romanelli and M. L. Tushman, "Organizational Transformation as Punctuated Equilibrium: An Empirical Test," (October 1994), pp. 1141–1166.

17. D. J. Hickson, R. J. Butler, D. Cray, G. R. Mallory, and D. C. Wilson, *Top Decisions: Strategic Decision-Making in Organizations* (San Francisco: Jossey-Bass, 1986), pp. 26–42.

18. H. Mintzberg, "Strategy-Making in Three Modes," *California Management Review* (Winter 1973), pp. 44–53.

19. W. H. Howell, "Leading Strategic Change: Something Old, Something New." *Planning Review* (September/October 1995), pp. 10–12.

20. J. B. Quinn, *Strategies for Change: Logical Incrementalism* (Homewood, Ill.: Irwin, 1980), p. 58.

21. R. L. Priem, A. M. A. Rasheed, and A. G. Kotulic, "Rationality in Strategic Decision Processes, Environmental Dynamism and Firm Performance," *Journal of Management*, Vol. 21, No. 5 (1995), pp. 913–929; J. W. Dean, Jr. and M. P. Sharfman, "Does Decision Process Matter? A Study of Strategic Decision-Making Effectiveness," *Academy of Management Journal* (April 1996), pp. 368–396.

22. J. Warner, "21st Century Capitalism: Snapshot of the Next Century," *Business Week* (November 18, 1994), p. 194.

23. P. Jones and L. Kahaner, *Say It & Live It: 50 Corporate Mission Statements That Hit the Mark* (New York: Currency Doubleday, 1995), p. 53.

Chapter 2

Corporate Governance and Social Responsibility

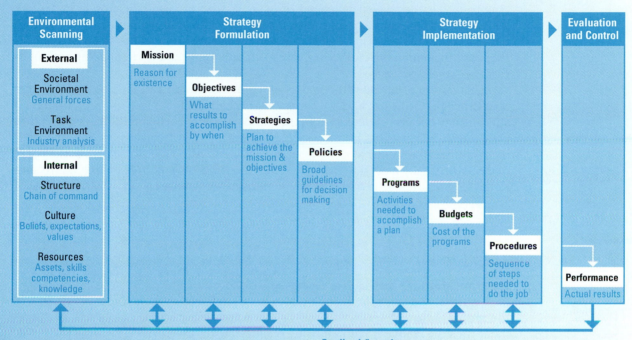

Environmental Scanning	Strategy Formulation	Strategy Implementation	Evaluation and Control

Environmental Scanning

External

Societal Environment
General forces

Task Environment
Industry analysis

Internal

Structure
Chain of command

Culture
Beliefs, expectations, values

Resources
Assets, skills competencies, knowledge

Strategy Formulation

Mission
Reason for existence

Objectives
What results to accomplish by when

Strategies
Plan to achieve the mission & objectives

Policies
Broad guidelines for decision making

Strategy Implementation

Programs
Activities needed to accomplish a plan

Budgets
Cost of the programs

Procedures
Sequence of steps needed to do the job

Evaluation and Control

Performance
Actual results

Feedback/Learning

At one time, the Eastman Kodak Company had been one of the most respected companies in the United States and perhaps the world. It was known for its excellent product quality and reliability. From 1983 to 1993, the company fell, however, from the top 10% to the bottom 18% of admired companies. Industry analysts portrayed the firm as bloated, slow-moving, myopic, and incapable of dealing effectively with its falling share of the photographic film market. Top management made strategic decisions based on protecting current products instead of developing future ones. For example, even though Kodak had been one of the first companies to develop a camcorder, management decided not to introduce it because it was costly and might detract from the current sales of its amateur film products. Profits were consistently below expectations. The company incurred billions of dollars in repeated one-time charges as it undertook incremental efforts to streamline and improve its performance.

Kodak's board of directors was extremely concerned with the inability of Chief Executive Officer Kay Whitmore to turn the company around. Whitmore had joined Kodak in 1957 as an engineer and epitomized the company's cautious home-grown management. On August 6, 1993, Kodak's board of directors, led by a group of outside directors, fired Whitmore. Instead of looking internally for a replacement, the board offered the CEO position to George Fisher, then Chairman and CEO of Motorola, Inc. Motorola had long been regarded a well-managed company, known for its dedication to hard work and quality. The board expected Fisher to deliver fast and deep cost cuts. Just four months later, however, Fisher stated that cost cutting alone would not be the answer. He proposed to commit the entire company to growth opportunities in imaging and to divest non-core businesses.[1]

This example illustrates the impact of top management and the board of directors on a firm's performance. Kodak's top managers had traditionally been promoted from within. They became so dedicated to the company's past in chemical imaging that they were unable to perceive a future in electronic imaging. As strategic managers, management had failed to adjust to a changing environment. Although slow to react, the board of directors finally moved to bring in some new blood. Would this be enough to save Kodak and return it to its past position of industry dominance?

2.1   *Corporate Governance: Role of the Board of Directors*

A **corporation** is a mechanism established to allow different parties to contribute capital, expertise, and labor, for their mutual benefit. The investor/shareholder participates in the profits of the enterprise without taking responsibility for the operations. Management runs the company without being responsible for personally providing the funds. To make this possible, laws have been passed so that shareholders have limited liability and, correspondingly, limited involvement in a corporation's activities. That involvement does include, however, the right to elect directors who have a legal duty to represent the shareholders and protect their interests. As representatives of the shareholders, directors have both the authority and the responsibility to establish basic corporate policies and to ensure that they are followed.[2]

The board of directors has, therefore, an obligation to approve all decisions that might affect the long-run performance of the corporation. This means that the corporation is fundamentally governed by the *board of directors* overseeing *top management*, with the concurrence of the *shareholder*. The term **corporate governance** refers to the relationship among these three groups in determining the direction and performance of the corporation.[3]

Over the past decade, shareholders and various interest groups have seriously questioned the role of the board of directors in corporations. They are concerned that outside board members often lack sufficient knowledge, involvement, and enthusiasm to do an adequate job of providing guidance to top management. For example, when officials of the California Public Employees' Retirement System—a key shareholder group—criticized IBM's board of directors in the early 1990s for not doing more to prevent the company's nosedive in earnings, the four outside members of the board's executive committee admitted that they did not know enough about the company's business to properly evaluate management. Like IBM's top management, they had missed the trend away from mainframe computers to personal computers. Board members actually admitted in the meeting that none of them felt comfortable using a personal computer. According to one director, "Not one of us has a PC in our home or office."[4]

The general public has not only become more aware and more critical of many boards' apparent lack of responsibility for corporate activities, it has begun to push government to demand accountability. As a result, the board as a rubber stamp of the CEO or as a bastion of the "old-boy" selection system is being replaced by more active, more professional boards.

Responsibilities of the Board

Laws and standards defining the responsibilities of boards of directors vary from country to country. For example, board members in Ontario, Canada, face more than 100 provincial and federal laws governing director liability. The United States, however, has no clear national standards or federal laws. Specific requirements of directors vary, depending on the state in which the corporate charter is issued. There is, nevertheless, a developing worldwide consensus concerning the major responsibilities of a board. Interviews with 200 directors from eight countries (Canada, France, Germany, Finland, Switzerland, the Netherlands, United Kingdom, and Venezuela) revealed strong agreement on the following five **board of director responsibilities,** listed in order of importance:

1. Setting corporate strategy, overall direction, mission or vision

2. Hiring and firing the CEO and top management

3. Controlling, monitoring, or supervising top management

4. Reviewing and approving the use of resources

5. Caring for shareholder interests[5]

Directors in the United States must make certain, in addition to the duties just listed, that the corporation is managed in accordance with the laws of the state in which it is incorporated. They must also ensure management's adherence to laws and regulations, such as those dealing with the issuance of securities, insider trading, and other conflict-of-interest situations. They must also be aware of the needs and demands of constituent groups so that they can achieve a judicious balance among the interests of these diverse groups while ensuring the continued functioning of the corporation.

In a legal sense, the board is required to direct the affairs of the corporation but not to manage them. It is charged by law to act with **due care,** or *due diligence*. If a director or the board as a whole fails to act with due care and, as a result, the corporation is in some way harmed, the careless director or directors can be held personally liable for the harm done. This is no small concern given that a recent survey of outside directors revealed that more than 40% have been named as part of a lawsuit against the corporation.[6]

Role of the Board in Strategic Management

How does a board of directors fulfill these many responsibilities? The **role of the board of directors in strategic management** is to carry out three basic tasks:

- **Monitor.** By acting through its committees, a board can keep abreast of developments inside and outside the corporation, bringing to management's attention developments it might have overlooked. A board should at least carry out this task.

- **Evaluate and influence.** A board can examine management's proposals, decisions, and actions; agree or disagree with them; give advice and offer suggestions; outline alternatives. More active boards perform this task in addition to the monitoring one.

- **Initiate and determine.** A board can delineate a corporation's mission and specify strategic options to its management. Only the most active boards take on this task in addition to the two previous ones.

Board of Directors Continuum

A board of directors is involved in strategic management to the extent that it carries out the three tasks of monitoring, evaluating and influencing, and initiating and determining. The **board of directors continuum** shown in Figure 2.1 shows the possible degree of involvement (from low to high) in the strategic management process. As types, boards can range from *phantom boards* with no real involvement to *catalyst boards* with a very high degree of involvement. Research does suggest that active board involvement in strategic management is positively related to corporate financial performance.[7]

Highly involved boards tend to be very active. They take their tasks of monitoring, evaluating, and influencing, plus initiating and determining very seriously; they provide advice when necessary and keep management alert. As depicted in Figure 2.1, their heavy involvement in the strategic management process places them in the active participation or even catalyst positions. At Zenith Electronics Corporation, for example, the board's executive committee of three outsiders meets monthly with Chief Executive Jerry Pearlman to discuss business issues. The board created an oversight system to track 20 performance measures. The CEO must explain to the board any deviation from the corporate plan in any of the variables. The board also linked all top management bonuses exclusively to Zenith's financial performance.[8] Other corporations with actively participating boards are Mead Corporation, Rolm and Haas, Whirlpool, Westinghouse, the Mallinckrodt Group, Dayton-Hudson, and General Motors.

As a board becomes less involved in the affairs of the corporation, it moves farther to the left on the continuum (see Figure 2.1). On the far left are passive phantom or rubber stamp boards that typically never initiate or determine strategy unless a crisis occurs. In these situations, the CEO also serves as Chairman of the Board, personally nominates all directors, and works to keep board members under his or her control by giving them the "mushroom treatment"—*throw manure on them and keep them in the dark!*

Generally, the smaller the corporation, the less active is its board of directors. In an entrepreneurial venture, for example, the privately-held corporation may be 100% owned by the founders—who also manage the company. In this case, there is no need for an active board to protect the interests of the owner-manager shareholders—the interests of the owners and the managers are identical. In this instance, a board is really unnecessary and only meets to satisfy legal requirements. If stock is sold to outsiders to finance growth, however, the board becomes more active. Key investors want seats on the board so they can oversee their investment. To the extent that they still control most of the stock, however, the founders dominate the board. Friends, family members, and key shareholders usually become members, but the board acts primarily as a rubber stamp for any proposals put forward by the owner-managers. This cozy relationship between the board and management should change, however, when the corporation goes public and stock is more widely dispersed. The founders, who are still acting as management, may sometimes make decisions that conflict with the needs of the other share-

Figure 2.1
Board of Directors Continuum

Source: T. L. Wheelen and J. D. Hunger, "Board of Directors Continuum." Copyright © 1994 by Wheelen and Hunger Associates. Reprinted by permission.

DEGREE OF INVOLVEMENT IN STRATEGIC MANAGEMENT

Low (Passive) ————————————————————————————— High (Active)

Phantom	Rubber Stamp	Minimal Review	Nominal Participation	Active Participation	Catalyst
Never knows what to do, if anything; no degree of involvement.	Permits officers to make all decisions. It votes as the officers recommend on action issues.	Formally reviews selected issues that officers bring to its attention.	Involved to a limited degree in the performance or review of selected key decisions, indicators, or programs of management.	Approves, questions, and makes final decisions on mission, strategy, policies, and objectives. Has active board committees. Performs fiscal and management audits.	Takes the leading role in establishing and modifying the mission, objectives, strategy, and policies. It has a very active strategy committee.

holders (especially if the founders own less than 50% of the common stock). In this instance, problems could occur if the board fails to become more active in terms of its roles and responsibilities.

Most large, publicly-owned corporations probably have boards that operate at some point between nominal and active participation. One study of boards ranging from hospitals to Fortune 500 firms found that:

- 30% of the boards actively worked with management to develop strategic direction (**active/catalyst**)

- 30% worked to revise as well as ratify management's proposals (**minimal/ nominal participation**)

- 40% merely ratified management's strategic proposals (**phantom/rubber stamp**).[9]

Members of a Board of Directors

The boards of most publicly owned corporations are composed of both inside and outside directors. **Inside directors** (sometimes called management directors) are typically officers or executives employed by the corporation. **Outside directors** may be executives of other firms but are not employees of the board's corporation. Although there is no clear evidence indicating that a high proportion of outsiders on a board results in improved corporate performance, there is a trend in the United States to increase the number of outsiders on boards. The typical large U.S. corporation has an average of eleven directors, of whom two are insiders.[10] Even though outsiders account for around 80% of the board members in these large U.S. corporations (approximately the same as in Canada), they only account for about 40% of board membership in small U.S. companies. People who favor a high proportion of outsiders state that outside directors are less biased and more likely to evaluate management's performance objectively than are inside directors. This is the main reason why the New York Stock Exchange requires that all companies listed on the exchange have an audit committee composed entirely of independent, outside members. This view is in agreement with **agency theory,** which states that problems arise in corporations because the agents (top management) are not willing to bear responsibility for their decisions unless they own a substantial amount of stock in the corporation. The theory suggests that a majority of a board needs to be from outside the firm so that top management is prevented from acting selfishly to the detriment of the shareholders. See the **Key Theory** feature for fuller discussion of Agency Theory.

In contrast, those who prefer inside over outside directors contend that outside directors are less effective than are insiders because the outsiders are less likely to have the necessary interest, availability, or competency. Directors may sometimes serve on so many boards that they spread their time and interest too thin to actively fulfill their responsibilities. They could also point out that the term "outsider" is too simplistic—some outsiders are not truly objective and should be considered more as insiders than as outsiders. For example, there can be:

1. *Affiliated* directors who, though not really employed by the corporation, handle the legal or insurance work for the company (thus dependent on the current management for a key part of their business).

2. *Retired* directors who used to work for the company, such as the past CEO (partly responsible for much of the corporation's current strategy and probably groomed the current CEO as his or her replacement).

3. *Family* directors who are descendants of the founder and own significant blocks of stock (with personal agendas based on a family relationship with the current CEO).[11]

The majority of outside directors are active or retired CEOs and COOs of other corporations. Others are academicians, attorneys, consultants, former government officials, major shareholders, and bankers. In Germany, bankers are represented on almost every board—primarily because they own large blocks of stock in German corporations. In Denmark, Sweden, Belgium, and Italy, however, investment companies assume this role. For example, the investment company Investor AB casts 42.5% of the Electrolux AB shareholder votes—thus guaranteeing itself positions on the Electrolux board. Nineteen ninety-five surveys of large U.S. corporations found that 69% of the boards had at least one woman director—up from 60% in 1992 and only 11% in 1972 with one-third now having two female directors.[12] Boards having at least one minority member increased from 9% in 1973 to 47% in 1995 (African-American: 34%; Latino: 9%; Asian: 4%).

The globalization of business has not yet had much impact on board membership. One study of U.S. boards found 37 international (non-U.S.) directors on only 30 out of 100 boards surveyed. Of these, five were insiders and 32 were outsiders.[13] The scarcity of international directors may be changing as more corporations increase their operations around the world. See the 🌐**21st Century Global Society** feature for recent board changes at Hoechst AG.

Outside directors serving on the boards of large U.S. corporations annually earned on average $33,000. Most companies also provided some form of payment through stock options.[14] Directors serving on the boards of small companies usually received much less (around $10,000).

The vast majority of inside directors includes the chief executive officer, chief operating officer, and presidents or vice-presidents of key operating divisions or functional units. Few, if any, inside directors receive any extra compensation for assuming this extra duty. Very rarely does a U.S. board include any lower level operating employees.

KEY THEORY

APPLICATION OF AGENCY THEORY TO CORPORATE GOVERNANCE

Managers of large, modern publicly-held corporations are typically not the owners. In fact, most of today's top managers own only nominal amounts of stock in the corporation they manage. The real owners (shareholders) elect boards of directors who hire managers as their agents to run the firm's day-to-day activities. As suggested in the classic study by Berle and Means, top managers are, in effect, "hired hands" who may very likely be more interested in their personal welfare than that of the shareholders. For example, management might emphasize strategies, such as acquisitions, that increase the size of the firm (to become more powerful and to demand increased pay and benefits) or that diversify the firm into unrelated businesses (to reduce short-term risk and to allow them to put less effort into a core product line that may be facing difficulty), but that result in a reduction in dividends and/or stock price.

Agency theory is concerned with analyzing and resolving two problems that occur in relationships between principals (owners/shareholders) and their agents (top management):

1. *The agency problem* that arises when (a) the desires or objectives of the owners and the agents conflict or (b) it is difficult or expensive for the owners to verify what the agent is actually doing.

2. *The risk sharing problem* that arises when the owners and agents have different attitudes toward risk.

The likelihood that these problems will occur increases when stock is widely held (no one shareholder owns more than a small percentage of the total common stock), when the board of directors is composed of people who know little of the company or who are personal friends of top management, and when a high percentage of board members are inside (management) directors.

To better align the interests of the agents with those of the owners and to increase the corporation's overall performance, agency theory suggests that top management have a significant degree of ownership in the firm and/or have a strong financial stake in its long-term performance. In support of this argument, research does indicate a positive relationship between corporate performance and the amount of stock owned by directors.[15]

Source: For a good summary of agency theory as applied to corporate governance, see J. P. Walsh and J. K. Seward, "On the Efficiency of Internal and External Corporate Control Mechanisms," *Academy of Management Review* (July 1990), pp. 421–458; K. M. Eisenhardt, "Agency Theory: An Assessment and Review," *Academy of Management Review* (January 1989), pp. 57–74; S. L. Oswald and J. S. Jahera, Jr., "The Influence of Ownership on Performance: An Empirical Study," *Strategic Management Journal* (May 1991), pp. 321–326. For background, see also A. A. Berle, Jr. and G. C. Means, *The Modern Corporation and Private Property* (New York: Macmillan, 1932).

Codetermination: Should Employees Serve on Boards?

Codetermination, the inclusion of a corporation's workers on its board, began only recently in the United States. Corporations such as Chrysler, Northwest Airlines, United Airlines (UAL), and Wheeling-Pittsburgh Steel have added representatives from employee associations to their boards as part of union agreements or Employee Stock Ownership Plans (ESOPs). For example, United Airline workers traded 15% in pay cuts for 55% of the company (through an ESOP) and three of the firm's twelve board seats. In this instance, workers represent themselves on the board not so much as employees, but primarily as owners. At Chrysler, however, the United Auto Workers obtained a seat on the board as part of a union contract agreement in exchange for changes in work

HOECHST AG ADDS INTERNATIONAL MEMBERS TO ITS BOARD

The world's biggest chemical firm is based in Germany, but it is increasingly becoming a globally oriented company. For example, two of its six major businesses are located in the United States. Hoechst (pronounced Herkst) now employs more people in the Americas than it does in its home country. According to Chairman Juergen Dormann, "We are not merely a German company with foreign interests. One could almost say we are a nonnational company."

Hoechst expects its sales in the Americas to rise to 40% of the company's total sales by 2000

compared to less than 6% in 1987. To provide an international orientation, Hoechst has added an American and a Brazilian to its nine-member management board. One of their contributions has been to recommend performance-based pay for managers—common in the United States, but very unusual in German corporations.

Source: G. Steinmetz and M. Marshall, "How a Chemical Giant Goes About Becoming a Lot Less German," *Wall Street Journal* (February 18, 1997), pp. A1, A14.

rules and reductions in benefits. In situations like this when a director represents an internal stakeholder, critics raise the issue of conflict of interest. Can a member of the board, who is privy to confidential managerial information, function, for example, as a union leader whose primary duty is to fight for the best benefits for his or her members?

Although the movement to place employees on the boards of directors of U.S. companies shows little likelihood of increasing (except through employee stock ownership), the European experience reveals an increasing acceptance of worker participation (without ownership) on corporate boards. Germany pioneered codetermination during the 1950s with a two-tiered system: a *supervisory board* elected by shareholders and employees to approve or decide corporate strategy and policy and a *management board* (composed primarily of top management) appointed by the supervisory board to manage the company's activities. Worker representatives in specific industries such as coal, iron, and steel were given equal status with management on policy-making supervisory boards. In other industries, however, workers only elect one-third of supervisory board membership. At Siemens AG, for example, shareholders only elect ten people to the supervisory board. Employees of Siemens and "dependent" firms elect seven members with employee labor unions electing three more members for a total of ten. This 20-member supervisory board elects a 17-member management board to actually run the company.[16]

Most other western European countries have either passed similar codetermination legislation (as in Sweden, Denmark, Norway, and Austria) or use worker councils to work closely with management (as in Belgium, Luxembourg, France, Italy, Ireland, and the Netherlands). Nevertheless research on German codetermination found that legislation requiring firms to put employee representatives on their boards lowered dividend payments, led to a more conservative investment policy, and reduced firm values.[17]

Interlocking Directorates

CEOs often nominate chief executives (as well as board members) from other firms to membership on their own boards in order to create an interlocking directorate. A *direct*

interlocking directorate occurs when two firms share a director or when an executive of one firm sits on the board of a second firm. An *indirect* interlock occurs when two corporations have directors who also serve on the board of a third firm, such as a bank.

Although the Clayton Act and the Banking Act of 1933 prohibit interlocking directorates by U.S. companies competing in the same industry, interlocking continues to occur in almost all corporations, especially large ones. Interlocking occurs because large firms have a large impact on other corporations; and these other corporations, in turn, have some control over the firm's inputs and marketplace. For example, most large corporations in the United States, Japan, and Germany are interlocked either directly or indirectly with financial institutions.[18] Interlocking directorates are also a useful method for gaining both inside information about an uncertain environment and objective expertise about potential strategies and tactics. Family-owned corporations, however, are less likely to have interlocking directorates than are corporations with highly dispersed stock ownership, probably because family-owned corporations do not like to dilute their corporate control by adding outsiders to boardroom discussions. Nevertheless some evidence indicates that well-interlocked corporations are better able to survive in a highly competitive environment.[19]

Nomination and Election of Board Members

Traditionally the CEO of the corporation decided whom to invite to board membership and merely asked the shareholders for approval in the annual proxy statement. All nominees were usually elected. There are some dangers, however, in allowing the CEO free rein in nominating directors. The CEO might select only board members who, in the CEO's opinion, will not disturb the company's policies and functioning. Given that the average length of service of a U.S. board member is 8.4 years, CEO-friendly, passive boards are likely to result.[20] Directors selected by the CEO often feel that they should go along with any proposal the CEO makes. Thus board members find themselves accountable to the very management they are charged to oversee. Because this is likely to happen, more boards are using a nominating committee to nominate new outside board members for the shareholders to elect. Approximately 73% of Fortune 500 U.S. corporations now use nominating committees to identify potential directors.

Virtually every corporation whose directors serve terms of more than one year divides the board into classes and staggers elections so that only a portion of the board stands for election each year. Arguments in favor of this practice are that it provides continuity by reducing the chance of an abrupt turnover in its membership and that it reduces the likelihood of electing people unfriendly to management (who might be interested in a hostile takeover) through cumulative voting. An argument against staggered boards is that they make it more difficult for concerned shareholders to curb a CEO's power—especially when that CEO is also Chairman of the Board. For example, out of dissatisfaction with the company's recent poor performance and their perception that the board was inactive, two unions supported a shareholder proposal in 1996 to cancel Kmart's staggered board so that the entire board would be elected annually.

Organization of the Board

The size of the board is determined by the corporation's charter and its bylaws in compliance with state laws. Although some states require a minimum number of board members, most corporations have quite a bit of discretion in determining board size. The average large, publicly-held firm has around 11 directors. The average small/medium size privately-held company has approximately seven to eight members.

In 1995, 68% of the top executives of large, U.S. publicly-held corporations held the dual designation of chairman and CEO, a drop from 72% just one year earlier. (The percentage of firms having the Chair/CEO position combined in Canada and the United Kingdom is 43% and 20%, respectively.)[21] The combined Chair/CEO position is being increasingly criticized because of the potential for conflict of interest. The CEO is supposed to concentrate on strategy, planning, external relations, and responsibility to the board. The chairman's responsibility is to ensure that the board and its committees perform their functions as stated in the board's charter. Further, the chairman schedules board meetings and presides over the annual shareholders' meeting. Critics of combining the two offices in one person ask how the board can properly oversee top management if the chairman is also top management. For this reason, the chairman and CEO roles are separated by law in Germany, the Netherlands, and Finland. A similar law is being considered in Britain and Australia. Although the majority of research does suggest that firms that separate the two positions outperform financially those firms that combine the offices, some studies have found no significant difference in operating performance.[22]

Many of those who prefer that the chairman and CEO positions be combined do agree that the outside directors should elect a **lead director.** This person would be consulted by the Chair/CEO regarding board affairs and would coordinate the annual evaluation of the CEO.[23] The lead director position is very popular in the United Kingdom where it originated. Of those U.S. companies combining the chair and CEO positions, 27% currently have a lead director. This is one way to give the board more power without undermining the power of the Chair/CEO.

The most effective boards accomplish much of their work through committees. Although they do not usually have legal duties, most committees are granted full power to act with the authority of the board between board meetings. Typical standing committees are the executive, audit, compensation, finance, and nominating committees. The executive committee is formed from local directors who can meet between board meetings to attend to matters that must be settled quickly. This committee acts as an extension of the board and, consequently, may have almost unrestricted authority in certain areas.

Trends in Corporate Governance

The role of the board of directors in the strategic management of the corporation is likely to be more active in the future. The change will probably be more evolutionary, however, rather than radical or revolutionary. Different boards are at different levels of maturity and will not be changing in the same direction or at the same speed.

Some of today's **trends in governance** that are likely to continue include:

- Institutional investors, such as pension funds, mutual funds, and insurance companies, are becoming active on boards and are putting increasing pressure on top management to improve corporate performance. For example, the California Public Employees' Retirement System (CalPERS), the largest pension system in the United States, annually publishes a list of poorly performing companies, hoping to embarrass management into remedial action.

- As corporations become more global, they will increasingly add international directors to their boards.

- Shareholders are demanding that directors and top managers own more than token amounts of stock in the corporation. Stock is increasingly being used as part of a director's compensation.

- Outside or nonmanagement directors are increasing their numbers and power in publicly-held corporations as CEOs loosen their grip on boards. Outsiders are now taking charge of annual CEO evaluations.

- Boards will continue to take more control of board functions by either splitting the combined Chair/CEO into two separate positions or establishing a lead outside director position.

- Society, in the form of special interest groups, increasingly expects boards of directors to balance the economic goal of profitability with the social needs of society. Issues dealing with workforce diversity and the environment are now reaching the board level. For example, the board of Chase Manhattan Corporation recently questioned top management about its efforts to improve the sparse number of women and minorities in senior management.[24] Although many CEOs are resisting such issues, the battle is only just beginning. See the **Strategy in a Changing World** feature for one CEO's heated argument with a nun regarding her suggestion to add women to his company's board of directors.

2.2 Corporate Governance: The Role of Top Management

The top management function is usually conducted by the CEO of the corporation in coordination with the COO (Chief Operating Officer) or president, executive vice-president, and vice-presidents of divisions and functional areas. Even though strategic management involves everyone in the organization, the board of directors holds top management primarily responsible for the strategic management of the firm.[25]

Responsibilities of Top Management

Top management responsibilities, especially those of the CEO, involve getting things accomplished through and with others in order to meet the corporate objectives. Top management's job is thus multidimensional and is oriented toward the welfare of the total organization. Specific top management tasks vary from firm to firm and are developed from an analysis of the mission, objectives, strategies, and key activities of the corporation. The chief executive officer, in particular, must successfully handle two responsibilities crucial to the effective strategic management of the corporation: (1) *provide executive leadership and a strategic vision,* and (2) *manage the strategic planning process.*

Executive Leadership and Strategic Vision

Executive leadership is the directing of activities toward the accomplishment of corporate objectives. Executive leadership is important because it sets the tone for the entire corporation. A **strategic vision** is a description of what the company is capable of becoming. It is often communicated in the mission statement. People in an organization want to have a sense of mission, but only top management is in the position to specify and communicate this strategic vision to the general workforce. Top management's enthusiasm (or lack of it) about the corporation tends to be contagious. The importance of executive leadership is illustrated by John Welch, Jr., the successful Chairman and CEO of General Electric Company (GE). According to Welch: "Good business leaders create a vision, articulate the vision, passionately own the vision, and relentlessly drive it to completion."[26]

BOARD QUALIFICATIONS: DIVERSITY OR TECHNICAL COMPETENCE?

In her position as Director of Corporate Social Responsibility, Sister Doris Gormley of the Sisters of St. Francis of Philadelphia is responsible for ensuring that investments by her order of nuns—investments selected by professional financial advisers—don't violate the order's principles of social responsibility. The order, composed of 1,000 nuns, has a portfolio that is primarily used to support aging and retired nuns. Among other things, she examines proxy statements (asking shareholders to vote on nominees to the board and other proposals) to ascertain if a corporation's board of directors includes women and minorities. If a corporation does not, she sends it a form letter explaining the order's policy to withhold voting on any nominees or proposals by boards that don't contain qualified women and minorities. The letter, routinely sent each year to about 200 of the corporations in which the order owns stock, says in part:

> We believe that a company is best represented by a Board of qualified Directors reflecting the equality of the sexes, races, and ethnic groups. As women and minorities continue to move into upper level management positions of economic, educational, and cultural institutions, the number of qualified Board candidates also increases.

In the twelve years that Sister Doris has been sending this letter, most companies have responded politely, either explaining why they weren't pursuing board diversity or that they would keep her thoughts in mind when board vacancies occurred.

T. J. Rodgers, CEO of Cypress Semiconductor Corporation, however, took exception to the April 1996 letter. He was so incensed by her suggestion, he wrote her a six-page letter, which he distributed to Cypress shareholders. According to Rodgers, "a 'woman's view' on how to run our

semiconductor company does not help us, unless that woman has an advanced technical degree and experience as a CEO." He goes on to say that few women or minorities fit that description. A search for a director "usually yields a male who is 50-plus years old." Rodgers continues by saying:

> You ought to get down from your moral high horse. Your views seem more accurately described as 'politically correct' than 'Christian.' Choosing a Board of Directors based on race and gender is a lousy way to run a company. Cypress will never do it. . . . Bowing to special interest groups is an immoral way to run a company.

In little over a month after writing his response to Sister Doris, Rodgers received over 200 letters—only 15 of which were critical. The chairmen of Hewlett-Packard and Advanced Micro Devices as well as other corporate executives wrote to congratulate him. "Splendid letter," responded economist Milton Friedman.

For her part, Sister Doris was surprised by all the furor. She indicated that her form letter had nothing to do with "political correctness," but simply reflected "concern for the social integrity of business." Because her order owned 7,000 shares of Cypress stock at the time, Sister Doris felt that Rodgers' letter had failed to respect her shareholder rights. Stating that Rodgers' perspective on desired qualifications for a board position were extremely narrow, Sister Doris contended that the company might benefit from the views of other kinds of competent business people. "I would think that in 1996, even in the semiconductor industry, there are beginning to be qualified women and people of color."

Source: E. J. Pollock, "CEO Takes On a Nun in a Crusade Against 'Political Correctness,'" *Wall Street Journal* (July 15, 1996), pp. A1 and A7.

Chief executive officers with a clear strategic vision are often perceived as dynamic and charismatic leaders. For instance, the positive attitude characterizing many well-known industrial leaders—such as Bill Gates at Microsoft, Anita Roddick at The Body Shop, Ted Turner at CNN, Herb Kelleher at Southwest Airlines, and Andy Grove at Intel—has energized their respective corporations. They are able to command respect and to influence strategy formulation and implementation because they tend to have three key characteristics:

1. **The CEO articulates a strategic vision** for the corporation. The CEO envisions the company not as it currently is, but as it can become. The new perspective that the CEO's vision brings to activities and conflicts gives renewed meaning to everyone's work and enables employees to see beyond the details of their own jobs to the functioning of the total corporation.

2. **The CEO presents a role** for others to identify with and to follow. The leader sets an example in terms of behavior and dress. The CEO's attitudes and values concerning the corporation's purpose and activities are clear-cut and constantly communicated in words and deeds.

3. **The CEO communicates high performance standards but also shows confidence in the followers' abilities** to meet these standards. No leader ever improved performance by setting easily attainable goals that provided no challenge. The CEO must be willing to follow through by coaching people.

See the **Strategy in a Changing World** feature to learn how George Fisher provided executive leadership to Kodak.

Manage the Strategic Planning Process

As business corporations adopt more of the characteristics of the learning organization, strategic planning initiatives can now come from any part of an organization. However, unless top management encourages and supports the planning process, strategic management is not likely to result. In most corporations, top management must initiate and manage the strategic planning process. It may do so by first asking business units and functional areas to propose strategic plans for themselves, or it may begin by drafting an overall corporate plan within which the units can then build their own plans. Other organizations engage in concurrent strategic planning in which all the organization's units draft plans for themselves after they have been provided with the organization's overall mission and objectives.

Regardless of the approach taken, the typical board of directors expects top management to manage the overall strategic planning process so that the plans of all the units and functional areas fit together into an overall corporate plan. Top management's job therefore includes the tasks of evaluating unit plans and providing feedback. To do this, it may require each unit to justify its proposed objectives, strategies, and programs in terms of how well they satisfy the organization's overall objectives in light of available resources.[27]

Many large organizations have a **strategic planning staff** charged with supporting both top management and the business units in the strategic planning process. This planning staff typically consists of just under ten people, headed by a senior vice-president or director of corporate planning. The staff's major responsibilities are to:

1. Identify and analyze companywide strategic issues, and suggest corporate strategic alternatives to top management.

STRATEGY IN A CHANGING WORLD

EXECUTIVE LEADERSHIP AT EASTMAN KODAK

When George Fisher replaced Kay Whitmore as CEO of Eastman Kodak in 1993, the outlook for the company was dismal. The workforce had been dispirited by the loss of 40,000 jobs in five downsizings. Despite $10 billion in investments over the past decade, Kodak's nearly 100% U.S. market share in film had fallen to 70%, earnings per share had only grown 12¢, and long-term debt had risen to 66% of capital. Rather than simply cut costs quickly, as expected by the board of directors, Fisher committed the company to new imaging opportunities and the divestment of non-core businesses. He had a new vision for Kodak's future, one in which the company gave up its dedication to chemical-based film technology in favor of new electronic photography. The Wall Street community, however, was not only unimpressed, it questioned Kodak's very ability to undertake meaningful strategic change.

During the next three years, Fisher worked hard to turn Kodak around. He sold unrelated businesses that had been acquired during an earlier diversification and poured money into new product development. He successfully pushed for improvements in quality and efficiency.

Fisher is aware that in addition to obtaining profitable growth from today's chemistry-based photo products, he must ensure that the company is researching, developing, and marketing digital-electronic systems for the future. As a result, he is attempting to boost motivation for growing current products by encouraging the company's employees to innovate, differentiate products from competitors', and be more aggressive internationally. He also supports and encourages new developments in digital imaging that won't even begin to be profitable until 1997.

Nevertheless, during the 1995 fiscal year, Kodak earned a respectable $1.3 billion on sales of $15 billion and debt fell to only 11.5% of capital. In 1996, analyst Alex Henderson even advised clients to buy Eastman Kodak's stock. In 1997, after another year of improved corporate performance, the board increased Fisher's compensation package and extended his contract (which was to have expired in 1998) until 2000. Wall Street is no longer betting against George Fisher!

Source: L. Grant, "The Bears Back Off Kodak," *Fortune* (June 24, 1996), pp. 24–25; E. Nelson, "Eastman Kodak CEO Fisher Extends Employment Contract Through 2000," *Wall Street Journal* (February 27, 1997), p. B9.

2. Work as facilitators with business units to guide them through the strategic planning process.

To fulfill these responsibilities, the planning staff must have an in-depth knowledge of the principal techniques used in the strategic planning process. One recent survey of nearly 50 corporations from a variety of countries and industries listed the most popular strategic planning techniques in order of general usage:

- Core competencies analysis—72%
- Scenario planning—69%
- Benchmarking—56%
- Total Quality Management—44%
- Shareholder value analysis—44%

- Value chain analysis—44%

- Business process redesign (re-engineering)—33%

- Time-based competition—25%[28]

2.3   *Social Responsibilities of Strategic Decision Makers*

Should strategic decision makers be responsible only to shareholders or do they have broader responsibilities? The concept of **social responsibility** proposes that a private corporation has responsibilities to society that extend beyond making a profit. Strategic decisions often affect more than just the corporation. A decision to retrench by closing some plants and discontinuing product lines, for example, affects not only the firm's workforce, but also the communities where the plants are located and the customers with no other source of the discontinued product. Such situations raise questions of the appropriateness of certain missions, objectives, and strategies of business corporations. Managers must be able to deal with these conflicting interests in an ethical manner to formulate a viable strategic plan.

Responsibilities of a Business Firm

What are the responsibilities of a business firm and how much of them must be fulfilled? Milton Friedman and Archie Carroll offer two contrasting views of the responsibilities of business firms to society.

Friedman's Traditional View of Business Responsibility

Urging a return to a laissez-faire worldwide economy with a minimum of government regulation, Milton Friedman argues against the concept of social responsibility. A business person who acts "responsibly" by cutting the price of the firm's product to prevent inflation, or by making expenditures to reduce pollution, or by hiring the hard-core unemployed, according to Friedman, is spending the shareholder's money for a general social interest. Even if the business person has shareholder permission or encouragement to do so, he or she is still acting from motives other than economic and may, in the long run, harm the very society the firm is trying to help. By taking on the burden of these social costs, the business becomes less efficient—either prices go up to pay for the increased costs or investment in new activities and research is postponed. These results negatively affect—perhaps fatally—the long-term efficiency of a business. Friedman thus referred to the social responsibility of business as a "fundamentally subversive doctrine" and stated that:

> There is one and only one social responsibility of business—to use its resources and engage in activities designed to increase its profits so long as it stays within the rules of the game, which is to say, engages in open and free competition without deception or fraud.[29]

Carroll's Four Responsibilities of Business

As shown in Figure 2.2, Archie Carroll proposes that the managers of business organizations have **four responsibilities**: economic, legal, ethical, and discretionary.[30]

Figure 2.2
Responsibilities of Business

Source: Adapted from A. B. Carroll, "A Three Dimensional Conceptual Model of Corporate Performance," *Academy of Management Review* (October 1979), p. 499. Reprinted with permission.

1. **Economic** responsibilities of a business organization's management are to produce goods and services of value to society so that the firm may repay its creditors and shareholders.

2. **Legal** responsibilities are defined by governments in laws that management is expected to obey. For example, U.S. business firms are required to hire and promote people based on their credentials rather than to discriminate on non–job-related characteristics such as race, gender, or religion.

3. **Ethical** responsibilities of an organization's management are to follow the generally held beliefs about behavior in a society. For example, society generally expects firms to work with the employees and the community in planning for layoffs, even though no law may require this. The affected people can get very upset if an organization's management fails to act according to generally prevailing ethical values.

4. **Discretionary** responsibilities are the purely voluntary obligations a corporation assumes. Examples are philanthropic contributions, training the hard-core unemployed, and providing day-care centers. The difference between ethical and discretionary responsibilities is that few people expect an organization to fulfill discretionary responsibilities, whereas many expect an organization to fulfill ethical ones.[31]

Carroll lists these four responsibilities *in order of priority.* A business firm must first make a profit to satisfy its economic responsibilities. To continue in existence, the firm must follow the laws—thus fulfilling its legal responsibilities. To this point Carroll and Friedman are in agreement. Carroll, however, goes further by arguing that business managers have responsibilities beyond the economic and legal ones.

Having satisfied the two basic responsibilities, according to Carroll, the firm should look to fulfilling its social responsibilities. **Social responsibility,** *therefore, includes both ethical and discretionary, but not economic and legal responsibilities.* A firm can fulfill its ethical responsibilities by taking actions that society tends to value but has not yet put into law. When ethical responsibilities are satisfied, a firm can focus on discretionary responsibilities—purely voluntary actions that society has not yet decided are important.

The discretionary responsibilities of today may become the ethical responsibilities of tomorrow. The provision of day-care facilities is, for example, moving rapidly from a discretionary to an ethical responsibility. Carroll suggests that to the extent that business corporations fail to acknowledge discretionary or ethical responsibilities, society, through government, will act, making them legal responsibilities. Government may do this, moreover, without regard to an organization's economic responsibilities. As a result, the organization may have greater difficulty in earning a profit than it would have had if it had voluntarily assumed some ethical and discretionary responsibilities.

Both Friedman and Carroll argue their positions based on the impact of socially responsible actions on a firm's profits. Friedman says that socially responsible actions hurt a firm's efficiency. Carroll proposes that a lack of social responsibility results in increased government regulations, which reduce a firm's efficiency. Research has failed, unfortunately, to consistently support either position. There is no clear relationship between social responsibility and financial performance.[32]

As a matter of fact, refusing to live up to the expectations of society can sometimes pay off. For example, three firms that remained in segregated South Africa during the economic sanctions of the 1980s—Colgate-Palmolive, Johnson & Johnson, and 3M—were damned in shareholder resolutions, college demonstrations, and informal boycotts of their products. They were, however, able to expand their base quickly once apartheid ended and now dominate their South African markets. Firms that lived up to society's expectations by leaving are finding it very difficult to return to South Africa because they are now at a competitive disadvantage. McDonald's, which pulled its operations out of South Africa during apartheid, lost its right to its trademark during the firm's absence.

In contrast, firms that are known to be ethical and socially responsible often enjoy some benefits that may even provide them a competitive advantage. Some examples of these benefits are:

- Their environmental concerns may enable them to charge premium prices and gain brand loyalty (Ben & Jerry's Ice Cream).

- Their trustworthiness may help them generate enduring relationships with suppliers and distributors without needing to spend a lot of time and money policing contracts (Maytag).

- They can attract outstanding employees at less than the market rate (Procter & Gamble).

- They are more likely to be welcomed into a foreign country (Levi Strauss).

- They can utilize the goodwill of public officials for support in difficult times (Minnesota supported Dayton-Hudson's fight to avoid being acquired by Dart Industries of Maryland).

- They are more likely to attract capital infusions from investors who view reputable companies as desirable long-term investments (Rubbermaid).[33]

Corporate Stakeholders

The concept that business must be socially responsible sounds appealing until we ask, "Responsible to whom?" A corporation's task environment includes a large number of groups with interest in a business organization's activities. These groups are referred to as **corporate stakeholders** because they affect or are affected by the achievement of the firm's objectives.[34] Should a corporation be responsible only to some of these groups, or does business have an equal responsibility to all of them?

In any one strategic decision, the interests of one stakeholder group can conflict with another. For example, a business firm's decision to use only recycled materials in its manufacturing process may have a positive effect on environmental groups but a

COMPANY SPOTLIGHT

Location Decision

Throughout its history, Maytag Corporation has tried to act responsibly in light of the various concerns of its many stakeholder groups. Even though the corporation has kept its headquarters in Newton, Iowa, the acquisitions of Magic Chef and Hoover had meant that Maytag Corporation had to view things differently from Maytag Company. The company previously made only Maytag-brand major appliances in Newton, Iowa. The corporation now makes Maytag, Admiral, Magic Chef, Jenn-Air, Hardwick, Norge, and Hoover brand appliances, as well as Dixie-Narco vending machines, throughout North America and the world. Maytag Corporation's top management (many of whom came from Maytag Company) has to consider not only their responsibilities to the stakeholders of Maytag Company, but also their responsibilities to the various stakeholders of Magic Chef, Jenn-Air, Hoover, Admiral, and Dixie-Narco, as well as those stakeholders of the corporation as a whole. This has not been easy.

Maytag's reputation as a good corporate citizen was tarnished in 1990 by its decision to move dishwasher manufacturing from Newton to Jackson, Tennessee. Chairman and CEO Daniel Krumm announced that Maytag would consolidate the manufacturing of all the brands marketed by the corporation into one large, highly efficient plant.

Lonnie White, President of United Auto Workers Local 997 (the bargaining unit representing Maytag Company unionized employees in Newton, Iowa), responded with dismay to top management's decision. "Where is their commitment to the community and the state of Iowa?" asked White. "They can add a facility here in Newton to do the same thing that they're doing in Jackson, Tennessee." Pointing out that Maytag owned plenty of unused land in Newton, White contended that there could be only three reasons management would move dishwasher production to Tennessee: (1) to escape union shop, (2) to reduce wage costs, and (3) to cut benefits. "The Newton dishwasher line is only running one shift. Other lines run two shifts," said White in response to the statement that the line was near capacity. He indicated that the union was not so much concerned with itself as it was with the impact on local communities and the need to avoid "community cannibalism."

MAYTAG CORPORATION

negative effect on shareholder dividends. See the **Company Spotlight on Maytag Corporation** feature for a description of the firm's decision to move dishwasher production from Iowa to a lower wage location. On the one hand, shareholders were generally pleased with the decision because it would lower costs. On the other hand, Iowa officials and local union people were very unhappy at what they called "community cannibalism." Which group's interests should have priority?

Given the wide range of interests and concerns present in any organization's task environment, one or more groups, at any one time, probably will be dissatisfied with an organization's activities—even if management is trying to be socially responsible. As shown in the **Strategy in a Changing World** feature on Kathy Lee Gifford, a company may have some stakeholders of which it is only marginally aware. Therefore, before making a strategic decision, strategic managers should consider how each alternative will affect various stakeholder groups. What seems at first to be the best decision because it appears to be the most profitable may actually result in the worst set of consequences to the corporation.

KATHY LEE GIFFORD HAS SOME BAD DAYS

Should a company be concerned if some of its suppliers in developing countries are abusing their workers, employing child labor, and paying near starvation wages? Many companies would probably say that although such practices are regrettable, the internal practices of other companies (especially in other countries) is not their concern. In 1996, however, a human rights advocacy group accused U.S. clothing manufacturers and retailers Eddie Bauer, J. Crew, Kmart, and Wal-Mart of selling products made by underage Honduran workers under sweatshop conditions. Charles Kernaghan, executive director of the National Labor Committee Education Fund in Support of Worker and Human Rights in Central America, charged television personality Kathy Lee Gifford with supporting Wal-Mart's use of sweatshop suppliers by advertising the clothing.

Upon learning of these practices in the national media, Ms. Gifford and Wal-Mart severed ties with the Honduran plant employing children and with a New York sweatshop producing goods in Gifford's name. Following the uproar, President Clinton announced a labeling agreement with ten manufacturers stating that they would ensure that their products are manufactured under decent conditions and that they will identify clothes not made under these exploitative conditions.

Very little attention was paid by the media to an argument raised by Lucy Martinez-Mont, a professor of economics in Guatemala:

> The likely impact of Ms. Gifford's crusade on Central America frightens me. If it drives businesses to leave the region altogether, it will kill jobs and worsen living conditions for the poor. . . . People choose to work in the maquila shops of their own free will, because these are the best jobs available to them. Given that unemployment compensation is unheard of in Central America, a lousy job is always better than no job at all.[35]

Following the resolution of the sweatshop incidents, Gifford received a letter from a marine ministry association urging her to disassociate herself from the cruise industry (Gifford appears in ads for Carnival Cruise Lines) because of its exploitation of foreign crew members.

2.4 *Ethical Decision Making*

Some people joke that there is no such thing as "business ethics." They call it an oxymoron—a concept that combines opposite or contradictory ideas. Unfortunately there is some truth to this sarcastic comment. For example, a 1996 survey by the Ethics Resource Center of 1,324 employees of 747 American companies found that 48% of employees surveyed said that they had engaged in one or more unethical and/or illegal actions during the past year. The most common questionable behavior involved cutting corners on quality (16%), covering up incidents (14%), abusing or lying about sick days (11%), and lying to or deceiving customers (9%). Some 56% of workers reported pressure to act unethically or illegally on the job.[36]

Some Reasons for Unethical Behavior

Why are many business people perceived to be acting unethically? It may be that the involved people are not even aware that they are doing something questionable. There is no worldwide standard of conduct for business people. Cultural norms and values vary between countries and even between different geographic regions and ethnic groups within a country. For example, what is considered in one country to be a bribe to expedite service is sometimes considered in another country to be normal business practice.

Another possible reason for what is often perceived to be unethical behavior lies in differences in values between business people and key stakeholders. Some business people may believe profit maximization is the key goal of their firm, whereas concerned interest groups may have other priorities, such as the hiring of minorities and women or the safety of their neighborhoods. Of the six values measured by the Allport-Vernon-Lindzey Study of Values test (*aesthetic, economic, political, religious, social,* and *theoretical*), both U.S. and British executives consistently score highest on economic and political values and lowest on social and religious ones. This is similar to the value profile of managers from Japan, Korea, India, and Australia, as well as those of American business school students. U.S. Protestant ministers, in contrast, score highest on religious and social values and very low on economic values.[37]

This difference in values can make it difficult for one group of people to understand another's actions. For example, even though some people feel that the advertising of cigarettes (especially to youth) is unethical, the people managing these companies respond that they are simply offering a product—"*Let the buyer beware*" is a traditional saying in free market capitalism. They argue that customers in a free market democracy have the right to choose how they spend their money and live their lives. Social progressives may contend that business people working in tobacco, alcoholic beverages, and gambling industries are acting unethically by making and advertising products with potentially dangerous and expensive side effects, such as cancer, alcoholism, and addiction. People working in these industries could respond by asking if it is ethical for people who don't smoke, drink, or gamble to reject another person's right to do so.

Moral Relativism

Some people justify their seeming unethical positions by arguing that there is no one absolute code of ethics and that morality is relative. Simply put, **moral relativism** claims that morality is relative to some personal, social, or cultural standard and that there is no method for deciding whether one decision is better than another.

Adherents of moral relativism may believe that all moral decisions are deeply personal and that individuals have the right to run their own lives; each person should be allowed to interpret situations and act on his or her own moral values. They may also argue that social roles carry with them certain obligations to those roles only. A manager in charge of a department, for example, must put aside his or her personal beliefs and do instead what the role requires, that is, act in the best interests of the department. They could also argue that a decision is legitimate if it is common practice regardless of other considerations ("Everyone's doing it"). Some propose that morality itself is relative to a particular culture, society, or community. People should therefore "understand" the practices of other countries, but not judge them. If the citizens of another country share certain norms and customs, what right does an outsider have to criticize them?

Although these arguments make some sense, moral relativism could enable a person to justify almost any sort of decision or action, so long as it is not declared illegal.

Kohlberg's Levels of Moral Development

Another reason why some business people might be seen as unethical is that they may have no well-developed personal sense of ethics. A person's ethical behavior will be affected by his or her level of moral development, certain personality variables, and such situational factors as the job itself, the supervisor, and the organizational culture.[38] Kohlberg proposes that a person progresses through three levels of moral development.[39] Similar in some ways to Maslow's hierarchy of needs, the individual moves from total self-centeredness to a concern for universal values. Kohlberg's three levels are as follows:

1. **The preconventional level** is characterized by a concern for *self*. Small children and others who have not progressed beyond this stage evaluate behaviors on the basis of personal interest—avoiding punishment or quid pro quo.

2. **The conventional level** is characterized by considerations of society's *laws* and *norms*. Actions are justified by an external code of conduct.

3. **The principled level** is characterized by a person's adherence to an *internal moral code*. The individual at this level looks beyond norms or laws to find universal values or principles.

Kohlberg places most people in the conventional level, with less than 20% of U.S. adults in the principled level of development.[40]

Encouraging Ethical Behavior

Following Carroll's work, if business people do not act ethically, government will be forced to pass laws regulating their actions—and usually increasing their costs. For self interest, if for no other reason, managers should be more ethical in their decision making. One way to do that is by encouraging codes of ethics. Another is by providing guidelines for ethical behavior.

Codes of Ethics

Codes of ethics specify how an organization expects its employees to behave while on the job. Developing codes of ethics can be a useful way to promote ethical behavior, especially for people who are operating at Kohlberg's conventional level of moral development. Such codes are currently being used by about half of American business corporations. According to a report by the Business Roundtable, an association of CEOs from 200 major U.S. corporations, the importance of a code is that it (1) clarifies company expectations of employee conduct in various situations and (2) makes clear that the company expects its people to recognize the ethical dimensions in decisions and actions.[41]

Various studies do indicate that an increasing number of companies are developing codes of ethics and implementing ethics training workshops and seminars. However, research also indicates that when faced with a question of ethics, managers tend to ignore codes of ethics and try to solve their dilemma on their own.[42] To combat this tendency, the management of a company that wants to improve its employees' ethical behavior should not only develop a comprehensive code of ethics, but also communicate the code in its training programs, performance appraisal system, in policies and procedures, and through its own actions. It may also want to do the same for those companies with which it does business. For example, Reebok International has developed a set of production standards for the manufacturers that supply the company with its athletic shoes on a contract basis. See the **Strategy in a Changing World** feature for Reebok's human rights standards.

REEBOK DEMANDS HUMAN RIGHTS STANDARDS FROM ITS SUPPLIERS

Reebok International, the well-known athletic shoe company, contracts with independent companies in Asia to manufacture all of its footwear products. Although low cost and high-quality production are important to Reebok, the company is also concerned with the human rights record of its suppliers. Consequently it requires its suppliers to follow the following Human Rights Production Standards:

- **Non-Discrimination.** Reebok will seek business partners that do not discriminate in hiring and employment practices on grounds of race, color, national origin, gender, religion, or political or other opinion.

- **Working Hours/Overtime.** Reebok will seek business partners who do not require more than 60-hour work weeks on a regularly scheduled basis, except for appropriately compensated overtime in compliance with local laws, and will favor business partners who use 48-hour work weeks as their maximum normal requirement.

- **Forced or Compulsory Labor.** Reebok will not work with business partners that use forced or other compulsory labor, including labor that was required as a means of political coercion or as punishment for peacefully expressing political views, in the manufacture of its products. Reebok will not purchase materials that were produced by forced prison or other compulsory labor and will terminate business relationships with any sources found to utilize such labor.

- **Fair Wages.** Reebok will seek business partners who share a commitment to the betterment of wage and benefit levels that address the basic needs of workers and their families so far as is possible and appropriate in light of national practices and conditions. Reebok will not select business partners that pay less than the minimum wage required by local law or that pay less than prevailing local industry practices (whichever was higher).

- **Child Labor.** Reebok will not work with business partners that use child labor. The term "child" generally refers to a person who was less than 14 years of age, or younger than the age for completing compulsory education if that age was higher than 14. In countries where the law defines "child" to include individuals who were older than 14, Reebok will apply that definition.

- **Freedom of Association.** Reebok will seek business partners that share its commitment to the right of employees to establish and join organizations of their own choosing. Reebok will seek to assure that no employee was penalized because of his or her nonviolent exercise of this right. Reebok recognizes and respects the right of all employees to organize and bargain collectively.

- **Safe and Healthy Work Environment.** Reebok will seek business partners that strive to assure employees a safe and healthy workplace and that do not expose workers to hazardous conditions.

Source: Reebok International, Ltd., "Reebok Human Rights Production Standards," company document.

Guidelines for Ethical Behavior

According to Von der Embse and Wagley, **ethics** is defined as the consensually accepted standards of behavior for an occupation, trade, or profession. **Morality,** in contrast, is the precepts of personal behavior based on religious or philosophical grounds. **Law** refers to formal codes that permit or forbid certain behaviors and may or may not enforce ethics or morality.[43] Given these definitions, how do we arrive at a comprehensive statement of ethics to use in making decisions in a specific occupation, trade, or profession? A starting point for such a code of ethics is to consider the *three basic approaches to ethical behavior*:[44]

1. **Utilitarian approach:** This approach proposes that actions and plans should be judged by their consequences. People should therefore behave in such a way that will produce the greatest benefit to society and produce the least harm or the lowest cost. A problem with this approach is the difficulty in recognizing all the benefits and the costs of any particular decision. It is likely that only the most obvious stakeholders may be considered, and others may be "conveniently" forgotten.

2. **Individual rights approach:** This approach proposes that human beings have certain fundamental rights that should be respected in all decisions. A particular decision or behavior should be avoided if it interferes with the rights of others. A problem with this approach is in defining "fundamental rights." The U.S. Constitution includes a Bill of Rights that may or may not be accepted throughout the world. The approach can also encourage selfish behavior when a person defines a personal need or want as a "right."

3. **Justice approach:** This approach proposes that decision makers be equitable, fair, and impartial in the distribution of costs and benefits to individuals and groups. It follows the principles of *distributive justice* (people who are similar on relevant dimensions such as job seniority should be treated in the same way) and *fairness* (liberty should be equal for all persons). The justice approach can also include the concepts of *retributive justice* (punishment should be proportional to the "crime") and *compensatory justice* (wrongs should be compensated in proportion to the offense). Affirmative action issues such as reverse discrimination are examples of conflicts between distributive and compensatory justice.

Cavanagh proposes that we solve ethical problems by asking the following three questions regarding an act or decision:

1. **Utility:** Does it optimize the satisfactions of all stakeholders?

2. **Rights:** Does it respect the rights of the individuals involved?

3. **Justice:** Is it consistent with the canons of justice?

For example, is padding an expense account ethical or not? Using the utility criterion, this action increases the company's costs and thus does not optimize benefits for shareholders or customers. Using the rights approach, a person has no right to the money (otherwise we wouldn't call it "padding"). Using the justice criterion, salary and commissions constitute ordinary compensation, but expense accounts only compensate a person for expenses incurred in doing his or her job—expenses that the person would not normally incur except in doing this job.[45]

Another approach to resolving ethical dilemmas is by applying the logic of the philosopher Immanual Kant. Kant presents two principles (called categorical imperatives) to guide our actions:

1. *A person's action is ethical only if that person is willing for that same action to be taken by everyone who is in a similar situation.* This is same as the *Golden Rule*: Treat others as you would like them to treat you. For example, padding an expense account would be considered ethical if the person were also willing for everyone to do the same if

he or she were the boss. Because it is very doubtful that any manager would be pleased with expense account padding, the action must be considered unethical.

2. *A person should never treat another human being simply as a means, but always as an end.* This means that an action is morally wrong for a person if that person uses others merely as means for advancing his or her own interests. To be moral, the act should not restrict another people's actions so that they are left disadvantaged in some way.[46]

2.5 *Global Issues for the 21st Century*

- The **21st Century Global Society** feature in this chapter described a German-based corporation adding non-Germans to its board of directors. As business firms become increasingly global, their boards of directors may need to become more international in terms of their composition and orientation.

- Although codetermination seems to be primarily a European experience, it is likely that employees at all levels will continue to become more involved in strategic management.

- When making and approving strategic decisions, boards of directors will find that they must consider the interests of *all* key stakeholders and not just those of the people who own stock in the corporation. To avoid unwanted government interference, boards must ensure that management's actions do not antagonize any important stakeholders.

- Questions of diversity in the workplace and the human rights of employees are beginning to impact strategic decision making. Companies such as Reebok and Nike have been criticized for paying low wages to female workers in emerging economies.

- The ability to articulate a strategic vision and motivate people to achieve it may soon be the most important characteristic required of a chief executive officer.

- As business firms become increasingly multinational in scope, they will need to justify their strategic and operational decisions on a basis other than self-interest through moral relativism.

Projections for the 21st Century

- From 1994 to 2010, the world population will grow from 5.607 billion to 7.32 billion.

- From 1994 to 2010, the number of nations will increase from 192 to 202.[47]

Discussion Questions

1. Does a corporation really need a board of directors?

2. What recommendations would you make to improve the effectiveness of today's boards of directors?

3. What is the relationship between corporate governance and social responsibility?

4. What is your opinion of Reebok's production standards of human rights for its suppliers? What would Milton Friedman say? Contrast his view with Archie Carroll's view.

5. Does a company have to act selflessly to be considered socially responsible? For example, when building a new plant, a corporation voluntarily invested in additional equipment enabling it to reduce its pollution emissions beyond any current laws. Knowing that it would be very expensive for its competitors to do the same, the firm lobbied the government to make pollution regulations more restrictive on the entire industry. Is this company socially responsible? Were its managers acting ethically?

Key Terms

active board (p. 29)
agency theory (p. 30)
board of directors continuum (p. 28)
board of director responsibilities (p. 27)
board role in strategic management (p. 27)
Carroll's four responsibilities (p. 39)
catalyst board (p. 29)
codes of ethics (p. 45)
codetermination (p. 31)
corporate governance (p. 26)
corporate stakeholders (p. 41)

corporation (p. 26)
due care (p. 27)
ethics (p. 46)
executive leadership (p. 35)
individual rights approach (p. 47)
inside directors (p. 29)
interlocking directorate (p. 33)
justice approach (p. 47)
law (p. 46)
lead director (p. 34)
levels of moral development (p. 44)
minimal participation board (p. 29)
moral relativism (p. 44)

morality (p. 46)
nominal participation board (p. 29)
outside directors (p. 29)
phantom board (p. 29)
rubber stamp board (p. 29)
social responsibility (p. 40)
strategic planning staff (p. 37)
strategic vision (p. 35)
top management responsibilities (p. 35)
trends in governance (p. 34)
utilitarian approach (p. 47)

Strategic Practice Exercise

How far should people in a business firm go in gathering competitive intelligence? Where do *you* draw the line?

   Evaluate each of the following approaches that a business firm could use to gather information about competition. For each approach, mark your feeling about its appropriateness: **1** *(definitely not appropriate)*, **2** *(probably not appropriate)*, **3** *(undecided)*, **4** *(probably appropriate)*, or **5** *(definitely appropriate)*.

   The business firm should try to get useful information about competitors by:

_____ Careful study of trade journals.

_____ Wiretapping the telephones of competitors.

_____ Posing as a potential customer to competitors.

_____ Getting loyal customers to put out a phoney "request for proposal" soliciting competitors' bids.

_____ Buying competitors' products and taking them apart.

_____ Hiring management consultants who have worked for competitors.

_____ Rewarding competitors' employees for useful "tips."

_____ Questioning competitors' customers and/or suppliers.

_____ Buying and analyzing competitors' garbage.

_____ Advertising and interviewing for nonexistent jobs.

_____ Taking public tours of competitors' facilities.

_____ Releasing false information about the company in order to confuse competitors.

_____ Questioning competitors' technical people at trade shows and conferences.

_____ Hiring key people away from competitors.

_____ Analyzing competitors' labor union contracts.

_____ Having employees date persons who work for competitors.

_____ Studying aerial photographs of competitors' facilities.

After marking each of the preceding approaches, compare your responses to those of other people in your class. For each approach, the *people marking* **4** *or* **5** *should say why they thought this particular act would be appropriate. Those who marked* **1** *or* **2** *should then state why they thought this act would be inappropriate.*

What does this tell us about ethics and socially responsible behavior?

_____

Source: Developed from W. A. Jones, Jr. and N. B. Bryan, Jr., "Business Ethics and Business Intelligence: An Empirical Study of Information-Gathering Alternatives," *International Journal of Management* (June 1995), pp. 204–208.

Notes

1. J. A. Kidney, *Eastman Kodak Company* (December 5, 1995).
2. A. G. Monks, and N. Minow, *Corporate Governance* (Cambridge, Mass.: Blackwell Business, 1995), pp. 8–32.
3. *Ibid.*, p. 1.
4. J. H. Dobrzynski, "These Board Members Aren't IBM-Compatible," *Business Week* (August 2, 1992), p. 23.
5. A. Demb, and F. F. Neubauer, "The Corporate Board: Confronting the Paradoxes," *Long Range Planning* (June 1992), p. 13. These results are supported by a 1995 Korn/Ferry International survey in which chairmen and directors agreed that strategy and management succession, in that order, are the most important issues the board expects to face.
6. L. Light, "Why Outside Directors Have Nightmares," *Business Week* (October 23, 1996), p. 6.
7. W. Q. Judge, Jr., and C. P. Zeithaml, "Institutional and Strategic Choice Perspectives on Board Involvement in the Strategic Choice Process," *Academy of Management Journal* (October 1992), 766–794; J. A. Pearce II, and S. A. Zahra, "Effective Power-Sharing Between the Board of Directors and the CEO," *Handbook of Business Strategy, 1992/93 Yearbook* (Boston: Warren, Gorham, and Lamont, 1992), pp. 1.1–1.16.
8. J. H. Dobrzynski, "How to Handle a CEO," *Business Week* (February 21, 1994), pp. 64–65.
9. Judge and Zeithaml.
10. Statistics on boards of directors are taken from *23rd Annual Board of Directors Study* (New York: Korn/Ferry International, 1996); *Corporate Directors' Compensation, 1996 Edition* (New York: Conference Board, 1995); *Corporate Boards: CEO Selection, Evaluation and Succession* (New York: Conference Board, 1995) and were gathered during 1995.
11. See S. Finkelstein, and D. C. Hambrick, *Strategic Leadership: Top Executives and Their Impact on Organizations* (St. Paul: West, 1996), p. 213.
12. Reported by Korn/Ferry International and J. S. Lublin, "Survey Finds More Fortune 500 Firms Have At Least Two Female Directors," *Wall Street Journal* (September 25, 1995), p. A5.
13. T. J. Neff, "Boards Make Steady Progress in Key Areas," *Directors & Boards* (Summer 1994), p. 54.
14. According to 1995 proxy information gathered by Korn/Ferry International and surveys by The Conference Board.
15. D. J. McLaughlin, "The Director's Stake in the Enterprise," *Directors & Boards* (Winter 1994), pp. 53–59; R. Stobaugh, "The Positive Effects of Stock Ownership," *Directors & Boards* (Spring 1996), pp. 33–34.
16. R. E. Berenbeim, *Corporate Boards: CEO Selection, Evaluation and Succession: A Research Report* (New York: The Conference Board, 1995), p. 15.
17. L. H. Clark, Jr., "What Economists Say About Business—and Baboons," *Wall Street Journal* (June 7, 1983), p. 33. Article summarizes a research paper presented to the Interlaken Seminar on Analysis and Ideology, Interlaken, Switzerland, 1983.
18. M. L. Gerlach, "The Japanese Corporate Network: A Blockmodel Analysis," *Administrative Science Quarterly* (March 1992), pp. 105–139.
19. J. A. C. Baum, and C. Oliver, "Institutional Linkages and Organizational Mortality," *Administrative Science Quarterly* (June 1991) pp. 187–218; J. P. Sheppard, "Strategy and Bankruptcy: An Exploration into Organizational Death," *Journal of Management* (Winter 1994), pp. 795–833.
20. D. O'Neal, and H. Thomas, "Developing the Strategic Board," *Long Range Planning* (June 1996), p. 317.
21. The Conference Board reported that although 18% had an outsider as chair, 9% had another employee as chair.
22. See P. L. Rechner, and D. R. Dalton, "CEO Duality and Organizational Performance: A Longitudinal Analysis," *Strategic Management Journal* (February 1991), pp. 155–160 and C. M. Daily and D. R. Dalton, "Corporate Governance and the Bankrupt Firm: An Empirical Assessment," *Strategic Management Journal* (October 1994), pp. 643–654 for evidence favoring separation of Chair and CEO positions.

See also B. R. Baliga, R. C. Moyer, and R. S. Rao, "CEO Duality and Firm Performance: What's the Fuss?" *Strategic Management Journal* (January 1996), pp. 41–53 and A. Campbell, "The Cost of Independent Chairmen," *Long Range Planning* (December 1995), pp. 107–108 for evidence against separating the combined Chair/CEO position.

23. M. Lipton, and J. W. Lorsch, "The Lead Director," *Directors & Boards* (Spring 1993), pp. 28–31.

24. J. S. Lublin, "Texaco Case Causes a Stir in Boardrooms," *Wall Street Journal* (November 22, 1996), p. B1.

25. For an in-depth analysis of top management, see Finkelstein and Hambrick.

26. N. Tichy, and R. Charan, "Speed, Simplicity, Self-Confidence: An Interview with Jack Welch," *Harvard Business Review* (September-October 1989), p. 113.

27. For an in-depth guide to conducting the strategic planning process, see C. D. Fogg, *Team-Based Strategic Planning* (New York: AMACOM, 1994).

28. I. Wilson, "Strategic Planning Isn't Dead—It Changed," *Long Range Planning* (August 1994), pp. 12–24.

29. M. Friedman, "The Social Responsibility of Business Is to Increase Its Profits," *New York Times Magazine* (September 13, 1970), pp. 30, 126–127; and *Capitalism and Freedom* (Chicago: University of Chicago Press, 1963), p. 133.

30. A. B. Carroll, "A Three-Dimensional Conceptual Model of Corporate Performance," *Academy of Management Review* (October 1979), pp. 497–505.

31. Carroll refers to discretionary responsibilities as philanthropic responsibilities in A. B. Carroll, "The Pyramid of Corporate Social Responsibility: Toward the Moral Management of Organizational Stakeholders," *Business Horizons* (July-August 1991), pp. 39–48.

32. P. Rechner, and K. Roth, "Social Responsibility and Financial Performance: A Structural Equation Methodology," *International Journal of Management* (December 1990), pp. 382–391; K. E. Aupperle, A. B. Carroll, and J. D. Hatfield, "An Empirical Examination of the Relationship Between Corporate Social Responsibility and Profitability," *Academy of Management Journal* (June 1985), p. 459.

33. S. Preece, C. Fleisher, and J. Toccacelli, "Building a Reputation Along the Value Chain at Levi Strauss," *Long Range Planning* (December 1995), pp. 88–98; J. B. Barney and M. H. Hansen, "Trustworthiness as a Source of Competitive Advantage," *Strategic Management Journal* (Special Winter Issue, 1994), pp. 175–190.

34. R. E. Freeman, and D. R. Gilbert, *Corporate Strategy and the Search for Ethics* (Englewood Cliffs, N.J.: Prentice-Hall, 1988), p. 6.

35. L. Martinez-Mont, "Sweatshops Are Better Than No Shops," *Wall Street Journal* (June 25, 1996), p. A14.

36. "Nearly Half of Workers Take Unethical Actions—Survey," *Des Moines Register* (April 7, 1997), p. 18B.

37. K. Kumar, "Ethical Orientation of Future American Executives: What the Value Profiles of Business School Students Portend," *SAM Advanced Management Journal* (Autumn 1995), pp. 32–36, 47; M. Gable, and P. Arlow, "A Comparative Examination of the Value Orientations of British and American Executives," *International Journal of Management* (September 1986), pp. 97–106; W. D. Guth, and R. Tagiuri, "Personal Values and Corporate Strategy," *Harvard Business Review* (September-October 1965), pp. 126–127; G. W. England, "Managers and Their Value Systems: A Five Country Comparative Study," *Columbia Journal of World Business* (Summer 1978), p. 35.

38. L. K. Trevino, "Ethical Decision Making in Organizations: A Person-Situation Interactionist Model," *Academy of Management Review* (July 1986), pp. 601–617.

39. L. Kohlberg, "Moral Stage and Moralization: The Cognitive-Development Approach," in *Moral Development and Behavior,* edited by T. Lickona (New York: Holt, Rinehart & Winston, 1976).

40. Trevino, p. 606.

41. J. Keogh, ed., *Corporate Ethics: A Prime Business Asset* (New York: The Business Roundtable, 1988), p. 5.

42. G. F. Kohut, and S. E. Corriher, "The Relationship of Age, Gender, Experience and Awareness of Written Ethics Policies to Business Decision Making," *SAM Advanced Management Journal* (Winter 1994), pp. 32–39.

43. T. J. Von der Embse, and R. A. Wagley, "Managerial Ethics: Hard Decisions on Soft Criteria," *SAM Advanced Management Journal* (Winter 1988), p. 6.

44. G. F. Cavanagh, *American Business Values,* 3rd ed. (Englewood Cliffs, N.J.: Prentice Hall, 1990), pp. 186–199.

45. *Ibid.,* pp. 195–196.

46. I. Kant, "The Foundations of the Metaphysic of Morals," in *Ethical Theory: Classical and Contemporary Readings,* 2d ed., by L. P. Pojman (Belmont, Calif.: Wadsworth Publishing, 1995), pp. 255–279.

47. J. Warner, "21st Century Capitalism: Snapshot of the Next Century," *Business Week* (November 18, 1994), p. 194.

Chapter 3

Environmental Scanning and Industry Analysis

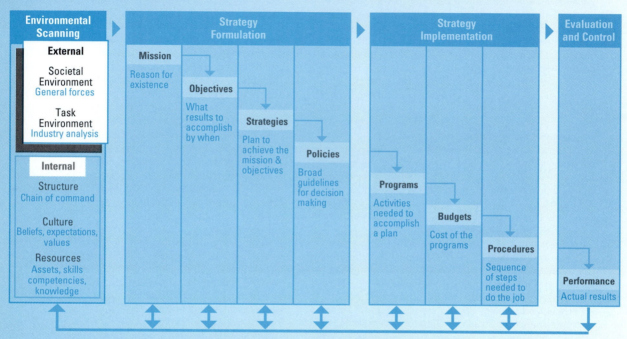

The decades of the 1960s and 1970s were exciting days for Tupperware, the company that originated airtight, easy-to-use plastic food-storage containers. Housewives gathered ten at a time in each others' homes to socialize and play games at Tupperware parties. The local Tupperware lady demonstrated and sold new products at these parties. The party concept as a marketing and distribution device was a huge success—company sales nearly doubled every five years.

During this same time period, however, the company's environment changed—with serious implications for Tupperware. By 1980, divorce was more common and more women had full-time jobs. More customers were single, childless, and working outside the home. As a result, Tupperware parties began to lose their popularity. Tupperware's North American sales slipped from 60% to 40% of the market, in contrast to Rubbermaid's increase from 5% to 40% of units sold during this same time period. The number of Tupperware dealers dropped from 32,000 to 24,000. By the early 1990s, most American women had either no idea how to find Tupperware or no desire to go to a Tupperware party. About 40% of the company's sales were from people who skipped the parties but sent orders along with friends who attended. Still hoping that these environmental changes were only temporary, management refused to change its marketing system. Tupperware's president actually predicted that before the end of the 1990s, the party concept would return to popularity because women and families will be spending more time at home—a forecast that by 1996 showed no indication of occurring. In contrast, Rubbermaid and other competitors, who had switched to marketing their containers in grocery and discount stores, continued to grow at the expense of Tupperware.[1]

Contrast Tupperware's experience with that of Chefs Unlimited, a company founded in 1992 by Dodd and Michelle Aldred of Raleigh, North Carolina. As husband and wife veterans of the restaurant industry, they knew how difficult it was to work long hours and still allow time to prepare home-cooked meals. That was one reason why people were spending more at restaurants during the 1990s. (The percentage of food dollars spent away from home increased from 36% in 1980 to 44% in 1995.) The Aldreds felt that many people were beginning to tire with eating out and would be willing to pay for a quality meal eaten in their own home. They offered people the opportunity to order entrees for either a one- or two-week period. Doing their own cooking in a 3,000 square foot commercial kitchen, the Aldreds delivered meals to customers for subsequent reheating. Although more expensive, these meals were of higher quality than the typical frozen dinner. By 1996, Chefs Unlimited was so successful catering to modern families that the Aldreds were planning to air express their meals to a nationwide audience the next year. Meanwhile, the U.S. Personal Chef Association was predicting the number of personal chef entrepreneurs in the United States and Canada to increase from 1,000 in 1996 to 5,000 in 2001.[2]

The Tupperware example shows how quickly a pioneering company can become an also-ran by failing to adapt to environmental change or, even worse, by failing to create change. The Chefs Unlimited example shows how a changing environment can create new opportunities at the same time it destroys old ones. The lesson is simple. To be successful over time, an organization needs to be in tune with its external environment. There must be a *strategic fit* between what the environment wants and what the corporation has to offer, as well as between what the corporation needs and what the environment can provide.

Current predictions are that the environment for all organizations will become even more uncertain as the world enters the twenty-first century.[3] **Environmental uncertainty** is the degree of *complexity* plus the degree of *change* existing in an organization's external environment. Environmental uncertainty is a threat to strategic managers because it hampers their ability to develop long-range plans and to make strategic decisions to keep the corporation in equilibrium with its external environment.

3.1 Environmental Scanning

Before an organization can begin strategy formulation, it must scan the external environment to identify possible opportunities and threats and its internal environment for strengths and weaknesses. **Environmental scanning** is the monitoring, evaluating, and disseminating of information from the external and internal environments to key people within the corporation. A corporation uses this tool to avoid strategic surprise and to ensure its long-term health. Research has found a positive relationship between environmental scanning and profits.[4]

Identifying External Environmental Variables

In undertaking environmental scanning, strategic managers must first be aware of the many variables within a corporation's societal and task environments. The **societal environment** includes general forces that do not directly touch on the short-run activities of the organization but that can, and often do, influence its long-run decisions. These, shown in Figure 1.3 on page 10, are as follows:

- **Economic** forces that regulate the exchange of materials, money, energy, and information.

- **Technological** forces that generate problem-solving inventions.

- **Political-legal** forces that allocate power and provide constraining and protecting laws and regulations.

- **Sociocultural** forces that regulate the values, mores, and customs of society.

The **task environment** includes those elements or groups that directly affect the corporation and, in turn, are affected by it. These are governments, local communities, suppliers, competitors, customers, creditors, employees/labor unions, special-interest groups, and trade associations. A corporation's task environment is typically the industry within which that firm operates. **Industry analysis** refers to an in-depth examination of key factors within a corporation's task environment. Both the societal and task environments must be monitored to detect the strategic factors that are likely to have a strong impact on corporate success or failure.

Scanning the Societal Environment

The number of possible strategic factors in the societal environment is very high. The number becomes enormous when we realize that, generally speaking, each country in the world can be represented by its own unique set of societal forces—some of which are very similar to neighboring countries and some of which are very different.

For example, even though Korea and China share Asia's Pacific Rim area with Thailand, Taiwan, and Hong Kong (sharing many similar cultural values), they have very different views about the role of business in society. It is generally believed in Korea and China (and to a lesser extent in Japan) that the role of business is primarily to contribute to national development; whereas in Hong Kong, Taiwan, and Thailand (and to a lesser extent in the Philippines, Indonesia, Singapore, and Malaysia), the role of business is primarily to make profits for the shareholders.[5] Such differences may translate into different trade regulations and varying difficulty in the **repatriation of profits** (transferring profits from a foreign subsidiary to a corporation's headquarters) from one group of Pacific Rim countries to another.

Monitoring Societal Trends   As noted in Table 3.1, large corporations categorize the societal environment in any one geographic region into four areas and focus their scanning in each area on trends with corporatewide relevance. Obviously trends in any one area may be very important to the firms in one industry but of lesser importance to firms in other industries.

Table 3.1   **Some Important Variables in the Societal Environment**

Economic	Technological	Political-Legal	Sociocultural
GDP trends	Total government spending for R&D	Antitrust regulations	Lifestyle changes
Interest rates	Total industry spending for R&D	Environmental protection laws	Career expectations
Money supply	Focus of technological efforts	Tax laws	Consumer activism
Inflation rates	Patent protection	Special incentives	Rate of family formation
Unemployment levels	New products	Foreign trade regulations	Growth rate of population
Wage/price controls	New developments in technology transfer from lab to marketplace	Attitudes toward foreign companies	Age distribution of population
Devaluation/revaluation		Laws on hiring and promotion	Regional shifts in population
Energy availability and cost	Productivity improvements through automation	Stability of government	Life expectancies
Disposable and discretionary income			Birth rates

Trends in the *economic* part of the societal environment can have an obvious impact on business activity. For example, an increase in interest rates means fewer sales of major home appliances. *Why?* Because a rising interest rate tends to be reflected in higher mortgage rates. Because higher mortgage rates increase the cost of buying a house, the demand for new and used houses tends to fall. Because most major home appliances are sold when people change houses, a reduction in house sales soon translates into a decline in sales of refrigerators, stoves, and dishwashers and reduced profits for everyone in that industry.

Changes in the *technological* part of the societal environment can also have a great impact on multiple industries. For example, improvements in computer microprocessors have not only led to the widespread use of home computers, but also to better automobile engine performance in terms of power and fuel economy through the use of microprocessors to monitor fuel injection.

Trends in the *political-legal* part of the societal environment have a significant impact on business firms. For example, periods of strict enforcement of U.S. antitrust laws directly affect corporate growth strategy. As large companies find it more difficult to acquire another firm in the same or in a related industry, they are typically driven to diversify into unrelated industries.[6] In Europe, the formation of the European Union has led to an increase in merger activity across national boundaries.

Demographic trends are part of the *sociocultural* aspect of the societal environment. The demographic bulge in the U.S. population caused by the "baby boom" in the 1950s strongly affects market demand in many industries. For example, between 1995 and 2005, an average of 4,400 Americans will turn 50 every day. This over-50 age group has become the fastest growing age group in all developed countries. Companies with an eye on the future can find many opportunities offering products and services to the growing number of "woofies" (well-off old folks)—defined as people over 50 with money to spend. These people are very likely to purchase recreational vehicles, take ocean cruises, and enjoy leisure sports such as boating, fishing, and bowling, in addition to needing financial services and health care.

This trend can mean increasing sales for firms like Winnebago (RVs), Carnival Cruise Lines, and Brunswick (sports equipment), among others.[7] To attract older customers, retailers will need to place seats in their larger stores so aging shoppers can rest. Washrooms need to be more accessible. Signs need to be larger. Restaurants need to raise the level of lighting so people can read their menus. Home appliances need simpler and larger controls. Already, the market for road bikes is declining as sales for tread mills and massagers for aching muscles increase.

Seven sociocultural trends in the United States that are helping to define what North America and the world will look like at the beginning of the next century are:

1. **Increasing environmental awareness.** Recycling and conservation are becoming more than slogans. Busch Gardens, for example, eliminated the use of disposable styrofoam trays in favor of washing and reusing plastic trays.

2. **Growth of the seniors market.** As their numbers increase, people over age 55 will become an even more important market. Already some companies are segmenting the senior population into Young Matures, Older Matures, and the Elderly—each having a different set of attitudes and interests.

3. **Generation Y boomlet.** Born after 1980 to the boomer and X generations, this cohort may end up being as large as the boomer generation. In 1957, the peak year of the postwar boom, 4.3 million babies were born. In 1990, there were 4.2 million births. By the mid 1990s, elementary schools were becoming overcrowded.[8] The U.S. census bureau projects generation Y to crest at 30.8 million births by 2005.

4. **Decline of the mass market.** Niche markets are beginning to define the marketers' environment. People want products and services that are adapted more to their personal needs. For example, Estee Lauder's "All Skin" and Maybelline's "Shades of You" line of cosmetic products are specifically made for African-American women. "Mass customization"—the making and marketing of products tailored to a person's requirements (Dell Computers)—is replacing the mass production and marketing of the same product in some markets.

5. **Pace and location of life.** Instant communication via facsimile machines, car telephones, and overnight mail enhances efficiency, but it also puts more pressure on people. Merging the personal computer with the communication and entertainment industry through telephone lines, satellite dishes, and cable television increases consumers' choices and allows workers to leave overcrowded urban areas for small towns and "telecommute" via personal computers and modems.

6. **Changing household.** Single-person households could become the most common household type in the United States after the year 2005. By 2005, only households composed of married couples with no children will be larger.[9] Although the Y generation baby boomlet may alter this estimate, a household clearly will no longer be the same as it was once portrayed in "The Brady Bunch" in the 1970s or even "The Cosby Show" in the 1980s.

7. **Diversity of workforce and markets.** Minority groups are increasing as a percentage of the total U.S. population. From 1996 to 2050, group percentages are expected by the U.S. Census Bureau to change as follows: *Whites*—from 83% to 75%; *Blacks*—from 13% to 15%; *Asian*—from 4% to 9%; *American Indian*—slight increase. *Hispanics*, which can be of any race, are projected to grow from 10% to 25% during this time period.[10] Traditional minority groups are increasing their numbers in the workforce and are being identified as desirable target markets. For example, the South Dekalb Mall in Atlanta, Georgia, recently restyled itself as an "Afrocentric retail center" in response to the rapid growth of the African-American 18-to-34 age group.[11]

Table 3.2   **Some Important Variables in International Societal Environments**

Economic	Technological	Political-Legal	Sociocultural
Economic development	Regulations on technology transfer	Form of government	Customs, norms, values
Per capita income	Energy availability/cost	Political ideology	Language
Climate	Natural resource availability	Tax laws	Demographics
GDP trends	Transportation network	Stability of government	Life expectancies
Monetary and fiscal policies	Skill level of work force	Government attitude toward foreign companies	Social institutions
Unemployment level	Patent-trademark protection	Regulations on foreign ownership of assets	Status symbols
Currency convertibility	Information-flow infrastructure	Strength of opposition groups	Life-style
Wage levels		Trade regulations	Religious beliefs
Nature of competition		Protectionist sentiment	Attitudes toward foreigners
Membership in regional economic associations		Foreign policies	Literacy level
		Terrorist activity	Human rights
		Legal system	Environmentalism

International Societal Considerations   Each country or group of countries in which a company operates presents a whole new societal environment with a different set of economic, technological, political-legal, and sociocultural variables for the company to face. International societal environments vary so widely that a corporation's internal environment and strategic management process must be very flexible. Cultural trends in Germany, for example, have resulted in the inclusion of worker representatives in corporate strategic planning. Differences in societal environments strongly affect the ways in which a **multinational corporation (MNC),** a company operating in multiple countries, conducts its marketing, financial, manufacturing, and other functional activities. For example, the existence of regional associations like the European Union, the North American Free Trade Zone, and Mercosur in South America has a significant impact on the competitive "rules of the game" both for those MNCs operating within and for those MNCs wanting to enter these areas.

To account for the many differences among societal environments from one country to another, consider Table 3.2. It includes a list of economic, technological, political-legal, and sociocultural variables for any particular country or region. For example, an important economic variable for any firm investing in a foreign country is currency convertibility. Without convertibility, a company operating in Russia cannot convert its profits from rubles to dollars. In terms of sociocultural variables, many Asian cultures (especially China) are less concerned with the values of human rights than are European and North American cultures. Some Asians actually contend that American companies are trying to impose Western human rights requirements on them in an attempt to make Asian products less competitive by raising their costs.[12]

Before planning its strategy for a particular international location, a company must scan the particular country environment(s) in question for opportunities and threats, and compare these with its own organizational strengths and weaknesses. For example, to operate successfully in a global industry such as automobiles, tires, electronics, or watches, a company must be prepared to establish a significant presence in the three developed areas of the world known collectively as the **Triad**. This term was coined by the Japanese management expert, Kenichi Ohmae, and it refers to the three developed markets of Japan, North America, and Western Europe, which now form a single market with common needs.[13] Focusing on the Triad is essential for an MNC pursuing success in a global industry, according to Ohmae, because close to 90% of all high–value-added, high-technology manufactured goods are produced and consumed in North America, Western Europe, and Japan. Ideally a company should have a significant presence in each of these regions so that it can produce and market its products simultaneously in all three areas. Otherwise, it will lose competitive advantage to Triad-oriented MNCs. No longer can an MNC develop and market a new product in one part of the world before it exports it to other developed countries.

Focusing only on the developed nations, however, causes a corporation to miss important market opportunities in the developing nations of the world. Although these nations may not have developed to the point that they have significant demand for a broad spectrum of products, they may very likely be on the threshold of rapid growth in the demand for specific products. This would be the ideal time for a company to enter this market—before competition is established. The key is to be able to identify the "trigger point" when demand for a particular product or service is ready to boom. See the **Key Theory** feature for an in-depth explanation of a technique to identify the optimum time to enter a particular market in a developing nation.

Scanning the Task Environment

As shown in Figure 3.1, a corporation's scanning of the environment will include analyses of all the relevant elements in the task environment. These analyses take the form of individual reports written by various people in different parts of the firm. At Procter & Gamble (P&G), for example, people from each of the brand management teams work with key people from the sales and market research departments to research and write a "competitive activity report" each quarter on each of the product categories in which P&G competes. People in purchasing also write similar reports concerning new developments in the industries that supply P&G. These and other reports are then summarized and transmitted up the corporate hierarchy for top management to use in strategic decision making. If a new development is reported regarding a particular product category, top management may then send memos asking people throughout the organization to watch for and report on developments in related product areas. The many reports resulting from these scanning efforts, when boiled down to their essentials, act as a detailed list of external strategic factors.

Identifying External Strategic Factors

Why do companies often respond differently to the same environmental changes? One reason is because of differences in the ability of managers to recognize and understand external strategic issues and factors. Few firms can successfully monitor all important external factors. Even though managers agree that strategic importance determines what variables are consistently tracked, they sometimes miss or choose to ignore crucial new developments.[14] Personal values of a corporation's managers as well as the success of current strategies are likely to bias both their perception of what is important to monitor in the external environment and their interpretations of what they perceive.[15]

In Tupperware's case, even though a number of top managers were generally aware that women were leaving the house in favor of careers, they chose to discount its importance in the marketing of the company's products. This willingness to reject unfamiliar

KEY THEORY

USING PPP TO IDENTIFY POTENTIAL MARKETS IN DEVELOPING NATIONS

Research by the Deloitte & Touche Consulting Group reveals that the demand for a specific product increases exponentially at certain points in a country's development. Identifying this trigger point of demand is thus critical to entering emerging markets at the best time—the time when enough people have enough money to buy what a company has to sell, but before competition is established. This can be done by using the concept of **purchasing power parity (PPP),** which measures the cost in dollars of the U.S.-produced equivalent volume of goods that an economy produces.

PPP offers an estimate of the material wealth a nation can purchase, rather than the financial wealth it creates as typically measured by Gross Domestic Product (GDP). As a result, restating a nation's GDP in PPP terms reveals much greater spending power than market exchange rates would suggest. For example, a shoe shine costing $5 to $10 in New York City can be purchased for 50¢ in Mexico City. Consequently the people of Mexico City can enjoy the same standard of living (with respect to shoe shines) as people in New York City with only 5% to 10% of the money. Correcting for PPP restates all Mexican shoe shines at their U.S. purchase value of $5. If one million shoe shines were purchased in Mexico last year, using the PPP model would effectively increase Mexican GDP by $5 million–$10 million. Using PPP, China becomes the world's second largest economy after the United States, with Brazil, Mexico, and India moving ahead of Canada into the top ten world markets.

Trigger points identify when demand for a particular product is about to rapidly increase in a country. This can be a very useful technique to identify when to enter a new market in a developing nation. Trigger points vary for different products. For example, an apparent trigger point for long-distance telephone services is at $7,500 in GDP per capita—a point when demand for telecommunications services increases rapidly. Once national wealth surpasses $15,000 per capita, demand increases at a much slower rate with further increases in wealth. The trigger point for life insurance is around $8,000 in GDP per capita. At this point, the demand for life insurance increases between 200% and 300% above those countries with GDP per capita below the trigger point.

Source: Summarized from D. Fraser and M. Raynor, "The Power of Parity," *Forecast* (May/June, 1996), pp. 8–12.

as well as negative information is called **strategic myopia.**[16] If a firm needs to change its strategy, it might not be gathering the appropriate external information to change strategies successfully.

One way to identify and analyze developments in the external environment is to use the **issues priority matrix** (Figure 3.2) in this way:

1. Identify a number of likely trends emerging in the societal and task environments. These are strategic environmental issues—those important trends that, if they occur, determine what the industry or the world will look like.

2. Assess the probability of these trends actually occurring from low to high.

3. Attempt to ascertain the likely impact (from low to high) of each of these trends on the corporation being examined.

A corporation's **external strategic factors** are those key environmental trends that are judged to have both a *medium to high probability of occurrence* and a *medium to*

Figure 3.1
Scanning the External Environment

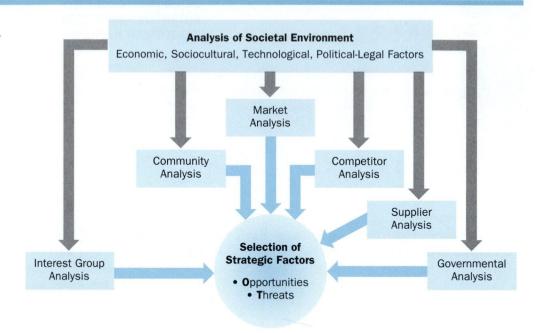

high probability of impact on the corporation. The issues priority matrix can then be used to help managers decide which environmental trends should be merely scanned (low priority) and which should be monitored as strategic factors (high priority). Those environmental trends judged to be a corporation's strategic factors are then categorized as *opportunities* and *threats* and are included in strategy formulation.

3.2   Industry Analysis: Analyzing the Task Environment

An **industry** is a group of firms producing a similar product or service, such as soft drinks or financial services. An examination of the important stakeholder groups, such as suppliers and customers, in a particular corporation's task environment is a part of industry analysis.

Porter's Approach to Industry Analysis

Michael Porter, an authority on competitive strategy, contends that a corporation is most concerned with the intensity of competition within its industry. The level of this intensity is determined by basic competitive forces, which are depicted in Figure 3.3. "The collective strength of these forces," he contends, "determines the ultimate profit potential in the industry, where profit potential is measured in terms of long-run return on invested capital."[17] In carefully scanning its industry, the corporation must assess the importance to its success of each of the six forces: *threat of new entrants, rivalry among existing firms, threat of substitute products or services, bargaining power of buyers, bargaining power of suppliers, and relative power of other stakeholders.*[18] The stronger each of these forces, the more limited companies are in their ability to raise prices and earn greater profits. Although Porter mentions only five forces, a sixth—other stakeholders—is added here to reflect

**Figure 3.2
Issues Priority
Matrix**

Source: Adapted from
L. L. Lederman, "Fore-
sight Activities in the
U.S.A.: Time for a Re-
Assessment?" *Long-
Range Planning* (June
1984), p. 46. Copyright
© 1984 by Pergamon
Press, Ltd. Reprinted by
permission.

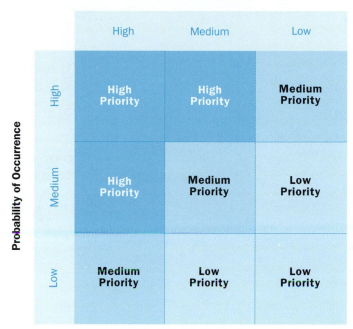

the power that governments, local communities, and other groups from the task environment wield over industry activities.

Using the model in Figure 3.3, a high force can be regarded as a threat because it is
likely to reduce profits. A low force, in contrast, can be viewed as an opportunity because
it may allow the company to earn greater profits. In the short run, these forces act as
constraints on a company's activities. In the long run, however, it may be possible for a
company, through its choice of strategy, to change the strength of one or more of the
forces to the company's advantage.

A strategist can analyze any industry by rating each competitive force as *high,
medium,* or *low* in strength. For example, the athletic shoe industry could be currently
rated as follows: rivalry is high (Nike, Reebok, Adidas, and Converse are strong competitors), threat of potential entrants is low (industry is reaching maturity), threat of substitutes is low (other shoes don't provide support for sports activities), bargaining power of
suppliers is medium but rising (suppliers in Asian countries are increasing in size and
ability), bargaining power of buyers is medium to low (advertising is more important
than distribution channels), threat of other stakeholders is medium to high (government
regulations and human rights concerns are growing). Based on current trends in each of
these competitive forces, the industry appears to be increasing in its level of competitive
intensity—meaning profit margins will likely fall for the industry as a whole.

Threat of New Entrants

New entrants to an industry typically bring to it new capacity, a desire to gain market
share, and substantial resources. They are, therefore, threats to an established corporation. The threat of entry depends on the presence of entry barriers and the reaction that
can be expected from existing competitors. An **entry barrier** is an obstruction that

Figure 3.3
Forces Driving
Industry Competition

Source: Adapted/reprinted with permission of The Free Press, an imprint of Simon & Schuster, from *Competitive Strategy: Techniques for Analyzing Industries and Competitors* by Michael E. Porter. Copyright © 1980 by The Free Press.

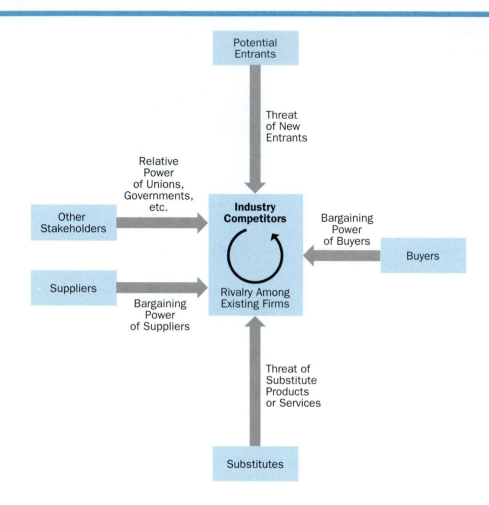

makes it difficult for a company to enter an industry. For example, no new domestic automobile companies have been successfully established in the United States since the 1930s because of the high capital requirements to build production facilities and to develop a dealer distribution network. Some of the possible barriers to entry are:

- **Economies of Scale.** Scale economies in the production and sale of mainframe computers, for example, gave IBM a significant cost advantage over any new rival.

- **Product Differentiation.** Corporations like Procter & Gamble and General Mills, which manufacture products like Tide and Cheerios, create high entry barriers through their high levels of advertising and promotion.

- **Capital Requirements.** The need to invest huge financial resources in manufacturing facilities in order to produce computer microprocessors creates a significant barrier to entry to any competitor for Intel.

- **Switching Costs.** Once a software program like Excel or Word becomes established in an office, office managers are very reluctant to switch to a new program because of the high training costs.

- **Access to Distribution Channels.** Small entrepreneurs often have difficulty obtaining supermarket shelf space for their goods because large retailers charge for space on their shelves and give priority to the established firms who can pay for the advertising needed to generate high customer demand.

- **Cost Disadvantages Independent of Size.** Microsoft's development of the first widely adopted operating system (MS-DOS) for the IBM-type personal computer gave it a significant advantage over potential competitors. Its introduction of Windows helped to cement that advantage.

- **Government Policy.** Governments can limit entry into an industry through licensing requirements by restricting access to raw materials, such as off-shore oil drilling sites.

Rivalry Among Existing Firms

In most industries, corporations are mutually dependent. A competitive move by one firm can be expected to have a noticeable effect on its competitors and thus may cause retaliation or countereffor. For example, the entry by mail order companies such as Dell and Gateway into a PC industry previously dominated by IBM, Apple, and Compaq increased the level of competitive activity to such an extent that any price reduction or new product introduction is now quickly followed by similar moves from other PC makers. According to Porter, intense rivalry is related to the presence of several factors, including:

- **Number of Competitors.** When competitors are few and roughly equal in size, such as in the U.S. auto and major home appliance industries, they watch each other carefully to make sure that any move by another firm is matched by an equal countermove.

- **Rate of Industry Growth.** Any slowing in passenger traffic tends to set off price wars in the airline industry because the only path to growth is to take sales away from a competitor.

- **Product or Service Characteristics.** Many people choose a videotape rental store based on location, variety of selection, and pricing because they view videotapes as a *commodity*—a product whose characteristics are the same regardless of who sells it.

- **Amount of Fixed Costs.** Because airlines must fly their planes on a schedule regardless of the number of paying passengers for any one flight, they offer cheap standby fares whenever a plane has empty seats.

- **Capacity.** If the only way a manufacturer can increase capacity is in a large increment by building a new plant (as in the paper industry), it will run that new plant at full capacity to keep its unit costs as low as possible—thus producing so much that the selling price falls throughout the industry.

- **Height of Exit Barriers.** Exit barriers keep a company from leaving an industry. The brewing industry, for example, has a low percentage of companies that leave the industry because breweries are specialized assets with few uses except for making beer.

- **Diversity of Rivals.** Rivals that have very different ideas of how to compete are likely to cross paths often and unknowingly challenge each other's position.

Threat of Substitute Products or Services

Substitute products are those products that appear to be different but can satisfy the same need as another product. For example, the fax is a substitute for Fed Ex,

Nutrasweet is a substitute for sugar, and bottled water is a substitute for a cola. According to Porter, "Substitutes limit the potential returns of an industry by placing a ceiling on the prices firms in the industry can profitably charge."[19] To the extent that switching costs are low, substitutes may have a strong effect on an industry. Tea can be considered a substitute for coffee. If the price of coffee goes up high enough, coffee drinkers will slowly begin switching to tea. The price of tea thus puts a price ceiling on the price of coffee. Sometimes a difficult task, the identification of possible substitute products or services means searching for products or services that can perform the same function, even though they may not appear to be easily substitutable.

Bargaining Power of Buyers

Buyers affect an industry through their ability to force down prices, bargain for higher quality or more services, and play competitors against each other. A buyer or a group of buyers is powerful if some of the following factors hold true:

- A buyer purchases a large proportion of the seller's product or service (for example, oil filters purchased by a major automaker).

- A buyer has the potential to integrate backward by producing the product itself (for example, a newspaper chain could make its own paper).

- Alternative suppliers are plentiful because the product is standard or undifferentiated (for example, motorists can choose among many gas stations).

- Changing suppliers costs very little (for example, office supplies are easy to find).

- The purchased product represents a high percentage of a buyer's costs, thus providing an incentive to shop around for a lower price (for example, gasoline purchased for resale by convenience stores makes up half their costs).

- A buyer earns low profits and is thus very sensitive to costs and service differences (for example, grocery stores have very small margins).

- The purchased product is unimportant to the final quality or price of a buyer's products or services and thus can be easily substituted without affecting the final product adversely (for example, electric wire bought for use in lamps).

Bargaining Power of Suppliers

Suppliers can affect an industry through their ability to raise prices or reduce the quality of purchased goods and services. A supplier or supplier group is powerful if some of the following factors apply:

- The supplier industry is dominated by a few companies, but it sells to many (for example, the petroleum industry).

- Its product or service is unique and/or it has built up switching costs (for example, word processing software).

- Substitutes are not readily available (for example, electricity).

- Suppliers are able to integrate forward and compete directly with their present customers (for example, a microprocessor producer like Intel can make PCs).

- A purchasing industry buys only a small portion of the supplier group's goods and services and is thus unimportant to the supplier (for example, sales of lawn mower tires are less important to the tire industry than are sales of auto tires).

Relative Power of Other Stakeholders

A sixth force should be added to Porter's list to include a variety of stakeholder groups from the task environment. Some of these groups are governments (if not explicitly included elsewhere), local communities, creditors (if not included with suppliers), trade associations, special-interest groups, and shareholders. The importance of these stakeholders varies by industry. For example, environmental groups in Maine, Michigan, Oregon, and Iowa successfully fought to pass bills outlawing disposable bottles and cans, and thus deposits for most drink containers are now required. This effectively raised costs across the board, with the most impact on the marginal producers who could not internally absorb all of these costs.

Industry Evolution

Over time most industries evolve through a series of stages from growth through maturity to eventual decline. The strength of each of the six forces mentioned earlier varies according to the stage of industry evolution. The industry life cycle is useful for explaining and predicting trends among the six forces driving industry competition. For example, when an industry is new, people often buy the product regardless of price because it fulfills a unique need. This is probably a **fragmented industry**—no firm has large market share and each firm serves only a small piece of the total market in competition with others (for example, Chinese restaurants). As new competitors enter the industry, prices drop as a result of competition. Companies use the experience curve (to be discussed in Chapter 4) and economies of scale to reduce costs faster than the competition. Companies integrate to reduce costs even further by acquiring their suppliers and distributors. Competitors try to differentiate their products from one another in order to avoid the fierce price competition common to a maturing industry.

By the time an industry enters maturity, products tend to become more like commodities. This is now a **consolidated industry**—dominated by a few large firms, each of which struggles to differentiate its products from the competition. As buyers become more sophisticated over time, purchasing decisions are based on better information. Price becomes a dominant concern, given a minimum level of quality and features. One example of this trend is the videocassette recorder industry. By the 1990s, VCRs had reached the point where there were few major differences among them. Consumers realized that because slight improvements cost significantly more money, it made little sense to pay more than the minimum for a VCR. The same is true of gasoline.

As an industry moves through maturity toward possible decline, its products' growth rate of sales slows and may even begin to decrease. To the extent that exit barriers are low, firms will begin converting their facilities to alternate uses or will sell them to another firm. The industry tends to consolidate around fewer but larger competitors. As in the case of the U.S. major home appliance industry described in the **Company Spotlight on Maytag Corporation** feature, the industry changed from being a fragmented industry (pure competition) composed of hundreds of appliance manufacturers in the industry's early years to a consolidated industry (mature oligopoly) composed of five companies (including Maytag) controlling over 98% of U.S. appliance sales. A similar consolidation was occurring in European major home appliances during the 1990s.

Categorizing International Industries

World industries vary on a continuum from multidomestic to global (see Figure 3.4).[20] **Multidomestic industries** are specific to each country or group of countries. This type of international industry is a collection of essentially domestic industries, like retailing

COMPANY SPOTLIGHT

Evolution of the U.S. Major Home Appliance Industry

In 1945, there were approximately 300 major home appliance manufacturers in the United States. By 1996, however, the "big five"—Whirlpool, General Electric, A.B. Electrolux (*no* relation to Electrolux Corporation, a U.S. company selling Electrolux brand vacuum cleaners), Maytag, and Raytheon—controlled over 98% of the U.S. market. The consolidation of the industry over the period was a result of fierce domestic competition. Emphasis on quality and durability coupled with strong price competition drove the surviving firms to increased efficiencies and a strong concern for customer satisfaction.

Prior to World War II, most appliance manufacturers produced a limited line of appliances deriving from one successful product. General Electric made refrigerators. Maytag focused on washing machines. Hotpoint produced electric ranges. Each offered variations of its basic product, but not until 1945 did firms begin to offer full lines of various appliances. By 1955, the major appliance industry began experiencing overcapacity, leading to mergers and acquisitions and a proliferation of national and private brands. Product reliability improved even though real prices (adjusted for inflation) declined about 10%.

Acknowledging that the U.S. major home appliance industry had reached maturity—future U.S. unit sales were expected to grow only 1%–2% annually on average for the foreseeable future—U.S. appliance makers decided to expand into Europe (where unit sales were expected to grow 5% annually). With Whirlpool's acquisition of the appliance business of Philips (The Netherlands), GE's joint venture with GEC (United Kingdom), AB Electrolux's (Sweden) purchase of White in the United States, and Maytag's acquisition of Hoover (vacuum cleaners worldwide plus major home appliances in the UK), the level of competition increased dramatically in both Europe and North America during the 1990s. In addition, rapid economic growth in Asia as well as in Mexico and South America had tremendous implications for the emerging global appliance industry. Environmental scanning and industry analysis had to be international in scope if a firm was to succeed in the 21st century.

MAYTAG CORPORATION

and insurance. The activities in a subsidiary of a multinational corporation (MNC) in this type of industry are essentially independent of the activities of the MNC's subsidiaries in other countries. In each country, the MNC tailors its products or services to the very specific needs of consumers in that particular country.

Global industries, in contrast, operate worldwide, with MNCs making only small adjustments for country-specific circumstances. A global industry is one in which an MNC's activities in one country are significantly affected by its activities in other countries. MNCs produce products or services in various locations throughout the world and sell them, making only minor adjustments for specific country requirements. Examples of global industries are commercial aircraft, television sets, semiconductors, copiers, automobiles, watches, and tires. The largest industrial corporations in the world in terms of dollar sales are, for the most part, multinational corporations operating in global industries.

The factors that tend to determine whether an industry will be primarily multidomestic or primarily global are:

1. *Pressure for coordination* within the multinational corporations operating in that industry.

2. *Pressure for local responsiveness* on the part of individual country markets.

Figure 3.4
Continuum of
International
Industries

Multidomestic ←	→ Global
Industry in which companies tailor their products to the specific needs of consumers in a particular country.	Industry in which companies manufacture and sell the same products, with only minor adjustments made for individual countries around the world.
• Retailing	• Automobiles
• Insurance	• Tires
• Banking	• Television sets

To the extent that the pressure for coordination is strong and the pressure for local responsiveness is weak for multinational corporations within a particular industry, that industry will tend to become global. In contrast, when the pressure for local responsiveness is strong and the pressure for coordination is weak for multinational corporations in an industry, that industry will tend to be multidomestic. Between these two extremes lie a number of industries with varying characteristics of both multidomestic and global industries. The dynamic tension between these two factors is contained in the phrase: *Think globally, but act locally.*

International Risk Assessment

Some firms, such as American Can Company and Mitsubishi Trading Company, develop elaborate information networks and computerized systems to evaluate and rank investment risks. Small companies can hire outside consultants such as Chicago's Associated Consultants International or Boston's Arthur D. Little, Inc., to provide political-risk assessments. Among the many systems that exist to assess political and economic risks are the Political System Stability Index, the Business Environment Risk Index, Business International's Country Assessment Service, and Frost and Sullivan's World Political Risk Forecasts.[21] Business International provides subscribers with continuously updated information on conditions in 63 countries. A Boston company called International Strategies offers an Export Hotline (800 USA-XPORT) that faxes information to callers for only the cost of the call.[22] Regardless of the source of data, a firm must develop its own method of assessing risk. It must decide on its most important risk factors and then assign weights to each.

Strategic Groups

A **strategic group** is a set of business units or firms that "pursue similar strategies with similar resources."[23] Categorizing firms in any one industry into a set of strategic groups is very useful as a way of better understanding the competitive environment.[24] Because a corporation's structure and culture tend to reflect the kinds of strategies it follows, companies or business units belonging to a particular strategic group within the same industry tend to be strong rivals and tend to be more similar to each other than to competitors in other strategic groups within the same industry.

For example, although McDonald's and Olive Garden are a part of the same restaurant industry, they have different missions, objectives, and strategies, and thus belong to different strategic groups. They generally have very little in common and pay little attention to each other when planning competitive actions. Burger King and Hardee's, however, have a great deal in common with McDonald's in terms of their similar strategy of producing a high volume of low-priced meals targeted for sale to the average family. Consequently they are strong rivals and are organized to operate similarly.

Figure 3.5
Mapping Strategic Groups in the U.S. Restaurant Chain Industry

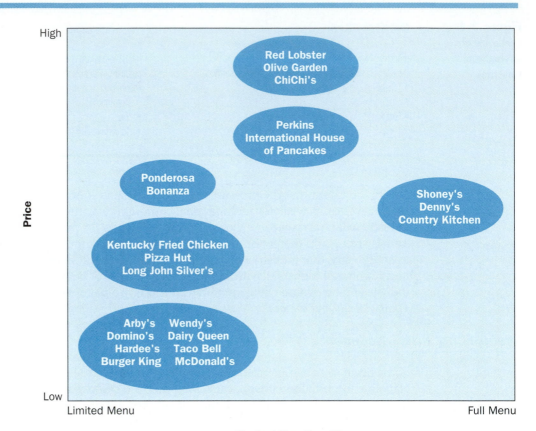

Strategic groups in a particular industry can be *mapped* by plotting the market positions of industry competitors on a two-dimensional graph using two strategic variables as the vertical and horizontal axes. (See Figure 3.5.)

1. Select two broad characteristics, such as price and menu, that differentiate the companies in an industry from one another.

2. Plot the firms using these two characteristics as the dimensions.

3. Draw a circle around those companies that are closest to one another as one strategic group, varying the size of the circle in proportion to the group's share of total industry sales. (You could also name each strategic group in the restaurant industry with an identifying title, such as quick fast food or buffet style service.)

Other dimensions, such as quality and degree of vertical integration, can also be used in additional graphs of the restaurant industry to gain a better understanding of how the various firms in the industry compete. Keep in mind, however, that when choosing the two dimensions, they should not be highly correlated; otherwise, the circles on the map will simply lie along the diagonal, providing very little new information other than the obvious.

Strategic Types

In analyzing the level of competitive intensity within a particular industry or strategic group, it is useful to characterize the various competitors for predictive purposes. A **strategic type** is a category of firms based on a common strategic orientation and a combination of structure, culture, and processes consistent with that strategy. According to Miles and Snow, competing firms within a single industry can be categorized on the basis of their general strategic orientation into one of four basic types.[25] This distinction helps explain why companies facing similar situations behave differently and why they continue to do so over a long period of time. These general types have the following characteristics:

- **Defenders** are companies with a limited product line that *focus on improving the efficiency of their existing operations*. This cost orientation makes them unlikely to innovate in new areas. An example is the Adolph Coors Company, which for many years emphasized production efficiency in its one Colorado brewery and virtually ignored marketing.

- **Prospectors** are companies with fairly broad product lines that *focus on product innovation and market opportunities*. This sales orientation makes them somewhat inefficient. They tend to emphasize creativity over efficiency. An example is the Miller Brewing Company, which successfully promoted "light" beer and generated aggressive, innovative advertising campaigns, but had to close a brand-new brewery when management overestimated market demand.

- **Analyzers** are corporations that *operate in at least two different product-market areas*, one stable and one variable. In the stable areas, efficiency is emphasized. In the variable areas, innovation is emphasized. An example is Anheuser-Busch, which can take a defender orientation to protect its massive market share in U.S. beer and a prospector orientation to generate sales in its amusement parks.

- **Reactors** are corporations that *lack a consistent strategy-structure-culture relationship*. Their (often ineffective) responses to environmental pressures tend to be piecemeal strategic changes. An example is the Pabst Brewing Company, which, because of numerous takeover attempts, has been unable to generate a consistent strategy to keep its sales from dropping.

Dividing the competition into these four categories enables the strategic manager not only to monitor the effectiveness of certain strategic orientations, but also to develop scenarios of future industry developments (discussed later in this chapter).

Hypercompetition

Most industries today are facing an ever-increasing level of environmental uncertainty. They are becoming more complex and more dynamic. Industries that used to be multidomestic are becoming global. New flexible, aggressive, innovative competitors are moving into established markets to rapidly erode the advantages of large previously dominant firms. Distribution channels vary from country to country and are being altered daily through the use of sophisticated information systems. Closer relationships with suppliers are being forged to reduce costs, increase quality, and gain access to new technology. Companies learn to quickly imitate the successful strategies of market leaders, and it becomes harder to sustain any competitive advantage for very long. Consequently, the level of competitive intensity is increasing in most industries.

Richard D'Aveni contends that as this type of environmental turbulence reaches more industries, competition becomes **hypercompetition**. According to D'Aveni:

In hypercompetition the frequency, boldness, and aggressiveness of dynamic movement by the players accelerates to create a condition of constant disequilibrium and change. Market stability is threatened by short product life cycles, short product design cycles, new

MICROSOFT OPERATES IN A HYPERCOMPETITIVE INDUSTRY

Microsoft is a hypercompetitive firm operating in a hypercompetitive industry. It has used its dominance in operating systems (DOS and Windows) to move into a very strong position in application programs like word processing and spreadsheets (Word and Excel). Even though Microsoft held 90% of the market for personal computer operating systems in 1992, it still invested millions in developing the next generation—Windows 95 and Windows NT. Instead of trying to protect its advantage in the profitable DOS operating system, Microsoft actively sought to replace DOS with various versions of Windows. Before hypercompetition, most experts argued against cannibalization of a company's own product line because it destroys a very profitable product instead of harvesting it like a "cash cow." According to this line of thought, a company would be better off defending its older products. New products would only be introduced if it could be proven that they would not take sales away from current products. Microsoft was one of the first companies to disprove this argument against cannibalization.

Bill Gates, Microsoft's co-founder, Chairman, and CEO, realized that if his company didn't replace its own DOS product line with a better product, someone else would (such as IBM with OS/2 Warp). He knew that success in the software industry depends not so much on company size but on moving aggressively to the next competitive advantage before a competitor does. "This is a hypercompetitive market," explained Gates. "Scale is not all positive in this business. Cleverness is the position in this business." By 1997, Microsoft still controlled over 90% of operating systems software and had achieved a dominant position in applications software as well.

Source: R. A. D'Aveni, *HyperCompetition* (New York: Free Press, 1994), p. 2.

technologies, frequent entry by unexpected outsiders, repositioning by incumbents, and tactical redefinitions of market boundaries as diverse industries merge. In other words, environments escalate toward higher and higher levels of uncertainty, dynamism, heterogeneity of the players and hostility.[26]

In hypercompetitive industries such as computers, competitive advantage comes from an up-to-date knowledge of environmental trends and competitive activity coupled with a willingness to risk a current advantage for a possible new advantage. Companies must be willing to *cannibalize* their own products (replacing popular products before competitors do so) in order to sustain their competitive advantage. As a result, industry or competitive intelligence has never been more important. See the **Strategy in a Changing World** feature to see how Microsoft is operating in the hypercompetitive industry of computer software. (Hypercompetition is discussed in more detail in Chapter 5.)

Creating an Industry Matrix

An **industry matrix** summarizes the external strategic factors (opportunities and threats) facing a particular industry. As shown in Table 3.3, the matrix gives a weight for each factor based on how important that factor is to the future of the industry. The matrix also specifies how well various competitors in the industry are responding to each factor. To generate an industry matrix using two industry competitors (called A and B), complete the following steps for the industry being analyzed:

Table 3.3   **Industry Matrix**

Strategic Factors	Weight	Company A Rating	Company A Weighted Score	Company B Rating	Company B Weighted Score
	1	2	3	4	5	6
Total	1.00				

- In **Column 1** (*Strategic Factors*) list the eight to ten most important opportunities and threats facing the industry as a whole.

- In **Column 2** (*Weight*) assign a weight to each factor from **1.0** (*Most Important*) to **0.0** (*Not Important*) based on that factor's probable impact on the overall industry's future success. **(All weights must sum to 1.0 regardless of the number of strategic factors.)**

- In **Column 3** (*Company A Rating*) examine a particular company within the industry—for example, Company A. Assign a rating to each factor from **5** (*Outstanding*) to **1** (*Poor*) based on Company A's current response to that particular factor. Each rating is a judgment regarding how well that company is currently dealing with each strategic factor.

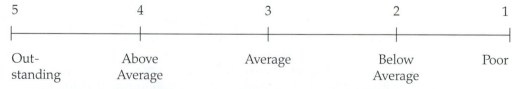

5	4	3	2	1
Out-standing	Above Average	Average	Below Average	Poor

- In **Column 4** (*Company A Weighted Score*) multiply the *weight* in **Column 2** for each factor times its rating in **Column 3** to obtain that factor's *weighted score* for Company A. This results in a weighted score for each factor ranging from **5.0** (*Outstanding*) to **1.0** (*Poor*) with 3.0 as the *average*.

- In **Column 5** (*Company B Rating*) examine a second company within the industry—in this case, Company B. Assign a rating to each factor from **5** (*Outstanding*) to **1** (*Poor*) based on Company B's current response to each particular factor.

- In **Column 6** (*Company B Weighted Score*) multiply the *weight* in **Column 2** for each factor times its rating in **Column 5** to obtain that factor's *weighted score* for Company B.

Finally, add the weighted scores for all the factors in **Columns 4** and **6** to determine the total weighted scores for companies A and B. The *total weighted score* indicates how well each company is responding to current and expected factors in the industry's environment. The industry matrix can be expanded to include all the major competitors within an industry simply by adding two additional columns for each additional competitor.

3.3 Industry/Competitive Intelligence

Much external environmental scanning is done on an informal and individual basis. Information is obtained from a variety of sources—customers, suppliers, bankers, consultants, publications, personal observations, subordinates, superiors, and peers. For example, scientists and engineers working in a firm's R&D lab can learn about new products and competitors' ideas at professional meetings; someone from the purchasing department, speaking with supplier-representatives' personnel, may also uncover valuable bits of information about a competitor. A study of product innovation in the scientific instrument and machine tool industries found that 80% of all product innovations were initiated by the customer in the form of inquiries and complaints.[27] In these industries, the sales force and service departments must be especially vigilant.

Industry (or **competitive**) **intelligence** is a formal program of gathering information on a company's competitors. Only 7% of large U.S. corporations have fully developed intelligence programs. In contrast, all Japanese corporations involved in international business and most large European companies have active intelligence programs.[28] This situation is changing, however. At General Mills, for example, all employees have been trained to recognize and tap sources of competitive information. Janitors no longer simply place orders with suppliers of cleaning materials, they also ask about relevant practices at competing firms!

Most corporations rely on outside organizations to provide them with environmental data. Firms such as A. C. Nielsen Co. provide subscribers with bimonthly data on brand share, retail prices, percentages of stores stocking an item, and percentages of stock-out stores. Strategists can use this data to spot regional and national trends as well as to assess market share. Information on market conditions, government regulations, competitors, and new products can be bought from "information brokers" such as FIND/SVP and Finsbury Data Services. Company and industry profiles are generally available from the Reference Press at Hoover's On Line site on the World Wide Web (*http://www.hoovers.com*). Many business corporations have established their own in-house libraries and computerized information systems to deal with the growing mass of available information.

Some companies, however, choose to use industrial espionage or other intelligence-gathering techniques to get their information straight from their competitors. Theft of proprietary R&D has risen 260% from 1985 to 1995. Using current or former competitors' employees and by using private contractors, some firms attempt to steal trade secrets, technology, business plans, and pricing strategies.[29] For example, Avon Products hired private investigators to retrieve from a public dumpster documents (some of them shredded) that Mary Kay Corporation had thrown away. Even Procter & Gamble, which defends itself like a fortress from information leaks, is vulnerable. A competitor was able to learn the precise launch date of a concentrated laundry detergent in Europe when one of its people visited the factory where machinery was being made. Simply asking a few questions about what a certain machine did, whom it was for, and when it would be delivered was all that was necessary.

3.4 *Forecasting*

Environmental scanning provides reasonably hard data on the present situation and current trends, but intuition and luck are needed to accurately predict if these trends will continue. The resulting forecasts are, however, usually based on a set of assumptions that may or may not be valid.

Danger of Assumptions

Faulty underlying assumptions are the most frequent cause of forecasting errors. Nevertheless many managers who formulate and implement strategic plans rarely consider that their success is based on a series of assumptions. Many long-range plans are simply based on projections of the current situation. One example of what can happen when a corporate strategy rests on the very questionable assumption that the future will simply be an extension of the present is that of Tupperware. Management not only assumed in the 1960s and 1970s that Tupperware parties would continue being an excellent distribution channel, its faith in this assumption also blinded it to information about America's changing lifestyles and their likely impact on sales. Even in the 1990s, when Tupperware executives realized that their extrapolated sales forecasts were no longer justified, they were unable to improve their forecasting techniques until they changed their assumptions.

Useful Forecasting Techniques

Various techniques are used to forecast future situations. Each has its proponents and critics. A study of nearly 500 of the world's largest corporations revealed trend extrapolation to be the most widely practiced form of forecasting—over 70% use this technique either occasionally or frequently.[30] Simply stated, **extrapolation** is the extension of present trends into the future. It rests on the assumption that the world is reasonably consistent and changes slowly in the short run. Time-series methods are approaches of this type; they attempt to carry a series of historical events forward into the future. The basic problem with extrapolation is that a historical trend is based on a series of patterns or relationships among so many different variables that a change in any one can drastically alter the future direction of the trend. As a rule of thumb, the further back into the past you can find relevant data supporting the trend, the more confidence you can have in the prediction.

Brainstorming, expert opinion, and statistical modeling are also very popular forecasting techniques. **Brainstorming** is a nonquantitative approach requiring simply the presence of people with some knowledge of the situation to be predicted. The basic ground rule is to propose ideas without first mentally screening them. No criticism is allowed. Ideas tend to build on previous ideas until a consensus is reached. This is a good technique to use with operating managers who have more faith in "gut feel" than in more quantitative "number-crunching" techniques. **Expert opinion** is a nonquantitative technique in which experts in a particular area attempt to forecast likely developments. This type of forecast is based on the ability of a knowledgeable person(s) to construct probable future developments based on the interaction of key variables. See the **🌐21st Century Global Society** feature for a prediction of the immediate future of Eastern Europe based on expert opinion. **Statistical modeling** is a quantitative technique that attempts to discover causal or at least explanatory factors that link two or more time series together. Examples of statistical modeling are regression analysis and other econometric methods. Although very useful in the grasping of historic trends, statistical modeling, like trend extrapolation, is based on historical data. As the patterns of

21ST CENTURY GLOBAL SOCIETY

EXPERT OPINION ON THE FUTURE OF EASTERN EUROPE

Based on his many years in the region, Edward Lucas, Eastern European correspondent for *The Economist*, predicted the likely future of a number of Eastern European nations. According to Lucas, it will soon become clear that the entrenched political and economic system in these countries would be a form of "crony capitalism," in which the communist elites have made a quiet shift from power to wealth. Although they will overtly support capitalism, political connections will be crucial for anyone wanting to do serious business. Output will rise, but according to Lucas, the amount will be based on some key factors: a nation's competitive advantage and its political and financial institutions. The region's current competitive advantage lay in cheap labor and high skills, but these are already being eroded.

A crucial distinction will thus emerge between those nations that keep their education system intact (as in Estonia, Czech Republic, and Slovenia) and where they are practically collapsing (as in Kazakhstan and Georgia). In addition, the likelihood of high taxes, capricious customs rules, and irresponsible politicians reinforced by public apathy in some countries will lead to a bad investment climate. Lucas made country-by-country predictions based on his score of some key factors ranging from 5=Outstanding to 1=Deplorable with a mid-point of 3=Tolerable.

	Democracy	Economic Performance	Internal Stability	Relations with Neighbors	Human Rights	Overall Outlook
Albania	2	3	3	3	2	Good
Azerbaijan	2	3	2	2	2	Good
Belarus	1	1	2	3	1	Poor
Bosnia-Herzegovina	2	1	1	1	2	Poor
Czech Republic	4	4	5	4	4	Good
Estonia	4	5	3	2	3	Good
Georgia	2	2	2	2	2	Good
Hungary	4	4	4	5	4	Good
Poland	4	5	4	5	4	Good
Serbia-Montenegro	1	1	2	1	1	Poor
Slovenia	4	4	5	4	4	Good
Tajikistan	1	1	1	2	1	Poor

Source: E. Lucas, "The Good Life After Communism," *The World in 1997* (London: The Economist Group, 1996), p. 42.

relationships change, the accuracy of the forecast deteriorates. Other forecasting techniques, such as *cross-impact analysis (CIA)* and *trend-impact analysis (TIA)*, have not established themselves successfully as regularly employed tools.

Scenario writing appears to be the most widely used forecasting technique after trend extrapolation. Originated by Royal Dutch Shell, scenarios are focused descriptions of different likely futures presented in a narrative fashion. The scenario thus may be merely a written description of some future state, in terms of key variables and issues, or it may be generated in combination with other forecasting techniques.

An **industry scenario** is a forecasted description of a particular industry's likely future. Such a scenario is developed by analyzing the probable impact of future societal forces on key groups in a particular industry. The process may operate as follows:[31]

1. Examine possible shifts in the societal variables globally.

2. Identify uncertainties in each of the six forces of the task environment (for example, potential entrants, competitors, likely substitutes, buyers, suppliers, and other key stakeholders).

3. Make a range of plausible assumptions about future trends.

4. Combine assumptions about individual trends into internally consistent scenarios.

5. Analyze the industry situation that would prevail under each scenario.

6. Determine the sources of competitive advantage under each scenario.

7. Predict competitors' behavior under each scenario.

8. Select the scenarios that are either most likely to occur or most likely to have a strong impact on the future of the company. Use these scenarios in strategy formulation.

3.5 Synthesis of External Factors—EFAS

After strategic managers have scanned the societal and task environments and identified a number of likely external factors for their particular corporation, they may want to refine their analysis of these factors using a form such as that given in Table 3.4. The **EFAS Table** (*External Factors Analysis Summary*) is one way to organize the external factors into the generally accepted categories of opportunities and threats as well as to analyze how well a particular company's management (rating) is responding to these specific factors in light of the perceived importance (weight) of these factors to the company. To generate an EFAS Table for the company being analyzed, complete the following steps:

- In **Column 1** (*External Factors*), list the eight to ten most important opportunities and threats facing the company.

- In **Column 2** (*Weight*), assign a weight to each factor from **1.0** (*Most Important*) to **0.0** (*Not Important*) based on that factor's probable impact on a particular company's current strategic position. The higher the weight, the more important is this factor to the current and future success of the company. **(All weights must sum to 1.0 regardless of the number of strategic factors.)**

- In **Column 3** (*Rating*), assign a rating to each factor from **5** (*Outstanding*) to **1** (*Poor*) based on that particular company's current response to that particular factor. Each rating is a judgment regarding how well the company is currently dealing with each external factor.

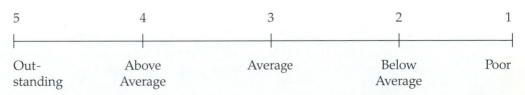

Table 3.4 External Factor Analysis Summary (EFAS): Maytag as Example

External Factors	Weight	Rating	Weighted Score	Comments
	1	2	3	4	5
Opportunities				
• Economic integration of European Community	.20	4	.80	Acquisition of Hoover
• Demographics favor quality appliances	.10	5	.50	Maytag quality
• Economic development of Asia	.05	1	.05	Low Maytag presence
• Opening of Eastern Europe	.05	2	.10	Will take time
• Trend to "Super Stores"	.10	2	.20	Maytag weak in this channel
Threats				
• Increasing government regulations	.10	4	.40	Well positioned
• Strong U.S. competition	.10	4	.40	Well positioned
• Whirlpool and Electrolux strong globally	.15	3	.45	Hoover weak globally
• New product advances	.05	1	.05	Questionable
• Japanese appliance companies	.10	2	.20	Only Asian presence is Australia
Total Scores	1.00		3.15	

Notes:
1. List opportunities and threats (5–10 each) in column 1.
2. Weight each factor from 1.0 (Most Important) to 0.0 (Not Important) in Column 2 based on that factor's probable impact on the company's strategic position. **The total weights must sum to 1.00**.
3. Rate each factor from 5 (Outstanding) to 1 (Poor) in Column 3 based on the company's response to that factor.
4. Multiply each factor's weight times its rating to obtain each factor's weighted score in Column 4.
5. Use Column 5 (comments) for rationale used for each factor.
6. Add the weighted scores to obtain the total weighted score for the company in Column 4. This tells how well the company is responding to the strategic factors in its external environment.

Source: T. L. Wheelen and J. D. Hunger, "External Strategic Factors Analysis Summary (EFAS)." Copyright © 1991 by Wheelen and Hunger Associates. Reprinted by permission.

- In **Column 4** (*Weighted Score*), multiply the *weight* in **Column 2** for each factor times its *rating* in **Column 3** to obtain that factor's *weighted score*. This results in a weighted score for each factor ranging from **5.0** (*Outstanding*) to **1.0** (*Poor*) with **3.0** as *average*.

- In **Column 5** (*Comments*), note why a particular factor was selected and how its weight and rating were estimated.

Finally, add the weighted scores for all the external factors in **Column 4** to determine the total weighted score for that particular company. The **total weighted score** indicates how well a particular company is responding to current and expected factors in its external environment. The score can be used to compare that firm to other firms in its industry. *The total weighted score for an average firm in an industry is always 3.0.*

As an example of this procedure, Table 3.4 includes a number of external factors for Maytag Corporation with corresponding weights, ratings, and weighted scores provided. This table is appropriate for 1995 *before* Maytag sold its European and Australian operations. Note that Maytag's total weight is 3.15, meaning that the corporation is slightly above average in the major home appliance industry.

🌐 3.6   *Global Issues for the 21st Century*

- The **21st Century Global Society** feature in this chapter explained how the economic outlook for some countries in Eastern Europe is poor, even though the region, as a whole, has great promise. Those countries that are able to build on their quality educational system and relatively low wages with solid political and financial institutions should be able to attract foreign investment and joint ventures.

- Increasing environmental uncertainty means that environmental scanning will become an important part of everyone's job. For companies to remain competitive, they will need to develop better methods of gathering, evaluating, and disseminating intelligence to those who need it.

- To manage strategically, organizations will have to become more attuned to the concerns of the many stakeholder groups who are affected by the company's actions. Shareholders will be only one part of the equation.

- The distinction made between the *developed* and *developing* nations will slowly begin to fade as the developing nations take on a greater proportion of world trade. The economic growth of the next century will be in Asia and Latin America, not in Western Europe or northern North America.

- As more industries become hypercompetitive, strategy will become increasingly short term in orientation—thus creating a paradox: Can strategic management exist with only a short-term time horizon?

Projections for the 21st Century

- From 1994 to 2010, the number of people living in poverty will increase from 3.7 billion to 3.9 billion.

- From 1994 to 2010, the average number of children per woman will decrease from 3.2 to 2.7.[32]

Discussion Questions

1. Discuss how a development in a corporation's societal environment can affect the corporation through its task environment.

2. According to Porter, what determines the level of competitive intensity in an industry?

3. According to Porter's discussion of industry analysis, is Pepsi Cola a substitute for Coca-Cola?

4. How can a decision maker identify strategic factors in the corporation's external international environment?

5. Compare and contrast trend extrapolation with the writing of scenarios as forecasting techniques.

Key Terms

brainstorming (p. 73)
consolidated industry (p. 65)
EFAS Table (p. 75)
entry barriers (p. 61)
environmental scanning (p. 53)
environmental uncertainty (p. 53)
expert opinion (p. 73)
external strategic factors (p. 59)
extrapolation (p. 73)
fragmented industry (p. 65)
global industry (p. 66)

hypercompetition (p. 69)
industry (p. 60)
industry analysis (p. 54)
industry intelligence (p. 72)
industry matrix (p. 70)
industry scenario (p. 75)
issues priority matrix (p. 59)
multidomestic industry (p. 65)
multinational corporation (MNC)
  (p. 57)
new entrants (p. 61)

purchasing power parity (p. 59)
repatriation of profits (p. 54)
scenario writing (p. 74)
societal environment (p. 54)
statistical modeling (p. 73)
strategic group (p. 67)
strategic myopia (p. 59)
strategic type (p. 68)
substitute products (p. 63)
task environment (p. 54)
the Triad (p. 58)

Strategic Practice Exercise

What are the forces driving industry competition in the airline industry? Read the following paragraphs. Using Porter's approach to industry analysis, evaluate each of the six forces to ascertain what drives the level of competitive intensity in this industry.

In recent years, the airline industry has become increasingly competitive. Since being deregulated during the 1970s in the United States, long established airlines such as Pan American and Eastern have gone out of business as new upstarts like US West and Southwest have successfully entered the market. It appeared that almost anyone could buy a few used planes to serve the smaller cities that the larger airlines no longer wanted to serve. These low-cost, small-capacity commuter planes were able to make healthy profits in these markets where it was too expensive to land large jets. Rail and bus transportation either did not exist or was undesirable in many locations. Eventually the low-cost local commuter airlines expanded service to major cities and grabbed market share from the majors by offering cheaper fares with no-frills service. In order to be competitive with these lower cost upstarts, United Airlines and Northwest Airlines offered stock in the company and seats on the board of directors to their unionized employees in exchange for wage and benefit reductions. Delta and American Airlines, among other major carriers, reduced their costs by instituting a cap on travel agent commissions. Travel agencies were livid at this cut in their livelihood, but they needed the airlines' business in order to offer customers a total travel package.

Globally it seemed as though every nation had to have its own airline for national prestige. These state-owned airlines were expensive, but the governments subsidized them with money and supporting regulations. For example, a foreign airline was normally only allowed to fly into one of a country's airports—forcing travelers to switch to the national airline to go to other cities. During the 1970s and 1980s, however, many countries began privatizing their airlines as governments tried to improve their budgets. To be viable in an increasingly global industry, national or regional airlines were forced to form alliances and even purchase an airline in another country or region. For example, the Dutch KLM Airline acquired half interest in the U.S Northwest Airlines in order to obtain not only U.S. destinations, but also Northwest's Asian travel routes, thus making it one of the few global airlines.

Costs were still relatively high for all of the world's major airlines because of the high cost of new airplanes. Just one new jet plane cost anywhere from $25 million to $100 million. By the 1990s, only three airframe manufacturers provided almost all of the commercial airliners: Boeing, Airbus, and McDonnell Douglas. Major airlines were forced to purchase new planes because they were more fuel efficient, safer, and easier to maintain. Airlines that chose to stay with an older fleet of planes had to deal with higher fuel and maintenance costs—factors that often made it cheaper to buy new planes.

1. Evaluate each of the forces driving competition in the airline industry:

   Threat of New Entrants   High, Medium, or Low? _____

   Rivalry Among Existing Firms   High, Medium, or Low? _____

   Threat of Substitutes   High, Medium, or Low? _____

   Bargaining Power of Buyers/Distributors   High, Medium, or Low? _____

   Bargaining Power of Suppliers   High, Medium, or Low? _____

   Relative Power of Other Stakeholders   High, Medium, or Low? _____

2. *Which of these forces is changing?* What will this mean to the overall level of competitive intensity in the airline industry in the future? Would you invest or look for a job in this industry?

Notes

1. L. M. Grossman, "Families Have Changed But Tupperware Keeps Holding Its Parties," *Wall Street Journal* (July 21, 1992), pp. A1, A13.

2. D. Phillips, "Special Delivery," *Entrepreneur* (September 1996), pp. 98–100; B. Saporito, "What's For Dinner?" *Fortune* (May 15, 1995), pp. 50–64.

3. S. H. Haeckel, "Adaptive Enterprise Design: The Sense-and-Respond Model," *Planning Review* (May/June 1995), pp. 6–13, 42.

4. J. B. Thomas, S. M. Clark, and D. A. Gioia, "Strategic Sensemaking and Organizational Performance: Linkages Among Scanning, Interpretation, Action, Outcomes," *Academy of Management Journal* (April 1993), pp. 239–270; M. A. Reynolds, G. Lindstrom, and C. Despres, "Strategy, Performance and the Use of Environmental Information: Evidence from a Computer Simulation," *American Business Review* (January 1994), pp. 45–52.

5. P. Lasserre, and J. Probert, "Competing on the Pacific Rim: High Risks and High Returns," *Long Range Planning* (April 1994), pp. 12–35.

6. A. Shleifer, and R. W. Viskny, "Takeovers in the 1960s and the 1980s: Evidence and Implications," in *Fundamental Issues in Strategy: A Research Agenda*, edited by R. P. Rumelt, D. E. Schendel, and D. J. Teece (Boston: Harvard Business School Press, 1994), pp. 403–418.

7. J. Wyatt, "Playing the Woofie Card," *Fortune* (February 6, 1995), pp. 130–132.

8. J. Greco, "Meet Generation Y," *Forecast* (May/June, 1996), pp. 48–54; J. Fletcher, "A Generation Asks: 'Can the Boom Last?'" *Wall Street Journal* (June 14, 1996), p. B10.

9. "Alone in America," *The Futurist* (September-October 1995), pp. 56–57.

10. "Population Growth Slowing as Nation Ages," *The* (Ames, IA) *Daily Tribune* (March 14, 1996), p. A7.

11. L. M. Grossman, "After Demographic Shift, Atlanta Mall Restyles Itself as Black Shopping Center," *Wall Street Journal* (February 26, 1992), p. B1.

12. J. Naisbitt, *Megatrends Asia* (New York: Simon & Schuster, 1996), p. 79.

13. K. Ohmae, "The Triad World View," *Journal of Business Strategy* (Spring 1987), pp. 8–19.

14. B. K. Boyd, and J. Fulk, "Executive Scanning and Perceived Uncertainty: A Multidimensional Model," *Journal of Management*, Vol. 22, No. 1 (1996), pp. 1–21.

15. R. A. Bettis and C. K. Prahalad, "The Dominant Logic: Retrospective and Extension," *Strategic Management Journal* (January 1995), pp. 5–14; J. M. Stofford and C. W. F. Baden-Fuller, "Creating Corporate Entrepreneurship," *Strategic Management Journal* (September 1994), pp. 521–536.

16. H. I. Ansoff, "Strategic Management in a Historical Perspective," in *International Review of Strategic Management*, Vol. 2, No. 1 (1991), edited by D. E. Hussey (Chichester, England: Wiley, 1991), p. 61.

17. M. E. Porter, *Competitive Strategy* (New York: Free Press, 1980), p. 3.

18. This summary of the forces driving competitive strategy is taken from Porter, *Competitive Strategy*, pp. 7–29.

19. *Ibid.*, p. 23.

20. M. E. Porter, "Changing Patterns of International Competition," *California Management Review* (Winter 1986), pp. 9–40.

21. T. N. Gladwin, "Assessing the Multinational Environment for Corporate Opportunity," in *Handbook of Business Strategy*, edited by W. D. Guth (Boston: Warren, Gorham and Lamont, 1985), pp. 7.28–7.41.

22. B. Holstein, "An Export Service of Great Import," *Business Week* (September 28, 1992), p. 138.

23. K. J. Hatten, and M. L. Hatten, "Strategic Groups, Asymmetrical Mobility Barriers, and Contestability," *Strategic Management Journal* (July-August 1987), p. 329.

24. A. Fiegenbaum, and H. Thomas, "Strategic Groups as Reference Groups: Theory, Modeling and Empirical Examination of Industry and Competitive Strategy," *Strategic Management Journal* (September 1995), pp. 461–476.

25. R. E. Miles, and C. C. Snow, *Organizational Strategy, Structure, and Process* (New York: McGraw-Hill, 1978).

26. R. A. D'Aveni, *HyperCompetition* (New York: The Free Press, 1994), pp. xiii–xiv.

27. R. T. Pascale, "Perspective on Strategy: The Real Story Behind Honda's Success," *California Management Review* (Spring 1981), p. 70.

28. L. Kahaner, *Competitive Intelligence* (New York: Simon & Schuster, 1996).

29. "Spooks Should Scare Corporate America," *Journal of Business Strategy* (July/August 1995), pp. 14–15; "Tips from Top Spies," *Journal of Business Strategy* (September/October 1996), p. 6.

30. H. E. Klein, and R. E. Linneman, "Environmental Assessment: An International Study of Corporate Practices," *Journal of Business Strategy* (Summer 1984), p. 72.

31. This process of scenario development is adapted from M. E. Porter, *Competitive Advantage* (New York: Free Press, 1985), pp. 448–470.

32. J. Warner, "21st Century Capitalism: Snapshot of the Next Century," *Business Week* (November 18, 1994), p. 194.

Chapter 4

Internal Scanning: Organizational Analysis

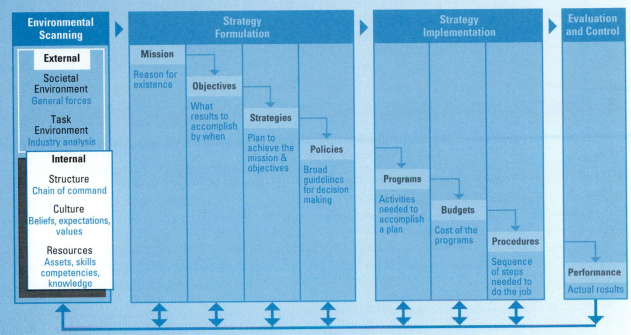

Environmental Scanning

External

Societal Environment
General forces

Task Environment
Industry analysis

Internal

Structure
Chain of command

Culture
Beliefs, expectations, values

Resources
Assets, skills competencies, knowledge

Strategy Formulation

Mission
Reason for existence

Objectives
What results to accomplish by when

Strategies
Plan to achieve the mission & objectives

Policies
Broad guidelines for decision making

Strategy Implementation

Programs
Activities needed to accomplish a plan

Budgets
Cost of the programs

Procedures
Sequence of steps needed to do the job

Evaluation and Control

Performance
Actual results

Feedback/Learning

United Airlines is a very successful, full-service international airline. It was not happy, however, about losing its traditional market share dominance in California to upstart Southwest Airlines. To regain this lucrative market, it took direct aim at Southwest in 1994 by launching on the West Coast its own low-cost carrier, Shuttle by United. It tried to imitate what it thought were Southwest's advantages. It used a fleet of Boeing 737s, the same plane Southwest used. It was able to obtain looser union work rules and a lower wage scale from those at its United Airlines' parent. To compete effectively, the Shuttle aimed to reduce United's cost of flying from the main airline's 10.5¢ to 7.4¢ per passenger mile. It planned to fly planes longer, speed up passenger boarding and takeoffs, and reduce idle time on the ground. By February 1996, however, Shuttle by United had only been able to reduce its costs to 8¢ per passenger mile contrasted with

Southwest's 7.1¢. To keep from losing money, the Shuttle was forced to raise fares and to pull out of all routes that did not connect with the carrier's hubs in San Francisco and Los Angeles. Its rate from San Francisco to Southern California was often $30 more than was Southwest's rate of $69. After 16 months of competition, Southwest had not only regained traffic it had lost initially to the Shuttle, but had actually increased its share of the California market! In addition to Southwest's low costs, it had a well-earned reputation for flying passengers safely to their destination on time. Even United's most loyal customers were taking Southwest for short flights. According to David Kliman, Director of Travel Management for Fireman's Fund Insurance of San Francisco, "We have a real bias to United all things being equal. But when fares are different, we book Southwest because it's cheaper."[1]

What gave Southwest Airlines this kind of advantage in a very competitive industry? So far no U.S. airline seems able to copy the secret of its success.

4.1   A Resource-Based Approach to Organizational Analysis

Scanning and analyzing the external environment for opportunities and threats is not enough to provide an organization a competitive advantage. Analysts must also look within the corporation itself to identify **internal strategic factors**—those critical *strengths* and *weaknesses* that are likely to determine if the firm will be able to take advantage of opportunities while avoiding threats. This internal scanning is often referred to as **organizational analysis** and is concerned with identifying and developing an organization's resources.

A **resource** is an asset, competency, process, skill, or knowledge controlled by the corporation. A resource is a strength if it provides a company with a competitive advantage. It is something the firm does or has the potential to do particularly well relative to the abilities of existing or potential competitors. A resource is a weakness if it is something the corporation does poorly or doesn't have the capacity to do although its competitors have that capacity. Barney, in his **VRIO framework** of analysis, proposes four questions to evaluate each of a firm's key resources:

1. **Value:** Does it provide competitive advantage?
2. **Rareness:** Do other competitors possess it?
3. **Imitability:** Is it costly for others to imitate?
4. **Organization:** Is the firm organized to exploit the resource?

If the answer to these questions is "yes" for a particular resource, that resource is considered a strength and a distinctive competence.[2]

Evaluate the importance of these resources to ascertain if they are internal strategic factors—those particular strengths and weaknesses that will help determine the future of the company. This can be done by comparing measures of these resources with measures of (1) *the company's past performance,* (2) *the company's key competitors,* and (3) *the industry as a whole.* To the extent that a resource (such as a firm's financial situation) is significantly different from the firm's own past, its key competitors, or the industry average, the resource is likely to be a strategic factor and should be considered in strategic decisions.

Using Resources to Gain Competitive Advantage

Proposing that a company's sustained competitive advantage is primarily determined by its resource endowments, Grant proposes a five-step, resource-based approach to strategy analysis.

1. Identify and classify the firm's resources in terms of strengths and weaknesses.

2. Combine the firm's strengths into specific capabilities. **Corporate capabilities** (often called **core competencies**) are the things that a corporation can do exceedingly well. When these capabilities/competencies are superior to those of competitors, they are often called **distinctive competencies.**

3. Appraise the profit potential of these resources and capabilities in terms of their potential for sustainable competitive advantage and the ability to harvest the profits resulting from the use of these resources and capabilities.

4. Select the strategy that best exploits the firm's resources and capabilities relative to external opportunities.

5. Identify resource gaps and invest in upgrading weaknesses.[3]

As indicated in Step 2, when an organization's resources are combined, they form a number of capabilities. In the earlier example, Southwest Airlines has two identifiable capabilities: low costs per passenger mile, and the capability for energizing its people to provide safe, on-time flight service.

Determining the Sustainability of an Advantage

Just because a firm is able to use its resources and capabilities to develop a competitive advantage does not mean it will be able to sustain it. Two characteristics determine the sustainability of a firm's distinctive competency(ies): durability and imitability.

Durability is the rate at which a firm's underlying resources and capabilities (core competencies) depreciate or become obsolete. New technology can make a company's core competency obsolete or irrelevant. For example, Intel's skills in using basic technology developed by others to manufacture and market quality microprocessors was a crucial capability until management realized that the firm had taken current technology as far as possible with the Pentium chip. Without basic R&D of its own, it would slowly lose its competitive advantage to others.

Imitability is the rate at which a firm's underlying resources and capabilities (core competencies) can be duplicated by others. To the extent that a firm's distinctive competency gives it competitive advantage in the marketplace, competitors will do what they can to imitate that set of skills and capabilities. Competitors' efforts may range from reverse engineering to hiring employees from the competitor to outright patent infringement. A core competency can be easily imitated to the extent that it is transparent, transferable, and replicable.

- **Transparency**—the speed with which other firms can understand the relationship of resources and capabilities supporting a successful firm's strategy. For example, Gillette has always supported its dominance in the marketing of razors with excellent R&D. A competitor could never understand how the Sensor razor was produced simply by taking one apart. Gillette's Sensor razor design was very difficult to copy, partially because the manufacturing equipment needed to produce it was so expensive and complicated.

- **Transferability**—the ability of competitors to gather the resources and capabilities necessary to support a competitive challenge. For example, it may be very difficult for a wine maker to duplicate a French winery's key resources of land and climate, especially if the imitator is located in Iowa.

- **Replicability**—the ability of competitors to use duplicated resources and capabilities to imitate the other firm's success. For example, even though many companies

**Figure 4.1
Continuum of
Resource
Sustainability**

Source: Suggested by J. R. Wiliams, "How Sustainable Is Your Competitive Advantage?" *California Management Review* (Spring 1992), p. 33.

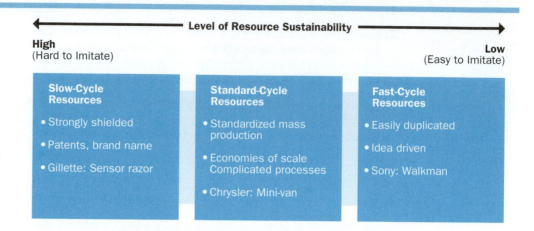

have tried to imitate Procter & Gamble's success with brand management by hiring brand managers away from P&G, they have often failed to duplicate P&G's success. The competitors failed to identify less visible P&G coordination mechanisms or to realize that P&G's brand management style conflicted with the competitor's own corporate culture.[4]

An organization's resources and capabilities can be placed on a continuum to the extent they are durable and can't be imitated (that is, aren't transparent, transferable, or replicable) by another firm. This **continuum of sustainability** is depicted in Figure 4.1. At one extreme are *slow-cycle resources,* which are sustainable because they are shielded by patents, geography, strong brand names, and the like. These resources and capabilities are distinctive competencies because they provide a sustainable competitive advantage. Gillette's Sensor razor is a good example of a product built around slow-cycle resources. The other extreme includes *fast-cycle resources,* which face the highest imitation pressures because they are based on a concept or technology that can be easily duplicated, such as Sony's Walkman. To the extent that a company has fast-cycle resources, the primary way it can compete successfully is through increased speed from lab to marketplace. Otherwise, it has no real sustainable competitive advantage.

With its low-cost position, reputation for safe, on-time flights, and its dedicated workforce, Southwest Airlines has successfully built a sustainable competitive advantage based on relatively slow-cycle resources—resources that are durable and can't be easily imitated because they lack transparency, transferability, and replicability.

4.2 *Value-Chain Analysis*

A good way to begin an organizational analysis is to ascertain where a firm's products are located in the overall value chain. A **value chain** is a linked set of value-creating activities beginning with basic raw materials coming from suppliers, moving on to a series of value-added activities involved in producing and marketing a product or service, and ending with distributors getting the final goods into the hands of the ultimate consumer. See Figure 4.2 for an example of a typical value chain for a manufactured product. The focus of value-chain analysis is to examine the corporation in the context of the overall chain of value-creating activities, of which the firm may only be a small part.

Figure 4.2
Typical Value Chain for a Manufactured Product

Source: Suggested by J. R. Galbraith, "Strategy and Organization Planning," in *The Strategy Process: Concepts, Contexts, Cases,* 2nd ed., edited by H. Mintzberg and J. B. Quinn (Englewood Cliffs, N.J.: Prentice Hall, 1991), p. 316.

Raw Materials → Primary Manufacturing → Fabrication → Product Producer → Distributor → Retailer

Very few corporations include a product's entire value chain, although Ford Motor Company did when it was run by its founder, Henry Ford I. During the 1920s and 1930s, the company owned its own iron mines, ore-carrying ships, and a small rail line to bring ore to its mile-long River Rouge plant in Detroit. Visitors to the plant would walk along an elevated walkway where they could watch iron ore being dumped from the rail cars into huge furnaces. The resulting steel was poured and rolled out onto a moving belt to be fabricated into auto frames and parts while the visitors watched in awe. As a group of visitors walked along the walkway, they observed an automobile being built piece by piece. Reaching the end of the moving line, the finished automobile was driven out of the plant into a vast adjoining parking lot. Ford trucks would then load the cars for delivery to dealers. Although the Ford dealers were not employees of the company, they had almost no power in the arrangement. Dealerships were awarded by the company and taken away if a dealer was at all disloyal. Ford Motor Company at that time was completely vertically integrated, that is, it controlled (usually by ownership) every stage of the value chain from the iron mines to the retailers.

Industry Value-Chain Analysis

The value chains of most industries can be split into two segments, *upstream* and *downstream* halves. In the petroleum industry, for example, upstream refers to oil exploration, drilling, and moving the crude oil to the refinery, and downstream refers to refining the oil plus the transporting and marketing of gasoline and refined oil to distributors and gas station retailers. Even though most large oil companies are completely integrated, they often vary in the amount of expertise they have at each part of the value chain. Texaco, for example, has its greatest expertise downstream in marketing and retailing. Others, such as British Petroleum, are more dominant in upstream activities like exploration.

In analyzing the complete value chain of a product, note that even if a firm operates up and down the entire industry chain, it usually has an area of primary expertise where its primary activities lie. A company's **center of gravity** is the part of the chain that is most important to the company and the point where its greatest expertise and capabilities lie—its core competencies. According to Galbraith, a company's center of gravity is usually the point at which the company started. After a firm successfully establishes itself at this point by obtaining a competitive advantage, one of its first strategic moves is to move forward or backward along the value chain in order to reduce costs, guarantee access to key raw materials, or to guarantee distribution.[5] This process is called *vertical integration.*

In the paper industry, for example, Weyerhauser's center of gravity is in the raw materials and primary manufacturing parts of the value chain in Figure 4.2. Weyerhauser's expertise is in lumbering and pulp mills, which is where the company started. It integrated forward by using its wood pulp to make paper and boxes, but its greatest capability still lay in getting the greatest return from its lumbering activities. In contrast, Procter & Gamble is primarily a consumer products company that also owned timberland and operated pulp mills. Its expertise is in the product producer and marketer distributor parts of the Figure 4.2 value chain. P & G purchased these assets to guarantee access to the large quantities of wood pulp it needed to expand its disposable diaper, toilet tissue, and napkin products. P & G's strongest capabilities have always been in the downstream activities of product development, marketing, and brand management. It has never been as efficient in upstream paper activities as Weyerhauser. It had no real distinctive competence on that part of the value chain. When paper supplies became more plentiful (and competition got rougher), P & G gladly sold its land and mills to focus more on that part of the value chain where it could provide the greatest value at the lowest cost—creating and marketing innovative consumer products.

Corporate Value-Chain Analysis

Each corporation has its own internal value chain of activities. See Figure 4.3 for an example of a corporate value chain. Porter proposes that a manufacturing firm's **primary activities** usually begin with *inbound logistics* (raw materials handling and warehousing), go through an *operations process* in which a product is manufactured, and continue on to *outbound logistics* (warehousing and distribution), *marketing and sales*, and finally to *service* (installation, repair, and sale of parts). Several **support activities,** such as *procurement* (purchasing), *technology development* (R&D), *human resource management*, and *firm infrastructure* (accounting, finance, strategic planning), ensure that the primary value-chain activities operate effectively and efficiently. Each of a company's product lines has its own distinctive value chain. Because most corporations make several different products or services, an internal analysis of the firm involves analyzing a series of different value chains.

The systematic examination of individual value activities can lead to a better understanding of a corporation's strengths and weaknesses. According to Porter, "Differences among competitor value chains are a key source of competitive advantage."[6] Corporate value chain analysis involves the following steps:

1. Examine each product line's value chain in terms of the various activities involved in producing that product or service. Which activities can be considered strengths or weaknesses?

2. Examine the "linkages" within each product line's value chain. **Linkages** are the connections between the way one value activity (for example, marketing) is performed and the cost of performance of another activity (for example, quality control). In seeking ways for a corporation to gain competitive advantage in the marketplace, the same function can be performed in different ways with different results. For example, quality inspection of 100% of output by the workers themselves instead of the usual 10% by quality control inspectors might increase production costs, but that increase could be more than offset by the savings obtained from reducing the number of repair people needed to fix defective products and increasing the amount of salespeople's time devoted to selling instead of exchanging already-sold, but defective, products.

3. Examine the potential synergies among the value chains of different product lines or business units. Each value element, such as advertising or manufacturing, has an inherent economy of scale in which activities are conducted at their lowest possible cost per unit of output. If a particular product is not being produced at a high enough level to reach economies of scale in distribution, another product could be used to share the same distribution channel. This is an example of **economies of**

Figure 4.3
A Corporation's Value Chain

Source: Adapted/reprinted with the permission of the The Free Press, an imprint of Simon & Schuster, from *Competitive Advantage: Creating and Sustaining Superior Performance* by Michael E. Porter, p. 37. Copyright © 1985 by Michael E. Porter.

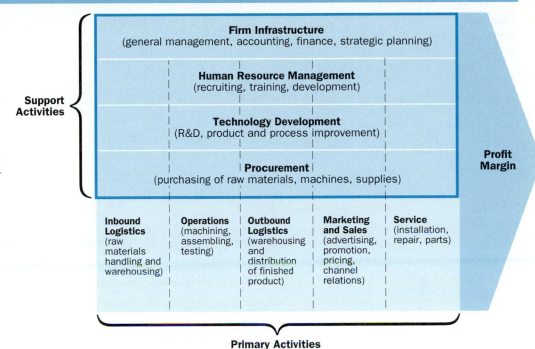

scope, which result when the value chains of two separate products or services share activities, such as the same marketing channels or manufacturing facilities. For example, the cost of joint production of multiple products can be less than the cost of separate production.

4.3 Scanning Functional Resources

The simplest way to begin an analysis of a corporation's value chain is by carefully examining its traditional functional areas for strengths and weaknesses. Functional resources include not only the financial, physical, and human assets in each area, but also the ability of the people in each area to formulate and implement the necessary functional objectives, strategies, and policies. The resources include the knowledge of analytical concepts and procedural techniques common to each area as well as the ability of the people in each area to use them effectively. If used properly, these resources serve as strengths to carry out value-added activities and support strategic decisions. In addition to the usual business functions of marketing, finance, R&D, operations, human resources, and information systems, we also discuss structure and culture as key parts of a business corporation's value chain.

Basic Organizational Structures

Although there is an almost infinite variety of structural forms, certain basic types predominate in modern complex organizations. Figure 4.4 illustrates three basic **organizational structures.** The conglomerate structure is a variant of divisional structure and is

Figure 4.4
Basic Structures of Corporations

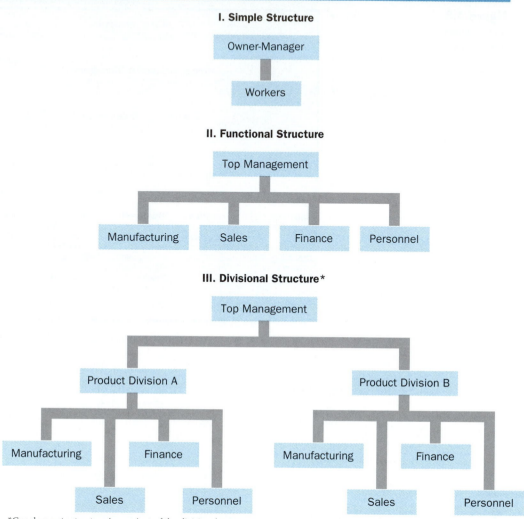

I. Simple Structure

Owner-Manager

Workers

II. Functional Structure

Top Management

Manufacturing   Sales   Finance   Personnel

III. Divisional Structure*

Top Management

Product Division A

Manufacturing   Finance

Sales   Personnel

Product Division B

Manufacturing   Finance

Sales   Personnel

*Conglomerate structure is a variant of the divisional structure.

thus not depicted as a fourth structure. Generally speaking, each structure tends to support some corporate strategies over others.

- **Simple structure** has no functional or product categories and is appropriate for a small, entrepreneur-dominated company with one or two product lines that operates in a reasonably small, easily identifiable market niche. Employees tend to be generalists and jacks-of-all-trades.

- **Functional structure** is appropriate for a medium-sized firm with several product lines in one industry. Employees tend to be specialists in the business functions important to that industry, such as manufacturing, marketing, finance, and human resources.

- **Divisional structure** is appropriate for a large corporation with many product lines in several related industries. Employees tend to be functional specialists organized according to product/market distinctions. General Motors, for example, groups its various auto lines into the separate divisions of Chevrolet, Pontiac,

Oldsmobile, Buick, and Cadillac. Management attempts to find some synergy among divisional activities through the use of committees and horizontal linkages.

- **Strategic business units (SBUs)** are a recent modification to the divisional structure. Strategic business units are divisions or groups of divisions composed of independent product-market segments that are given primary responsibility and authority for the management of their own functional areas. An SBU may be of any size or level, but it must have (1) *a unique mission,* (2) *identifiable competitors,* (3) *an external market focus,* and (4) *control of its business functions.*[7] The idea is to decentralize on the basis of strategic elements rather than on the basis of size, product characteristics, or span of control and to create horizontal linkages among units previously kept separate. For example, rather than organize products on the basis of packaging technology like frozen foods, canned foods, and bagged foods, General Foods organized its products into SBUs on the basis of consumer-oriented menu segments: breakfast food, beverage, main meal, dessert, and pet foods.

- **Conglomerate structure** is appropriate for a large corporation with many product lines in several unrelated industries. A variant of the divisional structure, the conglomerate structure (sometimes called a *holding company*) is typically an assemblage of legally independent firms (subsidiaries) operating under one corporate umbrella but controlled through the subsidiaries' boards of directors. The unrelated nature of the subsidiaries prevents any attempt at gaining synergy among them.

If the current basic structure of a corporation does not easily support a strategy under consideration, top management must decide if the proposed strategy is feasible or if the structure should be changed to a more advanced structure such as the matrix or network. (Advanced structural designs are discussed in Chapter 7.)

Corporate Culture: The Company Way

There is an oft-told story of a person new to a company asking an experienced co-worker what an employee should do when a customer calls. The old-timer responded: "There are three ways to do any job—the right way, the wrong way, and the company way. Around here, we always do things the company way." In most organizations, the "company way" is derived from the corporation's culture. **Corporate culture** is the collection of *beliefs, expectations,* and *values* learned and shared by a corporation's members and transmitted from one generation of employees to another. The corporate culture generally reflects the values of the founder(s) and the mission of the firm. It gives a company a sense of identity: "This is who we are. This is what we do. This is what we stand for." The culture includes the dominant orientation of the company, such as research and development at Hewlett-Packard, customer service at Nordstrom's, or product quality at Maytag. It often includes a number of informal work rules (forming the "company way") that employees follow without question. These work practices over time become part of a company's unquestioned tradition.

Corporate culture has two distinct attributes, intensity and integration.[8] **Cultural intensity** is the degree to which members of a unit accept the norms, values, or other culture content associated with the unit. This shows the culture's depth. Organizations with strong norms promoting a particular value, such as quality at Maytag, have intensive cultures, whereas new firms (or those in transition) have weaker, less intensive cultures. Employees in an intensive culture tend to exhibit consistent behavior, that is, they tend to act similarly over time. **Cultural integration** is the extent to which units throughout an organization share a common culture. This is the culture's breadth.

Organizations with a pervasive dominant culture may be hierarchically controlled and power oriented, such as a military unit, and have highly integrated cultures. All employees tend to hold the same cultural values and norms. In contrast, a company that is structured into diverse units by functions or divisions usually exhibits some strong subcultures (for example, R&D versus manufacturing) and a less integrated corporate culture.

Corporate culture fulfills several important functions in an organization:

1. Conveys a sense of identity for employees.

2. Helps generate employee commitment to something greater than themselves.

3. Adds to the stability of the organization as a social system.

4. Serves as a frame of reference for employees to use to make sense out of organizational activities and to use as a guide for appropriate behavior.[9]

Corporate culture shapes the behavior of people in the corporation. Because these cultures have a powerful influence on the behavior of people at all levels, they can strongly affect a corporation's ability to shift its strategic direction. A strong culture should not only promote survival, but it should also create the basis for a superior competitive position. See the 🌐**21st Century Global Society** feature to see how the Swiss company ABB Asea Brown Boveri AG uses its corporate culture to obtain competitive advantage. To the extent that a corporation's distinctive competence is embedded in an organization's culture, it will be very hard for a competitor to imitate it.[10]

A change in mission, objectives, strategies, or policies is not likely to be successful if it is in opposition to the accepted culture of the firm. Foot-dragging and even sabotage may result, as employees fight to resist a radical change in corporate philosophy. Like structure, if an organization's culture is compatible with a new strategy, it is an internal strength. But if the corporate culture is not compatible with the proposed strategy, it is a serious weakness. See the **Company Spotlight on Maytag Corporation** feature for how its corporate culture affects the company's orientation and activities.

Strategic Marketing Issues

The marketing manager is the company's primary link to the customer and the competition. The manager, therefore, must be especially concerned with the market position and marketing mix of the firm.

Market Position and Segmentation

Market position deals with the question, "Who are our customers?" It refers to the selection of specific areas for marketing concentration and can be expressed in terms of market, product, and geographical locations. Through market research, corporations are able to practice **market segmentation** with various products or services so that managers can discover what niches to seek, which new types of products to develop, and how to ensure that a company's many products do not directly compete with one another.

Marketing Mix

The **marketing mix** refers to the particular combination of key variables under the corporation's control that can be used to affect demand and to gain competitive advantage. These variables are *product, place, promotion,* and *price*. Within each of these four variables

21ST CENTURY GLOBAL SOCIETY

ABB USES CORPORATE CULTURE AS A COMPETITIVE ADVANTAGE

Zurich-based ABB Asea Brown Boveri AG is a worldwide builder of power plants, electrical equipment, and industrial factories in 140 countries. By establishing one set of values throughout its global operations, ABB's management believes that the company will gain an advantage over its rivals Siemens AG of Germany, France's Alcatel-Alsthom NV, and the U.S.'s General Electric Company.

Percy Barnevik, Swedish Chairman of ABB, managed the 1988 merger that created ABB from Sweden's Asea AB and Switzerland's BBC Brown Boveri Ltd. At that time both companies were far behind the world leaders in electrical equipment and engineering. Barnevik introduced his concept of a company with no geographic base—one that had many "home" markets that could draw on expertise from around the globe. To do this, he created a set of 500 global managers who could adapt to local cultures while executing ABB's global strategies. These people are multilingual and move around each of ABB's 5,000 profit cen-

ters in 140 countries. Their assignment is to cut costs, improve efficiency, and integrate local businesses with the ABB world view.

ABB requires local business units, such as Mexico's motor factory, to report both to one of ABB's traveling global managers and to a business area manager who sets global motor strategy for ABB. When the goals of the local factory conflict with worldwide priorities, it is up to the global manager to resolve it.

Few multinational corporations are as successful as ABB in getting global strategies to work with local operations. In agreement with the resource-based view of the firm, Barnevik states, "Our strength comes from pulling together. . . . If you can make this work real well, then you get a competitive edge out of the organization which is very, very difficult to copy."

Source: J. Guyon, "ABB Fuses Units With One Set of Values," *Wall Street Journal* (October 2, 1996), p. A15.

---

are several subvariables, listed in Table 4.1, that should be analyzed in terms of their effects on divisional and corporate performance.

Product Life Cycle

One of the most useful concepts in marketing, insofar as strategic management is concerned, is that of the product life cycle. As depicted in Figure 4.5, the **product life cycle** is a graph showing time plotted against the dollar sales of a product as it moves from introduction through growth and maturity to decline. This concept enables a marketing manager to examine the marketing mix of a particular product or group of products in terms of its position in its life cycle.

Strategic Financial Issues

The financial manager must ascertain the best sources of funds, uses of funds, and control of funds. Cash must be raised from internal or external (local and global) sources and allocated for different uses. The flow of funds in the operations of the organization must be monitored. To the extent that a corporation is involved in international activities, currency fluctuations must be dealt with to ensure that profits aren't wiped out by the rise or fall of the dollar versus the yen, deutsche mark, and other currencies. Bene-

COMPANY SPOTLIGHT

Culture as a Key Strength

F. L. Maytag, founder of the company, made a direct impact on Maytag Corporation's philosophy of management. He strongly valued (among other things) a commitment to quality, promotion from within, dedication to hard work, and an emphasis on performance. For example, in the company's first year of operation, almost half the products sold were defective in some way. In F. L. Maytag's words: "It was then that we learned that *nothing was actually 'sold' until it was in the hands of a satisfied user,* no matter if it had been paid for." His insistence on fixing or purchasing back the faulty products resulted in losses for the new company. The resulting commitment to quality became a key aspect of the corporate culture and a strength of the organization.

In the 1990s, Maytag Corporation still reflected F. L. Maytag's beliefs that hard work and performance are more important than management perquisites. For example, the corporate headquarters is housed on the second floor of a relatively small and modest building. Built in 1961, the Newton, Iowa, building also housed Maytag Company administrative offices on the first floor. Responding to a comment from outside observers that the corporation had spartan offices, Leonard Hadley, then–Chief Operating Officer, looked around at his rather small, windowless office and said, "See for yourself. We want to keep corporate staff to a minimum." Hadley felt that the headquarters' location, coupled with the fact that most of the corporate officers had originally been with the Maytag Company, resulted in an overall top management concern for product quality and financial conservatism.

Maytag purchased Magic Chef partially to obtain access to Admiral's refrigeration operations. Maytag needed Admiral to help it build a high-quality Maytag brand refrigerator. Unfortunately there were some doubts about Admiral's ability to produce quality products. Prior to its acquisition, Admiral had been owned by three different corporations. These previous owners had invested very little into the operation, and production quality had dropped significantly. Employee morale was low. When Leonard Hadley first visited Admiral's facilities in Galesburg, Illinois, to discuss the design of a Maytag line of refrigerators, employees wondered how Admiral was going to be integrated in the new Maytag Corporation. When Admiral personnel asked Hadley when the name on the plant water tower would be changed from Admiral to Maytag, Hadley responded: *"When you earn it!"* This story is widely told throughout Maytag Corporation not only to show Maytag's commitment to quality, but also to show how acquired companies were expected to also adopt this value.

MAYTAG CORPORATION

---

fits in the form of returns, repayments, or products and services must be given to the sources of outside financing. All these tasks must be handled in a way that complements and supports overall corporate strategy.

Financial Leverage

The mix of externally generated short-term and long-term funds in relation to the amount and timing of internally generated funds should be appropriate to the corporate objectives, strategies, and policies. The concept of **financial leverage** (the ratio of total debt to total assets) is helpful in describing how debt is used to increase the earnings available to common shareholders. When the company finances its activities by sales of bonds or notes instead of through stock, the earnings per share are boosted: the interest

Table 4.1   **Marketing Mix Variables**

Product	Place	Promotion	Price
Quality	Channels	Advertising	List price
Features	Coverage	Personal selling	Discounts
Options	Locations	Sales promotion	Allowances
Style	Inventory	Publicity	Payment periods
Brand name	Transport		Credit terms
Packaging			
Sizes			
Services			
Warranties			
Returns			

Source: Philip Kotler, *Marketing Management: Analysis, Planning, and Control,* 4th ed. (Englewood Cliffs, N.J.: Prentice-Hall, 1980), p. 89. Copyright © 1980. Reprinted by permission of Prentice-Hall, Inc.

paid on the debt reduces taxable income, but fewer shareholders share the profits than if the company had sold more stock to finance its activities. The debt, however, does raise the firm's break-even point above what it would have been if the firm had financed from internally generated funds only. High leverage may therefore be perceived as a corporate strength in times of prosperity and ever-increasing sales, or as a weakness in times of a recession and falling sales. This is because leverage acts to magnify the effect on earnings per share of an increase or decrease in dollar sales.

Capital Budgeting

Capital budgeting is the analyzing and ranking of possible investments in fixed assets such as land, buildings, and equipment in terms of the additional outlays and additional receipts that will result from each investment. A good finance department will be able to prepare such capital budgets and to rank them on the basis of some accepted criteria or *hurdle rate* (for example, years to pay back investment, rate of return, or time to break-even point) for the purpose of strategic decision making.

Strategic Research and Development (R&D) Issues

The R&D manager is responsible for suggesting and implementing a company's technological strategy in light of its corporate objectives and policies. The manager's job, therefore, involves (1) choosing among alternative new technologies to use within the corporation, (2) developing methods of embodying the new technology in new products and processes, and (3) deploying resources so that the new technology can be successfully implemented.

R&D Intensity, Technological Competence, and Technology Transfer

The company must make available the resources necessary for effective research and development. A company's **R&D intensity** (its spending on R&D as a percentage of sales revenue) is a principal means of gaining market share in global competition. The amount spent on R&D often varies by industry. For example, the U.S. computer software indus-

Figure 4.5
Product Life Cycle

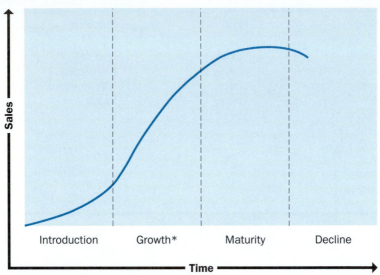

* The right end of the Growth stage is often called Competitive Turbulence because of price and distribution competition that shakes out the weaker competitiors. For further information, see C. R. Wasson, *Dynamic Competitive Strategy and Product Life Cycles,* 3rd ed. (Austin, Tex.: Austin Press, 1978).

try spends an average of 13.5% of its sales dollar for R&D, whereas the paper and forest products industry spends only 1.0%.[11] A good rule of thumb for R&D spending is that a corporation should spend at a "normal" rate for that particular industry unless its strategic plan calls for unusual expenditures.

Simply spending money on R&D or new projects does not mean, however, that the money will produce useful results. For example, Pharmacia Upjohn spent more of its revenues on research than any other company in any industry (18%), but it was ranked low in innovation.[12] A company's R&D unit should be evaluated for **technological competence** in both the development and the use of innovative technology. Not only should the corporation make a consistent research effort (as measured by reasonably constant corporate expenditures that result in usable innovations), it should also be proficient in managing research personnel and integrating their innovations into its day-to-day operations. If a company is not proficient in **technology transfer**, the process of taking a new technology from the laboratory to the marketplace, it will not gain much advantage from new technological advances. For example, Xerox Corporation has been criticized for failing to take advantage of various innovations (such as the mouse and the graphical user interface for personal computers) developed originally in its sophisticated Palo Alto Research Center. See the **Strategy in a Changing World** feature for a classic example of how Apple Computer's ability to imitate a core competency of Xerox gave it a competitive advantage (sustainable until Microsoft launched Windows 3.0).

R&D Mix

Basic R&D is conducted by scientists in well-equipped laboratories where the focus is on theoretical problem areas. The best indicators of a company's capability in this area are its patents and research publications. **Product R&D** concentrates on marketing and is concerned with product or product-packaging improvements. The best measurements of ability in this area are the number of successful new products introduced and the per-

A PROBLEM OF TECHNOLOGY TRANSFER AT XEROX CORPORATION

In the mid 1970s, Xerox Corporation's Palo Alto Research Center (PARC) had developed Alto, a new type of computer with some innovative features. Although Alto was supposed to serve as a research prototype, it became so popular among PARC personnel that some researchers began to develop Alto as a commercial product. Unfortunately this put PARC into direct conflict with Xerox's product development group, which was at the same time developing a rival machine called the Star. Because the Star was in line with the company's expressed product development strategy, top management, who placed all its emphasis on the Star, ignored Alto.

In 1979, Steve Jobs, co-founder of Apple Computer, Inc., made a now-legendary tour of the normally very secretive PARC. Researchers gave Jobs a demonstration of the Alto. Unlike the computers that Apple was then building, Alto had the power of a minicomputer. Its user-friendly software generated crisp text and bright graphics. Jobs fell in love with the machine. He promptly asked Apple's engineers to duplicate the look and feel of Alto. The result was the Macintosh—a personal computer that soon revolutionized the industry.

centage of total sales and profits coming from products introduced within the past five years. **Engineering** (or **process**) **R&D** is concerned with engineering, concentrating on quality control, and the development of design specifications and improved production equipment. A company's capability in this area can be measured by consistent reductions in unit manufacturing costs and by the number of product defects.

Most corporations will have a mix of basic, product, and process R&D, which varies by industry, company, and product line. The balance of these types of research is known as the **R&D mix** and should be appropriate to the strategy being considered and to each product's life cycle. For example, it is generally accepted that product R&D normally dominates the early stages of a product's life cycle (when the product's optimal form and features are still being debated), whereas process R&D becomes especially important in the later stages (when the product's design is solidified and the emphasis is on reducing costs and improving quality).

Impact of Technological Discontinuity on Strategy

The R&D manager must determine when to abandon present technology and when to develop or adopt new technology. Richard Foster of McKinsey and Company states that the displacement of one technology by another (**technological discontinuity**) is a frequent and strategically important phenomenon. Such a discontinuity occurs when a new technology cannot simply be used to enhance the current technology, but actually substitutes for that technology to yield better performance. For each technology within a given field or industry, according to Foster, the plotting of product performance against research effort/expenditures on a graph results in an S-shaped curve. He describes the process depicted in Figure 4.6:

Early in the development of the technology a knowledge base is being built and progress requires a relatively large amount of effort. Later, progress comes more easily. And then, as the

Figure 4.6
Technological
Discontinuity

Source: P. Pascarella,
"Are You Investing in
the Wrong Technol-
ogy?" *Industry Week*
(July 25, 1983), p. 38.
Copyright © 1983
Penton/IPC. All rights
reserved. Reprinted
by permission.

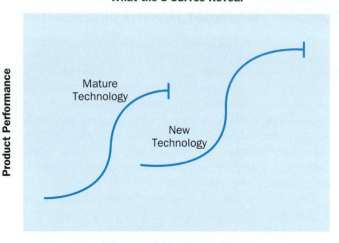

What the S-Curves Reveal

In the corporate planning process, it is generally assumed that incremental progress in technology will occur. But past developments in a given technology cannot be extrapolated into the future, because every technology has its limits. The key to competitiveness is to determine when to shift resources to a technology with more potential.

limits of that technology are approached, progress becomes slow and expensive. That is when R&D dollars should be allocated to technology with more potential. That is also—not so incidentally—when a competitor who has bet on a new technology can sweep away your business or topple an entire industry.[13]

The presence of a technological discontinuity in the world's steel industry during the 1960s explains why the large capital expenditures by U.S. steel companies failed to keep them competitive with the Japanese firms that adopted the new technologies. As Foster points out, "History has shown that as one technology nears the end of its S-curve, competitive leadership in a market generally changes hands."[14]

Strategic Operations Issues

The primary task of the operations (manufacturing or service) manager is to develop and operate a system that will produce the required number of products or services, with a certain quality, at a given cost, within an allotted time. Many of the key concepts and techniques popularly used in manufacturing can be applied to service businesses.

In very general terms, manufacturing can be intermittent or continuous. In **intermittent systems** (job shops), the item is normally processed sequentially, but the work and sequence of the process vary. An example is an auto body repair shop. At each location, the tasks determine the details of processing and the time required for them. These job shops can be very labor intensive. For example, a job shop usually has little automated machinery and thus a small amount of fixed costs. It has a fairly low break-even point, but its variable cost line (composed of wages and costs of special parts) has a relatively steep slope. Because most of the costs associated with the product are variable (many employees earn piece-rate wages), a job shop's variable costs are higher than those of automated firms. Its advantage over other firms is that it can operate at low levels and still be profitable. After a job shop's sales reach break-even, however, the huge variable costs as a percentage of total costs keep the profit per unit at a relatively low level. In terms of strategy, this firm should look for a niche in the marketplace for which it can produce and sell a reasonably small quantity of goods.

In contrast, **continuous systems** are those laid out as lines on which products can be continuously assembled or processed. An example is an automobile assembly line. A firm using continuous systems invests heavily in fixed investments such as automated processes and highly sophisticated machinery. Its labor force, relatively small but highly skilled, earns salaries rather than piece-rate wages. Consequently this firm has a high amount of fixed costs. It also has a relatively high break-even point, but its variable cost line rises slowly. Its advantage is that once it reaches break-even, its profits rise faster than do those of less automated firms. It reaps benefits from economies of scale. In terms of strategy, this firm needs to find a high-demand niche in the marketplace for which it can produce and sell a large quantity of goods. However, this type of firm is likely to suffer huge losses during a recession. During an economic downturn, the firm with less automation and thus less leverage is more likely to survive comfortably because a drop in sales primarily affects variable costs. It is often easier to lay off labor than to sell off specialized plants and machines.

Experience Curve

A conceptual framework that many large corporations have used successfully is the experience curve (originally called the learning curve). The **experience curve** suggests that unit production costs decline by some fixed percentage (commonly 20%–30%) each time the total accumulated volume of production in units doubles. The actual percentage varies by industry and is based on many variables: the amount of time it takes a person to learn a new task, scale economies, product and process improvements, and lower raw materials costs, among others. For example, in an industry with an 85% experience curve, a corporation might expect a 15% reduction in unit costs for every doubling of volume. The total costs per unit can be expected to drop from $100 when the total production is 10 units, to $85 ($100 × 85%) when production increases to 20 units, and to $72.25 ($85 × 85%) when it reaches 40 units. Achieving these results often means investing in R&D and fixed assets; higher fixed costs and less flexibility thus result. Nevertheless the manufacturing strategy is one of building capacity ahead of demand in order to achieve the lower unit costs that develop from the experience curve. On the basis of some future point on the experience curve, the corporation should price the product or service very low to preempt competition and increase market demand. The resulting high number of units sold and high market share should result in high profits, based on the low unit costs.

Management commonly uses the experience curve in estimating the production costs of (1) a product never before made with the present techniques and processes or (2) current products produced by newly introduced techniques or processes. The concept was first applied in the airframe industry and can be applied in the service industry as well. For example, a cleaning company can reduce its costs per employee by having its workers use the same equipment and techniques to clean many adjacent offices in one office building rather than just cleaning a few offices in multiple buildings. Although many firms have used experience curves extensively, an unquestioning acceptance of the industry norm (such as 80% for the airframe industry or 70% for integrated circuits) is very risky. The experience curve of the industry as a whole might not hold true for a particular company for a variety of reasons.

Flexible Manufacturing for Mass Customization

Recently the use of large, continuous, mass-production facilities to take advantage of experience-curve economies has been criticized. The use of Computer-Assisted Design and Computer-Assisted Manufacturing (CAD/CAM) and robot technology means that learning times are shorter and products can be economically manufactured in small, customized batches in a process called **mass customization**—the low-cost production of individually customized goods and services.[15] **Economies of scope** (in which common parts of the manufacturing activities of various products are combined to gain economies even though small numbers of each product are made) replace **economies of scale** (in which unit costs are reduced by making large numbers of the same product) in flexible manufacturing. **Flexible manufacturing** permits the low-volume output of custom-tailored products at relatively low unit costs through economies of scope. It is thus possible to have the cost advantages of continuous systems with the customer-oriented advantages of intermittent systems.

Strategic Human Resource (HRM) Issues

The primary task of the manager of human resources is to improve the match between individuals and jobs. A good HRM department should know how to use attitude surveys and other feedback devices to assess employees' satisfaction with their jobs and with the corporation as a whole. HRM managers should also use job analysis to obtain job description information about what each job needs to accomplish in terms of quality and quantity. Up-to-date job descriptions are essential not only for proper employee selection, appraisal, training, and development for wage and salary administration, and for labor negotiations, but also for summarizing the corporatewide human resources in terms of employee-skill categories. Just as a company must know the number, type, and quality of its manufacturing facilities, it must also know the kinds of people it employs and the skills they possess. The best strategies are meaningless if employees do not have the skills to carry them out or if jobs cannot be designed to accommodate the available workers. Hewlett-Packard, for example, uses employee profiles to ensure that it has the right mix of talents to implement its planned strategies.

Use of Teams

Management is beginning to realize that it must be more flexible in its utilization of employees in order for human resources to be a strength. Human resource managers, therefore, need to be knowledgeable about work options such as part-time work, job sharing, flex-time, extended leaves, and contract work, and especially about the proper use of teams. Over two-thirds of large U.S. companies are successfully using **autonomous work teams** in which a group of people work together without a supervisor to plan, coordinate, and evaluate their own work. Nevertheless only 10% of workers are currently in these teams.[16] Northern Telecom found productivity and quality to increase with work teams to such an extent that it was able to reduce the number of quality inspectors by 40%.[17]

As a way to move a product more quickly through its development stage, companies like Motorola, Chrysler, NCR, Boeing, and General Electric have begun using *cross-functional* work teams. Instead of developing products in a series of steps—beginning with a request from sales, which leads to design, then to engineering and on to purchasing, and finally to manufacturing (and often resulting in a costly product rejected by the customer)—companies are tearing down the traditional walls separating the departments so that people from each discipline can get involved in projects early on. In a process called **concurrent engineering,** the once-isolated specialists now work side by side and compare notes constantly in an effort to design cost-effective products with features customers want. Taking this approach enabled Chrysler Corporation to reduce its product development cycle from 60 to 36 months.[18]

Union Relations and Temporary Workers

If the corporation is unionized, a good human resource manager should be able to work closely with the union. Although union membership in the United States has dropped to less than 10% of private sector workers in the mid 1990s from over 23% in the 1970s, unions still represent around 20% of workers in manufacturing in the United States.[19] To save jobs, U.S. unions are increasingly willing to support employee involvement programs designed to increase worker participation in decision making.

Outside the United States, the average proportion of unionized workers among major industrialized nations is around 50%. European unions tend to be militant, politically oriented, and much less interested in working with management to increase efficiency. Nationwide strikes can occur quickly. Japanese unions are typically tied to individual companies and are usually supportive of management. These differences among countries have significant implications for the management of multinational corporations.

To increase flexibility, avoid layoffs, and reduce labor costs, corporations are using more temporary workers. According to a survey of 93 major multinational corporations (MNCs), 35% of the MNCs expect "contingent" workers to account for at least 10% of their workforce by the year 2000. For example, one out of five French workers were on a temporary or part-time contract in 1996.[20] Labor unions are concerned that companies are using temps to avoid hiring unionized workers. According to John Kinloch, vice-president of Communications Workers of America local 1058, "Corporations are trying to create a disposable workforce with low wages and no benefits."[21]

Quality of Work Life and Human Diversity

Human resource departments have found that to reduce employee dissatisfaction and unionization efforts (or, conversely, to improve employee satisfaction and existing union relations), they must consider the quality of work life in the design of jobs. Partially a reaction to the traditionally heavy emphasis on technical and economic factors in job design, **quality of work life** emphasizes improving the human dimension of work. The knowledgeable human resource manager, therefore, should be able to improve the corporation's quality of work life by (1) introducing participative problem solving, (2) restructuring work, (3) introducing innovative reward systems, and (4) improving the work environment. It is hoped that these improvements will lead to a more participative corporate culture and thus higher productivity and quality products.

Human diversity refers to the mix in the workplace of people from different races, cultures, and backgrounds. This is a hot issue in HRM. Realizing that the demographics are changing toward an increasing percentage of minorities and women in the U.S. workforce, companies are now concerned with hiring and promoting people without regard to ethnic background. Good human resource managers should be working to ensure that people are treated fairly on the job and not harassed by prejudiced co-workers or managers. According to one survey of 645 companies, 74% are concerned with issues in diversity and one-third believe that diversity will affect their corporate strategies.[22]

An organization's human resources are especially important in today's world of global communication and transportation systems. Advances in technology are copied almost immediately by competitors around the world. People are not as willing to move to other companies in other countries. This means that the only long-term resource advantage remaining to corporations operating in the industrialized nations may lie in the area of skilled human resources.

Strategic Information Systems Issues

The primary task of the manager of information systems (IS) is to design and manage the flow of information in an organization in ways that improve productivity and decision making. Information must be collected, stored, and synthesized in such a manner that it will answer important operating and strategic questions. This function is growing in importance.

A corporation's information system can be a strength or a weakness in all three elements of strategic management. It can not only aid in environmental scanning and in controlling a company's many activities, it can also be used as a strategic weapon in gaining competitive advantage. For example, American Hospital Supply (AHS), a leading manufacturer and distributor of a broad line of products for doctors, laboratories, and hospitals, developed an order entry distribution system that directly linked the majority of its customers to AHS computers. The system was successful because it simplified ordering processes for customers, reduced costs for both AHS and the customer, and allowed AHS to provide pricing incentives to the customer. As a result, customer loyalty was high and AHS's share of the market became large.

A trend in corporate information systems is the increasing use of the Internet for marketing and intranets for internal communication. For example, Federal Express found that by allowing customers to directly access its package-tracking database via the Fed Ex Web site instead of their having to ask a human operator, the company saved up to $2 million annually.[23] An **intranet** is an information network within an organization that also has access to the external worldwide Internet. The percentage of large and mid-size firms using an intranet soared to 55% in 1996 from just 11% the previous year. Intranets typically begin as ways to provide employees with company information such as lists of product prices, fringe benefits, and company policies. The networks are then gradually extended to major suppliers and customers. Few companies have taken the next step—to allow employees, customers, and suppliers to conduct business on the Internet in a completely automated manner.[24] By connecting these groups, companies hope to obtain a competitive advantage by reducing the time needed to design and bring new products to market, slashing inventories, customizing manufacturing, and entering new markets.[25]

4.4 The Strategic Audit: A Checklist for Organizational Analysis

One way of conducting an organizational analysis to ascertain a company's strengths and weakness is by using the **Strategic Audit found in Table 10.5 in Chapter 10.** The audit provides a checklist of questions by area of concern. For example, Part IV of the audit examines corporate structure, culture, and resources. It looks at resources in terms of the functional areas of marketing, finance, R&D, operations, human resources, and information systems, among others.

4.5 *Synthesis of Internal Factors—IFAS*

After strategists have scanned the internal organizational environment and identified factors for their particular corporation, they may want to summarize their analysis of these factors using a form such as that given in Table 4.2. This **IFAS Table** (*Internal Factor Analysis Summary*) is one way to organize the internal factors into the generally accepted categories of strengths and weaknesses as well as to analyze how well a particular company's management is responding to these specific factors in light of the perceived importance of these factors to the company. Except for its internal orientation, this IFAS Table is built the same way as the EFAS Table described in Chapter 3 (in Table 3.4). To use the IFAS Table, complete the following steps:

- In **Column 1** (*Internal Strategic Factors*), list the eight to ten most important strengths and weaknesses facing the company.

- In **Column 2** (*Weight*), assign a weight to each factor from **1.0** (*Most Important*) to **0.0** (*Not Important*) based on that factor's probable impact on a particular company's current strategic position. The higher the weight, the more important is this factor to the current and future success of the company. *All weights must sum to 1.0 regardless of the number of factors.*

- In **Column 3** (*Rating*), assign a rating to each factor from **5** (*Outstanding*) to **1** (*Poor*) based on management's current response to that particular factor. Each rating is a judgment regarding how well the company's management is currently dealing with each internal factor.

5	4	3	2	1
Out-standing	Above Average	Average	Below Average	Poor

- In **Column 4** (*Weighted Score*), multiply the *weight* in **Column 2** for each factor times its *rating* in Column 3 to obtain that factor's *weighted score*. This results in a weighted score for each factor ranging from **5.0** (*Outstanding*) to **1.0** (*Poor*) with 3.0 as *Average*.

- In **Column 5** (*Comments*), note why a particular factor was selected and how its weight and rating were estimated.

Finally, add the weighted scores for all the internal factors in Column 4 to determine the total weighted score for that particular company. The *total weighted score* indicates how well a particular company is responding to current and expected factors in its internal environment. The score can be used to compare that firm to other firms in its industry. *The total weighted score for an average firm in an industry is always 3.0.*

As an example of this procedure, Table 4.2 includes a number of internal factors for Maytag Corporation with corresponding weights, ratings, and weighted scores provided. This table is appropriate for 1995 *before* Maytag sold its European and Australian operations. Note that Maytag's total weighted score is 3.05, meaning that the corporation is about average compared to the strengths and weaknesses of others in the major home appliance industry.

Table 4.2   **Internal Factor Analysis Summary (IFAS): Maytag as Example**

Internal Factors	Weight	Rating	Weighted Score	Comments
	1	**2**	**3**	**4**	**5**
Strengths				
• Quality Maytag culture	.15	5	.75	Quality key to success
• Experienced top management	.05	4	.20	Know appliances
• Vertical integration	.10	4	.40	Dedicated factories
• Employee relations	.05	3	.15	Good, but deteriorating
• Hoover's international orientation	.15	3	.45	Hoover name in cleaners
Weaknesses				
• Process-oriented R&D	.05	2	.10	Slow on new products
• Distribution channels	.05	2	.10	Superstores replacing small dealers
• Financial position	.15	2	.30	High debt load
• Global positioning	.20	2	.40	Hoover weak outside the United Kingdom and Australia
• Manufacturing facilities	.05	4	.20	Investing now
Total Scores	**1.00**		**3.05**	

Notes:
1. List strengths and weaknesses (5–10 each) in Column 1.
2. Weight each factor from 1.0 (Most Important) to 0.0 (Not Important) in Column 2 based on that factor's probable impact on the company's strategic position. **The total weights must sum to 1.00.**
3. Rate each factor from 5 (Outstanding) to 1 (Poor) in Column 3 based on the company's response to that factor.
4. Multiply each factor's weight times its rating to obtain each factor's weighted score in Column 4.
5. Use Column 5 (comments) for rationale used for each factor.
6. Add the weighted scores to obtain the total weighted score for the company in Column 4. This tells how well the company is responding to the strategic factors in its internal environment.

Source: T. L. Wheelen and J. D. Hunger, "Internal Strategic Factor Analysis Summary (IFAS)." Copyright © 1991 by Wheelen and Hunger Associates. Reprinted by permission.

4.6   *Global Issues for the 21st Century*

• The **21st Century Global Society** feature in this chapter illustrated how business corporations are hiring a more diverse workforce with multilingual abilities in order to gain competitive advantage in a global environment. A number of firms, from American Express to Delta Airlines, have established international service centers in Utah, for example, because of the high level of multilingual talent within the state. Primarily because Mormons have sent their young people on missions around the world, the people of Utah can collectively speak 90% of the world's written languages. According to Fred Ball, head of a local Chamber of Commerce, "I can make one phone call and get a foreign language speaker in 30 minutes."[26]

• As more and more industries become hypercompetitive, it will become harder to sustain a competitive advantage unless a company has a distinctive competency that is not only durable but also hard to imitate. Durability has little value, however, in a global industry during a time of technological discontinuity.

• Expect an increasing number of corporations to contract various functions to suppliers or distributors in an effort to reduce costs and be globally competitive. For example, the manufacturing of athletic shoes is now exclusively done by Asian contractors for Nike, Reebok, and other global competitors. Corporations are downsizing in an attempt to focus on those parts of the industry value chain where they have distinctive competencies.

- Although the SBU structure has become widespread in most large corporations around the world, such a decentralized structure makes it difficult to take advantage of a corporation's core competencies. This problem will increase as more industries become global with longer communication and logistical networks.

- Expect corporate culture and human resources to increase in importance in hyper-competitive global industries. New products and new technologies are easier to duplicate than are the *intangible* aspects of corporate culture and human resources.

- Autonomous work teams should lead not only to greater efficiency through a reduction of supervisors, but also to greater effectiveness as work teams act to integrate functional specialties at the task level rather than at managerial levels. With supervisors no longer available to deal with disagreements, work teams will need increased training in conflict management.

Projections for the 21st Century

- From 1994 to 2010, the average income per capita in the *developed* nations will rise from $16,610 to $22,802.

- From 1994 to 2010, the average income per capita in the *developing* nations will increase from $950 to $2,563.[27]

Discussion Questions

1. What is the relevance of the resource-based view of the firm to strategic management in a global environment?

2. How can value-chain analysis help identify a company's strengths and weaknesses?

3. In what ways can a corporation's structure and culture be internal strengths or weaknesses?

4. What are the pros and cons of management's using the experience curve to determine strategy?

5. How might a firm's management decide whether it should continue to invest in current known technology or in new, but untested technology? What factors might encourage or discourage such a shift?

Key Terms

autonomous work teams (p. 98)
basic R&D (p. 94)
capital budgeting (p. 93)
center of gravity (p. 85)
concurrent engineering (p. 99)
continuous systems (p. 97)
continuum of sustainability (p. 84)

core competencies (p. 83)
corporate capabilities (p. 83)
corporate culture (p. 89)
cultural integration (p. 89)
cultural intensity (p. 89)
distinctive competencies (p. 83)
durability (p. 83)

economies of scale (p. 98)
economies of scope (p. 86)
engineering (or process) R&D (p. 95)
experience curve (p. 97)
financial leverage (p. 92)
flexible manufacturing (p. 98)

human diversity (p. 99)
IFAS Table (p. 101)
imitability (p. 83)
intermittent systems (p. 96)
internal strategic factors (p. 82)
intranet (p. 100)
linkages (p. 86)
market position (p. 90)
market segmentation (p. 90)
marketing mix (p. 90)

mass customization (p. 98)
organizational analysis (p. 82)
organizational structures (p. 87)
primary activities (p. 86)
product life cycle (p. 91)
product R&D (p. 94)
quality of work life (p. 99)
R&D intensity (p. 93)
R&D mix (p. 95)
resource (p. 82)

strategic business units (SBUs) (p. 89)
support activities (p. 86)
technological competence (p. 94)
technological discontinuity (p. 95)
technology transfer (p. 94)
value chain (p. 84)
VRIO framework (p. 82)
value-chain linkages (p. 86)

Strategic Practice Exercise

Does your college or university have a corporate culture? If it has survived for more than a decade, it probably has one. What are its characteristics? How intense is it? How well integrated?

Before the next class, interview a long-time employee and find some tangible items (like a mission statement, printed philosophy, or honor system policies) that illustrate the culture of your school. What aspect of the culture does your item illustrate? Try to answer the following questions:

____ 1. What are some key beliefs or values that faculty, staff (including administrators), and students share?

____ 2. Is there a story that people tell one another to illustrate a key value of the school? How long ago did this event occur?

____ 3. Does the school have a dominant orientation regarding teaching, research, and service? What does it communicate to its key stakeholders? Is it truthful or just advertising what it thinks stakeholders want from it?

____ 4. Are there any work practices that have become part of the school's unquestioned tradition, but no one seems to know why things are done that way?

Discuss in class what you have discovered. Do your fellow students agree with you? Is there anything about your school's culture you would like to see changed? Why?

Notes

1. S. McCartney, and M. J. McCarthy, "Southwest Flies Circles Around United's Shuttle," *Wall Street Journal* (February 20, 1996), pp. B1 and B8.
2. J. B. Barney, *Gaining and Sustaining Competitive Advantage* (Reading, Mass.: Addison-Wesley, 1997), pp. 145–164.
3. R. M. Grant, "The Resource-Based Theory of Competitive Advantage: Implications for Strategy Formulation," *California Management Review* (Spring 1991), pp. 114–135.
4. *Ibid*, pp. 123–128.
5. J. R. Galbraith, "Strategy and Organization Planning," in *The Strategy Process: Concepts, Contexts, and Cases,* 2nd ed., edited by H. Mintzberg and J. B. Quinn (Englewood Cliffs, N.J.: Prentice Hall, 1991), pp. 315–324.
6. M. Porter, *Competitive Advantage: Creating and Sustaining Superior Performance* (New York: The Free Press, 1985), p. 36.
7. M. Leontiades, "A Diagnostic Framework for Planning," *Strategic Management Journal* (January-March 1983), p. 14.
8. D. M. Rousseau, "Assessing Organizational Culture: The Case for Multiple Methods," in *Organizational Climate and Culture,* edited by B. Schneider (San Francisco: Jossey-Bass, 1990), pp. 153–192.
9. L. Smircich, "Concepts of Culture and Organizational Analysis," *Administrative Science Quarterly* (September 1983), pp. 345–346.
10. Barney, p. 155.
11. "R&D Scoreboard," *Business Week* (June 27, 1994), pp. 81–103.
12. B. O'Reilly, "The Secrets of America's Most Admired Corporations: New Ideas and New Products," *Fortune* (March 3, 1997), p. 62.
13. P. Pascarella, "Are You Investing in the Wrong Technology?" *Industry Week* (July 25, 1983), p. 37.
14. *Ibid.*, p. 38.
15. B. J. Pine, *Mass Customization: The New Frontier in Business Competition* (Boston: Harvard Business School Press, 1993).
16. B. Dumaine, "The Trouble with Teams," *Fortune* (September 5, 1994), p. 86.

17. A. Versteeg, "Self-Directed Work Teams Yield Long-Term Benefits," *Journal of Business Strategy* (November/December 1990), pp. 9–12.

18. R. Sanchez, "Strategic Flexibility in Product Competition," *Strategic Management Journal* (Summer 1995), p. 147.

19. The percentage of unionized government employees is 38.7%. See "Uncle Sam Gompers," *Wall Street Journal* (October 25, 1994), p. A20.

20. G. Koretz, "U.S. Labor Gets Flexible," *Business Week* (January 15, 1996), p. 22; J. Templeman, M. Trinephi, and S. Toy, "A Continent Swarming with Temps," *Business Week* (April 8, 1996), p. 54.

21. D. L. Boroughs, "The New Migrant Workers," *U.S. News & World Report* (July 4, 1994), p. 53.

22. D. S. Hames, "Training in the Land of Doone: An Exercise in Understanding Cultural Differences," *Journal of Management Education* (May 1996), p. 258.

23. A. Cortese, "Here Comes the Intranet," *Business Week* (February 26, 1996), p. 76.

24. B. Richards, "Inside Story," *Wall Street Journal* (June 17, 1996), p. R23.

25. D. Bartholomew, "Blue-Collar Computing," *Information-Week* (June 19, 1995), pp. 34–43.

26. S. B. Donnelly, "The State of Many Tongues," *Time* (April 13, 1992), p. 51.

27. J. Warner, "21st Century Capitalism: Snapshot of the Next Century," *Business Week* (November 18, 1994), p 194.

Chapter 5

Strategy Formulation: Situation Analysis and Business Strategy

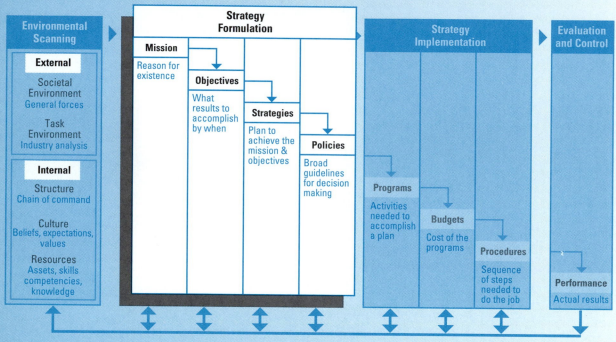

Environmental Scanning							

Environmental Scanning

External

Societal Environment
General forces

Task Environment
Industry analysis

Internal

Structure
Chain of command

Culture
Beliefs, expectations, values

Resources
Assets, skills competencies, knowledge

Strategy Formulation

Mission
Reason for existence

Objectives
What results to accomplish by when

Strategies
Plan to achieve the mission & objectives

Policies
Broad guidelines for decision making

Strategy Implementation

Programs
Activities needed to accomplish a plan

Budgets
Cost of the programs

Procedures
Sequence of steps needed to do the job

Evaluation and Control

Performance
Actual results

Feedback/Learning

When Donald Lamberti incorporated Casey's General Stores in 1967 in Des Moines, Iowa, he formulated a strategy unknown at that time in the convenience store industry. Instead of targeting the large, growing metropolitan areas of the eastern, western, and southern United States where potential sales were high, he chose to focus on the small towns in the agricultural heartland of the Midwest. Contrary to all the conventional wisdom arguing against beginning a business in a declining market, Lamberti avoided direct competition with Seven-Eleven and moved into these increasingly ignored small markets. The company expanded its offerings from just gasoline and basic groceries to include fast food and bakeries. In many small midwestern towns, Casey's was now the only retail business left. These were towns too small for even Wal-Mart to covet. Like any convenience store, prices were somewhat higher than in larger, more specialized stores in the cities. But small-town people did not want to have to drive 10 to 20 miles for a loaf of bread or a pizza.

By autumn 1996, Casey's was opening an average of six new convenience stores a month for a total of just over 1,000 stores in the upper midwestern United States. At a time when other convenience stores were struggling to show a profit and avoid bankruptcy, Casey's recorded continuing growth and profitability. (*For further information, see Caseys.com on the World Wide Web.*)

Casey's General Stores is successful because its strategic managers formulated a new strategy designed to give it an advantage in a very competitive industry. Casey's is an example of a differentiation focus competitive strategy in which a company focuses on a particular market area to provide a differentiated product or service. This strategy is one of the business competitive strategies discussed in this chapter.

5.1   *Situational Analysis: SWOT*

Strategy formulation is often referred to as strategic planning or long-range planning and is concerned with developing a corporation's mission, objectives, strategies, and policies. It begins with situation analysis: the process of finding a strategic fit between external opportunities and internal strengths while working around external threats and internal weaknesses. As shown in the Strategic Decision-Making Process in Figure 1.5, this is step 5(a): analyzing strategic factors in light of the current situation using SWOT analysis. **SWOT** is an acronym used to describe the particular **S**trengths, **W**eaknesses, **O**pportunities, and **T**hreats that are strategic factors for a specific company. SWOT analysis should not only result in the identification of a corporation's **distinctive competencies**—the particular capabilities and resources that a firm possesses and the superior way in which they are used—but also in the identification of opportunities that the firm is not currently able to take advantage of due to a lack of appropriate resources.

Generating a Strategic Factors Analysis Summary (SFAS) Matrix

The **SFAS (Strategic Factors Analysis Summary) Matrix** summarizes an organization's strategic factors by combining the *external* factors from the EFAS Table with the *internal* factors from the IFAS Table. The EFAS and IFAS examples given of Maytag Corporation (as it was in 1995) in Tables 3.4 and 4.2 list a total of 20 internal and external factors. These are too many factors for most people to use in strategy formulation. The SFAS Matrix requires the strategic decision maker to condense these strengths, weaknesses, opportunities, and threats into fewer than ten strategic factors. This is done by reviewing and revising the weight given each factor. The revised weights reflect the priority of each factor as a determinant of the company's future success. The highest weighted EFAS and IFAS factors should appear in the SFAS Matrix.

As shown in Figure 5.1, you can create an SFAS Matrix by following these steps:

- In the **Key Strategic Factors** column (column 1), list the most important EFAS and IFAS items. After each factor, indicate whether it is a strength (S), weakness (W), opportunity (O), or threat (T).

- In the **Weight** column (column 2), enter the weights for all of the internal and external strategic factors. As with the EFAS and IFAS Tables presented earlier, the **weight column must still total 1.00**. *This means that the weights calculated earlier for EFAS and IFAS will probably have to be adjusted.*

Table 4.2   **Internal Factor Analysis Summary (IFAS): Maytag as Example (Selection of Strategic Factors)***

Internal Strategic Factors	Weight	Rating	Weighted Score	Comments
	1	2	3	4	5
Strengths				
S1 Quality Maytag culture	.15	5	.75	Quality key to success
S2 Experienced top management	.05	4	.20	Know appliances
S3 Vertical integration	.10	4	.40	Dedicated factories
S4 Employee relations	.05	3	.15	Good, but deteriorating
S5 Hoover's international orientation	.15	3	.45	Hoover name in cleaners
Weaknesses				
W1 Process-oriented R&D	.05	2	.10	Slow on new products
W2 Distribution channels	.05	2	.10	Superstores replacing small dealers
W3 Financial position	.15	2	.30	High debt load
W4 Global positioning	.20	2	.40	Hoover weak outside the United Kingdom and Australia
W5 Manufacturing facilities	.05	4	.20	Investing now
Total	1.00		3.05	

Table 3.4   **External Factor Analysis Summary (EFAS): Maytag as Example (Selection of Strategic Factors)***

External Strategic Factors	Weight	Rating	Weighted Score	Comments
	1	2	3	4	5
Opportunities				
O1 Economic integration of European Community	.20	4	.80	Acquisition of Hoover
O2 Demographics favor quality appliances	.10	5	.50	Maytag quality
O3 Economic development of Asia	.05	1	.05	Low Maytag presence
O4 Opening of Eastern Europe	.05	2	.10	Will take time
O5 Trend to "Super Stores"	.10	2	.20	Maytag weak in this channel
Threats				
T1 Increasing government regulations	.10	4	.40	Well positioned
T2 Strong U.S. competition	.10	4	.40	Well positioned
T3 Whirlpool and Electrolux strong globally	.15	3	.45	Hoover weak globally
T4 New product advances	.05	1	.05	Questionable
T5 Japanese appliance companies	.10	2	.20	Only Asian presence is Australia
Total	1.00		3.15	

*The most important external and internal factors are identified in the EFAS and IFAS tables as shown here by shading these factors.

Figure 5.1   **Strategic Factor Analysis Summary (SFAS) Matrix**

Key Strategic Factors (Select the most important opportunities/threats from EFAS, Table 3.4 and the most important strengths and weaknesses from IFAS, Table 4.2)	Weight [1]	Rating [2]	Weighted Score [3]	Duration [4] SHORT	INTERMEDIATE [5]	LONG	Comments [6]
S1 Quality Maytag culture (S)	.10	5	.50			X	Quality key to success
S3 Hoover's international orientation (S)	.10	3	.30		X		Name recognition
W3 Financial position (W)	.10	2	.20		X		High debt
W4 Global positioning (W)	.15	2	.30			X	Only in N.A., U.K., and Australia
O1 Economic integration of European Community (O)	.10	4	.40			X	Acquisition of Hoover
O2 Demographics favor quality (O)	.10	5	.50		X		Maytag quality
O5 Trend to super stores (O + T)	.10	2	.20	X			Weak in this channel
T3 Whirlpool and Electrolux (T)	.15	3	.45	X			Dominate industry
T5 Japanese appliance companies (T)	.10	2	.20			X	Asian presence
Total Score	1.00		3.05				

Notes:
1. List each of your key strategic features developed in your IFAS and EFAS tables in Column 1.
2. Weight each factor from 1.0 (Most Important) to 0.0 (Not Important) in Column 2 based on that factor's probable impact on the company's strategic position. **The total weights must sum to 1.00.**
3. Rate each factor from 5 (Outstanding) to 1 (Poor) in Column 3 based on the company's response to that factor.
4. Multiply each factor's weight times its rating to obtain each factor's weighted score in Column 4.
5. For duration in Column 5, check appropriate column (short term—less than 1 year; intermediate—1 to 3 years; long term—over 3 years.)
6. Use Column 6 (comments) for rationale used for each factor.

Source: T. L. Wheelen and J. D. Hunger, "Strategic Factors Analysis Summary (SFAS)." Copyright © 1997 by Wheelen and Hunger Associates. Reprinted by permission.

- In the **Rating** column (column 3), enter the ratings of how the company's management is responding to each of the strategic factors. These ratings will probably (but not always) be the same as those listed in the EFAS and IFAS Tables.

- In the **Weighted Score** column (column 4), calculate the weighted scores as done earlier for EFAS and IFAS.

- In the new **Duration** column (column 5), depicted in Figure 5.1, indicate short-term (less than one year), intermediate-term (one to three years), or long-term (three years and beyond).

- In the **Comments** column (column 6), repeat or revise your comments for each strategic factor from the previous EFAS and IFAS Tables.

The resulting SFAS Matrix is a listing of the firm's external and internal strategic factors in one table. The example given is that of Maytag Corporation in 1995 *before the firm sold its European and Australian operations.* The SFAS Matrix includes only the most important factors gathered from environmental scanning and thus provides the information essential for strategy formulation.

Finding a Propitious Niche

One desired outcome of analyzing strategic factors is identifying a niche where an organization can use its core competencies to take advantage of a particular market opportunity. A niche is a need in the marketplace that is currently unsatisfied. The goal is to find a **propitious niche**—an extremely favorable niche—that is so well suited to the firm's internal and external environment that other corporations are not likely to challenge or dislodge it.[1] A niche is propitious to the extent that it currently is just large enough for one firm to satisfy its demand. After a firm has found and filled that niche, it is not worth a potential competitor's time or money to also go after the same niche.

Finding such a niche is not always easy. A firm's management must be always looking for a **strategic window**, that is, a unique market opportunity that is available only for a particular time. The first firm through a strategic window can occupy a propitious niche and discourage competition (if the firm has the required internal strengths). One company that has successfully found a propitious niche is Frank J. Zamboni & Company, the manufacturer of the machines that smooth the ice at ice skating rinks. Frank Zamboni invented the unique tractor-like machine in 1949 and no one has found a substitute for what it does. Before the machine was invented, people had to clean and scrape the ice by hand to prepare the surface for skating. Now hockey fans look forward to intermissions just to watch "the Zamboni" slowly drive up and down the ice rink turning rough, scraped ice into a smooth mirror surface—almost like magic. So long as Zamboni's company is able to produce the machines in the quantity and quality desired at a reasonable price, it's not worth another company's while to go after Frank Zamboni & Company's propitious niche.

As the niche grows, so can the company within that niche—by increasing its operations' capacity or through alliances with larger firms. The key is to identify a market opportunity in which the first firm to reach that market segment can obtain and keep dominant market share. For example, Church & Dwight was the first company in the United States to successfully market sodium bicarbonate for use in cooking. Its Arm & Hammer brand baking soda is still found in 95% of all U.S. households. The propitious niche concept is crucial to the software industry. Small initial demand in emerging markets allows new entrepreneurial ventures to go after niches too small to be noticed by established companies. When Microsoft developed its first disk operating system (DOS) in 1980 for IBM's personal computers, for example, the demand for such open systems software was very small—a small niche for a then very small Microsoft. The company was able to fill that niche and to successfully grow with it.

Niches can also change—sometimes faster than a firm can adapt to that change. A company may discover in its situation analysis that it needs to invest heavily in its capabilities to keep them competitively strong in a changing niche. Cummins Engine took this approach when it realized that it did not have what was needed to take advantage of a developing opportunity in the diesel engine market. It invested $1 billion—more than three times the market value of its stock—in two new lines of engines in the early 1980s. Ten years later, eager customers such as Ford and Chrysler were purchasing so many of the fuel-efficient motors for their trucks that Cummins had to build a second plant to meet demand. "Competence has given us an economic opportunity," explained CEO Henry Schacht. In retrospect, the CEO pointed out that if in 1981 the company had not chosen to invest heavily, "we would be in decline if not out of business."[2]

5.2   Review of Mission and Objectives

A reexamination of an organization's current mission and objectives must be made before alternative strategies can be generated and evaluated. Even when formulating strategy, decision makers tend to concentrate on the alternatives—the action possibilities—rather than on a mission to be fulfilled and objectives to be achieved. This tendency is so attractive because it is much easier to deal with alternative courses of action that exist right here and now than to really think about what you want to accomplish in the future. The end result is that we often choose strategies that set our objectives for us, rather than having our choices incorporate clear objectives and a mission statement.

Problems in performance can derive from an inappropriate statement of mission, which may be too narrow or too broad. If the mission does not provide a common thread (a unifying theme) for a corporation's businesses, managers may be unclear about where the company is heading. Objectives and strategies might be in conflict with each other. Divisions might be competing against one another, rather than against outside competition—to the detriment of the corporation as a whole.

A company's objectives can also be inappropriately stated. They can either focus too much on short-term operational goals or be so general that they provide little real guidance. There may be a gap between planned and achieved objectives. When such a gap occurs, either the strategies have to be changed to improve performance or the objectives need to be adjusted downward to be more realistic. Consequently objectives should be constantly reviewed to ensure their usefulness. This is what happened at Toyota Motor Corporation when top management realized that its "Global 10" objective of aiming for 10% of the global vehicle market by the end of the century was no longer feasible. Emphasis was then shifted from market share to profits. Interestingly, at the same time that both Toyota and General Motors were deemphasizing market share as a key corporate objective, Ford Motor Company was stating that it wanted to be Number One in sales worldwide. No longer content with being in second place, Alexander Trotman, Ford's Chairman of the Board, contends: "Have you ever seen a team run out on the field and say, 'We're going to be No. 2'"?[3]

5.3   Generating Alternative Strategies Using a TOWS Matrix

Thus far we have discussed how a firm uses SWOT analysis to assess its situation. *SWOT can also be used to generate a number of possible alternative strategies.* The **TOWS Matrix** (TOWS is just another way of saying SWOT) illustrates how the external opportunities and threats facing a particular corporation can be matched with that company's internal strengths and weaknesses to result in four sets of possible strategic alternatives. (See Figure 5.2.) This is a good way to use brainstorming to create alternative strategies that might not otherwise be considered. It forces strategic managers to create various kinds of growth as well as retrenchment strategies. It can be used to generate corporate as well as business strategies.

To generate a TOWS Matrix for Maytag Corporation in 1995, for example, use the *External Factor Analysis Summary* (EFAS) listed in Table 3.4 from Chapter 3 and the *Internal Factor Analysis Summary* (IFAS) listed in Table 4.2 from Chapter 4. To build Figure 5.3, take the following steps:

Figure 5.2
TOWS Matrix

Source: Adapted from *Long-Range Planning,* April 1982, H. Weihrich, "The TOWS Matrix—A Tool for Situational Analysis" p. 60. Copyright 1982, with kind permission from H. Weihrich and Elsevier Science Ltd. The Boulevard, Langford Lane, Kidlington OX5 1GB, UK.

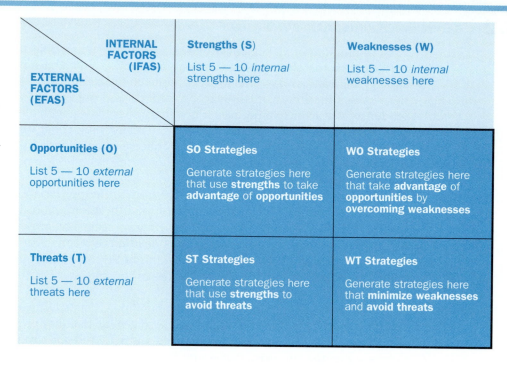

1. In the **Opportunities** (**O**) block, list the external opportunities available in the company's or business unit's current and future environment from the *EFAS Table* (Table 3.4).

2. In the **Threats** (**T**) block, list the external threats facing the company or unit now and in the future from the *EFAS Table* (Table 3.2).

3. In the **Strengths** (**S**) block, list the specific areas of current and future strength for the company or unit from the *IFAS Table* (Table 4.2).

4. In the **Weaknesses** (**W**) block, list the specific areas of current and future weakness for the company or unit from the *IFAS Table* (Table 4.2).

5. Generate a series of possible strategies for the company or business unit under consideration based on particular combinations of the four sets of strategic factors:

   - **SO Strategies** are generated by thinking of ways in which a company or business unit could use its strengths to take advantage of opportunities.

   - **ST Strategies** consider a company's or unit's strengths as a way to avoid threats.

   - **WO Strategies** attempt to take advantage of opportunities by overcoming weaknesses.

   - **WT Strategies** are basically defensive and primarily act to minimize weaknesses and avoid threats.

The TOWS Matrix is very useful for generating a series of alternatives that the decision makers of a company or business unit might not otherwise have considered. It can be used for the corporation as a whole (as was done in Figure 5.3 with Maytag Corporation before it sold Hoover Europe), or it can be used for a specific business unit within a corporation (like Hoover's floor care products). Nevertheless the TOWS Matrix is only one of many ways to generate alternative strategies. Another approach is to evaluate each business unit within a corporation in terms of possible competitive and cooperative strategies.

5.4 Business Strategies

Business strategy focuses on improving the competitive position of a company's or business unit's products or services within the specific industry or market segment that the company or business unit serves. Business strategy can be competitive (battling against all competitors for advantage) and/or cooperative (working with one or more competitors to gain advantage against other competitors). Just as corporate strategy asks *what* industry(ies) the company should be in, business strategy asks *how* the company or its units should compete or cooperate in each industry.

Porter's Competitive Strategies

Competitive strategy raises the following questions:

- Should we compete on the basis of low cost (and thus price), or should we differentiate our products or services on some basis other than cost, such as quality or service?

- Should we compete head to head with our major competitors for the biggest but most sought-after share of the market, or should we focus on a niche in which we can satisfy a less sought-after but also profitable segment of the market?

Michael Porter proposes two "generic" competitive strategies for outperforming other corporations in a particular industry: lower cost and differentiation.[4] These strategies are called generic because they can be pursued by any type or size of business firm, even by not-for-profit organizations.

- **Lower cost strategy** is the ability of a company or a business unit to design, produce, and market a comparable product more efficiently than its competitors.

- **Differentiation strategy** is the ability to provide unique and superior value to the buyer in terms of product quality, special features, or after-sale service.

Porter further proposes that a firm's competitive advantage in an industry is determined by its **competitive scope**, that is, the breadth of the company's or business unit's target market. Before using one of the two generic competitive strategies (lower cost or differentiation), the firm or unit must choose the range of product varieties it will produce, the distribution channels it will employ, the types of buyers it will serve, the geographic areas in which it will sell, and the array of related industries in which it will also compete. This should reflect an understanding of the firm's unique resources. Simply put, a company or business unit can choose a *broad target* (that is, aim at the middle of the mass market) or a *narrow target* (that is, aim at a market niche). Combining these two types of target markets with the two competitive strategies results in the four variations of generic strategies depicted in Figure 5.4. When the lower cost and differentiation strategies have a broad mass-market target, they are simply called *cost leadership* and *differentiation*. When they are focused on a market niche (narrow target), however, they are called *cost focus* and *differentiation focus*.

Table 4.2   Internal Factor Analysis Summary (IFAS): Maytag as Example

Internal Strategic Factors	Weight	Rating	Weighted Score	Comments
	1	2	3	4
Strengths				
S1 Quality Maytag culture	.15	5	.75	Quality key to success
S2 Experienced top management	.05	4	.20	Know appliances
S3 Vertical integration	.10	4	.40	Dedicated factories
S4 Employee relations	.05	3	.15	Good, but deteriorating
S5 Hoover's international orientation	.15	3	.45	Hoover name in cleaners
Weaknesses				
W1 Process-oriented R&D	.05	2	.10	Slow on new products
W2 Distribution channels	.05	2	.10	Superstores replacing small dealers
W3 Financial position	.15	2	.30	High debt load
W4 Global positioning	.20	2	.40	Hoover weak outside the United Kingdom and Australia
W5 Manufacturing facilities	.05	4	.20	Investing now
Total	**1.00**		**3.05**	

Table 3.4   External Factor Analysis Summary (EFAS): Maytag as Example

External Strategic Factors	Weight	Rating	Weighted Score	Comments
	1	2	3	4
Opportunities				
O1 Economic integration of European Community	.20	4	.80	Acquisition of Hoover
O2 Demographics favor quality appliances	.10	5	.50	Maytag quality
O3 Economic development of Asia	.05	1	.05	Low Maytag presence
O4 Opening of Eastern Europe	.05	2	.10	Will take time
O5 Trend to "Super Stores"	.10	2	.20	Maytag weak in this channel
Threats				
T1 Increasing government regulations	.10	4	.40	Well positioned
T2 Strong U.S. competition	.10	4	.40	Well positioned
T3 Whirlpool and Electrolux strong globally	.15	3	.45	Hoover weak globally
T4 New product advances	.05	1	.05	Questionable
T5 Japanese appliance companies	.10	2	.20	Only Asian presence is Australia
Total	**1.00**		**3.15**	

Figure 5.3 **Generating a TOWS Matrix for Maytag Corporation**

Internal Factors (IFAS Table 4.2)	Strengths (S)	Weaknesses (W)
External Factors (EFAS Table 3.4)	S1 Quality Maytag culture S2 Experienced top management S3 Vertical integration S4 Employee relations S5 Hoover's international orientation	W1 Process-oriented R&D W2 Distribution channels W3 Financial position W4 Global positioning W5 Manufacturing facilities
Opportunities (O) O1 Economic integration of European Community O2 Demographics favor quality O3 Economic development of Asia O4 Opening of Eastern Europe O5 Trend toward super stores	**SO Strategies** ■ Use worldwide Hoover distribution channels to sell both Hoover and Maytag major appliances. ■ Find joint venture partners in Eastern Europe and Asia.	**WO Strategies** ■ Expand Hoover's presence in continental Europe by improving Hoover quality and reducing manufacturing and distribution costs. ■ Emphasize superstore channel for all non-Maytag brands
Threats (T) T1 Increasing government regulation T2 Strong U.S. competition T3 Whirlpool and Electrolux positioned for global economy T4 New product advances T5 Japanese appliance companies	**ST Strategies** ■ Acquire Raytheon's appliance business to increase U.S. market share. ■ Merge with a Japanese major home appliance company ■ Sell off all non-Maytag brands and strongly defend Maytag's U.S. niche.	**WT Strategies** ■ Sell off Dixie-Narco Division to reduce debt. ■ Emphasize cost reduction to reduce break-even point. ■ Sell out to Raytheon or a Japanese firm.

Cost leadership is a low-cost competitive strategy that aims at the broad mass market and requires "aggressive construction of efficient-scale facilities, vigorous pursuit of cost reductions from experience, tight cost and overhead control, avoidance of marginal customer accounts, and cost minimization in areas like R&D, service, sales force, advertising, and so on."[5] Because of its lower costs, the cost leader is able to charge a lower price for its products than its competitors and still make a satisfactory profit. Some companies successfully following this strategy are Wal-Mart, Alamo Rent-A-Car, Southwest Airlines, Timex, and Gateway 2000. Having a low-cost position also gives a company or business unit a defense against rivals. Its lower costs allow it to continue to earn profits during times of heavy competition. Its high market share means that it will have high bargaining power relative to its suppliers (because it buys in large quantities). Its low price will also serve as a barrier to entry because few new entrants will be able to match the leader's cost advantage. As a result, cost leaders are likely to earn above-average returns on investment.

Differentiation is aimed at the broad mass market and involves the creation of a product or service that is perceived throughout its industry as unique. The company or

Figure 5.4
Porter's Generic Competitive Strategies

Source: Reprinted with permission of The Free Press, an imprint of Simon & Schuster, from *The Competitive Advantage of Nations* by Michael E. Porter, p. 39. Copyright © 1990 by Michael E. Porter.

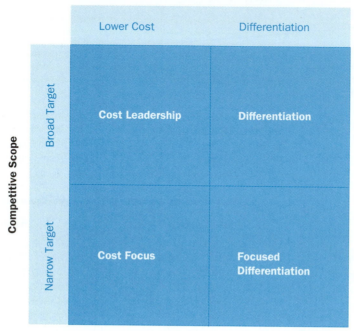

business unit may then charge a premium for its product. This specialty can be associated with design or brand image, technology, features, dealer network, or customer service. Differentiation is a viable strategy for earning above-average returns in a specific business because the resulting brand loyalty lowers customers' sensitivity to price. Increased costs can usually be passed on to the buyers. Buyer loyalty also serves as an entry barrier—new firms must develop their own distinctive competence to differentiate their products in some way in order to compete successfully. Examples of the successful use of a differentiation strategy are Walt Disney Productions, Maytag appliances, Nike athletic shoes, and Mercedes-Benz automobiles. Research does suggest that a differentiation strategy is more likely to generate higher profits than is a low-cost strategy because differentiation creates a better entry barrier. A low-cost strategy is more likely, however, to generate increases in market share.[6]

Cost focus is a low-cost competitive strategy that focuses on a particular buyer group or geographic market and attempts to serve only this niche, to the exclusion of others. In using cost focus, the company or business unit seeks a cost advantage in its target segment. A good example of this strategy is Fadal Engineering. Fadal focuses its efforts on building and selling no-frills machine tools to small manufacturers. Fadal achieved cost focus by keeping overhead and R&D to a minimum and by focusing its marketing efforts strictly on its market niche. The cost focus strategy is valued by those who believe that a company or business unit that focuses its efforts is better able to serve its narrow strategic target more efficiently than can its competition. It does, however, require a tradeoff between profitability and overall market share.

Differentiation focus, like cost focus, concentrates on a particular buyer group, product line segment, or geographic market. This is the strategy successfully followed by Casey's General Stores, Morgan Motor Car Company (manufacturer of classic British sports cars), and local health food stores. In using differentiation focus, the company or business unit seeks differentiation in a targeted market segment. This strategy is valued

DIFFERENTIATION FOCUS STRATEGY AT MORGAN MOTOR CAR COMPANY

By focusing on the values of traditional British, top-down, sports car motoring, the Morgan Motor Car Company has successfully found a way to differentiate itself from all competitors. Once competing with the respected British marques of MG, Triumph, Austin-Healey, Jaguar, and Aston Martin, the Morgan is now the sole occupant of a small, but durable propitious niche. Founded in 1919 by Henry F. S. Morgan, the company continues to use the same factory in England's West Midlands to produce automobiles seemingly unchanged from those produced before World War II. Although Morgans (known as "mogs" by admirers) have state-of-the-art engines with fuel injection, electronic ignition, and pollution control devices, the basic front-end suspension design has remained relatively unchanged since the company's founder built the first Morgan by hand in 1908. Although the chassis is based on a simple steel frame, the body is still constructed on a hand-built wooden frame of specially aged ash. The Morgan's hand-cut body panel must be fitted by hand onto the car.

The company makes three models, ranging in price from $35,000 to $50,000. The company has no long-term debt and enjoys steady growth in sales and profits. Sports cars with reputations comparable to that of the Morgan sell for $150,000 and up. For the person wanting a personalized car, the Morgan is available in 35,000 hand-painted colors. The company employs just enough skilled workers to build ten cars a week for an annual capacity of fewer than 500 cars. Because the company receives about 600 to 800 new orders each year, the current waiting list for a new Morgan is about 2,500 to 5,000 cars—about 10 years' production! The firm's response to a rapidly changing automobile industry seems perfectly tuned to staying in its propitious niche. According to Charles Morgan, grandson of the founder, "We . . . believe the Morgan policy of gradual and carefully considered change will enable us to maintain the car's qualities and unique appeal, and thereby ensure its survival for the foreseeable future."

Source: P. G. Goulet and A. Rappaport, "The Morgan Motor Car Company: The Last of the Great Independents," in Wheelen and Hunger, *Strategic Management and Business Policy,* 5th ed. (Reading, Mass.: Addison-Wesley, 1995), pp. 1126–1138.

by those who believe that a company or a unit that focuses its efforts is better able to serve the special needs of a narrow strategic target more effectively than can its competition. See the **Strategy in a Changing World** feature for Morgan Motors' ability to prosper in a changing global industry by sticking to British tradition.

Risks in Competitive Strategies

No one competitive strategy is guaranteed to achieve success, and some companies that have successfully implemented one of Porter's competitive strategies have found that they could not sustain the strategy. As shown in Table 5.1, each of the generic strategies has its risks. For example, a company following a differentiation strategy must ensure that the higher price it charges for its higher quality is not priced too far above the competition, otherwise customers will not see the extra quality as worth the extra cost. This is what is meant in Table 5.1 by the term **cost proximity.** Procter & Gamble's use of R&D and advertising to differentiate its products had been very successful for many years until customers in the value-conscious 1990s turned to cheaper private brands. As a result, P & G was forced to reduce costs until it could get prices back in line with customer expectations.

Table 5.1 **Risks of Generic Competitive Strategies**

Risks of Cost Leadership	Risks of Differentiation	Risks of Focus
Cost leadership is not sustained: • Competitors imitate. • Technology changes. • Other bases for cost leadership erode. Proximity in differentiation is lost.	Differentiation is not sustained: • Competitors imitate. • Bases for differentiation become less important to buyers. Cost proximity is lost.	The focus strategy is imitated: The target segment becomes structurally unattractive: • Structure erodes. • Demand disappears. Broadly targeted competitors overwhelm the segment: • The segment's differences from other segments narrow. • The advantages of a broad line increase.
Cost focusers achieve even lower cost in segments.	Differentiation focusers achieve even greater differentiation in segments.	New focusers subsegment the industry.

Source: Adapted/reprinted with permission of The Free Press, an imprint of Simon & Schuster, from *Competitive Advantage: Creating and Sustaining Superior Performance* by Michael E. Porter, p. 21. Copyright © 1985 by Michael E. Porter.

Issues in Competitive Strategies

Porter argues that to be successful, a company or business unit must achieve one of the preceding generic competitive strategies. Otherwise, the company or business unit is **stuck in the middle** of the competitive marketplace with no competitive advantage and is doomed to below-average performance. An example of a company stuck in the middle was Tandy Corporation. Tandy's strategy of selling personal computers to the average person had failed to generate the large amount of sales and profits top management had desired. Its computers had neither the exciting new features found on Compaq's products nor the low price of the PC clones like those sold through the mail by Dell or Gateway. Sales were stagnating. Attempting to increase its sales to business through its GRID Systems subsidiary while keeping up its Radio Shack sales, Tandy was confronted with the dilemma of trying to be all things to all people—and failing. Deciding at last that computers were distracting it from its primary business of consumer electronics retailing, management sold the company's computer operations to AST Research.

Research generally supports Porter's contention that a firm that fails to achieve a generic strategy is going to be stuck in the middle with no competitive advantage. But what about companies that attempt to achieve both a low-cost *and* a high differentiation position? The Japanese auto companies of Toyota, Nissan, and Honda are often presented as examples of successful firms able to achieve both of these generic strategies. Although Porter agrees that it is possible for a company or a business unit to achieve low cost and differentiation simultaneously, he argues that this state is often temporary. Porter does admit, however, that many different kinds of potentially profitable competitive strategies exist. Although there is generally room for only one company to successfully pursue the mass market cost leadership strategy (because it is so dependent on achieving dominant market share), there is room for an almost unlimited number of differentiation and focus strategies (depending on the range of possible desirable features and the number of identifiable market niches). Quality, alone, has eight different dimensions—each with the potential of providing a product with a competitive advantage (see Table 5.2).

Table 5.2   The Eight Dimensions of Quality

1. Performance.	Primary operating characteristics, such as a washing machine's cleaning ability.
2. Features.	"Bells and whistles," like cruise control in a car, that supplement the basic functions.
3. Reliability.	Probability that the product will continue functioning without any significant maintenance.
4. Conformance.	Degree to which a product meets standards. When a customer buys a product out of the warehouse, it will perform identically to that viewed on the showroom floor.
5. Durability.	Number of years of service a consumer can expect from a product before it significantly deteriorates. Differs from reliability in that a product can be durable, but still need a lot of maintenance.
6. Serviceability.	Product's ease of repair.
7. Aesthetics.	How a product looks, feels, sounds, tastes, or smells.
8. Perceived Quality.	Product's overall reputation. Especially important if there are no objective, easily used measures of quality.

Source: Adapted from D. A. Garvin, *Managing Quality: The Strategic and Competitive Edge* (New York: Free Press, 1988).

Most entrepreneurial ventures follow focus strategies. The successful ones differentiate their product from those of other competitors in the areas of quality and service, and they focus the product on customer needs in a segment of the market, thereby achieving a dominant share of that part of the market. Adopting guerrilla warfare tactics, these companies go after opportunities in market niches too small to justify retaliation from the market leaders.

Industry Structure and Competitive Strategy

Although each of Porter's generic competitive strategies may be used in any industry, certain strategies are more likely to succeed than others in some instances. In a **fragmented industry**, for example, where many small- and medium-sized local companies compete for relatively small shares of the total market, focus strategies will likely predominate. Fragmented industries are typical for products in the early stages of their life cycle. If few economies are to be gained through size, no large firms will emerge and entry barriers will be low—allowing a stream of new entrants into the industry. Chinese restaurants and funeral homes are examples. Over 85% of funeral homes in the United States are independently owned.[7]

If a company is able to overcome the limitations of a fragmented market, however, it can reap the benefits of a broadly targeted cost leadership or differentiation strategy. Until Pizza Hut was able to use advertising to differentiate itself from local competitors, the pizza fast-food business was a fragmented industry composed primarily of locally owned pizza parlors, each with its own distinctive product and service offering. Subsequently Domino's used the cost leader strategy to achieve U.S. national market share. Currently Sears is attempting to dominate the traditionally fragmented household repair and home improvement industry. Operating on the assumption that people have less time to fix things around the house, Sears is spending $30 million to emphasize "the service side of Sears" tied to "one phone call to Sears Home Central (800) 4-Repair."[8]

As an industry matures, fragmentation is overcome and the industry tends to become a **consolidated industry** dominated by a few large companies. Although many industries begin fragmented, battles for market share and creative attempts to overcome local or niche market boundaries often increase the market share of a few companies. After product standards become established for minimum quality and features, competition shifts to a greater emphasis on cost and service. Slower growth, overcapacity, and knowledgeable buyers combine to put a premium on a firm's ability to achieve cost leadership or differentiation along the dimensions most desired by the market. Research and development shifts from product to process improvements. Overall product quality improves, and costs are reduced significantly.

The industry has now become one in which cost leadership and differentiation tend to be combined to various degrees. A firm can no longer gain high market share simply through low price. The buyers are more sophisticated and demand a certain minimum level of quality for price paid. The same is true for firms emphasizing high quality. Either the quality must be high enough and valued by the customer enough to justify the higher price or the price must be dropped (through lowering costs) to compete effectively with the lower priced products. This consolidation is taking place worldwide in the automobile, airline, and home appliance industries.

Hypercompetition and Competitive Strategy

In his book *HyperCompetition,* D'Aveni proposes that it is becoming increasingly difficult to sustain a competitive advantage for very long. "Market stability is threatened by short product life cycles, short product design cycles, new technologies, frequent entry by unexpected outsiders, repositioning by incumbents, and tactical redefinitions of market boundaries as diverse industries merge."[9] Consequently a company or business unit must constantly work to improve its competitive advantage. It is not enough to be just the lowest cost competitor. Through continuous improvement programs, competitors are usually working to lower their costs as well. Firms must find new ways not only to reduce costs further, but also to add value to the product or service being provided.

The same is true of a firm or unit that is following a differentiation strategy. Maytag Company (a unit of Maytag Corporation), for example, was successful for many years by offering the most durable brand in major home appliances. It was able to charge the highest prices for Maytag brand washing machines. When other competitors improved the quality of their products, however, it became increasingly harder for customers to justify Maytag's significantly higher price. Consequently Maytag Company was forced not only to add new features to its products, but also to reduce costs through improved manufacturing processes so that its prices were no longer out of line with those of the competition.

D'Aveni contends that when industries become **hypercompetitive,** they tend to go through escalating stages of competition. Firms initially compete on cost and quality until an abundance of high-quality, low-priced goods result. This occurred in the U.S. major home appliance industry by 1980. In a second stage of competition, the competitors move into untapped markets. Others usually imitate these moves until the moves become too risky or expensive. This epitomized the major home appliance industry during the 1980s and 1990s as firms moved first to Europe and then into Asia and South America.

According to D'Aveni, firms then raise entry barriers to limit competitors. Economies of scale, distribution agreements, and strategic alliances make it all but impossible for a new firm to enter the major home appliance industry by the turn of the century. After the established players have entered and consolidated all new markets, the next stage is for the remaining firms to attack and destroy the strongholds of other firms. Maytag's 1995 decision to divest its European division and concentrate on improving its position in North America could be a prelude to building a North American stronghold while Whirlpool, GE, and Electrolux are distracted by European and worldwide investments. Eventually, according to D'Aveni, the remaining large global competitors work their way to a situation of perfect competition in which no one has any advantage and profits are minimal.

Before hypercompetition, strategic initiatives provided competitive advantage for many years, perhaps for decades. This is no longer the case. According to D'Aveni, as industries become hypercompetitive, there is no such thing as a sustainable competitive advantage. Successful strategic initiatives in this type of industry typically last only months to a few years. According to D'Aveni, the only way a firm in this kind of dynamic industry can sustain any competitive advantage is through a continuous series of multiple short-term initiatives aimed at replacing a firm's current successful products with the next generation of products before the competitors can do so. Intel and Microsoft are taking this approach in the hypercompetitive computer industry.

Hypercompetition views competition, in effect, as a distinct series of ocean waves on what used to be a fairly calm stretch of water. As industry competition becomes more intense, the waves grow higher and require more dexterity to handle. Although a strategy is still needed to sail from point A to point B, more turbulent water means that a craft must continually adjust course to suit each new large wave. One danger of D'Aveni's concept of hypercompetition, however, is that it may lead to an overemphasis on short-term tactics (to be discussed in the next section) over long-term strategy. Too much of an orientation on the individual waves of hypercompetition could cause a company to focus too much on short-term temporary advantage and not enough on achieving its long-term objectives through building sustainable competitive advantage.

Which Competitive Strategy Is Best?

Before selecting one of Porter's generic competitive strategies for a company or business unit, management should assess its feasibility in terms of company or business unit resources and capabilities. Porter lists some of the commonly required skills and resources, as well as organizational requirements, in Table 5.3.

Competitive Tactics

A **tactic** is a specific operating plan detailing how a strategy is to be implemented in terms of *when* and *where* it is to be put into action. By their nature, tactics are narrower in their scope and shorter in their time horizon than are strategies. Tactics, therefore, may be viewed (like policies) as a link between the formulation and implementation of strategy. Some of the tactics available to implement competitive strategies are **timing tactics** (when) and **market location tactics** (where).

Timing Tactics: When to Compete

The first company to manufacture and sell a new product or service is called the **first mover** (or pioneer). Some of the advantages of being a first mover are that the company is able to establish a reputation as an industry leader, move down the learning curve to assume the cost leader position, and earn temporarily high profits from buyers who value the product or service very highly. A successful first mover can also set the standard for all subsequent products in the industry. A company that sets the standard "locks in" customers and is then able to offer further products based on that standard.[10] Microsoft was able to do this in software with its Windows operating system, and Netscape garnered over 80% share of the Internet browser market by being first to commercialize the product successfully.

Being a first mover does, however, have its disadvantages. These disadvantages can be, conversely, advantages enjoyed by late mover firms. **Late movers** may be able to imitate the technological advances of others (and thus keep R&D costs low), keep risks

Table 5.3   **Requirements for Generic Competitive Strategies**

Generic Strategy	Commonly Required Skills and Resources	Common Organizational Requirements
Overall Cost Leadership	• Sustained capital investment and access to capital • Process engineering skills • Intense supervision of labor • Products designed for ease of manufacture • Low-cost distribution system	• Tight cost control • Frequent, detailed control reports • Structured organization and responsibilities • Incentives based on meeting strict quantitative targets.
Differentiation	• Strong marketing abilities • Product engineering • Creative flair • Strong capability in basic research • Corporate reputation for quality or technological leadership • Long tradition in the industry or unique combination of skills drawn from other businesses • Strong cooperation from channels	• Strong coordination among functions in R&D, product development, and marketing • Subjective measurement and incentives instead of quantitative measures • Amenities to attract highly skilled labor, scientists, or creative people
Focus	• Combination of the above policies directed at the particular strategic target	• Combination of the above policies directed at the particular strategic target

Source: Adapted/reprinted with permission of The Free Press, an imprint of Simon & Schuster, from *Competitive Strategy: Techniques for Analyzing Industries and Competitors* by Michael E. Porter, pp. 40–41. Copyright © 1980 by The Free Press.

down by waiting until a new market is established, and take advantage of the first mover's natural inclination to ignore market segments. Once Netscape had established itself as the standard for Internet browsers, Microsoft used its huge resources to directly attack Netscape's position. It did not want Netscape to also set the standard in the developing and highly lucrative intranet market inside corporations.

Market Location Tactics: Where to Compete

A company or business unit can implement a competitive strategy either offensively or defensively. An **offensive tactic** usually takes place in an established competitor's market location. A defensive tactic usually takes place in the firm's own current market position as a defense against possible attack by a rival.[11]

Offensive Tactics   Some of the methods used to attack a competitor's position are:

- **Frontal Assault.**   The attacking firm goes head to head with its competitor. It matches the competitor in every category from price to promotion to distribution channel. To be successful, the attacker must not only have superior resources, but also the willingness to persevere. This is generally a very expensive tactic and may serve to awaken a sleeping giant (as MCI and Sprint did to AT&T in long distance telephone service), depressing profits for the whole industry.

- **Flanking Maneuver.**   Rather than going straight for a competitor's position of strength with a frontal assault, a firm may attack a part of the market where the competitor is weak. Cyrix Corporation followed this tactic with its entry into the microprocessor market—a market then almost totally dominated by Intel. Rather than going directly after Intel's microprocessor business, Cyrix developed a math co-processor for Intel's 386 chip that would run 20 times faster than Intel's microprocessor. To be successful, the flanker must be patient and willing to carefully expand out of the relatively undefended market niche or else face retaliation by an established competitor.

- **Bypass Attack.** Rather than directly attacking the established competitor frontally or on its flanks, a company or business unit may choose to change the rules of the game. This tactic attempts to cut the market out from under the established defender by offering a new type of product that makes the competitor's product unnecessary. For example, instead of competing directly against Microsoft's Windows 95 operating system, Netscape chose to use Java "applets" in its Internet browser so that an operating system and specialized programs were no longer necessary to run applications on a personal computer.

- **Encirclement.** Usually evolving out of a frontal assault or flanking maneuver, encirclement occurs as an attacking company or unit encircles the competitor's position in terms of products or markets or both. The encircler has greater product variety (a complete product line ranging from low to high price) and/or serves more markets (it dominates every secondary market). Microsoft is following this tactic as it attacks Netscape's Internet browser business with its "embrace and extend" strategy. By embracing Netscape's use of cross-platform Internet applets and quickly extending it into multiple applications, Microsoft attempted to dominate the browser market.

- **Guerrilla Warfare.** Instead of a continual and extensive resource-expensive attack on a competitor, a firm or business unit may choose to "hit and run." Guerrilla warfare is characterized by the use of small, intermittent assaults on different market segments held by the competitor. In this way, a new entrant or small firm can make some gains without seriously threatening a large, established competitor and evoking some form of retaliation. To be successful, the firm or unit conducting guerrilla warfare must be patient enough to accept small gains and to avoid pushing the established competitor to the point that it must respond or else lose face. Microbreweries, which make beer for sale to local customers, use this tactic against national brewers like Anheuser-Busch.

Defensive Tactics According to Porter, **defensive tactics** aim to lower the probability of attack, divert attacks to less threatening avenues, or lessen the intensity of an attack. Instead of increasing competitive advantage per se, they make a company's or business unit's competitive advantage more sustainable by causing a challenger to conclude that an attack is unattractive. These tactics deliberately reduce short-term profitability to ensure long-term profitability.[12]

- **Raise Structural Barriers.** Entry barriers act to block a challenger's logical avenues of attack. Some of the most important according to Porter are to:

  (1) offer a full line of products in every profitable market segment to close off any entry points;

  (2) block channel access by signing exclusive agreements with distributors;

  (3) raise buyer switching costs by offering low-cost training to users;

  (4) raise the cost of gaining trial users by keeping prices low on items new users are most likely to purchase;

  (5) increase scale economies to reduce unit costs;

(6) foreclose alternative technologies through patenting or licensing;

(7) limit outside access to facilities and personnel;

(8) tie up suppliers by obtaining exclusive contracts or purchasing key locations;

(9) avoid suppliers that also serve competitors; and

(10) encourage the government to raise barriers such as safety and pollution standards or favorable trade policies.

- **Increase Expected Retaliation.** This tactic is any action that increases the perceived threat of retaliation for an attack. For example, management may strongly defend any erosion of market share by drastically cutting prices or matching a challenger's promotion through a policy of accepting any price-reduction coupons for a competitor's product. This counterattack is especially important in markets that are very important to the defending company or business unit. For example, when Clorox Company challenged Procter & Gamble Company in the detergent market with Clorox Super Detergent, P&G retaliated by test marketing its liquid bleach, Lemon Fresh Comet, in an attempt to scare Clorox into retreating from the detergent market.

- **Lower the Inducement for Attack.** A third type of defensive tactic is to reduce a challenger's expectations of future profits in the industry. Like Southwest Airlines, a company can deliberately keep prices low and constantly invest in cost-reducing measures. With prices kept very low, there is little profit incentive for a new entrant.

Cooperative Strategies

Competitive strategies and tactics are used to gain competitive advantage within an industry by *battling against* other firms. These are not, however, the only business strategy options available to a company or business unit for competing successfully within an industry. **Cooperative strategies** can also be used to gain competitive advantage within an industry by *working with* other firms.

Collusion

The two general types of cooperative strategies are collusion and strategic alliances. **Collusion** is the active cooperation of firms within an industry to reduce output and raise prices in order to get around the normal economic law of supply and demand. Collusion may be *explicit*, in which firms cooperate through direct communication and negotiation, or *tacit*, in which firms cooperate indirectly through an informal system of signals. Explicit collusion is illegal in most countries. For example, Archer Daniels Midland (ADM), the large U.S. agricultural products firm, has been accused of conspiring with its competitors to limit the sales volume and raise the price of the food additive lysine. Executives from three Japanese and South Korean lysine manufacturers admitted meeting in hotels in major cities throughout the world to form a "lysine trade association." By the end of 1996, the three companies had been fined more than $20 million by the U.S. federal government. Although ADM had earlier agreed to pay $25 million to settle a lawsuit on behalf of 600 lysine customers, U.S. federal prosecutors sought a grand jury indictment of the company and two of its senior executives.[13]

Collusion can also be tacit, in which there is no direct communication among competing firms. According to Barney, tacit collusion in an industry is most likely to be successful if (1) there are a small number of identifiable competitors, (2) costs are similar among firms, (3) one firm tends to act as the "price leader," (4) there is a common industry culture that accepts cooperation, (5) sales are characterized by a high frequency of small orders, (6) large inventories and order backlogs are normal ways of dealing with fluctuations in demand, and (7) there are high entry barriers to keep out new competitors.[14]

Even tacit collusion can, however, be illegal. For example, when General Electric wanted to ease price competition in the steam turbine industry, it widely advertised its prices and publicly committed not to sell below these prices. Customers were even told that if GE reduced turbine prices in the future, it would give customers a refund equal to the price reduction. GE's message was not lost on Westinghouse, the major competitor in steam turbines. Both prices and profit margins remained stable for the next ten years in this industry. The U.S. Department of Justice then sued both firms for engaging in "conscious parallelism" (following each other's lead to reduce the level of competition) in order to reduce competition.

Strategic Alliances

A **strategic alliance** is a partnership of two or more corporations or business units to achieve strategically significant objectives that are mutually beneficial.[15] Alliances between companies or business units have become a fact of life in modern business. Some alliances are very short term, only lasting long enough for one partner to establish a beachhead in a new market. Others are more long lasting and may even be the prelude to a full merger between two companies.

Companies or business units may form a strategic alliance for a number of reasons, including:

1. **To obtain technology and/or manufacturing capabilities.** For example, Intel formed a partnership with Hewlett-Packard to use HP's capabilities in RISC technology in order to develop the successor to Intel's Pentium microprocessor.

2. **To obtain access to specific markets.** Rather than buy a foreign company or build breweries of its own in other countries, Anheuser-Busch chose to license the right to brew and market Budweiser to other brewers, such as Labatt in Canada, Modelo in Mexico, and Kirin in Japan.

3. **To reduce financial risk.** For example, because the costs of developing a new large jet airplane were becoming too high for any one manufacturer, Boeing, Aerospatiale of France, British Aerospace, Construcciones Aeronáuticas of Spain, and Deutsche Aerospace of Germany planned a joint venture to design such a plane.

4. **To reduce political risk.** To gain access to China while ensuring a positive relationship with the often restrictive Chinese government, Maytag Corporation formed a joint venture with the Chinese appliance maker, RSD. See the **Company Spotlight on Maytag Corporation** feature to learn what both companies hoped to obtain from this strategic alliance.

5. **To achieve or ensure competitive advantage.** General Motors and Toyota formed Nummi Corporation as a joint venture to provide Toyota a manufacturing facility in the United States and GM access to Toyota's low-cost, high-quality manufacturing expertise.[16]

Cooperative arrangements between companies and business units fall along a continuum from weak and distant to strong and close. (See Figure 5.5.) The types of alliances range from mutual service consortia to joint ventures and licensing arrangements to value-chain partnerships.[17]

Maytag Forms a Joint Venture in China

Asia had become the world's second largest home appliance market (after Europe) by the mid 1990s and opportunities were still emerging. China and India, in particular, offered phenomenal growth opportunities. For example, the saturation level of washing machines (percentage of homes having a washer) in China was only 10% compared to 54% in Mexico and 75% in the United States. Although Japanese and Korean appliance manufacturers dominated the Asian market overall, the industry was still fragmented with no single dominant company in terms of market share. Matsushita was the overall market leader in Asia, but it had a market share of less than 10% outside Japan. U.S. and European appliance manufacturers were using acquisitions and joint ventures to establish a presence in this part of the world. AB Electrolux was establishing a full line of appliance facilities in China and India, among other Asian locations. In addition to its distributors in Australia, Malaysia, Japan, Singapore, Thailand, and Taiwan, Whirlpool established joint ventures in China and India. General Electric had part ownership of Philcor in the Philippines and a joint venture with Godrej & Boyce, India's largest appliance maker.

Realizing the vast potential of the Chinese market, Maytag Corporation formed two joint ventures in 1996 with Hefei Rongshida Group Corporation, known as RSD, to manufacturer and market washing machines and refrigerators. RSD was among the market leaders in China in laundry products and was a widely recognized brand throughout the country. It produced about 1.1 million washers in 1995 out of a total of 9.5 million sold in China. Maytag invested $35 million in a joint laundry products facility to sell washers and dryers throughout the country and some Pacific Rim areas. To help RSD enter the refrigerator business, Maytag invested another $35 million in the construction of a jointly-owned refrigeration products facility in the city of Hefei. Maytag owned 50.5% of both joint ventures through two wholly-owned subsidiaries. According to Leonard Hadley, Maytag Corporation's Chairman and CEO: "This is a focused investment for Maytag aimed at profitable growth in a market that is growing at double-digit rates."

MAYTAG CORPORATION

Mutual Service Consortia   A **mutual service consortium** is a partnership of similar companies in similar industries who pool their resources to gain a benefit that is too expensive to develop alone, such as access to advanced technology. For example, IBM of the United States, Toshiba of Japan, and Siemens of Germany formed a consortium to develop new generations of computer chips. As part of this alliance, IBM offered Toshiba its expertise in chemical mechanical polishing to help develop a new manufacturing process using ultraviolet lithography to etch tiny circuits in silicon chips. IBM then transferred the new technology to a facility in the United States.[18]

In another example, General Motors, Procter & Gamble, and six other companies purchased $20 million of equity in a small artificial intelligence company called Teknowledge. GM hoped that Teknowledge's expert systems software would help it to design cars and to prepare factory schedules. The other members of the consortium had similar hopes. The mutual service consortia is a fairly weak and distant alliance. There is very little interaction or communication among the partners.

Joint Venture   A **joint venture** is a "cooperative business activity, formed by two or more separate organizations for strategic purposes, that creates an independent busi-

| Mutual Service Consortia | Joint Venture Licensing Arrangement | Value-Chain Partnership |

Weak and Distant   **Strong and Close**

Figure 5.5
Continuum of Strategic Alliances

Source: Suggested by R. M. Kanter, "Collaborative Advantage: The Art of Alliances," *Harvard Business Review* (July-August 1994), pp. 96–108.

ness entity and allocates ownership, operational responsibilities, and financial risks and rewards to each member, while preserving their separate identity/autonomy."[19] Along with licensing arrangements, joint ventures lay at the mid-point of the continuum and are formed to pursue an opportunity that needs a capability from two companies or business units, such as the technology of one and the distribution channels of another.

Joint ventures are the most popular form of strategic alliance. They often occur because the companies involved do not want to or cannot legally merge permanently. Joint ventures provide a way to temporarily combine the different strengths of partners to achieve an outcome of value to both. For example, the pharmaceutical firm Merck & Company agreed with the chemical giant DuPont Company to form, under joint ownership, a new company called DuPont Merck Pharmaceutical Company. Merck provided the new company with its foreign marketing rights to some prescription medicines plus some cash. In return, Merck got access to all of DuPont's experimental drugs and its small but productive research operation.

Extremely popular in international undertakings because of financial and political-legal constraints, joint ventures are a convenient way for corporations to work together without losing their independence. See the 🌐 **21st Century Global Society** feature for an example of such a joint venture between a U.S. and a Mexican company.

Disadvantages of joint ventures include loss of control, lower profits, probability of conflicts with partners, and the likely transfer of technological advantage to the partner. Joint ventures are often meant to be temporary, especially by some companies who may view them as a way to rectify a competitive weakness until they can achieve long-term dominance in the partnership. Partially for this reason, joint ventures have a high failure rate.[20] Research does indicate, however, that joint ventures tend to be more successful when both partners have equal ownership in the venture and are mutually dependent on each other for results.[21]

Licensing Arrangement   A **licensing arrangement** is an agreement in which the licensing firm grants rights to another firm in another country or market to produce and/or sell a product. The licensee pays compensation to the licensing firm in return for technical expertise. Licensing is an especially useful strategy if the trademark or brand name is well known, but the MNC does not have sufficient funds to finance its entering the country directly. Anheuser-Busch is using this strategy to produce and market Budweiser beer in the United Kingdom, Japan, Israel, Australia, Korea, and the Philippines. This strategy also becomes important if the country makes entry via investment either difficult or impossible. The danger always exists, however, that the licensee might develop its competence to the point that it becomes a competitor to the licensing firm. Therefore, a company should never license its distinctive competence, even for some short-run advantage.

21ST CENTURY GLOBAL SOCIETY

DEAN FOODS FINDS A JOINT VENTURE PARTNER IN MEXICO

Half of all the citizens of Mexico are under the age of 18. To the management of the Chicago-based Dean Foods Company, this meant that Mexico was a potential market for milk and milk products. The country had withstood a chronic shortage of fresh milk due to government-set price ceilings, which reduced the incentive for local producers to provide the product. When trade barriers began dropping in 1991, Dean's El Paso dairy teamed with a Mexican distributor to truck milk and ice cream to border towns. By 1992, Mexico consumed one-third of that dairy's output. Dean also began purchasing broccoli and cauliflower from Mexico for its processing plants in Texas and New Mexico. The company assigned two of its corporate staff people to research the Mexican market. Based on their findings, Dean Foods planned to first emphasize dairy products and then vegetables. The company would eventually like to sell products that aren't native to Mexico, such as canned sweet corn, peas, and green beans.

Although Dean Foods could buy an existing Mexican dairy or simply export products from the United States, the company decided to ask its current dairy products distributor if it would be interested in a joint venture. Dean's managers toured the distributor's facilities; the distributor's managers toured one of Dean Foods' plants in Rockford, Illinois. Even with a joint venture, huge problems still existed. For example, only about half of all households in Mexico had refrigerators. Instead of selling milk in gallon jugs, Dean Foods would need to use small cartons. Some supermarkets turned off their electricity overnight. Dean Foods would have to set up refrigerated cases in supermarkets and pay the stores to maintain the electricity 24 hours a day. Because dairy farms were scarce in Mexico, Dean Foods would probably have to encourage the development of new ones. The company would probably also have to establish special quality control standards because 40% of all milk sold in the country was unpasteurized.

For Howard Dean, CEO of the company, the allure of Mexico was not in shifting plants to cut labor costs, but in the market potential for his products. "We've got to move quickly. The opportunity is now," concluded the grandson of the company's founder.

Source: L. Therrein and S. Baker, "Market Share Con Leche?" *Business Week* (Reinventing America, 1992 edition), p. 122.

Value-Chain Partnership   The **value-chain partnership** is a strong and close alliance in which one company or unit forms a long-term arrangement with a key supplier or distributor for mutual advantage. Value-chain partnerships are becoming extremely popular as more companies and business units outsource activities that were previously done within the company or business unit. For example, DuPont contracts out project engineering and design to Morrison Knudsen; AT&T, its credit card processing to Total System Services; Northern Telecom, its electronic component manufacturing to Comptronix; and Eastman Kodak, its computer support services to Businessland.

Another example of a value-chain partnership is the long-term relationship between a company or business unit with a supplier or distributor. To improve the quality of parts it purchases, companies in the U.S. auto industry, for example, have decided to work more closely with fewer suppliers and to involve them more in product design decisions. Such partnerships are also a way for a firm to acquire new technology to use in its own products. For example, Maytag Company was approached by one of its suppliers, Honeywell's Microswitch Division, which offered its expertise in fuzzy logic technology—a technology Maytag did not have at that time. The resulting partnership in product development resulted in Maytag's new IntelliSense™ dishwasher. Unlike previous dishwashers that the operator had to set, Maytag's fuzzy logic dishwasher automatically selected the proper cleaning cycle based on a series of factors such as the amount of dirt and presence of detergent.

According to Paul Ludwig, business development manager for Honeywell's Microswitch division, "Had Maytag not included us on the design team, we don't believe the two companies would have achieved the same innovative solution, nor would we have completed the project in such a short amount of time."[22] The benefits of such relationships do not just accrue to the purchasing firm. Research suggests that suppliers who engage in long-term relationships are more profitable than suppliers with multiple short-term contracts.[23]

5.5   Global Issues for the 21st Century

- The **21st Century Global Society** feature in this chapter illustrated how Dean Foods formed a joint venture with its Mexican distributor in order to expand its business in Mexico. Even though individual joint ventures are often short-lived, this type of strategic alliance is an extremely popular way of expanding globally. As countries become less fearful of foreign-based multinational corporations, they may begin to allow more cross-border mergers and acquisitions in addition to strategic alliances.

- As a corporation becomes more involved internationally, it will need to constantly review the appropriateness of its current mission and objectives. The huge investment required to become a global competitor means that return on investment objectives will need to be reduced while other objectives are expanded.

- One set of business strategies may not be sufficient for success in a global industry. A company may need to tailor its business strategies to each nation in which it operates.

- To be competitive in a global industry, companies are discovering that they must raise the quality of their products and reduce the prices. Although this does not mean that a company must follow both a differentiation and a low-cost strategy simultaneously, it does mean that international competition usually requires a higher level of performance in terms of cost and quality than does domestic competition.

- As more industries become increasingly global and hypercompetitive, fewer companies will survive unless they are able to adapt to changing conditions. For example, European companies in 1997 were falling behind many U.S. and some Asian companies in the use of networked personal computers. According to Intel CEO Andy Grove, European companies "operate like old-line U.S. companies did ten years ago." He warned of a "growing technology deficit."[24]

Projections for the 21st Century

- From 1994 to 2010, the average life expectancy for women will rise from 67 to 71 and for men will increase from 63 to 67.

- From 1994 to 2010, the number of AIDS cases worldwide will increase from 20 million to 38 million.[25]

Discussion Questions

1. What industry forces might cause a propitious niche to disappear?

2. Is it possible for a company or business unit to follow a cost leadership strategy and a differentiation strategy simultaneously? Why or why not?

3. Is it possible for a company to have a sustainable competitive advantage when its industry becomes hypercompetitive?

4. What are the advantages and disadvantages of being a first mover in an industry? Give some examples of first mover and late mover firms. Were they successful?

5. Why are most strategic alliances temporary?

Key Terms

business strategy (p. 113)
collusion (p. 124)
competitive scope (p. 113)
competitive strategy (p. 113)
consolidated industry (p. 119)
cooperative strategies (p. 124)
cost focus (p. 116)
cost leadership (p. 115)
cost proximity (p. 117)
defensive tactics (p. 123)
differentiation (p. 115)
differentiation focus (p. 116)

differentiation strategy (p. 113)
distinctive competencies (p. 107)
first mover (p. 121)
fragmented industry (p. 119)
hypercompetitive (p. 120)
joint venture (p. 126)
late mover (p. 121)
licensing arrangement (p. 127)
lower cost strategy (p. 113)
market location tactics (p. 121)
mutual service consortium (p. 126)
offensive tactics (p. 122)

propitious niche (p. 110)
SFAS Matrix (p. 107)
SO, ST, WO, WT Strategies (p. 112)
strategic alliances (p. 125)
strategic window (p. 110)
stuck in the middle (p. 118)
SWOT (p. 107)
tactics (p. 121)
timing tactics (p. 121)
TOWS Matrix (p. 111)
value-chain partnership (p. 128)

Strategic Practice Exercise

Read the following paragraph about a successful company in a newly emerging business. What should this company do if it wants to continue competing successfully in the future? Form a group with 3–4 other people in your class. Consider the questions posed at the end of the paragraph. Compare your group's recommendations with those of other groups.

    E*Trade Group, Inc., was a pioneer in the on-line trading of securities. Led by CEO Christos Cotsakos,

the discount brokerage firm had the largest volume of Internet trades—2,500 daily during 1996. Seventy-five percent of its business was conducted online. Even though only 80,000 investors traded online in 1996, that number was expected to grow to 1.3 million in just two years. E*Trade has been successful not only by being the first on the Internet, but also by charging only $12 per trade. Revenue, totaling $23.3 million in 1995, has grown an average of 125% annually since 1991. While E*Trade was preparing to go public, it was dealing with several problems. A computer hardware failure in May 1996 left many customers unable to access their accounts for 2½ hours. That led to a $1.7 million payment to clients who lost money in the market. An increase in accounts from 38,000 to 65,000, with trading volume tripling from 50 million to 170 million shares during the first five months of 1996, left the company struggling to keep up. Established brokerage firms, such as Charles Schwab and Fidelity Investments, were reducing their commissions and gearing up to compete for a share of this emerging Internet market.[26]

1. What competitive strategy is E*Trade following?

2. Does E*Trade have a sustainable competitive advantage?

3. Given the increasing level of competition in this industry, what do you think E*Trade should do to continue competing successfully?

Notes

1. W. H. Newman, "Shaping the Master Strategy of Your Firm," *California Management Review,* Vol. 9, No. 3 (1967), pp. 77–88.

2. K. Kelly, "Henry Schacht," *The 1993 Business Week 1000* (1993), p. 80.

3. R. L. Simpson, and O. Suris, "Alex Trotman's Goal: To Make Ford No. 1 in World Auto Sales," *Wall Street Journal* (July 18, 1995), p. A5.

4. M. E. Porter, *Competitive Strategy* (New York: The Free Press, 1980), pp. 34–41 as revised in M. E. Porter, *The Competitive Advantage of Nations* (New York: The Free Press, 1990), pp. 37–40.

5. Porter, *Competitive Strategy,* p. 35.

6. R. E. Caves, and P. Ghemawat, "Identifying Mobility Barriers," *Strategic Management Journal* (January 1992), pp. 1–12.

7. R. Tomsho, "Funeral Parlors Become Big Business," *Wall Street Journal* (September 18, 1996), pp. B1 & B4.

8. G. Buck, "If It Ain't Broke, Don't Fix It! It Is? Call Sears," *Des Moines Register* (March 2, 1997), p. G3.

9. R. A. D'Aveni, *HyperCompetition* (New York: The Free Press, 1994), pp. xiii–xiv.

10. Some refer to this as the economic concept of "increasing returns." Instead of reaching a point of diminishing returns when a product saturates a market and the curve levels off, the curve continues to go up as the company takes advantage of setting the standard to spin off new products that use the new standard to achieve higher performance than competitors. See J. Alley, "The Theory That Made Microsoft," *Fortune* (April 29, 1996), pp. 65–66.

11. Summarized from various articles by L. Fahey in *The Strategic Management Reader,* edited by L. Fahey (Englewood Cliffs, N.J.: Prentice-Hall, 1989), pp. 178–205.

12. This information on defensive tactics is summarized from M. E. Porter, *Competitive Advantage* (New York: Free Press, 1985), pp. 482–512.

13. T. M. Burton, "Archer-Daniels Faces a Potential Blow As Three Firms Admit Price-Fixing Plot," *Wall Street Journal* (August 28, 1996), pp. A3 & A6; R. Henkoff, "The ADM Tale Gets Even Stranger," *Fortune* (May 13, 1996), pp. 113–120.

14. Much of the content on cooperative strategies was summarized from J. B. Barney, *Gaining and Sustaining Competitive Advantage* (Reading, Mass.: Addison-Wesley, 1997), pp. 255–278.

15. E. A. Murray, Jr., and J. F. Mahon, "Strategic Alliances: Gateway to the New Europe?" *Long Range Planning* (August 1993), p. 103.

16. *Ibid,* pp. 105–106.

17. R. M. Kanter, "Collaborative Advantage: The Art of Alliances," *Harvard Business Review* (July-August 1994), pp. 96–108.

18. B. Bremner, Z. Schiller, T. Smart, and W. J. Holstein, "Keiretsu Connections," *Business Week* (July 22, 1996), pp. 52–54.

19. R. P. Lynch, *The Practical Guide to Joint Ventures and Corporate Alliances* (New York: John Wiley and Sons, 1989), p. 7.

20. One study of 880 alliances revealed only 45% were felt to be successful by both parties and 40% of the cases failed to last four years. See B. J. James, "Strategic Alliances," in *International Review of Strategic Management,* Vol. 2, No. 2, edited by D. E. Hussey (New York: John Wiley & Sons, 1992), pp. 63–72.

21. L. L. Blodgett, "Factors in the Instability of International Joint Ventures: An Event History Analysis," *Strategic Management Journal* (September 1992), pp. 475–481; J. Bleeke and D. Ernst, "The Way to Win in Cross-Border Alliances," *Harvard Business Review* (November-December 1991), pp. 127–135; J. M. Geringer, "Partner Selection Criteria for Developed Country Joint Ventures," in *International Management Behavior,* 2nd ed., edited by H. W. Lane and J. J. DiStephano (Boston: PWS-Kent, 1992), pp. 206–216.

22. S. Stevens, "Speeding the Signals of Change," *Appliance* (February 1995), p. 7.

23. K. Z. Andrews, "Manufacturer/Supplier Relationships: The Supplier Payoff," *Harvard Business Review* (September-October 1995), pp. 14–15.

24. D. Kirkpatrick, "Europe's Technology Gap Is Getting Scary," *Fortune* (March 17, 1997), pp. 26–27.

25. J. Warner, "21st Century Capitalism: Snapshot of the Next Century," *Business Week* (November 18, 1994), p. 194.

26. L. Himelstein, "This Virtual Broker Has Real Competition," *Business Week* (July 22, 1996), pp. 91–92.

Chapter 6

Strategy Formulation: Corporate Strategy

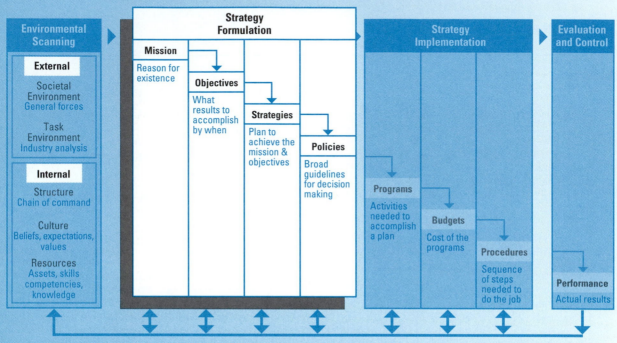

| Environmental Scanning | Strategy Formulation | | | | Strategy Implementation | Evaluation and Control |

When Lewis Platt became CEO of Hewlett-Packard Company in the early 1990s, he soon realized that the company was in danger of missing critical opportunities. Computers, communications, and consumer electronics were rapidly converging into one interrelated industry. Unfortunately Hewlett-Packard was not involved in the strategic alliances and acquisitions that other companies were using to take advantage of this development. A close look internally at Hewlett-Packard's strengths revealed a unique mix of core technologies that no single competitor could match. HP offered a broad and well-regarded family of computers; it was a leader in test and measurement instruments; and it was strong in computer networking. Management proposed that the company blend these three technologies to create new product categories.

Following this idea, Hewlett-Packard developed a diagnostic system for Ford Motor Company's dealers that combined instruments that monitor a car's internal operations with an HP computer. HP also began developing other products that could take advantage of its core competencies—video servers, interactive TV devices, digital cable TV decoders, video printers, interactive notepads, health monitors, and a physician's workstation, among others. It also formed a partnership with Intel Corporation to develop next-generation processors using HP's RISC expertise. According to Platt, the Intel relationship is "the key, the heart" of HP's hardware future. This strategy is already paying off for the company in terms of increased sales and profits.[1]

6.1   Corporate Strategy

Corporate strategy deals with three key issues facing the corporation as a whole:

1. The firm's overall orientation toward growth, stability, or retrenchment (*directional strategy*)

2. The industries or markets in which the firm competes through its products and business units (*portfolio strategy*)

3. The manner in which management coordinates activities and transfers resources and cultivates capabilities among product lines and business units (*parenting strategy*)

Corporate strategy is primarily about the choice of direction for the firm as a whole.[2] This is true whether the firm is a small, one-product company or a large multinational corporation. In a large multibusiness company, however, corporate strategy is also about managing various product lines and business units for maximum value. In this instance, corporate headquarters must play the role of the organizational "parent," in that it must deal with various product and business unit "children." Even though each product line or business unit has its own competitive or cooperative strategy that it uses to obtain it own competitive advantage in the marketplace, the corporation must coordinate these different business strategies so that the corporation as a whole succeeds as a "family."[3]

Corporate strategy, therefore, includes decisions regarding the flow of financial and other resources to and from a company's product lines and business units. Through a series of coordinating devices, a company transfers skills and capabilities developed in one unit to other units that need such resources. In this way, it attempts to obtain synergies among numerous product lines and business units so that the corporate whole is greater than the sum of its individual business unit parts.[4] All corporations, from the smallest company offering one product in only one industry to the largest conglomerate operating in many industries with many products must, at one time or another, consider one or more of these issues.

To deal with each of the key issues, this chapter is organized into **three parts** that examine corporate strategy in terms of *directional strategy* (orientation toward growth), *portfolio analysis* (coordination of cash flow among units), and *corporate parenting* (building corporate synergies through resource sharing and development).

6.2   Directional Strategy

Just as every product or business unit must follow a business strategy to improve its competitive position, every corporation must decide its orientation toward growth by asking the following three questions:

- Should we expand, cut back, or continue our operations unchanged?

- Should we concentrate our activities within our current industry or should we diversify into other industries?

- If we want to grow and expand nationally and/or globally, should we do so through *internal* development or through *external* acquisitions, mergers, or strategic alliances?

A corporation's **directional strategy** is composed of three general orientations (sometimes called grand strategies):

- **Growth strategies** expand the company's activities.

- **Stability strategies** make no change to the company's current activities.

- **Retrenchment strategies** reduce the company's level of activities.

Having chosen the general orientation (such as growth), a company's managers can select from several more specific corporate strategies such as concentration within one product line/industry or diversification into other products/industries. (See Figure 6.1.) These strategies are useful both to corporations operating in only one industry with one product line and to those operating in many industries with many product lines.

Growth Strategies

By far the most widely pursued corporate directional strategies are those designed to achieve growth in sales, assets, profits, or some combination. Companies that do business in expanding industries must grow to survive. Continuing growth means increasing sales and a chance to take advantage of the experience curve to reduce the per-unit cost of products sold, thereby increasing profits. This cost reduction becomes extremely important if a corporation's industry is growing quickly and competitors are engaging in price wars in attempts to increase their shares of the market. Firms that have not reached "critical mass" (that is, gained the necessary economy of large-scale production) will face large losses unless they can find and fill a small, but profitable, niche where higher prices can be offset by special product or service features. That is why Motorola, Inc., continued to spend large sums on the product development of cellular phones, pagers, and two-way radios, despite a serious drop in profits. According to Motorola's Chairman George Fisher, "What's at stake here is leadership." Even though the industry was changing quickly, the company was working to avoid the erosion of its market share by jumping into new wireless markets as quickly as possible. Continuing as the market leader in this industry would almost guarantee Motorola enormous future returns.

A corporation can grow internally by expanding its operations both globally and domestically, or it can grow externally through mergers, acquisitions, and strategic alliances. A **merger** is a transaction involving two or more corporations in which stock is exchanged, but from which only one corporation survives. Mergers usually occur between firms of somewhat similar size and are usually "friendly." The resulting firm is likely to have a name derived from its composite firms. One example is the merging of Allied Corporation and Signal Companies to form Allied Signal. An **acquisition** is the purchase of a company that is completely absorbed as an operating subsidiary or division of the acquiring corporation. Examples are Procter & Gamble's acquisition of Richardson-Vicks, known for its Oil of Olay and Vidal Sassoon brands, and Noxell Cor-

Figure 6.1
Corporate Directional Strategies

- **GROWTH**
  Concentration
    Vertical Growth
    Horizontal Growth
  Diversification
    Concentric
    Conglomerate

- **STABILITY**
  Pause/Proceed with Caution
  No Change
  Profit

- **RETRENCHMENT**
  Turnaround
  Captive Company
  Sell-Out/Divestment
  Bankruptcy/Liquidation

poration, known for Noxema and Cover Girl. Acquisitions usually occur between firms of different sizes and can be either friendly or hostile. Hostile acquisitions are often called takeovers. A **strategic alliance** is a partnership of two or more corporations or business units to achieve strategically significant objectives that are mutually beneficial. See Chapter 5 for a detailed discussion of strategic alliances.

Growth is a very attractive strategy for two key reasons:

- Growth based on increasing market demand may mask flaws in a company—flaws that would be immediately evident in a stable or declining market. A growing flow of revenue into a highly leveraged corporation can create a large amount of **organization slack** (unused resources) that can be used to quickly resolve problems and conflicts between departments and divisions. Growth also provides a big cushion for a turnaround in case a strategic error is made. Larger firms also have more bargaining power than do small firms and are more likely to obtain support from key stakeholders in case of difficulty.

- A growing firm offers more opportunities for advancement, promotion, and interesting jobs. Growth itself is exciting and ego-enhancing for CEOs. The marketplace and potential investors tend to view a growing corporation as a "winner" or "on the move." Executive compensation tends to get bigger as an organization increases in size. Large firms are also more difficult to acquire than are smaller ones; thus an executive's job is more secure.

The two basic growth strategies are **concentration** on the current product line(s) in one industry and **diversification** into other product lines in other industries.

Concentration

If a company's current product lines have real growth potential, concentration of resources on those product lines makes sense as a strategy for growth. The two basic concentration strategies are vertical growth and horizontal growth. Growing firms in a growing industry tend to choose these strategies before they try diversification.

Vertical Growth   Vertical growth can be achieved by taking over a function previously provided by a supplier or by a distributor. The company, in effect, grows by making its own supplies and/or by distributing its own products. This growth can be achieved either *internally* by expanding current operations or *externally* through acquisitions. Henry Ford, for example, used internal company resources to build his River Rouge Plant outside Detroit. The manufacturing process was integrated to the point that iron ore entered one end of the long plant and finished automobiles rolled out the other end into a huge parking lot. In contrast, DuPont, the huge chemical company, chose the external route to vertical growth by acquiring Conoco for the oil DuPont needed to produce synthetic fabrics.

Vertical growth results in **vertical integration**—the degree to which a firm operates vertically in multiple locations on an industry's value chain from extracting raw materials to manufacturing to retailing. More specifically, assuming a function previously provided by a *supplier* is called **backward integration** (going backward on an industry's value chain), whereas assuming a function previously provided by a *distributor* is labeled **forward integration** (going forward on an industry's value chain). Micron, for example, used forward integration when it expanded out of its successful memory manufacturing business to make and market its own personal computers.

Vertical growth is a logical strategy for a corporation or business unit with a strong competitive position in a highly attractive industry—especially when technology is predictable and markets are growing.[5] To keep and even improve its competitive position, the company may use backward integration to minimize resource acquisition costs and inefficient operations as well as forward integration to gain more control over product distribution. The firm, in effect, builds on its distinctive competence by expanding along the industry's value chain to gain greater competitive advantage.

Although backward integration is usually more profitable than forward integration, it can reduce a corporation's strategic flexibility. The resulting encumbrance of expensive assets that might be hard to sell could create an *exit barrier,* preventing the corporation from leaving that particular industry. When sales of its autos were declining, General Motors, for example, resorted to offering outside parts suppliers the use of its idle factories and workers.

Transaction cost economics proposes that vertical integration is more efficient than contracting for goods and services in the marketplace when the transaction costs of buying goods on the open market become too great. When highly vertically integrated firms become excessively large and bureaucratic, however, the costs of managing the internal transactions may become greater than simply purchasing the needed goods externally—thus justifying outsourcing over vertical integration. See the **Key Theory** feature for more information on transaction cost economics.

Harrigan proposes that a company's degree of vertical integration can range from total ownership of the value chain needed to make and sell a product to no ownership at all.[6] Under **full integration**, a firm internally makes 100% of its key supplies and completely controls its distributors. Large oil companies such as British Petroleum, Royal Dutch Shell, and Texaco are fully integrated. If a corporation does not want the disadvantages of full vertical integration, it may choose either taper or quasi-integration strategies. With **taper integration**, a firm internally produces less than half of its own requirements and buys the rest from outside suppliers. In terms of distributors, it sells part of its goods through company-owned stores and the rest through general wholesalers. With **quasi-integration**, a company does not make any of its key supplies, but purchases most of its requirements from outside suppliers that are under its partial control. For example, by purchasing 20% of the common stock of In Focus Systems, Motorola guaranteed its access to In Focus' revolutionary technology and enabled Motorola to establish a joint venture with In Focus to manufacture flat-panel video displays.[7] An example of forward quasi-integration would be a large pharmaceutical firm that acquires part interest in a

KEY THEORY

TRANSACTION COST ECONOMICS ANALYZES VERTICAL GROWTH STRATEGY

Why do corporations use vertical growth to permanently own suppliers or distributors when they could simply purchase individual items when needed on the open market? Transaction cost economics is a branch of institutional economics that attempts to answer this question. Beginning with work by Coase and extended by Williamson, transaction cost economics proposes that ownership of resources through vertical growth is more efficient than contracting for goods and services in the marketplace when the transaction costs of buying goods on the open market become too great. Transaction costs include the basic costs of drafting, negotiating, and safeguarding a market agreement (a contract) as well as the later managerial costs when the agreement is creating problems (goods aren't being delivered on time or quality is lower than needed), renegotiation costs (costs of meetings and phone calls), and the costs of settling disputes (lawyers' fees and court costs).

According to Williamson, three conditions must be met before a corporation will prefer internalizing a vertical transaction through ownership over contracting for the transaction in the marketplace: (1) a high level of uncertainty must surround the transaction; (2) assets involved in the transaction must be highly specialized to the transaction; and (3) the transaction must occur frequently. If there is a high level of uncertainty, it will be impossible to write a contract covering all contingencies and it is likely that the contractor will act opportunistically to exploit any gaps in the written agreement—thus creating problems and increasing costs. If the assets being

contracted for are highly specialized (goods or services with few alternate uses), there are likely to be few alternative suppliers—thus allowing the contractor to take advantage of the situation and increase costs. The more frequent the transactions, the more opportunity for the contractor to demand special treatment and thus increase costs further.

Vertical integration is not always more efficient than the marketplace, however. When highly vertically integrated firms become excessively large and bureaucratic, the costs of managing the internal transactions may become greater than simply purchasing the needed goods externally—thus justifying outsourcing over ownership. The usually hidden management costs (excessive layers of management, endless committee meetings needed for interdepartmental coordination, and delayed decision making due to excessively detailed rules and policies) add to the internal transaction costs—thus reducing the effectiveness and efficiency of vertical integration. The decision to own or to contract is, therefore, based on the particular situation surrounding the transaction and the ability of the corporation to manage the transaction internally both effectively and efficiently.

Sources: O. E. Williamson and S. G. Winter, eds., *The Nature of the Firm: Origins, Evolution, and Development* (New York: Oxford University Press, 1991); E. Mosakowski, "Organizational Boundaries and Economic Performance: An Empirical Study of Entrepreneurial Computer Firms," *Strategic Management Journal* (February 1991), pp. 115–133; P. S. Ring and A. H. Van De Ven, "Structuring Cooperative Relationships Between Organizations," *Strategic Management Journal* (October 1992), pp. 483–498.

drugstore chain in order to guarantee that its drugs have access to the distribution channel. Purchasing part interest in a key supplier or distributor usually provides a company with a seat on the other firm's board of directors, thus guaranteeing the acquiring firm both information and control. A company may not want to invest in suppliers or distributors, but it still wants to guarantee access to needed supplies or distribution channels. In this case, it may use contractual agreements. **Long-term contracts** are agreements between two separate firms to provide agreed-upon goods and services to each other for a specified period of time. This cannot really be considered to be vertical integration unless the contract specifies that the supplier or distributor cannot have a similar relationship with a competitive firm. In this case, the supplier or distributor is really a "captive company" that, although officially independent, does most of its business with the contracted firm and is formally tied to the other company through a long-term contract.

During the 1990s, there has been a movement away from vertical growth strategies (and thus vertical integration) toward cooperative contractual relationships with suppliers and even with competitors. These relationships range from **outsourcing**, in which resources are purchased from outsiders through long-term contracts instead of being made in-house (for example, Hewlett-Packard buys all its laser engines from Canon for HP's laser jet printers), to strategic alliances, in which partnerships, technology licensing agreements, and joint ventures supplement a firm's capabilities (for example, Toshiba has used strategic alliances with GE, Siemens, Motorola, and Ericsson to become one of the world's leading electronic companies).[8]

Horizontal Growth Horizontal growth can be achieved by expanding the firm's products into other geographic locations and/or by increasing the range of products and services offered to current markets. In this case, the company expands sideways at the same location on the industry's value chain. For example, Dell Computers followed a horizontal growth strategy when it extended its mail order business to the European continent. A company can grow horizontally through internal development or externally through acquisitions or strategic alliances with another firm in the same industry.

Horizontal growth results in **horizontal integration**—the degree to which a firm operates in multiple geographic locations at the same point in an industry's value chain. Horizontal integration for a firm may range from full to partial ownership to long-term contracts. For example, KLM, the Dutch airline, purchased a controlling stake (partial ownership) in Northwest Airlines to obtain access to American and Asian markets. KLM was unable to acquire all of Northwest's stock because of U.S. government regulations forbidding foreign ownership of a domestic airline (for defense reasons). Many small commuter airlines engage in long-term contracts with major airlines in order to offer a complete arrangement for travelers. For example, Mesa Airlines arranged a five-year agreement with United Airlines to be listed on United's computer reservations as United Express through the Denver airport. See also the **Company Spotlight on Maytag Corporation** feature for a discussion of Maytag's use of horizontal growth through acquisitions.

Diversification Strategies

When an industry consolidates and becomes mature, most of the surviving firms have reached the limits of growth using vertical and horizontal growth strategies. Unless the competitors are able to expand internationally into less mature markets (as was the case in the major home appliance industry), they may have no choice but to diversify into different industries if they want to continue growing. The two basic diversification strategies are concentric and conglomerate.

Concentric (Related) Diversification Growth through **concentric diversification** into a related industry may be a very appropriate corporate strategy when a firm has a strong competitive position but industry attractiveness is low. By focusing on the characteristics that have given the company its distinctive competence, the company uses those very strengths as its means of diversification. The firm attempts to secure strategic fit in a new industry where the firm's product knowledge, its manufacturing capabilities, and the

A Growth Strategy Of Horizontal Growth Through Acquisitions

Maytag management realized in 1978 that the company would be unable to continue competing effectively in the U.S. major home appliance industry if it remained only a high-quality niche manufacturer of automatic washers and dryers. The industry was rapidly consolidating around those appliance companies with a complete line of products at all price and quality levels in all three key lines of "white goods": laundry (washers and dryers), cooking (stoves and ovens), and cooling (refrigerators and freezers) appliances. Previously most companies made appliances deriving from one or two successful products: General Electric made refrigerators; Maytag focused on washing machines; and Hotpoint produced electric ranges. A company would fill the gaps in its line by putting its own brand name on products it purchased from other manufacturers. This was done because stoves could not be made in a plant making refrigerators and vice versa. Purchasing from others was cheaper than building a new plant. To keep unit costs low, companies had to build larger plants than its own sales justified (to obtain economies of scale). To keep the plants running at close to 100% capacity (thus keeping unit costs as low as possible), a firm would produce other brands' products through contracts until its own brand's sales caught up with plant capacity. Nevertheless it was significantly cheaper to be vertically integrated than to buy appliances from another appliance company, especially a competitor. The need to own plants in all three lines of white goods led to a series of acquisitions and mergers within the industry—growth through horizontal integration throughout the United States and Canada.

Maytag's top management concluded that it would soon have to acquire other companies or risk being bought out itself. Given the long timeframe needed to acquire the technology as well as the manufacturing and marketing expertise necessary to produce and sell these other lines of appliances, Maytag chose to grow externally by acquiring Jenn-Air and Magic Chef in the mid 1980s. It was thus able to obtain Jenn-Air's popular down-draft ranges and Magic Chef's gas stoves and other appliances plus Admiral's refrigeration facilities—products Maytag needed to be a full-line home appliance manufacturer. Similarly Maytag's management concluded that the best way to ensure a global presence in major home appliances was to purchase Hoover, the well-known vacuum cleaner company with a solid position in white goods in Europe and Australia. Competitors like GE, Whirlpool, and AB Electrolux were growing through horizontal integration across the globe. Maytag felt that it needed to be part of this growth.

MAYTAG CORPORATION

marketing skills it used so effectively in the original industry can be put to good use.[9] The corporation's products or processes are related in some way: they possess some common thread. The search is for **synergy**, the concept that two businesses will generate more profits together than they could separately. The point of commonality may be similar technology, customer usage, distribution, managerial skills, or product similarity.

The firm may choose to diversify concentrically through either internal or external means. American Airlines, for example, has diversified both internally and externally out of the increasingly unprofitable airline business into a series of related businesses run by the parent company AMR Corporation. Building on the expertise of its SABRE Travel Information Network, it built a computer reservations system for the French high-speed rail network and for the tunnel under the English Channel.

Conglomerate (Unrelated) Diversification When management realizes that the current industry is unattractive and that the firm lacks outstanding abilities or skills that it could easily transfer to related products or services in other industries, the most likely strategy is **conglomerate diversification**—diversifying into an industry unrelated to its current one. Rather than maintaining a common thread throughout their organization, strategic managers who adopt this strategy are primarily concerned with financial considerations of cash flow or risk reduction.

The emphasis in conglomerate diversification is on financial considerations rather than on the product-market synergy common to concentric diversification. A cash-rich company with few opportunities for growth in its industry might, for example, move into another industry where opportunities are great, but cash is hard to find. Another instance of conglomerate diversification might be when a company with a seasonal and, therefore, uneven cash flow purchases a firm in an unrelated industry with complementing seasonal sales that will level out the cash flow. CSX management considered the purchase of a natural gas transmission business (Texas Gas Resources) by CSX Corporation (a railroad-dominated transportation company) to be a good fit because most of the gas transmission revenue was realized in the winter months—the railroads' lean period.

International Entry Options

In today's world, growth usually has international implications. A corporation can select from several strategic options the most appropriate method for it to use in entering a foreign market or establishing manufacturing facilities in another country. The options vary from simple exporting to acquisitions to management contracts. As in the case of KLM's purchase of stock in Northwest Airlines, this can be a part of the corporate strategies previously discussed. See the 🌐 **21st Century Global Society** feature to see how the South Korean firm Daewoo is using multiple international entry options in a horizontal growth strategy. Some of the more popular options for international entry are as follows:

- **Exporting. Exporting,** shipping goods produced in the company's home country to other countries for marketing, is a good way to minimize risk and experiment with a specific product. The company could choose to handle all critical functions itself, or it could contract these functions to an export management company. Exporting is becoming increasingly popular for small businesses because of fax machines, 800 numbers, and overnight air express services, which reduce the once formidable costs of going international.

- **Licensing.** Under a **licensing** agreement, the licensing firm grants rights to another firm in the host country to produce and/or sell a product. The licensee pays compensation to the licensing firm in return for technical expertise. This is an especially useful strategy if the trademark or brand name is well known, but the company does not have sufficient funds to finance its entering the country directly. Anheuser-Busch is using this strategy to produce and market Budweiser beer in the United Kingdom, Japan, Israel, Australia, Korea, and the Philippines. This strategy also becomes important if the country makes entry via investment either difficult or impossible. The danger always exists, however, that the licensee might develop its competence to the point that it becomes a competitor to the licensing firm. Therefore, a company should never license its distinctive competence, even for some short-run advantage.

- **Joint Ventures.** The rate of **joint venture** formation between U.S. companies and international partners has been growing 27% annually since 1985.[10] Companies often form joint ventures to combine the resources and expertise needed to develop

DAEWOO EXPANDS ITS CORPORATE GROWTH STRATEGY INTERNATIONALLY

Daewoo, the South Korean conglomerate, is spending $18 billion to become the world's largest consumer electronics company and one of the top ten automakers by 2002. It has formed joint ventures with companies in the emerging markets of Vietnam, Poland, and Uzbekistan. In 1997, it introduced new car models in Europe and entered the U.S. auto market for the first time. Daewoo also hopes to acquire France's Thomson Multimedia and become the biggest seller of television sets in the United States.

Daewoo's low-price products using fairly simple technology have sold well in emerging nations. Management is concerned, however, that the company does not yet have the technology to compete with established U.S. and Japanese competitors. As a result, it has tripled its auto engineering staff at its Worthing Technical Center (purchased in 1992) in the United Kingdom. It is also working to improve the quality of its electronics at its color television plant in Kumi, South Korea.

Chairman Kim Woo Choong believes Daewoo can make the money-losing French television maker Thomson Multimedia profitable in two years. "We will have full economies of scale, so we can invest more in research and development," states Mr. Kim. Skeptics doubt if Daewoo has both the money and the capabilities needed to make meaningful inroads into markets in the developed nations. Kim responded that it is a goal worth attaining. "No one believed that we could make so much progress. Now, nobody's laughing."

Source: M. Schuman, "Daewoo Lifts Its Sights to U.S. and Europe," *Wall Street Journal* (March 3, 1997), p. A15.

---

new products or technologies. It also enables a firm to enter a country that restricts foreign ownership. The corporation can enter another country with fewer assets at stake and thus lower risk. For example, because the costs of developing a new large jet were becoming too high for any one manufacturer, Boeing, Aerospatiale of France, British Aerospace, Construcciones Aeronáuticas of Spain, and Deutsche Aerospace of Germany planned a joint venture to design such a plane. A joint venture may be an association between a company and a firm in the host country or a government agency in that country. A quick method of obtaining local management, it also reduces the risks of expropriation and harassment by host country officials.

- **Acquisitions.** A relatively quick way to move into an international area is through **acquisitions**—purchasing another company already operating in that area. Synergistic benefits can result if the company acquires a firm with strong complementary product lines and a good distribution network. Maytag Corporation's acquisition of Hoover gave it entry into Europe through Hoover's strength in home appliances in the United Kingdom and in its vacuum cleaner distribution centers on the European continent. To expand into North America, the Swedish appliance maker, A.B. Electrolux, purchased the major home appliance operations of White Consolidated Industries and renamed them Frigidaire. Research does suggest that wholly-owned subsidiaries are more successful in international undertakings than are strategic alliances, such as joint ventures.[11] In some countries, however, acquisitions can be difficult to arrange because of a lack of available information about potential candidates. Government restrictions on ownership, such as the U.S. requirement that limits foreign ownership of U.S. airlines to 49% of nonvoting and 25% of voting stock, can also discourage acquisitions.

- **Green-Field Development.** If a company doesn't want to purchase another company's problems along with its assets (as Japan's Bridgestone did when it acquired Firestone in the United States) it may choose **green-field development**—building its own manufacturing plant and distribution system. This is usually a far more complicated and expensive operation than acquisition, but it allows a company more freedom in designing the plant, choosing suppliers, and hiring a workforce. For example, Nissan, Honda, and Toyota built auto factories in rural areas of Great Britain and then hired a young workforce with no experience in the industry.

- **Production Sharing.** Coined by Peter Drucker, the term **production sharing** means the process of combining the higher labor skills and technology available in the developed countries with the lower-cost labor available in developing countries. The current trend is to move data processing and programming activities "offshore" to places such as Ireland, India, Barbados, Jamaica, the Philippines, and Singapore where wages are lower, English is spoken, and telecommunications are in place.

- **Turnkey Operations. Turnkey operations** are typically contracts for the construction of operating facilities in exchange for a fee. The facilities are transferred to the host country or firm when they are complete. The customer is usually a government agency of, for example, a Middle Eastern country that has decreed that a particular product must be produced locally and under its control. For example, Fiat built an auto plant in Russia to produce an older model of Fiat under a Russian brand name. MNCs that perform turnkey operations are frequently industrial equipment manufacturers that supply some of their own equipment for the project and that commonly sell replacement parts and maintenance services to the host country. They thereby create customers as well as future competitors.

- **BOT Concept.** The **BOT** (build, operate, transfer) concept is a variation of the turnkey operation. Instead of turning the facility (usually a power plant or toll road) over to the host country when completed, the company operates the facility for a fixed period of time during which it earns back its investment, plus a profit. It then turns the facility over to the government at little or no cost to the host country.[12]

- **Management Contracts.** A large corporation operating throughout the world is likely to have a large amount of management talent at its disposal. **Management contracts** offer a means through which a corporation may use some of its personnel to assist a firm in a host country for a specified fee and period of time. Management contracts are common when a host government expropriates part or all of a foreign-owned company's holdings in its country. The contracts allow the firm to continue to earn some income from its investment and keep the operations going until local management is trained.

Controversies in Directional Growth Strategies

Is vertical growth better than horizontal growth? Is concentric diversification better than conglomerate diversification? Although the research is not in complete agreement, growth into areas related to a company's current product lines is generally more successful than is growth into completely unrelated areas. For example, one study of various growth projects examined how many were considered successful, that is, still in existence after 22 years. The results were: vertical growth, 80%; horizontal growth, 50%; concentric diversification, 35%; and conglomerate diversification, 28%.[13]

In terms of diversification strategies, research suggests that the relationship between relatedness and performance is curvilinear. If a new business is very similar to that of the acquiring firm, it adds little new to the corporation and only marginally improves performance. If the new business is completely different from the acquiring company's businesses, there may be very little potential for any synergy. If, however, the new business provides new resources and capabilities in a different, but similar, business, the likelihood of a significant performance improvement is high.[14]

Is internal growth better than external growth? Corporations can follow the growth strategies of either concentration or diversification through the internal development of new products and services, or through external acquisitions, mergers, and strategic alliances. Although not yet conclusive, the research indicates that firms that grow through acquisitions do not perform financially as well as firms that grow through internal means.[15] Other research indicates, however, that acquisitions have a higher survival rate than do new internally generated business ventures.[16]

Stability Strategies

A corporation may choose stability over growth by continuing its current activities without any significant change in direction. Although sometimes viewed as a lack of strategy, the stability family of corporate strategies can be appropriate for a successful corporation operating in a reasonably predictable environment.[17] They are very popular with small business owners who have found a niche and are happy with their success and the manageable size of their firms. Stability strategies can be very useful in the short run, but they can be dangerous if followed for too long (as many small-town businesses discovered when Wal-Mart came to town). Some of the more popular of these strategies are the pause/proceed with caution, no change, and profit strategies.

Pause/Proceed with Caution Strategy

A **pause/proceed with caution strategy** is, in effect, a timeout—an opportunity to rest before continuing a growth or retrenchment strategy. It is a very deliberate attempt to make only incremental improvements until a particular environmental situation changes. It is typically conceived as a *temporary strategy* to be used until the environment becomes more hospitable or to enable a company to consolidate its resources after prolonged rapid growth. This was the strategy Dell Computer Corporation followed in 1993 after its growth strategy had resulted in more growth than it could handle. Explained CEO Michael Dell, "We grew 285% in two years, and we're having some growing pains." Selling personal computers by mail enabled it to underprice Compaq Computer and IBM, but it could not keep up with the needs of the $2 billion, 5,600-employee company selling PCs in 95 countries. Dell was not giving up on its growth strategy; it was merely putting it temporarily in limbo until the company could hire new managers, improve the structure, and build new facilities.

No Change Strategy

A **no change strategy** is a decision to do nothing new—a choice to continue current operations and policies for the foreseeable future. Rarely articulated as a definite strategy, a no change strategy's success depends on a lack of significant change in a corporation's situation. The relative stability created by the firm's modest competitive position in an industry facing little or no growth encourages the company to continue on its current course, making only small adjustments for inflation in its sales and profit objectives. There are no obvious opportunities or threats nor much in the way of significant strengths or weaknesses. Few aggressive new competitors are likely to enter such an industry. The corporation has probably found a reasonably profitable and stable niche for its products. Unless the industry is undergoing consolidation, the relative comfort a company in this situation experiences is likely to encourage the company to follow a no change strategy in which the future is expected to continue as an extension of the present. Most small-town businesses probably follow this strategy before Wal-Mart moves into their areas.

Profit Strategy

A **profit strategy** is a decision to do nothing new in a worsening situation, but instead to act as though the company's problems are only temporary. The profit strategy is an attempt to artificially support profits when a company's sales are declining by reducing investment and short-term discretionary expenditures. Rather than announcing the company's poor position to shareholders and the investment community at large, top management may be tempted to follow this very seductive strategy. Blaming the company's problems on a hostile environment (such as anti-business government policies, unethical competitors, finicky customers, and/or greedy lenders), management defers investments and/or cuts expenses (such as R&D, maintenance, and advertising) to stabilize profits during this period. It may even sell one of its product lines for the cash flow benefits. Obviously the profit strategy is useful only to help a company get through a temporary difficulty. Unfortunately the strategy is seductive and if continued long enough will lead to a serious deterioration in a corporation's competitive position. The profit strategy is thus usually top management's passive, short-term, and often self-serving response to the situation.

Retrenchment Strategies

A company may pursue retrenchment strategies when it has a weak competitive position in some or all of its product lines resulting in poor performance—sales are down and profits are becoming losses. These strategies impose a great deal of pressure to improve performance. In an attempt to eliminate the weaknesses that are dragging the company down, management may follow one of several retrenchment strategies ranging from turnaround or becoming a captive company to selling out, bankruptcy, or liquidation.

Turnaround Strategy

The **turnaround strategy** emphasizes the improvement of operational efficiency and is probably most appropriate when a corporation's problems are pervasive, but not yet critical. Analogous to a weight reduction diet, the two basic phases of a turnaround strategy are contraction and consolidation.[18]

Contraction is the initial effort to quickly "stop the bleeding" with a general across-the-board cutback in size and costs. The second phase, *consolidation*, implements a program to stabilize the now-leaner corporation. To streamline the company, plans are developed to reduce unnecessary overhead and to make functional activities cost-justified. This is a crucial time for the organization. If the consolidation phase is not conducted in a positive manner, many of the best people leave the organization. If, however, all employees are encouraged to get involved in productivity improvements, the firm is likely to emerge from this retrenchment period a much stronger and better organized company. It has improved its competitive position and is able once again to expand the business. See the **Strategy in a Changing World** feature for a description of IBM's effective use of the turnaround strategy.

IBM FOLLOWS A TURNAROUND STRATEGY

During the 1970s and 1980s, IBM dominated the computer industry worldwide. It was the market leader in both large mainframe and small personal computers. Along with Apple Computer, IBM set the standard for all personal computers. Even now—when IBM no longer dominates the field—personal computers are still identified as being either Apple or IBM-style PCs.

IBM's problems came to a head in the early 1990s. The company's computer sales were falling. More companies were choosing to replace their large, expensive mainframe computers with personal computers, but they weren't buying the PCs from IBM. An increasing number of firms like Hewlett-Packard, Dell, Gateway, and Compaq had entered the industry. They offered IBM-style PC "clones" that were considerably cheaper and often more advanced than IBM's PCs. IBM's falling revenues meant corporate losses in 1992 and 1993. Industry experts perceived the company as a bureaucratic dinosaur that could no longer adapt to changing conditions. Its stock price fell to $40 with no end in sight.

IBM's board of directors hired a new CEO, Louis Gerstner, to lead a corporate turnaround strategy at "Big Blue" (the nickname IBM earned from its rigid dress code policies). To stop the flow of red ink, the company violated its long-held "no layoffs" policy by reducing its workforce 40%. Under Gerstner, IBM reorganized its sales force around specific industries such as retailing and banking. Decision making was made easier. Previously, according to Joseph Formichelli, a top executive with the PC division, he "had to go through seven layers to get things done." Firing incompetent employees could take a year, "so

you pawned them off on another group." Strategy presentations were hashed over so many times "they got watered down to nothing." Under Gerstner, however, formal presentations were no longer desired. The emphasis switched to quicker decision making and a stronger customer orientation.

In 1987, customers had been forced to wait five to seven years for a new mainframe series. Now IBM produces a new line almost every year. Gerstner personally talks with at least one customer every day. The company's PC business, which had lost market share and generated huge losses in the early 1990s, has become profitable. Its market share rose almost one point to 8.9% in 1996—second place in global market share. Its stock price topped $140 by the end of 1996. Customers have been pleased with the company's improved products and better customer service. "Over the last couple of years they have been going out of their way to have a contact person you could call with any issue," reported Linda Wiersema, Chief Information Officer at LTV Corporation's LTV Steel unit.

The corporation still has a long way to go to complete its turnaround. Even though revenue increased 40% over the past decade, profits increased only 3.2%. In 1996, IBM's revenue increased just 5.6% compared to 19% at Hewlett-Packard and 29% at Intel. According to Chief Financial Officer Richard Thoman, "We've done a lot, but we still have a lot to do."

Source: B. Ziegler, "Gerstner's IBM Revival: Impressive, Incomplete," *Wall Street Journal* (March 25, 1997), pp. B1, B4.

Captive Company Strategy

A **captive company strategy** is the giving up of independence in exchange for security. A company with a weak competitive position may not be able to engage in a full-blown turnaround strategy. The industry may not be sufficiently attractive to justify such an effort from either the current management or from investors. Nevertheless a company in this situation faces poor sales and increasing losses unless it takes some action.

Management desperately searches for an "angel" by offering to be a captive company to one of its larger customers in order to guarantee the company's continued existence with a long-term contract. In this way, the corporation may be able to reduce the scope of some of its functional activities, such as marketing, thus reducing costs significantly. The weaker company gains certainty of sales and production in return for becoming heavily dependent on one firm for at least 75% of its sales. For example, to become the sole supplier of an auto part to General Motors, Simpson Industries of Birmingham, Michigan, agreed to let a special team from GM inspect its engine parts facilities and books and interview its employees. In return, nearly 80% of the company's production was sold to GM through long-term contracts.[19]

Sell-Out/Divestment Strategy

If a corporation with a weak competitive position in this industry is unable either to pull itself up by its bootstraps or to find a customer to which it can become a captive company, it may have no choice but to **sell out** and leave the industry completely. The sell-out strategy makes sense if management can still obtain a good price for its shareholders by selling the entire company to another firm. For example, Johnson Products, a pioneer in hair care products for African-American and other ethnic markets, found that over time it had lost its competitive position to larger cosmetics companies who had entered Johnson Products' niche. After numerous attempts to turn the company around, the Johnson family finally decided to sell out to Ivax Corporation while they could still get a decent price for the firm.

If the corporation has multiple business lines and it chooses to sell off a division with low growth potential, this is called **divestment**. Monsanto is one example of a company using this strategy. Founded in 1901, Monsanto recently realized that the very chemical business for which it had been known was hurting its growth as a corporation. The chemical division's performance had been overshadowed in the past ten years by advances in biotechnology and agricultural products such as Roundup. Divestment seemed a viable decision in 1997.

Bankruptcy/Liquidation Strategy

When a company finds itself in the worst possible situation with a poor competitive position in an industry with few prospects, management has only a few alternatives—all of them distasteful. Because no one is interested in buying a weak company in an unattractive industry, the firm must pursue a bankruptcy or liquidation strategy. **Bankruptcy** involves giving up management of the firm to the courts in return for some settlement of the corporation's obligations. Top management hopes that once the court decides the claims on the company, the company will be stronger and better able to compete in a more attractive industry. Wang Laboratories, Inc., took this approach in 1992. Founded by An Wang, the company had been unable to make the transition from word processors to personal computers and finally collapsed after the death of its founder. The company emerged from bankruptcy in 1993 under a court-supervised reorganization plan requiring that the company focus on office software.

In contrast to bankruptcy, which seeks to perpetuate the corporation, **liquidation** is the termination of the firm. Because the industry is unattractive and the company too weak to be sold as a going concern, management may choose to convert as many saleable assets as possible to cash, which is then distributed to the shareholders after all obligations are paid. The benefit of liquidation over bankruptcy is that the board of directors, as representatives of the shareholders, together with top management make the decisions instead of turning them over to the court, which may choose to ignore share-holders completely.

At times, top management must be willing to select one of these less desirable retrenchment strategies. Unfortunately, many top managers are unwilling to admit that their company has serious weaknesses for fear that they may be personally blamed. Even worse, top management may not even perceive that crises are developing. When these top managers do eventually notice trouble, they are prone to attribute the problems to temporary environmental disturbances and tend to follow profit strategies. Even when things are going terribly wrong, top management is greatly tempted to avoid liquidation in the hope of a miracle. Thus, a corporation needs a strong board of directors who, to safeguard shareholders' interests, can tell top management when to quit.

6.3 Portfolio Analysis

Chapter 5 dealt with how individual product lines and business units can gain competitive advantage in the marketplace by using competitive and cooperative strategies. Companies with multiple product lines or business units must also ask themselves how these various products and business units should be managed to boost overall corporate performance.

- How much of our time and money should we spend on our best products and business units to ensure that they continue to be successful?

- How much of our time and money should we spend developing new costly products, most of which will never be successful?

One of the most popular aids to developing corporate strategy in a multibusiness corporation is portfolio analysis. Although its popularity has dropped since the 1970s and 1980s when over half of the largest business corporations used portfolio analysis, it is still used by 27% of Fortune 500 firms in corporate strategy formulation.[20] Portfolio analysis puts corporate headquarters into the role of an internal banker. In **portfolio analysis**, top management views its product lines and business units as a series of investments from which it expects a profitable return. The product lines/business units form a portfolio of investments that top management must constantly juggle to ensure the best return on the corporation's invested money. Two of the most popular approaches are the BCG Growth-Share Matrix and GE Business Screen. This concept can also be used to develop strategies for international markets.

BCG Growth-Share Matrix

The **BCG (Boston Consulting Group) Growth-Share Matrix** depicted in Figure 6.2 is the simplest way to portray a corporation's portfolio of investments. Each of the corporation's product lines or business units is plotted on the matrix according to both the growth rate of the industry in which it competes and its relative market share. A unit's relative competitive position is defined as its market share in the industry divided by that of the largest other competitor. By this calculation, a relative market share above 1.0 belongs to the market leader. The business growth rate is the percentage of market growth, that is, the percentage by which sales of a particular business unit classification of products have increased. The matrix assumes that, other things being equal, a growing market is attractive.

Figure 6.2
BCG Growth-Share Matrix

Source: B. Hedley, "Strategy and the Business Portfolio," *Long Range Planning* (February 1997), p. 12. Reprinted with permission.

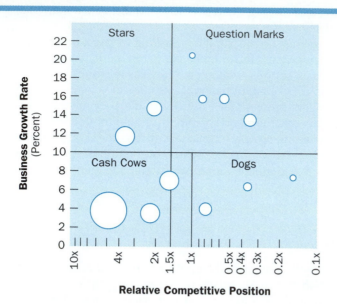

The line separating areas of high and low relative competitive position is set at 1.5 times. A product line or business unit must have relative strengths of this magnitude to ensure that it will have the dominant position needed to be a "star" or "cash cow." On the other hand, a product line or unit having a relative competitive position less than 1.0 has "dog" status.[21] Each product or unit is represented in Figure 6.2 by a circle. The area of the circle represents the relative significance of each business unit or product line to the corporation in terms of assets used or sales generated.

The BCG Growth-Share Matrix has a lot in common with the product life cycle. As a product moves through its life cycle, it is categorized into one of four types for the purpose of funding decisions:

- **Question marks** (sometimes called "problem children" or "wildcats") are new products with the potential for success, but they need a lot of cash for development. If such a product is to gain enough market share to become a market leader and thus a star, money must be taken from more mature products and spent on a question mark.

- **Stars** are market leaders typically at the peak of their product life cycle and are usually able to generate enough cash to maintain their high share of the market. When their market growth rate slows, stars become cash cows.

- **Cash cows** typically bring in far more money than is needed to maintain their market share. In this declining stage of their life cycle, these products are "milked" for cash that will be invested in new question marks. Question marks unable to obtain a dominant market share (and thus become stars) by the time the industry growth rate inevitably slows become dogs.

- **Dogs** have low market share and do not have the potential (because they are in an unattractive industry) to bring in much cash. According to the BCG Growth-Share Matrix, dogs should be either sold off or managed carefully for the small amount of cash they can generate.

Underlying the BCG Growth-Share Matrix is the concept of the experience curve (discussed in Chapter 4). The key to success is assumed to be market share. Firms with the highest market share tend to have a cost leadership position based on economies of scale, among other things. If a company is able to use the experience curve to its advantage, it should be able to manufacture and sell new products at a price low enough to garner early market share leadership (assuming no successful imitation by competitors). Once the product becomes a star, it is destined to be very profitable, considering its inevitable future as a cash cow.

Having plotted the current positions of its product lines or business units on a matrix, a company can project their future positions, assuming no change in strategy. Present and projected matrixes can thus be used to help identify major strategic issues facing the organization. The goal of any company is to maintain a balanced portfolio so it can be self-sufficient in cash and always working to harvest mature products in declining industries to support new ones in growing industries.

The BCG Growth-Share Matrix is a very well-known portfolio concept with some clear advantages. It is quantifiable and easy to use. Cash cows, dogs, and stars are an easy to remember way to refer to a corporation's business units or products. Unfortunately the BCG Growth-Share Matrix also has some serious limitations:

- The use of highs and lows to form four categories is too simplistic.

- The link between market share and profitability is not necessarily strong. Low-share businesses can also be profitable.

- Growth rate is only one aspect of industry attractiveness.

- Product lines or business units are considered only in relation to one competitor: the market leader. Small competitors with fast-growing market shares are ignored.

- Market share is only one aspect of overall competitive position.

GE Business Screen

General Electric, with the assistance of the McKinsey and Company consulting firm, developed a more complicated matrix. As depicted in Figure 6.3, the **GE Business Screen** includes nine cells based on long-term industry attractiveness and business strength/competitive position. The GE Business Screen, in contrast to the BCG Growth-Share Matrix, includes much more data in its two key factors than just business growth rate and comparable market share. For example, at GE, industry attractiveness includes market growth rate, industry profitability, size, and pricing practices, among other possible opportunities and threats. Business strength or competitive position includes market share as well as technological position, profitability, and size, among other possible strengths and weaknesses.[22]

The individual product lines or business units are identified by a letter and plotted as circles on the GE Business Screen. The area of each circle is in proportion to the size of the industry in terms of sales. The pie slices within the circles depict the market share of each product line or business unit.

To plot product lines or business units on the GE Business Screen, follow these four steps:

Step 1.   Select criteria to rate the industry for each product line or business unit. Assess overall industry attractiveness for each product line or business unit on a scale from 1 (very unattractive) to 5 (very attractive).

Step 2.   Select the key factors needed for success in each product line or business unit. Assess business strength/competitive position for each product line or business unit on a scale of 1 (very weak) to 5 (very strong).

Figure 6.3
General Electric's
Business Screen

Source: Adapted from *Strategic Management in GE*, Corporate Planning and Development, General Electric Corporation. Used by permission of General Electric Company.

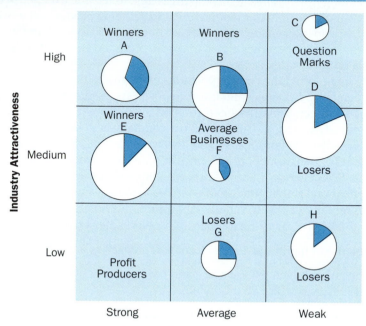

Step 3. Plot each product line's or business unit's current position on a matrix like that depicted in Figure 6.3.

Step 4. Plot the firm's future portfolio assuming that present corporate and business strategies remain unchanged. Is there a performance gap between projected and desired portfolios? If so, this gap should serve as a stimulus to seriously review the corporation's current mission, objectives, strategies, and policies.

Overall the nine-cell GE Business Screen is an improvement over the BCG Growth-Share Matrix. The GE Business Screen considers many more variables and does not lead to such simplistic conclusions. It recognizes, for example, that the attractiveness of an industry can be assessed in many different ways (other than simply using growth rate), and it thus allows users to select whatever criteria they feel are most appropriate to their situation. This portfolio matrix, however, does have some shortcomings:

• It can get quite complicated and cumbersome.

• The numerical estimates of industry attractiveness and business strength/competitive position give the appearance of objectivity, but they are in reality subjective judgments that may vary from one person to another.

• It cannot effectively depict the positions of new products or business units in developing industries.

International Portfolio Analysis

To aid international strategic planning, portfolio analysis can be applied to international markets.[23] Two factors form the axes of the matrix in Figure 6.4. A **country's attractiveness** is composed of its market size, the market rate of growth, the extent and type of government regulation, and economic and political factors. A **product's competitive**

Figure 6.4
Portfolio Matrix for Plotting Products by Country

Source: G. D. Harrell and R. O. Kiefer, "Multinational Strategic Market Portfolios," *MSU Business Topics* (Winter 1981), p. 7. Reprinted by permission.

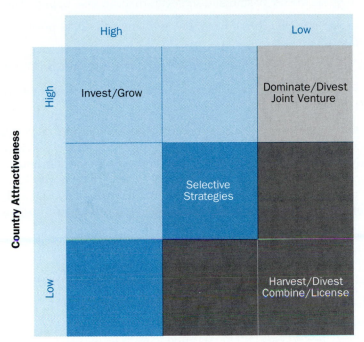

Competitive Strengths

strength is composed of its market share, product fit, contribution margin, and market support. Depending on where a product fits on the matrix, it should either receive more funding or be harvested for cash.

Portfolio analysis might not be useful, however, to corporations operating in a global industry rather than a multidomestic one. In discussing the importance of global industries, Porter argues against the use of portfolio analysis on a country-by-country basis:

> In a global industry, however, managing international activities like a portfolio will undermine the possibility of achieving competitive advantage. In a global industry, a firm must in some way integrate its activities on a worldwide basis to capture the linkage among countries.[24]

Advantages and Limitations of Portfolio Analysis

Portfolio analysis is commonly used in strategy formulation because it offers certain *advantages:*

- It encourages top management to evaluate each of the corporation's businesses individually and to set objectives and allocate resources for each.

- It stimulates the use of externally oriented data to supplement management's judgment.

- It raises the issue of cash flow availability for use in expansion and growth.

- Its graphic depiction facilitates communication.

Portfolio analysis does, however, have some very real *limitations* that have caused some companies to reduce their use of this approach:

- It is not easy to define product/market segments.

- It suggests the use of standard strategies that can miss opportunities or be impractical.

- It provides an illusion of scientific rigor when in reality positions are based on subjective judgments.

- Its value-laden terms like cash cow and dog can lead to self-fulfilling prophecies.

- It is not always clear what makes an industry attractive or where a product is in its life cycle.

- Naively following the prescriptions of a portfolio model may actually reduce corporate profits if they are used inappropriately. For example, General Mills' Chief Executive H. Brewster Atwater cites his company's Bisquick brand of flour as a product that would have been written off years ago based on portfolio analysis."This product is 57 years old. By all rights it should have been overtaken by newer products. But with the proper research to improve the product and promotion to keep customers excited, it's doing very well."[25]

6.4 *Corporate Parenting*

Campbell, Goold, and Alexander, authors of *Corporate-Level Strategy: Creating Value in the Multibusiness Company,* contend that corporate strategists must address two crucial questions:

- What businesses should this company own and why?

- What organizational structure, management processes, and philosophy will foster superior performance from the company's business units?[26]

Portfolio analysis attempts to answer these questions by examining the attractiveness of various industries and by managing business units for cash flow, that is, by using cash generated from mature units to build new product lines. Unfortunately portfolio analysis fails to deal with the question of what industries a corporation should enter or with how a corporation can attain synergy among its product lines and business units. As suggested by its name, portfolio analysis tends to primarily view matters financially, regarding business units and product lines as separate and independent investments.

Corporate parenting, in contrast, views the corporation in terms of resources and capabilities that can be used to build business unit value as well as generate synergies across business units. According to Campbell, Goold, and Alexander:

> Multibusiness companies create value by influencing—or parenting—the businesses they own. The best parent companies create more value than any of their rivals would if they owned the same businesses. Those companies have what we call *parenting advantage.*[27]

Corporate parenting generates corporate strategy by focusing on the core competencies of the parent corporation and on the value created from the relationship between the parent and its businesses. In the form of corporate headquarters, the parent has a great deal of power in this relationship. If there is a good fit between the parent's skills and resources and the needs and opportunities of the business units, the corporation is likely to create value. If, however, there is not a good fit, the corporation is likely to destroy value.[28] This approach to corporate strategy is useful not only in deciding what new businesses to acquire, but also in choosing how each existing business unit should be best managed. The primary job of corporate headquarters is, therefore, to obtain synergy among the business units by providing needed resources to units, transferring skills and capabilities among the units, and by coordinating the activities of shared unit functions to attain economies of scope (as in centralized purchasing).[29]

Developing a Corporate Parenting Strategy

Campbell, Goold, and Alexander recommend that the search for appropriate corporate strategy involves three analytical steps.

First, examine each business unit (or target firm in the case of acquisition) in terms of its critical success factors. **Critical success factors** are those elements of a company that determine its strategic success or failure. They emphasize its distinctive competence to ensure competitive advantage. Critical success factors will likely vary from company to company and from one business unit to another. People in the business units probably identified the critical success factors when they were generating business strategies for their units.

Second, examine each business unit (or target firm) in terms of areas in which performance can be improved. These are considered to be parenting opportunities. For example, two business units might be able to gain economies of scope by combining their sales forces. In another instance, a unit may have good, but not great, manufacturing and logistics skills. A parent company having world-class expertise in these areas can improve that unit's performance. The corporate parent could also transfer some people from one business unit having the desired skills to another unit in need of those skills. People at corporate headquarters may, because of their experience in many industries, spot areas where improvements are possible that even people in the business unit may not have noticed. Unless specific areas are significantly weaker than the competition, people in the business units may not even be aware that these areas could be improved, especially if each business unit only monitors its own particular industry.

Third, analyze how well the parent corporation fits with the business unit (or target firm). Corporate headquarters must be aware of its own strengths and weaknesses in terms of resources, skills, and capabilities. To do this, the corporate parent must ask if it has the characteristics that fit the parenting opportunities in each business unit. It must also ask if there is a misfit between the parent's characteristics and the critical success factors of each business unit.

Parenting-Fit Matrix

Campbell, Goold, and Alexander further recommend the use of a **parenting-fit matrix** which summarizes the various judgments regarding corporate/business unit fit for the corporation as a whole. Instead of describing business units in terms of their growth potential, competitive position, or industry structure, such a matrix emphasizes their fit with the corporate parent. As shown in Figure 6.5, the parenting-fit matrix is composed of two dimensions: the *positive contributions* that the parent can make and the *negative effects* the parent can make. The combination of these two dimensions creates five different positions—each with its own implications for corporate strategy.

Heartland Businesses

According to Campbell, Goold, and Alexander, business units that lie in the top right corner of the matrix should be at the heart of the corporation's future. These **heartland businesses** have opportunities for improvement by the parent, and the parent understands their critical success factors well. These businesses should have priority for all corporate activities.

Figure 6.5
Parenting-Fit Matrix

Source: Adapted from M. Alexander, A. Campbell, and M. Goold, "A New Model for Reforming the Planning Review Process," *Planning Review* (January/February 1995), p. 17. Reprinted with permission from Planning Reveiw, © 1995 The Planning Forum..

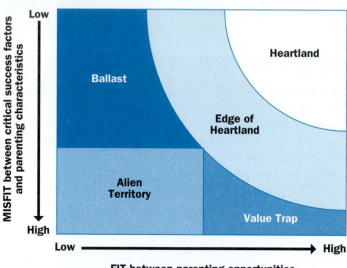

Edge-of-Heartland Businesses

For **edge-of-heartland businesses**, some parenting characteristics fit the business, but others do not. The parent may not have all the characteristics needed by a unit, or the parent may not really understand all of the unit's critical success factors. For example, a unit in this area may be very strong in creating its own image through advertising—a critical success factor in its industry (such as in perfumes). The corporate parent may, however, not have this strength and tends to leave this to its advertising agency. If the parent forced the unit to abandon its own creative efforts in favor of using the corporation's favorite ad agency, the unit may flounder. Such business units are likely to consume much of the parent's attention, as the parent tries to understand them better and transform them into heartland businesses. In this instance, the parent needs to know when to interfere in business unit activities and strategies and when to keep at arm's length.

Ballast Businesses

Ballast businesses fit very comfortably with the parent corporation but contain very few opportunities to be improved by the parent. This is likely to be the case in units that have been with the corporation for many years and have been very successful. The parent may have added value in the past, but it can no longer find further parenting opportunities. Like cash cows, ballast businesses may be important sources of stability and earnings. They can, however, also be a drag on the corporation as a whole by slowing growth and distracting the parent from more productive activities. Some analysts might put IBM's mainframe business units in this category. Because there is always a danger that environmental changes could move a ballast business unit into alien territory, corporate decision makers should consider divesting this unit as soon as they can get a price that exceeds the expected value of future cash flows.

Alien Territory Businesses

Alien territory businesses have little opportunity to be improved by the corporate parent, and a misfit exists between the parenting characteristics and the units' critical success factors. There is little potential for value creation, but high potential for value destruction on the part of the parent. These units are usually small and are often remnants of past experiments with diversification, businesses acquired as part of a larger purchase, or pet projects of senior managers. Even though corporate headquarters may admit that there is little fit, there may be reasons for keeping a unit: it is currently profitable, there are few buyers, the parent has made commitments to the unit's managers, or it is a favorite of the chairman. Because the corporate parent is probably destroying value in its attempts to improve fit, Campbell, Goold, and Alexander recommend that the corporation divest this unit while it still has value.

Value Trap Businesses

Value trap businesses fit well with parenting opportunities, but they are a misfit with the parent's understanding of the units' critical success factors. This is where corporate headquarters can make its biggest error. It mistakes what it sees as opportunities for ways to improve the business unit's profitability or competitive position. For example, in its zeal to make the unit a world-class manufacturer (because the parent has world-class manufacturing skills), it may not notice that the unit is primarily successful because of its unique product development and niche marketing expertise. The potential for possible gain blinds the parent to the downside risks of doing the wrong thing and destroying the unit's core competencies.

Horizontal Strategy: Corporate Competitive Strategy

A **horizontal strategy** is a corporate strategy that cuts across business unit boundaries to build synergy across business units and to improve the competitive position of one or more business units. When used to build synergy, it acts like a parenting strategy. When used to improve the competitive position of one or more business units, it can be thought of as a corporate competitive strategy. Large multibusiness corporations often compete against other large multibusiness firms in a number of markets. These **multipoint competitors** are firms that compete with each other not only in one business unit, but also in a number of business units. At one time or another, a cash-rich competitor may choose to build its own market share in a particular market to the disadvantage of another corporation's business unit. Although each business unit has primary responsibility for its own business strategy, it may sometimes need some help from its corporate parent, especially if the competitor business unit is getting heavy financial support from its corporate parent. In this instance, corporate headquarters develops a horizontal strategy to coordinate the various goals and strategies of related business units.[30]

For example, Procter & Gamble, Kimberly-Clark, Scott Paper, and Johnson and Johnson compete with one another in varying combinations of consumer paper products, from disposable diapers to facial tissue. If (purely hypothetically) Johnson and Johnson had just developed a toilet tissue with which it chose to challenge Procter & Gamble's high-share Charmin brand in a particular district, it might charge a low price for its new brand to build sales quickly. Procter & Gamble might not choose to respond to this attack on its share by cutting prices on Charmin. Because of Charmin's high market share, Procter & Gamble would lose significantly more sales dollars in a price war than Johnson and Johnson would with its initially low-share brand. To retaliate, Procter & Gamble might thus challenge Johnson and Johnson's high-share baby shampoo with Procter & Gamble's own low-share brand of baby shampoo in a different district. Once Johnson and Johnson had perceived Procter & Gamble's response, it might choose to stop challenging Charmin so that Procter & Gamble would stop challenging Johnson and Johnson's baby shampoo.

⬤ 6.5   *Global Issues for the 21st Century*

- The **21st Century Global Society** feature in this chapter illustrates how the South Korean firm Daewoo is using a combination of international entry options to become a global player in both the automobile and consumer electronics industries. Expect more Asian corporations to become major world players in the coming decades.

- The international implications of corporate growth strategies are increasing. Even if a firm is not planning to enter an international market, many of its suppliers and some of its manufacturing will probably be located in other nations.

- A disadvantage of a vertical growth strategy for a corporation operating in a global industry is that its functional value chain will be spread over the world, making logistics and communication especially important. A natural disaster or national revolution in any part of the world could temporarily halt the production of a company's products worldwide.

- Conglomerate diversification has been criticized as providing less value than has concentric diversification, primarily because it is more difficult to keep track of unrelated business units than related ones. Partially because of this, many companies are currently divesting units unrelated to their primary business. As more corporations become involved in international operations through acquisitions, strategic alliances, and other options (thus complicating management further), expect conglomerate diversification to become even less popular.

- Expect corporate parenting to become the dominant model in corporate strategy for evaluating business units and working to achieve synergies across unit boundaries. The parenting concept is based on the idea of the corporation as a learning organization that can transfer knowledge, skills, resources, and capabilities from a high-performing to an under-performing unit.

Projections for the 21st Century

- From 1994 to 2010, the number of wired telephone lines in the world will increase from 607 million to 1.4 billion.

- From 1994 to 2010, the number of wireless telephone lines in the world will increase from 34 million to 1.3 billion.[31]

Discussion Questions

1. How does horizontal growth differ from vertical growth as a corporate strategy? From concentric diversification?

2. What are the tradeoffs between an internal and an external growth strategy? Which approach is best as an international entry strategy?

3. Is stability really a strategy or just a term for no strategy?

4. Compare and contrast SWOT analysis with portfolio analysis.

5. How is corporate parenting different from portfolio analysis? How is it alike? Is it a useful concept in a global industry?

Key Terms

acquisition (p. 134, 141)
alien territory businesses (p. 154)
backward integration (p. 136)
ballast businesses (p. 154)
bankruptcy (p. 146)
BCG Growth-Share Matrix (p. 147)
BOT (p. 142)
captive company strategy (p. 145)
cash cows (p. 148)
concentration (p. 135)
concentric diversification (p. 138)
conglomerate diversification (p. 140)
corporate parenting (p. 152)
corporate strategy (p. 133)
country's attractiveness (p. 150)
critical success factors (p. 153)
directional strategy (p. 134)
diversification (p. 135)
divestment (p. 146)
dogs (p. 148)
edge-of-heartland businesses
   (p. 154)
exporting (p. 140)

forward integration (p. 136)
full integration (p. 136)
GE Business Screen (p. 149)
green-field development
   (p. 142)
growth strategies (p. 134)
heartland businesses (p. 153)
horizontal growth (p. 138)
horizontal integration (p. 138)
horizontal strategy (p. 155)
joint ventures (p. 140)
licensing (p. 140)
liquidation (p. 146)
long-term contracts (p. 137)
management contracts (p. 142)
merger (p. 134)
multipoint competitors (p. 155)
no change strategy (p. 143)
organization slack (p. 135)
outsourcing (p. 138)
parenting-fit matrix (p. 153)
pause/proceed with caution
   strategy (p. 143)

portfolio analysis (p. 147)
production sharing (p. 142)
product's competitive strength
   (p. 150-151)
profit strategy (p. 144)
quasi-integration (p. 136)
question marks (p. 148)
retrenchment strategies (p. 134)
sell out (p. 146)
stability strategies (p. 134)
stars (p. 148)
strategic alliance (p. 135)
synergy (p. 139)
taper integration (p. 136)
transaction cost economics
   (p. 136)
turnaround strategy (p. 144)
turnkey operations (p. 142)
value trap businesses (p. 155)
vertical growth (p. 135)
vertical integration (p. 136)

Strategic Practice Exercise

Read the following example of a company that has had its share of successes and failures in a very unique industry. Consider the questions at the end of the paragraph and discuss them with others.

> KinderCare Learning Centers had been founded to take advantage of the increasing numbers of dual-career couples who were turning to day-care centers to watch their children while they were at work. In comparison to some centers that were nothing more than babysitting services providing only minimal attention to the needs of the children, Kinder-Care offered pleasant surroundings staffed by well-trained personnel. Soon KinderCare had over 1,000 centers in almost 40 states in the United States. Not satisfied with its success, however, KinderCare's top management decided to take advantage of its relationship with working parents to diversify into the somewhat related businesses of banking, insurance, and retailing. Financed through junk bonds, the strategy failed to bring in enough cash to pay for its implementation. After years of losses, the company was driven to bankruptcy in the late 1980s. It emerged from bankruptcy in 1993, divested itself of its acquisitions and pledged to stay away from diversification. The new CEO initiated a concentration strategy with an emphasis on horizontal growth. KinderCare opened its first center catering expressly to commuters in a renovated supermarket near the Metro line to Chicago. It also offered to build child-care centers for big employers or to run existing facilities for a fee. It opened its first overseas center in Britain. By 1996, the company was earning $21.7 million on revenues of $506.5 million with centers in 38 states and the United Kingdom.[32]

____ What did this company do right?

____ What mistakes did it make?

____ Do you think it made the right decision to grow internationally?

____ Should it expand further? If so, what corporate strategy should it use?

Notes

1. R. D. Hof, "Hewlett-Packard Digs Deep for a Digital Future," *Business Week* (October 18, 1993), pp. 72–75; B. Gillooly, "HP's New Course," *InformationWeek* (March 20, 1996), pp. 45–56.

2. R. P. Rumelt, D. E. Schendel, and D. J. Teece, "Fundamental Issues in Strategy," in *Fundamental Issues in Strategy: A Research Agenda,* edited by R. P. Rumelt, D. E. Schendel, and D. J. Teece (Boston: HBS Press, 1994), p. 42.

3. This analogy of corporate parent and business unit children was initially proposed by A. Campbell, M. Goold, and M. Alexander. See "Corporate Strategy: The Quest for Parenting Advantage," *Harvard Business Review* (March-April, 1995), pp. 120–132.

4. M. E. Porter, "From Competitive Strategy to Corporate Strategy," in *International Review of Strategic Management,* Vol. 1, edited by D. E. Husey (Chicester, England: John Wiley & Sons, 1990), p. 29.

5. J. W. Slocum, Jr., M. McGill, and D. T. Lei, "The New Learning Strategy: Anytime, Anything, Anywhere," *Organizational Dynamics* (Autumn 1994), p. 36.

6. K. R. Harrigan, *Strategies for Vertical Integration* (Lexington, Mass.: Lexington Books, D. C. Heath, 1983), pp. 16–21.

7. L. Grant, "Partners in Profit," *U. S. News and World Report* (September 20, 1993), pp. 65–66.

8. For a discussion of the pros and cons of contracting versus vertical integration, see J. T. Mahoney, "The Choice of Organizational Form: Vertical Financial Ownership Versus Other Methods of Vertical Integration," *Strategic Management Journal* (November 1992), pp. 559–584.

9. A. Y. Ilinich, and C. P. Zeithaml, "Operationalizing and Testing Galbraith's Center of Gravity Theory," *Strategic Management Journal* (June 1995), pp. 401–410.

10. S. Sherman, "Are Strategic Alliances Working?" *Fortune* (September 21, 1992), p. 77.

11. B. Voss, "Strategic Federations Frequently Falter in Far East," *Journal of Business Strategy* (July/August 1993), p. 6; S. Douma, "Success and Failure in New Ventures," *Long Range Planning* (April 1991), pp. 54–60.

12. J. Naisbitt, *Megatrends Asia* (New York: Simon & Schuster, 1996), p. 143.

13. J. M. Pennings, H. Barkema, and S. Douma, "Organizational Learning and Diversification," *Academy of Management Journal* (June 1994), pp. 608–640.

14. C. C. Markides, "Consequences of Corporate Refocusing: Ex Ante Evidence," *Academy of Management Journal* (June 1992), pp. 398–412; M. Lubatkin, and S. Chatterjee, "Extending Modern Portfolio Theory into the Domain of Corporate Diversification: Does It Apply?" *Academy of Management Journal* (February 1994), pp. 109–136; J. S. Harrison, M. A. Hitt, R. E. Hoskisson, and R. D. Ireland, "Synergies and Post-Acquisition Performance: Differences Versus Similarities in Resource Allocations," *Journal of Management* (March 1991), pp. 173–190; J. Robins, and M. F. Wiersema, "A Resource-Based Approach to the Multibusiness Firm: Empirical Analysis of Portfolio Interrelationships and Corporate Financial Performance," *Strategic Management Journal* (May 1995), pp. 277–299.

15. W. B. Carper, "Corporate Acquisitions and Shareholder Wealth: A Review and Exploratory Analysis," *Journal of Management* (December 1990), pp. 807–823; P. G. Simmonds, "Using Diversification as a Tool for Effective Performance," *Handbook of Business Strategy, 1992/93 Yearbook,* edited by H. E. Glass and M. A. Hovde (Boston: Warren, Gorham & Lamont, 1992), pp. 3.1–3.7; B. T. Lamont and C. A. Anderson, "Mode of Corporate Diversification and Economic Performance," *Academy of Management Journal* (December 1985), pp. 926–936.

16. J. M. Pennings, H. Barkema, and S. Douma, "Organizational Learning and Diversification," *Academy of Management Journal* (June 1994), pp. 608–640.

17. A. Inkpen, and N. Choudhury, "The Seeking of Strategy Where It Is Not: Towards a Theory of Strategy Absence," *Strategic Management Journal* (May 1995), pp. 313–323.

18. J. A. Pearce II and D. K. Robbins, "Retrenchment Remains the Foundation of Business Turnaround," *Strategic Management Journal* (June 1994), pp. 407–417.

19. J. B. Treece, "U.S. Parts Makers Just Won't Say 'Uncle,'" *Business Week* (August 10, 1987), pp. 76–77.

20. B. C. Reimann, and A. Reichert, "Portfolio Planning Methods for Strategic Capital Allocation: A Survey of Fortune 500 Firms," *International Journal of Management* (March 1996), pp. 84–93; D. K. Sinha, "Strategic Planning in the Fortune 500," *Handbook of Business Strategy, 1991/92 Yearbook,* edited by H. E. Glass and M. A. Hovde (Boston: Warren Gorham & Lamont, 1991), p. 9.6.

21. B. Hedley, "Strategy and the Business Portfolio," *Long Range Planning* (February 1977), p. 9.

22. R. G. Hamermesh, *Making Strategy Work* (New York: John Wiley and Sons, 1986), p. 14.

23. G. D. Harrell, and R. O. Kiefer, "Multinational Strategic Market Portfolios," *MSU Business Topics* (Winter 1981), p. 5.

24. M. E. Porter, "Changing Patterns of International Competition," *California Management Review* (Winter 1986), p. 12.

25. J. J. Curran, "Companies That Rob the Future," *Fortune* (July 4, 1988), p. 84.

26. A. Campbell, M. Goold, and M. Alexander, *Corporate-Level Strategy: Creating Value in the Multibusiness Company* (New York: John Wiley & Sons, 1994).

27. A. Campbell, M. Goold, and M. Alexander, "Corporate Strategy: The Quest for Parenting Advantage," *Harvard Business Review* (March-April 1995), p. 121.

28. *Ibid.,* p. 122.

29. D. J. Collis, "Corporate Strategy in Multibusiness Firms," *Long Range Planning* (June 1996), pp. 416–418; D. Lei, M. A. Hitt, and R. Bettis, "Dynamic Core Competencies Through Meta-Learning and Strategic Context," *Journal of Management,* Vol. 22, No. 4 (1996), pp. 549–569.

30. M. E. Porter, *Competitive Advantage* (New York: Free Press, 1985), pp. 317–382.

31. J. Warner, "21st Century Capitalism: Snapshot of the Next Century," *Business Week* (November 18, 1994), p. 194.

32. S. Lipin, "KKR, On Buying Spree, to Acquire KinderCare," *Wall Street Journal* (October 4, 1996), p. A3.

Chapter 7

Strategy Formulation: Functional Strategy and Strategic Choice

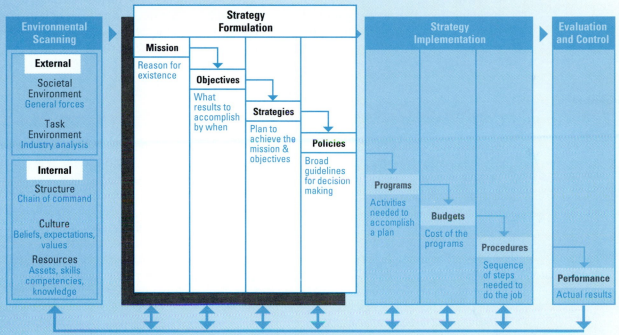

For almost 150 years, the Church & Dwight Company has been building market share on a brand name whose products are in 95% of all U.S. households. Yet if you asked the average person what products this company made, few would know. Although Church & Dwight may not be a household name, the company's ubiquitous orange box of Arm & Hammer[1] brand baking soda is cherished throughout North America. Church & Dwight is a classic example of a marketing functional strategy called product development. Shortly after its introduction in 1878, Arm & Hammer Baking Soda became a fundamental item on the pantry shelf as people found many uses for sodium bicarbonate other than baking, such as cleaning, deodorizing, and tooth brushing. Hearing of the many uses people were finding for its product, the company advertised that its baking soda was good not only for baking, but also for deodorizing refrigerators—simply by leaving an open box in the refrigerator. In a brilliant marketing move, the firm then suggested that consumers buy the product and throw it away—deodorize a kitchen sink by dumping Arm & Hammer baking soda down the drain! The company did not stop here. It looked for other uses of its sodium bicarbonate in new products. Church & Dwight has achieved consistent growth in sales and earnings through the use of "line extensions"—putting the Arm & Hammer brand first on baking soda, then on laundry detergents, toothpaste, and deodorants. By the mid 1990s, Church & Dwight had become a significant competitor in markets previously dominated only by giants like Procter & Gamble, Lever Brothers, and Colgate—using only one brand name. Was there a limit to this growth? Was there a point at which these continuous line extensions would begin to eat away at the integrity of the Arm & Hammer name?

7.1   Functional Strategy

Functional strategy is the approach a functional area takes to achieve corporate and business unit objectives and strategies by maximizing resource productivity. It is concerned with developing and nurturing a distinctive competence to provide a company or business unit with a competitive advantage. For example, just as a multidivisional corporation has several business units, each with its own business strategy, each business unit has its own set of departments, each with its own functional strategy.

The orientation of the functional strategy is dictated by its parent business unit's strategy. For example, a business unit following a competitive strategy of differentiation through high quality needs a manufacturing functional strategy that emphasizes expensive, quality assurance processes over cheaper, high-volume production; a human resource functional strategy that emphasizes the hiring and training of a highly skilled, but costly, workforce; and a marketing functional strategy that emphasizes distribution channel "pull" using advertising to increase consumer demand over "push" using promotional allowances to retailers. If a business unit were to follow a low-cost competitive strategy, however, a different set of functional strategies would be needed to support the business strategy.

Core Competencies

As defined earlier in Chapter 4, a **core competency** is something that a corporation can do exceedingly well. It is a key strength. It may also be called a **core capability** because it includes a number of constituent skills. When these competencies or capabilities are superior to those of the competition, they are called **distinctive competencies**. Although it is typically not an asset in the accounting sense, it is a very valuable capability—it does not "wear out." In general, the more core competencies are used, the more refined they get and the more valuable they become. To be considered a *distinctive* competency, the competency must meet three tests:

1. **Customer Value:** It must make a disproportionate contribution to customer-perceived value.

2. **Competitor Unique:** It must be unique and superior to competitor capabilities.

3. **Extendibility:** It must be something that can be used to develop new products/ services or enter new markets.[2]

Even though a distinctive competency is certainly considered a corporation's key strength, a key strength is not always considered to be a distinctive competency. As competitors attempt to imitate another company's competence in a particular functional area, what was once a distinctive competency becomes a minimum requirement to compete in the industry.[3] Even though the competency may still be a core competency and thus a strength, it is no longer unique. For example, when Maytag Company alone had high-quality products, Maytag's ability to make exceedingly reliable and durable washing machines was a distinctive competency. As other appliance makers imitated its quality control and design processes, this continued to be a key strength (that is, a core competency and a strategic factor) of Maytag, but it was less and less a distinctive competency.

Where do these competencies come from? A corporation can gain access to a distinctive competency in four ways:

- It may be an asset endowment, such as a key patent, coming from the founding of the company—Xerox grew on the basis of its original copying patent.

- It may be acquired from someone else—Whirlpool bought a worldwide distribution system when it purchased Philips's appliance division.

- It may be shared with another business unit or alliance partner—Apple Computer worked with a design firm to create the special appeal of its Apple II and Mac computers.

- It may be carefully built and accumulated over time within the company—Honda carefully extended its expertise in small motor manufacturing from motorcycles to autos and lawnmowers.[4]

For a functional strategy to have the best chance of success, it should be built on a distinctive competency residing within that functional area. If a corporation does not have a distinctive competency in a particular functional area, that functional area could be a candidate for outsourcing.

The Sourcing Decision: Where Should Functions Be Housed?

Where should a function be housed? Should it be integrated within the organization or purchased from an outside contractor? **Outsourcing** is purchasing from someone else a product or service that had been previously provided internally. For example, DuPont contracts out project engineering and design to Morrison Knudsen; AT&T contracts its credit card processing to Total System Services; Northern Telecom, its electronic component manufacturing to Comptronix; and Eastman Kodak, its computer support services to Businessland. Outsourcing is becoming an increasingly important part of strategic decision making and an important way to increase efficiency and often quality. Firms competing in global industries must in particular search worldwide for the most appropriate suppliers. In a study of 30 firms, outsourcing resulted on average in a 9% reduction in costs and a 15% increase in capacity and quality.[5]

Management services and information systems were the first functional areas to be heavily outsourced. In a 1995 survey of 314 large U.S. firms, 26% outsourced benefits administration, 87% outsourced recordkeeping, and 59% outsourced administration and service.[6] Approximately 20% of U.S. companies now use some form of information technology outsourcing.[7] Sales, marketing, and customer service are now becoming likely candidates for outsourcing.[8] For example, United Parcel Service has turned to outside sources to run 65 customer service "call centers" employing 5,000 people.[9]

Sophisticated strategists, according to Quinn, are no longer thinking just of market share or vertical integration as the keys to strategic planning:

> Instead they concentrate on identifying those few core service activities where the company has or can develop: (1) a continuing strategic edge and (2) long-term streams of new products to satisfy future customer demands. They develop these competencies in greater depth than anyone else in the world. Then they seek to eliminate, minimize, or outsource activities where the company cannot be preeminent, unless those activities are essential to support or protect the chosen areas of strategic focus.[10]

The key to outsourcing is to purchase from outside only those activities that are not key to the company's distinctive competencies. Otherwise, the company may give up the very capabilities that made it successful in the first place—thus putting itself on the road to eventual decline. Therefore, in determining functional strategy, the strategist must:

- Identify the company's or business unit's core competencies.

- Ensure that the competencies are continually being strengthened.

- Manage the competencies in such a way that best preserves the competitive advantage they create.

An outsourcing decision depends on the fraction of total value added that the activity under consideration represents and by the amount of potential competitive advantage in that activity for the company or business unit. See a proposed outsourcing matrix in Figure 7.1. A firm should consider outsourcing any activity or function that has low potential for competitive advantage. If that activity constitutes only a small part of the total value of the firm's products or services, it should be purchased on the open market (assuming that quality providers of the activity are plentiful). If, however, the activity contributes highly to the company's products or services, the firm should purchase it through long-term contracts with trusted suppliers or distributors. A firm should always produce at least some of the activity or function (taper vertical integration) if that activity has the potential for providing the company some competitive advantage. Full vertical integration should only be considered, however, when that activity or function adds significant value to the company's products or services in addition to providing competitive advantage.

Outsourcing does, however, have some disadvantages. For example, GE's introduction of a new washing machine was delayed three weeks by production problems at a supplier's company to whom it had contracted out key work. Some companies have found themselves locked into long-term contracts with outside suppliers that are no longer competitive.[11] Some authorities propose that the cumulative effects of continued outsourcing steadily reduces a firm's ability to learn new skills and to develop new core competencies.[12] A study of 30 firms with outsourcing experience revealed that unsuccessful outsourcing efforts had three common characteristics:

- The firms' finance and legal departments and their vendors dominated the decision process.

- Vendors were not prequalified based on total capabilities.

- Short-term benefits dominated decision making.[13]

Marketing Strategy

Marketing strategy deals with pricing, selling, and distributing a product. Using a **market development** strategy, a company or business unit can (1) capture a larger share of an existing market for current products through market saturation and market penetra-

Figure 7.1
Proposed
Outsourcing
Matrix

Source: J. D. Hunger
and T. L. Wheelen,
"Proposed Outsourcing
Matrix." Copyright ©
1996 by Wheelen and
Hunger Associates.
Reprinted by
permission.

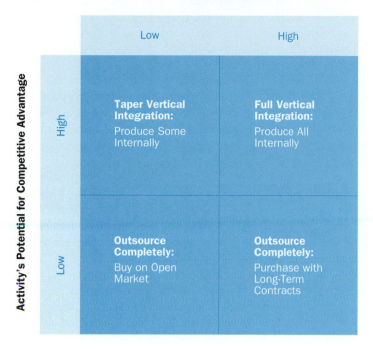

Activity's Total Value-Added to Firm's Products and Services

tion or (2) develop new markets for current products. Consumer product giants such as Procter & Gamble, Colgate-Palmolive, and Unilever are experts at using advertising and promotion to implement a market saturation/penetration strategy to gain the dominant market share in a product category. As seeming masters of the product life cycle, these companies are able to extend product life almost indefinitely through "new and improved" variations of product and packaging that appeal to most market niches. These companies also follow the second market development strategy by taking a successful product they market in one part of the world and marketing it elsewhere. Noting the success of their presoak detergents in Europe, for example, both P&G and Colgate successfully introduced this type of laundry product to North America under the trade names of Biz and Axion.

Using the **product development** strategy, a company or unit can (1) develop new products for *existing markets* or (2) develop new products for *new markets*. Church & Dwight has had great success following the first product development strategy by developing new products to sell to its current customers. Acknowledging the widespread appeal of its Arm & Hammer brand baking soda, the company generated new uses for its sodium bicarbonate by reformulating it as toothpaste, deodorant, and detergent. The company has also successfully followed the second product development strategy by developing pollution reduction products (using sodium bicarbonate compounds) for sale to coal-fired electric utility plants.

There are numerous other marketing strategies. For advertising and promotion, for example, a company or business unit can choose between a "push" or a "pull" marketing strategy. Many large food and consumer products companies in the United States and Canada have followed a **push strategy** by spending a large amount of money on trade promotion in order to gain or hold shelf space in retail outlets. Trade promotion includes discounts, in-store special offers, and advertising allowances designed to "push" products through the distribution system. The Kellogg Company recently decided to change its emphasis from a push to a **pull strategy**, in which advertising "pulls" the products through the distribution channels. The company now spends more money on consumer advertising designed to build brand awareness so that shoppers will ask for the products. Research has indicated that a high level of advertising (a key part of a pull strategy) is most beneficial to leading brands in a market.[14]

Other marketing strategies deal with distribution and pricing. Should a company use distributors and dealers to sell its products or should it sell directly to retailers? Gateway 2000, noted for only selling computers directly to the customer via telephone, decided in 1996 to sell "Destination," its combination computer television set, through CompUSA and Nobody Beats the Wiz chains of retail stores. The product was so novel that people were unwilling to buy the product unless they could personally view it in action. Another example was Sears Roebuck's decision to market brands of major home appliances other than its own Kenmore brand. Most appliance makers were very happy to sell their products through Sears' "Brand Central." After all, Sears sold one out of every four major home appliances sold in the United States. Maytag Corporation, however, had its reservations about changing its traditional distribution channels. As shown in the **Company Spotlight on Maytag Corporation** feature, the corporation chose not to sell its Maytag brand home appliances through Sears because management did not want to alienate existing Maytag dealers.

When pricing a new product, a company or business unit can follow one of two strategies. For new-product pioneers, **skim pricing** offers the opportunity to "skim the cream" from the top of the demand curve with a high price while the product is novel and competitors are few. **Penetration pricing**, in contrast, attempts to hasten market development and offers the pioneer the opportunity to use the experience curve to gain market share with a low price and dominate the industry. Depending on corporate and business unit objectives and strategies, either of these choices may be desirable to a particular company or unit. Penetration pricing is, however, more likely than skim pricing to raise a unit's operating profit in the long term.[15]

Financial Strategy

Financial strategy examines the financial implications of corporate and business-level strategic options and identifies the best financial course of action. It can also provide competitive advantage through a lower cost of funds and a flexible ability to raise capital to support a business strategy. Financial strategy usually attempts to maximize the financial value of the firm.

The tradeoff between achieving the desired debt-to-equity ratio and relying on internal long-term financing via cash flow is a key issue in financial strategy. Many small- and medium-sized companies such as Urschel Laboratories try to avoid all external sources of funds in order to avoid outside entanglements and to keep control of the company within the family. Many financial analysts believe, however, that only by financing through long-term debt can a corporation use financial leverage to boost earnings per share—thus raising stock price and the overall value of the company.

The desired level of current versus long-term investments has become a strategic issue. Although most companies usually choose to invest cash instead of hoarding it (to obtain a better return on investment), there are some exceptions. During the mid 1990s, U.S. auto companies together held more than $30 million in cash in short-term U.S. Treasury and corporate instruments. In past years, the auto firms had used cash earned during prosperous times to diversify into financial services, car rental, and aerospace companies. When the inevitable downturn occurred, the auto firms had been forced to divest their acquisitions and cut product development programs. This time, managers in

Maytag Supports Dealers as Part of Its Marketing Strategy

In the late 1980s, Sears instituted its new "Brand Central" format to sell white goods. In addition to offering its own private brands, the retail giant planned to offer nationally known brands such as General Electric, Whirlpool, Amana, Jenn-Air, and Speedqueen. Except for its Jenn-Air products, Maytag Corporation chose not to join Sears' Brand Central concept. Some industry experts thought this to be a strange decision given that Sears alone sold one out of every four U.S. major home appliances. Why would Maytag ignore this key sales outlet?

Leonard Hadley, Chief Operating Officer of Maytag Corporation at the time, explained that the company did not want to antagonize its carefully nurtured appliance dealers who had always considered Sears their major retail competition. Maytag Company's emphasis on quality and higher price rather than market share as its business competitive strategy made the Maytag brand more dependent on appliance dealers than either General Electric or Whirlpool were. In addition, some Maytag people feared that Sears might use the Maytag brand's image to attract customers into the stores, but then persuade them to buy a less-expensive Sears brand carrying a higher markup.

MAYTAG CORPORATION

all three U.S. auto companies decided to save their money to get through the next recession. In response to arguments from financial analysts and shareholders that cash was not a very productive asset, Ford's Treasurer, Malcolm MacDonald, responded that the corporation wanted immediate access to cash for strategic reasons.[16]

A very popular financial strategy is the leveraged buy out (LBO). In a **leveraged buy out**, a company is acquired in a transaction financed largely by debt—usually obtained from a third party, such as an insurance company. Ultimately the debt is paid with money generated from the acquired company's operations or by sales of its assets. The acquired company, in effect, pays for its own acquisition! Management of the LBO is then under tremendous pressure to keep the highly leveraged company profitable. Unfortunately the huge amount of debt on the acquired company's books may actually cause its eventual decline unless it goes public once again.

The management of dividends to shareholders is an important part of a corporation's financial strategy. Corporations in fast-growing industries such as computers and computer software often do not declare dividends. They use the money they might have spent on dividends to finance rapid growth. If the company is successful, its growth in sales and profits is reflected in a higher stock price—eventually resulting in a hefty capital gain when shareholders sell their common stock. Other corporations such as electric utilities that do not face rapid growth must support the value of their stock by offering generous and consistent dividends.

Research and Development (R&D) Strategy

R&D strategy deals with product and process innovation and improvement. It also deals with the appropriate mix of different types of R&D (basic, product, or process) and with the question of how new technology should be accessed—internal development, external acquisition, or through strategic alliances.

Table 7.1   Research and Development Strategy and Competitive Advantage

	Technological Leadership	Technological Followership
Cost Advantage	Pioneer the lowest cost product design. Be the first firm down the learning curve. Create low-cost ways of performing value activities.	Lower the cost of the product or value activities by learning from the leader's experience. Avoid R&D costs through imitation.
Differentiation	Pioneer a unique product that increases buyer value. Innovate in other activities to increase buyer value.	Adapt the product or delivery system more closely to buyer needs by learning from the leader's experience.

Source: Adapted/reprinted with the permission of The Free Press, an imprint of Simon & Schuster, from *Competitive Advantage: Creating and Sustaining Superior Performance* by Michael E. Porter, p. 181. Copyright © 1985 by Michael E. Porter.

One of the R&D choices is to be either a **technological leader** in which one pioneers an innovation or a **technological follower** in which one imitates the products of competitors. Porter suggests that deciding to become a technological leader or follower can be a way of achieving either overall low cost or differentiation. (See Table 7.1.)

One example of an effective use of the *leader* R&D functional strategy to achieve a differentiation competitive advantage is Nike, Inc. Nike spends more than most in the industry on R&D to differentiate the performance of its athletic shoes from that of its competitors. As a result, its products have become the favorite of the serious athlete. An example of the use of the *follower* R&D functional strategy to achieve a low-cost competitive advantage is Dean Foods Company. "We're able to have the customer come to us and say, 'If you can produce X, Y, and Z product for the same quality and service, but at a lower price and without that expensive label on it, you can have the business,'" says Howard Dean, president of the company.[17]

An increasing number of companies are working with their suppliers to help them keep up with changing technology. They are beginning to realize that a firm cannot be competitive technologically only through internal development. For example, Chrysler Corporation's skillful use of parts suppliers to design everything from car seats to drive shafts has enabled it to spend consistently less money than its competitors to develop new car models. Strategic technology alliances are one way to combine the R&D capabilities of two companies. As mentioned earlier in Chapter 5, Maytag Company worked with one of its suppliers to apply fuzzy logic technology to its new IntelliSense™ dishwasher. The partnership enabled Maytag to complete the project in a shorter amount of time than if it had tried to do it alone.[18]

Operations Strategy

Operations strategy determines how and where a product or service is to be manufactured, the level of vertical integration in the production process, the deployment of physical resources, and relationships with suppliers. It should also deal with the optimum level of technology the firm should use in its operations processes. See the 🌐 **21st Century Global Society** feature to see how differences in national conditions can lead to differences in product design and manufacturing facilities from one country to another.

Advanced Manufacturing Technology (AMT) is revolutionizing operations world-wide and should continue to have a major impact as corporations strive to integrate diverse business activities using computer integrated design and manufacturing (CAD/CAM) principles. The use of CAD/CAM, flexible manufacturing systems, computer numerically controlled systems, automatically guided vehicles, robotics, manufacturing resource planning (MRP II), optimized production technology, and just-in-time contribute to increased flexibility, quick response time, and higher productivity. Such investments also act to increase the company's fixed costs and could cause significant problems if the company is unable to achieve economies of scale or scope.

A firm's manufacturing strategy is often affected by a product's life cycle. As the sales of a product increase, there will be an increase in production volume ranging from lot sizes as low as one in a **job shop** (one-of-a-kind production using skilled labor) through **connected line batch flow** (components are standardized; each machine functions like a job shop but is positioned in the same order as the parts are processed) to lot sizes as high as 100,000 or more per year for **flexible manufacturing systems** (parts are grouped into manufacturing families to produce a wide variety of mass-produced items) and **dedicated transfer lines** (highly automated assembly lines making one mass-produced product using little human labor). According to this concept, the product becomes standardized into a commodity over time in conjunction with increasing demand. Flexibility thus gives way to efficiency.[19] This concept of eventual reduced flexibility is, however, being increasingly challenged by the new concept of mass customization.

Increasing competitive intensity in many industries has forced companies to switch from traditional mass production using dedicated transfer lines to a continuous improvement production strategy. A **mass production** system was an excellent method to produce a large amount of low-cost, standard goods and services. Employees worked on narrowly defined, repetitive tasks under close supervision in a bureaucratic and hierarchical structure. Quality, however, often tended to be fairly low. Learning how to do something better was the prerogative of management; workers were expected only to learn what was assigned to them. This system tended to dominate manufacturing until the 1970s. Under the **continuous improvement** system developed by Japanese firms, empowered cross-functional teams strive constantly to improve production processes. Managers become more like coaches. The result is a large quantity of low-cost, standard goods and services, but with high quality. The key to continuous improvement is the acknowledgment that workers' experience and knowledge can help managers solve production problems and contribute toward tightening variances and reducing errors. Because continuous improvement enables firms to use the same low-cost competitive strategy as do mass production firms but at a significantly higher level of quality, it is rapidly replacing mass production as an operations strategy.

According to B. Joseph Pine in his book *Mass Customization: The New Frontier in Business Competition*, a number of companies are now experimenting with **mass customization** as an operations strategy.[20] In contrast to continuous improvement, mass customization requires flexibility and quick responsiveness. Appropriate for an ever-changing environment, mass customization requires that people, processes, units, and technology reconfigure themselves to give customers exactly what they want, when they want it. Managers coordinate independent, capable individuals. An efficient linkage system is crucial. The result is low-cost, high-quality, customized goods and services. Mass customization is having a significant impact on product development. Under a true mass customization system, no one knows exactly what the next customer will want. Therefore, no one can know exactly what product the company will be creating/producing next. Because it is becoming increasingly difficult to predict what product-market opportunity will

WHIRLPOOL ADJUSTS ITS MANUFACTURING STRATEGY TO LOCAL CONDITIONS

To better penetrate the growing markets in developing nations, Whirlpool decided to build a "world washer." This new type of washing machine was to be produced in Brazil, Mexico, and India. Lightweight, with substantially fewer parts than its U.S. counterpart, its performance was to be equal to or better than anything on the world market while being competitive in price with the most popular models in these markets. The goal was to develop a complete product, process, and facility design package that could be used in different countries with low initial investment. Originally the plan had been to make the same low-cost washer in identical plants in each of the three countries.

Significant differences in each of the three countries forced Whirlpool to change its product design to suit each nation's situation. According to Lawrence Kremer, Senior Vice-President of Global Technology and Operations, "Our Mexican affiliate, Vitromatic, has porcelain and glassmaking capabilities. Porcelain baskets made sense for them. Stainless steel became the preferred material for the others." Costs also affected decisions. "In India, for example, material costs may run as much as

200% to 800% higher than elsewhere, while labor and overhead costs are comparatively minimal," added Kremer. Another consideration were the garments to be washed in each country. For example, saris—the 18-foot lengths of cotton or silk with which Indian women drape themselves—needed special treatment in an Indian washing machine, forcing additional modifications.

Manufacturing facilities also varied from country to country. Brastemp, Whirlpool's Brazilian partner, built its plant of precast concrete to address the problems of high humidity. In India, however, the construction crew cast the concrete, allowed it to cure, and then using chain, block, and tackle, five or six men raised each three-ton slab into place. Instead of using one building, Mexican operations used two, one housing the flexible assembly lines and stamping operations, and an adjacent facility housing the injection molding and extrusion processes.

Source: A. A. Ullmann, "Whirlpool Corporation, 1993: A Metamorphosis," in Wheelen and Hunger, *Strategic Management and Business Policy*, 5th ed. (Reading, Mass.: Addison-Wesley, 1995), pp. 713–715.

open up next, it is harder to create a long-term vision of the company's products. Companies using mass customization often say "anything," "anywhere," and "any time." Peter Kann, CEO of Dow Jones, describes his company as providing "business and financial news and information however, wherever, and whenever customers want to receive it."[21] Another example of mass customization is the new "Personal Pair" system Levi Strauss introduced to combat the growing competition from private label jeans. The customer is measured at one of the company's Personal Pair outlets, the measurements are sent to Levi's by computer, and the made-to-order jeans arrive a few days later. The jeans cost about $10 more than an off-the-shelf pair.[22]

Purchasing Strategy

Purchasing strategy deals with obtaining the raw materials, parts, and supplies needed to perform the operations function. Some purchasing choices are multiple, sole, and parallel sourcing. Under **multiple sourcing**, the purchasing company orders a particular part from several vendors. Multiple sourcing has traditionally been considered superior to other purchasing approaches because (1) it forces suppliers to compete for the business of an important buyer, thus reducing purchasing costs; and (2) if one supplier could not deliver, another usually could, thus guaranteeing that parts and supplies would always be on hand when needed. Multiple sourcing was one way a purchasing firm could control the relationship with its suppliers. So long as suppliers could provide evidence that they could meet the product specifications, they were kept on the purchaser's list of acceptable vendors for specific parts and supplies. Unfortunately the common practice of accepting the lowest bid often compromised quality.

W. Edward Deming, a well-known management consultant, strongly recommended sole sourcing as the only manageable way to obtain high supplier quality. **Sole sourcing** relies on only one supplier for a particular part. Given his concern with designing quality into a product in its early stages of development, Deming argued that the buyer should work closely with the supplier at all stages. This reduces both cost and time spent on product design as well as improving quality. It can also simplify the purchasing company's production process by using the *just-in-time (JIT)* concept of the purchased parts arriving at the plant just when they are needed rather than keeping inventories. The concept of sole sourcing is being taken one step further in *JIT II,* in which vendor sales representatives actually have desks next to the purchasing company's factory floor, attend production status meetings, visit the R&D lab, and analyze the purchasing company's sales forecasts. These in-house suppliers then write sales orders for which the purchasing company is billed. Developed by Lance Dixon at Bose Corporation, JIT II is also being used at IBM, Honeywell, and Ingersoll-Rand. Karen Dale, purchasing manager for Honeywell's office supplies, said she was very concerned about confidentiality when JIT II was first suggested to her. Now she has five suppliers working with her 20 buyers and reports few problems.[23]

Sole sourcing reduces transactions costs and builds quality by having purchaser and supplier work together as partners rather than as adversaries. Sole sourcing means that more companies are going to have longer relationships with fewer suppliers. For example, the average computer company obtained 80% of its material from 22 suppliers in 1995 compared to 31 suppliers in 1992.[24] Sole sourcing does, however, have its limitations. If a supplier is unable to deliver a part, the purchaser has no alternative but to delay production. Multiple suppliers can provide the purchaser with better information about new technology and performance capabilities. The limitations of sole sourcing have led to the development of parallel sourcing. In **parallel sourcing,** two suppliers are the sole suppliers of two different parts, but they are also backup suppliers for each other's parts. In case one vendor cannot supply all of its parts on time, the other vendor would be asked to make up the difference.[25]

Logistics Strategy

Logistics strategy deals with the flow of products into and out of the manufacturing process. During the 1990s, two trends were evident: centralization and outsourcing. To gain logistical synergies across business units, corporations began centralizing logistics in the headquarters group. This centralized logistics group usually contains specialists with expertise in different transportation modes such as rail or trucking. They work to aggregate shipping volumes across the entire corporation to gain better contracts with shippers. Companies like Amoco Chemical, Georgia-Pacific, Marriott, and Union Carbide view the logistics function as an important way to differentiate themselves from the competition, to add value, and to reduce costs. As in purchasing, long-term relationships between carriers and shippers coupled with sophisticated information systems are part of this logistics strategy.[26]

Many companies have found that outsourcing of logistics reduces costs and improves delivery time. For example, Hewlett-Packard contracted with Roadway Logistics to manage its in-bound raw materials warehousing in Vancouver, Canada. Nearly 140 Roadway employees replaced 250 HP workers, who were transferred to other HP activities. According to George Gecowets, Executive Director of the Council of Logistics Management, increasing global competition should motivate U.S. companies to increase their outsourcing of the logistics function from 12% in 1995 to as much as 30% in a few years.[27]

Human Resource Management (HRM) Strategy

HRM strategy, among other things, addresses the issue of whether a company or business unit should hire a large number of low-skilled employees who receive low pay, perform repetitive jobs, and most likely quit after a short time (the McDonald's restaurant strategy) or hire skilled employees who receive relatively high pay and are crosstrained to participate in *self-managed work teams*. As work increases in complexity, the more suited it is for teams, especially in the case of innovative product development efforts. A recent survey of 476 Fortune 1000 U.S. companies revealed that although only 7% of their workforce was organized into self-managed teams, half the companies reported that they would be relying significantly more on them in the years ahead.[28] Research indicates that the use of work teams leads to increased quality and productivity.[29]

Many North American and European companies are not only using an increasing amount of part-time and *temporary employees*, they are also experimenting with leasing temporary employees from employee leasing companies. To reduce costs and obtain increased flexibility, companies in the United States hired around two million temporary workers in 1994 (up from 600 thousand in 1984).[30] This number is expected to double by the end of the century.

Companies are finding that having a *diverse workforce* can be a competitive advantage. DuPont, for example, found that a group of African-American employees were able to create promising new markets for its agricultural products by focusing on black farmers. DuPont's use of multinational teams has helped the company develop and market products internationally. McDonald's has discovered that older workers perform as well, if not better, than younger employees. According to Edward Rensi, CEO of McDonald's USA: "We find these people to be particularly well motivated, with a sort of discipline and work habits hard to find in younger employees."[31]

Information Systems Strategy

Corporations are increasingly adopting **information systems strategies** in that they are turning to information systems technology to provide business units with competitive advantage. When Federal Express first provided its customers with *PowerShip* computer software to store addresses, print shipping labels, and track package location, its sales jumped significantly. UPS soon followed with its own *MaxiShips* software. Viewing its information system as a distinctive competency, Federal Express continued to push for further advantage against UPS by using its web site to enable customers to track their packages.

Many companies are also attempting to use information systems to form closer relationships with both their customers and suppliers through sophisticated intranets. For example, General Electric's Trading Process Network allows suppliers to electronically download GE's requests for proposals, view diagrams of parts specifications, and communicate with GE purchasing managers. According to Robert Livingston, GE's head of worldwide sourcing for the Lighting Division, going on the web reduces processing time by one-third.[32]

7.2 Strategies to Avoid

Several strategies, which could be considered corporate, business, or functional, are very dangerous. Managers who have made a poor analysis or lack creativity may be trapped into considering some of the following **strategies to avoid:**

- **Follow the Leader.** Imitating a leading competitor's strategy might seem to be a good idea, but it ignores a firm's particular strengths and weaknesses and the possibility that the leader may be wrong. Fujitsu Ltd., the world's second-largest computer maker, was driven since the 1960s by the sole ambition of catching up to IBM. Like IBM, Fujitsu competed primarily as a mainframe computer maker. So devoted was it to catching IBM, however, that it failed to notice that the mainframe business was reaching maturity and by the 1990s was no longer growing.

- **Hit Another Home Run.** If a company is successful because it pioneered an extremely successful product, it tends to search for another superproduct that will ensure growth and prosperity. Like betting on long shots at the horse races, the probability of finding a second winner is slight. Polaroid spent a lot of money developing an "instant" movie camera, but the public ignored it.

- **Arms Race.** Entering into a spirited battle with another firm for increased market share might increase sales revenue, but that increase will probably be more than offset by increases in advertising, promotion, R&D, and manufacturing costs. Since the deregulation of airlines, price wars and rate "specials" have contributed to the low profit margins or bankruptcy of many major airlines such as Eastern and Continental.

- **Do Everything.** When faced with several interesting opportunities, management might tend to leap at all of them. At first, a corporation might have enough resources to develop each idea into a project, but money, time, and energy are soon exhausted as the many projects demand large infusions of resources.

- **Losing Hand.** A corporation might have invested so much in a particular strategy that top management is unwilling to accept its failure. Believing that it has too much invested to quit, the corporation continues to throw "good money after bad." Pan American Airlines, for example, chose to sell its Pan Am Building and Intercontinental Hotels, the most profitable parts of the corporation, to keep its money-losing airline flying. Continuing to suffer losses, the company followed this strategy of shedding assets for cash, until it had sold off everything and went bankrupt.

7.3 Strategic Choice: Selection of the Best Strategy

After the *pros* and *cons* of the potential strategic alternatives have been identified and evaluated, one must be selected for implementation. By now, it is likely that many feasible alternatives will have emerged. How is the best strategy determined?

Perhaps the most important criterion is the ability of the proposed strategy to deal with the specific strategic factors developed earlier in the SWOT analysis. If the alternative doesn't take advantage of environmental opportunities and corporate strengths, and lead away from environmental threats and corporate weaknesses, it will probably fail.

Another important consideration in the selection of a strategy is the ability of each alternative to satisfy agreed-on objectives with the least resources and the fewest negative side effects. It is, therefore, important to develop a tentative implementation plan so that the difficulties that management is likely to face are addressed. This should be done in light of societal trends, the industry, and the company's situation based on the construction of scenarios.

Constructing Corporate Scenarios

Corporate scenarios are *pro forma* balance sheets and income statements that forecast the effect each alternative strategy and its various programs will likely have on division and corporate return on investment. In a survey of Fortune 500 firms, 84% reported using computer simulation models in strategic planning. Most of these were simply spreadsheet-based simulation models dealing with "what if" questions.[33]

The recommended scenarios are simply extensions of the industry scenarios discussed in Chapter 3. If, for example, industry scenarios suggest the probable emergence of a strong market demand in a specific country for certain products, a series of alternative strategy scenarios can be developed. The alternative of acquiring another firm having these products in that country can be compared with the alternative of a green-field development (building new operations in that country). Using three sets of estimated sales figures (optimistic, pessimistic, and most likely) for the new products over the next five years, the two alternatives can be evaluated in terms of their effect on future company performance as reflected in its probable future financial statements. *Pro forma* (estimated future) balance sheets and income statements can be generated with spreadsheet software, such as Lotus 1-2-3 or Excel, on a personal computer.

To construct a scenario, follow these steps:

- **First**, use *industry scenarios* (discussed earlier in Chapter 3) to develop a set of assumptions about the task environment (in the specific country under consideration). For example, 3M requires the general manager of each business unit to describe annually what his or her industry will look like in 15 years. List *optimistic, pessimistic,* and *most likely* assumptions for key economic factors such as the GDP (Gross Domestic Product), CPI (Consumer Price Index), and prime interest rate, and for other key external strategic factors such as governmental regulation and industry trends. *This needs to be done for every country/region in which the corporation has significant operations that will be affected by each strategic alternative.* These same underlying assumptions should be listed for each of the alternative scenarios to be developed.

- **Second**, develop *common-size financial statements* (discussed in Chapter 10) for the company's or business unit's previous years, to serve as the basis for the trend analysis projections of pro forma financial statements. Use the *Scenario Box* form in Table 7.2.
  - (a) Use the historical common-size percentages to estimate the level of revenues, expenses, and other categories in estimated pro forma statements for future years.
  - (b) Develop for each strategic alternative a set of *optimistic, pessimistic,* and *most likely* assumptions about the impact of key variables on the company's future financial statements.
  - (c) Forecast three sets of sales and cost of goods sold figures for at least five years into the future.
  - (d) Analyze historical data and make adjustments based on the environmental assumptions listed earlier. Do the same for other figures that can vary significantly.
  - (e) Assume for other figures that they will continue in their historical relationship to sales or some other key determining factor. Plug in expected inventory levels, accounts receivable, accounts payable, R&D expenses, advertising and promotion expenses, capital expenditures, and debt payments (assuming that debt is used to finance the strategy), among others.

Table 7.2 Scenario Box for Use in Generating Financial Pro Forma Statements

Factor	Last Year	Historical Average	Trend Analysis	Projections[1] 19—			19—			19—			Comments
				O	P	ML	O	P	ML	O	P	ML	
GDP													
CPI													
Other													
Sales units													
Dollars													
COGS													
Advertising and marketing													
Interest expense													
Plant expansion													
Dividends													
Net profits													
EPS													
ROI													
ROE													
Other													

Note:
1. **O** = Optimistic; **P** = Pessimistic; **ML** = Most Likely.

Source: T. L. Wheelen and J. D. Hunger. Copyright © 1993 by Wheelen and Hunger Associates. Reprinted by permission.

(f) Consider not only historical trends, but also programs that might be needed to implement each alternative strategy (such as building a new manufacturing facility or expanding the sales force).

- **Third**, construct detailed **pro forma financial statements** for each strategic alternative.
  (a) List the actual figures from this year's financial statements in the left column of the spreadsheet.
  (b) List to the right of this column the optimistic figures for years one through five.
  (c) Go through this same process with the same strategic alternative, but now list the pessimistic figures for the next five years.
  (d) Do the same with the most likely figures.
  (e) Develop a similar set of *optimistic* (O), *pessimistic* (P), and *most likely* (ML) pro forma statements for the second strategic alternative. This process generates six different pro forma scenarios reflecting three different situations (O, P, and ML) for two strategic alternatives.
  (f) Calculate financial ratios and common-size income statements, and balance sheets to accompany the pro formas.
  (g) Compare the assumptions underlying the scenarios with these financial statements and ratios to determine the feasibility of the scenarios. For example, if cost of goods sold drops from 70% to 50% of total sales revenue in the pro forma income statements, this drop should result from a change in the production process or a shift to cheaper raw materials or labor costs, rather than from a failure to keep the cost of goods sold in its usual

percentage relationship to sales revenue when the predicted statement was developed.

The result of this detailed scenario construction should be anticipated net profits, cash flow, and net working capital for each of three versions of the two alternatives for five years into the future. A strategist might want to go further into the future if the strategy is expected to have a major impact on the company's financial statements beyond five years. The result of this work should provide sufficient information on which forecasts of the likely feasibility and probable profitability of each of the strategic alternatives could be based.

Obviously these scenarios can quickly become very complicated, especially if three sets of acquisition prices and development costs are calculated. Nevertheless this sort of detailed "what if" analysis is needed to realistically compare the projected outcome of each reasonable alternative strategy and its attendant programs, budgets, and procedures. Regardless of the quantifiable pros and cons of each alternative, the actual decision will probably be influenced by several subjective factors like those described in the following sections.

Management's Attitude Toward Risk

The attractiveness of a particular strategic alternative is partially a function of the amount of risk it entails. **Risk** is composed not only of the *probability* that the strategy will be effective, but also of the *amount of assets* the corporation must allocate to that strategy and the *length of time* the assets will be unavailable for other uses. Because of variation among countries in terms of customs, regulations, and resources, companies operating in global industries must deal with a greater amount of risk than firms operating only in one country. The greater the assets involved and the longer they are committed, the more likely top management is to demand a high probability of success.

This might be one reason that innovations seem to occur more often in small firms than in large, established corporations. The small firm managed by an entrepreneur is willing to accept greater risk than would a large firm of diversified ownership run by professional managers. It is one thing to take a chance if you are the primary shareholder and are not concerned with periodic changes in the value of the company's common stock. It is something else if the corporation's stock is widely held and acquisition-hungry competitors or takeover artists surround the company like sharks every time the company's stock price falls below some external assessment of the firm's value!

Pressures from the External Environment

The attractiveness of a strategic alternative is affected by its perceived compatibility with the key stakeholders in a corporation's task environment. Creditors want to be paid on time. Unions exert pressure for comparable wage and employment security. Governments and interest groups demand social responsibility. Shareholders want dividends. All of these pressures must be considered in the selection of the best alternative.

Strategic managers should ask four questions to assess the importance of stakeholder concerns in a particular decision:

1. What stakeholders are most crucial for corporate success?

2. How much of what they want are they likely to get under this alternative?

3. What are they likely to do if they don't get what they want?

4. What is the probability that they will do it?

Strategy makers should be better able to choose strategic alternatives that minimize external pressures and maximize the probability of gaining stakeholder support. In addition, top management can propose a **political strategy** to influence its key stakeholders. Some of the most commonly used political strategies are constituency building, political action committee contributions, advocacy advertising, lobbying, and coalition building.

Pressures from the Corporate Culture

If a strategy is incompatible with the corporate culture, the likelihood of its success is very low. Foot-dragging and even sabotage will result as employees fight to resist a radical change in corporate philosophy. Precedents from the past tend to restrict the kinds of objectives and strategies that can be seriously considered. The "aura" of the founders of a corporation can linger long past their lifetimes because their values have been imprinted on a corporation's members.

In evaluating a strategic alternative, the strategy makers must consider **corporate culture pressures** and assess the strategy's compatibility with the corporate culture. If there is little fit, management must decide if it should:

- Take a chance on ignoring the culture.

- Manage around the culture and change the implementation plan.

- Try to change the culture to fit the strategy.

- Change the strategy to fit the culture.

Further, a decision to proceed with a particular strategy without a commitment to change the culture or manage around the culture (both very tricky and time consuming) is dangerous. Nevertheless restricting a corporation to only those strategies that are completely compatible with its culture might eliminate from consideration the most profitable alternatives. (See Chapter 9 for more information on managing corporate culture.)

Needs and Desires of Key Managers

Even the most attractive alternative might not be selected if it is contrary to the needs and desires of important top managers. Personal characteristics and experience do affect a person's assessment of an alternative's attractiveness.[34] A person's ego may be tied to a particular proposal to the extent that all other alternatives are strongly lobbied against. As a result, he or she may have unfavorable forecasts altered so that they are more in agreement with the desired alternative.[35] A key executive might influence other people in top management to favor a particular alternative so that objections to it are ignored. For example, Nextel's CEO, Daniel Akerson, decided that the best place to locate the corporation's 500-person national headquarters would be the Washington, D.C., area, close to his own home.[36]

There is a tendency to maintain the status quo, which means that decision makers continue with existing goals and plans beyond the point when an objective observer would recommend a change in course. Some executives show a self-serving tendency to attribute the firm's problems not to their own poor decisions, but to environmental events out of their control such as government policies or a poor economic climate.[37] Negative information about a particular course of action to which a person is committed may be ignored because of a desire to appear competent or because of strongly held values regarding consistency. It may take a crisis or an unlikely event to cause strategic decision makers to seriously consider an alternative they had previously ignored or discounted.[38] For example, it wasn't until the CEO of ConAgra, a multinational food products company, had a heart attack that ConAgra started producing the Healthy Choice line of low-fat, low-cholesterol, low-sodium frozen-food entrees.

Process of Strategic Choice

There is an old story at General Motors:

> At a meeting with his key executives, CEO Alfred Sloan proposed a controversial strategic decision. When asked for comments, each executive responded with supportive comments and praise. After announcing that they were all in apparent agreement, Sloan stated that they were not going to proceed with the decision. Either his executives didn't know enough to point out potential downsides of the decision, or they were agreeing to avoid upsetting the boss and disrupting the cohesion of the group. The decision was delayed until a debate could occur over the pros and cons.[39]

Strategic choice is the evaluation of alternative strategies and selection of the best alternative. There is mounting evidence that when an organization is facing a dynamic environment, the best strategic decisions are not arrived at through **consensus** when everyone agrees on one alternative. They actually involve a certain amount of heated disagreement, and even conflict. This is certainly the case for firms operating in a global industry. See the **Strategy in a Changing World** feature for how Intel made a decision of critical significance to its future. Because unmanaged conflict often carries a high emotional cost, authorities in decision making propose that strategic managers use "programmed conflict" to raise different opinions, regardless of the personal feelings of the people involved.[40] Two techniques help strategic managers avoid the consensus trap that Alfred Sloan found:

1. **Devil's Advocate.** The devil's advocate originated in the medieval Roman Catholic Church as a way of ensuring that impostors were not canonized as saints. One trusted person was selected to find and present all reasons why the person should *not* be canonized. When applied to strategic decision making, the **devil's advocate** (who may be an individual or a group) is assigned to identify potential pitfalls and problems with a proposed alternative strategy in a formal presentation.

2. **Dialectical Inquiry.** The dialectic philosophy, which can be traced back to Plato and Aristotle and more recently to Hegel, involves combining two conflicting views—the *thesis* and the *antithesis*—into a *synthesis*. When applied to strategic decision making, **dialectical inquiry** requires that two proposals using different assumptions be generated for each alternative strategy under consideration. After advocates of each position present and debate the merits of their arguments before key decision makers, either one of the alternatives or a new compromise alternative is selected as the strategy to be implemented.

Research generally supports the conclusion that both the devil's advocate and dialectical inquiry are equally superior to consensus in decision making, especially when the firm's environment is dynamic. The debate itself, rather than its particular format, appears to improve the quality of decisions by formalizing and legitimizing constructive conflict and by encouraging critical evaluation. Both lead to better assumptions and recommendations and to a higher level of critical thinking among the people involved.[41]

INTEL MAKES A STRATEGIC DECISION

The board of directors of Intel Corporation met in 1991 to decide the future of the company. They were being asked to vote on a proposal to commit $5 billion to making the next generation of microprocessor chip—five times the amount previously needed for the 486 chip and 50 times that for the earlier 386 chip. By 1991, Intel was already the world's largest manufacturer of microprocessors, the brains of personal computers. Its latest chip, the 486, was just beginning to take off. Its successor, the Pentium, was still in design. Intel's CEO, Andy Grove, received the startling estimate of the capital spending needed to make the Pentium just before the start of the board meeting. Grove hastily drew the spending curve on graph paper as the directors looked on.

In looking back on that board meeting, Grove remarked, "I remember people's eyes looking at that chart and getting big. I wasn't even sure I believed those numbers at the time." The proposal committed the company to build-

ing new factories—something Intel had been slow to do during the 1980s. According to Intel director Arthur Rock, a wrong decision would mean that the company would end up with a killing amount of overcapacity. "You had to have faith," said Rock. Based on Grove's presentation, the board decided to take the gamble. As a result, Intel's manufacturing expansion consumed $10 billion from 1991 through 1995. It was, however, timed perfectly for the boom in personal computer sales. Although rivals Motorola and IBM also began to add manufacturing capacity, none has been able to yet match the cash generated by Intel's 75% share of the microprocessor business. In this one crucial decision, Intel was able to turn the spiraling cost of competition into a competitive weapon.

Source: D. Clark, "All the Chips: A Big Bet Made Intel What It Is Today; Now It Wagers Again," *Wall Street Journal* (June 6, 1995), pp. A1, A5.

7.4 Development of Policies

The selection of the best strategic alternative is not the end of strategy formulation. The organization must now engage in **developing policies**. Policies define the broad guidelines for implementation. Flowing from the selected strategy, policies provide guidance for decision making and actions throughout the organization. At General Electric, for example, Chairman Welch insists that GE be Number One or Number Two wherever it competes. This policy gives clear guidance to managers throughout the organization. Another example of such a policy is Casey's General Stores' policy that a new service or product line may be added to its stores only when the product or service can be justified in terms of increasing store traffic.

Policies tend to be rather long lived and can even outlast the particular strategy that created them. Interestingly these general policies—such as "The customer is always right" or "Research and development should get first priority on all budget requests"—can become, in time, part of a corporation's culture. Such policies can make the implementation of specific strategies easier. They can also restrict top management's strategic options in the future. Thus a change in strategy should be followed quickly by a change in policies. Managing policy is one way to manage the corporate culture.

7.5   *Global Issues for the 21st Century*

- The **21st Century Global Society** feature in this chapter illustrates how Whirlpool adjusted its manufacturing strategy to suit local conditions in different parts of the world. Corporations operating internationally will constantly need to deal with the tradeoffs involved in producing one uniform, low-cost product for sale in all countries or producing a series of higher cost products modified to individual country tastes.

- For core competencies to be distinctive competencies, they must be superior to those of the competition. As more industries become hypercompetitive (discussed in Chapter 3), it will be increasingly difficult to keep a core competence distinctive. These resources are likely either to be imitated or made obsolete by new technologies.

- Outsourcing has become an important issue in all industries, especially in global industries such as automobiles where cost competition is fierce. General Motors, for example, was faced with a strike by its Canadian unions during 1996 when it wanted to outsource some operations. The Canadian unions were very concerned that such outsourcing would reduce union employment and increase the number of low-paying jobs. Expect this issue to continue in importance throughout the world as more industries become global.

- Just as a competitive strategy may need to vary from one region of the world to another, functional strategies may need to vary from region to region. When Mr. Donut expanded into Japan, for example, it had to market donuts not as breakfast, but as snack food. Because the Japanese had no breakfast coffee and donut custom, they preferred to eat the donuts in the afternoon or evening. Mr. Donut restaurants were thus located near railroad stations and supermarkets. All signs were in English to appeal to the Western interests of the Japanese.

- Even though shifting costly functions to the developing countries (either through outsourcing or transferring operations) has become an accepted way to reduce human resource costs, such a functional strategy is creating some problems. The United Nations enacted a convention in 1973 that called on nations to set 15 as the basic minimum work age, with 13 being the minimum for light work and 18 the minimum for hazardous work. Although many countries have ratified some parts of the agreement, some developing nations are ignoring it. Citing that as many as 250 million children between the ages of 5 and 14 work in low-paying jobs, the International Labor Organization is working to outlaw the practice beginning in 2000.[42]

Projections for the 21st Century

- From 1994 to 2010, the number of desktop PCs worldwide will double from 132 million to 278 million.

- From 1994 to 2010, the number of mobile PCs worldwide will more than triple from 18 million to 47 million.[43]

Discussion Questions

1. How can a corporation identify its core competencies? Its distinctive competencies?

2. When should a corporation or business unit outsource a function or activity?

3. Why is penetration pricing more likely than skim pricing to raise a company's or a business unit's operating profit in the long run?

4. How does mass customization support a business unit's competitive strategy?

5. What is the relationship of policies to strategies?

Key Terms

connected line batch flow (p. 167)
consensus (p. 176)
continuous improvement (p. 167)
core capability (p. 160)
core competency (p. 160)
corporate culture pressures (p. 175)
corporate scenarios (p. 172)
dedicated transfer lines (p. 167)
developing policies (p. 177)
devil's advocate (p. 176)
dialectical inquiry (p. 176)
distinctive competency (p. 160)
financial strategy (p. 164)
flexible manufacturing
   systems (p. 167)

functional strategy (p. 160)
HRM strategy (p. 170)
information systems strategy (p. 170)
job shop (p. 167)
leveraged buy out (p. 165)
logistics strategy (p. 169)
market development (p. 162)
marketing strategy (p. 162)
mass customization (p. 167)
mass production (p. 167)
multiple sourcing (p. 168)
operations strategy (p. 166)
outsourcing (p. 161)
parallel sourcing (p. 169)
penetration pricing (p. 164)

political strategy (p. 175)
pro forma financial statements (p. 173)
product development (p. 163)
pull strategy (p. 164)
purchasing strategy (p. 168)
push strategy (p. 163)
R&D strategy (p. 165)
risk (p. 173)
skim pricing (p. 164)
sole sourcing (p. 169)
strategic choice (p. 176)
strategies to avoid (p. 171)
technological follower (p. 166)
technological leader (p. 166)

Strategic Practice Exercise

Read the following example of a company that is attempting to use its functional expertise in information system technology to obtain a competitive advantage in its industry. Do you think it will succeed?

In October 1996 Federal Express (FedEx) announced plans to give away its "BusinessLink" software early in 1997 to enable thousands of companies to buy and sell goods on the Internet. The system was to allow businesses to tap into FedEx's central computer to build web sites promoting their goods on the World Wide Web. Customers would be able to view the catalogue on-line and order goods, pay for them, and arrange delivery—through FedEx, of course! FedEx had a highly regarded web site for

tracking its own delivery system, but this was its first venture into offering companies a way of doing business electronically.

FedEx planned to charge customers a transaction fee each time Federal Express processed an order made through the system. This fee was to average less than the average of a "few dollars" made to telephone order centers. There might also be a small setup fee when each customer went on-line. The company declined to specify how many customers it expected to sign up, except to say that it hoped to see thousands of software packages in use during 1997. The prime candidates were perceived to be rapidly growing businesses that already supplied a substantial volume of products to other businesses and whose products had a short shelf life. In 1996, approximately 425,000 customers shipped via FedEx using its Internet web site or other software.

At the time, analysts viewed FedEx's move as an unorthodox attempt to stake out a position on the crowded frontier of Internet commerce—an area predicted to grow from $40 million in 1995 to perhaps hundreds of billions of dollars in a decade. By offering free software and an easy route to Internet business, FedEx apparently hoped to lock up customers by using the software to capture shipping business. Critics thought the strategy to be far afield for a business based on moving parcels via airplanes and trucks. They remembered when FedEx introduced Zap Mail, a way to transmit document facsimiles, in the 1980s. The introduction of inexpensive fax machines forced FedEx to abandon Zap Mail, at a cost of $190 million.

Nevertheless FedEx executives were committed to doing something radical. The company had not been having the same rate of growth recently enjoyed by UPS, its major rival. Although not abandoning its primary logistics business, executives

contended that the future of the company was in BusinessLink. According to Laurie Tucker, Senior Vice-President of Logistics and Electronic Commerce: "You're not going to see us going out buying up property and building million-square-foot warehouses. Been there. Done that."

Interestingly both AT&T and Microsoft also thought Internet commerce to be a good opportunity. Within the same month that FedEx announced its plan, AT&T and Microsoft announced their intentions to develop and provide software allowing Internet transactions.[44]

____ Does Federal Express need to have a core competency in information systems technology to achieve its strategy?

____ What are the pros and cons of FedEx's BusinessLink software strategy?

____ Will BusinessLink have any impact on FedEx's primary logistics business of moving packages?

____ What are the odds that FedEx will succeed with BusinessLink?

Notes

1. Arm & Hammer is a registered trademark of Church & Dwight Company, Inc.
2. G. Hamel, and S. K. Prahalad, *Competing for the Future* (Boston: Harvard Business School Press, 1994), pp. 202–207.
3. *Ibid*, p. 211.
4. P. J. Verdin, and P. J. Williamson, "Core Competencies, Competitive Advantage and Market Analysis: Forging the Links," in *Competence-Based Competition,* edited by G. Hamel and A. Heene (New York: John Wiley and Sons, 1994), pp. 83–84.
5. B. Kelley, "Outsourcing Marches On," *Journal of Business Strategy* (July/August 1995), p. 40.
6. T. A. Stewart, "Taking On the Last Bureaucracy," *Fortune* (January 15, 1996), pp. 105–106.
7. J. W. Verity, "Let's Order Out for Technology," *Business Week* (May 13, 1996), p. 47.
8. "Taking Outsourcing to Higher Strategic Levels," *1996 Strategic Outsourcing Conference* (The Conference Board: New York City, June 13, 1996).
9. R. Frank, "Efficient UPS Tries to Increase Efficiency," *Wall Street Journal* (May 24, 1995), pp. B1, B4.
10. J. B. Quinn, "The Intelligent Enterprise: A New Paradigm," *Academy of Management Executive* (November 1992), pp. 48–63.
11. J. A. Byrne, "Has Outsourcing Gone Too Far?" *Business Week* (April 1, 1996), pp. 26–28.
12. D. Lei, and M. A. Hitt, "Strategic Restructuring and Outsourcing: The Effect of Mergers and Acquisitions and LBOs on Building Firm Skills and Capabilities," *Journal of Management,* Vol. 21, No. 5 (1995), pp. 835–859.
13. Kelley, "Outsourcing Marches On," p. 40.
14. S. M. Oster, *Modern Competitive Analysis,* 2d ed. (New York: Oxford University Press, 1994), p. 93.
15. W. Redmond, "The Strategic Pricing of Innovative Products," *Handbook of Business Strategy, 1992/1993 Yearbook,* edited by H. E. Glass and M. A. Hovde (Boston: Warren, Gorham and Lamont, 1992), pp. 16.1–16.13.
16. G. Stern, and R. L. Simison, "Big Three Auto Companies Are Parked on a Cash Cache Exceeding $30 Billion," *Wall Street Journal* (February 7, 1996), p. A2.
17. T. Due, "Dean Foods Thrives on Regional Off-Brand Products," *Wall Street Journal* (September 17, 1987), p. A6.
18. S. Stevens, "Speeding the Signals of Change," *Appliance* (February 1995), p. 7.
19. J. R. Williams, and R. S. Novak, "Aligning CIM Strategies to Different Markets," *Long Range Planning* (February 1990), pp. 126–135.
20. B. J. Pine, *Mass Customization: The New Frontier in Business Competition* (Boston: Harvard Business School Press, 1993).
21. B. J. Pine II, B. Victor, and A. C. Boynton, "Making Mass Customization Work," *Harvard Business Review* (September-October 1993), p. 119.
22. G. Hamel, "Strategy as Revolution," *Harvard Business Review* (July-August, 1996), p. 73.
23. F. R. Bleakley, "Some Companies Let Supplies Work on Site and Even Place Orders," *Wall Street Journal* (January 13, 1995), pp. A1, A6.

24. "Quality News," *The Quality Observer* (March 1996), p. 24.

25. J. Richardson, "Parallel Sourcing and Supplier Performance in the Japanese Automobile Industry," *Strategic Management Journal* (July 1993), pp. 339–350.

26. T. Richman, "Logistics Management: How 20 Best-Practice Companies Do It," *Harvard Business Review* (September-October 1995), pp. 11–12.

27. J. Bigness, "In Today's Economy, There Is Big Money To Be Made in Logistics," *Wall Street Journal* (September 6, 1995), pp. A1, A9.

28. B Dumaine, "Who Needs a Boss?" *Fortune* (May 7, 1990), pp. 52–60.

29. R. D. Banker, J. M. Field, R. G. Schroeder, and K. K. Sinha, "Impact of Work Teams on Manufacturing Performance: A Longitudinal Field Study," *Academy of Management Journal* (August 1996), pp. 867–890.

30. M. Cadden, and B. Laird, "Rising Market for Temps," *USA Today* (May 8, 1995), p. B1; J. Fierman, "The Contingency Work Force," *Fortune* (January 24, 1994), pp. 30–36.

31. K. Labich, "Making Diversity Pay," *Fortune* (September 9, 1996), pp. 177–180.

32. T. Smart, "Jack Welch's Cyber-Czar," *Business Week* (August 5, 1996), p. 83.

33. D. K. Sinha, "Strategic Planning in the Fortune 500," *Handbook of Business Strategy, 1991/1992 Yearbook,* edited by H. E. Glass and M. A. Hovde (Boston: Warren, Gorham and Lamont, 1991), pp. 9.6–9.8.

34. B. B. Tyler, and H. K. Steensma. "Evaluating Technological Collaborative Opportunities: A Cognitive Modeling Perspective," *Strategic Management Journal* (Summer 1995), pp. 43–70.

35. C. S. Galbraith, and G. B. Merrill, "The Politics of Forecasting: Managing the Truth," *California Management Review* (Winter 1996), pp. 29–43.

36. M. Leuchter, "The Rules of the Game," *Forecast* (May/June 1996), pp. 16–23.

37. V. L. Barker III, and P. S. Barr, "Why Is Performance Declining and What Road Leads to Recovery? An Empirical Examination of the Link Between Top Management Causal Attributions and Strategic Change During Turnaround Attempts," paper presented to *Academy of Management,* Dallas, Texas (August 1994).

38. J. Ross, and B. M. Staw, "Organizational Escalation and Exit: Lessons from the Shoreham Nuclear Power Plant," *Academy of Management Journal* (August 1993), pp. 701–732; P. W. Mulvey, J. F. Veiga, and P. M. Elsass, "When Teammates Raise a White Flag," *Academy of Management Executive* (February 1996), pp. 40–49.

39. R. A. Cosier, and C. R. Schwenk, "Agreement and Thinking Alike: Ingredients for Poor Decisions," *Academy of Management Executive* (February 1990), p. 69.

40. A. C. Amason, "Distinguishing the Effects of Functional and Dysfunctional Conflict On Strategic Decision Making: Resolving a Paradox for Top Management Teams," *Academy of Management Journal* (February 1996), pp. 123–148.

41. D. M. Schweiger, W. R. Sandberg, and P. L. Rechner, "Experiential Effects of Dialectical Inquiry, Devil's Advocacy, and Consensus Approaches to Strategic Decision Making," *Academy of Management Journal* (December 1989), pp. 745–772; G. Whyte, "Decision Failures: Why They Occur and How to Prevent Them," *Academy of Management Executive* (August 1991), pp. 23–31; R. L. Priem, D. A. Harrison, and N. K. Muir, "Structured Conflict and Consensus Outcomes in Group Decision Making," *Journal of Management,* Vol. 21, No. 4 (1995), pp. 691–710.

42. "30 Nations Want Rules to Restrict Child Labor," *St. Petersburg Times* (February 27, 1997), p. 6E.

43. J. Warner, "21st Century Capitalism: Snapshot of the Next Century," *Business Week* (November 18, 1994), p. 194.

44. Based on information in D. A. Blackmon, "FedEx Plans to Establish a Marketplace in Cyberspace," *Wall Street Journal* (October 9, 1996), p. B4.

Chapter 8

Strategy Implementation: Organizing for Action

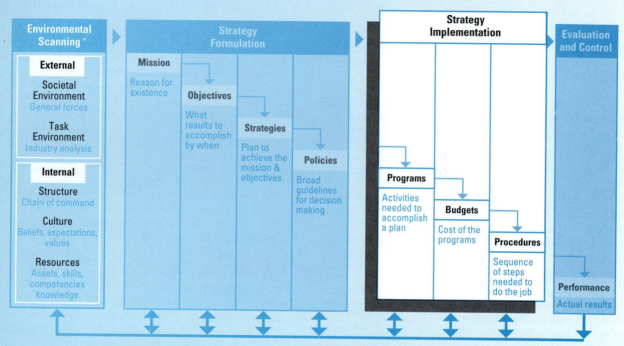

Environmental Scanning °

External

Societal Environment
General forces

Task Environment
Industry analysis

Internal

Structure
Chain of command

Culture
Beliefs, expectations, values

Resources
Assets, skills, competencies knowledge

Strategy Formulation

Mission
Reason for existence

Objectives
What results to accomplish by when

Strategies
Plan to achieve the mission & objectives

Policies
Broad guidelines for decision making

Strategy Implementation

Programs
Activities needed to accomplish a plan

Budgets
Cost of the programs

Procedures
Sequence of steps needed to do the job

Evaluation and Control

Performance
Actual results

Feedback/Learning

Pepsico, Inc., the maker of Pepsi Cola, was not pleased with only having 10% of the soft drink market in Brazil—the third largest soft-drink market in the world after the United States and Mexico. Coca-Cola, in contrast, controlled more than 50% of the market. Coke had successfully consolidated its many independent local bottlers into a set of regional bottlers that worked well together. The new regional Coke bottlers had close local connections, large capital budgets, and a solid distribution system. To combat Coke's entrenched position, Pepsico formulated an ambitious growth strategy in 1994. It wanted to achieve at least 20% share of Brazil's main urban markets by selling more than 250 million cases annually. To manage this growth strategy, Pepsico selected Charles Beach as its partner. After successfully building Pepsico's market shares in both Puerto Rico and Argentina, Beach was offered the Brazilian franchise as well. Beach used his bottling company, Buenos Aires Embotelladora SA (known simply as Baesa) to expand soft drink production and market share. With Pepsico's encouragement, Baesa built four Brazilian plants with a total capacity of 250 million cases of soft drinks—more than twice Pepsico's highest amount of sales in Brazil. Rather than distributing its products via beer trucks (as did most of the soft-drink companies in Brazil), Baesa built its own distribution fleet by purchasing 700 new trucks. The company introduced four new flavors of its Kas line of juice-based sodas that Pepsico had formulated especially for Brazil—offering them not just in the usual returnable bottles, but also in cans and plastic containers. To the amazement of analysts, Baesa and Pepsico pledged to have the Brazilian operations running within a year.

Operating problems plagued the company from the start. The new bottling plants were often forced to close down lines because of rushed installation and insufficient employee training. Baesa found itself discarding ten times as many bent or punctured cans as did its competitors. Management turnover was a serious problem. Many managers were unable to keep up with Baesa's fast pace and Beach's conflicting signals. At one point, Beach fired more than 20 executives who had been hired from other multinationals after they had been on the job only three months! Even though Baesa's debt had increased from $15.4 million in 1993 (before the Brazilian expansion) to $374 million in 1995, it planned to purchase two additional Brazilian bottling plants. By 1996, Baesa's debt reached $745 million.

In May 1996, Pepsico announced that Beach had been relieved of operational responsibility and that it would assume control of Baesa's operations. In August, Baesa announced a quarterly loss of $250 million. The bottler defaulted on $34 million in debt payments. Sales had not met expectations. In addition to selling some of its franchises, Baesa closed one of its new plants and laid off more than 1,500 workers. Pepsico's aggressive Brazilian growth strategy had failed. According to Craig Weatherup, Pepsico's new head of global beverages, "I guess we got a little ahead of our headlights. We may have gone too fast."[1]

8.1 *Strategy Implementation*

Strategy implementation is the sum total of the activities and choices required for the execution of a strategic plan. It is *the process by which strategies and policies are put into action through the development of programs, budgets, and procedures.* Although implementation is usually considered after strategy has been formulated, implementation is a key part of strategic management. Strategy formulation and strategy implementation should thus be considered as two sides of the same coin. Poor implementation has been blamed for a number of strategic failures. For example, half of all acquisitions fail to achieve what was expected of them, and one out of four international ventures do not succeed.[2] Pepsico's failed expansion in Brazil is one example of how a good strategy can result in a disaster through poor strategy implementation.

To begin the implementation process, strategy makers must consider these questions:

- *Who* are the people who will carry out the strategic plan?

- *What* must be done to align the company's operations in the new intended direction?

- *How* is everyone going to do what is needed?

These questions and similar ones should have been addressed initially when the pros and cons of strategic alternatives were analyzed. They must also be addressed again before appropriate implementation plans can be made. Unless top management can answer these basic questions satisfactorily, even the best planned strategy is unlikely to provide the desired outcome.

A survey of 93 Fortune 500 firms revealed that over half of the corporations experienced the following ten problems when they attempted to implement a strategic change. These problems are listed in order of frequency.

1. Implementation took more time than originally planned.

2. Unanticipated major problems arose.

3. Activities were ineffectively coordinated.

4. Competing activities and crises took attention away from implementation.

5. The involved employees had insufficient capabilities to perform their jobs.

6. Lower-level employees were inadequately trained.

7. Uncontrollable external environmental factors created problems.

8. Departmental managers provided inadequate leadership and direction.

9. Key implementation tasks and activities were poorly defined.

10. The information system inadequately monitored activities.[3]

Pepsico experienced almost all of these problems in its Brazilian expansion—all except the first one. Pepsico's "ready, fire, aim" corporate culture would not tolerate a slow deliberate implementation process. Most of its Brazilian problems resulted from the corporation's unwillingness to implement its strategy at anything but break-neck speed.

- Pepsico selected a relatively inexperienced manager to implement its expansion strategy. In a hurry to begin implementation, it failed to question Charles Beach's past. As a manager at a North Carolina Coca-Cola bottler, Beach had pleaded no contest in 1987 to a price-fixing charge. Beach's optimistic aggressiveness fit well with Pepsico's high-pressured, fast-moving corporate culture.

- Pepsico pushed Beach too fast. After building the Puerto Rican franchise, Beach was awarded the Argentina franchise in 1989. By 1994, Beach had been awarded the entire Southern Cone of South America—ten times the size of the market he had managed the year before. In contrast, Coca-Cola seasons even its largest bottlers over several years, letting them add to their territory slowly. According to one Salomon Brothers analyst, "Beach was a good operator, but he didn't have the management experience to take on the whole Southern Cone in one year."

- Both Pepsico and Beach's Baesa company assumed that a hard-hitting, fast-moving expansion strategy would make up for any slippage in implementation details. Over one year's time, Baesa built four new state-of-the-art bottling plants and a completely new distribution system to sell untested soft-drink products. People were hired quickly and put into key positions with insufficient training. No time was allowed to develop and coordinate implementation procedures. Even the infusion of money and talent from Pepsico was unable to keep the Brazilian operations from deteriorating into chaos.[4]

8.2   Who Implements Strategy?

Depending on how the corporation is organized, those who implement strategy will probably be a much more diverse set of people than those who formulate it. In most large, multi-industry corporations, the implementers are everyone in the organization. Vice-presidents of functional areas and directors of divisions or SBUs work with their subordinates to put together large-scale implementation plans. Plant managers, project managers, and unit heads put together plans for their specific plants, departments, and units. Therefore, every operational manager down to the first-line supervisor and every employee is involved in some way in the implementing of corporate, business, and functional strategies.

Many of the people in the organization who are crucial to successful strategy implementation probably have little to do with the development of the corporate and even business strategy. Therefore, they might be entirely ignorant of the vast amount of data and work that went into the formulation process. Unless changes in mission, objectives, strategies, and policies and their importance to the company are communicated clearly to all operational managers, there can be a lot of resistance and foot-dragging. Managers might hope to influence top management into abandoning its new plans and returning to its old ways. This is one reason why involving people from all organizational levels in the formulation and in the implementation of strategy tends to result in better organizational performance.

8.3   What Must Be Done?

The managers of divisions and functional areas work with their fellow managers to develop programs, budgets, and procedures for the implementation of strategy. They also work to achieve synergy among the divisions and functional areas in order to establish and maintain a company's distinctive competence.

Developing Programs, Budgets, and Procedures

Programs

The purpose of a **program** is to make the strategy action-oriented. For example, assume Ajax Continental chose forward vertical integration as its best strategy for growth. It purchased existing retail outlets from another firm (Jones Surplus) instead of building its own. To integrate the new stores into the company, various programs would now have to be developed:

1. A restructuring program to move the Jones Surplus stores into Ajax Continental's marketing chain of command so that store managers report to regional managers, who report to the merchandising manager, who reports to the vice-president in charge of marketing.

2. An advertising program. ("Jones Surplus is now a part of Ajax Continental. Prices are lower. Selection is better.")

3. A training program for newly hired store managers and for those Jones Surplus managers the corporation has chosen to keep.

4. A program to develop reporting procedures that will integrate the Jones Surplus stores into Ajax Continental's accounting system.

5. A program to modernize the Jones Surplus stores and to prepare them for a "grand opening."

Budgets

After programs have been developed, the **budget** process begins. Planning a budget is the last real check a corporation has on the feasibility of its selected strategy. An ideal strategy might be found to be completely impractical only after specific implementation programs are costed in detail.

Procedures

After the program, divisional, and corporate budgets are approved, standard operating **procedures (SOPs)** must be developed. They typically detail the various activities that must be carried out to complete a corporation's programs. Once in place, they must be updated to reflect any changes in technology as well as in strategy. In the case of Ajax Corporation's acquisition of Jones Surplus' retail outlets, new operating procedures must be established for, among others, in-store promotions, inventory ordering, stock selection, customer relations, credits and collections, warehouse distribution, pricing, paycheck timing, grievance handling, and raises and promotions. These procedures ensure that the day-to-day store operations will be consistent over time (that is, next week's work activities will be the same as this week's) and consistent among stores (that is, each store will operate in the same manner as the others). For example, to ensure that its policies are carried out to the letter in every one of its fast-food retail outlets, McDonald's has done an excellent job of developing very detailed procedures (and policing them!).

Achieving Synergy

One of the goals to be achieved in strategy implementation is synergy between and among functions and business units. This is the reason why corporations commonly reorganize after an acquisition. **Synergy** is said to exist for a divisional corporation if the return on investment (ROI) of each division is greater than what the return would be if each division were an independent business. The acquisition or development of additional product lines is often justified on the basis of achieving some advantages of scale in one or more of a company's functional areas. For example, when Ralston Purina acquired Union Carbide's Eveready and Energizer lines of batteries, Ralston's CEO argued that his company would earn better profit margins on batteries than Union Carbide because of Ralston's expertise in developing and marketing branded consumer products. Ralston Purina felt it could lower the costs of the batteries by taking advantage of synergies in advertising, promotion, and distribution.

8.4 How Is Strategy to Be Implemented? Organizing for Action

Before plans can lead to actual performance, a corporation should be appropriately organized, programs should be adequately staffed, and activities should be directed toward achieving desired objectives. *(Organizing activities are reviewed briefly in this chapter; staffing, directing, and control activities are discussed in Chapters 9 and 10.)*

Any change in corporate strategy is very likely to require some sort of change in the way an organization is structured and in the kind of skills needed in particular positions. Managers must, therefore, closely examine the way their company is structured in order to decide what, if any, changes should be made in the way work is accomplished. Should activities be grouped differently? Should the authority to make key decisions be centralized at headquarters or decentralized to managers in distant locations? Should the company be managed like a "tight ship" with many rules and controls, or "loosely" with few rules and controls? Should the corporation be organized into a "tall" structure with many layers of managers, each having a narrow span of control (that is, few employees per supervisor) to better control his or her subordinates; or should it be organized into a "flat" structure with fewer layers of managers, each having a wide span of control (that is, more employees per supervisor) to give more freedom to his or her subordinates? For example, Ford had a fairly tall structure with 15 layers of managers, whereas Toyota had a relatively flat structure (for an automaker) composed of seven layers. Was Toyota's or Ford's structure "better"?

Structure Follows Strategy

In a classic study of large U.S. corporations such as DuPont, General Motors, Sears, and Standard Oil, Alfred Chandler concluded that **structure follows strategy**—that is, changes in corporate strategy lead to changes in organizational structure.[5] He also concluded that organizations follow a pattern of development from one kind of structural arrangement to another as they expand. According to Chandler, these structural changes occur because the old structure, having been pushed too far, has caused inefficiencies that have become too obviously detrimental to bear. Chandler, therefore, proposed the following as the sequence of what occurs:

1. New strategy is created.

2. New administrative problems emerge.

3. Economic performance declines.

4. New appropriate structure is invented.

5. Profit returns to its previous level.

Chandler found that in their early years, corporations such as DuPont tend to have a centralized functional organizational structure that is well suited to producing and selling a limited range of products. As they add new product lines, purchase their own sources of supply, and create their own distribution networks, they become too complex for highly centralized structures. To remain successful, this type of organization needs to shift to a decentralized structure with several semiautonomous divisions (referred to in Chapter 4 as divisional structure).

Alfred P. Sloan, past CEO of General Motors, detailed how GM conducted such structural changes in the 1920s.[6] He saw decentralization of structure as "centralized policy determination coupled with decentralized operating management." After top management had developed a strategy for the total corporation, the individual divisions (Chevrolet, Buick, and so on) were free to choose how to implement that strategy. Patterned after DuPont, GM found the decentralized multidivisional structure to be extremely effective in allowing the maximum amount of freedom for product development. Return on investment was used as a financial control. (*This measure is discussed in more detail in Chapter 10.*)

Research generally supports Chandler's proposition that structure follows strategy (as well as the reverse proposition that structure influences strategy).[7] As mentioned earlier, changes in the environment tend to be reflected in changes in a corporation's strategy, thus leading to changes in a corporation's structure. Strategy, structure, and the environment need to be closely aligned; otherwise, organizational performance will likely suffer.[8] For example, a business unit following a differentiation strategy needs more freedom from headquarters to be successful than does another unit following a low-cost strategy.[9]

Although it is agreed that organizational structure must vary with different environmental conditions, which, in turn, affect an organization's strategy, there is no agreement about an optimal organizational design. What was appropriate for DuPont and General Motors in the 1920s might not be appropriate today. Firms in the same industry do, however, tend to organize themselves similarly. For example, automobile manufacturers tend to emulate General Motors' divisional concept, whereas consumer-goods producers tend to emulate the brand-management concept (a type of matrix structure) pioneered by Procter & Gamble Company. The general conclusion seems to be that firms following similar strategies in similar industries tend to adopt similar structures.

Stages of Corporate Development

Successful corporations tend to follow a pattern of structural development as they grow and expand. Beginning with the simple structure of the entrepreneurial firm (in which everybody does everything), they usually (if they are successful) get larger and organize along functional lines with marketing, production, and finance departments. With continuing success, the company adds new product lines in different industries and organizes itself into interconnected divisions. The differences among these three structural **stages of corporate development** in terms of typical problems, objectives, strategies, reward systems and other characteristics are specified in detail in Table 8.1.

Stage I: Simple Structure

Stage I is typified by the entrepreneur, who founds the company to promote an idea (product or service). The entrepreneur tends to make all the important decisions personally and is involved in every detail and phase of the organization. The Stage I company has little formal structure, which allows the entrepreneur to directly supervise the activities of every employee (see Figure 4.4 for an illustration of the simple, functional, and divisional structures). Planning is usually short range or reactive. The typical managerial functions of planning, organizing, directing, staffing, and controlling are usually performed to a very limited degree, if at all. The greatest strengths of a Stage I corporation are its flexibility and dynamism. The drive of the entrepreneur energizes the organization in its struggle for growth. Its greatest weakness is its extreme reliance on the entrepreneur to decide general strategies as well as detailed procedures. If the entrepreneur falters, the company usually flounders. This is often referred to as a **crisis of leadership**.[10]

Stage I describes Oracle Corporation, the computer software firm, under the management of its co-founder and CEO Lawrence Ellison. The company adopted a pioneering approach to retrieving data called structured query language (SQL). When IBM made SQL its standard, Oracle's success was assured. Unfortunately Ellison's technical wizardry was not sufficient to manage the company. Often working at home, he lost sight of details outside his technical interests. Although the company's sales were rapidly increasing, its financial controls were so weak that management had to restate an entire year's results to rectify irregularities. After the company recorded its first loss, Ellison hired a set of functional managers to run the company while he retreated to focus on new product development.

Table 8.1   **Factors Differentiating Stage I, II, and III Companies**

Function	Stage I	Stage II	Stage III
1. Sizing up: Major problems	Survival and growth dealing with short-term operating problems.	Growth, rationalization, and expansion of resources, providing for adequate attention to product problems.	Trusteeship in management and investment and control of large, increasing, and diversified resources. Also, important to diagnose and take action on problems at division level.
2. Objectives	Personal and subjective.	Profits and meeting functionally oriented budgets and performance targets.	ROI, profits, earnings per share.
3. Strategy	Implicit and personal; exploitation of immediate opportunities seen by owner-manager.	Functionally oriented moves restricted to "one product" scope; exploitation of one basic product or service field.	Growth and product diversification; exploitation of general business opportunities.
4. Organization: Major characteristic of structure	One unit, "one-man show."	One unit, functionally specialized group.	Multiunit general staff office and decentralized operating divisions.
5. (a) Measurement and control	Personal, subjective control based on simple accounting system and daily communication and observation.	Control grows beyond one person; assessment of functional operations necessary; structured control systems evolve.	Complex formal system geared to comparative assessment of performance measures, indicating problems and opportunities and assessing management ability of division managers.
5. (b) Key performance indicators	Personal criteria, relationships with owner, operating efficiency, ability to solve operating problems.	Functional and internal criteria such as sales, performance compared to budget, size of empire, status in group, personal relationships, etc.	More impersonal application of comparisons such as profits, ROI, P/E ratio, sales, market share, productivity, product leadership, personnel development, employee attitudes, public responsibility.
6. Reward-punishment system	Informal, personal, subjective; used to maintain control and divide small pool of resources to provide personal incentives for key performers.	More structured; usually based to a greater extent on agreed policies as opposed to personal opinion and relationships.	Allotment by "due process" of a wide variety of different rewards and punishments on a formal and systematic basis. Companywide policies usually apply to many different classes of managers and workers with few major exceptions for individual cases.

Source: D. H. Thain, "Stages of Corporate Development," *Business Quarterly* (Winter 1969), p. 37. Copyright © 1969 by *Business Quarterly*. Reprinted by permission.

Stage II: Functional Structure

Stage II is the point when the entrepreneur is replaced by a team of managers who have functional specializations. The transition to this stage requires a substantial managerial style change for the chief officer of the company, especially if he or she was the Stage I entrepreneur. He or she must learn to delegate; otherwise, having additional staff members yields no benefits to the organization. The previous example of Lawrence Ellison's retreat from top management at Oracle Corporation to new product development manager is one way that technically brilliant founders are able to get out of the way of the newly empowered functional managers. Once into Stage II, the corporate strategy favors protectionism through dominance of the industry, often through vertical and horizontal growth. The great strength of a Stage II corporation lies in its concentration and specialization in one industry. Its great weakness is that all of its eggs are in one basket.

By concentrating on one industry while that industry remains attractive, a Stage II company, like Oracle Corporation in computer software, can be very successful. Once a functionally structured firm diversifies into other products in different industries, however, the advantages of the functional structure break down. A **crisis of autonomy** can now develop, in which people managing diversified product lines need more decision-making freedom than top management is willing to delegate to them. The company needs to move to a different structure.

Stage III: Divisional Structure

Stage III is typified by the corporation's managing diverse product lines in numerous industries; it decentralizes the decision-making authority. These organizations grow by diversifying their product lines and expanding to cover wider geographical areas. They move to a divisional structure with a central headquarters and decentralized operating divisions—each division or business unit is a functionally organized Stage II company. They may also use a conglomerate structure if top management chooses to keep its collection of Stage II subsidiaries operating autonomously.

Recently divisions have been evolving into strategic business units (SBUs) to better reflect product-market considerations. Headquarters attempts to coordinate the activities of its operating divisions or SBUs through performance- and results-oriented control and reporting systems, and by stressing corporate planning techniques. The units are not tightly controlled but are held responsible for their own performance results. Therefore, to be effective, the company has to have a decentralized decision process. The greatest strength of a Stage III corporation is its almost unlimited resources. Its most significant weakness is that it is usually so large and complex that it tends to become relatively inflexible. General Electric, DuPont, and General Motors are Stage III corporations.

Stage IV: Beyond SBUs

Even with its evolution into strategic business units during the 1970s and 1980s, the divisional form is not the last word in organization structure. Under conditions of (1) increasing environmental uncertainty, (2) greater use of sophisticated technological production methods and information systems, (3) the increasing size and scope of worldwide business corporations, (4) a greater emphasis on multi-industry competitive strategy, and (5) a more educated cadre of managers and employees, new advanced forms of organizational structure have emerged and are continuing to emerge during the latter half of the twentieth century. The *matrix* and the *network* are two possible candidates for a fourth stage in corporate development—a stage that not only emphasizes horizontal over vertical connections between people and groups, but also organizes work around temporary projects in which sophisticated information systems support collaborative activities.

Blocks to Changing Stages

Corporations often find themselves in difficulty because they are blocked from moving into the next logical stage of development. Blocks to development may be internal (such as lack of resources, lack of ability, or a refusal of top management to delegate decision

THE FOUNDER OF THE MODEM BLOCKS THE TRANSITION TO STAGE II

Dennis Hayes is legendary not only for inventing the personal computer modem, but also for driving his company into bankruptcy. Hayes and retired partner Dale Heatherington founded Hayes Microcomputer Products 20 years ago when they invented a device that allowed personal computers to communicate with each other through telephone lines. Business boomed from $4.8 million in sales in 1981 to $150 million in 1985. When competitors developed low-cost modems, Hayes delayed until the early 1990s to respond with its own low-priced version. Sales and profits plummeted. Hayes lost its dominant position to U.S. Robotics. Management problems mounted. Creditors and potential investors looking into the company's books and operations found them a shambles. According to one investment banker, "The factory was in complete disarray." The company reported its first loss in 1994, by which time the company had nearly $70 million in debt. In November 1994, Hayes applied for protection from creditors under Chapter 11 of the U.S. Bankruptcy Code.

Still under the leadership of its founder, the company underwent a turnaround during 1995.

Still in second place with a 9.3% market share of modem sales in North America, Dennis Hayes put his company up for sale. He turned down a bid of $140 million from rival Diamond Multimedia Systems and instead accepted only $30 million for 49% of the company from Asian investors. Although the offer required Mr. Hayes to relinquish the title of chief executive, Hayes would still be a part of the company. He explained his decision as deriving from his unwillingness to completely let go of his baby. "I'll be able to have input, through the board and as chairman, that will best use my abilities. What I was concerned about was that someone would come in and . . . slash a part of the company without understanding how it fit in." Somewhat resigned to a lesser role, yet pleased to still have his name on the company, Dennis Hayes has finally accepted the need to let others help him manage the company. "Now I can hand over those day-to-day operations," smiled Hayes.

Source: D. McDermott, "Asians Rejuvenate Hayes Microcomputer," *Wall Street Journal* (May 6, 1996), p. A10.

making to others) or they may be external (such as economic conditions, labor shortages, and lack of market growth). For example, Chandler noted in his study that the successful founder/CEO in one stage was rarely the person who created the new structure to fit the new strategy, and that, as a result, the transition from one stage to another was often painful. This was true of General Motors Corporation under the management of William Durant, Ford Motor Company under Henry Ford I, Polaroid Corporation under Edwin Land, Apple Computer under Steven Jobs, and Hayes Microcomputer Products under Dennis Hayes. (See the **Strategy in a Changing World** feature for what happened to the inventor of the modem.)

This difficulty in moving to a new stage is compounded by the founder's tendency to maneuver around the need to delegate by carefully hiring, training, and grooming his or her own team of managers. The team tends to maintain the founder's influence throughout the organization long after the founder is gone. This is what happened at Walt Disney Productions when the family continued to emphasize Walt's policies and plans long after he was dead. Although this may often be an organization's strength, it may also be a weakness—to the extent that the culture supports the status quo and blocks needed change.

Organizational Life Cycle

Instead of considering stages of development in terms of structure, the organizational life cycle approach places the primary emphasis on the dominant issue facing the corporation. Organizational structure is only a secondary concern. The **organizational life cycle** describes how organizations grow, develop, and eventually decline. It is the organizational equivalent of the product life cycle in marketing. These stages are *Birth* (Stage I), *Growth* (Stage II), *Maturity* (Stage III), *Decline* (Stage IV), and *Death* (Stage V). The impact of these stages on corporate strategy and structure is summarized in Table 8.2. Note that the first three stages of the organizational life cycle are similar to the three commonly accepted stages of corporate development mentioned previously. The only significant difference is the addition of Decline and Death stages to complete the cycle. Even though a company's strategy may still be sound, its aging structure, culture, and processes may be such that they prevent the strategy from being executed properly—thus the company moves into Decline.

Movement from Growth to Maturity to Decline and finally to Death is not, however, inevitable. A *Revival* phase may occur sometime during the Maturity or Decline stages. The corporation's life cycle can be extended by managerial and product innovations.[11] This often occurs during the implementation of a turnaround strategy. At Maytag Corporation, for example, the Revival phase was initiated in the 1970s under the leadership of Daniel Krumm while Maytag was still in its Maturity stage of development. As pointed out in the **Company Spotlight on Maytag Corporation** feature, the transition from aggressive growth to a rather passive and complacent maturity in the 1950s and 1960s left the company vulnerable to competitive advances and the possibility of being acquired.

Unless a company is able to resolve the critical issues facing it in the Decline stage, it is likely to move into Stage V, corporate death—also known as bankruptcy. This is what happened to Pan American Airlines, Macy's Department Stores, Baldwin-United, Eastern Airlines, Colt's Manufacturing, Orion Pictures, and Wheeling-Pittsburgh Steel, as well as to many other firms. As in the cases of Johns-Manville, International Harvester, and Macy's—all of which went bankrupt—a corporation might nevertheless rise like a phoenix from its own ashes and live again under the same or a different name. The company may be reorganized or liquidated, depending on individual circumstances. Unfortunately less than 20% of firms entering Chapter 11 bankruptcy in the U.S. emerge as going concerns; the rest are forced into liquidation.[12]

Few corporations will move through these five stages in order. Some corporations, for example, might never move past Stage II. Others, like General Motors, might go directly from Stage I to Stage III. A large number of entrepreneurial ventures jump from Stage I or II directly into Stage IV or V. Hayes Microcomputer Products, for example, went from a Growth to a Decline stage under its founder Dennis Hayes. The key is to be able to identify indications that a firm is in the process of changing stages and to make the appropriate strategic and structural adjustments to ensure that corporate performance is maintained or even improved. Only time will tell if Hayes Microcomputer Products' new investors will be able to work with Dennis Hayes to take the company through a Revival phase—and successfully move it back to a growing, professionally managed Stage II firm.

Advanced Types of Organizational Structures

The basic structures (simple, functional, divisional, and conglomerate) were discussed earlier in Chapter 4 and summarized under the first three stages of corporate development. A new strategy may require more flexible characteristics than the traditional functional or divisional structure can offer. Today's business organizations are becoming less

Table 8.2   **Organizational Life Cycle**

	Stage I	**Stage II**	**Stage III**[1]	**Stage IV**	**Stage V**
Dominant Issue	Birth	Growth	Maturity	Decline	Death
Popular Strategies	Concentration in a niche	Horizontal and vertical growth	Concentric and conglomerate diversification	Profit strategy followed by retrenchment	Liquidation or bankruptcy
Likely Structure	Entrepreneur-dominated	Functional management emphasized	Decentralization into profit or investment centers	Structural surgery	Dismemberment of structure

Note:

1. An organization may enter a *Revival Phase* either during the Maturity or Decline Stages and thus extend the organization's life.

centralized with a greater use of cross-functional work teams. Table 8.3 depicts some of the changing structural characteristics of modern corporations. Although many variations and hybrid structures contain these characteristics, two forms stand out: the *matrix structure* and the *network structure*.

Matrix Structure

Most organizations find that organizing around either functions (in the functional structure) or around products and geography (in the divisional structure) provides an appropriate organizational structure. The matrix structure, in contrast, may be very appropriate when organizations conclude that neither functional nor divisional forms, even when combined with horizontal linking mechanisms like strategic business units, are right for their situations. In **matrix structures**, functional and product forms are combined simultaneously at the same level of the organization. (See Figure 8.1.) Employees have two superiors, a product or project manager and a functional manager. The "home" department—that is, engineering, manufacturing, or sales—is usually functional and is reasonably permanent. People from these functional units are often assigned temporarily to one or more product units or projects. The product units or projects are usually temporary and act like divisions in that they are differentiated on a product-market basis.

Pioneered in the aerospace industry, the matrix structure was developed to combine the stability of the functional structure with the flexibility of the product form. The matrix structure is very useful when the external environment (especially its technological and market aspects) is very complex and changeable. It does, however, produce conflicts revolving around duties, authority, and resource allocation. To the extent that the goals to be achieved are vague and the technology used is poorly understood, a continuous battle for power between product and functional managers is likely. The matrix structure is often found in an organization or within an SBU when the following three conditions exist:

- Ideas need to be cross-fertilized across projects or products.

- Resources are scarce.

- Abilities to process information and to make decisions need to be improved.[13]

Davis and Lawrence, authorities on the matrix form of organization, propose that *three distinct phases* exist in the development of the matrix structure.[14]

COMPANY SPOTLIGHT

Initiating a Revival Phase

Maytag Company expanded during the 1920s into a national company. In terms of the organizational life cycle, this was Maytag Company's *Growth stage.* Throughout the 1920s and 1930s, Maytag Company had an average U.S. market share of over 40% in washing machines. During the Great Depression of the 1930s, Maytag never suffered a loss. By World War II, Maytag had become the most successful washing machine company in the U.S. and had reached its *Maturity stage.* Unfortunately the innovative genius and entrepreneurial drive of the company's early years were no longer present. In the 1950s, Bendix, a newcomer to the industry, introduced an automatic washing machine that used an automatic spin cycle instead of a hand-cranked wringer to squeeze excess rinse water out of clothes. Maytag, however, was reluctant to convert to automatic washers. This reluctance cost the company its leadership of the industry. By 1954, Maytag's share of the U.S. washer market had dropped to only 8%. It continued through the 1960s as a relatively small (compared to its competition), but profitable company.

Taking over as company president in 1972, Daniel Krumm was not satisfied with Maytag's situation. Although the company had added products to its original line of washers, Krumm saw Maytag as merely a successful niche manufacturer in a maturing U.S. market and vulnerable to aggressive actions by larger competitors. Consequently Maytag's management adopted a strategy to become a full-line manufacturer and develop a stronger position in the U.S. appliance industry. The decision was made to grow by acquisition within the appliance industry. The *Revival phase* of Maytag's organizational life had begun.

In 1981, Maytag purchased Hardwick Stove, followed by Jenn-Air a year later, and Magic Chef in 1986. These acquisitions provided Maytag Corporation a full line of home appliances in the key three categories of laundry, cooking, and refrigeration appliances. This revitalized the firm and enabled it to solidify its position as one of the "Big Five" U.S. major home appliance manufacturers. It then began to look for growth opportunities in other parts of the world.

MAYTAG CORPORATION

1. *Temporary cross-functional task forces* are initially used when a new product line is being introduced. A project manager is in charge as the key horizontal link. Chrysler has extensively used this approach in product development.

2. *Product/brand management.* If the cross-functional task forces become more permanent, the project manager becomes a product or brand manager and a second phase begins. In this arrangement, function is still the primary organizational structure, but *product or brand managers act as the integrators of semipermanent products or brands.* Considered by many a key to the success of Procter & Gamble, brand management has been widely imitated by other consumer products firms around the world.

3. *Mature matrix.* The third and final phase of matrix development involves a *true dual-authority structure.* Both the functional and product structures are permanent. All employees are connected to both a vertical functional superior and a horizontal product manager. Functional and product managers have equal authority and must work well together to resolve disagreements over resources and priorities. TRW Systems, the aerospace company, is an example of a company that uses a mature matrix.

Table 8.3 **Changing Structural Characteristics of Modern Corporations**

Old Organizational Design	New Organizational Design
One large corporation	Mini-business units & cooperative relationships
Vertical communication	Horizontal communication
Centralized top-down decision making	Decentralized participative decision making
Vertical integration	Outsourcing & virtual organizations
Work/quality teams	Autonomous work teams
Functional work teams	Cross-functional work teams
Minimal training	Extensive training
Specialized job design focused on individual	Value-chain team-focused job design

Source: Adapted from B. Macy and H. Izumi, "Organizational Change, Design, and Work Innovation: A Meta-Analysis of 131 North American Field Studies—1961–1991," *Research in Organizational Change and Development*, Vol. 7, JAI Press (1993), p. 298. Reprinted with permission of JAI Press, Inc., Greenwich, CT and London, England.

Network Structure

A newer and somewhat more radical organizational design, the **network structure** (see Figure 8.1) is an example of what could be termed a "nonstructure" by its virtual elimination of in-house business functions. Many activities are outsourced. A corporation organized in this manner is often called a *virtual organization* because it is composed of a series of project groups or collaborations linked by constantly changing nonhierarchical, cobweb-like networks.[15] The network structure becomes most useful when the environment of a firm is unstable and is expected to remain so. Under such conditions, there is usually a strong need for innovation and quick response. Instead of having salaried employees, it may contract with people for a specific project or length of time. Long-term contracts with suppliers and distributors replace services that the company could provide for itself through vertical integration. Electronic markets and sophisticated information systems reduce the transaction costs of the marketplace, thus justifying a "buy" over a "make" decision. Rather than being located in a single building or area, an organization's business functions are scattered worldwide. The organization is, in effect, only a shell, with a small headquarters acting as a "broker," electronically connected to some completely owned divisions, partially owned subsidiaries, and other independent companies. In its ultimate form, the network organization is a series of independent firms or business units linked together by computers in an information system that designs, produces, and markets a product or service.[16]

An example of a complete network organization is Just Toys. The New York City company licenses characters like Disney's Little Mermaid, Hanna-Barbera's Flintstones, and Marvel Entertainment's Spiderman to make bendable polyvinyl chloride figures called Bend-Ems. The manufacturing and administrative work for Bend-Ems is contracted out. The company only employs 30 employees. If a toy isn't selling well, production can be reduced and shipments stopped almost immediately. It would take Mattel and Hasbro months to react in a similar situation.

Other companies like Nike, Reebok, and Benetton use the network structure in their operations function by subcontracting manufacturing to other companies in low-cost locations around the world. For control purposes, the Italian-based Benetton maintains what it calls an "umbilical cord" by assuring production planning for all its subcontractors, planning materials requirements for them, and providing them with bills of labor and standard prices and costs, as well as technical assistance to make sure their quality is up to Benetton's standards.

Figure 8.1
Matrix and Network Structures

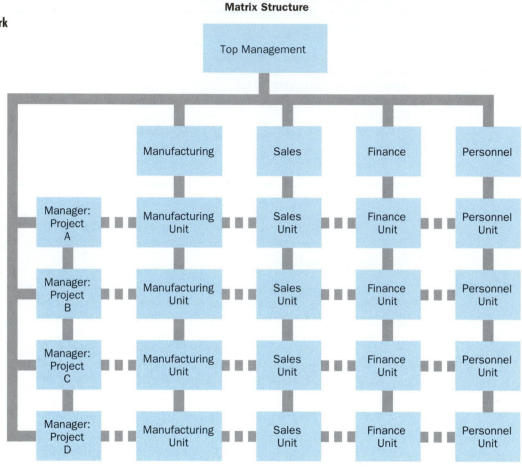

Matrix Structure

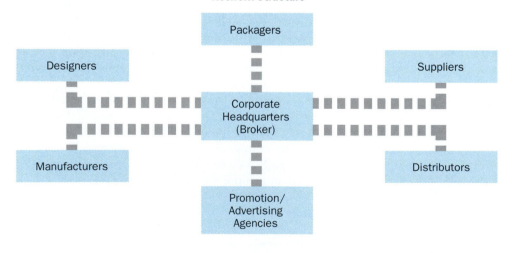

Network Structure

The network organization structure provides an organization with increased flexibility and adaptability to cope with rapid technological change and shifting patterns of international trade and competition. It allows a company to concentrate on its distinctive competencies, while gathering efficiencies from other firms who are concentrating their efforts in their areas of expertise. The network does, however, have disadvantages. The availability of numerous potential partners can be a source of trouble. Contracting out functions to separate suppliers/distributors may keep the firm from discovering any synergies by combining activities. If a particular firm overspecializes on only a few functions, it runs the risk of choosing the wrong functions and thus becoming noncompetitive.

Reengineering and Strategy Implementation

A recent approach to strategy implementation used to improve operations is called reengineering. **Reengineering** is the radical redesign of business processes to achieve major gains in cost, service, or time. It is not in itself a type of structure, but it is an effective way to implement a turnaround strategy.

Reengineering strives to break away from the old rules and procedures that develop and become ingrained in every organization over the years. These may be a combination of policies, rules, and procedures that have never been seriously questioned because they were established years earlier. These may range from "Credit decisions are made by the credit department" to "Local inventory is needed for good customer service." These rules of organization and work design were based on assumptions about technology, people, and organizational goals that may no longer be relevant. Rather than attempting to fix existing problems through minor adjustments and fine-tuning existing processes, the key to reengineering is to ask "If this were a new company, how would we run this place?"

Michael Hammer, who popularized the concept, suggests the following principles for reengineering:

- **Organize around outcomes, not tasks.** Design a person's or a department's job around an objective or outcome instead of a single task or series of tasks.

- **Have those who use the output of the process perform the process.** With computer-based information systems, processes can now be reengineered so that the people who need the result of the process can do it themselves.

- **Subsume information-processing work into the real work that produces the information.** People or departments that produce information can also process it for use instead of just sending raw data to others in the organization to interpret.

- **Treat geographically dispersed resources as though they were centralized.** With modern information systems, companies can provide flexible service locally while keeping the actual resources in a centralized location for coordination purposes.

- **Link parallel activities instead of integrating their results.** Instead of having separate units perform different activities that must eventually come together, have them communicate while they work so that *they* can do the integrating.

- **Put the decision point where the work is performed, and build control into the process.** The people who do the work should make the decisions and be self-controlling.

- **Capture information once and at the source.** Instead of having each unit develop its own database and information processing activities, the information can be put on a network so that all can access it.[17]

Several companies have had success with reengineering. For example, Pratt & Whitney, a jet engine manufacturer, used reengineering to overhaul its inefficient assembly lines. Independent product centers were established to replace old, mile-long "flow lines" to support an efficient work flow. In each center, old clusters of identical machines were regrouped into new clusters of different machines that together could manufacture one engine part in a simple continuous flow. Employees were cross-trained so that every person could operate every machine. This effort saved the company $5 billion and resulted in a 70% faster manufacturing process.[18] Nevertheless, because reengineering is almost always accompanied by a significant amount of pain, it is estimated that between 50% and 70% of reengineering efforts fail to achieve their goals.[19]

Designing Jobs to Implement Strategy

Organizing a company's activities and people to implement strategy involves more than simply redesigning a corporation's overall structure; it also involves redesigning the way jobs are done. With the increasing emphasis on reengineering, many companies are beginning to rethink their work processes with an eye toward phasing unnecessary people and activities out of the process. Process steps that had traditionally been performed sequentially can be improved by performing them concurrently using cross-functional work teams. Harley-Davidson, for example, has managed to reduce total plant employment by 25% while reducing by 50% the time needed to build a motorcycle. Restructuring through fewer people requires broadening the scope of jobs and encouraging teamwork. The design of jobs and subsequent job performance are, therefore, increasingly being considered as sources of competitive advantage.

Job design refers to the study of individual tasks in an attempt to make them more relevant to the company and to the employee(s). To minimize some of the adverse consequences of task specialization, corporations have turned to new job design techniques: **job enlargement** (combining tasks to give a worker more of the same type of duties to perform), **job rotation** (moving workers through several jobs to increase variety), and **job enrichment** (altering the jobs by giving the worker more autonomy and control over activities). The **job characteristics model** is a good example of job enrichment. (See the **Key Theory** feature.) Although each of these methods has its adherents, no one method seems to work in all situations.

A good example of modern job design is the introduction of team-based production by Corning, Inc., the glass manufacturer, in its Blacksburg, Virginia, plant. With union approval, Corning reduced job classifications from 47 to 4 to enable production workers to rotate jobs after learning new skills. The workers were divided into 14-member teams that, in effect, managed themselves. The plant had only two levels of management: Plant Manager Robert Hoover and two line leaders who only advised the teams. Employees worked demanding 12½ hour shifts, alternating three-day and four-day weeks. The teams made managerial decisions, imposed discipline on fellow workers, and were required to learn three "skill modules" within two years or else lose their jobs. As a result of this new job design, a Blacksburg team, made up of workers with interchangeable skills, can retool a line to produce a different type of filter in only ten minutes—six times faster than workers in a traditionally designed filter plant. The Blacksburg plant earned a $2 million profit in its first eight months of production, instead of losing the $2.3 million projected for the start-up period. The plant performed so well that Corning's top management acted to convert the company's 27 other factories to team-based production.[20]

KEY THEORY

DESIGNING JOBS WITH THE JOB CHARACTERISTICS MODEL

The job characteristics model is an advanced approach to job design based on the belief that tasks can be described in terms of certain objective characteristics and that these characteristics affect employee motivation. In order for the job to be motivating, (1) the worker needs to feel a sense of responsibility, feel the task to be meaningful, and receive useful feedback on his or her performance, and (2) the job has to satisfy needs that are important to the worker. The model proposes that managers follow five principles for redesigning work:

1. *Combine tasks* to increase task variety and to enable workers to identify with what they are doing.

2. *Form natural work units* to make a worker more responsible and accountable for the performance of the job.

3. *Establish client relationships* so the worker will know what performance is required and why.

4. *Vertically load the job* by giving workers increased authority and responsibility over their activities.

5. *Open feedback channels* by providing workers with information on how they are performing.

Research supports the job characteristics model as a way to improve job performance through job enrichment. Although there are several other approaches to job design, practicing managers seem increasingly to follow the prescriptions of this model as a way of improving productivity and product quality.

Source: J. R. Hackman and G. R. Oldham, *Work Redesign* (Reading, Mass.: Addison-Wesley, 1980), pp. 135–141; G. Johns, J. L. Xie, and Y. Fang, "Mediating and Moderating Effects in Job Design," *Journal of Management* (December 1992), pp. 657–676; R. W. Griffin, "Effects of Work Redesign on Employee Perceptions, Attitudes, and Behaviors: A Long-Term Investigation," *Academy of Management Journal* (June 1991), pp. 425–435.

8.5 International Issues in Strategy Implementation

An international company is one that engages in any combination of activities, from exporting/importing to full-scale manufacturing, in foreign countries. The **multinational corporation (MNC)**, in contrast, is a highly developed international company with a deep involvement throughout the world, plus a worldwide perspective in its management and decision making. For a multinational corporation to be considered global, it must manage its worldwide operations as if they were totally interconnected. This approach works best when the industry has moved from being multidomestic (each country's industry is essentially separate from the same industry in other countries; an example is retailing) to global (each country is a part of one worldwide industry; an example is consumer electronics).

Strategic alliances, such as joint ventures and licensing agreements, between a multinational company (MNC) and a local partner in a host country are becoming increasingly popular as a means by which a corporation can gain entry into other countries, especially less developed countries. The key to the successful implementation of these strategies is the selection of the local partner. Each party needs to assess not only the strategic fit of each company's project strategy, but also the fit of each company's respective resources. A successful joint venture may require as much as two years of prior contacts between both parties.

The design of an organization's structure is strongly affected by the company's stage of development in international activities and the types of industries in which the company is involved. The issue of centralization versus decentralization becomes especially important for a multinational corporation operating in both multidomestic and global industries.

Stages of International Development

Corporations operating internationally tend to evolve through five common stages, both in their relationships with widely dispersed geographic markets and in the manner in which they structure their operations and programs. These **stages of international development** are:

- **Stage 1 (Domestic Company).** The primarily domestic company exports some of its products through local dealers and distributors in the foreign countries. The impact on the organization's structure is minimal because an export department at corporate headquarters handles everything.

- **Stage 2 (Domestic Company with Export Division).** Success in Stage 1 leads the company to establish its own sales company with offices in other countries to eliminate the middlemen and to better control marketing. Because exports have now become more important, the company establishes an export division to oversee foreign sales offices.

- **Stage 3 (Primarily Domestic Company with International Division).** Success in earlier stages leads the company to establish manufacturing facilities in addition to sales and service offices in key countries. The company now adds an international division with responsibilities for most of the business functions conducted in other countries.

- **Stage 4 (Multinational Corporation with Multidomestic Emphasis).** Now a full-fledged multinational corporation, the company increases its investments in other countries. The company establishes a local operating division or company in the host country, such as Ford of Britain, to better serve the market. The product line is expanded, and local manufacturing capacity is established. Managerial functions (product development, finance, marketing, and so on) are organized locally. Over time, the parent company acquires other related businesses, broadening the base of the local operating division. As the subsidiary in the host country successfully develops a strong regional presence, it achieves greater autonomy and self-sufficiency. The operations in each country are, nevertheless, managed separately as if each is a domestic company.

- **Stage 5 (Multinational Corporation with Global Emphasis).** The most successful multinational corporations move into a fifth stage in which they have worldwide personnel, R&D, and financing strategies. Typically operating in a global industry, the MNC denationalizes its operations and plans product design, manufacturing, and marketing around worldwide considerations. Global considerations now dominate organizational design. The global MNC structures itself in a matrix form around some combination of geographic areas, product lines, and functions. All managers are now responsible for dealing with international as well as domestic issues.

Research provides some support for the stages of international development concept, but it does not necessarily support the preceding sequence of stages. For example,

21ST CENTURY GLOBAL SOCIETY

THE INTERNET: INSTANT ENTRY INTO THE INTERNATIONAL MARKETPLACE

A few years ago, The Doll Collection was a barely profitable neighborhood retail shop in Louisville, Kentucky, with a staff of three people. Looking for an inexpensive way to boost its sales, one of the employees, Jason Walters, suggested putting a web page on the Internet. After spending two weeks learning the Internet computer language, html, Walters designed a simple site showcasing well-known dolls like Barbie and Madam Alexander to attract buyers. Employees of The Doll Collection were amazed by the response—much of which came from outside North America. Sales jumped 375%. By 1997, the shop had become a global retailer, marketing Barbie and Madam Alexander dolls to people in almost every country, including Japan, China, and Australia. (Try The Doll Collection's web site at *http://www.dollpage.com.*)

This story is no isolated example. The transaction value of goods and services purchased using the Internet is predicted to rise from $100 million in 1995 to $186 billion by the turn of the century. Even though 75% of web users live in North America, it is becoming a global phenom-enon. New translation software is being developed to make the web more accessible to non-English speaking users. The World Trade Organization is working on a free trade framework for telecommunications. The European Union has set a January 1998 deadline for the full opening of its telecom markets in the majority of its member countries. Companies are expected to use the Internet to expand brand identification, access markets worldwide, and communicate effectively with customers. Soon e-mail transmitted over the Internet will rival the telephone and replace the fax machine. Videoconferencing will enable people to hold virtual meetings with people in different parts of the globe. If nothing else, the growth of the Internet is providing impetus for the globalization of 21st-century society.

Source: L. Beresford, "Global Smarts: Toy Story," *Entrepreneur* (February 1997), p. 38; W. Gates, "The Internet Grows Out of Nappies," *The World in 1997* (London: The Economist Group, 1996), p. 103; J. Chalmers, "Telecom Titans," *The World in 1997* (London: The Economist Group, 1996), p. 104–106.

a company may initiate production and sales in multiple countries without having gone through the steps of exporting or having local sales subsidiaries. In addition, any one corporation can be at different stages simultaneously, with different products in different markets at different levels. Firms may also leapfrog across stages to a global emphasis. The widespread growth of the Internet is changing the way business is being done internationally. See the **21st Century Global Society** feature for an example of how the Internet is enabling companies of all sizes to access the increasingly global marketplace. Nevertheless the stages concept provides a useful way to illustrate some of the structural changes corporations undergo when they increase their involvement in international activities.

Centralization versus Decentralization

A basic dilemma a multinational corporation faces is how to organize authority centrally so that it operates as a vast interlocking system that achieves synergy, and at the same time decentralize authority so that local managers can make the decisions necessary to meet the demands of the local market or host government. To deal with this problem, MNCs tend to structure themselves either along product groups or geographic areas.

Figure 8.2
Geographic Area Structure for a Multinational Corporation

*Note: Because of space limitations, product groups for only Europe and Asia are shown here.

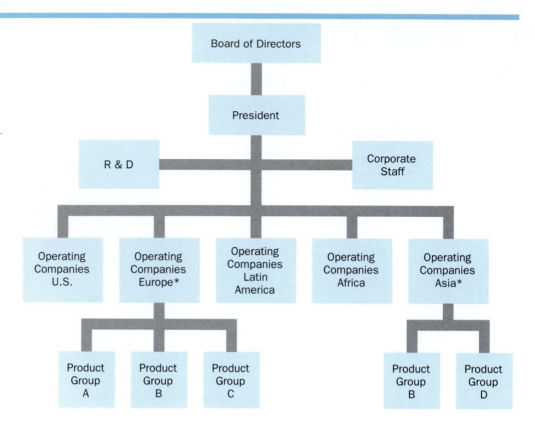

They may even combine both in a matrix structure—the design chosen by 3M Corporation and Asea Brown Boveri (ABB), among others.[21] One side of 3M's matrix represents the company's product divisions; the other side includes the company's international country and regional subsidiaries.

Two examples of the usual international structures are Nestlé and American Cyanamid. Nestlé's structure is one in which significant power and authority have been decentralized to geographic entities. This structure is similar to that depicted in Figure 8.2, in which each geographic set of operating companies has a different group of products. In contrast, American Cyanamid has a series of centralized product groups with worldwide responsibilities. To depict Cyanamid's structure, the geographical entities in Figure 8.2 would have to be replaced by product groups or strategic business units.

The **product-group structure** of American Cyanamid enables the company to introduce and manage a similar line of products around the world. This enables the corporation to *centralize* decision making along product lines and to reduce costs. The **geographic-area structure** of Nestlé, in contrast, allows the company to tailor products to regional differences and to achieve regional coordination. This *decentralizes* decision making to the local subsidiaries. As industries move from being multidomestic to more globally integrated, multinational corporations are increasingly switching from the geographic-area to the product-group structure. Texaco, Inc., for example, changed to a product-group structure in 1996 by consolidating its international, U.S., and new business opportunities under each line of business at its White Plains, New York, headquarters. According to Chairman Peter Bijur, "By placing groups which will perform similar work in the same location, they will be able to share information, ideas, and resources more readily—and move critical information throughout the organization."[22]

Simultaneous pressures for decentralization to be locally responsive and centralization to be maximally efficient are causing interesting structural adjustments in most large corporations. This is what is meant by the phrase "Think globally, act locally." Companies are attempting to decentralize those operations that are culturally oriented and closest to the customers—manufacturing, marketing, and human resources. At the same time, the companies are consolidating less visible internal functions, such as research and development, finance, and information systems, where there can be significant economies of scale.

🌐 **8.6** *Global Issues for the 21st Century*

- The **21st Century Global Society** feature in this chapter illustrates how the Internet is changing the way business is being conducted around the world. Small, local businesses can now access the international marketplace in a way undreamed of previously. The growth of the Internet is likely to stimulate the growth of an increasingly global society.

- Strategy implementation is likely to become an even more important issue to corporations engaging in international operations. Pepsico's bad experience in South America is one reason why, compared to the internationally successful Coca Cola, the company is struggling internationally.

- Strategic business units have become the most popular structural design in today's large multidivisional corporations. With more companies becoming multinational, expect them to take on many of the characteristics of the matrix and network organization.

- Many U.S. corporations have gone through the renewal phase of the organizational life cycle during the 1980s and 1990s by converting to more flexible organizational structures with cross-functional activities. This is making them more competitive in global industries. Most European corporations have yet to enter this phase and are beginning to lose their competitive advantages. Expect reengineering, job redesign, and other change techniques to soon become popular in Europe.

- As more industries become global, expect multinational corporations to adopt the matrix organization structure focusing on a centralized product group with various functions being decentralized to various regions for maximum efficiency and effectiveness.

Projections for the 21st Century

- From 1994 to 2010, the number of automobiles produced in the developed countries will increase from 20 million to 30 million vehicles.

- From 1994 to 2010, the number of automobiles produced in the emerging market nations will jump from 8 million to 30 million vehicles.[23]

Discussion Questions

1. How should a corporation attempt to achieve synergy among functions and business units?

2. How should an owner-manager prepare a company for its movement from Stage I to Stage II?

3. How can a corporation keep from sliding into the Decline stage of the organizational life cycle?

4. Is reengineering just another management fad or does it offer something of lasting value?

5. What are the advantages and disadvantages of the network structure?

Key Terms

budget (p. 186)
crisis of autonomy (p. 190)
crisis of leadership (p. 188)
divisional structure (p. 190)
functional structure (p. 189)
geographic-area structure (p. 201)
job characteristics model (p. 198)
job design (p. 198)
job enlargement (p. 198)
job enrichment (p. 198)

job rotation (p. 198)
matrix structure (p. 193)
multinational corporation (MNC) (p. 199)
network structure (p. 195)
organizational life cycle (p. 192)
procedures (p. 186)
product-group structure (p. 202)
program (p. 185)
reengineering (p. 197)

simple structure (p. 186)
SOPs (p. 186)
stages of corporate development (p. 188)
stages of international development (p. 200)
strategy implementation (p. 183)
structure follows strategy (p. 187)
synergy (p. 186)

Strategic Practice Exercise

One of today's trends is for large corporations to divide themselves into smaller units, eliminate layers of middle managers, and outsource many activities previously done internally—in order to better implement their strategies. One such company is Dana Corporation, a $5 billion auto-parts manufacturer. A big supplier to the large U.S., European, and Japanese automakers, Dana likes to operate as a series of small units. Only a handful of Dana's 120 plants employ more than 200 people. When a division of the company gets too big, it simply splits in half. "Plant managers should know the name and personal circumstances of everyone," insisted Dana Chairman Southwood Morcott.[24]

____ What kind of organizational structure does Dana use?

____ What is Dana Corporation trying to accomplish by breaking itself into a series of small units?

____ By keeping plant size so small, isn't Dana giving up economies of scale and thus potential cost advantages?

____ Would Dana be better off divesting many of its business units and using a network structure to contract for its supplies and raw materials in the marketplace?

Notes

1. R. Frank, and J. Friedland, "How Pepsi's Charge Into Brazil Fell Short of Its Ambitious Goals," *Wall Street Journal* (August 30, 1996), pp. A1, A6.

2. J. W. Gadella, "Avoiding Expensive Mistakes in Capital Investment," *Long Range Planning* (April 1994), pp. 103–110; B. Voss, "World Market Is Not for Everyone," *Journal of Business Strategy* (July/August 1993), p. 4.

3. L. D. Alexander, "Strategy Implementation: Nature of the Problem," *International Review of Strategic Management,*

Vol. 2, No. 1, edited by D. E. Hussey (New York: John Wiley & Sons, 1991), pp. 73–113.

4. Frank and Friedland.

5. A. D. Chandler, *Strategy and Structure* (Cambridge, Mass.: MIT Press, 1962).

6. A. P. Sloan, Jr., *My Years with General Motors* (Garden City, N.Y.: Doubleday, 1964).

7. T. L. Amburgey, and T. Dacin, "As the Left Foot Follows the Right? The Dynamics of Strategic and Structural

Change," *Academy of Management Journal* (December 1994), pp. 1427–1452; M. Ollinger, "The Limits of Growth of the Multidivisional Firm: A Case Study of the U.S. Oil Industry from 1930–90," *Strategic Management Journal* (September 1994), pp. 503–520.

8. D. F. Jennings, and S. L. Seaman, "High and Low Levels of Organizational Adaptation: An Empirical Analysis of Strategy, Structure, and Performance," *Strategic Management Journal* (July 1994), pp. 459–475.

9. A. K. Gupta, "SBU Strategies, Corporate-SBU Relations, and SBU Effectiveness in Strategy Implementation," *Academy of Management Journal* (September 1987), pp. 477–500.

10. L. E. Greiner, "Evolution and Revolution as Organizations Grow," *Harvard Business Review* (July-August 1972), pp. 37–46.

11. D. Miller, and P. H. Friesen, "A Longitudinal Study of the Corporate Life Cycle," *Management Science* (October 1984), pp. 1161–1183.

12. H. Tavakolian, "Bankruptcy: An Emerging Corporate Strategy," *SAM Advanced Management Journal* (Spring 1995), p. 19.

13. L. G. Hrebiniak, and W. F. Joyce, *Implementing Strategy* (New York: Macmillan, 1984), pp. 85–86.

14. S. M. Davis, and P. R. Lawrence, *Matrix* (Reading, Mass.: Addison-Wesley, 1977), pp. 11–24.

15. J. G. March, "The Future Disposable Organizations and the Rigidities of Imagination," *Organization* (August/November 1995), p. 434.

16. For more information on managing a network organization, see G. Lorenzoni and C. Baden-Fuller, "Creating a Strategic Center to Manage a Web of Partners," *California Management Review* (Spring 1995), pp. 146–163.

17. Summarized from M. Hammer, "Reengineering Work: Don't Automate, Obliterate," *Harvard Business Review* (July-August 1990), pp. 104–112.

18. J. Champy, *Managing Successful Reengineering* (Boston: HBS Management Productions, 1995). This is a videotape.

19. T. A. Stewart, "Reengineering: The Hot New Managing Tool," *Fortune* (August 23, 1993), pp. 41–42.

20. J. Hoerr, "Sharpening Minds for a Competitive Edge," *Business Week* (December 17, 1990), pp. 72–78.

21. C. A. Bartlett, and S. Ghoshal, "Beyond the M-Form: Toward a Managerial Theory of the Firm," *Strategic Management Journal* (Winter 1993), pp. 23–46.

22. A. Sullivan, "Texaco Revamps Executive Structure to Focus on Business, Not Geography," *Wall Street Journal* (October 3, 1996), p. B15.

23. J. Warner, "21st Century Capitalism: Snapshot of the Next Century," *Business Week* (November 18, 1994), p. 194.

24. R. A. Melcher, "How Goliaths Can Act Like Davids," *Business Week* (Enterprise 1993), p. 195.

Chapter 9

Strategy Implementation: Staffing and Directing

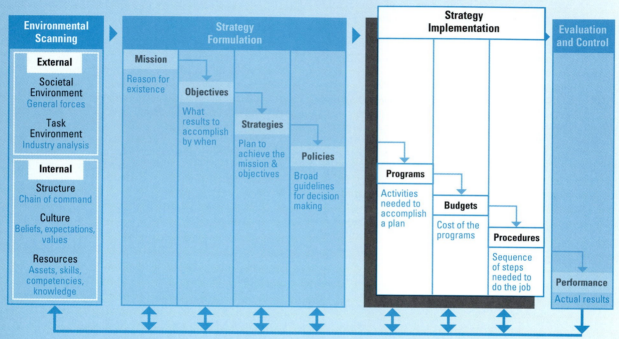

Have you heard of Enterprise Rent-A-Car? You won't find it at the airport with Hertz, Avis, or National car rental operations. Yet Enterprise owns more cars and operates in more locations than Hertz. The company accounts for over 20% of the $15 billion per year U.S. car rental market compared to 17% for Hertz and 12% for Avis. In ignoring the highly competitive airport market, Enterprise has chosen a differentiation competitive strategy by marketing to people in need of a spare car. Instead of locating many cars at a few high-priced locations at airports, Enterprise sets up inexpensive offices throughout metropolitan areas. As a result, cars are rented for 30% less than they cost at airports. As soon as one branch office grows to about 150 cars, the company opens another rental office a few miles away. People are increasingly renting from Enterprise even when their current car works fine. According to CEO Andy Taylor, "We call it a 'virtual car.' Small-business people who have to pick up clients call us when they want something better than their own car." Why is Enterprise able to follow this competitive strategy so successfully without attracting Hertz and Avis into its market?

The secret to Enterprise's success is its well-executed strategy implementation. Clearly laid out programs, budgets, and procedures support the company's competitive strategy by making Enterprise stand out in the mind of the consumer. When a new rental office opens, employees spend time developing relationships with the service managers of every auto dealership and body shop in the area. Enterprise employees bring pizza and doughnuts to workers at the auto garages across the country. Enterprise forms agreements with dealers to provide replacements for cars brought in for service. At major accounts, the company actually staffs an office at the dealership and has cars parked outside so customers don't have to go to an Enterprise office to complete paperwork.

One key to implementation at Enterprise is staffing—through hiring and promoting a certain kind of person. Virtually every Enterprise employee is a college graduate, usually from the bottom half of the class. According to COO Donald Ross, "We hire from the half of the college class that makes the upper half possible. We want athletes, fraternity types—especially fraternity presidents and social directors. People people." These new employees begin as management trainees in the $20,000–$25,000 salary range. Instead of regular raises, their pay is tied to branch office profits.

Another key to implementation at Enterprise is leading—through specifying clear performance objectives and promoting a team-oriented corporate culture. The company stresses promotion from within. Every Enterprise employee, including top executives, starts at the bottom. As a result, a bond of shared experience connects all employees and managers. To reinforce a cohesive culture of camaraderie, senior executives routinely do "grunt work" at branch offices. Even Andy Taylor, the CEO, joins the work. "We were visiting an office in Berkeley and it was mobbed, so I started cleaning cars," says Taylor. "As it was happening, I wondered if it was a good use of my time, but the effect on morale was tremendous." Because the financial results of every branch office and every region are available to all, the collegial culture stimulates good-natured competition. "We're this close to beating out Middlesex," grins Woody Erhardt, an area manager in New Jersey. "I want to pound them into the ground. If they lose, they have to throw a party for us, and we get to decide what they wear."[1]

This example from Enterprise Rent-A-Car illustrates how a competitive strategy must be implemented with carefully considered programs in order to succeed. This chapter discusses strategy implementation in terms of staffing and leading. *Staffing* focuses on the selection and use of employees. *Leading* emphasizes the use of programs to better align employee interests and attitudes with a new strategy.

9.1   Staffing

The implementation of new strategies and policies often calls for new human resource management priorities and a different use of personnel. Such **staffing** issues can involve hiring new people with new skills, firing people with inappropriate or substandard skills, and/or training existing employees to learn new skills.

If growth strategies are to be implemented, new people may need to be hired and trained. Experienced people with the necessary skills need to be found for promotion to newly created managerial positions. When a corporation follows a growth through acquisition strategy, it may find that it needs to replace several managers in the acquired company. Research by Walsh of 102 companies following an acquisition revealed that the percentage of the acquired company's top management team that either quit or was asked to leave was 26% after the first year and 61% after five years.[2]

If a corporation adopts a retrenchment strategy, however, a large number of people may need to be laid off or fired; and top management, as well as the divisional managers, needs to specify the criteria to be used in making these personnel decisions. Should employees be fired on the basis of low seniority or on the basis of poor performance? Sometimes corporations find it easier to close an entire division than to choose which individuals to fire.

Staffing Follows Strategy

As in the case of structure, staffing requirements are likely to follow a change in strategy. For example, promotions should be based not only on current job performance, but also on whether a person has the skills and abilities to do what is needed to implement the new strategy.

Hiring and Training Requirements Change

Having formulated a new strategy, a corporation may find that it needs to either hire different people or retrain current employees to implement the new strategy. Consider the introduction of team-based production at Corning's filter plant mentioned earlier in Chapter 8. Employee selection and training were crucial to the success of the new manufacturing strategy. Plant Manager Robert Hoover sorted through 8,000 job applications before hiring 150 people with the best problem-solving ability and a willingness to work in a team setting. Those selected received extensive training in technical and interpersonal skills. During the first year of production, 25% of all hours worked were devoted to training at a cost of $750,000.[3]

One way to implement a company's business strategy, such as overall low cost, is through training and development. One study of 155 manufacturing firms revealed that those with training programs had 19% higher productivity than did those without such a program. Another study found that a doubling of formal training per employee resulted in a 7% reduction in scrap.[4] Training is especially important for a differentiation strategy emphasizing quality or customer service. For example, Motorola, with annual sales of $17 billion, spends 4% of its payroll on training by providing at least 40 hours of training a year to its employees. It hopes to quadruple that within a few years at an annual cost of $600 million. There is a very strong connection between strategy and training at Motorola. For example, after setting a goal to reduce product development cycle time, Motorola created a course to teach its employees how to accomplish that goal. The company is especially concerned with attaining the highest quality possible in all its operations. Realizing that it couldn't hit quality targets with poor parts, Motorola developed a class for its suppliers on statistical process control. The company estimates that every $1 it spends on training delivers $30 in productivity gains within three years.[5]

Training is also important when implementing a retrenchment strategy. As suggested earlier, successful downsizing means that the company has to invest in its remaining employees. General Electric's Aircraft Engine Group used training to maintain its share of the market even though it had cut its workforce from 42,000 to 33,000 between 1991 and 1993.[6]

Matching the Manager to the Strategy

The most appropriate type of general manager needed to effectively implement a new corporate or business strategy depends on the desired strategic direction of that firm or business unit. Executives with a particular mix of skills and experiences may be classified as an **executive type** and paired with a specific corporate strategy. For example, a corporation following a concentration strategy emphasizing vertical or horizontal growth would probably want an aggressive new chief executive with a great deal of experience in that particular industry—a ***dynamic industry expert***. A diversification strategy, in contrast, might call for someone with an analytical mind who is highly knowledgeable in other industries and can manage diverse product lines—an ***analytical portfolio manager***. A corporation choosing to follow a stability strategy would probably want as its CEO a ***cautious profit planner***, a person with a conservative style, a production or engineering background, and experience with controlling budgets, capital expenditures, inventories, and standardization procedures. Weak companies in a relatively attractive industry tend to turn to a type of challenge-oriented executive known as the ***turnaround specialist*** to save the company. See the **Strategy in a Changing World** feature for a description of Ann Iverson, one such turnaround specialist. If a company cannot be saved, a **professional liquidator** might be called on by a bankruptcy court to close the firm and liquidate its assets. Research tends to support the conclusion that as a firm's environment changes, it tends to change the type of top executive to implement a new strategy.[7]

This approach is in agreement with Chandler, who proposed in Chapter 8 that the most appropriate CEO of a company changes as a firm moves from one stage of development to another. Because priorities certainly change over an organization's life, successful corporations need to select managers who have skills and characteristics appropriate to the organization's particular stage of development and position in its life cycle. For example, founders of firms tend to have functional backgrounds in technological specialties; whereas successors tend to have backgrounds in marketing and administration.[8]

Other studies have found a link between the type of CEO and the firm's overall strategic type. For example, successful prospector firms tended to be headed by CEOs from research/engineering and general management backgrounds. High performance defenders tended to have CEOs with accounting/finance, manufacturing/production, and general management experience. Analyzers tended to have CEOs with a marketing/sales background.[9]

A study of 173 firms over a 25-year period revealed that CEOs in these companies tended to have the same functional specialization as the former CEO, especially when the past CEO's strategy continued to be successful. This may be a pattern for successful corporations.[10] In particular, it explains why so many prosperous companies tend to recruit their top executives from one particular area. At Procter & Gamble (a good example of an analyzer firm), for example, the route to the CEO's position has always been through brand management with a strong emphasis on marketing. In other firms, the route may be through manufacturing, marketing, accounting, or finance—depending on what the corporation has always considered its key area (and its overall strategic orientation).

Selection and Management Development

Selection and development are important not only to ensure that people with the right mix of skills and experiences are initially hired, but also to help them grow on the job so that they might be prepared for future promotions.

ANN IVERSON IMPLEMENTS A TURNAROUND STRATEGY AT LAURA ASHLEY

When Sir Bernard Ashley visited a North Carolina shopping mall to see a prototype of an expanded Laura Ashley store, he was amazed and delighted. As the company's largest shareholder and co-founder, Ashley was well aware of how poorly the $512 million apparel and home furnishings company has fared since his wife Laura died in 1985. Unlike other Ashley shops, this one was packed with customers. "I almost cried, it was so marvelous," he exclaimed.

The credit for this change belongs to Ann Iverson. Since becoming CEO in July 1995, she had replaced most of top management, cut the payroll, slashed costs, and proposed an aggressive U.S. expansion plan. "I'm the kind of person who has a steamroller behind her back," explained Iverson. The board of directors of Laura Ashley Holdings PLC selected Iverson because of her ability to implement a turnaround strategy. Earlier Iverson had helped improve the profits of British Home Stores, a division of Storehouse PLC. She then moved to the CEO position of Storehouse's Mothercare Ltd. and introduced attractions such as talking trees and singing clocks to lure children and their mothers back into the stores. When Mothercare became profitable, she joined Melville Corporation in the United States to run its Kay-Bee Toy & Hobby Shops. At the same time, she agreed to serve on the Laura Ashley board of

directors. Her in-depth knowledge of retailing soon led the board to pick her to manage the company.

Iverson is a hands-on manager. She answers her own phone and gets into discussions regarding what kind of wood flooring should be used in the stores. To save expenses, she moved headquarters into a converted London bus depot. Acknowledging the dated Victorian look of the company's apparel, Iverson hired a new clothes designer, Basha Cohen, to freshen the line, but keep the flowing, romantic look. She also expanded the size of the stores to 7,200 from 2,500 square feet to expand home furnishings. One of her objectives is to increase revenue from home furnishings to 65% from its current 50% of total sales by the end of the decade. The company's wallpaper, bedspreads, linens, and curtains are less dependent on changing fashions than is its apparel line, with its floral prints and long, girlish dresses. Since Iverson's appointment as CEO, the company's stock has more than doubled to $3.20 per share. If her turnaround strategy succeeds, Iverson could earn $5.2 million over a three-year period.

Source: J. Flynn, and C. Power, "Giving Laura Ashley a Yank," *Business Week* (May 27, 1996), p. 147.

Executive Succession: Insiders versus Outsiders

Executive succession is the process of replacing a key top manager. Given that almost half of all CEOs are replaced within five years, it is important that the firm plan for this eventuality.[11] It is especially important for a company that usually promotes from within to prepare its current managers for promotion. Prosperous firms tend to look outside for CEO candidates only if they have no obvious internal candidates. Firms in trouble, however, tend to choose outsiders to lead them. For example, one study of 22 firms undertaking a turnaround strategy over a 13-year period found that the CEO was replaced in all but two companies. Of 27 changes of CEO (several firms had more than one CEO during this period), only seven were insiders—20 were outsiders.[12] The probability of an outsider being chosen to lead a firm in difficulty increases if there is no internal heir apparent, the last CEO was fired, and if the board of directors is composed of a large percentage of outsiders.[13] Boards realize that the best way to force a change in strategy is to hire a new CEO with no connections to the current strategy.

Identifying Abilities and Potential

A company can identify and prepare its people for important positions in several ways. One approach is to establish a sound **performance appraisal system** to identify good performers with promotion potential. A survey of 34 corporate planners and human resource executives from 24 large U.S. corporations revealed that approximately 80% made some attempt to identify managers' talents and behavioral tendencies so that they could place a manager with a likely fit to a given competitive strategy.[14] A company should examine its human resource system to ensure not only that people are being hired without regard to their racial, ethnic, or religious background, but also that they are being identified for training and promotion in the same manner. Management diversity could be a competitive advantage in a multiethnic world.

Many large organizations are using **assessment centers** to evaluate a person's suitability for an advanced position. Corporations such as AT&T, Standard Oil, IBM, Sears, and GE have successfully used assessment centers. Because each is specifically tailored to its corporation, these assessment centers are unique. They use special interviews, management games, in-basket exercises, leaderless group discussions, case analyses, decision-making exercises, and oral presentations to assess the potential of employees for specific positions. Promotions into these positions are based on performance levels in the assessment center. Many assessment centers have been able to accurately predict subsequent job performance.

Job rotation—moving people from one job to another—is also used in many large corporations to ensure that employees are gaining the appropriate mix of experiences to prepare them for future responsibilities. Rotating people among divisions is one way that the corporation can improve the level of organizational learning. For example, companies that pursue related diversification strategies through internal development make greater use of interdivisional transfers of people than do companies that grow through unrelated acquisitions. Apparently the companies that grow internally attempt to transfer important knowledge and skills throughout the corporation in order to achieve some sort of synergy.[15]

Problems in Retrenchment

Downsizing (sometimes called "rightsizing") refers to the planned elimination of positions or jobs. This program is often used to implement retrenchment strategies. Because the financial community is likely to react favorably to announcements of downsizing from a company in difficulty, such a program may provide some short-term benefits such as raising the company's stock price. If not done properly, however, downsizing may result in less, rather than more, productivity. One study of downsizing revealed that at 20 out of 30 automobile-related U.S. industrial companies, either the wrong jobs were eliminated or blanket offers of early retirement prompted managers, even those considered invaluable, to leave. After the layoffs, the remaining employees had to do not only their work, but also the work of the people who had gone. Because the survivors often didn't know how to do the departeds' work, morale and productivity plummeted.[16] In addition, cost-conscious executives tend to defer maintenance, skimp on training, delay new product introductions, and avoid risky new businesses—all of which leads to lower sales and eventually to lower profits.

A good retrenchment strategy can thus be implemented well in terms of organizing, but poorly in terms of staffing. A situation can develop in which retrenchment feeds on itself and acts to further weaken instead of strengthening the company. Research indicates that companies undertaking cost-cutting programs are four times more likely than others to cut costs again, typically by reducing staff.[17] In contrast, successful downsizing firms undertake a strategic reorientation, not just a bloodletting of employees. Research shows that when companies use downsizing as part of a larger restructuring program to narrow company focus, they enjoy better performance.[18]

Consider the following guidelines that have been proposed for successful downsizing:

- **Eliminate unnecessary work instead of making across-the-board cuts.** Spend the time to research where money is going and eliminate the task, not the workers, if it doesn't add value to what the firm is producing. Reduce the number of administrative levels rather than the number of individual positions. Look for interdependent relationships before eliminating activities. Identify and protect core competencies.

- **Contract out work that others can do cheaper.** For example, Bankers Trust of New York contracts out its mail room and printing services and some of its payroll and accounts payable activities to a division of Xerox. Outsourcing may be cheaper than vertical integration.

- **Plan for long-run efficiencies.** Don't simply eliminate all postponable expenses, such as maintenance, R&D, and advertising, in the unjustifiable hope that the environment will become more supportive. Continue to hire, grow, and develop—particularly in critical areas.

- **Communicate the reasons for actions.** Tell employees not only why the company is downsizing, but also what the company is trying to achieve. Promote educational programs.

- **Invest in the remaining employees.** Because most "survivors" in a corporate downsizing will probably be doing different tasks from what they were doing before the change, firms need to draft new job specifications, performance standards, appraisal techniques, and compensation packages. Additional training is needed to ensure that everyone has the proper skills to deal with expanded jobs and responsibilities. Empower key individuals/groups and emphasize team building. Identify, protect, and mentor people with leadership talent.

- **Develop value-added jobs to balance out job elimination.** When no other jobs are currently available within the organization to transfer employees to, management must consider other staffing alternatives. Harley-Davidson, for example, worked with the company's unions to find other work for surplus employees by moving work into Harley plants that was previously done by suppliers.[19]

International Issues in Staffing

Because of cultural differences, managerial style and human resource practices must be tailored to fit the particular situations in other countries. Most multinational corporations (MNCs) attempt to fill managerial positions in their subsidiaries with well-qualified citizens of the host countries. Unilever and IBM take this approach to international staffing. This policy serves to placate nationalistic governments and to better attune management practices to the host country's culture. The danger in using primarily foreign nationals to staff managerial positions in subsidiaries is the increased likelihood of suboptimization (the local subsidiary ignores the needs of the larger parent corporation). This makes it difficult for a multinational corporation to meet its long-term, worldwide objectives. To a local national in an MNC subsidiary, the corporation as a whole is an abstraction. Communication and coordination across subsidiaries become more difficult. As it becomes harder to coordinate the activities of several international subsidiaries, an MNC will have serious problems operating in a global industry.

Another approach to staffing the managerial positions of multinational corporations is to use people with an "international" orientation, regardless of their country of origin or host country assignment. This is a widespread practice among European firms. For example, Electrolux, a Swedish firm, had a French director in its Singapore factory. Using third-country "nationals" can allow for more opportunities for promotion than does Unilever's policy of hiring local people, but it can also result in more misunderstandings and conflicts with the local employees and with the host country's government.

To improve organizational learning, many multinational corporations are providing their managers with international assignments lasting as long as five years. Upon their return to headquarters, these expatriates will have an in-depth understanding of the company's operations in another part of the world. This has value to the extent that these employees communicate this understanding to others in decision-making positions. Unfortunately not all corporations appropriately manage international assignments. One mistake is failing to educate the person about the customs in other countries. While out of the country, a person may be overlooked for an important promotion (out of sight, out of mind). Upon his or her return to the home country, co-workers may deprecate the out-of-country experience as a waste of time. To improve their chances of success using expatriates, multinational corporations are now putting more emphasis on intercultural training for those managers being sent on an assignment to a foreign country. This training is one of the commonly cited reasons for the lower expatriate failure rates—6% or less—for European and Japanese MNCs, which have emphasized cross-cultural experiences, compared with a 35% failure rate for U.S.-based MNCs.[20]

Multinational corporations with a high level of international interdependence among activities need to provide their managers with significant international assignments and experiences as part of their training and development. Such assignments provide future corporate leaders with a series of valuable international contacts in additional to a better personal understanding of international issues and global linkages among corporate activities.[21] Daniel Krumm, for example, was Maytag Corporation's CEO when the corporation acquired Hoover to expand its international operations. One of Krumm's earlier assignments had been five years in Belgium and Germany as manager of Maytag's European operations. Executive recruiters report that compared to 1990, a greater percentage of major corporations are now requiring candidates to have international experience.[22]

U.S. corporations are also attempting to take advantage of immigrants and their children to staff key positions when negotiating entry into another country and when selecting an executive to manage the company's new foreign operations. For example, when General Motors wanted to learn more about business opportunities in China, it turned to its Chinese-American employees. See the 🌐 **21st Century Global Society** feature to learn how Shirley Young, a Chinese-American, helped negotiate a joint venture with a Chinese company to manufacture midsize Buicks in Shanghai.

Staffing international positions with immigrants or descendants of immigrants from that country may not necessarily be appropriate. AT&T, for example, has had mixed results with relocating around 50 ethnic employees to their home countries. The person may not understand the country's business practices because they either left long ago or never lived there. Local employees, in turn, often resent the newcomers' "foreign" manners and higher pay.[23]

21ST CENTURY GLOBAL SOCIETY

GENERAL MOTORS USES CHINESE-AMERICANS IN CHINESE JOINT VENTURE

Shirley Young, a Vice-President of Marketing at General Motors, was instrumental in helping GM negotiate a $1 billion joint venture with Shanghai Automotive to build a Buick plant in China. Uniquely qualified for this assignment, Young had been born in Shanghai, had relatives in China, and was fluent in Chinese. Her father, a hero in China, had been that country's Consul General to the Philippines during World War II. When GM wanted to establish links with China in 1992, it asked Young to help its people become acquainted with influential people in China's government and industrial circles. Young and other Chinese-Americans formed a committee to advise GM on relations with China. Although just a part of a larger team of GM employees working on the joint venture, Young coached GM employees on Chinese customs and traditions. Rather than eating together after transacting business, for example, she suggested that GM follow the Chinese practice of dining first. "These are little things that are just differences in the way each one looks at the world," says Ms. Young. "My being Chinese helps in that regard."

Source: G. Stern, "GM Executive's Ties to Native Country Help Auto Maker Clinch Deal in China," *Wall Street Journal* (November 2, 1995), p. B7.

9.2 *Leading*

Implementation also involves **leading** people to use their abilities and skills most effectively and efficiently to achieve organizational objectives. Without direction, people tend to do their work according to their personal view of what tasks should be done, how, and in what order. They may approach their work as they have in the past or emphasize those tasks that they most enjoy—regardless of the corporation's priorities. This can create real problems, particularly if the company is operating internationally and must adjust to customs and traditions in other countries. This direction may take the form of management leadership, communicated norms of behavior from the corporate culture, or agreements among workers in autonomous work groups. It may also be accomplished more formally through action planning, or through programs such as Management By Objectives and Total Quality Management.

Managing Corporate Culture

Because an organization's culture can exert a powerful influence on the behavior of all employees, it can strongly affect a company's ability to shift its strategic direction. A problem for a strong culture is that a change in mission, objectives, strategies, or policies is not likely to be successful if it is in opposition to the accepted culture of the company. Corporate culture has a strong tendency to resist change because its very reason for existence often rests on preserving stable relationships and patterns of behavior. For example, the male-dominated, Japanese-centered corporate culture of the giant Mitsubishi Corporation has created problems for the company as it tries to implement its growth strategy in North America. The alleged sexual harassment of its female employees by male supervisors resulted in a law suit by the U.S. Equal Employment Opportunity

Commission and a boycott of the company's automobiles by the National Organization for Women in 1996.[24]

There is no one best corporate culture. An optimal culture is one that best supports the mission and strategy of the company of which it is a part. This means that, like structure and staffing, *corporate culture should support the strategy*. Unless strategy is in complete agreement with the culture, any significant change in strategy should be followed by a modification of the organization's culture. Although corporate culture can be changed, it may often take a long time and it requires much effort. A key job of management involves **managing corporate culture.** In doing so, management must evaluate what a particular change in strategy means to the corporate culture, assess if a change in culture is needed, and decide if an attempt to change the culture is worth the likely costs.

Assessing Strategy-Culture Compatibility

When implementing a new strategy, a company should take the time to assess **strategy-culture compatibility.** (See Figure 9.1.) Consider the following questions regarding the corporation's culture:

1. **Is the planned strategy compatible with the company's current culture?** If *yes*, full steam ahead. Tie organizational changes into the company's culture by identifying how the new strategy will achieve the mission better than the current strategy does. *If not . . .*

2. **Can the culture be easily modified to make it more compatible with the new strategy?** If *yes*, move forward carefully by introducing a set of culture-changing activities such as minor structural modifications, training and development activities, and/or hiring new managers who are more compatible with the new strategy. When Procter & Gamble's top management decided to implement a strategy aimed at reducing costs, for example, it made some changes in how things were done, but it did not eliminate its brand-management system. The culture adapted to these modifications over a couple years and productivity increased. *If not . . .*

3. **Is management willing and able to make major organizational changes and accept probable delays and a likely increase in costs?** If *yes*, manage around the culture by establishing a new structural unit to implement the new strategy. At General Motors, for example, top management realized the company had to make some radical changes to be more competitive. Because the current structure, culture, and procedures were very inflexible, management decided to establish a completely new division (GM's first new division since 1918) called Saturn to build its new auto. In cooperation with the United Auto Workers, an entirely new labor agreement was developed, based on decisions reached by consensus. Carefully selected employees received from 100 to 750 hours of training, and a whole new culture was built piece by piece. *If not . . .*

4. **Is management still committed to implementing the strategy?** If *yes*, find a joint-venture partner or contract with another company to carry out the strategy. *If not,* **formulate a different strategy.**

Managing Cultural Change Through Communication

Communication is key to the effective management of change. Rationale for strategic changes should be communicated to workers not only in newsletters and speeches, but

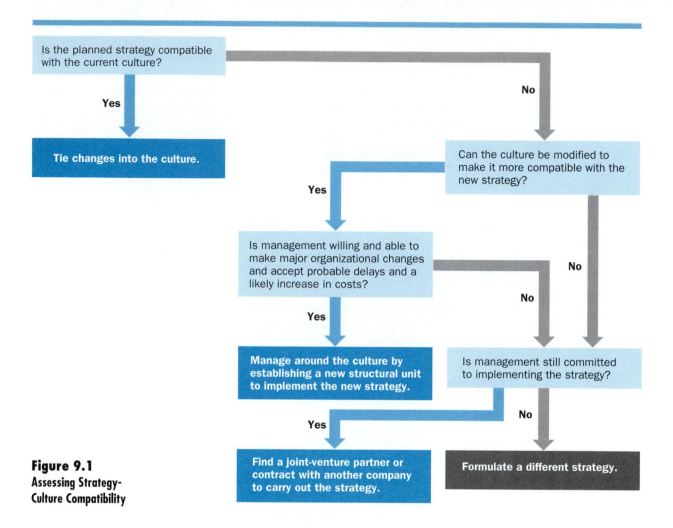

Figure 9.1
**Assessing Strategy-
Culture Compatibility**

also in training and development programs. Companies in which major cultural changes have taken place successfully had the following characteristics in common:

- The CEO and other top managers had a strategic vision of what the company could become and communicated this vision to employees at all levels. The current performance of the company was compared to that of its competition and constantly updated.

- The vision was translated into the key elements necessary to accomplish that vision. For example, if the vision called for the company to become a leader in quality or service, aspects of quality and service were pinpointed for improvement and appropriate measurement systems were developed to monitor them. These measures were communicated widely through contests, formal and informal recognition, and monetary rewards, among other devices.[25]

Managing Diverse Cultures Following an Acquisition

When merging with or acquiring another company, top management must give some consideration to a potential clash of corporate cultures. It's dangerous to assume that the firms can simply be integrated into the same reporting structure. The greater the gap between the cultures of the acquired firm and the acquiring firm, the faster executives in the acquired firm quit their jobs and valuable talent is lost.

Figure 9.2
Methods of Managing the Culture of an Acquired Firm

Source: A. Nahavardi and A. R. Malekzadeh, "Accultutation in Mergers and Acquisitions," *Academy of Management Review* (January 1988), p. 83. Copyright © 1988 by the Academy of Management. Reprinted by permission.

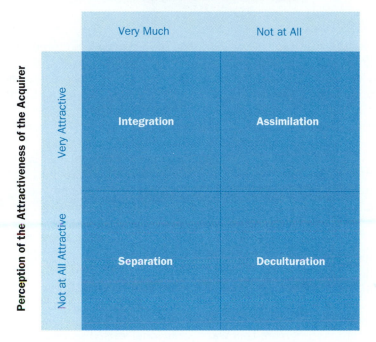

There are four general methods of managing two different cultures. (See Figure 9.2.) The choice of which method to use should be based on (1) *how much members of the acquired firm value preserving their own culture* and (2) *how attractive they perceive the culture of the acquirer to be.*[26]

1. **Integration** involves a relatively balanced give-and-take of cultural and managerial practices between the merger partners, and no strong imposition of cultural change on either company. It merges the two cultures in such a way that the separate cultures of both firms are preserved in the resulting culture. This is what occurred when the Seaboard and Chesapeake & Ohio railroads merged to form CSX Corporation. The top executives were so concerned that both cultures be equally respected that they kept referring to the company as a "partnership of equals."

2. **Assimilation** involves the domination of one organization over the other. The domination is not forced, but it is welcomed by members of the acquired firm, who may feel for many reasons that their culture and managerial practices have not produced success. The acquired firm surrenders its culture and adopts the culture of the acquiring company. The **Company Spotlight on Maytag Corporation** feature describes this method of acculturation when Admiral, a subsidiary of Magic Chef, joined Maytag Corporation.

3. **Separation** is characterized by a separation of the two companies' cultures. They are structurally separated, without cultural exchange. In the Shearson-American Express merger, both parties agreed to keep the fast-paced Shearson completely separate from the planning-oriented American Express. This approach allowed American Express to easily divest Shearson once it discovered that the merger was not working.

Maytag's corporate culture had been dominated almost from the beginning of the company by the concept of quality. Maytag employees took great pride in being known as the "dependability people." Over the years, Maytag Company consistently advertised that their repairmen were "lonely" because Maytag products rarely, if ever, needed repair.

Admiral's history had, however, been quite different. Prior to Maytag's purchase of Magic Chef (and thus Admiral) in 1986, Admiral had been owned by three different corporations. Its manufacturing plant in Galesburg, Illinois, had deteriorated to a dismal level by the time Maytag acquired it. Refrigerators sometimes rolled off the assembly line with screws driven in crooked and temperature balances askew!

Maytag's management had always wanted to have its own Maytag brand refrigerator. That was one reason why it purchased Magic Chef. But it was worried that Admiral might not be able to produce a quality product to Maytag's specifications. To improve Admiral's quality, Maytag's top management decided to integrate Admiral directly into Maytag Company operations. As a result, all Admiral functional departments, except marketing, reported directly to the Maytag Company president.

Under the direction of Leonard Hadley, while he was serving as Maytag Company President, a project was initiated to design and manufacture a refrigerator for the Maytag brand at the Admiral plant. When Hadley first visited Admiral's facilities to discuss the design of a Maytag line of refrigerators, Admiral personnel asked Hadley when the name on their plant's water tower would be changed from Admiral to Maytag. Hadley (acknowledging Maytag's cultural concerns regarding quality) responded: "When you earn it."

The refrigerator resulting from the Maytag-Admiral collaboration was a huge success. The project crystallized corporate management's philosophy for forging synergies among the Maytag companies, while simultaneously allowing the individual expertise of those units to flourish. Admiral's employees were willing to accept the dominance of Maytag's strong quality-oriented culture because they respected it. In turn, they expected to be treated with some respect for their tradition of skill in refrigeration technology.

MAYTAG CORPORATION

4. **Deculturation** involves the disintegration of one company's culture resulting from unwanted and extreme pressure from the other to impose its culture and practices. This is the most common and most destructive method of dealing with two different cultures. It is often accompanied by much confusion, conflict, resentment, and stress. Such a merger typically results in poor performance by the acquired company and its eventual divestment. This is what happened when AT&T acquired NCR Corporation in 1990 for its computer business. It replaced NCR managers with an AT&T management team, reorganized sales, forced employees to adhere to the AT&T code of values (called the "Common Bond"), and even dropped the proud NCR name (successor to National Cash Register) in favor of a sterile GIS (Global Information Solutions) nonidentity. By 1995, AT&T was forced to take a $1.2 billion loss and lay off 10,000 people.[27] The NCR unit was put up for sale in 1996.

Action Planning

Activities can be directed toward accomplishing strategic goals through action planning. At a minimum, an **action plan** states what actions are going to be taken, by whom,

Table 9.1 Example of an Action Plan

Action Plan for Jan Lewis, Advertising Manager, Ajax Continental

Program Objective: To Run a New Advertising and Promotion Campaign for the Combined Jones Surplus/Ajax Continental Retail Stores for the Coming Christmas Season Within a Budget of $XX.

Program Activities:
1. Identify Three Best Ad Agencies for New Campaign.
2. Ask Three Ad Agencies to Submit a Proposal for a New Advertising and Promotion Campaign for Combined Stores.
3. Agencies Present Proposals to Marketing Manager.
4. Select Best Proposal and Inform Agencies of Decision.
5. Agency Presents Winning Proposal to Top Management.
6. Ads Air on TV and Promotions Appear in Stores.
7. Measure Results of Campaign in Terms of Viewer Recall and Increase in Store Sales.

Action Steps	Responsibility	Start-End
1. A. Review previous programs	Lewis & Carter	1/1–2/1
B. Discuss with boss	Lewis & Smith	2/1–2/3
C. Decide on 3 agencies	Lewis	2/4
2. A. Write specifications for ad	Lewis	1/15–1/20
B. Assistant writes ad request	Carter	1/20–1/30
C. Contact ad agencies	Lewis	2/5–2/8
D. Send request to 3 agencies	Carter	2/10
E. Meet with agency acct. execs	Lewis & Carter	2/16–2/20
3. A. Agencies work on proposals	Acct. Execs	2/23–5/1
B. Agencies present proposals	Carter	5/1–5/15
4. A. Select best proposal	Lewis	5/15–5/20
B. Meet with winning agency	Lewis	5/22–5/30
C. Inform losers	Carter	6/1
5. A. Fine-tune proposal	Acct. Exec	6/1–7/1
B. Presentation to management	Lewis	7/1–7/3
6. A. Ads air on TV	Lewis	9/1–12/24
B. Floor displays in stores	Carter	8/20–8/30
7. A. Gather recall measures of ads	Carter	9/1–12/24
B. Evaluate sales data	Carter	1/1–1/10
C. Prepare analysis of campaign	Carter	1/10–2/15

during what timeframe, and with what expected results. After a program has been selected to implement a particular strategy, an action plan should be developed to put the program in place. See Table 9.1 for an example of an action plan for a new advertising and promotion program.

Take the example of a company choosing forward vertical integration through the acquisition of a retailing chain as its growth strategy. Now that it owns its own retail outlets, it must integrate the stores into the company. One of the many programs it would have to develop is a new advertising program for the stores. The resulting action plan to develop a new advertising program should include much of the following information:

1. **Specific actions to be taken to make the program operational.** One action might be to contact three reputable advertising agencies and ask them to prepare

a proposal for a new radio and newspaper ad campaign based on the theme "Jones Surplus is now a part of Ajax Continental. Prices are lower. Selection is better."

2. **Dates to begin and end each action.** Time would have to be allotted not only to select and contact three agencies, but to allow them sufficient time to prepare a detailed proposal. For example, allow one week to select and contact the agencies plus three months for them to prepare detailed proposals to present to the company's marketing director. Also allow some time to decide which proposal to accept.

3. **Person (identified by name and title) responsible for carrying out each action.** List someone—such as Jan Lewis, advertising manager—who can be put in charge of the program.

4. **Person responsible for monitoring the timeliness and effectiveness of each action.** Indicate that Jan Lewis is responsible for ensuring that the proposals are of good quality and are priced within the planned program budget. She will be the primary company contact for the ad agencies and will report on the progress of the program once a week to the company's marketing director.

5. **Expected financial and physical consequences of each action.** Estimate when a completed ad campaign will be ready to show top management and how long it will take after approval to begin to air the ads. Estimate also the expected increase in store sales over the six-month period after the ads are first aired. Indicate if "recall" measures will be used to help assess the ad campaign's effectiveness plus how, when, and by whom the recall data will be collected and analyzed.

6. **Contingency plans.** Indicate how long it will take to get an acceptable ad campaign to show top management if none of the initial proposals is acceptable.

Action plans are important for several reasons. First, action plans serve as a link between strategy formulation and evaluation and control. Second, the action plan specifies what needs to be done differently from the way operations are currently carried out. Third, during the evaluation and control process that comes later, an action plan helps in both the appraisal of performance and in the identification of any remedial actions, as needed. In addition, the explicit assignment of responsibilities for implementing and monitoring the programs may contribute to better motivation.

Management By Objectives

Management By Objectives (MBO) is an organizationwide approach to help ensure purposeful action toward desired objectives. MBO links organizational objectives and the behavior of individuals. Because it is a system that links plans with performance, it is a powerful implementation technique.

The MBO process involves:

1. Establishing and communicating organizational objectives.

2. Setting individual objectives (through superior-subordinate interaction) that help implement organizational ones.

3. Developing an action plan of activities needed to achieve the objectives.

4. Periodically (at least quarterly) reviewing performance as it relates to the objectives and including the results in the annual performance appraisal.

MBO provides an opportunity for the corporation to connect the objectives of people at each level to those at the next higher level. MBO, therefore, acts to tie together corprate, business, and functional objectives, as well as the strategies developed to achieve them.

One of the real benefits of MBO is that it can reduce the amount of internal politics operating within a large corporation. Political actions within a firm can cause conflict and create divisions between the very people and groups who should be working together to implement strategy. People are less likely to jockey for position if the company's mission and objectives are clear and they know that the reward system is based not on game playing, but on achieving clearly communicated, measurable objectives.

Total Quality Management

Total Quality Management (TQM) is an operational philosophy committed to *customer satisfaction* and *continuous improvement*. TQM is committed to quality/excellence and to being the best in all functions. TQM has four objectives:

1. Better, less variable quality of the product and service.

2. Quicker, less variable response in processes to customer needs.

3. Greater flexibility in adjusting to customers' shifting requirements.

4. Lower cost through quality improvement and elimination of non–value adding work.[28]

Because TQM aims to reduce costs and improve quality, it can be used as a program to implement both an overall low-cost or a differentiation business strategy. About 92% of manufacturing companies and 69% of service firms have implemented some form of quality management practices.[29]

According to TQM, faulty processes, not poorly motivated employees, are the cause of defects in quality. The program involves a significant change in corporate culture, requiring strong leadership from top management, employee training, empowerment of lower level employees (giving people more control over their work), and teamwork for it to succeed in a company. TQM emphasizes prevention, not correction. Inspection for quality still takes place, but the emphasis is on improving the process to prevent errors and deficiencies. Thus quality circles or quality improvement teams are formed to identify problems and to suggest how to improve the processes that may be causing the problems.

TQM's essential *ingredients* are:

- **An intense focus on customer satisfaction.** Everyone (not just people in the sales and marketing departments) understands that their jobs exist only because of customer needs. Thus all jobs must be approached in terms of how it will affect customer satisfaction.

- **Internal as well as external customers.** An employee in the shipping department may be the internal customer of another employee who completes the assembly of a product, just as a person who buys the product is a customer of the entire company. An employee must be just as concerned with pleasing the internal customer as in satisfying the external customer.

- **Accurate measurement of every critical variable in a company's operations.** This means that employees have to be trained in what to measure, how to measure, and how to interpret the data. A rule of TQM is "you only improve what you measure."

- **Continuous improvement of products and services.** Everyone realizes that operations need to be continuously monitored to find ways to improve products and services.

- **New work relationships based on trust and teamwork.** Important is the idea of *empowerment*—giving employees wide latitude in how they go about in achieving the company's goals. Research indicates that the key to TQM success lies in executive commitment, an open organizational culture, and employee empowerment.[30]

International Considerations in Leading

In a study of 53 different national cultures, Hofstede found that each nation's unique culture could be identified using five dimensions. He found that national culture is so influential that it tends to overwhelm even a strong corporate culture. In measuring the differences among these **dimensions of national culture** from country to country, he was able to explain why a certain management practice might be successful in one nation, but fail in another.[31]

1. **Power distance (PD)** is the *extent to which a society accepts an unequal distribution of power in organizations.* Malaysia and Mexico scored highest, whereas Germany and Austria scored lowest. People in those countries scoring high on this dimension tend to prefer autocratic to more participative managers.

2. **Uncertainty avoidance (UA)** is the *extent to which a society feels threatened by uncertain and ambiguous situations.* Greece and Japan scored highest on disliking ambiguity, whereas the United States and Singapore scored lowest. People in those nations scoring high on this dimension tend to want career stability, formal rules, and clear-cut measures of performance.

3. **Individualism-collectivism (I-C)** is the *extent to which a society values individual freedom and independence of action compared with a tight social framework and loyalty to the group.* The United States and Canada scored highest on individualism, whereas Mexico and Guatemala scored lowest. People in those nations scoring high on individualism tend to value individual success through competition, whereas people scoring low on individualism (thus high on collectivism) tend to value group success through collective cooperation.

4. **Masculinity-femininity (M-F)** is the *extent to which society is oriented toward money and things* (which Hofstede labels masculine) *or toward people* (which Hofstede labels feminine). Japan and Mexico scored highest on masculinity, whereas France and Sweden scored lowest (thus highest on femininity). People in those nations scoring high on masculinity tend to value clearly defined sex roles where men dominate and to emphasize performance and independence, whereas people scoring low on masculinity (and thus high on femininity) tend to value equality of the sexes where power is shared and to emphasize the quality of life and interdependence.

5. **Long-term orientation (LT)** is the *extent to which society is oriented toward the long versus the short term.* Hong Kong and Japan scored highest on long-term orientation, whereas Pakistan scored the lowest. A long-term time orientation emphasizes the importance of hard work, education, and persistence as well as the importance of thrift. Nations with a long-term time orientation should value strategic planning and other management techniques with a long-term payback.

These dimensions of national culture may help to explain why some management practices work well in some countries, but not in others. For example, Management By Objectives (MBO), which originated in the United States, has succeeded in Germany, according to Hofstede, because the idea of replacing the arbitrary authority of the boss with the impersonal authority of mutually agreed-upon objectives fits the low power distance that is a dimension of the German culture. It has failed in France, however, because the French are used to high power distances—to accepting orders from a highly personalized authority. In addition, some of the difficulties experienced by U.S. companies in using Japanese-style quality circles in Total Quality Management may stem from the extremely high value U.S. culture places on individualism. The differences between the U.S and Mexico on power distance (Mexico 104 vs. U.S. 46) and individualism-collectivism (U.S. 91 vs. Mexico 30) dimensions may help explain why some companies operating in both countries have difficulty adapting to the differences in customs.[32]

When one successful company in one country merges with another successful company in another country, the clash of corporate cultures is compounded by the clash of national cultures. In Maytag's case, the acquisition of Hoover's North American vacuum cleaner business created few problems because the quality-oriented corporate cultures were so similar. Problems arose when Maytag executives began interacting with their Hoover Europe colleagues in the United Kingdom. Maytag people were viewed by the British as demanding and "rigid," whereas the Hoover-Europe people were viewed as more laid back and "collegial." With cross-border mergers and acquisitions increasing to 6,377 by 1996, the management of cultures is becoming a key issue in strategy implementation.[33] See the 🌐 **21st Century Global Society** feature to learn how differences in national and corporate cultures created conflict when Upjohn Company of the U.S. and Pharmacia AB of Sweden merged.

Multinational corporations must pay attention to the many differences in cultural dimensions around the world and adjust their management practices accordingly. Cultural differences can easily go unrecognized by a headquarters staff that may interpret these differences as personality defects, whether the people in the subsidiaries are locals or expatriates. Hofstede and Bond conclude: "Whether they like it or not, the headquarters of multinationals are in the business of multicultural management."[34]

🌐 9.3 Global Issues for the 21st Century

- The first **21st Century Global Society** feature in this chapter illustrates how General Motors is using the diversity of its workforce to help it obtain entry into China. This is one reason why those companies hiring people of all races, religions, and national backgrounds will have an advantage in the world of the future.

- The second **21st Century Global Society** feature illustrates the difficulty of merging two companies—not only because of differences in corporate, but also in national culture. With the number of cross-border mergers and acquisitions increasing, expect companies to value international work experience more highly.

- Given the importance of technology in global business, companies will need to spend more time and money hiring skilled labor and training these employees to deal with emerging technologies.

- Differences in corporate and national cultures may explain why many companies prefer to work with a local partner in a strategic alliance rather than simply

CULTURAL DIFFERENCES CREATE IMPLEMENTATION PROBLEMS IN MERGER

When Upjohn Pharmaceuticals of Kalamazoo, Michigan, and Pharmacia AB of Stockholm, Sweden, merged in 1995, employees of both sides were optimistic for the newly formed Pharmacia & Upjohn, Inc. Both companies were second-tier competitors fighting for survival in a global industry. Together, the firms would create a global company that could compete scientifically with its bigger rivals.

Because Pharmacia had acquired an Italian firm in 1993, it also had a large operation in Milan. American executives scheduled meetings throughout the summer of 1996—only to cancel them when their European counterparts could not attend. Although it was common knowledge in Europe that most Swedes take the entire month of July for vacation and that Italians take off all of August, this was not common knowledge in Michigan. Differences in management styles became a special irritant. Swedes were used to an open system with autonomous work teams. Executives sought the whole group's approval before making an important decision. Upjohn executives followed the more traditional American top-down approach. Upon taking command of the newly merged firm, Dr. Zabriskie (who had been Upjohn's CEO), divided the company into departments reporting to the new London headquarters. He required frequent reports, budgets, and staffing updates. The Swedes reacted negatively to this top-down management hierarchical style. "It was degrading," said Stener Kvinnsland, head of Pharmacia's cancer research in Italy before he quit the new company.

The Italian operations baffled the Americans, even though the Italians felt comfortable with a hierarchical management style. Italy's laws and unions made layoffs difficult. Italian data and accounting were often inaccurate. Because the Americans didn't trust the data, they were constantly asking for verification. In turn, the Italians were concerned that the Americans were trying to take over Italian operations. At Upjohn, all workers were subject to testing for drug and alcohol abuse. Upjohn also banned smoking. At Pharmacia's Italian business center, however, waiters poured wine freely every afternoon in the company dining room. Pharmacia's boardrooms were stocked with humidors for executives who smoked cigars during long meetings. After a brief attempt to enforce Upjohn's policies, the company dropped both of the no-drinking and no-smoking policies for European workers.

Although the combined company had cut annual costs by $200 million, overall costs of the merger reached $800 million, some $200 million more than projected. Nevertheless, Jan Eckberg, CEO of Pharmacia before the merger, remained confident of the new company's ability to succeed. He admitted, however, that "we have to make some smaller changes to release the full power of the two companies."

Source: R. Frank and T. M. Burton, "Cross-Border Merger Results in Headaches for a Drug Company," *Wall Street Journal* (February 4, 1997), pp. A1, A12.

acquiring a company in another country. Alliances may be similar to a courtship period between two large companies and, if successful, may lead to an eventual merger.

- Improvements in communications (satellites, cell phones, Internet) and logistics are making it easier to interact with people of other nations. As more industries become global, it is possible that differences in national culture may become less important.

Nations do, however, want to keep some of their differences, yet be part of the world community. The British want to remain British. The same is true of the Chinese, the Italians, and the Canadians. Multinational corporations will be forced to deal with this paradox so long as different peoples want to be a part of a larger community, yet have their differences respected.

Projections for the 21st Century

- From 1994 to 2010, movie screens will increase in the United States from 25,105 to 74,114.

- From 1994 to 2010, movie screens will grow worldwide from 86,902 to 162,766.[35]

Discussion Questions

1. What skills should a person have for managing a business unit following a differentiation strategy? Why? What should a company do if no one is available internally and the company has a policy of promotion from within?

2. When should someone from outside the company be hired to manage the company or one of its business units?

3. What are some ways to implement a retrenchment strategy without creating a lot of resentment and conflict with labor unions?

4. How can corporate culture be changed?

5. Why is an understanding of national cultures important in strategic management?

Key Terms

action plan (p. 218)
assessment centers (p. 211)
assimilation (p. 217)
deculturation (p. 218)
dimensions of national
    culture (p. 222)
downsizing (p. 211)
executive succession (p. 210)
executive type (p. 209)
individualism-collectivism
    (I-C) (p. 222)

integration (p. 217)
international staffing (p. 212)
job rotation (p. 211)
leading (p. 214)
long-term orientation (LT)
    (p. 222)
Management By Objectives
    (MBO) (p. 220)
managing corporate culture (p. 215)
masculinity-femininity (M-F) (p. 222)

performance appraisal system (p. 211)
power distance (PD) (p. 222)
professional liquidator (p. 209)
separation (p. 217)
staffing (p. 207)
staffing follows strategy (p. 208)
strategy-culture compatibility (p. 215)
Total Quality Management (TQM) (p. 221)
turnaround specialist (p. 209)
uncertainty avoidance (UA) (p. 222)

Strategic Practice Exercise

Staffing involves finding the person with the right blend of characteristics, such as personality, training, and experience, to implement a particular strategy. Based on psychologist Carl Jung's work, Isabel Myers and Katheryn Briggs developed a way to measure two key dimensions of an individual's personality: (1) sensing and intuition and (2) thinking and feeling. Data about the world are obtained along a continuum with sensing at one end and intuition at the other. A **sensing person** *strives for logic and order*. An **intuitive in-**

dividual *works according to inspiration, flashes of insight, and hunches.* Judgments about the world are applied along a continuum with thinking at one end and feeling at the other. The **thinking person** *makes assessments in a logical and analytical manner.* A **feeling person** *makes assessments based on values and subjective emotions.* Engage in the following exercise to assess these characteristics of your personality and their impact on your decision making.

1. Fill out the form. Respond to the following 20 items in terms of your personal concerns and behavior. For each item, indicate which of the two alternative statements (*A or B*) is most characteristic of you. **Distribute 5 points between each set of two statements.** You may put all 5 points on A and none on B, or you may put some points on A and the rest on B. *The amount of points for each item (A and B) should sum to 5.*

1. Are you more	(a) pragmatic (b) idealistic	A	B
2. Are you more impressed by	(a) standards (b) sentiments	A	B
3. Are you more interested in that which	(a) convinces you by facts (b) emotionally moves you	A	B
4. It is worse to be	(a) impractical (b) having a boring routine	A	B
5. Are you more attracted to	(a) a person with good common sense (b) a creative person	A	B
6. In judging others, are you more swayed by	(a) the rules (b) the situation	A	B
7. Are you more interested in	(a) what has happened (b) what can happen	A	B
8. Do you more often have	(a) presence of mind (b) warm emotions	A	B
9. Are you more frequently	(a) a realistic sort of person (b) an imaginative sort of person	A	B
10. Are you more	(a) faithful (b) logical	A	B
11. Are you more	(a) action-oriented (b) creation-oriented	A	B
12. Which guides you more	(a) your brain (b) your heart	A	B
13. Do you take pride in your	(a) realistic outlook (b) imaginative ability	A	B
14. Which is more of a personal compliment	(a) you are consistent in your reasoning (b) you are considerate of others	A	B
15. Are you more drawn to	(a) basics (b) implications	A	B
16. Is it better to be	(a) fair (b) sentimental	A	B
17. Would you rather spend time with	(a) realistic people (b) imaginative people	A	B
18. Would you describe yourself as	(a) hard (b) soft	A	B
19. Would your friends say that you are	(a) someone who is filled with new ideas (b) someone who is a realist	A	B
20. It is better to be called a person who shows	(a) feelings (b) reasonable consistency	A	B

2. Score the form. Enter the numbers for your response to each item in the appropriate column of the following chart. Then add each of the four columns to obtain a total for each. **Circle** the *highest* of the **S** or **N** column totals. Then **circle** the *highest* of the **T** or **F** col-

umn totals. S = sensation. N = intuitive. T = thinking. F = feeling. This will tell you which of the *four decision-making styles you tend to favor*: **Sensation-Thinking (ST), Sensation-Feeling (SF), Intuitive-Thinking (NT),** or **Intuitive-Feeling (IF).**

Item #	A	B	Item #	A	B
1			2		
3			4		
5			6		
7			8		
9			10		
11			12		
13			14		
15			16		
17			18		
19			20		
Totals					
	S = Sensation	N =Intuitive		T = Thinking	F = Feeling

3. Form groups to do the exercise. Form into groups of about 4–6 people based on your decision-making style. Each group should be composed of people with the same decision-making style (**ST**, **SF**, **NT**, or **NF**). Your assignment is to form a new business venture. You have 30 minutes to discuss this in your group. When 30 minutes is over, a spokesperson from each group should present each group's ideas.

4. Analyze the group differences. How did the groups differ in terms of their ideas for a new venture?

How did each group handle the assignment? What does this tell you about how staffing should follow strategy?

Source: Questionnaire taken from D. Hellriegel, J. W. Slocum, and R. W. Woodman, *Organizational Behavior*, 7th ed. (Cincinatti: South-Western, 1995), pp. 108–134. Reprinted by permission. Exercise suggested by F. Ramsoomair, "Relating Theoretical Concepts to Life in the Classroom: Applying the Myers-Briggs Type Indicator," *Journal of Management Education* (February 1994), pp. 111–116.

Notes

1. B. O'Reilly, "The Rent-A-Car Jocks Who Made Enterprise #1," *Fortune* (October 28, 1996), pp. 125–128.
2. J. P. Walsh, "Doing a Deal: Merger and Acquisition Negotiations and Their Impact Upon Target Company Top Management Turnover," *Strategic Management Journal* (July-August 1989), pp. 307–322.
3. J. Hoerr, "Sharpening Minds for a Competitive Edge," *Business Week* (December 17, 1990), pp. 72–78.
4. *High Performance Work Practices and Firm Performance* (Washington, D.C.: U.S. Department of Labor, Office of the American Workplace, 1993), pp. i, 4.
5. K. Kelly, "Motorola: Training for the Millennium," *Business Week* (March 28, 1996), pp. 158–161.
6. R. Henkoff, "Companies That Train Best," *Fortune* (March 22, 1993), pp. 62–75.
7. A. S. Thomas, and K. Ramaswamy, "Environmental Change and Management Staffing: A Comment," *Journal of Management* (Winter 1993), pp. 877–887; J. P. Guthrie, C. M. Grimm, and K. G. Smith, "Environmental Change and Management Staffing: An Empirical Study," *Journal of Management* (December 1991), pp. 735–748.
8. R. Drazin, and R. K. Kazanjian, "Applying the Del Technique to the Analysis of Cross-Classification Data: A Test of CEO Succession and Top Management Team Development," *Academy of Management Journal* (December 1993), pp. 1374–1399; W. E. Rothschild, "A Portfolio of Strategic

Leaders," *Planning Review* (January/February 1996), pp. 16–19.

9. J. A. Parnell, "Functional Background and Business Strategy: The Impact of Executive-Strategy Fit on Performance," *Journal of Business Strategies* (Spring 1994), pp. 49–62.

10. M. Smith and M. C. White, "Strategy, CEO Specialization, and Succession," *Administrative Science Quarterly* (June 1987), pp. 263–280.

11. C. M. Farkas, and S. Wetlaufer, "The Ways Chief Executive Officers Lead," *Harvard Business Review* (May/June, 1996), p. 110.

12. C. Gopinath, "Turnaround: Recognizing Decline and Initiating Intervention," *Long Range Planning* (December 1991), pp. 96–101.

13. K. B. Schwartz, and K. Menon, "Executive Succession in Failing Firms," *Academy of Management Journal* (September 1985), pp. 680–686; A. A. Cannella, Jr., and M. Lubatkin, "Succession as a Sociopolitical Process: Internal Impediments to Outsider Selection," *Academy of Management Journal* (August 1993), pp. 763–793; W. Boeker and J. Goodstein, "Performance and Succession Choice: The Moderating Effects of Governance and Ownership," *Academy of Management Journal* (February 1993), pp. 172–186.

14. P. Lorange, and D. Murphy, "Bringing Human Resources Into Strategic Planning: System Design Characteristics," in *Strategic Human Resource Management*, edited by C. J. Fombrun, N. M. Tichy, and M. A. Devanna (New York: John Wiley and Sons, 1984), pp. 281–283.

15. R. A. Pitts, "Strategies and Structures for Diversification," *Academy of Management Journal* (June 1997), pp. 197–208.

16. B. O'Reilly, "Is Your Company Asking Too Much?" *Fortune* (March 12, 1990), p. 41.

17. *Wall Street Journal* (December 22, 1992), p. B1.

18. G. D. Bruton, J. K. Keels, and C. L. Shook, "Downsizing the Firm: Answering the Strategic Questions," *Academy of Management Executive* (May 1996), pp. 38–45.

19. M. A. Hitt, B. W. Keats, H. F. Harback, and R. D. Nixon, "Rightsizing: Building and Maintaining Strategic Leadership and Long-Term Competitiveness," *Organizational Dynamics* (Autumn 1994), pp. 18–32.

20. R. L. Tung, *The New Expatriates* (Cambridge, Mass.: Ballinger, 1988); J. S. Black, M. Mendenhall, and G. Oddou, "Toward a Comprehensive Model of International Adjustment: An Integration of Multiple Theoretical Perspectives," *Academy of Management Review* (April 1991), pp. 291–317.

21. K. Roth, "Managing International Interdependence: CEO Characteristics in a Resource-Based Framework," *Academy of Management Journal* (February 1995), pp. 200–231.

22. J. S. Lublin, "An Overseas Stint Can Be a Ticket to the Top," *Wall Street Journal* (January 29, 1996), pp. B1, B2.

23. J. S. Lublin, "Is Transfer to Native Land a Passport to Trouble?" *Wall Street Journal* (June 3, 1996), pp. B1, B5.

24. P. Elstrom, and S. V. Brull, "Mitsubishi's Morass," *Business Week* (June 3, 1996), p. 35.

25. G. G. Gordon, "The Relationship of Corporate Culture to Industry Sector and Corporate Performance," in *Gaining Control of the Corporate Culture,* edited by R. H. Kilmann, M. J. Saxton, R. Serpa, and Associates (San Francisco: Jossey-Bass, 1985), p. 123; T. Kono, "Corporate Culture and Long-Range Planning," *Long Range Planning* (August 1990), pp. 9–19.

26. A. R. Malekzadeh, and A. Nahavandi, "Making Mergers Work by Managing Cultures," *Journal of Business Strategy* (May/June 1990), pp. 53–57; A. Nahavandi, and A. R. Malekzadeh, "Acculturation in Mergers and Acquisitions," *Academy of Management Review* (January 1988), pp. 79–90.

27. J. J. Keller, "Why AT&T Takeover of NCR Hasn't Been a Real Bell Ringer," *Wall Street Journal* (September 19, 1995), pp. A1, A5.

28. R. J. Schonberger, "Total Quality Management Cuts a Broad Swath—Through Manufacturing and Beyond," *Organizational Dynamics* (Spring 1992), pp. 16–28.

29. S. S. Masterson, and M. S. Taylor, "Total Quality Management and Performance Appraisal: An Integrative Perspective," *Journal of Quality Management,* Vol. 1, No. 1 (1996), pp. 67–89.

30. T. C. Powell, "Total Quality Management as Competitive Advantage: A Review and Empirical Study," *Strategic Management Journal* (January 1995), pp. 15–37.

31. G. Hofstede, *Cultures and Organizations: Software of the Mind* (London: McGraw-Hill, 1991); G. Hofstede and M. H. Bond, "The Confucius Connection: From Cultural Roots to Economic Growth," *Organizational Dynamics* (Spring 1988), pp. 5–21; R. Hodgetts, "A Conversation with Geert Hofstede," *Organizational Dynamics* (Spring 1993), pp. 53–61.

32. See Hofstede and Bond, "The Confucius Connection," pp. 12–13.

33. R. Frank, and T. M. Burton, "Cross-Border Merger Results in Headaches for a Drug Company," *Wall Street Journal* (February 4, 1997), p. A1.

34. Hofstede and Bond, "The Confucius Connection," p. 20.

35. J. Warner, "21st Century Capitalism: Snapshot of the Next Century," *Business Week* (November 18, 1994), p. 194.

Chapter 10

Evaluation and Control

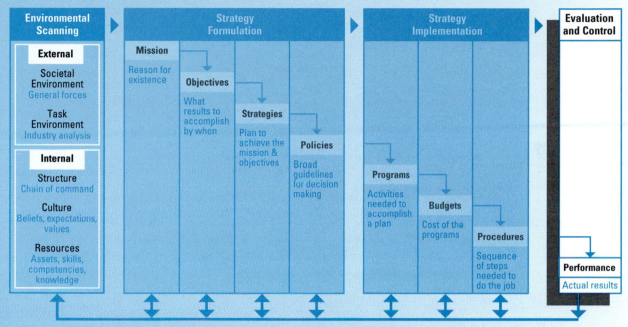

Environmental Scanning

External

Societal Environment
General forces

Task Environment
Industry analysis

Internal

Structure
Chain of command

Culture
Beliefs, expectations, values

Resources
Assets, skills, competencies, knowledge

Strategy Formulation

Mission
Reason for existence

Objectives
What results to accomplish by when

Strategies
Plan to achieve the mission & objectives

Policies
Broad guidelines for decision making

Strategy Implementation

Programs
Activities needed to accomplish a plan

Budgets
Cost of the programs

Procedures
Sequence of steps needed to do the job

Evaluation and Control

Performance
Actual results

Feedback/Learning

During the spring of 1992, Jim Cannavino, the manager in charge of IBM's personal computer business, insisted that his was the most profitable PC business in the world. Unfortunately his comment was based on the very strange way IBM allocated its costs to products. For example, IBM's system of accounting allocated all of a particular technology's R&D spending to the first group that used the technology; other IBM units then were able to use that technology free. As IBM found itself facing declining profits, it changed its cost allocation system to one that was more realistic. By the fall of 1992, IBM disclosed that its PC business was actually unprofitable. IBM's competitors commented that the business had probably been losing money on and off for years— IBM just didn't know it![1]

The **evaluation and control process** ensures that the company is achieving what it set out to accomplish. It compares performance with desired results and provides the feedback necessary for management to evaluate results and take corrective action, as needed. This process can be viewed as a five-step feedback model, as depicted in Figure 10.1.

1. **Determine what to measure.** Top managers and operational managers need to specify what implementation processes and results will be monitored and evaluated. The processes and results must be capable of being measured in a reasonably objective and consistent manner. The focus should be on the most significant elements in a process—the ones that account for the highest proportion of expense or the greatest number of problems. Measurements must be found for all important areas, regardless of difficulty.

2. **Establish standards of performance.** Standards used to measure performance are detailed expressions of strategic objectives. They are *measures* of acceptable performance results. Each standard usually includes a **tolerance range**, which defines acceptable deviations. Standards can be set not only for final output, but also for intermediate stages of production output.

3. **Measure actual performance.** Measurements must be made at predetermined times.

4. **Compare actual performance with the standard.** If actual performance results are within the desired tolerance range, the measurement process stops here.

5. **Take corrective action.** If actual results fall outside the desired tolerance range, action must be taken to correct the deviation. The following questions must be answered:

   a. Is the deviation only a chance fluctuation?

   b. Are the processes being carried out incorrectly?

   c. Are the processes appropriate to the achievement of the desired standard? Action must be taken that will not only correct the deviation, but will also prevent its happening again.

Top management is often better at the first two steps of the control model than it is in the last three follow-through steps. It tends to establish a control system and then delegate the implementation to others. This can have unfortunate results.

10.1 Evaluation and Control in Strategic Management

Evaluation and control information consists of performance data and activity reports (gathered in Step 3 of Figure 10.1). If undesired performance results because the strategic management processes were inappropriately used, operational managers must know about it so that they can correct the employee activity. Top management need not be involved. If, however, undesired performance results from the processes themselves, top managers, as well as operational managers, must know about it so that they can develop new implementation programs or procedures.

Evaluation and control information must be relevant to what is being monitored. The IBM example demonstrates how inappropriate data clouded the perceptions of the PC unit's manager and may have led to poor strategic decision making. Evaluation and control is not an easy process. One of the obstacles to effective control is the difficulty in developing appropriate measures of important activities and outputs.

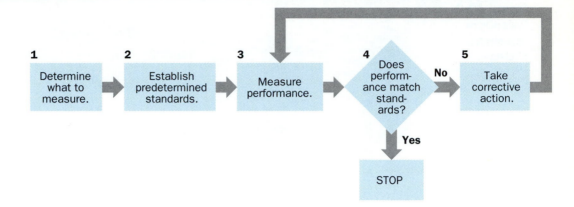

Figure 10.1
Evaluation and Control Process

An application of the control process to strategic management is depicted in Figure 10.2. It provides strategic managers with a series of questions to use in evaluating an implemented strategy. Such a strategy review is usually initiated when a gap appears between a company's financial objectives and the expected results of current activities. After answering the proposed set of questions, a manager should have a good idea of where the problem originated and what must be done to correct the situation.

10.2 Measuring Performance

Performance is the end result of activity. Which measures to select to assess performance depends on the organizational unit to be appraised and the objectives to be achieved. The objectives that were established earlier in the strategy formulation part of the strategic management process (dealing with profitability, market share, and cost reduction, among others) should certainly be used to measure corporate performance once the strategies have been implemented.

Appropriate Measures

Some measures, such as return on investment (ROI), are appropriate for evaluating the corporation's or division's ability to achieve a profitability objective. This type of measure, however, is inadequate for evaluating additional corporate objectives such as social responsibility or employee development. Even though profitability is a corporation's major objective, ROI can be computed only *after* profits are totaled for a period. It tells what happened after the fact—not what *is* happening or what *will* happen. A firm, therefore, needs to develop measures that predict *likely* profitability. These are referred to as **steering controls** because they measure variables that influence future profitability. One example of this type of control is the use of control charts in Statistical Process Control (SPC). In SPC, workers and managers maintain charts and graphs detailing quality and productivity on a daily basis. They are thus able to make adjustments to the system before it gets out of control.[2]

Behavior and Output Controls

Controls can be established to focus either on actual performance results (output) or on the activities that generate the performance (behavior). **Behavior controls** specify *how*

Figure 10.2
Evaluating an Implemented Strategy

Source: Jeffery A. Schmidt, "The Strategic Review," *Planning Review* (July/August 1988), p. 15. Copyright © 1988 by The Planning Forum, Oxford, Ohio.

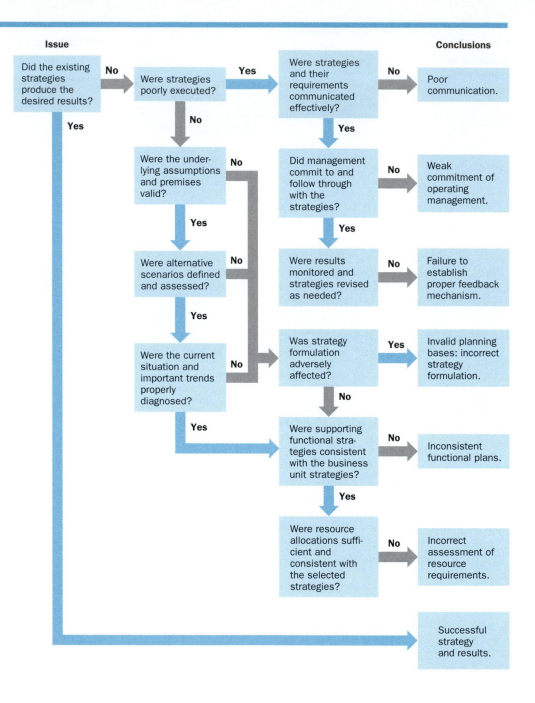

something is to be done through policies, rules, standard operating procedures, and orders from a superior. **Output controls** specify *what* is to be accomplished by focusing on the end result of the behaviors through the use of objectives and performance targets or milestones.

Behavior and output controls are not interchangeable. Behavior controls (such as following company procedures, making sales calls to potential customers, and getting to work on time) are most appropriate when performance results are hard to measure but the cause-effect connection between activities and results is clear. Output controls (such as sales quotas, specific cost reduction or profit objectives, and surveys of customer satisfaction) are most appropriate when specific output measures have been agreed on but the cause-effect connection between activities and results is not clear.

One example of an increasingly popular behavior control is the **ISO 9000 Standards Series** on quality management and assurance developed by the International Standards Association of Geneva, Switzerland. The ISO 9000 series (composed of five sections from 9000 to 9004) is a way of objectively documenting a company's high level of quality operations. ISO 9000 and 9004 contain guidelines for use with the other sections; 9001 is the most comprehensive standard; 9002 is less stringent; 9003 is only used for inspecting and testing procedures. A company wanting certification would probably document its process for product introductions, among other things. ISO 9001 would require this firm to separately document design input, design process, design output, and design verification—a large amount of work.

Many corporations view ISO 9000 certification as assurance that a supplier sells quality products. Firms such as DuPont, Hewlett-Packard, and 3M have facilities registered to ISO standards. Companies in over 60 countries, including Canada, Mexico, Japan, the United States (including the entire U.S. auto industry), and the European Union, are requiring ISO 9000 certification of their suppliers. In one survey of manufacturing executives, 51% of the executives found that certification increased their international competitiveness. Other executives noted that it signaled their commitment to quality and gave them a strategic advantage over noncertified competitors.[3]

Activity-Based Costing

Activity-based costing (ABC) is a new accounting method for allocating indirect and fixed costs to individual products or product lines based on the value-added activities going into that product.[4] This accounting method is thus very useful in doing a *value-chain analysis* of a firm's activities for making outsourcing decisions. Traditional cost accounting, in contrast, focuses on valuing a company's inventory for financial reporting purposes. To obtain a unit's cost, cost accountants typically add direct labor to the cost of materials. Then they compute overhead from rent to R&D expenses, based on the number of direct labor hours it takes to make a product. To obtain unit cost, they divide the total by the number of items made during the period under consideration.

Traditional cost accounting is useful when direct labor accounts for most of total costs and a company produces just a few products requiring the same processes. This may have been true of companies during the early part of the twentieth century, but it is no longer relevant today when overhead may account for as much as 70% of manufacturing costs. The appropriate allocation of indirect costs and overhead has thus become crucial for decision making. As mentioned at the beginning of this chapter, the use of traditional cost accounting at IBM blinded management to the true costs of its PC business. As PCs became a larger part of IBM's sales during the 1980s, corporate profits actually declined!

ABC accounting allows accountants to charge costs more accurately than the traditional method because it allocates overhead far more precisely. For example, imagine a production line in a pen factory where black pens are made in high volume and blue pens in low volume. Assume it takes eight hours to retool (reprogram the machinery) to shift production from one kind of pen to the other. The total costs include supplies (the same for both pens), the direct labor of the line workers, and factory overhead. In this instance, a very significant part of the overhead cost is the cost of reprogramming the machinery to switch from one pen to another. If the company produces ten times as many black pens as blue pens, ten times the cost of the reprogramming expenses will be allocated to the black pens as to the blue pens under traditional cost accounting methods. This approach underestimates, however, the true cost of making the blue pens (like IBM's personal computers).

ABC accounting, in contrast, first breaks down pen manufacturing into its activities. It is then very easy to see that it is the activity of changing pens that triggers the cost of retooling. The ABC accountant calculates an average cost of setting up the machinery and charges it against each batch of pens that requires retooling regardless of the size of the run. Thus a product carries only those costs for the overhead it actually consumes. Management is now able to discover that its blue pens cost almost twice as much as do the black pens. Unless the company is able to charge a higher price for its blue pens, it cannot make a profit on these pens. Unless there is a strategic reason why it must offer blue pens (such as a key customer who must have a small number of blue pens with every large order of black pens or a marketing trend away from black to blue pens), the company will earn significantly greater profits if it completely stops making blue pens.[5]

Activity-based costing can be used in many types of industries. For example, a bakery may use standard costs to allocate costs to products and to price customers' orders. Under the traditional standard cost system, overhead costs such as selling, advertising, warehousing, shipping, and administration are allocated to products and spread over the entire customer base. Under a traditional standard cost system, a bakery would allocate order handling charges on a percentage of sales basis. When this is done, profitable accounts tend to subsidize unprofitable ones—without anyone's knowledge. What is ignored is that the amount of time and expense spent processing an order is usually the same, regardless of whether the order is for 200 or 2000 donuts. The cost driver is not the number of cases ordered but the number of separate sales orders that must be processed. By assigning costs based on the number of orders that have to be processed, instead of by the dollar value of the order, the bakery can calculate a much more accurate cost for processing each customer's order. This information is crucial if management is to assess the profitability of different customers and to make strategic decisions regarding growth or retrenchment.[6]

Primary Measures of Corporate Performance

The days when simple financial measures such as ROI or EPS were used alone to assess overall corporate performance are coming to an end. Analysts now recommend a broad range of methods to evaluate the success or failure of a strategy. Some of these methods are stakeholder measures, shareholder value, and the balanced scorecard approach. Even though each of these methods has its supporters as well as detractors, the current trend is clearly toward more complicated financial measures and an increasing use of nonfinancial measures of corporate performance.[7] For example, research indicates that companies pursuing strategies founded on innovation and new product development now tend to favor nonfinancial over financial measures.[8]

Traditional Financial Measures

The most commonly used measure of corporate performance (in terms of profits) is **return on investment (ROI)**. It is simply the result of dividing net income before taxes by total assets. Although using ROI has several advantages, it also has several distinct limitations. (See Table 10.1.) Although ROI gives the impression of objectivity and precision, it can be easily manipulated.

Table 10.1   **Advantages and Limitations of Using ROI as a Measure of Corporate Performance**

Advantages

1. ROI is a single comprehensive figure influenced by everything that happens.
2. It measures how well the division manager uses the property of the company to generate profits. It is also a good way to check on the accuracy of capital investment proposals.
3. It is a common denominator that can be compared with many entities.
4. It provides an incentive to use existing assets efficiently.
5. It provides an incentive to acquire new assets only when doing so would increase the return.

Limitations

1. ROI is very sensitive to depreciation policy. Depreciation write-off variances between divisions affect ROI performance. Accelerated depreciation techniques increase ROI, conflicting with capital budgeting discounted cash-flow analysis.
2. ROI is sensitive to book value. Older plants with more depreciated assets have relatively lower investment bases than newer plants (note also the effect of inflation), thus increasing ROI. Note that asset investment may be held down or assets disposed of in order to increase ROI performance.
3. In many firms that use ROI, one division sells to another. As a result, transfer pricing must occur. Expenses incurred affect profit. Since, in theory, the transfer price should be based on the total impact on firm profit, some investment center managers are bound to suffer. Equitable transfer prices are difficult to determine.
4. If one division operates in an industry that has favorable conditions and another division operates in an industry that has unfavorable conditions, the former division will automatically "look" better than the other.
5. The time span of concern here is short range. The performance of division managers should be measured in the long run. This is top management's timespan capacity.
6. The business cycle strongly affects ROI performance, often despite managerial performance.

Source: "Advantages and Limitations of ROI as a Measure of Corporate Performance" from *Organizational Policy and Strategic Management: Text and Cases,* 2nd ed. by James M. Higgins, copyright © 1984 by The Dryden Press. Reproduced by permission of the publisher.

Earnings per share (EPS), dividing net earnings by the amount of common stock, also has several deficiencies as an evaluation of past and future performance. First, because alternative accounting principles are available, EPS can have several different but equally acceptable values, depending on the principle selected for its computation. Second, because EPS is based on accrual income, the conversion of income to cash can be near term or delayed. Therefore, EPS does not consider the time value of money. **Return on equity (ROE),** dividing net income by total equity, also has its share of limitations because it is also derived from accounting-based data. In addition, EPS and ROE are often unrelated to a company's stock price. Because of these and other limitations, EPS and ROE by themselves are not adequate measures of corporate performance.

Stakeholder Measures

Each stakeholder has its own set of criteria to determine how well the corporation is performing. These criteria typically deal with the direct and indirect impact of corporate activities on stakeholder interests. Top management should establish one or more simple **stakeholder measures** for each stakeholder category so that it can keep track of stakeholder concerns. (See Table 10.2.)

Shareholder Value

Because of the belief that accounting-based numbers such as return on investment, return on equity, and earnings per share are not reliable indicators of a corporation's economic value, many corporations are using shareholder value as a better measure of corporate performance and strategic management effectiveness. Real **shareholder value** can be defined as the present value of the anticipated future stream of cash flows from the business plus the value of the company if liquidated. Arguing that the purpose

Table 10.2 **A Sample Scorecard for "Keeping Score" with Stakeholders**

Stakeholder Category	Possible Near-Term Measures	Possible Long-Term Measures
Customers	Sales ($ and volume) New customers Number of new customer needs met ("tries")	Growth in sales Turnover of customer base Ability to control price

Suppliers	Cost of raw material
	Delivery time
	Inventory
	Availability of raw material
		Growth rates of:
		  Raw material costs
		  Delivery time
		  Inventory
		New ideas from suppliers

Financial community	EPS Stock price Number of "buy" lists ROE	Ability to convince Wall Street of strategy Growth in ROE
Employees	Number of suggestions Productivity Number of grievances	Number of internal promotions Turnover
Congress	Number of new pieces of legislation that affect the firm Access to key members and staff	Number of new regulations that affect industry Ratio of "cooperative" vs. "competitive" encounters
Consumer advocate (CA)	Number of meetings Number of "hostile" encounters Number of times coalitions formed Number of legal actions	Number of changes in policy due to C. A. Number of C. A.-initiated "calls for help"
Environmentalists	Number of meetings Number of hostile encounters Number of times coalitions formed Number of EPA complaints Number of legal actions	Number of changes in policy due to environmentalists Number of environmentalist "calls for help"

Source: R. E. Freeman, *Strategic Management: A Stakeholder Approach* (Boston: Ballinger Publishing Company, 1984), p. 179. Copyright © 1984 by R. E. Freeman. Reprinted by permission.

of a company is to increase shareholder wealth, shareholder value analysis concentrates on cash flow as the key measure of performance. The value of a corporation is thus the value of its cash flows discounted back to their present value, using the business's cost of capital as the discount rate. As long as the returns from a business exceed its cost of capital, the business will create value and be worth more than the capital invested in it.

The New York consulting firm Stern Stewart & Company devised and popularized two shareholder value measures: economic value added (EVA) and market value added (MVA). Well-known companies, such as Coca-Cola, General Electric, AT&T, Whirlpool, Quaker Oats, Eli Lily, Georgia-Pacific, Polaroid, Sprint, Teledyne, and Tenneco have adopted MVA and/or EVA as the best yardstick for corporate performance. According to Sprint's CFO, Art Krause, "Unlike EPS, which measures accounting results, MVA gauges true economic performance."[9]

Economic value added (EVA) has become an extremely popular shareholder value method of measuring corporate and divisional performance and may be on its way to replacing ROI as the standard performance measure. EVA measures the difference between the pre-strategy and post-strategy value for the business. Simply put, EVA is after-tax operating profit minus the total annual cost of capital.

- The annual cost of borrowed capital is the interest charged by the firm's banks and bondholders.

- To calculate the cost of equity, assume that shareholders generally earn about 6% more on stocks than on government bonds. If long-term treasury bills are selling at 7.5%, the firm's cost of equity should be 13.5%—more if the firm is in a risky industry. *A corporation's overall cost of capital is the weighted-average cost of the firm's debt and equity capital.*

- Total the amount of capital invested in the business, including buildings, machines, computers, and investments in R&D and training (allocating costs annually over their useful life).

- Multiply the firm's total capital by the weighted-average cost of capital.

- Compare that figure to pretax operating earnings. If the difference is positive, the strategy (and the management employing it) is generating value for the shareholders. If it is negative, the strategy is destroying shareholder value. [10]

Roberto Goizueta, CEO of Coca Cola, explains, "We raise capital to make concentrate, and sell it at an operating profit. Then we pay the cost of that capital. Shareholders pocket the difference."[11] Unlike ROI, ROE, or ROS, one of EVA's most powerful properties is its strong relationship to stock price.[12] Managers can improve their company's or business unit's EVA by: (1) earning more profit without using more capital, (2) using less capital, and (3) investing capital in high-return projects.

Market value added (MVA) measures the stock market's estimate of the net present value of a firm's past and expected capital investment projects. To calculate MVA,

1. First add all the capital that has been put into a company—from shareholders, bondholders, and retained earnings.

2. Reclassify certain accounting expenses, such as R&D, to reflect that they are actually investments in future earnings. This provides the firm's total capital. So far, this is the same approach taken in calculating EVA.

3. Using the current stock price, total the value of all outstanding stock, adding it to the company's debt. This is the company's market value. If the company's market value is greater than all the capital invested in it, the firm has a positive MVA— meaning that management (and the strategy it is following) has created wealth. In some cases, however, the market value of the company is actually less than the capital put into it—shareholder wealth is being destroyed.

Coca-Cola and General Electric tend to have the highest MVAs. In 1993, IBM had the lowest MVA of 200 large U.S. firms—a negative $23.7 billion. In 1995, that honor went to General Motors with a negative MVA of $17,803 billion. Studies have shown that EVA is a predictor of MVA. Consecutive years of positive EVA generally lead to a soaring MVA.[13] Research also reveals that CEO turnover is significantly correlated with MVA and EVA, whereas ROA and ROE are not. This suggests that EVA and MVA are more appropriate measures of the market's evaluation of a firm's strategy and its management than are the traditional measures of corporate performance.[14]

Balanced Scorecard Approach: Using Key Performance Measures

Rather than evaluate a corporation using a few financial measures, Kaplan and Norton argue for a "balanced scorecard," including nonfinancial as well as financial measures.[15]

The **balanced scorecard** combines financial measures that tell the results of actions already taken with operational measures on customer satisfaction, internal processes, and the corporation's innovation and improvement activities—the drivers of future financial performance. Management should develop goals or objectives in each of four areas:

1. **Financial:** How do we appear to shareholders?

2. **Customer:** How do customers view us?

3. **Internal Business Perspective:** What must we excel at?

4. **Innovation and Learning:** Can we continue to improve and create value?

Each goal in each area (for example, avoiding bankruptcy in the financial area) is then assigned one or more measures, as well as a target and an initiative. These measures can be thought of as **key performance measures**—measures that are essential for achieving a desired strategic option.[16] For example, a company could include cash flow, quarterly sales growth, and ROE as measures for success in the financial area. It could include market share (competitive position goal) and percentage of new sales coming from new products (customer acceptance goal) as measures under the customer perspective. It could include cycle time and unit cost (manufacturing excellence goal) as measures under the internal business perspective. It could include time to develop next generation products (technology leadership objective) under the innovation and learning perspective.

Evaluating Top Management

Through its strategy, audit, and compensation committees, a board of directors closely evaluates the job performance of the CEO and the top management team. Of course, it is concerned primarily with overall corporate profitability as measured quantitatively by return on investment, return on equity, earnings per share, and shareholder value. The absence of short-run profitability certainly contributes to the firing of any CEO. The board, however, is also concerned with other factors.

Members of the compensation committees of today's boards of directors generally agree that a CEO's ability to establish strategic direction, build a management team, and provide leadership are more critical in the long run than are a few quantitative measures. The board should evaluate top management not only on the typical output-oriented quantitative measures, but also on behavioral measures–factors relating to its strategic management practices. Unfortunately it is estimated that less than 30% of companies systematically evaluate their CEO's performance.[17]

The specific items that a board uses to evaluate its top management should be derived from the objectives that both the board and top management agreed on earlier. If better relations with the local community and improved safety practices in work areas were selected as objectives for the year (or for five years), these items should be included in the evaluation. In addition, other factors that tend to lead to profitability might be included, such as market share, product quality, or investment intensity.

Management audits are very useful to boards of directors in evaluating management's handling of various corporate activities. Management audits have been developed to evaluate activities such as corporate social responsibility, functional areas such as the marketing department, and divisions such as the international division, as well as to evaluate the corporation itself in a strategic audit. The strategic audit is explained in detail later in this chapter.

Primary Measures of Divisional and Functional Performance

Companies use a variety of techniques to evaluate and control performance in divisions, SBUs, and functional areas. If a corporation is composed of SBUs or divisions, it will use many of the same performance measures (ROI or EVA, for instance) that it uses to assess overall corporate performance. To the extent that it can isolate specific functional units such as R&D, the corporation may develop responsibility centers. It will also use typical functional measures such as market share and sales per employee (marketing), unit costs and percentage of defects (operations), percentage of sales from new products and number of patents (R&D), and turnover and job satisfaction (HRM).

During strategy formulation and implementation, top management approves a series of programs and supporting **operating budgets** from its business units. During evaluation and control, actual expenses are contrasted with planned expenditures and the degree of variance is assessed. This is typically done on a monthly basis. In addition, top management will probably require **periodic statistical reports** summarizing data on such key factors as the number of new customer contracts, volume of received orders, and productivity figures.

Responsibility Centers

Control systems can be established to monitor specific functions, projects, or divisions. Budgets are one type of control system that is typically used to control the financial indicators of performance. **Responsibility centers** are used to isolate a unit so that it can be evaluated separately from the rest of the corporation. Each responsibility center, therefore, has its own budget and is evaluated on its use of budgeted resources. It is headed by the manager responsible for the center's performance. The center uses resources (measured in terms of costs or expenses) to produce a service or a product (measured in terms of volume or revenues). There are five major types of responsibility centers. The type is determined by the way the corporation's control system measures these resources and services or products.

1. **Standard cost centers.** Primarily used in manufacturing facilities, standard (or expected) costs are computed for each operation on the basis of historical data. In evaluating the center's performance, its total standard costs are multiplied by the units produced. The result is the expected cost of production, which is then compared to the actual cost of production.

2. **Revenue centers.** Production, usually in terms of unit or dollar sales, is measured without consideration of resource costs (for example, salaries). The center is thus judged in terms of effectiveness rather than efficiency. The effectiveness of a sales region, for example, is determined by comparing its actual sales to its projected or previous year's sales. Profits are not considered because sales departments have very limited influence over the cost of the products they sell.

3. **Expense centers.** Resources are measured in dollars without consideration for service or product costs. Thus budgets will have been prepared for *engineered* expenses (those costs that can be calculated) and for *discretionary* expenses (those costs that can be only estimated). Typical expense centers are administrative, service, and research departments. They cost an organization money, but they only indirectly contribute to revenues.

4. **Profit centers.** Performance is measured in terms of the difference between revenues (which measure production) and expenditures (which measure resources). A

profit center is typically established whenever an organizational unit has control over both its resources and its products or services. By having such centers, a company can be organized into divisions of separate product lines. The manager of each division is given autonomy to the extent that she or he is able to keep profits at a satisfactory (or better) level.

Some organizational units that are not usually considered potentially autonomous can, for the purpose of profit center evaluations, be made so. A manufacturing department, for example, can be converted from a standard cost center (or expense center) into a profit center: it is allowed to charge a **transfer price** for each product it "sells" to the sales department. The difference between the manufacturing cost per unit and the agreed-upon transfer price is the unit's "profit."

Transfer pricing is commonly used in vertically integrated corporations and can work well when a price can be easily determined for a designated amount of product. Even though most experts agree that market-based transfer prices are the best choice, only 30%–40% of companies use market price to set the transfer price. (Of the rest, 50% use cost; 10%–20% use negotiation.)[18] When a price cannot be set easily, however, the relative bargaining power of the centers, rather than strategic considerations, tends to influence the agreed-upon price. Top management has an obligation to make sure that these political considerations do not overwhelm the strategic ones. Otherwise, profit figures for each center will be biased and provide poor information for strategic decisions at both corporate and divisional levels.

5. **Investment centers.** Because many divisions in large manufacturing corporations use significant assets to make their products, their asset base should be factored into their performance evaluation. Thus it is insufficient to focus only on profits, as in the case of profit centers. An investment center's performance is measured in terms of the difference between its resources and its services or products. For example, two divisions in a corporation made identical profits, but one division owns a $3 million plant, whereas the other owns a $1 million plant. Both make the same profits, but one is obviously more efficient: the smaller plant provides the shareholders with a better return on their investment. The most widely used measure of investment center performance is return on investment (ROI).

Most single-business corporations, such as Apple Computer, tend to use a combination of cost, expense, and revenue centers. In these corporations, most managers are functional specialists and manage against a budget. Total profitability is integrated at the corporate level. Multidivisional corporations with one dominating product line, such as Anheuser-Busch, which have diversified into a few businesses but which still depend on a single product line (such as beer) for most of their revenue and income, generally use a combination of cost, expense, revenue, plus profit centers. Multidivisional corporations, such as General Electric, tend to emphasize investment centers—although in various units throughout the corporation other types of responsibility centers are also used. One problem with using responsibility centers, however, is that the separation needed to measure and evaluate a division's performance can diminish the level of cooperation among divisions that is needed to attain synergy for the corporation as a whole. (This problem is discussed later in this chapter under "Suboptimization.")

Using Benchmarking to Evaluate Performance

According to Xerox Corporation, the company that pioneered this concept in the United States, **benchmarking** is "the continual process of measuring products, services, and practices against the toughest competitors or those companies recognized as industry leaders."[19] Benchmarking, an increasingly popular program, is based on the concept that it makes no sense to reinvent something that someone else is already using. It involves openly learning how others do something better than one's own company so that one not only can imitate, but perhaps even improve on their current techniques. The benchmarking process usually involves the following steps:

- **Identify the area or process to be examined.** It should be an activity that has the potential to determine a business unit's competitive advantage.

- **Find behavioral and output measures of the area or process and obtain measurements.**

- **Select an accessible set of competitors and best-in-class companies against which to benchmark.** These may very often be companies that are in completely different industries, but perform similar activities. For example, when Xerox wanted to improve its order fulfillment, it went to L. L. Bean, the successful mail order firm, to learn how it achieved excellence in this area.

- **Calculate the differences among the company's performance measurements and those of the best-in-class and determine** *why* **the differences exist.**

- **Develop tactical programs for closing performance gaps**.

- **Implement the programs and then compare the resulting new measurements with those of the best-in-class companies.**

Benchmarking has been found to produce best results in companies that are already well managed. Apparently poorer performing firms tend to be overwhelmed by the discrepancy between their performance and the benchmark—and tend to view the benchmark as too difficult to reach.[20] Nevertheless, a recent survey by Bain & Company of 460 companies of various sizes across all U.S. industries indicated that over 70% were using benchmarking in either a major or limited manner.[21] Manco, Inc., a small Cleveland-area producer of duct tape regularly benchmarks itself against Wal-Mart, Rubbermaid, and Pepsico to enable it to better compete with giant 3M. The American Productivity & Quality Center, a Houston research group, recently established a "best practices database" of 600 leading techniques from 250 companies.[22] See the **Strategy in a Changing World** feature to see how Seitz Corporation used benchmarking to implement its turnaround strategy.

International Measurement Issues

The three most widely used techniques for international performance evaluation are *return on investment*, *budget analysis*, and *historical comparisons*. In one study, 95% of the corporate officers interviewed stated that they use the same evaluation techniques for foreign and domestic operations. Rate of return was mentioned as the single most important measure.[23] However, ROI can cause problems when it is applied to international operations: Because of foreign currencies, different rates of inflation, different tax laws, and the use of transfer pricing, both the net income figure and the investment base may be seriously distorted.[24]

A study of 79 MNCs revealed that **international transfer pricing** from one country unit to another is primarily used *not* to evaluate performance, but to minimize taxes.[25] For example, the U.S. Internal Revenue Service contends that many Japanese firms doing business in the United States artificially inflate the value of U.S. deliveries in order to

STRATEGY IN A CHANGING WORLD

SEITZ CORPORATION USES BENCHMARKING IN STRATEGY IMPLEMENTATION

Seitz Corporation of Torrington, Connecticut, was a family-owned company that grew from a garage-based tool shop into a major supplier of the gears and bearings that circulate paper in copiers and dot matrix printers. By the mid 1980s, however, laser and ink jet printers were starting to replace dot matrix printers. Seitz was forced to lay off all but 80 employees as sales dropped significantly. Facing greater losses, management embarked on a major overhaul, using benchmarking. After first identifying the firms and the activities for study, they proceeded to adopt several of the practices that were examined. Among the measures incorporated were techniques to re-

duce new-product-to-market cycle time and just-in-time manufacturing. Cycle time was reduced from around nine weeks to three weeks. The use of just-in-time cut inventories—thus increasing floor space by 30%. With these and other improvements, Seitz's annual revenue reached a record $21 million by 1992 and employment climbed back to 190 people. Seitz's management group agreed that benchmarking had been key in implementing its turnaround strategy.

_____

Source: H. Rothman, "You Need Not Be Big to Benchmark," _Nation's Business_ (December 1992), p. 64.

reduce the profits and thus the taxes of their American subsidiaries.[26] Parts made in a subsidiary of a Japanese MNC in a low-tax country like Singapore can be shipped to its subsidiary in a high-tax country like the U.S. at such a high price that the U.S. subsidiary reports very little profit (and thus pays few taxes), while the Singapore subsidiary reports a very high profit (but also pays few taxes because of the lower tax rate). A Japanese MNC can, therefore, earn more profit worldwide by reporting less profit in high-tax countries and more profit in low-tax countries. Transfer pricing is an important factor, given that 56% of all trade in the triad and one-third of all international trade is composed of intercompany transactions.[27] Transfer pricing can thus be one way the parent company can reduce taxes and "capture profits" from a subsidiary. Other common ways of transferring profits to the parent company (often referred to as the **repatriation of profits**) are through dividends, royalties, and management fees.[28]

Transfer pricing and the repatriation of profits are complicated by constantly fluctuating currency exchange rates among nations. To make it easier for goods, services, and profits to move easily across the national borders of its member nations, the European Union is attempting to form a new economic and monetary union by 1998. The goal is to have one common currency, the _euro_, managed by a central bank. To be a part of this economic and monetary union, European Union members must meet four convergence criteria:

1. Government debt no larger than 60% of a country's GDP.

2. Government deficit no greater than 3% of GDP.

3. An inflation rate not exceeding 3.1%.

4. Government bonds yielding 8.5%.[29]

See the 🌐 **21st Century Global Society** feature to see how well each country was meeting the criteria in 1997.

Authorities in international business recommend that the control and reward systems used by a global MNC be different from those used by a multidomestic MNC.[30]

21ST CENTURY GLOBAL SOCIETY

EUROPEAN UNION'S PROBLEMS WITH FORMING A SINGLE CURRENCY

In the 1992 Maastricht treaty, the members of the European Union agreed to form an economic and monetary union in which there would be one currency, the euro, managed by a central bank. A single currency would allow goods, services, and profits to move easily across the national borders of the Union's member nations. To be a part of this economic and monetary union, members agreed to meet four criteria by 1998:

1. government debt no larger than 60% of a country's GDP;

2. government deficit no greater than 3% of GDP;

3. an inflation rate not exceeding 3.1%; and

4. government bonds yielding 8.5%. The following table shows how well each member country was meeting these criteria in 1997.

Only one member country (Luxembourg) in 1997 seemed able to meet all of these standards. Even Germany, the traditional economic powerhouse of Europe, was in difficulty. Some of the member countries were considering the exclusion of Italy and other Mediterranean countries until 2001 or 2002 because of their poor recent economic history. Spain, Portugal, and Italy were, however, in no mood to accept such a delay. It seemed likely that the move to a single European currency might be delayed until the end of the century.

Source: Table taken from "A Little EMU Enlightenment," *The Economist* (February 22, 1997), p. 88. Reprinted by permission. Other information from "Sweating for That Euro," *The Economist* (February 15, 1997), pp. 45–46.

	Govt Debt as % of GDP	Govt Deficit as % of GDP	Inflation Rate %	Govt Bond Yield %
Criteria[1]	no greater than 60	no greater than 3.0	no greater than 3.1	no greater than 8.5
Luxembourg	7	1.2	1.9	5.6
Austria	74	3.0	2.2	5.9
Belgium	127	3.0	1.5	6.7
Britain	59	4.0	2.8	8.3
Denmark	70	0.5	2.5	7.8
Finland	62	2.5	1.4	7.0
France	58	3.7	2.0	5.8
Ireland	80	2.8	3.0	7.4
Netherlands	78	2.4	2.3	5.8
Sweden	80	2.8	2.4	8.2
Germany	62	3.4	2.0	5.7
Portugal	72	3.5	2.8	8.0
Spain	70	3.5	3.0	8.0
Italy	125	4.3	3.0	8.8
Greece	108	6.2	7.5	13.0

Note:
1. Shaded areas indicate where criteria are not currently met.

The *multidomestic MNC* should use loose controls on its foreign units. The management of each geographic unit should be given considerable operational latitude, but it should be expected to meet some performance targets. Because profit and ROI measures are often unreliable in international operations, it is recommended that the MNC's top management, in this instance, emphasize budgets and nonfinancial measures of performance such as market share, productivity, public image, employee morale, and relations with the host country government.[31] Multiple measures should be used to differentiate between the worth of the subsidiary and the performance of its management.

The *global MNC*, however, needs tight controls over its many units. To reduce costs and gain competitive advantage, it is trying to spread the manufacturing and marketing operations of a few fairly uniform products around the world. Therefore, its key operational decisions must be centralized. Its environmental scanning must include research not only into each of the national markets in which the MNC competes, but also into the "global arena" of the interaction between markets. Foreign units are thus evaluated more as cost centers, revenue centers, or expense centers than as investment or profit centers because MNCs operating in a global industry do not often make the entire product in the country in which it is sold.

10.3 Strategic Information Systems

Before performance measures can have any impact on strategic management, they must first be communicated to those people responsible for formulating and implementing strategic plans. Strategic information systems can perform this function. They can be computer-based or manual, formal or informal. One of the key reasons given for the bankruptcy of International Harvester was the inability of the corporation's top management to precisely determine its income by major class of similar products. Because of this inability, management kept trying to fix ailing businesses and was unable to respond flexibly to major changes and unexpected events. In contrast, one of the key reasons for the success of Toys "R" Us has been management's use of the company's sophisticated information system to control purchasing decisions. Cash registers in the 300-plus U.S. Toys "R" Us stores transmit information daily to computers at the company's headquarters. Consequently managers know every morning exactly how many of each item have been sold the day before, how many have been sold so far in the year, and how this year's sales compare to last year's. The information system allows all reordering to be done automatically by computers without any managerial input. It also allows the company to experiment with new toys without committing to big orders in advance. In effect, the system allows the customers to decide through their purchases what gets reordered.

Multinational corporations are adopting a complex software system called R/3 from the German company SAP AG. The **R/3 software system** integrates and automates order taking, credit checking, payment verification, and book balancing. Because of R/3's ability to use a common information system throughout a company's many operations around the world, it is becoming the business information systems' global standard. Microsoft, for example, is using R/3 to replace a tangle of 33 financial tracking systems in 26 subsidiaries. Even though it cost the company $25 million and took 10 months to install, R/3 annually saves Microsoft $18 million. Coca Cola uses the R/3 system to enable a manager in Atlanta to use her personal computer to check the latest sales of 20-ounce bottles of Coke Classic in India. Owens-Corning envisions that its R/3 system will allow sales people to learn what is available at any plant or warehouse and to quickly assemble orders for customers.

R/3 is, nevertheless, not for every company. The system is extremely complicated and demands a high level of standardization throughout a corporation. Its demanding nature often forces companies to change the way they do business. Over the two-year period of installing R/3, Owens-Corning had to completely overhaul its operations. Because R/3 was incompatible with Apple Computer's very organic corporate culture, the company was only able to apply it to its order management and financial operations, but not to manufacturing. Dell Computer canceled its R/3 project after the installation budget reached $150 million and the system was still unable to handle Dell's sales volume.[32]

At the divisional or SBU level of a corporation, the information system should be used to support, reinforce, or enlarge its business-level strategy through its decision support system. An SBU pursuing a strategy of *overall cost leadership* could use its information system to reduce costs either by improving labor productivity or improving the use of other resources such as inventory or machinery. Merrill Lynch took this approach when it developed PRISM software to provide its 500 U.S. retail offices with quick access to financial information in order to boost brokers' efficiency. Another SBU, in contrast, might want to pursue a *differentiation* strategy. It could use its information system to add uniqueness to the product or service and contribute to quality, service, or image through the functional areas. Federal Express wanted to use superior service to gain a competitive advantage. It invested significantly in several types of information systems to measure and track the performance of its delivery service. Together, these information systems gave Federal Express the fastest error-response time in the overnight delivery business.

Increasingly, corporations are connecting their internal information networks (intranets) to other firms via "extranets" to implement strategic decisions and monitor their results. For example, Chicago-based Navistar no longer maintains a tire-and-rim inventory at its Springfield, Ohio, truck assembly plant. That responsibility is now being handled electronically by Goodyear Tire & Rubber, one of Navistar's suppliers. A Goodyear office in New York receives Navistar's manufacturing schedule and tire-and-rim requirements by electronic data interchange. The information is then sent to a Goodyear plant in Ohio where tires are mounted on rims. The completed assemblies are shipped to Navistar's Springfield plant—arriving just eight hours ahead of when they are needed.[33]

10.4   Problems in Measuring Performance

The measurement of performance is a crucial part of evaluation and control. The lack of quantifiable objectives or performance standards and the inability of the information system to provide timely and valid information are two obvious control problems. Without objective and timely measurements, it would be extremely difficult to make operational, let alone strategic, decisions. Nevertheless, the use of timely, quantifiable standards does not guarantee good performance. The very act of monitoring and measuring performance can cause side effects that interfere with overall corporate performance. Among the most frequent negative side effects are a short-term orientation and goal displacement.

Short-Term Orientation

Top executives report that in many situations they analyze *neither* the long-term implications of present operations on the strategy they have adopted *nor* the operational impact of a strategy on the corporate mission. Long-run evaluations are often not conducted because executives (1) don't realize their importance, (2) believe that short-run considerations are more important than long-run considerations, (3) aren't personally evaluated on a long-term basis, or (4) don't have the time to make a long-run analysis. [34] There is no real justification for the first and last "reasons." If executives realize the importance of long-run evaluations, they make the time needed to conduct them. Even though many chief executives point to immediate pressures from the investment community and to short-term incentive and promotion plans to support the second and third reasons, evidence does not always support their claims. [35]

Nevertheless, there are times when the stock market does not value a particular strategic investment. See the **Company Spotlight on Maytag Corporation** feature for the response of the investment community to Maytag's acquisition and subsequent divestiture of Hoover (in terms of Maytag's stock market price).

Many accounting-based measures do, however, encourage a **short-term orientation**. Table 10.1 indicates that one of the limitations of ROI as a performance measure is its short-term nature. In theory, ROI is not limited to the short run, but in practice it is often difficult to use this measure to realize long-term benefits for the company. Because managers can often manipulate both the numerator (earnings) and the denominator (investment), the resulting ROI figure can be meaningless. Advertising, maintenance, and research efforts can be reduced. Mergers can be undertaken that will do more for this year's earnings (and next year's paycheck) than for the division's or corporation's future profits. (Research of 55 firms that engaged in major acquisitions revealed that even though the firms performed poorly after the acquisition, the acquiring firms' top management still received significant increases in compensation!) [36] Expensive retooling and plant modernization can be delayed as long as a manager can manipulate figures on production defects and absenteeism.

Goal Displacement

Monitoring and measuring of performance (if not carefully done) can actually result in a decline in overall corporate performance. **Goal displacement** is the confusion of means with ends and occurs when activities originally intended to help managers attain corporate objectives become ends in themselves—or are adapted to meet ends other than those for which they were intended. Two types of goal displacement are behavior substitution and suboptimization.

Behavior Substitution

Behavior substitution refers to a phenomenon when people substitute activities that do not lead to goal accomplishment for activities that do lead to goal accomplishment because the wrong activities are being rewarded. Managers, like most people, tend to focus more of their attention on those behaviors that are clearly measurable than on those that are not. Employees often receive little to no reward for engaging in hard-to-measure activities such as cooperation and initiative. However, easy-to-measure activities might have little to no relationship to the desired good performance. Rational people, nevertheless, tend to work for the rewards that the system has to offer. Therefore, people tend to substitute behaviors that are recognized and rewarded for those behaviors that are ignored, without regard to their contribution to goal accomplishment. A U.S. Navy quip sums up this situation: "What you inspect (or reward) is what you get." In 1992, Sears, Roebuck & Co. thought that it would improve employee productivity by tying performance to rewards. It, therefore, paid commissions to its auto shop employees as a percentage of each repair bill. Behavior substitution resulted as employees altered their behavior to fit the reward system. The result was overbilled customers, charges for work never done, and a scandal that tarnished Sears' reputation. [37]

The law governing the effect of measurement on behavior seems to be that *quantifiable measures drive out nonquantifiable measures.*

COMPANY SPOTLIGHT

**The Impact
of Hoover
on Maytag's
Financial
Performance**

When Maytag Corporation purchased Hoover for its international appliance business, Maytag's debt soared to $923 million from $134 million just nine months earlier. Maytag's total outstanding shares swelled to 105 million from 75 million during the same time period. Interest payments leaped to $70 million in 1989 from $20 million the year before.

The corporation no longer had the best profit margin in the industry. Return on equity had been over 25% before the Magic Chef merger in 1986, peaked at over 30% in 1988, and was nearly halved to 18.3% in 1989 after the Hoover acquisition. By 1991, Maytag was earning just 8% on equity. In 1992, for the first time since the 1920s, the company showed a net loss. The stock price had dropped from $26.50 per share in 1988 to $13 in 1993. Shareholders were extremely unhappy with the company's performance and stated their feelings in the 1993 annual meeting. One angry stockholder asked CEO Leonard Hadley (who was conducting the meeting): *"How long will it be before earnings get back to the 1988 level of $1.77 per share from continuing operations? And along with that,"* he added, *"why should we have any confidence in your answer, given the performance of the past five years?"*

Even though Maytag showed a profit in 1994, the stock price only rose to around $15 a share—far below the $29 per share that one financial analyst thought it was worth.

Some investment analysts thought the corporation might soon be forced to sell Hoover or have no choice but to sell out to a competitor by the end of the decade.

Maytag finally decided to divest its Australian operations in December 1994 and its Hoover Europe operations in May 1995. In retrospect, management was forced to admit that Maytag had paid far too much for a very marginal European business. Neither the Australian nor the European operations had provided any profits until recently—and then only relatively small amounts. Selling off the overseas operations had meant big after-tax book losses and meant that Maytag reported another loss in 1995. The sales had, however, provided the cash for the corporation to reduce its heavy debt load. As a result, Maytag's stock price rose to $19 per share by February 1996. Financial analysts realized that without the various write-offs, the corporation would have shown a healthy profit in 1995. Nevertheless, Maytag's stock price continued to fluctuate around $20 per share throughout 1996—lower than what many analysts thought the corporation might actually be worth.

**MAYTAG
CORPORATION**

Suboptimization

Suboptimization refers to the phenomenon when a unit optimizes its goal accomplishment to the detriment of the organization as a whole. The emphasis in large corporations on developing separate responsibility centers can create some problems for the corporation as a whole. To the extent that a division or functional unit views itself as a separate entity, it might refuse to cooperate with other units or divisions in the same corporation if cooperation could in some way negatively affect its performance evaluation. The competition between divisions to achieve a high ROI can result in one division's refusal to share its new technology or work process improvements. One division's attempt to optimize the accomplishment of its goals can cause other divisions to fall behind and thus negatively affect overall corporate performance. One common example of suboptimization occurs when a marketing department approves an early shipment date to a customer as a means of getting an order and forces the manufacturing department into overtime production for this one order. Production costs are raised, which reduces the manufacturing department's overall efficiency. The end result might be that, although marketing achieves its sales goal, the corporation as a whole fails to achieve its expected profitability.

10.5 Guidelines for Proper Control

In designing a control system, top management should remember that *controls should follow strategy*. Unless controls ensure the use of the proper strategy to achieve objectives, there is a strong likelihood that dysfunctional side effects will completely undermine the implementation of the objectives. The following guidelines are recommended:

1. **Control should involve only the minimum amount of information** needed to give a reliable picture of events. Too many controls create confusion. Focus on the **critical success factors**: *those 20% of the factors that determine 80% of the results*.

2. **Controls should monitor only meaningful activities and results**, regardless of measurement difficulty. If cooperation between divisions is important to corporate performance, some form of qualitative or quantitative measure should be established to monitor cooperation.

3. **Controls should be timely** so that corrective action can be taken before it is too late. Steering controls, controls that monitor or measure the factors influencing performance, should be stressed so that advance notice of problems is given.

4. **Long-term and short-term controls should be used.** If only short-term measures are emphasized, a short-term managerial orientation is likely.

5. **Controls should aim at pinpointing exceptions.** Only those activities or results that fall outside a predetermined tolerance range should call for action.

6. **Emphasize the reward of meeting or exceeding standards** rather than punishment for failing to meet standards. Heavy punishment of failure typically results in goal displacement. Managers will "fudge" reports and lobby for lower standards.

To the extent that the culture complements and reinforces the strategic orientation of the firm, there is less need for an extensive formal control system. In their book *In Search of Excellence*, Peters and Waterman state that "the stronger the culture and the more it was directed toward the marketplace, the less need was there for policy manuals, organization charts, or detailed procedures and rules. In these companies, people way down the line know what they are supposed to do in most situations because the handful of guiding values is crystal clear."[38] The **Strategy in a Changing World** feature illustrates how the corporate culture at Southwest Airlines enabled the company to achieve its strategic objectives without a lot of detailed rules, regulations, and costly reporting procedures.

10.6 Strategic Incentive Management

To ensure congruence between the needs of the corporation as a whole and the needs of the employees as individuals, management and the board of directors should develop an incentive program that rewards desired performance. This reduces the likelihood of *agency problems* (when employees act to feather their own nest instead of

SOUTHWEST AIRLINES' CORPORATE CULTURE MAKES CONTROL EASIER

What is the secret behind Southwest Airlines's highly productive workforce that enables the company to achieve its low-cost competitive strategy even when it is expanding across the United States? Instead of using a lot of rules and inspectors, it uses corporate culture to ensure quality low-cost performance.

Colleen Barrett, the No. 2 executive at Southwest Airlines, is the keeper of the corporate culture. Though the airline doubled in size from 1991 to 1995, Barrett has devised ways to preserve Southwest's small company work ethic and its "can-do" spirit. Personifying the "empowerment" concept, Barrett gives employees freedom from centralized policies and constantly reinforces the message that employees should be treated like customers. She celebrates workers who go above and beyond the call of duty.

According to Barrett, job applicants are often misled by Southwest's zany reputation. "People get this image—fun, different, party place, Herb's (Founder and CEO Herb Kellehher) half nuts," she explains. "We have to remind them first and foremost, you have to work." Finding young, industrious workers who fit Southwest's culture is so difficult that the company interviews 50 applicants for every open position.

Fearing that the company might be losing its small company, underdog spirit, Barrett formed a culture committee. When Southwest was having problems with workers at its Los Angeles International Airport station, the culture committee swung into action. It dispatched employees to fill in for local supervisors so the supervisors could address morale and efficiency problems. That station is now considered one of Southwest's most efficient.

Barrett believes that building loyalty builds better performance. Employees are well paid compared to other airlines. Celebrations, ranging from spontaneous "fun sessions" to Christmas parties, are an important part of work. At the same time, employees are expected to work harder than their counterparts at other airlines. This approach has enabled Southwest to avoid the bureaucracy and mediocrity that develop in companies that have outgrown their entrepreneurial roots.

Source: S. McCartney, "Airline Industry's Top-Ranked Woman Keeps Southwest's Small-Fry Spirit Alive," *Wall Street Journal* (November 30, 1995), pp. B1–B2.

building shareholder value) mentioned earlier in Chapter 2. Incentive plans should be linked in some way to corporate and divisional strategy. For example, a survey of 600 business units indicates that the pay mix associated with a growth strategy emphasizes bonuses and other incentives over salary and benefits, whereas the pay mix associated with a stability strategy has the reverse emphasis.[39] Research does indicate that SBU managers having long-term performance elements in their compensation program favor a long-term perspective and thus greater investments in R&D, capital equipment, and employee training.[40]

The following three approaches are tailored to help match measurements and rewards with explicit strategic objectives and timeframes. [41]

1. **Weighted-factor method.** This method is particularly appropriate for measuring and rewarding the performance of top SBU managers and group level executives when performance factors and their importance vary from one SBU to another. One corporation's measurements might contain the following variations: the performance of high-growth SBUs is measured in terms of market share, sales growth, designated future payoff, and progress on several future-oriented strategic projects; the

Table 10.3   Weighted-Factor Approach to Strategic Incentive Management

Strategic Business Unit Category	Factor	Weight
High Growth	Return on assets	10%
	Cash flow	0%
	Strategic-funds programs (developmental expenses)	45%
	Market-share increase	45%
		100%
Medium Growth	Return on assets	25%
	Cash flow	25%
	Strategic-funds programs (developmental expenses)	25%
	Market-share increase	25%
		100%
Low Growth	Return on assets	50%
	Cash flow	50%
	Strategic-funds programs (developmental expenses)	0%
	Market-share increase	0%
		100%

Source: Reprinted by permission of the publisher from "The Performance Measurement and Reward System: Critical to Strategic Management," by Paul J. Stonich, from *Organizational Dynamics* (Winter 1984), p. 51. Copyright © 1984 by American Management Association, New York. All rights reserved.

performance of low-growth SBUs, in contrast, is measured in terms of ROI and cash generation; and the performance of medium-growth SBUs is measured for a combination of these factors. (Refer to Table 10.3.)

2. **Long-term evaluation method.** This method compensates managers for achieving objectives set over a multiyear period. An executive is promised some company stock or "performance units" (convertible into money) in amounts to be based on long-term performance. An executive committee, for example, might set a particular objective in terms of growth in earnings per share during a five-year period. The giving of awards would be contingent on the corporation's meeting that objective within the designated time. Any executive who leaves the corporation before the objective is met receives nothing. The typical emphasis on stock price makes this approach more applicable to top management than to business unit managers.

3. **Strategic-funds method.** This method encourages executives to look at developmental expenses as being different from expenses required for current operations. The accounting statement for a corporate unit enters strategic funds as a separate entry below the current ROI. It is, therefore, possible to distinguish between those expense dollars consumed in the generation of current revenues and those invested in the future of the business. Therefore, the manager can be evaluated on both a short- and a long-term basis and has an incentive to invest strategic funds in the future. (See Table 10.4.)

An effective way to achieve the desired strategic results through a reward system is to combine the three approaches:

1. Segregate strategic funds from short-term funds, as is done in the strategic-funds method.

Table 10.4   **Strategic-Funds Approach to an SBU's Profit-and-Loss Statement**

Sales	$12,300,000
Cost of sales	−6,900,000
Gross margin	$ 5,400,000
General and administrative expenses	−3,700,000
Operating profit (return on sales)	$ 1,700,000
Strategic funds (development expenses)	−1,000,000
Pretax profit	$ 700,000

Source: Reprinted by permission of the publisher from "The Performance Measurement and Reward System: Critical to Strategic Management," by Paul J. Stonich, from *Organizational Dynamics* (Winter 1984), p. 51. Copyright © 1984 by American Management Association, New York. All rights reserved.

2. Develop a weighted-factor chart for each SBU.

3. Measure performance on three bases: The pretax profit indicted by the strategic-funds approach, the weighted factors, and the long-term evaluation of the SBUs' and the corporation's performance.

General Electric and Westinghouse are two firms using a version of these measures.

10.7   *Using the Strategic Audit to Evaluate Corporate Performance*

The **strategic audit** provides a checklist of questions, by area or issue, that enables a systematic analysis of various corporate functions and activities to be made. (See Table 10.5.) It is a type of management audit and is extremely useful as a diagnostic tool to pinpoint corporatewide problem areas and to highlight organizational strengths and weaknesses.[42] The strategic audit can help determine why a certain area is creating problems for a corporation and help generate solutions to the problem.

The strategic audit is not an all-inclusive list, but it presents many of the critical questions needed for a detailed strategic analysis of any business corporation. Some questions or even some areas might be inappropriate for a particular company; in other cases, the questions may be insufficient for a complete analysis. However, each question in a particular area of the strategic audit can be broken down into an additional series of subquestions. Develop these subquestions when they are needed.

The strategic audit summarizes the key topics in the Strategic Management Model discussed in Chapters 1 through 10. As you look through the major headings of the audit in Table 10.5, note that it identifies by chapter, section, and page numbers where information about each topic can be found.

The strategic audit puts into action the strategic decision-making process illustrated in Figure 1.5 on pages 20-21. The headings in the audit are the same as those shown in Figure 1.5:

1. Evaluate current performance results

2. Review corporate governance

3. Scan and assess the *external* environment

4. Scan and assess the *internal* environment

5. Analyze strategic factors using SWOT

6. Generate and evaluate strategic alternatives

7. Implement strategies

8. Evaluate and control

Table 10.5 **Strategic Audit of a Corporation**

I. Current Situation

A. Current Performance   See Section 10.2 on pages 234–238.

How did the corporation perform the past year overall in terms of return on investment, market share, and profitability?

B. Strategic Posture   See Section 1.3 on pages 10–14.

What are the corporation's current mission, objectives, strategies, and policies?

1. Are they clearly stated or are they merely implied from performance?

2. **Mission:** What business(es) is the corporation in? Why?

3. **Objectives:** What are the corporate, business, and functional objectives? Are they consistent with each other, with the mission, and with the internal and external environments?

4. **Strategies:** What strategy or mix of strategies is the corporation following? Are they consistent with each other, with the mission and objectives, and with the internal and external environments?

5. **Policies:** What are they? Are they consistent with each other, with the mission, objectives, and strategies, and with the internal and external environments?

6. Do the current mission, objectives, strategies, and policies reflect the corporation's international operations—whether global or multidomestic?

II. Corporate Governance

A. Board of Directors   See Section 2.1 on pages 26–35.

1. Who are they? Are they internal or external?

2. Do they own significant shares of stock?

3. Is the stock privately held or publicly traded? Are there different classes of stock with different voting rights?

4. What do they contribute to the corporation in terms of knowledge, skills, background, and connections? If the corporation has international operations, do board members have international experience?

5. How long have they served on the board?

6. What is their level of involvement in strategic management? Do they merely rubber-stamp top management's proposals or do they actively participate and suggest future directions?

Source: T. L. Wheelen and J. D. Hunger, "Strategic Audit of a Corporation." Copyright © 1982 by Wheelen and Hunger Associates. Reprinted by permission. Revised 1988, 1991, 1994, and 1997.

Table 10.5   **Strategic Audit of a Corporation** *(continued)*

B. Top Management   See Sections 2.2 to 2.4 on pages 35–48.

1. What person or group constitutes top management?

2. What are top management's chief characteristics in terms of knowledge, skills, background, and style? If the corporation has international operations, does top management have international experience? Are executives from acquired companies considered part of the top management team?

3. Has top management been responsible for the corporation's performance over the past few years? How many managers have been in their current position for less than 3 years? Were they internal promotions or external hires?

4. Has it established a systematic approach to strategic management?

5. What is its level of involvement in the strategic management process?

6. How well does top management interact with lower level managers and with the board of directors?

7. Are strategic decisions made ethically in a socially responsible manner?

8. Is top management sufficiently skilled to cope with likely future challenges?

III. External Environment: Opportunities and Threats (SW**OT**)

A. Societal Environment   See Section 3.1 on pages 53–60.

1. What general environmental forces are currently affecting both the corporation and the industries in which it competes? Which present current or future threats? Opportunities? *See Table 3.1 on page 55.*

    a) Economic
    b) Technological
    c) Political-legal
    d) Sociocultural

2. Are these forces different in other regions of the world?

B. Task Environment   See Section 3.2 on pages 60–72.

1. What forces drive industry competition? Are these forces the same globally or do they vary from country to country?

    a) Threat of new entrants
    b) Bargaining power of buyers
    c) Threat of substitute products or services
    d) Bargaining power of suppliers
    e) Rivalry among competing firms
    f) Relative power of unions, governments, special interest groups, etc.

2. What key factors in the immediate environment (that is, customers, competitors, suppliers, creditors, labor unions, governments, trade associations, interest groups, local communities, and shareholders) are currently affecting the corporation? Which are current or future threats? Opportunities?

Table 10.5   **Strategic Audit of a Corporation** (continued)

C. Summary of External Factors   See EFAS Table on pages 75–76.

Which of these forces and factors are the most important to the corporation and to the industries in which it competes at the present time? Which will be important in the future?

IV. Internal Environment: Strengths and Weaknesses (**SW**OT)

A. Corporate Structure   See Sections 4.3 and 8.4 on pages 87–89 and 192–197.

1. How is the corporation structured at present?

   a) Is the decision-making authority centralized around one group or decentralized to many units?
   b) Is it organized on the basis of functions, projects, geography, or some combination of these?

2. Is the structure clearly understood by everyone in the corporation?

3. Is the present structure consistent with current corporate objectives, strategies, policies, and programs as well as with the firm's international operations?

4. In what ways does this structure compare with those of similar corporations?

B. Corporate Culture   See Section 4.3 on pages 89–90.

1. Is there a well-defined or emerging culture composed of shared beliefs, expectations, and values?

2. Is the culture consistent with the current objectives, strategies, policies, and programs?

3. What is the culture's position on important issues facing the corporation (that is, on productivity, quality of performance, adaptability to changing conditions, and internationalization)?

4 Is the culture compatible with the employees' diversity of backgrounds?

5. Does the company take into consideration the values of each nation's culture in which the firm operates?

C. Corporate Resources

1. Marketing   See Section 4.3 on pages 90–91.

a) What are the corporation's current marketing objectives, strategies, policies, and programs?

   i) Are they clearly stated, or merely implied from performance and/or budgets?
   ii) Are they consistent with the corporation's mission, objectives, strategies, policies, and with internal and external environments?

b) How well is the corporation performing in terms of analysis of market position and marketing mix (that is, product, price, place, and promotion) in both domestic and international markets? What percentage of sales comes from foreign operations?

   i) What trends emerge from this analysis?
   ii) What impact have these trends had on past performance and how will they probably affect future performance?
   iii) Does this analysis support the corporation's past and pending strategic decisions?
   iv) Does marketing provide the company with a competitive advantage?

Table 10.5   **Strategic Audit of a Corporation** (continued)

c) How well does this corporation's marketing performance compare with that of similar corporations?

d) Are marketing managers using accepted marketing concepts and techniques to evaluate and improve product performance? (Consider product life cycle, market segmentation, market research, and product portfolios.)

e) Does marketing adjust to the conditions in each country in which it operates?

f) What is the role of the marketing manager in the strategic management process?

2. Finance   *See Sections 4.3 and 14.3 on pages 91–93 and 320–326.*

a) What are the corporation's current financial objectives, strategies, policies, and programs?

  i) Are they clearly stated or merely implied from performance and/or budgets?

  ii) Are they consistent with the corporation's mission, objectives, strategies, policies, and with internal and external environments?

b) How well is the corporation performing in terms of financial analysis? (Consider ratios, common size statements, and capitalization structure.)

  i)   What trends emerge from this analysis?

  ii) Are there any significant differences when statements are calculated in constant versus reported dollars?

  iii) What impact have these trends had on past performance and how will they probably affect future performance?

  iv) Does this analysis support the corporation's past and pending strategic decisions?

  v)   Does finance provide the company with a competitive advantage?

c) How well does this corporation's financial performance compare with that of similar corporations?

d) Are financial managers using accepted financial concepts and techniques to evaluate and improve current corporate and divisional performance? (Consider financial leverage, capital budgeting, ratio analysis, and managing foreign currencies.)

e) Does finance adjust to the conditions in each country in which the company operates?

f) What is the role of the financial manager in the strategic management process?

3. Research and Development (R&D)   *See Section 4.3 on pages 93–96.*

a) What are the corporation's current R&D objectives, strategies, policies, and programs?

  i)   Are they clearly stated, or merely implied from performance and/or budgets?

  ii) Are they consistent with the corporation's mission, objectives, strategies, policies, and with internal and external environments?

  iii) What is the role of technology in corporate performance?

  iv) Is the mix of basic, applied, and engineering research appropriate given the corporate mission and strategies?

  v)   Does R&D provide the company with a competitive advantage?

b) What return is the corporation receiving from its investment in R&D?

c) Is the corporation competent in technology transfer? Does it use concurrent engineering and cross-functional work teams in product and process design?

d) What role does technological discontinuity play in the company's products?

e) How well does the corporation's investment in R&D compare with the investments of similar corporations?

f) Does R&D adjust to the conditions in each country in which the company operates?

g) What is the role of the R&D manager in the strategic management process?

Table 10.5 **Strategic Audit of a Corporation** (continued)

4. Operations and Logistics See Section 4.3 on pages 96–98.

a) What are the corporation's current manufacturing/service objectives, strategies, policies, and programs?

   i) Are they clearly stated, or merely implied from performance and/or budgets?

   ii) Are they consistent with the corporation's mission, objectives, strategies, policies, and with internal and external environments?

b) What is the type and extent of operations capabilities of the corporation? How much is done domestically versus internationally? Is the amount of outsourcing appropriate to be competitive? Is purchasing being handled appropriately?

   i) If product-oriented, consider plant facilities, type of manufacturing system (continuous mass production, intermittent job shop, or flexible manufacturing), age and type of equipment, degree and role of automation and/or robots, plant capacities and utilization, productivity ratings, availability and type of transportation.

   ii) If service-oriented, consider service facilities (hospital, theater, or school buildings), type of operations systems (continuous service over time to same clientele or intermittent service over time to varied clientele), age and type of supporting equipment, degree and role of automation and/or use of mass communication devices (diagnostic machinery, videotape machines), facility capacities and utilization rates, efficiency ratings of professional/service personnel, availability and type of transportation to bring service staff and clientele together.

c) Are manufacturing or service facilities vulnerable to natural disasters, local or national strikes, reduction or limitation of resources from suppliers, substantial cost increases of materials, or nationalization by governments?

d) Is there an appropriate mix of people and machines, in manufacturing firms, or of support staff to professionals, in service firms?

e) How well does the corporation perform relative to the competition? Is it balancing inventory costs (warehousing) with logistical costs (just-in-time)? Consider costs per unit of labor, material, and overhead; downtime; inventory control management and/or scheduling of service staff; production ratings; facility utilization percentages; and number of clients successfully treated by category (if service firm) or percentage of orders shipped on time (if product firm).

   i) What trends emerge from this analysis?

   ii) What impact have these trends had on past performance and how will they probably affect future performance?

   iii) Does this analysis support the corporation's past and pending strategic decisions?

   iv) Does operations provide the company with a competitive advantage?

f) Are operations managers using appropriate concepts and techniques to evaluate and improve current performance? Consider cost systems, quality control and reliability systems, inventory control management, personnel scheduling, TQM, learning curves, safety programs, and engineering programs that can improve efficiency of manufacturing or of service.

g) Does operations adjust to the conditions in each country in which it has facilities?

h) What is the role of the operations manager in the strategic management process?

5. Human Resources Management (HRM) See Section 4.3 on pages 98–100.

a) What are the corporation's current HRM objectives, strategies, policies, and programs?

   i) Are they clearly stated, or merely implied from performance and/or budgets?

Table 10.5 **Strategic Audit of a Corporation** *(continued)*

---

    ii) Are they consistent with the corporation's mission, objectives, strategies, policies, and with internal and external environments?

b) How well is the corporation's HRM performing in terms of improving the fit between the individual employee and the job? Consider turnover, grievances, strikes, layoffs, employee training, and quality of work life.

    i)   What trends emerge from this analysis?
    ii) What impact have these trends had on past performance and how will they probably affect future performance?
    iii) Does this analysis support the corporation's past and pending strategic decisions?
    iv) Does HRM provide the company with a competitive advantage?

c) How does this corporation's HRM performance compare with that of similar corporations?

d) Are HRM managers using appropriate concepts and techniques to evaluate and improve corporate performance? Consider the job analysis program, performance appraisal system, up-to-date job descriptions, training and development programs, attitude surveys, job design programs, quality of relationship with unions, and use of autonomous work teams.

e) How well is the company managing the diversity of its workforce?

f) Does HRM adjust to the conditions in each country in which the company operates? Does the company have a code of conduct for HRM in developing nations? Are employees receiving international assignments to prepare them for managerial positions?

g) What is the role of the HRM manager in the strategic management process?

6. Information Systems (IS)   *See Section 4.3 on page 100.*

a) What are the corporation's current IS objectives, strategies, policies, and programs?

    i)   Are they clearly stated, or merely implied from performance and/or budgets?
    ii) Are they consistent with the corporation's mission, objectives, strategies, policies, and with internal and external environments?

b) How well is the corporation's IS performing in terms of providing a useful database, automating routine clerical operations, assisting managers in making routine decisions, and providing information necessary for strategic decisions?

    i)   What trends emerge from this analysis?
    ii) What impact have these trends had on past performance and how will they probably affect future performance?
    iii) Does this analysis support the corporation's past and pending strategic decisions?
    iv) Does IS provide the company with a competitive advantage?

c) How does this corporation's IS performance and stage of development compare with that of similar corporations?

d) Are IS managers using appropriate concepts and techniques to evaluate and improve corporate performance? Do they know how to build and manage a complex database, conduct system analyses, and implement interactive decision-support systems?

e) Does the company have a global IS? Does it have difficulty with getting data across national boundaries?

f) What is the role of the IS manager in the strategic management process?

D. Summary of Internal Factors   *See IFAS Table on pages 101–102.*

Which of these factors are the most important to the corporation and to the industries in which it competes at the present time? Which will be important in the future?

Table 10.5   **Strategic Audit of a Corporation** (*continued*)

V. Analysis of Strategic Factors (SWOT)   See Sections 5.1 and 5.2 on pages 107–111.

A. Situational Analysis   See SFAS Table on pages 108–110.

What are the most important internal and external factors (**Strengths, Weaknesses, Opportunities, Threats**) that strongly affect the corporation's present and future performance? List five to ten *strategic factors*.

B. Review of Mission and Objectives   See Section 5.2 on page 111.

1. Are the current mission and objectives appropriate in light of the key strategic factors and problems?

2. Should the mission and objectives be changed? If so, how?

3. If changed, what will the effects on the firm be?

VI. Strategic Alternatives and Recommended Strategy

A. Strategic Alternatives   See Sections 5.3, 5.4, 6.2, and 7.1 on pages 111–129, 133–147 and 162–170.

1. Can the current or revised objectives be met by the simple, more careful implementing of those strategies presently in use (for example, fine-tuning the strategies)?

2. What are the major feasible alternative strategies available to this corporation? What are the pros and cons of each? Can corporate scenarios be developed and agreed upon?
   a) Consider *cost leadership* and *differentiation* as business strategies.
   b) Consider *stability, growth,* and *retrenchment* as corporate strategies.
   c) Consider any functional strategic alternatives that might be needed for reinforcement of an important corporate or business strategic alternative.

B. Recommended Strategy   See Sections 7.3 and 7.4 on pages 171–177.

1. Specify which of the strategic alternatives you are recommending for the corporate, business, and functional levels of the corporation. Do you recommend different business or functional strategies for different units of the corporation?

2. Justify your recommendation in terms of its ability to resolve both long- and short-term problems and effectively deal with the strategic factors.

3. What **policies** should be developed or revised to guide effective implementation?

VII. Implementation   See Chapters 8 and 9.

A. What kinds of **programs** (for example, restructuring the corporation or instituting TQM) should be developed to implement the recommended strategy?

Table 10.5   **Strategic Audit of a Corporation** (continued)

 1. Who should develop these programs?

 2. Who should be in charge of these programs?

B. Are the programs financially feasible? Can pro forma **budgets** be developed and agreed upon? Are priorities and timetables appropriate to individual programs?

C. Will new standard operating **procedures** need to be developed?

VIII. Evaluation and Control   *See Chapter 10.*

A. Is the current information system capable of providing sufficient feedback on implementation activities and performance? Can it measure *critical success factors*?

 1. Can performance results be pinpointed by area, unit, project, or function?

 2. Is the information timely?

B. Are adequate control measures in place to ensure conformance with the recommended strategic plan?

 1. Are appropriate standards and measures being used?

 2. Are reward systems capable of recognizing and rewarding good performance?

10.8   Global Issues for the 21st Century

- The **21st Century Global Society** feature in this chapter illustrates how difficult it is for a regional trading bloc to form a single currency for its member countries. Although the reality of the euro may be delayed until the turn of the century, its inevitable appearance may serve as an impetus to other trading blocs, such as NAFTA, to also move to a single currency among member nations.

- The International Standards Organization is going beyond ISO 9000 to develop ISO 14000, which focuses on environmental standards. Given the high level of environmental concern in the developed nations, this set of standards may eventually rival ISO 9000 in its global impact on business activities.

- The balanced scorecard approach to evaluating performance is increasingly being accepted by corporations. One benefit of this approach is its emphasis on evaluating the ability of the corporation to learn from its experience, especially in international activities. Given that "what you inspect is what you get," the balanced scorecard should help improve the learning capabilities of organizations.

- Activity-based costing (ABC) supports value-chain analysis by identifying the value provided by each step in a firm's value chain of activities. A clear understanding of each activity's or function's value can help in outsourcing decisions. As more industries become global, firms will need ABC to evaluate the efficiency of their operations in different parts of the world.

- The continuing evolution of European, American, and Asian trade blocs means that companies will need to have a presence in each bloc in order to be internationally competitive and to avoid customs duties. Given that at least one-third of all international trade takes place internally among individual units of multinational corporations, transfer pricing will continue to be a contentious issue for most countries and most multinational corporations.

Projections for the 21st Century

- From 1994 to 2010, the number of miles traveled by air will double from 1.5 trillion to 3 trillion.

- From 1994 to 2010, the number of credit card transactions will increase from 1.5 trillion to 2 trillion.[43]

Discussion Questions

1. Is Figure 10.1 a realistic model of the evaluation and control process?

2. What are some examples of behavior controls? Output controls?

3. Is EVA an improvement over ROI, ROE, or EPS?

4. How much faith can a manager place in a transfer price as a substitute for a market price in measuring a profit center's performance?

5. Is the evaluation and control process appropriate for a corporation that emphasizes creativity? Are control and creativity compatible?

Key Terms

activity-based costing (ABC) (p. 233)
balanced scorecard (p. 238)
behavior controls (p. 231)
behavior substitution (p. 246)
benchmarking (p. 240)
critical success factors (p. 248)
earnings per share (EPS) (p. 235)
economic value added (EVA) (p. 236)
evaluation and control information (p. 230)
evaluation and control process (p. 230)

goal displacement (p. 246)
international transfer pricing (p. 241)
ISO 9000 Standards Series (p. 233)
key performance measures (p. 238)
long-term evaluation method (p. 250)
management audits (p. 238)
market value added (MVA) (p. 237)
operating budgets (p. 239)
output controls (p. 232)
performance (p. 231)
periodic statistical reports (p. 239)
R/3 software system (p. 244)

repatriation of profits (p. 242)
responsibility centers (p. 239)
return on equity (ROE) (p. 235)
return on investment (ROI) (p. 234)
shareholder value (p. 235)
short-term orientation (p. 246)
stakeholder measures (p. 235)
steering controls (p. 231)
strategic audit (p. 251)
strategic-funds method (p. 250)
suboptimization (p. 247)
tolerance range (p. 230)
transfer prices (p. 240)
weighted-factor method (p. 249)

Strategic Practice Exercise

Have you ever heard a person say that something "was built like a Mack truck?" The Mack name and bulldog mascot are among the most recognized trademarks in the world. As recently as 1980, Mack held more than 20% of the North American heavy-duty truck market and employed 17,000 people. By the late 1980s, however, its well-known slogan was beginning to ring hollow. Market share dipped to 13% in 1989 and employment fell to 6,500 people. The company lost $185 million in that year—followed by four more years of losses. According to Elios Pascual, Chairman, President, and Chief Executive Officer of Mack Trucks Inc., of Allentown, Pennsylvania, "Our quality was suffering, but we didn't know how badly because we weren't really measuring it. Our pride had deteriorated into an arrogance that blinded us to the severity of the situation." What had happened to such a well-known and previously successful company?

In analyzing the situation, Chairman Pascual felt that the most important reason for this drop was the disappearance of the kind of teamwork that had built the company. "Mack had become tied into a segregated, departmental organization that discouraged people from talking to one another. The disconnection and frustration were apparent everywhere—from suppliers to employees." Coordination processes fell

apart. For example, some 1,200 partially assembled trucks at the company's Winnsboro, South Carolina, plant had to be parked in nearby fields while the plant waited for needed parts. Relations with labor (represented by the United Auto Workers union) became so bad that when the new general manager of Mack's Macungie, Pennsylvania, assembly plant visited the operation in 1990, an angry employee threw a bolt at him!

Pascual reported, "By 1991 the company was hovering near bankruptcy and we needed teamwork more than ever. It was at that point that we decided that unless we got everyone involved in the game, it would soon be over."[44]

1. What could have been some of the causes of the problems at Mack Trucks?

2. If you were the CEO of Mack Trucks in 1991, what would you do to improve the situation and stop the string of losses?

Notes

1. P. B. Carroll, "The Failures of Central Planning—at IBM," *Wall Street Journal* (January 28, 1993), p. A14.
2. D. Pickton, M. Starkey, and M. Bradford, "Understand Business Variation for Improved Business Performance," *Long Range Planning* (June 1996), pp. 412–415.
3. A. M. Hormozi, "Understanding and Implementing ISO 9000: A Manager's Guide," *SAM Advanced Management Journal* (Autumn 1995), pp. 4–11.
4. J. K. Shank, and V. Govindarajan, *Strategic Cost Management* (New York: The Free Press, 1993).
5. T. P. Pare, "A New Tool For Managing Costs," *Fortune* (June 14, 1993), pp. 124–129.
6. T. R. V. Davis, and B. L. Darling, "ABC in a Virtual Corporation," *Management Accounting* (October 1996), pp. 18–26.
7. C. K. Brancato, *New Corporate Performance Measures* (New York: The Conference Board, 1995).
8. C. D. Ittner, D. F. Larcker, and M. V. Rajan, "The Choice of Performance Measures in Annual Bonus Contracts," Working paper reported by K. Z. Andrews in "Executive Bonuses," *Harvard Business Review* (January–February 1996), pp. 8–9.
9. S. Tully, "America's Best Wealth Creators," *Fortune* (November 28, 1994), p. 143.
10. G. B. Stewart III, "EVA Works—But Not If You Make These Common Mistakes," *Fortune* (May 1, 1995), pp. 117–118.
11. S. Tully, "The Real Key to Creating Wealth," *Fortune* (September 20, 1993), p. 38.
12. K. Lehn, and A. K. Makhija, "EVA & MVA As Performance Measures and Signals for Strategic Change," *Strategy & Leadership* (May/June 1996), pp. 34–38.

13. A. B. Fisher, "Creating Stockholder Wealth: Market Value Added," *Fortune* (December 11, 1995), pp. 105–116.
14. Lehn and Makhija, p. 37.
15. R. S. Kaplan, and D. P. Norton, "Using the Balanced Scorecard as a Strategic Management System," *Harvard Business Review* (January–February 1996), pp. 75–85; R. S. Kaplan, and D. P. Norton, "The Balanced Scorecard—Measures That Drive Performance," *Harvard Business Review* (January–February, 1992), pp. 71–79.
16. C. K. Brancato, *New Performance Measures* (New York: The Conference Board, 1995).
17. J. S. Lublin, "Corporate Chiefs Polish Their Relations with Directors," *Wall Street Journal* (October 15, 1993), p. B1.
18. Z. U. Khan, S. K. Chawla, M. F. Smith, and M. F. Sharif, "Transfer Pricing Policy Issues in Europe 1992," *International Journal of Management* (September 1992), pp. 230–241.
19. H. Rothman, "You Need Not Be Big to Benchmark," *Nation's Business* (December 1992), p. 64.
20. C. W. Von Bergen, and B. Soper, "A Problem With Benchmarking: Using Shaping as a Solution," *SAM Advanced Management Journal* (Autumn 1995), pp. 16–19.
21. "Tool Usage Rates," *Journal of Business Strategy* (March/April 1995), p. 12.
22. G. Fuchsberg, "Here's Help in Finding Corporate Role Models," *Wall Street Journal* (June 1, 1993), p. B1.
23. S. M. Robbins, and R. B. Stobaugh, "The Bent Measuring Stick for Foreign Subsidiaries," *Harvard Business Review* (September–October 1973), p. 82.
24. J. D. Daniels, and L. H. Radebaugh, *International Business*, 5th ed. (Reading, Mass.: Addison-Wesley, 1989), pp. 673–674.

25. W. A. Johnson, and R. J. Kirsch, "International Transfer Pricing and Decision Making in United States Multinationals," *International Journal of Management* (June 1991), pp. 554–561.

26. "Fixing the Bottom Line," *Time* (November 23, 1992), p. 20.

27. T. A. Stewart, "The New Face of American Power," *Fortune* (July 26, 1993), p. 72; G. P. Zachary, "Behind Stocks' Surge Is an Economy in Which Big U.S. Firms Thrive," *Wall Street Journal* (November 22, 1995), pp. A1, A5.

28. J. M. L. Poon, R. Ainuddin, and H. Affrim, "Management Policies and Practices of American, British, European, and Japanese Subsidiaries in Malaysia: A Comparative Study," *International Journal of Management* (December 1990), pp. 467–474.

29. "A Little EMU Enlightenment," *The Economist* (February 22, 1997), p. 88.

30. C. W. L. Hill, P. Hwang, and W. C. Kim, "An Eclectic Theory of the Choice of International Entry Mode," *Strategic Management Journal* (February 1990), pp. 117–128; D. Lei, J. W. Slocum, Jr., and R. W. Slater, "Global Strategy and Reward Systems: The Key Roles of Management Development and Corporate Culture," *Organizational Dynamics* (Autumn 1990), pp. 27–41; W. R. Fannin, and A. F. Rodriques, "National or Global?—Control vs. Flexibility," *Long Range Planning* (October 1986), pp. 84–188.

31. A. V. Phatak, *International Dimensions of Management,* 2nd ed. (Boston: Kent, 1989), pp. 155–157.

32. J. B. White, D. Clark, and S. Ascarelli, "This German Software Is Complex, Expensive—and Wildly Popular," *Wall Street Journal* (March 14, 1997), pp. A1, A8.

33. B. Richards, "The Business Plan," *Wall Street Journal* (November 11, 1996), p. R10.

34. R. M. Hodgetts, and M. S. Wortman, *Administrative Policy,* 2nd ed. (New York: John Wiley and Sons, 1980), p. 128.

35. J. R. Wooldridge, and C. C. Snow, "Stock Market Reaction to Strategic Investment Decisions," *Strategic Management Journal* (September 1990), pp. 353–363.

36. D. R. Schmidt, and K. L. Fowler, "Post-Acquisition Financial Performance and Executive Compensation," *Strategic Management Journal* (November-December 1990), pp. 559–569.

37. W. Zellner, E. Schine, and G. Smith, "Trickle-Down Is Trickling Down at Work," *Business Week* (March 18, 1996), p. 34.

38. T. J. Peters, and R. H. Waterman, *In Search of Excellence* (New York: HarperCollins, 1982), pp. 75–76.

39. D. B. Balkin, and L. R. Gomez-Mejia, "Matching Compensation and Organizational Strategies," *Strategic Management Journal* (February 1990), pp. 153–169.

40. C. S. Galbraith, "The Effect of Compensation Programs and Structure on SBU Competitive Strategy: A Study of Technology-Intensive Firms," *Strategic Management Journal* (July 1991), pp. 353–370.

41. P. J. Stonich, "The Performance Measurement and Reward System: Critical to Strategic Management," *Organizational Dynamics* (Winter 1984), pp. 45–57.

42. G. Donaldson, "A New Tool for Boards: The Strategic Audit," *Harvard Business Review* (July-August 1995), pp. 99–107.

43. J. Warner, "21st Century Capitalism: Snapshot of the Next Century," *Business Week* (November 18, 1994), p. 194.

44. E. Pascual, "Mack Learns the Error of False Pride," *Wall Street Journal* (July 11, 1994), p. A10.

11

Strategic Issues in Managing Technology and Innovation

The DuPont Company has long been known for its excellence in basic corporate research. In the early 1990s, for example, it led the nation's chemical companies in patents applied for and granted. The company spent more than $13 billion on chemical and related research during the 1980s, but management admitted that the company failed to develop much in the way of major innovations. "They've been like the space program: the technology is great, but where's the payoff?" commented industry analyst John Garcia. CEO Edgar Woolard admitted that the company took too long to "convert research into products that can benefit our customers." In major established products, the company lost ground to competitors that spent more on improving manufacturing. Customers who wanted changes in Zytel nylon-resin products often had to wait six months for an answer. DuPont had become a secure place to work, said Woolard, but "we have too much bureaucracy running these businesses."

According to Joseph Miller, director of DuPont's polymers research, the emphasis in R&D was to find another "big bang" like its invention of nylon. As a result, the company introduced a series of new products—excellently designed, but rejected by the marketplace. Among them were Kevlar, stronger than steel, but too expensive for widespread usage; Corfam, a synthetic leather that didn't "breathe" and thus made shoes uncomfortable (costing DuPont $250 million); Qiana, a synthetic silk that was ignored because of increasing interest in natural fibers; plus many millions spent unsuccessfully on electronic imaging and pharmaceuticals. To focus "more intensity on customer needs," CEO Woolard announced that the company was shifting about 30% of its research budget (approximately $400 million annually) toward speeding new products to customers.[1]

This example from DuPont illustrates how a successful, established company can have difficulty in developing and marketing new products when it fails to make technology a part of its strategic management process. Companies that aren't knowledgeable about strategically managing technology and innovation have the potential to destroy the very capabilities that originally provided them with distinctive competence. In this chapter, we examine strategic issues in technology and innovation as they impact environmental scanning, strategy formulation, strategy implementation, and evaluation and control.

11.1   *Role of Management*

Due to increased competition and accelerated product development cycles, innovation and the management of technology is becoming crucial to corporate success. Approximately half the profits of all U.S. companies come from products launched in the previous 10 years.[2] What is less obvious is how a company can generate a significant return from investment in R&D as well as an overall sense of enthusiasm for innovative behavior and risk taking. One way is to include innovation in the corporation's mission statement. See the **Strategy in a Changing World** feature for some examples from well-known companies. Another way is by establishing policies that support the innovative process. For example, 3M has set a policy of generating at least 25% of its revenue from products introduced in the preceding three years. To support this policy, this $13 billion corporation annually spends nearly $1 billion.[3]

The importance of technology and innovation must be emphasized by people at the very top and reinforced by people throughout the corporation. If top management and the board are not interested in these topics, managers below them tend to echo their lack of interest. When Akio Morita, Chairman of Sony Corporation, visited the United Kingdom, he expressed disbelief at the number of accountants leading that country's companies. Uncomfortable because they lacked familiarity with science or technology, these top managers too often limited their role to approving next year's budget. Constrained by what the company could afford and guided by how much the competition was spending, they perceived R&D as a line expense item instead of as an investment in the future.[4]

Management has an obligation to not only encourage new product development, but also to develop a system to ensure that technology is being used most effectively with the consumer in mind. A study by Chicago consultants Kuczmarski & Associates of 11,000 new products marketed by 77 manufacturing, service, and consumer-product firms revealed that only 56% of all newly introduced products were still being sold five years later. Only one in 13 new product ideas ever made it into test markets. Although some authorities argue that this percentage of successful new products needs to be improved, others contend that too high a percentage means that a company isn't taking the risks necessary to develop a really new product.[5]

The importance of top management's providing appropriate direction is exemplified by Chairman Morita's statement of his philosophy for Sony Corporation:

> The key to success for Sony, and to everything in business, science, and technology for that matter, is never to follow the others. . . . Our basic concept has always been this—to give new convenience, or new methods, or new benefits, to the general public with our technology.

STRATEGY IN A CHANGING WORLD

EXAMPLES OF INNOVATION EMPHASIS IN MISSION STATEMENTS

To emphasize the importance of technology, creativity, and innovation to overall future corporate success, some well-known firms have added sections to this effect in their published mission statements. Some of these are listed here.

AT&T: "We believe innovation is the engine that will keep us vital and growing. Our culture embraces creativity, seeks different perspectives and risks pursuing new opportunities. We create and rapidly convert technology into products and services, constantly searching for new ways to make technology more useful to customers."

General Mills: "Innovation is the principal driver of growth. . . . To be first among our competitors, we must constantly challenge the status quo and be willing to experiment. . . . Our motivation system will strongly reward successful risk-taking, while not penalizing an innovative idea that did not work."

Gerber: "[The mission will be achieved by] investing in continued product and body-of-knowledge, innovation, and research in the areas of infant nutrition, care, and development."

Gillette: "We will invest in and master the key technologies vital to category success."

Hallmark: "[We believe] that creativity and quality—in our concept, products and services—are essential to our success."

Intel: "To succeed we must maintain our innovative environment. We strive to: embrace change, challenge the status quo, listen to all ideas and viewpoints, encourage and reward informed risk taking, and learn from our successes and mistakes."

Merck & Co.: "We are dedicated to achieving the highest level of scientific excellence and commit our research to maintaining human health and improving the quality of life."

Source: P. Jones and L. Kahaner, *Say It and Live It: The 50 Corporate Mission Statements That Hit the Mark* (New York: Currency Doubleday, 1995).

Morita and his co-founder, Masuru Ibuka, always looked for ways to turn ideas into clear targets. Says Morita, "When Ibuka was first describing his idea for the Betamax videocassette, he gave the engineers a paperback book and said, 'Make it this size.' Those were his only instructions."[6]

11.2 Environmental Scanning

External Scanning

Corporations need to continually scan their external societal and task environments for new developments in technology that may have some application to their current or potential products.

Technology Research

Motorola, a company well known for its ability to invest in profitable new technologies and manufacturing improvements, has a sophisticated scanning system. Its intelligence department monitors the latest technology developments introduced at scientific conferences, in journals, and in trade gossip. This information helps it build "technology roadmaps" that assess where breakthroughs are likely to occur, when they can be incorporated into new products, how much money their development will cost, and which of the developments is being worked on by the competition.[7]

Focusing one's scanning efforts too closely on one's own industry is dangerous. Most new developments that threaten existing business practices and technologies do not come from existing competitors or even from within traditional industries.[8] A new technology that can substitute for an existing technology at a lower cost and provide higher quality can change the very basis for competition in an industry. Consider, for example, the impact of Internet technology on the personal computer software industry. Microsoft Corporation had ignored the developing Internet technology while the company battled successfully with IBM, Lotus, and WordPerfect to dominate operating system software via Windows 95 as well as word processing and spreadsheet programs via Microsoft Office. Ironically, just as Microsoft introduced its new Windows 95 operating system, newcomer Netscape used Java applets in its user-friendly, graphically oriented browser program with the potential to make operating systems unnecessary. By the time Microsoft realized this threat to its business, Netscape had already established itself as the industry standard for browsers. Microsoft was forced to spend huge amounts of time and resources trying to catch up to Netscape's dominant market share with its own Internet Explorer browser.

Disadvantages of Market Research

Contrasted with **technology research** engaged in by Motorola and other companies, traditional **market research** may not always provide useful information on new product directions. According to Sony executive Kozo Ohsone, "When you introduce products that have never been invented before, what good is market research?" For example, Hal Sperlich took the concept of the minivan from Ford to Chrysler when Ford refused to develop the concept. According to Sperlich,

> [Ford] lacked confidence that a market existed because the product didn't exist. The auto industry places great value on historical studies of market segments. Well, we couldn't prove there was a market for the minivan because there was no historical segment to cite. In Detroit most product-development dollars are spent on modest improvements to existing products, and most market research money is spent on studying what customers like among available products. In ten years of developing the minivan we never once got a letter from a housewife asking us to invent one. To the skeptics, that proved there wasn't a market out there.[9]

A heavy emphasis on being customer-driven could actually prevent companies from developing innovative new products. A study of the impact of **technological discontinuity** (explained earlier in Chapter 4) in various industries revealed that the leading firms failed to switch to the new technology *not* because management was ignorant of the new development, but rather because they listened too closely to their current customers. In all of these firms, a key task of management was to decide which of the many product and development programs continually being proposed to them should receive financial resources. The criterion used for the decision was the total return perceived in each project, adjusted by the perceived riskiness of the project. Projects targeted at the known needs of key customers in established markets consistently won the most resources. Sophisticated systems for planning and compensation favored this type of project every time. As a result, the leading companies continued to use the established technology to make the products its current customers demanded, allowing smaller entrepreneurial competitors to develop the new, more risky technology.[10]

Because the market for the innovative products based on the new technology was fairly small at first, new ventures had time to fine-tune product design, build sufficient manufacturing capacity, and establish the product as the industry standard (as Netscape did with its Internet browser). As the marketplace began to embrace the new standard, the customers of the leading companies began to ask for products based on the new technology. Although some established manufacturers were able to defend their market share positions through aggressive product development and marketing activity (as Microsoft did against Netscape), many firms, finding that the new entrants had developed insurmountable advantages in manufacturing cost and design experience, were forced out of the market. Even the established manufacturers that converted to the new technology were unable to win a significant share of the new market.[11]

Instead of standard market research to test the potential of innovative products, some successful companies are using speed and flexibility to gain market information. These companies developed their products by "probing" potential markets with early versions of the products, learning from the probes, and probing again.[12] For example, Seiko's only market research is surprisingly simple. The company introduces hundreds of new models of watches into the marketplace. It makes more of the models that sell; it drops those that don't.

The consulting firm Arthur D. Little found that the use of standard market research techniques has only resulted in a success rate of 8% for new cereals—92% of all new cereals fail. As a result, innovative firms, such as Keebler and the leading cereal makers, are reducing their expenditures for market research and working to reduce the cost of launching new products by making their manufacturing processes more flexible.[13]

Internal Scanning

In addition to scanning the external environment, strategists should also assess their company's ability to innovate effectively by asking the following questions:

1. Has the company developed the resources needed to try new ideas?

2. Do the managers allow experimentation with new products or services?

3. Does the corporation encourage risk taking and tolerate mistakes?

4. Are people more concerned with new ideas or with defending their turf?

5. Is it easy to form autonomous project teams?[14]

In addition to answering these questions, strategists should assess how well company resources are internally allocated and evaluate the organization's ability to develop and transfer new technology in a timely manner into the generation of innovative products and services.

Resource Allocation Issues

The company must make available the resources necessary for effective research and development. Research indicates that a company's **R&D intensity** (its spending on R&D as a percentage of sales revenue) is a principal means of gaining market share in global competition.[15] The amount of money spent on R&D often varies by industry. For example, the computer software and drug industries spend an average of 11% to 13% of their sales dollar for R&D. Others, such as the food and the containers and packaging industries, spend less than 1%. A good rule of thumb for R&D spending is that a corporation should spend at a "normal" rate for that particular industry, unless its competitive strategy dictates otherwise.[16] Research indicates that consistency in R&D strategy and resource allocation across lines of business improves corporate performance by enabling the firm to better develop synergies among product lines and business units.[17]

Simply spending money on R&D or new projects does not, however, guarantee useful results. One study found that although large firms spent almost twice as much per R&D patent than did smaller firms, the smaller firms used more of their patents. The innovation rate of small businesses was 322 innovations per million employees versus 225 per million for large companies.[18] One explanation for this phenomenon is that large firms tend to spend development money to increase the efficiency of existing performance with a primary goal of reducing costs and downsizing. In contrast, small firms tend to apply technology to improving effectiveness with a goal of improving quality and customer satisfaction.[19] Other studies reveal that the maximum innovator in various industries often was the middle-sized firm. These firms were generally more effective and efficient in technology transfer. Very small firms often do not have sufficient resources to exploit new concepts, whereas the bureaucracy present in large firms rewards consistency over creativity.[20] From these studies, Hitt, Hoskisson, and Harrison propose the existence of an inverted U-shaped relationship between size and innovation. According to Hitt et al., "This suggests that organizations are flexible and responsive up to some threshold size but encounter inertia after that point."[21]

Sometimes most of the firms in an industry can waste their R&D spending. For example, between 1950 and 1979, the U.S. steel industry spent 20% more on plant maintenance and upgrading for each ton of production capacity added or replaced than did the Japanese steel industry. Nevertheless the top managements of U.S. steel firms failed to recognize and adopt two breakthroughs in steelmaking—the basic oxygen furnace and continuous casting. Their hesitancy to adopt new technology caused them to lose the world steel market.[22]

Time to Market Issues

In addition to money, another important consideration in the effective management of research and development is **time to market**. A decade ago, the time from inception to profitability of a specific R&D program was generally accepted to be 7 to 11 years. According to Karlheinz Kaske, CEO of Siemens AG, however, the time available to complete the cycle is getting shorter. Companies no longer can assume that competitors will allow them the number of years needed to recoup their investment. In the past, Kaske says, "ten to fifteen years went by before old products were replaced by new ones . . . now, it takes only four or five years."[23] Time to market is an important issue because *60% of patented innovations are generally imitated within four years at 65% of the cost of innovation.*[24] In the 1980s, Japanese auto manufacturers gained incredible competitive advantage over U.S. manufacturers by reducing new products' time to market to only three years. (U.S. auto companies needed five years.)[25]

Andy Grove, CEO of Intel, agrees with the increasing importance of time to market as a competitive weapon by stating, "Ultimately 'speed' is the only weapon we have." With $5 billion in annual sales, the company spends $1.2 billion a year on plant and equipment and $800 million on R&D. Intel is no longer content to introduce one or two new-generation microprocessors annually and a completely new family of computer microchips every four years. Previously Intel would introduce a new family of chips (such as the 386) only when the current market was sufficiently saturated with one family of chips (such as the 286). The advent of lower cost microprocessor clone manufacturers, such as Cyrix and AMD, meant that Intel had to give up the 386 market prematurely to focus on the emerging 486 market in 1992. The introduction of the Pentium (586 chip) microprocessor followed quickly in 1993, the Pentium Pro in 1995, and the Pentium II in

1997. Intel plans to continue developing new chip families every two years. Grove believes that this fast pace of development will keep chip cloners from ever catching up with Intel.[26]

11.3   Strategy Formulation

Research and development strategy deals not only with the decision to be a leader or a follower in terms of technology and market entry (discussed earlier in Chapter 7 under R&D strategy), but also with the source of the technology. Should a company develop its own technology or purchase it from others? The strategy also takes into account a company's particular mix of basic versus applied and product versus process R&D (discussed earlier in Chapter 4). The particular mix should suit the level of industry development and the firm's particular corporate and business strategies. The 🌐 **21st Century Global Society** feature illustrates how a company's competence in different aspects of R&D can affect its competitive strategy and its ability to successfully enter new markets. R&D strategy in a large corporation also deals with the proper balance of its product portfolio based on the life cycle of the products.

Product versus Process R&D

As illustrated in Figure 11.1, the proportion of product and process R&D tends to vary as a product moves along its life cycle. In the early stages, **product innovations** are most important because the product's physical attributes and capabilities most affect financial performance. Later, **process innovations** such as improved manufacturing facilities, increasing product quality, and faster distribution become important to maintaining the product's economic returns. Generally product R&D has been key to achieving differentiation strategies, whereas process R&D has been at the core of successful cost leadership strategies.

Historically, U.S. corporations have not been as skillful at process innovations as have German and Japanese companies. The primary reason has been a function of the amount of money invested in each form of R&D. U.S. firms spend, on the average, 70% of their R&D budgets on product R&D and only 30% on process R&D; German firms, 50% on each form; and Japanese firms, 30% on product and 70% on process R&D.[27] The emphasis by U.S. major home appliance manufacturers on process over product R&D may be one reason why they have such a strong position in the industry worldwide. (See the **Company Spotlight on Maytag Corporation** feature.)

Technology Sourcing

Technology sourcing, typically a make-or-buy decision, can be important in a firm's R&D strategy. Although in-house R&D has traditionally been an important source of technical knowledge for companies, firms can also tap the R&D capabilities of competitors, suppliers, and other organizations through contractual agreements (such as licensing, R&D agreements, and joint ventures). One example is Matsushita's licensing of Iomega's zip drive technology in 1996 so that Matshusita could also manufacture and sell removable cartridges for personal computers. When technological cycles were longer, a company was more likely to choose an independent R&D strategy not only because it gave the firm a longer lead time before competitors copied it, but also because it was more profitable in the long run. In today's world of shorter innovation life cycles and global competition, a company may no longer have the luxury of waiting to reap a long-term profit.

21ST CENTURY GLOBAL SOCIETY

THE IMPACT OF R&D ON COMPETITIVE ADVANTAGE IN CHINA

China is one of the ten largest economies in the world. Average income has tripled since 1978 for most rural people. Urban incomes have risen even faster, as the country's economy has grown at an annual rate of 9% in real terms for the past 15 years. As income increases, people are using it to improve their standard of living.

China is the world's fastest growing and potentially most profitable market for bathroom fixture manufacturers. Western-style toilets, which are easier to keep clean and use less water than the traditional Chinese fixtures, have become the standard in thousands of new apartment and office buildings. Two globally oriented companies attempting to dominate this lucrative market are American Standard of the United States and Toto Ltd. of Japan. Both design their products in their home country, manufacture them in Thailand using low-cost labor, and then ship the products to China for sale.

Product design has a significant impact on each company's competitive strategy in China. Toto has an advantage in one part of the design process because its designers in Japan use computers to generate models from blocks of foam. Engineering design is its distinctive competency. Blueprints can be in the hands of factory engineers in four weeks. In contrast, American Standard's process takes two months, on average. Models are crafted by hand by Jack Kaiser, an acknowledged design expert, and six associates. The personal touch is part of Standard's distinctive competency. Although the designers domi-

nate the process, they work closely with marketing and production to develop a product to suit consumers' needs. In contrast, Toto's engineers dominate the process—building for production, but limiting creativity and neglecting markets in other countries. This limits Toto's ability to successfully enter a new market with unusual needs.

Toto dominates the luxury bathroom market in China, but it has been slow to adapt to the fast-growing low end of the market. "To ask a Japanese engineer to make something cheaper is harder than to ask him to make something better," explained Thibault Danjou, a Toto marketing manager. American Standard has another advantage in its flexible manufacturing facility in Thailand. It only stocks 14 days' worth of inventory. Its production process is flexible enough to produce to order. Toto, in contrast, has a much more rigid production process and must keep two months' inventory on hand. American Standard can also fill odd size orders that Toto finds too difficult to fill. In selling new-style toilets to China, manufacturers must customize toilets to line up with existing sewage pipes. Selling close to half of the bathroom fixtures imported into China, American Standard is certainly cleaning up!

Source: S. Glain, "Top Toilet Makers from U.S. and Japan Vie for Chinese Market," *Wall Street Journal* (December 19, 1996), pp. A1, A11; "Deng's China: The Last Emperor," *The Economist* (February 22, 1997), pp. 21–25.

During a time of technological discontinuity in an industry, a company may have no choice but to purchase the new technology from others if it wants to remain competitive. For example, Ford Motor Company paid $100 million for 10.8% of the common stock of Cummins Engine Co., an expert in diesel engine technology. In return for its money, Ford got exclusive access to Cummins's truck engine technology. This allowed Ford to forgo the $300 million expense of designing a new engine on its own to meet U.S. emission standards.[28]

Firms that are unable to finance alone the huge costs of developing a new technology may coordinate their R&D with other firms through a **strategic alliance**. By the

Figure 11.1

Product and Process R&D in the Innovation Life Cycle

Source: Adapted from M. L. Patterson, "Lessons from the Assembly Line," *Journal of Business Strategy* (May/June 1993), p. 43. Permission granted by Faulkner & Gray, Eleven Penn Plaza, NY, NY 10001.

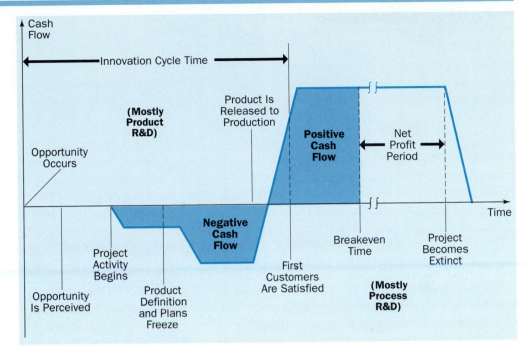

1990s, more than 150 cooperative alliances involving 1,000 companies were operating in the United States and many more were operating throughout Europe and Asia.[29] These alliances can be (a) *joint programs or contracts* to develop a new technology, (b) *joint ventures* establishing a separate company to take a new product to market, or (c) *minority investments* in innovative firms wherein the innovator obtains needed capital and the investor obtains access to valuable research. For example, Hewlett-Packard Company formed an alliance in 1996 with Microsoft, Oracle, and Netscape Communications to create an "electronic business framework" to bring together several Internet-related technologies. Some of their goals are to develop the remote installation and upgrading of software by network administrators, systems for secure electronic payments over the Internet, and integrate the Internet with telephone-based services such as telemarketing and customer service.

When should a company buy or license technology from others instead of developing it internally? Following the resource-based view of the firm discussed previously in Chapter 4, a company should *buy* technologies that are commonly available, but *make* (and protect) those that are rare, valuable, hard to imitate, and having no close substitutes. In addition, *outsourcing technology may be appropriate when:*

- The technology is of low significance to competitive advantage.
- The supplier has proprietary technology.
- The supplier's technology is better and/or cheaper and reasonably easy to integrate into the current system.
- The company's strategy is based on system design, marketing, distribution, and service—not on development and manufacturing.
- The technology development process requires special expertise.
- The technology development process requires new people and new resources.[30]

COMPANY SPOTLIGHT

Importance of Product and Process R&D in the Major Home Appliance Industry

Product innovation is being used in the major home appliance industry to provide consumers with new products as well as to add newer functions and features to existing products. The microwave oven was the last completely new product in this industry. Fuzzy logic technology is now being used to provide more effective, consumer-friendly appliances. Japanese appliance makers were the first to use this new technology to replace the many selector switches on an appliance with one start button. With fuzzy logic, a sophisticated set of electronic sensors and self-diagnostic software could measure the amount of detergent placed in a washing machine, check water temperature, gauge the amount of dirt on clothes, and decide not only how long the wash and rinse cycles should run, but also how vigorous the agitator should swish the water to get the clothes clean. By 1996, most major home appliance manufacturers had added fuzzy logic technology to top-end appliances in at least one of their product categories. Whirlpool added fuzzy logic to its VIP series of microwave ovens. Maytag did the same to its Intellisense™ line of dishwashers.

Process innovation for more efficient manufacturing of current products (as compared to new product development) has dominated research and development efforts in the U.S. major home appliance industry since the 1950s. Even though a refrigerator or a washing machine still looks and acts very much the same today as it did in the 1950s, it is built in a far different and more efficient manner. The components inside the appliances are being produced in highly automated plants using computer integrated manufacturing processes. An example of this emphasis on product simplification was Maytag's "Dependable Drive" washer transmission, which was designed to have 40.6% fewer parts than the transmission it replaced. Fewer parts meant simplified manufacturing and less chance of a breakdown. The result was lower manufacturing costs and higher product quality.

Most industry analysts agreed that continual process improvements have kept U.S. major home appliance manufacturers dominant in their industry. The emphasis on quality and durability, coupled with a reluctance to make major design changes simply for the sake of change, resulted in products with an average life expectancy of 20 years for refrigerators and 15 years for washers and dryers. Even though quality has improved significantly over the past 20 years, the average washer, dryer, and refrigerator cost no more than they did 20 years ago and yet last almost twice as long. If only the same could be said of the automobile industry!

Importance of Technological Competence

Firms that emphasize growth through acquisitions over internal development tend to be less innovative in the long run.[31] Research suggests that companies must have at least a minimal R&D capability if they are to correctly assess the value of technology developed by others. R&D creates a capacity in a firm to assimilate and exploit new knowledge. This is called a company's **absorptive capacity** and is a valuable by-product of routine in-house R&D activity.[32] Further, without this capacity, firms could become locked out in their ability to assimilate the technology at a later time.

Those corporations that do purchase an innovative technology must have the **technological competence** to make good use of it. Some companies that introduce the latest technology into their processes do not adequately assess the competence of their people to handle it. For example, a survey conducted in the United Kingdom found that 44% of all companies that started to use robots met with initial failure, and that 22% of these firms abandoned the use of robots altogether, mainly because of inadequate technological knowledge and skills.[33] One U.S. company built a new plant equipped with computer-integrated manufacturing and statistical process controls, but the employees could not operate the equipment because 25% of them were illiterate.[34]

Product Portfolio

Developed by Hofer and based on the product life cycle, the 15-cell **product/market evolution matrix** (shown in Figure 11.2) depicts the types of developing products that cannot be easily shown on other portfolio matrixes. Products are plotted in terms of their competitive positions and their stages of product/market evolution. As on the GE Business Screen, the circles represent the sizes of the industries involved, and the pie wedges represent the market shares of the firm's business product lines. Present and future matrixes can be developed to identify strategic issues. In response to Figure 11.2, for example, we could ask why product B does not have a greater share of the market, given its strong competitive position. We could also ask why the company only has one product in the developmental stage. A limitation of this matrix is that the product life cycle does not always hold for every product. Many products, for example, do not inevitably fall into decline but (like Tide detergent and Colgate toothpaste) are revitalized and put back on a growth track.

11.4   *Strategy Implementation*

If a corporation decides to develop innovations internally, it must make sure that its corporate system and culture are suitable for such a strategy. It must make sufficient resources available for new products, provide collaborative structures and processes, and incorporate innovation into its overall corporate strategy.[35] It must ensure that its R&D operations are managed appropriately. It must establish procedures to support all five **stages of new product development**. (See Table 11.1.) If, like most large corporations, the culture is too bureaucratic and rigid to support entrepreneurial projects, top management must reorganize so that innovative projects can be free to develop.

Developing an Innovative Entrepreneurial Culture

To create a more innovative corporation, top management must develop an entrepreneurial culture—one that is open to the transfer of new technology into company activities and products and services. The company must be flexible and accepting of change. It should include a willingness to withstand a certain percentage of product failures on the way to success. Such a culture has been noted in 3M Corporation and Texas Instruments, among others. Research and development in these companies is managed quite differently from traditional methods. First, employees are dedicated to a particular project outcome rather than to innovation in general. Second, employees are often responsible for all functional activities and for all phases of the innovation process. Time is allowed to be sacrificed from regular duties to spend on innovative ideas. If the ideas are feasible, employees are temporarily reassigned to help develop them. They may become project champions who fight for resources to make the project a success. Third, these internal ventures are often separated from the rest of the company to provide them with greater independence, freedom for short-term pressures, different rewards, improved visibility, and access to key decision makers.[36]

Figure 11.2
Product/Market Evolution Portfolio Matrix

Source: C. W. Hofer and D. Schendel, *Strategy Formulation: Analytical Concepts* (St. Paul, Minn,: West Publishing Co., 1978), p. 34. From C. W. Hofer, "Conceptual Constructs for Formulating Corporate and Business Strategies" (Dover, Mass.: Case Publishing), no. BP-0041, p. 3. Copyright © 1977 by Charles W. Hofer. Reprinted by permission.

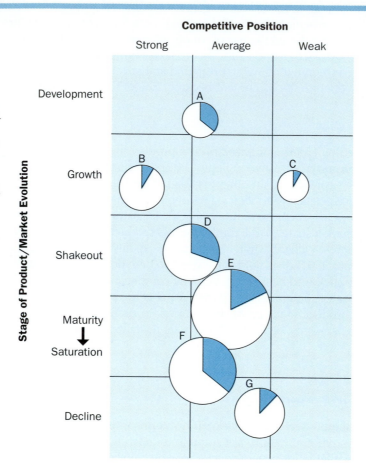

The innovative process often involves individuals at different organizational levels who fulfill three different types of entrepreneurial roles: product champion, sponsor, and orchestrator. A **product champion** is a person who generates a new idea and supports it through many organizational obstacles. A **sponsor** is usually a department manager who recognizes the value of the idea, helps obtain funding to develop the innovation, and facilitates its implementation. An **orchestrator** is someone in top management who articulates the need for innovation, provides funding for innovating activities, creates incentives for middle managers to sponsor new ideas, and protects idea/product champions from suspicious or jealous executives. Unless all of these roles are present in a company, major innovations are less likely to occur.[37]

Companies are finding that one way to overcome the barriers to successful product innovation is by using multifunctional teams with significant autonomy dedicated to a project. See the **Strategy in a Changing World** feature to learn how DuPont used this approach to improve its ability to convert research into successful new products. In a survey of 701 companies from Europe, the United States, and Japan, 85% of the respondents have used this approach with 62% rating it as successful.[38] Research reveals that cross-functional teams are best for designing and developing innovative new products, whereas the more traditional bureaucratic structures seem to be best for developing modifications to existing products, line extensions, and me-too products.[39] Chrysler Corporation was able to reduce the development time for new vehicles by 40% by using cross-functional teams and by developing a partnership approach to new projects.[40] International Specialty Products, a maker of polymers, used "product express" teams composed of chemists

Table 11.1   **Five Stages of New Product Development**

The Product Development & Management Association, based at Indiana University, has identified five stages of new product development:

- **Stage One: Idea Generation.** A new product concept is identified and refined. A team is formed to determine the idea's validity and market opportunity.
- **Stage Two: Concept Development and Screening.** The concept undergoes a feasibility study. Preliminary market research is conducted and a strategy is developed. If the product is not feasible, it's dropped.
- **Stage Three: Design and Development.** Using computer-aided design techniques, engineering and manufacturing turn the concept into a functioning product.
- **Stage Four: Market Testing.** Prototypes are now tested in the marketplace to learn if anyone is willing to purchase the product and at what price. Suggestions from consumers are fed back to the design team for possible inclusion.
- **Stage Five: Commercialization.** The entire company is energized to launch the new product.

Source: B. W. Mattimore, "Eureka! How to Invent a New Product," *The Futurist* (March-April 1995), p. 38.

and representatives from manufacturing and engineering to cut development time in half."Instead of passing a baton, we bring everyone into the commercialization process at the same time," explained John Tancredi, Vice-president for R&D. "We are moving laterally, like rugby players, instead of like runners in a relay race."[41]

Organizing for Innovation: Corporate Entrepreneurship

Corporate entrepreneurship (also called *intrapreneurship*) is defined by Guth and Ginsburg as "the birth of new businesses within existing organizations, that is, internal innovation or venturing; and the transformation of organizations through renewal of the key ideas on which they are built, that is, strategic renewal."[42] A large corporation that wants to encourage innovation and creativity within its firm must choose a structure that will give the new business unit an appropriate amount of freedom while maintaining some degree of control at headquarters.

Burgelman proposes (see Figure 11.3) that the use of a particular organizational design should be determined by the *strategic importance of the new business* to the corporation and the *relatedness of the unit's operations* to those of the corporation.[43] The combination of these two factors results in nine organizational designs for corporate entrepreneurship.

1. **Direct integration.** A new business with a great deal of strategic importance and operational relatedness must be a part of the corporation's mainstream. Product champions—people who are respected by others in the corporation and who know how to work the system—are needed to manage these projects. Hal Sperlich, for example, championed the development of the minivan both at Ford and Chrysler Corporation.

2. **New product business department.** A new business with a great deal of strategic importance and partial operational relatedness should be a separate department, organized around an entrepreneurial project in the division where skills and capabilities can be shared. Maytag Corporation did this when it built a new plant near its current Newton, Iowa, washer plant to manufacture a wholly new line of energy and water efficient front-loading dishwashers.

3. **Special business units.** A new business with a great deal of strategic importance and low operational relatedness should be a special new business unit with specific objectives and time horizons. General Motors did this with Saturn because GM wanted to set up an entirely new management, manufacturing, and marketing system.

DUPONT USES CROSS-FUNCTIONAL TEAMS TO IMPROVE INNOVATION

Once CEO Edgar Woolard pointed out the failure of DuPont to convert research into successful new products, the company began to change the way it conducted its R&D. To speed up the new product process, departments created small, interdisciplinary teams to deal with all new product ideas. These teams were allowed just two weeks to make a go or no-go decision. If they decided to go ahead with the concept, they were given two more weeks to form another team to begin the project. This cut the time needed to move from idea to prototype stage to just two months.

The company also started working more closely with its customers to do a better job of handling their requests. For example, Fluorware,

Inc., wanted DuPont to make a purer version of a Teflon basket that Fluorware used to hold silicon wafers during production. The two companies formed a joint team to find a solution. DuPont later brought out a commercial version of the product to sell to other companies. According to John Goodman, Fluorware's senior director for corporate technology, the Fluorware-DuPont team continues to hold regular meetings, "which we hope will lead to breakthroughs in materials science."

Source: S. McMurray, "DuPont Tries to Make Its Research Wizardry Serve the Bottom Line," *Wall Street Journal* (March 27, 1992), pp. A1, A4.

4. **Micro new ventures department.** A new business with uncertain strategic importance and high operational relatedness should be a peripheral project, which is likely to emerge in the operating divisions on a continuous basis. Each division thus has its own new ventures department. Xerox Corporation, for example, uses its SBUs to generate and nurture new ideas. Small product-synthesis teams within each SBU test the feasibility of new ideas. Those concepts receiving a "go" are managed by an SBU product-delivery team, headed by a chief engineer, that takes the prototype from development through manufacturing.

5. **New venture division.** A new business with uncertain strategic importance that is only partly related to present corporate operations belongs in a new venture division. It brings together projects that either exist in various parts of the corporation or can be acquired externally; sizable new businesses are built. R.J. Reynolds Industries, for example, established a separate company, R.J. Reynolds Development, to evaluate new business concepts with growth potential. The development company nurtures and develops businesses that might have the potential to become one of RJR's core businesses.

6. **Independent business units.** Uncertain strategic importance coupled with no relationship to present corporate activities can make external arrangements attractive. Hewlett-Packard established printers as an independent business unit in Boise, Idaho (far from its Palo Alto, California, headquarters) because management was unsure of the desktop printer's future. According to Richard Belluzzo, head of HP's printer business, "We had the resources of a big company, but we were off on our own. There wasn't central planning . . . , so we could make decisions really fast."[44]

7. **Nurturing and contracting.** When an entrepreneurial proposal might not be important strategically to the corporation but is strongly related to present opera-

Figure 11.3
Organizational Designs for Corporate Entrepreneurship

Source: Reprinted from R. A. Burgelman, "Designs for Corporate Entrepreneurship in Established Firms." Copyright © 1984 by the Regents of the University of California. Reprinted/condensed from *California Management Review*, Vol. 26, No. 3, p. 161. By permission of The Regents.

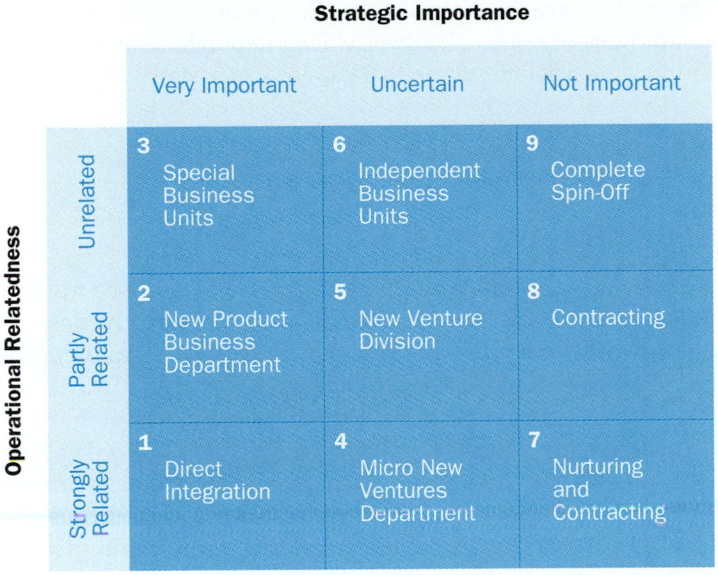

Strategic Importance

		Very Important	Uncertain	Not Important
Operational Relatedness	Unrelated	**3** Special Business Units	**6** Independent Business Units	**9** Complete Spin-Off
	Partly Related	**2** New Product Business Department	**5** New Venture Division	**8** Contracting
	Strongly Related	**1** Direct Integration	**4** Micro New Ventures Department	**7** Nurturing and Contracting

tions, top management might help the entrepreneurial unit to spin off from the corporation. This allows a friendly competitor, instead of one of the corporation's major rivals, to capture a small niche. Techtronix has extensively used this approach. Because of research revealing that related spin-offs tend to be poorer performers than nonrelated spin-offs (presumably owing to the loss of benefits enjoyed with a larger company), it is especially important that the parent company continue to support the development of the spun-off unit in this cell.[45]

8. **Contracting.** As the required capabilities and skills of the new business are less related to those of the corporation, the parent corporation may spin off the strategically unimportant unit, yet keep some relationship through a contractual arrangement with the new firm. The connection is useful in case the new firm eventually develops something of value to the corporation. For example, B.F. Goodrich offered manufacturing rights plus a long-term purchasing agreement to a couple of its managers for a specific raw material Goodrich still used (in declining quantities) in its production process, but no longer wanted to manufacture internally.

9. **Complete spin-off.** If both the strategic importance and the operational relatedness of the new business are negligible, the corporation is likely to completely sell off the business to another firm or to the present employees in some form of ESOP (Employee Stock Ownership Plan). The corporation also could sell off the unit through a leveraged buy-out (executives of the unit buy the unit from the parent company with money from a third source, to be repaid out of the unit's anticipated earnings). Because 3M wanted to focus its development money on areas with more profit potential, it decided to spin off its money-losing data storage and medical imaging divisions in 1996 as a new company called Imation.

Organizing for innovation has become especially important for those corporations that want to become more innovative, but their age and size have made them highly bureaucratic with a culture that discourages creative thinking. These new structural designs for corporate entrepreneurship cannot work by themselves, however. The entrepreneurial units must also have the support of management and sufficient resources. They must also have employees who are risk takers, willing to purchase an ownership interest in the new venture, and a corporate culture that supports new ventures.

11.5   Evaluation and Control

Companies want to gain more productivity at a faster pace from their research and development activities. But how do we measure the effectiveness or efficiency of a company's R&D? This is a problem given that a company shouldn't expect more than 1 in 20 product ideas from basic research to make it to the marketplace. Some companies measure the proportion of their sales attributable to new products. For example, 72% of Hewlett-Packard's revenues come from products introduced in the past three years.[46] At BellCore, the research part of seven regional Bell telephone companies, the effectiveness of basic research is measured by how often the lab's research is cited in other scientists' work. This measure is compiled and published by the Institute for Scientific Information. Other companies judge the quality of research by counting how many patents are filed annually.

Pittiglio Rabin Todd McGrath (PRTM), a high-tech consulting firm, proposes an **index of R&D effectiveness.** The index is calculated by dividing the percentage of total revenue spent on R&D into new product profitability, which is expressed as a percentage. When applying this measure to 45 large electronics manufacturers, only nine companies scored 1.0 or higher, indicating that only 20% received a positive payback from their R&D spending. The top companies kept spending on marginal products to a minimum by running frequent checks on product versus market opportunities and canceling questionable products quickly. They also moved new products to market in half the time of the others. As a result, revenue growth among the top 20% of the companies was double the average of all 45 companies.[47]

A study of 15 multinational companies with successful R&D operations focused on three measures of R&D success: (1) improving technology transfer from R&D to business units, (2) accelerating time to market for new products and processes, and (3) institutionalizing cross-functional participation in R&D. The companies participated in basic, applied, and developmental research activities. The study revealed 13 **best practices** that all of the companies followed.[48] Listed in Table 11.2, they provide a benchmark for a company's R&D activities.

11.6   Global Issues for the 21st Century

- The **21st Century Global Society** feature in this chapter illustrates not only how distinctive competencies in R&D can affect a company's competitive strategy, but also how emerging markets, such as China, are crucial to corporate growth strategies. Toto Ltd. is able to get from design to market quickly, but American Standard is able to design a product to better suit the needs of a new market. Expect both of these global competitors to do very well in China in the near future.

- Companies throughout the world are beginning to realize the benefits from cross-

Table 11.2   **Thirteen "Best Practices" for Improving R&D**

1. Corporate and business unit strategies are well defined and clearly communicated.
2. Core technologies are defined and communicated to R&D.
3. Investments are made in developing multinational R&D capabilities to tap ideas throughout the world.
4. Funding for basic research comes from corporate sources to ensure a long-term focus; funding for development comes from business units to ensure accountability.
5. Basic and applied research are performed either at a central facility or at a small number of labs, each focused on a particular discipline of science or technology. Development work is usually performed at business unit sites.
6. Formal, cross-functional teams are created for basic, applied, and developmental projects.
7. Formal mechanisms exist for regular interaction among scientists, and between R&D and other functions.
8. Analytical tools are used for selecting projects as well as for on-going project evaluation.
9. The transfer of technology to business units is the most important measure of R&D performance.
10. Effective measures of career development are in place at all levels of R&D.
11. Recruiting of new people is from diverse universities and from other companies when specific experience or skills are required that would take long to develop internally.
12. Some basic research is performed internally, but there are also many university and third-party relationships.
13. Formal mechanisms are used for monitoring external technological developments.

Source: I. Krause, and J. Liu, "Benchmarking R&D Productivity," *Planning Review* (January/February 1993), pp. 16–21, 52–53, with permission from The Planning Forum, The International Society for Strategic Management and Planning.

functional teams in product development activities. This should become the dominant design model in the coming years.

- To be competitive, companies must find the proper mix of product and process R&D. Even though the key to the success of the U.S. major home appliance industry has been its emphasis on process innovation, significant product innovation is more likely to result in a first mover advantage. For example, the first company to successfully use sound waves to clean clothes (instead of water and detergent) may very likely change the entire dynamics of the industry. At this moment, the Japanese appear most likely to develop product innovations in this industry.

- The inability of standard marketing research to properly evaluate the market potential of novel products suggests that many firms will be adopting Sony's approach of continually developing new products to be tested in the marketplace with sophisticated information systems market feedback. If it sells, make more. If it doesn't, cancel production and try another product.

- The inability of established firms to be as innovative as smaller firms indicates that companies may continue to break themselves down into smaller units to encourage creativity and innovation. The next issue will deal with balancing the efficiency rationale for centralizing R&D at corporate headquarters with the effectiveness rationale for decentralizing R&D to the business units. This has serious implications for multinational corporations.

Projections for the 21st Century

- From 1994 to 2010, the number of communications satellites worldwide will grow from 1,100 to 2,260.

- From 1994 to 2010, the number of McDonald's fast food restaurants will increase from 14,000 to 31,000—many of them outside the U.S. [49]

Discussion Questions

1. How should a corporation scan the external environment for new technological developments? Who should be responsible?

2. What is technology research and how does it differ from market research?

3. What is the importance of product and process R&D to competitive strategy?

4. What factors help determine whether a company should outsource a technology?

5. How can a company develop an entrepreneurial culture?

Key Terms

absorptive capacity (p. 272)
best practices (p. 278)
corporate entrepreneurship (p. 275)
index of R&D effectiveness (p. 278)
market research (p. 266)
orchestrator (p. 274)
process innovations (p. 269)
product champion (p. 274)

product innovations (p. 269)
product/market evolution matrix (p. 273)
R&D intensity (p. 267)
sponsor (p. 274)
stages of new product development (p. 273)
strategic alliance (p. 270)

technological competence (p. 272)
technological discontinuity (p. 266)
technology research (p. 266)
technology sourcing (p. 269)
time to market (p. 268)

Strategic Practice Exercise

Mary Clare had to make a decision on a new product idea and wasn't sure how to proceed. She worked as an Editor in the Business and Economics College Textbook Division of Addison Wesley Longman Publishing Company. Two of her current authors, David Hunger and Thomas Wheelen, had proposed an idea for a new book project to her. They were the authors of the successful hard-bound *Strategic Management and Business Policy* textbook. Based on their sense of the marketplace, they were proposing that the company publish a slimmed-down, paperback version of just the chapters (no case studies) of the hard-bound textbook. This new book would be called *Essentials of Strategic Management*. It was to be fairly short at about 200 pages (the current chapters had about 400 pages) and inexpensive—selling to students at around $20–$25. It would include no boxed examples or exercises and would be printed in simple black type. This was compared to the usual 1,000-page strategy textbook that included both text chapters and cases printed in multiple colors and selling for around $60 in campus bookstores. *Essentials* would be half the length of Hunger and Wheelen's paperback, *Strategic Marketing*, which was composed of the complete 14 chapters from *Strategic Management and Business Policy*, and selling at around $35–$40 retail.

Essentials would have a minimal Instructor's Manual compared to the usual large manual provided free to instructors who adopted a text.

The authors felt that there was a market for this product based on certain observations. First, they believed that some instructors preferred to select cases from other sources and didn't want a book that included cases. Second, they felt that some instructors at both the graduate and undergraduate levels wanted a small book that students could read quickly. The instructors could then spend most of the course analyzing cases and/or conducting a management simulation. Third, some instructors were heard to comment that students were no longer bringing their books to class because the books were too large and heavy to carry. The push to make textbooks more user-friendly had meant the addition of so many "bells and whistles" that the books had doubled in size over the past few years. Fourth, they felt increasing pressure from students who wanted cheaper textbooks.

Mary Clare wondered if Wheelen and Hunger were seeing the whole picture. She knew from previous market research that both students and professors strongly preferred textbooks done in multiple colors and including a lot of interesting boxed stories and exercises over the more traditional (but duller) textbooks. Unfortunately these improvements added considerably to both the cost and size of books. The breakeven point for a new textbook was getting higher and higher. An editor could no longer base a decision on a new project just on gut feel. A new book had to pay its own development costs.

One problem was: *What if the market doesn't accept this new type of strategy textbook?* Other publishers had been successful with *Essentials* books in the "Introduction To . . . (Management, Marketing, etc.)" markets, but no one yet had tried an *Essentials* book in strategy. Should Addison Wesley Longman be the first? Maybe it

would be better to let some other publisher try this idea first. On the other hand, *what if the* Essentials *book is a big success?* It might cannibalize the hard-cover textbook if current users of *Strategic Management and Business Policy* converted to the less expensive *Essentials* book. The company makes three times as much money on the large hardcover book than it would on the smaller paperback. But what if the market switches to smaller, simpler, cheaper textbooks and Addison Wesley Longman is left behind with no competitive products?

What should Mary Clare do?

Notes

1. S. McMurray, "DuPont Tries to Make Its Research Wizardry Serve the Bottom Line," *Wall Street Journal* (March 27, 1992), pp. A1, A4.
2. S. J. Towner, "Four Ways to Accelerate New Product Development," *Long Range Planning* (April 1994), p. 57.
3. R. Garud, and P. R. Nayyar, "Transformative Capacity: Continual Structuring by Intertemporal Technology Transfer," *Strategic Management Journal* (June 1994), p. 379.
4. C. A. Ferland, book review of *Third Generation R&D—Managing the Link to Corporate Strategy* by Roussel, Saad, and Erickson, in *Long Range Planning* (April 1993), p. 128.
5. C. Power, K. Kerwin, R. Grover, K. Alexander, and R. D. Hof, "Flops," *Business Week* (August 16, 1993), pp. 76–82.
6. B. R. Schlender, "How Sony Keeps the Magic Going," *Fortune* (February 24, 1992), p. 77.
7. G. C. Hill, and K. Yamada, "Motorola Illustrates How an Aged Giant Can Remain Vibrant," *Wall Street Journal* (December 9, 1992), pp. A1, A14.
8. N. Snyder, "Environmental Volatility, Scanning Intensity and Organizational Performance," *Journal of Contemporary Business* (September 1981), p. 16.
9. G. Hamel, and C. K. Prahalad, "Seeing the Future First," *Fortune* (September 5, 1995), p. 70.
10. J. Wade, "A Community-Level Analysis of Sources and Rates of Technological Variation in the Microprocessor Market," *Academy of Management Journal* (October 1996), pp. 1218–1244.
11. C. M. Christensen, and J. L. Bower, "Customer Power, Strategic Investment, and the Failure of Leading Firms," *Strategic Management Journal* (March 1996), pp. 197–218.
12. G. S. Lynn, J. G. Morone, and A. S. Paulson, "Marketing and Discontinuous Innovation: The Probe and Learn Process," *California Management Review* (Spring 1996), pp. 8–37.
13. W. I. Zangwill, "When Customer Research Is a Lousy Idea," *Wall Street Journal* (March 8, 1993), p. A10.
14. D. F. Kuratko, J. S. Hornsby, D. W. Naffziger, and R. V. Montagno, "Implement Entrepreneurial Thinking in Established Organizations," *SAM Advanced Management Journal* (Winter 1993), p. 29.
15. L. G. Franko, "Global Corporate Competition: Who's Winning, Who's Losing, and the R&D Factor as One Reason Why," *Strategic Management Journal* (September-October 1989), pp. 449–474; See also P. S. Chan, E. J. Flynn, and R. Chinta, "The Strategies of Growing and Turnaround Firms: A Multiple Discriminant Analysis," *International Journal of Management* (September 1991), pp. 669–675.
16. M. J. Chussil, "How Much to Spend on R&D?" *The PIMSletter of Business Strategy*, No. 13 (Cambridge, Mass.: The Strategic Planning Institute, 1978), p. 5.
17. J. S. Harrison, E. H. Hall, Jr., and R. Nargundkar, "Resource Allocation as an Outcropping of Strategic Consistency: Performance Implications," *Academy of Management Journal* (October 1993), pp. 1026–1051.
18. S. B. Graves, and N. S. Langowitz, "Innovative Productivity and Returns to Scale in the Pharmaceutical Industry," *Strategic Management Journal* (November 1993), pp. 593–605; A. Brady, "Small Is as Small Does," *Journal of Business Strategy* (March/April 1995), pp. 44–52.
19. D. H. Freedman, "Through the Looking Glass," in "The State of Small Business," *Inc.* (May 21, 1996), pp. 48–54.
20. N. Nohria, and R. Gulati, "Is Slack Good or Bad for Innovation?" *Academy of Management Journal* (October 1996), pp. 1245–1264.
21. M. A. Hitt, R. E. Hoskisson, and J. S. Harrison, "Strategic Competitiveness in the 1990s: Challenges and Opportunities for U.S. Executives," *Academy of Management Executive* (May 1991), p. 13.
22. T. F. O'Boyle, "Steel's Management Has Itself to Blame," *Wall Street Journal* (May 17, 1983), p. 32.
23. M. Silva, and B. Sjogren, *Europe 1992 and the New World Power Game* (New York: John Wiley and Sons, 1990), p. 231.
24. E. Mansfield, M. Schwartz, and S. Wagner, "Imitation Costs and Patents: An Empirical Study," *Economic Journal* (December 1981), pp. 907–918.
25. G. Stalk, Jr., and A. M. Webber, "Japan's Dark Side of Time," *Harvard Business Review* (July-August 1993), p. 99.
26. A. Deutschman, "If They're Gaining on You, Innovate," *Fortune* (November 2, 1992), p. 86; O. Port, A. Reinhardt, G. McWilliams, and S. V. Brull, "The Silicon Age? It's Just Dawning," *Business Week* (December 9, 1996), pp. 148–152.

27. M. Robert, "Market Fragmentation versus Market Seg-mentation," *Journal of Business Strategy* (September/Octo-ber 1992), p. 52.

28. K. Kelly, and M. Ivey, "Turning Cummins into the Engine Maker That Could," *Business Week* (July 30, 1990), pp. 20–21.

29. Silva and Sjogren, *Europe 1992 and the New World Power Game,* pp. 239–241. See also P. Nueno and J. Oosterveld, "Managing Technology Alliances," *Long Range Planning* (June 1988), pp. 11–17.

30. P. R. Nayak, "Should You Outsource Product Develop-ment?" *Journal of Business Strategy* (May/June 1993), pp. 44–45.

31. M. A. Hitt, R. E. Hoskisson, R. A. Johnson, and D. D. Moe-sel, "The Market for Corporate Control and Firm Innova-tion," *Academy of Management Journal* (October 1996), pp. 1084–1119.

32. W. M. Cohen, and D. A. Levinthal, "Absorptive Capacity: A New Perspective on Learning and Innovation," *Admin-istrative Science Quarterly* (March 1990), pp. 128–152.

33. "The Impact of Industrial Robotics on the World of Work," *International Labour Review,* Vol. 125, No. 1 (1986). Summarized in "The Risks of Robotization," *The Futurist* (May-June 1987), p. 56.

34. Hitt, Hoskisson, and Harrison, "Strategic Competitive-ness in the 1990s: Challenges and Opportunities for U.S. Executives," p. 9.

35. D. Dougherty, and C. Hardy, "Sustained Product Inno-vation in Large, Mature Organizations: Overcoming Innovation-to-Organization Problems," *Academy of Man-agement* (October 1996), pp. 1120–1153.

36. C. A. Lengnick-Hall, "Innovation and Competitive Ad-vantage: What We Know and What We Need to Know," *Journal of Management* (June 1992), pp. 399–429.

37. J. R. Galbraith, "Designing the Innovative Organization," *Organizational Dynamics* (Winter 1982), pp. 5–25.

38. P. R. Nayak, "Product Innovation Practices in Europe, Japan, and the U.S.," *Journal of Business Strategy* (May/June 1992), pp. 62–63.

39. E. M. Olson, "Organizing for Effective New Product De-velopment: The Moderating Role of Product Innovative-ness," *Journal of Marketing* (January 1995) as reported by K. Z. Andrews in *Harvard Business Review* (November-December, 1995), pp. 12–13.

40. D. Rowe, "Up and Running," *Journal of Business Strategy* (May/June 1993), pp. 48–50.

41. N. Freundlich, and M. Schroeder, "Getting Everybody Into the Act," *Business Week* (Quality 1991 edition), p. 152.

42. W. D. Guth, and A. Ginsberg, "Corporate Entrepreneur-ship," *Strategic Management Journal* (Summer 1990), p. 5.

43. R. A. Burgelman, "Designs for Corporate Entrepreneur-ship," *California Management Review* (Spring 1984), pp. 154–166; R. A. Burgelman and L. R. Sayles, *Inside Corpo-rate Innovation* (New York: The Free Press, 1986).

44. S. K. Yoder, "How H-P Used Tactics of the Japanese to Beat Them at Their Game," *Wall Street Journal* (September 8, 1994), pp. A1, A6.

45. C. Y. Woo, G. E. Willard, and S. M. Beckstead, "Spin-Offs: What Are the Gains?" *Journal of Business Strategy* (March-April 1989), pp. 29–32.

46. J. B. Levin, and R. D. Hof, "Has Philips Found Its Wizard?" *Business Week* (September 6, 1993), pp. 82–84.

47. O. Port, "Rating R&D: How Companies Get the Biggest Bang for the Buck," *Business Week* (July 5, 1993), p. 98.

48. I. Krause, and J. Liu, "Benchmarking R&D Productivity," *Planning Review* (January/February 1993), pp. 16–21, 52–53.

49. J. Warner, "21st Century Capitalism: Snapshots of the Next Century," *Business Week* (November 18, 1994), p. 194.

Chapter **12**

Strategic Issues in Entrepreneurial Ventures and Small Businesses

Debbie Giampapa was at a party juggling her food plate and drink. "This is ridiculous," she thought. "Why doesn't somebody make something to hold this?" When she got home she pulled a piece of cardboard out of the trash and cut a hole large enough to hold a standard 10-ounce plastic cup. Then she added a smaller hole for a wine glass. After much trial and error and a lot of perseverance in obtaining funding, plus deciding how to make and market her product, she established her own company, Fun-Zone. She went to die cutters and machinists to learn how machines could make her product. She told them she was doing door hangers because she didn't want them to steal her idea. Said Giampapa, "The more I understand what the machine can do, the better I can design the product." Giampapa is now selling thousands of "Party HOLDems" to customers like American Express, Walt Disney Company, and Coopers and Lybrand. When asked the secret of her success, she responded:

> It's not having the idea. It's believing in yourself and your product enough to put up the money and time for that. I've put in 16-hour days, seven-day weeks for two years.[1]

12.1 Importance of Small Business and Entrepreneurial Ventures

Strategic management as a field of study typically deals with large, established business corporations. However, small business cannot be ignored. There are 22 million small businesses—over 95% of all businesses in the United States. According to Dun & Bradstreet, 170,475 entrepreneurial ventures created 846,973 new jobs in the United States during 1996.[2] Research reveals that not only do small firms spend almost twice as much of their R&D dollars on fundamental research as do large firms, but also that small companies are responsible for a high proportion of innovations in products and services.[3] For example, new small firms produce 24 times more innovation per research dollar than do the much larger Fortune 500 firms.[4] The National Science Foundation estimates that 98% of "radical" product developments result from the research done in the labs of small companies.[5]

Despite the overall success of small businesses, however, every year tens of thousands of small companies fail. According to the U.S. Small Business Administration, 24% of all new businesses fail within two years and 63% fail within six years.[6] Similar failure rates occur in the United Kingdom, The Netherlands, Japan, Taiwan, and Hong Kong.[7] Although some studies are more positive regarding the survival rate of new entrepreneurial ventures, new businesses are definitely considered risky.[8] The causes of small-business failure (depending on the study cited) range from inadequate accounting systems to inability to cope with growth. The underlying problem appears to be an overall lack of strategic management—beginning with an inability to plan a strategy to reach the customer, and ending with a failure to develop a system of controls to keep track of performance.[9]

Definition of Small-Business Firms and Entrepreneurial Ventures

The most commonly accepted definition of a small-business firm is one that employs fewer than 500 people and that generates sales of less than $20 million annually.

Although the meanings of the terms "small business" and "entrepreneurship" overlap considerably, the concepts are different. The **small-business firm** is independently owned and operated, not dominant in its field, and does not engage in innovative practices. The **entrepreneurial venture**, in contrast, is any business whose primary goals are profitability and growth and that can be characterized by innovative strategic practices.[10] The basic difference between the small-business firm and the entrepreneurial venture, therefore, lies not in the type of goods or services provided, but in their fundamental views on growth and innovation. According to Donald Sexton, an authority on entrepreneurship, this explains why strategic planning is more likely to be present in an entrepreneurial venture than in the typical small-business firm:

> Most firms start with just a single product. Those oriented toward growth immediately start looking for another one. It's that planning approach that separates the entrepreneur from the small-business owner.[11]

The Entrepreneur as Strategist

Often defined as a person who organizes and manages a business undertaking and who assumes risk for the sake of a profit, the **entrepreneur** is the ultimate strategist. He or she makes all the strategic as well as operational decisions. All three levels of strategy—corporate, business, and functional—are the concerns of this founder and owner-manager of a company. As one entrepreneur puts it: "Entrepreneurs are strategic planners without realizing it."

The founding of FunZone described earlier captures the key elements of the entrepreneurial venture: a basic business idea that has not yet been successfully tried and a gutsy entrepreneur who, while working on borrowed capital and a shoestring budget, creates a new business through a lot of trial and error and persistent hard work. Similar stories can be told of other people, such as Debbie Fields, who created Mrs. Fields Cookies, and Will Parish, who founded National Energy Associates. Both were ridiculed at one time or another for their desire to start a business. Friends and family told Debbie Fields that starting a business to sell chocolate chip cookies "was a stupid idea." Will Parish, who built a power plant in California's Imperial Valley that burns "pasture patties," is called an "entre-manure." Every day the plant burns 900 tons of manure collected from nearby feedlots to generate 15 megawatts of electricity—enough to light 20,000 homes. The power is sold to Southern California Edison. Parish got the idea from a trip to India where the fuel used to heat a meal was cow dung. Now that the plant is earning a profit, Parish is building a larger plant nearby that will burn wheat straw and other crop wastes. The plants provide an environmentally sound as well as profitable way to dispose of waste. Very interested in conservation, Parish says, "I wanted to combine doing well with doing good."[12]

12.2   Use of Strategic Planning and Strategic Management

Research shows that strategic planning is strongly related to small-business financial performance.[13] A survey of the high growth *Inc. 500* firms revealed that 86% performed strategic planning. Of those performing strategic planning, 94% reported improved profits.[14] Nevertheless, many small companies still do not use the process. The reasons often cited for the apparent lack of strategic planning practices in many small-business firms are fourfold:

- **Not enough time.** Day-to-day operating problems take up the time necessary for long-term planning. It's relatively easy to justify avoiding strategic planning on the basis of day-to-day crisis management. Some will ask: "How can I be expected to do strategic planning when I don't know if I'm going to be in business next week?"

- **Unfamiliar with strategic planning.** The small-business CEO may be unaware of strategic planning or may view it as irrelevant to the small-business situation. Planning may be viewed as a straitjacket that limits flexibility.

- **Lack of skills.** Small-business managers often lack the skills necessary to begin strategic planning and do not have or want to spend the money necessary to import trained consultants. Future uncertainty may be used to justify a lack of planning. One entrepreneur admits, "Deep down, I know I should plan. But I don't know what to do. I'm the leader but I don't know how to lead the planning process."

- **Lack of trust and openness.** Many small-business owner-managers are very sensitive regarding key information about the business and are thus unwilling to share strategic planning with employees or outsiders. For this reason, boards of directors are often composed only of close friends and relatives of the owner-manager—people unlikely to provide an objective viewpoint or professional advice.

Degree of Formality

Research generally concludes that the *strategic planning process should be far more informal in small companies* than it is in large corporations.[15] Some studies have even found that too much formalization of the strategic planning process may actually result in reduced performance.[16] It is possible that a heavy emphasis on structured, written plans can be dysfunctional to the small entrepreneurial firm because it detracts from the very flexibility that is a benefit of small size. *The process of strategic planning, not the plan itself, is probably the key to improving business performance.*

These observations suggest that new entrepreneurial ventures begin life in Mintzberg's entrepreneurial mode of strategic planning (explained in Chapter 1) and move toward the planning mode as the company becomes established and wants to continue its strong growth. If, after becoming successfully established, the entrepreneur instead chooses stability over growth, the venture moves more toward the adaptive mode so common to many small businesses.

Usefulness of Strategic Management Model

The model of strategic management (presented in Figure 1.2) is also relevant to entrepreneurial ventures and small businesses. This basic model holds for both an established small company and a new entrepreneurial venture. As the research mentioned earlier concluded, small and developing companies increase their chances of success if they make a serious attempt to work through the strategic issues embedded in the strategic management model. The key is to focus on what's important—the set of managerial decisions and actions that determines the long-run performance of the company. The list of informal questions presented in Table 12.1 may be more useful to a small entrepreneurial company than their more formal counterparts used by large established corporations.

Usefulness of Strategic Decision-Making Process

As mentioned in Chapter 1, one way in which the strategic management model can be made action oriented is to follow the strategic decision-making model presented in Figure 1.5. The eight steps presented in that model are just as appropriate for small companies as they are for large corporations. Unfortunately the process does not fit new entrepreneurial ventures. These companies must develop new missions, objectives, strategies, and policies out of a comparison of its external opportunities and threats to its potential strengths and weaknesses. Consequently we propose in Figure 12.1 a modified version of the strategic decision-making process; this version more closely suits the new entrepreneurial business.

The proposed **strategic decision-making process for entrepreneurial ventures** is composed of the following eight interrelated steps:

1. **Develop the basic business idea**—a product and/or service having target customers and/or markets. The idea can be developed from a person's experience or generated in a moment of creative insight. For example, Debbie Giampapa conceived of the beverage-holding party tray long before such a product was feasible.

Table 12.1 Informal Questions to Begin the Strategic Management Process in a Small Company or Entrepreneurial Venture

Formal	Informal
Define mission	What do we stand for?
Set objectives	What are we trying to achieve?
Formulate strategy	How are we going to get there? How can we beat the competition?
Determine policies	What sort of ground rules should we all be following to get the job done right?
Establish programs	How should we organize this operation to get what we want done as cheaply as possible with the highest quality possible?
Prepare *pro forma* **budgets**	How much is it going to cost us and where can we get the cash?
Specify procedures	In how much detail do we have to lay things out, so that everybody knows what to do?
Determine performance measures	What are those few key things that will determine whether we can make it? How can we keep track of them?

2. **Scan and assess the external environment,** to locate factors in the societal and task environments that pose opportunities and threats. The scanning should focus particularly on market potential and resource accessibility.

3. **Scan and assess the internal factors** relevant to the new business. The entrepreneur should objectively consider personal assets, areas of expertise, abilities, and experience, all in terms of the organizational needs of the new venture.

4. **Analyze the strategic factors** in light of the current situation using SWOT. The venture's potential strengths and weaknesses must be evaluated in light of opportunities and threats. Develop a SFAS Table (Figure 5.1) of the strategic factors.

5. **Decide go or no go.** If the basic business idea appears to be a feasible business opportunity, the process should be continued. Otherwise, further development of the idea should be canceled unless the strategic factors change.

6. **Generate a business plan** specifying how the idea will be transformed into reality. See Table 12.2 for the suggested contents of a strategic **business plan**. The proposed venture's mission, objectives, strategies, and policies, as well as its likely board of directors (if a corporation) and key managers should be developed. Key internal factors should be specified and performance projections generated. The business plan serves as a vehicle through which financial support is obtained from potential investors and creditors. Starting a business without a business plan is the quickest way to kill a new venture. For example, one study of 270 clothing retailers found that 80% of the successful stores had written a business plan, whereas 65% of the failed businesses had not.[17]

The *strategic audit* (see Table 10.5 on pages 252–259) can be used to develop a formal business plan. The audit's sections and subsections, along with the questions within them, provide a useful framework. Instead of analyzing the historical events of an existing company, use the questions to project the proposed company's future. The questions can be reoriented to follow the outline in Table 10.5. A crucial building block of a sound business plan is the construction of realistic scenarios for the pro forma financials. The pro formas must reflect the impact of seasonality on the cash flows of the proposed new venture.

Figure 12.1
Strategic Decision-Making Process for New Ventures

Source: T. L. Wheelen and C. E. Michaels, Jr., "Model for Strategic Decision-Making Process for New Ventures." Copyright © 1987 by T. L. Wheelen. Reprinted by permission.

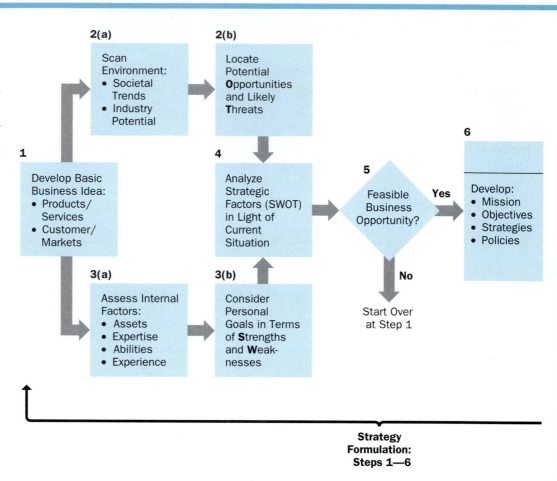

7. **Implement the business plan** through the use of action plans and procedures.

8. **Evaluate the implemented business plan** through comparison of actual performance against projected performance results. This step leads to Step 1(b) of the strategic decision-making process shown in Figure 1.5 on pages 20–21. To the extent that actual results are less than or much greater than the anticipated results, the entrepreneur needs to reconsider the company's current mission, objectives, strategies, policies, and programs, and possibly make changes to the original business plan.

12.3 *Issues in Environmental Scanning and Strategy Formulation*

Environmental scanning in small businesses is much less sophisticated than it is in large corporations. The business is usually too small to justify hiring someone to do only environmental scanning or strategic planning. Top managers, especially if they are the founders, tend to believe that they know the business and can follow it better than anyone else. A study of 220 small rapid-growth companies revealed that the majority of CEOs were actively and personally involved in all phases of the planning process, but

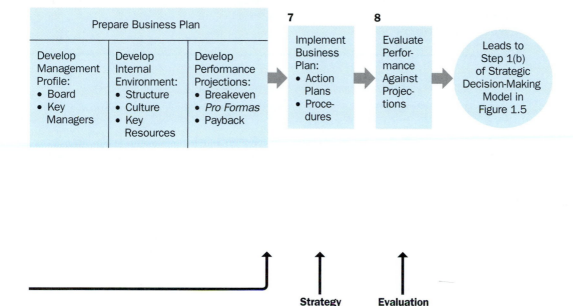

especially in the setting of objectives. Only 15% of the companies used a planning officer or formed a planning group to assist in the planning process. In the rest of the firms, operating managers who participated in strategic planning provided input only to the CEO, who then formulated the plan.[18] Unfortunately the literature suggests that few small businesses do much competitor analysis.

A fundamental reason for differences in *strategy formulation* between large and small entrepreneurial companies lies in the relationship between owners and managers. The CEO of a large corporation has to consider and balance the varied needs of the corporation's many stakeholders. The CEO of a small business, however, is very likely also to be the owner—the company's primary stakeholder. Personal and family needs can thus strongly affect the company's mission and objectives and can overrule other considerations.[19] For example, the **21st Century Global Society** feature illustrates how Anita Roddick's personal social and environmental values determined the policies and mission statement of her entrepreneurial venture, The Body Shop.

Size can affect the selection of an appropriate corporate strategy. Large corporations often choose growth strategies for their many side benefits for management as well as for shareholders. A small company may, however, choose a stability strategy because the entrepreneur is interested mostly in (1) generating employment for family members, (2) providing the family a "decent living," and (3) being the "boss" of a firm small enough

Table 12.2 **Contents of a Strategic Business Plan for an Entrepreneurial Venture**

I. Table of Contents	X. Human Resources Plan
II. Executive Summary	XI. Ownership
III. Nature of the Business	XII. Risk Analysis
IV. Strategy Formulation	XIII. Timetables and Milestones
V. Market Analysis	XIV. Strategy Implementation—Action Plans
VI. Marketing Plan	XV. Evaluation and Control
VII. Operational Plans—Service/Product	XVI. Summary
VIII. Financial Plans	XVII. Appendixes
IX. Organization and Management	

Note:
The strategic audit can be used to develop a business plan. It provides detailed questions to serve as a checklist.

Source: Thomas L. Wheelen, "Contents of a Strategic Business Plan for an Entrepreneurial Venture." Copyright © 1988 by Thomas L. Wheelen. Reprinted by permission.

that he or she can manage it comfortably. Thus the goals of a small business are likely to be the same as the goals of the owner-manager.

The basic SWOT analysis is just as relevant to small entrepreneurial businesses as it is to established large ones. Both the greatest strength and the greatest weakness of the small firm, at least in the beginning, rest with the entrepreneur—the owner-manager of the business. The entrepreneur is *the* manager, the source of product/market strategy, and the dynamo who energizes the company. That is why the internal assessment of a new venture's strengths and weaknesses focuses in Figure 12.1 on the founder's personal characteristics—his or her assets, expertise, abilities, and experience. Just as an entrepreneur's strengths can be the key to company success, personal weaknesses can be a primary cause of failure. For example, the study of clothing retailers mentioned earlier showed that the owner-managers of 85% of the failed stores had no prior retailing experience.

Sources of Innovation

Peter Drucker, in his book *Innovation and Entrepreneurship*, proposes seven sources for innovative opportunity that should be monitored by those interested in starting an entrepreneurial venture, either within an established company or as an independent small business.[20] The first four **sources of innovation** lie within the industry itself; the last three arise in the societal environment. These seven sources are:

1. **The unexpected.** An unexpected success, an unexpected failure, or an unexpected outside event can be a symptom of a unique opportunity. When Don Cullen of Transmet Corporation spilled a box of very fine aluminum flakes onto his company's parking lot, he discovered that their presence in the asphalt prevented it from turning sticky in high temperatures. His company now produces aluminum chips for use in roofing. Sales have doubled every year since the product's introduction and his company will soon dominate the business.

2. **The incongruity.** A discrepancy between reality and what everyone assumes it to be, or between what is and what ought to be, can create an opportunity for innovation. Realizing that the real costs of ocean freighter haulage were not in crew wages but in the time spent loading and unloading at port, Sea-Land changed the entire industry by introducing efficient containerized shipping to reduce handling time and costs.

MISSION AND POLICIES OF THE BODY SHOP REFLECT ENTREPRENEUR'S PERSONAL VALUES AND EXPERIENCES

Anita Roddick wanted to open a shop of her own to sell cosmetics and lotions. She had been dissatisfied with her inability to try a cream or a lotion before purchasing it in a large bottle. She wanted to sell naturally based cosmetics in five sizes so her customers could have a choice. Although the environmental "green" movement had not yet begun in Britain, Roddick was worried about the use of synthetic chemicals in cosmetics.

Roddick opened her first Body Shop in Brighton in 1976. Two nearby funeral homes threatened to sue her over the shop's name. Roddick then informed the local newspaper about the controversy. The resulting article was free publicity for her new shop. Based on this experience, Roddick developed a company policy of never spending a cent on advertising. The focus was instead to be on publicizing company values. Even though marketing experts in the United States doubted if The Body Shop could be successfully established in America without advertising, Roddick refused to change her policy. (By 1995, there were 235 shops in the United States plus hundreds more throughout the world!) Because Roddick used her firm as an expression of her concerns on social issues and the environment, the company received around 2,000 pounds

worth of free publicity annually. The company's mission statement is an extension of Anita Roddick's personal philosophy. It clearly tells that this now-global company is in business for more than just the sales of naturally based cosmetics.

- To creatively balance the financial and human needs of our stakeholders.

- To courageously ensure that our business is ecologically sustainable, meeting the needs of the present without compromising the future.

- To meaningfully contribute to local, national, and international communities in which we trade, adopting a code of conduct that ensures care, honesty, fairness and respect.

- To passionately campaign for the protection of the environment and human and civil rights, and against animal testing within the cosmetics and toiletries industry.

- To tirelessly work to narrow the gap between principle and practice, while making fun, passion, and care part of our daily lives.

Source: *Our Reason for Being.* Handout from The Body Shop.

3. **Innovation based on process need.** When a weak link is evident in a particular process, but people work around it instead of doing something about it, an opportunity is present for the person or company willing to forge a stronger one. For example, Alcon Laboratories was developed based on the discovery that a specific enzyme could enable doctors to avoid cutting a particular ligament when performing eye surgery.

4. **Changes in industry or market structure.** A business is ready for an innovative product, service, or approach to the business when the underlying foundation of the industry or market shifts. Black Entertainment Television, Inc. (BET), was born when Robert Johnson noticed that no television programmer was targeting the increasing number of black viewers. Johnson then successfully expanded into print with *Young Sisters & Brothers*, a monthly magazine aimed at black teenagers.

5. **Demographics.** Changes in the population's size, age structure, composition, employment, level of education, and income can create opportunities for innovation. For

example, Pam Henderson started a company called Kids Kab to shuttle children and teenagers to private schools, doctor and dental appointments, lessons, and extracurricular activities. With the trend to dual careers, parents were no longer always available to provide personal transportation for their own children and needed such a service.

6. **Changes in perception, mood, and meaning.** Opportunities for innovation can develop when a society's general assumptions, attitudes, and beliefs change. For example, the increasing dominance of a few national brewers have caused beer drinkers to look for alternatives to the same old national brands. By positioning Yuengling, a local Pennsylvania beer, as a full-flavored beer and providing it with an artsy, nostalgic-looking label, the small company was able to catch the fancy of young, trendy consumers who viewed it as Pennsylvania's version of Anchor Steam, the successful San Francisco beer.

7. **New knowledge.** Advances in scientific and nonscientific knowledge can create new products and new markets. Advances in two different areas can sometimes be integrated to form the basis of a new product. For example, Tuck Rickards opened The Virtual Emporium in Santa Monica's trendy Third Street Promenade shopping area to combine retailing excitement with information technology. The shop has a decor of an overgrown "Friends" TV set with 30 Gateway personal computers that connect to 80 Internet shopping sites. According to Rickards, "Most people are still intimidated by the Internet and many still want to go to a fun place to shop."[21]

Factors Affecting a New Venture's Success

According to Hofer and Sandberg, three factors have a substantial impact on a new venture's performance. In order of importance, these **factors affecting new venture success** are (1) the structure of the industry entered, (2) the new venture's business strategy, and (3) behavioral characteristics of the entrepreneur.[22]

Industry Structure

Research shows that the chances for success are greater for entrepreneurial ventures that enter rapidly changing industries than for those that enter stable industries. In addition, prospects are better in industries that are in the early, high-growth stages of development. Competition is often less intense. Fast market growth also allows new ventures to make some mistakes without serious penalty. New ventures also increase their chances of success when they enter markets in which they can erect entry barriers to keep out competitors.

Contrary to popular wisdom, however, patents may not always provide competitive advantage, especially for new ventures in a high-tech or hypercompetitive industry. A well-financed competitor could examine a newly filed application for a patent, work around the patent, and beat the pioneering firm to market with a similar product. In addition, the time and cost of filing and defending a patent may not be worth the effort. According to Connie Bagley, author of *The Entrepreneur's Guide to Business Law*:

> It might take 18 months to get a patent on a product that has a 12-month life cycle. By the time you finally get the damn thing litigated, it's meaningless. So people are focusing less on proprietary assurance and more on first-mover advantage. . . . The law is just too slow for this high-speed economy.[23]

Research further reveals that a new venture is more likely to be successful entering an industry in which one dominant competitor has a 50% or more market share than entering an industry in which the largest competitor has less than a 25% market share.

To explain this phenomenon, Hofer and Sandberg point out that when an industry has one dominant firm, the remaining competitors are relatively weak and are easy prey for an aggressive entrepreneur. To avoid direct competition with a major rival, the new venture can focus on a market segment that is being ignored.

Industry product characteristics also have a significant impact on a new venture's success. First, a new venture is more likely to be successful when it enters an industry with heterogeneous (different) products than when it enters one with homogeneous (similar) products. In a heterogeneous industry, a new venture can differentiate itself from competitors with a unique product; or, by focusing on the unique needs of a market segment, it can find a market niche. Second, a new venture is, according to research data, more likely to be successful if the product is relatively unimportant to the customer's total purchasing needs than if it is important. Customers are more likely to experiment with a new product if its cost is low and product failure will not create a problem.

Business Strategy

According to Hofer and Sandberg, the key to success for most new ventures is (1) to differentiate the product from those of other competitors in the areas of quality and service and (2) to focus the product on customer needs in a segment of the market in order to achieve a dominant share of that part of the market (Porter's focused differentiation competitive strategy). Adopting guerrilla-warfare tactics, these companies go after opportunities in market niches too small or too localized to justify retaliation from the market leaders.

To continue its growth once it has found a niche, the entrepreneurial firm can emphasize continued innovation and pursue natural growth in its current markets. It can expand into related markets in which the company's core skills, resources, and facilities offer the keys to further success.[24]

Entrepreneurial Characteristics

Four **entrepreneurial characteristics** are key to a new venture's success. Successful entrepreneurs have:

1. *The ability to identify potential venture opportunities better than most people.* They focus on opportunities—not on problems—and try to learn from failure. Entrepreneurs are goal oriented and have a strong impact on the emerging culture of an organization. They are able to envision where the company is going and are thus able to provide a strong overall sense of strategic direction. See the **Strategy in a Changing World** feature for Cherrill Farnsworth's ability to spot new entrepreneurial opportunities.

2. *A sense of urgency that makes them action oriented.* They have a high need for achievement, which motivates them to put their ideas into action. They tend to have an internal locus of control that leads them to believe that they can determine their own fate through their own behavior. They also have a significantly greater capacity to tolerate ambiguity and stress than do many in established organizations.[25] They also have a strong need for control and may even be viewed as "misfits who need to create their own environment." They tend to distrust others and often have a need "to show others that they amount to something, that they cannot be ignored."[26]

3. *A detailed knowledge of the keys to success in the industry and the physical stamina to make their work their lives.* They have better than average education and significant work experience in the industry in which they start their business. They often work with partners to form a new venture. (70% of new high-tech ventures are started by

STRATEGY IN A CHANGING WORLD

CHERRILL FARNSWORTH'S ENTREPRENEURIAL PERSONALITY

Cherrill Farnsworth is an example of a classic entrepreneur. She likes to form new ventures. Farnsworth is currently the CEO of TME, Inc., the fifth company she has founded. She founded her first company, a bus line, in 1974. After her husband was transferred to Houston in 1970, she noticed that people had no way to get downtown from her northwestern suburb. "Wherever there's angst, there's an opportunity," comments Farnsworth. Despite heavy opposition from major bus operators, she won a franchise to run a bus line. Soon, however, running the bus line became boring. After two years, she sold it for a profit. Remembers Farnsworth, "I realized at that point what value you could get by working hard and creating something new—especially if there's no competition." In her next three new ventures, she leased luxury vehicles, office equipment, and then oil field equipment.

In the early 1980s, Farnsworth was attracted to MRI machines—expensive machines used by hospitals to view the inside of a person's body without the use of x-rays. At the time, hospitals couldn't buy the machines because Medicare had not yet approved reimbursements from health insurers for the service. According to Farnsworth, when she first proposed to hospital administrators that she provide the service, "they found the idea shocking. They giggled and rolled their eyes." Once they reviewed the financials, however, they agreed. Financial backers soon followed.

In assessing her skills as an entrepreneur, Farnsworth sees herself not so much as a manager, but as someone who builds something and then moves on to another challenge. She comments on the future of TME, Inc.:

> I'm not a 20-year player. I've got to develop an exit strategy, probably by going public. I'm very transaction oriented. I love to put something together, build stockholder value, and then raise money again for another venture. Nothing makes me happier.

Source: C. Burck, "The Real World of the Entrepreneur: The Rewards of Angst," *Fortune* (April 5, 1993), pp. 64–65.

more than one founder.)[27] More than half of all entrepreneurs work at least 60 hours a week in the start-up year, according to a National Federation of Independent Business study.[28]

4. *Access to outside help to supplement their skills, knowledge, and abilities.* Over time, they develop a network of people having key skills and knowledge whom the entrepreneurs can call upon for support. Through their enthusiasm, these entrepreneurs are able to attract key investors, partners, creditors, and employees. For example, Mitch Kapor, founder of Lotus Development Corporation, did not hesitate to bring in Jim Manzi as President because Manzi had the managerial skills that Kapor lacked.

In summarizing their conclusions regarding factors affecting the success of entrepreneurial ventures, Hofer and Sandberg propose the guidelines presented in Table 12.3.

12.4 Issues in Strategy Implementation

Two key implementation issues in small companies are organizing and staffing the growing company and transferring ownership of the company to the next generation.

Table 12.3   Some Guidelines for New Venture Success

- Focus on industries facing substantial technological or regulatory changes, especially those with recent exits by established competitors.
- Seek industries whose smaller firms have relatively weak competitive positions.
- Seek industries that are in early, high-growth stages of evolution.
- Seek industries in which it is possible to create high barriers to subsequent entry.
- Seek industries with heterogeneous products that are relatively unimportant to the customer's overall success.
- Seek to differentiate your products from those of your competitors in ways that are meaningful to your customers.
- Focus such differentiation efforts on product quality, marketing approaches, and customer service—and charge enough to cover the costs of doing so.
- Seek to dominate the market segments in which you compete. If necessary, either segment the market differently or change the nature and focus of your differentiation efforts to increase your domination of the segments you serve.
- Stress innovation, especially new product innovation, that is built on existing organizational capabilities.
- Seek natural, organic growth through flexibility and opportunism that builds on existing organizational strengths.

Source: C. W. Hofer and W. R. Sandberg, "Improving New Venture Performance: Some Guidelines for Success," *American Journal of Small Business* (Summer 1987), pp. 17, 19. Copyright © 1987 by C. W. Hofer and W. R. Sandberg. Reprinted by permission.

Substages of Small Business Development

The implementation problems of a small business change as the company grows and develops over time. Just as the decision-making process for entrepreneurial ventures is different from that of established businesses, the managerial systems in small companies often vary from those of large corporations. Those variations are based on their stage of development. The stages of corporate growth and development discussed in Chapter 8 suggest that all small businesses are either in Stage I or trying to move into Stage II. These models imply that all successful new ventures eventually become Stage II, functionally organized companies. This is not always true, however. In attempting to show clearly how small businesses develop, Churchill and Lewis propose five **substages of small business development:** (a) existence, (b) survival, (c) success, (d) take-off, and (e) resource maturity.[29] A review of these small-business substages shows in more detail how a company can move through the entrepreneurial Stage I into a functionally oriented, professionally managed Stage II.

Stage A: Existence

At this point, the entrepreneurial venture faces the problems of obtaining customers and delivering the promised product or service. The organizational structure is simple. The entrepreneur does everything and directly supervises subordinates. Systems are minimal. The owner *is* the business.

Stage B: Survival

Those ventures able to satisfy a sufficient number of customers enter this stage; the rest close when their owners run out of start-up capital. Those reaching the survival stage are concerned about generating the cash flow needed to repair and replace capital assets as they wear out and to finance the growth to continue satisfying the market segment they have found.

At this stage, the organizational structure is still simple, but it probably has a sales manager or general supervisor to carry out the owner's well-defined orders. A major problem of many small businesses at this stage is finding a person who is qualified to supervise the business when the owner can't be present, but who is still willing to work for a very modest salary. Entrepreneurs usually try to use family members rather than hiring an outsider who lacks the entrepreneur's dedication to the business and (in the words of one owner-manager) "steals them blind." A company that remains in this stage for a long time is often called a "mom and pop" firm. It earns marginal returns on invested time and capital (with lots of psychic income!) and eventually goes out of business when "mom and pop" give up or retire. This type of small business is viewed more as a **lifestyle company** in which the firm is purely an extension of the owner's lifestyle. Over 94% of small private companies are in this category.[30]

Stage C: Success

By this point, the company's sales have reached a level where the firm is not only profitable, but has sufficient cash flow to reinvest in itself. The key issue at this stage is whether the company should be used as a platform for growth or as a means of support for the owners as they completely or partially disengage from the company. The company is transforming into a functionally structured organization, but it still relies on the entrepreneur for all key decisions. The two options are disengagement and growth.

C(1) Disengagement. The company can now successfully follow a stability strategy and remain at this stage almost indefinitely—provided that environmental change does not destroy its niche or poor management reduce its competitive abilities. By now functional managers have taken over some of the entrepreneur's duties. The company at this stage may be incorporated, but it is still primarily owned by the founder or founder's family. Consequently the board of directors is either a rubber stamp for the entrepreneur or a forum for family squabbles. Growth strategies are not pursued because either the market niche will not allow growth or the owner is content with the company at a size he or she can still manage comfortably.

C(2) Growth. The entrepreneur risks all available cash and the established borrowing power of the company in financing further growth. Strategic as well as operational planning is extensive and deeply involves the owner. Managers with an eye to the company's future rather than for its current situation are hired. This is an entrepreneurial high-growth firm aiming to be included in the *Inc. 500*. The emphasis now is on teamwork rather than on the entrepreneur's personal actions and energy. As noted in the **Company Spotlight on Maytag Corporation** feature, a corporate culture based on the personal values and philosophy of the founder begins to form as the founder hires and trains a dedicated team of successors.

Stage D: Take-Off

The key problems in this stage are how to grow rapidly and how to finance that growth. By now the firm is incorporated and has sold or is planning to sell stock in its company via an initial public offering (IPO) or via a direct public offering (DPO).[31] The entrepreneur must learn to delegate to specialized professional managers or to a team of managers who now form the top management of the company. A functional structure of the organization should now be solidly in place. Operational and strategic planning greatly involve the hired managers, but the company is still dominated by the entrepreneur's presence and stock control. Vertical and horizontal growth strategies are being seriously

COMPANY SPOTLIGHT

Impact of F. L. Maytag on Maytag Corporation

On March 21, 1997, Maytag introduced its new "Neptune" horizontal axis washing machine at New York's Lincoln Center. This was the culmination of a five-year effort to build a new front-loading washer that uses 40% less water and 65% less energy than the usual vertical axis top-loading washer. The new washer began as a response to anticipated government standards. When those standards were delayed, Maytag went ahead with the horizontal axis washer, even though Whirlpool and GE stopped their efforts and continued to focus on vertical axis top loaders. Why did Maytag choose to go ahead with the concept? Part of the reason comes from values ingrained in the company by its founder, F. L. Maytag. This entrepreneur made a lasting impact on the Maytag Corporation's corporate culture through his commitment to quality, innovation, and hard work.

- **Commitment to quality.** In the company's first year of operation (selling attachments to threshing machines), almost half the products sold were defective in some way. F. L.'s insistence on fixing or buying back the faulty products resulted in losses for the new company, but it set a strong example in emphasizing the importance of quality. F. L. commented that *"nothing was actually 'sold' until it was in the hands of a satisfied user."*

- **View of innovation.** In the company's early years when the factory itself sent service people out to far-flung dealers to repair defective products, F. L. Maytag noted that few calls ever came from a Minnesota dealer that employed a mechanic named Howard Snyder. Consequently he hired Snyder to improve the company's products. Snyder was not interested in cosmetic changes for the sake of sales, but in internal improvements related to quality, durability, and safety. This emphasis became the company's dominant view of research and development.

- **Dedication to hard work.** Imbued with the strong work ethic of the Midwest, F. L. Maytag spent huge amounts of time to establish and maintain the company. His trip West while Chairman of the Board to personally sell a traincar load of washers set an example to his sales force and became a permanent part of company lore.

- **Emphasis on performance.** F. L. Maytag did not like to boast about himself or his company. Preferring to be judged by his work rather than by his words, he was quoted in a company newsletter as saying: *"It's a good idea for a fellow to have a fair opinion of himself. . . . But it doesn't sound well to hear him broadcast it. It's a better idea to let his associates discover it by his deeds."*

MAYTAG CORPORATION

considered as the firm's management debates when and how to grow. The company is now included in the *Inc. 500* select group of firms.

At this point, the entrepreneur either is able to manage the transition from a small to a large company or recognizes personal limitations, sells his or her stock for a profit, and leaves the firm. The composition of the board of directors changes from dominance by friends and relatives of the owner to a large percentage of outsiders with managerial experience who can help the owner during the transition to a professionally managed company. The biggest danger facing the firm in this stage is the owner's desire to remain in total control (not willing to delegate) as if it were still a small entrepreneurial venture, even though he or she lacks the managerial skills necessary to run an established corporation.

Stage E: Resource Maturity

It is at this point that the small company has adopted most of the characteristics of an established, large company. It may still be a small-to-medium-sized company, but it is recognized as an important force in the industry and a possible candidate for the *Fortune 500* someday. The greatest concerns of a company at this stage are controlling the financial gains brought on by rapid growth and retaining its flexibility and entrepreneurial spirit. In terms of the stages of organizational growth and development discussed in Chapter 8, the company has become a full-fledged Stage II functional corporation.

Transfer of Power and Wealth in Family Businesses

Small businesses are often **family businesses.** Even though the founders of the companies are the primary forces in starting the entrepreneurial ventures, their needs for business support and financial assistance will cause them to turn to family members, who can be trusted, over unknown outsiders of questionable integrity, who may demand more salary than the enterprise can afford. Sooner or later, the founder's spouse and children are drafted into business operations either because the family standard of living is directly tied to the business or the entrepreneur desperately needs help just to staff the operation. The children are guaranteed summer jobs, and the business changes from dad's or mom's company to "our" company. The family members are extremely valuable assets to the entrepreneur because they are often also willing to put in long hours at low pay to help the business succeed. Even though the spouse and children might have no official stock in the company, they know that they will somehow share in its future and perhaps even inherit the business. The problem is that only 30% of family firms in the United States make it to the second generation, and just 13% survive to the third generation.[32]

Churchill and Hatten propose that family businesses go through four sequential phases from the time in which the venture is strictly managed by the founder to the time in which the next generation takes charge.[33] These phases are detailed in Table 12.4. Each of these phases must be well managed if the company is to survive past the third generation. Some of the reasons why family businesses may fail to successfully transfer ownership to the next generation are (1) inherited wealth destroys entrepreneurial drive, (2) the entrepreneur doesn't allow for a changing firm, (3) emphasis on business means the family is neglected, (4) the business' financial growth can't keep up with rising family lifestyles, (5) family members are not prepared to run a business, and (6) the business becomes an arena for family conflicts.[34] In addition, succession planning may be ignored because of the founder's or family's refusal to think about the founder's death, the founder's unwillingness to let go of the firm, the fear of sibling rivalry, or intergenerational envy.

12.5   Issues in Evaluation and Control

As a means by which the corporation's implementation of strategy can be evaluated, the control systems of large corporations have evolved over a long period of time in response to pressures from the environment (particularly the government). Conversely the entrepreneur creates what is needed as the business grows. Because of a personal involvement in decision making, the entrepreneur managing a small business has little need for a formal, detailed reporting system. Thus the founder who has little under-

Table 12.4   **Transfer of Power in a Family Business**

Phase 1.   **Owner-managed business.** Phase 1 begins at start-up and continues until the entrance of another family member into the business on a full-time basis. Family considerations influence but are not yet a directing part of the firm. At this point, the founder (entrepreneur) and the business are one.

Phase 2.   **Training and development of new generation.** The children begin to learn the business at the dining room table during early childhood and then through part-time and vacation employment. The family and the business become one. Just as the entrepreneur identified with the business earlier, the family now begins to identify itself with the business.

Phase 3.   **Partnership between generations.** At this point, a son or daughter of the founder has acquired sufficient business and managerial competence so that he or she can be involved in key decisions for at least a part of the company. The entrepreneur's offspring, however, has to first gain respect from the firm's employees and other managers and show that he or she can do the job right. Another issue is the lack of willingness of the founder to share authority with the son or daughter. Consequently a common tactic taken by sons and daughters in family businesses is to take a job in a large, established corporation where they can gain valuable experience and respect for their skills.

Phase 4.   **Transfer of power.** Instead of being forced to sell the company when he or she can no longer manage the business, the founder has the option in a family business of turning it over to the next generation as part of their inheritance. Often the founder moves to the position of Chairman of the Board and promotes one of the children to the position of CEO. Unfortunately some founders cannot resist meddling in operating affairs and unintentionally undermine the leadership position of the son or daughter. To avoid this problem, the founder should sell his or her stock (probably through a leveraged buy-out to the children) and physically leave the company and allow the next generation the freedom it needs to adapt to changing conditions.

Source: N. C. Churchill and K. J. Hatten, "Non-Market-Based Transfer of Wealth and Power: A Research Framework for Family Businesses," *American Journal of Small Business* (Winter 1987), pp. 51–64. Reprinted with permission.

standing of accounting and a shortage of cash might employ a bookkeeper instead of an accountant. A formal personnel function might never appear because the entrepreneur lumps it in with simple bookkeeping and uses a secretary to handle personnel files. As an entrepreneurial venture becomes more established, it will develop more complex evaluation and control systems, but they are often not the kind used in large corporations and are probably used for different purposes.

Financial statements, in particular, tell only half the story in small, privately owned companies. The formality of the financial reporting system in such a company is usually a result of pressures from government tax agencies, not from management's desire for an objective evaluation and control system. For example, the absence of taxes in Bermuda has been given as the reason why business owners keep little documentation—thus finding it nearly impossible to keep track of inventory, monitor sales, or calculate how much they are owed.[35]

Because balance sheets and income statements do not always give an accurate picture, standard ratios such as return on assets and debt-equity are unreliable. *Cash flow is widely regarded as more important for an entrepreneurial business than is the traditional balance sheet or income statement.* Even though a small business may be profitable in the accounting sense, a negative cash flow could bankrupt the company. Levin and Travis provide five reasons why owners, operators, and outside observers should be wary of using standard financial methods to indicate the health of a small, privately owned company.[36]

- **The line between debt and equity is blurred.** In some instances, what appears as a loan is really an easy-to-retrieve equity investment. The entrepreneur in this instance doesn't want to lose his or her investment if the company fails. Another condition is that retained earnings seldom reflect the amount of internal financing needed for the company's growth. This account may merely be a place in which cash is left so that the owner can avoid double taxation. To avoid other taxes, owner-managers may own fixed assets that they lease to the corporation. The equity that was used to buy those assets is really the company's equity, but it doesn't appear on the books.

- **Lifestyle is a part of financial statements.** The lifestyle of the owner and the owner's family is often reflected in the balance sheet. The assets of some firms include beach cottages, mountain chalets, and automobiles. In others, plants and warehouses that are used for company operations are not shown because they are held separately by the family. Income statements may not reflect how well the company is operating. Profitability is not so important in decision making in small, private companies as it is in large, publicly held corporations. For example, spending for recreation or transportation and paying rents or salaries above market rates to relatives put artificially high costs on the books of small firms. The business might appear to be poorly managed to an outsider, but the owner is acting rationally. The owner-manager wants dependable income or its equivalent with the least painful tax consequences. Because the standard profitability measures such as ROI are not useful in the evaluation of such a firm, Levin and Travis recommend return on current assets as a better measure of corporate productivity.

- **Standard financial formulas don't always apply.** Following practices that are in contrast to standard financial recommendations, small companies often use short-term debt to finance fixed assets. The absence of well-organized capital markets for small businesses, along with the typical banker's resistance to making loans without personal guarantees, leaves the private owner little choice.

- **Personal preference determines financial policies.** Because the owner is often the manager of the small firm, dividend policy is largely irrelevant. Dividend decisions are based not on stock price (which is usually unknown because the stock is not traded), but on the owner's lifestyle and the tradeoff between taking wealth from the corporation and double taxation.

- **Banks combine personal and business wealth.** Because of the large percentage of small businesses that go bankrupt every year, bank loan officers are reluctant to lend money to a small business unless the owner also provides some personal guarantees for the loan. In some instances, part of the loan may be composed of a second mortgage on the owner's house. If the owner does not want to succumb to this pressure by lenders to include the owner's personal assets as part of the collateral, the owner-manager must be willing to pay high interest rates for a loan that does not put the family's assets at risk.

12.6 *Global Issues for the 21st Century*

- The **21st Century Global Society** feature in this chapter illustrates how an entrepreneur's personal values and beliefs can become part of a new venture's mission statement and policies. In this way, entrepreneurs are change agents—leading the way to the future. Anita Roddick incorporated concern for the environment long before it became fashionable. The founders of Apple Computer changed an industry (and perhaps the world) in their effort to make a user-friendly computer widely available.

- Entrepreneurship is becoming increasingly important throughout the world. True to economist Joseph Schumpeter's view of entrepreneurship as "creative destruction," much of the world from Eastern Europe to South America to Asia envisions entrepreneurial ventures as the means to build successful free market economies. New entrepreneurial ventures are emerging daily in these countries.

- Given the inability of large corporations to adapt successfully to technological discontinuities, current technological advances should provide an increasing number of opportunities for entrepreneurial ventures in the near future. For example, entrepreneurs worldwide are using the Internet to advertise and sell their products as well as to find suppliers and distributors.

- Multinational corporations have discovered that forming a joint venture with a local entrepreneur is an excellent strategy to enter a country. Developing nations, in particular, are very wary of foreign-owned companies that don't use their profits to further develop the country. The globalization of industries can thus stimulate entrepreneurial ventures worldwide.

- The inability of most entrepreneurial ventures to have access to financial and other resources means that they need to engage in strategic alliances to obtain adequate supplies and distribution. IBM, for example, invests in new ventures working to develop new technologies in order to gain access to the technologies when they are developed.

Projections for the 21st Century

- From 1994 to 2010, the number of golf courses in the U.S. will increase from 14,648 to 16,800.

- From 1994 to 2010, gambling revenues will grow in the U.S. from $39.5 billion to $125.6 billion.[37]

Discussion Questions

1. In terms of strategic management, how does a new venture's situation differ from that of an ongoing small company?

2. How should a small entrepreneurial company engage in environmental scanning? To what aspects of the environment should management pay most attention?

3. What are the characteristics of an attractive industry from an entrepreneur's point of view? What role does innovation play?

4. What considerations should small-business entrepreneurs keep in mind when they are deciding if a company should follow a growth or a stability strategy?

5. How does being family owned (as compared to being publicly owned) affect a firm's strategic management?

Key Terms

business plan (p. 287)
entrepreneur (p. 284)
entrepreneurial characteristics (p. 293)
entrepreneurial venture (p. 284)
factors affecting new venture success (p. 292)

family businesses (p. 298)
lifestyle company (p. 296)
small-business firm (p. 284)
sources of innovation (p. 290)
strategic decision-making process for entrepreneurial ventures (p. 286)

substages of small business development (p. 295)

Strategic Practice Exercise

In December 1991, after a day of snowboarding at Squaw Valley, Erik Anderson and Jeff Sand sat on the cold ground working to remove their boots from the large, complicated bindings holding their feet to the snowboards. As they released their boots from the plastic straps, they wondered if there was a better way to attach boots to a snowboard, say, a simple step-in method. Alpine skiers had been using step-in bindings for more than 20 years, but nothing like it had yet been developed for snowboarding—an industry with sales of $750 million in 1996 and projected to top $2 billion by 2000. Although the primary users of snowboards, teenage boys, so far didn't seem to care much about the inconvenient strap-in bindings, a step-in system might attract more people to the sport.

During the spring of 1992, Anderson and Sand began two years of evening and weekend research and development (keeping their day jobs designing retail stores), funded primarily by $200,000 in loans from family and friends. Their goal was to make a product that would eliminate the complicated straps and high-backed plastic frames of conventional bindings, yet provide enough support to preserve control and flexibility. They developed a design incorporating a steel rod on either side of the boot to hold the rider's boot tightly to the board. Because the new binding did away with the high-backed frame, the boots would now have to furnish all the support. This meant that Anderson and Sand's newly formed company, Switch Manufacturing, would have to produce not only the *Autolock binding*, but also its companion, *Flexible boot*, as well.

Anderson and Sand brought their pioneering product to market in early 1995, but competition was not far behind. The giant American ski-maker K2, in partnership with the Japanese bicycle maker Shimano, introduced a step-in product, the *Clicker*. At about the same time, two other step-in systems, *Device* and *T-Bone*, were introduced by other competitors.

Step-in sales grew to 5% of the snowboard-binding market by 1995. Even though Anderson optimistically expected step-ins to soon account for 95% of the market, serious snowboarders had their doubts. Steve Klassen, world extreme snowboarding champion, felt that the product was not yet perfected. "As soon as I find a step-in binding that equals the performance of the strap systems, I'll switch myself. Switch's current design, which has metal bolts hanging off the side of the boot, won't become the standard. But that's not to say that Switch might not come up with the right system in the future."

Because of retailer reluctance to stock multiple lines of step-ins, Anderson predicted that the market would soon have to settle on only three to four step-in systems. Success for Switch meant that it had to be one of these basic standards or face being closed out of distribution.

With little money to spend on marketing, Anderson and Sand decided to license their boot technology to a large number of boot makers as a way to establish the Autolock binding as the de facto standard in this fast-growing industry. Shimano had successfully done this in 1990 when it had licensed its integrated shoe-and-pedal clip-in system to makers of bike shoes around the world. Even though Switch would receive a $5,000 licensing fee plus a $1 royalty on each pair of boots sold, the founders realized that this would cut into sales of Switch's own Flexible boot line. Commented Anderson, "by licensing their technology, Shimano lost a lot of shoe sales, but it was offset incredibly by the increase in their pedal sales." If the boot makers would use Switch's boot technology, they would have to buy the step-in binding from Switch—and success would be assured.

Switch Manufacturing had 1995 sales of $1.5 million. Anderson and Sands projected sales of $9 million for 1996 and $19 million for 1997 with a projected pre-tax 1997 profit of $2.8 million. Co-founder Anderson claimed that his company's sales and market share in 1996 were the same as those of K2. By year-end 1996, Switch's system was being used by the boot makers Vans, Gordo, Nice, Titan, Duffs, and Flexible.[38] (See Switch's web site at *Switch-sf.com*.)

1. What do you think of Switch's chances to make its binding one of the industry standards?

2. What has Switch done right?

3. Should it have done anything differently?

4. Will Switch survive the competition?

5. What are your recommendations to Switch's management?

Notes

1. J. Norman, "Great Idea? That's the Easy Part," *Des Moines Register* (November 12, 1995), p. 3G.
2. "StartUps: Still a Job Engine," *Business Week* (March 24, 1997), p. 26.
3. *The State of Small Business: A Report to the President,* (Washington, D.C.: U.S. Government Printing Office, 1987), p. 117.
4. B. Keats, and J. Bracker, "Toward a Theory of Small Firm Performance: A Conceptual Model," *American Journal of Small Business* (Spring 1988), pp. 41–58; D. Dougherty, "A Practice-Centered Model of Organizational Renewal Through Product Innovation," *Strategic Management Journal* (Summer 1992), pp. 77–92.
5. J. Castro, J. McDowell, and W. McWhirter, "Big vs. Small," *Time* (September 5, 1988), p. 49.
6. B. Bowers, "This Store Is a Hit But Somehow Cash Flow Is Missing," *Wall Street Journal* (April 13, 1993), p. B2.
7. M. J. Foster, "Scenario Planning for Small Businesses," *Long Range Planning* (February 1993), p. 123; M. S. S. El-Namacki, "Small Business—The Myth and the Reality," *Long Range Planning* (August 1990), p. 79.
8. According to a study by Dun & Bradstreet of 800,000 small U.S. businesses started in 1985, 70% were still in business in March 1994. Contrary to other studies, this study only counted firms as failures if they owed money at the time of their demise. Also see J. Aley, "Debunking the Failure Fallacy," *Fortune* (September 6, 1993), p. 21.
9. R. N. Lussier, "Startup Business Advice from Business Owners to Would-Be Entrepreneurs," *SAM Advanced Management Journal* (Winter 1995), pp. 10–13.
10. J. W. Carland, F. Hoy, W. R. Boulton, and J. A. C. Carland, "Differentiating Entrepreneurs from Small Business Owners: A Conceptualization," *Academy of Management Review* (April 1984), p. 358; J. W. Carland, J. C. Carland, F. Hoy, and W. R. Boulton, "Distinctions Between Entrepreneurial and Small Business Ventures," *International Journal of Management* (March 1988), pp. 98–103.
11. S. P. Galante, "Counting on a Narrow Market Can Cloud Company's Future," *Wall Street Journal* (January 20, 1986), p. 17.
12. D. Fields, "Mrs. Fields' Weekends," *USA Weekend* (February 3–5, 1989), p. 16; M. Alpert, "In the Chips," *Fortune* (July 17, 1989), pp. 115–116.
13. J. S. Bracker, B. W. Keats, and J. N. Pearson, "Planning and Financial Performance Among Small Firms in a Growth Industry," *Strategic Management Journal* (November-December 1988), pp. 591–603; J. Kargar and J. A. Parnell, "Strategic Planning Emphasis and Planning Satisfaction in Small Firms: An Empirical Investigation," *Journal of Business Strategies* (Spring 1996), pp. 1–20.
14. W. H. Baker, H. Lon, and B. Davis, "Business Planning in Successful Small Firms," *Long Range Planning* (December 1993), pp. 82–88.
15. A. Thomas, "Less Is More: How Less Formal Planning Can Be Best," in *The Strategic Planning Management Reader,* edited by L. Fahey (Englewood Cliffs, N.J.: Prentice Hall, 1989), pp. 331–336; C. B. Shrader, C. L. Mulford, and V. L. Blackburn, "Strategic and Operational Planning, Uncertainty, and Performance in Small Firms," *Journal of Small Business Management* (October 1989), pp. 45–60.
16. R. B. Robinson, Jr., and J. A. Pearce II, "The Impact of Formalized Strategic Planning on Financial Performance in Small Organizations," *Strategic Management Journal* (July-September 1983), pp. 197–207; R. Ackelsberg and P. Arlow, "Small Businesses Do Plan and It Pays Off," *Long Range Planning* (October 1985), pp. 61–67.
17. V. Fowler, "Business Study Focuses on Failures," *Des Moines Register* (August 9, 1992), p. G1. For information on preparing a business plan, see J. T. Broome, Jr., "How to Write a Business Plan," *Nation's Business* (February 1993), pp. 29–30, and P. D. O'Hara, *The Total Business Plan* (Boston: Wiley & Sons, 1990). For information on business plan software, see B. McWilliams, "Garbage In, Garbage Out," *Inc.* (August 1996), pp. 41–44.
18. J. C. Shuman, and J. A. Seeger, "The Theory and Practice of Strategic Management in Smaller Rapid Growth Firms," *American Journal of Small Business* (Summer 1986), p. 14.
19. S. Birley, and P. Westhead, "Growth and Performance Contrasts Between 'Types' of Small Firms," *Strategic Management Journal* (November-December 1990), pp. 535–557; J. L. Ward and C. E. Aronloff, "How Family Affects Strategy," *Small Business Forum* (Fall 1994), pp. 85–90.
20. P. F. Drucker, *Innovation and Entrepreneurship* (New York: HarperCollins, 1985), pp. 30–129.
21. "The Virtual Emporium Is Your . . . One-Stop Shop," *GW2k: Gateway Magazine* (Spring 1997), p. 37.
22. C. W. Hofer, and W. R. Sandberg, "Improving New Venture Performance: Some Guidelines for Success," *American Journal of Small Business* (Summer 1987), pp. 12–23. See also J. J. Chrisman and A. Bauerschmidt, "New Venture Performance: Some Critical Extensions to the Model," Paper presented to *State-of-the-Art Symposium on Entrepreneurship,* Iowa State University (April 12–14, 1992).
23. Interview with C. Bagley by J. Useem, "Forget Patents, Says Stanford Prof," *Inc.* (October 1996), p. 23.
24. Some studies do indicate that new ventures can also be successful following strategies other than going after an undefended niche with a focus strategy. See A. C. Cooper, G. E. Willard, and C. Y. Woo, "A Reexamination of the Niche Concept," in *The Strategy Process: Concepts, Contexts, and Cases,* 2nd edition, edited by H. Mintzberg and J. B. Quinn (Englewood Cliffs, N.J.: Prentice-Hall, 1991), pp. 619–628; P. P. McDougal, J. G. Covin, R. B. Robinson, Jr., and L. Herron, "The Effects of Industry Growth and Strategic Breadth on New Venture Performance and Strategy Content," *Strategic Management Journal* (September 1994), pp. 537–554.
25. H. P. Welsch, "Entrepreneurs' Personal Characteristics: Causal Models," Paper presented to *State-of-the-Art Symposium on Entrepreneurship,* Iowa State University (April

12–14, 1992); A. Rahim, "Stress, Strain, and Their Moderators: An Empirical Comparison of Entrepreneurs and Managers," *Journal of Small Business Management* (January 1996), pp. 46–58.

26. M. Kets de Vries, "The Dark Side of Entrepreneurship," *Harvard Business Review* (November-December 1985), pp. 160–167.

27. A. C. Cooper, F. J. Gimeno-Gascon, and C.Y. Woo, "Initial Human and Financial Capital as Predictors of New Venture Performance," *Journal of Business Venturing* (Volume 9, 1994), pp. 371–395; H. R. Feeser, and G. E. Willard, "Founding Strategies and Performance in High-Tech Firms," in *Handbook of Business Strategy, 1991/92 Yearbook,* edited by H. E. Glass, and M. A. Hovde (Boston: Warren, Gorham & Lamont, 1991), pp. 2.1–2.18.

28. R. Ricklefs, and U. Gupta, "Traumas of a New Entrepreneur," *Wall Street Journal* (May 10, 1989), p. B1.

29. N. C. Churchill, and V. L. Lewis, "The Five Stages of Small Business Growth," *Harvard Business Review* (May-June 1983), pp. 30–50.

30. J. W. Petty, and W. D. Bygrave, "What Does Finance Have to Say to the Entrepreneur?" *Journal of Small Business Finance* (Spring 1993), pp. 125–137.

31. See C. Farrell, K. Rebello, R. D. Hof, and M. Maremont, "The Boom in IPOs," *Business Week* (December 18, 1995), pp. 64–72; S. Gruner, "When Mom & Pop Go Public," *Inc.* (December 1996), pp. 66–73.

32. J. Ward, *Keeping the Family Business Healthy* (San Francisco: Jossey-Bass, 1987), as reported by U. Gupta and M. Robichaux, "Reins Tangle Easily at Family Firms," *Wall Street Journal* (August 9, 1989), p. B1.

33. N. C. Churchill, and K. J. Hatten, "Non-Market-Based Transfers of Wealth and Power: A Research Framework for Family Businesses," *American Journal of Small Business* (Winter 1987), pp. 51–64.

34. J. L. Ward, and C. E. Aronoff, "Shirt Sleeves to Shirt Sleeves," *Nation's Business* (September 1992), pp. 62–63.

35. J. Applegate, "Business People in Bermuda Get Sloppy Without Taxes," *Des Moines Register* (July 6, 1992), p. 8B.

36. R. I. Levin, and V. R. Travis, "Small Company Finance: What the Books Don't Say," *Harvard Business Review* (November-December 1987), pp. 30–32.

37. J. Warner, "21st Century Capitalism: Snapshot of the Next Century," *Business Week* (November 18, 1994), p. 194.

38. C. Caggiano, "Kings of the Hill," *Inc.* (August 1996), pp. 46–53.

Chapter 13

Strategic Issues in Not-for-Profit Organizations

The New York City Chapter of the American Heart Association (AHA) was in a difficult situation. Although it was one of 56 affiliates of the AHA, it had to generate revenue to put into its own projects. In recent years, the number of charitable organizations asking for corporate and foundation funds had proliferated at the same time that government dollars for human services and the arts were being drastically cut. Increasing costs had meant that the chapter would have to either increase its funding through more donations or drop some of its programs. The chapter's board of directors and management was unwilling to cut the chapter's programs on reducing death and disability from heart attacks and strokes. Unfortunately they would then have to raise an additional $1 million on top of the current budget—an impossible goal.[1] What should the organization do?

The American Heart Association was not alone in this situation. By the mid-1990s, most not-for-profit organizations were turning to strategic management and other concepts from business to ensure their survival. This was a significant change because most not-for-profit managers had traditionally felt that business concepts were not relevant to their situation. According to Peter Drucker:

> Twenty years ago, management was a dirty word for those involved in nonprofit organizations. It meant business, and nonprofits prided themselves on being free of the taint of commercialism and above such

sordid considerations as the bottom line. Now most of them have learned that nonprofits need management even more than business does, precisely because they lack the discipline of the bottom line.[2]

A knowledge of not-for-profit organizations is important if only for the sole reason that they employ over 25% of the U.S. workforce and own approximately 15% of the nation's private wealth.[3] In the United States alone, in addition to various federal, state, and local government agencies, there are about 10,000 not-for-profit hospitals and nursing homes (84% of all hospitals), 4,600 colleges and universities, over 100,000 private and public elementary and secondary schools, and almost 350,000 churches and synagogues, plus many thousands of charities and service organizations.[4]

Typically **not-for-profit organizations** include **private nonprofit corporations** (such as hospitals, institutes, private colleges, and organized charities) as well as **public governmental units** or **agencies** (such as welfare departments, prisons, and state universities). Traditionally studies in strategic management have dealt with profit-making firms to the exclusion of nonprofit or governmental organizations. This, however, is changing. Not-for-profit organizations are adopting strategic management in increasing numbers.

Scholars and practitioners are concluding that many strategic management concepts and techniques can be successfully adapted for not-for-profit organizations.[5] Although the evidence is not yet conclusive, there appears to be an association between strategic planning efforts and performance measures such as growth.[6] The purpose of this chapter is, therefore, to highlight briefly the major differences between the profit-making and the not-for-profit organization, so that the effects of their differences on the strategic management process can be understood.

13.1   Why Not-for-Profit?

The not-for-profit sector of an economy is important for several reasons. First, society desires certain goods and services that profit-making firms cannot or will not provide. These are referred to as **public or collective goods** because people who might not have paid for the goods receive benefits from them. Paved roads, police protection, museums, and schools are examples of public goods. A person cannot use a private good unless she or he pays for it. Generally once a public good is provided, however, anyone can use or enjoy it. See the ⬤ **21st Century Global Society** feature for those aspects of society most suited to being served by not-for-profit organizations rather than by profit-making business firms.

Second, a private nonprofit organization tends to receive benefits from society that a private profit-making firm cannot obtain. Preferred tax status to nonstock corporations is given in section 501(c)(3) of the U.S. Internal Revenue code in the form of exemptions from corporate income taxes. Private nonprofit firms also enjoy exemptions from various other state, local, and federal taxes. Under certain conditions, these firms also benefit from the tax deductibility of donors' contributions and membership dues. In addition, they qualify for special third-class mailing privileges.[7] These benefits are allowed because private nonprofit organizations are typically service organizations, which are expected to use any excess of revenue over costs and expenses (a *surplus* rather than a *profit*) either to improve service or to reduce the price of their service. This service orientation is reflected in the fact that not-for-profit organizations do not use the term "customer" to refer to the recipient of the service. The recipient is typically referred to as a patient, student, client, case, or simply "the public."

21ST CENTURY GLOBAL SOCIETY

ASPECTS OF LIFE MOST SUITED FOR NOT-FOR-PROFITS

Certain aspects of life do *not* appear to be served appropriately by profit-making business firms, yet are often crucial to the well-being of society. These aspects include areas in which society as a whole benefits from a particular service, but in which a particular individual only benefits indirectly. It is in these areas that not-for-profit organizations have traditionally been most effective. Libraries and museums are examples. Although most people do not visit libraries or museums very often, they are usually willing to pay taxes and/or donate funds to support their existence. They do so because these people believe that these organizations act to uplift the culture and quality of life of the region. To fulfill their mission, entrance fees (if any) must be set low enough to allow everyone admission. These fees, however, are not profitable—they rarely even cover the costs of the service. The same is true of animal shelters managed by the Humane Society. Although few people want abandoned pets running wild through city streets, fees charged from the sale of these animals cannot alone pay the costs of finding and caring for them. Additional revenue is needed—either in the form of donations or public taxation. Such public or collective services cannot generate a profit, yet they are necessary for any successful civilization.

Many nations throughout the world are attempting to privatize state-owned enterprises to balance their budgets. **Privatization** is (1) the selling of state-owned enterprises to private individuals or corporations or (2) the hiring of a private business to provide services previously offered by a state agency. Problems can result, however, if privatization goes too far. For example, in converting from a communist-oriented, centrally managed economy to a more democratic, free-market economy, Eastern European countries are finding that profit-making business firms are unable to satisfy all of society's needs. What used to be provided by the state free of charge (tax-supported) in Russia and other countries may now be provided only for the rich or not at all. The same problem is evident in the United States in the controversy over the provision of health care.

Some of the aspects of life that cannot easily be privatized and are often better managed by not-for-profit organizations are as follows:

- Religion
- Education
- Charities
- Clubs, interest groups, unions
- Health care
- Government

Although society's need for these aspects of life should continue and even increase in the 21st century, business firms seeking a profit have little incentive to satisfy the needs, with the possible exception of health care.

13.2 Importance of Revenue Source

The feature that best differentiates not-for-profit (NFP) organizations from each other as well as from profit-making corporations is their **source of revenue**.[8] The **profit-making firm** depends on revenues obtained from the sale of its goods and services to customers, who typically pay for the costs and expenses of providing the product or service plus a profit. The not-for-profit organization, in contrast, depends heavily on dues, assessments, or donations from its membership, or on funding from a sponsoring agency such as the United Way or the federal government to pay for much of its costs and expenses.

Sources of Not-for-Profit Revenue

Revenue is generated from a variety of sources—not just from clients receiving the product or service from the NFP. It can come from people who do not even receive the services they are subsidizing. One study of Minnesota nonprofits found that donations accounted for almost 40%, government grants for around 25%, and program service fees for about 35% of total revenues.[9] In other types of not-for-profit organizations—such as unions and voluntary medical plans—revenue comes mostly from the members, the people who receive the service. Nevertheless, the members typically pay dues in advance and must accept later whatever service is provided whether they choose it or not, whether it is what they expected or not. The service is often received long after the dues are paid.

In profit-making corporations, there is typically a simple and direct connection between the customer or client and the organization. The organization tends to be totally dependent on sales of its products or services to the customer for revenue and is therefore extremely interested in pleasing the customer. As shown in Figure 13.1, the profit-making organization *(organization A)* tries to influence the customer (through advertising and promotion) to continue to buy and use its services. Either by buying or not buying the item offered, the customer, in turn, directly influences the organization's decision-making process. The business is thus market oriented.

In the case of the typical not-for-profit organization, however, there is likely to be a very different sort of relationship between the organization providing and the person receiving the service. Because the recipient of the service typically does not pay the entire cost of the service, outside sponsors are required. In most instances, the sponsors receive none of the service but provide partial to total funding for the needed revenues. As indicated earlier, these sponsors can be the government (using taxpayers' money) or charitable organizations, such as the United Way (using voluntary donations). As shown in Figure 13.1, the not-for-profit organization can be partially dependent on sponsors for funding *(organizations B and C)* or totally dependent on the sponsors *(organization D)*. The less money it receives from clients receiving the service or product, the less market oriented is the not-for-profit organization.

Patterns of Influence on Strategic Decision Making

The **pattern of influence** on the organization's strategic decision making derives from its sources of revenue. As shown in Figure 13.1, a private university *(organization B)* is heavily dependent on student tuition and other client-generated funds for about 70% of its revenue. Therefore, the students' desires are likely to have a stronger influence (as shown by an unbroken line) on the university's decision making than are the desires of the various sponsors such as alumni and private foundations. The sponsors' relatively marginal influence on the organization is reflected by a broken line. In contrast, a public university *(organization C)* is more heavily dependent on outside sponsors such as a state legislature for revenue funding. Student tuition and other client-generated funds form a small percentage (typically less than 40%) of total revenue. Therefore, the university's decision making is heavily influenced by the sponsors (unbroken line) and only marginally influenced directly by the students (broken line).

In the case of *organization D*, however, the client has no direct influence on the organization because the client pays nothing for the services received. In this situation, the organization tends to measure its effectiveness in terms of sponsor satisfaction. It has no real measure of its efficiency other than its ability to carry out its mission and achieve its objectives within the dollar contributions it has received from its sponsors. In contrast to

Figure 13.1
The Effects of Sources of Revenue on Patterns of Client-Organization Influence

Source: Thomas L. Wheelen and J. David Hunger, "The Effect of Revenue Upon Patterns of Client-Organization Influence." Copyright © 1982 by Wheelen and Hunger Associates. Revised 1991. Reprinted by permission.

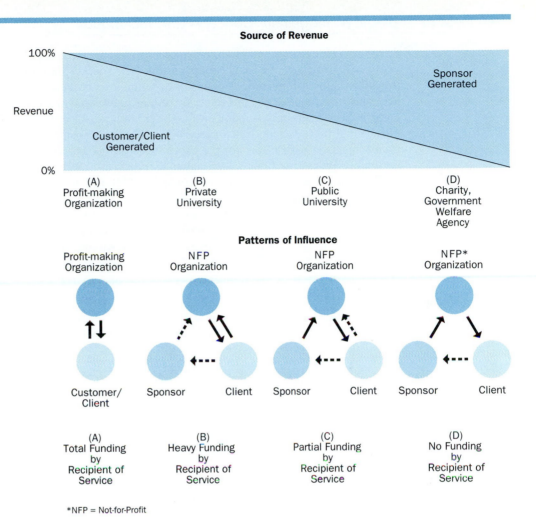

other organizations in which the client contributes a significant proportion of the needed revenue, *organization D* actually might be able to increase its revenue by heavily lobbying its sponsors while reducing the level of its service to its clients!

Regardless of the percentage of total funding that the client generates, the client may attempt to indirectly influence the not-for-profit organization through the sponsors. This is depicted by the broken lines connecting the client and the sponsor in *organizations B, C, and D* in Figure 13.1. Welfare clients or prison inmates, for example, may be able to indirectly improve the services they receive if they pressure government officials by writing to legislators or even by rioting. And students at public universities can lobby state officials for student representation on governing boards.

The key to understanding the management of a not-for-profit organization is thus learning who pays for the delivered services. If the recipients of the service pay only a small proportion of the total cost of the service, strategic managers are likely to be more concerned with satisfying the needs and desires of the funding sponsors or agency than those of the people receiving the service. The acquisition of resources can become an end in itself.

Usefulness of Strategic Management Concepts and Techniques

Some strategic management concepts can be equally applied to business and not-for-profit organizations, whereas others cannot. The marketplace orientation underlying portfolio analysis, for example, does not translate into situations in which client satisfaction and revenue are only indirectly linked. Industry analysis and competitive strategy are primarily relevant to not-for-profits that obtain most of their revenue from user fees rather than from donors or taxpayers. For example, as hospitals find themselves relying increasingly on patient fees for their revenue, they use competitive strategy to gain advantage versus other hospitals. Smaller NFP hospitals stress the "high touch" of their staff over the "high tech" of competitors having better diagnostic machinery.

SWOT analysis, mission statements, stakeholder analysis, and corporate governance are, however, just as relevant to a not-for-profit as they are to a profit-making organization.[10] As with any corporation, nonprofits usually have boards of directors whose job is to ensure that the paid executive director and staff work to fulfill the organization's mission and objectives. Many not-for-profits are finding a well-crafted mission statement not only helps in finding donors, but also in attracting volunteers. Take the example of the mission statement of a local animal shelter:

> To shelter and care for stray, lost, or abandoned animals and to responsibly place animals in new homes and enforce animal laws. We are also here to better educate people in ways to be solutions to animal problems, not causes.[11]

Strategic management is difficult to apply when the organization's output is difficult to measure objectively, as is the case with most not-for-profit organizations. Thus it is very likely that many not-for-profit organizations have *not* used strategic management because its concepts, techniques, and prescriptions did not lend themselves to situations where sponsors, rather than the marketplace, determined revenue. The situation, however, is changing. The trend toward privatizing public organizations, such as converting subsidized community hospitals to independent (nonsubsidized) status, usually means that the clients pay a larger percentage of the costs. As these not-for-profits become more market oriented (and thus client oriented), strategic management becomes more applicable and more increasingly used.[12] Nevertheless, various constraints on not-for-profits mean that strategic management concepts and techniques must be modified to be effective.[13]

13.3 Impact of Constraints on Strategic Management

Several characteristics peculiar to the not-for-profit organization constrain its behavior and affect its strategic management. Newman and Wallender list the following five **constraints on strategic management**:

1. **Service is often intangible and hard to measure.** This difficulty is typically compounded by the existence of multiple service objectives developed to satisfy multiple sponsors.

2. **Client influence may be weak.** Often the organization has a local monopoly, and clients' payments may be a very small source of funds.

3. **Strong employee commitments to professions or to a cause may undermine allegiance** to the organization employing them.

4. **Resource contributors may intrude on the organization's internal management.** Such contributors include fund contributors and government.

5. **Restraints on the use of rewards and punishments** may result from constraints 1, 3, and 4.[14]

It is true that several of these characteristics can be found in profit-making as well as in not-for-profit organizations. Nevertheless, as Newman and Wallender state, the ". . . frequency of strong impact is much higher in not-for-profit enterprises."[15]

Impact on Strategy Formulation

The long-range planning and decision making affected by the listed constraints serve to add at least four **complications to strategy formulation.**

1. **Goal conflicts interfere with rational planning.** Because the not-for-profit organization typically lacks a single clear-cut performance criterion (such as profits), divergent goals and objectives are likely, especially with multiple sponsors. Differences in the concerns of various important sponsors can prevent management from stating the organization's mission in anything but very broad terms, if they fear that a sponsor who disagrees with a particular, narrow definition of mission might cancel its funding. For example, a study of 227 public Canadian hospitals found that over half had very general, ambiguous, and unquantified objectives.[16] According to Heffron, an authority in public administration:"The greater openness within which they are compelled to operate—the fishbowl atmosphere—impedes thorough discussion of issues and discourages long-range plans that might alienate stakeholders."[17] In such organizations, it is the reduced influence of the clients that permits this diversity of values and goals to occur without a clear market check. For example, when a city council considers changing zoning to implement a strategic plan for the city, all sorts of people (including the press) will demand to be heard. A decision might be made based on pressure from a few stakeholders (who make significant contributions or who threaten to stir up trouble) to the detriment of the community as a whole.

2. **An integrated planning focus tends to shift from results to resources.** Because not-for-profit organizations tend to provide services that are hard to measure, they rarely have a net bottom line. Planning, therefore, becomes more concerned with resource inputs, which can easily be measured, than with service, which cannot. Goal displacement (explained earlier in Chapter 10) becomes even more likely than it is in business organizations.[18]

3. **Ambiguous operating objectives create opportunities for internal politics and goal displacement.** The combination of vague objectives and a heavy concern with resources allows managers considerable leeway in their activities. Such leeway makes possible political maneuvering for personal ends. In addition, because the effectiveness of the not-for-profit organization hinges on the satisfaction of the sponsoring group, management tends to ignore the needs of the client while focusing on the desires of a powerful sponsor. University administrators commonly say that people will donate money for a new building (which will carry the donor's name), but not for other more pressing needs, such as the maintenance of existing buildings. In this situation, powerful department heads might wine and dine the donor, hoping to get the money for their pet projects. This problem is compounded by the common practice of selecting people to boards of trustees/directors not on

the basis of their managerial experience, but on the basis of their ability to contribute money, raise funds, and work with politicians. Their lack of interest in overseeing management is reflected in an overall not-for-profit board-meeting attendance rate of only 50%, compared with 90% for boards of directors of business corporations. Board members of not-for-profit organizations, therefore, tend to ignore the task of determining strategies and policies—often leaving this to the paid (or sometimes unpaid) executive director. The larger the board, the less likely it is to exercise control over top management.[19]

4. **Professionalization simplifies detailed planning but adds rigidity.** In not-for-profit organizations in which professionals play important roles (as in hospitals or colleges), professional values and traditions can prevent the organization from changing its conventional behavior patterns to fit new service missions tuned to changing social needs. This rigidity, of course, can occur in any organization that hires professionals. The strong service orientation of most not-for-profit organizations, however, tends to encourage the development of static professional norms and attitudes. As not-for-profits attempt to become more business-like, this may be changing. One study of Minnesota nonprofits revealed that 29% of the program directors and 15% of the staff had degrees or experience in business administration.[20]

Impact on Strategy Implementation

The five constraining characteristics also affect how a not-for-profit organization is organized in both its structure and job design. Three **complications to strategy implementation** in particular can be highlighted:

1. **Decentralization is complicated.** The difficulty of setting objectives for an intangible, hard-to-measure service mission complicates the delegation of decision-making authority. Because of the heavy dependence on sponsors for revenue support, the top management of a not-for-profit organization must be always alert to the sponsors' view of an organizational activity. This necessary caution leads to **defensive centralization**, in which top management retains all decision-making authority so that low-level managers cannot take any actions to which the sponsors may object.

2. **Linking pins for external-internal integration become important.** Because of the heavy dependence on outside sponsors, a special need arises for people in buffer roles to relate to both inside and outside groups. This role is especially necessary when the sponsors are diverse (revenue comes from donations, membership fees, and federal funds) and the service is intangible (for instance, a "good" education) with a broad mission and multiple shifting objectives. The job of a "Dean for External Affairs," for example, consists primarily of working with the school's alumnae and raising funds.

3. **Job enlargement and executive development can be restrained by professionalism.** In organizations that employ a large number of professionals, managers must design jobs that appeal to prevailing professional norms. Professionals have rather clear ideas about which activities are, and which are not, within their province. Enriching a nurse's job by expanding his or her decision-making authority for drug dosage, for example, can cause conflict with medical doctors who believe that such authority is theirs alone. Because a professional often views managerial jobs as nonprofessional and merely supportive, promotion into a management position is not always viewed positively.

Impact on Evaluation and Control

Special **complications to evaluation and control** arising from the constraining characteristics also affect how behavior is motivated and performance is controlled. Two problems, in particular, are often noticed:

1. **Rewards and penalties have little or no relation to performance.** When desired results are vague and the judgment of success is subjective, predictable and impersonal feedback cannot be established. Performance is judged either intuitively ("You don't seem to be taking your job seriously") or on the basis of whatever small aspects of a job can be measured ("You were late to work twice last month").

2. **Inputs rather than outputs are heavily controlled.** Because its inputs can be measured much more easily than outputs, the not-for-profit organization tends to focus more on the resources going into performance than on the performance itself.[21] The emphasis is thus on setting maximum limits for costs and expenses. Because there is little to no reward for staying under these limits, people usually respond negatively to such controls.

13.4 Popular Not-for-Profit Strategies

Because of various pressures on not-for-profit organizations to provide more services than the sponsors and clients can pay for, these organizations are developing strategies to help them meet their desired service objectives. In addition to a heavy use of volunteers to keep costs low, NFPs are choosing the strategies of strategic piggybacking, mergers, and strategic alliances.

Strategic Piggybacking

Coined by Nielsen, the term **strategic piggybacking** refers to the development of a new activity for the not-for-profit organization that would generate the funds needed to make up the difference between revenues and expenses.[22] The new activity is related typically in some manner to the not-for-profit's mission, but its purpose is to help subsidize the primary service programs. It appears to be a form of concentric diversification, but it is engaged in not as part of the mission, but only for its money-generating value. In an inverted use of portfolio analysis, the organization invests in new, safe cash cows to fund its current cash-hungry stars, question marks, and dogs.

Although this strategy is not new, it has recently become very popular. As early as 1874, for example, the Metropolitan Museum of Art retained a professional to photograph its collections and to sell copies of the prints. Profits were used to defray the museum's operating costs. More recently, various income-generating ventures have appeared under various auspices, from the Girl Scouts to UNICEF, and in numerous forms, from cookies and small gift shops to vast real estate developments. A study by the U.S. General Accounting Office revealed that the amount of funds resulting from income-producing activities has significantly increased since the 1970s. Hospitals are offering wellness programs, ranging from meditation classes to aerobics. Some 70% of colleges and universities now offer "auxiliary" services, such as bookstores, conference rooms, and computer centers as sources of income.[23] The Small Business Administration, however, views this activity as "unfair competition." The Internal Revenue Service

(IRS) advises that a not-for-profit that engages in a business "not substantially related" to the organization's exempt purposes may jeopardize its tax-exempt status, particularly if the income from the business exceeds approximately 20% of total organizational revenues. The IRS is enforcing a law requiring charities to pay taxes on income from businesses that aren't related to their charitable activities. Nevertheless, not-for-profits are exempt if their businesses are staffed by volunteers or if almost all their merchandise is donated.[24]

Although strategic piggybacks can help not-for-profit organizations self-subsidize their primary missions and better use their resources, according to Nielsen, there are several potential drawbacks.[25] First, the revenue-generating venture could actually lose money, especially in the short run. Second, the venture could subvert, interfere with, or even take over the primary mission. Third, the public, as well as the sponsors, could reduce their contributions because of negative responses to such "money-grubbing activities" or because of a mistaken belief that the organization is becoming self-supporting. Fourth, the venture could interfere with the internal operations of the not-for-profit organization. To avoid these drawbacks, a not-for-profit should first carefully evaluate its resources before choosing this strategy. See the **Strategy in a Changing World** feature for necessary resources.

Mergers

Dwindling resources are leading an increasing number of not-for-profits to consider **mergers** as a way of reducing costs. For example, the merger of Baptist Health Systems and Research Health Services created Health Midwest in Kansas City. The New York Hospital–Cornell Medical Center and Columbia-Presbyterian Medical Center combined to form the New York and Presbyterian Hospitals Health Care System. Between 1980 and 1991, more than 400 U.S. hospitals were involved in mergers and consolidations— more than half of them happening after 1987.[26]

Strategic Alliances

Strategic alliances involve developing cooperative ties with other organizations. Alliances are often used by not-for-profit organizations as a way to enhance their capacity to serve clients or to acquire resources while still enabling them to keep their identity.[27] Services can be purchased and provided more efficiently through cooperation with other organizations than if they were done alone. For example, four Ohio universities agreed to create and jointly operate a new school of international business. Alone, none of the business schools could afford the $30 million to build the school.

13.5 Global Issues for the 21st Century

- The **21st Century Global Society** feature in this chapter describes how some aspects of society may best be provided by not-for-profit organizations than by business firms. As more countries adopt a free market economy and their governments attempt to balance their budgets, expect the debate over what should be business' sphere of influence and what should be that of not-for-profits' to escalate.

- The U.S. National Association of College and University Business Officers predicts that within a few years over 90% of colleges and universities in the United States

STRATEGY IN A CHANGING WORLD

RESOURCES NEEDED FOR SUCCESSFUL STRATEGIC PIGGYBACKING

Based on his experience as a consultant to not-for-profit organizations, Edward Skloot suggests that a not-for-profit should have five resources before engaging in strategic piggybacking:

1. **Something to sell.** The organization should assess its resources to see if people might be willing to pay for goods or services closely related to the organization's primary activity. Repackaging the Boston Symphony into the less formal Boston Pops Orchestra created a way to subsidize the deficit-creating symphony and provide year-round work for the musicians.

2. **Critical mass of management talent.** Enough people must be available to nurture and sustain an income venture over the long haul. This can be very difficult, given that the most competent not-for-profit professionals often don't want to be managers.

3. **Trustee support.** If the trustees have strong feelings against earned-income ventures, they could actively or passively resist commercial involvement. When the Children's Television Workshop began licensing its Sesame Street characters to toy companies and theme parks, many people criticized it for joining business in selling more things to children.

4. **Entrepreneurial attitude.** Management must be able to combine an interest in innovative ideas with business-like practicality.

5. **Venture capital.** Because it often takes money to make money, engaging in a joint venture with a business corporation can provide the necessary start-up funds as well as the marketing and management support. For example, Massachusetts General Hospital receives $50 million from Hoechst, the German chemical company, for biological research in exchange for exclusive licenses to develop commercial products from particular research discoveries.

Source: E. Skloot, "Should Not-for-Profits Go into Business?" *Harvard Business Review* (January-February 1983), pp. 20–24.

will be using strategic piggybacks. Expect a similar trend for other not-for-profits that heavily rely on donations and taxpayer support for their revenue.

- In 1995, the President of the United Way of America was convicted of misusing the charity's money. Although United Way's board of directors was not charged with any wrongdoing, this incident showed that NFP boards could be just as derelict in their duties as were some of the boards of business corporations. This has prompted many nonprofits to evaluate the effectiveness of their corporate governance structure. In the future, expect more nonprofits to be just as concerned about corporate governance as they are about using board members for fund-raising and political connections.

- The privatization of state-owned business enterprises (such as the sale of British Airways stock to the public by the U. K. government) is likely to continue globally because most of these enterprises must expand internationally in order to survive in the increasing global environment. They cannot compete successfully if they are forced to follow inefficient, socially oriented policies and regulations (emphasizing employment over efficiency) rather than economically oriented, international practices (emphasizing efficiency over employment). The global trend toward privatization should continue until each country reaches the point where the efficiency of business is counterbalanced by the effectiveness of the not-for-profit sector of the economy. As political motives overcome economic ones, government will likely intervene in that decision.

• Strategic alliances and mergers are becoming commonplace among not-for-profit organizations. The next logical step is strategic alliances between business firms and not-for-profits. Already business corporations are forming alliances with universities to fund university research in exchange for options on the results of that research. Business firms find it cheaper to pay universities to do basic research than to do it themselves. Universities are in need of research funds to attract top professors and to maintain expensive labs. Such alliances of convenience are being criticized, but they are likely to continue.

Projections for the 21st Century

• From 1994 to 2010, the number of AIDS cases worldwide will grow from 20 million to 38 million.

• From 1994 to 2010, the cost of a Wharton MBA will increase from $84,200 to $257,200.[28]

Discussion Questions

1. Are not-for-profit organizations less efficient than profit-making organizations? Why or why not?

2. How does the lack of a clear-cut performance measure, such as profits, affect the strategic management of a not-for-profit organization?

3. What are the pros and cons of strategic piggybacking? In what way is it "unfair competition" for NFPs to engage in revenue generating activity?

4. What are the pros and cons of mergers and strategic alliances? Should not-for-profits engage in alliances with business firms?

5. Recently, however, many not-for-profit organizations in the United States have been converting to profit making. Why would a not-for-profit organization want to change its status to profit making?

Key Terms

complications to evaluation and control (p. 313)
complications to strategy formulation (p. 311)
complications to strategy implementation (p. 312)
constraints on strategic management (p. 310)

defensive centralization (p. 312)
mergers (p. 314)
not-for-profit organization (p. 306)
patterns of influence (p. 308)
private nonprofit corporations (p. 306)
privatization (p. 307)
profit-making firm (p. 307)

public governmental units or agencies (p. 306)
public or collective goods (p. 306)
source of revenue (p. 307)
strategic alliances (p. 314)
strategic piggybacking (p. 313)

Strategic Practice Exercises

1. Read the **21st Century Global Society** feature in this chapter. It lists six aspects of society that it proposes are better managed by not-for-profit organizations than by profit-making organiza-

tions. Do you agree with this list? Should some aspects be deleted from the list? Should other aspects be added?

2. Examine a local college or university—perhaps the one you may be currently attending. What strategic issues is it facing? Develop a SFAS Table (Figure 5.1) of strategic factors. Is it attempting to use any strategic management concepts? If so, which ones? What sorts of strategies should it be considering for continued survival and future growth? Is it currently using strategic piggybacks to obtain additional funding? What sorts of additional piggybacks should it consider? Are strategic alliances with another college or university or business firm a possibility?

Notes

1. B. Wiesendanger, "Profitable Pointers from Non-Profits," *Journal of Business Strategy* (July/August 1994), pp. 33–39.

2. P. F. Drucker, "What Business Can Learn from Nonprofits," *Harvard Business Review* (July-August 1989), p. 89.

3. G. Rudney, "The Scope and Dimensions of Nonprofit Activity," in *The Nonprofit Sector: A Research Handbook,* edited by W. W. Powell (New Haven: Yale University Press, 1987), p. 56; C. P. McLaughlin, *The Management of Nonprofit Organizations* (New York: John Wiley and Sons, 1986), p. 4.

4. M. O'Neill, *The Third America* (San Francisco: Jossey-Bass, 1989).

5. K. Ascher, and B. Nare, "Strategic Planning in the Public Sector," *International Review of Strategic Management,* Vol. 1, edited by D. E. Hussey (New York: John Wiley & Sons, 1990), pp. 297–315; I. Unterman, and R. H. Davis, *Strategic Management of Not-for-Profit Organizations* (New York: Praeger Press, 1984), p. 2.

6. P. V. Jenster, and G. A. Overstreet, "Planning for a Non-Profit Service: A Study of U.S. Credit Unions," *Long Range Planning* (April 1990), pp. 103–111; G. J. Medley, "Strategic Planning for the World Wildlife Fund," *Long Range Planning* (February 1988), pp. 46–54.

7. J. G. Simon, "The Tax Treatment of Nonprofit Organizations: A Review of Federal and State Policies," in *The Nonprofit Sector: A Research Handbook,* edited by W. W. Powell (New Haven: Yale University Press, 1987), pp. 67–98.

8. B. P. Keating, and M. O. Keating, *Not-for-Profit* (Glen Ridge, N.J.: Thomas Horton & Daughters, 1980), p. 21.

9. K. A. Froelich, "Business Management in Nonprofit Organizations," paper presented to the *Midwest Management Society* (Chicago, 1995).

10. Ascher and Nare, "Strategic Planning in the Public Sector," pp. 297–315; R. McGill, "Planning for Strategic Performance in Local Government," *Long Range Planning* (October 1988), pp. 77–84.

11. Lorna Lavender, Supervisor of Ames (Iowa) Animal Shelter, quoted by K. Petty, "Animal Shelter Cares for Homeless," *ISU Daily* (July 25, 1996), p. 3.

12. E. Ferlie, "The Creation and Evolution of Quasi Markets in the Public Sector: A Problem for Strategic Management," *Strategic Management Journal* (Winter 1992), pp. 79–97; Research has found that for-profit hospitals have more mission statement components dealing with principal services, target customers, and geographic domain than do not-for-profit hospitals. See R. Subramanian, K. Kumar, and C. C. Yauger, "Mission Statements of Hospitals: An Empirical Analysis of Their Contents and Their Relationship to Organizational Factors," *Journal of Business Strategies* (Spring 1993), pp. 63–78.

13. J. D. Hunger, and T. L. Wheelen, "Is Strategic Management Appropriate for Not-for-Profit Organizations?" in *Handbook of Business Strategy, 1989/90 Yearbook,* edited by H. E. Glass (Boston: Warren, Gorham and Lamont, 1989), pp. 3.1–3.8; The contention that the pattern of environmental influence on the organization's strategic decision making derives from the organization's source(s) of income agrees with the authorities in the field. See R. E. Emerson, "Power-Dependence Relations," *American Sociological Review* (February 1962), pp. 31–41; J. D. Thompson, *Organizations in Action* (New York: McGraw-Hill, 1967), pp. 30–31; and J. Pfeffer, and G. R. Salancik, *The External Control of Organizations: A Resource Dependence Perspective* (New York: HarperCollins, 1978), p. 44.

14. W. H. Newman, and H. W. Wallender III, "Managing Not-for-Profit Enterprises," *Academy of Management Review* (January 1978), p. 26.

15. *Ibid.,* p. 27. The following discussion of the effects of these constraining characteristics is taken from pp. 27–31.

16. J. Denis, A. Langley, and D. Lozeau, "Formal Strategy in Public Hospitals," *Long Range Planning* (February 1991), pp. 71–82.

17. F. Heffron, *Organization Theory and Public Administration* (Englewood Cliffs, N.J.: Prentice-Hall, 1989), p. 132.

18. Heffron, pp. 103–115.

19. I. Unterman, and R. H. Davis, *Strategic Management of Not-for-Profit Organizations* (New York: Praeger Press, 1984), p. 174; J. A. Alexander, M. L. Fennell, and M. T. Halpern, "Leadership Instability in Hospitals: The Influence of Board-CEO Relations and Organizational Growth and Decline," *Administrative Science Quarterly* (March 1993), pp. 74–99.

20. Froelich, "Business Management in Nonprofit Organizations," p. 9.

21. R. M. Kanter, and D. V. Summers, "Doing Well While Doing Good: Dilemmas of Performance Measurement in Nonprofit Organizations and the Need for a Multiple-Constituency Approach," in *The Nonprofit Sector: A Research Handbook,* edited by W. W. Powell (New Haven: Yale University Press, 1987), p. 163.

22. R. P. Nielsen, "SMR Forum: Strategic Piggybacking—A Self-Subsidizing Strategy for Nonprofit Institutions," *Sloan Management Review* (Summer 1982), pp. 65–69; R. P. Nielsen, "Piggybacking for Business and Nonprofits: A

Strategy for Hard Times," *Long Range Planning* (April 1984), pp. 96–102.

23. D. C. Bacon, "Nonprofit Groups: An Unfair Edge?" *Nation's Business* (April 1989), pp. 33–34; "Universities Push Auxiliary Services to Generate More Revenue," *Wall Street Journal* (April 27, 1995), p. A1.

24. E. Skloot, "Should Not-for-Profits Go Into Business?" *Harvard Business Review* (January-February 1983), p. 21; E. Felsenthal, "As Nonprofits Add Sidelines, IRS Takes Aim," *Wall Street Journal* (May 3, 1996), p. B1.

25. R. P. Nielsen, "Piggybacking Strategies for Nonprofits: A Shared Costs Approach," *Strategic Management Journal* (May-June 1986), pp. 209–211.

26. S. Collins, "A Bitter Financial Pill," *U.S. News & World Report* (November 29, 1993), pp. 83–86.

27. K. G. Provan, "Interorganizational Cooperation and Decision Making Autonomy in a Consortium Multihospital System," *Academy of Management Review* (July 1984), pp. 494–504; R. D. Luke, J. W. Begun, and D. D. Pointer, "Quasi-Firms: Strategic Interorganizational Forms in the Health Care Industry," *Academy of Management Review* (January 1989), pp. 9–19.

28. J. Warner, "21st Century Capitalism: Snapshot of the Next Century," *Business Week* (November 18, 1994), p. 194.

Chapter 14

Suggestions for Case Analysis

In July 1996, AlliedSignal's free cash flow measure turned negative. Although the company reported a 16% gain in net income for the second quarter, the *free cash flow* was a negative $90 million. Top management dismissed the cash flow situation as only temporary, arguing that capital spending and increasing inventory during the first part of the year was needed to fuel the company's sales growth expected later in the year. A company spokesman predicted that the free cash flow for the year should hit $300 million and concluded, "There's no problem with cash flow here."

"Not so!" responded Jeffrey Fotta, President of Boston's Ernst Institutional Research. Fotta contended that Allied's growing sales and earnings masked a serious problem in the company. Over the past year, Allied's push to boost sales had caused it difficulty in meeting its cash needs from operations. "They're growing too fast and not getting the returns from capital investments they used to get. Allied peaked in mid 1995, and returns have been deteriorating since." Fotta predicted that without major changes, AlliedSignal would have increasing difficulty continuing its double-digit sales growth.[1]

This is an example of how one analyst used a performance measure to assess the overall health of a company. You can do the same type of in-depth analysis on a comprehensive strategic management case. This chapter provides you with various analytical techniques and suggestions for conducting this kind of case analysis.

14.1 The Case Method

The analysis and discussion of case problems has been the most popular method of teaching strategy and policy for many years. The case method provides the opportunity to move from a narrow, specialized view that emphasizes functional techniques to a broader, less precise analysis of the overall corporation. Cases present actual business situations and enable you to examine both successful and unsuccessful corporations. In case analysis, you might be asked to critically analyze a situation in which a manager had to make a decision of long-term corporate importance. This approach gives you a feel for what it is like to be faced with making and implementing strategic decisions.

14.2 Researching the Case Situation

Don't restrict yourself only to the information written in the case. You should undertake outside research into the environmental setting. Check the decision date of each case to find out when the situation occurred and then screen the business periodicals for that time period. Use computerized company and industry information services such as COMPUSTAT, Compact Disclosure, and CD/International, available on CD-Rom or on-line at the library. On the World Wide Web, Hoover's On Line Corporate Directory (*www.hoovers.com*) and the Security Exchange Commission's Edgar database (*www.sec.gov*) provide access to corporate annual reports and 10-K forms. This background will give you an appreciation for the situation as it was experienced by the participants in the case. See the **Strategy in a Changing World** feature for how to access the World Wide Web for business information.

A company's annual report and 10-K form from that year can be very helpful. Two-thirds of portfolio managers and 54% of security analysts agree that annual reports are the most important documents a public company can produce.[2] They contain not only the usual *income statements* and *balance sheets,* but also *cash flow statements* and notes to the financial statements indicating why certain actions were taken. 10-K forms include detailed information not usually available in an annual report. An understanding of the economy during that period will help you avoid making a serious error in your analysis, for example, suggesting a sale of stock when the stock market is at an all-time low or taking on more debt when the prime interest rate is over 15%. Information on the industry will provide insights on its competitive activities. Some resources available for research into the economy and a corporation's industry are suggested in Appendix 14.A.

14.3 Financial Analysis: A Place to Begin

Once you have read a case, a good place to begin your analysis is with the financial statements. **Ratio analysis** is the calculation of ratios from data in these statements. It is done to identify possible financial strengths or weaknesses. Thus it is a valuable part of SWOT analysis. A review of key financial ratios can help you assess the company's overall situation and pinpoint some problem areas. Ratios are useful regardless of firm size and enable you to compare a company's ratios with industry averages. Table 14.1 lists some of the most important financial ratios, which are (1) **liquidity ratios**, (2) **profitability ratios**, (3) **activity ratios**, and (4) **leverage ratios**.

STRATEGY IN A CHANGING WORLD

USING THE WORLD WIDE WEB TO OBTAIN INFORMATION

The **World Wide Web** is a part of the Internet and is an excellent source of information about industries as well as individual companies. To begin, you only need access to the Internet and a browser like Netscape Navigator or Microsoft's Internet Explorer.

Going Directly to the Company's Web Page

If you are looking for information about a particular company, you can first try using a simplified version of the firm's name to directly get to the firm's home (primary) web page. For example, first type in the protocol—the standard first part of the url (uniform resource locator)—*http://www.* Don't capitalize any letters in the url. Then type in a likely name for the firm, such as *maytag, ibm, toyota, hp* (Hewlett-Packard), *ti* (Texas Instruments), or *awl* (Addison Wesley Longman). This is referred to as the company's server name. Follow this name with the suffix *.com.* This is called a domain. In the United States, all business urls end with the domain name *.com.* University urls end with *.edu.* Government agencies' urls end with *.gov.* Outside of the United States each country has its own suffix, such as *.uk* for Great Britain, *.au* for Australia, *.ca* for Canada, *.de* for Germany, and *.pe* for Peru. This string of words and letters usually completes the url. For example, try typing *http://www.maytag.com* in the location line of your Internet browser and tap the Enter key. This takes you directly to Maytag's home web page. In some instances, the url may also contain a more specific web page beyond the company's home page. In this case, the *.com* is followed by */xxxx.html (xxxx* can be anything). This indicates that this is another web page that uses the html (hypertext markup language) language of the World Wide Web. Sometimes instead of *html*, it is abbreviated to simply *htm*.

Using a Search Tool

If typing in an obvious company name doesn't work, use a search tool. This is especially the case if you are investigating a non-U.S. corporation like AB Electrolux of Sweden. Search tools are services that act like a library's card file to help you find information on a topic. Some of the common search tools are:

- Yahoo (*http://www.yahoo.com*)
- AltaVista (*http://altavista.digital.com*)
- Galaxy (*http://galaxy.einet.net/galaxy.html*)
- Infoseek (*http://infoseek.go.com*)

The url will take you to the search tool's web page where you can type in the name of a company. The search tool uses its search engine to find any references to that firm. One of these references should include the company's url. Use it to get to the company's home web page.

Finding More Information

Getting to the company's home web page does not necessarily mean that you now have access to the firm's financials. For example, Maytag's home page doesn't provide access to its financial reports. In that case, try related business directories such as Hoover's On-Line (*http://www.hoovers.com*) or the U.S. Securities and Exchange Commission Edgar database (*http://www.sec.gov*). If the company's stock is publicly traded and listed on one of the major stock exchanges, these business directories should get you to the database containing the latest annual reports and 10-K reports, as well as quarterly reports. Other sites offering valuable information relating to business firms are:

- All Business Network (*http://www.all-biz.com/srch_abn.htm*)
- Web 100 (*http://www.w100.com*)
- Big Book (*http://www.bigbook.com*)
- Wall Street Research Net (*http://www.wsrn.com*)
- GTE Superpages (*http://superpages.gte.net*)

(continued)

USING THE WORLD WIDE WEB TO OBTAIN INFORMATION (*continued*)

- International Info (*http://www.nijenrode.nl.nbr/int*)

- Export Hotline & Trade Bank (*http://www. exporthotline.com*)

Additional web sites are listed at the end of Appendix 14.A. Note that web sites constantly change. Just because a particular url works one time does not mean that it will work a year or two later. If the company is doing a good job of managing its web sites, it will leave a message on its abandoned web page sending you to a new web page. If nothing works, simply go to one of the search tools and begin again. Good luck!

Note: Until recently, all Internet addresses in the U.S. ended with one of six domain names: .com for commercial businesses, .org for non-profit organizations, .net for networks, .edu for educational institutions, .gov for governmental bodies, and .mil for the military. Seven endings are being added: .store for businesses offering goods, .info for information services, .nom for personal sites, .firm for businesses, .web for specialized web sites, .arts for cultural groups, and .rec for recreational activities.

For additional information, see C. B. Leshin, *Management on the Web* (Upper Saddle River, N.J.: Prentice-Hall, 1997).

Analyzing Financial Statements

In your analysis, do not simply make an exhibit including all the ratios, but select and discuss only those ratios that have an impact on the company's problems. For instance, accounts receivable and inventory may provide a source of funds. If receivables and inventories are double the industry average, reducing them may provide needed cash. In this situation, the case report should include not only sources of funds, but also the number of dollars freed for use. Compare these ratios with industry averages to discover if the company is out of line with others in the industry.

A typical financial analysis of a firm would include a study of the operating statements for five or so years, including a trend analysis of sales, profits, earnings per share, debt to equity ratio, return on investment, and so on, plus a ratio study comparing the firm under study with industry standards.

- Scrutinize historical income statements and balance sheets. These two basic statements provide most of the data needed for analysis. Statements of cash flow may also be useful.

- Compare historical statements over time if a series of statements is available.

- Calculate changes that occur in individual categories from year to year, as well as the cumulative total change.

- Determine the change as a percentage as well as an absolute amount.

- Adjust for inflation if that was a significant factor.

Examination of this information may reveal developing trends. Compare trends in one category with trends in related categories. For example, an increase in sales of 15% over three years may appear to be satisfactory until you note an increase of 20% in the cost of goods sold during the same period. The outcome of this comparison might suggest that further investigation into the manufacturing process is necessary.

Table 14.1   **Financial Ratio Analysis**

	Formula	How Expressed	Meaning
1. Liquidity Ratios			
Current ratio	$\dfrac{\text{Current assets}}{\text{Current liabilities}}$	Decimal	A short-term indicator of the company's ability to pay its short-term liabilities from short-term assets; how much of current assets are available to cover each dollar of current liabilities.
Quick (acid test) ratio	$\dfrac{\text{Current assets} - \text{Inventory}}{\text{Current liabilities}}$	Decimal	Measures the company's ability to pay off its short-term obligations from current assets, excluding inventories.
Inventory to net working capital	$\dfrac{\text{Inventory}}{\text{Current assets} - \text{Current liabilities}}$	Decimal	A measure of inventory balance; measures the extent to which the cushion of excess current assets over current liabilities may be threatened by unfavorable changes in inventory.
Cash ratio	$\dfrac{\text{Cash} + \text{Cash equivalents}}{\text{Current liabilities}}$	Decimal	Measures the extent to which the company's capital is in cash or cash equivalents; shows how much of the current obligations can be paid from cash or near-cash assets.
2. Profitability Ratios			
Net profit margin	$\dfrac{\text{Net profit after taxes}}{\text{Net sales}}$	Percentage	Shows how much after-tax profits are generated by each dollar of sales.
Gross profit margin	$\dfrac{\text{Sales} - \text{Cost of goods sold}}{\text{Net sales}}$	Percentage	Indicates the total margin available to cover other expenses beyond cost of goods sold, and still yield a profit.
Return on investment (ROI)	$\dfrac{\text{Net profit after taxes}}{\text{Total assets}}$	Percentage	Measures the rate of return on the total assets utilized in the company; a measure of management's efficiency, it shows the return on all the assets under its control regardless of source of financing.
Return on equity (ROE)	$\dfrac{\text{Net profit after taxes}}{\text{Shareholders' equity}}$	Percentage	Measures the rate of return on the book value of shareholders' total investment in the company.

(continued)

Note that multinational corporations follow the accounting rules for their home country. As a result, their financial statements may be somewhat difficult to understand or to use for comparisons with competitors from other countries. For example, British firms such as British Petroleum and The Body Shop use the term "turnover" rather than sales revenue. In the case of AB Electrolux of Sweden, a footnote to the annual report indicates that the consolidated accounts have been prepared in accordance with Swedish accounting standards, which differ in certain significant respects from U.S. generally accepted accounting principles (U.S. GAAP). In this case, 1994 net income of

Table 14.1   Financial Ratio Analysis *(continued)*

	Formula	How Expressed	Meaning
Earnings per share (EPS)	$\dfrac{\text{Net profit after taxes} - \text{Preferred stock dividends}}{\text{Average number of common shares}}$	Dollars per share	Shows the after-tax earnings generated for each share of common stock.
3. Activity Ratios			
Inventory turnover	$\dfrac{\text{Net sales}}{\text{Inventory}}$	Decimal	Measures the number of times that average inventory of finished goods was turned over or sold during a period of time, usually a year.
Days of inventory	$\dfrac{\text{Inventory}}{\text{Cost of goods sold} \div 365}$	Days	Measures the number of one day's worth of inventory that a company has on hand at any given time.
Net working capital turnover	$\dfrac{\text{Net sales}}{\text{Net working capital}}$	Decimal	Measures how effectively the net working capital is used to generate sales.
Asset turnover	$\dfrac{\text{Sales}}{\text{Total assets}}$	Decimal	Measures the utilization of all the company's assets; measures how many sales are generated by each dollar of assets.
Fixed asset turnover	$\dfrac{\text{Sales}}{\text{Fixed assets}}$	Decimal	Measures the utilization of the company's fixed assets (i.e., plant and equipment); measures how many sales are generated by each dollar of fixed assets.
Average collection period	$\dfrac{\text{Accounts receivable}}{\text{Sales for year} \div 365}$	Days	Indicates the average length of time in days that a company must wait to collect a sale after making it; may be compared to the credit terms offered by the company to its customers.
Accounts receivable turnover	$\dfrac{\text{Annual credit sales}}{\text{Accounts receivable}}$	Decimal	Indicates the number of times that accounts receivable are cycled during the period (usually a year).
Accounts payable period	$\dfrac{\text{Accounts payable}}{\text{Purchases for year} \div 365}$	Days	Indicates the average length of time in days that the company takes to pay its credit purchases.
Days of cash	$\dfrac{\text{Cash}}{\text{Net sales for year} \div 365}$	Days	Indicates the number of days of cash on hand, at present sales levels.

(continued)

4,830m SEK (Swedish kronor) approximated 5,655 SEK according to U.S. GAAP. Total assets for the same period were 84,183m SEK according to Swedish principle, but 86,658 according to U.S. GAAP.

Common-Size Statements

Common-size statements are income statements and balance sheets in which the dollar figures have been converted into percentages. *For the income statement, net sales*

Table 14.1   **Financial Ratio Analysis** *(continued)*

	Formula	How Expressed	Meaning
4. Leverage Ratios			
Debt to asset ratio	$\dfrac{\text{Total debt}}{\text{Total assets}}$	Percentage	Measures the extent to which borrowed funds have been used to finance the company's assets.
Debt to equity ratio	$\dfrac{\text{Total debt}}{\text{Shareholders' equity}}$	Percentage	Measures the funds provided by creditors versus the funds provided by owners.
Long-term debt to capital structure	$\dfrac{\text{Long-term debt}}{\text{Shareholders' equity}}$	Percentage	Measures the long-term component of capital structure.
Times interest earned	$\dfrac{\text{Profit before taxes} + \text{Interest charges}}{\text{Interest charges}}$	Decimal	Indicates the ability of the company to meet its annual interest costs.
Coverage of fixed charges	$\dfrac{\text{Profit before taxes} + \text{Interest charges} + \text{Lease charges}}{\text{Interest charges} + \text{Lease obligations}}$	Decimal	A measure of the company's ability to meet all of its fixed-charge obligations.
Current liabilities to equity	$\dfrac{\text{Current liabilities}}{\text{Shareholders' equity}}$	Percentage	Measures the short-term financing portion versus that provided by owners.
5. Other Ratios			
Price/earnings ratio	$\dfrac{\text{Market price per share}}{\text{Earnings per share}}$	Decimal	Shows the current market's evaluation of a stock, based on its earnings; shows how much the investor is willing to pay for each dollar of earnings.
Divided payout ratio	$\dfrac{\text{Annual dividends per share}}{\text{Annual earnings per share}}$	Percentage	Indicates the percentage of profit that is paid out as dividends.
Dividend yield on common stock	$\dfrac{\text{Annual dividends per share}}{\text{Current market price per share}}$	Percentage	Indicates the dividend rate of return to common shareholders at the current market price.

Note:
In using ratios for analysis, calculate ratios for the corporation and compare them to the average and quartile ratios for the particular industry. Refer to Standard and Poor's and Robert Morris Associates for average industry data. Special thanks to Dr. Moustafa H. Abdelsamad, Dean, Business School, Texas A&M University–Corpus Christi, Corpus Christi, Texas, for his definitions of these ratios.

represent 100%: calculate the percentage of each category so that the categories sum to the net sales percentage (100%). For the balance sheet, give the total assets a value of 100%, and calculate other asset and liability categories as percentages of the total assets. (Individual asset and liability items, such as accounts receivable and accounts payable, can also be calculated as a percentage of net sales.)

When you convert statements to this form, it is relatively easy to note the percentage that each category represents of the total. Look for trends in specific items, such as cost of goods sold, when compared to the company's historical figures. To get a proper picture, however, make comparisons with industry data, if available, to see if fluctuations are merely reflecting industrywide trends. If a firm's trends are generally in line with those of the rest of the industry, problems are less likely than if the firm's trends are worse than industry averages. These statements are especially helpful in developing scenarios and pro forma statements because they provide a series of historical relationships (for example, cost of goods sold to sales, interest to sales, and inventories as a percentage of assets) from which you can estimate the future with your scenario assumptions for each year.

Z-value, Index of Sustainable Growth, and Free Cash Flow

If the corporation being studied appears to be in poor financial condition, use **Altman's Bankruptcy Formula** to calculate its Z-value. The **Z-value** formula combines five ratios by weighting them according to their importance to a corporation's financial strength. The formula is:

$$Z = 1.2x_1 + 1.4x_2 + 3.3x_3 + 0.6x_4 + 1.0x_5$$

where:

x_1 = Working capital/Total assets (%)

x_2 = Retained earnings/Total assets (%)

x_3 = Earnings before interest & taxes/Total assets (%)

x_4 = Market value of equity/Total liabilities (%)

x_5 = Sales/Total assets (number of times)

Scores below *1.81* indicate significant credit problems, whereas a score above *3.0* indicates a healthy firm. Scores between 1.81 and 3.0 indicate question marks.[3]

The **index of sustainable growth** is useful to learn if a company embarking on a growth strategy will need to take on debt to fund this growth. The index indicates how much of the growth rate of sales can be sustained by internally generated funds. The formula is:

$$g^* = \frac{[P(1-D)\ (1+L)]}{[T-P\ (1-D)\ (1+L)]}$$

where:

P = (Net profit before tax/Net sales) $\times$ 100

D = Target dividends/Profit after tax

L = Total liabilities/Net worth

T = (Total assets/Net sales) $\times$ 100

If the planned growth rate calls for a growth rate higher than its g^*, external capital will be needed to fund the growth unless management is able to find efficiencies, decrease dividends, increase the debt/equity ratio, or reduce assets by renting or leasing arrangements.[4]

Takeover artists and LBO (leveraged buy-out) specialists look at a corporation's financial statements for **operating cash flow**: the amount of money generated by a company before the cost of financing and taxes. This is the company's net income plus depreciation plus depletion, amortization, interest expense, and income tax expense. LBO specialists will take on as much debt as the company's operating cash flow can sup-

IS INFLATION DEAD OR JUST SLEEPING?

Inflation is a recent problem in the United States. Between 1800 and 1940, there was no clear trend up or down in the overall cost of living. A movie-goer in the late 1930s watching a drama set in the early 1800s would not notice prices to be unusual. For example, the cost of a loaf of bread in the late 1930s was roughly the same as in 1800. With the minor exceptions of 1949 and 1955, prices have risen every year since 1945. The Consumer Price Index (a generally used measure of the overall cost of living in the United States) increased nine times from 1945 to 1996. (Watch the movie *It's a Wonderful Life* to see how prices have changed.) From 1970 to 1980, the CPI more than doubled. After an average rate of 7.1% during the 1970s, inflation slowed to 5.5% in the 1980s, and 3.4% during the 1990s.

The rate of inflation in other countries varies and has a significant impact on a multinational corporation's profits. For example, the inflation rate in Brazil during 1987 was 545%. Bolivia's rate during 1985 was an astounding 25,000%! During the 1990s, Western Europe had an inflation rate of around 2%, while Eastern European countries were dealing with a rate ranging from 24% in Hungary to 52% in Russia to 91% in the Ukraine.

A report by the Boskin Commission recommended to Congress that the methodology used by the U.S. Bureau of Labor Statistics tends to overstate inflation and should be changed. Before inflation is declared dead by politicians anxious to reduce cost of living increases to Social Security payments (to reduce government expenditures and thus government debt), note what happens with a relatively constant 3.4% rate of inflation. Through the working of compound interest, the price level has already risen about 25% by 1996 and should reach 40% by the turn of the century. This means that companies have to be constantly monitoring not only their costs, but also the prices of the products they offer. *Unless a company's dollar sales are increasing over 3.5% annually, its sales are actually falling (in constant dollars)!* The same is true for net income. This point is often overlooked by the chief executive officers of troubled companies who are anxious to keep their jobs by fooling both the board and the shareholders.

Source: P. W. Boltz, "Is Inflation Dead?" *T. Rowe Price Report* (Winter 1997), pp. 10–11.

port. Although operating cash flow is a broad measure of a company's funds, some takeover artists look at a much narrower **free cash flow**: the amount of money a new owner can take out of the firm without harming the business. This is net income plus depreciation, depletion, and amortization less capital expenditures and dividends. The free cash flow ratio is very useful in evaluating the stability of an entrepreneurial venture.[5]

Useful Economic Measures

If you are analyzing a company over many years, you may want to adjust sales and net income for inflation to arrive at "true" financial performance in constant dollars. **Constant dollars** are dollars adjusted for inflation to make them comparable over various years. See the **Strategy in a Changing World** feature to learn why inflation is an important issue. One way to adjust for inflation in the U.S. is to use the Consumer Price Index (CPI), as given in Table 14.2. Dividing sales and net income by the CPI factor for that year will change the figures to 1982–1984 constant dollars.

Table 14.2 **U.S. Economic Indicators: Gross Domestic Product (GDP) in Billions of Dollars; Consumer Price Index for All Items (CPI) (1982–84 = 1.0); Prime Interest Rate (PIR)**

Year	GDP	CPI	PIR
1982	3,542.1	.965	14.86%
1983	3,514.5	.996	10.79
1984	3,902.4	1.039	12.04
1985	4,180.7	1.076	9.93
1986	4,422.2	1.096	8.33
1987	4,693.3	1.136	8.21
1988	5,049.6	1.183	9.32
1989	5,483.7	1.240	10.87
1990	5,743.8	1.307	10.01
1991	5,916.7	1.362	8.46
1992	6,244.4	1.403	6.25
1993	6,553.0	1.445	6.00
1994	6,935.7	1.482	7.15
1995	7,253.8	1.524	8.83
1996	7,661.6	1.569	8.27
1997	8,110.9	1.605	8.44
1998	8,537.9	1.630	8.50

Sources:

1. Gross Domestic Product from *Survey of Current Business* (January 1999), Vol. 79, No. 1, Table 1.1, p. D-2.

2. Consumer Price Index from U.S. Department of Commerce, *1997 Statistical Abstract of the United States*, 117th edition, Chart no. 752, p. 487; U.S. Bureau of Labor Statistics, *Monthly Labor Review* (October 1998), Chart no. 28, p. 74.

3. Prime Interest Rates from D. S. Benton, "Banking and Financial Information," Table 1-2, p. 3, in *Thorndike Encyclopedia of Banking and Financial Tables,* 3rd ed., 1998 Yearbook (Boston: Warren, Gorham and Lamont, 1998).

Another helpful analytical aid is **prime interest rate**, the rate of interest banks charge on their lowest risk loans. For better assessments of strategic decisions, it can be useful to note the level of the prime interest rate at the time of the case. (See Table 14.2.) A decision to borrow money to build a new plant would have been a good one in 1992, but less practical in 1989.

In preparing a scenario for your pro forma financial statements, you may want to use the **gross domestic product (GDP)** from Table 14.2. GDP is used worldwide and measures the total output of goods and services within a country's borders. Remember that scenarios have to be adjusted for a country's specific conditions. See the 🌐 **21st Century Global Society** feature for a list of the fastest growing economies in the world. These are the locations making a strong impact on strategic decision making in most corporations.

14.4 *Format for Case Analysis: The Strategic Audit*

There is no one best way to analyze or present a case report. Each instructor has personal preferences for format and approach. Nevertheless, we suggest an approach for both written and oral reports in Appendix 14.B, which provides a systematic method for suc-

21ST CENTURY GLOBAL SOCIETY

THE FASTEST GROWING ECONOMIES IN THE WORLD

Using a sophisticated scoring system based on measures of economic stability, human capital, free market policies, export orientation, and investment ratios, American Express Bank Ltd. publishes a list of the current economic world *tigers*—those countries demonstrating the capacity for rapid, sustained growth. These countries are: China, Hong Kong, Malaysia, Singapore, South Korea, and Thailand. They also calculate a list of *near-tigers*—those countries on the verge of rapid growth. These countries are: the Philippines, Czech Republic, Argentina, Chile, Taiwan, Vietnam, and Indonesia. Expect corporations to be seriously investing in these countries now and in the near future. The following table presents estimated figures for 1997 by country.

Country	GDP	GDP/ head	Population	GDP Growth	Inflation
Tigers:					
China	$897 bil	$720	1.24 bil	9.5%	12%
Hong Kong	$171 bil	$27,130	6.32 mil	5%	6.1%
Malaysia	$96 bil	$4,543	21.2 mil	7.8%	3.9%
Singapore	$102 bil	$32,878	3.1 mil	6.9%	1.6%
South Korea	$544 bil	$11,910	45.6 mil	7.3%	4.4%
Thailand	$202 bil	$3,250	62.1 mil	7.1%	4.4%
Near-Tigers:					
Philippines	$86 bil	$1,200	71.2 mil	5.8%	7.5%
Czech Republic	$57 bil	$5,570	10.3 mil	5.5%	8.2%
Argentina	$297 bil	$8,470	35 mil	2.2%	1.8%
Chile	$83 bil	$5,680	14.5 mil	5.5%	6.2%
Taiwan	$305 bil	$14,090	21.6 mil	5.7%	3.5%
Vietnam	$28 bil	$360	77.1 mil	7.9%	8.7%
Indonesia	$246 bil	$1,210	203.3 mil	7.2%	7.0%

Source: G. Koretz, "Look Who's Set to Pounce," *Business Week* (March 31, 1997), p. 30; D. Fishburn (ed.), "The World in Figures: Countries," *The World in 1997* (London: The Economist Group, 1996), pp. 83–89.

cessfully attacking a case. This approach is based on the **strategic audit**, which was presented in Chapter 10 as Table 10.5 (pages 252–259). We find that this approach provides structure and is very helpful for the typical student who may be a relative novice in case analysis. Regardless of the format chosen, be careful to include a complete analysis of key environmental variables—especially of trends in the industry and of the competition. Look at international developments as well.

If you choose to use the strategic audit as a guide to the analysis of complex strategy cases, you may want to use the strategic audit worksheet in Figure 14.1. Make a copy of the worksheet to use to take notes as you analyze a case. **You can also download the Strategic Audit Worksheet, from the *Strategic Management and Business* worldwide web site at http://www.prenhall.com/wheelen.** See Appendix 14.C for an example of a completed student-written analysis of a 1993 Maytag Corporation case *(not the 1996 version in the case portion of this book)* done in an outline form using the strategic audit format. This is an example of what a case analysis in outline form may look like.

Case discussion focuses on critical analysis and logical development of thought. A solution is satisfactory if it resolves important problems and is likely to be implemented successfully. How the corporation actually dealt with the case problems has no real bearing on the analysis because management might have analyzed its problems incorrectly or implemented a series of flawed solutions.

Figure 14.1
Strategic Audit Worksheet

Strategic Audit Heading	Analysis		Comments
	(+) Factors	(−) Factors	
I. Current Situation			
A. Past Corporate Performance Indexes			
B. Strategic Posture: Current Mission Current Objectives Current Strategies Current Policies			
SWOT Analysis Begins:			
II. Corporate Governance			
A. Board of Directors			
B. Top Management			
III. External Environment (EFAS): Opportunities and Threats (SWOT)			
A. Societal Environment			
B. Task Environment (Industry Analysis)			
IV. Internal Environment (IFAS): Strengths and Weaknesses (SWOT)			
A. Corporate Structure			
B. Corporate Culture			
C. Corporate Resources 1. Marketing			
2. Finance			
3. Research and Development			
4. Operations and Logistics			
5. Human Resources			
6. Information Systems			
V. Analysis of Strategic Factors (SFAS)			
A. Key Internal and External Strategic Factors (SWOT)			
B. Review of Mission and Objectives			

(continued)

Figure 14.1
Strategic Audit Worksheet
(continued)

SWOT Analysis Ends. Recommendation Begins:	
VI. Alternatives and Recommendations	
A. Strategic Alternatives	
B. Recommended Strategy	
VII. Implementation	
VIII. Evaluation and Control	

Note: See the complete Strategic Audit on pages 252–259. It lists the pages in the book that discuss each of the eight headings.

Source: T. L. Wheelen and J. D. Hunger, "Strategic Audit Worksheet." Copyright © 1989 by Wheelen and Hunger Associates. Revised 1991, 1994, and 1997. Reprinted by permission. Additional copies available for classroom use in Part D of *Case Instructors Manual* and on the Addison Wesley Longman web site (Use Passport).

14.5 *Global Issues for the 21st Century*

- The **21st Century Global Society** feature in this chapter lists the 13 fastest growing economies in the world. Expect an increasing amount of investment to be located in these countries in the near future. These are attractive locations for outsourcing and for international entry strategies. By the turn of the century, the economic tigers will include not only Asian, but also Eastern European and South American countries.

- Inflation will probably remain at a low but significant level during the near future for much of the developed world. As in the case of the European Union, regional blocs are realizing that inflation must be kept under control if there is to be prosperity.

- Expect the World Wide Web to soon become a dominant source of information throughout the world regarding industries, companies, and countries. It is an excellent way to obtain the latest information for competitive analysis.

- As multinational corporations increase their global presence, there will be increasing pressure for worldwide uniform accounting standards. The coming common currency in the European Union will eliminate some of the currency conversion problems and will support common standards. The next step may be one international stock exchange with subsidiary exchanges in each region or country.

- Standard financial ratios are of limited value for entrepreneurial ventures, especially small/family owned firms. With an increasing global emphasis on new business ventures, expect other measures, such as operating cash flow and free cash flow, to become equally important measures of financial health.

Projections for the 21st Century

- From 1994 to 2010, expect consumer inflation to decline from 4.3% to 2.5%.

- From 1994 to 2010, expect the international value of the U.S. dollar to increase from 1.0 to 9.33.[6]

Discussion Questions

1. Why should you begin a case analysis with a financial analysis? When are other approaches appropriate?

2. What are common-size financial statements? What is their value to case analysis? How are they calculated?

3. When should you gather information outside the case by going to the library or using the Internet? What should you be looking for?

4. When is inflation an important issue in conducting case analysis? Why bother?

5. How can you learn the date a case took place?

Key Terms

activity ratios (p. 320)
Altman's Bankruptcy Formula (p. 326)
common-size statements (p. 324)
constant dollars (p. 327)
free cash flow (p. 327)

gross domestic product (GDP) (p. 328)
index of sustainable growth (p. 326)
leverage ratios (p. 320)
liquidity ratios (p. 320)
operating cash flow (p. 326)

prime interest rate (p. 328)
profitability ratios (p. 320)
ratio analysis (p. 320)
strategic audit worksheet (p. 329)
World Wide Web (p. 321)
Z-value (p. 321)

Strategic Practice Exercise

Convert the following two years of income statements from the Maytag Corporation into common-size state-ments. The dollar figures are in thousands. What does converting to a common-size reveal?

	1992	%	1991	%
Net sales	$3,041,223		$2,970,626	
Cost of sales	2,339,406	_____	2,254,221	_____
Gross profits	701,817		716,405	
Selling, general, and admin. expenses	528,250		524,898	
Reorganization expenses	95,000	_____	—	_____
Operating income	78,567		191,507	
Interest expense	(75,004)		(75,159)	
Other—net	3,983		7,069	_____
Income before taxes and accounting changes	7,546		123,417	
Income taxes	(15,900)		(44,400)	
Income before accounting changes	(8,354)		79,017	
Effects of accounting changes for post-retirement benefits	(307,000)	_____	—	_____
Net income (loss)	$ (315,354)		$ 79,017	

RESOURCES FOR CASE LIBRARY RESEARCH

Company Information

1. Annual Reports
2. *Moody's Manuals on Investment* (a listing of companies within certain industries that contains a brief history and a five-year financial statement of each company)
3. Securities and Exchange Commission Annual Report Form 10-K (annually) and 10-Q (quarterly)
4. Standard and Poor's *Register of Corporations, Directors, and Executives*
5. Value Line's *Investment Survey*
6. *Findex: The Directory of Market Research Reports, Studies and Surveys* (a listing by Find/SVP of over 11,000 studies conducted by leading research firms)
7. *COMPUSTAT, Compact Disclosure, CD/International,* and *Hoover's Online Corporate Directory* (computerized operating and financial information on thousands of publicly held corporations)
8. Shareholders Meeting Notices.

Economic Information

1. Regional statistics and local forecasts from large banks
2. *Business Cycle Development* (Department of Commerce)
3. Chase Econometric Associates' publications
4. U.S. Census Bureau publications on population, transportation, and housing
5. *Current Business Reports* (U.S. Department of Commerce)
6. *Economic Indicators* (U.S. Joint Economic Committee)
7. *Economic Report of the President to Congress*
8. *Long-Term Economic Growth* (U.S. Department of Commerce)
9. *Monthly Labor Review* (U.S. Department of Labor)
10. *Monthly Bulletin of Statistics* (United Nations)
11. *Statistical Abstract of the United States* (U.S. Department of Commerce)
12. *Statistical Yearbook* (United Nations)
13. *Survey of Current Business* (U.S. Department of Commerce)
14. *U.S. Industrial Outlook* (U.S. Department of Defense)
15. *World Trade Annual* (United Nations)
16. *Overseas Business Reports* (by country, published by U.S. Department of Commerce)

Industry Information

1. Analyses of companies and industries by investment brokerage firms
2. *Business Week* (provides weekly economic and business information, and quarterly profit and sales rankings of corporations)
3. *Fortune* (each April publishes listings of financial information on corporations within certain industries)
4. *Industry Survey* (published quarterly by Standard and Poor's Corporation)
5. *Industry Week* (late March/early April issue provides information on 14 industry groups)
6. *Forbes* (mid-January issue provides performance data on firms in various industries)
7. *Inc.* (May and December issues give information on fast-growing entrepreneurial companies)

Directory and Index Information on Companies and Industries

1. *Business Periodical Index* (on computer in many libraries)
2. *Directory of National Trade Associations*
3. *Encyclopedia of Associations*
4. Funk and Scott's *Index of Corporations and Industries*
5. Thomas's *Register of American Manufacturers*
6. *Wall Street Journal Index*

Ratio Analysis Information

1. *Almanac of Business and Industrial Financial Ratios* (Prentice-Hall)
2. *Annual Statement Studies* (Robert Morris Associates)
3. *Dun's Review* (Dun and Bradstreet; published annually in September-December issues)
4. *Industry Norms and Key Business Ratios* (Dun and Bradstreet)

On-Line Information

1. *Hoover's Online*—Financial statements and profiles of public companies (*http://www.hoovers.com*)
2. *U.S. Securities & Exchange Commission*—Official filings of public companies in Edgar database (*http://www.sec.gov*)
3. *Fortune 500*—Statistics for largest U.S. corporations (*http://www.pathfinder.com*)
4. *Dun & Bradstreet's Online*—Short reports on 10 million public and private U.S. companies (*http://www.dbisna.com/dnb/dnbhome.htm*)
5. *Ecola's 24-Hour Newsstand*—Links to web sites of 2,000 newspapers, journals, and magazines (*http://www.ecola.com/news*)
6. *Competitive Intelligence Guide*—Information on company resources (*http://www.fuld.com*)
7. *The Economist*—Provides international information and surveys (*http://www.economist.com*)
8. *Web 100*—Information on 100 largest U.S. and international companies (*http://www.w100.com*).
9. *Nyenrode University* of the Netherlands—Provides European business information (*http://www.nyenrode.nl*).
10. *Bloomberg*—Information on interest rates, stock prices, currency conversion rates, and other general financial information (*http://www.bloomberg.com*)

SUGGESTED CASE ANALYSIS METHODOLOGY USING THE STRATEGIC AUDIT

1. READ CASE

First Reading of the Case

- Develop a general overview of the company and its external environment.

- Begin a list of the possible strategic factors facing the company at this time.

- List the research information you may need on the economy, industry, and competitors.

2. READ THE CASE WITH THE STRATEGIC AUDIT

Second Reading of the Case

- Read the case a second time using the strategic audit as a framework for in-depth analysis. (See Table 10.5. on pages 252–259.) You may want to make a copy of the strategic audit worksheet (Figure 14.1) to use to keep track of your comments as you read the case.

- The questions in the strategic audit parallel the strategic decision making process shown in Figure 1.3 (pages 20–21).

- The audit provides you with a conceptual framework to examine the company's mission, objectives, strategies, and policies as well as problems, symptoms, facts, opinions, and issues.

- Perform a financial analysis of the company using ratio analysis (see Table 14.1) and do the calculations necessary to convert key parts of the financial statements to a common-size basis.

3. DO OUTSIDE RESEARCH

Library and On-line Computer Services

- Each case has a decision date indicating when the case actually took place. Your research should be based on the time period for the case.

- See Appendix 14.A for resources for case research. Your research should include information about the environment at the time of the case. Find average industry ratios. You may also want to obtain further information regarding competitors and the company itself (10-K forms and annual reports). This information should help you conduct an industry analysis. Check with your instructor to see what kind of outside research is appropriate for your assignment.

- Don't try to learn what actually happened to the company discussed in the case. What management actually decided may not be the best solution. It will certainly bias your analysis and will probably cause your recommendation to lack proper justification.

4. BEGIN SWOT ANALYSIS

External Environmental Analysis: EFAS

- Analyze the four societal forces to see what trends are likely to affect the industry(s) in which the company is operating.

- Conduct an industry analysis using Porter's competitive forces from Chapter 3. Develop an Industry Matrix (Table 3.3 on page 71).

- Generate 8–10 external factors. These should be the *most important* opportunities and threats facing the company at the time of the case.

- Develop an EFAS Table, as shown in Table 3.3, for your list of external strategic factors.

- **Suggestion:** Rank the 8–10 factors from most to least important. Start by grouping the 3 top factors and then the 3 bottom factors.

Internal Organizational Analysis: IFAS

- Generate 8–10 internal factors. These should be the *most important* strengths and weaknesses of the company at the time of the case.

- Develop an IFAS Table, as shown in Table 4.2 (page 102), for your list of internal strategic factors.

- **Suggestion:** Rank the 8–10 factors from most to least important. Start by grouping the 3 top factors and then the 3 bottom factors.

5. WRITE YOUR STRATEGIC AUDIT: PARTS I–IV

First Draft of Your Strategic Audit

- Review the student-written audit of an old Maytag case in Appendix 14.C for an example.

- Write Parts I–IV of the strategic audit. Remember to include the factors from your IFAS and IFAS Tables in your audit.

6. WRITE YOUR STRATEGIC AUDIT: PART V

Strategic Factor Analysis Summary: SFAS

- Condense the list of factors from the 16–20 identified in your EFAS and IFAS Tables to only the 8-10 most important factors.

- Select the most important EFAS and IFAS factors. Reconsider the weights of each. The weights still need to add to 1.0.

- Develop a SFAS Table, as shown in Figure 5.1 (page 109), for your final list of strategic factors. Although the weights (indicating the importance of each factor) will probably change from the EFAS and IFAS Tables, the numerical rating (1–5) of each factor should remain the same. These ratings are your assessment of management's performance on each factor.

- This is a good time to reexamine what you wrote earlier in Parts I–IV. You may want to add to or delete some of what you wrote. Ensure that each one of the strategic factors you have included in your SFAS Table is discussed in the appropriate place in Parts I–IV. Part V of the audit is *not* the place to mention a strategic factor for the first time.

- Write Part V of your strategic audit. This completes your SWOT analysis.

- This is the place to suggest a revised mission statement and a better set of objectives for the company. The SWOT analysis coupled with revised mission and objectives for the company set the stage for the generation of strategic alternatives.

7. WRITE YOUR STRATEGIC AUDIT: PART VI

Strategic Alternatives and Recommendation

A. Alternatives

- Develop around three mutually exclusive strategic alternatives. If appropriate to the case you are analyzing, you might propose one alternative for growth, one for stability, and one for retrenchment. Within each corporate strategy, you should probably propose an appropriate business/competitive strategy. You may also want to include some functional strategies where appropriate.

- Construct a scenario for each alternative. Use the data from your outside research to project general societal trends (GDP, inflation, and so on) and industry trends. Use these as the basis of your assumptions to write pro forma financial statements (particularly income statements) for each strategic alternative for the next five years.

- List pros and cons for each alternative based on your scenarios.

B. Recommendation

- Specify which one of your alternative strategies you recommend. Justify your choice in terms of dealing with the strategic factors you listed in Part V of the audit.

- Develop policies to help implement your strategies.

8. WRITE YOUR STRATEGIC AUDIT: PART VII

Implementation

- Develop programs to implement your recommended strategy.

- Specify who is to be responsible for implementing each program and how long each program will take to complete.

An Example of an Action Plan

- Refer to the pro forma financial statement you developed earlier for your recommended strategy. Do the numbers still make sense? If not, this may be a good time to rethink the budget numbers to reflect your recommended programs.

9. WRITE YOUR STRATEGIC AUDIT: PART VIII

Evaluation and Control

- Specify the type of evaluation and controls that you need to ensure that your recommendation is carried out successfully. Specify who is responsible for monitoring these controls.

- Indicate if sufficient information is available to monitor how the strategy is being implemented. If not, suggest a change to the information system.

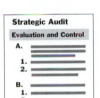

Strategic Audit — Evaluation and Control

10. PROOF AND FINE-TUNE YOUR AUDIT

Final Draft of Your Strategic Audit

- Check to ensure that your audit is within the page limits of your professor. You may need to cut some parts and expand others.

- Make sure that your recommendation clearly deals with the strategic factors.

- Attach your EFAS, IFAS, and SFAS Tables plus your ratio analysis and pro forma statements. Label them as numbered exhibits and refer to each of them within the body of the audit.

- Proof your work for errors. If on a computer, use a spell checker.

Special Note: Depending on your assignment, it is relatively easy to use the strategic audit you have just developed to write a written case analysis in essay form or to make an oral presentation. The strategic audit is just a detailed case analysis in an outline form and can be used as the basic framework for any sort of case analysis and presentation.

EXAMPLE OF STUDENT-WRITTEN STRATEGIC AUDIT

For 1993 Maytag Corporation Case

I. CURRENT SITUATION

A. Financial Performance—Currently poor, high debt load, first losses since 1920s, and price/earnings ratio negative.

B. Strategic Posture

1. **Mission**—Developed in 1989 for the Maytag Company: "To provide our customers with products of unsurpassed performance that last longer, need fewer repairs, and are produced at the lowest possible cost." Updated in 1991: "Our collective mission is world class quality." This expands Maytag's longstanding belief in product quality to all aspects of our operations.

2. **Objectives**—"To be profitability leader in industry for every product line Maytag manufactures." Choose increased profitability rather than market share. "To be number one in total customer satisfaction," and to "Grow the North American appliance business and become the third largest appliance manufacturer (in unit sales) in North America." Increase profitable market share growth in North American appliance and floor care business, 6.5% return on sales, 10% return on assets, 20% return on equity, beat competition in satisfying customers, dealer, builder and endorser, move into third place in total units shipped per year.

3. **Strategies**—Global growth through acquisition, and alliance with Bosch Siemens, consolidate dealer bases, preserve individual strong quality brand names as competitive advantage, but create synergy between companies, product improvement, investment in plant and equipment.

4. **Policies**—Maytag quality is the standard for the industry; although one goal is to make customer satisfaction second to none, policy to speed delivery is "in process," and Maytag is slow to respond to change in the marketplace or changes in consumer desires.

II. STRATEGIC MANAGERS

A. Board—Fourteen members, of whom 11 are outsiders. Well-respected Americans, most of whom have served on this board since 1986 or earlier...time for a change?

B. Top Management—Promoting from within results in a board that is knowledgeable and experienced in the appliance industry, but no one especially skilled in international business (Asian or Latin American affairs) is on the board—could be a problem.

III. EXTERNAL ENVIRONMENT (*EFAS* see Exhibit 1)

A. Societal environment is unstable but recession is ending, consumer confidence is growing, could increase spending for appliances.

1. North American market mature, but vigilant consumers still want value for money in safe, environmentally sound products—Maytag can do this.
2. NAFTA, European Union, and other regional trade pacts are opening doors to markets in Europe, Asia, Latin America, that offer enormous potential—economy truly becoming global in nature.

B. **Task Environment** very competitive, dominated by Big Global Conglomerates
   1. Whirlpool and AB Electrolux have enormous resources and truly global presence.
   2. Technology and materials used in manufacture same around the world, no comparative advantage, increased use of robotics.
   3. European design impacting everything, as is consumer desire for technologically advanced appliances using fuzzy logic.
   4. Quality and safety regulations standardization becoming reality.
   5. Super retailers are more important as a distribution channel, mom and pop dealers less.

IV. INTERNAL ENVIRONMENT (*IFAS* see Exhibit 2)

A. **Corporate Structure**
   1. Present structure is conglomerate of appliance manufacturing and vending machine companies in America and Europe, and a loose purchasing alliance with the German firm of Bosch Siemens.
   2. Decisions of major impact result from strategic plans made in Newton, Iowa, by Maytag Corporation by corporate staff, with a timeline of about three years.

B. **Corporate Culture**
   1. Quality is the key ingredient and a commitment to quality is shared by executives and workers.
   2. Much of corporate culture is based on founder F. L. Maytag's personal philosophy, including concern for quality, employees, local community, innovation, and performance.

C. **Corporate Resources**
   1. **Marketing** efforts streamlined to make them more profitable, combining three sales forces into two, to concentrate on major retailers (took $95 million in charges to do this reconstructing). Hoover also had well-publicized marketing fiasco involving airline tickets.
   2. **Finance (see Exhibits 4 and 5)**—Although revenues are up slightly, operating income is down significantly and some key ratios are troubling, such as a 57% debt/asset ratio, 132% long-term debt/equity ratio. Not to mention the fact that net income is 400% less than 1988, based on common-size income statements.
   3. **R&D**—Maytag appears to have become a follower, taking far too long to get product innovations to market (competitors put out more in last 6 months than prior 2 years combined) lagging in fuzzy logic and other technological areas.

4. **Operations**—Is where Maytag shines, and continual improvement process kept it dominant in the U.S. market for many years—it's just not enough now.

5. **Human Resources**—Labor relations are strained, with two salary raise delays, and layoffs of 4500 employees from Magic Chef. The unions express concern at new, more distant tone from Maytag Corporation since 1989.

6. **Information Systems** are not mentioned in this case, which makes the reader surmise they are not used efficiently, if at all. It represents another critical area where Maytag seems unwilling or unable to commit resources needed to stay competitive.

V. **ANALYSIS OF STRATEGIC FACTORS (*SFAS* see Exhibit 3)**
   A. **Key strategic factors are:**
      1. Financially Maytag does not have the resources of its competitors, so it must forge alliances with someone (like Bosch Siemens) who does in order to compete in the global market.
      2. Technologically Maytag has caught up with everyone else in terms of manufacturing capability, but product design and customer service innovation are areas of serious weakness.
      3. Evaluation and control issues, directly related to MIS areas, are only going to become more crucial as the company plants become flung all over the planet. (The Hoover Europe fiasco could happen again!)
      4. The good reputation of the Maytag name will continue to serve the company well in North America, quality still is a key factor.
   B. **Current Mission and Objectives:**
      1. Current mission appears appropriate.
      2. Some of the objectives are really goals and need to be quantified and given time horizons.

VI. **STRATEGIC ALTERNATIVES AND RECOMMENDED STRATEGY**
   A. **Strategic Alternatives**
      1. **Growth Through Concentric Diversification**: Acquire a company in a related industry like commercial appliances.
         a. **Pros:** Product/market synergy created by acquisition of related company.
         b. **Cons:** Maytag does not have the financial resources to play this game.
      2. **Pause Strategy**: Consolidate various acquisitions to find economies and to encourage innovation among the business units.
         a. **Pros:** Maytag needs to get its financial house in order and get administrative control over its recent acquisitions.
         b. **Cons:** Unless it can grow through a stronger alliance with Bosch Siemens or some other backer, Maytag is a prime candidate for takeover because of its poor financial performance in recent years and it is suffering from the initial reduction in efficiency inherent in this external growth strategy.

3. **Retrenchment**: Sell Hoover's foreign major home appliance businesses (Australia and UK) to emphasize increasing market share in North America.

   a. **Pros**: Divesting Hoover will improve the bottom line and enable Maytag Corp. to focus on the U.S. while Whirlpool, Electrolux, and GE are battling elsewhere.

   b. **Cons**: Maytag may be giving up its only opportunity to become a player in the coming global appliance industry.

B. **Recommended Strategy**

1. I recommend the pause strategy, at least for a year, so Maytag can get a grip on its European operation and consolidate the companies it has in a more synergistic way.

2. Maytag quality must be maintained and continued shortage of operating capital will take its toll, so investment must be made in R&D.

3. Maytag may be able to make the Hoover U.K. investment work better since the recession is ending and the E.C. countries are closer to integrating than ever before.

4. Because it is only an average competitor, Maytag needs the Hoover link to Europe to provide a jumping off place for negotiations with Bosch Siemens that could strengthen their alliance.

VII. IMPLEMENTATION

A. The only way to increase profitability in North America is to further involve Maytag with the superstore retailers, sure to anger the independent dealers, but necessary for Maytag to compete.

B. Board members with more global business experience should be recruited with an eye toward the future, especially with expertise in Asia and Latin America.

C. R&D needs to be improved, as does marketing, to get new products on line quickly. IS functions need to be developed for speedier evaluation and control.

VIII. EVALUATION AND CONTROL

A. While the question of controls vs. autonomy is "under review," another Hoover fiasco may easily be brewing.

B. The acquired companies do not all share the Midwestern work ethic or the Maytag Corporation culture and Maytag's managers must inculcate these values into all the new employees.

C. Systems should be developed to decide if the size and location of Maytag manufacturing plants is still correct and to plan for the future; industry analysis indicates that smaller automated plants may be more efficient now than in the past.

Note: The following exhibits were originally attached in their entirety to this strategic audit, but for reasons of space only their titles are listed here:
Exhibit 1: EFAS Table
Exhibit 2: IFAS Table
Exhibit 3: SFAS Table
Exhibit 4: Ratio Analysis for 5 Years
Exhibit 5: Common-size Income Statements

Notes

1. J. A. Sasseen, "Are Profits Shakier Than They Look?" *Business Week* (August 5, 1996), pp. 54–55.

2. J. Fulkerson, "How Investors Use Annual Reports," *American Demographics* (May 1996). Cited from American Demographics web site.

3. M. S. Fridson, *Financial Statement Analysis* (New York: John Wiley & Sons, 1991), pp. 192–194.

4. D. H. Bangs, *Managing by the Numbers* (Dover, N. H.: Upstart Publications, 1992), pp. 106–107.

5. J. M. Laderman, "Earnings, Schmernings Look at the Cash," *Business Week* (July 24, 1989), pp. 56–57.

6. J. Warner, "21st Century Capitalism: Snapshot of the Next Century," *Business Week* (November 18, 1994), p. 194.

Cases in Strategic Management

Section A

**Corporate Governance: Questions
of Executive Leadership**

Section B

**Environmental Issues: Questions of Social
Responsibility and Ethics**

Section C

Issues in Strategic Management

Industry One   Food
Industry Two   Computer/Internet/Software
Industry Three   Entertainment/Travel
Industry Four   Recreation Equipment
Industry Five   Major Home Appliances
Industry Six   Mass Merchandising/Department Stores
Industry Seven   Specialty Retailers
Industry Eight   Small/Medium Entrepreneurial Ventures
Industry Nine   Manufacturing

The Recalcitrant Director at Byte Products, Inc.: Corporate Legality versus Corporate Responsibility

Dan R. Dalton, Richard A. Cosier, and Cathy A. Enz

Byte Products, Inc., is primarily involved in the production of electronic components that are used in personal computers. Although such components might be found in a few computers in home use, Byte products are found most frequently in computers used for sophisticated business and engineering applications. Annual sales of these products have been steadily increasing over the past several years; Byte Products, Inc., currently has total sales of approximately $265 million.

Over the past six years increases in yearly revenues have consistently reached 12%. Byte Products, Inc., headquartered in the midwestern United States, is regarded as one of the largest volume suppliers of specialized components and is easily the industry leader with some 32% market share. Unfortunately for Byte, many new firms—domestic and foreign—have entered the industry. A dramatic surge in demand, high profitability, and the relative ease of a new firm's entry into the industry explain in part the increased number of competing firms.

Although Byte management—and presumably shareholders as well—is very pleased about the growth of its markets, it faces a major problem: Byte simply cannot meet the demand for these components. The company currently operates three manufacturing facilities in various locations throughout the United States. Each of these plants operates three production shifts (24 hours per day), seven days a week. This activity constitutes virtually all of the company's production capacity. Without an additional manufacturing plant, Byte simply cannot increase its output of components.

James M. Elliott, Chief Executive Officer and Chairman of the Board, recognizes the gravity of the problem. If Byte Products cannot continue to manufacture components in sufficient numbers to meet the demand, buyers will go elsewhere. Worse yet is the possibility that any continued lack of supply will encourage others to enter the market. As a long-term solution to this problem, the Board of Directors unanimously authorized the construction of a new, state-of-the-art manufacturing facility in the southwestern United States. When the planned capacity of this plant is added to that of the three current plants, Byte should be able to meet demand for many years to come. Unfortunately, an estimated three years will be required to complete the plant and bring it on line.

Jim Elliott believes very strongly that this three-year period is far too long and has insisted that there also be a shorter range, stopgap solution while the plant is under construction. The instability of the market and the pressure to maintain leader status are two factors contributing to Elliott's insistence on a more immediate solution. Without such a move, Byte management believes that it will lose market share and, again, attract competitors into the market.

This case was prepared by Professors Dan R. Dalton and Richard A. Cosier of the Graduate School of Business at Indiana University and Professor Cathy A. Enz of Cornell University. The names of the organization, individual, location, and/or financial information have been disguised to preserve the organization's desire for anonymity. This case was edited for SMBP–7th Edition. Reprinted by permission.

SEVERAL SOLUTIONS?

A number of suggestions for such a temporary measure were offered by various staff specialists, but rejected by Elliott. For example, licensing Byte's product and process technology to other manufacturers in the short run to meet immediate demand was possible. This licensing authorization would be short-term, or just until the new plant could come on line. Top management, as well as the board, was uncomfortable with this solution for several reasons. They thought it unlikely that any manufacturer would shoulder the fixed costs of producing appropriate components for such a short term. Any manufacturer that would do so would charge a premium to recover its costs. This suggestion, obviously, would make Byte's own products available to its customers at an unacceptable price. Nor did passing any price increase to its customers seem sensible, for this too would almost certainly reduce Byte's market share as well as encourage further competition.

Overseas facilities and licensing also were considered but rejected. Before it became a publicly traded company, Byte's founders decided that its manufacturing facilities would be domestic. Top management strongly felt that this strategy had served Byte well; moreover, Byte's majority stockholders (initial owners of the then privately held Byte) were not likely to endorse such a move. Beyond that, however, top management was reluctant to foreign license—or make available by any means the technologies for others to produce Byte products—as they could not then properly control patents. Top management feared that foreign licensing would essentially give away costly proprietary information regarding the company's highly efficient means of product development. There also was the potential for initial low product quality—whether produced domestically or otherwise—especially for such a short-run operation. Any reduction in quality, however brief, would threaten Byte's share of this sensitive market.

THE SOLUTION!

One recommendation that has come to the attention of the Chief Executive Officer could help solve Byte's problem in the short run. Certain members of his staff have notified him that an abandoned plant currently is available in Plainville, a small town in the northeastern United States. Before its closing eight years before, this plant was used primarily for the manufacture of electronic components. As is, it could not possibly be used to produce Byte products, but it could be inexpensively refitted to do so in as few as three months. Moreover, this plant is available at a very attractive price. In fact, discreet inquiries by Elliott's staff indicate that this plant could probably be leased immediately from its present owners because the building has been vacant for some eight years.

All the news about this temporary plant proposal, however, is not nearly so positive. Elliott's staff concedes that this plant will never be efficient and its profitability will be low. In addition, the Plainville location is a poor one in terms of high labor costs (the area is highly unionized), warehousing expenses, and inadequate transportation links to Byte's major markets and suppliers. Plainville is simply not a candidate for a long-term solution. Still, in the short run a temporary plant could help meet the demand and might forestall additional competition.

The staff is persuasive and notes that this option has several advantages: (1) there is no need for any licensing, foreign or domestic, (2) quality control remains firmly in the company's hands, and (3) an increase in the product price will be unnecessary. The temporary plant, then, would be used for three years or so until the new plant could be built. Then the temporary plant would be immediately closed.

CEO Elliott is convinced.

TAKING THE PLAN TO THE BOARD

The quarterly meeting of the Board of Directors is set to commence at 2:00 P.M. Jim Elliott has been reviewing his notes and agenda for the meeting most of the morning. The issue of the temporary plant is clearly the most important agenda item. Reviewing his detailed presentation of this matter, including the associated financial analyses, has occupied much of his time for several days. All the available information underscores his contention that the temporary plant in Plainville is the only responsible solution to the demand problems. No other option offers the same low level of risk and ensures Byte's status as industry leader.

At the meeting, after the board has dispensed with a number of routine matters, Jim Elliott turns his attention to the temporary plant. In short order, he advises the 11-member board (himself, three additional inside members, and seven outside members) of his proposal to obtain and refit the existing plant to ameliorate demand problems in the short run, authorize the construction of the new plant (the completion of which is estimated to take some three years), and plan to switch capacity from the temporary plant to the new one when it is operational. He also briefly reviews additional details concerning the costs involved, advantages of this proposal versus domestic or foreign licensing, and so on.

All the board members except one are in favor of the proposal. In fact, they are most enthusiastic; the overwhelming majority agree that the temporary plant is an excellent—even inspired—stopgap measure. Ten of the 11 board members seem relieved because the board was most reluctant to endorse any of the other alternatives that had been mentioned.

The single dissenter—T. Kevin Williams, an outside director—is, however, steadfast in his objections. He will not, under any circumstances, endorse the notion of the temporary plant and states rather strongly that "I will not be party to this nonsense, not now, not ever."

T. Kevin Williams, the senior executive of a major nonprofit organization, is normally a reserved and really quite agreeable person. This sudden, uncharacteristic burst of emotion clearly startles the remaining board members into silence. The following excerpt captures the ensuing, essentially one-on-one conversation between Williams and Elliott.

> WILLIAMS: How many workers do your people estimate will be employed in the temporary plant?
>
> ELLIOTT: Roughly 1,200, possibly a few more.
>
> WILLIAMS: I presume it would be fair, then, to say that, including spouses and children, something on the order of 4,000 people will be attracted to the community.
>
> ELLIOTT: I certainly would not be surprised.
>
> WILLIAMS: If I understand the situation correctly, this plant closed just over eight years ago and that closing had a catastrophic effect on Plainville. Isn't it true that a large portion of the community was employed by this plant?
>
> ELLIOTT: Yes, it was far and away the majority employer.

WILLIAMS: And most of these people have left the community presumably to find employment elsewhere.

ELLIOTT: Definitely, there was a drastic decrease in the area's population.

WILLIAMS: Are you concerned, then, that our company can attract the 1,200 employees to Plainville from other parts of New England?

ELLIOTT: Not in the least. We are absolutely confident that we will attract 1,200— even more, for that matter virtually any number we need. That, in fact, is one of the chief advantages of this proposal. I would think that the community would be very pleased to have us there.

WILLIAMS: On the contrary, I would suspect that the community will rue the day we arrived. Beyond that, though, this plan is totally unworkable if we are candid. On the other hand, if we are less than candid, the proposal will work for us, but only at great cost to Plainville. In fact, quite frankly the implications are appalling. Once again, I must enter my serious objections.

ELLIOTT: I don't follow you.

WILLIAMS: The temporary plant would employ some 1,200 people. Again, this means the infusion of over 4,000 to the community and surrounding areas. Byte Products, however, intends to close this plant in three years or less. If Byte informs the community or the employees that the jobs are temporary, the proposal simply won't work. When the new people arrive in the community, there will be a need for more schools, instructors, utilities, housing, restaurants, and so forth. Obviously, if the banks and local government know that the plant is temporary, no funding will be made available for these projects and certainly no credit for the new employees to buy homes, appliances, automobiles, and so forth.

If, on the other hand, Byte Products does not tell the community of its "temporary" plans, the project can go on. But, in several years when the plant closes (and we here have agreed today that it will close), we will have created a ghost town. The tax base of the community will have been destroyed; property values will decrease precipitously; practically the whole town will be unemployed. This proposal will place Byte Products in an untenable position and in extreme jeopardy.

ELLIOTT: Are you suggesting that this proposal jeopardizes us legally? If so, it should be noted that the legal department has reviewed this proposal in its entirety and has indicated no problem.

WILLIAMS: No! I don't think we are dealing with an issue of legality here. In fact, I don't doubt for a minute that this proposal is altogether legal. I do, however, resolutely believe that this proposal constitutes gross irresponsibility.

I think this decision has captured most of my major concerns. These along with a host of collateral problems associated with this project lead me to strongly suggest that you and the balance of the board reconsider and not endorse this proposal. Byte Products must find another way.

THE DILEMMA

After a short recess, the board meeting reconvened. Presumably because of some discussion during the recess, several other board members indicated that they were no longer inclined to support the proposal. After a short period of rather heated discussion, the following exchange took place.

ELLIOTT: It appears to me that any vote on this matter is likely to be very close. Given the gravity of our demand capacity problem, I must insist that the stockholders' equity be protected. We cannot wait three years; that is clearly out of the question. I still feel that licensing—domestic or foreign—is not in our long-term interests for any number of reasons, some of which have been discussed here. On the other hand, I do not want to take this project forward on the strength of a mixed vote. A vote of 6–5 or 7–4, for example, does not indicate that the board is remotely close to being of one mind. Mr. Williams, is there a compromise to be reached?

WILLIAMS: Respectfully, I have to say no. If we tell the truth, namely, the temporary nature of our operations, the proposal is simply not viable. If we are less than candid in this respect, we do grave damage to the community as well as to our image. It seems to me that we can only go one way or the other. I don't see a middle ground.

The Wallace Group

Laurence J. Stybel

Frances Rampar, President of Rampar Associates, drummed her fingers on the desk. Scattered before her were her notes. She had to put the pieces together in order to make an effective sales presentation to Harold Wallace.

Hal Wallace was the President of The Wallace Group. He had asked Rampar to conduct a series of interviews with some key Wallace Group employees, in preparation for a possible consulting assignment for Rampar Associates.

During the past three days, Rampar had been talking with some of these key people and had received background material about the company. The problem was not in finding the problem. The problem was that there were too many problems!

BACKGROUND OF THE WALLACE GROUP

The Wallace Group, Inc., is a diversified company dealing in the manufacture and development of technical products and systems (see Exhibit 1). The company currently consists of three operational groups and a corporate staff. The three groups include Electronics, Plastics, and Chemicals, each operating under the direction of a Group Vice-President (see Exhibits 2–4). The company generates $70 million in sales as a manufacturer of plastics, chemical products, and electronic components and systems. Principal sales are to large contractors in governmental and automotive markets. With respect to sales volume, Plastics and Chemicals are approximately equal in size, and both of them together equal the size of the Electronics Group.

Electronics offers competence in the areas of microelectronics, electromagnetic sensors, antennas, microwave, and minicomputers. Presently, these skills are devoted primarily to the engineering and manufacture of countermeasure equipment for aircraft. This includes radar detection systems that allow an aircraft crew to know that they are being tracked by radar units on the ground, on ships, or on other aircraft. Further, the company manufactures displays that provide the crew with a visual "fix" on where they are relative to the radar units that are tracking them.

In addition to manufacturing tested and proven systems developed in the past, The Wallace Group is currently involved in two major and two minor programs, all involving display systems. The Navy-A Program calls for the development of a display system for a tactical fighter plane; Air Force-B is another such system for an observation plane. Ongoing production orders are anticipated following flight testing. The other two programs, Army-LG and OBT-37, involve the incorporation of new technology into existing aircraft systems.

The Plastics Group manufactures plastic components used by the electronics, automotive, and other industries requiring plastic products. These include switches, knobs, keys, insulation materials, and so on, used in the manufacture of electronic equipment and other small made-to-order components installed in automobiles, planes, and other products.

Exhibit 1 An Excerpt from the Annual Report

To the Shareholders:

This past year was one of definite accomplishment for The Wallace Group, although with some admitted soft spots. This is a period of consolidation, of strengthening our internal capacity for future growth and development. Presently, we are in the process of creating a strong management team to meet the challenges we will set for the future.

Despite our failure to achieve some objectives, we turned a profit of $3,521,000 before taxes, which was a growth over the previous year's earnings. And we have declared a dividend for the fifth consecutive year, albeit one that is less than the year before. However, the retention of earnings is imperative if we are to lay a firm foundation for future accomplishment.

Currently, The Wallace Group has achieved a level of stability. We have a firm foothold in our current markets, and we could elect to simply enact strong internal controls and maximize our profits. However, this would not be a growth strategy. Instead, we have chosen to adopt a more aggressive posture for the future, to reach out into new markets wherever possible and to institute the controls necessary to move forward in a planned and orderly fashion.

The Electronics Group performed well this past year and is engaged in two major programs under Defense Department contracts. These are developmental programs that provide us with the opportunity for ongoing sales upon testing of the final product. Both involve the creation of tactical display systems for aircraft being built by Lombard Aircraft for the Navy and the Air Force. Future potential sales from these efforts could amount to approximately $56 million over the next five years. Additionally, we are developing technical refinements to older, already installed systems under Army Department contracts.

In the future, we will continue to offer our technological competence in such tactical display systems and anticipate additional breakthroughs and success in meeting the demands of this market. However, we also believe that we have unique contributions to make to other markets, and to that end we are making the investments necessary to expand our opportunities.

Plastics also turned in a solid performance this past year and has continued to be a major supplier to Chrysler, Martin Tool, Foster Electric, and, of course, to our Electronics Group. The market for this group continues to expand, and we believe that additional investments in this group will allow us to seize a larger share of the future.

Chemicals' performance, admittedly, has not been as satisfactory as anticipated during the past year. However, we have been able to realize a small amount of profit from this operation and to halt what was a potentially dangerous decline in profits. We believe that this situation is only temporary and that infusions of capital for developing new technology, plus the streamlining of operations, have stabilized the situation. The next step will be to begin more aggressive marketing to capitalize on the group's basic strengths.

Overall, the outlook seems to be one of modest but profitable growth. The near term will be one of creating the technology and controls necessary for developing our market offerings and growing in a planned and purposeful manner. Our improvement efforts in the various company groups can be expected to take hold over the years with positive effects on results.

We wish to express our appreciation to all those who participated in our efforts this past year.

Harold Wallace
Chairman and President

The Chemicals Group produces chemicals used in the development of plastics. It supplies bulk chemicals to the Plastics Group and other companies. These chemicals are then injected into molds or extruded to form a variety of finished products.

HISTORY OF THE WALLACE GROUP

Each of the three groups began as a sole proprietorship under the direct operating control of an owner/manager. Several years ago, Harold Wallace, owner of the original electronics company, determined to undertake a program of diversification. Initially, he attempted to expand his market by product development and line extensions entirely within the electronics industry. However, because of initial problems, he drew back and sought other opportunities. Wallace's primary concern was his almost total dependence

Exhibit 2 Organizational Chart: The Wallace Group

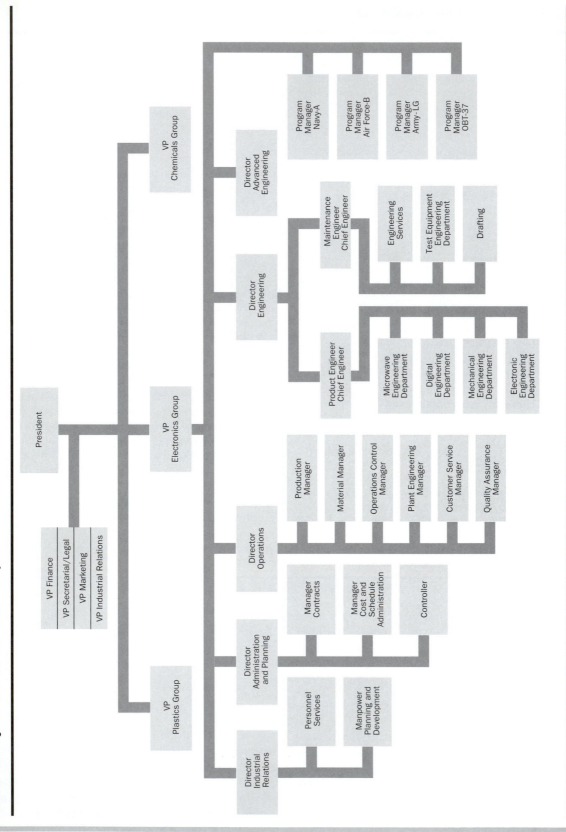

Exhibit 3   **The Wallace Group**

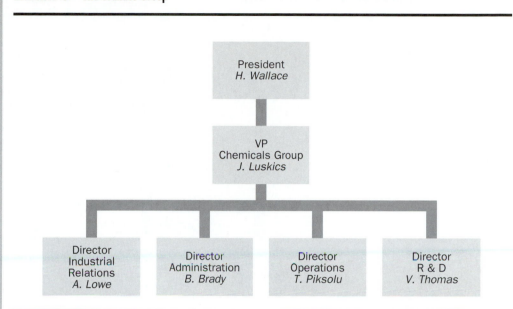

on defense-related contracts. He had felt for some time that he should take some strong action to gain a foothold in the private markets. The first major opportunity that seemed to satisfy his various requirements was the acquisition of a former supplier, a plastics company whose primary market was not defense-related. The company's owner desired to sell his operation and retire. At the time, Wallace's debt structure was such that he could not manage the acquisition, and so he had to attract equity capital. He was able to gather a relatively small group of investors and form a closed corporation. A Board of Directors was formed with Wallace as Chairman and President of the new corporate entity.

With respect to operations, little changed. Wallace continued direct operational control over the Electronics Group. As holder of 60% of the stock, he maintained effective control over policy and operations. However, because of his personal interests, the Plastics Group, now under the direction of a newly hired Vice-President, Martin Hempton, was left mainly to its own devices except for yearly progress reviews by the President. All Wallace asked at the time was that the Plastics Group continue its profitable operation, which it did.

Several years ago, Wallace and the Board decided to diversify further because two-thirds of their business was still defense-dependent. They learned that one of the major suppliers of the Plastics Group, a chemical company, was on the verge of bankruptcy. The company's owner, Jerome Luskics, agreed to sell. However, this acquisition required a public stock offering, with most of the funds going to pay off debts incurred by the three groups, especially the Chemicals Group. The net result was that Wallace now holds 45% of The Wallace Group and Jerome Luskics 5%, with the remainder distributed among the public.

ORGANIZATION AND PERSONNEL

Presently, Harold Wallace serves as Chairman and President of The Wallace Group. The Electronics Group had been run by LeRoy Tuscher, who just resigned as Vice-President. Hempton continued as Vice-President of Plastics, and Luskics served as Vice-President of the Chemicals Group.

Exhibit 4   **The Wallace Group**

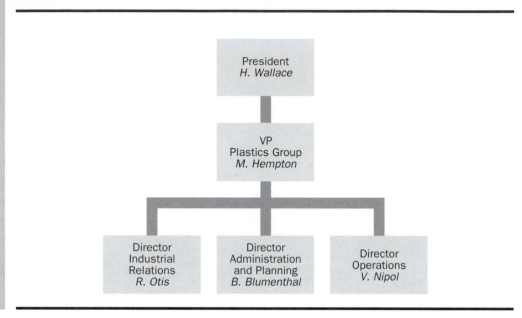

Reflecting the requirements of a corporate perspective and approach, a corporate staff has grown up, consisting of Vice-Presidents for Finance, Secretarial/Legal, Marketing, and Industrial Relations. This staff has assumed many functions formerly associated with the group offices.

Because these positions are recent additions, many of the job accountabilities are still being defined. Problems have arisen over the responsibilities and relationships between corporate and group positions. President Wallace has settled most of the disputes himself because of the inability of the various parties to resolve differences among themselves.

CURRENT TRENDS

Presently, there is a mood of lethargy and drift within The Wallace Group (see Exhibits 5–11). Most managers feel that each of the three groups functions as an independent company. And, with respect to group performance, not much change or progress has been made in recent years. Electronics and Plastics are still stable and profitable, but both lack growth in markets and profits. The infusion of capital breathed new life and hope into the Chemicals operation but did not solve most of the old problems and failings that had caused its initial decline. For all these reasons Wallace decided that strong action was necessary. His greatest disappointment was with the Electronics Group, in which he had placed high hopes for future development. Thus he acted by requesting and getting the Electronics Group Vice-President's resignation. Hired from a computer company to replace LeRoy Tuscher, Jason Matthews joined The Wallace Group a week ago.

Last week, Wallace's net sales were $70 million. By group they were:

Electronics	$35,000,000
Plastics	$20,000,000
Chemicals	$15,000,000

Exhibit 5   Selected Portions of a Transcribed Interview with H. Wallace

RAMPAR: What is your greatest problem right now?

WALLACE: That's why I called you in! Engineers are a high-strung, temperamental lot. Always complaining. It's hard to take them seriously.

Last month we had an annual stockholders' meeting. We have an Employee Stock Option Plan, and many of our long-term employees attended the meeting. One of my managers—and I won't mention any names—introduced a resolution calling for the resignation of the President—me!

The vote was defeated. But, of course, I own 45% of the stock!

Now I realize that there could be no serious attempt to get rid of me. Those who voted for the resolution were making a dramatic effort to show me how upset they are with the way things are going.

I could fire those employees who voted against me. I was surprised by how many did. Some of my key people were in that group. Perhaps I ought to stop and listen to what they are saying.

Businesswise, I think we're O.K. Not great, but O.K. Last year we turned in a profit of $3.5 million before taxes, which was a growth over previous years' earnings. We declared a dividend for the fifth consecutive year.

We're currently working on the creation of a tactical display system for aircraft being built by Lombard Aircraft for the Navy and the Air Force. If Lombard gets the contract to produce the prototype, future sales could amount to $56 million over the next five years.

Why are they complaining?

RAMPAR: You must have some thoughts on the matter.

WALLACE: I think the issue revolves around how we manage people. It's a personnel problem. You were highly recommended as someone with expertise in high-technology human-resource management.

I have some ideas on what is the problem. But I'd like you to do an independent investigation and give me your findings. Give me a plan of action.

Don't give me a laundry list of problems, Fran. Anyone can do that. I want a set of priorities I should focus on during the next year. I want a clear action plan from you. And I want to know how much this plan is going to cost me!

Other than that, I'll leave you alone and let you talk to anyone in the company you want.

On a consolidated basis, the financial highlights of the last two years are as follows:

	Last Year	Two Years Ago
Net sales	$70,434,000	$69,950,000
Income (pre-tax)	3,521,000	3,497,500
Income (after-tax)	2,760,500	1,748,750
Working capital	16,200,000	16,088,500
Shareholders' equity	39,000,000	38,647,000
Total assets	59,869,000	59,457,000
Long-term debt	4,350,000	3,500,000
Per Share of Common Stock		
Net income	$.37	$.36
Cash dividends paid	.15	.25

Of the net income, approximately 70% came from Electronics, 25% from Plastics, and 5% from Chemicals.

Exhibit 6 **Selected Portions of a Transcribed Interview with Frank Campbell, Vice-President of Industrial Relations**

RAMPAR: What is your greatest problem right now?

CAMPBELL: Trying to contain my enthusiasm over the fact that Wallace brought you in!

Morale is really poor here. Hal runs this place like a one-man operation, when it's grown too big for that. It took a palace revolt to finally get him to see the depths of the resentment. Whether he'll do anything about it, that's another matter.

RAMPAR: What would you like to see changed?

CAMPBELL: Other than a new President?

RAMPAR: Uh-huh.

CAMPBELL: We badly need a management development program for our group. Because of our growth, we have been forced to promote technical people to management positions who have had no prior managerial experience. Mr. Tuscher agreed on the need for a program, but Hal Wallace vetoed the idea because developing such a program would be too expensive. I think it is too expensive *not* to move ahead on this.

RAMPAR: Anything else ?

CAMPBELL: The IEWU negotiations have been extremely tough this time around, due to excessive demands they have been making. Union pay scales are already pushing up against our foreman salary levels, and foremen are being paid high in their salary ranges. This problem, coupled with union insistence on a no-layoff clause, is causing us fits. How can we keep all our workers when we have production equipment on order that will eliminate 20% of our assembly positions?

RAMPAR: Wow.

CAMPBELL: We have been sued by a rejected candidate for a position on the basis of discrimination. She claimed our entrance qualifications are excessive because we require shorthand. There is some basis for this statement since most reports are given to secretaries in handwritten form or on audio cassettes. In fact, we have always required it and our executives want their secretaries to have skill in taking dictation. Not only is this case taking time, but I need to reconsider if any of our position entrance requirements, in fact, are excessive. I am sure we do not want another case like this one.

RAMPAR: That puts The Wallace Group in a vulnerable position, considering the amount of government work you do.

CAMPBELL: We have a tremendous recruiting backlog, especially for engineering positions. Either our pay scales are too low, our job specs are too high, or we are using the wrong recruiting channels. Kane and Smith [Director of Engineering and Director of Advanced Systems] keep rejecting everyone we send down there as being unqualified.

RAMPAR: Gee.

CAMPBELL: Being head of Human Resources around here is a tough job. We don't act. We react.

Exhibit 7   Selected Portions of a Transcribed Interview with Matthew Smith, Director of Advanced Systems

RAMPAR: What is your greatest problem right now?

SMITH: Corporate brass keeps making demands on me and others that don't relate to the job we are trying to get done. They say that the information they need is to satisfy corporate planning and operations review requirements, but they don't seem to recognize how much time and effort is required to provide this information. Sometimes it seems like they are generating analyses, reports, and requests for data just to keep themselves busy. Someone should be evaluating how critical these corporate staff activities really are. To me and the Electronics Group, these activities are unnecessary.

An example is the Vice-President, Marketing (L. Holt), who keeps asking us for supporting data so he can prepare a corporate marketing strategy. As you know, we prepare our own group marketing strategic plans annually, but using data and formats that are oriented to our needs, rather than Corporate's. This planning activity, which occurs at the same time as Corporate's, coupled with heavy work loads on current projects, makes us appear to Holt as though we are being unresponsive.

Somehow we need to integrate our marketing planning efforts between our group and Corporate. This is especially true if our group is to successfully grow in nondefense-oriented markets and products. We do need corporate help, but not arbitrary demands for information that divert us from putting together effective marketing strategies for our group.

I am getting too old to keep fighting these battles.

RAMPAR: This is a long-standing problem?

SMITH: You bet! Our problems are fairly classic in the high-tech field. I've been at other companies and they're not much better. We spend so much time firefighting, we never really get organized. Everything is done on an ad hoc basis.

I'm still waiting for tomorrow.

Exhibit 8   Selected Portions of a Transcribed Interview with Ralph Kane, Director of Engineering

RAMPAR: What is your greatest problem right now?

KANE: Knowing you were coming, I wrote them down. They fall into four areas:

1. Our salary schedules are too low to attract good, experienced EEs. We have been told by our Vice-President (Frank Campbell) that corporate policy is to hire new people below the salary grade midpoint. All qualified candidates are making more than that now and in some cases are making more than our grade maximums. I think our Project Engineer job is rated too low.

2. Chemicals Group asked for and the former Electronics Vice-President (Tuscher) agreed to "lend" six of our best EEs to help solve problems it is having developing a new battery. That is great for the Chemicals Group, but meanwhile how do we solve the engineering problems that have cropped up in our Navy-A and OBT-37 programs?

3. As you know, Matt Smith (Director of Advanced Systems) is retiring in six months. I depend heavily on his group for technical expertise, and in some areas he depends heavily on some of my key engineers. I have lost some people to the Chemicals Group, and Matt has been trying to lend me some of his people to fill in. But he and his staff have been heavily involved in marketing planning and trying to identify or recruit a qualified successor long enough before his retirement to be able to train him. The result is that his people are up to their eyeballs in doing their own stuff and cannot continue to help me meet my needs.

4. IR has been preoccupied with union negotiations in the plant and has not had time to help me deal with this issue of management planning. Campbell is working on some kind of system that will help deal with this kind of problem and prevent them in the future. That is great, but I need help now—not when his "system" is ready.

Exhibit 9   Selected Portions of a Transcribed Interview with Brad Lowell, Program Manager, Navy-A

RAMPAR: What is your . . .?

LOWELL: . . . great problem? I'll tell you what it is. I still cannot get the support I need from Kane in Engineering. He commits and then doesn't deliver, and it has me quite concerned. The excuse now is that in "his judgment," Sid Wright needs the help for the Air Force program more than I do. Wright's program is one week ahead of schedule, so I disagree with "his judgment." Kane keeps complaining about not having enough people.

RAMPAR: Why do you think Kane says he doesn't have enough people?

LOWELL: Because Hal Wallace is a tight-fisted S.O.B. who won't let us hire the people we need!

Exhibit 10   Selected Portions of a Transcribed Interview with Phil Jones, Director, Administration and Planning

JONES: Wheel spinning—that's our problem! We talk about expansion, but we don't do anything about it. Are we serious or not?

For example, a bid request came in from a prime contractor seeking help in developing a countermeasure system for a medium-range aircraft. They needed an immediate response and a concept proposal in one week. Tuscher just sat on my urgent memo to him asking for a go/no go decision on bidding. I could not give the contractor an answer (because no decision came from Tuscher), so they gave up on us.

I am frustrated because (1) we lost an opportunity we were "naturals" to win, and (2) my personal reputation was damaged because I was unable to answer the bid request. Okay, Tuscher's gone now, but we need to develop some mechanism so an answer to such a request can be made quickly.

Another thing, our MIS is being developed by the Corporate Finance Group. More wheel spinning! They are telling us what information we need rather than asking us what we want! E. Kay (our Group Controller) is going crazy trying to sort out the input requirements they need for the system and understanding the complicated reports that come out. Maybe this new system is great as a technical achievement, but what good is it to us if we can't use it?

Exhibit 11   Selected Portions of a Transcribed Interview with Burt Williams, Director of Operations

RAMPAR: What is your biggest problem right now?

WILLIAMS: One of the biggest problems we face right now stems from corporate policy regarding transfer pricing. I realize we are "encouraged" to purchase our plastics and chemicals from our sister Wallace groups, but we are also committed to making a profit! Because manufacturing problems in those groups have forced them to raise their prices, should *we* suffer the consequences? We can get some materials cheaper from other suppliers. How can we meet our volume and profit targets when we are saddled with non-competitive material costs?

RAMPAR: And if that issue was settled to your satisfaction, then would things be O.K.?

WILLIAMS: Although out of my direct function, it occurs to me that we are not planning effectively our efforts to expand into nondefense areas. With minimal alteration to existing production methods, we can develop both end-use products (e.g., small motors, traffic control devices, and microwave transceivers for highway emergency communications) and components (e.g., LED and LCD displays, police radar tracking devices, and word processing system memory and control devices) with large potential markets.

The problems in this regard are:

1.   Matt Smith (Director, Advanced Systems) is retiring and has had only defense-related experience. Therefore he is not leading any product development efforts along these lines.

2.   We have no marketing function at the group level to develop a strategy, define markets, and research and develop product opportunities.

3.   Even if we had a marketing plan and products for industrial/commercial application, we have no sales force or rep network to sell the stuff.

    Maybe I am way off base, but it seems to me we need a Groups/Marketing/Sales function to lead us in this business expansion effort. It should be headed by an experienced technical marketing manager with a proven track record in developing such products and markets.

RAMPAR: Have you discussed your concerns with others?

WILLIAMS: I have brought these ideas up with Mr. Matthews and others at the Group Management Committee. No one else seems interested in pursuing this concept, but they won't say this outright and don't say why it should not be addressed. I guess that in raising the idea with you I am trying to relieve some of my frustrations.

THE PROBLEM CONFRONTING FRANCES RAMPAR

As Rampar finished reviewing her notes (see Exhibits 5–11), she kept reflecting on what Hal Wallace had told her:

Don't give me a laundry list of problems, Fran. Anyone can do that. I want a set of priorities I should focus on during the next year. I want a clear action plan from you. And I want to know how much this plan is going to cost me!

Fran Rampar again drummed her fingers on the desk.

Environmental Issues: Questions of Social Responsibility and Ethics

The Audit

John A. Kilpatrick, Gamewell D. Gantt, and George A. Johnson

Sue was puzzled as to what course of action to take. She had recently started her job with a national CPA firm, and she was already confronted with a problem that could affect her future with the firm. On an audit, she encountered a client who had been treating payments to a large number, but by no means a majority, of its workers as payments to independent contractors. This practice saves the client the payroll taxes that would otherwise be due on the payments if the workers were classified as employees. In Sue's judgment this was improper as well as illegal and should have been noted in the audit. She raised the issue with John, the senior accountant to whom she reported. He thought it was a possible problem but did not seem willing to do anything about it. He encouraged her to talk to the partner in charge if she didn't feel satisfied.

She thought about the problem for a considerable time before approaching the partner in charge. The ongoing professional education classes she had received from her employer emphasized the ethical responsibilities that she had as a CPA and the fact that her firm endorsed adherence to high ethical standards. This finally swayed her to pursue the issue with the partner in charge of the audit. The visit was most unsatisfactory. Paul, the partner, virtually confirmed her initial reaction that the practice was wrong, but he said that many other companies in the industry follow such a practice. He went on to say that if an issue was made of it, Sue would lose the account and he was not about to take such action. She came away from the meeting with the distinct feeling that had she chosen to pursue the issue she would have created an enemy.

Sue still felt disturbed and decided to discuss the problem with some of her co-workers. She approached Bill and Mike, both of whom had been working for the firm for a couple of years. They were familiar with the problem because they had encountered the same issue when doing the audit the previous year. They expressed considerable concern that if she went over the head of the partner in charge of the audit, they could be in big trouble since they had failed to question the practice during the previous audit. They said that they realized it was probably wrong, but they went ahead because it had been ignored in previous years and they knew their supervisor wanted them to ignore it again this year. They didn't want to cause problems. They encouraged Sue to be a "team player" and drop the issue.

This case was prepared by Professors John A. Kilpatrick, Gamewell D. Gantt, and George A. Johnson of the College of Business, Idaho State University. The names of the organization, individual, location, and/or financial information have been disguised to preserve the organization's desire for anonymity. This case was edited for SMBP–7th Edition. Presented to and accepted by the refereed Society for Case Research. All rights reserved to the authors and the SCR. Copyright © 1995 by John A. Kilpatrick, Gamewell D. Gantt, and George A. Johnson. Reprinted by permission.

Brookstone Hospice: Heel or Heroine?

Shirley F. Olson and Sharon Meadows

"To be profit oriented is acceptable for any business but when that profit is given priority over a patient's life . . . well—I've got problems with that," Kathy Bennett tearfully declared. Kathy's anger stemmed from an incident that had taken place earlier in the month. As the nursing supervisor for a large hospice located in the northeastern United States, she had seen many things that she questioned but nothing quite like this latest occurrence.

The hospice with which she was associated employed 35 people and operated under the same philosophy as that of all other hospices—its goal was to ensure that the terminally ill patient was as comfortable as possible during the last days of life. Its reason for existence was therefore not to cure in the traditional medical sense but to ensure the patient a relatively pain-free, dignified death. Its mission and purpose as outlined in the company manual was (a) to provide a holistic approach to the dying patients and their significant others (family, friends), (b) to help the surviving significant others back to an optimal level of functioning, and (c) to assist health care professionals dealing with dying patients and their significant others.

To achieve that purpose, Brookstone's described strategy was to offer care in the last six months of the terminally ill patient's life, with 24-hour, hands-on care if needed, for up to seven days. Otherwise care was limited to two visits per week by the RN and weekly visits from the chaplain and social worker. The hospice doctor made visits as needed. The organization also offered a hot line that patients' families could use for discussing their concerns with the chaplain and for pre-planning the funeral. Brookstone's home health aides were available as the family required for daily duties—patient baths, trips to and from the doctor and the grocery, and light housework. Thus, not only the patient but also the family received services in the form of support from the team. Unlike traditional care, the group members—with the exception of the doctor—continued to visit the family after the death of the patient and thus assured their well-being, as noted in the organization's mission/purpose statement. Team members always attended the funeral and even visited families on the first anniversary of the death, which was a very painful time.

The structure of the organization was quite loose, as was required by the very nature of the work being done. Essentially all employees were part of matrix-type structures with each patient constituting the center of that matrix. Needless to say, the nurses, chaplains, and so on were associated with more than one patient at any one time, but because the patients' needs were always changing, the components in the matrix also changed rapidly as different members were needed for their particular expertise.

The matrixes were coordinated by an overall administrator, Jim Cole, who prided himself on the organization's flexibility. Cole went so far as to indicate, "Our people are top-level professionals and need very little managing. I like to leave decisions—to the extent possible—to their discretion. Of course, I still see myself as the final authority. My nurse supervisor coordinates all the RNs, and the doctors are coordinated similarly by

This case was prepared by Professor Shirley F. Olson, Vice-President of J. J. Ferguson Companies, and Ms. Sharon Meadows, Nurse Practitioner. It was presented at the North American Case Research Association Meeting, 1986. Distributed by the North American Case Research Association. All rights reserved to the authors and the North American Case Research Association. The names of the organization, individual, location, and/or financial information have been disguised to preserve the organization's desire for anonymity. This case was edited for SMBP–7th Edition. Reprinted by permission of the authors and the North American Case Research Association.

our in-house physician. The social worker and chaplain also work through the nurse supervisor. My job essentially then is to watch all this happen. So far I've been pretty successful. Just this last year Brookstone grossed $2.5 million. And we are projecting $3.2 this year."

Despite Cole's quick overview of the hospice's structure, Kathy Bennett was one of many to note that although the company procedures manual had a segment devoted to structure, that page was blank. "My team director told me not to ask too many questions about who reported to whom. She said Cole liked the feeling of flexibility and did not want anything about Brookstone to appear bureaucratic. However, I do know that our Chief Team Operator, the Executive Medical Director, and the Marketing Director all answered to Cole. Answering to the Team Operator were the two team directors who directly supervised the RNs, aides, chaplains, and social workers. The hospice MDs reported to the Executive Medical Director, and the marketing representative reported to the Marketing Director." As Kathy noted, "The very nature of the work we do makes us such a close knit group. When you are faced with death every day and sometimes several times a day, you have a much greater appreciation for life and family, and people in general. I've been with this group almost seven years and up until this incident a few days ago, Brookstone has been ideal—not just for me as an employee but for our patients also. Their needs are so great and their time so short. When I leave here every night, I never have to wonder what we accomplished that day. At least that was the case until now."

THE EPISODE

The incident to which Kathy continued to refer involved an 86-year-old man, Sam Gardner, suffering from a malignancy of the kidney. Mr. Gardner had been accepted by Brookstone three weeks earlier and was being visited regularly. On Sunday, February 18, Gardner's daughter, Beverly, had contacted Brookstone's duty nurse saying that her father seemed to be bleeding profusely internally. Although the family had been told that this would happen in the latter stages of the illness, the bleeding was much worse than they had expected and had gone on for almost 16 hours.

In response, Bennett sent the on-call nurse to the Gardner home to assess the patient's condition. Within minutes of her arrival, the nurse phoned Kathy, the nursing supervisor, and indicated that Mr. Gardner needed to be admitted to a hospital's acute-care in-patient unit. While the nurse was on the phone with Kathy, the family became increasingly hysterical. At one point during the phone conversation, Kathy heard Beverly scream out, "I'll call an ambulance myself and take him. We just can't sit here and let him bleed to death while your bureaucratic organization has us on hold."

Realizing the urgency in the duty nurse's voice, Kathy immediately began the procedure for admitting Gardner to Covington General Hospital, the hospital with which Brookstone contracted. The procedure required by Brookstone Hospice was quite lengthy if Gardner was to be admitted to the Hospice Inpatient Unit at Covington General. Specifically:

1. The patient's primary doctor had to be contacted and had to approve admission.

2. The hospice doctor had to be contacted to act as the attending physician; if the patient's primary doctor refused the case, the hospice physician then performed as the primary doctor.

3. The hospital admissions office had to be notified of the incoming patient.

Although Kathy was more than familiar with the required procedure, several factors prevented it from being followed. First, the primary doctor refused to care for Gardner if he were transported to Covington General, stating that he would treat the patient if and only if he were taken to Catholic Charities Hospital. Brookstone had no contractual agreement with Catholic Charities.

As Kathy attempted to reason with the physician, the patient meanwhile had been placed in an ambulance that sat in the Gardners' driveway and waited for instructions from the duty nurse as to where the patient was to be taken. Kathy desperately continued her telephoning as she sought to follow established procedure, which required that no action on a hospice patient be taken without approval from the hospice's MDs. Despite the efforts she was not able to contact any of the four hospice doctors who were on call that weekend. "I called every answering service, home, and golf course I could think of at the time but to no avail. That went on for at least 45 minutes while my poor patient lay in the ambulance waiting on our 'procedure.' You can only imagine how I felt. Finally in my desperation I gave permission to transport Gardner to the nearest hospital—Covington General (C.G.H.)—and the story goes on from there," Kathy noted.

After Gardner was taken to C.G.H., he went directly to the emergency room where he was assessed by the E.R. physician, C. Wallace. Wallace immediately set Gardner up for urological surgery the following Monday morning. On that Monday, the urologist contacted one of Brookstone's team doctors to discuss the so-called "curative surgery." Brookstone had well-defined policies about how hospice patients were to be treated. Once a patient signed with the hospice, no other health care professional could take any action whatsoever without contacting the hospice. As the procedure manual noted, a paramedic could not even resuscitate a nonbreathing hospice patient until contact was made with Brookstone. Realizing these rules, Wallace knew he faced a battle when he made the call.

Because the hospice discouraged curative measures—surgical or otherwise—the hospice physician was forced to discuss the proposed surgery with his superior in the hospice office before giving the urologist his approval to go ahead with the procedure. Immediately the supervisor vigorously discouraged the proposal—primarily on the grounds that the urologist stated that the surgery would extend the patient's life. Kathy overheard one of the team doctors state, "The man is 86 years old and has cancer. Can't you people understand the situation? That surgery will cost the hospice a minimum of $7,800. We—you and me—will pay for that right out of our pockets. We don't want to do that, do we? After all, Gardner will be dead anyway in three months. Our purpose is not to extend life but to assure quality life even until death."

Needless to say Kathy could not believe what she was hearing. Affiliated with an organization that she perceived as one of the best in the nation, she suddenly saw Brookstone quite differently in just those few split seconds of that comment.

THE AFTERMATH

"At least something good finally came out of all the madness. Despite the discouragement from the hospice doctors, the Covington General urologist operated anyway. Five days later, the 86-year-old Gardner, who had been diagnosed as having only 3 months to live, was discharged from the hospital—with a prognosis of 3 years or more. Somehow he got my name from his duty nurse and called me here at the hospice yesterday. Gardner's voice was a bit weak, but his message was extremely clear. He told me in no uncertain terms that he credited me with saving his life and with giving him 3 years instead of 3 months. Gardner said he knew the chance I took by sending him to Covington General. His call meant everything to me, and I could use some good news. The same day he called, I was fired. A medical team doctor and Jim Cole called me in, showed me the surgical bill Brookstone received on Gardner, and informed me that I had seriously violated numerous policies and procedures. As a result, my termination was effective immediately. One of the doctors went so far as to remind me of the financial constraints facing the hospice and said, 'Kathy, you know as well as anyone the money difficulty we've been having. Only two weeks ago, our payroll was held up to two days because of our cash flow difficulties. That $7,800 we had to pay on Gardner would have gone a long way here in the organization. Yet you saw fit to spend it on a guy who is old and going to die anyway.'"

ARM & HAMMER[1] (1998): Poised for Growth?

Roy A. Cook

The arm of Vulcan, the mythical hammer-wielding god of fire, first appeared on baking soda packages produced by co-founder Austin Church in 1867. Since then, the ARM & HAMMER™ brand has earned the confidence of six generations of Americans and is recognized as one of the nation's best known and most trusted logos.[2]

BACKGROUND

For 150 years, Church & Dwight Company, Inc., worked to build market share on a brand name that was rarely associated with the company. This brand name became so pervasive that it could be found on a variety of consumer products in 95% of all U.S. households. As the world's largest producer and marketer of sodium bicarbonate–based products, Church & Dwight had until the early 1900s achieved fairly consistent growth in both sales and earnings as new and expanded uses were found for sodium bicarbonate. Sodium bicarbonate is used in many products because it can perform a variety of functions, including cleaning, deodorizing, leavening, and buffering. Although Church & Dwight may not be a household name, the company's ubiquitous yellow box of ARM & HAMMER Baking Soda is.

Shortly after its introduction in 1878, ARM & HAMMER Baking Soda became a fundamental item on the pantry shelf as homemakers found many uses for it other than baking, such as cleaning and deodorizing. It can also be used as a dentrifice, a chemical agent to absorb or neutralize odors and acidity, a kidney dialysis element, a blast medium, and a pollution control agent. It is also showing promise as a potential treatment for osteoporosis.

From the 1980s through the early 1990s, company sales, on average, increased almost 15% annually. However, the stated strategy of "selling related products in different markets all linked by common carbonate and bicarbonate technology"[3] faltered and sales growth plateaued in 1993. As the chairman of one investment company said, "The only thing they had going for them [was] their uniqueness and they lost it. They made poor marketing and operating decisions that cost them a lot of money."[4]

Faced with investment community concerns and a string of disappointing financial results, Robert A. Davies III, President and Chief Executive Officer (CEO), articulated two key financial objectives for the company in 1996. The first was to raise operating margins from around 7% to 10% by 1998. The second was to achieve annual sales gains in the high single- or low double-digit range.[5] The financial picture for Church & Dwight during these transitional years from 1994 to 1997 is captured in the financial statements shown in Exhibits 1 and 2.

This case was prepared by Professor Roy A. Cook of Fort Lewis College. This case was edited for SMBP–7th Edition. Copyright © 1998 by Roy A. Cook. Reprinted by permission.

Exhibit 1 **Consolidated Statements of Income: Church & Dwight Company, Inc.**
(Dollar amounts in thousands, except per-share data)

Year Ending December 31	1997	1996	1995	1994
Net sales	$574,906	$527,771	$485,759	$491,048
Cost of sales	330,682	306,047	289,734	281,271
Gross profit	244,224	221,724	196,025	209,777
Selling, general, and administrative expenses	213,668	194,461	183,669	201,362
Restructuring charges	—	—	3,987	6,941
Income from operations	30,556	27,263	8,369	1,474
Equity in joint venture income	6,057	5,140	7,389	7,874
Investment earnings	1,666	1,544	1,249	655
Gain on disposal of product lines	—	—	339	410
Other income	1,320	(424)	201	209
Interest expense	(912)	(352)	(1,255)	(890)
Income before taxes	38,687	33,171	16,292	9,732
Income taxes	14,181	11,943	6,140	3,615
Net income	$ 24,506	$ 21,228	$ 10,152	$ 6,117

MANAGEMENT

The historically slow but steady course that Church & Dwight has traveled reflects top management's efforts to focus the company's activities. The ability to remain focused may be attributable to the fact that more than 50% of the outstanding shares of common stock have been owned by descendants of the company's co-founders. Dwight C. Minton, a direct descendant of Austin Church, directed the company as CEO from 1969 through 1995. He became a member of the Board in 1965 and succeeded his father as Chairman of the Board in 1981. Although Minton remained on the Board, he stepped down as CEO and passed those duties on to the first nonfamily member in the company's history, Robert A. Davies, III.

Although Davies was a nonfamily member, he had a long history of service with Church & Dwight. He served as Vice-President, General Manager of the Arm & Hammer Division, and then as President/Chief Operating Officer from 1969 through 1984. Davies continued to expand his experiences by serving as President and CEO of California Home Brands (a group of canning companies). In 1995, he returned to Church & Dwight as President of the Arm & Hammer Division to put the division "back on track." [6] Commenting on the change in leadership, Minton stated, "The effect of [Davies'] presence with us today is seen in an improved marketing focus and tighter cost structure." [7]

Many companies with strong brand names in the consumer products field have been susceptible to leveraged buy-outs and hostile takeovers. However, a series of calculated actions spared Church & Dwight's management from having to make last-minute decisions to ward off unwelcome suitors. Besides maintaining majority control of the outstanding common stock, management proposed and the Board amended the company's charter in 1986. This amendment gave current shareholders four votes per share but required future shareholders to buy and hold shares for four years before receiving the same privilege. The Board of Directors was also structured into three classes containing four directors in each class to serve staggered three-year terms.

Exhibit 2   **Consolidated Balance Sheets: Church & Dwight Company, Inc.**
(Dollar amounts in thousands)

Year Ending December 31	1997	1996	1995	1994
Assets				
Current assets				
Cash and cash equivalents	$ 14,949	$ 22,902	$ 11,355	$ 4,659
Short-term investments	3,993	5,011	5,027	2,976
Accounts receivable, less allowances of				
$1,532, $1,478, $1,304, and $912	49,566	41,837	44,427	44,404
Inventories	61,275	48,887	41,349	55,078
Current portion of note receivable	4,131	—	—	—
Deferred income taxes	9,802	11,962	11,704	10,820
Prepaid expenses	5,727	4,920	5,313	5,268
Total current assets	149,443	135,519	119,175	123,205
Property, plant, and equipment (net)	142,343	138,371	144,339	138,460
Note receivable from joint venture	6,869	11,000	11,000	11,000
Equity investment in affiliates	26,871	16,211	11,258	13,868
Long-term supply contract	2,775	3,314	3,852	4,391
Intangibles and other assets	22,713	3,556	3,556	3,556
Total assets	$351,014	$307,971	$293,180	$294,480
Liabilities and Shareholders' Equity				
Current liabilities				
Short-term borrowings	$ 32,000	—	$ 5,000	$ 25,000
Accounts payable and accrued expenses	92,090	93,375	86,815	72,974
Current portion of long-term debt	685	—	—	—
Income taxes payable	1,456	5,379	5,286	1,802
Total current liabilities	126,231	98,754	97,101	99,776
Long-term debt	6,815	7,500	7,500	7,500
Deferred income taxes	20,578	20,005	19,573	18,887
Deferred income	—	—	—	339
Deferred liabilities	3,786	2,392	1,595	1,176
Nonpension postretirement and postemployment benefits	14,263	14,008	13,729	12,861
Shareholders' equity				
Common stock—$1 par value	23,330	23,330	23,330	23,330
Additional paid-in capital	34,097	33,364	33,061	32,823
Retained earnings	197,622	182,069	169,438	167,901
Cumulative translation adjustments	(591)	(194)	(686)	(741)
	254,458	238,569	225,143	223,313
Less common stock in treasury, at cost	(74,568)	(72,708)	(70,501)	(69,372)
Due from officers	(549)	(549)	(960)	—
Total shareholders' equity	179,341	165,312	153,682	153,941
Total liabilities and shareholders' equity	$351,014	$307,971	$293,180	$294,480

As a further deterrent to would-be suitors or unwelcome advances, the company entered into an employee severance agreement in 1989 with key officials. This agreement provided severance pay of up to three times the individual's highest annual salary and bonus plus benefits for the preceding three years if the individual were terminated within one year after a change in control of the company. Change of control was defined as "the acquisition by a person or group of 25% or more of company common stock; a change in the majority of the board of directors not approved by the pre-change board of directors; or the approval by the stockholders of the company or a merger, consolidation, liquidation, dissolution, or sale of all the assets of the company."[8]

As Church & Dwight pushed more aggressively into the consumer products field, several changes were made in key management positions. The current roster of key officers along with their ages, positions, and original dates of employment are shown in Exhibit 3. Several of these individuals, including Davies, Bendure, Crilly, Kornhauser, Koslow, and Wilcaukas, brought extensive marketing experience to the top management team.

In addition to the many changes that had taken place in key management positions, changes also began to be made in the composition of the Board of Directors. As of July 30, 1998, the Board of Directors was expanded from 12 to 13 members. Prior to this change, two new Board members were added in 1992 and one was added in 1995. Excluding these additions to the Board, the average length of service for the nine remaining members was 21 years. The mid-year 1998 change brought in a replacement for a retiring director who had served for over 29 years and one new Board member. Four of the five directors who were elected since 1992 brought significant experience in the consumer products field to the Board. They had gained these experiences from companies such as Frito-Lay, Pepsi-Cola International, California Home Brands, Diamond Crystal Salt, Lever Brothers Personal Products, Johnson & Johnson International, and McNeil Consumer Products.[9, 10]

CONSUMER PRODUCTS

Not only had the ARM & HAMMER logo become a trusted consumer trademark, but baking soda also became synonymous with environmental safety in consumers' minds. Church & Dwight had long been known for environmental education, conservation, and products that were environmentally sound, as can be seen in the following statement:

> From 19th-century trading cards and "Books of Valuable Recipes" to 20th-century print advertisements and radio and television commercials, a wide range of communication tools educated the public to the many attributes of baking soda. While the media have changed drastically since the early years, the message has been consistent: ARM & HAMMER Baking Soda is a safe, natural, pure-food product with a unique variety of applications.[11]

Church & Dwight has selected an overall family branding strategy to further penetrate the consumer products market in the United States and Canada by introducing additional products displaying the ARM & HAMMER logo. The ARM & HAMMER brand controls a commanding 85% of the baking soda market. By capitalizing on its easily recognizable brand name, logo, and established marketing channels, Church & Dwight has moved into such products as laundry detergent (approximately 4% of the market), carpet cleaners and deodorizers (approximately 28% of the market), air deodorizers (approximately 13% of the market), toothpaste (approximately 7% of the market), and deodorant/antiperspirants (less than 2% of the market). This strategy has allowed the company to promote multiple products using only one brand name.

The strategy to move more aggressively into the consumer products arena can be traced to Dwight Minton. From the company's founding until 1970, it produced and sold

**Exhibit 3   Key Officers and Their Management Positions:
Church & Dwight Company, Inc.**

Name	Age	Position	Anniversary Date
Robert A. Davies, III	62[1]	President & Chief Executive Officer	1995
Raymond L. Bendure, Ph.D.	54[1]	Vice-President Research & Development	1995
Mark A. Bilawsky	50[1]	Vice-President, General Counsel and Secretary	1976
Mark G. Conish	45[1]	Vice-President Manufacturing and Distribution	1993
James P. Crilly	55[1]	Vice-President Arm & Hammer Division	1995
Zvi Eiref	59[1]	Vice-President Finance & Chief Financial Officer	1995
Dennis M. Moore	47[1]	Vice-President/General Manager International Operations/Business Development	1980
Eugene F. Wilcaukas	55[1]	Vice-President, President & Chief Operating Officer Specialty Products Division	1997
Leo T. Belill	57[2]	Vice-President Specialty Products Division	1986
Alfred H. Falter	48[2]	Vice-President Corporate Purchasing	1979
W. Patrick Fiedler	49[2]	Vice-President Sales & Marketing, Specialty Products Division	1995
Gary P. Halker	47[2]	Vice-President, Controller and Chief Information Officer	1977
Jaap Ketting	46[2]	Vice-President—Brazil	1987
Henry Kornhauser	65[2]	Vice-President—Advertising	1997
Larry B. Koslow	46[2]	Vice-President Marketing Personal Care, Arm & Hammer Division	1995
Ronald D. Munson	55[2]	Vice-President International Operations, Specialty Products Division	1983
Joyce F. Srednicki	53[2]	Vice-President Marketing Household Products, Arm & Hammer Division	1997

1. Executive Officers serving for such term as the Board of Directors shall determine.
2. Executive Officers serving for such terms as determined and at the discretion of the Chief Executive Officer.

Source: Church & Dwight Co., Inc., *Notice of Annual Meeting of Stockholders and Proxy Statement*, 1998, p. 7.

only two consumer products: ARM & HAMMER Baking Soda and a laundry product marketed under the name Super Washing Soda. In 1970, under Minton, Church & Dwight began testing the consumer products market by introducing a phosphate-free, powdered laundry detergent which has since been reformulated. Several other products, including a liquid laundry detergent, fabric softener sheets, an all-fabric bleach, tooth powder and toothpaste, baking soda chewing gum, deodorant/antiperspirants, deodorizers (carpet, room, and pet) and clumping cat litter have been added to the expanding list of ARM & HAMMER brands. However, in a recent move, the company departed from its previous strategy of developing new product offerings in-house by buying several well-known consumer brands such as Brillo®, Parsons® Ammonia, Cameo® Aluminum & Stainless Steel Cleaner, Rain Drops® water softener, SNO BOWL® toilet bowl cleaner, and TOSS 'N SOFT® dryer sheets from The Dial Corporation.

The company's largest selling consumer product line continued to be laundry detergent, capturing approximately 4% of the market. "Despite a virtual absence of advertising, the detergent is positioned to offer quality cleaning at a substantial discount (15–20%) to Procter & Gamble's Tide."[12] The mature $4.3 billion domestic soap detergent market was growing at less than 1% annually, but it was far from tranquil. Environmental concerns continued to increase, and competition from the introduction of innovative products intensified. During 1992 and 1993, Church & Dwight allowed its laundry detergents pricing structure to move above its targeted differential of 15–20% discount without any supporting advertising, which resulted in market share erosion. "A ten-percent price decrease, implemented in December 1993, effectively corrected this price relationship by the middle of 1994." [13] Although this move stopped market share loss, growth in this highly competitive segment has been elusive. New low-cost entrants such as USA Detergents and Huish Detergents have shifted the playing field to a pricing emphasis. [14]

Faced with the problems of a mature domestic market, marketers often rely on a segmentation approach to gain market share. New consumer products must muscle their way into markets by taking market share from current offerings. Church & Dwight also began to focus its attention outside the United States and Canada. The key difference in the U.S. and Canadian markets was that they were both marketing driven, whereas the markets in the rest of the world were still product driven. [15]

The company's household consumer products have traditionally been heavily promoted (but not advertised) and sold at prices below market leaders. At times, these price differentials were as much as 25%. Church & Dwight had to modify this generic strategy somewhat as it rolled out ARM & HAMMER Dental Care from regional test markets into nationwide distribution.

The task of successfully implementing a nationwide marketing campaign is not new to the company. In 1972, with Davies heading up the Arm & Hammer Division, Church & Dwight made marketing history when it introduced ARM & HAMMER Baking Soda as a refrigerator deodorizer. A national television advertising campaign and point-of-sale promotions in grocery stores were used. The outcome was accelerated growth and a 74% increase in volume over a three-year period. [16]

The company's consumer products strategy has been focused on niche markets to avoid a head-on attack from competitors with more financial and marketing clout. In exploring new and existing markets, the common thread was to seek new uses of the basic baking soda ingredient for loyal users. To further this objective, Church & Dwight developed its own consumer research studies on trends in baking soda use for health care and household applications, identifying users by age, gender, income level, and education level. [17]

The company's most recent and aggressive entrants into the consumer products market have been its dental care products. Although it entered a crowded field of specialty products, Church & Dwight planned to ride the crest of increasing interest by both dentists and hygienists in baking soda as an important element in a regimen for maintaining dental health. [18] Church & Dwight was able to sneak up on the giants in the industry and moved rapidly from the position of a niche player in the toothpaste market (along with products such as Topol, Viadent, Check-Up, Zact, and Tom's of Maine) to that of a major competitor. In only five years, the company captured market share (almost 10%) and the attention of major competitors. These competitors were initially slow to react to this new category of dental care products, but they finally responded through new product offerings, heavy promotions, and price cuttings to stem market share loss.

Church & Dwight's dramatic success in penetrating the toothpaste market did not go unnoticed nor unchallenged. Both Procter & Gamble and Colgate introduced similar products. In addition, Procter & Gamble indicated that it would compete on a price basis (possibly lowering prices on baking soda toothpaste by as much as 30%) supported by heavy advertising. This fiercely competitive $2 billion market continues to attract a great deal of attention and marketing emphasis from a variety of key players, as can be seen in Exhibit 4. [19, 20]

Exhibit 4   Market Share of Niche Toothpaste Products

	Market Share		
Brand	**1997**	**1995**	**1992**
Crest	27%	30%	31%
Colgate	19	18	22
Mentadent	11	11	0
Aqua Fresh	11	8	9
ARM & HAMMER™	7	7	10

Sources: *Advertising Age,* April 21, 1997, p. 16; Zachary Schiller, *Business Week,* August 14, 1995, p. 48; and Kathleen Deveny, "Toothpaste Makers Tout New Packaging," *Wall Street Journal,* November 10, 1992, p. B-1.

Baking soda–based toothpastes accounted for 30% of all sales in the domestic toothpaste market. This phenomenal growth continued to attract new entrants such as Unilever PLC, Chesebrough-Pond Inc. (Mentadent), and Warner-Lambert Co. (Listerine Cool Mint). "Competition remains robust, as new brands continue to appear and existing brands expand into emerging category growth segments."[21] New and expanded consumer product offerings designed to promote improved oral care continued to drive sales growth.

Baking soda's success as a toothpaste ingredient resulted in its use in many other personal care products including mouthwash, shampoo, foot powder, and deodorant/antiperspirant. In 1994, the company rolled out an entry into the fiercely competitive deodorant/antiperspirant market with a $15 million launch of an antiperspirant with baking soda. In less than two years, ARM & HAMMER Deodorant Antiperspirant with Baking Soda gained almost 2.5% of an approximately $1½ billion market.[22, 23] But by 1998, its market share had eased to less than 2%.

As more and more products were added to Church & Dwight's consumer line-up, the need for additional marketing expertise grew. Along with the addition of Henry Kornhauser to the top management team in 1997, Church & Dwight brought many of its marketing tasks in house. Kornhauser brought 17 years of senior management and agency experience with him to Church & Dwight. The first major project undertaken by this new in-house function was the $15 million launch of ARM & HAMMER Dental Care Gum.[24]

For the most part, Church & Dwight's entries into the consumer products market met with success. However, some products failed to meet expectations or could even be termed failures. Most notable among the company's marketing missteps were an oven cleaner and a previously unsuccessful foray into underarm deodorants. The company eventually sold off the oven cleaner line and pulled the underarm deodorant from test markets during the mid 1970s. Another potential marketing problem may be looming on the horizon. ARM & HAMMER could be falling into the precarious line-extension snare. Placing a well-known brand name on a wide variety of products could cloud its position and cause it to lose marketing pull.[25] As the company officials looked toward the future prospects for consumer products, the following strategy was stated to guide their actions: "to establish Church & Dwight as a major factor in the $7 billion household products business, primarily using our famous trademark to market middle-priced brands acceptable to the great majority of American consumers. . . . To add to this, via acquisition, other strong brand equities capable of delivering the same objectives."[26]

SPECIALTY PRODUCTS

Church & Dwight was in an enviable position to profit from its dominant niche in the sodium bicarbonate products market because it controlled the primary raw material used in its production. The primary ingredient in sodium bicarbonate is produced from the mineral trona, which is extracted from the company's mines in southwestern Wyoming. The other ingredient, carbon dioxide, is a readily available chemical that can be obtained from a variety of sources.

The company maintained a dominant position in the production of the required raw materials for both its consumer and industrial products. It manufactured almost two-thirds of the sodium bicarbonate sold in the United States and, until 1995, was the only U.S. producer of ammonium bicarbonate and potassium carbonate. In 1998 the company had the largest share (approximately 60%) of the sodium bicarbonate capacity in the United States with 430,000 tons of annual capacity in addition to 11,000 tons of production capacity in Venezuela. Its closest competitor, FMC, had an estimated annual capacity of only 70,000 tons. A third competitor, NaTec, had an estimated annual capacity of 125,000 tons. In addition, 10,000 tons per year were imported from Mexico.[27,28,29]

The Specialty Products Division of Church & Dwight basically consisted of the manufacture and sale of sodium bicarbonate for three distinct market segments: performance products, animal nutrition products, and specialty cleaning products. Manufacturers use sodium bicarbonate performance products as a leavening agent for commercial baked goods; an antacid in pharmaceuticals; a chemical in kidney dialysis; a carbon dioxide release agent in fire extinguishers; and an alkaline in swimming pool chemicals, detergents, and various textile and tanning applications. Animal feed producers use sodium bicarbonate nutritional products predominantly as a buffer, or antacid, for dairy cattle feeds, and they make a nutritional supplement that enhances milk production of dairy cattle. Sodium bicarbonate has also recently been used as an additive to poultry feeds to enhance feed efficiency. Specialty cleaning products are found in blasting (similar to sand blasting applications) as well as many emerging aqueous-based cleaning technologies such as automotive parts cleaning and circuit board cleaning.

Although management has focused increased attention on consumer products, Exhibit 5 shows the relevant contributions of consumer products and continued importance of specialty products to total sales over a five-year period. The stated strategy for this segment is "to solidify worldwide leadership in sodium bicarbonate and potassium carbonate, while broadening our product offerings to other related chemicals. . . . to build a specialized high-margin specialty cleaning business, allying carbonate technology, the ARM & HAMMER trademark and environmental position."[30]

Fluctuations in the significance of specialty products sales can be traced to a series of acquisitions, partnership agreements, and divestitures. These included the acquisition of a 40% interest in Brotherton Chemicals Ltd., a United Kingdom producer of ammonium-based chemicals; a 49% interest in Sales y Oxidos, S.A., a Mexican producer of strontium carbonate; purchase of a 40% interest in two Brazilian bicarbonate and carbonate-related companies; a partnership agreement entered into with Occidental Petroleum Corp. to form Armand Products Co., which produces and markets potassium chemicals; and control of National Vitamin Products Co., which specializes in animal nutrition products. Although the flurry of chemical related acquisitions appeared to have the potential for accelerating growth, management decided to divest the National Vitamin Products Company and the 49% interest in Sales y Oxidos, S.A.

Just like the Consumer Products Division, the Specialty Products Division focused

Exhibit 5   **Percentage of Net Sales**

	1997	1996	1995	1994	1993
Consumer products	80	79	78	80	81
Specialty products	20	21	22	20	19

on developing new uses for the company's core product, sodium bicarbonate. With this goal in mind, a Specialty Cleaning Unit (now called Specialty Cleaning Products) was formed in 1994. This unit was created "in the anticipation that, over the next few years, many of the current solvent-based cleaning products will be regulated out of existence. This new unit will use our core, environmentally-friendly carbonate and bicarbonate technology in the industrial and precision-cleaning markets to build a major position both domestically and internationally.[31]

Pollution control processes at coal-fired electrical plants where sodium compounds are used to clean flue gases may open up an entirely new market for Church & Dwight's specialty products in the environmental area. The company has tested a process whereby dry injection rather than the typical wet scrubbers can be used to remove sulfur oxide and nitrogen oxides from smokestack emissions. The company is hoping that it may help to provide solutions to the country's acid rain problems. The process of dumping baking soda into incinerators of all types to neutralize various pollutants causing acid rain has been successfully tested[32] but has not been adopted on a commercial basis. Reducing sulfur dioxide from smokestack emissions also is being explored in waste incinerator applications.

To this point, utilities have opted to use lime because it is cheaper. However, lime poses disposal problems, and bicarbonate is still being considered for flue gas desulfurization because of its environmental superiority.[33] Experiments with municipalities' adding sodium bicarbonate to their water supplies to reduce lead content have proved to be very successful. Although water treatment applications are currently providing minimal revenues, the potential for future sales is enormous.

Additional opportunities are being explored for ARMEX Blast Media. This is a sodium bicarbonate–based product used as a paint stripping compound. It gained widespread recognition when it was used successfully for the delicate task of stripping the accumulation of years of paint and tar from the interior of the Statue of Liberty without damaging the fragile copper skin. It is now being considered for other specialized applications in the transportation and electronics industries and in industrial cleaning because of its apparent environmental safety. ARMEX also has been introduced into international markets.

The company launched another specialty chemical product, ARMAKLEEN, in 1992. It is an aqueous-based cleaner used for cleaning printed circuit boards. This potentially promising product may have an enormous market because it may be able to replace chlorofluorocarbon-based cleaning systems. "ARMAKLEEN, a carbonate and bicarbonate technology, is the first nonsolvent-based system for this market."[34] Sodium bicarbonate also has been used to remove lead from drinking water and, when added to water supplies, coats the inside of pipes and prevents lead from leaching into the water. This market could grow in significance with additions to the Clean Water Bill. The search for new uses of sodium bicarbonate continues in both the consumer and industrial products divisions.

INTERNATIONAL OPERATIONS

Church & Dwight has traditionally enjoyed a great deal of success in North American markets; however, less than 5% of sales are outside the United States and Canada. It has achieved full distribution in the U.S. and Canada and limited distribution in Mexico.[35] It was not until 1994 that the company entered into the United Kingdom market with its DENTAL CARE products.[36] "Moving into overseas markets will put Church & Dwight into heightened competition with major oral-care and household product marketers such as Procter & Gamble Company, Unilever, and Colgate-Palmolive Company."[37] The Specialty Products Division has established small footholds in Venezuela and Brazil. South American markets hold the promise of rapid growth and the company is also exploring opportunities in the Far East. According to Eugene Wilcaukas, Vice-President, "We've been a little late in Asia. We have a strong desire to be there and the financial ability to accomplish it."[38]

The company expanded its presence in the international consumer products markets with the acquisition of DeWitt International Corporation, which manufactures and markets personal care products including toothpaste. The DeWitt acquisition not only provided the company with increased international exposure but also with much needed toothpaste production facilities and technology. Even with this acquisition, the company still derives over 96% of its revenues from the United States and Canada. Owing to the perceived limited market potential of the DeWitt product line, Church & Dwight divested the subsidiary's brands and its overseas operations but retained its U.S. toothpaste manufacturing facilities in Greenville, South Carolina.

At the same time the company was testing the international waters for its consumer products, it was also continuing to pursue expansion of its specialty products into international markets. Attempts to enter international markets have met with limited success, probably for two reasons: (1) lack of name recognition and (2) transportation costs. Although ARM & HAMMER is one of the most recognized brand names in the United States (in the top ten), it does not enjoy the same name recognition elsewhere. In addition, "[i]nternational transportation represents 40 to 45% of Church & Dwight's sales expense, versus 5 to 10% domestically."[39] However, export opportunities continue to present themselves as 10% of all U.S. production of sodium bicarbonate is exported.

CHURCH & DWIGHT'S FUTURE

The company's stated mission for the 1990s was:

> We will supply customers quality ARM & HAMMER Sodium Bicarbonate and related products, while performing in the top quarter of American businesses.[40]

The core business and foundation on which the company was built remained the same after more than 150 years. However, as the new management team at Church & Dwight became established and looked to the future, they had to reflect on the successes and mistakes of the past as they planned for the future. With the proper strategic moves, the future held the opportunity to once again enhance shareholder wealth of this publicly traded, but family controlled, company.

Notes

1. ARM & HAMMER is a registered trademark of Church & Dwight Company, Inc.
2. Church & Dwight Company, Inc., *1995 Annual Report,* inside cover.
3. "C&D Sees Growth Despite Competitions," *Chemical Marketing Reporter* (December 11, 1989), 236, p. 9.
4. Andrea Adelson, "Arm and Hammer Names a New President," *New York Times* (February 2, 1995), p. D3.
5. Church & Dwight Company, Inc., *1996 Annual Report,* p. 4.
6. Adelson, p. D3.
7. Letter to Stockholders, November 14, 1995.
8. Church & Dwight Company, Inc., *Notice of Annual Meeting of Stockholders* (1989), p. 17.
9. Church & Dwight Co., Inc., *Notice of Annual Meeting of Stockholders and Proxy Statement* (1998).
10. "Church & Dwight Company, Inc., Announces New Board Members." *Company Press Release* (July 30, 1998).
11. *Marketing Milestones: 150th Anniversary* (1996), p. 2.
12. "C&D Sees Growth Despite Competition," p. 19.
13. Church & Dwight Company, Inc., *1994 Annual Report,* p. 1.
14. Kerri Walsh, "Soaps and Detergents," *Chemical Week* (January 29, 1998), pp. 27–29.
15. Pam Weisz, "Church & Dwight in Need of Next Big Idea," *Brandweek* (November 13, 1995), p. 8.
16. Church & Dwight Company, Inc., *1988 Annual Report.*
17. Carrie M. Wainwright, "Church & Dwight: Slow But Steady into Personal Care," *Drug & Cosmetic Industry* (February 1987), p. 28.
18. David Kiley, "Arm & Hammer Mixes Its Own," *Adweek's Marketing Week* (July 4, 1988), p. 3.
19. Based on information from Towne-Oller & Associates, New York.
20. Tara Parker-Pope, "Colgate's Total Grabs Bib Share of Toothpaste Sales," *The Wall Street Journal* (March 6, 1998), p. B3.
21. Church & Dwight Company, Inc., *1995 Annual Report,* p. 7.
22. *Brandweek* (January 31, 1994), p. 4.
23. Bear Stearns Report, 1996.
24. Judann Pollack, "Arm & Hammer Spending Soars to Back Dental Gum," *Advertising Age* (March 23, 1998), p. 49.
25. Ronald Alsop, "Arm & Hammer Baking Soda Going in Toothpaste as Well as Refrigerator," *Wall Street Journal* (June 24, 1988), pp. 2–24.
26. Church & Dwight Company, Inc., *1997 Annual Report,* p. 10.
27. "C&D Sees Growth Despite Competition," pp. 9, 19.
28. Gretchen Busch, "New Bicard Pact Could Have Impact on Supply Picture," *Chemical Marketing Reporter* (November 30, 1992), 242 (22).
29. *Chemical Marketing Reporter* (August 22, 1994), pp. 3+
30. Church & Dwight Company, Inc., *1997 Annual Report,* p. 13.
31. Church & Dwight Company, Inc., *1984 Annual Report,* p. 13.
32. Kathleen Deveny, "Marketing," *Wall Street Journal* (April 27, 1990), p. B-1.
33. "Lime Wins on Price," *Chemical Marketing Reporter* (August 22, 1994), p. 17.
34. Rick Mullin, "Soaps and Detergents: New Generation of Compacts," *Chemicalweek* (January 27, 1993), p. 29.
35. Riccardo A. Davis, "Arm & Hammer Seeks Growth Abroad," *Advertising Age* (August 17, 1992), pp. 3, 42.
36. "Arm & Hammer Set for Second TV Push," *Marketing* (July 7, 1994), p. 7.
37. Davis, p. 42.
38. Robert Westervelt, "Church & Dwight Takes Brazilian Stake," *Chemical Weekly* (June 18, 1997), p. 15.
39. Robert J. Bowman, "Quality Management Comes to Global Transportation," *World Trade* (February 1993), p. 38.
40. Church & Dwight Company, Inc., *1989 Annual Report.*

Tasty Baking Company (1998)

Ellie A. Fogarty, Joyce P. Vincelette, Thomas L. Wheelen, and Thomas M. Patrick

Carl S. Watts, President, CEO, and Chairman of Tasty Baking Company, was filled with mixed emotions when he looked at the date on his desk calendar. October 1, 1998, meant the beginning of Phase II of his company's broad-based planned rollout of Tasty-kakes to the Midwestern states. Since 1991, Tasty Baking Company had pursued a growth and geographic expansion strategy to move beyond its strong regional market on the East Coast. With Phase II, Tastykake brand snack cakes would be available in a total of 47 states! Watts couldn't help but smile as he colored in Nebraska and Kansas on his map of the United States.

What took the smile away was the realization that three months had passed since Interstate Bakeries, the largest wholesale bakery in the United States and maker of Hostess and Dolly Madison snack cakes, had announced its plan to acquire Drake Bakeries of New Jersey, maker of popular Northeast snack cakes Yodels and Devil Dogs and Tastykake's biggest regional competitor. This time, Tasty Baking Company had not questioned the acquisition during the 90-day period allowed for challenges and the deal was finalized the previous week. In 1987, Tasty Baking Company had successfully asserted violation of anti-trust laws when it asked the Federal Trade Commission to require the divestiture of Drake Bakeries by Ralston Purina (then owners of Continental Baking Company, makers of Hostess Snack Cakes).

The snack cake industry was consolidating faster than Watts could believe. Just last year, he had hired his own consultant to investigate acquisition possibilities for Tasty Baking Company. In the snack cake industry, it was cheaper to buy than build in terms of expansion. Watts's mind was distracted: how could he and his company concentrate on geographic expansion and the related growth pains he expected and, at the same time, confront the Interstate Bakeries competition in Tasty Baking Company's most secure market?

COMPANY HISTORY (1914–1998)

The Early Years

The Tasty Baking Company was incorporated on February 25, 1914, in Pennsylvania. Herbert C. Morris, a Boston egg salesman, and Philip J. Baur, a Pittsburgh baker, established a bakery in North Philadelphia to produce Tastykakes. These prewrapped, single-serving, white iced cakes were named by Morris's wife, Willavene, and retailed for ten cents at local grocers.

Morris and Baur only supplied retailers with as many cakes as they thought would sell quickly. This controlled distribution kept fresh products on the shelves and avoided losses resulting from stale goods. Their basic principle to use only the freshest ingredients to make the finest possible products continues to guide the company today.

This case was prepared by Ellie A. Fogarty, Business Librarian, and Professors Joyce P. Vincelette and Thomas M. Patrick of The College of New Jersey, and Professor Thomas L. Wheelen of the University of South Florida. This case was edited for SMBP–7th Edition. This case may not be reproduced in any form without written permission of the copyright holder, Thomas L. Wheelen. Copyright © 1999 by Thomas L. Wheelen. Reprinted by permission.

By 1918, sales exceeded $1 million and in 1923, a six-story plant on Hunting Park Avenue was opened. By 1930, the facility had been expanded to five times its original size. To increase dwindling sales during the Depression, company bakers discovered they could bake three chocolate cupcakes from the same amount of batter normally used for two. They packaged them together, kept the price at a nickel, and buyers thought they were getting a better bargain. During this time, Tasty Baking Company began selling its popular single-portion, rectangular pie, shaped to fit into a lunch box.

In 1951, Philip J. Baur suffered a stroke and died at the age of 66. Paul R. Kaiser, Baur's son-in-law, became President. Herbert C. Morris accepted the post of Chairman of the Board, a position he maintained until his death in 1960.[1] Tasty Baking Company began trading on the American Stock Exchange in 1965.

Acquisitions and Divestitures

In 1965, Tasty Baking Company purchased Philip and Jacobs, Inc., a family graphic arts supply business founded in the mid 1880s, as part of a diversification move. At that time, Tasty Baking Company was made up of two separate divisions, Tastykake and Philip and Jacobs, Inc. Through subsequent acquisitions, Philip and Jacobs, Inc., grew to become one of the largest distributors of supplies and equipment to the printing industry in the United States. Philip and Jacobs, Inc., was spun off to Tasty Baking Company shareholders on August 1, 1993, so that Philip and Jacobs, Inc., could pursue an expansion policy and the Tastykake Division, now the only business of the Tasty Baking Company, could focus on its core business of snack cakes. Tasty Baking Company shareholders received two shares of Philip and Jacobs, Inc., common stock for every three shares of Tasty Baking Company common stock. In September 1994, Philip and Jacobs, Inc., merged with Momentum Corporation of Washington to form PrimeSource Corporation.

Continuing to grow and diversify, Tasty Baking Company acquired Buckeye Biscuit Co. in 1966. Larami Corporation, a Philadelphia toy manufacturer, was purchased in 1970. In 1976, Tasty Baking Company acquired Ole South Foods Co., a frozen dessert manufacturer. Ole South Food's operations were then discontinued in 1979.

In 1981, Philip J. Baur, Jr., son of the Tastykake founder, became Chairman of the Board. Nelson G. Harris was named President and CEO. Harris implemented a strategic planning process, the beginning of the company's five-year plans, and explored new products and markets. Harris upgraded the factory and equipment in the plant for $40 million. He also sold off the company's extraneous businesses: Larami Corporation in 1981 and Buckeye Biscuit Company in 1986.

Owner/Operators

In 1986, as the company began its second five-year plan, Tasty Baking Company's 460 sales routes were sold. Sales representatives were given the opportunity to purchase the exclusive right to sell and distribute Tastykake products in defined geographical territories in the Mid-Atlantic states and become independent owner/operators. However, many interested drivers were unable to obtain financing at the bank (in some cases, routes cost as much as $50,000). To assist the independent owner/operators in the purchase of the routes, the company arranged financing with a group of Philadelphia banks. Each owner/operator who elected to accept this financing signed a note for the purchase of the route and placed the route as security on the loan. In addition, Tasty Baking Company agreed that, at the bank's option, the company would repurchase any route in loan default. Selling the routes raised $16 million for the company. The owner/operators grasped this entrepreneurial opportunity and worked harder, faster, and better with a resulting increase in sales. In 1997, a route sold for ten times its weekly sales. Five thousand dollars in weekly sales was typical of most routes. Tasty Baking Company provided financial assistance through its subsidiary, Tasty Baking Company Financial Services, Inc. As the route grew and prospered, parts could be sold to new owner/operators. Approval from Tasty Baking Company was needed before any existing routes or parts of routes were sold.

In 1995, the company was contacted by the IRS regarding the owner/operators' employee status. Tasty Baking Company treated them as independent contractors and did not pay FICA taxes on them. The IRS argued that independent contractors could take the jobs they wanted and decline the ones they didn't want. They could work for several companies at a time. This was not the case with Tasty Baking Company's owner/operators. By 1997, the dispute was resolved. Tasty Baking Company took a $1.95 million charge in its fourth quarter to cover penalties assessed by the IRS for unpaid taxes from 1990 to 1997. Tasty Baking Company now treats its owner/operators as "statutory employees" for payroll tax purposes only.[2]

Dutch Mill

In 1995, Tasty Baking Company completed its first acquisition of a competing bakery in the company's 81-year history. Tasty Baking Company, the fourth largest baking company in the United States and the Mid-Atlantic region's leading snack cake producer, purchased Dutch Mill Baking Company for $1.87 million. Dutch Mill, a New Jersey–based baker of donuts, all-natural muffins, cookies, and fat-free angel food cake, maintained an 11% market share (ranked number three) in northern New Jersey and metropolitan New York City, the largest retail food market in the United States. Tasty Baking Company had only a 1% share of the $100 million snack cake market in New York City at the time.[3]

Carl S. Watts, who was elected President and CEO after Harris retired in 1992, stated that, "the acquisition of Dutch Mill Baking Company supplements our core strategic plan which is to build our baseline business through geographic expansion and new product development. Dutch Mill will complement our efforts quite nicely and will allow for possible sales and marketing synergies to be exchanged between the two brands."[4]

Strategic Alliances

Although the Schmidt Baking Company in Baltimore has been delivering Tastykakes along the Eastern shore of Maryland for over 40 years, the 1990s marked the beginning of an era of strategic distribution alliances for Tasty Baking Company. In 1991, when the company's management team drafted its third five-year plan, the company was looking to geographically expand its markets.

In 1992, Tasty Baking Company formed a partnership with Kroger Stores, one of the nation's largest grocery chains, to distribute Tastykake products to its 1,200 supermarkets in the Southeast and Midwest. Kroger baked English muffins that Tasty Baking Company bought and distributed on its routes under the Tastykake name. In exchange, Tasty Baking Company bought 600,000 to 700,000 pounds of peanut butter annually from a Kroger subsidiary. The Kroger arrangement gave the Tastykake brand legitimacy as it established a distribution foothold in new territories. In 1993, Tasty Baking Company joined up with Merita Bakery, a division of Interstate Bakeries Corporation, to sell Tastykake cakes and pies in Florida and Georgia and in Fry's Food & Drug Stores in Phoenix, Arizona.[5]

In an attempt to penetrate the largest snack cake market, metropolitan New York City, Tasty Baking Company entered into a distribution agreement with Frito-Lay in January 1994. This marked the first time Tastykakes were delivered on a route operated by a non-bakery company. Frito-Lay, the food division of PepsiCo Inc., distributed Tasty Baking Company's snack cakes, donuts, and cookies to supermarkets, convenience stores, and other retail outlets along the company's 200 routes. However, the potato chips and other salty snacks produced by Frito-Lay had a 30–90 day shelf-life, much longer than a snack cake, which had a 4–7 day shelf-life. Incompatible delivery schedules led to the termination of Tasty Baking Company's agreement with Frito-Lay in 1995.

In April 1994, Tasty Baking Company negotiated a marketing agreement that made it the exclusive supplier of snack cakes to 500 Wawa convenience stores in Connecticut, Pennsylvania, New Jersey, Delaware, and Maryland, pushing out Hostess, Dolly Madison, and some other brands.

Westward Expansion

Chicago

Tastykakes made their way into the Chicago market during the summer of 1997. In June, 187 Jewel Food Stores began offering a ten-item line of family packs shipped fresh three times a week via tractor trailer. Direct-store delivery was handled by Chicago-based Alpha Baking company with additional support by The Sell Group, a food brokerage company. Tasty Baking Company leveraged its high market share in the Philadelphia area in its negotiations with Jewel. Jewel and ACME Markets, a major grocery chain in the Northeast with whom Tasty Baking Company had an established, strong relationship, were owned by American Stores of Salt Lake City, Utah. Tasty Baking Company worked with national product people in Utah to put together the comprehensive distribution program. Tasty Baking Company picked products from its portfolio of 100 SKUs to optimize the product mix to guarantee the success of the brand over time and to ensure that the products didn't duplicate one another in icings, fillings, and form.[6]

By August 1997, Tastykakes had entered 177 of Southland Corporation's 7-Eleven convenience stores in Chicago. Tasty Baking Company was participating in 7-Eleven's Combined Distribution Center (CDC) program. In the past, the CDC concept had encountered difficulties with short shelf-life products like snack cakes, which perform significantly better with a direct-store door (DSD) system due to the relatively perishable nature of the product. Fortunately Tasty Baking Company switched to a new packaging film that had become available to extend the shelf-life of its snack cakes to 21 days from 7–10 days.

In January 1998, Tasty Baking Company made its Tastykakes available in all 104 Dominick's Supermarkets in Chicago. Tasty Baking Company kicked off its entry into Chicago with broadcast and print ad campaigns using radio, free-standing inserts (FSIs), and in-store media. Later, Tasty Baking Company added Eagle and Kroger Supermarkets to its account list in Chicago. By the spring of 1998, on an annual run rate, Tasty Baking Company had a 5% market share in Chicago, taking share from Hostess, the category leader.[7]

Colorado

Continuing its relationship with 7-Eleven, Tasty Baking Company entered 240-plus 7-Eleven stores from Denver and Colorado Springs to Pueblo, Fort Collins, and Grand Junction in October 1997. Tasty Baking Company supported this move with 405 spot radio ads in the Denver/Boulder metropolitan area.[8]

Ohio

Tastykakes were introduced to 100 Super K-Mart, Sparkle, Heinen's, Food Centre, and other stores from Youngstown to Lorain (Cleveland area) in May 1998. Only one-fourth of Tastykake's product line was selected to distribute to Ohio with the direct route sales method. Tastykake fruit pies were considered too fragile to ship and would be available only on the East Coast.[9]

West Coast

Tasty Baking Company began a rollout to the 249 Luck Stores in Southern California and Nevada in the summer of 1998. This was seen as a key market for Tastykake's Tropical Delights line of snack cakes, a refreshing tasting vanilla cake filled with guava, coconut, papaya, or pineapple filling and topped with coconut, which was targeted to the Latino consumer and those in warmer climates. Tasty Baking Company reached others on the West Coast and the Pacific Northwest through a wholesaler network with Coremark International, the number two wholesaler in the nation.

Midwest Expansion

In August 1998, Tasty Baking Company began Phase I of a broad-based planned rollout of its products to the Dakotas, Minnesota, Wisconsin, Michigan, Illinois, and parts of Iowa. Metz Baking Company, a major manufacturer and distributor of bread, rolls, and other bakery products in the Midwest and North Central United States, distributed top-selling family packs of Tastykakes on approximately 650 of its direct-store delivery routes to grocery stores. The effort was supported with a major ad campaign including radio, consumer promotions, FSI-coupons, in-store displays, and consumer sampling. Phase II, begun in October 1998, included 300 more routes to Nebraska, Kansas, and more areas of Iowa.[10]

In 1998, Tasty Baking Company manufactured over 100 varieties of snack cakes, donuts, cookies, pies, and muffins. Independent owner/operators and distributors sold these products in 47 states, Washington D.C., and Puerto Rico. Tasty Baking Company dominated the Philadelphia market, holding 64% share of the snack cake segment.

CORPORATE GOVERNANCE

Board of Directors

Philip J. Baur, Jr., retired as Chairman of the Board on January 22, 1998, a position he had held since 1981. Mr. Baur had been a Director of the company since 1954. He was a Director of PrimeSource Corporation. Mr. Baur controlled 3%, or approximately 251,309 shares of common stock.[11] (See Exhibit 1 for the Board of Directors and the Executive Officers.)

Carl S. Watts was elected a Director in April 1992. In 1998, he held 2%, or 130,397 shares of common stock. Watts, who started at Tasty Baking Company in 1967 as a route driver and held a variety of positions in the Sales and Marketing Department before being appointed Vice-President of Sales and Marketing in 1985 and President of the Tastykake Division in 1989, was elected President and CEO and remains in that position today. On January 23, 1998, Watts succeeded Philip J. Baur, Jr., as Chairman of the Board of Directors.

Exhibit 1   Board of Directors and Executive Officers: Tasty Baking Company

Board of Directors	Executive Officers
Philip J. Baur, Jr. Retired Chairman of the Board	**Carl S. Watts** Chairman, President and Chief Executive Officer
Carl S. Watts Chairman, President and Chief Executive Officer	**John M. Pettine** Vice-President and Chief Financial Officer
Nelson G. Harris Chairman of the Executive Committee	**William E. Mahoney** Vice-President, Human Resources
Fred C. Aldridge, Jr., Esq. Attorney-at-law	**Elizabeth H. Gemmill, Esq.** Vice-President and Secretary
G. Fred DiBona, Jr. President and CEO, Independence Blue Cross	**Paul M. Woite** Vice-President, Manufacturing
John M. Pettine Vice-President and Chief Financial Officer	**W. Dan Nagle** Vice-President, Sales and Marketing
James L. Everett, III Retired Chairman of the Board PECO Energy Company	**Daniel J. Decina** Treasurer and Controller
Judith M. von Seldeneck Chief Executive Officer, Diversified Search Companies	**Eugene P. Malinowski** Assistant Treasurer
	Thomas M. Lubiski Assistant Controller
	Edward J. Delahunty Assistant Secretary
	Colleen M. Henderson Assistant Secretary

Source: Tasty Baking Company, *1995 Annual Report,* p. 32.

No other Director or Executive Officer controlled 1% or more of the company's common stock. All Directors and Executive Officers as a group owned approximately 8% of outstanding stock.

Nelson G. Harris was elected a Director of Tasty Baking Company in April 1979, President of the company in September 1979, CEO in April 1981, and Chairman and CEO in February 1991, in which capacity he served until his retirement on May 1, 1992. Harris served as Chairman of the Executive Committee of the Board of Directors. He was a Director of American Water Works Company, Inc., and Rittenhouse Trust Company.[12]

Judith M. von Seldeneck was elected a Director in July 1991. She was the CEO of Diversified Search Companies, a general executive search firm. Von Seldeneck was also a Director of CoreStates Financial Corporation, Keystone Insurance Company, and Triple A MidAtlantic. James L. Everett, III, a retired CEO of PECO Energy Company, served as a Director of Tasty Baking Company since 1970.[13]

Fred C. Aldridge, Jr., a retired senior partner of the Philadelphia law firm of Stradley, Ronon, Stevens & Young, was elected a Director in 1981. He was President of The Grace S. and W. Linton Nelson Foundation and President of Preston Drainage Company. John M. Pettine was elected a Director in April 1992. He had served as Vice-President, Finance, since December 1983 and had been elected Vice-President and Chief Financial Officer of the company in April 1991. Both Aldridge and Pettine were Directors of PrimeSource Corporation.[14]

G. Fred DiBona, Jr., was elected a Director in 1998. DiBona was president and CEO of Independence Blue Cross since 1990. He was also a Director of Philadelphia Suburban Corporation, Pennsylvania Savings Bank, and Magellan Health Services, Inc., and Chairman of the Blue Cross and Blue Shield Association.[15]

Executive Officers

William E. Mahoney was elected Vice-President, Human Resources in December 1984. He joined the company in 1972 and served as Director of Industrial Relations and Personnel from 1982 to 1984. Paul M. Woite was elected Vice-President, Manufacturing, on April 21, 1995. Woite was Manager, Maintenance Operations from May 1989 to October 1993 and Director, Engineering & Maintenance, from October 1993 to April 1995. He joined the company in 1963. W. Dan Nagle was elected Vice-President, Sales and Marketing, in November 1989. He joined the company in 1984 as Director of Marketing and became Director of National Sales in 1986.[16] (See Exhibit 1 for the Board of Directors and the Executive Officers.)

SNACK CAKE INDUSTRY

Consolidation

Dozens of companies, many of which operated only on a regional basis, supplied the snack cake market. That was why, until recently, the market for snack cakes had not seen a great deal of consolidation. This was primarily due to the perishability of the sweet baked goods. Because they go stale so quickly, they usually cannot be shipped over long distances and must therefore be baked near the markets in which they will be consumed. Thus national marketers had to operate multiple bakeries or use artificial preservatives in their products. As a result, economies of scale were limited—which in turn provided additional opportunities for regional and local bakeries.[17]

In the highly competitive snack cakes market, where overall growth in retail sales had been relatively flat during the early 1990s, competitors were looking for new ways to extend their marketing reach and cut their distribution expenses. One important new trend was consolidation between the leading players. For example, Interstate Bakeries Corporation (IBC) made strategic acquisitions in the 1990s to become the largest wholesale bakery in the United States. In 1995, IBC acquired Continental Baking, maker of Hostess snack cakes and Wonder Bread. In 1998, IBC acquired Drakes Bakery, maker of Yodels and Devil Dogs. IBC controlled almost 20% of the snack cake market with its powerhouse brands. In addition to acquiring brands, IBC acquired the John J. Nissen Baking company of Portland, Maine, and swapped its Grand Junction, Colorado, bakery plus cash for Earthgrains' Massachusetts bakery. This way, IBC could manufacture its snack cakes and breads closer to its markets.

Low-calorie/Low-fat Products

In 1993, shoppers moved away from low-calorie, fat-free, and low-fat foods in favor of "full-flavored" foods. Manufacturers responded by reducing the number of products aimed at health- and diet-conscious consumers. During 1994, however, shoppers took their cue from the Nutrition Labeling and Education laws that became effective that May by seeking out more healthful foods. Again, food manufacturers were quick to respond. As fast as they had disappeared, a wide array of low-fat and reduced-fat products re-appeared on store shelves packaged with calorie-revealing labels. These "new" products were among that year's most popular introductions.[18] By 1998, all the major snack cake brands included low- and reduced-fat varieties. However, emphasis was back on the sweet in sweet goods as snack cake companies noted a decline in the health-consciousness trend. With FDA approval of Procter & Gamble's Olestra as a GRAS (generally recognized as safe) ingredient, new possibilities existed for producers of fat- and calorie-laden foods. This no-fat fat substitute would make formulating healthy products that taste good much easier.

Demographics

Demographic trends affecting the snack cakes market included the teenage market, aging baby boomers, and the increase of single-parent homes and dual-career families. These trends created a greater demand for convenient bakery snacks. The appeal of a snack cake was that it saved time and effort, came in a single-serving package, and required no preparation. The use of snack cakes and cookies tended to rise with the presence of children between the ages of 2 and 11 in the household.[19] Research showed that, on average, the under-25s buy fewer bakery products than the over-40s. Snack cake manufacturers would have to reach this younger market segment to promote sales of bakery products. Younger customers were as concerned, if not more concerned, about fat and calories. As bakers roll out better-tasting low- and no-fat snack cakes, teenagers could turn to bakery foods in large numbers.[20]

Census forecasts indicated that by 2010, Hispanics will be the largest ethnic minority in the United States. Developing foods based on ethnic preferences to satisfy new consumers became important for all food manufacturers.

New Products

Breakfast products became the focus of many wholesale bakeries in the late 1990s. In 1997 and 1998, the top snack cake companies introduced branded varieties of donuts, pastries, buns, rolls, coffee cakes, muffins, cereal bars, and granola bars. Competition from in-store bakeries (ISBs), which had been making steady sales gains throughout the 1990s, caused wholesale manufacturers to secure new retail customers and prevent consumers from defecting to ISBs.

Sales Outlets

To make the purchase of snack cakes as easy as possible, the products were available in supermarkets, convenience stores, mass merchandisers, and vending machines. The popularity of gourmet coffee helped sales in convenience stores—commuters picked up a snack cake with their coffee on the way to the office. In 1997, sales of snack cakes by outlet were: $1,344.1 million, supermarkets; $409.0 million, convenience stores; $238.9 million, mass merchandisers; $92.5 million, vending machines. Another $495.6 million of snack cakes were sold in drug stores, mom and pop stores, and on military bases.[21] (See Exhibit 2.)

Exhibit 2 1997 Sales by Outlets

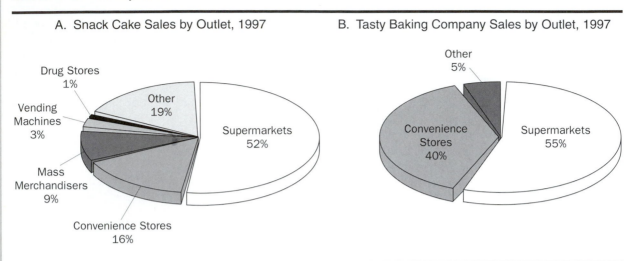

A. Snack Cake Sales by Outlet, 1997

Drug Stores
1%

Vending
Machines
3%

Other
19%

Supermarkets
52%

Mass
Merchandisers
9%

Convenience Stores
16%

B. Tasty Baking Company Sales by Outlet, 1997

Other
5%

Convenience
Stores
40%

Supermarkets
55%

Source: "Bakery Foods: Snack Cakes & Pies," *Snack Food & Wholesale Bakery* (June 1998), p. S1.

Source: Dan Malovany, "Sweet Expectations," *Snack Food & Wholesale Bakery* (January 1998), p. 18.

Forecasts

Analysts in the bakery industry were watching the impact of the 1996 Farm Act on wheat production and prices. According to the law, wheat farmers no longer had to grow wheat to receive payments from the government. Farmers may decide to allocate sizable acreage to alternative crops due to market forces. Other analysts considered whether farmers would forward-integrate into milling and other aspects of food manufacturing, including baking. A more distant possibility considered was the thought that millers and bakers would backward-integrate into wheat production to ensure a supply of desired product. Gyrations in commodity prices for wheat and flour could be affected by export demand from China, the world's largest importer of wheat. China's imports could expand from 50% to 100% over the next ten years. Bakers would have to keep an eye on flour prices to see the future impact on production costs.

COMPETITION

Tasty Baking Company characterized its competition as "everything . . . that you might consume as a snack," for example, in the summer months, ice cream and frozen yogurt or for sports fans, pretzels, potato chips, and peanuts. By 1998, Tasty Baking Company was competing with cookie, donut, and snack bar makers, as well as institutional and private label bakeries. Competition also included other regional or local bakeries and in-store bakeries. However, snack cakes accounted for over 80% of Tasty Baking Company's sales in 1997, so its most immediate competition came from other snack cake producers. The primary brands that competed with Tastykakes were Interstate Bakeries (Hostess, Dolly Madison, and Drake), McKee (Little Debbie), and Entenmann's (Bestfoods) (see Exhibit 3).

Hostess

Continental Baking Company, maker of Wonder Bread and Hostess Twinkies, was the nation's largest baker until it was acquired by Interstate Bakeries Corporation (IBC), a Kansas City, Missouri–based company and maker of Home Pride Bread and Dolly Madison snack cakes, in July 1995. Besides Twinkies, the Hostess line included Ho Ho's, Ding Dong's, Suzy Q's, assorted donuts, coffee cake, and a collection of fruit pies. The "light" product line included Twinkie Lights, Cupcake Lights, and fat-free Crumb Coffee Cakes.

Dolly Madison

The Dolly Madison snack cakes did not lose sales to the Hostess line once the acquisition was completed. The Dolly Madison line was targeted toward young men and convenience stores, whereas Hostess targeted kids and moms who shopped in supermarkets. In 1997, IBC's market share for Hostess and Dolly Madison snack cakes was 16% (see Exhibit 3).

Drakes

IBC completed an acquisition in 1998 of Drake Bakeries, formerly owned by Culinar of Canada, increasing its ownership of bakeries to 70. Drake Bakeries, maker of Yodels and Devil Dogs, competed with Tasty Baking Company for the Northeast and Mid-Atlantic region. The combination of Drake's and Hostess would give IBC a dominant market share in many of Tasty Baking Company's strong regions. In 1997, Drake's market share was 4% (see Exhibit 3).

Little Debbie's

Little Debbie's producer, McKee Foods, was a privately held, Tennessee company that marketed 60 varieties of snack cakes and 20 varieties of Sunbelt bread and cereal to 44 states. It was the number one snack cake in sales in 1997. Examples of Little Debbie products include Chocolate Twins, Swiss Cake Rolls, Nutty Bars, Donut Sticks, Jelly Rolls, and Marshmallow Pies. Its 1997 market share for snack cakes was 24% (see Exhibit 3).

Entenmann's

Bestfoods, maker of Entenmann's cakes, had 10% market share in 1997 (see Exhibit 3). Bestfoods was a global consumer foods company that operated in 60 countries. Its best known brands included Knorr, Hellmann's, Thomas' English Muffins, and Skippy Peanut Butter.

Tasty Baking and Others

Tasty Baking Company's market share in 1997 was 5%. Private label brands had 20% market share with the remaining 21% belonging to many small companies (see Exhibit 3).

Exhibit 3 Snack Cake U.S. Market Share, 1997

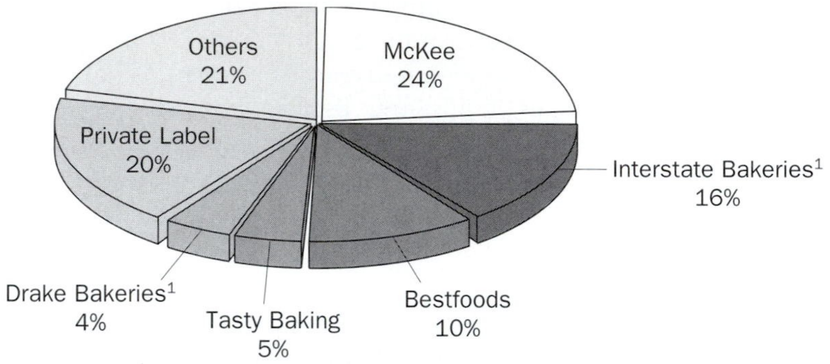

Others 21%
McKee 24%
Interstate Bakeries[1] 16%
Private Label 20%
Drake Bakeries[1] 4%
Tasty Baking 5%
Bestfoods 10%

Note: 1. Drake Bakeries acquired by Interstate Bakeries in 1998.

Source: "Bakery Foods: Snack Cakes/Pies," *Snack Food Wholesale Bakery* (June 1998), p. S1.

COMPANY PROFILE

Corporate Structure

In 1994, Tasty Baking Company completed a restructuring program designed to enhance the company's overall competitiveness, productivity, and efficiency. To facilitate team work and communication, departments and responsibilities in every area within the company were realigned vertically by product line rather than horizontally across lines. Previously each functional area had its own supervisory hierarchy, objectives, responsibilities, and budgets. Conflicts and turf battles resulted, and mistakes and oversights by one group were blamed on the other.

To break down barriers between employees in different departments, Tasty Baking Company had set up a series of programs to open communications and broadened duties to give its people more responsibility. At monthly meetings, teams of employees on a particular line were brought together to discuss costs, operations, and budgets. This resulted in broader participation in problem solving and gave the company full benefit of the innovative ideas of its employees.

Corporate Culture

Tasty Baking Company's conservative corporate culture stemmed largely from its founders, Morris and Baur. Throughout their careers, they had conducted their business honestly and ethically. Morris and Baur instilled in Tasty Baking Company a commitment to the finest ingredients, highest quality, and daily delivery of fresh products.

Tasty Baking Company was a family-oriented company, and workers were encouraged to suggest friends and family members for employment positions. This, and the fact that Tasty Baking Company tried to promote from within, contributed to a very low turnover rate. Employees' opinions were taken seriously. In 1994, Tasty Baking Company changed its award for implemented suggestions from $50 to $75, and usable ideas from workers increased 400%.[22]

Tasty Baking Company was dedicated to the community in which it operated. The Allegheny West Community Development Project, started by Tasty Baking Company in 1968, built or rehabilitated over 400 homes for low-income families in North Philadelphia.[23] The Allegheny West Foundation, run by President Ron Hinton, was started to promote stability and improvement of the local neighborhood. Tasty Baking Company was also involved in the work of the United Way, the Greater Philadelphia Food Bank, the Philadelphia Committee for the Homeless, various educational programs, and soup kitchens.

Human Resources

Following the example of its founders, Tasty Baking Company highly valued its employees. The company employed approximately 1,060 full-time and 100 part-time workers. The company considered its employee relations to be good. No employee of the company was represented by a union. In 1994 and 1995, Teamsters Local 115 led an eight-month organizing drive, which ended on April 5, 1995. Employees rejected the appeal to join the union in a 442 to 223 vote. In 1969, the Bakery, Confectionery & Tobacco Workers also conducted an unsuccessful campaign at Tasty Baking Company.[24]

The company participated in a funded noncontributory pension plan providing retirement benefits for substantially all employees. The Tasty Baking Company Thrift Plan permitted participants to make contributions to the Plan on a pretax salary reduction basis. The company contributed one dollar for each one dollar contributed by an employee up to a specified limit. The company's contribution was invested in Tasty Baking Company common stock, and participants chose from a selection of Dreyfus Corporation investment options for their contributions. The company contributed $355,077 to the Plan in 1997, $369,169 in 1996, and $370,124 in 1995.[25] Over 93% of Tasty Baking Company employees owned company shares through the 401-K program.[26]

Marketing

Because Tasty Baking Company considered its competition to be all types of snack foods, it wanted to change the company's marketing strategy. In the 1980s, the strategy developed around taste—"Nobody bakes a cake as tasty as a Tastykake!" Tasty Baking Company involved consumers, store managers, trade buyers, and the company's ad agency, the Weightman Group of Philadelphia, in a process called "Brand Planning" to gain a better understanding of its brand and how it competed in the whole universe of snack products.

Tasty Baking Company followed its products from the shelf to the home to see how they were consumed and what role the snacks played in people's lives. The results of this study, which would either revalidate the current "taste" strategy or point the company in a new strategic direction, set the course for Tasty Baking Company's next advertising campaign.[27] When taste emerged as the main reason people bought Tastykakes, the study led to the first major advertising effort since 1989.

The "Moments" campaign included three 15-second vignettes featuring family members enjoying a Tastykake together, with the popular "Nobody Bakes a Cake as Tasty as a Tastykake" jingle recorded in a variety of soundtracks including country, urban gospel, and contemporary.

Tasty Baking Company made use of strategically placed in-store displays, billboards, transit ads, product samples, business publications, newspapers, coupons, spot radio and television advertising, and sporting events to promote its products. In 1997, Tasty Baking Company spent $210,000 advertising its products. When entering new markets, Tasty Baking Company used free-standing inserts (FSIs) in Sunday newspapers, promotions, and heavy in-store sampling to generate trial of the products.

In 1989, Tasty Baking Company introduced "Tastykare," a direct marketing program to serve displaced Philadelphians who longed for Tastykakes. By calling a toll-free number, customers throughout the United States could have Tastykake products delivered via second-day air service. This service was also available on the Internet.

Products

Tasty Baking Company produced over 100 different varieties of snack cakes, donuts, cookies, pies, and muffins (see Exhibit 4). The availability of some products varied according to the season of the year. The cakes, cookies, and donuts principally sold at retail prices for individual packages ranging from 33 cents to 99 cents and family convenience packages and jumbo packs ranging from $2.39 to $3.99. The pies sold at retail for 75 cents each.[28] Tasty Baking Company developed its best known and most loved varieties in the 1920s and 1930s—chocolate cupcakes, Butterscotch Krimpets, rectangular Tasty pies, and Kandy Kakes. These products remained the most popular items throughout the company's history.

A Tasty Baking Company analysis of snack cake consumption that focused on how sales fluctuated during certain times of the year led to the introduction of a holiday- and seasonal-themed line of products. This analysis noted the increase in home baking during the major holidays—Easter, Christmas—as well as the sharp increases in candy sales during those times of the year. To attract holiday business, Tasty Baking Company introduced Coconut Kandy Kakes for Easter. The response was very favorable, and the line was expanded. Unlike the company's traditional products, all the holiday-themed items were more targeted toward children and impulse sales. Even the wrappers were decorated to tie in with the theme. So far, the company's regular line had been cannibalized very little.[29]

Tasty Lites, a line of reduced-fat, reduced-calorie products, was introduced in 1991. To circumvent the new FDA rulings on light/lite foods, the line was renamed TastyToos in 1992. In 1995, Tasty Baking Company reengineered its ingredients and processes to retain the taste but remove the fat in its product line. Even the film used to wrap the low-fat product was changed to keep in more moisture and flavor. This new low-fat line, with less than 2 grams of fat, included eight varieties. Although he did not cite specific sales figures, Gary G. Kyle, Director of Marketing, said sales of the new products went beyond original sales expectations. The raspberry-filled Koffee Kakes emerged as the strongest seller, followed by the Creme Filled Chocolate Cupcakes.[30]

In 1998, Tasty Baking Company's Snak Bars were the result of a reworking of the cookie bar recipe that was not performing well. The new product was 33% larger than the previous product. Tasty Baking Company added vitamins and minerals for the nutrition-conscious consumer. Snak Bars were packaged in metallic wrappers with distinctive graphics. They were targeted to men and women with busy schedules who were looking for grab-and-go snacks. The five varieties were strawberry-iced, lemon-iced, chocolate chip, oatmeal raisin, and fudge-iced.

Tropical Delights, or Delicias Tropicales on the bilingual packaging, were introduced first to the Puerto Rico market and later expanded to all of Tasty Baking Company's markets. Taste panels were conducted in Puerto Rico to ensure authenticity. Tropical Delights were distributed by Holsum Bakery in Puerto Rico. Varieties included coconut-topped

Exhibit 4   Tastykake Products—1998: Tasty Baking Company

Sugar Wafers	Chocolate Juniors	**Holiday Theme Varieties**
Tasty Klairs	Butterscotch Krimpets	Coconut Kandy Kakes
Brownies	Peanut Butter Kandy Kakes	Witchy Good Treats
Koffee Kakes	Creme-filled Chocolate Cupcakes	Frosty Kandy Kakes
P.B. Krunch	Chocolate Kandy Kakes	Sparkle Kakes
Jelly Krimpets	Coconut Juniors	Bunny Trail Treats
Honey Buns	Creme-filled Buttercream Cupcakes	Cupid Kakes
Whirly Twirls	Cinnamon Raisin Breakfast Buns	Kringle Kakes
Kreme Krimpies	Chocolate Cupcakes	St. Patty's Treats
Pecan Twirls	Creme-filled Koffee Kakes	Santa Snacks
Lemon Juniors	Orange Juniors	Bunny Bars
PoundKake	Chocolate Covered Pretzels	Ghostly Goodies
Bear Claws		Tasty Tweets
		Sweetie Kakes

Low Fat	**Mini Donuts**	**Pies**
Lemon Krimpets	Powdered Sugar	Apple
Apple Krimpets	Rich Frosted	Blueberry
Raspberry Krimpets	Honey Wheat	Cherry
Lemon-filled Koffee Kakes	Chocolate	Pumpkin
Apple-filled Koffee Kakes		Lemon
Raspberry-filled Koffee Kakes	**Gold Collection**	Strawberry
Creme-filled Vanilla Cupcakes	Chocolate Royale	Peach
Creme-filled Chocolate Cupcakes	Carrot Cake	Lemon-Lime
	Chocolate Chuck Macadamia Cookie	Coconut Cream

Pastry Pockets—apple, lemon, cheese
Tasty Mini Muffins—blueberry, banana nut, carrot, raisin, nut
Tastykake English Muffins—traditional, sourdough, cinnamon raisin
Tasty Mini Cupcakes—4 varieties
Kreme Bars—chocolate and peanut butter
Cookies—oatmeal raisin and chocolate chip
Snak Bars—strawberry-, lemon-, fudge-iced, oatmeal raisin, chocolate chip
Danish—cheese, raspberry, lemon
Tropical Delights—guava, papaya, pineapple, coconut

Source: Tasty Baking Company documents.

vanilla cakes with guava, papaya, pineapple, or coconut filling. The packaging featured palm trees and tropical fruit in addition to bilingual wording of nutritional information. Although created to appeal to the Hispanic market, these refreshing cakes became popular in warmer climates and with members of Generation X.

In April 1998, three varieties of Danish products debuted at the Oxford facility: cheese, raspberry, and lemon. New varieties, such as blueberry or cherry, could easily be created in the future.

Also in 1998, Tasty Baking Company rolled out chocolate and peanut butter varieties of Kreme Bars, chocolate cakes filled with vanilla or peanut butter and covered with a dark or milk chocolate coating. They were sold in 12-cake Family Packs and individual two-cake packs. In addition, Tasty Baking Company brought out premium Tasty Collection chocolate chip and oatmeal raisin cookies, the number one and two preferred varieties of cookies.

Tasty Baking Company instituted two new brands, Aunt Sweetie's Bakery and Snak n' Fresh, which allowed Tasty Baking Company to enter the private label, food service, and institutional marketplaces with yeast raised and other products without compromising the integrity of its Tastykake brand.

Production

In the 1960s, Tasty Baking Company automated the production systems at its Hunting Park plant, which cut the mixing, baking, icing, wrapping, and packaging time from 12 hours to 45 minutes and the truck loading time from 5 hours to 3 minutes. From 1986 to 1990, the company's 565,000 square foot, six-story production facility received $50 million worth of upgrades, which included a complete renovation of its Kandy Kake line and a second donut line. In 1989, the company reduced its dependence on conventional energy sources by building an on-site 3.5-megawatt cogeneration system in order to run its facilities with minimal use of petroleum-based products.

The Hunting Park plant had 16 production lines (14 ovens and two donut fryers). Each line had its own bulk handling system, depositor, oven, icing system, metal detector, wrapper, cartoner, ink-jet coder, caser, and bar coder. Production occurred six days a week for two to two and a half shifts a day with an annual output in excess of 100 million pounds. Tasty Baking Company baked over 3.5 million individual cakes and pies each day and 2.5 million donuts every week.

In 1995, with the acquisition of Dutch Mill Baking Company, Tasty Baking Company expanded its product lines and distribution. The Dutch Mill facility produced boxed donuts, muffins, and fat-free angel food cake.

The Oxford facility operated as a wholly-owned subsidiary of Tasty Baking Company and allowed the company to produce the products that had been made for them by other companies. The 160,000-square-foot facility produced a variety of yeast-raised donuts, bear claws, Danish, and cinnamon or fruit-filled sweet rolls. Tasty Baking Company was investigating how to use this facility to serve the in-store bakery and food-service segment of the bakery industry. Whereas the Hunting Park facility was a multilevel maze of ingredient handling, mixing, and dedicated lines, production at the single-level Oxford plant ran in a relatively straight line that was designed for flexibility and short runs. All equipment was on wheels for quick changes.

True to its guiding principle of consistent quality and fresh products, Tasty Baking Company set up a rigorous vendor certification program. It began with a series of formal audits, starting with raw material evaluation. If the vendor's product passed this analysis, a small quantity of ingredients was used in a production run. If the ingredients met expectations, Tasty Baking Company would bring in a partial order. The vendor and Tasty Baking Company worked on the specifications together. Three consecutive trials were run before ordering a full shipment. Even after certification, virtually every raw material was analyzed from a biological, chemical, physical, and organoleptic/sensory aspect before it was accepted in production. All results were recorded in a database for monthly reports that were distributed to the purchasing department and vendors.[31]

Technicians checked cocoa samples every morning for color, flavor, aroma, fineness, moisture, and butterfat content. Surprise sampling could occur at any time. Random sampling was conducted approximately every 15 minutes on some lines.

Tasty Baking Company employed tasters to ensure the proper color, size, icing, and distribution of the filling. They also checked the aroma, the flavor release, and the quantity and quality of the flavor. One taster typically sampled 60 to 70 bites of snack cakes each day. Rejections were rare, once every few years, because the production staff had its own quality-control levels. Several times a year, a panel of eight to ten testers met to make sure their palates agreed and that the company's products were true to their original form.[32]

Tasty Baking Company used three natural preservatives in the production of its snack cakes: sorbic acid, citric acid, and potassium sorbate. According to the *Foods & Nutrition Encyclopedia,* the food industry used additives for one or more of the following four appropriate purposes:

1. To maintain or improve nutritional value.

2. To maintain freshness.

3. To help in processing or preparation.

4. To make food more appealing.

On the other hand, the following uses of food additives were considered inappropriate:

1. To disguise faulty or inferior processes.

2. To conceal damaged, inferior, or spoiled foods.

3. To gain some functional property at the expense of nutritional quality.

4. To replace economical, well-recognized manufacturing processes and practices.

5. To use in excess of the minimum required to achieve the intended effects.[33]

Sorbic acid is a food additive possessing antimicrobial benefits; it prevents food spoilage from bacteria, molds, fungi, and yeast. It is commonly used in the form of sodium sorbate or potassium sorbate. In the body, it is metabolized like other fatty acids. It is on the GRAS (generally recognized as safe) list of approved food additives when used at low concentrations. Higher concentrations were regulated by the U.S. Food and Drug Administration. Besides baked goods, sorbic acid was used in beverages, cheese, fish, jams, salads, and wine. Citric acid had been used in food preparation for over 100 years and was used as a flavoring agent in foods.[34] Tasty Baking Company complied with federal regulations concerning food additives and used proper quantities to maintain freshness in its products.

To avoid using preservatives and to expand geographically, Tasty Baking Company used a special film developed by Mobil. The high-barrier coating of Mobil BICORO 110 AXT delivered excellent moisture, oxygen, and aroma barrier characteristics as well as good seal performance for improved shelf-life. This film provided good machinability as well as excellent printing characteristics for the aesthetics needed in the increasingly competitive battle for shelf space. AXT film, first used only on low-fat products, increased the shelf-life of the product to 21 days versus 7 to 10 days and provided management with flexibility with the products. The company could extend its geographic reach because this packaging would maintain the freshness of the product. Improvements in profitability were also noticeable because fewer products needed to be discarded before reaching customers' hands. Although the cost of the film was higher, these costs were compensated by increased sales.[35]

Distribution

Tasty Baking Company's products were available in 47 states, Washington D.C., and Puerto Rico. These products were sold primarily by 487 independent owner/operators through distribution routes to approximately 30,000 retail outlets in a six-state region from New York to Virginia, which was the company's principal market. Tasty Baking Company also distributed its products through its strategic alliances. In addition, products were available through the Tastykare program, whereby consumers called a toll-free number to order the delivery of a variety of Tastykake gift packs.[36]

Outside of the store-door routes, Tasty Baking Company found a way to flash-freeze its baked goods without affecting quality or taste. They shipped the products frozen to retailers' warehouses where they were allowed to thaw and then coded with a 21-day shelf-life.[37]

Tasty Baking Company's strategic alliance with Merita Bakery moved Tastykake cakes and cookies into Florida and southern Georgia on the 1,200 routes Merita runs in those areas. Tastykake products were shipped frozen via tractor-trailer to five Kroger manufacturing/warehouse locations: Anderson, South Carolina; Columbus, Ohio; Memphis, Tennessee; Houston, Texas; and Indianapolis, Indiana. The products were sold in Kroger's 1,200 supermarkets in the Southwest and Midwest.

After signing a distribution agreement with Fry's Food & Drug Stores in 1993, Tasty Baking Company wrote to all its Tastykare customers in Arizona telling them where they could find Tastykakes. Fry's, which had originally ordered only five or six items from Tasty Baking Company, was inundated with requests from consumers and increased the number of items ordered as well as the amount of each item.[38]

Tasty Baking Company's main distribution channel was through supermarkets (55% of sales). However, the company made 40% of its sales through convenience stores. The remaining 5% came from vending machines and other channels (see Exhibit 2).[39]

Information Systems

Computer technology continued to revolutionize the food industry. Investment in automation was essential to remain competitive and to meet increasingly demanding customer expectations for electronic data interchange. In 1993, Tasty Baking Company made a $3 million investment in hand-held computers for the owner/operator delivery routes. By keeping track of inventory as well as credit and billing, these devices cut paperwork by hours a week and improved billing and inventory accuracy. All owner/operators were trained to use these computers, which made their operations more efficient and provided timely sales information to management. Some of Tasty Baking Company's customers indicated that in the near future they would require suppliers to have hand-held computers capable of downloading inventory and billing information directly into their stores' computer system whenever a product delivery was made.[40]

In 1997, Tasty Baking Company engaged in a project to upgrade its computer hardware and software in order to improve its operating performance and avoid any potential year 2000 problems. The company expected to complete the project in 1999.[41]

Tasty Baking Company entered an agreement with Ross Systems Inc. for software and services valued at nearly $1.6 million. The licensed product, Ross' Renaissance CS Enterprise Resource Planning & Supply Chain System, helped Tasty Baking Company manage current projects as well as implement its aggressive growth plans.[42]

Finance

Exhibits 5 and 6 provide financial information for Tasty Baking Company. Net sales for 1997 were 8% higher than they were for 1992. Unfortunately net income dropped by 29% for the same time period. These numbers do not depict an accurate picture for Tasty Baking Company.

In 1997, several favorable events took place for the shareholders. The company moved to the New York Stock Exchange. Such a move increased the liquidity of Tasty Baking Company common stock as well as raising its profile among institutional investors. The Board of Directors increased the dividend by 7.1% and authorized a 5-for-4 stock split. These actions helped push Tasty Baking Company stock up by 75.6% in 1997.

After a lengthy legal battle, Tasty Baking Company took a pretax charge of $1,950,000 ($1,171,170 after taxes) in connection with its dispute with the IRS related to the treatment of Tasty Baking Company owner/operators for payroll tax purposes. Excluding this charge, Tasty Baking Company's 1997 net income was up by $933,000, or 15%, over 1996. This increase was due in part to increased productivity, stable commodity prices, expense control, and increased sales. Gross sales increased by 4.5% in 1997 over 1996, and net sales increased by 2% for the same time period.

Tasty Baking Company was successful in reducing its cost of sales as a percentage of net sales. This figure was 60.8%, 62.0%, and 63% for 1997, 1996, and 1995, respectively. This was brought about by improvements in manufacturing efficiencies, reduced utility costs, and product price increase. Selling and administrative expenses increased by $1,576,509 (4.1%) in 1997 due to increased advertising costs and an increase in selling expense.

Long-term debt increased in 1997 by $2,470,637 to $7,773,053 due to facility modernization. However this amount was only 55% as great as it was in 1992. Current interest expense is less than half of what it was in 1992.

Return on sales (net income/sales) remained fairly stable. It was 4.1%, 4.3%, 4.0%, and 4.1% for 1997, 1996, 1995, and 1994, respectively. Return on equity exhibited a downward trend. It was 14.6%, 16.2%, 15.7%, and 17.6% for 1997, 1996, 1995, and 1994, respectively.

Tasty Baking Company leased most of its facilities. The company contributed property to the Tasty Baking Company Pension Plan and in turn leased this property back from its employees at market rates. The company retained the option to repurchase the property at any time at its then fair market value.

In August 1995, Tasty Baking Company exchanged 578,435 shares of stock (worth $649,000) for the purchase of Dutch Mill Baking Company. The purchase price exceeded the fair market value of its assets by $303,000. This amount will be amortized on a straight-line basis over 15 years.

On July 1, 1996, Tasty Baking Company purchased a 160,000-square-foot manufacturing facility in Oxford, Pennsylvania, for $4 million. This purchase allowed Tasty Baking Company to manufacture products that had been previously made by other suppliers. This step helped Tasty Baking Company increase margins and expand new product offerings.

Exhibit 5 **Consolidated Highlights of Operating Results (Unaudited): Tasty Baking Company**

Year Ending December 31	1997	1996	1995	1994	1993	1992
Net sales	$149,291,974	$146,718,391	$141,831,073	$142,055,111	$137,772,730	$138,381,391
Costs and expenses						
Cost of sales	90,754,876	90,955,370	89,403,295	84,921,787	82,603,806	84,598,553
Depreciation	7,214,997	7,267,639	7,463,311	7,327,385	6,784,732	6,991,671
Selling, general and administrative	40,198,649	38,622,140	37,040,622	40,713,980	40,684,291	40,644,071
Payroll tax settlement and severance charges	1,950,000	—	—	—	—	—
Restructure charge (early retirement program 1990)	—	—	950,000	1,240,000	—	—
Interest expense	536,820	520,375	675,613	803,688	838,184	1,175,164
Provision for doubtful accounts	499,787	825,145	785,036	592,040	530,980	245,012
Other income, net	(1,607,522)	(1,742,863)	(4,901,455)	(3,164,684)	(3,262,708)	(3,414,411)
Total cost and expenses	139,547,607	136,447,806	131,416,422	132,434,196	128,179,285	130,240,060
Income from continuing operations before provision for income taxes	9,744,367	10,270,585	10,414,651	9,620,915	9,593,445	8,141,331
Provision for income taxes						
Federal	3,183,866	3,528,932	2,345,811	3,086,954	2,988,595	2,203,537
State	881,528	784,352	500,319	942,330	633,530	438,116
Deferred	(388,204)	(347,278)	1,377,541	(209,113)	284,316	477,270
Decrease in net deferred tax asset due to change in tax rate	—	—	550,868	—	—	—
Total income taxes	3,677,190	3,966,006	4,774,539	3,819,871	3,906,441	3,118,923
Income from continuing operations before cumulative effect of changes in accounting principles	3,677,190	3,966,006	5,640,112	5,800,744	5,687,004	5,022,408
Discontinued operations						
Income from spun-off subsidiary, net of income taxes	—	—	—	—	2,253,366	3,554,002
Provision for cost spin-off, net of income taxes	—	—	—	—	(804,569)	—
Cumulative effect of changes in accounting principles on spun-off subsidiary	—	—	—	—	(805,264)	—
Cumulative effect of changes in accounting principles for						
Income taxes	—	—	—	—	1,003,507	—
Postretirement benefits other than pensions	—	—	—	—	(11,708,989)	—
Net income (loss)	$6,067,177	$6,304,579	$5,640,112	$5,800,744	($4,374,945)	$8,576,410
Retained earnings						
Balance, beginning of year	22,265,220	19,425,849	17,228,764	14,680,877	45,851,426	42,119,726
Dividend of P&J common shares	—	—	—	—	(22,806,526)	—
Cash dividends paid on common shares	(3,544,121)	(3,465,208)	(3,443,027)	(3,252,857)	(3,989,078)	(4,844,710)
Balance, end of year	24,788,276	22,265,220	19,425,849	17,228,764	14,680,877	45,851,426

Exhibit 5 **Consolidated Highlights of Operating Results (Unaudited): Tasty Baking Company** *(continued)*

Year Ending December 31	1997	1996	1995	1994	1993	1992
Earnings per common share						
Increase from continuing operations before cumulative effect of changes in accounting principles	$0.78[1]	$0.82[1]	$0.92	$0.94	$0.93	$0.83
Income from spun-off subsidiary, net of income taxes	—	—	—	—	$0.37	$0.58
Provision for cost of spin-off, net of income taxes	—	—	—	—	($0.13)	—
Cumulative effect for changes in accounting principles on spun-off subsidiary	—	—	—	—	($0.13)	—
Cumulative effect of changes in accounting principles for:						
Income taxes	—	—	—	—	$0.16	—
Postretirement benefits other than pensions	—	—	—	—	($1.92)	—
Net income (loss) per common share	$0.78[1]	$0.82[1]	$0.92	$0.94	($0.72)	$1.41

Note: 1. Reflects 5-for-4 stock split.

Source: Tasty Baking Company, *1997, 1996, 1995, 1994 Annual Reports.*

Notes

1. Tasty Baking Company, *1988 Annual Report,* p. 3.
2. Rosland Briggs, "Tasty Baking Settles 3-Year Tax Battle," *Philadelphia Inquirer* (January 16, 1998), p. C1.
3. M. B. Pinheiro, "Baked Goods Industry," *Janney Montgomery Scott Industry Report* (September 5, 1995), p. 17.
4. Kathleen M. Grim, "Tasty Baking Company Acquires Dutch Mill Baking Company, Inc," *PR Newswire* (August 29, 1995), p. 1.
5. Julia C. Martinez, "Philadelphia's Tasty Baking Co. Considers Buying Another Bakery," *Philadelphia Inquirer* (April 23, 1994), p. D1.
6. Dan Malovany, "Sweet Expectations," *Snack Food & Wholesale Bakery* (January 1998), p. 18.
7. E. R. Katzman, "Global Food Industry." *Merrill Lynch Capital Markets Report* (April 13, 1998), p. 81.
8. "Philadelphia's Tastiest Treasures Now Appearing on Store Shelves in 7-Eleven Stores in Colorado," *PR Newswire* (October 2, 1997).
9. Michael Sangiacomo, "Tastykakes Come to Northeast Ohio," *The Plain Dealer* (May 22, 1998), p. 1B.
10. "Tasty Baking Company Continues Midwest Expansion," *Business Wire* (September 24, 1998).
11. Tasty Baking Company, *1998 Proxy Statement,* pp. 3, 8.
12. *Ibid.,* p. 8.
13. *Ibid.*
14. *Ibid.*
15. *Ibid.*
16. *Ibid.*
17. "Market for Bakery Snacks: Industry Overview," *FIND\SVP Report* (January 1995), p. 1.
18. *Standard and Poor's Industry Survey* (April 13, 1995), p. F2.
19. "Market for Bakery Snacks: The Consumer," *FIND\SVP Report* (January 1995), p. 2.
20. Carol Meres Krosky, "It's a Brave New World," *Bakery Production and Marketing* (January 15, 1996), p. 36.
21. "Bakery Foods: Snack Cakes/Pies," *Snack Food & Wholesale Bakery* (June 1998), pp. S1–21.
22. Robert Carey, "Employee Ideas Get Unboxed," *Incentive Performance Supplement* (June 4, 1995), p. 4.
23. Alan J. Heavens, "Open Door to Homeownership," *Philadelphia Inquirer* (September 24, 1995), p. R1.
24. Francesca Chapman, "Tasty Bakers Won't Go Union Route," *Philadelphia Daily News* (April 7, 1995), p. 45.
25. Tasty Baking Company, *1997 Annual Report,* p. 27.
26. Malovany, "Sweet Expectations," p. 18.
27. "Complete Competitor," *Snack Food* (July 1994), p. 27.
28. Tasty Baking Company, *Form 10-K* (1997), p. 2.
29. "Happy Holidays: Introduced New Holiday-Theme Products in Its Tastykake Product Line," *Snack Food* (July 1994), p. 28.
30. Maria Gallagher, "But Are They Tasty?" *Philadelphia Daily News* (January 31, 1996), p. F1.
31. "Fast and Fresh: Implements a Strict Quality Control Program Starting from Its Raw Materials to Final Products," *Snack Food* (July 1994), p. 35.
32. "Quality, a Matter of Taste," *The Orlando Sentinel* (September 17, 1996), p. B5.

Exhibit 6　Consolidated Balance Sheets: Tasty Baking Company

Year Ending December 31	1997	1996	1995	1994	1993	1992
Assets						
Current assets						
Cash	$ 748,117	$ 233,366	$ 85,104	$ 147,251	$ 141,026	$ 449,626
Receivables	18,661,411	16,962,591	18,630,903	17,574,423	17,361,496	18,304,372
Inventories	3,296,202	2,855,512	3,263,282	2,937,060	2,952,719	3,466,721
Deferred income taxes, prepayments and other	2,241,587	2,726,014	3,349,314	3,681,528	3,130,000	2,488,753
Total current assets	24,947,317	22,777,483	25,328,603	24,340,262	23,585,241	24,709,472
Property, plant, and equipment						
Land	1,267,095	1,267,095	697,987	697,987	697,987	697,987
Buildings and improvements	27,843,342	27,366,281	24,797,546	23,937,822	23,921,821	23,821,084
Machinery and equipment	120,598,909	110,715,679	101,374,855	97,366,055	93,677,286	88,446,734
	149,709,346	139,349,055	126,870,388	122,001,864	118,297,094	112,965,805
Less accumulated depreciation	(105,501,230)	(98,375,648)	(91,230,770)	(84,063,636)	(76,736,251)	(72,054,686)
	44,208,116	40,973,407	35,639,618	37,938,228	41,560,843	40,911,119
Net assets of discontinued operations	—	—	—	—	—	29,047,734
Other assets	25,163,945	23,677,474	24,334,762	24,858,106	25,358,935	17,427,948
Total assets	$ 94,319,378	$ 87,428,364	$ 85,302,983	$ 87,136,596	$ 90,505,019	$112,096,273
Liabilities and Shareholders' Equity						
Current liabilities						
Current portion of long-term debt	$29,354	$58,340	$127,720	$222,831	$185,742	$221,789
Current obligations under capital leases	543,962	587,336	513,159	455,712	426,800	373,170
Notes payable, banks	900,000	—	700,000	1,800,000	1,800,000	6,400,000
Accounts payable	4,345,944	3,963,610	4,699,747	4,075,343	5,684,555	4,800,391
Accrued payrolls and employee benefits	6,817,319	5,608,274	4,310,550	3,565,536	3,664,585	3,975,443
Accrued income taxes	—	1,474,887	—	893,111	679,028	982,997
Other	1,826,981	925,338	1,033,612	987,307	368,546	533,570
Total current liabilities	14,463,560	12,617,785	11,384,788	11,999,840	12,809,256	17,287,360
Long-term debt, less current portion	7,773,053	5,302,416	4,576,385	5,349,558	8,572,389	14,255,701
Long-term obligations under capital leases less current portion	587,156	1,131,118	1,653,134	2,166,293	2,634,101	2,929,256
Deferred income	—	—	—	3,271,268	4,642,445	6,117,343
Accrued pensions and other liabilities	11,771,540	11,203,178	13,129,760	11,691,444	11,554,424	10,721,376
Postretirement benefits other than pensions	18,129,226	18,267,013	18,620,763	19,707,364	20,049,638	—
Shareholders' equity						
Common stock, par value $.50 per share, Authorized 15,000,000 shares, issued 7,289,087 shares	4,558,243	4,555,680	3,644,544	3,644,544	3,644,544	3,554,344
Capital in excess of par value of stock	29,337,938	28,831,377	29,662,330	29,175,510	29,105,725	23,424,543
Retained earnings	24,788,276	22,265,220	19,425,849	17,228,764	14,680,877	45,851,426
	58,684,457	55,652,277	52,732,723	50,048,818	47,431,146	72,830,313
Less—Treasury stock, at cost	16,738,364	16,329,055	16,364,757	16,601,793	16,579,825	11,280,132
Management Stock Purchase Plan receivables and deferrals	351,250	416,368	429,813	496,196	608,555	764,944
Total shareholders' equity	41,594,843	38,906,854	35,938,153	32,950,829	30,242,766	60,785,237
Total liabilities and shareholders' equity	$ 94,319,378	$ 87,428,364	$85,302,983	$ 87,136,596	$ 90,505,019	$112,096,273

Source: Tasty Baking Company, *1997, 1996, 1995, 1994 Annual Reports.*

33. *Food & Nutrition Encyclopedia,* 2nd ed. Boca Raton, FL: CRC Press, p. 10.

34. *Ibid.,* p. 2005.

35. Judy Rice, "Live Long and Prosper," *Prepared Foods* (August 1996), p. 128.

36. Tasty Baking Company, *Form 10-K* (1994), p. 2.

37. Mary Ellen Kuhn, "Bakeries on the Brink," *Food Processing* (March 1995), p. 35.

38. Paul Rogers, "Tasty Obsession," *Snack Food* (July 1994), p. 24.

39. Malovany, "Sweet Expectations," p. 18.

40. Tasty Baking Company, *1993 Annual Report,* pp. 8–9.

41. Tasty Baking Company, *1997 Annual Report,* p. 14.

42. "Ross Systems, Inc. Announces $1.6 Million Agreement," *PR Newswire* (August 7, 1997).

Microsoft Corporation (1998): Growth versus Antitrust

David B. Croll, Gordon P. Croll, and Andrew J. Croll

ANTITRUST PROCEEDINGS

On May 22, 1998, U.S. District Judge Thomas Jackson set the trial date of September 8, 1998, for the antitrust lawsuit by the U.S. Department of Justice (DOJ) and 20 state attorneys general against Microsoft.[1] The lawsuit was filed on May 18, 1998, after negotiations between the two sides reached an impasse on May 16, 1998.[2]

Exhibit 1 is a full-page newspaper ad by Bill Gates to Microsoft's customers, partners, and shareholders. Microsoft's lawyers had requested that Judge Jackson schedule the preliminary hearing for the government injunction in January 1999 and the full trial at a later date. Judge Jackson rejected Microsoft's request and ordered the trial to be put on a fast-track schedule. David Boies, DOJ lawyer, said, "And it lays to rest any comparisons to the IBM case."[3] The IBM case was a landmark antitrust case that dragged on for 13 years until the DOJ finally dropped the case in 1982 because the issues had become technologically irrelevant.

On May 18, 1998, the lawsuit by DOJ and 20 states asked the Federal court to force Microsoft to change its practices so that Microsoft's competitors, both Internet browsers (Netscape and others) and software companies, could compete on a level playing field. They wanted Microsoft to:

- Remove its Explorer browser from Windows or offer Netscape's browser, too.

- Let PC makers modify opening screens so they can promote browsers and software other than Microsoft's.

- Allow Internet providers and websites to tout browsers other than Explorer.[4]

On May 12, the U.S. District Court of Appeals for the District of Columbia ruled that Judge Jackson's injunction (of December 15, 1997) on Windows 95 did not extend to Windows 98. So, Microsoft announced that Windows 98 would be released on June 25, 1998. According to Susan Gregory Thomas, technology writer, Windows 98 was a tune-up of Windows 95. She said Windows 98 offered "more efficient use of hard-disk space, faster performance overall, fewer system crashes, automatic support of new peripherals, and the ability to watch TV on your computer."[5] To get the TV feature required the purchase of a $100 television tuner board. Microsoft will sell about two million copies of Windows 98 each month. This became a major issue in Judge Jackson's selecting September for the trial. Judge Jackson told Microsoft's attorneys, "By the time you propose to be ready, 16 to 18 million horses will already be out of the barn, and that's too late."[6]

Exhibit 1   Bill Gates's Letter to Customers, Partners, and Shareholders: Microsoft Corporation

When Microsoft was formed 23 years ago, we made a commitment to innovation—to creating software that would bring the benefits of affordable, accessible computing into every home and office. Today, PCs are helping people be more productive at work, helping children learn and get access to the Internet at school, and helping families communicate with each other. This is an industry built on innovation, competition, and consumer choice—principles that America's antitrust laws were designed to promote, and that have always been a cornerstone of Microsoft's business practices.

Yet, as you have probably heard, on May 18th the Department of Justice and a number of state Attorneys General filed antitrust lawsuits against us in federal court. We believe that the allegations made in these lawsuits are without merit—and the litigation, if it were to succeed, would hurt consumers and high-tech companies everywhere, not to mention the U.S. economy.

During the past two weeks, Microsoft engaged in serious discussions with federal and state officials in an effort to avoid a protracted lawsuit. But their key demands—that Microsoft incorporate Netscape's competing Web-browser software in every copy of Windows, or that we license PC makers to emasculate Windows by hiding its entire user interface and removing access to its Internet technology—appear to benefit a single competitor at the expense of consumers.

We do not believe that the government should be in the business of designing software products—particularly if its goal is to hide innovative new technology from consumers. We are working hard to make computers easier to use, not more difficult. Hiding cool new technology does not help consumers.

PC makers are already free to install Web-browsing software from any company on their computers, and to display that software prominently. Windows users can already choose between Microsoft's Internet Explorer and any other Web browser—most of them free. Because we share extensive data about Windows with software developers—among them competitors such as Netscape and Sun Microsystems—consumers can choose from thousands of different software applications, confident that all will run on their PC. And with Windows 98, the applications they choose will run better than ever.

I want you to know that Microsoft will vigorously defend the fundamental principle at stake in this litigation. The freedom to innovate, improve, and integrate new features into products has been the mainstay of our industry for more than two decades, and has helped turn it into one of the most vibrant and competitive industries the world has seen. Without it, today's PCs would lack integrated modem support, memory management, task switching, and countless other features we all now take for granted.

We plan to move ahead with the release of Windows 98 on schedule. It's a great new product that will benefit PC users both at work and at home. Microsoft remains passionately committed to providing the best solutions to your software needs by constantly improving Windows and supporting open Internet standards. Without the ability to create and improve new products, no high-tech company could survive—and consumers everywhere would be worse off.

Sincerely,

Bill Gates

Source: Bill Gates, Microsoft company document, *USA Today* (May 19, 1998), p. 9A

Below are other key dates in this antitrust action.

March 3, 1998:   Bill Gates spent three hours testifying before the Senate Judiciary Committee concerning the Microsoft monopolistic tactics it employed in order to restrict its Internet partners' dealings with Microsoft's rivals. The "Who's Who" of information technology were called to testify: (1) Scott McNealy, Chairman of Sun Microsystems;

(2) Michael Dell, CEO of Dell Computer Corporation; (3) Jim Barksdale, CEO of Netscape Communications, and others.[7]

December 11, 1997: Judge Thomas Penfield Jackson issued a preliminary injunction ordering Microsoft to sell Windows 95 to computer makers without the browser.

October 20, 1997: The Justice Department sued Microsoft, alleging that the company violated the 1994 consent decree by forcing computer makers to use Explorer as a condition of licensing Windows 95.

September 1997: Microsoft launched Internet Explorer 4.0 in a stepped-up challenge to Netscape, whose share of the browser market slipped from 90% to about 60%.

July 1994: Microsoft, in a consent decree, agreed not to "tie" Microsoft operating systems to other products but reserved the right to integrate new features into its software.

1993: The FTC deadlocked on two votes to file a formal complaint and closed its investigation. Antitrust investigators at the U.S. Department of Justice and the European Commission began their own probes.

1991: Federal Trade Commission began to look into complaints that Microsoft abused its monopoly in PC operating systems.[8]

The major areas of disagreement between Microsoft and DOJ and the 20 states were:

1. **The Browser:** Could Microsoft integrate Internet software into its operating system?

2. **The Desktop:** Could PC makers decide which products to feature on their own machines?

3. **The Future:** Who will control the evolution of Windows—Microsoft or a federal judge?[9]

INTERVIEW WITH BILL GATES

Late Saturday (May 16, 1998) evening, after talks with the Justice Department had broken down, Microsoft Chairman Bill Gates spoke by phone from Redmond, Washington, with Managing Editor Walter Isaacson of *Time*.

QUESTION: *This suit is going to be messy. Are you upset?*

ANSWER: It's amazing it got to this point. It's very disappointing the government would do this.

QUESTION: *The government wants you to include Netscape's browser as well as Microsoft's with Windows. What's wrong with that?*

ANSWER: When they demanded that, we asked them to repeat it out loud. The government was trying to advantage a competitor of ours. That's really unprecedented. Netscape was able to get the government working on its behalf.

QUESTION: *Can Netscape compete if the browser is in the operating system?*

ANSWER: In fact, Netscape seeks to use their browser to beat us as an operating system. That's what they're trying to create.

QUESTION: *That's why it's important for you to build a browser in?*

ANSWER: It's a huge priority for us to integrate browsing technology into Windows. When we talk to consumers and to computer manufacturers, they ask us to make the system simpler. That requires more integration. Preventing us from doing that would be a step backward.

QUESTION: *By that argument, you could integrate whatever you want into new versions of Windows.*

ANSWER: Innovation is part of the process of building a better operating system. The heart of this dispute is that the Justice Department wants to make it illegal for us to be able to put new functions into our operating system. When we asked them, "What will you let us put in?" they never had an answer. The only right we've asked for is to be able to listen to customers and add new capabilities based on that input. Was putting a graphical interface in Windows a good thing? Font management? File-system management? I think so.

QUESTION: *But isn't such tying or bundling illegal?*

ANSWER: The law is 100% on our side. The ability of a successful company to add functionality to its product has long been upheld. There is no precedent for taking a technology product and breaking it into pieces.

QUESTION: *Does that mean you'll someday tie such products as speech recognition into Windows?*

ANSWER: A natural interface is part of what an operating system should have. The future of Windows is to let the computer see, listen, and even learn. That is why this company is spending billions to develop new functions.

QUESTION: *But won't that wipe out any other company trying to develop speech recognition?*

ANSWER: We work with a lot of partners. But it's like building car engines. If you want to build engines, you've got to team up with someone building cars or be prepared to build the car yourself.

QUESTION: *What about Justice's demand that you not require computer makers to display Windows when a computer is turned on?*

ANSWER: Computer manufacturers display quite a lot of things when a computer is turned on. But when you get Windows running, you should get to the Windows desktop.

QUESTION: *What will happen if the government gets an injunction?*

ANSWER: Blocking Windows 98 would be a bad thing for consumers and the industry. They say the Microsoft browser should be ripped out. We don't have time to do the engineering of that.

QUESTION: *What do you think the government's motive is?*

ANSWER: I'm not an expert in politics. I do sometimes shake my head and wonder why this is happening. I just don't understand.

QUESTION: *Any chance for a settlement now?*

ANSWER: We worked hard to settle. I wish we had been able to. I'll seize every opportunity to do so.[10]

OTHER LEGAL ISSUES

In October 1994, Microsoft made plans to acquire Intuit Inc., a developer of personal finance, tax preparation, and small business accounting software, for about 27 million shares of Microsoft's stock. However, the U.S. Department of Justice filed suit to stop this purchase. The DOJ felt that with the purchase of Intuit by Microsoft, Microsoft would monopolize the online banking industry. Microsoft decided it was not worth the time and effort of litigation, and therefore withdrew its offer. Many believe that Microsoft will still be able to be a major force in on-line banking even without the acquisition of Intuit Inc.

In early 1995, Apple Computer Inc. expanded its lawsuit with the San Francisco Canyon Company to include Microsoft Corporation and Intel Corporation. Apple's allegations were that Canyon furnished Intel with a program expediting Video for Windows that included code duplicated word-for-word from Apple's QuickTime for Windows. Intel then gave the code to Microsoft for use in a cooperatively developed product titled Display Control Interface.[11] The lawsuit was settled out of court.

In April 1997, Ticketmaster sued Microsoft over Internet link. Ticketmaster alleged that Microsoft was engaging in "electronic piracy" by offering a link to Ticketmaster's website against the company's stated wishes. Ticketmaster claimed that Microsoft needed to make a formal legal agreement to make the link. They were negotiating an agreement, but the talks had failed. According to experts, these types of links are everywhere in cyberspace, but Ticketmaster wanted Microsoft to pay to offer a link to their website.[12] Paul Allen, co-founder of Microsoft, was a Director of Ticketmaster.

On October 7, 1997, Sun sued Microsoft in Federal court with a breach-of-contract suit. Sun charged that Microsoft was using its software language, Java, on its Internet Explorer 4.0 that violated its licensing agreement. The licensing agreement to Java was signed in December 1995. Microsoft may have needed Sun's Java in 1995, but in the next two years Microsoft had made major advancements into cybersoftware. Internet Explorer 4.0 was introduced in late September. The lawsuit came after several months of discussion between the two companies on how Microsoft would use Sun's Java.[13]

Java, according to an analyst, was perhaps the only technology that could challenge Microsoft's dominance. Java had the backing of IBM, Oracle, Netscape, and some 700,000 programmers at software companies.

In early November 1997, the State of Texas sued Microsoft "charging that terms of the company's software licenses are impeding the State's anti-trust investigation of Microsoft business practices." It was a similar suit to the U.S. Department of Justice lawsuit. Dan Morales, Texas Attorney General "alleged that provisions of Microsoft's licensing agreement require companies that buy its software to inform Microsoft before providing information to State or Federal investigators."[14]

In early December, attorneys general from some of the nation's most populous states held a secret three-day meeting to develop strategies for a possible anti-trust lawsuit against Microsoft's marketing practices.[15] This was similar to what the states did before suing the tobacco industry. California, Connecticut, Massachusetts, and Oregon had opened independent investigations of Microsoft's business practices.[16] At the filing of the lawsuit against Microsoft, a total of 20 states were on board.

MICROSOFT'S TWENTY-THREE YEAR HISTORY (1975–1998)

From his earliest years, Bill Gates had excellent concentration, reading, and memory powers. He had read the entire encyclopedia by age 8. At Lakeside High School in Seattle, he demonstrated his competitive spirit to his classmates. Bill could solve math problems faster than any of his classmates.[17]

While at Lakeside, Bill Gates and his friend, Paul Allen, spent all of their free time on the teletype machine linked into a PEP-10 computer, which Digital Equipment Corporation (DEC) manufactured, that General Electric operated at a nearby Computer Center Corporation (CCC). BASIC was the time-sharing language that they used. Gates and Allen earned money by debugging programs for CCC, TRW, and local companies. During these years, Gates developed his passion to learn and compete successfully. Before graduating, Gates said, "I'm going to make my first million by the time I'm 25." [18] In order for Gates to graduate, his mother had to pay $200 for his excessive computer usage.

In 1973, Gates entered Harvard. Allen was a student at Washington State University but dropped out. He accompanied his friend Bill Gates to Boston, where he took a programmer's job with Honeywell. When Allen left school, he had wanted to form a company. While at Harvard, Gates spent many long stretches (up to 36 hours) at the computer center, restocking his energy with pizza and Coke. He had developed this diet for survival while at Lakeside. Gates and Allen both left Boston in 1975. [19]

They read an announcement for the Altair 8080, the first microcomputer kit, manufactured by MITS of Albuquerque, New Mexico. Gates and Allen contacted Ed Roberts, owner of MITS, and told him that they had developed a program that allowed his Altair microcomputer to be programmed in BASIC. Roberts expressed an interest in their project. So, they spent the next eight weeks, both day and night, on the project. They did not have an Altair microcomputer, so they programmed it on an Intel 8080 chip. They were still writing a "boot strap" program during the flight to Albuquerque to demonstrate their program to Roberts. The demonstration was successful. They signed a contract with MITS to license their BASIC software. The software became known as Microsoft BASIC. Gates said, "When I showed up in Albuquerque, I had to take an advance from MITS because I had no money to pay for a hotel room. The plane ticket took all my money." [20]

In July 1975, Gates and Allen formed a partnership, Microsoft, with the mission of developing computer languages for Altair and other microcomputer companies. They opened operations in Seattle. Gates also developed Disk BASIC for Altair. He offered to sell BASIC to Roberts for $6,500 because everyone was pirating Microsoft's BASIC. Roberts declined that offer. [21]

In 1976, General Electric, Citicorp, and National Cash Register signed contracts for Microsoft BASIC. At this point, Gates assembled his "Micro-Kids—high IQ insomniacs who wanted to join the personal computer crusade, kids with a passion for computers who would drive themselves to the limits of their ability and endurance, pushing the outside of the software envelope." [22] Gates had to break his contract with MITS in order to make money. Gates developed a strategy for a complex out-of-court settlement whereby Microsoft was determined the legal owner of BASIC. [23] An analyst said, "This was the first of many times when Bill Gates's negotiation skills were underestimated." During the period 1976–1981, Gates took two vacation days per year.

In 1980, IBM entered the microcomputer business with a machine based on Intel's 8086 memory chip. They contracted with Microsoft to write a BASIC program for IBM's 8-bit memory. IBM also asked Microsoft to furnish other languages—FORTRAN, Pascal, and COBOL—for other IBM machines. Microsoft had to gain access to Digital Research's CP/M operating system to develop these languages. Both IBM and Microsoft representatives tried to negotiate with Digital Research but with no success. Finally, Bill Gates offered to build the operating system, MS-DOS, and the languages. IBM accepted the offer. [24] During this time, Paul Allen negotiated the purchase of an obscure operating system, Q-DOS, from Seattle Computer, Inc., for $50,000. This acquisition has been called the deal of the decade. It was an operating system for the Intel 8086 chip and became the basis for Microsoft MS-DOS. Before IBM introduced its computer in 1981, CP/M was an excellent operating system and nearly all existing hardware and software employed it. Eventually 99% of the IBM compatibles had MS-DOS as their operating system. In 1981, revenues topped $16 million, and the Microsoft staff grew from 85 to 125.

The company's basic strategy during this period, according to Gates, was "to charge a price so low that microcomputer makers couldn't do the software internally for that cheap." They bid a job to Texas Instruments at $99,000 because "we were too shy to make a bid in the six figures." [25]

Microsoft's collaboration with IBM throughout the 1980s created the world's first mass market phenomenon in the computer industry based on the availability of computer chips, parts, and the MS-DOS operating system. The acceptance of MS-DOS as a software standard for the PC industry (MS-DOS was used on over 100 million computers worldwide) led to Microsoft's increasingly important role in the industry. During the last 15 years, they made many enhancements to the original operating system, crowning in the most recent release stand-alone, MS-DOS 6.22.

In 1985, Microsoft started work on a graphical computer interface that used icons instead of word commands, which resembled the user-friendly Macintosh interface. This revolutionary new operating environment for the personal computer came into its own with the release of Windows 3.0 in 1990. Apple, the maker of Macintosh, believed this was an infringement on their copyrights and filed a lawsuit accordingly. [26]

In 1991, Microsoft and IBM ended a decade of partnership when they went their separate ways on the next generation of operating systems for personal computers. IBM chose to pursue a former joint venture with Microsoft on the OS/2 operating system, while Microsoft continued to improve its Windows operating system. Microsoft announced Windows 3.0 in May 1990 and followed with Windows 3.1 in April 1992. Microsoft targeted Windows software for all kinds of computers, ranging from tiny hand-held devices to giant multiprocessor systems. It is now used on 15 million computers worldwide. Microsoft continued the work on the operating systems and developed Windows NT, an operating system designed to run as a server in a demanding network environment, which Microsoft released in July 1993. [27] Microsoft's latest and greatest accomplishment was to turn Windows into a true 32-bit multitasking environment with greater ease of use. This answered IBM's Warp, the latest generation of OS/2 32-bit operating systems that long went unchallenged. Microsoft accomplished this in August 1995 with the release of Windows 95.

Another significant aspect of Microsoft's business has been its application software business. In 1984, Microsoft was one of the few established software companies to develop application software for the original Apple Macintosh. Microsoft's early support for the Macintosh resulted in tremendous success for Microsoft's word processing and spreadsheet programs for the Macintosh. When Microsoft later released Windows, the graphical operating system for the IBM personal computer, Microsoft's experience on graphical applications for the Macintosh led to success with the Windows applications like Microsoft Excel and Microsoft Word. Today these applications are designed to behave similarly on Windows and the Macintosh. [28]

In 1994, Gates made a personal investment of $10 million for a 30% stake in Teledesic, which was building a network of satellites for delivering high-speed data around the world. [29]

Microsoft invested $30 million in 1994 in DreamWorks SKG, which was a new megaventure entertainment company. The company was founded by Steven Spielberg, Jeffrey Katzenberg (a former Disney executive), and David Geffen. The founders invested $100 million ($33.3 million each) in return for 67% of the profits and 100% of the voting control. Paul Allen purchased $500 million of the $684 million of a special class of stock, which was reserved for big investors. Allen was appointed a director in the new company. Microsoft purchased a second class of stock, which was designated for smallish "strategic" investors. DreamWorks SKG intended to issue $216 million in this class of stock. [30]

This relationship resulted in DreamWorks SKG's forming a joint venture with

Microsoft to produce interactive games. Microsoft formed a subsidiary, DreamWorks Interactive L.L.C., of which the company owned 50%. Microsoft had a strong interest in developing content programming. The company was investing in entertainment programming.

In 1995, the company's "simultaneous launch of Windows 95 and the Microsoft Office for Windows 95 was not only the most successful retail launch in our business," noted Bob Herbold, COO, "but also one of the most successful launches ever of any consumer product in any industry. This is an important milestone because it introduces users to a new generation of personal computing and represents a key achievement in enhancing the Microsoft brand worldwide." Windows 95 was the most tested program in history— 400,000 beta testers helped Microsoft management to fully debug the new program.[31]

Gates paid $10 million to the Rolling Stones to use their 1981 hit song "Start Me Up." Microsoft bought the entire daily run of the *London Times* and gave the paper away "free" as an advertising strategy. It was the first time the *London Times* ever allowed anyone to purchase the entire run of its paper. *Forbes* gave the company the 1995 Crafty Marketing Campaign award for its overall marketing strategy for Windows 95. Microsoft spent about $200 million on Windows 95.[32]

In 1995, the company shipped version 4.0 of Windows NT. Jeff Raikes, Group Vice-President, Sales and Marketing, said, "the momentum behind [this] . . . product is outstanding."[33] He further stated that "corporate customers made decisions to adopt Windows NT servers and workstations in record numbers, driving 19% revenue growth."[34]

Microsoft Internet Explorer 3.0 was introduced in 1996. Bob Herbold, COO, said, "It was released to rave reviews, winning seven of eight (tied the eighth) major head-to-head product reviews by industry and business publications. More than three million customers have downloaded Internet Explorer in just eight weeks, and major corporations are beginning to standardize on it."[35] AT&T and Microsoft agreed to jointly promote and distribute Microsoft Internet Explorer 3.0 with AT&T WorldNet service.

In May 1997, Microsoft acquired Dimension X, which was a Java programming and multimedia company. This acquisition allowed Java programmers to create software for the Internet, which could help Microsoft persuade third-party developers to write software using the Java version that worked best with Microsoft Windows.[36]

On June 9, 1997, Microsoft purchased an 11.5% stake in Comcast Corporation, the nation's fourth largest cable operator. The company paid $1 billion for this investment. Comcast owned 14% of At Home (this relationship is developed later in the case). According to an analyst, Gates "had repeatedly expressed frustration with the pace of cable and telephone companies in upgrading their systems to make new interactive business feasible."[37] This acquisition may allow Microsoft to prod the nation's largest operators to accelerate their investment in high-speed Internet access to homes. Comcast had 4.3 million subscribers. Microsoft had a 15% stake in UUNet, an Internet service provider, that now is a unit of WorldCom, Inc.

In July 1997, it was rumored that Microsoft was going to make an offer to acquire CBS from Westinghouse Electric Corporation. Microsoft did not acquire CBS. Microsoft and General Electric became cable news partners in MSNBC.[38]

In August 1997, Microsoft invested $150 million in Apple Computer stock, and they agreed to continue application developments for the Macintosh. They agreed that Internet Explorer would be included in the Macintosh operating system.

On August 1, 1997, Microsoft acquired WebTV for approximately $450 million in cash and stock. WebTV was an on-line service that allowed its customers to use their television with a set-top box terminal based on proprietary technology to receive the Internet. A director of Microsoft owned 10% of WebTV. Steve Perlman, CEO of WebTV, expected to sell 250,000 set-top boxes by Christmas 1997 and a million by the end of 1998. At the time of the acquisition, WebTV had over 50,000 subscribers, which means Gates paid about $8,500 per customer. The company was acquired because of the product and management team.[39]

On September 16, 1997, Microsoft unveiled a new, souped-up version of its WebTV system for surfing the Net via television. This investment allowed access to the 98% of U.S. homes that have a television as opposed to the 40% that have a PC. This 40% penetration rate of homes had remained constant for several years. It is estimated that 1,000,000 net-ready TVs will be in U.S. homes by 2000. Some of the major companies in the Internet battle for net TVs are Sun Microsystem, Netchannel, and Oracle.[40]

During September 1997, Microsoft announced that the introduction of Windows 98 was moved back from January to May 1998. Microsoft was under pressure from retailers and PC makers who feared that the January introduction would postpone Christmas sales. Windows 98 was to be a modest updating of Windows 95, which had been a major revision. Windows 98 was scheduled to include the Internet Explorer. The bundling of the Internet Explorer into Windows was the center of an anti-trust investigation of Microsoft.[41]

Bob Herbold, COO, summarized Microsoft's 23 years when he said, "For 23 years, Microsoft has grown by listening to our customers and helping them be more productive at work, at school, and at home. We've succeeded by working to use the power of personal computing to improve the quality of people's lives."[42] He further stated that, "The strong [financial] results . . . are testimony that our customers think we are on the right track."[43]

CORPORATE GOVERNANCE

Top Management

On June 1, 1990, Jon Shirley, President and COO since 1983, retired and was replaced by Michael R. Hallman, who was a 20-year veteran of IBM. Hallman left after two years. He "was not passionate enough about PC software to suit Gates."[44] After Hallman's departure in 1992, Gates did not hire another President; instead he created the Office of the President. It was referred to as the BOOP, Bill and the Office of the President. The group consisted of three Executive Vice-Presidents: Steve Ballmer, Bob Herbold, and Mike Maples, who retired in July 1995. Gates reorganized the company into four operating groups: (1) Applications and Content Product Group, (2) Platform Product Group, (3) Sales and Support, and (4) Operations Group. He appointed both Frank M. (Pete) Higgins and Nathan P. Myhrvold as Group Vice-Presidents, Applications and Content Group.

The executive officers of Microsoft were:[45]

- **William H. Gates,** 41, co-founded Microsoft in 1975 and has been its Chief Executive Officer and Chairman of the Board since the original partnership in 1981. His annual compensation in salary was $349,992, $340,618, and $275,000 with bonuses of $241,360, $221,970, and $140,580 for 1997, 1996, and 1995, respectively. He received no stock options. Gates owned 270,797,000 shares (22.3%). He was selected as the 1995 Performance of the Year CEO by *Forbes*.

- **Steven A. Ballmer,** 36, was named Executive Vice-President, Sales and Support, in February 1992. He has been Senior Vice-President, Systems Software, since 1989. From 1984 until 1989, Mr. Ballmer served as Vice-President, Systems Software. He joined Microsoft in 1980. His annual compensation in salary was $316,242, $271,869, and $249,174 with bonuses of $265,472, $212,905, and $162,800 for 1997, 1996, and 1995, respectively. He received other compensation of approximately $5,000 for each of these years. He owned 59,906,647 shares (4.9%).

- **Robert J. Herbold,** 55, joined Microsoft as Executive Vice-President and Chief Operating Officer in November 1994. Herbold had been with Procter & Gamble since 1968, with experience in information services, advertising, and market research. Most recently, he was P&G's Senior Vice-President, Information Services and Advertising. His annual compensation in salary was $536,127, $471,672, and $286,442, with bonuses of $265,472, $212,905, and $453,961 for 1997, 1996, and 1995, respectively. He received 650,000 stock options when he joined the company and is not eligible for additional stock options until 1999.

- **Paul A. Maritz,** 42, was named Group Vice-President, Platforms and Applications, in October 1996 and had been Group Vice-President, Platforms, since May 1995. He had been Senior Vice-President, Product and Technology Strategy, in November 1994 and had been Senior Vice-President, Systems Division, since February 1992. He had been Vice-President, Advanced Operating Systems, since 1989. Mr. Maritz joined Microsoft in 1986. His total compensation in salary was $282,084, $244,382, and $203,750 with bonuses of $243,105, $222,300, and $138,794 for 1997, 1996, and 1995, respectively. He owned 917,931 shares of stock and 1,251,500 stock options with a market value of $142,536,046.

- **Bernard Vergnes,** 50, was a Senior Vice-President of Microsoft and was named President, Microsoft Europe, in April 1992, and Chairman, Microsoft Europe, on July 1, 1997. He had been Vice-President, Europe, since 1989. Mr. Vergnes served as General Manager of Microsoft's French subsidiary since its inception in 1983. His annual compensation was $384,088, $398,001, and $356,660 with bonuses of $329,842, $226,191, and $169,785 for 1997, 1996, and 1995, respectively. He owned 857,500 shares of common and stock options of 342,500 shares with a market value of $35,352,438.

These executives were the five highest paid executives. The executives and directors owned 436,013,437 (35.8%) shares of common stock.

Corporate executives were as follows:[46]

Name	Age	Title
William H. Gates	41	Chairman of the Board; Chief Executive Officer
Steven A. Ballmer	41	Executive Vice-President, Sales and Support
Robert J. Herbold	55	Executive Vice-President; Chief Operating Officer
Frank M. (Pete) Higgins	39	Group Vice-President, Interactive Media
Paul A. Maritz	42	Group Vice-President, Platforms and Applications
Nathan P. Myhrvold	38	Group Vice-President, Chief Technology Officer
Jeffrey S. Raikes	39	Group Vice-President, Sales and Marketing
James E. Allchin	45	Senior Vice-President, Personal and Business Systems Division
Joachim Kempin	55	Senior Vice-President, OEM Sales
Michel Lacombe	46	Senior Vice-President, Microsoft; President, Microsoft Europe
Craig J. Mundie	48	Senior Vice-President, Consumer Platforms Division
William H. Neukom	55	Senior Vice-President, Law and Corporate Affairs; Secretary
Brad A. Silverberg	43	Senior Vice-President, Applications and Internet Client
Gregory B. Maffei	37	Vice-President, Finance; Chief Financial Officer

Board of Directors

The seven directors were:[47]

- **William H. Gates,** 41, co-founded Microsoft in 1975 and has been its Chief Executive Officer and Chairman of the Board since the original partnership was incorporated in 1981. From 1975 to 1981, Mr. Gates was a partner with Paul Allen, Microsoft's other founder, in the predecessor partnership. Mr. Gates was also a director of ICOS Corporation.

- **Paul G. Allen,** 44, had been a Director of the company since 1990, and also served on the Board from 1981 to 1984. Mr. Allen was a co-founder of the company and worked at Microsoft from 1975 to 1984. Mr. Allen owned and invested in a suite of companies exploring the potential of multimedia digital communications. His wholly-owned companies include Asymetrix Corporation, Interval Research Corp., and Vulcan Ventures, Inc. He was also the owner of the Portland Trail Blazers basketball team and the Seattle Seahawks football team, a partner in the entertainment studio DreamWorks SKG, and held investments in more than 35 technology companies. Mr. Allen was also a Director of both HSN, Inc., and Ticketmaster Corp. In 1998, Mr. Allen purchased Marcus Cable, the nation's largest closely-held operator of cable television systems, for $2 billion and assumed $1 billion in debt.

- **Jill E. Barad,** 46, had been a Director of the company since 1996. Ms. Barad had been the President and Chief Executive Officer of Mattel, Inc., since January 1997. Starting as a product manager at Mattel in 1981, she was named Executive Vice-President of Marketing and Worldwide Product Development in 1986 and, in 1989, President of the Girls and Activity Toys Division. In 1990, she was named President of Mattel USA and in 1992, President and Chief Operating Officer of Mattel, Inc. Ms. Barad was also a director of Mattel, Inc., Pixar Animation Studios, and BankAmerica Corporation.

- **Richard A. Hackborn,** 50, had been a Director of the company since 1994. Mr. Hackborn retired in 1993 from Hewlett-Packard Company, which designs, manufactures, and services electronic products and systems for measurement, computation, and communications, and currently serves on that company's Board of Directors. From 1990 to 1993, he was Hewlett-Packard's Executive Vice-President, Computer Products Organization, and from 1984 through 1990, he was its Vice-President and General Manager, Peripherals Group.

- **David F. Marquardt,** 46, had served as a Director of the company since 1981. Mr. Marquardt had been a general partner of various Technology Venture Investors entities, which were private venture capital limited partnerships, since August 1980. He was a director of Auspex Systems, Inc., Farallon Communications, Inc., Vioneer, Inc., and various privately-held companies.

- **William G. Reed, Jr.,** 58, had been a Director of the company since 1987. From 1971 to 1986, Mr. Reed was Chairman of the Board of Simpson Timber Company, a forest products company. Since 1986, Mr. Reed had served as Chairman of the Board of Simpson Investment Company, a forest products holding company, which was the parent of Simpson Timber Company. He was also a Director of Safeco Corporation, Washington Mutual Savings Bank, and The Seattle Times Company.

- **Jon A. Shirley,** 59, served as President and Chief Operating Officer of Microsoft from 1983 to 1990. He had been a Director of the company since 1983. Mr. Shirley also served as Chairman of the Board of Directors of Mentor Graphics Corporation.

Gates and Allen received no compensation for serving on the Board. The outside directors were paid $8,000 per year plus $1,000 for each board meeting and $500 for committee meetings. Allen, Marquardt, O'Brien (a director since 1986, resigned on date of the 1998 annual board meeting), Reed, and Shirley received an annual option to purchase 5,000 shares.[48]

OPERATIONAL GROUPS

The company recently reorganized into the following four groups:[49]

- **Platforms Product Group** was comprised of five primary divisions, each responsible for a particular area of platform software development and marketing. The Personal Systems Division developed PC operating systems. The Business Systems Division developed server operating systems and server applications. The Internet Client and Collaboration Division developed Web browser technologies and e-mail, editing, and collaboration products. The Developer Tools Division created software development tools. The Consumer Platforms Division developed system software for non-PC devices, multimedia devices, and digital authorizing environments. This group grew 27% in 1996 and 18% in 1997. Windows 95 released in 1996, and Microsoft Windows released in 1997. Platforms Product Group revenues were $5.97 billion, $4.11 billion, and $2.36 billion in 1997, 1996, and 1995, respectively. Paul A. Maritz was named Group Vice-President in May 1995.

- **Applications and Content Product Group** had four divisions that created and marketed productivity programs, interactive entertainment, information products, desktop finance products, and PC input devices. The Desktop Applications Division created business productivity applications and products designed for the home, school, and the small business market. Interactive Media offerings included children's titles, games, reference sources, online informational services, and MSN. The Desktop Finance Division developed personal finance products. The Input Device Division created PC peripherals. Microsoft Research was a research lab for creating new technology in support of the company vision or the evolution of personal computing. Applications and Content Product Group revenues were $5.39 billion, $4.56 billion, and $3.58 billion in 1997, 1996, and 1995, respectively.

- **Sales and Support Group** was responsible for building long-term business relationships with customers of three types: OEM (original equipment manufacturers), end users, and organizations. The Sales and Support Group managed the channels that served those customers. These included the OEM channel and the following geographic channels: United States and Canada, Europe, and Other International. The group also provided support for the company's products through Product Support Services, Consulting Services, and Solution Providers. OEM channel revenues were $3.48 billion, $2.50 billion, and $1.65 billion in 1997, 1996, and 1995, respectively. The primary source of OEM revenues was from licensing of desktop operating systems. OEM channel revenues were highly dependent on PC shipment volume Steven A. Ballmer has served as Executive Vice-President since 1992.

- **Operations Group** was responsible for managing business operations and overall business planning. This included the process of manufacturing and delivering finished goods and licenses; corporate functions such as finance, administration, human resources, and legal; the publishing efforts of Microsoft Press; and other corporate functions. Robert J. Herbold joined Microsoft in 1994 as Executive Vice-President and Chief Operating Officer.

Microsoft could be described as a collection of small development centers, typically with no more than 300 or 400 people each. Of course, this was much larger than when Microsoft first began operations and the projects had only four or five people, but it was still much smaller than competing organizations that have a thousand or more people on a project. According to Gates, "It's very important to me and to the guys that work for us that Microsoft feel like a small company, even though it isn't one anymore. I remember how much fun it is to be small and the business units help preserve that feeling."[50]

CULTURE AND MANAGEMENT STYLE

Corporate Culture

Gates expected Microsoft programmers to work as hard as he did, that is, a 60–80 hour work week. It was expected, but unwritten, that employees work evenings and weekends. If employees took a vacation, it was very short. Dave Moore, Director of Development, described a usual day: "The Microsoft Way: Wake up, go to work, do some work. 'Oh, I'm hungry,' Go down, eat some breakfast. Do some work. 'Oh, I'm hungry,' Eat some lunch. Work until you drop. Drive home. Sleep."[51] Another employee, Jim Conner, a Program Manager, said, "They're outstanding at hiring workaholics . . . I think a lot of that has to do with our interview process. And they're really, really good at motivating people. My own perception, speaking to some degree about myself, I suppose, is that we're really good at finding people who are trying to hit that final home run . . . And man, they give you a lot of bats here. So they're very happy to load you up to death. And people accept that challenge."[52]

Most of the employees had individual offices with windows. The corporate headquarters at Redmond looked more like a college campus than the home of a Fortune 500 company. Employees could be seen jogging, playing music, and juggling. Working hours were extremely flexible. Dress and appearance were extremely casual (for example, working in bare feet). Most employees were rarely seen wearing a suit and tie. When Microsoft staff attended off-site events, they dressed more conventionally. But if Microsoft was the host, they dressed informally. At one function hosted by Microsoft, an IBM'er who could not remember a programmer's name referred to him as "the guy without shoes."[53]

Very few successfully made it through the interview process. Microsoft only hired approximately 2%–3% of the people it interviewed. Each potential employee was subjected to several intense interview sessions in which he or she was questioned on technical issues and evaluated for determination and dedication. The interview was developed to ascertain how smart a person was in an abstract sense. Gates said he looked for the following qualities in prospective employees: ambition, IQ (most important), technical expertise, and business judgment. An example of a question asked in a Microsoft interview was to estimate the volume of water flowing down the Mississippi River. The interviewer's primary purpose was to assess the approach the recruit took to analyze the problem.[54]

In 1997, *Fortune* ranked Microsoft as the fifth "Most Admired Company," which was two higher than the previous year. Microsoft's overall score was 8.29. *Fortune* said, "The winners chart a course of constant renewal and work to sustain a culture that produces the very best products and people." The other top companies were Coca-Cola, Mirage Resorts, and United Parcel Service. The companies were rated in eight categories. Microsoft was ranked first in the "Ability to Attract, Develop and Keep Talented People" category. More than 10,000 senior executives, outside directors, and financial analysts were surveyed.[55]

Bill Gates's Management Style[56]

In 1997, *Fortune* listed Microsoft on its honor roll of the "World's Most Admired Companies," and Gates was recognized as one of the Top 25 Managers in 1996 by *Business Week*. Gates's management style was legendary. He would constantly challenge his programmers. He wanted them to argue with him over issues and concepts. He was very aggressive and vocal in arguing with his employees. But he would change his mind if an employee had a convincing argument. Many felt he created this atmosphere because of his competitive nature. He believed that every employee should come to work thinking—"I want to win."[57]

One of his first acquisitions after signing the MITS contract was a Porsche 911. Gates and Allen would compete over who could get from one place to another the quickest. He still drives a Porsche and garners many speeding tickets and fines. He was known for pushing his Porsche to the limits, while always being in control.[58]

The tenacity, competitiveness, passion, and formidable intellect that drove Gates in high school now allowed him to conquer his competitors. His technical competence allowed him to find a flaw in a program or an argument. Once he had determined a flaw in a presentation, he would rip the presenter apart.[59]

Gates did not believe in paying high base salaries, but instead gave high incentive compensation in the form of bonuses and stock options. The company had a low turnover rate for employees. Compensation included a semi-annual bonus of up to 15%, stock options, and payroll deductions for stock purchases. Many employees became paper millionaires after 1986 when Microsoft went public.[60] Senior managers did not receive a base salary very much higher than the company average. Bill Gates received $349,992 in salary and $241,360 in a bonus in 1997.

In 1983, Gates hired Jon A. Shirley as President and CEO. He recognized the need for professional management. Steve Jobs, founder and CEO of NeXT Computer, Inc., and founder and Chairman of Apple Computer, said about Gates's management style that "Bill has done a great job of cloning himself as the company has grown. Now there are all these 'Little Bills' running various product groups and divisions, and they keep coming at you and coming at you . . . They're not afraid to stumble, and they have all this money so they can afford to hire anyone they want. So now they can really keep coming at you."[61] Although Gates had many talented, capable individuals at Microsoft, he himself continued to drive one of the world's most profitable enterprises to an even higher level.

In 1997, he and his family took possession of his new $60 million-plus waterfront mansion. Square footage for all structures was more than 66,000 square feet (equal to 1.5 acres). Estimated property taxes for 1998 were $620,183.[62] The original proposed house was to cost $10 million and be completed in 1992. The project caused problems for his neighbors, so he tried many creative ways to reduce their problems. Gates considered appealing his property tax and supposedly stopped when he found out that Paul Allen's property taxes were higher.

He still went away alone to his beach house for one week twice a year. He used the time for personal renewal. He read books and reviewed company projects. An analyst said, "This may be one of his secrets to his continual revising of his vision. He is a major visionary."

BILL GATES BUILDS HIS BRAIN TRUST

From 1990 to 1997, Bill Gates and Nathan Myhrvold quietly hired 245 of the brightest researchers from around the world. Gates intended to hire another 400 researchers over the next three years. Gates and Myhrvold wanted to build one of the all-time great basic research institutions like the Bell Laboratory, IBM's Thomas J. Watson Laboratory, Xerox's Palo Alto Research Center (PARC), and Sarnoff Corporation (formerly the RCA Labs). At the same time, other corporations were pulling back from basic research.

Beside the Redmond Lab, Gates intended to build complementary research labs around the world. A new center was being developed in Cambridge, England. Gates and Myhrvold's vision was ambitious, but Gates said, "The future of computer is the computer that talks, listens, sees, and learns. This is what is being created at Microsoft Research." [63] Myhrvold said, "It's a lot easier to understand why Microsoft would invest, say, $1 billion in Comcast TV-cable business or spend $425 million to buy WebTV Networks." [64]

Jennifer Tour Chayes, statistical physicist, recently joined Microsoft with her husband. When she met Bill Gates, she commended him for investing in research that "won't pay off for one hundred years." [65]

Here are a few of the major research projects: (1) doing away with keyboards by creating PCs that understand speech and even talk back; (2) helping programmers become more productive; (3) creating software that lives on networks, not on PCs. [66]

A recent survey by the National Science Foundation found that U.S. corporate spending on basic research, running about $6 billion a year in the 1990s, had declined as a percentage of sales. [67] When Myhrvold was asked if there was any scenario in which Gates would pull back on basic research, he responded, "Alzheimers." He added, "Bill isn't going to pull the plug on research any more than he will pull the plug on Microsoft." [68] He summarized the issue on basic research when he said, "We're either really smart or really stupid. Whenever you're greatly at odds with the rest of the world, one of those two things are true." [69]

Myhrvold defined his job as "doing things others agree are theoretically possible but have not been built before." [70] When he was offered the job of basic research, he jumped at the offer and viewed it as "attempting to do something only an investigator thinks is possible." [71]

THE INTERNET SUPERHIGHWAY

The future that is the "Superhighway" has started to become a reality, where consumers and businesses will be provided with affordable high-speed Internet access. The federal government, since 1996, has been using digital subscriber line (DSL) technology where data was processed over conventional basic copper phone wires 30 times faster than today's fastest modems. Gates was a major supporter of the phone companies' or cable companies' making investments in high-speed digital lines. Access to the Internet was in three modes: (1) phone lines connected to the consumer's PC and a DSL modem,

Exhibit 2 **The Superhighway**

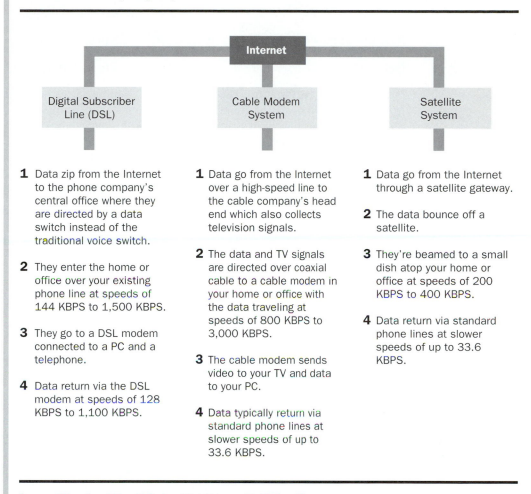

Digital Subscriber Line (DSL)

1 Data zip from the Internet to the phone company's central office where they are directed by a data switch instead of the traditional voice switch.

2 They enter the home or office over your existing phone line at speeds of 144 KBPS to 1,500 KBPS.

3 They go to a DSL modem connected to a PC and a telephone.

4 Data return via the DSL modem at speeds of 128 KBPS to 1,100 KBPS.

Cable Modem System

1 Data go from the Internet over a high-speed line to the cable company's head end which also collects television signals.

2 The data and TV signals are directed over coaxial cable to a cable modem in your home or office with the data traveling at speeds of 800 KBPS to 3,000 KBPS.

3 The cable modem sends video to your TV and data to your PC.

4 Data typically return via standard phone lines at slower speeds of up to 33.6 KBPS.

Satellite System

1 Data go from the Internet through a satellite gateway.

2 The data bounce off a satellite.

3 They're beamed to a small dish atop your home or office at speeds of 200 KBPS to 400 KBPS.

4 Data return via standard phone lines at slower speeds of up to 33.6 KBPS.

Source: "Warp Speed Ahead," *Business Week* (February 16, 1998), p. 80.

(2) coaxial cables from cable company to cable modem which dispatches it to the consumer's PC and/or TV, and (3) satellites used to send data to the consumer's PC.[72] See Exhibit 2 for a fuller understanding of these methods to deliver the Internet to a home or business.

Companies in the business of delivering the Internet have been investing billions of dollars in new forms of technology to link the consumer to the Internet at warp speed—"as high as 250 times faster than the standard modem."[73] Gates wanted to develop and build a new set-top box that brought the Internet to the TV—that is faster and cheaper. Each of the major companies was exploring acquisitions and/or joint ventures to hasten the development of new technologies.

The major online services and Internet access providers in 1997 were:[74]

Provider	Subscribers	Monthly Cost
America Online (AOL)	8,000,000	$19.95 (unlimited)
CompuServe	5,300,000	$9.95 for 1st 5 hours $2.95 per hour

Microsoft Network	2,000,000	$19.95 (unlimited)
Prodigy	1,000,000	$19.95 (unlimited)
AT&T WorldNet	600,000	$19.95 (unlimited)
Netcom	562,000	$19.95 (unlimited)

From September to January 1997, AOL (America Online) customers' daily visits increased from 6 million to nearly 11 million. The customer's time online doubled to 34 minutes. Steve Case, Chairman of AOL, expected that AOL would have 10 million customers by the end of 1997. The ever-growing customer base caused longer and longer delays for getting online. This caused serious complaints, which led 20 state attorneys general to propose legal action against AOL. On January 22, 1997, AOL met with the attorneys general, and a week later AOL made concessions. AOL made it easier for disgruntled customers to stop the service.[75]

CABLE/HDTV BATTLE

In January 1998, Telecommunications, Inc. (TCI) selected Microsoft to supply at least five million units of Windows CE operating system, which was a scaled-down version of the operating system used in almost all of the PCs.

At the same time, TCI announced a license agreement with Scott McNealy, CEO of Sun Microsystems, to provide Sun's Personal Java software. This would provide another way for software programmers to create applications.[76]

These products were to be incorporated in TCI's new digital set-top boxes, which were expected to be available by early 1999. The boxes were being designed not only to deliver hundreds of new channels, but to provide high-speed Internet access. They offered web-based enhancements to traditional television programming, interactive advertising, electronic programming, and other new services.

These alliances may allow TCI influence in setting standards not only for the cable industry but also for the broadcast television industry. On the horizon, the standards for HDTV (high-definition television) are to be established.

Gates would like television broadcasters to abandon HDTV and select a lower resolution transmission format when digital broadcasting begins. Most broadcasters have rejected Gates's proposed alternative. The TCI agreement gave Microsoft a small foothold because it will be supplying the operating systems, Windows CE, for TCI's new digital boxes. This agreement has angered the broadcasters, television makers, and government officials.[77]

Most industry observers felt that John Malone, Chairman of TCI, pulled off a major coup in getting archrivals Gates and McNealy to reach simultaneous agreements to provide products for TCI's new digital box. There were rumors that Microsoft would make an equity investment in TCI. Malone said this was an "arms-length technology licensing agreement" and not conditioned on a Microsoft equity investment in TCI.[78]

Microsoft acquired WebTV in August 1997 and Comcast in June. These acquisitions and the TCI agreement may enhance Microsoft's influence in setting the HDTV standards battle.

Microsoft had held discussions with Time Warner and U.S. West, two of the nation's largest cable operators, to develop a high-speed Internet access system.[79] This service would provide web pages, e-mail, and other Internet services over cable modems at speeds faster than existing systems allow over standard phone lines. This new company would compete with At Home Corp., a start-up company that was controlled by TCI. At Home reached about 44 million homes and 2 million already served by upgraded two-way systems. Microsoft may decide to compete with At Home, so in its purchase agreement with Comcast, a clause allowed Microsoft to force Comcast to break its exclusive agreement with At Home. Microsoft believed that At Home had allied with its rivals—Sun, Oracle, and Netscape. Dean Gilbert, Senior Vice-President and General Manager of At Home, said they had been in discussions with both Time Warner and U.S. West. He stated, "It remains to be seen whether they will become affiliates of At Home."[80]

Brian Roberts, President of Comcast, was viewed as an innovator and the first in the cable industry to take Microsoft's money. He was believed to be uneasy about the potential for a software lock-in.[81]

Gates's wish list to become the cable leader included: (1) combine the functions of a digital set-top box and the cable modem into one device; (2) reduce the cost for a box to about $300 and be assured that he could design it (present cable modems cost $200 to $300 and set-top boxes were $450); (3) allow him to set the industry standards and specifications for the device that will link both TVs and PCs to information providers; and (4) use Microsoft software, including Windows CE operating system for hand-held computers, and other consumer products. An analyst said, "There are a lot of similarities with the battle for cable, and when Gates and Allen created MS-DOS, which became the standard for the PC." Another analyst said Gates wants "to make sure the cable guys do not develop an independent base without him to do this."[82]

Another aspect of the battle for the Internet by phone lines was that Internet grid-lock may be on the immediate horizon. Pacific Bell expects that homes with online access in California will go from 19% in 1997 to 33% in 2001. The company also expects that more than half of home phone traffic by 2001 will be via PCs rather than voice. This potential gridlock of phone lines was one of the major reasons phone companies used to add three more digits to telephone numbers. Phone numbers will go to 10 digits instead of the current 7, plus the local area code. Even for local calls, the user will have to dial the local area code (10 numbers versus 7 at the present time). So, for a long distance call, the user will have to dial 13 numbers. Phone consumers have actively been protesting these changes.

PRODUCTS [83]

Personal Systems

The Personal Systems Division had overall responsibility for the Microsoft Windows PC operating systems. Operating systems software performed a variety of functions, such as allocating computer memory, scheduling applications software execution, managing information and communication flow among the various PC components, and enabling endusers to access files and information.

- **Windows 95/98.** Microsoft's primary personal operating system, the successor to MS-DOS and Windows 3.1, Windows 95 was released commercially in August 1995. Its successor, Windows 98, was released in May 1998. Windows 95/98 was a fully integrated, multitasking, 32-bit operating system designed to be compatible with Intel microprocessor-based PCs, most hardware devices, and Windows 3.1 and MS-DOS applications.

- **Windows NT Workstation.** Also a fully integrated, multitasking, 32-bit operating system, Windows NT Workstation provided greater security, robustness, and portability. Windows NT Workstation was a multithreaded operating system for mission-critical computing that provided the same features and applications programming interfaces (APIs) for Intel and Alpha AXP microprocessors.

- **MS-DOS** was a single-user, single-tasking operating system designed for Intel microprocessor-based PCs. MS-DOS was introduced in 1981 and was pre-installed by OEMs on most PCs shipped prior to the release of Windows 95. Even though version 6.22 was the last version to be released, MS-DOS continues to be included within Windows 95 and 98 to ensure compatibility with older software applications.

- **Windows 3.1/3.11.** Microsoft Windows 3.1 and 3.11 provided a graphical user interface and other enhancements for MS-DOS–based PCs. Not an operating system in itself, it worked in partnership with the MS-DOS operating system. The Windows 3.1/3.11 line has been superceded by the Windows 95/98 and NT lines. Windows 3.1 supported 16-bit Windows-based applications and offered ease of use, aesthetic appeal, and straightforward integration into corporate computing environments. Windows for Workgroups 3.11 integrated network and workgroup functionality directly into the Windows operating system.

Business Systems

The Business Systems Division developed and marketed Windows NT Server and related Microsoft BackOffice and Internet server-based applications. Server operating systems were enterprise-wide platforms for building and deploying distributed applications for networked PCs.

- **Windows NT Server.** Windows NT Server was a powerful operating system foundation for both server applications and file and print sharing, with extensive network management features, administration tools, security, and high availability. Windows NT Server provided a platform for business-critical applications and databases, connectivity, system management, and e-mail servers. The operating system integrated web services such as Microsoft Internet Information Server, a server used to manage intranet and Internet functionality, and Microsoft FrontPage, a website creation and management tool.

- **Microsoft BackOffice.** Based on Windows NT Server, the Microsoft BackOffice family of server applications was an integrated series of software products that included services for file and print, applications, database, messaging, groupware, desktop management, Internet access, transaction processing, and host connectivity. BackOffice enabled organizations to share information, collaborate, and manage and deploy business-critical applications. Microsoft Exchange Server provided e-mail, group scheduling, and integrated groupware capabilities; Microsoft SQL Server managed and stored data; Microsoft Proxy Server created a single, secure gateway to the Internet, Microsoft SNA Server provided connectivity to host data and applications; and Microsoft Systems Management Server centrally managed this distributed environment.

- **Internet Server Tools.** The company also offered Internet servers based on Windows NT Server. In addition to the web services technologies included in Windows NT Server, the company also offered Microsoft Site Server, which allowed a comprehensive management of sophisticated websites and their content. Microsoft Transaction Server was a component-based transaction processing system for developing, deploying, and managing scalable enterprise, Internet, and intranet server applications.

Developer Tools

The Developer Tools Division provided software development tools and technical information to Windows and Internet applications developers. These products and services empowered independent software developers, corporate developers, solutions developers, and webmasters to create a broad spectrum of applications, primarily for Windows 95 and Windows NT, but also for the platform-independent Internet and intranets.

- **Software Development Tools and Computer Languages.** Software development tools and computer languages allowed software developers to write programs in a particular computer language and translate programs into a binary machine-readable set of commands that activate and instruct PC hardware. The company developed and marketed a number of software development environments and language compilers. Microsoft Visual C++ was the company's development system for Windows application development. The Microsoft Visual Basic programming system provided easy access to a wide variety of data sources by integrating the Microsoft Access database engine and the ability to take advantage of investments in commercial applications through ActiveX controls. Microsoft Visual J++, a development environment for Java applications and Internet applets, contained a high productivity Integrated Development Environment and a collection of integrated components to create, test, tune, and deploy Java code on multiple platforms using ActiveX controls.

- **Developer Information.** The company provided third-party software developers with a wide range of technical and support information that assists them in developing software products intended to run on Windows operating systems, taking advantage of key technologies such as ActiveX controls and Windows 32-bit APIs. Developers could subscribe to the Microsoft Developer Network (MSDN) information service and receive periodic updates via CD-ROMs, magazines, and several online information services.

Desktop Applications Software

The Desktop Applications Division developed applications software, which provided the PC with instructions for the performance of productivity tasks such as manipulating text, numbers, or graphics. The company's desktop applications software was designed for use by a broad class of end users, regardless of business, industry, or market segment. Primary examples of desktop applications software were word processing, spreadsheet, and presentation graphics programs. The company's desktop applications programs were developed principally for Windows and Macintosh operating systems.

- **Microsoft Office.** Microsoft Office was a suite of software programs featuring seamless integration of the most commonly used desktop applications. Microsoft Office was based on a document-centric concept, with common commands and extensive use of cross-application capabilities. Microsoft Office was available in several versions, with certain combinations of products available for the various operating system platforms. The most recent version for Windows, Microsoft Office 97, had enhanced Internet features such as integration with Microsoft Internet Explorer, a web toolbar, the ability to save as an HTML format, connectivity to other Office documents or websites via hyperlinks, and support for ActiveX controls. Products offered in the various versions included Microsoft Word (word processing), Microsoft Excel (spreadsheet), Microsoft PowerPoint (presentation graphics), Microsoft Outlook (scheduling), Microsoft Access (database), Microsoft Bookshelf (reference), and others. The Microsoft Home Essentials version of the suite was marketed primarily toward users in the home.

- **Microsoft Word.** The company's principal word processing program was Microsoft Word. Versions of Microsoft Word provided graphical word processing features plus the ability to handle graphics, tables, spreadsheet data, charts, and images imported from other software programs.

- **Microsoft Excel.** The company's spreadsheet program was Microsoft Excel. It was an integrated spreadsheet with pivot table, database, and business graphics capabilities. Microsoft Excel allowed full linking and embedding of objects that permitted users to view and edit graphics or charts from other programs in the worksheet in which the object was stored. Microsoft Excel graphics capabilities could be linked to its spreadsheets to allow simultaneous changes to charts as changes were made to the spreadsheets.

- **Microsoft PowerPoint.** Microsoft PowerPoint was a presentation graphics program for producing transparencies, slides, overheads, and prints.

- **Microsoft Access.** Microsoft Access was a relational database management application that provided access to structured business data. Database products controlled the maintenance and utilization of structured data organized into a set of records or files.

- **Microsoft Outlook.** This division also developed the Microsoft Outlook desktop information management program, which managed e-mail, calendars, contacts, tasks, and files on the PC. Outlook helped users communicate through e-mail and share information by means of public folders, forms, and Internet connectivity.

- **Other Productivity Products.** The company also offered other productivity products, including Microsoft Works, Microsoft Publisher, and Microsoft FrontPage. Microsoft Works was an integrated software program that contained basic word processing, spreadsheet, and database capabilities that allowed the easy exchange of information from one tool to another. Microsoft Publisher was an easy-to-use, entry-level desktop publishing program. Microsoft FrontPage was a website creation and management tool for websites on the Internet or intranet.

Consumer Products

The Consumer Platforms Division developed software for non-PC devices, the Broadcast PC, multimedia devices, and network multimedia.

- **Non-PC Devices.** The division developed Windows CE, a scalable Windows platform for a broad range of communications, entertainment, and mobile computing devices. The Windows CE operating system enabled information appliances to communicate with each other, share information with Windows PCs, and connect to the Internet. Handheld PCs based on Windows CE were manufactured and sold by various hardware OEMs and were designed to be companions to Windows-based PCs.

- **Multimedia Devices.** In August 1997, Microsoft acquired WebTV Networks, Inc., an online service that enabled consumers to experience the Internet through their televisions via set-top terminals based on WebTV technologies. Future versions of the set-top terminals will use the Windows CE operating system.

The Consumer Platforms Division was also responsible for Softimage, which developed, marketed, and supported a family of interactive software products enabling digital media producers to create and edit two- and three-dimensional content for digital media productions. Softimage supplied 3D visualization software for broadcast, film production, and other high-end animation applications. In addition, Softimage had a product line of 2D visualization software for use on high-end applications, including postproduction editing and the integration of visual images, text, sound, and special effects technology. These products were designed for the Windows NT and IRIX operating systems.

- **Softimage 3D.** Softimage 3D provided three-dimensional animation software for film and video professionals, animators, and artists who created and produced high-end, three-dimensional imagery for traditional and new media.

- **Softimage DS.** Softimage DS was a digital authoring environment blending 2D and 3D graphics, digital video, and digital audio. The digital studio environment accommodated many types of projects for digital multimedia such as high-end advertising, entertainment, games, and integrated interactive multimedia.

Interactive Media

The Interactive Media Division developed and marketed interactive entertainment and information products across a variety of media, including the Internet, the Microsoft Network, and CD-ROM.

- **Learning and Entertainment.** Reference titles included Microsoft Encarta and Microsoft Bookshelf. The Encarta multimedia encyclopedia blended text in articles with a wealth of innovative, interactive information presented through animations, videos, maps, charts, sounds, and pictures. Bookshelf was a multimedia reference library that integrated seven well-respected and authoritative works, including a dictionary, world atlas, world almanac, thesaurus, concise encyclopedia, and two books of quotations.

  Personal interest titles included Microsoft Cinemania, an interactive guide to the movies with entries for 19,000 films, Microsoft Dinosaurs, musical titles, and many others.

  Titles for children included Microsoft Creative Writer, a full-featured creative writing and publishing program. The company also had a series of products based on the popular children's book and television series, Scholastic's *The Magic School Bus*.

  The company offered a line of entertainment products. Microsoft Flight Simulator was a popular aircraft flight simulation product available for Windows, MS-DOS, and Macintosh operating systems. Games included Monster Truck Madness, Microsoft Golf, and other sports and action titles. Most games were available for the Windows 95/98 environment.

- **Interactive Service Media.** The company was developing an online decision support infrastructure for end users in such fields as automobiles, retail, entertainment, and travel. Microsoft CarPoint provided current and objective information for new car purchases, including test drive reviews, dealer invoices, and surround videos. Additionally, CarPoint featured a new car buying service. Comprised of a national network of dealers, this service referred customers to nearby dealers. Microsoft Sidewalk was a personalized city guide to local entertainment. The Sidewalk editorial team provided previews, reviews, and even customized suggestions about entertainment events in Seattle, New York, Boston, and Minneapolis, with city guides scheduled to launch in San Francisco, Houston, Washington, D.C., San Diego, Denver, and Sydney, Australia. Microsoft Expedia was a free travel service on the World Wide Web and MSN that enabled users to find low fares, book flights, make hotel reservations, and rent cars. Expedia also offered a comprehensive source of information for more than 300 destinations including photos, historical information, and local details. Expedia Streets 98 and Expedia Trip Planner 98 were comprehensive route-planning programs with detailed maps and road information for routes in North America.

- **The Microsoft Network.** MSN was a web-based interactive online service. MSN provided easy and inexpensive access for users to a wide range of graphically rich online content. The online service provided access to the Internet, electronic mail, bulletin boards, and myriad additional services offered by Microsoft and by independent content providers (ICPs).

- **Joint Ventures.** The company had entered into joint venture arrangements to take advantage of creative talent and content from other organizations. Microsoft owned 50% of DreamWorks Interactive L.L.C., a software company that developed interactive and multimedia products. DreamWorks SKG owned the remaining 50%.

Internet Client and Collaboration

The Internet Client and Collaboration Division developed Internet browser technology and e-mail and group collaboration products.

- **Internet Software.** The division had overall development and marketing responsibility for Microsoft Internet Explorer, the company's Internet browser. It also provided products for developing, running, and managing Internet and intranet applications and content, including ActiveX controls. Formerly known as object linking and embedding (OLE) controls, ActiveX controls were components (or objects) that could be inserted into a web page or another application that allowed packaged functionality programmed elsewhere to be reused and enabled real-time, active content.

Desktop Finance

Microsoft Money was a financial organization product that allowed users to computerize their household finances. Microsoft Money was available for systems running Windows 95/98 and provided online home-banking services with numerous banks in the United States.

Microsoft Investor was an online investing site that provided a comprehensive offering of information and services designed to help personal investors make investment decisions, track their securities, and understand the market. A blend of free and subscription-basis services, Investor provided portfolio tracking and analysis, company and mutual fund research, an investment finder, daily editorial and market summaries, e-mail notifications and alerts, and access to online trading through leading financial services firms.

PC Input Devices

The company's major input device was the Microsoft Mouse, a handheld pointing device that facilitated the use of a PC. It could be used with MS-DOS and Windows operating systems and worked with most applications products from Microsoft and other companies. Microsoft also offered a mouse designed for the home and a mouse for young children. The company also marketed the Microsoft Natural Keyboard, an ergonomically designed keyboard. Additionally, Microsoft sold joysticks and gamepads for use with PC games.

Microsoft Press [84]

Microsoft Press published books about software products from Microsoft and other software developers and about current developments in the industry. Microsoft Press typically published books that were written and copyrighted by independent authors who submitted their manuscripts to the company for publication and who received royalties based on net revenues the book generated.

Microsoft Press contracted with an independent commercial printer for the manufacturing of its books. Publisher's Resources, Inc., acted as the company's main fulfillment house in the United States, maintaining the majority of the inventory of Microsoft Press books. Books were marketed by independent sales representatives and by Microsoft Press sales personnel. Internationally, Microsoft Press had numerous agreements with publishers for the worldwide distribution of its books. Microsoft Press had granted a publisher in England the right to distribute English-language versions of its books in all countries except the United States, Canada, Central and South America, and certain Asian countries. In most cases, Microsoft Press provided each publisher with a book's manuscript, and the publisher arranged for its translation and the printing, marketing, and distribution of the translated version.

Product Development [85]

The PC software industry was characterized by extremely rapid technological change, which required constant attention to software technology trends, shifting consumer demand, and rapid product innovation. The pace of change had recently become even greater due to the surge of interest in the Internet, other forms of online services, PC server-based networking, and new programming languages such as Java.

Most of the company software products were developed internally. The company also purchased technology, licensed intellectual property rights, and oversaw third-party development and localization of certain products. Whenever the company noted a new development in the industry, it strove to quickly obtain access to that development and to improve upon it. This was often referred to as Microsoft's "embrace and extend" approach to new product development. Internal development enabled Microsoft to maintain closer technical control over the products and gave the company the freedom to designate which modifications and enhancements were most important and when they should be implemented. The company had created a substantial body of proprietary development tools and had evolved development methodologies for creating and enhancing its products. These tools and methodologies were also designed to simplify a product's portability among different operating systems, microprocessors, or computers. Product documentation was generally created internally.

The company believed that a crucial factor in the success of a new product was getting it to market quickly to respond to new user needs or advances in PCs, servers, peripherals, and the Internet, without compromising product quality. The company strove to become informed at the earliest possible time about changing usage patterns and hardware advances that might have affected software design.

During fiscal years 1995, 1996, and 1997, the company spent $860 million, $1.43 billion, and $1.93 billion, respectively, on product research and development activities. Those amounts represented 14.5%, 16.5%, and 16.9%, respectively, of revenue in each of those years, excluding funding of joint venture activity. The company was committed to continue high expenditures for research and product development.

Localization [86]

To best serve the needs of users in foreign countries, Microsoft "localized" many of its products to reflect local languages and conventions. In France, for example, all user messages and documentation were in French and all monetary references were in French francs, and in the United Kingdom, monetary references were in British pounds and user messages and documentation reflected certain British conventions. Various Microsoft products have been localized into more than 30 languages.

MARKETING/DISTRIBUTION [87]

Microsoft aligned its sales and marketing staff with several customer types, including OEMs, end users, organizations, enterprises, applications developers, Internet content providers (ICPs), and infrastructure owners. The company's sales and marketing group sought to build long-term relationships with customers of Microsoft products. In addition to the OEM channel, Microsoft had three major geographic sales and marketing organizations: the U.S. and Canada; Europe; and elsewhere in the world (Other International).

The OEM customer unit included the sales force that worked with original equipment manufacturers that pre-installed Microsoft software on their PCs.

The end-user customer unit had responsibility for activities that targeted end users who made individual buying decisions for the PCs they used at work or home. Most sales and marketing activities aimed at end-user customers were performed by this unit, including developing and administering reseller relationships; reseller sales terms and conditions; channel marketing and promotions; end-user marketing programs; support policies; and seminars, events, and sales training for resellers. The key products marketed by the end-user customer unit were the company's desktop operating systems, desktop applications, and interactive media products.

The organization customer unit had responsibility for activities that targeted groups of users in small and medium-sized organizations. The unit worked with channel partners such as distributors, aggregators, value-added resellers, and Solution Providers to provide complete business solutions to this customer segment. The unit's sales and marketing activities included providing technical training to Solution Providers (described below) and channel resellers; developing support policies; and supporting and providing seminars, events, and sales training for channel partners.

The enterprise customer unit had responsibility for sales and marketing activities that target large organizations. The unit worked directly with these organizations and through large account resellers to create and support enterprise-wide, mission-critical solutions for business computing needs.

The applications developer customer unit targeted corporate developers and independent software vendors (ISVs) who built business applications with a development platform based on Microsoft Windows and BackOffice architecture. The unit's sales and marketing activities included providing industry-specific technical training, seminars, and events for ISVs.

The Internet customer unit was responsible for introducing the company's products and technologies to the public infrastructure owners and ICPs. Infrastructure owners included network operators (telephone companies, cable companies, Internet service providers, etc.) who build, own, and operate the public networks and ICPs who provide content for the Web.

Finished Goods Channels

- **Distributors and Resellers.** The company marketed its products in the finished goods channels primarily through independent, non-exclusive distributors and resellers. Distributors included CHS Electronics, Computer 2000, Ingram Micro, Softbank, Tech Data, and Merisel. Resellers included Software Spectrum and Stream International. Microsoft has a network of field sales representatives and field support personnel who solicit orders from distributors and resellers and provide product training and sales support.

- **Large Accounts.** The Microsoft Select program offered flexible software acquisition, licensing, and maintenance options specially customized to meet the needs of large, multinational organizations. Targeted audiences included technology specialists and influential end users in large enterprises. Marketing efforts and fulfillment were generally coordinated with the Microsoft network of large account resellers.

- **Solution Providers.** Microsoft's Solution Providers program was a comprehensive support relationship with independent organizations that provided network and system integration, custom development, training, and technical support for business computing solutions. The program supported value-added resellers (VARs), system integrators, consultants, custom application developers, solution developers, Internet service and hosting organizations, independent content providers, and sitebuilders (companies that build websites for other companies) as well as technical support and training organizations. Under this business partnership strategy, the company provided sales and product information, development services, early access to Microsoft products, and customer support tools, including priority telephone support, education, and business development support. To ensure high-quality technical services for the company's products, Microsoft Solution Providers were required to have Microsoft-certified professionals on staff.

- **Consulting Services.** The company's Consulting Services Division assisted customers in using the company's computer operating systems, applications, and communications products. The group worked with Solution Providers and helped create enterprise-wide computing solutions for large corporate accounts.

- **International Sales Sites.** The company has established marketing and/or support subsidiaries in more than 60 countries. Product was generally delivered by the company's owned or outsourced manufacturing operations.

The company's international operations, both OEM and finished goods, were subject to certain risks common to foreign operations in general, such as governmental regulations, import restrictions, and foreign exchange rate fluctuations. Microsoft hedged a portion of its foreign exchange risk.

OEM Channel

Microsoft operating systems were licensed primarily to OEMs under agreements that granted the OEMs the right to distribute copies of the company's products with their computers. The company also marketed certain desktop applications and interactive media programs to OEMs under similar arrangements. In addition, the company marketed the Microsoft Mouse and Natural Keyboard to OEMs for distribution to buyers of their computers. In almost all cases, the products were distributed under Microsoft trademarks. The company had OEM agreements covering one or more of its products with virtually all of the major PC OEMs, including AST Research, Acer, Compaq, Digital Equipment Corporation, Dell, Fujitsu, Gateway 2000, Hewlett-Packard, IBM, NEC, Packard Bell, Siemens, Toshiba, and Vobis.

Advertising

The company worked closely with large advertising and direct marketing firms. Advertising, direct marketing, worldwide packaging, and marketing materials were targeted to various end-user segments. The company used broad consumer media (television, radio, and business publications) and trade publications. Microsoft had programs under which qualifying resellers and OEMs were reimbursed for certain advertising expenditures. The company maintained a broad advertising campaign emphasizing the Microsoft brand identity.

CUSTOMERS[88]

The company's customers included end users, organizations, enterprises, ISPs, application developers, and OEMs. Most end users of Microsoft products were individuals in business, government agencies, educational institutions, and at home. These end users obtained Microsoft products primarily through distributors, resellers, and OEMs that included certain Microsoft products with their hardware. The company's practice was to ship its products promptly upon receipt of purchase orders from its customers and, consequently, backlog was not significant.

PRODUCT SUPPORT[89]

The company provided product support coverage options to meet the needs of users of Microsoft products. Support personnel were located in various sites in the United States and around the world. Certain support was also supplied by qualified third-party support organizations. The company hired individuals with product expertise and provided them with productivity tools, continuous product education and training, and consistent processes to deliver quality support for Microsoft products. Coverage options ranged from standard no-charge toll telephone support to fee-based offerings providing unlimited 800 number telephone and electronic technical support for all Microsoft products 24 hours per day, 7 days per week.

Users had access to troubleshooting "wizards" and Microsoft's KnowledgeBase, a library of thousands of technical articles that was updated regularly with useful information regarding Microsoft products. Microsoft provided access to KnowledgeBase via MSN, America Online, CompuServe, Prodigy, and the Internet. Additionally, several support offerings included Microsoft Technet and Microsoft Developer Network information subscription services.

As a supplement or alternative to direct support, the company enhanced the third-party support channel by providing Microsoft Solution Providers with education, training, tools, and support. Microsoft Solution Providers included Authorized Training Centers, which offered advanced product education and certification on Microsoft products; and Authorized Support Centers, which provided a wide spectrum of multinational support and integration services.

SOFTWARE COMPETITORS[90]

The PC software business was intensely competitive and subject to extremely rapid technological change. Microsoft faced formidable competition in all areas of its business activity, including competition from many companies much larger than Microsoft. The rapid pace of technological change constantly created new opportunities for existing competitors and start-ups and could quickly render existing technologies less valuable. The company also faced constant competition from software pirates who unlawfully copied and distributed Microsoft's copyrighted software products.

- **Operating systems.** Microsoft's operating system products faced substantial competition from a wide variety of companies. Major competitors such as IBM, Apple Computer, Digital Equipment Corporation, Hewlett-Packard, and Sun Microsystems were vertically integrated in both software development and hardware manufacturing and had developed operating systems that they preinstalled on computers of their own manufacture. Many of these operating system software products were also licensed to third-party OEMs for preinstallation on their machines. Microsoft's operating system products competed with UNIX-based operating systems from a wide range of companies, including IBM, AT&T, Hewlett-Packard, Sun, and The Santa Cruz Operation. Variants of UNIX such as Lynx (a text-based operating system) ran on a wide variety of computer platforms and had gained increasing acceptance as desktop operating systems. As PC technology increasingly moved toward connectivity and communications, Microsoft's operating system products faced increased competition from network server operating systems such as Novell's NetWare, Banyan's Vines, the many variants of UNIX, IBM's OS/2, "middleware" products such as IBM's Lotus Notes, and intranet servers from Netscape, IBM, Sun, and others.

- **Business systems.** The company was a fairly recent entrant into the business of providing enterprise-wide computing solutions. Several competitors enjoyed a larger share of sales and larger installed bases. Many companies offered operating system software for mainframes and midrange computers, including IBM, Digital Equipment [owned by Compaq Computer], Hewlett-Packard, and Sun. Because legacy business systems were typically support intensive, these competitors also offered substantive support services. Software developers that provided competing server applications for PC-based distributed client/server environments included Oracle, IBM, Computer Associates, Sybase, and Informix. Several software vendors offered connectivity servers. As mentioned, numerous companies and organizations offered Internet and intranet server software that competed against the company's business systems. Additionally, IBM had a large installed base of Lotus Notes and cc:Mail, both of which competed with the company's workgroups and mail products.

- **Desktop applications.** The company's competitors included many software application vendors such as IBM (Lotus), Oracle, Apple (Claris), Corel (WordPerfect), and local application developers in Europe and the Far East. IBM and Corel had large installed bases with their spreadsheet and word processor products, respectively, and both had aggressive pricing strategies. Also, IBM and Apple pre-installed certain of their software products on various models of their PCs, competing directly with Microsoft desktop application software.

- **Developer tools.** The company's developer products competed against offerings from Borland, Macromedia, Oracle, Sun, Sybase, Symantec, and other companies.

- **News services.** The company's MSNBC joint ventures faced formidable competition from other 24-hour cable and new Internet organizations such as CNN and Fox News Network. MSNBC also competed with traditional news media such as newspapers and broadcast TV and Internet news services.

- **Consumer platforms.** A wide variety of companies developed operating systems for information appliances, including Apple, Motorola, 3Com, and Psion Software. The company's nascent WebTV offerings and other multimedia consumer products faced such competitors as Sun, Oracle, and NetChannel. An enormous range of companies, including media conglomerates, telephone companies, cable companies, retailers, hardware manufacturers, and software developers, were competing to make interactive services widely available to the home.

- **Internet platforms and services.** The advent of the Internet as a computing, communication, and collaboration platform as well as a low-cost and efficient distribution vehicle increased competition and created uncertainty as to future technology directions. The company faced intense competition in the development and marketing of Internet (and intranet) software from a wide variety of companies and organizations, including IBM, Netscape, Novell, Oracle, Sun, and many others. In addition, the very low barriers to entry on the Internet also have allowed numerous web-based service companies to build significant businesses in such areas as electronic mail, electronic commerce, web search engines, and information of numerous types. Competitors included Netscape, Lycos, Yahoo, Excit, Infoseek, CitySearch, and many others.

- **Online services.** Microsoft's online services network, MSN, faced formidable competition from America Online and other online networks such as CompuServe (acquired by AOL), Prodigy, and impending entrants. Additionally, MSN faced competition from online services that are offered to users directly via the World Wide Web.

- **Interactive media.** The company's Interactive Media division faced many smaller but focused and branded competitors, particularly in the areas of entertainment and education. Consolidation in this area of software development had made certain competitors even stronger. Competitors included Intuit, Broderbund, Electronic Arts, The Learning Company (including Softkey, MECC, and Compton's), Voyager, CUC International (including Sierra On Line, Knowledge Adventures, and Davidson Associates), and Dorling Kindersley. Still other competitors own branded content, such as Disney and Lucas Arts.

Additionally, PC-based games were increasingly competing head to head against games created for proprietary systems such as Nintendo, Sony PlayStation, and Sega. Input devices faced substantial competition from computer manufacturers because computers were typically sold with a keyboard and mouse.

Several of Microsoft's most significant competitors, including IBM, Sun, Oracle, and Netscape, had jointly embarked upon various technology development and marketing initiatives that were intended to increase customer demand for products from these companies. These initiatives related in part to efforts to move software from individual PCs to centrally managed servers. Although the likely technological and business success of such "thin client" strategies is currently unknown, widespread adoption of such computing systems would present significant challenge to the company's historical business model of decentralized computing via individual PCs.

The company's competitive position may be adversely affected by one or more of these factors in the future, particularly in view of the fast pace of technological change in the software industry.

DATAMATION 1995 SURVEY[91]

For 1995, Microsoft's software received mixed reviews. Exhibit 3 shows the top 12 sellers of software according to *Datamation*. Microsoft had the highest score and ranked eighth with an overall score of 3.28. Users rated its service and support at a low 2.90 and the degree to which it was easy to deal with at 3.01. Its highest score (3.78) and ranking (second) were for price and performance. *Datamation* viewed Microsoft's performance as "lacklustered."

Hewlett-Packard (HP) received the highest overall rating in five of the six market segments that were rated. Hewlett-Packard received a number one overall rating in Workstations, Software, Peripherals, Service & Support, and Midrange Services. Software sales were 5% of its total sales, $19.2 billion in 1994. HP placed second in the PC market segment, behind Compaq.

Computer Associates received the lowest overall rating (2.52) and came in last in five out of the six categories. *Datamation* stated that "CA, which manages to keep growing its revenues by buying up small competitors, doesn't seem to satisfy its customers."[92]

MSNBC—24-HOUR NEWS CHANNEL

On December 15, 1995, NBC and Microsoft became partners in a new 24-hour news cable channel, MSNBC Cable, and an online news source to be carried on the Internet. There was no contract, just a letter of intent for the venture. Microsoft paid NBC $220 million for a 50% share of MSNBC Cable. Both companies were to invest about $200 million each over a five-year period to fund the two services. John F. Welch, Chairman of General Electric, expected the venture to break even within five years. General Electric owned NBC and CNBC.[93]

"This is the very beginning of an interactive world," said Bill Gates, speaking via satellite from Hong Kong. "By bringing the power of these two operations to bear on this, we'll be able to be a leader and make the news far more attractive than it's been." He further stated, "We're taking the long-term view here that, over time, video will be an important data type, as well as the audio and text that are already available."[94]

MSNBC On-line's "goal is to provide NBC News video, sound, graphics, and text via the Internet's World Wide Web. The Web will become accessible through high-speed

Exhibit 3   1995 *Datamation* 100 Survey

Software	Overall Rating	Product Quality/ Reliability	Service/ Support	Supports Industry Standards	Price/ Performance	Easy to Deal With
HP	3.70	4.19	3.81	3.71	3.33	3.43
Digital	3.46	3.81	3.62	3.36	3.31	3.19
Borland	3.42	3.69	3.00	3.42	3.85	3.12
Novell	3.36	4.00	3.16	3.48	3.16	3.00
Lotus	3.32	3.88	3.00	3.27	3.30	3.12
SAS	3.31	4.21	3.57	3.31	2.69	2.79
IBM	3.29	3.93	3.46	3.22	2.88	2.95
Microsoft	**3.28**	**3.59**	**2.90**	**3.14**	**3.78**	**3.01**
Unisys	3.27	3.81	3.33	3.00	3.00	3.20
Legent	3.25	3.70	3.27	3.64	2.90	2.73
Oracle	2.82	3.48	2.64	3.30	2.29	2.41
CA	2.52	2.97	2.44	2.73	2.38	2.06

Note: Rating scale 5 (highest) to 1 (lowest).
Source: Chris Staiti and Nancy Meachum, "Users Give HP Top Rating," *Datamation* (June 1, 1995), p. 44.

cable modems which will soon reach the market."[95] A viewer could see a story on NBC's "Dateline" and then explore it in depth on MSNBC On-line. NBC had exclusive editorial control over both services.

Bill Gates and Jack Welch were rated the number one and two 1995 Performance of the Year CEO's by *Forbes*.[96] An analyst said this should make for a most interesting alliance between these two high-achieving executives.

Previously, Turner Corporation announced it was creating a new financial channel, CNNfn, in January 1996, to compete with NBC's CNBC financial channel. CNN was not impressed by MSNBC. "Every service they announced today, we've already got out there," said Steve Haworth, a CNN spokesman. "Our homepage on the Internet . . . is getting 3 million hits a day."[97] CNN was received in 67.5 million households in the United States and millions more around the world.

MSNBC's goal for U.S. subscribers was approximately 20 million homes in 2000. Overseas, it had the potential to reach 200 million homes through NBC Super Channel in Europe, CNBC in Asia and Europe, Canal de Noticeas NBC in Latin America, and NBC Asia, which was scheduled to begin operations in January.

NBC dropped its existing cable service, America's Talking, a talk network that was carried in about 20 million cable homes and had agreements for 15 million more by 2000. This meant that the major cable systems, Time Warner and Tele-Communications, had to decide to keep or drop NBC's service after the two new services were introduced.

Capital Cities/ABC recently unveiled its own plans to develop a 24-hour news channel by mid-1997, and it expected to reach 5 million homes. Capital Cities/ABC merged with the Walt Disney Company on January 4, 1996. The Federal Communications Commission (FCC) unanimously approved the $19 billion merger on February 8, 1996. ABC decided not to go ahead with the new channel. In November 1996, Rupert Murdoch, Chairman of News Corporation, said he would launch an all-news channel. Fox Broadcasting Company was owned by the News Corporation and was to be the vehicle to develop the new channel. News Corporation, of which the Murdoch family controls 30% of the voting stock, was one of the world's great media empires, operating on five continents. Marc Gunther of *Fortune* said,"News Corp. [was] . . . the most global of the entertainment giants and the only one created, built, and thoroughly dominated by one man [Rupert Murdoch]." [98] Murdoch encountered serious problems with starting this all-news channel. News Corporation owned and operated 22 TV stations and owned several cable networks.

MANUFACTURING [99]

Microsoft contracted most of its manufacturing activity to third parties. Outside manufacturers produced various retail software packaged products, documentation, and hardware such as mouse pointing devices, keyboards, and joysticks. There were other custom manufacturers in the event that outsourced manufacturing became unavailable from current sources.

In recent years, the company's sales mix had shifted to OEM and corporate and organizational licenses from packaged products. Online distribution of software may increase in the future. During July 1996, Microsoft sold its domestic manufacturing and distribution operation.

The company's remaining manufacturing facilities were located in Puerto Rico and Ireland. The Irish manufacturing facility replicated disks, assembled other purchased parts, and packaged final product. The Puerto Rican facility manufactured CD-ROMs, assembled other purchased parts, and packaged final product. Quality control tests were performed on purchased parts, finished disks and CD-ROMs, and other products. The chief materials and components used in Microsoft products included disks or CD-ROMs, books, and multicolor printed materials. The company was often able to acquire component parts and materials on a volume discount basis. The company had multiple sources for raw materials, supplies, and components.

HUMAN RESOURCES/EMPLOYEES—MILLIONAIRE CLUB

Microsoft employed 22,232 people, 15,835 domestically and 6,397 internationally. There were 8,059 employees in product research and development; 11,074 in sales, marketing, and support; 1,115 in manufacturing and distribution; and 1,984 in finance and administration. The company management stated,"Microsoft's success is highly dependent on its ability to attract and retain qualified employees. To date, the company believes it has been successful in its efforts to recruit qualified employees, but there is no assurance that it will continue to be successful in the future." [100] No unions represented the company's employees. Every employee was eligible to become a shareholder through the employee stock purchase and stock option plan. The employees' and directors' shares and options comprised 42% of the shares outstanding. The directors and executive officers as a group owned about 35.8%.

Microsoft offered stock options to its employees. The paper profits for stock options in December 1997 were approximately $1.1 million for each employee. Allan Sloan said, "If Microsoft were to issue all 259 million option shares today, existing holders' stake in the company would drop to about 83% from the current 100%." [101] This would dilute the stock price. According to Sloan, in the three months ended September 30, Microsoft spent $913 million buying its own shares—more than it spent on sales and marketing ($788 million) or research and development ($567 million) or any other single cost item.[102] This prevented the dilution of shareholders' wealth. The company purchased stock on the exchange versus issuing new stock.

Sloan discovered that Microsoft sold *put options* on its stock. A put option was sold to outsiders, which gives the put option holder the right to sell stock to Microsoft at a fixed price on a specific day. Through June 30, the company had raised $270 million selling puts that had expired. This was tax-free money for the corporation.[103] Robert Williams, tax expert at Lehman Brothers, said, "Corporations never have to pay tax on transactions involving their stock or options on their stock."[104]

The stock price adversely affected Microsoft's employees from acquiring the company stock options. Some analysts felt this was one of the prime reasons for all the stock splits. The latest 2-for-1 split was in January 1998.

ASIAN FLU: ECONOMIC COLLAPSE

In the fall of 1997, the major Asian economic powers suffered a major collapse in their stock markets and their individual currencies (see Exhibit 4). U.S. computer manufacturers received a benefit, in that local wages in each of these companies were substantially decreased. The cost to these companies were reduced sales in these countries. On CNBC, in 1997 they discussed the impact of the "Asian Flu" on U.S. computer companies for the fourth quarter sales and net profit with experts. To about everyone's surprise, the impact was small in the fourth quarter of 1997. The ripple effects of the "Asian Flu" started to show up in the first quarter of 1998 and were expected to last for one or two more quarters of 1998. Compaq claimed its drop in financial performance, both sales and profit, was the result of the Asian Flu.[105]

An analyst said, "The ripple effects of the Asian Flu will affect sales of Microsoft products to computer manufacturers and to Asian corporate clients." U.S. exports of computers to Asia was expected to be $7.6 billion before the Asian Flu.

All exported consumer products to these Asian markets were being impacted. Nike, in the first quarter of 1998, announced profits down 70% and 1,600 people were laid off because of the economic collapse in Asia.[106] The economic collapse caused a financial bailout package for several of these Asian countries by the International Monetary Fund. On May 21, 1998, President Suharto of Indonesia resigned after 32 years in office. The collapse of the Indonesian economy brought down President Suharto.

FINANCE

Revenues for the second quarter of fiscal year 1998 (ending December 31, 1997) were up 34% over the same quarter in 1997. Revenues were $3.5 billion versus $2.68 billion in 1997. Net income was $1,126 million and $740 million for 1997 and 1996 second quarters respectively. Sales were driven by the introduction of Office 97.

Sales by product group changed this period. Platform Product Group revenues grew 26% to $1.88 billion in the second quarter. Applications and Content Product Group revenues grew 43% to $1.7 billion for the same quarter. Revenues from licenses to OEMs who pre-installed Microsoft products on hardware were at a record high at $1.21 million. During this quarter, Microsoft released several new products, including Microsoft BackOffice Small Business Server 4.0 and Microsoft SQL Server 6.5 and other products.

Exhibit 4 **Asian Flu: Currencies and Stock Prices Tumble in the Fall of 1997**

Country	Stock Price Changes (%)	Currency Changes (%)
Hong Kong	(19.5)	0.04
Indonesia	(21.6)	(53.00)
Malaysia	(46.0)	(32.80)
Philippines	(42.4)	(33.40)
Singapore	(28.7)	(12.30)
South Korea	(28.0)	(14.30)
Taiwan	6.9	(12.10)
Thailand	(45.4)	(58.00)

Source: Adapted from Neel Chowdhury and Anthony Paul, "Where Asia Goes from Here," *Fortune* (November 24, 1997), pp. 96–97.

Research and development expenses increased 29% in the second quarter to $627 million, primarily driven by higher development headcount-related costs, third-party development, and charges from purchased R&D.

On August 1, 1997, the company acquired WebTV Networks, Inc. (WebTV), an on-line service that enabled consumers to experience the Internet through their televisions via set-top terminals. Microsoft paid $425 million in stock and cash for WebTV. Year-to-date results reflected a one-time write-off of in-process technologies under development by WebTV of $295 million, which was recorded in the first quarter.

Sales and marketing expenses were $876 million in the December quarter, which represented 24.4% of revenue, compared to 27.5% in the second quarter of the prior year. The total expense as a percentage of revenue decreased due to lower relative support costs.

General and administrative costs increased to $106 million in the second quarter, compared to $81 million in the December quarter of the prior year, due in part to higher legal costs.[107]

The 1997 financial results are shown in Exhibits 5 and 6. Revenues were $11,358 million, $8,671 million, $5,937 million, $4,694 million, and $3,753 million for 1997, 1996, 1995, 1994, and 1993 respectively. Net income was $3,454 million, $2,195 million, $1,453 million, $1,146 million, and $953 million for the same five years (see Exhibit 5).

Exhibit 7 shows annual financial results by geographical regions. U.S. operational revenues comprised 78.1%, 77.7%, 75.7%, 74.6%, and 70.7% of total revenues for 1997, 1996, 1995, 1994, and 1993, respectively. U.S. operational revenues comprised 72.8%, 69.4%, 83.6%, 80.8%, and 72.4% of total operating revenues for the same period.

Greg Maffei, Chief Financial Officer, said, "European revenues were up 33% over same quarter (2nd) last year and OEM revenues exploded 40%."[108] Approximately 37%, 34%, and 32% of Microsoft's revenues were collected in foreign currencies in 1997, 1996, and 1995, respectively.

Office 97 posted impressive sales for the third consecutive quarter, while Microsoft Windows 95 sales were seasonally strong. John DeVaan, Vice-President, Desktop Application Division, said "Office 97 continues to be a success because it offers the customer ease of use, reduced cost of ownership, and true integration."[109]

During February 23, 1998, Gates and nine other Microsoft executives sold about

$1.69 billion of stock. The stock price was at a record high. Gates sold $322 million. The company's stock prices for the past five years were as follows:

Stock Prices		
Year	High	Low
1997	150.8	80.6
1996	86.1	39.9
1995	54.6	29.1
1994	32.6	19.5
1993	24.5	17.6

FUTURE FOR INTELLECTUAL PROPERTIES

In May 1998, many analysts were discussing the Senate investigation of Microsoft, and the DOJ and 20 states' law suit of Microsoft. One analyst said, "DOJ may have to redefine the word 'monopoly.' They are using a historical concept of antitrust that was defined in the late 1890s. There are major differences from a monopoly of iron, coal, oil, and railroad companies, and an intellectual property company (Intel, Microsoft) of today. Intellectual properties are created in a dynamic and globally competitive environment. Today's product is quickly surpassed by newer intellectual properties. These intellectual properties of today compete in a global business environment, which is the opposite of the old monopolies. The life cycle of coal or oil is endless, whereas the life shelf of an intellectual property would be measured in terms of days. Companies in today's markets spend millions or billions on R&D to develop new intellectual properties. So, we need a new, clear definition of monopolies for intellectual property companies and a way to protect their copyrighted products."

INTEL—FTC FILES ANTITRUST CHARGES

On June 8, 1998, the Federal Trade Commission (FTC) filed antitrust charges against Intel Corporation. The FTC in its findings alleged that:

1. Intel illegally used its monopoly share of the microprocessor business to punish customers and rivals by denying them information on vital Intel chips.

2. Intel cut off Digital Equipment Corp.'s access to technical information after Digital filed a patent-infringement lawsuit against Intel.

3. Intel denied key information to Intergraph Corp. after it refused to grant Intel a royalty-free license to use certain Intergraph technology.

4. Intel refused to supply crucial information to Compaq Computer Corp. after Compaq asserted its intellectual property rights to certain technology.[110]

The FTC's 11-page complaint charged that Intel had retaliated against Compaq Computer, Digital Equipment, and Intergraph when they tried to enforce patents against Intel or other companies allied with Intel.

Exhibit 5   Balance Sheet: Microsoft Corporation
(Dollar amounts in millions, except per-share data)

Year Ending June 30	1997	1996
Assets		
Current assets		
Cash and short-term investments	$ 8,966	$ 6,940
Accounts receivable	980	639
Other	427	260
Total current assets	10,373	7,839
Property, plant, and equipment	1,465	1,326
Equity investments	2,346	675
Other assets	203	253
Total assets	$14,387	$10,093
Liabilities and Shareholders' Equity		
Current liabilities		
Accounts payable	$ 721	$ 808
Accrued compensation	336	202
Income taxes payable	466	484
Unearned revenue	1,418	560
Other	669	371
Total current liabilities	3,610	2,425
Minority interest	—	125
Put warrants	—	635
Commitments and contingencies		
Shareholders' equity		
Convertible preferred stock—shares authorized 0 and 100; shares issued and outstanding 0 and 13	980	—
Common stock and paid-in capital—shares authorized 4,000; shares issued and outstanding 1,194 and 1,204	4,509	2,924
Retained earnings	5,288	3,984
Total shareholders' equity	10,777	6,908
Total liabilities and shareholders' equity	$14,387	$10,093

Source: Microsoft Corporation, *1997 Annual Report,* p. 24.

An analyst found it interesting that both Intel and Microsoft had 90% market shares in their segments of the market and both were being charged with antitrust allegations. This could be the first legal step in the process to label Intel as a monopoly.

Notes

1. "Judge: No Delay for Microsoft," *St. Petersburg Times* (May 22, 1998), p. 1E.
2. Paul Davidson,"Suit Outlines Case Against Microsoft," (May 19, 1997), p. 1A.
3. "Judge: No Delay for Microsoft," *St. Petersburg Times* (May 22, 1998), p. 1E.
4. Davidson, p. 1A.
5. Susan Gregory Thomas,"The Waiting Game,"*U.S. News & World Report* (May 25, 1998), p. 1998.

Exhibit 6 **Income Statement: Microsoft Corporation**
(Dollar amounts in millions, except per-share data)

Year Ending June 30	1997	1996	1995	1994	1993
Net revenues	$11,358	$ 8,671	$5,937	$4,649	$3,753
Operating expenses					
Cost of revenues	1,085	1,188	877	763	633
Research and development	1,925	1,432	860	610	470
Sales and marketing	2,856	2,657	1,895	1,384	1,205
General and administrative	362	316	267	166	119
Total operating expenses	6,228	5,593	3,899	2,923	2,427
Operating income	5,130	3,078	2,038	1,726	1,326
Interest income, net	443	320	191	102	82
Non-continuing items	—	—	(46)	(90)	—
Other expenses	(259)	(19)	(16)	(16)	(7)
Income before taxes	5,314	3,379	2,167	1,722	1,401
Provision for income taxes	(1,860)	(1,184)	(714)	(576)	(448)
Net income	$ 3,454	$ 2,195	$1,453	$1,146	$ 953
Earnings per share	$2.62	$1.71	$1.16	$0.94	$0.785
Weighted average shares outstanding	1,312	1,281	1,254	1,220	1,212

Source: Microsoft Corporation, *1995 Annual Report*, p. 17, and *1997 Annual Report*, p. 24.

6. Davidson, p. 1A.
7. John R. Wilke and David Bank, "Microsoft's Chief Concedes Hardball Tactics," *The Wall Street Journal* (March 4, 1998), p. B1.
8. "PC Makers Push Ahead on Windows 98," *The Wall Street Journal* (May 19, 1998), p. B6.
9. Davidson, p. 1A.
10. Michael Krantz, "Headed for Battle," *Time* (May 25, 1998), pp. 58–59. The questions and answers were directly quoted from this article.
11. Dan Clark, "A Master Programmer Updates His Code," *The Wall Street Journal*, p. B6.
12. "Ticketmaster vs. Microsoft," *Business Week* (May 12, 1997), p. 48, and Bruce Orwell, "Ticketmaster Sues Microsoft Corp. Over Internet Link," *The Wall Street Journal* (April 12, 1997), p. B11.
13. Robert D. Hof, Steve Hamm, and Peter Burrows, "Behind the Brawl Over Java," *Business Week* (October 20, 1997), pp. 34–35.
14. "Texas Sues Microsoft, Alleging Licenses Impede State's Probe," *The Wall Street Journal* (November 11, 1997), p. A4.
15. *Ibid.*
16. "States Meet to Consider Microsoft Lawsuit," *St. Petersburg Times* (December 17, 1997), p. 1E.
17. J. Wallace and J. Erickson, *Hard Drive* (New York: Harper, 1993); pp. 50–61.
18. *Ibid.*
19. *Ibid.*, p. 61.
20. *Ibid.*, and Henry Goldblatt, "Bill Gates & Paul Allen Talk," *Fortune* (October 2, 1995), p. 72.
21. *Ibid.*
22. Wallace, p. 107.
23. *Ibid.*
24. *Ibid.*
25. Goldblatt, p. 72.
26. James Day, "Apple Looks to Include Windows 3.0 in Lawsuit," *Computerworld* (April 22, 1991), p. 4.
27. *Microsoft Encarta*, 1995 ed., s.v. "Microsoft Corporation."
28. *Ibid.*
29. David Bank, "Microsoft Casts a Wider Communications Net," *The Wall Street Journal* (June 10, 1997), p. B5.
30. Andrew E. Serwer, "Analyzing the Dream," *Fortune* (April 17, 1995), p. 71.
31. Microsoft Corporation, *Microsoft News Release* (October 7, 1995), pp. 1–2.
32. David C. Kaufman, "Windows 95: Do You Need the Most Overhyped Product of the Decade?" *Fortune* (September 18, 1995), p. 192.
33. *Microsoft Investor Relations News Release* (October 21, 1996), p. 1.
34. *Ibid.*
35. *Ibid.*, p. 3.
36. "Microsoft Deal," *USA Today* (May 8, 1997), p. B1.
37. Mark Robichaux and Don Clark, "Microsoft May Put $1 Billion into Comcast," *The Wall Street Journal* (June 9, 1997), p. A3.
38. "Microsoft Denies CBS Bid Rumors," *Tampa Tribune* (July 2, 1997), p. 2 Business.
39. Amy Cortese, Steve Hamm, and Robert Hof, "Why Microsoft Is Glued to the Tube," *Business Week* (September 22, 1997), pp. 96 and 100.
40. *Ibid.*, p. 86.

Exhibit 7 **Financial Information by Geographic Areas: Microsoft Corporation**
(Dollar amounts in millions, except per-share data)

	1997	1996	1995	1994
A. Net Revenues				
U.S. operations	$ 8,877	$ 6,739	$4,495	$3,472
European operations	2,770	2,215	1,607	1,401
Other international operations	1,757	1,267	821	375
Eliminations	(2,046)	(1,550)	(986)	(599)
Total net revenues	$11,358	$ 8,671	$5,937	$4,649
B. Operating Income				
U.S. operations	$ 3,733	$ 2,137	$1,414	$1,394
European operations	1,013	649	444	346
Other international operations	469	297	163	31
Eliminations	(85)	(5)	17	(45)
Total operating income	$ 5,130	$3,078	$2,038	$1,726
C. Identifiable Assets				
U.S. operations	$11,630	$8,193	$5,862	$4,397
European operations	3,395	2,280	1,806	1,366
Other international operations	705	1,042	689	423
Eliminations	(1,343)	(1,422)	(1,147)	(823)
Total identifiable assets	$14,387	$10,093	$7,210	$5,363

Source: Microsoft Corporation, *Form 10-K* (June 30, 1995), p. 28, and *1997 Annual Report*, p. 41.

41. Steve Hamm and Amy Cortese, "Why Win98's Delay Is O.K.," *Business Week* (September 29, 1997), p. 80.
42. *Microsoft Investor Relations News Release* (June 21, 1998), p. 2.
43. *Ibid.*
44. Brent Schlender, "What Does Bill Gates Want," *Fortune* (January 16, 1995), p. 54.
45. *Notice of Annual Shareholders Meeting,* pp. 3–4 and *Form 10-K* (June 30, 1997), pp. 13–14.
46. *Form 10-K* (June 30, 1997), p. 13.
47. *Notice of Annual Shareholders Meeting,* pp. 3–4 and Leslie Cauley and Kara Swisher, *Wall Street Journal* (April 6, 1998), p. A3.
48. *Ibid.*
49. *Form 10-K* (June 30, 1997), p. 1. The material directly quoted, except for minor editing.
50. *Form 10-K* (June 30, 1995), pp. 1, 14–15.
51. Michael A. Cusumano and Richard Selby, *Microsoft Secrets* (New York: The Free Press, 1995), p. 46.
52. *Ibid.*
53. Richard Brandt, "The Billion-Dollar Whiz Kid," *Business Week* (April 13, 1987), p. 70.
54. Stephen Manes and Paul Andrews, *Gates: How Microsoft's Mogul Reinvented an Industry and Made Himself the Richest Man in America* (New York: Doubleday, 1996), p. 396.
55. Rahul Jacob, "Corporate Reputation," *Fortune* (March 6, 1995), pp. 54–57.
56. Wallace and Erickson, pp. 254–256.
57. *Ibid.*, p. 369.
58. Goldblatt, p. 82.
59. Wallace and Erickson, pp. 254–256.
60. Brent Schlender, "How Bill Gates Keeps the Magic Going," *Fortune* (June 18, 1990), p. 84.
61. *Ibid.*, p. 83.
62. J. Martin Mcomber, "Gates' Neighbors Can't Wait for Quiet," *St. Petersburg Times* (July 10, 1997), p. 4A.
63. Randall E. Stross, "Mr. Gates Builds His Brain Trust," *Fortune* (December 8, 1997), p. 84.
64. *Ibid.*
65. *Ibid.*
66. *Ibid.*, p. 86.
67. *Ibid.*, p. 98.
68. *Ibid.*
69. *Ibid.*
70. *Ibid.*, p. 87.
71. *Ibid.*
72. "Warp Speed Ahead," *Business Week* (February 14, 1998), p. 80.
73. *Ibid.*
74. Adapted from "Where You Can Connect," *Business Week* (February 10, 1997), p. 50.
75. *Ibid.*
76. David Bank and Leslie Cauley, "TCI Set-Up-Box Pacts Put Microsoft Against Sun," *The Wall Street Journal* (January 12, 1998), p. A3.

77. "Microsoft Strikes Stealthy Blow in HDTV Battle," *St. Petersburg Times* (March 2, 1998), p.18.

78. Bank and Cauley, p. A3.

79. David Bank, "Microsoft, Time Warner and U.S. West Discuss High-Speed Internet Service," *The Wall Street Journal* (November 6, 1997), p. B8.

80. *Ibid.*

81. David Bank, "Why Microsoft Wants to Hook into Cable TV," *The Wall Street Journal* (October 16, 1997), p. B1.

82. "Bill Gates, The Cable Guy," *Fortune* (July 14, 1997), p. 220.

83. *Form 10-K* (June 30, 1997), pp. 1–5. The material in this section, Products, was directly abstracted. Windows 98 information was added. The verb tense was changed and minor editing done.

84. *Form 10-K* (June 30, 1997), pp. 5–6. The material in this section, Microsoft Press, was abstracted. The verb tense was changed.

85. *Ibid.,* (June 30, 1997), p. 6. The material in this section, Product Development, was abstracted. The verb tense was changed.

86. *Ibid.,* (June 30, 1995) The material in this section, Localization, was abstracted. The verb tense was changed.

87. *Ibid.,* (June 30, 1997), pp. 6–8. The material in this section, Marketing/Distribution, was abstracted. The verb tense was changed and edited.

88. *Ibid.,* p. 8. The material in this section, Customers, was abstracted. The verb tense was changed.

89. *Ibid.* The material in this section, Product Support, was abstracted. The verb tense was changed.

90. *Ibid.,* pp. 9–10. The material in this section, Competition, was abstracted. The verb tense was changed.

91. "DATAMATION 100," *Datamation* (June 1, 1995), p. 69.

92. *Ibid.,* p. 40.

93. "Microsoft NBC Team for Cable," *St. Petersburg Times* (December 15, 1995), p. B1.

94. *Ibid.*

95. *Ibid.*

96. "The Short List of 1995's Best Performers," *Forbes* (January 1, 1996), p. 71.

97. "Microsoft NBC Team for Cable," *St. Petersburg Times* (December 15, 1995), p. B1.

98. Marc Gunther, "The Rules According to Rupert," *Fortune* (October 26, 1998), p. 94.

99. *Form 10-K* (June 30, 1997), p. 6. The material in this section, "Manufacturing," was abstracted. The verb tense was changed.

100. *Form 10-K* (June 30, 1995), p. 10.

101. Allan Sloan, "Millionaires Next Door," *Newsweek* (December 8, 1997), p. 56.

102. *Ibid.*

103. *Ibid.*

104. *Ibid.*

105. Steven Butler, Phillip J. Longman, and Matthew Miller, "Pacific Grim," *U.S. News & World Report* (December 6, 1997), pp. 26, 27, and 30.

106. "Amid Glut of Swooshes, Nike Tries to Pump Up Profit," *St. Petersburg Times* (March 20, 1998), p. 6E.

107. *Microsoft Investor Relations News Release* (January 21, 1998), pp. 7–8. This was abstracted.

108. *Microsoft Investor Relations News Release* (January 21, 1998), p. 1.

109. *Ibid.*

110. John R. Wilke and Dean Takahaski, "Intel Is Hit with FTC Antitrust Charges," *Wall Street Journal* (June 9, 1998), p. A3.

Apple Computer, Inc. (1997): The Second Time Around

David B. Croll and Thomas L. Wheelen

THE SECOND TIME AROUND

It was September 26, 1997, and Apple Computer, Inc., had just closed its fiscal 1997 books. It had not been a good three months. For the fourth-fiscal quarter, 1997, Apple's revenues were $1.6 billion, a decrease of 30% from the fourth quarter a year ago. The company's net loss for the quarter was $161 million, or $(1.26) per share, compared with a net profit of $25 million, or $0.20 per share, in the same quarter a year ago.[1] (See Exhibit 1.)[2] Steven Jobs, who had founded the firm along with Steve Wozniak in Jobs's parents' garage in 1976, was back as CEO 14 years after being replaced in that position by John Sculley. Although only holding the title of Acting CEO, Steve Jobs was clearly the man in charge once again. While Apple Computer, Inc., was caught up in a search for a new chief executive, computer industry executives everywhere agreed that what Apple needed most was a radical new survival plan.

Steve Jobs was not without suggestions, some wanted and some not so wanted. Prince Alwaleed, a 5% shareholder in Apple advised "Let's consider any alliance that makes sense. I'm willing to listen to anything."[3] But hopes of a white knight to buy Apple and fix it were all but extinguished. Former suitors, a list that once included IBM and Sun Microsystems Inc., were long gone. Many experts were urging Apple to finally take the most radical step of all, stop fighting the Intel/Microsoft PC standard. That would mean continuing to make Macs for the loyal legions, while also building a new business in "Wintel," PCs using Intel Computer chips and Windows operating system. Scott McNealy, Sun Microsystems' CEO who came close to buying Apple 21 months earlier, agreed, "At this point, they need somebody who will just walk in and say 'We're going to be a Compaq' or 'We're going to be a [Sun-compatible] player.' They are down to Tyson-Holyfield. . . . It's better to have your ear chewed on than to be sitting outside the ring."[4] However, for this plan to work, experts suggested Apple also would need to sell off its ailing operating-system (OS) software operations.

PaineWebber Inc. calculated Apple's breakup value in 1996 when Sun Microsystems was considering buying Apple. Although some time had passed since these values were calculated, they remained basically the same in late 1997. (See Exhibit 2.)[5]

"Apple has lost the OS war, and there's no point fighting it again and again," said David B. Yoffie, a professor at Harvard Business School and a Director of Intel.[6] He was not alone in that sentiment. In June 1997, all 160 industry executives at a Harvard executive seminar studying Apple voted that it should be broken up. That was not necessarily bad news for Apple, as it would end the conflict between Apple and makers of Mac clones. Selling off software would also help Apple focus on its last remaining strengths—its world-renowned brand and catchy hardware design.

This case was prepared by Professor David B. Croll of the McIntire School of Commerce at the University of Virginia and by Professor Thomas L. Wheelen of the University of South Florida. All rights are reserved to the authors. This case may not be reproduced in any form without written permission of the copyright holder, David B. Croll. This case was edited for SMBP–7th Edition. Copyright © 1998 by David B. Croll. Reprinted by permission.

Exhibit 1   **Another Bruise for Apple**

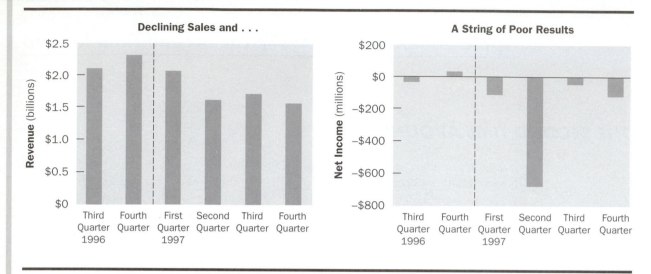

Even former Apple CEO John Sculley had advice for Jobs. He thought Apple should partner with a PC maker to attack the education market, where Apple was fast losing ground, while selling Macs to the faithful. If the stock dipped below 10, Jobs might not have a chance to try any of these strategies or strategies of his own. (See Exhibit 3.)[7] An investor group including Microsoft director and venture capitalist David F. Marquardt would consider a run at Apple if the stock fell into single digits, according to an individual close to the group.[8] Time was not on Apple's side; Steven Jobs had to come up with a strategy fast.

BACKGROUND TO THE CURRENT DECLINE

In July 1997, Gilbert Amelio resigned as Chief Executive Officer of Apple Computer, Inc. At a company renowned for its populist egalitarianism, Dr. Amelio had a reputation as arrogant, isolated, and out of touch. Instead of slowing Apple's decline, Amelio's regime presided over an accelerated loss of market share, deteriorating earnings, and a stock that had lost half of its value. In short, Amelio's forced resignation had all the signs of a classic Apple blunder: too late, too little, and providing too few answers. Would Apple itself follow Amelio into oblivion?[9]

Apple had failed to license the Mac operating system to other manufacturers early enough that it might today be as ubiquitous as Windows. Both Amelio and his immediate predecessor, Michael Spindler, failed to accept any of the buyout offers proposed to Apple. In late 1994, IBM offered $40 a share for the company, payable in shares of IBM. Apple refused because Apple's board reviewed IBM as "going nowhere." Apple turned down a second offer from IBM in the spring of 1995 and rebuffed overtures from Sun Microsystems, including one early the previous year for between $18 and $21 a share. These days, sources say, Sun chairman Scott McNealy heaves a sigh of relief that Apple turned him down.[10] To compound the error, Apple began to license Macs to a number of new cloners in 1996, too late to do anything but cannibalize Apple's own sales. This helped drag down its U.S. market share from 11% in 1996 to about 4% in 1998.

Exhibit 2   An Analysis of the Computer Maker's Breakup Value

Slices of the Apple	1996 Sales[1] (in billions)	Multiple[2]	Valuation (in billions)
Computer hardware	$11.0	0.2	$2.20
Operating systems	0.32	2.0	.064
Claris systems	0.25	1.0	0.25
Printers, scanners	1.0	0.2	0.20
Newton, other	0.03	5.0	0.15
Total	12.72	0.27	3.44
Breakup share value			$27.96
Share price Jan. 31			$27.25

Notes:
1. Projected
2. Based on comparisons with poorly performing peers

Source: Peter Burrows, "How Much for One Apple, Slightly Bruised," *Business Week* (February 12, 1996), p. 35.

Data Source: PaineWebber, Inc.

Amelio spent $400 million in early 1997 to acquire NeXT software from Steve Jobs. The rumor in the computer industry was that Amelio, seduced by Jobs's legendary sales-manship, hugely overpaid for a technology that Apple might never be able to put to use. It was also widely rumored that Jobs himself had lost faith in NeXT's innovative software and wanted desperately to find a buyer.[11]

By the end of Amelio's tenure, Apple seemed to be in utter disarray. One chief executive approached Apple with a plan to buy its $1.5 billion imaging division. "I couldn't find anyone who could make the decision," he said, ultimately giving up. Amelio's fate was sealed when Jobs and other executives arrived from NeXT.[12] They knew Apple and the industry, and they seemed focused, impassioned, and full of vision.

Even strong Apple fanatics were convinced that only draconian remedies could save Apple. Many thought the company, desperate for a bailout, could be bought cheaply. Some often-mentioned buyers were Oracle Corp. or Taiwan's Umax Data Systems. Even Jean-Louis Gassee, head of a software maker and ex-senior Vice President of Apple Products Division, concluded that "Apple doesn't need a CEO. They need a messiah."[13]

HISTORICAL BACKGROUND

Founded in a California garage in 1976, Apple created the personal computer revolution with powerful, yet easy-to use, machines for the desktop. Steve Jobs sold his Volkswagen van and Steve Wozniak hocked his programmable calculator to raise seed money to begin the business. Not long afterward, a mutual friend helped recruit A.C. "Mike" Markkula to help market the company and give it a million-dollar image. All three founders had left the company's management team, but Mike Markkula remained as a member of the Board of Directors until August 1997.

The early success of Apple was attributed largely to marketing and technological innovation. In the high growth industry of personal computers in the early 1980s, Apple grew quickly. It stayed ahead of its competitors by contributing key products that stimulated the development of software specifically for the computers. Landmark programs

Exhibit 3 **The Amelio Era**

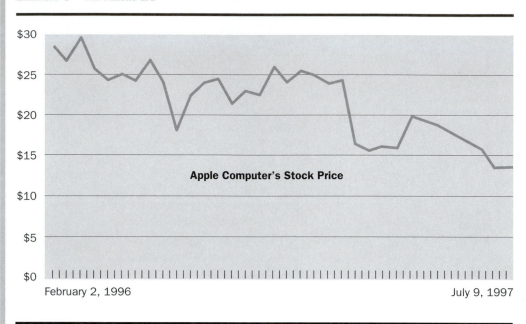

Apple Computer's Stock Price

February 2, 1996 — July 9, 1997

Source: *Business Week* (July 21, 1997), p. 32.

such as Visicalc (forerunner of Lotus 1-2-3 and other spreadsheet programs) were developed first for the Apple II. Apple also secured early dominance in the education and consumer markets by awarding hundreds of thousands of dollars in grants to schools and individuals for the development of educational software.

Even with enormous competition, Apple's revenues continued to grow at unprecedented rates, reaching $583.1 million by fiscal 1982. The introduction of the Macintosh graphical user interface in 1984, which included icons, pull-down menus, and windows, became the catalyst for desktop publishing and instigated the second technological revolution attributable to Apple. Apple kept the architecture of the Macintosh proprietary, i.e., it could not be cloned like the "open system" IBM PC. This allowed the company to charge a premium for its distinctive "user-friendly" features.

A shake-out in the personal computer industry began in 1983, when IBM entered the PC market, first affecting companies selling low-priced machines to consumers. Companies that made strategic blunders or that lacked sufficient distribution or brand awareness for their products disappeared. By 1985, only the largest computer and software companies seemed positioned to survive.

In 1985, amid a slumping market, Apple saw the departure of its founders, Jobs and Wozniak, and instituted a massive reorganization to streamline operations and expenses. Under the leadership of John Sculley, Chief Executive Officer and Chairman of the Board, the company engineered a remarkable turnaround. Macintosh sales gained momentum throughout 1986 and into 1987. Sales increased 40% from $1.9 billion in fiscal 1986 to $2.7 billion in fiscal 1987, and earnings jumped 41% from $154 million in $217 million. Nearly half the company's sales and most of its profits came from the business sector. Dozens of new software and peripheral products were introduced. The new technology carried over into 1988, which saw the introduction of products specifically designed for improving the networking and connectivity capabilities of Apple computers.

In the early 1990s, Apple Computer sold more personal computers than any other computer company. Net sales grew to over $7 billion, net income to over $530 million, and earnings per share to $4.33. On October 2, 1991, Apple and IBM signed a series of agreements, including the establishment of joint ventures in multimedia and object-based system software and other joint product development initiatives.[14]

The period from 1993 to 1995 was a time of considerable change in the management of Apple Computer. In June 1993, John Sculley was forced to resign and Michael H. Spindler was appointed CEO of the company. CFO Joseph A. Graziano, a strong advocate of Apple's merging with another company, was asked to resign, citing differences of opinion between Graziano and Spindler. Daniel L. Eilers, Senior Vice-President of Apple Computer, Inc., also resigned. It was rumored that Eilers was forced to resign when he sided with Graziano and a buyout, alienating Spindler.

In December 1995, Apple and IBM announced that they were folding Kaleida Labs Inc., a joint venture set up in 1991 to develop software that would enable consumers to play any kind of multimedia program on personal computers. This move was the first formal recognition by the two companies that at least part of the strategic alliance that Apple and IBM had entered into several years earlier was not working. Taligent, a much larger joint project, was also in trouble.

CURRENT SITUATION[15]

During 1996 and 1997, Apple experienced declines in net sales, units shipped, and share of the personal computer market compared to prior years. The decline in demand and the resulting losses, coupled with intense price competition throughout the industry, led to the company's decision to continue to restructure its business during 1997 aimed at reducing its core structure, improving its competitiveness, and restoring sustainable profitability. Apple's restructuring efforts included a large number of layoffs, simplification of the product lines, increases in the proportion of products manufactured under outsourcing arrangements, and the implementation of an online store in the continental United States. In addition, Apple planned to increase the proportion of products manufactured on a made-to-order basis.

In February 1997, Apple acquired NeXT. The programmers at NeXT had developed software that enabled customers to implement business applications on the Internet/World Wide Web and enterprise-wide client/server networks. The acquisition was accounted for as a purchase and accordingly the operating results were included in Apple's consolidated operating results. The total purchase price was $427 million. The purchase of NeXT brought Steve Jobs back into the company.

According to industry analysts, Apple's future operating results and financial condition depended on its ability to successfully develop, manufacture, and market technologically innovative products to meet customer demand patterns. Apple's future also depended on its ability to effect a change in marketplace perception of the company's prospects, including the viability of the Macintosh platform. Apple should be able to deliver planned enhancements to the current MacOS and make timely delivery of a new and substantially backward-compatible operating system. It must attract, motivate, and retain employees, including a new Chief Executive Officer, maintain the availability of third-party software for particular applications, and, at the same time, wind down its MacOS licensing program.

ECONOMIC SITUATION

The U.S. economy continued to roll along in 1997. Growth in GDP, which nominally exceeded 4% in the first half of the year, was expected to slow to 2.5% to 3% in the latter half of 1997. (See Exhibits 4 and 5.) [16, 17] Importantly, that rate of growth probably was not sufficient to cause the Federal Reserve to push interest rates to levels that would choke off the upward economic trend. Economic forecasters thought spending on durable equipment, which included computer gear, would rise at a brisk 10% pace during 1998 and continue at a 6.0%–8.0% annual rate until the year 2002. Consumers would also be able to continue spending on computers and related products such as printers and equipment to connect to the Internet.

Overseas the conditions were mixed. (See Exhibit 6.) [18] The emerging markets in the former Soviet Union and Eastern Europe offered the potential for rapid growth. But the developed countries in Europe were experiencing relatively slow growth. The economic recovery that appeared to be building in Japan in the first quarter of 1997 did occur. That country's GDP contracted sharply in the June quarter. The currency turmoil that embroiled Southeast Asia was expected to impede the rapid growth that the region's countries had been enjoying. [19]

MANAGEMENT

On July 9, 1997, Apple announced that Dr. Gilbert F. Amelio had resigned as Chairman of the Board and Chief Executive Officer. (See Exhibit 7.) [20] A search was started for a new CEO, and in the interim Steve Jobs assumed the position of acting CEO. Other members of Dr. Amelio's senior management saw little chance that they would be successfully assimilated into the new management team. Guerrino De Luca, Apple's Executive Vice-President of Marketing, resigned in September. He had held this position since February 1997. Dave Manovich, Senior Vice-President of International Sales, and James McCluney, Senior Vice-President of Worldwide Operations, resigned from Apple in October. James McCluney had been with Apple since July 1996 and Dave Manovich since February 1997. On the same day that Dr. Amelio resigned, Ellen Hancock, a well-known industry executive who worked for Dr. Amelio at National Semiconductor Corp., resigned her position as Executive Vice-President of Technology.

Apple announced significant changes to its Board of Directors on August 6, 1997, replacing all but two directors. (See Exhibit 8.) [21] The continuing directors were Gareth C.C. Chang, President of Hughes International, and Edgar S. Woolard, Jr., retired Chairman of E.I. DuPont de Nemours & Company. The new directors were William V. Campbell, President and CEO of Intuit Corp.; Lawrence J. Ellison, Chairman and Chief Executive Officer of Oracle Corp.; Steven P. Jobs, Chairman and Chief Executive Officer of Pixar Animation Studios; and Jerome B. York, Vice-Chairman of Tracinda Corporation and former Chief Financial Officer of IBM and Chrysler Corporation. Many critics blamed the old Board more than the CEOs and in particular Mike Markkula, who had served on the Board from the beginning. "It's the Board of Directors who drove the company into the ground," said Jim Clark, Chairman of Netscape Communications Corp. "Who is at fault here? It's not Sculley and Amelio. The real fault lies with Mike Markkula and the people who have been running the company from day one." [22]

Exhibit 4 In the U.S., a Picture of Economic Strength

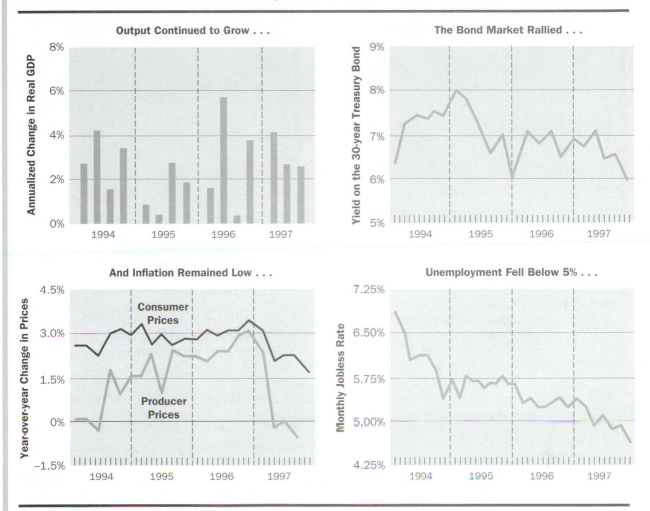

Source: *WSJ* (January 2, 1998), p. B36.

CLONES

Apple previously entered into agreements to license its MacOS to other personal computer vendors (the "clone vendors") as part of an effort to increase the installed base for the Macintosh platform. Then it determined that the benefits of licensing the MacOS to clone vendors were more than offset by the impact and costs of the licensing program. As a result, Apple agreed to acquire the Mac-related assets and license to distribute the MacOS of Power Computer Corporation, a clone vendor, for $100 million, but it had no plans to renew its other MacOS licensing agreements.[23] Jobs also disclosed that he offered the other cloners, including Motorola Inc., Umax Data Systems Inc. of Taiwan, and sub-licensees of International Business Machines Corp., new licenses to Apple's future technology in return for substantially higher fees.

The reason for reversing the clone strategy, Apple executives said, "is that Mac compatibles didn't boost the market—they only took share from Apple."[24] "The original ob-

Exhibit 5   Economic Job and Wage Information

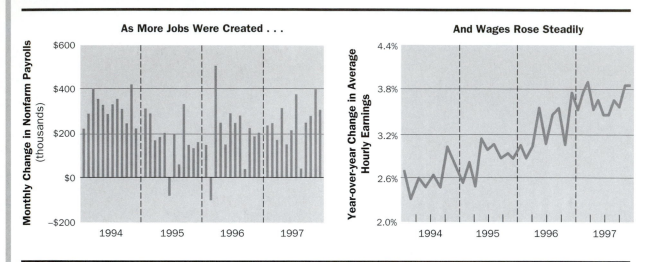

Source: *WSJ* (January 2, 1998), p. B36.

jective was to expand the Mac customer base," explained Chief Financial Officer Fred D. Anderson Jr. Abandoning the clone strategy created fresh problems. Many Mac fans now professed loyalty to cloners, which typically offered better performance at lower prices than Apple.

Apple's management said the company would honor existing contracts, and Anderson said Apple was open to new deals that would expand the Mac market. But cloners were suspicious. An Apple insider said: "Steve's not about to let clones eat any more of Apple's lunch." [25] (See Exhibit 9.) [26]

Cloning helped the Mac market. Dataquest Inc. analyst James B. Staten said, "Competition from Power Computer and Motorola has led to lower prices for buyers." Rivalry was giving buyers more choices. Apple and Power Computer, for instance, used different versions of PowerPC chips. "It has brought technological choice in the marketplace," said Staten. Cutting off cloners seemed to reverse Apple's customer image. "The message to the marketplace would be: We can't compete; our only chance is to sell to people who are so fanatical that they're willing to buy overpriced boxes," said Eric Lewis, an analyst at International Data Corp. [27]

In Jobs's view, the upstarts were not creating new Mac customers. They were boring into Mac strongholds that Jobs felt Apple must defend to survive. His position, according to a clonemaker executive who had met with Jobs recently: "Either stay out of Apple's core markets or fork over licensing fees of more then $200 per machine, up from $50 or less today. As long as he's in charge, cloners must play by Jobs's rules." [28]

MICROSOFT AND APPLE MAKE A DEAL

Bill Gates, CEO of Microsoft, announced in mid October 1997 that he would pay $150 million for a minority nonvoting stake in Apple. The deal permitted Microsoft to maintain its dominance as the number one supplier of business software to Apple customers and to continue the advancement of its web strategy of pushing its browser into every desktop. Quite possibly, Microsoft also gained an ally in its campaign against Sun's

Exhibit 6   *Performance of the World's Major Government Bond Markets*

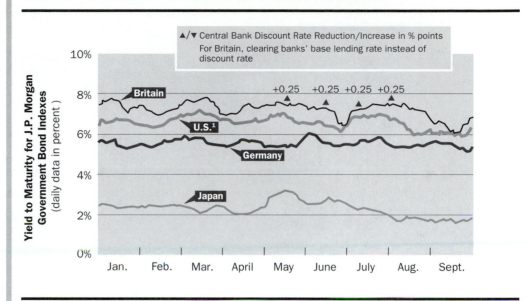

1. Federal funds target rate, discount rate unchanged.

Source: Datastream, *WSJ* (January 2, 1998), p. B36.

and Oracle's efforts to convert corporate users and consumers to networked computers that used Java rather than Microsoft Windows. Apple gained renewed industry confidence and Microsoft software support.

Besides cash infusion, Apple received an undisclosed sum, estimated in the hundreds of millions, to resolve long-standing disputes with Microsoft over software patents. Apple also secured a five-year commitment from Microsoft to ship a Mac version of Office, the business package that included Microsoft Word, the best-selling word processor for Macs. Office 98, developed for the new Mac OS 8, was expected to be available at the end of 1997.

On balance, Microsoft seemed to be the bigger winner. Its Internet Explorer would be installed as the default browser on all Macintosh systems. Although rival Netscape still claimed to hold 70% of the browser market, it had been losing ground steadily to Microsoft, and for Netscape this deal represented another setback. Apple and Microsoft also agreed to make sure their efforts with Java and other programming languages were compatible. Java, which was well suited to allowing inexpensive, stripped-down computers to run on software delivered via an in-house network or the World Wide Web, had been attracting software developers because of its flexibility in creating programs that worked in several environments. Microsoft preferred to see Java promoted as a programming language for coding new Windows applications, not as a potential rival standard. Apple's support could help Microsoft toward this end.[29]

PRODUCT INTRODUCTIONS[30]

To remain competitive, Apple would have to continually introduce new products and technologies and enhance existing products. Recent introductions included new Power-Book and Power Macintosh add-ons and the MacOS 8. The success of these new prod-

Exhibit 7 **Reality Bytes**

Apple's Previous Board

Dr. Gilbert F. Amelio, age 53, Chairman and CEO Apple Computer; Director since 1996, resigned July 9, 1997
Gareth C. C. Chang, 53, Corporate Senior Vice-President Marketing, Hughes Electronics; Director since 1996[1]
Bernard Goldstein, 66, Managing Director, Boradview Associates; Director since 1991
Katherine M. Hudson, 49, President and CEO W. H. Brady Co.; Director since 1994
Delano E. Lewis, 58, President and CEO National Public Radio; Director since 1994
A. C. Markkula, Jr., 54, Vice-Chairman Apple; Director since 1977
Edgar S. Woolard, Jr., 62, Chairman E.I. duPont De Nemours; Director since 1996[1]

Note: 1. Remained on Board of Directors after Jobs returned.
Source: *Apple's Dec. 27, 1996 Proxy Statement*

Time Capsule

- **April 1976:** Steve Jobs and Steve Wozniak form Apple in Jobs's parents' garage.
- **April 1977:** The Apple II is introduced at the West Coast Computer Faire.
- **April 1983:** Former PepsiCo executive John Sculley becomes Apple CEO.
- **January 1984:** The Macintosh debuts in a celebrated commercial during the Super Bowl.
- **May 1985:** Steve Jobs resigns after power struggle with Sculley.
- **June 1993:** Sculley forced out and replaced by Michael Spindler.
- **October 1995:** Apple profits drop by 48% amid problems that include shrinking market share and inability to meet demand.
- **January 1996:** Apple posts $69 million loss in December quarter, lays off 1,300 workers.
- **February 1996:** Spindler is forced out in favor of Gilbert Amelio, a board member and then-CEO of National Semiconductor.
- **December 1996:** Apple buys Jobs's NeXT Software Inc. for $400 million, and Jobs returns as adviser to the company.
- **January 1997:** Apple's turnaround falters. After profit in September quarter, it posts $120 million loss for December period.
- **July 1997:** Amelio ousted in an overhaul that expands Jobs's role in running the company.

Source: *WSJ* (July 11, 1997), p. B1.

ucts depended on market acceptance, the availability of application software for new products, and the ability of the company to manage inventory levels in line with anticipated demand. Although the number of new introductions might decrease as a result of restructuring, the risks and uncertainties associated with new introductions might increase as Apple refocuses its offerings on key growth segments.

The rate of shipments immediately following the introduction of a new product was not necessarily an indication of the future rate of shipments for the product. The initial large purchases by a small segment of the user population that tended to purchase new technology prior to its acceptance by the majority of users tended to drive up early shipments. In the past, Apple experienced difficulty in anticipating demand for new products, resulting in shortages, which adversely affected its operating results.

Apple hinted that in November 1997 it could unveil three super-fast Macintosh computers that would be built to order. The three computers would use the new G3 microprocessor, which ran complex software applications such as graphic design programs faster than previous models. Apple also planned to introduce two desktop computers, priced at $1,999 to $2,999, as well as a fast notebook computer called the PowerBook G3 at about $5,700. The G3 processor would be available in two models, running at 233 megahertz and 266 megahertz.

Additionally Apple announced plans for two operating systems. It planned to introduce major upgrades to the current MacOS and later, a new operating system (code

Exhibit 8   New Board of Directors: Apple Computer, Inc.

Director		Joined Board
Steven P. Jobs	(Interim) CEO, Apple Computer	1997
Fred D. Anderson	Executive VP, Apple Computer	1997
Gareth C. C. Chang	Senior VP, Hughes Electronics	1996
William V. Campbell	CEO, Intuit Corp.	1997
Lawrence Ellison	CEO, Oracle Corp.	1997
Jerome B. York	Chairman, Tracinda Corp.	1997
Edgar S. Woolard, Jr.	Former CEO, DuPont	1996

Source: Apple Computer, Inc., *1997 Form 10-K,* p. 25. (Data: Company reports)

named "Rhapsody"), which was expected to offer advanced functionality based on Apple and NeXT software technologies. Apple expected Rhapsody to complement MacOS in the company's overall operating system strategy. MacOS would move forward as Apple's volume operating system, delivering market leading ease-of-use, multimedia and Internet integration, whereas Rhapsody initially would be targeted at server and high-end desktop applications. Rhapsody aimed to integrate MacOS ease of use and functionality with the market-leading technologies pioneered by NeXT Software in OPENSTEP. However, the NeXT software technologies that Apple planned to use in the development of Rhapsody were not originally designed to be compatible with the MacOS. As a result, there could be no assurance that the development of Rhapsody could be completed at reasonable cost or at all. Rhapsody might not be fully backward compatible with all existing applications, which would result in a loss of existing customers. Finally, it was uncertain whether Rhapsody or the planned enhancements to the current MacOS would gain developer support and market acceptance.

COMPETITION[31]

Apple Computer, Inc. was the primary maker of hardware that used the Mac Operating System. The MacOS had a minority market share in the personal computer market, which was dominated by makers of computers that run on Microsoft Windows 95 and Windows NT operating systems (Wintel). (See Exhibits 10 and 11.) [32, 33] Apple believed that the MacOS, with its perceived advantages over Windows, and the general reluctance of the Macintosh installed user base to incur the costs of switching platforms had been the driving forces behind sales of Apple's personal computer hardware for the past several years. Recent innovations in the Windows platform, including those in Windows 95, Windows NT, and Windows 98, had added features to the Windows platform that made the differences between the MacOS and Microsoft's operating systems less significant.

To meet competition from Windows and other platforms, Apple had previously devoted substantial resources toward developing personal computer products capable of running application software designed for the Windows operating systems. These products included an add-on card containing a Pentium or 586-class microprocessor that enabled users to run applications concurrently that required the MacOS, Windows 3.1, or Windows 95 operating systems. Apple planned to outsource the cross-platform business in 1998.

Exhibit 9 **Apple Struggles to Take Back Mac Market**
(Share of U.S. Market for Macintosh Systems; Quarterly Data)

	1996			1997	
	Q2	Q3	Q4	Q1	Q2
Apple Computer	90.62%	88.30%	75.37%	71.15%	80.98%
Power Computing	7.05	8.23	10.31	12.20	9.73
Motorola	—	—	8.23	9.34	5.10
UMAX	2.33	3.47	6.09	7.31	4.18

Source: Dataquest Inc., *WSJ* (September 3, 1997), p. 3.

Several Apple competitors had either targeted or announced their intention to target certain of Apple's key market segments, including education and publishing. (See Exhibit 12.)[34] Many of these companies had greater financial, marketing, manufacturing, and technological resources than Apple.

COMPUTER AND PERIPHERALS INDUSTRY

The computer and peripherals industry as a group was expected to do well in 1998 with a few exceptions. At the low end of the market, sales of personal computers had been boosted by the introduction of machines selling for under $1,000. The $1,000 price appeared to have brought out consumers who previously had been put off by higher prices. This augured well for the Christmas season when many consumers do their computer shopping. But the always competitive PC business was likely to become more so. The major PC manufacturers were moving to a build-to-order model, which reduced costs and further narrowed the range of prices between top-tier and bottom-tier vendors, putting pressure on the smaller companies. The large operators, such as Compaq, Dell, Hewlett-Packard, and IBM promised to gain market share at the expense of the smaller companies.

In the mid-range, the ever more powerful PCs were putting pressure on low-end workstations. However, high-end workstations still provided power that PC-based machines could not match. Likewise, servers that acted as the hubs for networks of personal computers and workstations were selling extremely well. Here, too, machines based on Intel processors running Microsoft's Windows NT operating system were making inroads on the other operating systems.

At the high end, mainframes were making a strong comeback. New studies found that the big machines often were actually less expensive to operate than were networks of servers and personal computers. Sales were also being spurred by a new generation of mainframes that were less expensive to manufacture and operate than older models.[35]

Compaq Computer

Compaq Computer Corporation produced laptop and desktop personal computers that were IBM compatible. The company was a leading player in the market for portable computers and PC servers and has a leading share of the IBM-compatible desktop market. Compaq sold its products through mail order and over 38,000 outlets worldwide. Foreign business accounted for 47% of their total sales.

Exhibit 10   Worldwide Server Operating Systems Market Share

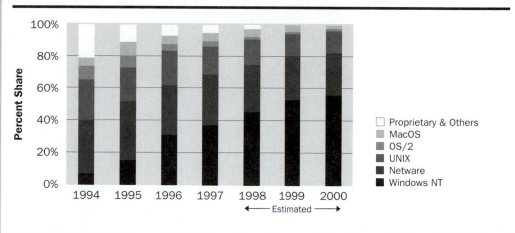

Source: Dataquest Inc., 1996, Technology Forecast: 1997, Price Waterhouse, p. 165.

Compaq recently forecasted that they would have over $50 billion in sales by the year 2000. Moreover, this goal did not take into account Compaq's merger with Tandem Computer Corp., a maker of mainframe computers with annual sales of $2 billion. This forecast was based on Compaq's average annual unit sales growth already at two to three times the 20% rate for the PC industry as a whole. In the third (July–September) quarter of 1997, Compaq's sales volumes rose 54% over the previous year. The surge was due to a good demand environment stimulated by lower prices as corporations continued to shift toward networking and the Internet and consumers were attracted to the sub-$1,000 desktops Compaq had begun to offer. Compaq's adoption of build-to-order manufacturing lowered costs, enabling it to sell at competitive prices without hurting profit margins.

In the U.S. market, Compaq was easily taking market share from second-tier PC makers, but not from major players like Dell and Hewlett-Packard. These companies tended to meet or beat Compaq's pricing moves. There was some fear that Compaq's sales spurt would not last long, given market saturation. In the overseas market, Compaq continued to face domestic rivals and local manufacturers that were favored by the local populaces. Still Compaq's operating profit margins were expected to continue to grow, despite competitive pricing and increases in sales, service, and support personnel. This growth was due to improving sales mix, with servers and workstations accounting for a rising proportion of revenues.[36]

Dell Computer

Dell Computer Corp. made notebook and desktop computers, servers, and workstations compatible with IBM. They sold their products to corporations, government, and education customers via sales teams; they marketed to individuals and smaller institutional buyers through direct marketing. Dell provided on-site service through BancTec service and Digital Equipment Corporation. Foreign sales accounted for 32% of their total sales.

In 1997, Dell's revenues grew 67% over 1996 as compared to the industry-wide annualized average gains of 20%. Their top-of-the-line product was benefiting from the growing tendency of both corporations and consumers toward purchasing from direct suppliers. Certainly, it helped that Dell's PC products, desktops, laptops, and serv-

Exhibit 11   **Worldwide Server Operating Systems Unit Sales**

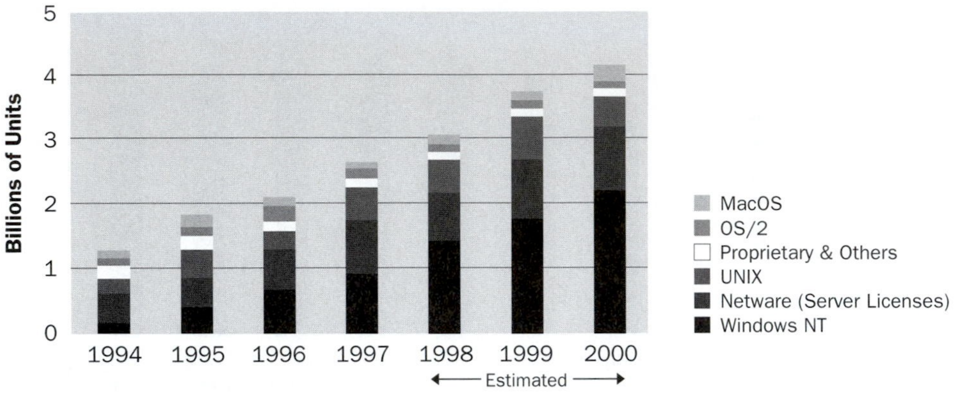

Source: Dataquest Inc., 1996, Technology Forecast, 1997, Price Waterhouse, p. 165.

ers were competitively priced and had a reputation for quality. Dell was the number three PC maker in both the United States and worldwide in unit shipments in 1997. It grabbed the top spot among PC desktop suppliers to medium and large U.S. corporations. Compaq held the top slot for total PC sales to that market. Adding to Dell's revenues was its push into value-added services, such as asset management and leasing and the use of the Internet for direct sales. Dell gained an increasing number of consumers who wanted to trade up their PCs but no longer required retail hand-holding.

The built-to-order model of Dell proved to be very beneficial. Its biggest advantage was that it resulted in a relatively small finished goods inventory. This allowed Dell to expand into next-generation products faster than rivals selling through third parties. The low inventory level also enabled Dell to incorporate declining components' costs and pass some of the savings to customers more quickly than rivals, a positive for both margins and market share. Recently, other PC makers have adopted build-to-order models. To hold its own, Dell had been investing more in marketing and support services, and these added costs so far had been offset by an improving sales mix.[37]

Hewlett-Packard

Hewlett-Packard Company was a designer and manufacturer of precision electronic products and systems for measurement and computation. Its major product categories were: measurement, design, information, and manufacturing equipment; peripherals and network products and instrumentation. In 1997, Hewlett-Packard foreign sales accounted for 56% of its total sales.

H-P continued to roll out new products. In July 1997, it released color copiers based on ink jet technology that were less expensive than laser copiers. A month later, it announced a machine that combined a color printer, copier, fax, and scanner. In September, it unveiled a line of very powerful Intel processor-based workstations, as well as new UNIX workstations and two new families of UNIX-based servers. In the fall, the company planned to revamp its Pavilion family of home computers, including an entry in the

Exhibit 12   Making Art and Teaching Johnny
Despite Apple's mere 4% overall market share, the Mac still rules among loyal graphics pros and teachers.

Mac Market Share of U.S. Graphics Software Sales, 1997		Top PC Vendors in U.S. Education Market, First Quarter, 1997	
Desktop Publishing Software	62.4%	Apple	29.6%
		Dell	9.6%
		Compaq	9.1%
Presentation Software	51.6%	IBM	7.3%
		Gateway 2000	6.6%
Drawing and Painting Software	43.9%		

Source: Steven Terry, "Big Brother?" *Newsweek* (August 18, 1997), p. 27.

fast-growing under-$1,000 market. It also planned to introduce new portables aimed to increase its share of that rapidly expanding market. The company announced a plan to speed its personal computers to market and to trim inventories; it would ship parts to selected resellers who would do the final assembly and distribution of the machines. H-P was also moving into new fields. It had a line of digital cameras and printers aimed at the home photographer.[38]

International Business Machines

IBM Corporation was the world's largest supplier of advance information processing technology and communication systems. In 1996, the revenue breakdown for IBM was 48% sales; 17% software; 9% maintenance; 21% services; and 5% rentals and financing. Foreign sales accounted for 48% of its total sales. Fiscal 1997 was IBM's best year ever. Demand was good for the company's new System 390 mainframes, given the more powerful versions of the machine that were now available. Sales of IBM's commercial personal computers and PC-based servers also were strong, and the semiconductor business improved. A new family of machines that was introduced in September 1997 boosted the PC-server business further. The company's services business, paced by strong demand for IBM's outsourcing and systems integration services, soared.

At the high end of the market, mainframes continued to be in demand because companies were moving to consolidate data centers and to save money and improve management control. Sales were expected to grow as IBM rolled out new, more powerful versions of its mainframes based on new technology, which were less expensive to manufacture and maintain. The new families of RS/6000 and AS/400 servers also continued to generate better sales. IBM aimed to be one of the leaders in the field of electronic business. It was well positioned because of its knowledge of customers' businesses and its extensive experience with worldwide networks, which were a plus for services and hardware sales.[39]

Gateway 2000

Gateway 2000, Inc., manufactured, marketed and supported a product line of IBM-compatible desktop, notebook, and subnotebook personal computers. It marketed directly to businesses, individuals, government agencies, and educational institutions. Foreign sales accounted for only 15.7% of the total in fiscal 1996.

Gateway had two quarters of falling earnings. Management blamed the shortfall on the added SG&A costs meant to support optimistic forecasts of corporate sales that had yet to materialize, as well as on sharp price cuts due to an excess of older inventory. With a slowdown in its traditional consumer and small business markets, Gateway was attempting to add a greater amount of high-growth corporate business to its product mix, though this would put it in direct competition with entrenched industry leaders IBM, Dell, and Compaq.

Several problems presented near-term obstacles to rapid corporate sales. First, Gateway had yet to build a first-rate major account sales force. This disadvantage would not likely be overcome for at least several quarters and possibly longer. Furthermore the company's brand recognition, although strong in consumer markets, was weaker with corporate procurement organizations. Last, and of more importance to corporate decision makers, was the company's lack of its own on-site service and support organization, though in some areas it partnered with established third-party service companies.[40]

OTHER COMPETITORS[41]

Apple did not simply compete in the computer and peripherals industry but was substantially affected by the competition in the computer software and services industry and to a lesser extent by that in the semiconductor industry. Decisions by customers to purchase Apple's personal computers, as opposed to Windows-based systems, were often based on the availability of third-party software for particular applications. Apple believed that the availability of third-party application software for Apple's hardware products depended in part on third-party developers' perception and analysis of the relative benefits of developing Apple software products versus software for the larger Windows market. The recent financial losses and declining licensing program caused software developers to question Apple's prospects in the personal computer market. Moreover, Apple's plan to introduce a new operating system (code named "Rhapsody") might cause software developers to stop developing software for the current MacOS.

Microsoft was an important developer of application software for Apple's products. Although Apple had entered into a relationship with Microsoft, which included Microsoft's agreement to develop and ship future versions of its Microsoft Office and Internet Explorer products and certain other Microsoft tools for the MacOS, the relationship was for a limited term and did not cover many areas in which Apple directly competed with Microsoft.

COMPUTER SOFTWARE AND SERVICES

The industry had been growing at a rapid pace and was expected to continue to grow for the foreseeable future. The personal computer market, which had shown some signs of slowing growth, had taken off, spurred by demand for machines selling for less than

$1,000. That growth spurt would boost demand for operating systems, applications, and games to use on the new machines. This was very good for companies such as Microsoft and Intuit. Many of those newly purchased computers would undoubtedly be used to access the Internet, which would lead to more sales of Microsoft's browser and server software.

Some companies in this industry depended a great deal on overseas markets. As a whole, foreign sales accounted for nearly a third of software companies' revenues and a similar percentage of their profits. The turmoil in some of the previously very fast-growing areas of Asia seemed sure to slow growth and, consequently, demand for computer hardware and software.

The corporate market was growing rapidly. Companies were moving to tie together their computing resources so that users could share data and gear. As businesses grappled with the problems of converting their systems to correctly recognize dates after 1999, they were upgrading applications and turning to the providers of outsourcing services to help them. A shortage of programmers and application developers could be a problem for this industry group, but it was more likely to lead to additional demand for outsourcing services and prepackaged applications.[42]

Microsoft

Microsoft Corp. was the largest independent maker of software. Over half of Microsoft's 1997 revenues, 53%, were derived from sales of operating systems and server applications, Internet products, and non-PC software. The remaining 47% of revenues were derived from sales of productivity programs, PC input devices, and interactive entertainment and information products. Non-U.S. sales represented 40% of total sales and pretax profits in 1997.

Microsoft's September 1997 quarter was very good. There was strong demand across the product line, with notable strength in the overseas markets and in demand for Microsoft's Office 97 suite of applications and the Windows 95 and Windows NT Workstation operating systems. New versions of Windows and Windows NT were expected to lift sales and earnings starting in fiscal 1999. Microsoft also was moving into new areas, such as cable television, aiming to speed up the move to use cable to connect homes with the Internet.

Microsoft had most of the computer industry under its control, but that could change if the technology shifted. Most new PCs came with Microsoft software the computer buyers got as part of the basic purchase price but for which computer makers pay a considerable fee to Microsoft. If a purchaser wanted to use Intuit's Quicken instead of Money or Netscape's Navigator instead of Explorer, they had to pay additional money.[43]

Microsoft's stranglehold could loosen quickly if web browsers evolved into substitutes for computer operating systems, as some analysts predicted. That's why Microsoft got so upset when Netscape and the Internet suddenly exploded on the scene a few years ago. Netscape's goal was to establish browser dominance and use it to build an empire in the same way that Microsoft used its dominance of operating systems to create the colossus it became.[44]

Microsoft had problems from other sources. In October, the U.S. Justice Department filed a complaint claiming that Microsoft's bundling of its Internet browser, Explorer, with Windows 95 violated the company's 1995 consent decree with the Department. Microsoft contended that the agreement gave it the right to add new features to Windows and that the Department knew that it intended to bundle the browser. Sun Microsystems sued, claiming that Microsoft was attempting to disrupt the development of

Sun's programming language, Java, as an industry standard. Microsoft counter-sued, alleging breach of contract and unfair competition. A number of states initiated antitrust action against Microsoft. Obviously there was no way to determine the outcome of these actions, but Microsoft believed that the matters would not have a material adverse impact on its financial condition.[45]

Netscape Communications

Netscape Communications was a provider of a comprehensive line of Internet client and server applications software and applications development software tools designed to enhance online communications for individual users and organizations. Non-U.S. sales represented 30% of Netscape's total sales.

Netscape may be the primary beneficiary of the Justice Department's antitrust action against Microsoft. Many believed that Microsoft's actions reflected its fear that Netscape might gain control of the desktop market and its browser would evolve into an alternative platform to Windows.

Netscape's income in 1997 increased 53% over 1996; however, the revenue mix shift caused some consternation. Significant increases in advertising revenue accounted for much of the gain, while software license revenues were up only 8% and server licenses, the company's lifeblood, only up 9%.

Netscape was moving from a product-oriented sales approach to a solutions selling approach. Targeting large, enterprise-wide sales required a solutions selling approach. This required staff consultants to help design and deploy complex Internet-driven intranets and extranets. This was expected to be one of Netscape's new directions for the year. Netscape anticipated consulting to account for 15% of its total revenues by the end of 1998.[46]

SEMICONDUCTOR INDUSTRY

Until recently, Intel's almost total domination of the personal computer market for microprocessors enabled the industry giant to base its pricing policies on supply and demand factors. Recently it had to acknowledge the rising competitive threat to market shares from rivals. Despite the emergence of serious competition, producing microprocessors for PCs was still a highly profitable business.[47] (See Exhibit 13.)[48]

Intel

Intel Corporation was a leading manufacturer of integrated circuits. Its main products were microprocessors, most notably the Pentium series, microcontrollers, and memory chips. Foreign sales made up about 58% of total sales.

Intel's primary strategy had been, and continued to be, to introduce ever-higher performance microprocessors. To implement this strategy, the company planned to cultivate new businesses and continue to work with the software industry to develop compelling applications that could take advantage of this higher performance, thus driving demand toward the newer products. In line with this strategy, the company announced that the first member of its new family of 64-bit microprocessors, code-named "Merced," was scheduled for production in 1999.[49]

Intel could not control all aspects of the market it dominated. The Federal Trade Commission wanted to make sure of that by looking into Intel's agreement to acquire

Exhibit 13   Semiconductor Revenues

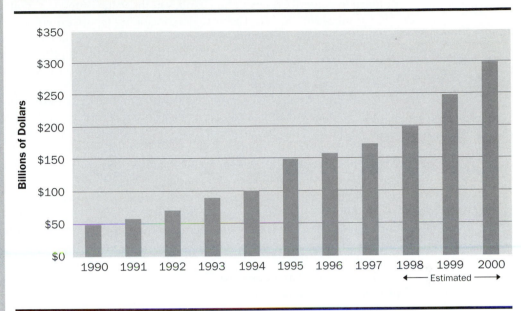

Source: Dataquest, 1996, Technology Forecast, Price Waterhouse, p. 50.

other companies. New competition in the market for microprocessors forced Intel to lower Pentium prices more aggressively than it would have liked. In line with the company's strategy to introduce ever-higher performance microprocessors, Intel introduced the PentiumPro processor with MMX media enhancement technology, followed by the PentiumII.

Motorola

Motorola, Inc., was a leading manufacturer of electronic equipment and components, with semiconductors representing 26% of its total sales. Foreign sales represented 60% of Motorola total sales. Profitability improved in 1997 on semiconductors as compared to a year earlier.[50]

Semiconductor sales were up 3% in 1997 to 2.0 billion, and orders rose 36% from 1996. The semiconductor segment, however, continued to report an operating loss. However, excluding the impact of charges related to phasing out participation in the dynamic random access memory (DRAM) market, operating profits would have been positive. Orders increased significantly in the Asia-Pacific region, Europe, and the Americas, and were higher in Japan. The semiconductor segment of Motorola planned to reallocate resources from the DRAM technology to other technologies, including proprietary fast static random access memories (FSRAM) and integrated memories such as flash and electronically erasable programmable read-only memory (EEPROM).[51]

GLOBAL MARKET RISKS[52]

A large portion of Apple's revenue was derived from its international operations. As a result, the consolidated operations and financial results could have been significantly affected by risks associated with international activities, including economic conditions, political instability, tax laws, and changes in the value of the U.S. dollar.

Countries in the Asia-Pacific region, including Japan, experienced weakness in their currency, banking, and equity markets in 1997. These weaknesses could have adversely affected consumer demand for Apple's products and the supply of product components. Overall, Apple was a net receiver of currencies other than the U.S. dollar and, as such, benefited from a weaker dollar.

Although Apple was exposed to fluctuations in the interest rates of many of the world's leading industrialized countries, its interest income and expense was most sensitive to fluctuations in the general level of U.S. interest rates. To mitigate the impact of fluctuations in U.S. interest rates, the company has entered into interest rate swaps. Apple, however, did not engage in leveraged hedging. Apple's current financial condition might increase the costs of its hedging transactions, as well as affect the nature of the hedging transactions into which others were willing to enter.

To reduce some market risk, Apple Computer International Ltd. and Zi Corporation announced a joint development memorandum of understanding for future collaboration on Chinese-language products for the MacOS and Apple's next-generation operating system, Rhapsody. Under the memorandum, Apple was to assist Zi to develop and market Chinese-language products in the following areas: Internet and intranet; word processing, education, and document processing and publishing.[53]

INVENTORY AND SUPPLY [54]

Apple made an accounting provision for inventories of products that had become obsolete or were in excess of anticipated demand. The company had to order components for its products and build inventory well in advance of product shipments. Because markets were volatile and subject to rapid technology and price changes, there was a risk that the company would forecast incorrectly and produce excess or insufficient inventories of particular products. Apple's consolidated operating results and financial condition had been in the past and could in the future be materially adversely affected by its ability to manage inventory levels and respond to short-term shifts in customer demand.

Third-party manufacturers produced some of Apple's products. As part of its restructuring, Apple sold its Fountain, Colorado, manufacturing facility to SCI and entered into an outsourcing agreement. It also sold its Singapore printed circuit board manufacturing assets to NatSteel Electronics, which was expected to supply Apple its main logic boards. As a result of these actions, the proportion of Apple's products produced and distributed under outsourcing arrangements had increased greatly. Even though some products were produced elsewhere, Apple remained at least initially responsible to the ultimate consumer for warranty service and, in event of product defects, may remain primarily liable.

Apple's ability to produce and market competitive products also depended on the ability and desire of IBM and Motorola, the sole suppliers of the PowerPC RISC microprocessor, for its Macintosh computers. These companies must continue to supply adequate numbers of microprocessors that produce superior price and performance results compared with those supplied to competitors by Intel Corporation. The desire of IBM and Motorola to continue producing these microprocessors might be influenced by Microsoft's decision not to adapt its Windows NT operating system software to run on the PowerPC microprocessor. IBM produced personal computers based on Intel microprocessors as well as workstations based on the PowerPC microprocessor, and it was also the developer of OS/2, a competing operating system to Apple's MacOS. Motorola recently announced its intention to stop producing Mac clones. As a result, Motorola may be less inclined to continue to produce PowerPC microprocessors.

Apple's current financial condition and uncertainties related to recent events could affect the terms on which suppliers are willing to supply their products. There can be no assurance that the current suppliers will continue to supply the company on terms acceptable to it or that Apple will be able to obtain comparable products from alternative sources.

MARKETING AND DISTRIBUTION

Currently Apple distributed its products through wholesalers, resellers, mass merchants, and cataloguers and directly to educational institutions. In addition, Apple planned in November 1997 to begin selling many of its products directly to end users in the United States through an online store. Many of Apple's significant resellers operated on narrow product margins. Most such resellers also distributed products from competing manufacturers.[55]

Apple announced a new U.S. production distribution strategy that would reduce channel inventory, increase Apple advocacy, and streamline channel operations. The company would leverage long-standing relationships with Ingram Micro Inc. and Micro-Age, Inc., to more effectively manage inventory and secure products to resellers and therefore customers faster than ever before. "We're working with distributors who have made a sizable investment and commitment to Apple and are focused on helping us to get our products into the channel faster," said Mitch Mandich, Senior Vice-President of the Americas. "Ingram Micro and MicroAge are both increasing the number of resources they dedicate to Apple and improving their advocacy of our products." This move was good news for the channel. "As Apple's largest distributor in the world and long-time authorized distributor, we have always supported Apple and their customers, and will continue to do so," said Jeff Rodek, Worldwide President and CEO of Ingram Micro.[56]

Uncertainty over demand for Apple's products may continue to cause resellers to reduce their ordering and marketing of the products. In addition, Apple experienced delays in ordering by resellers in light of uncertain demand. Under the arrangements with resellers, resellers had the option to reduce or eliminate unfilled orders previously placed. Apple recently revised its channel program, including decreasing the number of resellers and reducing returns, price protection, and certain rebate programs, in an effort to reduce channel inventory, increase inventory turns, increase product support within the channel, and improve gross margins.

LITIGATION[57]

In January 1996, a shareholder class action suit was filed naming Apple and its then-directors as defendants. The complaint sought injunctive relief and damages for alleged acts of mismanagement resulting in a depressed stock price. This suit was later amended to add a former director as a defendant and to add purported claims based on breach of fiduciary duty, misrepresentation, and insider trading.

In March 1996, a second suit was filed alleging that the defendants, the Board of Directors of Apple, had breached their fiduciary duty by allegedly rejecting an offer from a computer company to acquire the company at a price in excess of $50 per share. This suit has also been amended to add Apple Corp. as a defendant.

Apple was named in approximately 60 lawsuits, alleging that plaintiffs incurred so-called "repetitive stress" injuries to their upper extremities as a result of using keyboards and mouse input devices sold by the company. These actions were similar to those filed against other major suppliers of personal computers. In October 1996, Apple prevailed in the first full trial to go to verdict. Since then, approximately ten lawsuits were dismissed and two others were dismissed by court order.

In *Exponential Technology* v. *Apple* the plaintiff alleged that Apple, which was an investor in Exponential, breached its fiduciary duty by misusing confidential information about Exponential's financial situation to cause them to fail. The suit also alleged that Apple fraudulently misrepresented the facts about allowing Exponential to sell its processors to the company's MacOS licensees.

FINANCIALS

Net sales decreased 28% in 1997 as compared to 1996. Revenues were $7.1 billion, with a net loss for the year of $1.0 billion, or $(8.29) per share. Total Macintosh computer unit sales and peripheral unit sales decreased 27% and 28%, respectively, as a result of a decline in worldwide demand for most of the company's products. (See Exhibits 14,[58] 15,[59] and 16.[60]) Apple believes that this was due principally to continued customer concerns regarding the company's strategic direction, financial condition, and future prospects, and the viability of the Macintosh platform.

The 1997 Annual Report and Form 10-K were not released until 90 days after closing or some time in late December 1997. There should be no material difference between the unaudited results and the audited numbers reported later. The quarterly returns traditionally do not provide a cash flow statement. However, the unaudited numbers showed no short-term cash flow problems in 1997. There were no short-term cash flow problems prior to the cash infusion from Microsoft in August 1997.

International net sales represented 50% of total net sales in 1997 compared with 52% of net sales in 1996. International net sales declined 30% in 1997 compared with 1996. Net sales in European markets and Japan decreased during 1997 as a result of decreases in Macintosh computer and peripheral unit sales and the average aggregate revenue per Macintosh unit in Japan.[61]

Domestic net sales declined 26% during 1997 due to decreases in unit sales of Macintosh computers and peripheral products and in the average aggregate revenue per peripheral unit. Apple's estimated share of the worldwide and U.S. personal computer markets declined to 3.8% from 5.7% and 4.5% from 7.4%, respectively. (See Exhibits 17[62] and 18.[63]) The most troubling aspect of the results was the sales weakness. "It is very bad," said Michael Kwatinetz, managing director of DMG Technology Group in New York. "They've got to stabilize the sales line, or else it doesn't matter what they do."[64]

FUTURE

Apple insiders, former employees, and suppliers were talking about the big changes Steve Jobs was planning. He apparently planned to recast Apple from industry has-been

Exhibit 14   **Two Years of Woe for Apple and Its Shareholders**

Things were bad under Michael Spindler, the CEO who left in February 1996. Under Gil Amelio, the situation has deteriorated. Despite a blip of profitability in the fourth quarter of fiscal 1996, Apple is, on the whole, a money-losing venture whose sales are tanking while the share price falls toward an all-time low.

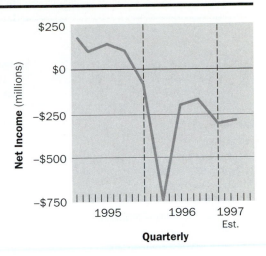

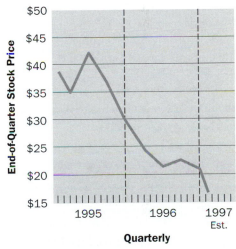

Source: (See footnote 58.)

to a highflier like Dell Computer Corp. Apple may take the first step when it launches a line of blazingly fast Macintoshes that not only should rival the fastest PCs but also would be the first Macs that Apple sells directly to consumers over the phone and the Internet.

Apple was expected to take a quantum leap forward in adopting Dell's direct-sales approach to building these speedy new Macs to match orders as they were placed. This build-to-order strategy has been a huge success for Dell.

Even that may just be a warm-up. In the future, Jobs had an even bigger event planned. Rather than build a future solely around Apple's 13-year old Macintosh computer, Jobs concentrated on the nascent market for so-called network computers. These computers called NCs were diskless machines that would sell for around $500 and run applications dispatched by big computer servers. Engineers worked overtime on a sleek new design for a MacNC scheduled for release in early 1998.

Exhibit 15   Consolidated Statements of Operations: Apple Computer, Inc.
(Dollar amounts in millions, except per-share data)

	Three Months Ending		Twelve Months Ending	
	September 26, 1997 (Unaudited)	September 27, 1996 (Unaudited)	September 26, 1997	September 27, 1996
Net sales	$ 1,614	$ 2,321	$ 7,081	$ 9,833
Costs and expenses				
Cost of sales	1,294	1,810	5,713	8,865
Research and development	94	146	485	604
Selling, general and administrative	259	359	1,286	1,568
Special charges				
In-process research and development	—	—	375	—
Restructuring costs	62	(28)	217	179
Termination of license agreement	75	—	75	—
	1,784	2,287	8,151	11,216
Operating income (loss)	(170)	34	(1,070)	(1,383)
Interest and other income (expense), net	9	6	25	88
Income (loss) before provisions for income taxes	(161)	40	(1,045)	(1,295)
Provisions for income taxes	—	15	—	(479)
Net income (loss)	$ (161)	$ 25	$ (1,045)	$ (816)
Earnings (loss) per common and common equivalent share	$ (1.26)	$ 0.20	$ (8.29)	$ (6.59)
Cash dividends paid per common share	$ —	$ —	$ —	$ 0.12
Common and common equivalent shares used in the calculations of earnings (loss) per share (in thousands)	127,607	124,819	126,062	123,734

By January 1998, at the annual MacWorld trade show, Jobs planned to be ready to unveil his key to the future: Apple's first network computer, expected to be priced initially from $700 to $900. This effort was more like a halfway step because the MacNC still would run Apple's operating software. That way, customers could use their existing Mac applications as well as slimmed-down applets based on the Java programming language. But if NCs took off, Apple could move to a pure NC, which would have very little resident software but would download applications and data off the network. That could allow Apple to cut back on some of the more than $200 million it spent on operating-system software and focus instead on exploiting its brand and loyal-customer base in the education and publishing markets.[65]

Insiders said Jobs and Oracle Corp. CEO Lawrence J. Ellison, a close friend whom Jobs named to Apple's board in August 1997, were talking about how Apple and Oracle might work together. One possibility was an investment from Oracle to help fund the development of Apple network computers that would run Oracle software. This plan was bold and a far cry from the go-slow approach of Apple's former CEOs Amelio and Spindler. But it begged the question that had been bandied about Silicon Valley for half a year: Is Jobs going to stop playing at CEO and actually take the job? Or if he did step down as Acting CEO, would he stay around and look over the shoulder of the new CEO?[66]

Some analysts hoped for a quick rebound in corporate profits. Jobs had captured the

Exhibit 16 **Consolidated Balance Sheets: Apple Computer, Inc.**
(Dollar amounts in millions, except per-share data)

	September 26, 1997	September 27, 1996
Assets		
Current assets		
Cash and cash equivalents	$1,230	$1,552
Short-term investments	229	193
Accounts receivable, net of allowance for doubtful accounts of $99 ($91 in 1996)	1,035	1,496
Inventories		
Purchased parts	141	213
Work in progress	15	43
Finished goods	281	406
	437	662
Deferred tax assets	259	342
Other current assets	234	270
Total current assets	3,424	4,515
Property, plant, and equipment		
Land and buildings	453	480
Machinery and equipment	460	544
Office furniture and equipment	110	136
Leasehold improvements	172	188
	1,195	1,348
Accumulated depreciation and amortization	(709)	(750)
Net property, plant, and equipment	486	598
Other assets	323	251
Total assets	$4,233	$5,364
Liabilities and Shareholders' Equity		
Current liabilities		
Notes payable to banks	$ 25	$ 186
Accounts payable	685	791
Accrued compensation and employee benefits	99	120
Accrued marketing and distribution	278	257
Accrued warranty and related	128	181
Accrued restructuring costs	180	117
Other current liabilities	423	351
Total current liabilities	1,818	2,003
Long-term debt	951	949
Deferred tax liabilities	264	354
Shareholders' equity		
Series A non-voting convertible preferred stock, no par value; 150,000 shares issued and outstanding	150	—
Common stock, no par value; 320,000,000 shares authorized; 127,949,220 shares issued and outstanding in 1997 (124,496,972 shares in 1996)	498	439
Retained earnings	589	1,634
Other	(37)	(15)
Total shareholders' equity	1,200	2,058
Total liabilities and shareholders' equity	$4,233	$5,364

Exhibit 17   **Apple's Slice of the PC Market**

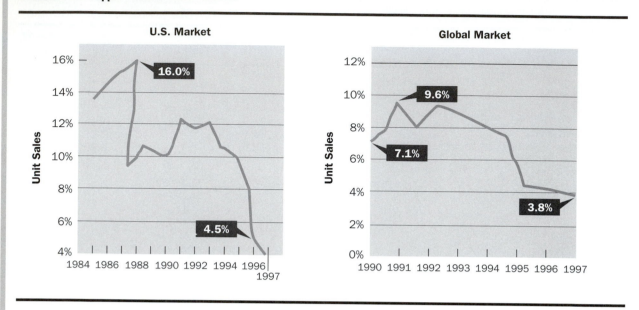

*Note: 1997 figures are second quarter (preliminary).

Source: International Data Corp., *U.S. News & World Report* (August 18 & 25, 1997), p. 20.

Exhibit 18   **Apple's Smaller Piece of a Shrinking Pie**

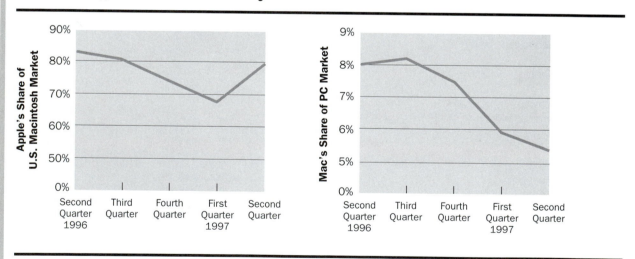

Source: *Business Week* (September 1, 1997).

Exhibit 19   **Apple: Up, Down, Up, Breakeven?**

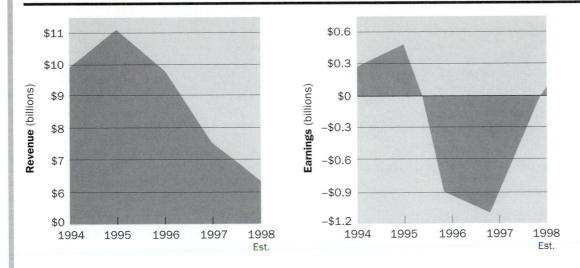

Source: *Business Week* (November 17, 1997), p. 146.

(Data Company reports, estimates by Deutsche Morgan Grenfell)

support of Apple's most important cast: its engineers. Staffers said Jobs was at last proposing a game plan that might pull Apple out of its downward spiral. Deutsche Morgan Grenfell, a European investment banking firm, estimated a continued drop in total revenues in the short term for Apple but a return to profitability in fiscal year 1998. (See Exhibit 19.) [67]

Notes

1. Apple Computer Inc., Fourth Quarter Press Release, October 15, 1997.
2. Jim Carlton, "Apple Posts Smaller-Than-Expected Loss," *Wall Street Journal* (July 17, 1997), p. B8.
3. Peter Burrows, "Is Apple Mincemeat?" *Business Week* (July 28, 1997), p. 32.
4. *Ibid.*
5. Peter Burrows, "How Much for One Apple, Slightly Bruised," *Business Week* (February 12, 1996), p. 35.
6. Burrows, "Is Apple Mincemeat?" p. 32.
7. Peter Burrows, "Dangerous Limbo at Apple," *Business Week* (July 21, 1997), p. 32.
8. Burrows, "Is Apple Mincemeat?" p. 32.
9. Burrows, "Dangerous Limbo at Apple," p. 32.
10. Michael Meyer, "A Death Spiral?" *Newsweek* (August 18, 1997), pp. 48–50.
11. *Ibid.*
12. *Ibid.*
13. *Ibid.*
14. Apple Computer, Inc., *1992 Form 10-K*, p. 6.
15. Apple Computer, Inc., *1997 Form 10-K*, pp. 9–13. The material in this section, Current Situation, was directly abstracted. The verb tense was changed and some material altered.
16. *Wall Street Journal* (January 2, 1998), p. 36.
17. *Ibid.*
18. *Ibid.*
19. Computer and Peripherals Industry, *Value Line* (October 24, 1997), p. 1080.
20. *Wall Street Journal* (July 11, 1997), p. B1.
21. Peter Burrows, "Will Apple Slide into High-tech Irrelevance?" *Business Week* (February 17, 1997), p. 36.
22. Jim Carlton, "Apple's Board Finally Gets Aggresive as DuPont's Woolard Takes Lead Role," *Wall Street Journal* (July 14, 1997), p. B10.
23. Apple Computer, Inc., *1997 Form 10-K*, p. 46.
24. Peter Burrows, "Hell Hath No Fury Like a Cloner Scorned?" *Business Week* (September 1, 1997), pp. 31–32.

25. *Ibid.*

26. Jim Carlton and G. Christian Hill, "Apple Moves to Shut Down Cloners of Mac Line," *Wall Street Journal* (September 3, 1997), p. 3.

27. Burrows, "Hell Hath No Fury," pp. 31–32.

28. *Ibid.*

29. Susan Gregory Thomas, "Why Bill Gates and Steve Jobs Made Up." *U.S. News & World Report* (August 18/August 25, 1997), pp. 19–20.

30. Apple Computer, Inc., *1997 Form 10-K*, pp. 18–19. The material in this section, Production Introductions, was directly abstracted. The verb tense was changed and some material altered.

31. *Ibid.* pp. 19–21. The material in this section, Competition, was directly abstracted. The verb tense was changed and some material altered.

32. Price Waterhouse, Technology Forecast–1997, p. 165.

33. *Ibid.*

34. Steven Levy, "Big Brother?" *Newsweek* (August 18, 1997), p. 27.

35. Computer and Peripherals Industry, *Value Line* (October 24, 1997), p. 1080.

36. Compaq Computer, *Value Line* (October 24, 1997), p. 1089.

37. Dell Computer, *Value Line* (October 24, 1997), p. 1091.

38. Hewlett-Packard, *Value Line* (October 24, 1997), p. 1096.

39. International Business Machines, *Value Line* (October 24, 1997), p. 1099.

40. Gateway 2000, *Value Line* (October 24, 1997), p. 1094.

41. Apple Computer, Inc., *1997 Form 10-K*, pp. 20–21. The material in this section, Other Competitors, was directly abstracted. The verb tense was changed and some material altered.

42. Computer Software & Services, *Value Line* (December 5, 1997), p. 2192.

43. Microsoft, *Value Line* (December 5, 1997), p. 2217.

44. Allan Sloan, "Bill Does What's Good for Bill," *Newsweek* (August 18, 1997), p. 31.

45. Microsoft, *Value Line* (December 5, 1997), p. 2217.

46. Netscape Communications, *Value Line* (December 5, 1997), p. 2219.

47. Semiconductor Industry, *Value Line* (October 24, 1997), p. 1052.

48. Price Waterhouse, Technology Forecast–1997, p. 50.

49. Intel, *Value Line* (October 24, 1997), p. 1060.

50. Motorola, *Value Line* (October 24, 1997), p. 1067.

51. Motorola Inc., Quarterly Report, *Form 10-Q* (July 16, 1997), p. 2.

52. Apple Computer, Inc., *1997 Form 10-K*, pp. 21–22. The material in this section, Global Market Risks, was directly abstracted. The verb tense was changed and edited.

53. Apple Computer, Inc., Press Release, June 6, 1997.

54. Apple Computer, Inc., *1997 Form 10-K*, pp. 22–24. The material in this section, Inventory and Supply, was directly abstracted. The verb tense was changed and edited.

55. Apple Computer, Inc., *1997 Form 10-K*, p. 24. The material in this paragraph, Marketing and Distribution, was directly abstracted. The verb tense was changed and edited.

56. Apple Computer, Inc., Press Release, November 3, 1997.

57. Apple Computer, Inc., *1997 Form 10-K*, pp. 53–55. The material in this section, Litigation, was directly abstracted. The verb tense was changed and edited.

58. Brent Schlender, "Something's Rotten in Cupertino," *Fortune Magazine* (March 3, 1997), p. 104.

59. Apple Computer, Inc., Press Release, "Apple Reports Fourth Fiscal Quarter Results," October 15, 1997.

60. *Ibid.*

61. Apple Computer, Inc., *1997 Form 10-K*, p. 11.

62. *U.S. News & World Report* (August 18 and 25, 1997), p. 20.

63. Burrows, "Hell Hath No Fury," pp. 31–32.

64. Jim Carlton, "Apple's Loss Proves Wider Than Forecast," *Wall Street Journal* (December 16, 1997), p. A3.

65. Peter Burrows, "A Peek at Steve Jobs's Plan," *Business Week* (November 17, 1997), pp. 144–145.

66. *Ibid.*

67. *Business Week* (November 17, 1997), p. 146.

Cisco Systems, Inc. (1998)

Michael I. Eizenberg, Donna M. Gallo, Irene Hagenbuch, and Alan N. Hoffman

COMPANY BACKGROUND

Internet giant Cisco Systems, Inc., had its humble beginnings in 1984 as the brainchild of Leonard Bosack and Sandy Learner, a husband and wife team, both of whom were computer scientists at Stanford University. Together, they had designed a new networking device that made it dramatically easier for computers to communicate data with each other. It was their plan to integrate this technology into local area and wide area networks (LANs and WANs). Their vision was to bring the ideas and technology they had used in developing the campus-wide computer network at Stanford to a broader marketplace.

Cisco's original customers were universities, the aerospace industry, and government agencies. Bosack and Learner hired John P. Morgridge to run their growing company. Morgridge, now Chairman of the Board, established a culture at Cisco that stressed frugality and rapid, ongoing innovation. In 1986, the company shipped its first multiprotocol router; in 1987, revenues reached $1.5 million.

Since 1987, Cisco had pioneered the development of router and switch technology that enabled the development and connectivity of larger and larger computer networks, which in a few short years combined to form the burgeoning World Wide Web of today. Throughout a period of rampant Internet and intranet development, Cisco had remained the market leader and held either number one or number two market share in almost every segment in which it participated. In 1998, Cisco stood at the threshold of a sea of unparalleled opportunities as all forms of communication, whether data, voice, or video, were converging on the Internet as the multimedia superhighway of the future.

Cisco's key to growth was its position as the innovative leader in providing an ever broader and more powerful range of intranet and Internet products, primarily routers, switches, and related services. Expandability was a critical aspect as customers moved from small office networks to huge intranet- and Internet-based network solutions that transmit data as well as voice and full motion video. Potential prospects now saw Cisco Systems as forming the strategic backbone of their enterprises with completely integrated end-to-end solutions capable of expanding as business requirements changed or networking capabilities increased.

This case was prepared by Michael I. Eizenberg, Donna M. Gallo, Irene Hagenbuch, and Professor Alan N. Hoffman of Bentley College. This case was edited for SMBP–7th Edition. Copyright © 1998 Michael I. Eizenberg, Donna M. Gallo, Irene Hagenbuch, and Professor Alan N. Hoffman. Reprinted by permission.

CORPORATE GOVERNANCE

John Chambers, CEO

Within one year of Cisco's going public, Morgridge hired John T. Chambers as Senior Vice-President of Worldwide Operations. Chambers was the son of two physicians and had thoughts of entering the medical field himself, but opted for "running his own business." He held a JD (law degree) as well as BS and BA degrees in business from West Virginia University and an MBA from Indiana University. His career in the computer industry began with IBM in 1977 where he spent six years. Subsequently he worked at Wang Laboratories for eight years. Since 1994, Chambers had been President and CEO of Cisco Systems Inc. He led Cisco through a period of huge expansion in the face of extremely tough competition. His personal and corporate business philosophy remained customer oriented.

Chambers spent as much as 40% of his working hours dealing directly with Cisco's customers. He saw at least two and as many as 12 customers every day. He said, "The two things that get companies into trouble is that they get too far away from their customers and too far away from their employees." Chambers was committed to staying close to customers and employees. His method was simple. Every employee associated with a Cisco account marked an account as critical when it was associated with an upcoming decision that might go against Cisco. Chambers still personally checked out each of the company's critical accounts every day, always with the employee, and often with the company itself.

Exhibit 1 lists other corporate executives. Exhibit 2 provides a biographical sketch of the company's Board of Directors.

John Chambers Goes to China

In September 1998, John Chambers embarked on a five-day tour of Asia that included meetings with Prime Minister Goh Chok Tong of Singapore, Prime Minister Mahathir Mohamad of Malaysia, and Chief Executive Tung Chee Hwa of the Hong Kong SAR. On September 21, 1998, Chambers met with China's President Jiang Zemin at the Diaoyutai State Guesthouse in Beijing, the final stop of his Asian tour.

During the 90-minute meeting, President Jiang and Chambers exchanged views on a broad range of topics, including the development of the China market economy, the importance of IT and education on the future development of China, the impact of networking technology on the globalization of economies, and China's leadership role during the Asian financial crisis.

President Jiang expressed his desire to see more multinational companies such as Cisco Systems cooperate with, and invest in, China. However, he further stressed that although investment in manufacturing is important, even greater synergy would arise from intellectual exchange. To this end, he said the Chinese government would set legislation and policies to create a beneficial environment to facilitate the technology transfer process.

Said Chambers, "Rapid innovations in networking and telecommunications technologies have accelerated the pace of globalization of the emerging Internet Economy. These technological innovations have created unprecedented opportunities for companies in emerging nations such as China to compete globally by leveling the playing field."

He continued, "At a time [1998] when multinational corporations are withdrawing from Asia due to the recent financial crisis, Cisco Systems is taking a long-term view and

Exhibit 1   **Corporate Executives: Cisco Systems, Inc.**

A. Officers	B. Other Senior Vice-Presidents
Larry R. Carter	**Douglas C. Allred**
Senior Vice-President, Finance and Administration	Senior Vice-President, Customer Advocacy
Chief Financial Officer and Secretary	**Barbara Beck**
John T. Chambers	Senior Vice-President, Human Resources
President and Chief Executive Officer	**William Carrico**
Gary J. Daichendt	Senior Vice-President,
Executive Vice-President	Small/Medium Business Line of Business
Worldwide Operations	**Howard S. Charney**
Judith Estrin	Senior Vice-President, Office of the President
Senior Vice-President, Business Development	**Charles H. Giancarlo**
Chief Technology Officer	Senior Vice-President, Global Alliances
Edward R. Kozel	**Richard J. Justice**
Senior Vice-President, Corporate Development	Senior Vice-President, Americas
Donald J. Listwin	**Kevin J. Kennedy**
Executive Vice-President	Senior Vice-President
Service Provider and Consumer Lines of Business	Service Provider Line of Business
Mario Mazzola	**Clifford B. Meltzer**
Senior Vice-President	Senior Vice-President/General Manager
Enterprise Line of Business	IOS Technology and Engineering Operations
Carl Redfield	**James Richardson**
Senior Vice-President	Senior Vice-President, EMEA/AN Operations
Manufacturing and Logistics	**F. Selby Wellman**
	Senior Vice-President/General Manager
	InterWorks Business Unit and RTP Site Executive

Source: Cisco Systems, Inc., *1998 Annual Report.*

increasing our investment in Asia, leveraging our position as the worldwide leader in networking for the Internet and the converging telecommunications market."

Chambers further noted, "As a business leader I would like to express my thanks to President Jiang for his leadership role in the recent Asian financial crisis. I would also like to reaffirm Cisco Systems' long-term commitment to China, with continued investments in the form of technology laboratories, Cisco Networking Academy education program, joint research and development programs, and local manufacturing alliances. Through these investments, we aim to cooperate with the Chinese government in training a new generation of knowledge workers who can take on the challenges of the emerging Internet Economy." In conclusion, President Jiang Zemin wished Cisco continued success in China, and reemphasized his desire to see further cooperation between the Chinese government and Cisco Systems, as part of his government's efforts to strengthen the IT industry and further accelerate the pace of modernization.

Cisco, the largest networking company in China, enjoyed tremendous growth in this market, achieving a year-on-year revenue growth of over 100% for two years. In a 12-month period, Cisco increased its China staff by 500%, and continued to invest heavily in this country.

Exhibit 2   Board of Directors: Cisco Systems, Inc.

Ms. Bartz, 50, has been a member of the Board of Directors since November 1996. She has been Chairman and Chief Executive Officer of Autodesk, Inc., since September 1996. From April 1992 to September 1996 she was Chairman, Chief Executive Officer, and President of Autodesk, Inc. Prior to that, she was with Sun Microsystems from August 1983 to April 1992, most recently as Vice-President of Worldwide Field Operations. Ms. Bartz also currently serves on the Board of Directors of Airtouch Communications, Inc., BEA Systems, Inc., Cadence Design Systems, Inc., and Network Appliance, Inc.

Mr. Chambers, 49, has been a member of the Board of Directors since November 1993. He joined the company as Senior Vice-President in January 1991 and became Executive Vice-President in June 1994. Mr. Chambers became President and Chief Executive Officer of the Company as of January 31, 1995. Prior to his services at Cisco, he was with Wang Laboratories for eight years, most recently as Senior Vice-President of U.S. Operations.

Ms. Cirillo, 51, has been a member of the Board of Directors since February 1998. She has been at Bankers Trust as Executive Vice-President and Managing Director since July 1997. Prior to joining Bankers Trust, she was with Citibank for 20 years, most recently as Senior Vice-President. Ms. Cirillo also currently serves on the Board of Directors of Quest Diagnostics, Inc.

Dr. Gibbons, 67, has been a member of the Board of Directors since May 1992. He is a Professor of Electrical Engineering at Stanford University and also Special Consul to the Stanford President for Industrial Relations. He was Dean of the Stanford University School of Engineering from 1984 to 1996. Dr. Gibbons also currently serves on the Board of Directors of Lockheed Martin Corporation, Centigram Communications Corporation, El Paso Natural Gas Company, and Raychem Corporation.

Mr. Kozel, 43, has been a member of the Board of Directors since November 1996. He joined the Company as Director, Program Management in March 1989. In April 1992, he became Director of Field Operations, and in February 1993, he became Vice-President of Business Development. From January 1996 to April 1998, he was Senior Vice-President and Chief Technical Officer. In April 1998, Mr. Kozel became Senior Vice-President, Corporate Development of the Company. Mr. Kozel currently serves on the Board of Directors of Centigram Communications Corporation.

Mr. Morgan, 60, has been a member of the Board of Directors since February 1998. He has been Chief Executive Officer of Applied Materials, Inc., since 1977 and also Chairman of the Board since 1987. He was President of Applied Materials, Inc., from 1976 to 1987. He was previously a senior partner with West Ven Management, a private venture capital partnership affiliated with Bank of America Corporation.

Mr. Morgridge, 65, joined the Company as President and Chief Executive Officer and was elected to the Board of Directors in October 1988. Mr. Morgridge became Chairman of the Board on January 31, 1995. From 1986 to 1988 he was President and Chief Operating Officer at GRiD Systems, a manufacturer of laptop computer systems. Mr. Morgridge currently serves on the Board of Directors of Polycom, Inc.

Mr. Puette, 56, has been a member of the Board of Directors since January 1991. He has been President, Chief Executive Officer, and on the Board of Directors of Centigram Communications Corporation since September 1997. Prior to this, he was Chairman of the Board of Directors of NetFRAME Systems, Inc., from January 1996 to September 1997 and was President, Chief Executive Officer, and on the Board of Directors of NetFRAME Systems, Inc., from January 1995 to September 1997. He was a consultant from November 1993 to December 1994. Prior to that, he was Senior Vice-President of Apple Computer, Inc., and President of the Apple USA Division from June 1990 to October 1993. Mr. Puette also currently serves on the Board of Directors of Quality Semiconductor, Inc.

Mr. Son, 41, has been a member of the Board of Directors since July 26, 1995. He has been the President and Chief Executive Officer of SOFTBANK Corporation since September 1981.

Mr. Valentine, 66, has been a member of the Board of Directors of the company since December 1987 and was elected Chairman of the Board of Directors in December 1988. He became Vice-Chairman of the Board on January 31, 1995. He has been a general partner of Sequoia Capital since 1974. Mr. Valentine currently serves as Chairman of the Board of Directors of C-Cube Microsystems Inc., a semiconductor video compression company, and as Chairman of the Board of Network Appliance, Inc., a company in the network file server business.

Mr. West, 43, has been a member of the Board of Directors of the company since April 1996. He has been President and Chief Executive Officer of Hitachi Data Systems, a joint venture computer hardware services company owned by Hitachi, Ltd., and Electronic Data Systems Corporation, since June 1996. Prior to that, Mr. West was at Electronic Data Systems Corporation from 1984 to June of 1996, most recently as President of Electronic Data Systems Corporation Infotainment Business Unit.

Source: Cisco Systems, Inc., *1998 Form 10-K.*

CISCO'S BUSINESS PLAN

During three and one-half years as President and CEO of Cisco Systems, Chambers grew Cisco Systems revenue from $1.2 billion to more than $8.5 billion in annual revenues. Cisco became the fastest growing company in the history of the computer industry.

Unlike most technology companies, Cisco had never taken a restrictive approach that favored one technology over another. The company's philosophy was to pay close attention to its customers' requests, monitor all technological alternatives, and provide customers a range of options from which to choose. Cisco designed and developed its products to encompass all widely accepted industry standards. Some of its technological solutions were so broad that they became industry standards themselves.

Cisco was the world's largest supplier of high-performance computer Internet working systems. Its routers and other communication products connected and managed local and wide area networks (LANs and WANs). The work entailed many protocols, media interfaces, network topologies, and cabling systems, which allowed customers to connect different computer networks by using a variety of hardware and software across offices, countries, and continents. Cisco's products were sold in 90 countries through a direct sales force, distributors, and value-added resellers (VARs). They were supported through a worldwide network of direct sales representatives and business partners. Their products included backbone and remote access routers, LAN and asynchronous transfer mode (ATM) switches, dial-up access servers, and network management software.

All these products upheld multiprotocol multiple media connectivity in a multitude of vendor environments. Cisco's Gigabit Switch Router (GSR), which provided Internet routing and switching at gigabit speed, was introduced to answer criticism that routers created bottlenecks in the Internet backbone, the network's core. It was targeted at the Internet–service provider market and was designed to substantially outperform Ascend Technologies' GRF high-speed router. The GSR supported several hundred thousand routes compared to the GRF, which was limited to supporting about 150,000 routes.

CISCO'S TARGET MARKET

Cisco sold to three target markets: large enterprises, service providers (SPs) and small/medium businesses. Enterprises that used Cisco's products were large corporations, government agencies, utilities, and educational institutions that had complex networking requirements. In these environments, Cisco's products connected multiple locations and types of computer systems into one large network. SPs were companies that provided information services such as telecommunications carriers, Internet service providers, cable companies, and wireless communication providers. The small and medium-sized businesses that Cisco targeted needed data networks for connections to the Internet and their business partners.

Selling to these target markets had become more complex as technology developed. The industry trend during the mid 1990s had been for high-tech companies to provide consultation services when selling their products. For Cisco this meant that each sale had the potential of becoming a technical consulting assignment. This often resulted in a system integration issue to be addressed from the level of overall business strategy. Cisco consultants would become an integral part of this process. Selling became a highly value added service where a company could not solely depend "on selling the box." In response to this demand, Cisco began to build its network application consulting service. This service, headed by Sue Bostrom, who came to Cisco with extensive consulting experience from McKinsey, consisted of the Networked Application Group of 12 people that began expanding in late 1997.

CISCO'S STOCK

Cisco's stock had been a strong point of the company's history. Cisco Systems went public on February 16, 1990, in an initial public offering underwritten by Morgan Stanley & Co. with Smith Barney, Harris Upham & Co., of 90.4 million shares at a split-adjusted price of $0.5625 per share. Cisco's annual revenues increased from $69 million in 1990 to $6.44 billion in fiscal 1997. This represented a nearly 100-fold growth in seven years. Cisco was the third largest company on NASDAQ and among the top 40 in the world measured by market capitalization. The stock had split six times since the initial public offering. A share of Cisco common stock sold on February 16, 1990, for $18.00. That single share of stock on November 18, 1997, was worth $53.42, and the split history would yield 48 shares of stock for a total value of $2,564.16. In short, an investment of $1,000 in 1990 grew nearly 150 times to a value of slightly more than $142,000 by 1997. The fundamental challenge for Cisco's management was to maintain the phenomenal growth rate in revenue as well as profitability in the future. Where would the continuing growth opportunities come from?

GLOBALLY NETWORKED BUSINESSES

In the 1990s, the rapid emergence of networking technologies had changed the pace at which individuals and companies communicated. The speed of conducting business accelerated daily. A dynamic environment like this forced companies to vastly increase accessibility to all its relevant information in order to remain competitive.

Chris Sinton, Director of Cisco Connection, was convinced that, "The first challenge is moving beyond viewing the network only as an information-sharing tool to using the network as a foundation for applications linked to core business systems that serve all business constituents."

Cisco transformed itself using its own technology to its fullest advantage into a leading example of a globally networked business. Cisco positioned its network, together with its core business systems and operational information, and opened this information to prospects, customers, partners, suppliers, and employees. The company worked in an open, collaborative environment that transcended the traditional corporate barriers in business relationships. There were no communication channels for customers, employees, or suppliers to make their way through. Virtually all operational and business information was open to everybody online all the time, no matter what their geographic location or business relationship to Cisco. Through being globally networked, Cisco saved $250 million in 1997 business expenses by reducing servicing costs and improving customer/supplier relationships.

According to John Chambers, the globally networked business model was based on three core assumptions:

- The relationships a company maintains with its key constituencies can be as much of a competitive differentiation as its core products or services.

- The manner in which a company shares information and systems is a critical element in the strength of its relationships.

- Being "connected" is no longer adequate. Business relationships and the communications that support them must exist in a "networked" fabric.

John Chambers believed that globally networked business would set new standards on efficiency and productivity within business relationships by simplifying network infrastructures and deploying a unifying software fabric that supports end-to-end network services. This would allow companies to automate the fundamental ways in which they work together.

Global network applications provided Cisco Systems with a wide range of business opportunities. Cisco's prospects were presented with several attractive alternatives when they considered the purchase of a network system. Cisco noted that a key competitive differentiator was the ease with which prospects could access company information that simplifed and facilitated the purchasing processes. Hence Cisco provided its prospects with the Cisco Connection Online (CCO) web site. CCO was the foundation of the Cisco Connection suite of interactive, electronic services that provided immediate, open access to Cisco's information, resources, and systems any time, anywhere, allowing all constituents to streamline business processes and improve their productivity. Using CCO, prospects had immediate access to information on Cisco's products, services, and partners. CCO allowed potential customers to buy promotional merchandise and Internet software, read technical documentation, and download public software files. Almost one quarter of a million prospects logged on to CCO monthly.

Cisco's fast growth forced the company to find alternatives to traditional sales ordering methods. With rising expenses and a shortage in qualified sales people in the industry, Cisco created the Internetworking Product Center (IPC), part of CCO. IPC served as an online ordering system for direct customers as well as partners. It created better access to support capabilities that enabled the customers to solve problems in less time. Within six months of operation, IPC processed more than $100 million in orders. It led to an immense increase in the percentage of orders that Cisco received via the Web. Between September 1996 and September 1997, the percentage of orders increased by 800%. At the same time, the annualized dollar run rate of orders received climbed from $30 million to $2.734 billion, a 9,013% increase. In 1998, the company was receiving more than $9 million in orders per day. Through IPC, Cisco also assisted their direct customers and partners to configure equipment. This led to shorter delivery intervals and more precise orders than would have been the case if Cisco used traditional sales methods. In short, customers received exactly what they wanted in less time.

Cisco also assisted its worldwide clientele through the CCO with technical support. The online support service looked at over 20,000 support cases each month. The service hastened the resolution of problems, improved the support process, and gave immediate global access to Cisco's engineers and support systems around the clock.

For its partners, Cisco had a Partner-Initiated Customer Access (PICA) program. Partners had access to information and interactive applications that supported them in selling more effectively. PICA helped partners to in turn provide their customers with real-time access to the latest software releases. It lifted the resources of Cisco's partners and increased customer satisfaction and loyalty. Through CCO, partners could quickly address difficult customer questions and problems by using the self-help support solutions.

Being a globally networked company, Cisco relied heavily on successful partnerships with suppliers. To do that, Cisco created the Cisco Supplier Connection. This was an extranet application that increased the productivity and efficiency in the supply function. The Cisco Supplier Connection enabled suppliers and manufacturers to dial into Cisco's manufacturing resource planning. It allowed them to use this connection to reduce the order fulfillment cycle. Through the link, they could monitor orders and see them almost at the same time Cisco's customers placed them. The suppliers then could assemble the parts needed from stock and ship them right to the specific customer. After that, the system reminded Cisco to pay for the parts used. Through the Cisco Supplier Connection, the company was able to reduce the time- and labor-intensive functions of purchase ordering, billing, and delivery. The application allowed suppliers to better manage their manufacturing schedules, improve their cash management, and respond more quickly to Cisco's needs, which in turn benefited Cisco's customers. Cisco gained real-time access to suppliers' information, experienced lower business costs in processing orders (an estimated $46 per order), improved the productivity of its employees involved in purchasing (78% increase), and saw order cycles reduced substantially.

For its employees, Cisco created Cisco Employee Connection (CEC), an intranet web site that allowed them to fulfill their tasks more proficiently. The site contained the unique needs of its 10,000 networked employees and provided users with immediate access to current services and information and instant global communications. All of Cisco's employees could access the same information simultaneously through the power of networking regardless of where they were located. The CEC had been the primary mechanism for decreasing Cisco's communication cost and time to market.

Overall, by becoming a globally networked business, Cisco was able to react more quickly and compete more effectively. Becoming a globally networked business provided Cisco with a scalable (the ability to add on to), manageable business system that enabled them to do more with less. The technology allowed Cisco to reach the goals of improved productivity, reduced time to market, greater revenue, lower expenses, and stronger relationships. They would prosper as other businesses adopt the model it has successfully pioneered. As indicated by the market researcher International Data Corporation (IDC), sales on the Internet would grow to $116 billion by the year 2000. More than 70% of that amount would be from business-to-business transactions, which indicated that the Internet would become one of the key distribution channels for companies. Ultimate business success depended on the ability of companies to become online businesses, leveraging their networks and cultivating their interactive relationships with prospects, customers, partners, suppliers, and employees.

THE CONVERGENCE OF DATA, VOICE, AND VIDEO

In 1994, there were 3,000 web sites in the world, 3.2 million host computers, and 30 million Internet users. Four short years later, there were 2.5 million sites, 36.7 million hosts, and 134 million Internet users. During this time of rapid expansion, the question of which communication protocol would be the standard for linking the increasingly vast numbers of computer systems and networks was resolved. Internet Protocols (IP) have become the one fundamental language used in every type of interconnected computing. Two important questions remained unresolved: How pervasive will Internet-based communication become? Will it become the predominant means of converging data, voice, and video? That public communications in the year 2002 will be synonymous with the Internet, at this juncture, seems more realistic than strained.

The world is now experiencing exponential growth of communication via the Internet. This rapid rate of growth is accelerating because of the daily increase in the number of Internet users and because transmissions over the Internet have evolved from just text and data to include multi-media, audio, and full motion video.

Traditional phone companies, using proven and highly stable circuit switching, continue to make impressive technological gains. Northern Telecom's DMS stored program switch has been able to double its performance every six and one-half years without any increase in cost. IP routers and frame relay packet switches, such as the ones Cisco provides, have been able to double their performance every 10–20 months without cost increases. IP routers and switches can now transfer a higher number of bits per second at a lower cost than traditional circuit switches.

Tom Steinert-Threlkeld stated in his "Internet 2002" article that if you follow this trend to its most reasonable conclusion, the Internet will soon provide the underlying structure for all communication networks, including multimedia transmissions between individuals and businesses, local and long-distance phone service, and television broadcasts via cable or satellite. Given this perspective, we are barely at the beginning of the growth cycle in the networking industry.

Cisco executives are already talking about the day when the cost of moving data, voice, and video along IP networks will be so inexpensive that the price of bundled IP data services will include both long distance and local phone calls at a price substantially lower than what customers pay now for telephone services alone. Other included features will be as diverse as video conferencing, feature film and audio downloading, and voice mail messaging, including lengthy video and audio clips.

Cisco itself continued to provide fundamental solutions that would be enable data to move more efficiently along IP networks. Its new Tag Switching technology allowed data packets of various sizes to flow substantially faster and more reliably through routers directly past switches using the same unique Tag. This new technology enabled networks to handle more traffic, users, media-rich data, and bandwidth-intensive applications.

The opportunities in the networking industry were becoming vast as the Internet took its place as the platform for all forms of traditional and innovative communication. Cisco was positioned to be a major innovative force in the future generations of Internet technology. Many experts predicted a 100-fold increase in Internet usage within the next five years.

KEY COMPETITIVE ISSUES

Customers to the computer networking industry are seeking access to information that will set higher standards of efficiency and productivity, leading to higher profits. The objective is to heighten their competitive capabilities and give them a competitive advantage over their rivals. Central to this is the ability to manage constituent relationships through the sharing of critical information and the open exchange of resources and services. The need for seamless transmission of data and voice is important to the customer base. Accomplishing this necessitates broad-based suppliers of networking products. Competitors in the networking industry are shifting their focus toward becoming full-service providers in this rapidly growing industry in order to meet the needs of their growing customer base. Correctly assessing the current and, most importantly, the future informational needs of customers is a key factor to a firm's survival or extinction. Cisco Systems, Lucent Technologies, 3Com, Ascend Communications, and Bay Networks are the strongest forces in the push to dominate the market.

Industry growth is so dramatic that analysts and investors are having difficulty determining continuing and future growth rates. This leaves competitors scrambling to gain as much market share as their organizations can maintain and manage. High growth and profitability lead to intense competitive challenges. New entrants are possible from many segments of the high-tech community. New competitors could be from the telecommunications, data networking, software, and semiconductors industries. Companies from these industries are likely to enter based on their strengths in brand name recognition, technological knowledge and capabilities, and a strong financial background. Globalization and the growing strength of both domestic and foreign competitors in all these industries makes the competitive pressure even greater for existing companies.

THE CHALLENGERS

Commanding approximately 80% of its market put Cisco in an enviable competitive position. However, formidable competitors existed, and as the industry growth rates continued to accelerate, maintaining this market share could be a daunting task. As the industry moved toward the convergence of voice and data systems, competitors were expected to be positioning for growth through merger, acquisition, and/or joint venture partnering. End users were driving industry competitors to provide a full range of services as well as a high level of customization. The ability to create a total system that enabled customers to access information and enhanced their ability to efficiently facilitate their own business and communication processes with their vendors and customers would be a key factor for success. Escalating industry growth left Cisco faced with deciding how much internal growth it could sustain in order to hold its current percentage of a growing market. Its top competitors were sure to be opportunistic of any weaknes within Cisco.

Ascend Communications

Founded in 1989, Ascend Communications was the leading supplier of remote access solutions, supporting in excess of 30 million Internet connections daily. The company operated in over 30 countries worldwide through a distribution system that included direct sales, OEM relationships, strategic alliances, distributors, and VARs. Ascend's extensive service program, Ascend Advantage Services, was enhanced through an alliance with IBM's Availability Services, a segment of IBM Global Services. This allowed Ascend and its participating resellers to use the resources of IBM's worldwide service network to support Ascend products. Quality was an important strength for Ascend. The company held the prestigious Quality System Certificates ISO 9000 and ISO 9001 covering design, manufacture, sale, and service of data networking products.

Fiscal year 1997 proved to be prosperous for Ascend. Net sales increased 31% from $890.3 million in 1996 to $1.167 billion in 1997. Strengthening the company's competitive position and maintaining a leadership status in networking products and technologies was a high priority for top management. Several acquisitions throughout the year supported the company's transition from a recognized leading supplier of remote access solutions to a broad-based supplier of wide area networking products. The acquisition of Cascade Communications proved to be a significant link to becoming a full-service provider for global communications. Cascade's strength as a leader in broadband data communications products enabled Ascend to extensively broaden its product base. The company also acquired Whitetree, Inc., a pioneer in local area network switching technology, and InterCon, a developer of client software products for both the corporate and ISP markets. These two smaller acquisitions filled gaps in building a seamless networking system for their customers. Strong research and development, strategic alliances, and key acquisitions were the strategies Ascend used to position itself as a strong competitor in providing integrated networking solutions for its service provider customers and its enterprise customers.

Lucent Technologies

On February 1, 1996, AT&T transformed Lucent Technologies into a stand-alone entity by separating it from the parent corporation. The independent organization competed in three core businesses. The largest was network operating systems followed by business communications systems and microelectronics products. Lucent's technologies connect, route, manage, and store information across networks. In 1997, net income was reported as $541 million, compared to a net loss of $793 million for the previous 12 months.

Lucent faced serious challenges from both the intense competitive nature of the industry and its internal organization. Two significant factors played a role in the company's performance. The first was its heavy reliance on a limited number of large customers for a material portion of their revenues. One of its largest customers was the former parent AT&T. Increasingly Lucent's customer base was purchasing from fewer suppliers. Therefore, the contracts from these buyers were very large and tended to be highly seasonal, which was the second significant factor impacting Lucent's performance. Delaying capital expenditures until the fourth quarter of the calendar was typical purchasing behavior for Lucent's large customers. With a fiscal year ended September 30, the result was that a disproportionate share of Lucent's revenue stream was recognized in its first quarter. On a calendar-year basis, profitability was lower in each of the first three quarters than in the fourth quarter. Consequently investors may have concerns regarding the value of the stock throughout the year. In addition to fluctuations in its revenue stream, Lucent faced stringent demands from its large customers in terms of favorable pricing, financing, and payment terms that extend over multiyear contracts. Recognition of revenue from large cost outlays in the development of large-scale systems for its customers reflected harshly on the company's financial statements. The company encountered a material risk factor should any of its large purchasers reduce orders or move to a competitor.

To reduce the overall risk of dependence on a few large buyers, Lucent began to diversify its customer base by pursuing customers from other industries such as cable television network operators, access providers, and computer manufacturers. However, management did not anticipate that the company's customer base would broaden significantly in the near future. Beginning in fiscal year 1997, the company embarked on an acquisition strategy aimed at strengthening its core businesses and smoothing out the revenue stream. The first transaction in October 1996 was for Agile Networks, Inc., a provider of advanced intelligent data switching products that support both ethernet and ATM technology. In September 1997, Lucent embarked on a major transaction with the $1.8 million purchase of Octel Communications Corporation, a provider of voice, fax, and electronic messaging technologies. The products of Octel were viewed as complementary to the products and services Lucent was offering. Fiscal year 1998 began with two transactions. The company sought to further enhance and broaden R&D knowledge and the capabilities gained from the previous transactions. The acquisition of Livingston Enterprises, Inc., a global company that provided connection equipment to Internet service providers was a strategic step in this direction. Lucent continued to follow its strategy of strengthening its core businesses in a joint venture with Philips Electronics N.V. The joint venture, 40% owned by Lucent, was a global conveyor of personal communications products. The complete range of products included digital and analog wireless phones, corded and cordless phones, answering machines, screen phones, and pagers.

In an effort to focus on its core businesses, Lucent sold off some of its businesses. The subsidiary Paradyne and the company's interconnect products and Custom Manufacturing Services were sold in 1996. The company's Advanced Technology Systems unit was sold in October 1997. By the end of fiscal 1997, Lucent had positioned itself as a leader in the design, development, and manufacture of integrated systems and software applications for network operators and business enterprises.

3Com

3Com Corporation was the first organization to develop technology for networking personal computers. In the 20 years following its introduction of this new technology, the industry grew to be one of the largest in the world. 3Com remained one of the top industry competitors. Revenues in 1997 were approximately $3.2 billion, up from $2.3 billion in 1996. Net income rose from $177 million in 1996 to $373 million in 1997. Growth in fiscal 1997 focused on the introduction of new products to expand and strengthen its product breadth and establish the company in emerging market segments. New products were developed in its systems business, switching technology, client access business, and networking software. The new product introductions were supported through the bolstering of the company's sales and support functions and acquisition activity.

The first acquisition of 1997 was OnStream Networks, a leading provider of solutions for integrated video, voice, and data. This addition to 3Com's business portfolio strengthened its ATM/broadband wide-area focus. The most significant event of 1997 was the announcement of a merger between 3Com and U.S. Robotics, creating a $5.6 billion company. U.S. Robotics was a leader in remote access concentrators, modems, and connected handheld organizers. The addition of U.S. Robotics' products and technology to 3Com's product portfolio gave it strong representation in key business areas. Once the transaction was completed in early fiscal 1998, it was one of two networking companies with revenues over $5 billion. These acquisitions enabled 3Com to gain leverage as a full-service provider in each of the four key markets of the networking industry: enterprise networks, Internet service providers, business systems, and the consumer market. Further, the combined companies constituted a wider distribution channel, allowing for greater reach to the customer base.

3Com's management believed that flexible, faster, and simpler access to networks would be the most important features a networking company could offer and believed that through these acquisitions, the company was in a superior competitive position to its nearest competitors. They saw that the way to achieve this was by providing low-cost solutions to customers for fully integrated end-to-end connectivity that extends across local and wide area networks. 3Com was solidly positioned to provide that extensive service to the networking market.

Bay Networks

Bay Networks was a global company offering networking solutions to enterprise networks and Internet and telecommunications service providers. The company's fiscal position remained steady from 1996 to 1997 with little growth. Revenues in each year were just over $2.0 billion. The company adopted a strategy called Adaptive Networking to meet the changes and challenges of the high growth Internet services and networking segments of the industry. Its focus was on key technologies in switching/ATM services and network management. As with most of its competitors, Bay Networks used a merger and acquisition strategy to bolster its competitive position and become a full-service provider. However, the strategy failed to change the company's position. By the end of fiscal 1997, net income fell with a loss of $1.46 per share. A few months later, the company made a blockbuster announcement that would have a drastic effect on the competitive environment in the industry. Executives of the communications giant Northern Telecom and of Bay Networks announced a merger of the two organizations, to be called Nortel. This merger would combine telecommunications with the data equipment used to move information across networks, giving the combined entity a significant competitive advantage that no other competitor comes close to matching. Estimates set the value of Nortel at almost $18 billion, by far the largest company in the industry.

Niche Competitors

Cisco also faced competition from smaller networking companies specializing in specific niches of the industry. Company estimates placed the number of competitors in the ATM switching, frame relay, and workgroups segments to be between 30 and 50 in each segment. Customers with the need for specialties in these areas might find doing business with a small expert organization to be advantageous. However, as the industry moved toward mergers and consolidations, competitors from this segment were not a formidable threat.

The key challenge for Cisco Systems would be its ability to remain on top of a critical and growing industry in light of increasing competitive challenges and continuing weakness from foreign markets.

FINANCIAL PERFORMANCE

Exhibits 3 and 4 are the company's consolidated statement of operations, consolidated balance sheets, and selected financial information, respectively.

Exhibit 3 **Consolidated Statements of Operations: Cisco Systems, Inc.**
(Dollar amounts in thousands, except per-share data)

Year Ending	July 25, 1998	July 26, 1997	July 28, 1996
Net sales	$8,458,777	$6,440,171	$4,096,007
Cost of sales	2,917,617	2,241,378	1,409,862
Gross margin	5,541,160	4,198,793	2,686,145
Expenses			
Research and development	1,020,446	698,172	399,291
Sales and marketing	1,564,419	1,160,269	726,278
General and administrative	258,246	204,661	159,770
Purchased research and development	593,695	508,397	—
Total operating expenses	3,436,806	2,571,499	1,285,339
Operating income	2,104,354	1,627,294	1,400,806
Realized gains on sale of investment	5,411	152,689	—
Interest and other income, net	192,701	108,889	64,019
Income before provision for income taxes	2,302,466	1,888,872	1,464,825
Provision for income taxes	952,394	840,193	551,501
Net income	$1,350,072	$1,048,679	$ 913,324
Net income per share — basic	$ 0.88	$ 0.71	$ 0.64
Net income per share — diluted	$ 0.84	$ 0.68	$ 0.61
Shares used in per-share calculation — basic	1,533,869	1,485,986	1,437,030
Shares used in per-share calculation — diluted	1,608,173	1,551,039	1,490,078

Source: Cisco Systems, Inc., *1998 Annual Report,* p. 28.

Exhibit 4   **Consolidated Balance Sheets: Cisco Systems, Inc.**
(Dollar amounts in thousands, except par value)

Year Ending	July 25, 1998	July 26, 1997
Assets		
Current assets		
Cash and equivalents	$ 534,652	$ 269,608
Short-term investments	1,156,849	1,005,977
Accounts receivable, net of allowances for doubtful		
accounts of $39,842 in 1998 and $22,340 in 1997	1,297,867	1,170,401
Inventories, net	361,986	254,677
Deferred income taxes	344,905	312,132
Prepaid expenses and other current assets	65,665	88,471
Total current assets	3,761,924	3,101,266
Investments	3,463,279	1,267,174
Restricted investments	553,780	363,216
Property and equipment, net	595,349	466,352
Other assets	542,373	253,976
Total assets	$8,916,705	$5,451,984
Liabilities and Shareholders' Equity		
Current liabilities		
Accounts payable	$ 248,872	$ 207,178
Income taxes payable	410,363	256,224
Accrued payroll and related expenses	390,542	263,269
Other accrued liabilities	717,203	393,438
Total current liabilities	1,766,980	1,120,109
Commitments and contingencies		
Minority interest	43,107	42,253
Shareholders' equity		
Preferred stock, no par value, 5,000 shares authorized:		
none issued or outstanding in 1998 and 1997		
Common stock and additional paid-in capital,		
$0.001 par value (no par value—July 26,1997)		
2,700,000 shares authorized: 1,562,582 shares issued		
and outstanding in 1998 and 1,509,252 shares in 1997	3,220,205	1,763,200
Retained earnings	3,828,223	2,487,058
Unrealized gain on investments	78,314	49,628
Cumulative translation adjustments	(20,124)	(10,264)
Total shareholders' equity	7,106,618	4,289,622
Total liabilities and shareholders' equity	$8,916,705	$5,451,984

Source: Cisco Systems, Inc., *1998 Annual Report*, p. 29.

Sun Microsystems, Inc. (1998)

Irene Hagenbuch and Alan N. Hoffman

> The Network is the computer's means to make all the systems work together like one big re-source. Sun has always seen our customers' computing needs answered by a variety of com-puting resources in a heterogeneous network.
>
> —Scott G. McNealy, CEO, April 1987

COMPANY BACKGROUND

John Doerr, of Kleiner Perkins, described Sun Microsystems, Inc., with world headquar-ters in Palo Alto, California, as "the last standing, fully integrated computing company adding its own value at the chip, OS and systems level."

The company's history started in 1982, when Andreas Bechtolsheim, Bill Joy, Vinod Khosla, and Scott McNealy founded Sun Microsystems, Inc., for Stanford University Network. The same year, the first Sun system, the Sun-1, a high-performance computer based on readily available, inexpensive components and UNIX was produced. After a rocky two-year start, McNealy, who started out as Vice-President for Manufacturing and Operations, was appointed President in 1984 when Khosla left the company. By 1998, Sun had become a global Fortune 500 leader in enterprise network computing with op-erations in 150 countries and over $8 billion in revenues.

The company's philosophy was to enable customers to create breakaway business strategies by using their network computing products, solutions, and services. Sun fur-ther stated that in an age when information was power, it provided the technology, in-novation, and partnerships that enabled individuals or entire organizations to access information from anywhere to anything on any device allowing users to better differen-tiate and more effectively create breakaway business products and services.

Supporting and enforcing its philosophy where everything it brought to the market was predicated upon the existence of the network, where Java was on every client and every server, Sun had a vision statement. Its "vision is for a networked computing future driven by the needs and choices of the customer. It is a vision in which every man, woman, and child has access to the collective planetary wisdom that resides on the net-work." Sun further explained that the Internet represents the first environment through which the company's vision could actually start to be achieved. It saw its role as one of making the most of the opportunity, by delivering open, affordable, and useful products to help as many people as possible share in the power of the network around the world.

COMPETITION

Sun's competitors in the technical and scientific markets were primarily Hewlett-Packard (HP), International Business Machines Corporation (IBM), Compaq Computer Corporation (CPQ), and Silicon Graphics, Inc. (SGI).

The information technology industry, the market for Sun's services and products, was extremely competitive in 1998. The industry was characterized by rapid, continuous

---

This case was prepared by Irene Hagenbuch and Professor Alan N. Hoffman of Bentley College. This case was edited for SMBP–7th Edition. Copyright © 1998, Irene Hagenbuch and Professor Alan N. Hoffman. Reprinted by permission.

change, frequent product performance improvements, short product life cycles, and price reductions. This environment forced Sun to rapidly and continuously develop, introduce, and deliver in quantity new systems, software, and service products, in addition to new microprocessor technologies, to offer its customers improved performance at competitive prices. The company began to improve, change, and implement several new business practices, processes, and a series of related information systems. Jim Moore from GeoPartners Research in Cambridge, Mass., compared Sun to IBM in its glory days, when customers viewed it as the repository of wisdom and competence: "Sun has suddenly become a thought leader for the whole industry."

Compared to previous years, Sun was increasingly dependent on the ability of its suppliers. Their competence in designing, manufacturing, and delivering advanced components required for the timely introduction of new products was crucial to Sun's future competitiveness. The failure of any of these suppliers to deliver components on time or in sufficient quantities, or the failure of any of Sun's own designers to develop innovative products on a timely basis, could also have a serious impact on the company's operating results. To prevent any adverse affect on its net revenues and operating results, Sun frequently made advanced payments to specific suppliers and often entered into noncancelable purchase contracts with vendors early in the design process. The commitments helped secure components for the development, production, and introduction of new products. The computer systems that Sun sold were distributed through the company's own systems. No customer accounted for more than 10% of Sun's revenues in fiscal 1997, 1996, or 1995. Sun's vision and strategy stayed constant. With more market opportunities, an increasing number of companies realized the benefits of open network computing.

After Sun observed that sharing data between computers was crucial to key business tasks, McNealy worked extensively to transform Sun's product line in order to capitalize on networking. Its main products could be divided into six categories: Servers and Workstations, Solaris and Solstice, SunSpectrum, WorkShop and NEO, UltraSPARC and Java Processors, and Java Software (see Exhibit 1). This wide variety of products was used to implement the McNealy philosophy: "The network is the computer." Sun was reconfiguring its UNIX operating system for workstations, called Solaris, to run servers that coordinated work and stored data on networks.

The year 1994 was a big year in the computer industry. Sun faced the dramatic expansion of the Internet's World Wide Web. Millions of users came to believe that the network was indeed the computer. Because Sun had accepted this statement for a long time, the company had been faster in making the transition compared to its UNIX rivals IBM and Hewlett-Packard. Thus many customers turned to Sun for their workstations. According to Computer Intelligence, a research firm in La Jolla, California, 26% of all Web servers in use in the United States were made by Sun. This was more than any other company.

By 1998, Sun was the leading provider of UNIX-based servers. Java helped increase sales, even though the language does nothing yet to make Sun's servers better than those of its competitors. Using Java to sell servers was a necessity because the workstation—the computer Sun was built on—was going the way of the minicomputer. The more expensive machines made by Sun and others were being replaced by PCs incorporating cheaper Intel microprocessors. Although companies were having inexpensive Windows NT servers handle their simpler networking tasks, they still relied on UNIX for their most critical applications because Solaris servers crashed a lot less frequently than NT servers. Nonetheless, the PCs that ran Microsoft's Windows NT operating system, Compaq, Dell, and others would soon take over the market for workstations priced less than $10,000.

Exhibit 1   Products: Sun Microsystems

Servers and Workstations: The company offers a full line of Ultra Enterprise servers to support an immense database and mission-critical business applications. With its Netra server family, Sun delivers preconfigured solutions for intranet and Internet publishing. Its Ultra workstation series combines accelerated graphics, high-bandwidth networking, and fast processing to provide outstanding performance for technical applications.

Solaris and Solstice: With Sun's installed base of more than 2 million systems, Solaris software is the leading operating environment for open client-server networks. The Solstice products consist of a highly scalable and comprehensive suite of intranet management software, helping organizations securely access, administer, and manage rapidly changing intranet computing environments.

SunSpectrum: This newly developed portfolio of enterprise-wide support services connects Sun's customers to a highly responsive organization that supports more than half a million systems worldwide. That combination of hardware, system software, and application support with premium account-level services maximizes both system availability and customer satisfaction.

WorkShop and NEO: The WorkShop family, which includes the new Java WorkShop solution, delivers visual development tools that quickly and easily create multiplatform applications for the Internet, intranets, and enterprise networks. NEO delivers system administration tools, object-oriented development tools, and transparent networking in order to reduce the cost of creating, customizing, and maintaining applications.

UltraSPARC and Java Processors: Well-developed UltraSPARC microprocessors accelerate multimedia and networking applications with their innovative architecture and VIS media instruction set through powering networked systems from routers to supercomputers. The planned JavaChip microprocessor family will be optimized for Java-powered applications.

Java Software: It is the first software platform planned from start for the Internet and corporate intranets that will run on any computer.

Source: Sun Microsystems, Inc., *1998 Form 10-K.*

In January 1998, however, Sun announced sweeping innovations made to its award-winning power desktop line. This move, designed to capture new growth within the $19 billion market for high-end personal computers and powerful workstations, allowed the company to grow market share at both the low-end (less than $5,000) and the high-end (more than $15,000) of the workstation market. Putting its expertise in high-performance system design enabled the company to lower the price of advanced workstations and graphics technologies. Sun's announcement of new graphics capabilities as well as the fastest workstation, the Ultra 60 multiprocessing system, ideally positioned the company to take market share from competitors like Hewlett-Packard, IBM, DEC, and Silicon Graphics at the high-end of the market. Sun was pushing SGI's technology to the limits with its new price/performance levels and intended to overtake SGI's market share in the $25,000+ workstation market, which was approximately $3 billion in 1996. These new workstations allowed the users to run the most popular Microsoft Windows 95 applications alongside the Solaris applications. This meant that users could run the more than 12,000 Solaris applications, which offered proven UNIX reliability/uptime, handled larger data sets, and delivered faster real-world modeling capabilities than the NT environment, in addition to the PC applications like Microsoft Office.

The new Darwin line was designed to appeal to the growing base of desktop users who were demanding more reliability and power. When the Darwin systems were coupled with new accelerated graphics, Sun was able to focus more on the needs of the rapidly growing base of digital contents creators. This desktop line set a new low price point for workstation functionality, enabling Sun to grasp market share from Compaq and other PC vendors at the lower end of the market. Part of this move into the desktop markets was the announcement of a worldwide trade-in program designed to ensure investment protection for existing Sun customers and to attract new customers currently using other PCs and competitive workstations to the Sun platform. To specifically draw the attention of Silicon Graphics', Apple Computer's, Compaq's, and other PC vendors' customers toward the performance and speedy graphics advantages of Sun systems, Sun designed its "Jurassic-Back," "Mac-Back," and "Paq-Back" trade-in promotions.

FINANCIAL PERFORMANCE

Even though Sun's industry was fast changing and highly competitive, the company managed to have at least 10% sales growth over the last several years across its product line. Its net revenue in fiscal 1998 increased to $9.7 billion, or 13% compared to $8.6 billion in fiscal 1997 (see Exhibit 2). Net income was flat for fiscal 1998 at $762 million, the same as fiscal 1997. However, the product's gross margin was 53.8% for fiscal 1998, compared to 51.1% in fiscal 1997. Research and development (R&D) expenses increased $188 million, or 22.7%, in fiscal 1998. Sun has one of the strongest balance sheets in the industry, with $822 million in cash in the bank (see Exhibit 3.) Having been the world leader in workstation sales (with 39% in unit sales and 35% in revenues, per Dataquest), the company was successfully transforming itself into an enterprise-computing firm with a focus on global network computing. This move was necessary when Sun's workstation sales started to slip and its server sales to gain.

Between 1988 and 1998, the company's revenues grew an average of 34.1% annually as the demand for its open network computing products and services has risen. The revenues by geography have been well balanced. Approximately 49% of the total revenue was generated from outside the United States. Its net income grew 41% annually on average over the same time period.

CORPORATE GOVERNANCE

Exhibit 4 lists the company's Board of Directors and corporate executives, and outlines the corporate worldwide structure.

Scott G. McNealy

The story behind Sun's current Chairman of the Board, President, and Chief Executive Officer Scott G. McNealy was not very typical for a Silicon Valley entrepreneur. He didn't drop out of college to realize his idea for the PC business nor did he work his way up through engineering. His background in manufacturing made McNealy a fierce competitor who knew his business fundamentals, always kept score, and had good moves. He was smart, complex, and fiercely ambitious. Over the many years at Sun, McNealy had become one of the industry's most respected managers. Lawrence J. Ellison, CEO of Oracle, said, "There are two things I think about Scott. One is passionate leadership, and the other is his rigorous financial management. And that's uncommon to find in one person" (*Fortune,* October 13, 1997). Those talents, plus a competitive instinct and nonstop drive, kept Sun rolling through a decade of tremendous change in the computer industry.

McNealy grew up in a house where hard work and a fast-paced environment were part of the everyday life. As a child, Scott learned a great deal about manufacturing. His

Exhibit 2   Consolidated Statements of Income: Sun Microsystems, Inc.
(Dollar amounts in thousands, except per-share data)

Year Ending June 30	1998	1997	1996
Net revenues			
Products	$8,603,259	$7,747,115	$6,392,358
Services	1,187,581	851,231	702,393
Total net revenues	9,790,840	8,598,346	7,094,751
Costs and expenses			
Cost of sales—products	3,972,283	3,790,284	3,468,416
Cost of sales—services	721,053	530,176	452,812
Research and development	1,013,782	825,968	653,044
Selling, general, and administrative	2,777,264	2,402,442	1,787,567
Purchased in-process research and development	176,384	22,958	57,900
Total costs and expenses	8,660,766	7,571,828	6,419,739
Operating income	1,130,074	1,026,518	675,012
Gain on sale of equity investment	—	62,245	—
Interest income	47,663	39,899	42,976
Interest expense	(1,571)	(7,455)	(9,114)
Income before income taxes	1,176,166	1,121,207	708,874
Provision for income taxes	413,304	358,787	232,486
Net income	$ 762,862	$ 762,420	$ 476,388
Net income per common share—basic	$ 2.04	$ 2.07	$ 1.28
Net income per common share—diluted	$ 1.93	$ 1.96	$ 1.21
Shares used in the calculation of net income per common share—basic	373,728	368,426	371,134
Shares used in the calculation of net income per common share—diluted	394,274	388,967	393,380

Source: Sun Microsystems, Inc., *1998 Annual Report,* p. 26.

curiosity in his father's work, who was Vice-Chairman of American Motors Corp., led the grade-schooler to look into his dad's briefcase at night to inspect its contents. Many Saturdays, young McNealy went along to the plant and snooped around while his father caught up on paperwork. By the time he was a teenager, Scott was spending evenings with his father reading over memos and playing golf with industry leaders such as Lee A. Iacocca.

Graduating from Harvard University in economics, McNealy took a job for two years as a foreman at a Rockwell International Corp. plant in Ashtabula, Ohio, which made body panels for semi tractors. In 1978, he enrolled in Stanford University's business school where he focused on manufacturing at a time when finance and information technologies were the ways to the top. Although many of his classmates wanted to launch a Digital Age business, McNealy signed on as a manufacturing trainee for FMC Corp. The company assigned him to a factory in Silicon Valley where it was building Bradley fighting vehicles for the U.S. Army.

McNealy's career in the computer world started in 1981 when his mentor from Harvard asked him for help in the troubled production department of a workstation company called Onyx Systems. After only 10 months at Onyx, a former Stanford classmate, Vinod Khosla, contacted McNealy to join him and Bechtolsheim in starting Sun. In 1982, he joined Sun to head up manufacturing and operations. McNealy's manufacturing skills enabled the new company to keep up with the high demand as sales went from $9 million

Exhibit 3   Consolidated Balance Sheets: Sun Microsystems, Inc.
(Dollar amounts in thousands, except share and per-share data)

Year Ending June 30	1998	1997
Assets		
Current assets		
Cash and cash equivalents	$ 822,267	$ 660,170
Short-term investments	476,185	452,590
Accounts receivable, net of allowances of $235,563 in 1998 and $196,091 in 1997	1,845,765	1,666,523
Inventories	346,446	437,978
Deferred tax assets	371,841	286,720
Other current assets	285,021	224,469
Total current assets	4,147,525	3,728,450
Property, plant, and equipment		
Machinery and equipment	1,251,660	1,057,239
Furniture and fixtures	113,636	93,078
Leasehold improvements	256,233	166,745
Land and buildings	635,699	341,279
	2,257,228	1,658,341
Accumulated depreciation and amortization	(956,616)	(858,448)
	1,300,612	799,893
Other assets, net	262,925	168,931
Total assets	$5,711,062	$4,697,274
Liabilities and Shareholders' Equity		
Current liabilities		
Short-term borrowings	$ 7,169	$ 100,930
Accounts payable	495,603	468,912
Accrued payroll-related liabilities	315,929	337,412
Accrued liabilities and other	810,562	625,600
Deferred service revenues	264,967	197,616
Income taxes payable	188,641	118,568
Note payable	40,000	—
Total current liabilities	2,122,871	1,849,038
Deferred income taxes and other obligations	74,563	106,299
Commitments and contingencies		
Shareholders' equity		
Preferred stock, $0.001 par value, 10,000,000 shares authorized; no shares issued and outstanding	—	—
Common stock, $0.00067 par value, 950,000,000 shares authorized;		
issued: 430,311,441 shares in 1998 and 430,535,886 shares in 1997	288	288
Additional paid-in capital	1,345,508	1,229,797
Retained earnings	3,150,935	2,409,850
Treasury stock, at cost: 54,007,866 shares in 1998 and 60,050,380 shares in 1997	(1,003,191)	(915,426)
Currency translation adjustment and other	20,088	17,428
Total shareholders' equity	3,513,628	2,741,937
Total liabilities and shareholders' equity	$5,711,062	$4,697,274

Source: Sun Microsystems, Inc., *1998 Annual Report,* p. 27.

Exhibit 4 **Board of Directors, Corporate Officers, and Worldwide Corporate Structure: Sun Microsystems, Inc.**

A. Board of Directors
Scott G. McNealy
Chairman of the Board of Directors, President, and Chief Executive Officer, Sun Microsystems, Inc.
L. John Doerr
General Partner, Kleiner Perkins Caufield & Byers
Judith L. Estrin
President, Chief Executive Officer, Precept Software, Inc.
Robert J. Fisher
Executive Vice-President and Director, Gap, Inc., President, Gap Division, Gap, Inc.
Robert L. Long
Management Consultant
M. Kenneth Oshman
Chairman, President, and Chief Executive Officer, Echelon Corporation
A. Michael Spence
Dean, Graduate School of Business, Stanford University

B. Corporate Officers
Scott G. McNealy
Chairman of the Board of Directors, President, and Chief Executive Officer, Sun Microsystems, Inc.
Kenneth M. Alvares
Vice-President, Human Resources, Sun Microsystems, Inc., and Corporate Executive Officer
Alan E. Baratz
President, JavaSoft, and Corporate Executive Officer
Lawrence W. Hambly
President, SunService Division, and Corporate Executive Officer

Michael E. Lehman
Vice-President, Chief Financial Officer, Sun Microsystems, Inc., and Corporate Executive Officer
Michael H. Morris
Vice-President, General Counsel, and Secretary, Sun Microsystems, Inc.
Alton D. Page
Vice-President, Treasurer, Sun Microsystems, Inc.
William J. Raduchel
Vice-President, Corporate Planning and Development, and Chief Information Officer, Sun Microsystems, Inc., and Corporate Executive Officer
George Reyes
Vice-President, Controller, Sun Microsystems, Inc.
Janpieter T. Scheerder
President, SunSoft, Inc., and Corporate Executive Officer
Chester J. Silvestri
President, Sun Microelectronics, and Corporate Executive Officer
Edward J. Zander
President, Sun Microsystems Computer Company, and Corporate Executive Officer

Sun Worldwide
Manufacturing
2 countries
International Research & Development
8 countries
International Sales, Service, and Support
41 countries
International Distributors
Nearly 150 countries

Source: Sun Microsystems, Inc., *1998 Annual Report*, p. 47.

in 1983 to $39 million in 1984. Nonetheless, the high amount of new orders surpassed the cash available for expansion. McNealy then asked Sun's customer Eastman Kodak Co. to invest $20 million. As a condition of the investment, Kodak insisted that McNealy take over as President. In 1984, McNealy was officially named CEO of the company.

McNealy showed his ability as a CEO over the coming years. After the company went public in 1986, it took two years for Sun to outgrow its production capacities, which led to the company's first quarterly loss. Its troubled production facilities was reason enough for McNealy to move from Sun's executive suite to the floor of Sun's biggest factory and revamp the company's manufacturing. In the months after production was rolling again, he showed skills nobody expected. He deliberately pruned the product line, sharpening Sun's focus to workstations built around a high-powered processor of its own design. Realizing that fixing problems on the factory floor was no job for the CEO of a company of Sun's size led McNealy to reorganize the company. He pushed profit-and-loss responsibility down to individual product organizations, called planets, that let them feel the troubles if things went wrong.

At Sun's headquarters, McNealy, having an image in the industry of being brash, was building a corporate culture based on his own motto:"Kick butt and have fun." Soon after that, the company became known for its aggressive marketing, featuring Network, McNealy's Greater Swiss Mountain dog, and various juvenile behavior taking place within Sun's headquarters.

This humor had an important effect on the culture. During these competitive times in the computer industry when good positions and good workers were hard to find, it helped employees live with their demanding jobs and bound employees together. Carol A. Bartz, former Sales Vice-President of Sun, and Thomas J. Meredith, former Sun Treasurer, agreed that McNealy had a special gift. Using humor and a tremendous amount of energy, McNealy had the ability to raise employees enthusiastically to their feet.

Sun did not only consist of McNealy alone, however. According to Ellison, Scott McNealy complemented his leadership with very capable people."You don't find Scott surrounded by dummies. You find Scott surrounded by real smart people, like Bill Joy and Eric Schmidt [chief technology officer] and others who do wonderful work."

JAVA, THE PROGRAMMING LANGUAGE

Java originated from a 1990 programming language, code-named Oak, that would enable all computerized devices to run simple programs distributed to them over a network. At one point, Oak was part of the effort to develop a two-way interactive cable TV system (which Sun lost out to Silicon Graphics). By the end of 1994, Oak seemed to be going nowhere. During one last presentation of Oak, McNealy recognized the potential of the programming language—how to reach his ultimate goal of harnessing the Internet to stop Microsoft from swallowing all of them—and became Oak's biggest supporter. Soon after that, the language was renamed Java, a colloquial word for "coffee." The fact that the name was informal and generic, compared to previous programming language names that were obscure and somewhat daunting, implied that normal people should also care about Java, regardless of whether they knew what it did or not. By May 1995, McNealy informed the public, who at that point did not know what to make of the new concept. On January 12, 1996, Sun officially released Java—its new network software. With the announcement of Java, Sun entered a new era with a tremendous amount of public exposure and a hightened interest in the company.

The brand name Java referred to many things, including a programming language plus a set of components and tools. It was originally looked at as a language that would jazz up web pages with graphic animations—dancing icons, for example. To Microsoft's dismay, Java evolved to trick people into thinking it is a computing platform. Its most important part was what made Java a self-sufficient computing system: the Java Virtual Machine, or JVM. The JVM was a piece of software that imitated all the functions of the computing device. This allowed Java to run on any machine with a JVM, insensitive to the underlying operating system (Windows, Macintosh, UNIX, etc.), and it allowed applications written in Java to run on all machines without being changed. The Java digital language was the first universal software that would allow all computerized devices to share programs and communicate over a network. It made possible the rapid development of versatile programs for communicating and collaborating on the Internet.

Compared to ordinary software applications, Java applications, or "applets," were little programs that resided on the network in centralized servers. The network delivered the programs to the user's machine when needed. Because the applets were so much smaller, they required comparably less time to download. In other words, Java let programmers write small applications that could zip across the World Wide Web. Without leaving the browser, the user could print out attractive text and charts. The user always got the latest version of the applets. Because the software was stored in only one place, corporations could keep it updated more easily. Java's designers believed that in this new environment, the program's speed would be measured by how fast a program ran on a network and not by how fast a program ran on an individual computer. In this sense, being object oriented versus speed oriented made programs run faster or at least appear to. Java was developed to have its objects move quickly into and out of different machines and merge with other Java objects on the network, even when these objects appeared unexpectedly.

With the immense growth of the World Wide Web, Java's introduction was one of those magic moments where place and time seemed perfect. It appeared to be the language best suited for Internet computing. In addition to not only applying to all PCs, Java was also inherently virus-proof because the language was designed so that applets could not alter data in the user's computer's files or on its hard disk. Silicon Graphics and Macromedia partnered with Sun to jointly define a new set of open multimedia formats and application programming interfaces (APIs) to extend Sun's Java. The companies believed that these new API formats would enhance Java's capabilities for providing animation and interactivity, especially in the area of 3D rendering and multimedia over the Internet or corporate networks.

With the increasing importance of the Internet, McNealy once more was convinced that Java will alter the dynamics of the business. "Java opens up a whole new world for Sun," he said. It can be said that a part of the new world had already started. Java was well on its way to becoming the Internet software standard, which would put Sun as the leader in Internet computing. Millions of personal computer owners already had access to Java in 1998 because the software was built into the 1996 release of Netscape's web browser. As the "intelligent network" also started to include mobile phones, smart pagers, hand-held electronic assistants, and so on, in addition to the traditional computers, Java was set to become a standard language for these far-flung devices.

Although Sun was planning to eventually donate the software language to the computer world by publicizing all the specs and letting anybody use them, Java could continue to spur profitable growth for the company. According to management, Java should increase Sun's sale of Internet servers, priced at $25,000, and start its new line of JavaStation network computers. Java should also raise the demand for Sun's software development tools and for special Sun chips, which other computer makers could incorporate into their machines to run Java faster.

McNealy's view of the future was not shared universally, however. It was very unlikely that Java would change computing soon. The programming language was fairly immature, and its programs ran significantly slower than programs written specifically for a particular computer operating system. Furthermore, the system of distributing software on the web has raised security issues.

THE JAVA CONTROVERSY

By the first week of December 1995, many of the top names in computing from Netscape Communications to Oracle Systems, Apple, BulletProof Corporation, Wind River Systems, Inc., Toshiba, and IBM had endorsed Java. IBM had 2,500 programmers working to improve Java because it saw Java as the glue that could finally link its many lines of computers seamlessly. Because Java programs ran on any hardware or operating system, Java could bypass and therefore break Microsoft's cash cow, Microsoft Office. For Java to be present on further PCs, Sun tried to persuade Microsoft to incorporate a Java interpreter right into the Windows operating systems. After four months of negotiations, Sun received a fax from Microsoft in March 1996 agreeing to license Java on Sun's terms. Microsoft had changed its strategy of writing its own software for any interface or function (unless customers demanded that Microsoft adopted another) because of a software language. In its many years of business, Microsoft had rarely adopted anyone else's software or hardware standards. The company had agreed to license a product from Sun, because it did not have a lot of choices.

On October 7, 1997, however, Sun Microsystems announced that the company had filed a lawsuit in U.S. District Court, Northern District of California, San Jose Division, against Microsoft Corporation for breaching its contractual obligation to deliver a compatible implementation of Java technology on its products. More detailed, the complaint charged Microsoft with trademark infringement, false advertising, breach of contract, unfair competition, interference with prospective economic advantage, and inducing breach of contract. Sun claimed that Microsoft had deliberately violated its licensing agreement in its attempt to reduce the cross platform compatibility made possible by the Java technology and deliver a version of the technology that worked only with Microsoft's products. Sun also added an additional charge that Microsoft illegally placed Sun's software code on its World Wide Web site. Sun asked for $35 million in damages over that one issue.

Even though there had been threats about revoking Microsoft's Java licensing agreement, Sun did not plan to cancel Microsoft's license. The company's goal is to pressure Microsoft to fulfill the obligations created in that license. Sun was seeking a court order to hinder Microsoft from improperly using the Java-compatible logo and deceiving the marketplace. The logo appeared in different locations in and on Microsoft's consumer packaging and promotional materials. Sun was further seeking to hinder Microsoft from misleading Java developers and to prevent the company from delivering anything but fully compatible Java technology implementations. Sun saw itself as responsible for defending the integrity of Java. Michael Morris, Sun's VP/General Counsel, stated, "nowhere is the sanctity of a trademark more important than in the field of computer software. Our customers rely on the reputation and the goodwill of the trademark to make informed, efficient decisions about the technology they are using."

One of any Java licensee's most significant contractual obligations was to pass the Java compatibility tests. These tests determined if a licensee's technology conformed to the Java specifications and APIs. In Microsoft's case, the products that failed were the new Internet Explorer 4.0 browser and the company's Software Development Kit for Java (SDKJ). The new technology did not pass Sun's compatibility tests due to Microsoft's improper modification to the products. Hence, applications written using Microsoft's development tools had not run on all machines without making the necessary adjustments.

For the two companies the stakes were high. McNealy was convinced that Sun could win a lawsuit against Microsoft, the most powerful software company in the world, by having a court that looks at the case, not at the companies involved. Winning the suit would enable Sun to live up to the CEO's idea behind his drive to develop Java: To free the world of the duopolistic grip of Microsoft and Intel or so-called Wintel. It would open the market for Sun and other computer companies. As Microsoft was fully aware of McNealy's concept, its strategy behind the company's allegedly illegal behavior was to encourage developers to write Java programs that were tied to Windows. This would block Sun's efforts to expand the language into a possible full-blown operating system.

Sun and its CEO were very confident that the court would see the merits of the complaint and move to a speedy resolution. Sun seemed to ignore, however, that Microsoft, Intel Corp., Digital Equipment Corp., and Compaq Computer Corp. had all signed an open letter on September 11, 1997, that urged Sun to turn control of Java over to the International Standards Organization (ISO). This demand would put the Java logo in the public domain. Sun seemed to have missed that this suit was not solely about Microsoft. It was about whether Sun could respond to the standards body. If Sun lost, its previously forwarded plan where the ISO would have some oversight over Java might not get accepted and Sun would have to give up the control of the key components of Java and the Java brand. This, in turn, would lead to a huge future loss in revenue and a decline in any investments of many trustworthy companies like IBM, who had partnered with Sun in the development of Java. Furthermore, it would enable Microsoft to establish a Windows-only variant of Java, one that would only benefit Wintel (PCs based on Intel's microprocessor using the Windows operating system) machine users, as a competing standard that would block Sun from creating a uniform Java that could run equally well on any type of computer.

THE VENDETTA WITH MICROSOFT

The suit had developed into a public fight between Sun Microsystems and Microsoft, two extremely successful companies. This sniping between Sun and Microsoft was more about who controlled the future of computing than the surface spat over the Java Internet programming language. Microsoft had brought its weight into play to slow Sun down further. Microsoft was using its power, market visibility, and market presence to try to reposition Java as "just another programming language."

The rivalry between the two companies became so shrill that Aaron Goldberg of Computer Intelligence in La Jolla, California, called it a "urinary Olympics." After winning out over Apple, Lotus, and WordPerfect, Microsoft was convinced that it was on its way to win the browser war as well. Netscape was still growing and finding new customers; it could lose out to Microsoft as well. Thinking that Sun would succeed where others had failed was probably irrational.

At the same time, it had to be said that it might be smart to be perceived as the one company who was attacking Microsoft. Many CIOs (Chief Information Officers) started to worry about the increasing costs of information technology systems and software and their dependence on Microsoft and Intel. The incredibly high sums spent on equipment and maintenance increased the CIOs' willingness to support new alternatives. In addition to the CIOs, customers always liked to apply pressure to the market leaders in the hope of driving down prices. Consumers liked the concept that no user of Java needed to buy the software in a retail store or from an electronic catalogue; it was part of the economic transaction. There was also a willingness and availability of money in the industry to help anyone who might loosen Microsoft's control over the way things will be in the future. This was why there had been so much support for Java, even more than McNealy originally expected.

McNealy soon would have to decide if this almost personal vendetta to break Microsoft's power in the computer industry was in the best interest of Sun's shareholders and if it was a healthy path for Sun in the future. He could have considered cooperating with

Microsoft. This would have opened up Java to the masses and could have helped Sun sell even more highly profitable servers and workstations. Stating Sun's point of view that Java did not have to make money for the company as long as it helped the company break Microsoft's business model showed the intent of McNealy. Sadly enough, this might really not have been in the public's best interest. McNealy was convinced "if Java catches on big, the software lock-in of the Microsoft Windows/Intel design will end. Then, computer and software companies will once again be able to differentiate their products. Indeed, they will have to." If Java did not catch on or especially if Sun lost the suit, no one, including McNealy, would know what Sun's future would look like in the computer technology industry, especially if one considered that the lawsuit as well as Java itself did not affect Microsoft as much as originally thought. The fact that many people liked Java did not change how customers wanted to use those computers on their desks. They still wanted to calculate spreadsheets, process words, hold presentations, and manage personal information by using software that allowed people to do all of it as conveniently as possible. It did not seem to make a difference that the new programmers would use Java to create new software. Many of the present programmers would continue using conventional languages to develop commercial software as all the new languages would end up running on Windows machines anyway, if only because these are the machines the majority of the users already had.

SUN MICROSYSTEMS FACED REVOLT OVER JAVA CONTROL

Sun Microsystems was facing an industry revolt against its control of Java, the computer language that allowed programs to run on any system. On November 2, 1998, 14 companies, including Hewlett-Packard, Microsoft, Siemens, and Rockwell, announced they would start setting their own standards for creating Java programs that controlled devices such as cellphones and printers. The move followed several months of negotiations with Sun over industry complaints that it was being too slow at developing new software standards and was charging too much in licensing fees.

Joe Beyers, general manager of Internet Software at Hewlett-Packard, said, "We are trying to respond to customer needs, but Sun has been unwilling to relinquish control of Java. If they want to go in a different direction, they can, but I hope they can join us."

Sun focused on developing Java for mainstream computer programming to the frustration of companies wanting to develop other uses. Sun had yet to start selling its own system for running Java programs on embedded processors.

In 1998, Hewlett-Packard broke Sun's grip on Java by developing its own system for operating Java programs called Chai, which does not require a license from Sun. Beyers said several other companies were developing similar systems.

POSTSCRIPT

On November 24, 1998, America Online (AOL) announced it was purchasing Netscape Communications for $4.2 billion and entering into a multilayered strategic partnership with Sun Microsystems to develop new Internet Access devices (see Exhibit 5).

Exhibit 5   AOL, Netscape, and Sun Microsystems Announced a Union

America Online
- Reaches 60 million Internet users
- Controls Netcenter, the fastest growing gateway to the Web. AOL can offer businesses a one-stop shop for setting up storefronts in cyberspace and access to its customers.
- Earns revenue from Netscape corporate software sold by Sun
- Licenses Java technology from Sun for use in future Internet access devices

Netscape
- Gets AOL's financial, technological backing
- Gains wider distribution of its comporate and electronic-commerce software through Sun and AOL

Sun
- Broadens its product line by including Netscape's respected corporate and electronic-commerce software with Sun hardware
- Gets wider distribution of Java and other software technology
- Becomes a hardware supplier to AOL, the world's biggest online service

Microsoft
- Faces a stronger competitor for its Internet businesses
- Gets a major new argument against the Justice Department as Netscape, AOL, and Sun are now stronger competitiors

Source: Doug Levy, "AOL, Netscape Announced Union," *USA Today* (November 25, 1998), p. 2B.

References

Alsop, Stewart, "Warning to Scott McNealy: Don't Moon the Ogre," *Fortune* (October 13, 1997).

Alsop, Stewart, "Sun's Java: What's Hype, What's Real," *Fortune* (July 7, 1997).

Bank, David, "Sun Lawsuit Is Latest Shot at Microsoft," *Wall Street Journal* (October 9, 1997).

Bank, David, "Sun Suit Says Microsoft Disrupts Java," *Wall Street Journal* (October 10, 1997).

"BulletProof Releases JdesignerPro 2.32—Advanced RAD Application Development System for Java": biz.yahoo.com/prnews/980120/ca_bulletp_1.html. January 20, 1998

Fitzgerald, Michael, "Sun's Threat: Microsoft Could Lose Java License," *ZDNet* (September 23, 1997).

Gomes, Lee, "Sun Microsystems 1st-Period Net, Sales Miss Expectations Due to Currency Rates," *Wall Street Journal* (October 17, 1997).

Gomes, Lee, and Clark, Don, "Java Is Finding Niches But Isn't Yet Living Up To Its Early Promises," *Wall Street Journal* (August 27, 1997).

Gomes, Lee, "Profits at Sun Microsystems Increase 56%," *Wall Street Journal* (April 16, 1997).

Hamm, Steve with Robert Hof, "Operation Sunblock: Microsoft Goes to War," *Business Week* (October 27, 1997).

Hof, Robert D. with Peter Burrows and Kathy Rebello, "Scott McNealy's Rising Sun," *Business Week* (January 22, 1996).

Hof, Robert D. with John Verity, "Now, Sun Has To Keep Java Perking," *Business Week* (January 22, 1996).

Indiana Rigdon, Joan, "Sun Microsystems' Earnings Soar 41% Due to Strength at Top of Product Line," *Wall Street Journal* (January 16, 1997).

Kirkpatrick, David, "Meanwhile, Back at Headquarters . . . ," *Fortune* (October 13, 1997).

Mitchell, Russ, "Extreme Fighting, Silicon Valley Style," *U.S. News & World Report* (October 20, 1997).

Schlender, Brent, "The Adventures of Scott McNealy," *Fortune* (October 13, 1997).

Schlender, Brent, "Sun's Java: The Threat to Microsoft Is Real," *Fortune* (November 11, 1996).

Seminerio, Maria, "Java Jive: Microsoft vs. Sun Draws No Blood—Yet," *ZDNet* (September 23, 1997).

Sun Microsystems Seeks to Bar Microsoft from Unauthorized Use of 'Java Compatible' Logo": *www.java.sun.com/pr/1997/nov/sun.pr971118.html.* November 18, 1997

"Sun Microsystems, Silicon Graphics and Macomecia Intend to Define a New Set of Open 3D and Multimedia Interfaces for Java and the Web" from Sun's home page: *www.sun.com*

Sun Microsystems, Inc., *1996 Annual Report*

Sun Microsystems, Inc., *1997 Annual Report*

Sun Microsystems, Inc.'s home page: *www.sun.com*

"Sun Sues Microsoft for Breach of Java Contract": *www.sun.com/smi/Presssunflash/9710/sunflash.971007.10.html.* October 7, 1997

"Sun Unveils Plans to Grow Desktop Market at Expense of Compaq, H-P and SGI": *www.sun.com/smi/Press/sunflash/9801/sunflash.980113.3.html.* January 13, 1998

"Wind River System's Tornado for Java Passes Sun Microsystems' Java Compatibility Tests": biz.yahoo.com/prnews/980121/ca_wind_ri_1.html. January 21, 1998

Industry Three   Entertainment/Travel

Circus Circus Enterprises, Inc. (1998)

John K. Ross III, Michael J. Keeffe, and Bill J. Middlebrook

> We possess the resources to accomplish the big projects: the know-how, the financial power, and the places to invest. The renovation of our existing projects will soon be behind us, which last year represented the broadest scope of construction ever taken on by a gaming company. Now we are well positioned to originate new projects. Getting big projects right is the route to future wealth in gaming; big successful projects tend to prove long staying power in our business. When the counting is over, we think our customers and investors will hold the winning hand.
>
> —Circus Circus Enterprises, Inc., *1997 Annual Report*

Big projects and a winning hand. Circus Circus seemed to have both. And big projects they were, with huge pink and white striped concrete circus tents, a 600-foot-long riverboat replica, a giant castle, and a great pyramid. Its latest project, Mandalay Bay, would include a 3,700-room hotel/casino, an 11-acre aquatic environment with beaches, a snorkeling reef, and a swim-up shark exhibit.

Circus Circus Enterprises, Inc., (hereafter Circus) described itself as being in the business of entertainment and was one of the innovators in the theme resort concept that is popular in casino gaming. Their areas of operation were the glitzy vacation and convention meccas of Las Vegas, Reno, and Laughlin, Nevada, as well as other locations in the United States and abroad. Historically Circus's marketing of its products had been called "right out of the bargain basement" and had catered to "low rollers." Circus continued to broaden its market and now aimed more at the middle-income gambler and family-oriented vacationers as well as the more upscale traveler and player.

Circus was purchased in 1974 for $50,000 as a small and unprofitable casino operation by partners William G. Bennett, an aggressive cost-cutter who ran furniture stores before entering the gaming industry in 1965, and William N. Pennington (see Exhibit 1 for Board of Directors and Top Managers). The partners were able to rejuvenate Circus with fresh marketing, went public with a stock offering in October 1983, and experienced rapid growth and high profitability over time. Within the five-year period from 1993 to 1997, the average return on invested capital was 16.5% and Circus had generated over $1 billion in free cash flow. In 1998, Circus was one of the major players in the Las Vegas, Laughlin, and Reno markets in terms of square footage of casino space and number of hotel rooms—despite the incredible growth in both markets. For the first time in company history, casino gaming operations in 1997 provided slightly less than one-half of total revenues and that trend continued into 1998 (see Exhibit 2). On January 31, 1998, Circus reported a net income of approximately $89.9 million on revenues of $1.35 billion. This was down slightly from 1997's more than $100 million net income on revenues of $1.3 billion. Circus had invested over $585.8 million in capital expenditures during 1997, and another $663.3 million was invested in fiscal year 1998.

This case was prepared by Professors John K. Ross III, Michael J. Keeffe, and Bill J. Middlebrook of Southwest Texas State University. The case was edited for SMBP–7th Edition. Copyright © 1998 by John K. Ross III, Michael J. Keeffe, and Bill J. Middlebrook. Reprinted by permission.

Exhibit 1   Corporate Executives: Circus Circus Enterprises, Inc.

A. Directors

Name	Age	Title
Clyde T. Turner	59	Chairman of the Board and CEO Circus Circus Enterprises
Michael S. Ensign	59	Vice-Chairman of the Board and COO Circus Circus Enterprises
Glenn Schaeffer	43	President, CFO Circus Circus Enterprises
William A. Richardson	50	Vice-Chairman of the Board and Executive Vice-President Circus Circus Enterprises
Richard P. Banis	52	Former President and COO Circus Circus Enterprises
Arthur H. Bilger	44	Former President and COO New World Communications Group International
Richard A. Etter	58	Former Chairman and CEO Bank of America–Nevada
William E. Bannen, M.D.	48	Vice-President/Chief Medical Officer, Blue Cross Blue Shield of Nevada
Donna B. More	40	Partner, Law Firm of Freeborn & Peters
Michael D. McKee	51	Executive Vice-President The Irving Company

B. Officers

Name	Title
Clyde T. Turner	Chairman of the Board and Chief Executive Officer
Michael S. Ensign	Vice-Chairman of the Board and Chief Operating Officer
Glenn Schaeffer	President, Chief Financial Officer, and Treasurer
William A. Richardson	Vice-Chairman of the Board and Executive Vice-President Circus Circus Enterprises
Tony Alamo	Senior Vice-President, Operations
Gregg Solomon	Senior Vice-President, Operations
Kurt D. Sullivan	Senior Vice-President, Operations
Steve Greathouse	Senior Vice-President, Operations
Yvett Landau	Vice-President, General Counsel, and Secretary
Les Martin	Vice-President and Chief Accounting Officer

Source: Circus Circus Enterprises, Inc., *1998 Annual Report,* Proxy Statement (May 1, 1998).

CIRCUS CIRCUS OPERATIONS

Circus defined entertainment as pure play and fun, and it went out of its way to see that customers had plenty of opportunities for both. Each Circus location had a distinctive personality.

Circus Locations

Circus Circus–Las Vegas was the world of the Big Top, where live circus acts performed free every 30 minutes. Kids could cluster around video games, while the adults migrated to nickel slot machines and dollar game tables. Located at the north end of the Vegas strip, Circus Circus–Las Vegas sat on 69 acres of land with 3,744 hotel rooms, shopping areas, two specialty restaurants, a buffet with seating for 1,200, fast food shops, cocktail lounges, video arcades, and 109,000 square feet of casino space. It also included the Grand Slam Canyon, a 5-acre glass enclosed theme park with a four-loop roller coaster. Approximately 384 guests could also stay at nearby Circusland RV Park. For the year ending January 31, 1997, $126.7 million was invested in this property for new rooms and remodeling, with another $35.2 million invested in fiscal 1998.

Exhibit 2   **Sources of Revenues as a Percentage of Net Revenues: Circus Circus Enterprises, Inc.**

Source	1998	1997	1996	1995
Casinos	46.7%	49.2%	51.2%	52.3%
Food & Beverage	15.9	15.8	15.5	16.2
Hotel	24.4	22.0	21.4	19.9
Other	10.5	11.0	12.2	14.2
Unconsolidated	7.3	6.5	3.5	.5
Less Complimentary Allowances	(4.8)	(4.5)	(3.8)	(3.1)

Source: Circus Circus Enterprises, Inc., *1995–1998 Form 10-Ks.*

Luxor, an Egyptian-themed hotel and casino complex, opened on October 15, 1993, when 10,000 people entered to play the 2,245 slot and video poker games and the 110 table games in the 120,000-square-foot casino in the hotel atrium (reported to be the world's largest). By the end of the opening weekend, 40,000 people per day were visiting the 30-story bronze pyramid that encased the hotel and entertainment facilities.

Luxor featured a 30-story pyramid and two new 22-story hotel towers, including 492 suites. It was connected to the Excalibur casino by a climate-controlled skyway with moving walkways. Situated at the south end of the Las Vegas strip on a 64-acre site adjacent to Excalibur, Luxor featured a food and entertainment area on three levels beneath the hotel atrium. The pyramid's hotel rooms could be reached from the four corners of the building by state-of-the-art "inclinators," which traveled at a 39-degree angle. Parking was available for nearly 3,200 vehicles, including a covered garage with approximately 1,800 spaces.

The Luxor underwent major renovations costing $323.3 million during fiscal 1997 and another $116.5 million in fiscal 1998. The resulting complex contains 4,425 hotel rooms, extensively renovated casino space, an additional 20,000 square feet of convention area, an 800-seat buffet, a series of IMAX attractions, five theme restaurants, seven cocktail lounges, and a variety of specialty shops. Circus expected to draw significant walk-in traffic to the newly refurbished Luxor and was one of the principal components of the Masterplan Mile.

Located next to the Luxor, Excalibur was one of the first sights travelers saw as they exited I-15 (management was confident that the sight of a giant, colorful medieval castle would make a lasting impression on mainstream tourists and vacationing families arriving in Las Vegas). Guests crossed a drawbridge, with moat, onto a cobblestone walkway where multicolored spires, turrets, and battlements loomed above. The castle walls were four 28-story hotel towers containing 4,008 rooms. Inside was a medieval world complete with a Fantasy Faire inhabited by strolling jugglers, fire eaters, and acrobats, as well as a Royal Village complete with peasants, serfs, and ladies-in-waiting around medieval theme shops. The 110,000-square-foot casino encompassed 2,442 slot machines, more than 89 game tables, a sports book, and a poker and keno area. There were 12 restaurants, capable of feeding more than 20,000 people daily, and a 1,000-seat amphitheater. Excalibur, which opened in June 1990, was built for $294 million and primarily financed with internally generated funds. In the year ending January 31, 1997, Excalibur contributed 23% of the organization's revenues, down from 33% in 1993. Yet 1997 was a record year, generating the company's highest margins and over $100 million in operating cash flow. In fiscal 1998, Excalibur underwent $25.1 million in renovations and was connected to the Luxor by enclosed, moving walkways.

Situated between the two anchors on the Las Vegas strip (Circus Circus–Las Vegas at one end and Luxor/Excalibur at the other) were two smaller casinos owned and operated by Circus. The Silver City Casino and Slots-A-Fun primarily depended on the foot traffic along the strip for their gambling patrons. Combined, they offered more than 1,202 slot machines and 46 gaming tables on 34,900 square feet of casino floor.

Circus owned and operated ten properties in Nevada and one in Mississippi, and it had a 50% ownership in three others (see Exhibit 3).

All of Circus's operations did well in Las Vegas. However, Circus Circus's 1997 operational earnings for the Luxor and Circus Circus–Las Vegas were off 38% from the previous year. Management credited the disruption in services due to renovations for this decline.

However, Circus's combined hotel room occupancy rates had remained above 90% due, in part, to low room rates ($45 to $69 at Circus Circus–Las Vegas) and popular buffets. Each of the major properties contained large, inexpensive buffets that management believed made staying with Circus more attractive. Yet, recent results showed a room occupancy rate of 87.5%, due in part to the building boom in Las Vegas.

The company's other big-top facility was Circus Circus–Reno. With the addition of Skyway Tower in 1985, this big top offered a total of 1,605 hotel rooms, 60,600 square feet of casino, a buffet that could seat 700 people, shops, video arcades, cocktail lounges, midway games, and circus acts. Circus Circus–Reno had several marginal years, but it became one of the leaders in the Reno market. Circus anticipated that recent remodeling, at a cost of $25.6 million, would increase this property's revenue generating potential.

The Colorado Belle and the Edgewater Hotel were located in Laughlin, Nevada, on the banks of the Colorado River, a city 90 miles south of Las Vegas. The Colorado Belle, opened in 1987, featured a huge paddlewheel riverboat replica, buffet, cocktail lounges, and shops. The Edgewater, acquired in 1983, had a southwestern motif, a 57,000-square-foot casino, a bowling center, buffet, and cocktail lounges. Combined, these two properties contained 2,700 rooms and over 120,000 square feet of casino. These two operations contributed 12% of the company's revenues in the year ended January 31, 1997, and again in 1998, down from 21% in 1994. The extensive proliferation of casinos throughout the region, primarily on Indian land, and the development of mega-resorts in Las Vegas seriously eroded outlying markets such as Laughlin.

Three properties purchased in 1995 and located in Jean and Henderson, Nevada, represented Circus's continuing investments in outlying markets. The Gold Strike and Nevada Landing service the I-15 market between Las Vegas and southern California. These properties had over 73,000 square feet of casino space, 2,140 slot machines, and 42 gaming tables combined. Each had limited hotel space (1,116 rooms total) and depended heavily on I-15 traffic. The Railroad Pass was considered a local casino and was dependent on Henderson residents as its market. This smaller casino contained only 395 slot machines and 11 gaming tables.

Gold Strike–Tunica (formally Circus Circus–Tunica) was a dockside casino located in Tunica, Mississippi. It opened in 1994 on 24 acres of land located along the Mississippi River, approximately 20 miles south of Memphis. In 1997, operating income declined by more than 50% due to the increase in competition and lack of hotel rooms. Circus decided to renovate this property and add a 1,200-room tower hotel. The total cost for all remodeling was $119.8 million.

Joint Ventures

Circus was currently engaged in three joint ventures through the wholly-owned subsidiary Circus Participant. In Las Vegas, Circus joined with Mirage Resorts to build and op-

Exhibit 3   **Properties and Percentage of Total Revenues:
Circus Circus Enterprises, Inc.**

Properties	Percent Revenues			
	1998	1997	1996	1995
Las Vegas				
Circus Circus–Las Vegas	25%[1]	24%[1]	27%[1]	29%[1]
Excalibur	21	23	23	25
Luxor	23	17	20	24
Slots-A-Fun and Silver City				
Reno				
Circus Circus–Reno				
Laughlin				
Colorado Bell	12[2]	12[2]	13[2]	16[2]
Edgewater				
Jean, Nevada				
Gold Strike	6[3]	6[3]	4[3]	—
Nevada Landing				
Henderson, Nevada				
Railroad Pass				
Tunica, Mississippi				
Gold Strike	4	4	5	3
50% ownership				
Silver Legacy, Reno, Nevada	7.3	6.5[4]	3.5[4]	.5[4]
Monte Carlo, Las Vegas, Nevada				
Grand Victoria Riverboat Casino, Elgin, Illinois				

Notes:
1. Combined with revenues from Circus Circus–Reno.
2. Colorado Bell and Edgewater have been combined.
3. Gold Strike and Nevada Landing have been combined.
4. Revenues of unconsolidated affiliates have been combined. Revenues from Slots-A-Fun and Silver City, management fees, and other income were not separately reported.

erate the Monte Carlo, a hotel-casino with 3,002 rooms designed along the lines of the grand casinos of the Mediterranean. It was located on 46 acres (with 600 feet on the Las Vegas strip) between the New York-New York casino and the soon to be completed Bellagio, with all three casinos to be connected by monorail. The Monte Carlo featured a 90,000-square-foot casino containing 2,221 slot machines and 95 gaming tables, along with a 550-seat bingo parlor, high-tech arcade rides, restaurants and buffets, a microbrewery, approximately 15,000 square feet of meeting and convention space, and a 1,200-seat theater. Opened on June 21, 1996, the Monte Carlo generated $14.6 million as Circus's share in operating income for the first seven months of operation.

In Elgin, Illinois, Circus was in a 50% partnership with Hyatt Development Corporation in the Grand Victoria. Styled to resemble a Victorian riverboat, this floating casino and land-based entertainment complex included some 36,000 square feet of casino space, containing 977 slot machines and 56 gaming tables. The adjacent land-based complex contained two movie theaters, a 240-seat buffet, restaurants, and parking for approximately 2,000 vehicles. Built for $112 million, the Grand Victoria returned $44 million in operating income to Circus in 1996.

The third joint venture was a 50% partnership with Eldorado Limited in the Silver Legacy. Opened in 1995, this casino was located between Circus Circus–Reno and the Eldorado Hotel and Casino on two city blocks in downtown Reno, Nevada. The Silver Legacy had 1,711 hotel rooms, 85,000 square feet of casino, 2,275 slot machines, and 89 gaming tables. Management seemed to believe that the Silver Legacy held promise; however, the Reno market was suffering and the opening of the Silver Legacy had cannibalized the Circus Circus–Reno market.

Circus engaged in a fourth joint venture to penetrate the Canadian market, but on January 23, 1997, announced they had been bought out by Hilton Hotels Corporation, one of three partners in the venture.

Circus achieved success through an aggressive growth strategy and a corporate structure designed to enhance that growth. A strong cash position, innovative ideas, and attention to cost control allowed Circus to satisfy the bottom line during a period when competitors were typically taking on large debt obligations to finance new projects. (See Exhibits 4–7.) Yet the market was changing. Gambling of all kinds had spread across the country; no longer did the average individual need to go to Las Vegas or New Jersey. Instead, gambling could be found as close as the local quick market (lottery), bingo hall, many Indian reservations, the Mississippi River, and others. There were almost 300 casinos in Las Vegas alone, 60 in Colorado, and 160 in California. To maintain a competitive edge, Circus continued to invest heavily in the renovation of existing properties (a strategy common to the entertainment/amusement industry) and continued to develop new projects.

New Ventures

Circus currently had three new projects planned for opening within the near future. The largest project, Mandalay Bay, was scheduled for completion in the first quarter 1999 and was estimated to cost $950 million (excluding land). Circus owned a contiguous mile of the southern end of the Las Vegas strip, which they called their "Masterplan Mile" and which currently contains the Excalibur and Luxor resorts. Located next to the Luxor, Mandalay Bay is aimed at the upscale traveler and player and was to be styled as a South Seas adventure. The resort would contain a 43-story hotel-casino with over 3,700 rooms and an 11-acre aquatic environment. The aquatic environment would contain a surfing beach, swim-up shark tank, and snorkeling reef. A Four Seasons Hotel with 400 rooms would complement the remainder of Mandalay Bay. Circus anticipated that the remainder of the Masterplan Mile would eventually include at least one additional casino resort and several stand-alone hotels and amusement centers.

Circus also planned three other casino projects, provided all the necessary licenses and agreements could be obtained. In Detroit, Circus combined with the Atwater Casino Group in a joint venture to build a $600 million project. Although negotiations with the city to develop the project had been completed, the remainder of the appropriate licenses needed to be obtained before construction began.

Along the Mississippi Gulf, at the north end of the Bay of St. Louis, Circus planned to construct a casino resort containing 1,500 rooms at an estimated cost of $225 million. Circus had received all the necessary permits to begin construction, but these approvals had been challenged in court, delaying the project.

In Atlantic City, Circus had entered into an agreement with Mirage Resorts to develop a 181-acre site in the Marina District. Land title had been transferred to Mirage, but Mirage had purported to cancel its agreement with Circus. Circus had filed suit against Mirage seeking to enforce the contract, while others had filed suit to stop all development in the area.

Exhibit 4 **Selected Financial Information: Circus Circus Enterprises, Inc.**

Fiscal Year	1998	1997	1996	1995	1994	1993	1992	1991
Earnings per share ($)	0.40	0.99	1.33	1.59	1.34	2.05	1.84	1.39
Current ratio	.85	1.17	1.30	1.35	.95	.90	1.14	.88
Total liabilities/Total assets	.65	.62	.44	.54	.57	.48	.58	.77
Operating profit margin	17.4%	17.0%	19.0%	22.0%	21.0%	24.4%	24.9%	22.9%

Source: Circus Circus Enterprises, Inc., *Annual Reports* and *Form 10-Ks* (1991–1998).

Most of Circus's projects were being tailored to attract mainstream tourists and family vacationers. However, the addition of several joint ventures and the completion of the Masterplan Mile would also attract the more upscale customer.

THE GAMING INDUSTRY

By 1997, the gaming industry had captured a large amount of the vacation/leisure time dollars spent in the United States. Gamblers lost over $44.3 billion on legal wagering in 1995 (up from $29.9 billion in 1992), including wagers at racetracks, bingo parlors, lotteries, and casinos. This figure did not include dollars spent on lodging, food, transportation, and other related expenditures associated with visits to gaming facilities. Casino gambling accounted for 76% of all legal gambling expenditures, far ahead of second place Indian Reservation at 8.9% and lotteries at 7.1%. The popularity of casino gambling could be credited to a more frequent and somewhat higher pay out as compared to lotteries and racetracks; however, as winnings were recycled, the multiplier effect restored a high return to casino operators.

Geographic expansion had slowed considerably; no additional states had approved casino type gambling since 1993. Growth had occurred in developed locations, with Las Vegas, Nevada, and Atlantic City, New Jersey, leading the way.

Las Vegas remained the largest U.S. gaming market and one of the largest convention markets with more than 100,000 hotel rooms hosting more than 29.6 million visitors in 1996, up 2.2% over 1995. Casino operators were building to take advantage of this continued growth. Recent projects included the Monte Carlo ($350 million), New York-New York ($350 million), Bellagino ($1.4 billion), Hilton Hotels ($750 million), and Project Paradise ($800 million). Additionally, Harrah's was adding a 989-room tower and remodeling 500 current rooms, and Caesar's Palace had plans to add 2,000 rooms. Las Vegas hotel and casino capacity was expected to continue to expand with some 12,500 rooms opening within a year, beginning in the fall of 1998. According to the Las Vegas Convention and Visitor Authority, Las Vegas was a destination market with most visitors planning their trip more than a week in advance (81%), arriving by car (47%) or airplane (42%), and staying in a hotel (72%). Gamblers were typically return visitors (77%), averaging 2.2 trips per year for those who like playing the slots (65%).

For Atlantic City, besides the geographical separation, the primary differences in the two markets reflected the different types of consumers frequenting these markets. Las Vegas attracted overnight resort-seeking vacationers, whereas Atlantic City's clientele were predominantly day-trippers traveling by automobile or bus. Gaming revenues were expected to grow in 1997, to $4 billion split between 10 casino/hotels currently operat-

Exhibit 5   Twelve-Year Summary: Circus Circus Enterprises, Inc.

Fiscal Year	Revenues (in thousands)	Net Income
1998	$1,354,487	$ 89,908
1997	1,334,250	100,733
1996	1,299,596	128,898
1995	1,170,182	136,286
1994	954,923	116,189
1993	843,025	117,322
1992	806,023	103,348
1991	692,052	76,292
1990	522,376	76,064
1989	511,960	81,714
1988	458,856	55,900
1987	373,967	28,198
1986	306,993	37,375

Source: Circus Circus Enterprises, Inc., *Annual Reports* and *Form 10-Ks* (1986–1998).

ing. Growth in the Atlantic City area would be concentrated in the Marina section of town where Mirage Resorts had entered into an agreement with the city to develop 150 acres of the Marina as a destination resort. This development was to have included a resort wholly owned by Mirage, a casino/hotel developed by Circus, and a complex developed by a joint venture with Mirage and Boyd Corp. Currently in Atlantic City, Donald Trump's gaming empire held the largest market share with Trump's Castle, Trump Plaza, and the Taj Mahal (total market share was 30%). The next closest in market share was Caesar's (10.3%), Tropicana and Bally's (9.2% each), and Showboat (9.0%).

Several smaller markets were located around the United States, primarily in Mississippi, Louisiana, Illinois, Missouri, and Indiana. Each state had imposed various restrictions on the development of casino operations within their states. In some cases, for example, Illinois where only 10 gaming licenses are available, this had severely restricted the growth opportunities and hurt revenues. In Mississippi and Louisiana, revenues were up 8% and 15%, respectively, in riverboat operations. Native American casinos continued to be developed on federally controlled Indian land. These casinos were not publicly held but did tend to be managed by publicly held corporations. Overall these other locations presented a mix of opportunities and generally constituted only a small portion of overall gaming revenues.

MAJOR INDUSTRY PLAYERS

The past several years had seen numerous changes as mergers and acquisitions reshaped the gaming industry. As of year-end 1996, the industry was a combination of corporations ranging from those engaged solely in gaming to multinational conglomerates. The largest competitors, in terms of revenues, combined multiple industries to generate both large revenues and substantial profits (see Exhibit 8). However, those engaged primarily in gaming could also be extremely profitable.

In 1996, Hilton began a hostile acquisition attempt of ITT Corporation. As a result, ITT merged with Starwood Lodging Corporation and Starwood Lodging Trust. The

Exhibit 6 **Annual Income: Circus Circus Enterprises, Inc.**
(Dollar amounts in thousands)

Fiscal Year Ending January 31	1998	1997	1996	1995	1994
Revenues					
Casino	$ 632,122	$ 655,902	$ 664,772	$ 612,115	$538,813
Rooms	330,644	294,241	278,807	232,346	176,001
Food and beverage	215,584	210,384	201,385	189,664	152,469
Other	142,407	146,554	158,534	166,295	117,501
Earnings of unconsolidated affiliates	98,977	86,646	45,485	5,459	—
	1,419,734	1,393,727	1,348,983	1,205,879	984,784
Less complimentary allowances	(65,247)	(59,477)	(49,387)	(35,697)	(29,861)
Net revenue	1,354,487	1,334,250	1,299,596	1,170,182	954,923
Costs and expenses					
Casino	316,902	302,096	275,680	246,416	209,402
Rooms	122,934	116,508	110,362	94,257	78,932
Food and beverage	199,955	200,722	188,712	177,136	149,267
Other operating expenses	90,187	90,601	92,631	107,297	72,802
General and administrative	232,536	227,348	215,083	183,175	152,104
Depreciation and amortization	117,474	95,414	93,938	81,109	58,105
Preopening expense	3,447	—	—	3,012	16,506
Abandonment loss	—	48,309	45,148	—	—
Total costs and expenses	1,083,435	1,080,998	1,021,554	892,402	737,118
Operating profit before corporate expense	271,052	253,252	278,042	277,780	217,805
Corporate expense	34,552	31,083	26,669	21,773	16,744
Income from operations	236,500	222,169	251,373	256,007	201,061
Other income (expense)					
Interest, dividends, and other income (loss)	9,779	5,077	4,022	225	(683)
Interest income and guarantee fees from unconsolidated affiliate	6,041	6,865	7,517	992	—
Interest expense	(88,847)	(54,681)	(51,537)	(42,734)	(17,770)
Interest expense from unconsolidated affiliate	(15,551)	(15,567)	(5,616)	—	—
Income before taxes and extraordinary charges	(88,578)	(58,306)	(45,614)	(41,517)	(18,453)
Income before provision for income tax	147,922	163,863	205,759	214,490	182,608
Provision for income tax	58,014	63,130	76,861	78,204	66,419
Income before extraordinary loss	—	—	—	—	116,189
Extraordinary loss	—	—	—	—	—
Net income	$ 89,908	$ 100,733	$ 128,898	$ 136,286	$116,189
Earnings per share					
Income before extraordinary loss	.95	.99	1.33	1.59	1.34
Extraordinary loss	—	—	—	—	—
Net income per share	.94	.99	1.33	1.59	1.34

Source: Circus Circus Enterprises, Inc., *Annual Reports* and *Form 10-Ks* (1994–1998).

Exhibit 7   Consolidated Balance Sheets: Circus Circus Enterprises, Inc.
(Dollar amounts in thousands)

	January 31, 1998	January 31, 1997	January 31, 1996	January 31, 1995	January 31, 1994
Assets					
Current assets					
Cash and cash equivalents	$ 58,631	$ 69,516	$ 62,704	$ 53,764	$ 39,110
Receivables	33,640	34,434	16,527	8,931	8,673
Inventories	22,440	19,371	20,459	22,660	20,057
Prepaid expenses	20,281	19,951	19,418	20,103	20,062
Deferred income tax	7,871	8,577	7,272	5,463	—
Total current assets	142,863	151,849	124,380	110,921	87,902
Property, equipment	2,466,848	1,920,032	1,474,684	1,239,062	1,183,164
Other assets					
Excess of purchase price over fair market value	375,375	385,583	394,518	9,836	10,200
Notes receivable	1,075	36,443	27,508	68,083	—
Investments in unconsolidated affiliates	255,392	214,123	173,270	74,840	—
Deferred charges and other assets	21,995	21,081	17,533	9,806	16,658
Total other	653,837	657,230	612,829	162,565	26,858
Total assets	$3,263,548	$2,729,111	$2,213,503	$1,512,548	$1,297,924
Liabilities and Shareholders Equity					
Current liabilities					
Current portion of long-term debt	$ 3,071	$ 379	$ 863	$ 106	$ 169
Accounts and contracts payable					
Trade	22,103	22,658	16,824	12,102	14,804
Construction	40,670	21,144	—	1,101	13,844
Accrued liabilities					
Salaries, wages, and vacations	36,107	31,847	30,866	24,946	19,650
Progressive jackpots	7,511	6,799	8,151	7,447	4,881
Advance room deposits	6,217	7,383	7,517	8,701	6,981
Interest payable	17,828	9,004	3,169	2,331	2,278
Other	33,451	30,554	28,142	25,274	25,648
Income tax payable	—	—	—	—	3,806
Total current liabilities	166,958	129,768	95,532	82,008	92,061
Long-term debt	1,788,818	1,405,897	715,214	632,652	567,345
Other liabilities					
Deferred income tax	175,934	152,635	148,096	110,776	77,153
Other long-term liabilities	8,089	6,439	9,319	988	1,415
Total other liabilities	184,023	159,074	157,415	111,764	78,568
Total liabilities	2,139,799	1,694,739	968,161	826,424	737,974
Redeemable preferred stock	—	17,631	18,530	—	—
Temporary equity	—	44,950	—	—	—
Commitments and contingent liabilities					

Exhibit 7 **Consolidated Balance Sheets: Circus Circus Enterprises, Inc.** *(continued)*

	January 31, 1998	January 31, 1997	January 31, 1996	January 31, 1995	January 31, 1994
Shareholders equity					
Common stock	1,893	1,880	1,880	1,607	1,603
Preferred stock	—	—	—	—	—
Additional paid-in capital	558,658	498,893	527,205	124,960	120,135
Retained earnings	1,074,271	984,363	883,630	754,732	618,446
Treasury stock	(511,073)	(513,345)	(185,903)	(195,175)	(180,234)
Total shareholders equity	1,123,749	971,791	1,226,812	686,124	559,950
Total liabilities and shareholders' equity	$3,263,548	$2,729,111	$2,213,503	$1,512,548	$1,297,924

Source: Circus Circus Enterprises, Inc., *Annual Reports* and *Form 10-Ks* (1994–1998).

resulting corporation, Starwood/ITT, was one of the world's largest hotel and gaming corporations, owning the Sheraton, the Luxury Collection, the Four Points Hotels, and Caesar's, as well as communications and educational services. In 1996, ITT hosted approximately 50 million customer nights in locations worldwide. Gaming operations were located in Las Vegas, Atlantic City, Halifax and Sydney (Nova Scotia), Lake Tahoe, Tunica (Mississippi), Lima (Peru), Cairo (Egypt), Canada, and Australia. In 1996, ITT had a net income of $249 million on revenues of $6.579 billion. In June 1996, ITT announced plans to join with Planet Hollywood to develop casino/hotels with the Planet Hollywood theme in both Las Vegas and Atlantic City. However, these plans might be deferred as ITT became fully integrated into Starwood and management had the opportunity to refocus on the operations of the company.

Hilton Hotels owned (as of February 1, 1998) or leased and operated 25 hotels and managed 34 hotels partially or wholly owned by others along with 180 franchised hotels. Eleven of the hotels were also casinos: six in Nevada, two in Atlantic City, and three in Australia and Uruguay. In 1997, Hilton had a net income of $250.0 million on $5.31 billion in revenues. Hilton received 38% of total operating revenues from gaming operations and continues to expand in the market. Recent expansions included the Wild Wild West theme hotel casino in Atlantic City, the completed acquisition of all the assets of Bally's, and construction on a 2,900-room Paris Casino resort located next to Bally's Las Vegas.

Harrah's Entertainment, Inc., was primarily engaged in the gaming industry with casino/hotels in Reno, Lake Tahoe, Las Vegas, and Laughlin, Nevada and in Atlantic City, New Jersey; riverboats in Joliet, Illinois, Vicksburg and Tunica, Mississippi, Shreveport, Louisiana, and Kansas City, Kansas; two Indian casinos; and one in Auckland, New Zealand. In 1997, it operated a total of approximately 774,500 square feet of casino space with 19,835 slot machines and 934 table games. With this and some 8,197 hotel rooms, it had a net income of $99.3 million on $1.619 billion in revenues.

All of Mirage Resorts Inc.'s gaming operations were currently located in Nevada. It owned and operated the Golden Nugget–Downtown, Las Vegas, the Mirage on the strip in Las Vegas, Treasure Island, and the Golden Nugget–Laughlin. Additionally it was a 50% owner of the Monte Carlo with Circus Circus. Net income for Mirage Resorts in 1997 was $207 million on revenues of $1.546 billion. Current expansion plans included the

Exhibit 8   **Major U.S. Gaming, Lottery and Pari-mutuel Companies**
1996 Revenues and Net Income (in millions)

	1997 Revenues	1997 Income	1996 Revenues	1996 Net Income
Starwood/ITT	—	—	$6597.0	$249.0
Hilton Hotels	5316.0	250.0	3940.0	82.0
Harrah's Entertainment	1619.0	99.3	1586.0	98.9
Mirage Resorts	1546.0	207	1358.3	206.0
Circus Circus	1354.4	89.9	1247.0	100.7
Trump Hotel and Casino, Inc.	1399.3	−42.1	976.3	−4.9
MGM Grand	827.5	111.0	804.8	74.5
Aztar	782.3	4.4	777.5	20.6
Int. Game Technology	743.9	137.2	733.5	118.0

Source: Individual companies' *1996 Annual Reports* and *Form 10-Ks.*

development of the Bellagio in Las Vegas ($1.6 billion estimated cost) and the Beau Rivage in Biloxi, Mississippi ($600 million estimated cost). These two properties could add a total of 265,900 square feet of casino space to the current Mirage inventory and an additional 252 gaming tables and 4,746 slot machines. An additional project was the development of the Marina area in Atlantic City, New Jersey, in partnership with Boyd Gaming.

MGM Grand Hotel and Casino was located on approximately 114 acres at the northeast corner of Las Vegas Boulevard across the street from New York-New York Hotel and Casino. The casino was approximately 171,500 square feet in size and was one of the largest casinos in the world with 3,669 slot machines and 157 table games. Current plans call for extensive renovation costing $700 million. Through a wholly-owned subsidiary, MGM owned and operated the MGM Grand Diamond Beach Hotel and a hotel/casino resort in Darwin, Australia. Additionally, MGM and Primadonna Resorts, Inc., each owned 50% of New York-New York Hotel and Casino, a $460 million architecturally distinctive themed destination resort that opened on January 3, 1997. MGM also intended to construct and operate a destination resort hotel/casino, entertainment, and retail facility in Atlantic City on approximately 35 acres of land on the Atlantic City Boardwalk.

THE LEGAL ENVIRONMENT

Within the gaming industry, all current operators must consider compliance with extensive gaming regulations as a primary concern. Each state or country had its own specific regulations and regulatory boards requiring extensive reporting and licensing requirements. For example, in Las Vegas, Nevada, gambling operations were subject to regulatory control by the Nevada State Gaming Control Board, by the Clark County Nevada Gaming and Liquor Licensing Board, and by city government regulations. The laws, regulations, and supervisory procedures of virtually all gaming authorities were based on public policy primarily concerned with the prevention of unsavory or unsuitable persons from having a direct or indirect involvement with gaming at any time or in any capacity and the establishment and maintenance of responsible accounting practices and procedures. Additional regulations typically covered the maintenance of effective controls over the financial practices of licensees (establishing minimum procedures for internal fiscal affairs, safeguarding assets and revenues, providing reliable record keeping, and filing periodic reports), the prevention of cheating and fraudulent practices, and the provision of a source of state and local revenues through taxation and licensing fees. Changes in such laws, regulations, and procedures could have an adverse effect on gaming operations. All gaming companies must submit detailed operating and financial reports to authorities. Nearly all financial transactions, including loans, leases, and the sale of securities, must be reported. Some financial activities were subject to approval by regulatory agencies. As Circus moved into other locations outside of Nevada, it would need to adhere to local regulations.

FUTURE CONSIDERATIONS

Circus Circus stated that they were "in the business of entertainment, with . . . core strength in casino gaming," and that they intended to focus their efforts in Las Vegas, Atlantic City, and Mississippi. Circus further stated that the "future product in gaming, to be sure, is the entertainment resort" (Circus Circus, *1997 Annual Report*).

Circus was one of the innovators of the gaming resort concept and continued to be a leader in that field. However the mega-entertainment resort industry operated differently from the traditional casino gaming industry. In the past, consumers would visit a casino to experience the thrill of gambling. Now they not only gambled, but expected to be dazzled by enormous entertainment complexes that were costing in the billions of dollars to build. The competition had continued to increase at the same time that growth rates had been slowing.

For years, analysts had questioned the ability of the gaming industry to continue high growth in established markets as the industry matures. Through the 1970s and 1980s, the gaming industry experienced rapid growth. Through the 1990s, the industry began to experience a shake-out of marginal competitors and a consolidation phase. Circus Circus had been successful through this turmoil, but it now faced the task of maintaining high growth in a more mature industry.

References

Aztar Corp., *1997* and *1998 Form 10-Ks,* retrieved from EDGAR Data Base, http://www.sec.gov/Archives/edgar/data/.

"Casinos Move into New Areas," *Standard and Poors Industry Surveys* (March 11, 1993), pp. L35–L41.

Circus Circus Announces Promotion, *PR Newswire* (June 10, 1997).

Circus Circus Enterprises, Inc., *Annual Report to Shareholders* (January 31, 1989, January 31, 1990, January 31, 1993, January 31, 1994, January 31, 1995, January 31, 1996).

Circus Circus Enterprises, Inc., *Annual Report to Shareholders* (January 31, 1997).

Circus Circus Enterprises, Inc., *Annual Report to Shareholders* (January 31, 1998).

Corning, Blair, "Luxor: Egypt Opens in Vegas," *San Antonio Express News* (October 24, 1993).

"Economic Impacts of Casino Gaming in the United States," by Arthur Andersen for the American Gaming Association (May 1997).

Harrah's Entertainment, Inc., *1997* and *1998 Form 10-Ks,* retrieved from EDGAR Data Base, http://www.sec.gov/Archives/edgar/data/.

"Harrah's Survey of Casino Entertainment," Harrah's Entertainment, Inc. (1996).

Industry Surveys—Lodging and Gaming, *Standard and Poors Industry Surveys* (June 19, 1997).

Hilton Hotels Corp., *1997* and *1998 Form 10-Ks,* retrieved from EDGAR Data Base, http://www.sec.gov/Archives/edgar/data/.

"ITT Board Rejects Hilton's Offer as Inadequate, Reaffirms Belief That ITT's Comprehensive Plan Is in the Best Interest of ITT Shareholders," Press Release (August 14, 1997).

ITT Corp., *1997 Form 10-K*, retrieved from EDGAR Data Base, http://www.sec.gov/Archives/edgar/data/.

Lalli, Sergio, "Excalibur Awaiteth," *Hotel and Motel Management* (June 11, 1990).

MGM Grand, Inc., *1997* and *1998 Form 10-Ks*, retrieved from EDGAR Data Base, http://www.sec.gov/Archives/edgar/data/

Mirage Resorts, Inc., *1997* and *1998 Form 10-Ks*, retrieved from EDGAR Data Base, http://www.sec.gov/Archives/edgar/data/.

The Walt Disney Company (1996): Capital Cities/ABC Merger (Revised)

Paul P. Harasimowicz Jr., Martin J. Nicholson, John F. Talbot, John J. Tarpey, and Thomas L Wheelen

On February 8, 1996, the five-member panel of the Federal Communication Commission (FCC) unanimously approved the $19 billion merger of Walt Disney Company and Capital Cities/ABC, Inc., which created the world's largest entertainment company (see Exhibit 1). The FCC refused to grant Disney a waiver from its cross-ownership ban on owning a newspaper and radio station in the same city. The FCC required Disney to sell either a newspaper or a radio station in Detroit and Fort Worth. Disney was granted a year to sell these properties. The sale requirement could be lifted if the FCC scrapped its cross-ownership rules during the year. The new Telecommunications Laws just passed by Congress required the FCC to review its broadcast-ownership rules. Michael D. Eisner, Chairman and Chief Executive Officer (CEO), expressed disappointment that the FCC denied Disney's waiver requests. Disney must also sell its Los Angeles television station, KCAL, as part of the Department of Justice's (DOJ) earlier approval of this merger. The FCC also required the sale of KCAL for its approval.[1]

On January 4, 1996, the shareholders of Disney and Capital Cities had agreed to the merger. The final capital structure of the combined company depends on the choices of Capital Cities holders of their 153.9 million shares of common stock. Each shareholder could exchange each Capital Cities share for one Disney share plus $65 in cash or opt for all stock or all cash. In March 1996, Warren E. Buffet showed his support for the merged companies when he converted Berkshire Hathaway's 20,000,000 shares (13.0%) of Capital Cities stock into Disney stock. He served on the Board of Capital Cities and he voted Berkshire Hathaway's shares.

According to Michael Eisner, the deal developed out of a conversation with Warren Buffet at a meeting about Disney and Capital Cities. Buffet took Eisner to where Thomas S. Murphy, Chairman and CEO of Capital Cities, was about to start a golf match. Eisner and Murphy started talking in earnest, and a deal was quickly struck without the assistance of any investment bankers. Michael Eisner said he and Murphy had discussed this deal several times over the past few years but could not resolve the payment terms—stock, cash, or a combination.

Roy E. Disney, Vice-Chairman, said, "This is the only major acquisition we've [Disney] undertaken in the last 11 years."[2] He further stated, "It's a very conservative thing to do."[3]

A few weeks later, Major League Baseball Owners approved Disney's 25% acquisition of the California Angels American League team with the option to purchase the remainder of the stock at a later time. Disney received approval to manage the team

This case was prepared by Paul P. Harasimowicz Jr., DDS (self-employed dentist in Gardner, MA), Martin J. Nicholson (retired Civil Engineer with CALTRANS), John F. Talbot (retired teacher from Lunenburg High School), John J. Tarpey (retired from Gardner High School), and Professor Thomas L. Wheelen. All are graduates of Gardner High School in Gardner, MA. All except John J. Tarpey were the class of 1953, and Tarpey was the class of 1954. Marty, Jack Talbot, and Tom graduated from Sacred Heart School in 1949. Paul and Jack Tarpey graduated from Elm Street School in 1949 and 1950, respectively. Research was partially provided by the following graduate students: Roxanne Alexander, Christine Christian, Peter A. Christian, and Erika Schofer at USF. This case was edited for SMBP–7th Edition. This case may not be reproduced in any form without written permission of the copyright holder, Thomas L. Wheelen. Copyright © 1998 renewed by Thomas L. Wheelen.

Exhibit 1 **Disney and Capital Cities/ABC Merge: Walt Disney Company**

A. A Snapshot Overview of Disney After the Merger

Revenues	$19.3 billion
Cash flow	$4.6 billion
Employees	85,000
Production companies	Walt Disney Productions
	Touchstone Pictures
	ABC Productions
Distribution	11 company-owned TV stations
	228 TV affiliates
	21 radio stations
Cable	ESPN, Lifetime, A&E, Disney Channel
Publishing	Newspapers in 13 states
	Fairchild Publications
	Chilton Publications

B. Disney Perspective of the Merger as Stated in 1995 Annual Report

Cap Cities is a widely diversified broadcaster and publisher. It owns and operates the ABC Television Network Group, which distributes programming to 224 affiliated stations; 10 television stations, six of them in the nation's top 10 markets; ABC Radio Networks, serving more than 3,400 radio stations; and 21 AM and FM radio outlets, all in major U.S. markets.

The ABC Cable and International Broadcast Group is the majority owner of ESPN and ESPN2 here and overseas and is a partner in the A&E and Lifetime cable networks in the U.S. ESPN reaches more than 66 million cable subscribers, or about 70% of U.S. TV households, and is seen in 130 countries in 11 different languages.

Overseas, Cap Cities/ABC holds minority interests in the German production and distribution companies Tele-Munchen and RTL-2, Hamster Productions and TV Sport of France, Tesauro of Spain, the Scandinavian Broadcasting System, Eurosport of London, and the Japan Sports Channel. In addition, it has launched two children's television program services in China.

Cap Cities/ABC Publishing Group owns and operates 7 daily newspapers, including the nationally respected *Kansas City Star* and *Fort Worth Star-Telegram*. It also publishes weekly newspapers and shopping guides in several states.

The Company's Diversified Publishing Group produces more than 100 periodicals, including publications in fields as varied as automobile repair and ophthalmology, electronic components and industrial safety. Another subsidiary, Fairchild Publications, produces 14 periodicals, including *Women's Wear Daily* and *W*.

Source: Michael Oneal, Stephen Baker, and Ronald Grover, "Disney Kingdom," *Business Week* (August 14, 1995), p. 31; and Walt Disney Company, *1995 Annual Report*, pp. 8–9.

franchise. Gene Autry, legendary cowboy movie and radio star of the 1930s, 1940s, and 1950s, was the founder and owner of the California Angels. Disney already owned the National Hockey League's Mighty Ducks of Anaheim. There had been much discussion that the owners of the National Football League would like Disney to own a franchise in Los Angeles. The two football teams (the Los Angeles Raiders and the Los Angeles Rams) moved their franchises in 1995 to Oakland and St. Louis. The Seattle Seahawks announced their intention to move to Los Angeles, but the Commissioner of Football and the owners had not approved the move.

STRATEGIC MANAGEMENT

Board of Directors[4]

After the merger, the Board of Directors consisted of 17 members, of whom seven were internal members. Thomas S. Murphy, former Chairman and CEO of Capital Cities/ABC,

Exhibit 2   Board of Directors: Walt Disney Company

Stephen F. Bollenbach (1995)
Senior Executive Vice-President and
    Chief Financial Officer
The Walt Disney Company

Reveta F. Bowers [1,4] (1993)
Head of School
Center for Early Education

Roy E. Disney [3] (June 1984)
Vice-Chairman (1967–March 1984)
The Walt Disney Company

Michael D. Eisner [3] (1984)
Chairman and Chief Executive Officer
The Walt Disney Company

Stanley P. Gold [4] (1987) (June 1984–Sept.1984)
President and Chief Executive Officer
Shamrock Holding, Inc.

Sanford M. Litvack (1995)
Senior Executive Vice-President and
    Chief of Corporate Operations
The Walt Disney Company

Ignacio E. Lozano Jr. [1,2] (1981)
Editor-in-Chief
LA Opinion

George J. Mitchell [4] (1995)
Special Counsel
Verner, Liipfert, Bernard, McPherson and Hand

Thomas S. Murphy (1996)
Chairman and Chief Executive Officer
Capital Cities

Richard A. Nunis [3] (1981)
Chairman
Walt Disney Attractions

Michael Ovitz (1996)
President
The Walt Disney Company

Sidney Poitier [2] (1994)
Chief Executive Officer
Verdon-Cedric Productions

Irwin E. Russell [2]
Attorney at Law

Robert A. M. Stern (1992)
Senior Partner
Robert A. M. Stern Architects

E. Cardon Walker [1]
Former Chairman and Chief Executive Officer
The Walt Disney Company

Raymond L. Watson [1,2,3]
Vice-Chairman
The Irvine Company

Gary L. Wilson [3]
Co-Chairman
Northwest Airline Corporation

Directors Emeritus

Caroline Leonetti Ahmanson
Chairman Emeritus
Federal Reserve Bank of San Francisco

Joseph F. Cullman 3rd
Chairman Emeritus
Philip Morris Companies, Inc.

Notes:
1. Member of Audit Review Committee
2. Member of Compensation Committee
3. Member of Executive Committee
4. Member of Nominating Committee

Source: The Walt Disney Company, *Special Meeting of Stockholders* (January 4, 1996), pp. 99–101.

joined the Disney board, and Michael Ovitz, President of Disney since October 1, 1995, became a board member. Roy Disney, Vice-Chairman, was the nephew of Walt Disney. He also served as the head of Disney's Animation Department. Michael Eisner, Chairman and CEO, joined the board in 1984. Exhibit 2 lists the board members' shares in Disney. Thomas S. Murphy owned beneficially 1,024,260 (0.67%) shares in Capital Cities/ABC, which translates to 1,024,260 (0.15%) in Disney common stock, and he received $65 in cash for each share. Eisner and Roy Disney had beneficial ownership of 9,050,780 (1.33%) and 8,014,044 (1.18%) shares, respectively, after the acquisition. The new board and all executives as a group had beneficial ownerships of 19,818,902 (2.92%) shares.

Bass Management Trust owned beneficially 31,125,578 (5.95%) shares in Disney. Warren E. Buffet owned beneficially 20,000,000 shares of Capital Cities. These shares belonged to Berkshire Hathaway Inc., of which Warren E. Buffet owned directly or indirectly 43.25% of the outstanding stock. State Farm Mutual Automobile Insurance owned beneficially 9,041,000 (5.88%) of Capital Cities.

The non-employee directors were paid $30,000 annually and $1,000 per meeting attended. These board members were also granted the option to purchase 2,000 shares of common stock yearly.

Top Management

The corporate executive officers and chief executives of Disney's principal businesses are shown in Exhibit 3. Michael Ovitz, President, joined Disney on October 1, 1995. He was Chairman and co-founder of Creative Artists Agency.[5] He replaced Frank G. Wells, Chief Operating Officer (COO), who died in a helicopter accident in the spring of 1995. Wells had come to Disney with Michael D. Eisner in 1984. They had been best friends. Wells's death was a great personal loss for Michael Eisner. Jeffrey Katzenberg, the Studio Chief, resigned when he was not named the replacement for Frank G. Wells. He then joined Steven Spielberg and David Geffen to form a new mega-venture entertainment company called Dream Works SKG. The three founders invested $100 million ($33.3 million each) to form the company and will get 67% of the profits and 100% of the voting control. The company will have five classes of stock: A and S for outside investors, B and SKG for the principals, and E for the employees. The founders wanted to raise $900 million through stock offerings—$216 million in class S stock, which was designated for smallish, "strategic" investors like Microsoft, which invested $30 million, and $684 million in class A stock, which was reserved for the big investors. Paul Allen, co-founder of Microsoft, purchased $500 million of class A stock and was appointed to the board. The A shareholders will receive 25% of the profits, and the S shareholders will receive 8% of the profits.[6] Katzenberg initiated a $200 million lawsuit against Disney for past profit sharing on projects done while he was at Disney.

Richard More resigned and was replaced by Dennis F. Hightower as head of Walt Disney Television and Telecommunications. One analyst reported that he was "a curious choice given that he had no strengths. Does Eisner have the team to manage this mammoth acquisition?"[7] This analyst also noted that more than a dozen top executives, in addition to Jeffrey Katzenberg and Richard More, had left the company. Disney also lost two of its top TV animators. Eisner had undergone emergency heart surgery in 1994. The same analyst felt that Eisner had no clear successor at the merger time.

Robert A. Iger, President and COO of Capital Cities/ABC, joined the Disney management team as President of ABC. He had shared the leadership of Capital Cities/ABC with Thomas S. Murphy, who stated that they were a true management team.

Every Monday for the past 12 years, a staff lunch was held. This was a planning meeting where the past performance was reviewed to ascertain management's successes and failures and to plan the future.

Executive Compensation

Exhibit 4 provides a list of the five most highly compensated executives as of September 30, 1995.[8]

Michael Eisner's total compensation was $14,800,000. Disney's stock price had increased 28% during this fiscal year. Eisner's 1995 compensation package outpaced his 1994 plan by nearly 40%. Eisner had 6,000,000 exercisable share options and 2,000,000

Exhibit 3 **Corporate Executive Officers and Chief Executives of Principal Business: Walt Disney Company**

A. Corporate Executive Officers

Name and Year First Became an Executive Officer of Disney	Age	Office
Michael D. Eisner (1984)	53	Chairman of the Board and Chief Executive Officer of Disney. Prior to joining Disney in September 1984, Mr. Eisner was President and Chief Operating Officer of Paramount Pictures Corp., which was then a wholly-owned subsidiary of Gulf & Western Industries, Inc. Prior to joining Paramount in 1976 Mr. Eisner was Senior Vice-President, Prime Time Programming, for ABC Entertainment, a division of the American Broadcasting Company, Inc., with responsibility for the development and supervision of all prime-time series programming, limited series movies made for television, and the acquisition of talent. He had beneficial ownership of 9,050,780 (1.33%) shares.
Michael Ovitz (1995)	48	President of Disney beginning October 1, 1995. Mr. Ovitz co-founded Creative Artists Agency in 1975, serving most recently as its Chairman. Mr. Ovitz is a member of the Board of Trustees of the California Institute of the Arts, the Sundance Institute, and the Board of Advisors of the UCLA School of Theater, Film and Television. He also serves on the Board of Advisors of the Ziff-Davis Publishing Company and is a member of the boards of several medical and charitable organizations, including the Executive Board of the UCLA Hospital and Medical Center, of which he is Chairman. He had beneficial ownership of 203,506 (0.3%) shares.
Roy E. Disney (1984)	65	Has been Vice-Chairman of the Board of Directors of Disney since 1984, and since November 1985 has also served as head of Disney's animation department. In addition, Mr. Disney is Chairman of the Board of Shamrock Holding, Inc., which, through its subsidiaries, is engaged in real estate development and the making of investments. Mr. Disney is a nephew of the late Walt Disney. He had beneficial ownership of 8,014,044 (1.18%) shares.
Sanford M. Litvack (1991)	59	Senior Executive Vice-President and Chief of Corporate Operations of Disney since August 1994. From April 1991 through November 1991, Mr. Litvak served as Senior Vice-President—General Counsel of Disney. From November 1991 through June 1992, he served as General Counsel and from June 1992 through August 1994, as Executive Vice-President—Law and Human Resources of Disney. Mr. Litvack was a litigation partner with the law firm of Dewey Ballantine from 1987 until joining Disney in 1991. He had owned beneficially 345,498 (0.05%) shares.
Stephen F. Bollenbach (1995)	53	Senior Executive Vice-President and Chief Financial Officer of Disney since May 1, 1995. Mr. Bollenbach served as Chief Executive Officer and President of Host Marriott Corporation from October 1993 until he joined Disney. From March 1992 until October 1993, he served as the Chief Financial Officer of Marriott Corporation. During the two years prior to joining Marriott Corporation, Mr. Bollenbach was the Chief Financial Officer of the Trump Group. He served as Senior Vice-President and Chief of Directors of Holiday Corporation/Promus Companies prior thereto. In addition, Mr. Bollenbach is a member of the Board of Directors of American West Airlines, Inc. He had owned beneficially 150,000 (0.02%) shares.
John F. Cooke (1995)	53	Executive Vice-President—Corporate Affairs since February 1995. Prior thereto Mr. Cooke was President of the Disney Channel. Mr. Cooke is Chairman of the Board of Governors for the UCLA Center for Communication Policy and serves on the U.S. Advisory Council on the National Information Infrastructure.
Lawrence P. Murphy (1985)	43	Executive Vice-President and Chief Strategic Officer since February 1995. From November 1991 through February 1995, Executive Vice-President—Strategic Planning and Development. From February 1989 through November 1991, Senior Vice-President—Strategic Planning. He has owned beneficially 293,280 (0.04%) shares.
John J. Garand (1992)	48	Senior Vice-President—Planning and Control since June 1995. Vice-President—Planning and Control from April 1992 through June 1995. From April 1990 through March 1992, Senior Vice-President and Chief Financial Officer for Morse Shoe Inc.

(continued)

Exhibit 3   **Corporate Executive Officers and Chief Executives of Principal Business:**
Walt Disney Company *(continued)*

B. Principal Businesses With Chief Executives

Disney Consumer Products	Walt Disney Feature Animation
Barton K. Boyd	Roy E. Disney, Chairman
	Peter Schneider, President
Disney Design and Development	
Peter S. Rummell	Walt Disney Imagineering
	Martin A. Sklar
Disneyland Paris	
Phillippe Bourguignon	Walt Disney Motion Pictures
	Joseph E. Roth
Walt Disney Attractions	
Richard A. Nunis, Chairman	Walt Disney Television and Telecommunications
Judson C. Green, President	Dennis F. Hightower

Source: The Walt Disney Company, *Special Meeting of Stockholders* (January 4, 1996), pp. 94–98; and *1995 Annual Report*, p. 70.

unexercisable share options. The values of these options were $238,410,000 (exercisable options) and $79,470,000 (unexercisable options).[9]

HISTORY OF WALT DISNEY COMPANY

The origins of the Walt Disney Company can be traced back to 1923. Walt Disney and his brother Roy formed the Walt Disney Bros. Studio, which produced short animation clips. After much disappointment and many financial downfalls, the Walt Disney Bros. Studio finally produced the successful animated film *Steamboat Willie. Steamboat Willie* was the first animated movie to incorporate sound. Because Walt was the inspiration behind this animated movie and the inspiration for the whole studio, it seemed fitting that the studio was renamed Walt Disney Productions. The studio was characterized by many attributes that Walt Disney believed in, including great attention to detail and the constant striving for improvement and creativity.[10]

Disney quickly became the leading animation studio. By 1937, Disney's *Snow White and the Seven Dwarfs,* the first full-length feature animated film, made its debut. Through the years, Walt Disney Productions continued to grow and expand. From the very beginning, Walt dreamed of building an amusement park "for the enjoyment of honest American families."[11] Even though it took some creative financing on the part of Walt Disney, Walt Disney Productions opened up Disneyland in Anaheim, California, during 1955. Over the years, many disagreements arose between the "Walt Men" and the "Roy Men" about the future of the company. A feud transpired for a decade, but the brothers were able to reconcile their differences before Walt died of lung cancer in 1966.

During 1971, Walt Disney World was opened just outside of Orlando, Florida. Walt had envisioned this project before his death. The complex, which included rides, theme attractions, restaurants, and shops, was located on 29,000 acres of land. To accommodate the guests of the park, Walt Disney Productions developed eight resort hotels, villas, houses, and camping facilities around the theme park. Approximately one year after the opening of Walt Disney World, another tragedy struck. Roy Disney died and left the company without a strong leader. Up until that point, either Walt or Roy had per-

Exhibit 4   **Executive Compensation: Walt Disney Company**

Name and Principal Positions	Fiscal Year	Annual Compensation		Long-Term Compensation		
		Salary	Bonus	Number of Stock Options Granted	Restricted Stock Awards	All Other Compensation
Michael D. Eisner	1995	$750,000	$8,024,707	—	5,996,522	$ 6,877
Chief Executive Officer and	1994	$750,000	$7,268,807	—	2,638,394	$ 9,730
Chairman of the Board	1993	750,000	—	—	—	9,667
Sanford M. Litvack	1995	$647,115	$1,600,000	—	—	$ 6,820
Senior Executive Vice-	1994	500,000	1,600,000	200,000	—	9,731
President and Chief of	1993	500,000	375,000	—	—	9,992
Corporate Affairs						
John F. Cooke	1995	$569,616	$ 550,000	335,000	—	$ 6,840
Executive Vice-President	1994	523,751	575,000	—	—	7,859
and Chief Strategic Officer	1993	505,770	500,000	—	—	10,842
Lawrence P. Murphy	1995	$475,769	$ 550,000	150,000	—	$ 6,828
Executive Vice-President	1994	436,846	800,000	—	—	9,701
and Chief Strategic Officer	1993	408,558	500,000	—	—	10,151
Roy E. Disney	1995	$350,000	$ 550,000	200,000	—	$ 3,820
Vice-Chairman of the Board	1994	350,000	500,000	—	—	6,670
	1993	350,000	450,000	—	—	5,532

sonally supervised every aspect of the Disney projects. Now there was no one to look to for direction.

When Card Walker, a "Walt man," moved into the position of president, everything appeared to be under control. For the first few years, Walker stuck to the old Disney formulas that delivered predictable and wholesome entertainment that generated increasing revenues. But by 1979, Disney's market share of the motion picture industry had fallen to a mere 4%. As the company continued to slide, internal conflict began to eat away at the Walt Disney Production Company.

Even the much heralded opening of the Environmental Prototype Community of Tomorrow (EPCOT) continued to make matters worse. Walt Disney Company's management was determined to open EPCOT by 1982 and in so doing incurred tremendous costs and debt to finance this project. Faced with mounting problems, the management team was inflexible and refused to deviate from the old Disney pattern to alleviate some of the problems. Finally, Chairman Walker retired at the end of 1982. He still serves on the Board of Directors. He received $565,359 in 1995 for films in which he invested between 1963 and 1979 under a former company investment program.

Ron Miller, Walt's son-in-law, and Ray Watson took over the Disney operations on Walker's retirement. They had inherited a company that was filled with problems ranging from falling stock prices to a strong takeover bid by Saul Steinberg at a premium price. Disney found itself in a vulnerable position with no strong leadership. Disney's management team was "perceived to be weak, ineffectual, and divided." [12] The directors finally called for Miller's resignation during 1984.

After Miller's resignation, Michael Eisner (age 41) and Frank Wells joined the Disney Team. They both were highly regarded executives with Paramount Pictures Corporation. The team of Eisner and Wells was an "attractive and suitable combination for the task of resurrecting Disney." [13] Eisner provided the creativity and determination needed for Disney to expand and grow, and Wells provided a way to implement and profit from Eisner's ideas. Roy Disney, Walt's nephew, backed Eisner's bid for the office. Roy had resigned during 1984 over the management issues but had returned to the Board in June 1984. Many of the directors felt that Eisner was inexperienced at running such a large company, but Roy Disney's attorney, Stanley Gold, made an impassioned speech to the directors: "You see guys like Eisner as a little crazy . . . but every great studio in this business has been run by crazies. What do you think Walt Disney was? The guy was off the god-damned wall. This is a creative institution. It needs to be run by crazies again." [14] After that plea, the Board of Directors decided to give Eisner a chance. Eisner and Wells took that chance and ran with it.

Disney's first attempt at global expansion occurred during 1983 with the opening of Tokyo Disneyland. Disney entered into a joint venture with Oriental Land Company, Ltd., to build the theme park. Disney received 10% of the ticket sales, 5% of the concession sales, and 10% of any corporate sponsorship agreements. After opening, Tokyo Disneyland proved to be the most popular theme park in the Disney company. A second joint venture, this time with MGM, created the MGM-Studios in Orlando, Florida.

With the success of Tokyo Disneyland, Disney decided to attempt another global expansion, Disneyland Paris, in 1992. Unfortunately, the reviews for the Paris operation were dismal, and the Disney Company suffered losses in the deal. But with creative financing and dedication, the management team was able to survive the storm and turn Disneyland Paris into a small success. In 1994, Disneyland Paris lost $110.4 million, but in 1995 the loss was reduced to $35.1 million. [15]

During 1994, Disney recorded its billionth guest when approximately 28.9 million people visited its parks. [16]

Today Disney is a diversified international entertainment company with operations in three business segments: *filmed entertainment, theme parks and resorts,* and *consumer products.*

A fundamental component of the success that Disney has experienced was the concept of "synergy." Synergy can be described as using ideas generated in one part of the company to fuel ideas in other seemingly unrelated areas of the company. For example, Disney's construction of a motor speedway in Orlando and the decision to host Indy car races was viewed as merely another of the company's efforts to become a major player in the sports world. However, scheduling of the inaugural race was timed to coincide with the traditional slow period at nearby Walt Disney World in order to improve attendance at the parks and resorts. Doubtless Disney will also take advantage of the increased TV viewing during the same weekend (Super Bowl weekend) with its increased television access as a result of its recent acquisition of ESPN and ABC.

Exhibit 5 provides a list of new businesses added during Michael Eisner's tenure. The company has grown 610% over the last decade, and almost half of the company's growth has come from businesses that did not exist in 1985.

THE AMUSEMENT AND ENTERTAINMENT INDUSTRY

The entertainment and amusement industry was poised on the edge of a major spending boom during the last decade of the twentieth century. Consumer spending on entertainment and recreation as a percentage of nonmedical consumer spending had risen from 7.1% in 1979 to 9.4% in 1993. [17] A recent *Better Homes and Gardens* survey also showed that a record 92 million adults planned to take a family vacation in 1995—up

Exhibit 5   New Businesses Started Under Eisner's Leadership

Businesses

- International Film Distribution
- Television Broadcasting
- Television Station Ownership
- Expanded Ownership of Cable Systems
- Radio and Radio Network Broadcasting
- Ownership of Radio Stations
- Newspaper, Magazine, and Book Publishing
- Disney Stores
- Conventions
- Live Theatrical Entertainment
- Home Video Production
- Interactive Computer Programs and Games
- On-Line Computer Programs
- Sites on the World Wide Web
- Ownership of Professional Sports Teams
- Telephone Company Partnership (Americast) to produce and provide programming for distribution over home telephone lines (coming over the next 12–18 months)
- Disney Regional Entertainment, which will include a variety of new Disney entertainment and education ventures at locations around the country and world
- Disney Cruise Line

Source: The Walt Disney Company, *1996 Annual Report*, September 30, 1996, p. 4.

4% from 1994.[18] The survey also revealed that the decade-long trend of shorter trips may be reversing. Length of stay averaged 7.5 nights in 1994, up from 6.4 in 1993.[19] More families were traveling with kids as well. All were trends that were favorable to theme parks such as Disney's.

Global travel and tourism were also projected to experience strong mid- and long-term growth, with gross output increasing 55% by the year 2005.[20] The improving European economy, coupled with the recovering Japanese economy, also provided a ready market for the amusement giants.

Other economic indicators had also given hope to the entertainment goliaths. The faster-than-expected recoveries in Japan and Germany had helped in the sale of U.S. products, including vacations for foreigners. With a few exceptions, the weak dollar also encouraged American vacationers to stay home rather than engage in more expensive overseas travel. If these factors continued for all of 1995, the U.S. economy would see approximately a 3.0% increase in GDP.[21] The growing economy also resulted in a 3.4% increase in disposable income during 1994.[22] On a discouraging note, however, there were also claims that the "growth in leisure-time spending was likely to be tempered by increased consumer debt and higher interest rates."[23]

Emerging Industry Trends

Theme parks faced increasing competition on several fronts as the 1990s came to a close. The average family's entertainment dollar was being stretched in more directions than ever, forcing theme park operations to pay attention to previously ignored competitors. The *Better Homes and Gardens* survey also found that the beach was the favorite getaway for 50% of the families surveyed, with historical sites close behind at 42%.[24] This left the theme parks sharing an 8% segment of the vacation market with an increasing number of destinations. One such competitor had been the cruise industry. According to Thomas Elrod, President of Marketing and Entertainment at Walt Disney Attractions, "Disney's major competitor was not theme parks, but such trips as ski vacations, cruises, Caribbean trips, and European vacations."[25] Disney Cruise Lines will open in January 1998 with two ships.

Another substitute was the gaming industry, whose growth has also increased in recent years. Las Vegas had reportedly set out to "clean up its act" in order to promote itself as a "family destination vacation location." Its goal was to "shift its reputation from 'Sin City' to a sophisticated fun center for all ages."[26] Such a change in focus put Vegas head to head with amusement parks.

The industry must look at the increasing popularity of spectator sports as well. With the rise in the average ticket price for national football games and similar increases in both hockey and basketball, the cash outlay for a family had become significant. A day at the ballpark may soon replace a theme park outing.

The recent wave of mergers in the entertainment industry had also affected the competitive environment in which the theme parks operated. Although the mergers had decreased the number of competitors, they had improved the quality of the competition as well. Disney's recent purchase of Capital Cities/ABC momentarily made it the largest entertainment syndicate in the world. However, Time Warner's subsequent acquisition of the Turner network placed it on top. This acquisition had not yet received governmental approval in 1995. A few analysts doubted that Time Warner would get all the approvals required to make the deal. The result of these mergers could be fewer, but fatter, companies.[27] The concept of synergies, sometimes practiced as vertical integration, had driven the entertainment conglomerates in their quest for greater exposure and, hence, marketing opportunities for their products. The result was a small number of very powerful competitors with sufficient financial resources to carry out their plans.

The theme park industry must also face the changing demographics of its customer base. The traditional theme park audience, children under 15, was expected to decline from 21.9% of the population to only 19.9% during the next fifteen years.[28] At the same time, people 35 and over will increase from 48.9% in 1995 to 52.8% in 2010.[29] These projections had led to a marketing push among the industry giants aimed at attracting adults over 35 and childless families.

The face of the industry's audience was also changing. The racial composition of the United States was experiencing slight changes. By the year 2010, the percentage of whites will decrease from its present level of 82.8% to 79.6%, and African-Americans will increase from 12.6% to 13.6%. Asians will increase from 3.7% to 5.9%, and among all races, the percentage of Hispanics will increase from 10.1% to 13.2%.[30] To attract members of these racial groups, the theme parks' management needed to consider their cultural backgrounds and interests as well as traditional (white) "American" values, when designing the parks and rides.

An increasing number of theme park visitors were from overseas as well. Theme park operators needed to take care to consider societal values and customs of other cultures and use them in their marketing plans. They had to remember that what attracted Americans to a park would not always attract foreign visitors.

Another trend that may affect the industry was the recent movement in the corporate world to become more "socially responsible." Environmental awareness, a component of the corporate citizens' responsibility, had also become an issue for corporations, including theme parks. Management had been and would continue to be concerned about the effects of a project on the environment. Many companies had felt an anticorporate backlash. For example, the expansion plans of Wal-Mart and Home Depot had fallen victim to unreceptive communities. Vacationers' preferences had also been affected by the recent "green" movement. Eco-trips such as white rafting, hiking, or whale watching had never been more popular.

Some studies had also found societal expectations of longer vacations and more leisure time, whereas other authorities predicted that "the average American's work week has lengthened, leaving less free time for recreation."[31]

COMPETITOR PROFILES

Exhibit 6 shows the 1995 attendance for the top ten theme parks. Disney owned the top four parks. The combined attendance of the Disney parks was 47.2 million. The attendance for the three Busch parks was 12.5 million, the attendance for the two Universal Studios parks was 12.7 million, and Time Warner's park had 4.0 million customers.

Busch Entertainment

A member of the Anheuser-Busch Corporation, Busch Entertainment owned and operated Busch Gardens in Tampa, Florida; Busch Gardens in Williamsburg, Virginia; Sea-World of Florida in Orlando; SeaWorld of California in San Diego; and several other properties. The company had recently sold Cypress Gardens of Winter Haven, Florida, to a group of the park's managers and announced plans to expand its Tampa theme park. Although its core business was beer, the company's SeaWorld and Busch Gardens parks were enormously successful. The two SeaWorld parks alone attracted 8.7 million visitors in 1995.[32]

In 1995, attendance at SeaWorld of Florida was 4.95 million, which was a 4% increase over 1994; SeaWorld of California had 3.75 million visitors with a slight gain over 1994; and Busch Gardens had 3.8 million visitors and a 2% increase in attendance over 1994 (see Exhibit 6). Busch had three of the top ten amusement attractions.

MCA/Rank Organization

A joint venture between Matsushita's MCA (Matsushita recently sold its 80% interest in MCA to Seagram Co., a Canadian beverage company) and the British leisure development group, Rank Organization, operated the popular Universal Studios theme parks in Orlando, Florida, and Hollywood, California. The Universal parks brought in 12.7 million visitors in 1995, second only to the Walt Disney theme parks. The company recently announced plans to build Universal City Florida, a new theme park and entertainment complex set to open in 1999. MCA and Rank were also discussing plans to build five hotel properties. The parks' parent organization, Seagram Co., had been identified as one of the up-and-coming companies in the entertainment industry. In addition to its

Exhibit 6   Strategic Business Units: 1995 Theme Park Attendance

Park (Location)	1995 Attendance (in Millions)	% Change from 1994
1. Disneyland (Anaheim, Calif.)	14.10	+38%
2. Magic Kingdom (Orlando)	12.90	+15%
3. EPCOT (Orlando)	10.70	+10%
4. Disney-MGM Studios (Orlando)	9.50	+19%
5. Universal Studios Florida (Orlando)	8.00	+ 4%
6. SeaWorld of Florida (Orlando)	4.95	+ 8%
7. Universal Studios Adventure (Universal City, Calif.)	4.70	+ 2%
8. Six Flags Great Adventure (Jackson, N.J.)	4.00	+25%
9. Busch Gardens (Tampa)	3.80	+ 2%
10. SeaWorld of California (San Diego)	3.75	(slight gain)

Source: *St. Petersburg Times* (December 20, 1995), p. 6E.

interest in MCA, Seagram also owned 14.9% of Time Warner, giving it the flexibility and liquidity that many smaller companies lacked.[33]

In 1995, Universal Studios Florida had 8.0 million customers, which was a 4% increase over 1994, and Universal Studios Hollywood had 4.7 million customers, which was an increase of 2% over 1994 (see Exhibit 6).

Time Warner

Time Warner had operated the ten Six Flags amusement parks until a recent sale of 51% of the Six Flags Corp. to a group led by Boston Ventures Group. Six Flags entered the theme park industry in 1961, six years after Disneyland, and its revenues grew to $22 million in 1994.[34] Attendance also grew from 18 million in 1991 to 22 million in 1994.[35] Time Warner had begun using its cartoon characters to develop attractions in its parks. The recent sale, however, placed the management of the parks in the hands of the Boston Venture Group. Only Six Flags Great Adventure in Jackson, N.J., ranked among the top ten theme parks. In 1995, the attendance was 4.0 million, which was a 25% increase over 1994 (see Exhibit 6).

Viacom

Viacom recently acquired Paramount Communications, complete with its many theme parks, for $10 billion. Paramount Parks is the fourth largest theme park company in America, with more than 12 million visitors a year. The subsidiary operated Great America in Santa Clara, California; Carowinds in Charlotte, N.C.; Canada's Wonderland in Toronto; Raging Waters in San Jose, California; Kings Dominion in Richmond, Virginia; and Kings Island in Cincinnati, Ohio. The company thrived on thrilling roller coasters and other traditional rides and had recently announced plans to team with MGM to develop a ride based on the popular TV show, *Outer Limits.* Paramount had formed licensing agreements with MGM to expand its merchandising. Plans for a sports and entertainment park (dubbed Wayne's World because of its connections to Miami's Wayne Huizenga) near Miami were recently scuttled due to high costs and a lack of consistency with the strategic direction of its parent.[36]

STRATEGIC BUSINESS UNITS

The company's three strategic business units are: (1) Theme Parks and Resorts, (2) Filmed Entertainment, and (3) Consumer Products.

Theme Parks and Resorts

The revenues from Theme Parks and Resorts Unit were $3,959.8 million, $3,463.6 million, $3,440.7 million, and $3,306.9 million for 1995, 1994, 1993, and 1992, respectively (see Exhibit 7). Theme Parks and Resorts revenues increased by 19.6% over the four years. Film unit revenues increased by 96% over the same period, and Consumer Products Unit revenues increased 99%. Theme Parks and Resorts operating income was $860.8 million, $684.1 million, $746.9 million, and $644.0 million in 1995, 1994, 1993, and 1992, respectively (see Exhibit 7).

Theme Parks and Resorts operating revenue over these four years increased by 25.2%. Again, the other two strategic business units had better performance over these four years. Film's operating income was up approximately 80%. Theme Parks and Resorts revenues and operating income contribution to total revenues and total operating income were (1) 32.7% and 35.2% in 1995, (2) 34.4% and 34.8% in 1994, (3) 40.4% and 43.3% in 1993, (4) 44.1% and 44.9% in 1992 (see Exhibit 7).

Over the four years, the contribution to revenues and operating income decreased each year for the Theme Parks and Resorts unit. In 1983, the pre-Eisner era, Theme Parks and Resorts revenues were $1,031,202, which contributed 78.9% of total revenues. During the Eisner era, Theme Parks and Resorts revenues increased by approximately $2.9 billion but were only 32.7% of total 1995 revenues.

The company operated the Walt Disney World destination resort in Florida and the Disneyland Park and the Disneyland Hotel in California. The company earned royalties on revenues generated by the Disneyland Tokyo theme park.

All of the theme parks and most of the associated resort facilities were operated on a year-round basis. Historically the Theme Parks and Resorts business experienced fluctuations in park attendance and resort occupancy resulting from the nature of vacation travel. Peak attendance and resort occupancy generally occurred during the summer school vacation months and during early winter and the spring holiday period.[37]

Walt Disney World Destination Resort[38]

The Walt Disney World destination resort was located on approximately 29,900 acres of land owned by the company 15 miles southwest of Orlando, Florida. The resort included three theme parks (the Magic Kingdom, EPCOT, and the Disney-MGM Studios Theme Park), hotels and villas, an entertainment complex, a shopping village, conference centers, campgrounds, golf courses, water parks, and other recreational facilities designed to attract visitors for an extended stay. The company marketed the entire Walt Disney World destination resort through a variety of national, international, and local advertising promotional activities. A number of attractions in each of the theme parks were sponsored by corporate participants through long-term participation agreements.

Magic Kingdom

The Magic Kingdom, which opened in 1971, consisted of seven principal areas: *Main Street, Liberty Square, Frontierland, Tomorrowland, Fantasyland, Adventureland,* and *Mickey's Starland.* These areas featured themed rides and attractions, restaurants, refreshment

Exhibit 7 **Consolidated Statement of Income and Contributions by Strategic Business Units: Walt Disney Company**
(Dollar amounts in millions)

Year Ending September 30	1995		1994		1993		1992	
Revenues								
Filmed entertainment	$ 6,001.5	49.5%	$ 4,793.3	47.7%	$3,673.4	43.1%	$3,115.2	41.5%
Theme parks and resorts	3,959.8	32.7	3,463.6	34.4	3,440.7	40.4	3,306.9	44.1
Consumer products	2,150.8	17.8	1,798.2	17.9	1,415.1	16.5	1,081.9	14.4
	$12,112.1	100.0%	$10,055.1	100.0%	$8,529.2	100.0%	$7,504.0	100.0%
Costs and expenses								
Filmed entertainment	$ 4,927.1	51.0%	$ 3,937.2	48.7%	$3,051.2	44.8%	$2,606.9	42.9%
Theme parks and resorts	3,099.0	32.0	2,779.5	34.4	2,693.8	39.6	2,662.9	43.9
Consumer products	1,640.3	17.0	1,372.7	16.9	1,059.7	15.6	798.9	13.2
	$ 9,666.4	100.0%	$ 8,089.4	100.0%	$6,804.7	100.0%	$6,068.7	100.0%
Operating income								
Filmed entertainment	$ 1,074.4	43.9%	$ 856.1	43.6%	$ 622.2	36.1%	$ 508.3	35.4%
Theme parks and resorts	860.8	35.2	684.1	34.8	746.9	43.3	644.0	44.9
Consumer products	510.5	20.9	425.5	21.6	355.4	20.6	283.0	19.7
	$ 2,445.7	100.0%	$ 1,965.7	100.0%	$1,724.5	100.0%	$1,435.3	100.0%
Corporate activities								
General and administrative expenses	$ 183.6	62.4%	$ 162.2	106.6%	$ 164.2	120.9%	$ 148.2	100.3%
Interest expense	178.3	60.7	119.9	78.7	157.7	116.1	126.8	87.6
Investment and interest income	(68.0)	(23.1)	(129.9)	(85.3)	(186.1)	(137.0)	(130.3)	(87.9)
	$ 293.9	100.0%	$ 152.2	100.0%	$ 135.8	100.0%	$ 144.7	100.0%
Loss from investment in Euro Disney	$(35.1)		$(110.4)		$(514.7)		$11.2	
Income before income taxes and cumulative effect of accounting changes	$ 2,116.7		$ 1,703.1		$1,074.0		$1,301.8	
Income taxes	736.6		592.7		402.7		485.1	
Income before cumulative effect of accounting changes	$ 1,380.1		$ 1,110.4		$ 671.3		$ 816.7	
Cumulative effect of accounting changes								
Pre-opening costs	—		—		$(271.2)		—	
Post-retirement benefits	—		—		(130.3)		—	
Income taxes	—		—		30.0		—	
Net income	$ 1,380.1		$ 1,110.4		$ 299.8		$ 816.7	

Source: Adapted from The Walt Disney Company, *1995 Annual Report,* p. 54, and *1994 Annual Report,* p. 48.

stands, and merchandise shops. Its 1995 attendance was 12.9 million, an increase of 15% over 1994 (see Exhibit 6). It slipped into second place behind Disneyland.

EPCOT

EPCOT, which opened in 1982, consisted of two major themed areas: *Future World* and *World Showcase.* Future World dramatized certain historical developments and addressed the challenges facing the world today through major pavilions devoted to high-tech products of the future ("Innoventions"), communication and technological exhibitions

("Spaceship Earth"), and energy, transportation, imagination, life and health, and the land and seas. World Showcase presented a community of nations focusing on the culture, traditions, and accomplishments of people around the world. World Showcase included as a central showpiece the American Adventure pavilion, which highlighted the history of the American people. Other nations represented were Canada, Mexico, Japan, China, France, the United Kingdom, Germany, Italy, Morocco, and Norway. Both areas featured themed rides and attractions, restaurants, refreshment stands, and merchandise shops. Its 1995 attendance was 10.7 million, an increase of 10% over 1994 (see Exhibit 6).

Disney–MGM Studios Theme Park

The Disney–MGM Studios Theme Park, which opened in 1989, consisted of a theme park, an animation studio, and a production facility. The theme park centered around Hollywood as it was during the 1930s and 1940s and featured Disney animators at work and a backstage tour of the production facilities in addition to themed food service and merchandise shops and a back lot area. Currently it hosted both feature film and television productions. Its 1995 attendance was 9.5 million, an increase of 19% over 1994 (see Exhibit 6).

Resort Facilities

As of September 30, 1995, the company owned and operated 12 resort hotels and a complex of villas and suites at the Walt Disney World destination resort, with a total of approximately 14,300 rooms. Disney's Boardwalk Resort, a mixed-use resort built around a turn-of-the-century Atlantic boardwalk theme, offering approximately 380 hotel rooms and additional Disney Vacation Club villas, and The Disney Institute, a resort community offering participatory programs and enriching experiences, were expected to open in 1996. In addition, Disney's Fort Wilderness camping and recreational area offered approximately 1,200 campsites and wilderness homes. Several of the resort hotels also contained conference centers and related facilities.

Recreational activities available at the resort facilities included five championship golf courses, an animal sanctuary, tennis, sailing, water skiing, swimming, horseback riding, and a number of noncompetitive sports and leisure-time activities. The company also operated three water parks: Blizzard Beach, River Country, and Typhoon Lagoon.

The company had developed a shopping facility known as the Disney Village Marketplace. Pleasure Island, an entertainment center adjacent to Disney Village Marketplace, included restaurants, night clubs, and shopping facilities. Currently under development were Celebration, a 5,000-acre town; Disney Cruise Lines, a cruise vacation line that would include two ships; Disney's Animal Kingdom, a themed wild animal adventure park incorporating live animals in natural habitats; Disney's Coronado Springs Resort, designed to serve the moderately priced hotel/convention market; a sports complex featuring amateur sporting events; and a motor speedway that would host Indianapolis-style racing. The downtown area of Celebration was scheduled to open during 1996, when limited residential lot sales were also expected to begin. This was a town that Disney was developing, and it has been highly accepted by the public.

At the Disney Village Marketplace Hotel Plaza, seven independently operated hotels were situated on property leased from the company. These hotels have a capacity of approximately 3,700 rooms. Additionally two hotels—the Walt Disney World Swan and the Walt Disney World Dolphin, with an aggregate capacity of approximately 2,300 rooms—were independently operated on property leased from the company near EPCOT. Another hotel, the 290-room Shades of Green on Walt Disney World Resort, was leased from the company and operated by a nonprofit organization as an armed forces recreation center.

Disney Vacation Club

In October 1995, Disney Vacation Development, Inc., a wholly-owned subsidiary of the company, opened its 497-unit Disney Vacation Club in Vero Beach, Florida. A 102-unit Disney Vacation Club on Hilton Head Island, South Carolina, and 377 Disney Vacation Club Villas located at Disney's Boardwalk Resort were expected to open in 1996. Each facility was intended to be sold under a vacation ownership plan and operated partially as rental property until the units were completely sold. The company had also acquired property for a planned resort in Newport Beach, California.

Disneyland

The company owned 330 acres and had under long-term lease an additional 39 acres of land in Anaheim, California. Disneyland, which opened in 1955, consisted of eight principal areas: *Toontown, Fantasyland, Adventureland, Frontierland, Tomorrowland, New Orleans Square, Main Street,* and *Critter Country.* These areas featured themed rides and attractions, restaurants, refreshment stands, and merchandise shops. Several Disneyland attractions were sponsored by corporate participants. The company marketed Disneyland through national and local advertising and promotional activities. The company also owned and operated the 1,100-room Disneyland Hotel near Disneyland. In 1995, Disneyland moved into first place among theme parks with 14.1 million customers, an increase of 38% over 1994. Much of this attendance growth was attributed to the Indiana Jones ride (a new attraction).

Tokyo Disneyland

The company earned royalties on revenues generated by the Tokyo Disneyland theme park, which was owned and operated by Oriental Land Co., Ltd., an unrelated Japanese corporation. The park, which opened in 1983, was similar in size and concept to Disneyland and was located approximately six miles from downtown Tokyo.

Disney Design and Development

Disney Design and Development, encompassing the company's two major design and development organizations, Walt Disney Imagining and Disney Development Company, provided master planning, real estate development, attraction and show design, engineering support, production support, project management, and other development services for the company's operations.

Competitive Position

The company's theme parks and resorts competed with all other forms of entertainment, lodging, tourism, and recreational activities. The profitability of the leisure-time industry was influenced by various factors that could not be directly controlled such as economic conditions, amount of available leisure time, oil and transportation prices, and weather patterns. The company believed its theme parks and resorts benefited substantially from the company's reputation in the entertainment industry for excellent quality and from synergy with activities in other business segments of the company.

Theme Parks and Resorts Financial Results[39]

Revenues (1995 versus 1994) increased 14%, or $496.2 million, to $3.96 billion (see Exhibit 7), driven by growth of $288 million from higher theme park attendance at the parks in Florida and California and $127 million from an increase in occupied rooms at Florida resorts. Higher theme park attendance reflected increased domestic and international tourist visitation. The increase in occupied rooms reflected the openings of Disney's Wilderness Lodge and Disney's All-Stars Sports Resort in the third quarter of 1994 and the phased opening of All-Star Music Resort during 1995.

Operating income increased 26%, or $176.7 million, to $860.8 million in 1995 (see Exhibit 7), driven by higher theme park attendance and an increase in occupied rooms at Florida resorts. Costs and expenses—principally of labor; cost of merchandise, food, and beverages sold; depreciation; repairs and maintenance; entertainment; and marketing and sales expenses—increased 11%, or $319.5 million, to $3,099.0 million, primarily due to an expansion of theme park attractions and Florida resorts and increased marketing and sales expenses, partially offset by the impact of ongoing cost reduction initiatives.

Revenues (1994 versus 1993) of $3.46 billion in 1994 were substantially unchanged from the prior year (see Exhibit 7) as the growth of $22.7 million reflecting higher guest spending at Florida theme parks and resorts and $47 million from an increase in occupied rooms at Florida resorts offset the $114 million impact of lower attendance at Florida and California theme parks. Guest spending rose, primarily due to expanded product offering and certain price increases, and the increase in occupied rooms reflected the third quarter openings of Disney's Wilderness Lodge and Disney's All-Star Sports Resort and expansion at the Disney Vacation Club. Lower attendance at the parks was driven by reduced international tourism.

Operating income decreased 8%, or $62.8 million, to $684.1 million in 1994 (see Exhibit 7), reflecting the impact of reduced revenues from lower theme park attendance. Costs and expenses increased 3%, or $85.7 million, to $2,779.5 million, primarily due to the expansion of theme park attractions and resorts in Florida and a charge recorded in the fourth quarter to write off certain development costs associated with Disney's America, as a result of the company's decision to seek a new site for the theme park.

Highlights for 1995

Consider the following 1995 selected highlights for the Theme Parks and Resorts Unit:[40]

40th Anniversary

- *Walt Disney World* celebrated its fortieth anniversary with many special events.

Attendance

- *Disneyland* had attendance of 14.1 million, a 387% increase over 1994.

- *Magic Kingdom* had attendance of 12.9 million, a 15% increase over 1994.

- *EPCOT* had attendance of 10.7 million, a 10.7% increase over 1994.

- *Disney-MGM Studios* had attendance of 9.5 million, a 19% increase over 1994.

New Rides and Attractions

- Indiana Jones attraction at Disneyland was the primary reason that Disneyland surpassed the Magic Kingdom in attendance.

- Ground broken for Disney's Animal Kingdom on a 500-acre site at Walt Disney World. This was the number one requested attraction by visitors to Walt Disney World. It was scheduled to open in 1998.

- Space Mountain made its debut in Euro Disney.

- Tokyo Disneyland held its first wintertime special event, Alice's Wonderland Party.

- Planet Hollywood restaurant opened near Pleasure Island at Walt Disney World.

New Theme Parks

- Walt Disney Company and Oriental Land Company Ltd., owner of Tokyo Disneyland, announced plans to open a second theme park, Tokyo DisneySea.

New Hotel Acquisition

- Disney purchased the 502-room Pan Pacific Hotel, adjacent to the Disneyland Hotel. The two hotels had 1,638 rooms.

Donations

- Resorts donated $1 million to the new Orlando Science Center.

Cruise Ships

- Disney Cruise Line announced its first two ships—Disney Wonder and Disney Magic—which will enter service in January 1998. Each ship will carry up to 2,400 guests and be home ported in Port Canaveral, Florida.

Filmed Entertainment

The revenues for Filmed Entertainment were $6,001.5 million, $4,793.3 million, $3,673.4 million, and $3,115.2 million for 1995, 1994, 1993, and 1992, respectively (see Exhibit 7). Film revenues had increased by approximately 96% over the past four years. Operating income was $1,074.4 million, $856.1 million, $622.2 million, and $508.3 million, in 1995, 1994, 1993, and 1992, respectively (see Exhibit 7). So, Film operating income over these four years increased by approximately 113%. Film revenues and operating income contribution to total revenues and total operating income were (1) 49.5% and 43.9% in 1995, (2) 47.7% and 43.6% in 1994, (3) 43.1% and 36.1% in 1993, and (4) 41.5% and 35.4% in 1992 (see Exhibit 7).

In 1983, the pre-Eisner era, film revenues contributed $165,458,000 (1.2%) of total revenues of $1,307,357,000. Under the management of Eisner and Wells, the Film Unit accomplished a complete turnaround strategy and had seen revenues increase approximately $5.9 billion.

The company produced and acquired live-action and animated motion pictures for distribution to the theatrical, television, and home video markets and produced original television programming for the network and first-run syndication markets. In addition, the company provided programming for and operated the Disney Channel, a pay television programming service, and KCAL-TV, a Los Angeles television station. The company also produced music recordings and live stage plays.

The success of all the company's theatrical motion pictures and television programming was heavily dependent on public taste, which is unpredictable and subject to change without warning. In addition, Filmed Entertainment operating results fluctuated due to the timing of theatrical and home video periods and competition in the market.

Theatrical Films

Walt Disney Pictures and Television, a wholly-owned subsidiary of the company, produced and acquired live-action motion pictures that were distributed under the banners of *Walt Disney Pictures, Touchstone Pictures, Hollywood Pictures,* and *Caravan Pictures.* The company's *Miramax Film Corp.* subsidiary distributed films under its own banner. In addition, the company distributed films produced or acquired by the independent production companies Cinergi Pictures Entertainment, Interscope Communications, and Merchant-Ivory Productions. The company also produced animated motion pictures under the banner of *Walt Disney Pictures.*

The company generally sought to distribute approximately 20 to 30 feature films each year under the company's various banners, including several live-action family feature films, one to two full-length animated films under the Walt Disney Pictures banner, and between 15 and 25 teenage and adult films under the other motion picture banners. In addition, the company periodically reissued previously released animated films. As of September 30, 1995, the company had released 311 full-length live-action features (primarily color), 33 full-length animated color features, and approximately 536 cartoon shorts. The company also expected that Miramax would independently acquire and produce approximately 30 films per year. In 1994, Disney's *The Lion King* was the number one box office attraction for the year.

The company distributed and marketed its film products through its own distribution and marketing companies in the United States and certain foreign markets.

Home Video

The company directly distributed home video releases from each of its banners in the domestic market. In the international market, the company distributed both directly and through foreign distribution companies. In addition, the company acquired and produced original programming for direct-to-video release. As of September 30, 1995, approximately 657 titles, including 203 feature films and 193 cartoon shorts and animated features, were available to the domestic marketplace. Approximately 589 titles, including 293 feature films and 296 cartoon shorts and animated features, were available to the international home entertainment market.

Network Television

The company's network television operation developed, produced, and distributed television programming to network and other broadcasters under the *Buena Vista Television, Touchstone Television,* and *Walt Disney Television* labels. Program development was carried out in collaboration with several independent writers, producers, and creative teams under exclusive development arrangements. Since 1991, the company had focused on the development, production, and distribution of half-hour comedies for network prime-time broadcast, including such series as *Home Improvement, Ellen, If Not For You,*

Boy Meets World, and *Misery Loves Company.* The company sought to syndicate in the domestic market those series that produced enough programs to permit syndicated "strip" broadcasting on a five-days-per-week basis.

The company licensed television series developed for U.S. networks in a number of foreign markets, including Germany, Italy, the United Kingdom, France, Spain, and Canada.

Walt Disney Television currently distributed two animated cartoon series for Saturday morning: *Aladdin* and *Timon and Pumbaa.* The company also offered a variety of prime-time specials for exhibition on network television.

The company believed that its television programs complemented the marketing and distribution of its theatrical motion pictures, the Walt Disney World destination resort, Disneyland, and other businesses.

Pay Television and Television Syndication

The company licensed several feature films to pay-television services, including its wholly-owned subsidiary, the Disney Channel.

The company's Buena Vista Television subsidiary licensed the theatrical and television film library to the domestic television syndication market. Major packages of the company's feature films and television programming had been licensed for broadcast and basic cable continuing over several years.

The company licensed its feature films for pay-television on an output basis in several geographic markets, including the United Kingdom and Scandinavia, and had an arrangement with Showtime through 1996 for the United States. In 1993, the company entered into an agreement to license to the Encore pay-television service over a multi-year period, as well as exclusive domestic pay-television rights to Miramax films beginning in 1994 and to Touchstone Pictures and Hollywood Pictures films starting in 1997.

The company also produced first-run animated and live-action syndicated programming. The Disney Afternoon is a two-hour block of cartoons airing five days per week, including *Aladdin, Gargoyles, Darkwing Duck, Goof Troop,* and *Bonkers. Tail Spin, Duck Tales,* and *Chip'N Dale* were also syndicated nationally. Live-action programming included *Live with Regis and Kathie Lee* and *Kathie Lee and Danny!,* daily talk shows; *Siskel & Ebert,* a weekly motion picture review program; *Disney Presents Bill Nye the Science Guy* and *Sing Me a Story With Belle,* weekly educational programs for children; and *Land's End,* a weekly action program. *Home Improvement, Blossom,* and *Dinosaurs* entered syndication in September 1995, joining *The Golden Girls* and *Empty Nest* in off-network syndication.

Some of the company's television programs were also syndicated abroad, including *The Disney Club,* a weekly series that the company produced for foreign markets. The company's television programs were telecast regularly in many countries, including Australia, Brazil, Canada, China, France, Germany, Italy, Japan, Mexico, Spain, and the United Kingdom. The company teamed with Compagnie Luxembourgeoise de Télédiffusion S. A. to launch Super RTL, a new family-oriented channel in Germany in June 1995.

The Disney Channel

The Disney Channel, which had approximately 14.5 million subscribers, was the company's nationwide premium television service. New shows developed for original use by the Disney Channel included dramatic, adventure, comedy, and educational series, as well as documentaries and first-run television movies. In addition, entertainment specials included shows originating from both the Walt Disney World destination resort and Disneyland. The balance of the programming consisted of products acquired from third parties and products from the company's theatrical film and television programming library. The Disney Channel premiered in Taiwan in March 1995, with the launch of the Disney Channel (Taiwan), and in Europe in October 1995, with the launch of the Disney Channel UK. The company was scheduled to begin broadcasting the Disney Channel in Australia in late 1996 and was exploring the development of the Disney Channel in other countries around the world.

KCAL-TV

The company operated KCAL-TV, an independent commercial station on VHF Channel 9 in Los Angeles. Its revenues were derived from the sale of advertising time to local, regional, and national advertisers. This channel must be sold according to the FCC agreement on the merger with Capital Cities/ABC.

Walt Disney Theatrical Productions

In 1994, the company produced a Broadway-style stage musical based on the animated feature film *Beauty and the Beast.* The stage adaptation was playing in three cities in the United States and overseas and was scheduled to open in additional cities around the world beginning in 1996.

Hollywood Records

Hollywood Records sought to develop and market recordings from new talent across the spectrum of popular music, as well as soundtracks from the company's live-action motion pictures.

Competitive Position

The company's filmed entertainment businesses (including theatrical films; products distributed through the network, syndication, pay-television, and home video markets; and the Disney Channel) competed with all forms of entertainment. The company also competed to obtain creative talents, story properties, advertiser support, broadcast rights, and market share, which are essential to the success of all of the company's filmed entertainment businesses.

A significant number of companies produced and/or distributed theatrical and television films, exploited products in the home video market, and provided pay television programming service. The company produced and distributed films designed for family audiences and believed that it was a significant source of such films.[41]

Film Financial Results[42]

Revenues (1995 versus 1994) increased 25%, or $1.21 billion, to $6.00 billion in 1995 (see Exhibit 7), driven by growth of $605 million in worldwide home video revenues, $340 million in television revenues, and $106 million in worldwide theatrical revenues. Home video revenues increased primarily due to the domestic and initial international release of *The Lion King* and the worldwide release of *Snow White and the Seven Dwarfs,* compared to the worldwide release of *Aladdin,* the domestic release of *The Fox and the Hound* and the international release of *The Jungle Book* in the prior year. Television revenues grew primarily due to the release of *Home Improvement* in syndication and increased availability and success of titles in pay television. Theatrical revenues increased primarily due to the domestic rerelease and expanded international release of *The Lion King,* the domestic release of *Pocahontas,* and the domestic release of the live-action titles *The Santa Clause, While You Were Sleeping,* and *Pulp Fiction.*

Operating income increased 25%, or $218.3 million, to $1.07 billion in 1995 (see Exhibit 7), primarily due to growth in worldwide home video and television. Costs and expenses increased 25%, or $989.9 million, to $4,927.1 million, principally due to higher home video marketing and distribution costs reflecting the worldwide release of *Snow White and the Seven Dwarfs* and the domestic release of *The Lion King,* higher distribution costs related to theatrical releases, and costs associated with the syndication of *Home Improvement.*

Revenues (1994 versus 1993) increased 30%, or $1.12 billion, to $4.79 billion in 1994 (see Exhibit 7), driven by growth of $731 million in worldwide home video revenues, $224 million in worldwide theatrical revenues, and $99 million in television revenues. Domestic home video revenues were driven by *Aladdin, The Fox and the Hound,* and *The Return of Jafar* compared to *Beauty and the Beast* and *Pinocchio* in 1993, while international home video revenues were driven by *The Jungle Book, Aladdin,* and *Bambi* compared to *Beauty and the Beast* and *Cinderella* in the prior year. Theatrical revenues increased due to the worldwide release of *The Lion King* (except for Europe), *Aladdin* in Europe, and continued expansion of theatrical productions, including full-year operations of Miramax, which was acquired in June 1993. Television revenues grew due to increased title availabilities worldwide.

Operating income increased 38%, or $233.9 million, to $856.1 million in 1994 (see Exhibit 7), driven by growth in worldwide home video activity and television, partly offset by lower worldwide theatrical operating income, reflecting lower results per film in 1994. Theatrical results in 1993 were driven by the worldwide release of *Aladdin* (except for Europe) and international releases of *Beauty and the Beast, Sister Act,* and *The Jungle Book* compared to the 1994 release of *The Lion King,* the European release of *Aladdin,* and the international release of *Cool Runnings.* Costs and expenses increased 29%, or $886.0 million, to $3,937.2 million, principally due to higher film cost amortization and increased distribution and selling costs, resulting from increased home video and theatrical activities.

Highlights for 1995

Consider the following selected 1995 highlights for the Film Unit: [43]

1995 Oscars

- *The Lion King* received Oscars for the best original score and best original song.

- Martin Landau was named best supporting actor for *Ed Wood.*

- Dianne Wiest was named best supporting actress for *Bullets Over Broadway.*

- Miramax received 22 nominations, more than any other studio.

1995 People's Choice Awards

- Tim Allen as top male television performer *(Home Improvement).*

1995 Video Releases

- *The Lion King* home video released—sold 20 million copies in 6 days—fastest selling video of all time. It went on to sell 30 million copies. *The Lion King* was a major part of Disney's 20% growth in 1995 revenues over 1994.

- *The Lion King*—an additional 23 million copies shipped for international sales.

- *Aladdin*—sold 15 million units outside of North America and total worldwide sales were 40 million units.

- *Snow White and the Seven Dwarfs*—sales reached 16 million and total worldwide sales were 38 million units.

World's Largest Premiere

- *Pocahontas* had the world's largest premiere, held in New York's Central Park. About a million people attended.

Disney's Channel

- Reached 15 million subscribers.

- *Disney Club of India,* which is one of more than 35 Disney Club programs broadcast internationally with weekly audiences of approximately 30 million.

Consumer Products

The company licensed the name Walt Disney, as well as the company's characters, visual and literary properties, and songs and music, to various consumer manufacturers, retailers, show promoters, and publishers throughout the world. The company also engaged in direct retail distribution through the Disney Stores and consumer catalogs and published books, magazines, and comics in the United States and Europe. In addition, the company produced audio products for all markets, as well as film and video products for the educational marketplace. Operating results for the consumer products business were influenced by seasonal consumer purchasing behavior and by the timing of animated theatrical releases.[44]

The revenues for the Consumer Products Unit were $2,150.8 million, $1,798.2 million, $1,415.1 million, and $1,081.9 million for 1995, 1994, 1993, and 1992, respectively (see Exhibit 7). Consumer Products revenues increased approximately 99% over the past four years. Consumer Products operating income was $510.5 million, $425.5 million, $355.4 million, and $283.0 million for 1995, 1994, 1993, and 1992, respectively (see Exhibit 7). So, Consumer Products operating income over these four years increased by approximately 80%. Consumer Products revenues and operating income contribution to total revenues and total operating income were (1) 17.8% and 20.9% in 1995, (2) 17.9% and 21.6% in 1994, (3) 16.5% and 20.6% in 1993, and (4) 14.4% and 19.7% in 1992 (see Exhibit 7).

In 1983, Consumer Products revenues had been only $110,697,000 and contributed 8.5% to total revenues of $1,307,357,000. During the Eisner era, Consumer Products revenues had increased by approximately $2 billion.

Character Merchandise and Publications Licensing[45]

The company's domestic and foreign licensing activities generated royalties, which were usually based on a fixed percentage of the wholesale or retail selling price of the licensee's products. The company licensed characters based on traditional and newly created film properties. Character merchandise categories that had been licensed included apparel, watches, toys, gifts, housewares, stationery, sporting goods, and domestic items such as sheets and towels. Publication categories that had been licensed included continuity-series books, book sets, art and picture books, magazines, and newspaper comic strips.

In addition to receiving licensing fees, the company was actively involved in developing and approving licensed merchandise and in conceptualizing, developing, writing, and illustrating licensed publications. The company continually sought to create new characters to be used in licensed products.

Publishing

The company had book imprints in the United States offering trade books for children (Mouse Works, Disney Press, and Hyperion Books for Children) and adults (Hyperion Press). In addition, the company was a joint venture partner in Disney Hachette Editions, which produced children's books, and Disney Hachette Press, which produced children's magazines and computer software magazines in France. In Italy and France, the company published comic magazines for children. The company also published the children's magazine *Disney Adventures,* the general science magazine *Discover,* and the family entertainment and informational magazines *FamilyFun* and *FamilyPC.*

The Disney Stores

The company marketed Disney-related products directly through its retail facilities operated under "The Disney Store" name. These facilities were generally located in leading shopping malls and similar retail complexes. The stores carried a wide variety of Disney merchandise and promoted other businesses of the company. During fiscal 1995, the company opened 64 new Disney Stores in the United States and Canada, 26 in Europe, and 15 in the Asian–Pacific area, bringing the total number to 429 as of September 30, 1995. The company expected to open additional stores in the future in selected markets throughout the country, as well as in Asian–Pacific, European, and Latin American countries.

Audio Products and Music Publishing

The company produced and distributed compact discs, audiocassettes, and records primarily directed at the children's market in the United States and France. These products consisted primarily of soundtracks for animated films and read-along production, and licenses for the creation of similar products throughout the rest of the world. In addition, the company commissioned new music for its motion pictures, television programs, and records and exploited the song copyrights created for the company by licensing others to produce and distribute printed music, records, audiovisual devices, and public performances.

Domestic retail sales of compact discs, audiocassettes, records, and related materials were the largest source of revenues, whereas direct marketing, which uses catalogs, coupon packages, and television, was a secondary means of distribution for the company.

Other Activities

The company produced audiovisual materials for the educational market, including videocassettes and film strips. It also licensed the manufacture and sale of posters and other teaching aids. The company marketed and distributed, through various channels, animation cel art and other animation-related artwork.

Competitive Position

The company competed in its character merchandising and other licensing, publishing, and retail activities with other licensers, publishers, and retailers of character, brand, and celebrity names. In the record and music publishing business, the company competed with several other companies. Although public information was limited, the company believed it was the largest worldwide licenser of character-based merchandise and producer/distributor of children's audio products.

Consumer Products Financial Results[46]

Revenues (1995 versus 1994) increased 20%, or $352.6 million, to $2.15 billion in 1995 (see Exhibit 7), driven by growth of $237 million from the Disney Stores and $67 million from worldwide character merchandise licensing. In 1995, 105 new Disney Stores opened, bringing the total number of stores to 429. Comparable store sales grew 4%, and sales at new stores contributed $94 million of sales growth. Worldwide merchandise licensing growth was generated by increased demand for traditional Disney characters and recent animated film properties, principally *The Lion King* and *Pocahontas.*

Operating income increased 20%, or $85.0 million, to $510.5 million in 1995 (see Exhibit 7), primarily due to growth in worldwide character merchandise licensing and the Disney Stores. Costs and expenses, which consisted principally of costs of goods sold, labor, and publicity and promotion, increased 19%, or $267.6 million, to $1,640.3 (see Exhibit 7), primarily due to the ongoing expansion and revenue growth of the Disney Stores.

Revenues (1994 versus 1993) increased 27%, or $383.1 million, to $1.80 billion in 1994 (see Exhibit 7), driven by growth of $166 million from the Disney Stores, $109 million from worldwide character merchandise licensing, and $87 million from publications, catalogs, and records and audio entertainment. In 1994, 85 new Disney Stores opened, bringing the total number of stores to 324. Comparable store sales grew 7%, and sales at new stores contributed $70 million of sales growth. Worldwide merchandise licensing growth was generated by increased demand for traditional Disney characters and new animated film properties, including *Aladdin* and *The Lion King.*

Operating income increased 20%, or $70.1 million, to $425.5 million in 1994 (see Exhibit 7), primarily due to the worldwide success of character merchandise licensing and the expansion of the Disney Stores, partially offset by higher costs and expenses. Costs and expenses increased 30%, or $313.0 million, to $1,372.7 million (see Exhibit 7), primarily reflecting the expansion and revenue growth of the Disney Stores and higher expenses in the catalog businesses.

Highlights for 1995

Consider the following selected 1995 highlights for the Consumer Products Unit:[47]

Revenues

- Revenues reached $2 billion.

- Sales of *The Lion King* merchandise reached $1 billion, a record for film merchandise.

Book Sales

- Disney published the five top-selling children's books of 1994.

- Disney had more titles in the top 100 than any other company.

Argentina

- The Disney Animation Festival opened in Buenos Aires in a 500,000-square-foot exhibition space. It attracted nearly 600,000 attendees.

Family Fun Magazine

- Won the Acres of Diamond award from Temple University. It was cited as the best magazine launched in the past five years.

Australia

- Disney opened a Disney Store in Melbourne, Australia, which is the eleventh country.

- Disney planned to open more than 24 stores on that continent.

China

- 95 Mickey's Corner Boutiques developed by licensee Vigor International.

Other Operations[48]

Disney Interactive

Disney Interactive, organized in 1995, was a fully integrated software venture focused on product development and the marketing of entertainment and educational computer software and video game titles for home and school.

Disney Sports Enterprises

Disney Sports Enterprises provided management and development services for the company's National Hockey League franchise, the Mighty Ducks of Anaheim. The company recently acquired a 25% interest in the American League Baseball franchise, the California Angels.

Disneyland Paris

Disneyland Paris was located on a 4,800-acre site at Marne-la-Vallée, approximately 20 miles east of Paris. The project had been developed pursuant to a 1987 master agreement with the French government by Euro Disney S.C.A., a publicly held French company in which the company held a 39% equity interest and which was managed by a subsidiary of the company. In addition, the company had licensed various intellectual property rights to Euro Disney for use in connection with the project.

The Disneyland theme park, which opened in April 1992, drew on European traditions in its five themed lands. Six themed hotels, with a total of approximately 5,200 rooms, were part of the resort complex, together with an entertainment center offering a variety of retail, dining, and show facilities and a 595-space camping area. The complex was served by direct rail transport to Paris and by high-speed TGV train service.

In 1994, the company, Euro Disney, Euro Disney's principal creditors, and Euro Disney's shareholders approved a financial restructuring that included an offering of new shares, to which the company subscribed 49%, and various other contributions and concessions by and from the company and Euro Disney's creditors. In connection with the restructuring, the company agreed to waive its royalties and base management fees through September 30, 1998.

Exhibit 7 shows the losses from Disney's investment in Euro Disney as $35.1 million in 1995, $110.4 million in 1994, and $514.4 million in 1993, and a profit of $11.2 million in 1992. The four-year losses totaled $648.7 million.

HUMAN RESOURCES MANAGEMENT

The number of Disney's employees were 71,000, 65,000, 62,000, 58,000, and 58,000 for 1995, 1994, 1993, 1992, and 1991, respectively. After the merger, the company would have approximately 85,000 employees.

During fiscal year 1995, 27,435 Disney cast members worldwide, working through Disney Volunteers Program, donated 227,102 hours of community service in 361 separate projects (for example, American Cancer Society and Pediatrics AIDS). Disney management was proud that much of the volunteerism focused on children. Eisner stated that it "was appropriate for a company named Disney."

The company's pension plan covered most salaried and hourly employees not covered by a union and industrywide pension program.

Approximately 70% of job openings were filled with promotions from within. Every employee hired were required go through the same initial training program. Even new upper level executives had to participate in this program. Training was Disney's way of reinforcing its company's culture with new employees. Disney wanted its customers treated the Disney way, so training was very important.

The company put a lot of emphasis on the employment interview. They wanted to determine the correct fit for each person in the company. Management paid a great deal of attention to employees' suggestions on how to improve the facilities and the treatment of customers.

FINANCE[49]

Revenues (1995 versus 1994) increased 20%, or $2.06 billion, to a record $12.11 billion in 1995 (see Exhibit 7), reflecting growth in Filmed Entertainment, Theme Parks and Resorts, and Consumer Products revenues of $1.21 billion, $496.2 million, and $352.6 million, respectively. Revenues of $2.80 billion from foreign operations in all business segments increased 19%, or $443.6 million, in 1995 and represented 23% of total revenues.

Operating income rose 24%, or $480.0 million, to a record $2.45 billion in 1995 (see Exhibit 7), driven by increases in Filmed Entertainment, Theme Parks and Resorts, and Consumer Products operating income of $218.3 million, $176.7 million, and $85.0 million, respectively. Net income increased 24% to a record $1.38 billion, and earnings per share increased 27% to a record $2.60 from $1.11 billion and $2.04, respectively.

The company's investment (1995 versus 1994) in Euro Disney resulted in a loss of $35.1 million in 1995, compared to a loss of $110.4 million in 1994 (see Exhibit 7). Results for 1995 included a gain of $55 million from the sale of approximately 75 million

Exhibit 8   Selected Financial Information by Geographic Segment: Walt Disney Company
(Dollar amounts in millions)

Geographic Segment	1995	1994	1993
Domestic revenues			
United States	$ 9,311.0	$ 7,697.6	$ 6,710.8
United States export	547.8	458.0	399.8
International revenues			
Europe	1,552.1	1,344.8	984.6
Rest of world	701.2	554.7	434.0
Total	$12,112.1	$10,055.1	$ 8,529.2
Operating income			
United States	$ 1,745.8	$ 1,392.7	$ 1,591.7
Europe	464.1	405.0	121.8
Rest of world	323.2	226.0	82.5
Unallocated expenses	(87.4)	(58.0)	(71.5)
Total	$ 2,445.7	$ 1,965.7	$ 1,724.5
Identifiable assets			
United States	$13,437.5	$11,306.1	$11,084.5
Europe	1,060.2	1,237.8	519.7
Rest of world	108.1	282.4	146.9
Total	$14,605.8	$12,826.3	$11,751.1

Source: The Walt Disney Company, *1995 Annual Report,* pp. 64–65.

shares, or 20% of the company's investment in Euro Disney, to Prince Alwaleed Bin Talal Bin Abdulaziz Al Saud in the first quarter. The company currently held an ownership interest in Euro Disney of approximately 39% and had agreed, under certain conditions, to maintain ownership of at least 34% of the outstanding common stock of Euro Disney until June 1999, at least 25% for the subsequent five years, and at least 16.67% for an additional term thereafter. The prior-year loss consisted of a $52.8 million third-quarter charge reflecting the company's participation in the Euro Disney financial restructuring, and the company's equity share of Euro Disney's post-restructuring operating results.

Revenues (1994 versus 1993) increased 18%, or $1.53 billion, to a record $10.06 billion in 1994 (see Exhibit 7), driven by growth in Filmed Entertainment, Theme Parks and Resorts, and Consumer Products revenues of $1.12 billion, $22.7 million, and $383.1 million, respectively. Revenues of $2.36 billion from foreign operations in all business segments increased 30%, or $539.1 million, in 1994 and represented 23% of total revenues, an increase of two percentage points over 1993.

Operating income rose 14%, or $241.2 million, to a record $1.97 billion in 1994 (see Exhibit 7), driven by increases in Filmed Entertainment, and Consumer Products operating income of $233.9 million and $70.1 million, respectively, partially offset by Theme Parks and Resorts results, which declined $62.8 million. Net income increased 65% to a record $1.11 billion, and earnings per share increased 66% to a record $2.04 from $671.3 million and $1.23, respectively, before the cumulative effect of accounting

Exhibit 9 **Consolidated Balance Sheet: Walt Disney Company**
(Dollar amounts in millions)

Year Ending September 30	1995	1994
Assets		
Cash and cash equivalents	$ 1,076.5	$ 186.9
Investments	866.3	1,323.2
Receivables	1,792.8	1,670.5
Merchandise inventories	824.0	668.3
Film and television costs	2,099.4	1,596.2
Theme parks, resorts and other property, at cost		
Attractions, building and equipment	8,339.9	7,450.4
Accumulated depreciation	(3,038.5)	(2,627.1)
	5,301.4	4,823.3
Projects in progress	778.4	879.1
Land	110.5	112.1
	6,190.3	5,814.5
Investment in Euro Disney	532.9	629.9
Other assets	1,223.6	936.8
Total assets	$14,605.8	$12,826.3
Liabilities and Shareholders' Equity		
Accounts payable and other accrued liabilities	$ 2,842.5	$ 2,474.8
Income taxes payable	200.2	267.4
Borrowings	2,984.3	2,936.9
Unearned royalty and other advances	860.7	699.9
Deferred income taxes	1,067.3	939.0
Shareholders' equity		
Preferred stock, $.10 par value		
Authorized—100.0 million shares		
Issued—none		
Common stock, $.025 billion shares		
Authorized—1.2 billion shares		
Issued—575.4 million shares and 567.0 million shares	1,226.3	945.3
	6,990.4	5,790.3
Issued—578.4 million shares and 567.0 million shares	37.3	59.1
Retained earnings	8,254.0	6,794.7
Cumulative translation and other adjustments		
Less treasury stock, at cost—51.0 million shares and 42.9 million shares	1,603.2	1,286.4
	6,650.8	5,508.3
Total liabilities and shareholders' equity	$14,605.8	$12,826.3

Source: The Walt Disney Company, *1995 Annual Report,* p. 55.

changes in 1993. Excluding Euro Disney reserves, which negatively impacted 1993 results, net income and earnings per share grew 25%.

Exhibit 8 provides selected financial information by geographic region and Exhibit 9 is Disney's Balance Sheet. *Value Line* felt the merger could require Disney to borrow $7 billion to finance cash payments.

Notes

1. Albert R. Karr and Thomas R. King, "FCC to Consider Throwing Out Rules Barring Ownership of Competing Media," *Wall Street Journal* (February 8, 1996), p. 9.
2. Walt Disney Company, *1995 Annual Report,* p. 9.
3. *Ibid.*
4. Walt Disney Company, *Special Meeting of Stockholders,* pp. 94–106.
5. *Ibid.,* p. 96.
6. Andrew E. Serwer, "Analyzing the Dream," *Fortune* (April 17, 1995), p. 71.
7. Howard Gleckman, Mark Lewyn, and Larry Armstrong, "Disney's Kingdom," *Business Week* (August 14, 1995), p. 34.
8. Walt Disney Company, *Form 10-K* (September 30, 1995), p. 21.
9. *Ibid.,* p. 24.
10. Neil H. Snyder, "The Walt Disney Company," a previously published case.
11. *Ibid.*
12. *Ibid.*
13. *Ibid.*
14. Stephen Koepp, "So You Believe in Magic?" *Time* (April 25, 1988), pp. 66–73.
15. Thomas R. King, "Disney Posts Record Net But . . . ," *Wall Street Journal* (November 29, 1995), p. A3.
16. Vicki Vaughn, "Disney Says Park Attendance Strong," *The Reuter Business Report* (October 12, 1995).
17. *The Encyclopedia of American Industries* (New York: International Thomson Publishing, 1994), p. 1204.
18. Gene Sloan, "More Plan Vacations with Family," *USA Today* (April 20, 1995), p. D1.
19. *Ibid.*
20. *Hotel and Motel Management,* 209:19 (November 7, 1994), pp. 4, 42.
21. *Standard & Poor's Industry Surveys* (New York: S&P/McGraw-Hill, April 6, 1995), p. L15.
22. Jill Roth, "Predicting Trends," *American Printer,* 214:3 (December 1994), pp. 34, 35.
23. *Ibid.*
24. Sloan, "More Plan Vacations with Family."
25. Rance Crain, "Marketing the Disney Empire," *Advertising Age,* 63:48 (November 23, 1992).
26. *USA Today* (August 25, 1995), p. 7D.
27. Antonio Zerbisias, "Media Giants Tentacles Reaching Deeper . . . ," *The Toronto Star* (August 27, 1995), p. C6.
28. Cited in *Standard & Poor's Industry Surveys* (New York: S&P/McGraw-Hill, April 6, 1995), p. L15.
29. *Ibid.*
30. *Ibid.*
31. Dryden, Kemmerling, et al., "Length of Workweek in the USA in the Future," *IIE Transactions,* 25:3 (May 1993), pp. 99–104.
32. *Standard & Poor's Industry Surveys* (New York: S&P/McGraw-Hill, April 6, 1995), p. L15.
33. *Ibid.*
34. David Lieberman, "Time Warner Sells Control of Six Flags," *USA Today* (April 18, 1995), p. B4.
35. *Ibid.*
36. Cathy Dunkley, "TV-Inspired Thrills in Virginia," *The Hollywood Reporter* (August 18, 1995).
37. *Form 10-K* (September 30, 1995), p. 3. The preceding 2 paragraphs were taken directly from the source, with minor editing. The verb tenses were changed.
38. *Ibid.,* pp. 3–5. The following 13 paragraphs were taken directly from the source, with minor editing. The verb tenses were changed, and attendance figures and a note on celebration acceptances were added.
39. *Ibid.,* p. 11. The following 4 paragraphs were taken directly from the source, with minor editing. The verb tenses were changed, and Exhibit 7 references were added.
40. *1995 Annual Report,* pp. 16, 19, 20, and 25–26.
41. *Form 10-K* (September 30, 1995), pp. 1–3. The preceding 21 paragraphs were taken directly from the source, with minor editing. The verb tenses were changed, the exhibit reference was added, and parts of the text were highlighted.
42. *Ibid.,* pp. 10–11. The following 4 paragraphs were taken directly from the source, with minor editing. The verb tenses were changed, and Exhibit 7 reference was added.
43. *1995 Annual Report,* pp. 16, 19, 20, and 25–26.
44. *Form 10-K* (September 30, 1995), p. 6. The verb tenses were changed.
45. *Ibid.,* pp. 6–7. The following 8 paragraphs were taken directly from the source, with minor editing. The verb tenses were changed, and Exhibit 7 reference was added.
46. *Ibid.,* pp. 11–12. The following 4 paragraphs were taken directly from the source, with minor editing. The reference to Exhibit 7 was added.
47. *1995 Annual Report,* pp. 16, 19, 20, and 25–26.
48. *Form 10-K* (September 30, 1995), p. 7. The following 5 paragraphs were taken from the source with minor editing. The verb tenses were changed, and the sentence on the acquisition of the California Angels was added.
49. *Form 10-K* (September 30, 1995), pp. 10 and 12. The following 5 paragraphs were taken directly from the source, with minor editing. The verb tenses were changed, and the reference to Exhibit 7 was added.

Carnival Corporation (1998)

Michael J. Keeffe, John K. Ross III, and Bill J. Middlebrook

Carnival Corporation, in terms of passengers carried, revenues generated, and available capacity, was the largest cruise line in the world and considered the leader and innovator in the cruise travel industry. Given its inauspicious beginnings, Carnival has grown from two converted ocean liners to an organization with two cruise divisions (and a joint venture to operate a third cruise line) and a chain of Alaskan hotels and tour coaches. Corporate revenues for fiscal 1997 reached $2.4 billion with net income from operations of $666 million. The growth continued, with May 1998 revenues up $100 million over the same quarter in 1997 to $1.219 billion. Carnival has several "firsts" in the cruise industry: the first cruise line to carry over one million passengers in a single year and five million total passengers by fiscal 1994. In 1998, its market share of the cruise travel industry stood at approximately 26% overall.

Carnival Corporation CEO and Chairman Micky Arison and Carnival Cruise Lines President Bob Dickinson were prepared to maintain the company's reputation as the leader and innovator in the industry. They assembled one of the newest fleets catering to cruisers, with the introduction of several "superliners" built specifically for the Caribbean and Alaskan cruise markets, and expected to invest over $3.0 billion in new ships by the year 2002. Additionally the company had expanded its Holland American Lines fleet to cater to more established cruisers and planned to add three of the new ships to its fleet in the premium cruise segment. Strategically, Carnival Corporation seemed to have made the right moves at the right time, sometimes in direct contradiction to industry analysts and cruise trends.

The Cruise Lines International Association (CLIA), an industry trade group, tracked the growth of the cruise industry for over 25 years. In 1970, approximately 500,000 passengers took cruises for three consecutive nights or more, reaching a peak of 5 million passengers in 1997, an average annual compound growth rate of approximately 8.9% (this growth rate declined to approximately 2% per year over the period from 1991 to 1995). At the end of 1997, the industry had 136 ships in service, with an aggregate berth capacity of 119,000. CLIA estimated that the number of passengers carried in North America would increase from 4.6 million in 1996 to 5 million in 1997, or approximately 8.7%. CLIA expected the number of cruise passengers to increase to 5.3 million in 1998; and with new ships to be delivered, the North American market would have roughly 144 vessels with an aggregate capacity of 132,000 berths.

Carnival exceeded the recent industry trends, and the growth rate in the number of passengers carried was 11.2% per year over the 1992 to 1996 period. The company's passenger capacity in 1991 was 17,973 berths and had increased to 31,078 at the end of fiscal 1997. Capacity was added with the delivery of several new cruise ships, such as the Elation, which went into service in early 1998 and increased passenger capacity by 2,040.

Even with the growth in the cruise industry, the company believed that cruises represented only 2% of the applicable North American vacation market, defined as persons who travel for leisure purposes on trips of three nights or longer, involving at least one

This case was prepared by Professors Michael J. Keeffe, John K. Ross III, and Bill J. Middlebrook of Southwest Texas State University. The case was edited for SMBP–7th Edition. Copyright © 1998 by Michael J. Keeffe, John K. Ross III, and Bill J. Middlebrook. Reprinted by permission.

night's stay in a hotel. The Boston Consulting group, in a 1989 study, estimated that only 5% of persons in the North American target market have taken a cruise for leisure purposes and estimated the market potential to be in excess of $50 billion. Carnival's management believed that by 1996 only 7% of the North American population has ever cruised. Various cruise operators, including Carnival Corporation, had based their expansion and capital spending programs on the possibility of capturing part of the 93% of the North American population who had yet to take a cruise vacation.

THE EVOLUTION OF CRUISING

With the replacement of ocean liners by aircraft in the 1960s as the primary means of transoceanic travel, the opportunity for developing the modern cruise industry was created. Ships that were no longer required to ferry passengers from destination to destination became available to investors with visions of a new vacation alternative to complement the increasing affluence of Americans. Cruising, once the purview of the rich and leisure class, was targeted to the middle class, with services and amenities similar to the grand days of first-class ocean travel.

According to Robert Meyers, Editor and Publisher of *Cruise Travel* magazine, the increasing popularity of taking a cruise as a vacation can be traced to two serendipitously timed events. First, television's "Love Boat" series dispelled many myths associated with cruising and depicted people of all ages and backgrounds enjoying the cruise experience. This show was among the top ten shows on television for many years, according to Nielsen ratings, and provided extensive publicity for cruise operators. Second, the increasing affluence of Americans and the increased participation of women in the work force gave couples and families more disposable income for discretionary purposes, especially vacations. As the myths were dispelled and disposable income grew, younger couples and families "turned on" to the benefits of cruising as a vacation alternative, creating a large new target market for the cruise product, which accelerated the growth in the number of Americans taking cruises as a vacation.

CARNIVAL HISTORY

In 1972, Ted Arison, backed by American International Travel Services, Inc. (AITS), purchased an aging ocean liner from Canadian Pacific Empress Lines for $6.5 million. The new AITS subsidiary, Carnival Cruise Line, refurbished the vessel from bow to stern and renamed it the *Mardi Gras* to capture the party spirit. (Also included in the deal was another ship later renamed the *Carnivale.*) The company start was not promising, however. On its first voyage, the *Mardi Gras,* with over 300 invited travel agents aboard, ran aground in Miami Harbor. The ship was slow and guzzled expensive fuel, limiting the number of ports of call and lengthening the minimum stay of passengers on the ship to break even. Arison then bought another old ocean vessel from Union Castle Lines to complement the *Mardi Gras* and the *Carnivale* and named it the *Festivale.* To attract customers, Arison began adding on-board diversions such as planned activities, a casino, nightclubs, discos, and other forms of entertainment designed to enhance the shipboard experience.

Carnival lost money for the next three years, and in late 1974, Ted Arison bought out the Carnival Cruise subsidiary of AITS, Inc., for $1 cash and the assumption of $5 million in debt. One month later, the *Mardi Gras* began showing a profit and through the remainder of 1975 operated at more than 100% capacity. (Normal ship capacity is determined by the number of fixed berths available. Ships, like hotels, can operate beyond this fixed capacity by using rollaway beds, pullmans, and upper bunks.)

Ted Arison (then Chairman), along with Bob Dickinson (who was then Vice-President of Sales and Marketing) and his son Micky Arison (then President of Carnival), began to alter the current approach to cruise vacations. Carnival went after first-time and younger cruisers with a moderately priced vacation package that included air fare to the port of embarkation and home after the cruise. Per diem rates were very competitive with other vacation packages, and Carnival offered passage to multiple exotic Caribbean ports, several meals served daily with premier restaurant service, and all forms of entertainment and activities included in the base fare. Items of a personal nature, liquor purchases, gambling, and tips for the cabin steward, table waiter, and busboy were not included in the fare. Carnival continued to add to the shipboard experience with a greater variety of activities, nightclubs, and other forms of entertainment and varied ports of call to increase its attractiveness to potential customers.

Carnival was the first modern cruise operator to use multimedia advertising promotions and to establish the theme of "Fun Ship" cruises, primarily promoting the ship as the destination and ports of call as secondary. Carnival told the public that it was throwing a shipboard party and everyone was invited. The "Fun Ship" theme still permeated all Carnival Cruise ships.

Throughout the 1980s, Carnival was able to maintain a growth rate of approximately 30%, about three times that of the industry as a whole, and between 1982 and 1988, its ships sailed with an average of 104% capacity (currently they operate at 104% to 105% capacity, depending on the season). Targeting younger, first-time passengers by promoting the ship as a destination proved to be extremely successful. Carnival's 1987 customer profile showed that 30% of the passengers were between the ages of 25 and 39 with household incomes of $25,000 to $50,000.

In 1987, Ted Arison sold 20% of his shares in Carnival Cruise Lines and immediately generated over $400 million for further expansion. In 1988, Carnival acquired the Holland America Line, which had four cruise ships with 4,500 berths. Holland America was positioned to the higher income travelers, with cruise prices averaging 25–35% more than similar Carnival cruises. The deal also included two Holland America subsidiaries, Windstar Sail Cruises and Holland America Westours. This success, and the foresight of management, allowed Carnival to begin an aggressive "superliner" building campaign for its core subsidiary. By 1989, the cruise segments of Carnival Corporation carried over 750,000 passengers in one year, a "first" in the cruise industry.

Ted Arison relinquished the role of Chairman to his son Micky in 1990, a time when the explosive growth of the 1980s began to subside. Higher fuel prices and increased airline costs began to affect the industry as a whole. The Persian Gulf War caused many cruise operators to divert ships from European and Indian ports to the Caribbean area of operations, increasing the number of ships competing directly with Carnival. Carnival's stock price fell from $25 in June 1990 to $13 late in the year. The company also incurred a $25.5 million loss during fiscal 1990 for the operation of the Crystal Palace Resort and Casino in the Bahamas. In 1991, Carnival reached a settlement with the Bahamian government (effective March 1, 1992) to surrender the 672-room Riveria Towers to the Hotel Corporation of the Bahamas in exchange for the cancellation of some debt incurred in constructing and developing the resort. The corporation took a $135 million write-down on the Crystal Palace for that year.

The early 1990s, even with industry-wide demand slowing, were still a very exciting time. Carnival took delivery of its first two "superliners"; the *Fantasy* (1990) and the *Ecstasy* (1991), which were to further penetrate the three- and four-day cruise market and supplement the seven-day market. In early 1991, Carnival took delivery of the third "superliner," *Sensation* (inaugural sailing November 1, 1993), and later in the year contracted for the fourth "superliner" to be named the *Fascination* (inaugural sailing 1994).

In 1991, Carnival attempted to acquire Premier Cruise Lines, which was then the official cruise line for Walt Disney World in Orlando, Florida, for approximately $372 million. The deal was never consummated because the involved parties could not agree on price. In 1992, Carnival acquired 50% of Seabourn, gaining the cruise operations of K/S Seabourn Cruise Lines, and formed a partnership with Atle Byrnestad. Seabourn serves the ultra-luxury market with destinations in South America, the Mediterranean, Southeast Asia, and the Baltics.

The 1993 to 1995 period saw the addition of the "superliner" *Imagination* for Carnival Cruise Lines and the *Ryndam* for Holland America Lines. In 1994, the company discontinued operations of Fiestamarina Lines, which attempted to serve Spanish-speaking clientele. Fiestamarina was beset with marketing and operational problems and never reached continuous operations. Many industry analysts and observers were surprised at the failure of Carnival to successfully develop this market. In 1995, Carnival sold a 49% interest in the Epirotiki Line, a Greek cruise operation, for $25 million, and it purchased $101 million (face amount) of senior secured notes of Kloster Cruise Limited, the parent of competitor Norwegian Cruise Lines, for $81 million. Kloster was having financial difficulties and Carnival could not obtain common stock of the company in a negotiated agreement. If Kloster were to fail, Carnival Corporation would be in a good position to acquire some of the assets of Kloster.

Carnival Corporation expanded through internally generated growth, as evidenced by the number of new ships on order (Exhibit 1). Additionally Carnival seemed to be willing to continue with its external expansion through acquisitions if the right opportunity arose.

In June 1997, Royal Caribbean made a bid to buy Celebrity Cruise Lines for $500 million and assumption of $800 million in debt. Within a week, Carnival had responded by submitting a counter offer to Celebrity for $510 million and the assumption of debt, then two days later raising the bid to $525 million. However, Royal Caribbean seemed to have had the inside track and announced the final merger arrangements with Celebrity on June 30, 1997. The resulting company had 17 ships with approximately 30,000 berths.

However, not to be thwarted in their attempts at continued expansion, Carnival announced in June 1997 the purchase of Costa, an Italian cruise company and the largest European cruise line, for $141 million. External expansion continued when, on May 28, 1998, Carnival announced the acquisition of Cunard Line for $500 million from Kvaerner ASA. Cunard was then merged with Seabourn Cruise Line (50% owned by Carnival) with Carnival owning 68% of the resulting Cunard Line Limited.

THE CRUISE PRODUCT

Ted and Micky Arison envisioned a product in which the classical cruise elegance along with modern convenience could be had at a price comparable to land-based vacation packages sold by travel agents. Carnival's all-inclusive package, when compared to resorts or a theme park such as Walt Disney World, often was priced below these destinations; especially when the array of activities, entertainment, and meals was considered.

A typical vacation on a Carnival cruise ship starts when the bags are tagged for the ship at the airport. Upon arriving at the port of embarkation, passengers are ferried by air-conditioned buses to the ship for boarding, and luggage is delivered by the cruise

Exhibit 1 Carnival and Holland America Ships Under Construction

Vessel	Expected Delivery	Shipyard	Passenger Capacity [1]	Cost (millions)
Carnival Cruise Lines				
Elation	03/98	Masa-Yards	2,040	$ 300
Paradise	12/98	Masa-Yards	2,040	300
Carnival Triumph	07/99	Fincantieri	2,640	400
Carnival Victory	08/00	Fincantieri	2,640	430
CCL Newbuild	12/00	Masa-Yards	2,100	375
CCL Newbuild	2001	Masa-Yards	2,100	375
CCL Newbuild	2002	Masa-Yards	2,100	375
Total Carnival Cruise Lines			15,912	$2,437
Holland America Line				
Volendam	6/99	Fincantieri	1,440	274
Zaandam	12/99	Fincantieri	1,440	286
HAL Newbuild	9/00	Fincantieri	1,440	300
Total Holland America Line			4,260	$ 860
Windstar Cruises				
Wind Surf	5/98	Purchase	312	40
Total all vessels			20,484	$3,337

Note:

1. In accordance with industry practice, all capacities indicated are calculated based on two passengers per cabin even though some cabins can accommodate three or four passengers. (*Form 10-Q*, 5/31/98).

ship staff to the passenger's cabin. Waiters dot the ship offering tropical drinks to the backdrop of a Caribbean rhythm, while the cruise staff orients passengers to the various decks, cabins, and public rooms. In a few hours (most ships sail in the early evening), dinner is served in the main dining rooms, where wine selection rivals the finest restaurants and the variety of main dishes are designed to suit every palate. Diners can always order double portions if they decide not to save room for the variety of desserts and after-dinner specialties.

After dinner, cruisers can choose between many forms of entertainment, including live music, dancing, nightclubs, and a selection of movies; or they can sleep through the midnight buffet until breakfast. (Most ships have five or more distinct nightclubs.) During the night, a daily program of activities arrives at the passengers' cabins. The biggest decisions to be made for the duration of the vacation will be what to do (or not to do), what to eat and when (usually eight separate serving times, not including the 24-hour room service), and when to sleep. Service in all areas from dining to housekeeping is upscale and immediate. The service is so good that a common shipboard joke says that if you leave your bed during the night to visit the head (sea talk for bathroom), your cabin steward will have made the bed and placed chocolates on the pillow by the time you return.

After the cruise, passengers are transported back to the airport in air-conditioned buses for the flight home. Representatives of the cruise line are on hand at the airport to help cruisers meet their scheduled flights. When all amenities are considered, most vacation packages would be hard pressed to match Carnival's per diem prices that range from $125 to $250 per person/per day, depending on accommodations. (Holland America and Seabourn are higher, averaging $300 per person/per day.) Occasional specials allow for even lower prices and special suite accommodations can be had for an additional payment.

CARNIVAL OPERATIONS

Carnival Corporation, headquartered in Miami, was composed of Carnival Cruise Lines, Holland America Lines (which included Windstar Sail Cruises as a subsidiary), Holland America Westours, Westmark Hotels, Airtours, and the newly created Cunard Line Limited. Carnival Cruise Lines, Inc., was a Panamanian corporation, and its subsidiaries were incorporated in Panama, the Netherlands Antilles, the British Virgin Islands, Liberia, and the Bahamas. The ships were subject to inspection by the U.S. Coast Guard for compliance with the Convention for the Safety of Life at Sea (SOLAS), which required specific structural requirements for the safety of passengers at sea, and by the U.S. Public Health Service for sanitary standards. The company was also regulated in some aspects by the Federal Maritime Commission.

At its helm, Carnival Corporation was led by CEO and Chairman of the Board Micky Arison and Carnival Cruise Lines President and COO Bob Dickinson. A. Kirk Lanterman was the President and CEO of the Holland America cruise division, which included Holland America Westours and Windstar Sail Cruises. (A listing of corporate officers is presented in Exhibit 2.)

The company's product positioning stemmed from its belief that the cruise market actually comprises three primary segments with different passenger demographics, passenger characteristics, and growth requirements. The three segments were the *contemporary, premium,* and *luxury* segments. The contemporary segment was served by Carnival ships for cruises that are seven days or shorter in length and featured a casual ambiance. The premium segment, served by Holland America, served the seven-day and longer market and appealed to more affluent consumers. The luxury segment, although considerably smaller than the other segments, catered to experienced cruisers for seven-day and longer sailings and was served by Seabourn. Windstar Sail Cruises, a subsidiary of Holland America, provided specialty sailing cruises.

Corporate structure was built around the "profit center" concept and updated periodically when needed for control and coordination purposes. The cruise subsidiaries of Carnival gave the corporation a presence in most of the major cruise segments and provided for worldwide operations.

Carnival always placed a high priority on marketing in an attempt to promote cruises as an alternative to land-based vacations. It wanted customers to know that the ship in itself was the destination and the ports of call were important, but secondary, to the cruise experience. Education and the creation of awareness were critical to corporate marketing efforts. Carnival was the first cruise line to successfully break away from traditional print media and use television to reach a broader market. Even though other lines had followed Carnival's lead in selecting promotional media and were near in total advertising expenditures, the organization still led all cruise competitors in advertising and marketing expenditures.

Carnival wanted to remain the leader and innovator in the cruise industry and intended to do so with sophisticated promotional efforts and by gaining loyalty from former cruisers, by refurbishing ships, varying activities and ports of call, and being innovative in all aspects of ship operations. Management intended to build on the theme of the ship as a destination given the historical success with this promotional effort. The company capitalized and amortized direct-response advertising and expenses other ad-

Exhibit 2 **Corporate Officers of Carnival Corporation**

Micky Arison
Chairman of the Board
Chief Executive Officer
Carnival Corporation

Gerald R. Cahill
Senior Vice-President—Finance and CFO
Carnival Corporation

Robert H. Dickinson
President and COO
Carnival Cruise Lines

Howard S. Frank
Vice-Chairman and Chief Operating Officer
Carnival Corporation

Roderick K. McLeod
Senior Vice-President—Marketing
Carnival Corporation

Lowell Zemnick
Vice-President and Treasurer
Carnival Corporation

Meshulam Zonis
Senior Vice-President—Operations
Carnival Cruise Lines

A. Kirk Lanterman
Chairman of the Board
Chief Executive Officer
Holland America Lines

Peter T. McHugh
President and COO
Holland America Lines

Source: Carnival Corporation, 1998.

vertising costs as incurred. Advertising expense totaled $112 million in 1997, $109 million in 1996, $98 million in 1995, and $85 million in 1994.

FINANCIAL PERFORMANCE

Carnival retains Price Waterhouse as independent accountants, the Barnett Bank Trust Company–North America as the registrar and stock transfer agent, and its Class A Common stock trades on the New York Stock Exchange under the symbol CCL. In December 1996, Carnival amended the terms of its revolving credit facility primarily to combine two facilities into a single $1 billion unsecured revolving credit facility due in 2001. The borrowing rate on the One Billion Dollar Revolver is a maximum of LIBOR* plus

---

*"LIBOR Rate" means, for an Interest Period for each LIBOR (London Interbank Offer Rate) Rate Advance comprising part of the same Borrowing, the rate determined by the Agent to be the rate of interest per annum rounded upward to the nearest whole multiple of 1/100 of 1% per annum, appearing on the Telerate screen 3750 at 11:00 A.M. (London time) two business days before the first day of such interest period for a term equal to such interest period and in an amount substantially equal to such portion of the loan, or if the agent cannot so determine the LIBOR rate by reference screen 3750, then (ii) equal to the average (rounded upward to the nearest whole multiple of 1/100 of 1% per annum, if such average is not such a multiple) of the rate per annum at which deposits in United States dollars are offered by the principal office of each of the reference lenders in London, England, to prime banks in the London Interbank market at 11:00 A.M. (London time) two business days before the first day of such interest period for a term equal to such interest period and in an amount substantially equal to such portion of the loan. In the latter case, the LIBOR rate for an interest period shall be determined by the agent on the basis of applicable rates furnished to and received by the agent from the reference lenders two business days before the first day of such interest period, subject, however, to the provisions of Section 2.05. If at any time the agent shall determine that by reason of circumstances affecting the London Interbank market (i) adequate and reasonable means do not exist for ascertaining the LIBOR rate for the succeeding interest period or (ii) the making or continuance of any loan at the LIBOR rate has become impracticable as a result of a contingency occurring after the date of this agreement which materially and adversely affects the London Interbank market, the agent shall so notify the lenders and the borrower. Failing the availability of the LIBOR rate, the LIBOR rate shall mean the base rate thereafter in effect from time to time until such time as a LIBOR rate may be determined by reference to the London Interbank market.

Exhibit 3 **Consolidated Statements of Operations: Carnival Corporation**
(Dollar amounts in thousands)

	Six-Month Comparison			Year Ending November 30				
	May 31, 1998	May 31, 1997	1997	1996	1995	1994	1993
Revenues	$1,219,196	$1,117,696	$2,447,468	$2,212,572	$1,998,150	$1,806,016	$1,556,919
Costs and expenses							
Operating expense	669,951	634,622	1,322,669	1,241,269	1,131,113	1,028,475	907,925
Selling and administrative	163,784	156,219	296,533	274,855	248,566	223,272	207,995
Depreciation and amortization	89,266	82,658	167,287	144,987	128,433	110,595	93,333
	923,001	873,499	1,786,489	1,661,111	1,508,112	1,362,342	1,209,253
Operating income before affiliated	296,195	244,197	660,979	551,461	—	—	—
Income from affiliated	(13,034)	(11,694)	53,091	45,967	—	—	—
Operating income	283,161	232,503	714,070	597,428	490,038	443,674	347,666
Other income (expense)							
Interest income	5,885	3,382	8,675	18,597	14,403	8,668	11,527
Interest expense, net of capitalized interest	(24,735)	(31,536)	(55,898)	(64,092)	(63,080)	(51,378)	(34,325)
Other income (expense)	(662)	2,105	5,436	23,414	19,104	(9,146)	(1,201)
Income tax expense	6,861	6,353	(6,233)	(9,045)	(9,374)	(10,053)	(5,497)
	(12,651)	(19,696)	(48,020)	(31,126)	(38,947)	(61,909)	(29,496)
Income before extraordinary item	270,510	212,807	666,050	566,302	451,091	381,765	318,170
Extraordinary item							
Loss on early extinguishment of debt	—	—	—	—	—	—	—
Discontinued operations							
Hotel Casino operating loss	—	—	—	—	—	—	—
Loss on disposal of Hotel Casino	—	—	—	—	—	—	—
Net income	$ 270,510	$ 212,807	$ 666,050	$ 566,302	$ 451,091	$ 381,765	$ 318,170

Source: Carnival Corporation, *1997* and *1998 Form 10-K* and *Form 10-Q.*

14 basis points and the facility fee is 6 basis points. Carnival initiated a commercial paper program in October 1996, which is supported by the One Billion Dollar Revolver. As of November 30, 1996, the company had $307 million outstanding under its commercial paper program and $693 million available for borrowing under the One Billion Dollar Revolver.

The consolidated financial statements for Carnival Cruise Lines, Inc., are shown in Exhibits 3 and 4 and selected financial data are presented in Exhibit 5.

Customer cruise deposits, which represent unearned revenue, are included in the balance sheet when received and recognized as cruise revenues on completion of the voyage. Customers also are required to pay the full cruise fare (minus deposit) 60 days in advance, with the fares being recognized as cruise revenue on completion of the voyage.

Property and equipment on the financial statements is stated at cost. The depreciation and amortization amount is calculated using the straight-line method over the following estimated useful lives: vessels 25–30 years, buildings 20–40 years, equipment 2–20 years and leasehold improvements at the shorter of the "term of lease" or "related asset life." Goodwill of $275 million resulting from the acquisition of HAL Antillen, N.V. (Holland America Lines) is being amortized using the straight-line method over 40 years.

During 1995, Carnival received $40 million from the settlement of litigation with Metra Oy, the former parent company of Wartsila Marine Industries, related to losses suffered in connection with the construction of three cruise ships. (Wartsila declared bankruptcy in late 1994.) Of this amount, $14.4 million was recorded as "other income," with the remainder used to pay legal fees and reduce the cost basis of the three ships.

On June 25, 1996, Carnival reached an agreement with the trustees of Wartsila and creditors for the bankruptcy, which resulted in a cash payment of approximately $80 million. Of the $80 million received, $5 million was used to pay certain costs, $32 million was recorded as other income, and $43 million was used to reduce the cost basis of certain ships that had been affected by the bankruptcy.

By May 31, 1998, Carnival had outstanding long-term debt of $1.55 billion, with the current portion being $58.45 million. This debt was primarily composed of $306.8 million in commercial paper and several unsecured debentures and notes of less than $200 million each at rates ranging from 5.65% to 7.7%.

According to the Internal Revenue Code of 1986, Carnival was considered a "controlled foreign corporation (CFC)" because 50% of its stock was held by individuals who were residents of foreign countries and its countries of incorporation exempt shipping operations of U.S. persons from income tax. Because of CFC status, Carnival expected all of its income (with the exception of U.S. source income from the transportation, hotel, and tour businesses of Holland America) to be exempt from U.S. federal income taxes at the corporate level.

The primary financial consideration of importance to Carnival management involved the control of costs, both fixed and variable, for the maintenance of a healthy profit margin. Carnival had the lowest break-even point of any organization in the cruise industry (ships break even at approximately 60% of capacity) due to operational experience and economies of scale. Unfortunately, fixed costs, including depreciation, fuel, insurance, port charges, and crew costs, which represented more than 33% of the company's operating expenses, could not be significantly reduced in relation to decreases in passenger loads and aggregate passenger ticket revenue. (Major expense items were air fares (25–30%), travel agent fees (10%), and labor (13–15%) Increases in these costs could negatively affect the profitability of the organization.

Exhibit 4   **Consolidated Balance Sheets: Carnival Corporation**
(Dollar amounts in thousands)

	6 Months Ending	Year Ending November 30				
	May 31, 1998	1997	1996	1995	1994	1993
Assets						
Current assets						
Cash and cash equivalents	$ 120,600	$ 139,989	$ 111,629	$ 53,365	$ 54,105	$ 60,243
Short-term investments	9,414	9,738	12,486	50,395	70,115	88,677
Accounts receivable	66,503	57,090	38,109	33,080	20,789	19,310
Consumable inventories (average cost)	76,226	54,970	53,281	48,820	45,122	37,245
Prepaid expenses and other	102,754	74,238	75,428	70,718	50,318	48,323
Total current assets	375,497	336,025	290,933	256,378	240,449	253,798
Property and equipment (at cost)						
Less accumulated depreciation and amortization	5,469,814	4,327,413	4,099,038	3,414,823	3,071,431	2,588,009
Other assets						
Goodwill (less accumulated amortization)	403,077	212,607	219,589	226,571	233,553	237,327
Long-term notes receivable	—	—	—	78,907	76,876	29,136
Investment in affiliates and other assets	425,715	479,329	430,330	128,808	47,514	21,097
Net assets of discontinued operations	37,733	71,401	61,998	—	—	89,553
Total assets	$6,711,836	$5,426,775	$5,101,888	$4,105,487	$3,669,823	$3,218,920
Liabilities and Shareholders' Equity						
Current liabilities						
Current portion of long-term debt	$ 58,457	$ 59,620	$ 66,369	$ 72,752	$ 84,644	$ 91,621
Accounts payable	187,897	106,783	84,748	90,237	86,750	81,374
Accrued liabilities	169,048	154,253	126,511	113,483	114,868	94,830
Customer deposits	755,890	420,908	352,698	292,606	257,505	228,153
Dividends payable	44,619	44,578	32,416	25,632	21,190	19,763
Reserve for discontinued operations	—	—	—	—	—	34,253
Total current liabilities	1,215,911	786,142	662,742	594,710	564,957	549,994
Long-term debt	1,557,016	1,015,294	1,277,529	1,035,031	1,046,904	916,221
Convertible notes	—	—	39,103	115,000	115,000	115,000
Other long-term liabilities	23,907	20,241	91,630	15,873	14,028	10,499
Shareholders' equity						
Class A Common Stock (1 vote share)	5,949	2,972	2,397	2,298	2,276	2,274
Class B Common Stock (5 votes share)	—	—	550	550	550	550
Paid-in capital	871,676	866,097	819,610	594,811	544,947	541,194
Retained earnings	2,912,499	2,731,213	2,207,781	1,752,140	1,390,589	1,089,323
Other	1,799	4,816	546	(4,926)	(9,428)	(6,135)
Total shareholders' equity	3,791,923	3,605,098	3,030,884	2,344,873	1,928,934	1,627,206
Total liabilities and shareholders' equity	$6,711,836	$5,426,775	$5,101,888	$4,105,487	$3,669,823	$3,218,920

Source: Carnival Corporation, *1997* and *1998 Form 10-K* and *Form 10-Q*.

Exhibit 5   Selected Financial Data by Segment: Carnival Corporation
(Dollar amounts in thousands)

Year Ending November 30	1997	1996	1995	1994	1993
Revenues					
Cruise	$2,257,567	$2,003,458	$1,800,775	$1,623,069	$1,381,473
Tour	242,646	263,356	241,909	227,613	214,382
Intersegment revenues	(52,745)	(54,242)	(44,534)	(44,666)	(38,936)
Total	2,447,468	2,212,572	1,998,150	1,806,016	1,556,919
Gross operating profit					
Cruise	1,072,758	913,880	810,736	726,808	598,642
Tour	52,041	57,423	56,301	50,733	50,352
Total	1,124,799	971,303	867,037	777,541	648,994
Depreciation and amortization					
Cruise	157,454	135,694	120,304	101,146	84,228
Tour	8,862	8,317	8,129	9,449	9,105
Corporate	971	976	—	—	—
Total	167,287	144,987	128,433	110,595	93,333
Operating income					
Cruise	656,009	535,814	465,870	425,590	333,392
Tour	13,262	21,252	24,168	18,084	14,274
Corporate	44,799	40,362	—	—	—
Total	714,070	597,428	490,038	443,674	347,666
Identifiable assets					
Cruise	4,744,140	4,514,675	3,967,174	3,531,727	2,995,221
Tour	163,941	150,851	138,313	138,096	134,146
Discontinued resort and casino	—	—	—	—	89,553
Corporate	518,694	436,362	—	—	—
Total	5,426,775	5,101,888	4,105,487	3,669,823	3,218,920
Capital expenditures					
Cruise	414,963	841,871	456,920	587,249	705,196
Tour	42,507	14,964	8,747	9,963	10,281
Corporate	40,187	1,810	—	—	—
Total	$ 497,657	$ 858,645	$ 465,667	$ 597,212	$ 715,477

Source: Carnival Corporation, *1997* and *1998 Form 10-K* and *Form 10-Q's*.

PRINCIPAL SUBSIDIARIES

Carnival Cruise Lines

At the end of fiscal 1997, Carnival operated 11 ships with a total berth capacity of 20,332. Carnival operated principally in the Caribbean and had an assortment of ships and ports of call serving the three-, four-, and seven-day cruise markets (see Exhibit 6).

Each ship was a floating resort, including a full maritime staff, shopkeepers, casino operators, entertainers, and complete hotel staff. Approximately 14% of corporate reve-

Exhibit 6   The Ships of Carnival Corporation

Name	Registry	Built	First in Company	Service Cap[1]	Gross Tons	Length/Width	Areas of Operation
Carnival Cruise Lines							
Carnival Destiny	Panama	1996	1997	2,642	101,000	893/116	Caribbean
Inspiration	Panama	1996	1996	2,040	70,367	855/104	Caribbean
Imagination	Panama	1995	1995	2,040	70,367	855/104	Caribbean
Fascination	Panama	1994	1994	2,040	70,367	855/104	Caribbean
Sensation	Panama	1993	1993	2,040	70,367	855/104	Caribbean
Ecstasy	Liberia	1991	1991	2,040	70,367	855/104	Caribbean
Fantasy	Liberia	1990	1990	2,044	70,367	855/104	Bahamas
Celebration	Liberia	1987	1987	1,486	47,262	738/92	Caribbean
Jubilee	Panama	1986	1986	1,486	47,262	738/92	Mexican Riviera
Holiday	Panama	1985	1985	1,452	46,052	727/92	Mexican Riviera
Tropicale	Liberia	1982	1982	1,022	36,674	660/85	Alaska, Caribbean
Total Carnival Ships capacity = 20,332							
Holland America Lines							
Veendam	Bahamas	1996	1996	1,266	55,451	720/101	Alaska, Caribbean
Ryndam	Netherlands	1994	1994	1,266	55,451	720/101	Alaska, Caribbean
Maasdam	Netherlands	1993	1993	1,266	55,451	720/101	Europe, Caribbean
Statendam	Netherlands	1993	1993	1,266	55,451	720/101	Alaska, Caribbean
Westerdam	Netherlands	1986	1988	1,494	53,872	798/95	Canada, Caribbean
Noordam	Netherlands	1984	1984	1,214	33,930	704/89	Alaska, Caribbean
Nieuw Amsterdam	Netherlands	1983	1983	1,214	33,930	704/89	Alaska, Caribbean
Rotterdam IV	Netherlands	1997	1997	1,316	62,000	780/106	Alaska, Worldwide
Total HAL Ships capacity = 10,302							
Windstar Cruises							
Wind Spirit	Bahamas	1988	1988	148	5,736	440/52	Caribbean, Mediterranean
Wind Song	Bahamas	1987	1987	148	5,703	440/52	Costa Rica, Tahiti
Wind Star	Bahamas	1986	1986	148	5,703	440/52	Caribbean, Mediterranean
Total Windstar Ships capacity = 444							
Total capacity = 31,078							

Note:

1. In accordance with industry practice, passenger capacity is calculated based on two passengers per cabin even though some cabins can accommodate three or four passengers.

nue was generated from shipboard activities such as casino operations, liquor sales, and gift shop items. At various ports of call, passengers could also take advantage of tours, shore excursions, and duty-free shopping at their own expense. Shipboard operations were designed to provide maximum entertainment, activities, and service. The size of the company and the similarity in design of the new cruise ships allowed Carnival to achieve various economies of scale, and management was very cost conscious.

Although the Carnival Cruise Lines division was increasing its presence in the shorter cruise markets, its general marketing strategy was to use three-, four-, or seven-day moderately priced cruises to fit the time and budget constraints of the middle class. Shorter cruises could cost less than $500 per person (depending on accommodations) up to roughly $3000 per person in a luxury suite on a seven-day cruise, including port charges. (Per diem rates for shorter cruises were slightly higher, on average, than per diem rates for seven-day cruises.) Average rates per day were approximately $180, excluding gambling, liquor and soft drinks, and items of a personal nature. Guests were expected to tip their cabin steward and waiter at a suggested rate of $3 per person/per day and the bus boy at $1.50 per person/per day.

Some 99% of all Carnival cruises were sold through travel agents who receivd a standard commission of 10% (15% in Florida). Carnival worked extensively with travel agents to help promote cruises as an alternative to a Disney or European vacation. In addition to training travel agents from nonaffiliated travel/vacation firms to sell cruises, a special group of employees regularly visited travel agents posing as prospective clients. If the agent recommended a cruise before another vacation option, he or she received $100. If the travel agent specified a Carnival cruise before other options, he or she received $1000 on the spot. During fiscal 1995, Carnival took reservations from about 29,000 of the approximately 45,000 travel agencies in the United States and Canada, and no one travel agency accounted for more than 2% of Carnival revenues.

On-board service was labor intensive, employing help from some 51 nations—mostly third world countries—with reasonable returns to employees. For example, waiters on the *Jubilee* could earn approximately $18,000 to $27,000 per year (base salary and tips), significantly greater than could be earned in their home country for similar employment. Waiters typically worked 10 hours per day with approximately one day off per week for a specified contract period (usually three to nine months). Carnival records show that employees remained with the company for approximately eight years and that applicants exceeded demand for all cruise positions. Nonetheless, the American Maritime union had cited Carnival (and other cruise operators) several times for exploitation of its crew.

Holland America Lines

On January 17, 1989, Carnival acquired all the outstanding stock of HAL Antillen N.V. from Holland America Lines N.V. for $625 million in cash. Carnival financed the purchase through $250 million in retained earnings (cash account) and borrowed the other $375 million from banks at 0.25% over the prime rate. Carnival received the assets and operations of the Holland America Lines, Westours, Westmark Hotels, and Windstar Sail Cruises. Holland America currently had seven cruise ships with a capacity of 8,795 berths, with new ships to be delivered in the future.

Founded in 1873, Holland America Lines was an upscale (it charges an average of 25% more than similar Carnival cruises) line with principal destinations in Alaska during the summer months and the Caribbean during the fall and winter, with some worldwide cruises of up to 98 days. Holland America targeted an older, more sophisticated cruiser with fewer youth-oriented activities. On Holland America ships, passengers could dance to the sounds of the Big Band era and avoid the discos of Carnival ships. Passengers on Holland America ships enjoyed more service (a higher staff-to-passenger ratio than Carnival) and had more cabin and public space per person, and a "no tipping" shipboard policy. Holland America had not enjoyed the spectacular growth of Carnival cruise ships, but it sustained constant growth over the decade of the 1980s and early 1990s with high occupancy. The operation of these ships and the structure of the crew was similar to the Carnival cruise ship model, and the acquisition of the line gave the Carnival Corporation a presence in the Alaskan market where it had none before.

Holland America Westours was the largest tour operator in Alaska and the Canadian Rockies and provided vacation synergy with Holland America cruises. The transportation division of Westours included over 290 motor coaches comprised of the Gray

Line of Alaska, the Gray Line of Seattle, Westours motorcoaches, the McKinley Explorer railroad coaches, and three-day boats for tours to glaciers and other points of interest. Carnival management believed that Alaskan cruises and tours should increase for two reasons: (1) the aging "baby boomer" population segment increasingly will want relaxing vacations with scenic beauty, and (2) Alaska is a U.S. destination—meaning no custom or language difficulties.

Westmark Hotels consisted of 16 hotels in Alaska and the Yukon territories and also provided synergy with cruise operations and Westours. Westmark was the largest group of hotels in the region providing moderately priced rooms for the vacationer.

Windstar Sail Cruises was acquired by Holland America Lines in 1988 and consisted of three computer controlled sailing vessels with a berth capacity of 444. Windstar was very upscale and offered an alternative to traditional cruise liners with a more intimate, activity-oriented cruise. The ships operated primarily in the Mediterranean and the South Pacific, visiting ports not accessible to large cruise ships. Although catering to a small segment of the cruise vacation industry, Windstar helped with Carnival's commitment to participate in all segments of the cruise industry.

Seabourn Cruise Lines

In April 1992, Carnival acquired 25% of the capital stock of Seabourn. As part of the transaction, Carnival also made a subordinated secured 10-year loan of $15 million to Seabourn and a $10 million convertible loan to Seabourn. In December 1995, Carnival converted the $10 million convertible loan into an additional 25% equity interest in Seabourn.

Seabourn targeted the luxury market with three vessels providing 200 passengers per ship with all-suite accommodations. Seabourn was considered the "Rolls Royce" of the cruise industry and in 1992 was named the "World's Best Cruise Line" by the prestigious Condé Naste *Traveler's* Fifth Annual Readers' Choice poll. Seabourn cruised the Americas, Europe, Scandinavia, the Mediterranean, and the Far East.

Airtours

In April 1996, Carnival acquired a 29.5% interest in Airtours for approximately $307 million. Airtours and its subsidiaries was the largest air-inclusive tour operator in the world and was publicly traded on the London Stock Exchange. Airtours provided air-inclusive packaged holidays to the British, Scandinavian, and North American markets. Airtours provided holidays to approximately 5 million people per year and owned or operated 32 hotels, two cruise ships, and 31 aircraft.

Airtours operated 19 aircraft exclusively for its U.K. tour operators, providing a large proportion of their flying requirements. In addition, Airtours' subsidiary Premiair operated a fleet of 14 aircraft, which provided most of the flying requirements for Airtours' Scandinavian tour operators.

Airtours owned or operated 32 hotels (6,500 rooms), which provided rooms to Airtours' tour operators principally in the Mediterranean and the Canary Islands. In addition, Airtours had a 50% interest in Tenerife Sol, a joint venture with Sol Hotels Group of Spain, which owned and operated three additional hotels in the Canary Islands providing 1,300 rooms.

Through its subsidiary Sun Cruises, Airtours owned and operated three cruise ships. Both the 800-berth *MS Seawing* and the 1,062-berth *MS Carousel* commenced operations in 1995. Recently Airtours acquired a third ship, the *MS Sundream,* which was the sister ship of the *MS Carousel*. The ships operated in the Mediterranean, the Caribbean, and around the Canary Islands and were booked exclusively by Airtours' tour operators.

Costa Crociere S.p.A.

In June 1997, Carnival and Airtours purchased the equity securities of Costa from the Costa family at a cost of approximately $141 million. Costa was headquartered in Italy and was considered Europe's largest cruise line with seven ships and a 7,710-passenger capacity. Costa operated primarily in the Mediterranean, Northern Europe, the Caribbean, and South America. The major market for Costa was in southern Europe, mainly Italy, Spain, and France. In January 1998, Costa signed an agreement to construct an eighth ship with a capacity of approximately 2,100 passengers.

Cunard Line

Carnival's most recent acquisition had been the Cunard Line, announced on May 28, 1998. Comprised of five ships, the Cunard Line was considered a luxury line with strong brand name recognition. Carnival purchased 50% of Cunard for an estimated $255 million, with the other 50% being owned by Atle Brynestad. Cunard was immediately merged with Seabourn and the resulting Cunard Cruise Line Limited (68% owned by Carnival) with its now eight ships, was to be headed by the former President of Seabourn, Larry Pimentel.

Joint Venture with Hyundai Merchant Marine Co. Ltd.

In September 1996, the Carnival and Hyundai Merchant Marine (HMM) Co. Ltd. signed an agreement to form a 50/50 joint venture to develop the Asian cruise vacation market. Each contributed $4.8 million as the initial capital of the joint venture. In addition, in November 1996, Carnival sold the cruise ship *Tropicale* to the joint venture for approximately $95.5 million cash. Carnival then chartered the vessel from the joint venture until the joint venture was ready to begin cruise operations in the Asian market, targeting a start date in or around the spring of 1998. The joint venture borrowed the $95.5 million purchase price from a financial institution, and Carnival and HMM each guaranteed 50% of the borrowed funds.

This arrangement was, however, short lived as in September 1997 the joint venture was dissolved and Carnival repurchased the *Tropicale* for $93 million.

FUTURE CONSIDERATIONS

Carnival's management had to continue to monitor several strategic factors and issues for the next few years. The industry itself was expected to see further consolidation through mergers and buyouts, and the expansion of the industry could negatively affect the profitability of various cruise operators. Another factor of concern to management was how to reach the large North American market, of which only 5% to 7% have ever taken a cruise.

With the industry maturing, cruise competitors were becoming more sophisticated in their marketing efforts and price competition was the norm in most cruise segments. (For a partial listing of major industry competitors, see Exhibit 7.) Royal Caribbean Cruise Lines had also instituted a major shipbuilding program and was successfully

Exhibit 7   Major Industry Competitors

Celebrity Cruises, 5200 Blue Lagoon Drive, Miami, Fl 33126

Celebrity Cruises operates four modern cruise ships on four-, seven- and ten-day cruises to Bermuda, the Caribbean, the Panama Canal, and Alaska. Celebrity attracts first-time cruisers as well as seasoned cruisers. Purchase by Royal Caribbean on July 30, 1997.

Norwegian Cruise Lines, 95 Merrick Way, Coral Gables, Fl 33134

Norwegian Cruise Lines (NCL), formally Norwegian Caribbean Lines, was the first to base a modern fleet of cruise ships in the Port of Miami. It operates 10 modern cruise liners on three-, four-, and seven-day Eastern and Western Caribbean cruises and cruises to Bermuda. A wide variety of activities and entertainment attracts a diverse array of customers. NCL just completed reconstruction of two ships and is building the Norwegian Sky, a 2,000-passenger ship to be delivered in the summer of 1999.

Disney Cruise Line, 500 South Buena Vista Street, Burbank, CA 91521

Disney has just recently entered the cruise market with the introduction of the *Disney Magic* and *Disney Wonder.* Both ships cater to both children and adults and feature 875 staterooms each. Each cruise includes a visit to Disney's private island, Castaway Bay. Although Disney currently has only two ships and the cruise portion of Disney is small, the potential for future growth is substantial, with over $22 billion in revenues and $1.9 billion net profits in 1997.

Princess Cruises, 10100 Santa Monica Boulevard, Los Angeles, Ca 90067

Princess Cruises, with its fleet of nine "Love Boats," offers seven-day and extended cruises to the Caribbean, Alaska, Canada, Africa, the Far East, South America, and Europe. Princess's primary market is the upscale 50-plus experienced traveler, according to Mike Hannan, Senior Vice-President for Marketing Services. Princess ships have an ambiance best described as casual elegance and are famous for their Italian-style dining rooms and onboard entertainment.

Royal Caribbean Cruise Lines, 1050 Caribbean Way, Miami, Fl 33132

RCCL's nine ships have consistently been given high marks by passengers and travel agents over the past 21 years. RCCL's ships are built for the contemporary market, are large and modern, and offer three-, four-, and seven-day as well as extended cruises. RCCL prides itself on service and exceptional cuisine. With the purchase of Celebrity, RCCL becomes the largest cruise line in the world with 17 ships and a passenger capacity of over 31,100. Plans include the introduction of six additional ships by the year 2002. In 1997, RCCL had net income of $175 million on revenues of $1.93 billion.

Other Industry Competitors (Partial List)

American Hawaii Cruises	(2 Ships—Hawaiian Islands)
Club Med	(2 Ships—Europe, Caribbean)
Commodore Cruise Line	(1 Ship—Caribbean)
Cunard Line	(8 Ships—Caribbean, Worldwide)
Dolphin Cruise Line	(3 Ships—Caribbean, Bermuda)
Radisson Seven Seas Cruises	(3 Ships—Worldwide)
Royal Olympic Cruises	(6 Ships—Caribbean, Worldwide)
Royal Cruise Line	(4 Ships—Caribbean, Alaska, WW)

Source: Cruise Line International Association, *1996 Form 10-K* and *Annual Report.*

challenging Carnival Cruise Lines in the contemporary segment. The announcement that the Walt Disney Company was entering the cruise market with two 80,000-ton cruise liners in 1998 was expected to significantly impact the "family" cruise vacation segment.

With competition intensifying, industry observers believed the wave of failures, mergers, buyouts, and strategic alliances would increase. Regency Cruises ceased operations on October 29, 1995, and filed for Chapter 11 bankruptcy. American Family Cruises, a spin-off from Costa Cruise Lines, failed to reach the family market, and Carnival's Fiestamarina failed to reach the Spanish-speaking market. EffJohn International sold its Commodore Cruise subsidiary to a group of Miami-based investors, which then chartered one of its two ships to World Explorer Cruises/Semester At Sea. Sun Cruise Lines merged with Epirotiki Cruise Line under the name of Royal Olympic Cruises, and Cunard bought the Royal Viking Line and its name from Kloster Cruise Ltd., with one ship of its fleet being transferred to Kloster's Royal Cruise Line. All of these failures, mergers, and buyouts occurred in 1995, which was not an unusual year for changes in the cruise line industry.

The increasing industry capacity was also a source of concern to cruise operators. The slow growth in industry demand was occurring during a period when industry berth capacity continued to grow. The entry of Disney and the ships already on order by current operators was expected to increase industry berth capacity by over 10,000 per year for the next three years, a significant increase. The danger lay in cruise operators using the "price" weapon in their marketing campaigns to fill cabins. If cruise operators could not make a reasonable return on investment, operating costs would have to be reduced (affecting quality of services) to remain profitable. This would increase the likelihood of further industry acquisitions, mergers, and consolidations. A worst case scenario would be the financial failure of weaker lines.

Still, Carnival's management believed that demand should increase during the remainder of the 1990s. Considering that only 5% to 7% of the North American market has taken a cruise vacation, reaching more of the North American target market would improve industry profitability. Industry analysts stated that the problem was that an "assessment of market potential" was only an "educated guess"; and what if the current demand figures were reflective of the future?

American Council for International Studies (ACIS): Striving to Stay Small

Michael I. Eizenberg, Sharon Ungar Lane, and Alan N. Hoffman

In the spring of 1977, four young middle-level managers at American Leadership Study Groups decided they were unhappy with the way their company was being run. As they saw it, senior management was out of touch with the day-to-day running of the company and with long range planning. After thoroughly discussing their concerns, Michael Eizenberg (age 29), John Hannyngton (25), Peter Jones (27), and David Stitt (26) decided that they would leave ALSG and go out on their own. They were convinced they had the right combination of skills, experience, expertise, and commitment to build their own organization.

They soon enlisted the support of Linda Van Huss, American Leadership Study Group's leading field sales person. Clandestinely they created a business plan, sought legal advice, and among them invested $100,000 in cash. In addition, their close working relationships with Djohn Andersen and Miriam Zumpolle secured them $200,000 in backing from the Scandanavian Student Travel Service.

ACIS: THE EARLY YEARS

In August 1978, the American Council for International Studies (ACIS) was launched with a mailing to high schools throughout the United States. Its first brochure was a simple 32-page, black-and-white catalog whose prices were only a few percentage points lower than those in the glossy 100-page brochures of their much more established competition. The founders were counting on their personal relations with teachers, as well as their expertise, to bring in an initial base of customers. Sales during the first few months were much lower than they expected. Clients felt some personal loyalty, but were finally influenced by the feeling of stability they had working with a well-established organization.

ACIS was conceived of as an educational travel organization that enabled teachers to lead their students on educational trips abroad. Its goal was to create a highly efficient hands-on infrastructure that would foster close partnerships with teachers so they would return each year with a new group of student travelers. Senior managers' involvement in the day-to-day running of the organization to forge these partnerships was crucial and differentiated ACIS from its competitors.

"We didn't really understand the risk we were taking until we were actually out on our own," Michael Eizenberg, President of ACIS, recalls. "Within the organization we were extremely confident of ourselves and our abilities. It wasn't until we were actually in our own sparsely furnished offices that we understood how much we had depended on the infrastructure we had previously worked within. All of a sudden, we understood

---

This case was prepared by Michael I. Eizenberg, Sharon Ungar Lane, and Professor Alan N. Hoffman of Bentley College. This case was edited for SMBP–7th Edition. Copyright © 1998 Michael I. Eizenberg, Sharon Ungar Lane, and Professor Alan N. Hoffman. Reprinted by permission.

the risk we were taking. There was a moment of pause, but we became stronger and more focused. We pulled harder together, and there was added intensity and purpose to our work. We realized that if we were going to make it, it would be because we had the strength and determination to make it happen."

Business did not pour into ACIS. Linda Van Huss drove to high schools all over the south, virtually collaring teachers she knew to lead groups. New leads were followed up immediately with unprecedented levels of personal service. Despite their best efforts, when the sales season ended in January, ACIS had signed up only 2,300 participants, roughly 16% of what the established organizations were carrying, and about 30% below their own worst case projections. (See Exhibit 1.)

AIRLINE DEREGULATION

Throughout the 1960s and 1970s, all tour operators, including organizations offering educational trips, relied on the inexpensive flights to Europe offered by charter companies. Only when charter flights were full did organizations turn to the scheduled airlines for a few seats at significantly higher rates. The managers at ACIS were stunned to discover that they did not have enough passengers to make even the smallest charter flight operation possible. They had never considered having to rely totally on the scheduled carriers. Now they assumed they were going to have to grab a few seats here and there from a variety of carriers, at rates well above their budgets.

However, by the late 1970s, travelers' disenchantment with charter flights and the Airline Deregulation Act of 1978 began to have an impact. The skies were opening to new competition on routes between the United States and the United Kingdom. Laker Airways was already beginning to provide scheduled service between New York and London; and British Airways and the U.S. flag carriers were faced with significant low-priced competition in their most lucrative transatlantic market.

The ACIS managers had nurtured contacts at British Airways, but British Airways had in the past been reluctant to seek the lower priced traffic of customers such as ACIS. In early December 1978, a call came from British Airways indicating their willingness to reconsider its position. An exploratory breakfast the next day with District Manager Jim Kivlehan turned into an all-day session. By lunchtime, they had established that ACIS passengers could fly from all 13 British Airways gateways throughout the United States so that passengers did not have to fly to New York to board a charter flight. By late afternoon, British Airways had decided it would be willing to provide service to points beyond London, with convenient connections on British European Airways. By the end of the day, the majority of ACIS passengers were placed at rates below original budgets on British Airways scheduled 747s. The remaining passengers were placed with other foreign flag carriers in groups of 40 or 50 at higher rates. The end result was much better than originally anticipated.

Its early foothold selling scheduled service at new competitive rates from gateways throughout the United States suddenly gave ACIS a significant competitive advantage. Its small size in 1979 allowed ACIS to shift its passengers easily from charters to scheduled flights, and direct scheduled airline service from multiple U.S. gateways quickly became a defining characteristic of ACIS. Larger, more established companies lacked the impetus to change, and their existing infrastructures made such a major change difficult to implement. They had thrived with charters and controlled significant market share; they would only gradually make the shift that ACIS had made in one morning.

Exhibit 1   Overview of Educational Travel Organizations in 1979

Name	Year Founded	Est. No. of clients	Est. Revenue	Location
AIFS	1965	15,000	$25,000,000	Greenwich, CT
CHA	1966	17,000	$27,000,000	Philadelphia, PA
ALSG	1966	12,000	$20,000,000	Worcester, MA
ACIS	1978	2,300	$3,000,000	Boston, MA

IT'S GREAT TO BE SMALL

ACIS's organizational structure was simple. Mike Eizenberg was President. He handled flights, general management, and corporate functions. David Stitt and Peter Jones were responsible for telephone sales in Boston, Linda Van Huss was in charge of field sales throughout the southeast, and John Hannyngton directed overseas operations. All four were Vice-Presidents. There were three other full-time employees.

When a prospective trip leader spoke to Peter, David, or Linda, they had direct access to John Hannyngton's strong organizational abilities overseas and Mike Eizenberg's grasp of the emerging opportunities in the deregulated airline industry. All decisions were made within the small management group. When they disagreed, they considered various solutions until they found one that worked from all points of view. Everyone was on hand, accessible, and deeply committed to the common goal of doing their best for each customer.

The integration of sales, flight, and overseas arrangements was spontaneous. The whole organization, its customers, and suppliers benefited greatly from ACIS's quick and decisive commitment. Active communication led to constant and thorough review.

Close partnerships were forged with teachers who led groups. Especially careful attention was paid to selecting staff in Europe who would be ACIS's frontline representatives overseas and in day-to-day charge of all educational and operational components. ACIS executives were also always highly visible abroad, pitching in to ensure high levels of customer satisfaction. As the dollar strengthened during the early and mid 1980s, ACIS significantly improved hotel quality without passing on major price increases, adding substantially to its own bottom line. Teachers frequently commented that ACIS's programs kept improving every year.

The years from 1980 to 1985 were outstanding for ACIS. Enrollments grew 25–30% each year. Tangible excitement strummed through the organization. Everything kept getting better. Airline seats were plentiful, and the dollar had more and more purchasing power abroad. When Eurodollar interest rates soared to 20%, ACIS's bottom line rose substantially as well. Profitability was high enough each year to support building a larger organization with higher ongoing and infrastructure expenses. Most important, the word was spreading to high school teachers everywhere that ACIS offered a genuinely interesting educational experience, great quality, and exceptional personal service.

In 1981, ACIS began investing in a Data General computer system, and Mike Tenney was hired as system architect. Mike created an integrated database for sales, marketing, operations, and administration. Embedded "notepads" allowed sales and operations staff to modify ACIS's expanding range of preplanned itineraries and keep track of special customer requests and sales commitments, permitting the selling process to remain responsive to special customers and changing market conditions. By 1983, there was e-mail throughout the Boston office and a modem link with Atlanta. By 1984, many ACIS managers had Macintosh's on their desks and used emulation software to access travel information in the Data General computer system.

1985: GROWTH AND PROSPERITY

In 1985, ACIS had acquired a historic brownstone building for its headquarters in Boston and opened sales offices in Atlanta, Chicago, and Los Angeles. In addition, it had acquired a small office building for its European headquarters in London, opened an operations office in Paris, and invested in start-up companies to handle arrangements in Madrid and Rome. Its loyal and solid customer base enthusiastically referred new customers to ACIS. The organization had excellent working relationships with all major airlines. The overseas network provided high-quality services, and the educational experience was beneficial to all involved. However, ACIS's core infrastructure in 1985 remained surprisingly small: 17 people worked in Boston, 4 in Atlanta, 1 in Chicago and Los Angeles, and 2 in London and Paris. Revenues were now in the same range as its largest competitors, and it provided superior service with many fewer staff members.

"Both 1984 and 1985 were incredible years," recalls Michael Eizenberg. "The marketplace had a definite rhythm. The dollar was stronger than it had ever been. Suddenly it was 10 francs to the dollar, not 5. Everyone wanted to go to Europe, the airlines had plenty of seats to sell, and we had great trips to offer at very good prices. It was as if we were dancing to the beat of our customers and our suppliers. Each of us at ACIS had developed a lot of our own patterns, but we danced together. It felt like we all had parts in an amazing piece of choreography." ACIS's sales season for spring and summer 1986 ended just prior to the Christmas holidays 1985 and had set another record. Everyone in the organization felt great heading home for the holiday break. (See Exhibit 2.)

TERRORISM STRIKES THE ROME AIRPORT

On December 27, 1985, as terminals were jammed with hundreds of holiday travelers waiting at the check-in counters, Leonardo da Vinci Airport in Rome was attacked by terrorists. At 9:03 AM, a man threw a grenade toward an espresso bar. Other terrorists showered the 820-foot-long terminal with bullets. Within five minutes, the attack was over, leaving 15 people dead and 74 wounded. Minutes later the terror was repeated at Schwechat Airport in Vienna as terrorists opened fire with AK-47 automatic rifles and rolled three hand grenades across the floor like bowling balls toward their victims. The result: 37 dead, 47 wounded. The entire civilized world was outraged and feared what terrorists might do next.

Airport authorities had been on guard because of a November 26, 1985, U.S. Federal Aviation Administration (FAA) alert for "terrorist threats." Interpol, the international Paris-based anti-crime organization, had issued a similar warning. But heightened security at the airports in both Rome and Vienna had not prevented the attacks because precautions had been taken mainly in the boarding areas and around the planes themselves, while the terrorists attacked places away from the boarding gates where people were allowed to move freely. The massacre was aimed at innocent, defenseless civilians.

The impact on international travel was immediate. No one wanted to go to Europe. It seemed as though everyone who had signed up for an ACIS trip no longer had any intention of going. The switchboard was overwhelmed with phone calls insisting that

Exhibit 2   **Overview of Educational Travel Organizations in 1985**

Name	Year Founded	Est. No. of Clients	Est. Revenue	Location
AIFS	1965	14,000	$25,000,000	Greenwich, CT
CHA	1966	16,000	$27,000,000	Philadelphia, PA
ALSG	1966	13,000	$21,000,000	Worcester, MA
ACIS	1978	15,300	$24,000,000	Boston, MA

trips be cancelled and all monies refunded. ACIS received 7,000 cancellations and demands for refunds in just two days! Their remaining 8,000 passengers were likely to cancel as well.

For the first few days, everyone at ACIS was stunned trying to deal with the panic. "At first, we simply did our best to buy time and try to calm everybody down. We assured them that we were a responsible organization and could be counted on in this difficult situation," explains Michael Eizenberg. "No matter what we said, it was clear that the situation was far beyond anything we could control. A sense of panic prevailed that we increasingly felt helpless to do anything about. Cancellations kept streaming in, along with demands for full refunds."

Perhaps 30% of prospective participants were willing to adopt a wait-and-see attitude. The predominant view from the marketplace called for ACIS to cancel all trips and make full refunds. However, doing so would have had severe financial consequences. After all the work and money already expended, the whole of 1986 stood to be a total loss.

The ACIS participant contract contained clear language about cancellation penalties, entitling ACIS to keep $250 from the deposit of anyone who cancelled. Enforcing these penalties would give ACIS the same level of income from those who chose to cancel as it would earn from those who chose to participate.

The U.S. State Department informed ACIS there were no Travel Advisories indicating travel to Europe was unsafe nor a significant threat of future terrorist attacks, but ACIS could not sell this view in the marketplace. However, enforcing cancellation penalties would have alienated the goodwill ACIS had worked so hard to build up. After all its success and good luck, ACIS faced a no-win situation: either risk losing the market or face losing a significant percentage of its capital.

"After a week, even the most loyal ACIS teachers were growing impatient for answers. They needed an immediate solution that would work with students, parents, and school administrators," recalls Michael Eizenberg. "On January 7, we announced we were amending the cancellation policies stated in our catalogue and were offering full refunds of all monies except for a $35 registration/processing fee and a $150 credit which could be used on a future trip abroad with ACIS."

Everyone at ACIS felt that the offer was an extremely fair and generous solution under the circumstances. Most parents, teachers, and school administrators also acknowledged the good faith the offer represented. Still, processing the 8,000 cancellations was discouraging to everyone at ACIS. ACIS's fine reputation had been thoroughly tested, but not tarnished.

ACIS had built up financial reserves during its good years. Although these would have been dangerously drained had 1986 been a total loss, the year turned out quite well. The $35 per participant in registration/processing fees retained guaranteed the organization $500,000 in 1986 income. Interest income on deposits and future credits contributed another $350,000. Six thousand passengers ended up traveling, yielding $250,000 in operating income. Airlines eager to generate sales came through with $250,000 in promotional support. By the spring, the dollar had dropped 12% in value, and the organization sold off $3 million in excess foreign exchange contracts. This brought in an additional $350,000. By year's end, ACIS showed a respectable profit while preserving its greatest asset, the goodwill of its customers.

Although ACIS withstood the unprecedented events of 1986 quite well, an underlying feeling that it could not withstand two or three similar years in rapid succession persisted. When the sales season for 1987 began in September 1986, the market had not gotten over the shock either. The substantially weaker U.S. dollar and lower U.S. interest rates were not helping. By October, it was clear that the market would only recover to about 75% of its previous level and that profitability would be reduced by about half from 1985.

ACSI IS SOLD TO AIFS

In late October 1986, Michael Eizenberg spoke with Bertil Hult, owner of EF, the world's largest educational travel organization. EF had begun as a small language school for Swedish students who wanted to study English in the United Kingdom. By 1986, EF was operating various language and exchange programs for upwards of 50,000 participants worldwide. Hult wanted to expand his position in the U.S. market and asked if ACIS would be interested in becoming part of his large and diversified organization. He suggested that they meet at his offices in Santa Barbara.

"I really didn't expect much when I flew out. There were four of us with significant ownership positions in ACIS, and I knew that it would take $5 million for a deal to be worthwhile for all of us. I couldn't imagine anyone paying that much for ACIS in the current market environment. At the meetings, I was extremely impressed with Bertil and the other EF senior managers I met," recalls Michael Eizenberg. "Late the following afternoon we got around to discussing the number. Bertil's jaw dropped when I mentioned the $5 million figure. He'd thought we were in bad financial shape after 1986, but we weren't. I remember his saying that with EF's management, worldwide resources, and marketing expertise, he could quickly build a company much larger and more competitive than ACIS, for a lot less than $5 million. The meeting ended cordially, but I realized that EF was never going to pay the money it would take to make us all happy, and there was no way we were going to sell for less."

A week later, at the Council for Standards in International Education (CSIE) annual meeting in Washington, D.C., Mike Eizenberg sat with one of the EF executives he had met in Santa Barbara. Hank Kahn, a Divisional President of American Institute for Foreign Study (AIFS), observed Eizenberg's rapport with his EF colleagues and asked what was going on between him and EF. Eizenberg told Kahn that EF was interested in acquiring ACIS and added that the number being discussed was $5 million.

AIFS Inc. had become a publicly traded company (NASDAQ) in February 1986. At that time, it was the parent company of the American Institute for Foreign Study, Inc. The Institute operated a diversified group of programs all in the field of International Education. These included College Semester Summer Study Abroad, High School Academic and Travel programs, and several Inbound Programs (including Camp America, Homestay in America, Academic Year in America, and Au Pair in America). It also owned Richmond College, a fully accredited American University in London. In November 1986, AIFS Inc. acquired ELS English Language Schools as its second subsidiary. In the spring of 1987, Roger Walther, President and co-founder of AIFS Inc., announced his intention to acquire ACIS, one of his largest competitors in the outbound high school market, in order to propel the firm to dominance in the international student travel industry.

In June 1987, AIFS Inc. acquired ACIS for $4.75 million combined cash and stock, plus earn-out incentives worth an additional $1,500,000 over five years. ACIS thus became AIFS Inc.'s third subsidiary. The management of all AIFS outbound high school programs became the responsibility of the ACIS management team. ACIS became the single brand name for all ACIS and AIFS outbound high school programs.

Michael Eizenberg joined the Board of AIFS Inc., the Board of Trustees of Richmond College, and remained as President and CEO of ACIS. Peter Jones, John Hannyngton, and Linda Van Huss retained their positions as senior managers at ACIS, keeping intact the entrepreneurial team that had created ACIS.

The late 1980s were a time of expansive growth for AIFS Inc. With the acquisition of the two new subsidiaries, sales volume grew from $33,049,000 in 1986 to $95,604,000 in 1988. The high school subsidiary accounted for approximately 40% of gross sales in 1988, and AIFS Inc. returned to a leadership position in this important market area.

The original owners of ACIS stayed on as the management team of the organization. The ACIS subsidiary underwent regular review by the AIFS Inc. Board, but the subsidiary continued to function with a great deal of autonomy. ACIS achieved all of the performance goals established in the original acquisition agreement and received the maximum amount payable under the terms of the earn-out.

The 1990s brought new challenges and new opportunities for AIFS Inc. and for the management team of the ACIS subsidiary.

1990: WAR IN IRAQ/KUWAIT

On August 2, 1990, Iraqi military forces invaded and occupied small, neighboring Kuwait. At 0230 hours Baghdad time on January 17, Desert Storm began against Iraq. Iraq capitulated on February 28. ACIS enrollments in 1991 suffered much as they had in 1986. Enrollments had been low during the fall. When the war erupted in January, ACIS experienced a 50% cancellation rate. By the time the war ended, it was too late to renew interest in ACIS's 1991 programs. As in 1986, ACIS kept a small processing fee and refunded the balance of all monies paid except for $150, which could be used as a credit on a future trip with ACIS. However, ACIS recognized that the low participant numbers offered a chance to regroup and began looking at its 1992 planning with a new sense of urgency.

NEW LOOK, NEW IDEAS, NEW BUSINESS

In January 1992, Charlotte Dietz, Vice-President of Marketing, initiated a series of focus group meetings and several marketing initiatives that were destined to change the face of ACIS entirely. A "Partnership Committee" of 25 teachers came to Boston to discuss their views of international travel in general and ACIS in particular. The loyalty the teachers felt to ACIS was stronger than anyone within the organization had imagined. They reinforced the view that the quality of ACIS programs abroad and its level of personal service prior to departure was markedly superior to that of its competitors. The teachers were loyal and genuinely wanted to help spread the word about the superiority of ACIS programs. The problem was that CHA, EF, ACIS, and ALSG all had beautiful four-color brochures emphasizing the high quality each organization offered. All that differentiated them was price; and in this regard, ACIS was at a disadvantage.

ACIS's marketing plan for 1992 was a strategic breakthrough. It focused on three key areas:

1. Mobilizing ACIS's loyal customer base

2. Enhancing and differentiating ACIS's written materials

3. Making ACIS's commitment to quality tangible and accessible to new teachers

In early July, a personal letter of thanks was sent to the entire ACIS mailing list. The letter also solicited referrals, offering a $100 stipend for each new teacher enrolled. The mailing yielded new leads, which in turn yielded a lot of new business.

The 1992 ACIS catalog was published in late August 1991. Its look was revolutionary. The presentation was of the highest quality; it looked more like a "coffee table" book than a travel brochure. On the cover was a reproduction of Maximilien Luce's impressionist masterpiece "Le Quai St-Michel et Notre Dame." Beautiful four-color photographs adorned the inside pages. Interesting vignettes created exciting itineraries. Teacher testimonials expressed satisfaction and loyalty. ACIS's brochure finally conveyed its unique vision of educational travel.

Participant numbers skyrocketed in 1992. Flight costs were kept substantially below budget. More than 100 new couriers were selected and trained. All departments and overseas offices maintained very high levels of performance. Continuing airline and hotel over-capacity meant suppliers were genuinely grateful for any and all business and willingly helped solve any problems that arose. ACIS finished the year with record profitability. The original founders of ACIS received the balance of their earn-out.

A LONG-TIME COMPETITOR EXITS

In September 1991, Milestone Educational Institute acquired the assets of ALSG. In June 1993, Milestone went out of business leaving more than 5,000 students and teachers without trips at the last minute. The ACIS management team immediately set about helping the stranded travelers, supported by $100,000 of corporate funds to provide free or substantially reduced rates to the stranded groups. Continental Airlines provided free tickets for all passengers ALSG had booked with Continental. Several communities held local fund-raising events. EF also offered a reduced rate plan. Passports, a new entrant started by Gil Markle, the original founder of ALSG, provided support as well. Within ten days, the majority of stranded travelers were setting off on trips. ACIS benefited tremendously from the goodwill its actions during the crises created, adding substantially to its bottom line for many years to come.

THAT'S A GOOD IDEA!

In 1993, ACIS managers read Harvard Business School professors James Heskett, Earl Sasser, and Christopher Hart's book *Service Breakthroughs*. ACIS was already committed to providing high quality. *Service Breakthroughs* made high quality crucial and insisted that a key step to achieving it was establishing parameters so quality could be objectively measured. Questionnaires were individually prepared for each teacher to evaluate every service, measure overall satisfaction, and compare ACIS to other travel organizations.

The overall level of teacher satisfaction was exceptionally high: 96.5% indicated that they planned to travel with ACIS again, and 98% indicated they would recommend ACIS to a colleague. More than 75% of experienced teachers indicated that ACIS was "outstandingly better" than its lower priced competitors, and an additional 20% indicated that ACIS was "better."

The reports also collated statistical data about satisfaction ratings for each hotel and every meal, the performance of the courier, overall pre-departure service, and the educational content of the trip. Overall ratings were high, although there were some disparities. Statistical standards were established according to type of service. Hotels and restaurants were required to achieve a minimum of 80% good/excellent, 15% average, and not more than 5% poor to be retained. Couriers were required to achieve at least 80% excellent, 15% good, and 5% average. Educational content required an overall 95% excellent rating.

The Teacher Evaluation Report was distributed to all ACIS staff and immediately became the standard by which the organization measured itself. Key numbers from this report were published in ACIS's 1994 teacher brochure to emphasize teacher satisfaction.

EVERYTHING IS GREAT, BUT . . .

ACIS's 1994 results were outstanding. ACIS gained a significant amount of the market share that ALSG had previously controlled, and the dollar increased in value. Altogether it made for an extremely impressive bottom line.

Each of the functional departments maintained high levels of performance even with all the growth. However, the significant increase in volume began to strain internal systems. In its 1994 brochure, ACIS offered 92 different programs, many of which could be modified with extra days or additional features. Sales staff also regularly made minor adjustments at the request of teachers. The notepad feature of the now 10-year-old database allowed for these modifications and adjustments to be noted, but it did not integrate them in the actual database structure. At lower volume levels, it was feasible for all the departments to work with the notepads, but not as volume increased.

Until 75 days prior to departure, ACIS "free sold" from a wide open inventory of more than 90 itineraries. Some teachers had groups as small as five or six participants; others as large as 40 or 50. They all had to be divided into bus groups of 35–45 to operate efficiently in Europe. This happened 80% of the time as part of the natural flow of demand. However, significant numbers of teachers were asked to switch dates or change their programs to fit a coherent operational structure. The large variety of programs ACIS offered meant this consolidation process became more complex as the number of participants and the number of itineraries offered grew.

Airline and hotel capacity was beginning to show signs of tightening, and it was extremely challenging to find the space needed during the peak demand periods. The premise of unlimited capacity was questioned.

Twice in 1994, the organization ground to a virtual halt while the issues surrounding consolidating groups and finding the air and hotel capacity required were resolved. ACIS was uncharacteristically performing like a large unwieldy company. Often ACIS senior managers had to step in to solve problems that went beyond what staff members could meaningfully address.

The "hands on" work of ACIS senior staff during these periods went a long way toward maintaining overall morale within the organization and a high satisfaction level with teachers. Teachers were frequently given extra benefits because their trip plans needed to be changed. Customer satisfaction results were extremely high in 1994, with nearly 99% of teachers saying that they would recommend ACIS to a colleague. Enrollment figures and profitability came in at record levels. By the time of the 1995 Sales Meeting in August 1994, the intense months of the previous year were a distant memory. (See Exhibit 3.)

YIELD MANAGEMENT AND GLOBAL ALLIANCES

Prior to the Airline Deregulation Act of 1978, the U.S. government had carefully regulated the number of scheduled flights allowed on all international and domestic routes, and all airlines were required to charge the same governmentally regulated rates. As soon as the Deregulation Act took effect, upstarts such as People Express, Laker, New York Air, Southwest, and Midway moved into previously protected routes, and airline capacity more than doubled. The established carriers also scrambled to expand route systems. The extra capacity created a bonanza for travel industry wholesalers like ACIS. Airlines needed help filling all the seats that were coming onto the market. High-volume wholesalers were able to leverage huge discounts from carriers desperate for business. Wholesalers in every market segment prospered, while the airlines themselves lost billions year after year.

In response, the established carriers began to develop yield management systems. The early systems lacked the sophistication and the computer capability to manage seat inventory for maximum yield. Carriers either sold too many cheap seats and didn't hold back sufficient seat inventory for higher paying customers, or they held back too many high-priced seats and flew empty airplanes.

In 1988, Bell Laboratories patented a mathematical formula that could perform rapid calculations on fare problems with literally thousands of variables. During the next five years, further advances in software enabled the yield and inventory control departments at major airlines to perform complicated passenger demand and rate per seat calculations on a flight-by-flight basis. Computer-driven yield control calculations took control of the number of cheap seats available on every flight.

In 1991, the U.S. government granted antitrust immunity to a global alliance between Northwest Airlines and KLM Royal Dutch Airlines. This global alliance permitted Northwest and KLM to code share using the same aircraft on previously competitive routes and to enter into joint marketing agreements that covered their entire route systems. Delta Airlines entered into a similar global alliance with Swiss Air and Sabena, and United Airlines entered an alliance with Lufthansa and SAS. An alliance between British Airways and American Airlines awaited government approval. These alliances reduced the amount of capacity partners made available on competitive routes to passenger demand.

By 1994, the unprecedented airline losses, which occurred in the first 14 years after de-regulation, had turned into record profits.

1995: UPGRADING ACIS INFORMATION SYSTEMS

In 1995, senior management recognized that the problem of communication between the strong functional departments needed to be addressed. A core inventory of trips was established, and the Group Reservations Department was put in charge of overall coor-

Exhibit 3   Overview of Educational Travel Organizations in 1994

Name	Year Founded	Est. No. of Participants	Est. Revenue	Location
EF	1986	70,000	$120,000,000	Cambridge, MA
CHA	1966	35,000	$ 70,000,000	Philadelphia, PA
ACIS	1978	35,000	$ 80,000,000	Boston, MA
Passports	1993	2,300	$ 3,000,000	Spencer, MA

dination of the sales, flights, and overseas departments. But the two initiatives yielded only small improvements in overall coordination. The large variety of trips that ACIS offered made selling into the core inventory extremely difficult, especially in the competitive market in which ACIS was operating. Airlines were releasing less of their flight inventory to wholesale group sales. By the time the ACIS Group Reservations Department had the opportunity to provide overall coordination, a lot of the least expensive airline space was already gone.

Mike Tenney was at work on writing the code for a new Oracle database system. In the meantime each department was forced to find complex, inefficient, and undocumented "workarounds" to cope with the limitations of the now 12-year-old computer system. Annually there were two extremely difficult and stressful time periods at ACIS when the overall organizational flow ground to a halt while the expectations and demands of groups were made to fit within available airline and hotel space. In 1995, the two periods lasted six weeks instead of four. For the first time, significant airline cost overruns were incurred for about 3% of ACIS passengers. The dollar also weakened at a time when ACIS was "long" on dollars (the company had a large supply of U.S. dollars compared to foreign currencies). These two factors reduced ACIS profitability by about 20% from the record levels achieved the year before. Although 1995 was a good year, management was concerned that it would no longer always be easy to find the cheap airline seats ACIS's budgeting depended on.

Stephen Cummings installed a wide area network using frame relay technology. This gave all 100 ACIS employees in the United States and Europe instant access to the Business Basic database as well as several secondary databases developed in Lotus Notes. Microsoft Office Suite was installed on all ACIS servers worldwide. Lotus Notes Mail was used companywide, and ACIS began gathering teacher e-mail addresses to facilitate electronic communication with teachers. A website was established with basic information about ACIS and its most popular programs.

But it was increasingly clear that the overall organizational design of the company did not work effectively within the constraints of limited airline and hotel capacity, and there was as much of a battle for cheap seats as there was for passengers. The organization was being stretched to its limits for longer periods of time than ever before.

NEW CHALLENGES FOR 1996

ACIS faced new challenges at every turn. EF already had a mailing out that guaranteed extremely low prices for 1996. In addition, experienced employees from Milestone created a new competitor, National Educational Travel Council (NETC), which had secured substantial backing from a group of U.K. investors and offered high-quality, small company service at low prices.

ACIS senior managers also realized that the overall dynamics of the business were changing because cheap seats were becoming a scarce commodity and were often sold out, especially during busy periods. And it had become increasingly difficult to find well-located, high-quality hotels within ACIS's budgets. ACIS's commitment to maintaining consistently high quality also drove trip fees up because services receiving lower customer satisfaction had to be replaced with more expensive ones, increasing the price differential between ACIS and its lower priced competitors. Customers willing to pay the larger price differential were harder to find. At the same time, the dollar was dropping in value in Europe, and ACIS was long on dollars for the entire 1996 season.

Senior management was very concerned about losing market share, especially to NETC. Something had to be done to keep prices down. The best way to hold the line was to get more business in sooner to increase efficiency and ensure the best access to the maximum number of cheap seats and lowest priced, good-quality land arrangements.

ACIS: BEGINNING TO LOSE THAT "SMALL FEELING"

ACIS announced its most aggressive pricing strategy ever, contingent on participants' meeting early enrollment deadlines. They did, and by October 15, 1996, enrollments were at record levels. The deluge of registrations stretched ACIS processing capabilities to their limits. The new enrollment deadlines added another degree of complexity to the already strained computer system. When processing early registrations, there was definite advantage when the Group Reservations Department could position groups so that they meshed well with the expectations of teachers and the availability of flights and overseas arrangements. Frequently, however, there was no readily apparent solution, and it became extremely complex to negotiate an outcome that was acceptable to the different functional departments because each had limitations and requirements that it felt compelled to meet. In effect, this meant that 25% of all groups booked could not readily flow through the system. This was further complicated by the "notepad" structure of the old database system, which dealt with minor modifications to itineraries by noting them as text in an "exceptions" field and did not integrate them into the overall database structure.

The 1996 strategy worked only insofar as it preserved and expanded ACIS's market share. It kept NETC from gaining market share solely at the expense of ACIS. However, ACIS had begun to feel like a big company. The organization ground to a halt for extended periods to resolve discrepancies between teacher expectation and operational requirements. But as high quality remained a driving concern, ACIS again received extremely high teacher satisfaction ratings.

Despite the surge in enrollment numbers, profitability for 1996 dropped to its lowest level in several years—lower prices yielded decreased margins and high enrollment led to being long on dollars while the value of the dollar plummeted. In addition, the strategy of having participants book early so that ACIS would have better access to lower priced airline seats was only partially successful. The cost savings were more than offset by cost overages on the last 5% of passengers booked, reducing profitability.

THE NEED TO GET SMALL AGAIN

January 1996 was a crucial month at ACIS. Michael Eizenberg returned after spending three months in the Advanced Management Program at Harvard Business School.

Exhibit 4   AIFS, Inc.—1997

Board of Directors	Subsidiary Officers	

Board of Directors	American Institute for Foreign Study	American Council for International Studies
Cyril J. H. Taylor Chairman of the Board	**American Institute for Foreign Study**	**American Council for International Studies**
Robert N. Brennan Vice-Chairman President and COO, American Institute For Foreign Study, Inc.	Cyril J. H. Taylor Chairman and CEO	Michael I. Eizenberg President and CEO
	Robert N. Brennan President and COO	Peter Jones Managing Director
Michael I. Eizenberg President and CEO, American Council for International Studies, Inc.	Peter Lasalandra Senior Vice-President	Tom Jones Executive Vice-President
Walter McCann President, Richmond College	William Gertz Senior Vice-President	Rebecca Tabaczynski Executive Vice-President
Peter Tcherepnine Executive Vice-President Loeb Partners Corporation	John Linakis Senior Vice-President	Linda Van Huss Executive Vice-President
Headquarters AIFS, Inc. 102 Greenwich Avenue Greenwich, Connecticut 06830	Robert Cristadoro Vice-President	Charlotte Dietz Senior Vice-President
	Barbara Cartledge Vice-President	Stephen Cummings Senior Vice-President
Subsidiaries American Institute for Foreign Study 102 Greenwich Avenue Greenwich, Connecticut 06830	Dennis Regan Vice-President	Michael Tenney Senior Vice-President
37 Queens Gate London, SW7 5HR	Paul Moonves Senior Vice-President and Treasurer	
American Council for International Studies 19 Bay State Road Boston, Massachusetts 02181		

Note:
A de-merger occurred within AIFS Inc. in 1992, which resulted in ELS being "split off" under the leadership of Roger O. Walther.

Passenger numbers were at a record high, but airlines were increasingly imposing capacity limitations. Hotel space was tight. The 12-year-old reservation and group management system was being stretched to its limits. Consolidating groups into a workable structure was more complex than ever before. Everyone in the organization displayed incredible dedication, but there was also more than enough stress and frustration.

ACIS had five major functional departments: Administration, Flights, Group Reservations, Overseas, and Sales. (See Exhibit 4 for list of officers.)

Meetings were held to consider the challenges the organization faced. They began with a strategic overview of the growth and development of ACIS and proceeded to a discussion of how a combination of once extremely favorable external conditions had become much more challenging. Six common themes emerged:

1. Profitability needed to improve.

2. The database system caused a lot of problems.

3. There were difficulties communicating between departments and offices.

4. Staff in one department did not know what staff in another department did.

5. Competition made it hard to find new clients and low-cost airline seats.

6. Sometimes ACIS felt like a big clumsy company.

"The problems we faced would have been unthinkable in the early days of ACIS," recalled Michael Eizenberg. "Then profitability had increased year after year. In those days it was great when the computer had worked right, but we were close enough to what we were doing that it didn't matter as much when it didn't. Sure we had written memos to document what we were doing, but the most important communication happened spontaneously when we simply spoke to each other every day. When there were seven, eight, nine, ten of us, we worked so closely together that we always knew what the other was doing. Selling was much easier when we had a smaller number of programs. We knew the exact details of each program so well that it was simple to convince potential clients about our superior product. Years before, we could move the whole organization in an instant to take advantage of inexpensive airline seats when they became available. Back then, we proved that a highly motivated team working together with the right combination of capabilities and experience could accomplish just about anything. Peter Jones, my partner from the earliest days of the organization, was skeptical at first, but he climbed on board when I told him it was time to reinvent the old ACIS. The only difference was this time we'd be coaches."

1997—ANOTHER DIFFICULT YEAR FOR EDUCATIONAL TRAVEL

Sales started slowly for 1997. The crash of TWA Flight 800 in July 1996 had cast a shadow over educational travel. In addition, the dollar was weak when ACIS entered into foreign exchange contracts to establish pricing rates for its 1997 programs. This forced ACIS to significantly increase prices to bring its margins back to workable levels. There were also difficulties implementing the new Oracle database system. All of these factors together contributed to a significant decline in 1997 sales compared to the previous two years.

Harley-Davidson, Inc. (1998): The 95th Anniversary

Thomas L. Wheelen, Kathryn E. Wheelen, Thomas L. Wheelen II, and Richard D. Wheelen

On March 5, 1998, the Committee of the 95th Celebration met to discuss the route kick-offs for Canada, Mexico, the United States, and Latin America. The starting cities for the United States motorcycle routes were: Riverside, CA (June 2); Dallas, TX (June 5); Orlando, FL (June 5); York, PA (June 5); and Spokane, WA (June 3). The Canadian, Mexican, and Latin American starting cities were: Dartmouth, Nova Scotia (June 3); Vancouver, British Columbia (June 3); Edmonton, Alberta (June 4); Ottawa, Ontario (June 5); Mexico City, Mexico (June 1); and Miami, FL (June 5). Exhibit 1 shows the motorcycle routes for the United States participants. The riders were to meet on June 9 in Milwaukee. Over 100,000 were expected to participate in the 95th celebration on June 13. An analyst said, "this is the ultimate in customer loyalty." At the end of the meeting, the committee for the analysis of new competition was to meet to discuss how their individual research was progressing.

HISTORY [1]

In 1903, William Harley (age 21), a draftsman, and his friend, Arthur R. Davidson, began experimenting with ideas to design and build their own motorcycles. They were joined by Arthur's brothers, William, a machinist, and Walter, a skilled mechanic. The Harley-Davidson Motor Company started in a 10×15 foot shed in the Davidson family's backyard in Milwaukee, Wisconsin.

In 1903, three motorcycles were built and sold. The production increased to eight in 1904. The company then moved to Juneau Avenue, which is the site of the company's present offices. In 1907, the company was incorporated.

In 1969, AMF Inc., a leisure and industrial product conglomerate, acquired Harley-Davidson. The management team expanded production from 15,000 in 1969 to 40,000 motorcycles in 1974. AMF favored short-term profits instead of investing in research and development and retooling. During this time, Japanese competitors continued to improve the quality of their motorcycles, while Harley-Davidson began to turn out noisy, oil-leaking, heavily vibrating, poorly finished, and hard-to-handle machines. AMF ignored the Japanese competition. In 1975, Honda Motor Company introduced its "Gold Wing," which became the standard for large touring motorcycles. Harley-Davidson had controlled this segment of the market for years. There was a $2,000 price differential between Harley's top-of-the-line motorcycles and Honda's comparable Gold Wing. This caused American buyers of motorcycles to start switching to Japanese motorcycles. The Japanese companies (Suzuki and Yamaha) from this time until the middle 1980s continued to enter the heavyweight custom market with Harley lookalikes.

During AMF's ownership of the company, sales of motorcycles were strong, but prof-

Exhibit 1   **Motorcycle Routes for the 95th Anniversary Celebration in Milwaukee: Harley-Davidson, Inc.**

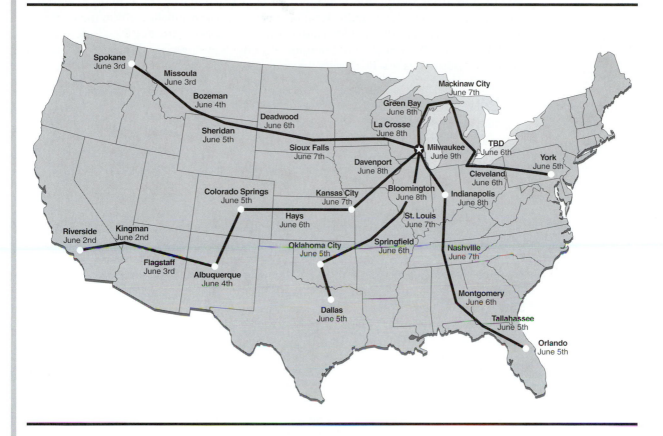

Source: Harley-Davidson, Inc., *1997 Annual Report*, pp. 75–76.

its were weak. The company had serious problems with poor quality manufacturing and strong Japanese competition. In 1981, Vaughn Beals, then head of the Harley Division, and 13 other managers conducted a leveraged buyout of the company for $65 million.

New management installed a Materials As Needed (MAN) system to reduce inventories and stabilize the production schedule. Also, this system forced production to work with marketing for more accurate forecasts. This led to precise production schedules for each month, allowing only a 10% variance. The company forced its suppliers to increase their quality in order to reduce customer complaints.

The management team invested in research and development. Management purchased a Computer-Aided Design (CAD) system that allowed the company to make changes in the entire product line and still maintain its traditional styling. These investments by management had a quick payoff in that the break-even point went from 53,000 motorcycles in 1982 to 35,000 in 1986.

In June 1993, over 100,000 members of the worldwide Harley-Davidson family came home (Milwaukee) to celebrate the company's 90th anniversary. Willie G. Davidson, Vice-President—Styling, grandson of the founder, said, "I was overwhelmed with emotion when our parade was rolling into downtown Milwaukee. I looked up to heaven and told the founding fathers, 'Thanks, guys.'"[2]

During 1993, the company acquired a 49% interest in Buell Motorcycle Company, a manufacturer of sport/performance motorcycles. This investment in Buell offered the company the possibility of gradually gaining entry into select niches within the performance motorcycle market. In 1998, Harley-Davidson owned most of the stock in Buell. Buell began distribution of a limited number of Buell motorcycles during 1994 to select Harley-Davidson dealers. Buell sales were:

Year	Sales	Units
1994	$ 6 million	576
1995	$14 million	1,407
1996	$23 million	2,762
1997	$40 million	4,415

Buell's mission "is to develop and employ innovative technology to enhance 'the ride' and give Buell owners a motorcycle experience that no other brand can provide." The European sport/performance market was four times larger than its U.S. counterpart. In 1997, there were 377 Buell dealers worldwide. In February 1998, Buell motorcycles placed first and third in the inaugural Pro Thunder series of racing; Buell had been racing motorcycles since 1996. The Buell motorcycles were priced at $5,245 and $8,399.

On November 14, 1995, the company acquired substantially all of the common stock and common stock equivalents of Eaglemark Financial Services, Inc., a company in which it held a 49% interest since 1993. Eaglemark provided credit to leisure product manufacturers, their dealers, and customers in the United States and Canada. The transaction was accounted for as a step acquisition under the purchase method. The purchase price for the shares and equivalents was approximately $45 million, which was paid from internally generated funds and short-term borrowings. The excess of the acquisition cost over the fair value of the net assets purchased resulted in approximately $43 million of goodwill, which was amortized on a straight-line basis over 20 years.

On January 22, 1996, the company announced its strategic decision to discontinue the operations of the Transportation Vehicles segment in order to concentrate its financial and human resources on its core motorcycle business. The Transportation Vehicles segment comprised the Recreational Vehicles division (Holliday Rambler trailers), the Commercial Vehicles division (small delivery vehicles), and B & B Molders, a manufacturer of custom or standard tooling and injection-molded plastic pieces. During 1996, the company completed the sale of the Transportation Vehicles segment for an aggregate sales price of approximately $105 million; approximately $100 million in cash and $5 million in notes and preferred stock.[3]

In the fall of 1997, GT Bicycles manufactured and distributed a 1,000 Harley Limited Edition at a list retail price of $1,700. The pedal-powered bike had a real Harley paint job, signature fenders, a fake gas tank, and chrome of a Harley Softail motorcycle. GT Bicycles manufactured the Velo Glide bikes and was licensed by Harley to produce the limited version. The four-speed bike weighed 40-plus pounds. Ken Alder, cycle shop owner, said, "It's a big clunker that no one would really want to ride." Nevertheless, the bicycles sold out in less than four months to buyers. The resale price for the Limited Edition jumped to $3,500, and one collector advertised his for $5,000. In contrast, a person could purchase an actual Harley XHL 883 Sportster motorcycle for $5,245.[4]

CORPORATE GOVERNANCE

Board of Directors

The Board of Directors consisted of ten members, of which three were internal members—Richard E. Teerlink, Chairman; Jeffrey E. Bleustein, President and Chief Executive Officer (CEO); and Vaughn L. Beals, Jr., Chairman Emeritus (see Exhibit 2).

The terms of the Board of Directors were a three-year stagger system: (a) terms expiring in 2000 were Vaughn L. Beals, Jr. (69), Donald A. James (53), and James A. Norling (55); (b) terms expiring in 1999 were Richard J. Hermon-Taylor (53), Sara L. Levinson (48), and Richard F. Teerlink (60); and (c) terms expiring in 1998 were Barry K. Allen (48), Richard I. Beattie (57), and Richard G. LeFauve (62). Sara L. Levinson, President of NFL Properties, Inc., joined the board in 1996.[5]

The company's vision was that: "Harley-Davidson, Inc., is an action-oriented, international company—a leader in its commitment to continuously improve the quality of profitable relationships with stakeholders (customers, dealers, employees, suppliers, shareholders, government, and society). Harley-Davidson believed the key to success was to balance stakeholders' interests through the empowerment of all employees to focus on value-added activities."[6]

Directors who were employees of the company did not receive any special compensation for their services as directors. Except for Beals, directors who were not employees of the company received in 1996 an annual fee of $25,000 plus $1,500 for each regular meeting of the Board, $750 for each special meeting of the Board, and $750 for each Board committee meeting, provided that directors did not receive any additional compensation for more than two Board committee meetings in connection with any Board meeting. The company reimbursed directors for any travel expenses incurred in connection with attending Board or Board committee meetings.

The company had a consulting contract with Beals pursuant to which Beals was paid $242,240 per year. The consulting term was to expire on June 30, 1998. The consulting contract also provided for supplemental retirement benefits of $159,840 per year after the consulting term expired until his death. In the event of Beals's death prior to the end of the consulting term, the consulting agreement provided, as a death benefit, the continuation of certain payments under the consulting agreement through July 1, 1999.

All directors and executive officers as a group (14 individuals) owned 2,126,498 shares (2.8%). Richard F. Teerlink owned 1,059,923 shares (1.4%), Jeffrey L. Bleustein owned 352,000 shares, and Vaughn L. Beals, Jr., owned 401,076 shares. Both the Bleustein and Beals ownership of shares was less than 1%. Ruane, Cunniff & Co., Inc. owned 4,284,345 shares (5.7%). This company was the largest owner of stock.[7]

TOP MANAGEMENT

Richard F. Teerlink has been a director of the company since 1982. He has been Chairman of the Board of the company since May 1996, Chief Executive Officer of the company since 1989, and President of the company since 1988. He was also a director of Johnson Controls, Inc. and Outboard Marine Corporation. His salary was $518,751, $486,303, and $440,901 and bonuses were $715,000, $500,000, and $700,000 for 1996, 1995, and 1994, respectively.

Jeffrey L. Bleustein has been a director of the company since December 1996. He

Exhibit 2   Board of Directors: Harley-Davidson, Inc.

Barry K. Allen, Executive Vice-President, Ameritech Corporation

Barry has been a member of the Board since 1992. His distinguished business career has taken him from the telecommunications industry to leading a medical equipment and systems business and back again. Barry's diverse experience has been particularly valuable to the Board in the areas of marketing and organizational transformation.

Vaughn L. Beals, Jr., Chairman Emeritus, Harley-Davidson, Inc.

This senior Director joined the company in 1975. He served as President, Chief Executive Officer, and Chairman during his years with the company. Vaughn led the group of 13 employees who took the company back to private ownership in 1981 and engineered the now famous "turnaround" following the LBO. Without Vaughn Beals, it is extremely unlikely that Harley-Davidson would exist today.

Richard I. Beattie, Chairman of the Executive Committee, Simpson Thacher & Bartlett

Dick has been a valued advisor to Harley-Davidson for nearly 20 years. His contributions evolved and grew with the company over time. In the early 1980s, he provided legal and strategic counsel to the 13 leaders who purchased Harley-Davidson from AMF, taking it back to private ownership. He also advised the team when it was time to take the company public again in 1986. Dick was elected to the Board in 1996.

Jeffrey L. Bleustein, President and Chief Executive Officer, Harley-Davidson, Inc.

Jeff began his association with Harley-Davidson in 1975 when he was asked to oversee the engineering group. During his tenure as Vice-President—Engineering, Harley-Davidson developed the Evolution engine and established the foundations of our current line of cruiser and touring motorcycles. Jeff has demonstrated creativity and vision across a wide range of senior leadership roles. In 1996 he was elected to the Board, and in June 1997 he was appointed to his current position.

Richard J. Hermon-Taylor, Group Vice-President, Abt Associates, Inc., President, BioScience International, Inc.

Richard joined the Board in 1986 and has been advising on marketing and manufacturing strategy for Harley-Davidson for nearly 20 years. His association with the company began when he was with the Boston Consulting Group in the mid 1970s and has been valued through the intervening years.

Donald A. James, Vice-Chairman, Chief Executive Officer, Fred Deeley Imports Ltd.

Don's wisdom and knowledge of the motorcycle industry have guided the Board since 1991. As a 31-year veteran of Harley-Davidson's exclusive distributor in Canada, he has a strong sense for our core products. Don has a particularly keen understanding of the retail issues involved with motorcycles and related products and the competitive advantage inherent in strong, long-lasting dealer relationships.

Richard G. Lefauve, President, GM University, Senior Vice-President, General Motors Corporation

Skip joined the Board in 1993. He has generously shared his vehicle industry experience with Harley-Davidson, including learning from his prior role as President of Saturn. Parallels in durable goods manufacturing, consumer trends, and life-long customer marketing strategy have provided considerable creative stimuli for Board discussion.

Sara L. Levinson, President, NFL Properties, Inc.

Sara joined the Board in 1996. She understands the value and power of strong brands, and her current senior leadership role in marketing and licensing, together with her previous experience at MTV, give her solid insights into the entertainment industries and younger customer segments.

Exhibit 2 **Board of Directors: Harley-Davidson, Inc.** *(continued)*

James A. Norling, President and General Manager, Messaging, Information and Media Sector, Motorola, Inc.

Jim has been a Board member since 1993. His career with Motorola has included extensive senior leadership assignments in Europe, the Middle East, and Africa, and he has generously shared his international experience and understanding of technological change to benefit Harley-Davidson.

Richard F. Teerlink, Chairman of the Board, Harley-Davidson, Inc.

Rich joined Harley-Davidson in 1981 and was elected to the Board in 1982. In 1988 he was appointed President of the company; in 1989, Chief Executive Officer. In 1996 he was named Chairman of the Board. Rich is credited with the financial restructuring of Harley-Davidson from private to public during the mid 1980s. His leadership was instrumental in creating a values-based culture at the company, which revolves around developing mutually beneficial relationships with all stakeholders.

Source: Direct quotation, Harley-Davidson, Inc., *1997 Annual Report*, p. 70.

has been Executive Vice-President of the company since 1991 and President and Chief Operating Officer of the Motor Company since 1993. He was also a director of Rexworks, Inc. His salary was $370,227, $318,183, and $283,257 and bonuses were $362,082, $269,183, and $265,297 for 1996, 1995, and 1994, respectively.[8]

Exhibit 3 shows the corporate officers for Harley-Davidson and its two business segments—Motorcycles and Related Products and Financial Services.

HARLEY OWNER GROUP (H.O.G.)

A special kind of camaraderie marked the Harley Owners Group rallies and other motorcycle events. At events and rallies around the globe, members of H.O.G. came together for fun, adventure, and a love of their machines and the open road. As the largest motorcycle club in the world, H.O.G. offered customers organized opportunities to ride. H.O.G. rallies and events visibly promoted the Harley-Davidson experience to potential new customers and strengthen the relationships among members, dealers, and Harley-Davidson employees.

Exhibit 4 provides a profile of the H.O.G. clubs. As of 1997, there were about 380,000 members of the H.O.G. clubs worldwide.

OTHER KEY RELATIONSHIPS[9]

Dealership Relationships

- **The Americas.** There were 595 Harley-Davidson dealerships in the United States and 41 MotorClothes apparel and collectible retail stores. In 1997, 35 dealerships were relocated; 71 dealerships were modernized or expanded; 6 new dealerships and 11 new apparel and collectibles retail stores were added to the U.S. network. In Canada, there were 76 Harley-Davidson dealerships serviced by the independent Canadian distributor, Fred Deeley Imports. In Latin America and Mexico, there were 16 dealerships and 7 MotorClothes apparel and collectible retail stores.

Exhibit 3   Corporate Officers: Harley-Davidson, Inc.

1. Corporate Officers, Harley-Davidson, Inc.

Richard F. Teerlink
Chairman

Jeffrey L. Bleustein
President and
Chief Executive Officer

James M. Brostowitz
Vice-President,
Controller and Treasurer

C. William Gray
Vice-President,
Human Resources

Gail A. Lione
Vice-President, General
Counsel and Secretary

James L. Ziemer
Vice-President and
Chief Financial Officer

2. Motor Company Leadership

Jeffrey L. Bleustein
President and
Chief Executive Officer

Garry S. Berryman
Vice-President, Purchasing

Joanne M. Bischmann
Vice-President, Marketing

James M. Brostowitz
Vice-President and
Controller

William B. Dannehl
General Manager,
York Operations

William G. Davidson
Vice-President,
Styling

Kathleen A. Demitros
Vice-President,
Communications

Karl M. Eberle
Vice-President, General Manager,
Kansas City Operations

Clyde Fessler
Vice-President, Business
Development

Jon R. Flickinger
General Sales Manager,
North America

John D. Goll
Vice-President,
Quality and Reliability

C. William Gray
Vice-President,
Human Resources

John A. Hevey
Vice-President, General
Manager, Asia/Pacific
and Latin American Regions

Timothy K. Hoelter
Vice-President, International Trade
and Regulatory Affairs

Ronald M. Hutchinson
Vice-President, Parts, Accessories,
and Customer Service

Michael D. Keefe
Director, Harley Owners Group

Brian P. Lies
Vice-President,
General Merchandise

Gail A. Lione
Vice-President and
General Counsel

James A. McCaslin
Vice-President,
Continuous Improvement

Steven R. Phillips
General Manager,
Tomahawk Operations

John K. Russell
Vice-President, Managing
Director, Europe

David J. Storm
Vice-President, Planning
and Information Services

W. Kenneth Sutton, Jr.
Vice-President, General Manager
Powertrain Operations

Earl K. Werner
Vice-President, Engineering

Jerry G. Wilke
Vice-President

3. Eaglemark Financial Services Leadership

Steven F. Deli
Chairman and
Chief Executive Officer

Christopher J. Anderson
Vice-President, Bankcards

Mark R. Budde
Vice-President, Insurance

Michael G. Case
Vice-President, Operations

Al C. Ely
Vice-President, Wholesale Operations

Glen J. Villano
Vice-President,
Sales and Marketing

Donna F. Zarcone
Vice-President and
Chief Financial Officer

4. Buell Motorcycle Company Leadership

Jeffrey L. Bleustein
Chief Executive Officer

Erik F. Buell
Chairman and
Chief Technical Officer

Jerry G. Wilke
President and
Chief Operating Officer

Source: Harley-Davidson, Inc., *1997 Annual Report*, p. 76.

Exhibit 4   1997 Profile of the H.O.G.: Harley-Davidson, Inc.

H.O.G. Sponsored Events: In 1997, U.S. national rallies were held in Portland, Maine; Oklahoma City, Oklahoma; and Portland, Oregon. There were two touring rallies and 46 state rallies in the U.S. H.O.G. also participated in events at Daytona and Sturgis Bike Weeks, factory open houses, and numerous motorcycle races. Internationally, H.O.G. held rallies in Norway, France, Japan, Canada, Australia, New Zealand, Brazil, and Mexico. There were also five state rallies in Australia, two provincial rallies in Canada, four touring rallies in Europe, and one touring rally in South Africa.

H.O.G. Membership: Any Harley-Davidson motorcycle owner could become a member of H.O.G. In fact, the first year of membership was included with the purchase of a new Harley-Davidson motorcycle. The number of H.O.G. members had grown rapidly since the motorcycle organization began in 1983 with 33,000 members in the United States and Canada. There were 380,000 H.O.G. members worldwide in more than 100 countries. Sponsorship of H.O.G. chapters by Harley-Davidson dealers grew from 49 chapters in 1985 to 988 chapters at the close of 1997. Worldwide membership renewal increased to 71% in 1997.

A Snapshot of H.O.G.

Worldwide members	380,000
Worldwide dealer-sponsored chapters	988
Countries with members	105
Worldwide rallies	70
Worldwide attendance at rallies	127,000
Miles logged by members attending U.S. rallies and events	41 million

Source: Harley-Davidson, Inc., *1997 Annual Report*, pp. 22–23.

- **Europe/Middle East/Africa.** There were in 1997 305 Harley-Davidson dealerships in the European Region, up from 253 dealerships in 1996. Growing the business in the European Region meant helping dealers there develop relationships with new customers. In 1998, Harley introduced two new motorcycle models for this market, specifically designed to appeal to the preferences of European cruiser motorcycle riders. Saudi Arabia and Oman were established as new markets in 1997.

- **Asia/Pacific.** Building relationships like the one between Tokyo dealership manager Masatoshi Ohtsubo and his customers was one of the keys to expanding Harley-Davidson's business in the Asia/Pacific region. There were 43 authorized dealers and 77 smaller "Live to Ride" shops serviced by the Japanese subsidiary. There were also 55 dealers in Australia and New Zealand that were serviced by three independent distributors, and direct deals in Malaysia, Singapore, Taiwan, and Thailand.

Supplier Relationships

More than 250 of Harley-Davidson's largest suppliers gathered at the annual supplier conference to share a vision of growing together. Through these meetings, the Supplier Advisory Council, and other efforts such as regular visits to suppliers by senior management, Harley-Davidson was successful in continuously reducing costs and increasing quality.

Family Relationships

Since the beginning of the Harley-Davidson Motor Company in 1903, Davidson family members have always been involved in the business. Many other families were also represented within the ranks of employees, like Alvin Burnett and his daughter Lynn Rhody, both of Tomahawk, Wisconsin.

Employee Relationships

According to management, all Harley-Davidson employees across the company worked to grow the business by delivering continuous improvements and first-rate quality. Harley-Davidson and their union partners developed long-lasting relationships to ensure continued success. For example, in 1996 the company and Lodge 175 of the International Association of Machinist and Aerospace Workers ratified a progressive long-term operating agreement for the York facility.

On-line

Harley-Davidson's website (www.harley-davidson.com) has been affectionately called the "anti-website" because it encourages visitors to get off-line and onto their Harleys. Nearly 1.5 million visitors in 1997 said the website provided easy access to information about the company and its national events.

BUSINESS SEGMENTS AND FOREIGN OPERATIONS[10]

The company operated in two business segments (excluding discontinued operations): Motorcycles and Related Products and Financial Services. The company's reportable segments were strategic business units that offered different products and services. They were managed separately, based on the fundamental differences in their operations.

Motorcycles and Related Products ("Motorcycles") (referred to as the Motor Company) consisted primarily of the company's wholly-owned subsidiary, H-D Michigan, Inc., and its wholly-owned subsidiary, Harley-Davidson Motor Company. The Motorcycles segment designed, manufactured, and sold primarily heavyweight (engine displacement of 651+ cc) touring and custom motorcycles and a broad range of related products that included motorcycle parts and accessories and riding apparel. The company, which was the only major American motorcycle manufacturer, had held the largest share of the United States heavyweight motorcycle market since 1986. The company held a smaller market share in the European market, which was a larger market than that of the United States, and in the Japanese market, which was a smaller market than that of the United States. In 1997, 132,300 motorcycles shipped and 147,000 were expected to ship in 1998.

Financial Services ("Eaglemark") consisted of the company's majority-owned subsidiary, Eaglemark Financial Services, Inc. Eaglemark provided motorcycle floor planning and parts and accessories financing to the company's participating North American dealers. Eaglemark also offered retail financing opportunities to the company's domestic motorcycle customers. In addition, Eaglemark had established the Harley-Davidson Chrome VISA Card for customers in the United States. Eaglemark also provided property and casualty insurance for motorcycles as well as extended service contracts. A smaller portion of its customers were in other leisure products businesses. Prior to 1995, Eaglemark carried on business only in the United States. In 1995, Eaglemark extended its operations to include Canada.

Exhibit 5 provides financial information on the company's two business segments.

Exhibit 5   **Information by Industry Segments: Harley-Davidson, Inc.**
(Dollar amounts in thousands)

A. Revenues and Income from Operations

Year Ending December 31	1997	1996	1995
Net sales			
Motorcycles and related products	$1,762,569	$1,531,227	$1,350,466
Financial services [1]	—	—	—
	$1,762,569	$1,531,227	$1,350,466
Income from operations			
Motorcycles and related products	$ 265,486	$ 228,093	$ 184,475
Financial services [1]	12,355	7,801	3,620
General corporate expenses	(7,838)	(7,448)	(7,299)
Operating income	$ 270,003	$ 228,446	$ 180,796

B. Assets, Depreciation, and Capital Expenditures

	Motorcycles and Related Products	Transportation Vehicles [2]	Financial Services [1]	Corporate	Consolidated
1997					
Identifiable assets	$856,779	—	$598,514	$143,608	$1,598,501
Depreciation and amortization	66,426	—	3,489	263	70,178
Net capital expenditures	183,194	—	2,834	143	186,171
1996					
Identifiable assets	$770,271	—	$387,666	$142,048	$1,299,985
Depreciation and amortization	51,657	—	3,367	258	55,282
Net capital expenditures	176,771	—	1,994	6	178,771
1995					
Identifiable assets	$575,118	$111,556	$269,461	$ 24,535	$ 980,670
Depreciation and amortization	41,754	—	320	255	42,329
Net capital expenditures	112,579	—	221	185	112,985

Notes:
1. The results of operations for the majority-owned financial services subsidiary are included as operating income from financial services in the statements of operations.
2. The results of operations for the Transportation Vehicles segment are clasified as discontinued operations in the statements of operations.

Source: Harley-Davidson, Inc., *1997 Annual Report,* p. 67.

MOTORCYCLES AND RELATED PRODUCTS SEGMENT

President and CEO's Comments [11]

Jeffrey L. Bleustein said in the *1997 Annual Report,* "At Harley-Davidson we are focused on growing our business, and I am very confident about our continued success. Consider these strengths:

- Our distinctive Harley-Davidson motorcycles are among the most admired in the world. These products, and those that come out of our new Product Development

Exhibit 6   Selected U.S. and World Financial and Sales Information: Harley-Davidson, Inc.

A. Motor Company Revenue, 1997
(Dollar amounts in millions)

$1,036.4	Domestic Motorcycles
389.2	Export Motorcycles
241.9	Worldwide Parts and Accessories
95.1	Worldwide General Merchandise
1,762.6	**Total**

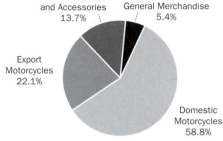

Worldwide Parts and Accessories 13.7%
Worldwide General Merchandise 5.4%
Export Motorcycles 22.1%
Domestic Motorcycles 58.8%

B. Worldwide Motorcycle Shipments
(Units in thousands)

	1986	1987	1988	1989	1990	1991	1992	1993	1994	1995	1996	1997
Total Worldwide	36.7	43.3	50.5	58.9	62.5	68.6	76.5	81.7	95.8	105.1	118.8	132.3
Export	6.8	8.6	11.6	15.3	19.3	21.6	23.3	24.5	29.3	32.1	34.7	36.1
Export Percentage	18.5%	19.9%	23.0%	26.0%	30.9%	31.5%	30.5%	30.0%	30.6%	30.5%	29.2%	27.3%

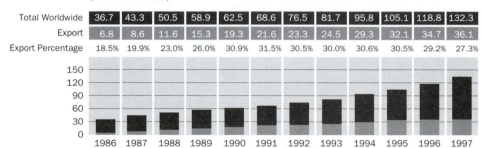

C. Worldwide Parts & Accessories and General Merchandise Revenue
(Dollar amounts in millions)

	1986	1987	1988	1989	1990	1991	1992	1993	1994	1995	1996	1997
Parts and Accessories	35.0	42.2	51.4	63.2	80.2	94.3	103.6	127.8	162.0	192.1	210.2	241.9
General Merchandise[1]	9.4	13.6	19.2	23.0	29.8	36.0	52.1	71.2	94.3	100.2	90.7	95.1

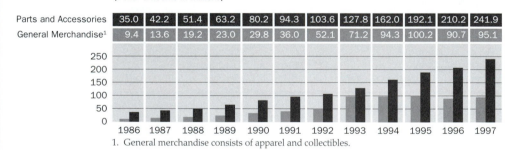

1. General merchandise consists of apparel and collectibles.

D. Operating Income
(Dollar amounts in millions)

1986	1987	1988	1989	1990	1991	1992	1993	1994	1995	1996	1997
21.3	30.6	50.4	63.2	90.2	89.6	102.3	136.2	163.5	184.5	228.1	265.5

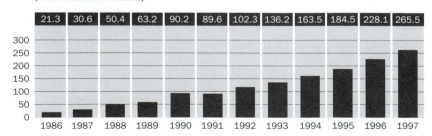

Exhibit 7   World Registrations: Harley-Davidson, Inc.

A. North American[1] 651+ cc Motorcycle Registrations
(Units in thousands)

100.7	112.0	132.8	150.4	163.1	178.5	205.4	Total Industry
48.3	56.0	63.4	69.5	77.0	85.1	99.3	Harley-Davidson
48.0%	50.0%	47.7%	46.2%	47.2%	47.6%	48.3%	Harley-Davidson Market Share

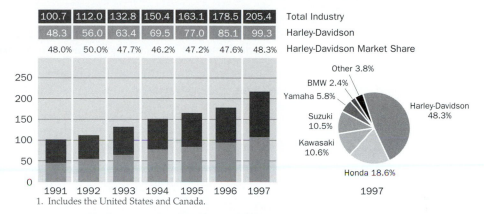

1. Includes the United States and Canada.

B. European[2] 651+ cc Motorcycle Registrations
(Units in thousands)

194.7	212.1	218.6	201.9	207.2	224.7	250.3	Total Industry
11.0	12.1	13.2	14.4	15.4	15.3	15.3	Harley-Davidson
5.6%	5.7%	6.1%	7.1%	7.4%	6.8%	6.1%	Harley-Davidson Market Share

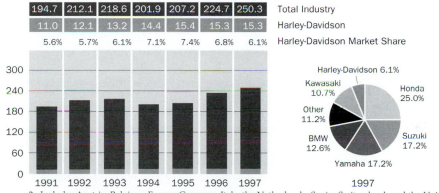

2. Includes Austria, Belgium, France, Germany, Italy, the Netherlands, Spain, Switzerland, and the United Kingdom.

C. Asia/Pacific[3] 651+ cc Motorcycle Registrations
(Units in thousands)

27.0	37.5	35.7	39.1	39.4	37.4	58.9	Total Industry
5.3	6.0	6.7	7.6	7.9	8.2	9.7	Harley-Davidson
19.5%	16.1%	18.7%	19.4%	20.1%	21.9%	16.5%	Harley-Davidson Market Share

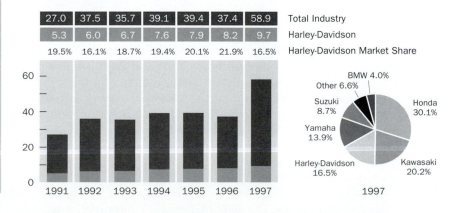

Center in the future, will continue to define leadership in our chosen market segments and enable us to reach out to new customers and new markets.

- Last year marked the sixth consecutive year of continued growth for the worldwide heavyweight motorcycle market. From the U.S. to Asia/Pacific, Europe to South America, the opportunities for Harley-Davidson have never been better. (See Exhibits 6 and 7.)

- We have developed long-lasting relationships, built on trust and mutual respect, with our customers, dealers, suppliers, and the employees of Harley-Davidson.

- We have a strong and widely admired brand that begins with the passion that our customers have for their Harley-Davidson motorcycles. This translates into unparalleled brand loyalty and a remarkably high repurchase intent.

- We have a proven management team with an excellent track record and a committed workforce dedicated to growing the business.

- We have demonstrated for twelve consecutive years that we can deliver sustained revenue growth and earnings growth at the levels of the finest high-performing companies.

No one can accurately predict the future. What I can predict with the utmost confidence are the things that won't change at Harley-Davidson—namely, our commitment to providing more great motorcycles; to enhancing the unparalleled Harley lifestyle experience; and to continuing to provide excellent financial performance.

Undoubtedly there will be some bumps in the road ahead as there have been in the road just traveled, but we will always seek to deliver a smooth ride."

Overview [12]

The primary business of the Motorcycles segment was to design, produce, and sell premium heavyweight motorcycles. The Motor Company's motorcycle products emphasized traditional styling, design simplicity, durability, ease of service, and evolutionary change. Studies by the company indicated that the typical U.S. Harley-Davidson motorcycle owner was a male in his mid-forties, with a household income of approximately $68,000, who purchased a motorcycle for recreational purposes rather than to provide transportation, and who was an experienced motorcycle rider. Over two-thirds of the Motor Company's sales were to buyers with at least one year of higher education beyond high school, and 34% of the buyers had college degrees. Approximately 9% of the Motor Company's U.S. retail sales were to female buyers. (See Exhibit 8.)

The heavyweight class of motorcycles comprised four types: *standard,* which emphasized simplicity and cost; *performance,* which emphasized handling and acceleration; *touring,* which emphasized comfort and amenities for long-distance travel; and *custom,* which emphasized styling and individual owner customization. The Motor Company manufactured and sold 20 models of touring and custom heavyweight motorcycles, with suggested domestic retail prices ranging from approximately $5,200 to $19,300. (See Exhibit 9.) The touring segment of the heavyweight market was pioneered by the company and included motorcycles equipped for long-distance touring with fairings, windshields, saddlebags, and Tour Paks®. The custom segment of the market included motorcycles featuring the distinctive styling associated with classic Harley-Davidson motorcycles. These motorcycles were highly customized through the use of trim and accessories. The Motor Company's motorcycles were based on variations of four basic chassis designs and were powered by one of three air-cooled, twin cylinder

Exhibit 8   **Purchaser Demographic Profile: Harley-Davidson, Inc.**

Demographic	1985	1987	1988	1989	1990	1991	1992	1993	1994	1995
Gender (%)										
Male	98%	98%	96%	96%	96%	95%	95%	93%	93%	91%
Female	2	2	4	4	4	5	5	7	7	9
Median age										
Years	34.1	34.7	34.6	34.6	36.7	38.5	38.4	41.6	42.1	42.5
Marital status (%)										
Married	54%	55%	59%	56%	56%	62%	59%	65%	68%	67%
Single	29	25	25	27	27	23	23	19	18	17
Widowed/Divorced	17	16	16	17	17	15	18	16	14	16
No answer	—	4	—	—	—	—	—	—	—	—
Children living at home (%)										
None	41%	55%	54%	57%	58%	57%	57%	53%	54%	53%
1–2	34	37	37	36	35	36	36	38	38	39
3 +	6	7	8	7	7	7	7	9	8	9
No Answer	19	1	1	—	—	—	—	—	—	—
Median income (Dollars in thousands)										
Personal	$28.0	$30.7	$31.3	$36.4	$38.5	$40.3	$42.7	—	—	—
Household	35.3	38.4	40.0	44.7	47.3	50.5	53.7	61.9	65.2	66.4
Education level (%)										
Non-high school grad	8%	9%	8%	8%	7%	6%	6%	5%	5%	4%
High school grad	41	32	34	33	34	27	28	26	25	24
Some college/trade school	31	41	37	38	38	40	38	39	39	38
College grad/post grad	19	18	20	21	22	26	29	31	31	34

Source: Harley-Davidson, Inc., *Background and History* (company document), p. 3.

engines of "V" configuration which had displacements of 883cc, 1200cc, and 1340cc. The Motor Company manufactured its own engines and frames.

Although there were some accessory differences between the Motor Company's top-of-the-line touring motorcycles and those of its competitors, suggested retail prices were generally comparable. The prices for the high end of the Motor Company's custom product line ranged from being competitive to 50% more than its competitors' custom motorcycles. The custom portion of the product line represented the Motor Company's highest unit volumes and continued to command a premium price because of its features, styling, and high resale value. The Motor Company's smallest displacement custom motorcycle (the 883cc Sportster®) was directly price competitive with comparable motorcycles available in the market. The Motor Company's surveys of retail purchasers indicated that, historically, over three-quarters of the purchasers of its Sportster model came from competitive-brand motorcycles, were people completely new to the sport of motorcycling, or were people who had not participated in the sport for at least five years. Since 1988, the Motor Company's research had consistently shown a repurchase intent in excess of 92% on the part of purchasers of Harley-Davidson motorcycles, and the Motor Company expected to see sales of its 883cc Sportster model partially translated into sales of its higher priced products in the normal two- to three-year ownership cycle. The Motor Company's worldwide motorcycle sales generated 78.5%, 78.3%, and 76.9% of revenues in the Motorcycles segment during 1997, 1996, and 1995, respectively.

Exhibit 9   1998 Motorcycles Product Line: Harley-Davidson, Inc.

Motorcycle	Suggested Selling Price ($)	
	States	California
XLH Sportster 1200	$ 7,610	$ 7,730
XL 1200S Sportster 1200 Sport	8,395	8,515
XL 1200C Sportster 1200 Custom	8,670	8,790
XLH Sportster 883	5,245	5,365
XLH Sportster 883 Hugger	5,945	6,065
FXDL Dyna Low Rider	13,750	14,035
FXD Dyna Super Glide	10,865	11,150
FXDS-CONV Dyna Convertible	14,100	14,385
FXDWG Dyna Wide Glide	14,775	15,060
FLSTC Heritage Softail Classic	15,275	15,565
FXSTC Softail Custom	14,125	14,145
FXSTS Heritage Springer	17,145	17,435
FLSTF Fat Boy	14,595	14,885
FXSTS Springer Softail	14,765	15,055
FLTR/FLTRI Road Glide	14,850	15,095
FLHT Electra Glide Standard	12,275	12,990
FLHTC/FLHTCI Electra Glide Classic	14,975	15,220
FLHTCUI Ultra Classic Electra Glide	18,065	18,165
FLHR Road King	14,725	14,990
FLHRCI Road King Classic	15,960	16,080
FLHRCI Road King with Sidecar	N/A	N/A

Source: Harley-Davidson, Inc., *Harley-Davidson 1998 Motorcycles.*

The major product categories for the Parts and Accessories (P&A) business were replacement parts (Genuine Motor Parts™) and mechanical accessories (Genuine Motor Accessories™). Worldwide net P&A sales comprised 13.7%, 13.7%, and 14.2% of net sales in the Motorcycles segment in 1997, 1996, and 1995, respectively. Worldwide P&A net sales had grown 49.3% over the last three years (since 1994).

Worldwide net sales of the General Merchandise business, which included Motor-Clothes® apparel and collectibles, comprised 5.4%, 5.9%, and 7.4% of net sales in the Motorcycles segment in 1997, 1996, and 1995 respectively.

The Motor Company also provided a variety of services to its dealers and retail customers, including service training schools, customized software packages for dealers, delivery of its motorcycles, membership in an owners club, and a Fly and Ride™ program through which a member could rent a motorcycle through a dealer at a vacation destination.

Exhibit 10 shows that motorcycle sales in units (excluding Buell) increased by 11.4% in 1997 and net sales for this business segment were up 15.1% in 1997.

Licensing[13]

In recent years, the company has endeavored to create an awareness of the Harley-Davidson brand among the non-riding public and provide a wide range of product for enthusiasts by licensing the name "Harley-Davidson" and numerous related trademarks owned by the company. The company had licensed the production and sale of a broad

Exhibit 10   **Motorcycle Unit Shipments and Net Sales: Harley-Davidson, Inc.**

	1997	1996	Increase	% Change
Motorcycle Units (excluding Buell)	132,285	118,771	13,514	11.4%
Net sales (in millions)				
Motorcycles (excluding Buell)	$1,382.8	$1,199.2	$183.6	15.3%
Motorcycle parts and accessories	241.9	211.2	30.7	14.5
General merchandise	95.1	90.7	4.4	4.8
Other	42.8	30.1	12.7	42.2
Total motorcycles and related products	$1,762.6	$1,531.2	$231.4	15.1%

Source: Harley-Davidson, Inc., *Form 10-K* (December 31, 1997), p. 20.

range of consumer items, including tee-shirts, jewelry, small leather goods, toys, and numerous other products. In 1993, the licensed Harley-Davidson Café opened in Manhattan, New York. In 1995, the company entered into an agreement to license three additional restaurants with the New York Café's owners. Under this agreement, a new Café in Las Vegas, Nevada, was opened in September 1997. Although the majority of licensing activity occured in the United States, the company continued to expand into international markets.

The company's licensing activity provided it with a valuable source of advertising and goodwill. Licensing also had proven to be an effective means for enhancing the company's image with consumers and provided an important tool for policing the unauthorized use of the company's trademarks, thereby protecting the Harley-Davidson brand and its use. Royalty revenues from licensing, included in motorcycle revenue, were approximately $24 million, $19 million, and $24 million during 1997, 1996, and 1995, respectively. Although royalty revenues from licensing activities were relatively small, the profitability of this business was relatively high.

Marketing and Distribution[14]

The company's basic channel of U.S. distribution for its motorcycles and related products consisted of approximately 600 independently owned, full-service dealerships to whom the company sold direct. With respect to sales of new motorcycles, approximately 77% of the U.S. dealerships sold the company's motorcycles exclusively. All dealerships carried the company's genuine replacement parts and aftermarket accessories and performed servicing of the company's motorcycle products.

The company's marketing efforts were divided among dealer promotions, customer events, magazine and direct mail advertising, public relations, and cooperative programs with Harley-Davidson dealers. The company also sponsored racing activities and special promotional events and participated in all major motorcycle consumer shows and rallies. In an effort to encourage Harley-Davidson owners to become more actively involved in the sport of motorcycling, the Motor Company formed a riders club in 1983. The Harley Owners Group®, or HOG®, was the industry's largest company-sponsored motorcycle enthusiast organization. The Motor Company's expenditures on domestic marketing, selling, and advertising were approximately $85.2 million, $75.4 million, and $71.5 million during 1997, 1996, and 1995, respectively.

Retail Customer and Dealer Financing[15]

The company believed Eaglemark and other financial services companies provided adequate retail and wholesale financing to the Motor Company's domestic and Canadian dealers and customers. In addition, to encourage its dealers to carry sufficient parts and accessories inventories and to counteract the seasonality of the parts and accessories business, the Motor Company, from time to time, offered its domestic dealers quarterly special discounts and/or 120-day delayed payment terms through Eaglemark. Eaglemark also began to provide wholesale financing to dealers supported by the company's European subsidiaries through a joint venture agreement with Transamerica Distribution Finance Corporation. Previously the company offered extended winter terms to certain European customers.

International Sales[16]

International sales were approximately $458 million, $421 million, and $401 million, accounting for approximately 26%, 27%, and 30% of net sales of the Motorcycles segment during 1997, 1996, and 1995, respectively. The international heavyweight (651+ cc) market was growing and was significantly larger than the U.S. heavyweight market. The Motor Company ended 1997 with an approximate 6.1% share of the European heavyweight (651+ cc) market and an approximate 16.5% share of the Asia/Pacific (Japan and Australia) heavyweight (651+ cc) market (see Exhibit 7).

In total, the Motor Company was represented internationally by 577 independent dealers in 55 countries. Japan, Germany, and Canada, in that order, represented the company's largest export markets and accounted for approximately 51% of export sales.

In the European Region (Europe/Middle East/Africa), there were currently 305 independent dealers serving 30 country markets. This network of dealers was served by nine independent distributors and four wholly-owned subsidiaries in France, Germany, the Netherlands, and the United Kingdom. The company had continued to build infrastructure in Europe, following the establishment of its United Kingdom–based European Headquarters in 1995. New information systems, linking all the European subsidiary markets, were successfully installed and began operating in early 1997. The European management team was continuing to build and develop distributor, dealer, and customer relationships. The company's focus was to expand and improve the distribution network, tailor product development to market needs, and attract new customers through coordinated Europe-wide and local marketing programs.

In the Asia/Pacific Region, there were currently 179 independent dealers serving eight country markets. During 1996, the company began to implement a strategic plan for the Asia/Pacific Region, which outlined growth objectives and strategies for achieving them. Although the economic crisis in Southeast Asia had currently curtailed the company's plans to open new markets in Southeast Asia, according to management, short-term growth should continue to come from existing markets in Japan and Australia. Long-term growth opportunities were expected to come from existing markets in Japan, Australia, and Southeast Asia and from new markets in the region.

The Americas market included Canada and a separate Latin American distribution network. The Latin American market consisted of 16 country markets managed from Milwaukee. The Latin American market had a diverse dealer network including 17 full-line dealers, as well as seven resort and mall stores focusing on selling General Merchandise. During 1997, the company's distribution network was expanded in Mexico and Argentina. In the future, the focus will be on improving distribution and volumes within the two largest Latin American markets, Mexico and Brazil. Management intended to expand advertising and promotion, and to investigate regional sourcing of General Merchandise to extend the customer reach of branded products in the region. In Canada, there were currently 76 full-line dealerships served by a single independent distributor.

Competition [17]

The U.S. and international heavyweight (651+ cc) motorcycle markets were highly competitive. The company's major competitors generally had financial and marketing resources that were substantially greater than those of the company. They also had larger overall sales volumes and were more diversified than the company. Harley management believed the heavyweight motorcycle market was the most profitable segment of the U.S. motorcycle market. During 1997, the heavyweight segment represented approximately 54% of the total U.S. motorcycle market (on- and off-highway motorcycles and scooters) in terms of new units registered. (See Exhibit 11.)

Domestically, the Motor Company competed in the touring and custom segments of the heavyweight motorcycle market, which together accounted for 80%, 80%, and 78% of total heavyweight retail unit sales in the United States during 1997, 1996, and 1995, respectively. The custom and touring motorcycles were generally the most expensive and most profitable vehicles in the market.

For the last ten years, the Motor Company had led the industry in domestic (United States) sales of heavyweight motorcycles. The Motor Company's share of the heavyweight market was 49.1% in 1997, up from 48.2% in 1996. This was significantly greater than the company's largest competitor (Honda) domestically, which had an 18.5% market share at the end of 1997. (See Exhibit 12.)

On a worldwide basis, the Motor Company measured its market share using the heavyweight classification. Although definitive market share information did not exist for many of the smaller foreign markets, the Motor Company estimated its worldwide competitive position using data reasonably available to it. (See Exhibit 11.)

Competition in the heavyweight motorcycle market was based on several factors, including price, quality, reliability, styling, product features, customer preference, and warranties. The Motor Company emphasized quality, reliability, and styling in its products and offered warranties for its motorcycles. The Motor Company regarded its support of a motorcycling lifestyle in the form of events, rides, rallies, and HOG as a competitive advantage. In general, resale prices for used Harley-Davidson motorcycles, as a percentage of prices when new, were significantly higher than resale prices for used motorcycles of the company's competitors.

Domestic heavyweight registrations increased 15% and 10% during 1997 and 1996, respectively. The company believed its ability to maintain its market share would depend primarily on its ability to increase its annual production capacity as discussed in the Motorcycle Manufacturing section of this case.

New Competitors

New competitors have entered the marketplace because Harley-Davidson has not been able to fully meet the demand for its heavyweight motorcycles. This backlog of customers was the primary reason that Harley-Davidson had increased units shipped from 81,696 in 1993 to 132,285 in 1997, which represented an increase of 50,589 motorcycles (61.9%) over the past five years. Over the past seven years, the demand for Harley-Davidson motorcycles had exceeded production. A few years ago, a potential customer would have to wait one or more years to purchase his or her new motorcycle. Some

Exhibit 11   **Worldwide Heavyweight Motorcycle Registration Data**
(Engine displacement of 651+ cc; units in thousands)

	1997	1996	1995
North America[1]			
Total registrations	205.4	178.5	163.1
Harley-Davidson registrations	99.3	85.1	77.0
Harley-Davidson market share percentage	48.3%	47.6%	47.2%
Europe[2]			
Total registrations	250.3	224.7	207.2
Harley-Davidson registrations	15.3	15.3	15.4
Harley-Davidson market share percentage	6.1%	6.9%	7.4%
Japan/Australia[3]			
Total registrations	58.9	37.4	39.4
Harley-Davidson registrations	9.7	8.2	7.9
Harley-Davidson market share percentage	16.5	21.9%	20.1%
Total			
Total registrations	514.6	440.6	409.7
Harley-Davidson registrations	124.3	108.6	100.3
Harley-Davidson market share percentage	24.2%	24.6%	24.5%

Notes:
1. Includes the United States and Canada.
2. Includes Austria, Belgium, France, Germany, Italy, the Netherlands, Spain, Switzerland, and United Kingdom. (Data provided by Giral S.A.)
3. Data provided by JAMA and ABS.

Source: Harley-Davidson, Inc., *Form 10-K* (December 31, 1997), p. 9.

potential customers, who did not want to wait for their turn on the waiting list for a new motorcycle, would offer thousands of dollars to acquire another person's motorcycle allotment. How lists were set up and maintained was solely the dealer's responsibility.

This backlog caused new entrants to start manufacturing cruiser motorcycles. These were:

1. *Big Dog Motorcycles* was expected to produce 2,000 motorcycles in 1998 and double that in 1999. These motorcycles should cost upward of $22,000 versus about $16,000 for Harley-Davidson. In 1997, the company had 55 employees who turned out 300 motorcycles. Sheldon Coleman, President, said, "When you buy a Harley, the factory bike is an anemic motorcycle." He further stated, "You have to put several thousands into it to get it up to real-world standards."[18]

2. *Polaris* was one of the largest manufacturers of all-terrain vehicles, snowmobiles, and personal watercraft. In 1997, the company introduced the Polaris Victory with a price tag of about $12,500. Polaris selected about 200 of its 2,000 dealers to sell the Victory. Matt Parks, General Manager of Polaris' Victory Motorcycle Division, said, "We're going to be a major player in the business."[19]

3. *Excelsior Supply* bought Henderson Co. in 1917, one of the "big three" U.S. manufacturers, along with Harley and Indian. Excelsior went bankrupt in 1931 but reappeared recently as Excelsior-Henderson. In 1993, Excelsior-Henderson decided to re-introduce the Excelsior motorcycles. The first motorcycle was scheduled to be out in October 1998 and expected to retail between $16,000 and $20,000. The com-

Exhibit 12   Shares of U.S. Heavyweight Motorcycle Market
(Above 750cc engine displacement)

Year Ending December 31	1997	1996	1995	1994	1993
New U.S. registrations (thousands of units)					
Total new registrations	190.2	165.7	151.2	140.8	123.8
Harley-Davidson new registrations	93.5	79.9	72.1	65.2	59.3
Percentage market share (%)					
Harley-Davidson	49.1%	48.2%	47.7%	46.3%	47.9%
Buell	1.0	1.0	0.5	0.1	0.0
Honda	18.5	18.8	20.2	22.5	20.1
Suzuki	10.1	8.7	9.6	10.6	12.1
Kawasaki	10.4	12.2	10.6	9.8	9.7
Yamaha	5.4	5.9	5.8	5.6	5.8
Other	5.5	5.2	5.6	5.1	4.4
Totals	100%	100%	100%	100%	100%

Note: Information in this report regarding motorcycle registrations and market shares has been derived from data published by R.L. Polk & Co.

Source: Harley-Davidson, Inc., *1997 Form 10-K*, p. 8.

pany was moving into new production facilities with a yearly 20,000 motorcycle capacity.

Industry analysts expected the cruiser sales to grow 12% to 15% a year for several years.

Ducati SpA, an Italian maker of deluxe motorcycles, was "mounting an ambitious push to market its bikes as a passport to a fast-paced lifestyle."[20] CEO Federino Minoli said, "That is not a mechanical industry thing. That is about exclusivity, luxury, having fun." He went on to say, "We want to create a Ducati way of life."[21] Neiman Marcus featured a limited-series Ducati 748 in its 1997 "wish list" catalog for men, along with other luxury merchandise such as a Porsche bicycle, Emporio Armani watches, and Gucci shoes. New York's Solomon R. Guggenheim Museum featured several Ducatis in its 1997 exhibit, "The Art of Motorcycling." Ducati's two top sellers were the $8,000 Monster and the $17,000 top-of-the-line 916. An analyst said, "The Ducati owners tended to be speed and racing fanatics, while Harley owners seek a custom look and comfortable ride." He further stated, "Still, as Ducati's strategy evolves, it's looking more and more like its Milwaukee-based cousin."[22]

A Tampa dealer for Polaris, Moto Guzzi, and other competitive foreign motorcycle said "about 35% of his customers are female." He further stated that the "average male buyer makes about eight visits to his store before purchasing his motorcycle, while the female buyer made only one or two visits." A car dealer of pre-owned Jaguars found these comments to be the opposite of his business. Men will call about the car advertisement in the paper and ask several questions about price, color, and model. About 90% of the men buyers come to his dealership and purchase the car after one or two visits. The majority of the men buyers come to the dealership and purchase on the first visit, and many never drive the car. Women usually make two to three visits before purchasing the car.[23]

Motorcycle Manufacturing [24]

To achieve cost and quality parity with its competitors, the company had incorporated manufacturing techniques to continuously improve its operations. These techniques, which included employee involvement, just-in-time inventory principles, and statistical process control, had significantly improved quality, productivity, and asset utilization.

The Motor Company's use of just-in-time inventory principles allowed it to minimize its inventories of raw materials and work-in-process as well as scrap and rework costs. This system also allowed quicker reaction to engineering design changes, quality improvements, and market demands. The Motor Company had trained the majority of its manufacturing employees in problem solving and statistical methods.

For the past two years, the Motor Company had been implementing a comprehensive motorcycle manufacturing strategy designed to, among other things, significantly increase its motorcycle production capacity. "Plan 2003" called for the enhancement of the Motor Company's ability to increase capacity, increase flexibility to adjust to changes in the marketplace, improve product quality, and reduce costs. The strategy called for the achievement of the increased capacity at the existing facilities combined with some new additions. The transition into a new engine plant in Milwaukee and the construction of a new assembly plant in Kansas City, Missouri, were both completed in 1997. The Motor Company believed the worldwide heavyweight (651+ cc) market would continue to grow and planned to continue to increase its motorcycle production capacity to be able to sustain its annual double-digit unit growth. For 1998, the Motor Company's production target was 147,000 units.

In 1997, the Motor Company and Dr. Ing. h.c. Porsche AG of Stuttgart, Germany, formed a joint venture to source and assemble powertrain components for use in potential new motorcycle products. The joint venture planned to operate out of one of the Motor Company's U.S. manufacturing facilities.

Raw Material and Purchase Components [25]

The Motor Company was proceeding aggressively to establish long-term mutually beneficial relationships with its suppliers. Through these relationships the Motor Company was gaining access to technical and commercial resources for application directly to product design, development, and manufacturing initiatives. This strategy was resulting in improved product technical integrity, application of new features and innovations, reduced lead times for product development, and smoother/faster manufacturing ramp-up of new vehicle introductions.

The Motor Company purchased all of its raw material, principally steel and aluminum castings, forgings, sheets and bars, and certain motorcycle components, including carburetors, batteries, tires, seats, electrical components, and instruments. The Motor Company anticipated no significant difficulties in obtaining raw materials or components for which it relied on a limited source of supply.

Research and Development [26]

The Motor Company believed research and development were significant factors in the Motor Company's ability to lead the market definition of touring and custom motorcycling. As a result, the Motor Company completed construction of a new 213,000-square-foot Product Development Center (PDC) in 1996. The PDC brought together employees from styling, purchasing, and manufacturing with regulatory professionals and supplier representatives to create a concurrent product and process development methodology. The Motor Company incurred research and development expenses of approximately $53.3 million, $37.7 million, and $27.2 million during 1997, 1996, and 1995, respectively.

The $40 million Product Development Center was headed by Willie G. Davidson, Vice-President—Styling. Davidson was the grandson of one of the founders.

Patents and Trademarks[27]

The company owned certain patents that related to its motorcycles and related products and processes for their production. Management had increased its efforts to patent its technology and to enforce those patents. The company saw such actions as important as it moved forward with new technologies. The company's goal was to make all of its intellectual property assets work together to achieve the greatest effect.

Trademarks were important to the company's motorcycle business and licensing activities. The company had a vigorous global program of trademark registration and enforcement to strengthen the value of the trademarks associated with its products, prevent the unauthorized use of those trademarks, and enhance its image and customer goodwill. Management believed the "Harley-Davidson®" trademark was highly recognizable by the general public and a very valuable asset. The Bar and Shield Design trademark was also highly recognizable by the general public. Additionally, the company used numerous trademarks, trade names, and logos, which were registered both in the United States and abroad. The "Harley-Davidson" trademark had been used since 1903 and the Bar and Shield trademark since 1907.

Seasonality

The company, in general, had not experienced significant seasonal fluctuations in motorcycle production. This had primarily been the result of a strong demand for the Motor Company's motorcycles and related products as well as the availability of floor plan financing arrangements for its North American independent dealers. Dealers had to pay for the motorcycles when they were delivered. Thus they needed "floor plan" financing to pay for inventory until they sold it. Floor plan financing allowed dealers to build their inventory levels in anticipation of the spring and summer selling seasons. The lack of floorplanning had caused foreign accounts receivable to be an issue of concern. Beginning in 1998, floorplanning for dealers supported by the company's European subsidiaries was made available.[28]

December 31	1997	1996
	(Dollar amounts in thousands)	
Accounts receivable		
Domestic	$ 15,189	$ 49,888
Foreign	87,608	91,427
	$102,797	$141,315

Domestic motorcycle sales were generally floorplanned by the purchasing dealers. Foreign motorcycle sales were sold on open account, letter of credit, draft, and payment in advance. Effective September 1, 1997, Eaglemark became responsible for all credit and collection activities for the Motorcycles segment's domestic receivables. As such, approximately $69 million of accounts receivable were classified as finance receivables as of

December 31, 1997. The presentation of finance receivables had been changed to classify receivables representing wholesale motorcycle and parts and accessories receivables and retail finance receivables with maturities of less than one year as current.

The allowance for doubtful accounts deducted from accounts receivable was $1.5 million and $1.9 million at December 31, 1997, and 1996, respectively.[29]

Regulations [30]

Both U.S. federal and state authorities had various environmental control requirements relating to air, water, and noise pollution that affected the business and operations of the company. The company endeavored to ensure that its facilities and products complied with all applicable environmental regulations and standards.

European Union Certification procedures ensured that the company's motorcycles complied with the lower European Union noise standards (80 dba). At the beginning of the next decade, there may be a further reduction of European Union noise standards. Accordingly, the company expected that it should continue to incur some level of research and development costs related to this matter over the next several years.

The company's motorcycles were subject to certification by the U.S. Environmental Protection Agency (EPA) for compliance with applicable emissions and noise standards and by the State of California Air Resources Board (ARB) with respect to the ARB's more stringent emissions standards. The company's motorcycles were subjected to the additional ARB tailpipe and evaporative emissions standards that required the company to build unique vehicles for sale exclusively in California. The company's motorcycle products had been certified to comply fully with all such applicable standards. The company anticipated there will be further reductions in the ARB's, and potentially in the EPA's, motorcycle emissions standards in the coming years. Accordingly, the company expected to incur some level of research and development costs related to this matter over the next several years.

The company, as a manufacturer of U.S. motorcycle products, was subject to the National Traffic and Motor Vehicle Safety Act (Safety Act), which was administered by the National Highway Traffic Safety Administration (NHTSA). The company had acknowledged to NHTSA that its motorcycle products complied fully with all applicable federal motor vehicle safety standards and related regulations.

In accordance with NHTSA policies, the Motor Company had, from time to time, initiated certain voluntary recalls. During the last three years, the Motor Company had initiated five voluntary recalls at a total cost of approximately $3.7 million. The company fully reserved for all estimated costs associated with recalls in the period that they are announced.

Federal, state, and local authorities had adopted various control standards relating to air, water, and noise pollution that affected the business and operations of the Motorcycles segment. Management did not anticipate that any of these standards would have a materially adverse impact on its capital expenditures, earnings, or competitive position.

Employees [31]

As of December 31, 1997, the Motorcycles segment had approximately 5,700 employees. Production workers at the motorcycle manufacturing facilities in Wauwatosa, Menomonee Falls, and Tomahawk, Wisconsin, and Kansas City, Missouri, were represented principally by the United Paperworkers International Union (UPIU) of the AFL-CIO as well as by the International Association of Machinist and Aerospace Workers (IAM). Production workers at the motorcycle manufacturing facility in York, Pennsylvania, were represented principally by the IAM. The collective bargaining agreement with the Wisconsin-UPIU and IAM will expire on March 31, 2001, the collective bargaining agreement with the Kansas City-UPIU and IAM will expire on December 31, 2003, and the collective bargaining agreement with the Pennsylvania-IAM will expire on February 2, 2002.

Commitments and Contingencies [32]

The company was involved with government agencies in various environmental matters, including a matter involving soil and groundwater contamination at its York, Pennsylvania, facility. The facility was formerly used by the U.S. Navy and AMF (the predecessor corporation of Minstar). The company purchased the facility from AMF in 1981. Although the company was not certain as to the extent of the environmental contamination at the facility, it was working with the Pennsylvania Department of Environmental Resources in undertaking certain investigation and remediation activities. In March 1995, the company entered into a settlement agreement with the Navy. The agreement called for the Navy and the company to contribute amounts into a trust equal to 53% and 47%, respectively, of future costs associated with investigation and remediation activities at the facility (response costs). The trust will administer the payment of the future response costs at the facility as covered by the agreement. In addition, in March 1991 the company entered into a settlement agreement with Minstar related to certain indemnification obligations assumed by Minstar in connection with the company's purchase of the facility. Pursuant to this settlement, Minstar was obligated to reimburse the company for a portion of its response costs at the facility. Although substantial uncertainty existed concerning the nature and scope of the environmental remediation that will ultimately be required at the facility, based on preliminary information then available to the company and taking into account the company's settlement agreement with the Navy and the settlement agreement with Minstar, the company estimated that it will incur approximately $6 million of net additional response costs at the facility. The company had established reserves for this amount. The company's estimate of additional response costs was based on reports of environmental consultants retained by the company, the actual costs incurred to date, and the estimated costs to complete the necessary investigation and remediation activities. Response costs were expected to be incurred over a period of approximately ten years.

Under the terms of the sale of the Commercial Vehicles Division, the company had agreed to indemnify Utilimaster Corporation for 12 years for certain claims related to environmental contamination present at the date of sale, up to $20 million. Based on the environmental studies performed as part of the sale of the Transportation Vehicles segment, the company did not expect to incur any material expenditure under this indemnification.

Since June 1996, the company self-insured its product liability losses in the United States up to $2.5 million ($3.0 million between June 1995 and June 1996). Catastrophic coverage was maintained for individual claims in excess of $2.5 million ($3.0 million between June 1995 and June 1996) up to $25 million. Prior to June 1995, the company was self-insured for all product liability losses in the United States. Outside the United States, the company was insured for product liability up to $25 million per individual claim and in the aggregate. The company accrued for claim exposures that were probable of occurrence and could be reasonably estimated.

At December 31, 1997, the company was contingently liable for $15.9 million related to letters of credit. The letters of credit typically act as a guarantee of payment to certain third parties in accordance with specified terms and conditions.

Lawsuit

A New Jersey jury awarded $9.9 million to a motorcyclist who claimed his cruise control stuck and caused him serious injury. This award was believed to be the largest one ever against a motorcycle company for product liability. He still rode his modified motorcyle with a sidecar.[33]

Properties

The Motor Company had five facilities that performed manufacturing operations: Wauwatosa and Menomonee Falls, Wisconsin, suburbs of Milwaukee (motorcycle powertrain production); Tomahawk, Wisconsin (fiberglass parts production and painting); York, Pennsylvania (motorcycle parts fabrication, painting, and assembly). The construction of a new 330,000-square-foot manufacturing facility in Kansas City, Missouri, was completed in 1997 and was expected to be producing all Sportster motorcycles by the end of the second quarter of 1998. As a result of the February acquisition of the remaining interest in BMC, the company had a manufacturing facility in East Troy, Wisconsin, dedicated to the production of Buell® motorcycles.

Expansion had also taken place at the company's powertrain operations in the Milwaukee area, its motorcycle assembly operations in York, Pennsylvania, and its fiberglass products plant in Tomahawk, Wisconsin, to enable the company to achieve its long-term goal of increased motorcycle production capacity.

The principal properties of the Motorcycles and Related Products segment as of March 20, 1998, are shown in Exhibit 13.[34]

HARLEY-DAVIDSON CAFÉS

In 1997, the second Harley-Davidson Café opened in Las Vegas. The first café had opened in New York City. These two restaurants represented another opportunity for riders and non-riders to immerse themselves in the energy and excitement of Harley-Davidson. These cafés were among the most visible brand-building tools the company had, and they generated licensing income for Harley-Davidson as they created an entertaining dining experience for customers. Road Burnin' Bar-B-Que, Big Bowl Roadside Greens, and some classic motorcycles and memorabilia were all part of the scene. Hundreds of thousands of diners had already savored the experience.[35]

FINANCIAL SERVICES SEGMENT[36]

Eaglemark provided financial services programs to leisure product manufacturers and their dealers and customers in the United States and Canada. The company had acquired a 49% interest in Eaglemark in 1993 and subsequently acquired substantially all of the remaining shares in 1995. Eaglemark commenced doing business in 1993 with the purchase of the Harley-Davidson wholesale financing portfolio from ITT Commercial Finance Corporation. In January 1998, Eaglemark entered the European market through a joint venture agreement with Transamerica Distribution Finance Corporation to provide wholesale financing to dealers supported by the Company's European subsidiaries.

Exhibit 13   Motorcycles and Related Products Segment Properties: Harley-Davidson, Inc.

Type of Facility	Location	Square Feet	Status
Office and Warehouse	Milwaukee, WI	512,100	Owned
Product Development Center	Wauwatosa, WI	213,000	Owned
Manufacturing	Wauwatosa, WI	443,000	Owned
Manufacturing	Menomonee Falls, WI	448,000	Owned
Manufacturing	Tomahawk, WI	112,250	Owned
Manufacturing	York, PA	1,033,060	Owned
Manufacturing	Kansas City, MO	330,000	Owned
Manufacturing	East Troy, WI	40,000	Lease expiring 1999
Distribution Center	York, PA	84,000	Lease expiring 2004
Distribution Center	Franklin, WI	250,000	Owned
Motorcycle Testing	Talladega, AL	23,500	Leases expiring 1998–1999
Office	Kansas City, MO	23,600	Lease expiring 1998
Office	Mukwanago, WI	4,800	Lease expiring 1998
Office	Ann Arbor, MI	2,300	Lease expiring 1999
Office and Warehouse	East Troy, WI	8,044	Lease expiring 1998
Office and Service Area	Morfelden-Walldorf, Germany	25,840	Lease expiring 2001
Office	Tokyo, Japan	13,048	Lease expiring 1999
Warehouse	Yokohama, Japan	10,652	Lease expiring 1999
Office	Brackley, England	2,845	Lease expiring 2005
Warehouse	Brackley, England	1,122	Lease expiring 2005
Office	Windsor, England	10,147	Lease expiring 2006
Office	Liederdorp, The Netherlands	8,400	Lease expiring 2001
Office	Paris, France	5,650	Lease expiring 2005

Source: Harley-Davidson, Inc., *Form 10-K* (December 31, 1997), p. 14.

Harley-Davidson

Eaglemark provided both wholesale and retail financial services to Harley-Davidson dealers and customers and operated under the trade names Harley-Davidson Credit and Harley-Davidson Insurance. Wholesale financial services included floorplan and open account financing of motorcycles, trade acceptance financing of motorcycle parts and accessories, computer loans, showroom remodeling loans, and the brokerage of a range of commercial insurance products, including property and casualty, general liability, and special events insurance policies. Eaglemark's wholesale financial services were offered to all Harley-Davidson dealers in the United States and Canada, and during 1997 were used one or more times by approximately 95% of such dealers. Eaglemark's wholesale finance operations were located in Plano, Texas.

Retail financial services included installment lending for new and used Harley-Davidson motorcycles; the Harley-Davidson Chrome®VISA® Card; the brokerage of a range of motorcycle insurance products, including liability, casualty and credit life and disability insurance policies; and extended service agreements. Eaglemark acted only as an insurance agent and did not assume any underwriting risk with regard to the various insurance policies and extended service agreements that it sold. Eaglemark's retail financial services were available through virtually all Harley-Davidson dealers in the United States and Canada. Eaglemark's retail finance operations were located in Carson City, Nevada.

Other Manufacturers

Eaglemark also provided wholesale and retail financial services through manufacturer participation programs to certain aircraft, marine, and recreational vehicle dealers and customers. These programs were similar to the Harley-Davidson program described above.

Funding

Eaglemark's growth had been funded through a combination of capital contributions from the company, unsecured commercial paper borrowings, revolving credit facilities borrowings, senior subordinated notes borrowing, and the securitization of its retail installment loans. Future growth was expected to be financed by using similar sources as well as internally generated funds.

Competition

Eaglemark believed that its ability to offer a package of wholesale and retail financial services using the name of the manufacturer provided a significant competitive advantage over its competitors. Its competitors competed for business based largely on price and, to a lesser extent, service. Eaglemark competed based on convenience, service, and, to a lesser extent, price.

The only significant national retail financing competitor for Harley-Davidson motorcycle installment loans was Greentree Financial. During 1997, Eaglemark financed 19% of new Harley-Davidson motorcycles retailed in the United States, up from 17% in 1996. In contrast, competition to provide retail financial services to aircraft, recreational vehicle, and watercraft dealers was substantial, with many competitors being much larger than Eaglemark. These competitors included The CIT Group, NationsCredit, BankOne, and KeyBank USA. Credit unions, banks, other financial institutions, and insurance agencies also competed for retail financial services business in their local markets.

Eaglemark faced little national competition for the Harley-Davidson wholesale financial business. Competitors were primarily banks and other financial institutions that provided wholesale financing to Harley-Davidson dealers in their local markets. In contrast, competition to provide wholesale financial services to aircraft, recreational vehicle, and watercraft dealers was substantial, with many competitors being much larger than Eaglemark. These competitors included Deutche Financial, NationsCredit, Bombardier, and Transamerica. They typically offered manufacturer-sponsored programs similar to Eaglemark's programs.

Patents and Trademarks

Eaglemark had registered trademarks for the name "Eaglemark" and the Eaglemark logo. All the other trademarks or trade names used by Eaglemark, such as Harley-Davidson Credit, were licensed from the manufacturer.

Seasonality

The leisure products for which Eaglemark currently provided financial services were used only during the warmer months of the year in the northern United States and

Canada, generally March through August. As a result, the business experienced significant seasonal variations. From September until mid March, dealer inventories increased and turned more slowly, increasing wholesale financing volume substantially. During this same time there was a corresponding decrease in the retail financing volume. Customers typically did not buy motorcycles, watercraft, and recreational vehicles until they could use them. From about mid March through August, retail financing volume increased and wholesale financing volume decreased.

Employees

As of December 31, 1997, the Financial Services segment had approximately 360 employees. None of Eaglemark's personnel was represented by labor unions.

Operating Income

Exhibit 14 shows the operating income and identifiable assets of Eaglemark under Financial Services.

IMPACT OF YEAR 2000 [37]

The company had completed an assessment and was modifing or replacing portions of its software so that its computer systems would function properly with respect to dates in the year 2000 and thereafter. The company also had initiated discussions with its significant suppliers and financial institutions to ensure that those parties had appropriate plans to remediate Year 2000 issues where their systems interfaced with the company's systems or otherwise impacted its operations. The company was assessing the extent to which operations were vulnerable should those organizations fail to properly remediate their computer systems.

The company's comprehensive Year 2000 initiative was being managed by a team of internal staff with the assistance of outside consultants. The team's activities were designed to ensure that there was no adverse effect on the company's core business operations and that transactions with suppliers and financial institutions were fully supported. The company was well underway with these efforts, which were scheduled to be completed by mid 1999. While the company believed its planning efforts were adequate to address its Year 2000 concerns, there could be no guarantee that the systems of other companies on which the company's systems and operations relied would be converted on a timely basis and would not have a material effect on the company. The cost of the Year 2000 initiatives was estimated to be approximately $11 million, of which $2 million was incurred in 1997.

The costs of the project and the date on which the company believed it would complete the Year 2000 modifications were forward-looking statements and were based on management's best estimates, which were derived using numerous assumptions of future events, including the continued availability of certain resources and other factors. However, there could be no guarantee that these estimates would be achieved, and the actual results could differ materially from those anticipated. Specific factors that might cause such material differences included, but were not limited to, the availability and cost of personnel trained in this area, the ability to locate and correct all relevant computer codes, and similar uncertainties.

Exhibit 14 Revenues, Operating Income, and Assets: Harley-Davidson, Inc.

	Motorcycles and Related Products	Transportation Vehicles [1]	Financial Services [2]	Corporate
1997				
Revenue	$1,762,569	—	—	—
Operating income (loss)	265,486	—	$ 12,355	$ (7,838)
Identifiable assets as of December 31	856,779	—	598,514	143,608
1996				
Revenue	$1,531,227	—	—	—
Operating income (loss)	228,093	—	$ 7,801	$ (7,448)
Identifiable assets as of December 31	770,271	—	387,666	142,048
1995				
Revenue	$1,350,466	—	—	—
Operating income (loss)	184,475	—	$ 3,620	$ (7,299)
Identifiable assets as of December 31	595,118	$111,556	269,461	24,535

Note:
1. The Transportation Vehicles segment was reported as discontinued operations commencing in 1995.
2. The Financial Services segment's results of operations are included in operating income.

Source: Harley-Davidson, Inc., *Form 10-K* (December 31, 1997), p. 3.

CORPORATE

Human Resources and Social Responsibility

Harley-Davidson employed approximately 6,060 people in 1997. This was approximately a 9% reduction from 6,700 employees in 1995. This reduction was principally due to the sale of the Transportation Segment. The employment details for the Motorcycles and Related Products segment and the Financial Services segment were discussed earlier in this case.

Some of the highlights and growth initiatives in community affairs according to management were:

1. In its 16 years as a national corporate sponsor of MDA, the Harley-Davidson family of employees, dealers, customers, and suppliers had raised more than $25 million for the fight against neuromuscular disease. Not included in that figure were hundreds of thousands of dollars raised for MDA through the European and Asian/Pacific families. In 1997, more than $2.6 million was raised for MDA.

2. Harley-Davidson dealers and HOG chapters had adopted many local charitable or civic organizations around the world.

3. Through the Motor Company's Volunteer Matching Hours Program, employees were encouraged to volunteer and become involved in charitable organizations. Harley-Davidson then matched volunteer hours with monetary grants to those organizations, giving all employees a voice in how the company invested in its communities.

Richard F. Teerlink said, "The employees of Harley-Davidson are committed to identifying new opportunities that will perpetuate our growth. And they're committed to developing these opportunities because it's fun! They want the excitement of remaining a

Exhibit 15   Consolidated Statements of Operations: Harley-Davidson, Inc.
(Dollar amounts in thousands, except per-share data)

Year Ending December 31	1997	1996	1995
Net sales	$1,762,569	$1,531,227	$1,350,466
Cost of goods sold	1,176,352	1,041,133	939,067
Gross profit	586,217	490,094	411,399
Operating income from financial services	12,355	7,801	3,620
Selling, administrative, and engineering	(328,569)	(269,449)	(234,223)
Income from operations	270,003	228,446	180,796
Interest income	7,871	3,309	1,446
Interest expense	—	—	(1,350)
Other—net	(1,572)	(4,133)	(4,903)
Income from continuing operations before provision for income taxes	276,302	227,622	175,989
Provision for income taxes	102,232	84,213	64,939
Income from continuing operations	174,070	143,409	111,050
Discontinued operations			
Income from operations, net of applicable income taxes	—	—	1,430
Gain on disposition of discontinued operations, net of applicable income taxes	—	22,619	—
Net income	$ 174,070	$ 166,028	$ 112,480
Basic earnings per common share:			
Income from continuing operations	$ 1.15	$ 0.95	$ 0.74
Income from discontinued operations	$ —	$ 0.15	$ 0.01
Net income	$ 1.15	$ 1.10	$ 0.75
Diluted earnings per common share:			
Income from continuing operations	$ 1.13	$ 0.94	$ 0.73
Income from discontinued operations	$ —	$ 0.15	$ 0.01
Net income	$ 1.13	$ 1.09	$ 0.74
Cash dividends per common share	$ 0.135	$ 0.11	$ 0.09

Source: Harley-Davidson, Inc., *1997 Annual Report*, p. 49.

growth company that is focused on continuously improving the mutually-beneficial relationships we have with all of our stakeholders over the long term. Their adherence to this simple philosophy has created positive results and a solid foundation for continued growth."[38]

Corporate Financial Performance

The net sales of the company had increased annually for the last five years. The net sales for the company were $1,762,569,000, $1,531,227,000, $1,350,446,000, $1,158,887,000, and $932,262,000 for 1997, 1996, 1995, 1994, and 1993, respectively.

Exhibit 16 **Consolidated Balance Sheets: Harley-Davidson, Inc.**
(Dollar amounts in thousands, except per-share data)

Year Ending December 31	1997	1996
Assets		
Current assets		
Cash and cash equivalents	$ 147,462	$ 142,479
Accounts receivable, net	102,797	141,315
Finance receivables, net	293,329	183,808
Inventories	117,475	101,386
Deferred income taxes	24,941	25,999
Prepaid expenses	18,017	18,142
Total current assets	704,021	613,129
Finance receivables, net	249,346	154,264
Property, plant and equipment, net	528,869	409,434
Deferred income taxes	3,001	4,691
Goodwill	38,707	40,900
Other assets	74,957	77,567
Total assets	$1,598,901	$1,299,985
Liabilities and Shareholders' Equity		
Current liabilities		
Accounts payable	$ 106,112	$ 100,699
Accrued and other liabilities	164,938	142,334
Current portion of finance debt	90,638	8,065
Total current liabilities	361,688	251,098
Finance debt	280,000	250,000
Long-term liabilities	62,131	70,366
Post-retirement healthcare benefits	68,414	65,801
Commitments and contingencies		
Shareholders' equity		
Series A Junior Participating preferred stock, none issued	—	0
Common stock, 157,241,441 and 156,252,182 shares issued in 1997 and 1996, respectively	1,572	1,562
Additional paid-in capital	187,180	174,371
Retained earnings	683,824	530,782
Cumulative foreign currency translation adjustment	(2,835)	(566)
	869,741	706,149
Less		
Treasury stock (4,916,488 and 4,914,368 shares in 1997 and 1996, respectively), at cost	(41,959)	(41,933)
Unearned compensation	(1,114)	(1,496)
Total shareholders' equity	826,668	662,720
Total liabilities and shareholders' equity	$1,598,901	$1,299,985

Source: Harley-Davidson, Inc., *1997 Annual Report*, p. 50.

Exhibit 17   Selected Financial Data: Harley-Davidson, Inc.
(Dollar amounts in thousands, except per-share data)

Year Ending December 31	1997	1996	1995	1994	1993
Income Statement Data					
Net sales	$1,762,569	$1,531,227	$1,350,466	$1,158,887	$933,262
Cost of goods sold	1,176,352	1,041,133	939,067	800,548	641,248
Gross profit	586,217	490,094	411,399	358,339	292,014
Operating income from financial services	12,355	7,801	3,620	—	—
Selling, administrative, and engineering	(328,569)	(269,449)	(234,223)	(204,777)	(162,675)
Income from operations	270,003	228,446	180,796	153,562	129,339
Interest income, net	7,871	3,309	96	1,682	994
Other income (expense), net	(1,572)	(4,133)	(4,903)	1,196	(3,249)
Income from continuing operations before provision for income taxes and accounting charges	276,302	227,622	175,989	156,440	127,084
Provision for income taxes	102,232	84,213	64,939	60,219	50,765
Income from continuing operations before accounting changes	174,070	143,409	111,050	96,221	76,319
Income (loss) from discontinued operations, net of tax	—	22,619	1,430	8,051	(57,904)
Income before accounting changes	174,070	166,028	112,480	104,272	18,415
Cumulative effect of accounting changes, net of tax	—	—	—	—	(30,300)
Net income (loss)	$ 174,070	$ 166,028	$ 112,480	$ 104,272	$ (11,885)
Weighted average common shares					
Basic	$ 151,650	$ 150,683	$ 149,972	$ 150,440	$149,048
Diluted	153,948	152,925	151,900	153,365	152,004
Earnings per common share from continuing operations					
Basic	$ 1.15	$ 0.95	$ 0.74	$ 0.64	$ 0.51
Diluted	1.13	0.94	0.73	0.63	0.50
Dividends paid	$ 0.135	$ 0.11	$ 0.09	$ 0.07	$ 0.03
Balance Sheet Data					
Working capital	$ 342,333	$ 362,031	$ 288,783	$ 189,358	$142,996
Current finance receivables, net	293,329	183,808	169,615	—	—
Long-term finance receivables, net	249,346	154,264	43,829	—	—
Total assets	1,598,901	1,299,985	980,670	676,663	527,958
Short-term debt, including current maturities of long-term debt	—	2,580	2,691	1,431	4,190
Long-term debt, less current maturities	20,934	25,122	18,207	9,021	2,919
Short-term finance debt	90,638	8,065	—	—	—
Long-term finance debt	280,000	250,000	164,330	—	—
Total debt	391,572	285,767	185,228	10,452	7,109
Shareholders' equity	$ 826,668	$ 662,720	$ 494,569	$ 433,232	$324,912

Note: The notes were deleted.
Source: Harley-Davidson, Inc., *1997 Annual Report*, p. 40.

Exhibit 18 Geographic Information: Harley-Davidson, Inc.
(Dollar amounts in thousands)

	1997	1996	1995
Revenues [1]			
United States	$1,304,748	$1,110,527	$949,415
Canada	62,717	58,053	48,046
Germany	81,541	82,800	102,638
Japan	90,243	79,401	69,350
Other foreign countries	223,320	200,446	181,017
Total revenues	$1,762,569	$1,531,227	$1,350,466
Long-lived assets [2]			
United States	$607,363	$492,054	$353,801
Other foreign countries	7,073	7,508	5,325
Total	$614,436	$499,562	$359,126

Notes:
1. Revenues are attributed to geographic regions based on location of customer.
2. Long-lived assets include all long-term assets except those specifically excluded under SFAS No. 131 such as deferred income taxes and financial instruments, including finance receivables.

Source: Harley-Davidson, Inc., *Form 10-K* (December 31, 1997), p. 53.

The net income for the company were $174,070,000, $166,028,000, $112,480,000, $104,272,000, and $(11,885,000) for 1997, 1996, 1995, 1994, and 1993, respectively. The 1993 loss was the result of a $55,600,000 (after-tax) write-down of goodwill and certain other assets at Holiday Rambler Corporation and a $30,300,000 (after-tax) one-time charge for accounting changes related to post-retirement health care benefits and income taxes. Net sales and earnings for 1997 and 1996 were at record levels.

The board had authorized the repurchasing of 8 million shares of common stock. In 1995, 3.3 million shares were purchased. The company was still able to repurchase another 4.7 million shares. As of March 20, 1998, there were approximately 52,578 shareholders of record.

On August 20, 1997, the company's Board of Directors declared a two-for-one stock split for shareholders of record on September 12, 1997. On December 31, 1997, the company had 157,241,441 shares of common stock issued.

The stock price ranged from $31.25 to $16.875 and $24.75 to $13.185 for 1997 and 1996. The company paid its first dividend in 1993. The dividends were 13.5¢, 11¢, 9¢, 7¢, and 3¢ for 1997, 1996, 1995, 1994, and 1993, respectively (see Exhibit 16).

Exhibits 15, 16, and 17 are the company's income statement, balance sheet, and selected financial data. Exhibit 18 provides geographic revenues and assets.

Notes

1. Stuart C. Henricks, Charles B. Shrader, and Allan N. Hoffman, "The Eagle Soars Alone," in *Strategic Management and Business Policy,* 3rd Ed., by Thomas L. Wheelen and J. David Hunger (Reading, Mass.: Addison-Wesley Publishing Company, 1989), pp. 453–458. Parts of this case were abstracted and rewritten from the case "The Eagle Soars Alone." Harley-Davidson, Inc., *1997 Annual Report,* pp. 9, 27, and 32; and Harley-Davidson, Inc., *Form 10-K,* December 31, 1997, p. 40.

2. Harley-Davidson, Inc., *1993 Annual Report,* p. 23.

3. Harley-Davidson, Inc., *Form 10-K* (December 31, 1997), p. 40. These above two paragraphs were directly quoted with minor editing.

4. Roy Furchgott, "Rebel Without an Engine," *Business Week* (September 15, 1997), p. 8.

5. Harley-Davidson, Inc., *1997 Notice of Annual Meeting,* pp. 3–5. Some paragraphs were directly quoted with minor editing.

6. Harley-Davidson, Inc., *1997 Annual Report,* p. i.

7. Harley-Davidson, Inc., *1997 Notice of Annual Meeting,* p. 2.

8. *Ibid.,* pp. 3, 4, and 6.

9. Harley-Davidson, Inc., *1997 Annual Report,* pp. 18–19. These three paragraphs were directly quoted with minor editing.

10. Harley-Davidson, Inc., *1997 Form 10-K,* p. 51. These two paragraphs were directly quoted with minor editing.

11. Harley-Davidson, Inc., *1997 Annual Report,* p. 3. The following section was directly quoted with minor editing.

12. Harley-Davidson, Inc., *1997 Form 10-K,* pp. 6–7. The following six paragraphs were directly quoted with minor editing.

13. *Ibid.* The following two paragraphs were directly quoted with minor editing.

14. *Ibid.* The following two paragraphs were directly quoted with minor editing.

15. *Ibid.* pp. 6–7. The following paragraph was directly quoted with minor editing.

16. *Ibid.* p. 7. The following five paragraphs were directly quoted with minor editing.

17. *Ibid.* pp. 7–9. The following six paragraphs were directly quoted with minor editing.

18. Ken Stevens and Dale Kurschner, "That Vroom! You Hear May Not Be a Harley," *Business Week* (October 20, 1997), p. 160.

19. *Ibid.*

20. Maureen Kline, "An Italian Motorcycle Maker Revs Up Luxury Image," *Wall Street Journal* (December 26, 1997), p. B1.

21. *Ibid.*

22. *Ibid.,* p. B3

23. Case author's conversation with these two dealers.

24. *Ibid.,* pp. 9–10. The below four paragraphs were directly quoted with minor editing.

25. *Ibid.,* p. 10. The below two paragraphs were directly quoted with minor editing.

26. *Ibid.* The below paragraph was directly quoted with minor editing.

27. *Ibid.,* pp. 10–11. The below two paragraphs were directly quoted with minor editing.

28. *Ibid.,* p. 11. The above paragraphs were directly quoted with minor editing.

29. *Ibid.,* p. 38. The table and above two paragraphs were directly quoted with minor editing.

30. *Ibid.,* p. 11. The below six paragraphs were directly quoted with minor editing.

31. *Ibid.,* p. 12. This paragraph was directly quoted with minor editing.

32. *Ibid.,* p. 44. The below four paragraphs were directly quoted with minor editing.

33. Richard Gibson, "Jury Finds Against Harley-Davidson in Accident Case," *Wall Street Journal* (February 2, 1997), p. B2.

34. *Ibid.,* pp. 14–15. The above three paragraphs were directly quoted with minor editing.

35. *Ibid.*

36. Harley-Davidson, Inc., *1997 Form 10-K,* pp. 12 and 13. The operating income paragraph was added. All other paragraphs were directly quoted with minor editing. Harley-Davidson, Inc., *1997 Annual Report,* p. 28.

37. *Ibid.,* p. 26. The below three paragraphs were directly quoted with minor editing.

38. Harley-Davidson, Inc., *1994 Annual Report,* p. 39.

Reebok International, Ltd. (1998): Customer Revolt

Thomas L. Wheelen, Moustafa H. Abdelsamad, and Stanley R. Sitnik

Paul Fireman, Chairman, President, and Chief Executive Officer (CEO) of Reebok, spelled out the company's situation in his letter to the shareholders in the *1997 Annual Report.*

> This isn't going to be a traditional shareholders' letter. I'm not going to spend a lot of time telling you what went up, down or sideways in 1997. Despite difficult market conditions, we improved our earnings per share but fell short of our financial goals for the year.
>
> Instead, I'd like to focus on the big picture. I'd like to talk with you about shifting consumer preferences. I'd like to share with you our multiple-brand strategy for achieving growth across a variety of market segments. But most importantly, I'd like to tell you about the future—my personal vision for where our company is headed—and why that should be important to you as an investor.
>
> **A significant market shift** If you follow our business, you've probably read stories about a "worldwide product glut" plaguing the athletic footwear and apparel industry—the primary market for our Reebok® brand, which accounts for approximately 84% of our revenues. I can tell you first-hand these reports are not exaggerated. It's tough out there, and we believe it is unlikely that conditions will improve significantly until the end of the year or later.
>
> Here's what I think is happening: Every ten years or so, consumers get bored with the status quo. People change, fashions change, sports trends change. Without much warning, a fundamental market shift occurs. And things are never the same again.
>
> In the 60s, canvas sneakers were king. In the 70s, track and field and tennis footwear grabbed the spotlight. This was followed by an explosion in running shoes and apparel. Reebok's heyday during the 80s was defined by fitness and aerobics. Throughout the past decade basketball shoes and big-name sports stars have dominated the industry.
>
> Now a new change is underway—a rebellion. Consumers appear to be turning their backs on marketing hype and superheroes. Prices are coming down; close-outs are common. Retail distribution channels are clogged with unsold inventory.
>
> While we haven't experienced excessive inventories or the need for major markdowns to date, the events surrounding the industry are having a significant impact on our business, and things could get worse before getting better. The market is being saturated with discounted products, making it difficult to increase market share. It could take retailers the rest of the year or longer to whittle down their excess inventories.
>
> **But here's the good news . . .** Change is good. The disruption in the marketplace provides an opportunity for us to separate ourselves from the competition. Retailers and consumers are looking for fresh ideas and new products. And Reebok has built a diversified portfolio of footwear, apparel, and lifestyle brands that we think will allow us to capitalize on the opportunity.
>
> I'm not suggesting a "right time, right place" scenario, by any means. But many factors are working in our favor. The market influences are moving away from tough, in-your-face urban culture, and clean-cut, all-American styles are enjoying popularity. Upscale, casual lifestyle brands are surging. Sleek running shoes are back in vogue. Classic styles have re-emerged.

Outdoor and adventure shoes are hot, as are many alternative sport products. Customers are choosing product quality and performance over flash.

We believe these trends play to our company's strengths. Over the past two years, we have worked tirelessly to revitalize our products, technologies, and marketing strategy. We've gone back to the fundamentals of developing distinctive products that make a real difference for our customers. We think our new DMX and 3D Ultralite athletic footwear technologies deliver unparalleled benefits to athletes, and our research shows a significant "intent to re-purchase" among initial buyers. We have plans to incorporate these breakthrough technolo-gies into many new products over the coming years.

Our multiple-brand strategy is also coming to the forefront. Our Rockport®, Ralph Lau-ren® Footwear, and Greg Norman® brands are now beginning to reap the rewards of chang-ing consumer demands for comfortable, stylish "brown shoes" and fashionable sportswear. And our Ralph Lauren Polo Sport® brand, which will be expanded over the course of 1998 and 1999, will continue to bring an exciting high-end fashionable athletic element to the mix. These valuable brands provide us with a diversified portfolio of products to pursue growth across a variety of markets and consumers.

Getting our internal house in order   We haven't been sitting around waiting for con-ditions to change. We have taken aggressive actions to maintain our profitability despite mar-ket challenges. Our Reebok® brand has improved inventory management, credit management, and customer service while reducing general and administrative type expenses. We have initiated a plan to consolidate our warehouse facilities and improve efficiencies throughout our supply chain. These initiatives should be enhanced with the installation of an enterprise-wide global management information system, which will be substantially completed dur-ing 1999.

We have also announced a number of actions to increase efficiency in the near-term. We will be simplifying our organizational structure by eliminating management layers, combin-ing business units, and centralizing operations, beginning in the first quarter of 1998. This is an effort to become more focused and to free up resources which can be allocated to near-term projects that we believe can generate immediate results.

One customer at a time   So what's the missing ingredient? What must we do to achieve success? Simply put: We have to get out there and tell our story more effectively. We need to have more consumers "try on the future" and experience the Reebok difference. We need to re-establish the Reebok® brand as a major influence in its marketplace, a brand which people can trust and rely upon.

I want consumers to buy the quality and value of our products, not the hype which sur-rounds them. We must win respect one customer and retailer at a time. To supplement our benefits-driven advertising, we will deploy a mobile marketing tour of our new technologies utilizing both try-on vans and special mall kiosks. These efforts are expected to result in mil-lions of new customer "try-ons" worldwide in 1998.

We will reposition the Reebok® brand around creating possibilities one athlete at a time. Our product will be the hero, enabling the customer to fulfill his or her dreams. Rather than creating sports stars, we will create the products and technologies of the future which sports stars choose to wear. We must separate ourselves from our competition, create a clear brand identity, and continually demonstrate and market the performance-enhancing benefits of our products.

I recognize that short-term difficulties lie ahead. But I feel confident that positive oppor-tunities line our path. We will work to rise above the noise and clatter to be a company that provides enduring value—both for our customers and our shareholders. And we will con-tinue to refocus our resources to take greater advantage of opportunities among our complete portfolio of brands. That is our strategy; that is our commitment; that is our formula for high-quality growth.[1]

An analyst said of Fireman's letter to the shareholders, "He didn't mention that Nike has increased its market share of 31.7% in 1993 to 47.0% in 1997, while Reebok's has decreased from 20.6% in 1993 to 16.0 in 1997; the Asian financial crisis and potential impact on athletic shoe sales; and the concern over cheap labor and human rights in Southeast Asia." Nike had received the most publicity over the Southeast Asia human rights concerns. Exhibit 1 shows Reebok's Human Rights Production Standards. Nike had taken a similar position and published it. Reebok, also, had stockholder unrest by large institutional investors over Paul Fireman's management style and turnover of executives, which they felt affected company performance.

BACKGROUND AND HISTORY

The history of Reebok began in England in the 1890s. Athletes wanted to run faster. To meet this demand, Joseph William Foster developed cleated running shoes. By 1895, he had formed J.W. Foster and Sons, which made hand-stitched athletic shoes for many of the top athletes of that time.

In 1958, two of J.W. Foster's grandsons started a companion company that they named Reebok International after an African gazelle. In time this new company would absorb the parent company.

In 1979, Paul Fireman purchased an exclusive North American distribution license from Reebok. That year he marketed three running shoes in the United States, and at $60 a pair they were the most expensive on the market. Sales increased slowly, exceeding $1.3 million in 1981, and eventually outgrew the production capacity of the U.K. plant. In 1981, needing financing for expansion, Reebok USA swapped 56% of its stock for $77,500 with Pentland Industries, a British shoe distributor, and established production facilities in Korea. That year, in a move that was to characterize the company, Reebok noted the popularity of a new fitness craze called aerobic dancing. It also noted that no one was making a shoe for this purpose. Thus it was the first company to market an athletic shoe just for women. Shortly, the "Freestyle" line, a fashion-oriented aerobic shoe, was introduced and sales took off. Company sales were $3.5 million, $13 million, and $3.6 billion in 1982, 1983, and 1997, respectively.

In 1985, Reebok USA and Reebok International merged to become Reebok International, Ltd. Four million shares of stock were offered to the public, and Pentland became a large shareholder. Paul Fireman continued as CEO and Chairman. This share offering was used to finance the company's growth strategy.

Reebok pursued a strategy of line extensions and acquisitions. In 1986, it acquired The Rockport Company for $118.5 million in cash. In 1987, Reebok purchased the outstanding common stock of Avia Group International for $181.0 million in cash and 194,000 shares of Reebok common shares. It also acquired ESE Sports for $18 million in cash. Rockport purchased John A. Frye Co. for $10 million cash. In 1988 and 1989, it acquired Ellesse USA, Inc. (for $25 million in cash) and Boston Whaler, respectively. In 1991, it purchased a large portion of Pentland Group's holdings in Reebok (Pentland still had an ownership interest of about 13% after the Reebok purchase) and acquired the assets of Above the Rim International. The following year, Reebok acquired Perfection Sports Fashions, which marketed under the Tinley brand name. In 1993, Reebok sold Ellesse USA, and Boston Whaler, Inc.

In the late 1980s, after five years of phenomenal growth in the United States, the decision was made to aggressively pursue expansion into overseas markets and achieve an objective of 50% sales internationally. In 1997, Reebok products were available in 140 countries, and about 45.1% of total shares were generated from international shares.

In 1992, Paul Fireman had set a bold goal for the company: to displace Nike as

Exhibit 1   **Human Rights Production Standards: Reebok International, Ltd.**

Non-Discrimination

Reebok will seek business partners that do not discriminate in hiring and employment practices on grounds of race, color, national origin, gender, religion, or political or other opinion.

Working Hours/Overtime

Reebok will seek business partners who do not require more than 60-hour work weeks on a regularly scheduled basis, except for appropriately compensated overtime in compliance with local laws, and we will favor business partners who use 48-hour work weeks as their maximum normal requirement.

Forced or Compulsory Labor

Reebok will not work with business partners that use forced or other compulsory labor, including labor that was required as a means of political coercion or as punishment for peacefully expressing political views, in the manufacture of its products. Reebok will not purchase materials that were produced by forced prison or other compulsory labor and will terminate business relationships with any sources found to utilize such labor.

Fair Wages

Reebok will seek business partners who share our commitment to the betterment of wage and benefit levels that address the basic needs of workers and their families so far as possible and appropriate in light of national practices and conditions. Reebok will not select business partners that pay less than the minimum wage required by local law or that pay less than prevailing local industry practices (whichever was higher).

Child Labor

Reebok will not work with business partners that use child labor. The term "child" generally refers to a person who was less than 14 years of age, or younger than the age for completing compulsory education if that age was higher than 14. In countries where the law defines "child" to include individuals who were older than 14, Reebok will apply that definition.

Freedom of Association

Reebok will seek business partners that share its commitment to the right of employees to establish and join organizations of their own choosing. Reebok will seek to assure that no employee was penalized because of his or her non-violent exercise of that right. Reebok recognizes and respects the right of all employees to organize and bargain collectively.

Safe and Healthy Work Environment

Reebok will seek business partners that strive to assure employees a safe and healthy workplace and that do not expose workers to hazardous conditions.

Source: Reebok International, Ltd., "Reebok Human Rights Production Standards," company document.

the top sports and fitness brand and become number one by 1995. By the end of 1994, Reebok's market share was 21.3%, a 3.4% increase over 1993. Nike's market share decreased by 6.3% from 31.7% to 29.7% during the same time. Since Fireman established this goal to be number one, public perceptions of the brand had noticeably changed. Reebok started out as a brand that focused on aerobics, walking, and women. Eventually, it began to receive real credence by serious athletes—but not to the extent received by Nike. "We've lost the Michael Jordan generation. That battle had been lost—Nike owns them,"[2] said Tom Carmody, Reebok's General Manager—North America. The next step was a two-year marketing offensive designed to bump Nike from number one. The project included more inspired and focused advertising, expansion of the apparel, business, and more cross-promotion with other marketers, like Wheaties, to enhance Reebok's image as a leading sports brand.[3] Reebok intended to establish a worldwide reputation in sports as a supplier of innovative, high-performance athletic footwear, apparel, and equipment.

In late 1995, Reebok was facing an open revolt by a group of institutional shareholders who owned about 15% of Reebok's stock. This group included Warren Buffet's Government Employees Insurance Company (GEICO) and Chieftain Capital Management.

These groups "were fed up with management missteps, rising costs, earning disappointments, and a sagging stock."[4] Some of the groups wanted Fireman to resign as CEO. Fireman said that he "isn't opposed to a new chief executive officer or chief operating officer." He further stated, "Titles don't mean anything."[5] Earlier in 1995, both Joint Presidents had resigned. Fireman announced that there had been "a consolidation of leadership and a focus."[6] Glenn Greenberg, Money Manager of Chieftain Capital, indicated that Chieftain had dumped 4.5 million shares of Reebok. Warburg Pincus Asset Management and GEICO had reportedly sold Reebok shares. Over the next year, the management team stabilized.

On June 7, 1996, Reebok sold its subsidiary, Avia Group International, Inc. The company recorded a special charge of $54,064,000 in the fourth quarter of 1995 for this sale. In 1987, Reebok had paid $181 million in cash and 194,000 shares of Reebok stock for Avia. The company sold the Avia Group to refocus the company's strategies back to its core brands. As part of this strategy, the company discontinued its Bok Division in November 1996. Bok products were aimed at four segments and targeting the 16- to 24-year-old market: "Freesport," characterized by activities such as skateboarding, surfing, snowboarding; "Clubsport," a fashion-oriented line; "Utility," with worker-boot influence; and "Classic," updated popular designs from earlier seasons.

On July 28, 1996, the Board of Directors authorized the repurchase of up to 24.0 million shares of the company's common stock. The offer to repurchase commenced on July 30, 1996, and expired on August 27, 1996, and the price range for repurchasing stock was $30.00 to $36.00 net per share in cash. The company repurchased approximately 17.0 million common stock at a price of $36.00. Reebok's Board of Directors also suspended the quarterly dividend.[7] An analyst felt these measures resulted from the earlier revolt by the institutional shareholders.

CORPORATE GOVERNANCE

Board of Directors

The Board of Directors of Reebok International, Ltd., as of December 31, 1997, were:[8]

Name	Company
Paul B. Fireman	Chairman, President & CEO Reebok International, Ltd.
Paul R. Duncan	Executive Vice-President Reebok International, Ltd.
M. Katherine Dwyer	President Revlon Consumer Products, USA Revlon, Inc.
William F. Glavin	President Emeritus Babson College
Mannie L. Jackson	Chairman & Chief Executive Officer Harlem Globetrotters International, Inc.
Bertram M. Lee, Sr.	Chairman of the Board Albimar Communications, Inc.
Richard G. Lesser	Executive Vice-President & Chief Operating Officer TJX Companies, Inc.
William M. Marcus	Executive Vice-President & Treasurer American Biltrite, Inc.

Robert Meers	Executive Vice-President
	Reebok International Ltd.
	President & Chief Executive Officer
	Reebok Division
Geoffery Nunes	Retired Senior Vice-President & General Counsel
	Millipore Corporation

During 1997, each director who was not an officer or employee of the company received $25,000 annually plus $2,000 for each committee chairmanship held, $2,000 for each directors' meeting, and $1,000 for each committee meeting attended, plus expenses. Beginning in 1998, as a part of a new policy adopted by the Board of Directors that required each director to own Reebok Common Stock with a market value of at least four times the amount of the annual retainer within five years from the date of the director's first election to the Board, a minimum of 40% of the annual retainer was paid to the directors in Reebok's common stock.[9]

Top Management

In 1995, both Joint Presidents, John H. Duerden and Roberto Muller, had resigned: John H. Duerden resigned on April 7 and Robert Muller resigned on May 26. On August 22, 1995, John Watson was named Senior Vice-President and General Manager of the company's Apparel Division. He previously worked for Esprit De B mgH of Duesseldorf, Germany, as head of European operations.[10] This was what partially caused the unrest of institutional investors in the fall of 1995.

The company's executives as of December 31, 1997, were:[11]

Paul B. Fireman (54) founded the company and served as its Chief Executive Officer and a Director since the company's founding in 1979 and its Chairman of the Board since 1986. With the exception of 1988, Fireman served as President of the company from 1979 to the present.

In the mid and late 1980s, Fireman was one of the highest paid executives in the country. His salary package included base pay of $357,200 plus 5% of the amount by which Reebok's pre-tax earnings topped $20 million. He averaged $13.6 million a year. In 1990, the Board of Directors decided that Mr. Fireman's compensation should be more closely tied to increases in value for Reebok shareholders. Fireman has a new employment contract that determines his annual salary, plus an annual bonus based on the company's earnings, with a maximum of $1 million. He also was given a one-time grant of options to purchase 2.5 million Reebok common shares. The options will become exercisable over a period of five years at exercise prices ranging from $17.32 to $18.37 per share and remain exercisable until July 24, 2000. In 1991, Reebok paid a $513,601 premium on a $50 million life insurance policy for Mr. Fireman and his wife, Phyllis. This was reduced to only $46,162 in 1996. Mr. Fireman paid the remainder of the premiums. There had been some shareholder criticism of the high level of Fireman's compensation.

Paul Fireman and his wife, Phyllis, have sold some of their stock through secondary offerings, lowering their ownership to 7.7 million and 5.0 million shares, respectively. This represented about a 21.04% ownership interest, worth approximately $383 million at $30 per share. This left the company insiders (other than Fireman) with a 2.1% ownership interest.

Fireman was known to have a problem in delegation, which contributed to management turnover. A former executive who was highly recruited and lasted less than a year said that "Paul was the sort of fellow who would make a great neighbor . . . But he was absolutely convinced that no one can do a job better than he can." [12] The institution investment groups felt that this caused some of the turmoil in the company management team.

Fireman was a strong advocate of "est training," the human-potential program founded by Werner Erhart in the 1970s. The Forum was the current version of est. His admiration for est was best summarized when he said, "I believe in anything that allows you to look at yourself and see what's possible." [13] A former Reebok executive said that "the company sometimes divides up between those who buy into the est message and those who don't." He further said, "Key employees, even top management, at times seem to be kept out of the loop, denied crucial new research or excluded from strategy meetings unless they accept the est outlook and methods. Fervent est adherents, meanwhile, form a sort of subculture with its own attitudes and jargon." [14]

Paul R. Duncan (54) was appointed Executive Vice-President in February 1990, with responsibility for special projects since November 1996. Prior to that, Duncan was President of the company's Specialty Business Group from October 1995 to November 1996, and Chief Operating Officer for the Reebok Division from June 1995 to October 1995. Previously, from 1985 to June 1995, he was Chief Financial Officer. He had served as a Director since March 1989.

Arthur I. Carver (47) has been the Senior Vice-President of Sourcing and Logistics of the Reebok Division since January 1996. Prior to that, Carver was Vice-President of Operations Development Worldwide for the Reebok Division since February 1994. Previously, from June 1992 through February 1994, he was Vice-President of North American Operations. Prior to that, he was Director of Sales Operations. Carver joined the company in 1990.

Roger Best (45) has been Senior Vice-President of the Reebok Division since February 1996. In July 1997, he became the General Manager of the Reebok Division's European Region. Prior to that, he was General Manager of Reebok North America since February 1996. Previously, from April 1995 through February 1996, he was Regional Vice-President of the Reebok Division's Northern Europe Operations and Managing Director of Reebok U.K. and, from January 1992 through April 1995, he was Managing Director of Reebok U.K. Best joined the company in 1992.

William M. Sweeney (40) has been Senior Vice-President of the Reebok Division and General Manager of Reebok North America since August 1997. Prior to that, Sweeney was Regional Vice-President of the Reebok Division's Asia/Pacific Region and President of Reebok Japan since November 1995. He joined Reebok in 1991 as marketing director for the Asia/Pacific Region and was based at the regional headquarters in Hong Kong.

James R. Jones, III (53) has been Senior Vice-President of Human Resources for the Reebok Division since April 1997. Prior to that, Jones was Vice-President of Human Resources of Inova Health System from May 1996 through April 1997. From July 1995 through May 1996, Jones was the Senior Vice-President of Human Resources of Franciscan Health System. Prior to that, since 1991, Jones was the Vice-President of Human Resources of The Johns Hopkins University.

Barry Nagler (41) has been Senior Vice-President of the Company since February 1998 and General Counsel since September 1995. Nagler was previously a Vice-President of the company since May 1995. Prior to that, Nagler was divisional Vice-President and Assistant General Counsel for the Company since September 1994. He joined the Company in June 1987 as Counsel. [15]

The directors and executive officers owned 9,022,592 shares (14.96%) of the company. William Marcus owned 612,373 shares, and is the only corporate person to own more than 1.0% beside Paul Fireman.

Executive Compensation

Exhibit 2 shows the aggregate compensation paid or accrued by the company for service rendered during the years ended December 1995, 1996, and 1997 for the Chief Executive Officer and the company's four other most highly compensated executive officers.[16]

CORPORATE ORGANIZATION

The three principal business group units of Reebok were Reebok Division, Rockport Company, Inc., and Greg Norman Division.

The Reebok Division

The Reebok Division designed, produced, and marketed sports and fitness footwear, apparel, and accessories as well as related sports and fitness products that combined the attributes of athletic performance and style. The Division's products included footwear for basketball, running, soccer, rugby, tennis, golf, track and field, volleyball, football, baseball, aerobics, cross training, outdoor and walking activities, and athletic apparel and accessories. The Division continued to expand its product scope through the development and marketing of related sports and fitness products and services, such as sports and fitness videos and programming, and through its strategic licensing program, pursuant to which the company's technologies and/or trademarks were licensed to third parties for fitness equipment, sporting goods, and related products and services.

The Reebok Division had targeted, as its primary customer base, athletes and others who believed that technical and other performance features were the critical attributes of athletic footwear and apparel. Over the past few years, the company had sought to increase Reebok's on-field presence and establish itself as an authentic sports brand. Through such effort, Reebok had gained increased visibility on playing fields worldwide through endorsement arrangements with such prominent athletes as NBA Rookie of the Year Allen Iverson of the Philadelphia 76ers, and with various sports and event sponsorships. Recently, given the diminishing influence of sports "icons" on consumer buying preferences and the increasing consumer appeal of "brown shoe" or "casual" footwear products, the company had been reevaluating its substantial investment in sports marketing deals and was in the process of eliminating or restructuring certain of its underperforming marketing contracts that the company believed no longer reflected the company's brand positioning. In 1998, the Reebok Division intended to focus its efforts on the performance of its products and, in particular, its proprietary technologies, and on bringing its message, both product and brand essence, directly to the consumer. Consistent with this focus, in 1998 the Reebok Division implemented a new direct-to-the-consumer campaign called "Try on the Future," a nationwide, mobile tour designed to give consumers the opportunity to experience and "try on" Reebok's new products and technologies.

As part of its commitment to offer leading athletic footwear technologies, the Division engaged in product research, development, and design activities in the company's Stoughton, Massachusetts, headquarters, where it had a state-of-the-art

Exhibit 2   Summary Compensation Table: Reebok International, Ltd.

Name and Principal Position	Year	Annual Compensation		Other Annual Compensation	Long-Term Compensation Awards		All Other Compensation ($)
		Salary ($)	Bonus ($)		Restricted Stock Awards	Options (#)	
Paul B. Fireman	1997	$1,038,474	$562,500	—	None	111,150	$ 54,112
Chairman, President and	1996	1,000,012	None	—	None	500,000	100,913
Chief Executive Officer	1995	1,000,000	None	—	None	87,300	96,645
Robert Meers	1997	769,227	365,625	—	None	35,000	39,749
Executive Vice-President;	1996	699,978	None	—	None	250,000	41,066
President and CEO,	1995	591,325	None	—	None	140,000	31,041
Reebok Division							
Angel Martinez	1997	467,328	325,078	—	None	None	29,001
Executive Vice-President;	1996	425,022	201,354	—	None	187,500	31,776
President and CEO	1995	400,010	60,000	$62,000	$21,483	25,000	28,889
The Rockport Company							
Kenneth I. Watchmaker	1997	509,600	281,250	—	None	None	29,769
Executive Vice-President and	1996	440,387	None	—	None	150,000	30,750
Chief Financial Officer	1995	400,000	60,000	—	$21,483	25,000	29,003
Roger Best	1997	379,972	85,000	—	None	None	17,875
Senior Vice-President	1996	344,515	100,000	—	None	220,550	17,883
of the Reebok Division	1995	195,000	75,075	—	None	6,950	30,389

Note: All notes were deleted.

50,000-square-foot product development facility that was dedicated to the design and development of technologically advanced athletic and fitness footwear, and in its various Far East offices. Recently, Reebok had opened development centers in the Far East to enable its development activities to be more closely integrated with production. Development centers were opened in Korea in May 1996 and in China in June 1997. New development centers were also scheduled to open in Taiwan and Thailand during 1998.[17]

The Reebok Division's worldwide sales (including Greg Norman) were $3.131 billion in 1997, an increase of 5.0% for comparable sales of $2.982 billion in 1996. The stronger U.S. dollar adversely impacted 1997 sales and profits for this division. In constant dollars, the sales for Reebok brand increased 8.3% in 1997, when compared with 1996. The increase in U.S. sales was attributed primarily to increases in running, walking, and men's cross-training categories. These increases were partially offset by decreasing sales of basketball, outdoor, and women's fitness shoes.

The Reebok Division U.S. apparel sales increased by 37.2% to $431.9 million from $314.9 million in 1996. The increase resulted primarily from increases in branded core basics, licensed, and graphic categories. Total international sales for Reebok Division were $1.471 billion and $1.474 billion, respectively, for 1997 and 1996. International sales in constant dollars showed a gain of 6.4%, and all regions generated sales increases over the prior year on a constant dollar basis.

The Rockport Company

The company's Rockport subsidiary, headquartered in Marlborough, Massachusetts, designed, produced, and distributed specially engineered comfort footwear for men and women worldwide under the ROCKPORT® brand, as well as apparel through a licensee. Rockport also developed, marketed, and sold footwear under the RALPH LAUREN® brand pursuant to a license agreement entered into in May 1996.

Rockport Brand

Designed to address different aspects of customers' lives, the Rockport product line included casual, dress, outdoor performance, golf, and fitness walking shoes. In 1997, Rockport focused on its men's business with the introduction of its Bourbon Street™ collection, refined footwear combining comfort with style and targeting an expanded customer base including younger consumers. Rockport also solidified its success with its ProWalker® World Tour Shoe, with an expanded product line.

Internationally, the Rockport brand continued to grow. In 1997, the Rockport brand's international revenues grew by 46%.

Rockport expanded its retail presence in 1997 with the opening of a "concept" shop in San Francisco, California, and an increase in the United States in the number of its Rockport shops—independent retail shops dedicated exclusively to the sale of Rockport products—from 15 to 21 (see discussions under "Retail Stores"). In addition, Rockport emphasized retail in its international business by opening additional "concept" or retail shops outside of the United States, operated by Rockport distributors or third-party retailers.

Rockport introduced an integrated marketing campaign in 1997 using the directive, "Be Comfortable. Uncompromise. Start with your feet."™ The campaign featured real individuals, unique for their nonconformity, wearing Rockport shoes with a statement of their unique comfort level. The "Uncompromise" campaign was used as the major marketing platform for the brand in the fall of 1997, encompassing television advertising, print advertising, public relations, and retail promotions. In 1997, Rockport continued to expand its offerings on its Internet website including the establishment of a business-to-business direct purchase program enabling employees at participating companies to purchase Rockport products through Rockport's website.

Rockport marketed its products to authorized retailers throughout the United States primarily through a locally based employee sales staff, although Rockport used independent sales agencies for certain products. Internationally Rockport marketed its products through approximately 30 locally based distributors in approximately 50 foreign countries and territories. A majority of the international distributors were either subsidiaries of the company or joint venture partners or independent distributors that also sold Reebok brand products.

Rockport distributed its products predominantly through select higher quality national and local shoe store chains, department stores, independent shoe stores, and outdoor outfitters, emphasizing retailers that provided substantial point-of-sale assistance and carried a full product line. Rockport also sold its products through independently owned Rockport dedicated retail shops as well as Rockport concept or company stores (see discussion under "Retail Stores"). Rockport had not pursued mass merchandisers or discount outlets for the distribution of its products.

Ralph Lauren Brand

In 1997, Rockport continued to develop the Ralph Lauren footwear business, which was acquired in May 1996. The Ralph Lauren footwear line was expanded in 1997 to include men's English dress shoes. In addition, Collection Classics were introduced for women's shoes and the Refined Casual segment for both men's and women's shoes was expanded. Also in 1997, Polo Sport athletic footwear products were offered. The Polo Sport athletic footwear product line was expected to expand over the next two years with the introduction of new product categories.

Ralph Lauren footwear was marketed to authorized retailers though a locally based employee staff. Products were distributed primarily through higher quality department stores. Products were also sold through space licensing and merchandising arrangements at Ralph Lauren Polo retail stores.

Rockport's sales increased by 14.5% to $512.5 million from $447.6 million in 1996. Exclusive of the Ralph Lauren footwear business, which was acquired in May 1996, Rockport's sales increased 7.3% in 1997. International revenues, which grew by 46.0%, accounted for approximately 21% of Rockport sales (excluding Ralph Lauren footwear) in 1997, as compared with 16.0% in 1996. Increased sales in the walking and men's categories were partially offset by decreased sales in women's lifestyle category. The decrease in the women's lifestyle category was the result of a strategic initiative to refocus the women's business around an outdoor, adventure, and travel positioning and reduce the product offerings in the refined women's dress shoe segment. Rockport continued to attract young customers to the brand with the introduction of a wider selection of dress and casual products. The Ralph Lauren footwear business performed well in 1997 and was beginning to generate sales growth in its traditional segments, reflecting the benefits of improved product design and development and increased distribution. Rockport planned to expand the current product line of Ralph Lauren Polo Sport athletic footwear during 1998 with additional products to be available at retail during 1999.[18]

Greg Norman Division

The company's Greg Norman Division produced a collection of apparel and accessories marketed under the Greg Norman® name and logo. The Greg Norman Collection had grown from a golf apparel line to a broader line of men's casual sportswear. The Greg Norman product line had been expanded to include a wide range of apparel products—from leather jackets and sweaters to activewear—at a variety of upper-end price points. The Greg Norman Division intended to grow the Greg Norman brand further by offering a variety of lifestyle products and expanding into international markets. It was anticipated that the Division would accomplish such expansion through various licensing and distribution arrangements. In 1997, Greg Norman footwear, leather, and hosiery products were sold through licensees of the company. The Division anticipated entering into a number of new agreements that would broaden the scope of products offered and expand distribution internationally.

The Greg Norman brand was marketed though its endorsement by pro golfer Greg Norman and a marketing and advertising campaign designed to emphasize his aggressive, bold, charismatic, and "winning" style. The current tag line for the brand and marketing focus was "Attack Life."

Greg Norman products were distributed principally at department and men's specialty stores, on-course pro shops, and golf specialty stores and were sold by a combination of independent and employee sales representatives. The Greg Norman Collection was also sold in Greg Norman dedicated shops within independently owned retail stores as well as Greg Norman concept or company stores.[19]

Reebok's strategy was to challenge the men's super brands. Greg Norman, celebrity golfer, finished 1997 ranked No. 1 in The Official World Golf Rankings. But Reebok's Greg Norman Collection may have had an even better year. Sales for the operating unit approximated $80 million, an increase of more than 50% compared with 1996. While remaining a strong leadership position within the golf industry, the Greg Norman Collection had expanded its retail distribution to 750 department stores, up from 550 the year before. With its high-quality product and bold styling, the brand continued to pursue a larger share of the growing upscale collection sportswear market. Three broad-based market trends were working in Reebok's favor: the maturing of the baby-boomer generation, strong growth in casual lifestyle apparel, and golf's surging popularity. In 1998, Reebok planned to build on its success by introducing new lines of clothing—from swimwear and volleyball apparel to high-fashion outerwear. Reebok also planned to continue to expand its retail presence and advertising to challenge the men's apparel super brands for increased floor space and market share.[20]

INTERNATIONAL OPERATIONS

The Reebok Division's international sales were coordinated from the company's corporate headquarters in Stoughton, Massachusetts, which was also where the Division's regional operations responsible for Latin America were located. There were also regional offices in Luesden, Holland, which was responsible for Europe; in Hong Kong, which was responsible for Far East operations; and in Denham Lock, England, which was responsible for the Middle East and Africa, although this office moved to Delhi, India, in March 1998. The Canadian operations of the Division were managed through a wholly-owned subsidiary headquartered outside of Toronto. The Division marketed Reebok products internationally through wholly-owned subsidiaries in Austria, Belgium, Canada, France, Germany, Ireland, the Netherlands, Italy, Poland, Portugal, Russia, Switzerland, and the United Kingdom, and through majority-owned subsidiaries in Japan, India, South Korea, Spain, and South Africa. Reebok products were also marketed internationally through 29 independent distributors and joint ventures in which the company held a minority interest. The company or its wholly-owned U.K. subsidiary held partial ownership interests in six of these international distributors, with its percentage of ownership ranging from 30% to 35%. Through this international distribution network, products bearing the Reebok brand were actively marketed internationally in approximately 170 countries and territories. The Division's International operations unit also had small design staffs that assisted in the design of Reebok apparel.

In 1997, Reebok finalized its plans to restructure its international logistics over the next several years. This global restructuring effort included reducing the number of European warehouses in operation from 19 to three, establishing a shared services company to centralize European administrative operations, and implementing a global management information system. The global restructuring initiative, which was expected to be completed in 1999, should enable the company to achieve operational efficiencies and to manage its business on a global basis more cost effectively. In connection with such restructuring, the company recorded a special pre-tax charge of $33.2 million in 1997.

During 1997, the contribution of the division's International operations unit to overall sales of Reebok products (including Greg Norman apparel) decreased to

$1.471 billion from $1.474 billion in 1996. The Division's 1997 international sales were negatively impacted by changes in foreign currency exchange rates. In addition, these sales figures did not reflect the full wholesale value of all Reebok products sold outside the United States in 1997 because some of the division's distributors were not subsidiaries and thus their sales to retailers were not included in the calculation of the Division's international sales. If the full wholesale value of all international sales of Reebok products were included, total sales of Reebok products outside the United States would represent approximately $1.779 billion in wholesale value, consisting of approximately 33.2 million pairs of shoes totaling approximately $1.098 billion in wholesale value of footwear sold outside the United States in 1997 (compared with approximately 35.7 million pairs totaling approximately $1.189 billion in 1996) and approximately $680.5 million in wholesale value of Reebok apparel (including Greg Norman apparel) sold outside the United States in 1997 (compared with approximately $613.8 million in 1996).[21] On a constant dollar basis, international sales increased by 6.4%.

International Sales and Production

A substantial portion of the company's products were manufactured abroad, and approximately 40% of the company's sales were made outside the United States. The company's footwear and apparel production and sales operations were thus subject to the usual risks of doing business abroad, such as currency fluctuations, longer payment terms, potentially adverse tax consequences, repatriation of earnings, import duties, tariffs, quotas, and other threats to free trade, labor unrest, political instability, and other problems linked to local production conditions and the difficulty of managing multinational operations. If such factors limited or prevented the company from selling products in any significant international market or prevented the company from acquiring products from its suppliers in China, Indonesia, Thailand, or the Philippines, or significantly increased the cost to the company of such products, the company's operations could be seriously disrupted until alternative suppliers were found or alternative markets were developed, with a significant negative impact.[22]

Trade Policy

For several years, imports from China to the United States, including footwear, have been threatened with higher or prohibitive tariff rates, either through statutory action or intervention by the Executive Branch, due to concern over China's trade policies, human rights, foreign weapons sales practices, and foreign policy. Further debate on these issues was expected to continue in 1998. However, the company did not anticipate that restrictions on imports from China would be imposed by the United States during 1998. If adverse action was taken with respect to imports from China, it could have an adverse effect on some or all of the company's product lines, which could result in a negative financial impact. The company had put in place contingency plans that would allow it to diversify some of its sourcing to countries other than China if any such adverse action occurred. In addition, the company did not believe that it would be more adversely impacted by any such adverse action than its major competitors. The actual effect of any such action, however, depended on several factors, including how reliant the company, as compared to its competitors, was on production in China and the effectiveness of the contingency plans put in place.

The European Union (EU) imposed quotas on certain footwear from China in 1994. The effect of such quota scheme on Reebok had not been significant because the quota scheme provided an exemption for certain higher priced special technology athletic footwear. Such exception was available for most Reebok products. This exemption did not, however, cover most of Rockport's products. Nevertheless, the volume of quota available to Reebok and Rockport in 1998 was expected to be sufficient to meet the anticipated sales for Rockport products in EU member countries. However, an insufficient quota could adversely affect Rockport's international sales.

In addition, the EU had imposed antidumping duties against certain textile upper footwear from China and Indonesia. A broad exemption from the dumping duties was provided for athletic textile footwear, which covered most Reebok models. If the athletic footwear exemption remained in its current form, few Reebok product lines would be affected by the duties; however, Rockport products would be subject to these duties. Nevertheless, the company believed that those Reebok and Rockport products affected by the duties could generally be sourced from other countries not subject to such duties. If, however, the company was unable to implement such alternative sourcing arrangements, certain of its product lines could be adversely affected by these duties.

The EU also had imposed antidumping duties on certain leather upper footwear from China, Thailand, and Indonesia. These duties applied only to low-cost footwear, below the import prices of most Reebok and Rockport products. Thus the company did not anticipate that its products would be impacted by such duties.

The EU continued to review the athletic footwear exemption that applied to both the quota scheme and antidumping duties discussed above. The company, through relevant trade associations, was working to prevent imposition of a more limited athletic footwear exception. If revisions were adopted narrowing such exemption, certain of the company's product lines could be affected adversely, although the company did not believe that its products would be more severely affected than those of its major competitors.

Various other countries had taken or were considering steps to restrict footwear imports or impose additional customs duties or other impediments, which actions would affect the company as well as other footwear importers. The company, in conjunction with other footwear importers, was aggressively challenging such restrictions. Such restrictions had, in some cases, had a significant adverse effect on the company's sales in some of such countries, most notably Argentina, although they had not had a material adverse effect on the company as a whole.[23]

Global Restructuring Activities

The company currently was undertaking various global restructuring activities designed to enable the company to achieve operating efficiencies, improve logistics, and reduce expenses. There could be no assurance that the company would be able to effectively execute on its restructuring plans or that such benefits would be achieved. In addition, in the short term, the company could experience difficulties in product delivery or other logistical operations as a result of its restructuring activities, which could have an adverse effect on the company's business. In the short term, the company could also be subject to increased expenditures and charges from such restructuring activities. The company was also in the process of eliminating or restructuring certain of its underperforming marketing contracts. There could be no assurance that the company would be able to successfully restructure such agreements or achieve the cost savings anticipated.[24]

INDUSTRY AND COMPETITION

Changing Markets

In 1997, U.S. athletic footwear sales were about $8 billion and they had experienced little growth over the past few years. In 1997, Nike had 47.0% of the U.S. market, which was a growth of 48.3% over its market share of 31.7% in 1993 (see Exhibit 3). Reebok had 16.0% of the U.S. market and had seen its market share decrease by 22.3% from 20.6% in 1993. The two companies combined had 63.0% and 52.3% of the U.S. market in 1997 and 1993, respectively. A major shift was Others at 30.5% in 1993 to 14.0% (a drop of 54.1%). New companies among the "top eight" were New Balance and Airwalk, both with 3.0% market share. Fila's market share had increased by 50% from 4.0% in 1993 to 6.0% in 1997. Adidas had the highest increase of 93.5% for this period. Keds was the biggest loser with a 65.5% decrease (5.8% to 2.0%) over these five years. Converse also suffered a 30.2% loss of market share (see Exhibit 3).

Adidas, a German corporation, had 6.0% and 3.1% of the U.S. market in 1997 and 1993, respectively. The potential customer liked the classic Adidas styling. In the mid 1990s, Adidas controlled more than 70% of the global market for soccer shoes and apparel. Both Nike and Reebok had made serious financial commitments to enter this market and to become number one. In 1997, Nike agreed to pay $120 million over eight years to sponsor the U.S. Soccer Foundation, the governing body for the top men's, women's, and youth teams. Nike had 12% of the U.S. soccer shoe market, and Adidas had 42%. In soccer apparel sales, Adidas led with 32%, Britain's Umbro was second with 24%, and Nike was third with 12%. During the past two years, Nike locked up the marketing rights to several multinational soccer foundations, including Brazil, Italy, Russia, Nigeria, Holland, and South Korea. Nike was paying about $200 million over 10 years to Brazil. Robert Muller, former Reebok International President, said, "Nike is saying, 'Let's get the top teams that we can win on a consistent basis and pay whatever it takes.'" He further stated, "By not letting anyone else in, they can maximize their global exposure." [25]

The women's market has been a growth market for athletic footwear companies. In 1994, women, for the first time, purchased more athletic footwear than men. This segment of the market had become the battleground because men's sales seemed to be flat. Women basketball players were a large segment of this market. High school girls played basketball more than other sports. Walking shoes, one of the biggest categories of women's sales, was also one of the fastest growth areas. [26]

In 1997, PCH Investments LLC purchased a 42% stake in L.A. Gear. A new board was elected and the board announced a restructuring that eliminated about 60% of the company's roughly 100 employees at headquarters. L.A. Gear had 5.1% and 3.1% market share in 1994 and 1993, respectively. PCH Investments' filing with the Security and Exchange Commission noted that the board was considering a number of measures to keep the company afloat. The filing also included "a merger, reorganization or liquidation" strategies as strategic choices for the board. Trefoil Investment, Disney family's investment group, had invested $100 million in the company in 1990 and had received some $25 to $30 million in dividends over the next seven years. Trefoil sold PCH Investments' controlling interest for $230,000. This was three weeks after PCH Investments acquired its 42% stake in L.A. Gear. [27]

Teenage Research Unlimited did its latest 1997 survey and found that 40% of teens named Nike as one of the "coolest" brands, but this was down from 52% (or 30% decrease) from just six months earlier. Kim Hastrieter of *Paper,* a New York magazine, said,

Exhibit 3 Share of the U.S. Athletic Footwear Market

	1997	1994	1993	% Change 1993–1997
Nike	47.0%	29.7%	31.7%	48.3%
Reebok	16.0	21.3	20.6	(22.3)
Adidas	6.0	5.1	3.1	93.5
Fila	6.0	4.7	4.0	50.0
Converse	3.0	4.6	4.3	(30.2)
New Balance	3.0	—	—	—
Airwalk	3.0	—	—	—
Keds	2.0	4.6	5.8	(65.5)
Others[1]	14.0	30.0	30.5	(54.1)

Note:
1. Other balances total to 100% for 1994 and 1993.

Source: *Business Week* (March 13, 1995), p. 7, and Bill Saporito "Can Nike Get Unstuck?" *Time* (March 30, 1998), p. 51.

"the coolest things around now are brilliantly colored suede sneakers by New Balance." Adidas, which was torpedoed by Reebok and Nike in the 80s, was staging a comeback. Candie's, a small maker of women's shoes, was running ads featuring former MTV star Jenny McCarthy with the slogan, "Just Screw It," while Nike had the slogan, "Just Do It." So, the new competitors (New Balance, Airwalk, and others; see Exhibit 3) were attacking Nike and Reebok straight on.[28]

In the fall of 1997, a new trend emerged as schools reopened—teens were turning their noses up at the "white shoe" that they had wanted in past years; instead, they were opting for "brown shoes." The 1997 casual footwear included clunky, huge, and caterpillar boots. So, the big winners could be: Wolverine, which made Caterpillar and Wolverine boots, and Hush Puppies—the latter two had strong fall sales—and Timberland, which made popular outdoor and casual brown-shoe styles. Reebok's Rockport division could supply some of the demand for this change in consumer buying preferences.

Susan Pulliam and Laura Bird, *Wall Street Journal* reporters, felt the big losers would be Nike, Fila, and Woolworth's Foot Locker unit. Brenda Gall, a Merrill Lynch analyst, wrote to her clients that "feedback from industry contacts suggests that basketball shoe sales have gotten off to a sluggish start for the important back-to-school season, and stronger demand for running models has not been enough of an offset."[29]

John Stanley, a retail analyst at Genesis Merchant Group Securities, predicted "that Woolworth's athletic shoe group will record another decline for August [1997] in sales at stores open at least a year, following an 8% decline in July."[30] Woolworth reported a same-store companywide sales decline of 5.8% in July 1997. In early 1998, sales trends had not reversed.

The "Asian Economic Crisis" started in the fall of 1997 and lasted for several years. The impact of the crisis on Reebok and Nike were two-fold. First, the cost of manufacturing athletic footwear was greatly reduced as the currencies in these countries devaluated and it could take several years or more to fully rebound. Second, the Asian consumer did not have sufficient funds to buy athletic footwear as they had in past years. Nike seemed to be taking a bigger hit from the Asian Economic Crisis. In 1997, Nike's revenues from the Asia/Pacific market were $1,245,217,000 (13.6% of total revenues), $735,094,000 (11.3%), and $515,652,000 (10.8%), and operating income was

$174,997,000 (13.3% of total operating revenue), $123,585,000 (13.7%), and $64,168,000 (9.9%) for 1997, 1996, and 1995, respectively. See Exhibit 4 for Reebok's sales, net income, and identifiable assets. The Asian/Pacific region was included in the geographic heading "Other countries." Other countries' revenues were 12.9% in 1997.

The Y Generation Rebellion

A survey of the U.S. Y generation found 6.5 million skateboarders, 4.5 million snowboarders, 1.5 million stunt bikers, 2 million wakeboarders, and 1 million all-terrain boarders, die-hards who rode down off-season ski slopes or other hills on 3½-foot-long boards with 6-inch wheels that looked like little inner-tubes.[31]

Over the next three years, experts expected the wakeboarders to increase sixfold and skateboard and snowboard users to double. Terry Dorner, World Sports & Marketing, said, "You ain't seen nothing yet."[32]

This shift by the Y generation had seen companies like Vans, Airwalk, Etonic, and DC have their annual sales increase by 20% to 50% over the previous two years. During this time, these niche companies' sales increased to $500 million, or 6.3% of the $8 billion U.S. sneaker market.

Their shoes were cheap. A pair of Vans cost $45 to $50, underpricing Nike's retail average of $70 to $75. The shoes had dimpled rubber soles, instead of waffled ones, and simple colors and designs. The logos were discreet versus the boisterous swoosh of Reebok's logo.

PepsiCo Inc.'s Mountain Dew sales increased 13% in 1996, and moved from No. 6 to No. 4, behind Coke, Pepsi-Cola, and Diet Coke, by featuring snowboarding in its advertisements. In fiscal 1997, Van's sales were up 26% to $159 million. In fiscal 1998, Van's sales were hit by the collapse of its Japanese distribution system, but analysts still predicted sales to be up 13% to $180 million. Much of the sales growth should come from footwear chains that in the past have not given its products much exposure. In 1998, Foot Locker was featuring Van shoes in window displays and started selling them in more than 1,000 stores, up from a few the previous year.

Van's had a cadre of 236 athletic endorsers. The endorsers were relatively unknown, compared with Nike's endorsers.

Van's had competed for years against Reebok and Nike in the basketball and running shoe segments of the market. The company was started in 1966, and had sales of only $35 million in 1995. Walter Schoenfeld, former owner of the Seattle Mariners and founder of Brittania jeans, and his son, Gary Schoenfeld, CEO, said, "I figure the most we could make do is $750 million in annual sales." He further stated, "After that, we run the risk of losing our core customers who do not want us to get too big."[33]

For Reebok's star athletes, ESPN was raising their profiles with shows featuring boarding sports in its twice-a-year X Games competition. MTV ran an extreme-sports festival in November 1997 and planned more such programming.

Snow Valley, formerly a struggling ski resort, changed its name to Mountain of Youth and doubled its attendance to 200,000. Snowboarders made up 70% of the customers.[34]

Competitors

Nike

Nike was the world's top marketer of high-quality footwear and sports apparel. The Foot Locker, a Woolworth's division, was Nike's largest customer (about 14%). The company's

Exhibit 4   Operations by Geographical Area: Reebok International, Ltd.
(Dollar amounts in thousands)

	1997		1996		1995		1994	
	Amount	%	Amount	%	Amount	%	Amount	%
Net sales								
United States	$2,000,883	54.9	$1,935,724	55.6	$2,027,080	58.2	$1,974,904	60.3
United Kingdom	661,358	18.2	566,196	16.3	492,843	14.2	506,658	15.4
Europe	510,981	14.0	623,209	17.9	642,622	18.4	502,029	15.3
Other countries	470,377	12.9	353,475	10.2	318,905	9.2	296,827	9.0
Total	$3,643,599	100.0	$3,478,604	100.0	$3,481,450	100.0	$3,280,418	100.0
Net income								
United States	$ 83,894	62.1	$ 41,522	29.9	$ 52,314	31.7	$ 126,916	49.9
United Kingdom	50,441	37.3	60,050	43.2	74,175	45.0	62,949	24.7
Europe	(567)	(0.4)	21,854	15.6	28,138	17.1	28,290	11.1
Other countries	1,351	1.0	15,524	11.3	10,171	6.2	36,323	14.3
Total	$ 135,119	100.0	$ 138,950	100.0	$ 164,798	100.0	$ 254,478	100.0
Identifiable assets								
United States	$ 938,027	53.4	$ 887,217	49.7	$ 813,935	49.3	$ 963,462	58.5
United Kingdom	372,526	21.2	391,865	21.9	291,825	17.7	282,795	17.1
Europe	278,606	15.8	282,057	15.8	311,903	18.9	221,771	13.4
Other countries	166,938	9.6	225,045	12.6	233,956	14.1	181,433	11.0
Total	$1,756,097	100.0	$1,786,184	100.0	$1,651,619	100.0	$1,649,461	100.0

Source: Reebok International, Ltd., *1997 Annual Report*, p. 36.

U.S. market share for athletic footwear was 47.0%, and up 48.2% (31.7% to 47.0% from 1993 (see Exhibit 3). Sales were $9,186.5 million (up 42.0%), $6,470.6 million (up 35%) and $4,760.8 million, and operating income was $1,295.2 million (up 44.1%), $899.1 million (up 38.3%), and $649.9 million for 1997, 1996, and 1995, respectively (see Exhibit 5).

On September 10, 1997, Nike announced that Michael Jordan would head his own Nike Division, Jordan Inc. Jordan discussed this with Phil Knight, Chairman and CEO, about 10 years ago, but at that time Knight scoffed at the notion. Jordan has been the heart and soul of Nike's presence in athletic footwear (Air Jordan) and athletic sportswear. Jordan saw the new company as part of his opportunity to stay with the game after he retired. Asked about his title and role he would play with the new division, Jordan said, "I don't have a title. They call me CEO, but my responsibilities are to help create the product, implement my feelings and my style."[35] The apparel suggested retail prices ranged from $30 to $140. Air Jordan would cost about $150.

Nike's company culture was based on dedicated corporate loyalty and fierce competition from its 9,700 employees. The company was located on a 74-acre corporate campus in Beaverton, Oregon. Phil Knight, Founder and Chairman, was a former University of Oregon track star and Stanford MBA. Knight wanted to base his company's culture on the deep loyalty that he had seen in Japan, and he wanted his employees to feel the adrenaline rush of athletes performing at their highest levels. Nike still had this culture 30 years later. When entering his office, Knight removed his shoes, Japanese style.[36]

Exhibit 5   Athletic Shoe Industry

A. Revenues (millions of dollars)

Company	Estimated		Actual			
	2000–2002	**1998**	**1997**	**1996**	**1995**	**1994**
Nike	$13,000.0	$9,750.0	$9,186.5	$6,470.6	$4,760.8	$3,789.7
Reebok	4,500.0	3,700.0	3,643.6	3,478.6	3,481.5	3,280.4
Stride Rite	800.0	565.0	516.7	448.3	496.4	523.9

B. Net Profits (millions of dollars)

Company	Estimated		Actual			
	2000–2002	**1998**	**1997**	**1996**	**1995**	**1994**
Nike	$ 950.0	$ 565.0	$ 795.8	$ 553.2	$ 406.7	$ 298.8
Reebok	240.0	135.0	134.3	139.0	209.7	254.5
Stride Rite	60.0	26.0	19.8	2.5	1.5	19.8

C. Operating Profit Margin (%)

Company	Estimated		Actual			
	2000–2002	**1998**	**1997**	**1996**	**1995**	**1994**
Nike	15.0%	12.5%	16.5%	16.6%	15.9%	15.3%
Reebok	10.5	8.5	8.8	8.9	11.6	13.9
Stride Rite	13.5	8.7	7.9	2.5	3.1	7.7

D. Net Profit Margins (%)

Company	Estimated		Actual			
	2000–2002	**1998**	**1997**	**1996**	**1995**	**1994**
Nike	7.3%	5.8%	8.7%	8.5%	8.5%	8.0%
Reebok	5.3	3.3	3.7	4.0	6.0	7.8
Stride Rite	7.5	4.6	3.8	0.6	0.3	3.8

Source: *Value Line* (February 20, 1998), pp. 1669, 1671, and 1672.

Knight found that consumers responded best "to athletes who combined passion to win with a maverick disregard for convention. Outlaws with morals!" [37] Some of his rules of business were: "Play by the rules, but be ferocious," and "It's all right to be Goliath, but always act like David." [38] Employees took two-hour workouts at midday at the Bo Jackson Sports and Fitness Center on campus, then worked late into the night at a relentless pace. Paul Fireman stated that "I think Nike was more of a cult, where people have to give up their individuality." [39]

On March 16, 1998, Nike announced the lay-off of about 450 employees. This was in addition to 300 temporary workers announced earlier. The lay-offs were caused by sales weakness in U.S. and Asian markets.

New Balance

New Balance had total sales of $560 million in 1997. This was an increase of 16% over 1996. The company ranked fifth with a market share of 3.0% (see Exhibit 3). The company's athletic footwear sales were $260 million.

Mike Kormas, President of Footwear Market Insights, said that New Balance "is becoming the Nike of the baby-boomer generation."[40] His company surveyed 25,000 households every four months on footwear purchasing preferences. He reckoned that "the average age of a Nike consumer is 25, the average age of a Reebok consumer is 33, and the average age of a New Balance consumer is 42."[41] New Balance offered five widths of shoes, from a narrow AA to an expansive EEEE. About 20% to 30% of the population had narrower or wider foot size than average. Most other companies offered two widths—medium and wide. Retailers for New Balance said they sold more EE or EEEE than the other three sizes.

The company in the past competed for the basketball shoe market, but efforts were disappointing. Jim Davis, President and CEO, said, "We chose not to be in a position where we live and die by basketball. We'd just as soon pass the $10 to $15 a pair we need in superstar endorsements to the consumer."[42] New Balance spent $4 million in advertising and promotion to generate sales of $560 million. The $4 million was less than 1% of Nike's or Reebok's budgets. In 1998, the company planned to increase the marketing budget to $13 million.

Stride Rite

Stride Rite was the leading marketer of quality children's footwear in the United States and one of the major marketers of boating and outdoor recreational shoes and athletic and casual footwear for children and adults. Major brand names included Stride Rite, Sperry Top-Sider, Keds, Pro-Keds, and Tommy Hilfiger lines for men and women. The company stabilized its previously falling Keds. Sales were down 10% from 1996 in the Keds lines, but profitability improved by approximately 50%, due primarily to fewer markdowns and aggressive cost cutting. The company's margins improved in 1997, which was primarily the result of shifting manufacturing overseas. The company operated 204 retail stores and leased children's shoe departments.[43] The company's market share dropped from 5.8% in 1994 to 2.0% (65.5%) in 1997 (see Exhibits 3 and 5).

Adidas AG

Adidas AG had seen its market share increase from 3.1% in 1993 to 6.0% in 1997. (See Exhibit 3.) Adidas's sales were $500 million. The German company had been founded in 1920. The company's profits had been squeezed by intense competition from Reebok and Nike on its home territories during the 1990s. Nike and Reebok had entered the soccer shoe segment of the world market to attack Adidas's dominance of this market. Joachim Bernsdorff, a consumer-goods expert with Bank Julius Bear in Frankfurt, said, "The basic mistake was Adidas's insistences on making athletic gear." He further stated, "They felt above selling style, colorful clothes—without seeing that's what young people want."[44] The company had restarted production of old models, as teenagers and trendsetters around the world rediscovered sneakers made by Adidas 20 years ago. It was being called the revival of a classic!

Fila

Fila had sales of $484 million and a market share of 6.0%, which was a 50% increase over 1993 (see Exhibit 3).

Converse

Converse was a sneaker company before Nike and Reebok were founded. The company's sales were $280 million, and it ranked tied for third place with 3.0% market share and down 30.2% since 1993 (see Exhibit 3).

Puma AG

Puma AG had suffered almost a decade of losses, but had profitable years beginning in 1994.

MARKETING AND PROMOTIONAL ACTIVITIES

The Reebok Division devoted significant resources to advertising its products to a variety of audiences through television, radio, and print media and used its relationships with major sports figures in a variety of sports to maintain and enhance visibility for the Reebok brand. The Reebok Division's advertising program in 1997 was directed toward both the trade and the ultimate consumers of Reebok products. The major advertising campaigns in 1997 included an ad campaign featuring real-life portraits of rookies Allen Iverson of the National Basketball League (NBA) and Saudia Roundtree of the American Basketball League (ABL) depicting their adjustment to professional sports, as well as real-life portraits of Reebok endorsers Shawn Kemp and Shaquille O'Neal, and a marketing campaign for the DMX® Run shoe featuring Spencer White, Reebok's director of research engineering.[45]

Advertising expense (including cooperative advertising) amounted to $164,870,000, $201,584,000, and $157,573,000 for 1997, 1996, and 1995, respectively. Advertising production costs were expensed the first time the advertisement was run. Selling, general, and administrative expenses decreased as a percentage of sales from 30.6% ($1,065,792,000) in 1996 to 29.4% ($1,069,433,000) in 1997.

Substantial resources were devoted to promotional activities in 1997, including endorsement agreements with athletes, teams, leagues, and sports federations; event sponsorships; in-store promotions; and point-of-sale materials. In 1997, the Reebok Division gained visibility for the Reebok brand through endorsement arrangements with such athletes as 1997 Rookie of the Year Allen Iverson of the Philadelphia 76ers, with whom Reebok marketed a signature line of footwear and apparel. Other endorsements in basketball in 1997 came from professional players such as Shaquille O'Neal, Shawn Kemp, Clyde Drexler, Nick Van Exel, and Steve Smith. In 1997, Reebok entered into a multiyear agreement with NBA Properties for a comprehensive licensed merchandise, marketing, and basketball development program in Latin America. In addition, Reebok sponsored a number of college basketball programs and had a sponsorship agreement with the Harlem Globetrotters. Reebok was also the founding sponsor of the ABL and the official footwear and apparel sponsor of the league. Reebok was the exclusive supplier of uniforms and practice gear to the league's nine teams and an official ABL licensee and had entered into endorsement agreements with a number of ABL players including Saudia Roundtree, Jennifer Azzi, and Carolyn Jones. Reebok was also an official footwear supplier to the Women's National Basketball Association (WNBA).

To promote the sale of its cross training footwear in 1997, Reebok used endorsements by prominent athletes such as National Football League (NFL) players Emmitt Smith, Derrick Thomas, John Elway, Ken Norton, Jr., Herman Moore, and Ben Coates, as well as Major League Baseball (MLB) players Frank Thomas, Mark McGwuire, Juan Gonzalez, and Roger Clemens. To promote its cleated football and baseball shoes, the company also had endorsement contracts with numerous MLB and NFL players, and sponsored a number of college football programs.

The company had a multiyear agreement with NFL Properties under which Reebok had been designated a "Pro Line" licensee for the U.S. and international markets with the right to produce and market uniforms and sideline apparel bearing NFL team logos. Pursuant to this agreement, in 1997 Reebok supplied uniforms and sideline apparel to the San Francisco 49ers, Detroit Lions, New York Giants, New Orleans Saints, Kansas City Chiefs, and Atlanta Falcons. In addition to the Pro Line license, Reebok had an agreement with the NFL under which Reebok was one of only three brands authorized to provide NFL players with footwear that had visible logos, and all NFL on-field game officials wore Reebok footwear exclusively.[46]

Jerry Jones, owner of the Dallas Cowboys, signed an exclusive contract with Nike. This contract had to be approved by the president of the NFL. Under current NFL rules, only a company licensed by the NFL to sell NFL's Pro Line products can do so for NFL teams. So the NFL sued Jerry Jones. He countersued the NFL. The NFL and Jerry Jones subsequently dropped their suits, allowing Jones to proceed.

In soccer, Reebok had a number of endorsement arrangements including contracts with Gabriel Batistuta of Fiorentina and the Argentinean national team, Ryan Giggs of Manchester United and Wales, Dennis Bergkamp of Arsenal and the Netherlands, and Guiseppe Signori of Lazio and Italy, as well as U.S. national team members Eric Wynalda, Brad Friedel, Michelle Akers, and Julie Foudy. The company also had major sponsorship agreements with the Liverpool Football Club, one of the world's best known soccer teams, and with the Argentina National Football Association, which took effect in 1999. In addition, Reebok had entered into sponsorship agreements with such soccer teams as Aston Villa, Borussia Moenchengladbach of Germany, Bastia of France, Palmeiras of Brazil, Brondby of Denmark, and IFK Gothenburg of Sweden. In 1997, the company extended its sponsorship of the Bolton Wanderers of England to include naming rights to the team's new soccer arena, the Reebok Stadium. Reebok was also the official uniform supplier of two U.S. major league soccer teams: the New England Revolution and the Colorado Rapids. In July 1997, the first-ever Reebok Cup, an international soccer tournament featuring four of the world's most powerful club teams, was held in the United States. In rugby, the company sponsored the national rugby teams of Australia and Italy.

Tennis promotions in 1997 included endorsement contracts with well-known professionals including Michael Chang, Venus Williams, Patrick Rafter, and Arantxa Sanchez-Vicario. Promotional efforts in running included endorsement contracts with such well-known runners as Ato Boldon, Derrick Adkins, Kim Batten, and Marie Jose Perec.

In February 1997, Reebok apologized for naming a shoe "Incubus." Incubus, according to legend, was a demon that had sex with sleeping women. The name received national media coverage and complaints from customers. Dave Fogelson, a Reebok spokesman, said, "Someone should have looked it [Incubus] up." He further stated, "There are no excuses, and we apologize." Reebok management hired a name consultant to avoid future mistakes.[47]

To promote its women's sports and fitness products, Reebok sponsored athletes such as Rebecca Lobo of the WNBA as well as Michelle Akers and Julie Foudy of the U.S. national soccer team, Lisa Fernandez of the U.S. national softball team, and Liz Masakayan, pro beach volleyball player. In addition, Reebok sponsored a variety of college basketball and volleyball teams and such organizations as the ABL and the WNBA.

In 1997, the Reebok Division also continued its promotional efforts in the fitness area. Reebok fitness programming was featured on Fit-TV, a 24-hour cable network, pursuant to a programming agreement. Through an agreement with Channel One Communications, in 1997 Reebok provided the programming for P.E. TV, an award-winning program designed to educate kids about physical fitness. Reebok had developed numerous fitness programs, such as its Versa Training program, designed to help consumers meet their varied fitness goals with aerobic, strength, and flexibility workouts, the Walk Reebok program, which promoted walking; its Cycle Reebok program that featured the Cycle Reebok studio cycle; and the Reebok Flexible Strength program that developed strength and flexibility simultaneously. These programs were complemented by the marketing and sale of a line of Reebok fitness videos, as well as the marketing and sale of Reebok fitness equipment products such as the Step Reebok exercise platform and the Cycle Reebok studio cycle.

To gain further visibility for the Reebok brand, Reebok had also entered into several key sport sponsorships such as an arrangement under which Reebok was designated the official footwear and apparel sponsor of the Russian Olympic Committee and approximately 25 individual associated Russian sports federations. This arrangement was recently extended through the Sydney 2000 Summer Olympic Games. Reebok will also be an official sponsor of the Sydney 2000 Olympic Games and the official sports brand of the 1998 and 2000 Australian Olympic teams, as well as an official sponsor and supplier of sports footwear and apparel to the national Olympic teams from Brazil, New Zealand, Poland, and South Africa. In addition, as an extension of its commitment to provide athletes with technologically advanced products, Reebok had entered into sponsorship agreements with the Team Scandia and Cristen Powell, a top fuel drag racer on the National Hod Rod Association circuit, as well as with Eliseo Salazar, one of the top drivers on the Indy Car racing circuit, and the R&S Indy Racing League (IRL) TEAM on the 1998 IRL circuit. Reebok also had school-wide sponsorship arrangements with colleges such as U.C.L.A., University of Texas, University of Virginia, and University of Wisconsin. In 1997, the Reebok Division also ran marketing promotions on its Internet website.[48]

Sales of the following categories of products contributed more than 10% to the company's total consolidated revenue in the years indicated: 1997, footwear (approximately 72%) and apparel (approximately 27%); 1996, footwear (approximately 75%) and apparel (approximately 24%); 1995, footwear (approximately 81%) and apparel (approximately 18%).[49]

Sales by the company of athletic and casual footwear tended to be seasonal in nature, with the strongest sales occurring in the first and third quarter. Apparel sales also generally varied during the course of the year, with the greatest demand occurring during the spring and fall seasons. Exhibit 6 shows sales by quarters.[50]

SPORTS AND FITNESS EQUIPMENT AND LICENSING

The company had continued to pursue its strategic trademark and technology licensing program begun in 1991. This program was designed to pursue opportunities for licens-

Exhibit 6 **Sales by Quarter**

Year Ending December 1997	First Quarter	Second Quarter	Third Quarter	Fourth Quarter
Net sales	$930,041	$841,059	$1,009,053	$863,446
Gross profit	356,229	323,511	370,211	299,599
Net income	40,184	20,322	73,968	645
Basic earnings per share	.72	.36	1.32	.01
Diluted earnings per share	.69	.35	1.26	.01

ing the company's trademarks, patents, and other intellectual property to third parties for sporting goods, apparel, and related products and services. The licensing program was focused on expanding the Reebok brand into new sports and fitness markets and enhancing the reputation of the company's brands and technologies. The company had pursued strategic alliances with licensees who Reebok believed were leaders and innovators in their product categories and who shared Reebok's commitment to offering superior, innovative products. The company believed that its licensing program reinforced Reebok's reputation as a market leader.

The company's licensing program included such products as a full line of athletic gloves, including baseball batting gloves, football gloves, running gloves, court/racquet-ball gloves, fitness/weightlifting gloves, cycling gloves, golf gloves, and winter gloves, all featuring the Reebok trademark and Reebok's Vector Logo; a collection of Reebok performance sports sunglasses; the Watch Reebok collection of sport watches, and a line of heart rate monitors and a pedometer and stopwatch; Reebok weight belts, both with and without Reebok's Instapump technology; and a line of gymnastic apparel including replicas of the U.S. gymnastics team uniforms. Reebok also had license agreements with Mead for a line of Reebok school supplies and with Haddad Apparel for a line of Reebok infant and toddler apparel. In addition, in 1997, Reebok entered into a licensing agreement with Fab-Knit, Ltd., to manufacture and sell a new line of Reebok team uniforms and jackets.

In 1997, Reebok entered into a new video license agreement with BMG Video, a unit of BMG Entertainment, to produce, market, and sell a line of Reebok fitness videos. Through a licensee, Reebok also sold Reebok fitness audio tapes. In the equipment area, in January 1998, the company signed a license agreement with industry leader Icon Health & Fitness, Inc. to develop, market, and sell a complete line of Reebok fitness equipment products for the home market. The initial home fitness products from this license debuted at the Super Show in Atlanta in February 1998. Reebok also had a license agreement with Cross Conditioning Systems under which Cross Conditioning Systems sold a line of Reebok fitness equipment products designed for use in health clubs and other institutional markets. In 1997 under this relationship the Reebok Body Mill, Reebok Body Tree, Reebok Body Peak, Reebok Studio Cycle, and Reebok Cycle Plus were sold to health clubs and other institutions.

In addition, as part of the company's licensing program, WEEBOK infant and toddler apparel and accessories and a line of WEEBOK footwear were sold by licensees. WEEBOK is a fashion-oriented, kid-specific brand that offered apparel in sizes 0–7 and footwear in sizes 0–12.[51]

RETAIL STORES

Woolworth's athletic division included Foot Locker, Lady Foot Locker, Kid Foot Locker, Champs, and Eastbay catalog, which had sales of $3.6 billion. In 1996, sales soared by 10.2% but grew at half this rate in 1997. Foot Locker was the hardest hit chain in 1997. Foot Locker's same-store sales for 1996 and 1997 had an 11.2% decrease. The decrease was attributed to the Y Generation shift in shoe purchasing and the brown versus white shoe rebellion by students.

In the summer of 1996, management of Woolworth decided to shut down its Woolworth retail chain. Roger N. Farah, CEO, decided to make Foot Locker the linchpin of his turnaround plan for the $7.1 billion retailer. Kurt Bernard, who published Bernard's Retail Trend Report, said, "They gave up a dead industry in favor of putting all the eggs in one basket."[52] He further stated, "And the basket is getting shaken up. They're going to have scrambled eggs."[53] To make things a little worse, Woolworth could not account for $43 million in inventory at its Woolworth stores. This shrinkage was 5.82%, which was three times the companywide average.

Foot Locker was also losing ground to newcomers that had superstores, which were as much as 10 times larger than its stores. At some competitors' stores, Just For Feet, Inc., and Sneaker Stadium, kids could try out gear on a real basketball court. Foot Action had sport shows on big-screen TVs and racks of spandex and sweats. Thomas E. Clark, President of Nike, said of the new competitors, "These larger formats give the retailer the opportunity to romance products better."[54]

CEO Roger N. Farah's response was to create 1,500 Foot Locker superstores by pushing back the storeroom walls. In late 1998, he expected to convert 100 of the old Woolworth stores into superstores that combined all the company's athletic products in one store.[55]

Reebok and Nike have been battling over dominance in sales in the Foot Locker. Tensions between Reebok and Foot Locker went back to the 1980s. At that time, Reebok's aerobic shoe sales were not in the stores. So, Foot Locker management asked Reebok to turn out a specialty line for Foot Locker. Josie Esquivel, an analyst at Morgan Stanley, said that "Reebok basically thumbed its nose" at the retailer. Reebok "was selling to whomever it wanted, including the discounter down the street from Foot Locker."[56] Foot Locker's strategy was to offer exclusive lines as a weapon against discounters and was receiving exclusive lines from other athletic shoe manufacturers. Nike agreed to make exclusive lines for Foot Locker. In 1996, Nike introduced Flight 65 and Flight 67, which were high-priced basketball shoes that sold only at Foot Locker. These shoes came in Nike's trademark black and white. Earlier in the year, Reebok had agreed to make shoes exclusively for Foot Locker, but none of the shoes had reached the store.

Fireman's views on the rocky relations with Foot Locker were that "Reebok wasn't as good a listener to [Foot Locker], which happens to have a good ear as to what's happening on the street and consumers."[57] Fireman was trying to repair the relationship, so he recently spent a few days with buyers of Woolworth's foot units, "trying to discern their needs."[58]

Over the past few years, "Reebok had hired an army of testers at Woolworth's shoe chains . . . to find out whether Reebok was getting equal treatment with other brands."[59] Reebok was disappointed with their findings. They found that Reebok had the most shoes on display in the stores but got little positive help from the stores' salespeople. A salesperson told one 17-year-old customer that "Nikes were hip."[60]

Reebok recognized that Foot Locker's customers were not Reebok's core clients, who were older customers and preteens unable to spend $80 to $90 for shoes. Foot Locker's target market were teens and Generation X customers, who spent $80 to $90 for shoes. Fireman said, "There's no question Nike owns that market," and "there's no one really in that market to compete against them in the high-end niche."[61]

Nike had a special salesforce, Elkins, which called on stores and spread the gospel of Nike. They were enthusiastic sponsors of Nike's product lines. They provided the company with excellent information on market trends and competition.

William De Vrues, who headed Woolworth's footwear units, dismissed talk about bad relations with Reebok. He said, "We're only selling what the customer wants."[62]

Reebok's Retail Stores

The company operated approximately 150 factory direct stores, including Reebok, Rockport, and Greg Norman stores which sold a variety of footwear, apparel, and accessories marketed under the company's various brands. The company intended to continue to open additional factory direct stores, although its policy was to locate and operate those retail outlets in such a way as to minimize disruption to its normal channels of distribution.

The company also operated Reebok "concept" or company retail stores located in New York City and King of Prussia, Pennsylvania. The company envisioned its concept stores as a model for innovative retailing of its products and as a potential proving ground for testing new products and marketing/merchandising techniques. The stores sold a wide selection of in-line Reebok footwear and apparel. Internationally, the company, its subsidiaries, or its independent distributors owned several Reebok retail stores. The company continued to open retail stores either directly or through its distributors in numerous international markets. Reebok retail shops were expected to be an important means of presenting the brand in relatively new markets such as China, India, and Russia and in other international markets.

The company was working to develop a retail store concept to showcase the Reebok brand at retail and was expected to incorporate this design into independently owned retail stores dedicated exclusively to the sale of Reebok products. In 1998, the company planned to test this concept in a few stores to be opened in markets around the world.

Rockport had concept or company retail stores in San Francisco, California; Boston, Massachusetts; Newport, Rhode Island; King of Prussia, Pennsylvania; and New York City. In addition, there were a number of Rockport shops—independent stores that sold Rockport products exclusively—in the U.S. as well as internationally. There were two Greg Norman concept or company retail stores in New York City. Rockport's Ralph Lauren footwear subsidiary operated "concept" footwear departments in Ralph Lauren/Polo stores in a number of locations in the United States, including New York City and Beverly Hills, California. In addition, the Ralph Lauren footwear subsidiary had footwear retail operations in approximately 19 Ralph Lauren/Polo factory direct stores and operated one factory direct store in Tannersville, Pennsylvania.

Reebok was also a partner in the Reebok Sports Club/NY, a premier sports and fitness complex in New York City featuring a wide array of fitness equipment, facilities, and services in a luxurious atmosphere. The club used approximately 125,000 square feet and occupied five floors of the Lincoln Square project. A Reebok concept store as well as Rockport and Greg Norman concept stores were also located in the building.[63]

MANUFACTURING AND PRODUCTION

Virtually all of the company's products were produced by independent manufacturers, almost all of which were outside the United States, except that some of the company's apparel and some of the component parts used in the company's footwear were sourced from independent manufacturers located in the United States. Each of the company's operating units generally contracted with its manufacturers on a purchase order basis, subject in most cases to the terms of a formal manufacturing agreement between the company and such manufacturers. All contract manufacturing was performed in accordance with detailed specifications furnished by the operating unit, subject to strict quality control standards, with a right to reject products that did not meet specifications. To date, the company had not encountered any significant problem with product rejection or customer returns. The company generally considered its relationships with its contract manufacturers to be good.

As part of its commitment to human rights, Reebok had adopted human rights standards and a monitoring program that applied to manufacturers of its products (see Exhibit 1). In conjunction with this program, the company required its supplier of soccer balls in Pakistan to end the use of child labor by centralizing all production, including ball stitching, so that the labor force could be adequately monitored to prevent the use of child labor. Reebok soccer balls were sold with a guarantee that the balls were made without child labor.

China, Indonesia, Thailand, and the Philippines were the company's primary sources for footwear, accounting for approximately 39%, 28%, 15%, and 8%, respectively, of the company's total footwear production during 1997 (based on the number of units produced). The company's largest manufacturer, which had several factory locations, accounted for approximately 13% of the company's total footwear production in 1997.

Reebok's wholly-owned Hong Kong subsidiary, and a network of affiliates in China, Indonesia, India, Thailand, Taiwan, South Korea, and the Philippines, provided quality assurance, quality control, and inspection services with respect to footwear purchased by the Reebok Division's U.S. and international operations. In addition, this network of affiliates inspected certain components and materials purchased by unrelated manufacturers for use in footwear production. The network of affiliates also facilitated the shipment of footwear from the shipping point to point of destination, as well as arranging for the issuance to the unrelated footwear manufacturers of letters of credit, which were the primary means used to pay manufacturers for finished products. The company's apparel group used the services of independent third parties, as well as the company's Hong Kong subsidiary and its network of affiliates in the Far East, to assist in the placement, inspection, and shipment of apparel and accessories orders internationally. Production of apparel in the United States was through independent contractors that the company's apparel group retained and managed. Rockport products were produced by independent contractors that were retained and managed through country managers employed by Rockport. The remainder of the company's order placement, quality control, and inspection work abroad was handled by a combination of employees and independent contractors in the various countries in which its products were made.[64]

When Reebok began manufacturing in a new location, it started with the simplest and least expensive lines. This procedure allowed the workers to learn the trade and Reebok to establish acceptable standards. The company had 480 employees involved in production who worked closely with the factories to provide detailed specifications for production and quality control. These employees also facilitated the shipment of footwear and arranged for the issuance of letters of credit, the primary means used to pay manufacturers for the finished product. Some of the apparel and some of the component parts of the footwear were sourced in the United States.

Since 1983, Reebok had used production facilities in South Korea (1983), Taiwan (1985), Philippines (1986), China (1987), Indonesia (1987), Thailand (1987), India (1994), and Vietnam (1995). Some of the plants in these countries had been closed.

Technology

Reebok placed a strong emphasis on technology and had continued to incorporate various proprietary performance technologies in its products, focusing on cushioning, stability, and lightweight features.

In 1995, Reebok introduced its propriety DMX® technology for superb cushioning. DMX® used a two-pod system that allowed air to flow from the heel to the forefoot. This technology continued to be used successfully in several Reebok walking shoes. In April 1997, the company debuted its DMX® 10 technology at retail with the introduction of the DMX Run shoe. This advanced technology incorporated a ten-pod, heel to forefoot, active air transfer system delivering cushioning when and where it was needed. The DMX® 10 technology was also introduced at retail in November 1997 in The Answer, an Allen Iverson signature basketball shoe. In February 1998, Reebok debuted at retail DMX® 6, a six-pod, heel to forefoot, active air transfer system, in a running shoe, Run DMX® 6. In addition, DMX® 6 was available at retail in February 1998 in The Lightning, a signature basketball shoe to be worn by NBA player Nick Van Exel and as a team shoe to be worn by many college athletes. The company also introduced a DMX® Sockliner, which was expected to debut at retail in a golf shoe in March 1998 and in a soccer shoe in April 1998.

3D Ultralite™ technology was Reebok's approach to lightweight performance footwear. 3D Ultralite was a proprietary material that allowed the midsole and outsole to be combined in one injection molded unit composed of foam and rubber, thus making the shoe lightweight, flexible, and durable. In 1997, the company introduced this technology in running, walking, basketball, and women's fitness shoes. In 1998, the company planned to continue to introduce 3D Ultralite technology at retail in additional footwear categories, including women's sports training and men's cross-training.

Reebok continued to incorporate Hexalite®, a honeycomb-shaped material, which provided stability and cushioning, in many of its shoes and in many different applications. Radial Hexalite®, one application of this technology, combined under-the-foot cushioning and lateral stabilization and was first available at retail in early 1997. Hexliner™, a PU foam sockliner that included reengineered Hexalite® material in the heel for a softer feel close to the foot, was first available at retail in June 1997.

Finally, Reebok has incorporated advanced technology into its apparel products with the introduction of Hydromove™ technology in certain performance apparel. This moisture management system helps keep athletes warm in cold weather and dry and cool in hot weather. Performance apparel incorporating the Hydromove™ technology first became available at retail at the end of 1996.[65]

Sources of Supply

The principal materials used in the company's footwear products were leather, nylon, rubber, ethylvinyl acetate, and polyurethane. Most of these materials could be obtained from a number of sources, although a loss of supply could temporarily disrupt production. Some of the components used in the company's technologies were obtained from only one or two sources, and thus a loss of supply could disrupt production. The principal materials used in the company's apparel products were cotton, fleece, nylon, and spandex. These materials could be obtained from a number of sources.

The footwear products of the company that were manufactured overseas and shipped to the United States for sale were subject to U.S. Customs duties. Duties on the footwear products imported by the company ranged from 6% to 37.5% (plus a unit charge, in some cases, of 90 cents), depending on whether the principal component was leather or some other material and on the construction.

As with its international sales operations, the company's footwear and apparel production operations were subject to the usual risks of doing business abroad, such as import duties, quotas and other threats to free trade, foreign currency fluctuations and restrictions, labor unrest, and political instability. Management believed that it had the ability to develop, over time, adequate substitute sources of supply for the products obtained from present foreign suppliers. If, however, events should prevent the company from acquiring products from its suppliers in China, Indonesia, Thailand, or the Philippines, or significantly increase the cost to the company of such products, the company's operations could be seriously disrupted until alternative suppliers were found, with a significant negative impact.[66]

Backlog

The company's backlog of orders at December 31, 1997 (many of which were cancelable by the purchaser), totaled approximately $1.224 billion, compared to $1.198 billion as of December 31, 1996. The company expected that substantially all of these orders would be shipped in 1998, although, as noted above, many of these orders were cancelable. The backlog position was not necessarily indicative of future sales because the ratio of future orders to "at once" shipments and sales by company-owned retail stores may vary from year to year.[67]

INFORMATION SYSTEMS

Year 2000

The company had conducted a global review of its computer systems to identify the systems that could be affected by the technical problems associated with the year 2000 and had developed an implementation plan to address the "year 2000" issue. As part of its global restructuring, in 1997 the company began its global implementation of SAP software, to substantially replace all legacy systems. The company believed that, with modifications to existing software and converting to SAP software, the year 2000 will not pose significant operational problems for the company's computer systems. The cost of such modifications was not expected to be material. The company expected its SAP programs to be substantially implemented by 1999 and the implementation was currently on schedule. However, if the modifications and conversions are not implemented or completed in a timely or effective manner, the year 2000 problem could have a material impact on company operations. In addition, in converting to SAP software, the company was relying on its software partner to develop new software applications and there could be problems in successfully developing such new applications.[68]

HUMAN RIGHTS

Reebok Human Rights Award

Reebok explained its stand on human rights in its *1997 Annual Report.*[69]

> Reebok International has a long-held commitment to human rights, and we require our partners and vendors to abide by an internationally recognized standard of human rights.

> In 1992 we adopted a worldwide code of conduct mandating the fair treatment of workers involved in making Reebok products. This code rejects the use of child labor, unsafe working conditions, unfair wages, and other threats to basic human rights. In addition, our commitment has resulted in a number of important human rights initiatives [cited below] of which we are proud.

Guarantee: "Manufactured Without Child Labor"

> In November 1996, Reebok announced a program to label its soccer balls with a guarantee that the balls are made without child labor. This was believed to be the first time a guarantee of this kind was placed on a widely distributed consumer product. We used a stringent monitoring program at a new soccer ball facility in Sialkot, Pakistan, to ensure that children did not enter the workplace and that soccer balls are not distributed to children for stitching. In addition, Reebok will commit $1,000,000 from the sale of soccer balls toward the educational and vocational needs of children in the Sialkot region, where the majority of the world's soccer balls are produced. The Reebok Educational Assistance to Pakistan program, together with the Pakistan-based group, Society for the Advancement of Education (SAHE), opened a school for former child workers, the first in a series of initiatives in this region.

Witness

> In 1993, the Reebok Foundation joined the Lawyers Committee for Human Rights and musician Peter Gabriel to create Witness, a program which supplies activists with communications equipment to document and expose human rights abuses.

Reebok Human Rights Award

> Since 1988, we have sponsored the annual Reebok Human Rights Awards to recognize young people who, early in their lives and against great odds, join the struggle for human rights. It is unique for being a human rights award sponsored by a corporation that recognizes activists 30 years of age and younger.

Human Rights Incidents and Resolves

In 1996 and 1997, both Reebok and Nike were accused by activists of worker abuse in Southeast Asian countries and China. Most of the heat was on Nike. Some of the accusations and resolves were:

- **Incident One:** Teenage girls were paid 20 cents an hour to make $180 Nike sneakers in Vietnam factories. At one plant, sex abuses were reported. Thuyen Nguyen, founder of Vietnam Labor Watch, issued the report. He said about 35,000 workers at five Vietnamese plants—almost all young women—put in 12-hour days making Nike shoes. Though labor costs amount to less than $2 a pair, the shoes retail up to $180 in the United States. So, the Vietnamese workers earn $2.40 a day, which was slightly more than the $2 it costs to buy three meals a day. McLain Ramsey, Nike spokeswoman, reported that the manager at that plant was suspended and that an accounting firm had been hired to inspect the factories for abuses. She asked, "What is Nike's responsibility?" and further stated, "But we have put in the time and energy to make what are in many cases good factories into better factories." [70]

- **Incident Two:** Subcontractors making shoes in China for Nike and Reebok used workers as young as 13 who earned as little as 10 cents an hour toiling up to 17 hours a day in enforced silence (a violator could be fined $1.20 to $3.60), the independent observers charged. The watchdog group, Global Exchange, provided a study of the Chinese factories to the Associated Press. The report described the companies' motives this way: "Where in the world can we find the cheapest labor, even if in the most repressed circumstances." [71] Nike said the report was erroneous. Reebok said it monitored work records at these plants. Global Exchange stated that the subcontractors at all four sites with about 80,000 employees violated not only "the most basic tenets of Chinese labor law, they're also flagrantly violating [Nike and Reebok's] own code of conduct," [72] which the companies formulated to regulate their practices overseas.

- **Resolve One:** Nike hired former U.N. Ambassador Andrew Young to review its labor practices in Asia. He acknowledged some incidents of worker abuse, such as forced overtime. But, he said, he found no pattern of widespread mistreatment. [73]

- **Resolve Two:** In September 1997, Chairman Phil Knight announced at the company's shareholders' meeting that Nike had severed contracts with four factories in Indonesia where wages being paid workers were the government minimum wage. [74]

- **Resolve Three:** In January 1998, Nike hired Maria Eitel, a former Microsoft public relations executive, to the newly created position of Vice-President, Corporate and Social Responsibility. Eitel would be responsible for Nike's labor practices, environmental affairs, and "global community involvement." Thomas Clarke, Nike's President and CEO, said the hiring of Eitel "signals Nike's commitment from the top to be a leader not only in developing footwear, apparel and equipment, but in global corporate citizenship." [75] Eitel said, "Nike has been an easy target [for critics] because of its high profile." She further stated, "we have to put this into perspective," and "This isn't just Nike's issue. It's an industry and government issue as well." [76]

- **Resolve Four:** On May 12, 1998, Phil Knight "pledged to raise the minimum worker age and let human rights groups help monitor its foreign plants, which employ half a million workers." [77] Nike used U.S. safety and health standards in these plants. Nike would also summarize the human rights groups' conclusion. An analyst felt Phil Knight's new labor policies would put pressure on other U.S. companies operating in developing nations.

FINANCIAL PERFORMANCE

Management Report on 1997 Operating Results

Net sales for the year ended December 31, 1997, were $3.644 billion, a 4.7% increase from the year ended December 31, 1996, sales of $3.479 billion, which included $49.4 million of sales from the company's Avia subsidiary that had been sold in June 1996. The Reebok Division's worldwide sales (including Greg Norman) were $3.131 billion in 1997, a

5.0% increase from comparable sales of $2.982 billion in 1996. The stronger U.S. dollar had adversely impacted Reebok Brand worldwide sales comparisons with the prior year. On a constant dollar basis, sales for the Reebok Brand worldwide increased 8.3% in 1997 as compared to 1996. The Reebok Division's U.S. footwear sales increased 3.0% to $1.229 billion in 1997 from $1.193 billion in 1996. The increase in the Reebok Division's U.S. footwear sales was attributed primarily to increases in the running, walking, and men's cross-training categories. The increase in sales in these categories was partially offset by decreases in Reebok's basketball, outdoor, and women's fitness categories. The underlying quality of Reebok footwear sales in the United States improved from 1996. Sales to athletic specialty accounts increased approximately 31%, and the amount of off-price sales declined from 7.6% of total Reebok footwear sales in 1996 to 3.2% of total Reebok footwear sales in 1997. The Reebok Division's U.S. apparel sales increased by 37.2% to $431.9 million from $314.9 million in 1996. The increase resulted primarily from increases in branded core basics, licensed, and graphic categories. The Reebok Division's international sales (including footwear and apparel) were $1.471 billion in 1997, approximately equal to the Division's international sales in 1996 of $1.474 billion. The international sales comparison was negatively impacted by changes in foreign currency exchange rates. On a constant dollar basis, for the year ended December 31, 1997, the international sales gain was 6.4%. All international regions generated sales increases over the prior year on a constant dollar basis. For international sales, increases in the running, classic, and walking categories were offset by decreases in the basketball and tennis categories. Generally in the industry there was in 1998 a slowdown in branded athletic footwear and apparel at retail, and there was a significant amount of promotional product offered across all distribution channels. As a result of this situation and the expected ongoing negative impact from currency fluctuations, it would be difficult to increase reported sales for the Reebok Brand in 1998.

Rockport's sales for 1997 increased by 14.5% to $512.5 million from $447.6 million in 1996. Exclusive of the Ralph Lauren footwear business, which was acquired in May 1996, Rockport's sales increased 7.3% in 1997. International revenues, which grew by 46.0%, accounted for approximately 21.0% of Rockport's sales (excluding Ralph Lauren Footwear) in 1997, as compared to 16.0% in 1996. Increased sales in the walking and men's categories were partially offset by decreased sales in the women's lifestyle category. The decrease in the women's lifestyle category was the result of a strategic initiative to refocus the women's business around an outdoor, adventure, and travel positioning and reduce the product offerings in the refined women's dress shoe segment. Rockport continued to attract younger customers to the brand with the introduction of a wider selection of dress and casual products. The Ralph Lauren footwear business performed well in 1997 and was beginning to generate sales growth in its traditional segments, reflecting the benefits of improved product design and development and increased distribution. Rockport planned to expand the current product line of Ralph Lauren Polo Sport athletic footwear during 1998 with additional products available at retail during 1999.

The company's gross margin declined from 38.4% in 1996 to 37.0% in 1997. Margins were being negatively impacted by both start-up costs and initially higher manufacturing costs on the company's new technology products (DMX 2000 and 3D Ultralite). In addition, the decline reflected a significant impact from currency fluctuations as a result of the stronger U.S. dollar and a decrease in full-margin, at-once business as a result of an over-inventoried promotional retail environment. The company estimated that 100 basis points of the margin decline was due to currency. Looking forward, the company expected margins to continue to be under pressure through at least the first half of 1998. However, the company believed that if the technology product line expanded and gained greater critical mass and with improving production capabilities, the new technology products were capable of generating margin improvement.

Selling, general, and administrative expenses decreased as a percentage of sales from 30.6% in 1996 to 29.4% in 1997. The reduction was primarily due to the absence of certain advertising and marketing expenses associated with the 1996 Summer Olympics. In addition, non-brand building general and administrative infrastructure expenses declined. Research, design, and development expenses increased 27.0% for the year and retail operating expenses increased in support of new store openings. At December 31, 1997, the company operated 157 Reebok, Rockport, and Greg Norman retail stores in the United States as compared to 141 at the end of 1996.

Interest expense increased as a result of the additional debt the company incurred to finance the shares acquired during the 1996 Dutch Auction share repurchase.[78]

Exhibits 7 and 8 are Reebok's Consolidated Statement of Income and Balance Sheets.

The highlights of the Reebok report of first quarter 1998 results are shown below:[79]

- Net sales in the 1998 first quarter were $880.1 million, a decrease of 5.4% from 1997's first quarter net sales of $930.0 million. Worldwide sales for the Reebok brand in the 1998 first quarter were $750.5 million, a decrease of 7.5% from 1997's first quarter sales of $811.6 million. Approximately half of the decline in the Reebok brand sales is due to currency fluctuations, primarily as a result of the strength of the U.S. dollar and the devaluation of certain Asian currencies.

- In the U.S., Reebok footwear sales in the current year quarter were $293.7 million, a decrease of 12.2% from 1997 U.S. footwear sales of $334.6 million. Reebok apparel sales in the United States were $96.8 million for the quarter, as compared with 1997's first quarter apparel sales of $97.9 million.

- Sales of the Reebok brand outside the United States—including both footwear and apparel—decreased 5.0% in the 1998 first quarter to $360.0 million from $379.1 million in 1997. On a constant dollar basis, international revenues grew approximately 2.0% in the first quarter of 1998 as compared to the first quarter of 1997.

- Sales for the company's Rockport subsidiary grew 9.5% to $129.6 million from $118.4 million in the first quarter of 1997.

- The company reported that its total backlog of open customer orders to be delivered from April 1998 through September 1998 for the Reebok brand was down 3.8%. North American backlog was down 9.0%, and international backlog increased 5.7%. On a constant dollar basis, worldwide Reebok brand backlog was down 2.6%, and international backlog was up 9.5%.

- As previously announced, the company recorded a special pre-tax charge of $35.0 million in the first quarter of 1998 for personnel-related expenses in connection with ongoing business re-engineering efforts and the restructuring of certain underperforming marketing contracts. As a result of this charge, the company reported a first quarter 1998 net loss of $3.4 million, or $0.06 per share. In 1997, the company had reported a profit of $40,184,000 or $0.72 per share.

Commenting on these poor first quarter results, Paul Fireman said,

The company's overall results were in line with our expectations and reflect the continuing difficult conditions in the athletic footwear and apparel industry, which is experiencing an

Exhibit 7   Consolidated Statements of Income: Reebok International, Ltd.
(Dollar amounts in thouands, except per-share data)

Year Ending December 31	1997	1996	1995
Net sales	$ 3,643,599	$ 3,478,604	$ 3,481,450
Other income (expense)	(6,158)	4,325	3,126
Total income	3,637,441	3,482,929	3,484,576
Costs and expenses			
Cost of sales	2,294,049	2,144,422	2,114,084
Selling, general, and administrative expenses	1,069,433	1,065,792	999,731
Special charges	58,161	—	72,098
Amortization of intangibles	4,157	3,410	4,067
Interest expense	64,366	42,246	25,725
Interest income	(10,810)	(10,609)	(7,103)
Total costs and expenses	3,479,356	3,245,261	3,208,602
Income before income taxes and minority interest	158,085	237,668	275,974
Income taxes	12,490	84,083	99,753
Income before minority interest	145,595	153,585	176,221
Minority interest	10,476	14,635	11,423
Net income	$ 135,119	$ 138,950	$ 164,798
Basic earnings per share	$ 2.41	$ 2.06	$ 2.10
Diluted earnings per share	$ 2.32	$ 2.03	$ 2.07
Dividends per common share	$ —	$ 0.225	$ 0.300
Common shares issued	93,115,835	92,556,295	111,015,133

Source: Reebok International, Ltd., *1997 Annual Report*, pp. 26–27.

over-inventoried and highly promotional environment. Despite these difficulties, however, we did achieve strong sell-throughs on several of our marquis product introductions during the quarter, including our 3D Ultralite product, the Shroud, and our new DMX 6 running shoe. We think these successes are indicative of our ability to apply our two new proprietary technologies, DMX and 3D Ultralite, and we will continue our efforts to market these technologies through unique direct-to-the-consumer campaigns that allow customers to experience our products first-hand. During the quarter we started the Reebok "Try on the Future" Tour using vans and kiosks in major malls to take our products direct to the consumer. Our experience is that when consumers try on our technologies, they are much more likely to buy our product. In addition to this marketing campaign, we will launch a brand image advertising campaign which will debut during the second quarter, and we are optimistic that this along with our product specific advertising will begin to generate excitement and momentum for the Reebok brand.[80]

Exhibit 8   Consolidated Balance Sheets: Reebok International, Ltd.
(Dollar amounts in thouands, except per-share data)

Year Ending December 31	1997	1996
Assets		
Current assets		
Cash and cash equivalents	$ 209,766	$ 232,365
Accounts receivable, net of allowance for doubtful accounts		
(1997: $44,003; 1996: $43,527)	561,729	590,504
Inventory	563,735	544,522
Deferred income taxes	75,186	69,422
Prepaid expenses and other current assets	54,404	26,275
Total current assets	1,464,820	1,463,088
Property and equipment, net	156,959	185,292
Non-current assets		
Intangibles, net of amortization	65,784	69,700
Deferred income taxes	19,371	7,850
Other	49,163	60,254
	134,318	137,804
Total assets	$1,756,097	$1,786,184
Liabilities and Shareholders' Equity		
Current liabilities		
Notes payable to banks	$ 40,665	$ 32,977
Current portion of long-term debt	121,000	52,684
Accounts payable	192,142	196,368
Accrued expenses	219,386	169,344
Income taxes payable	4,260	65,588
Total current liabilities	577,453	516,961
Long-term debt, net of currrent portion	639,355	854,099
Minority interest	32,132	33,890
Shareholders' equity		
Common stock, par value $.01; authorized 250,000,000 shares;		
issued 93,115,835 shares in 1997; 92,556,295 shares in 1996	931	926
Retained earnings	1,145,271	992,563
Less 36,716,227 shares in treasury at cost	(617,620)	(617,620)
Unearned compensation	(140)	(283)
Foreign currency translation adjustment	(21,285)	5,648
Total shareholders' equity	507,157	381,234
Total liabilities and shareholders' equity	$1,756,097	$1,786,184

Source: Reebok International, Ltd., *1997 Annual Report,* p. 28.

Notes

1. Reebok International, Ltd., *1997 Annual Report,* pp. 7–11. This letter was directly quoted and one sentence deleted.
2. *Footwear News,* May 8, 1995.
3. *Ibid.*
4. Joseph Pereira, "In Reebok—Nike War, Big Woolworth Chain Was a Major Battleground," *Wall Street Journal* (September 22, 1995), p. A-1.
5. *Ibid.*
6. *Ibid.*
7. Reebok International, Ltd., *1996 Annual Report,* p. 36.
8. Reebok International, Ltd., *1997 Annual Report,* p. 39.
9. Reebok International, Ltd., *1998 Notice of Annual Meeting of Shareholders,* p. 5. This was directly quoted.
10. *Wall Street Journal* (August 23, 1995), p. B-7.
11. Reebok International, Ltd., *Form 10-K* (December 31, 1997), pp. 18–20.
12. Kenneth Labich, "Nike vs. Reebok," *Fortune* (September 18, 1995), p. 104.
13. *Ibid.*
14. *Ibid.*
15. Reebok International, Ltd., *Form 10-K* (December 31, 1997), p. 20.
16. Reebok International, Ltd., *1998 Notice of Annual Meeting of Shareholders,* p. 8.
17. Reebok International, Ltd., *Form 10-K* (December 31, 1997), pp. 2–3. The above three paragraphs were directly quoted with minor editing.
18. *Ibid.,* pp. 8–9. The above ten paragraphs were directly quoted with minor editing.
19. Reebok International, Ltd., *Form 10-K* (December 31, 1997), p. 9. The above three paragraphs were directly quoted with minor editing.
20. Reebok International, Ltd., *1997 Annual Report,* p. 17. The above paragraph was directly quoted with minor editing.
21. Reebok International, Ltd., *Form 10-K* (December 31, 1997), pp. 6–7. The above three paragraphs were directly quoted with minor editing.
22. *Ibid.,* p. 16. The above paragraph was directly quoted with minor editing.
23. *Ibid.,* pp. 11–12. The above six paragraphs were directly quoted with minor editing.
24. *Ibid.,* p. 18. The above paragraph was directly quoted with minor editing.
25. Stefan Fatsis, "Nike Kicks in Millions to Sponsor Soccer in U.S.," *Wall Street Journal* (October 22, 1997), p. B-1.
26. Joseph Pereira, "Women Jump Ahead of Men in Purchase of Athletic Shoes," *Wall Street Journal* (May 26, 1995), p. B-1.
27. Kathryn Kranhold, "L.A. Gear Plans to Restructure, Cutting Jobs," *Wall Street Journal* (November 4, 1997), p. 6.
28. J. Solomon, "When Cool Goes Cold," *Newsweek* (March 30, 1998), p. 37.
29. Susan Pulliam and Laura Bird, "Season's Casual Shoe Trend Means Some Firms Will Get Stomped . . . ," *Wall Street Journal* (August 27, 1997), p. C-1.
30. *Ibid.*
31. "A Fast Ride Uphill," *St. Petersburg Times* (April 14, 1998), p. 10-A.
32. *Ibid.*
33. *Ibid.,* p. 9A–10A.
34. *Ibid.,* p. 10A.
35. Bill Meyers, "Jordan Inc.," *USA Today* (September 9, 1997), p. 1A, and Oscar Dixon, "Air Apparent Executive," *USA Today* (September 9, 1997), p. 3C.
36. Kenneth Labich, "Nike vs. Reebok," *Fortune* (September 18, 1995), pp. 14–16.
37. *Ibid.,* p. 92.
38. *Ibid.*
39. *Ibid.,* p. 100
40. Joseph Pereira, "Sneaker Company Tag Out-of-Breath Baby Boomers," *Wall Street Journal* (January 1, 1998), p. B-1.
41. *Ibid.*
42. *Ibid.*
43. Jonathan B. Chappell, "Stride Rite," *Value Line* (February 20, 1998), p. 1672.
44. Cecile Rohwedder and Matt Marshall, "Germany's Adidas Was Seen Sprinting Toward Making Initial Public Offering," *Wall Street Journal* (September 18, 1995), p. A7B.
45. Reebok International, Ltd., *Form 10-K* (December 31, 1997), p. 4. The above paragraph was directly quoted with minor editing.
46. *Ibid.* The above two paragraphs were cited directly with minor editing.
47. "Reebok Issues Apology for Naming Shoe 'Incubus'," *Wall Street Journal* (February 26, 1997), p. B12.
48. *Ibid.,* pp. 4–5. The above five paragraphs, not including note 47, were cited directly with minor editing.
49. *Ibid.,* p. 12.
50. *Ibid.,* p. 13, and *1997 Annual Report,* p. 39.
51. *Ibid.,* p. 7. The above four paragraphs were cited directly with minor editing.
52. I. Jeanne Dugan, "Why Foot Locker Is in a Sweat," *Business Week* (October 27, 1997), p. 52.
53. *Ibid.*
54. *Ibid.*
55. *Ibid.*
56. Joseph Pereira, "In Reebok-Nike War," p. A-1.
57. *Ibid.,* p. A-5
58. *Ibid.*
59. *Ibid.*
60. *Ibid.*
61. Labich, p. 104
62. Pereira, "In Reebok-Nike War," p. A-1.
63. Reebok International, Ltd., *Form 10-K* (December 31, 1997), pp. 9–10. The above five paragraphs were directly quoted with minor editing.
64. *Ibid.,* pp. 10–11. The above four paragraphs were directly quoted with minor editing.
65. *Ibid.,* pp. 3–4. The above five paragraphs were directly quoted with minor editing.
66. *Ibid.,* p. 11. The above three paragraphs were directly quoted with minor editing.

67. *Ibid.,* p. 13. The above paragraph was directly quoted with minor editing.
68. *Ibid.,* p. 18. The above paragraph was directly quoted with minor editing.
69. Reebok International, Ltd., *1997 Annual Report,* p. 18. The four below paragraphs were directly quoted with minor editing.
70. "Activist: Nike-makers Abused," *St. Petersburg Times* (March 28, 1997), p. 6-E.
71. "Report Blasts Nike, Reebok Subcontractors," *St. Petersburg Times* (July 21, 1997), p. 3-A.
72. *Ibid.*
73. "Nike Factory Manager Sentenced," *St. Petersburg Times* (June 29, 1997), p. E1.
74. "Nike Cancels Pacts with Indonesia Plants Over Wage Policies," *The Wall Street Journal* (September 23, 1997), p. B-6.
75. Bill Richards, "Nike Hires an Executive from Microsoft for New Post Focusing on Labor Policies," p. B-14.
76. *Ibid.*
77. Aaron Bernstein, "Nike Finally Does It," *Business Week* (May 25, 1998), p. 46.
78. Reebok International, Ltd., *1997 Annual Report,* pp. 20–21. The above five paragraphs were directly quoted with minor editing.
79. Reebok International, Ltd., *Reebok Report First Quarter 1998 Results* (April 22, 1998), pp. 1–2. The below six paragraphs were directly quoted with minor editing.
80. *Ibid.,* p. 3. The above paragraph was directly quoted with minor editing.

The U.S. Major Home Appliance Industry (1996): Domestic versus Global Strategies

J. David Hunger

The U.S. major home appliance industry in 1996 was an example of a very successful industry. Contrasted with the U.S. automobile and consumer electronics industries, U.S. major appliance manufacturers had been able to ward off Japanese competition and were actually on the offensive internationally. Imports to the United States of major home appliances (primarily microwave ovens and small refrigerators) were only a small proportion of total sales. For "white goods"—refrigerators, freezers, washing machines, dryers, ranges, microwave ovens, and dishwashers—over 84% of those sold in the United States were made domestically.[1] The industry had been very successful in keeping prices low and in improving the value of its products. Compared to 1982, major home appliance prices had increased more slowly than the increase in U.S. earnings and the consumer price index (CPI). Thus the average American consumer in 1996 could earn a new appliance in 80% fewer hours on the job than a half-century ago. For example, although the price of a Maytag automatic washing machine had risen from $280 in 1949 to $440 in 1995, it had actually declined when inflation was considered. In addition, the energy efficiency of the most common major appliances had increased every year since 1972. Sales had also been increasing. More appliances were made and sold in the United States in 1994 than in any preceding year. (See Exhibits 1 and 2.) Although shipments for 1995 were down slightly, most industry analysts predicted that 1996 shipments should be fairly stable.

Nevertheless, the major home appliance industry faced some significant threats, as well as opportunities, as it moved through the last decade of the twentieth century. After 50 years of rising sales in both units and dollars, the North American market had reached maturity. Aside from some normal short-term fluctuations, future unit sales were expected to grow only 1%–2% percent annually on average for the foreseeable future. Operating margins had been dropping as appliance manufacturers were forced to keep prices low to be competitive, even though costs kept increasing. In Western Europe, however, a market already 25% larger than the mature North American appliance market, unit sales were expected to grow 2%–3% annually on average. This figure was expected to increase significantly as Eastern European countries opened their economies to world trade. Economies in Asia and Latin America were becoming more important to world trade as more countries moved toward free-market economies. Industry analysts expected appliance markets in these areas to grow at a rate of 5%–6% annually.[2] The industry was under pressure from governments around the world to make environmentally safe products and significantly improve appliance energy efficiency.

DEVELOPMENT OF THE U.S. MAJOR HOME APPLIANCE INDUSTRY

In 1945, there were approximately 300 U.S. major appliance manufacturers in the United States. By 1996, however, the "big five" of Whirlpool, General Electric, Maytag, A.B.

This industry note was prepared by Professor J. David Hunger of Iowa State University. This case was edited for SMBP—7th Edition. All rights reserved to the author. Copyright © 1996 by J. David Hunger. Reprinted by permission.

Exhibit 1   **U.S. Manufacturers' Unit Shipments of Major Home Appliances**
(Unit amounts in thousands)

Product	2000[1]	1995	1994	1993	1992	1991	1990	1985	1980
Compactors	128	98	130	125	126	129	185	177	235
Dishwashers									
Built-in	4,713	4,327	4,326	3,891	3,619	3,360	3,419	3,327	2,354
Portable	243	226	254	208	201	211	217	248	384
Disposers	4,945	4,519	4,798	4,436	4,195	4,002	4,137	4,105	2,962
Dryers									
Compact	258	160	220	275	275	268	275	189	207
Electric	4,252	4,020	4,036	3,853	3,563	3,295	3,318	2,891	2,287
Gas	1,381	1,205	1,303	1,221	1,154	1,018	1,002	834	682
Freezers									
Chest	979	933	960	871	1,005	794	723	634	963
Compact	350	357	340	368	360	355	351	237	310
Upright	730	756	731	735	686	620	573	602	789
Microwave Ovens									
Comb. ranges[2]	88	80	86	94	110	128	146	314	265
Countertop	7,946	7,760	7,830	7,130	6,990	7,233	8,193	9,727	3,320
Microwave/Convect.	129	115	125	130	280	300	303	256	NA
Over-the-range	1,087	1,100	924	778	625	674	780	900	NA
Range/Oven Hoods	3,029	2,740	2,725	2,650	2,522	2,342	2,450	2,588	2,400
Ranges, Electric									
Built-in	740	619	699	659	624	568	631	574	555
Free-standing	3,234	3,004	3,024	2,731	2,508	2,332	2,358	2,567	1,975
Glass/Ceramic[2]	575	450	400	320	257	150	85	86	155
Surface units	466	425	446	458	442	409	455	409	NA
Ranges, Gas									
Built-in	95	86	87	90	91	92	106	84	102
Free-standing	2,671	2,490	2,534	2,343	2,221	2,041	2,061	1,729	1,437
Surface units	368	278	337	322	301	268	262	NA	NA
Refrigerators									
Built-in	NA	123	122	115	100	NA	NA	NA	NA
Compact[2]	1,325	1,032	950	1,030	950	925	932	783	543
Standard	8,851	8,670	8,652	8,109	7,761	7,273	7,101	6,080	5,124
Washers									
Automatic	7,190	6,901	7,035	6,792	6,515	6,197	6,192	5,278	4,426
Compact	295	200	275	365	365	358	344	303	266
Water Heaters									
Electric	4,034	3,917	3,897	3,609	3,399	3,170	3,226	3,452	2,451
Gas	5,098	4,453	4,750	4,470	4,241	3,936	3,906	3,529	2,818
Total Appliances[3]	66,200	60,159	61,174	57,396	54,759	51,814	53,152	51,268	37,010

Notes:
1. Estimated.
2. Duplications, not included in total. Numbers have been rounded off.
3. Data for major electric appliances include all imports and exports.
Source: *Appliance* (April 1990), p. 33; (April 1995), p. 45; (January 1996), p. 42; (April 1996), p. 43.

Exhibit 2 **U.S. Manufacturers' Unit Shipments of Floor Care Appliances**
(Unit amounts in thousands)

Product	1995	1994	1993	1992	1991	1990	1989	1988	1985
Polishers	180	185	NA	NA	NA	NA	NA	NA	NA
Shampooers	1,825	2,300	1,950	1,600	1,200	1,000	NA	NA	NA
Vacuum Cleaners									
Cannisters	1,840	1,963	1,700	2,100	2,385	2,741	3,010	3,177	2,998
Central	174	157	141	134	129	130	NA	NA	NA
Handheld electric	3,140	3,750	3,810	3,610	2,900	2,500	1,900	1,050	564
Handheld rechargeable	2,380	2,500	2,640	2,740	3,500	5,000	5,125	5,300	5,440
Stick	2,320	2,060	1,825	1,600	1,500	1,644	1,893	1,725	1,077
Upright	10,737	10,215	9,250	8,330	6,960	6,578	6,470	5,750	4,438
Total Floor Care	22,596	23,130	21,316	20,114	18,574	19,593	18,398	17,002	14,517

Source: *Appliance* (April 1990), p. 35; (April 1995), p. 46; (January 1996), p. 44; (April 1996), p. 44.

Electrolux (*no* relation to Electrolux Corporation, a U.S. company selling Electrolux brand vacuum cleaners), and Raytheon controlled over 98% of the U.S. market. The consolidation of the industry over the period was a result of fierce domestic competition. Emphasis on quality and durability coupled with strong price competition drove the surviving firms to increased efficiencies and a strong concern for customer satisfaction.

Industry History

All of the major U.S. automobile firms except Chrysler had participated at one time in the major home appliance industry. Giants in the consumer electronics industry had also been involved heavily in appliances. Some of the major auto, electronics, and diversified companies active at one time in the appliance industry were General Motors (Frigidaire), Ford (Philco), American Motors (Kelvinator), Studebaker (Franklin), Bendix, International Harvester, General Electric, RCA, Emerson Electric, Westinghouse, McGraw Edison, Rockwell, United Technologies, Raytheon, Litton, Borg-Warner, and Dart & Kraft. Only General Electric, Raytheon, and Emerson Electric remained in major home appliances in 1996. Emerson Electric continued through its In-Sink-Erator line of disposers and dishwashers, as well as being a major supplier of electronic parts to the remaining appliance makers. Most of the other firms divested their appliance business units, many of which were acquired by White Consolidated Industries, which itself was acquired by the Swedish firm A.B. Electrolux in 1986 and subsequently renamed Frigidaire.

Prior to World War II, most appliance manufacturers produced a limited line of appliances derived from one successful product. General Electric made refrigerators. Maytag focused on washing machines. Hotpoint produced electric ranges. Each offered variations of its basic product, but not until 1945 did firms begin to offer full lines of various appliances. By 1955, the major appliance industry began experiencing overcapacity, leading to mergers and acquisitions and a proliferation of national and private brands.

The industry almost doubled in size during the 1960s as sales of several products grew rapidly. Dishwasher unit sales almost quadrupled. Unit sales of clothes dryers more than tripled. Product reliability improved even though real prices (adjusted for inflation) declined by about 10%.

Although the 1970s were a time of high inflation and high interest rates, the major home appliance industry continued to increase its unit sales. Profit margins were squeezed even more, and the industry continued to consolidate around fewer firms. Although antitrust considerations prevented GE and Whirlpool from acquiring other appliance units, White was able to buy the troubled appliance divisions of all the automobile manufacturers, along with Westinghouse's, as they were put up for sale.

The market continued to expand in the 1980s, thanks partially to the acceptance by the U.S. consumer of the microwave oven. By the 1990s, U.S. appliance manufacturers offered a full range of products even if they did not make the item themselves. A company would fill the gaps in its line by putting its own brand name on products it purchased from another manufacturer. For example, Whirlpool made trash compactors for Frigidaire (A.B. Electrolux), In-Sink-Erator (Emerson Electric), Jenn-Air, Magic Chef (Maytag), and Sears. Caloric (Raytheon) not only made gas ranges for its in-house Amana brand, but also for Whirlpool. General Electric made some microwave ovens for Caloric (Raytheon), Jenn-Air, Magic Chef (Maytag), and its own Hotpoint and RCA brands.

Product and Process Design

Innovations in the industry tended to be of three types: (1) new products that expanded the appliance market, (2) new customer-oriented features, and (3) process improvements to reduce manufacturing costs. New products that had strongly increased industry unit sales were dishwashers in the 1960s and microwave ovens in the 1980s. The combination washer–dryer and compact versions of other appliances, such as refrigerators and washers, were not very popular in the United States but had been successful in Europe and Asia where household space was at a premium and cultural norms favored daily over weekly food shopping. One potential new product was the microwave clothes dryer. The use of microwave energy for drying meant that clothes could be dried faster at a lower temperature (thus less shrinkage and damage) with less energy use than a conventional dryer. Unfortunately, the technology needed further development before it could be marketed; microwaves have a tendency to heat metal objects to such a point that they cause fabric damage.

Customer-oriented features included the self-cleaning oven, pilotless gas range, automatic ice cube–making refrigerator, and others. In most cases, features were introduced on top-of-the-line models and made available on lower priced models later. Manufacturers' own brands usually had the newest and most elaborate features, followed by national retailers such as Sears Roebuck and Montgomery Ward whose offerings usually copied the most successful features from the previous year. In this competitive industry, aside from patented features, no one producer could successfully keep a new innovation to itself for more than a year.

In the mid 1990s, three trends were evident. First, European visual product design was having a strong impact on appliance design worldwide. Frigidaire, for example, introduced a "Euroflair" line of appliances. A soft, rounded appearance was replacing the block, sharp-cornered look. Second, manufacturers were introducing "smart" appliances with increasingly sophisticated electronic controls and self-diagnostic features. The Japanese firms of Matsushita, Hitachi, Toshiba, and Mitsubishi had pioneered the use of "fuzzy logic" computer software to replace the many selector switches on an appliance with one start button. By 1996, all of the major U.S. home appliance manufacturers were using fuzzy logic to some extent in making and marketing their products. Whirlpool's new "Sixth Sense" oven could determine the necessary settings for reheating or defrosting food with no guesswork from the cook. The user simply pressed a single button for defrost; the oven then calculated on its own the correct time and power output. The third trend was the increasing emphasis on environmentally safe products, such as the use of CFC-free refrigerant, and on greater efficiency in the use of water and energy. Maytag, among others, was actively involved in developing a "horizontal axis" washing machine that would use significantly less water and electricity than its typical "vertical axis" washer.

Process improvements for more efficient manufacturing of current products (compared to new-product development) has tended to dominate research and development efforts in the U.S. major home appliance industry. Although modern appliances were much more effective and efficient, a refrigerator or a washing machine in the 1990s still looked and acted very much the same as it did in the 1950s. It was built in a far different manner, however. Richard Topping, director of the Center for Product Development of the consulting firm Arthur D. Little, indicated that the appliance industry historically had been characterized by low intensity in research and development because of intense cost competition and demand for higher reliability. Topping went on to stress that the basis for effective competition in the future would be in producing the fewest basic components necessary in the most efficient plants. Although individual designs might vary, the components inside the appliances would become more universal and would be produced in highly automated plants, using computer integrated manufacturing processes.[3] Examples of this emphasis on product simplification were Maytag's "Dependable Drive" and Whirlpool's frame fabrication for its "Eye Level" ranges. Maytag's new washer transmission was designed to have 40.6% fewer parts than the transmission it replaced. Fewer parts meant simplified manufacturing and less chance of a breakdown. The result was lower manufacturing costs and higher product quality.

Most industry analysts agreed that continual process improvements had kept U.S. major home appliance manufacturers dominant in their industry. The emphasis on quality and durability, coupled with a reluctance to make major design changes simply for the sake of change, resulted in products with long average life expectancy. With the average useful life of a refrigerator or range approaching 18 years and those of washers and dryers approaching 15 years, it was easy to see one reason why the Japanese manufacturers had been less successful in entering the U.S. appliance market than with automobiles. (See Exhibit 3.) Another reason was a constant unrelenting pressure to reduce costs or be driven from the marketplace.

Manufacturing and Purchasing

Although many manufacturing operations took place in an appliance factory, much of the process focused on proper preparation of the metal frame within which the washing, drying, or cooking components and elements would be attached. Consequently, appliance manufacturers could be characterized as "metal benders" who fabricated different shapes of metal boxes out of long coils of metal. Sophisticated machines would form and even weld the frames, and automated assembly lines and robots would add porcelain to protect the metal and add color to the finish. People were usually still needed to install the internal components in the frame and to wire sophisticated electronic controls. Quality control was often a combination of electronic diagnostics and personal inspection by employees.

Manufacturing costs were generally in the range of 65%–75% of total operating costs. (See Exhibit 4.) Although direct labor costs were still an important part of the cost of completed goods (about 10%), most companies were carefully examining material costs, general administration, and overhead for cost reduction. Traditionally, the optimal size of an assembly plant was considered to be an annual capacity of 500,000 units for

Exhibit 3   **Average Life Expectancy of Major Home Appliances (in years)**

Compactors	8
Dishwashers	9
Disposers	9
Dryers—electric	13
Dryers—gas	14
Freezers	12
Microwave ovens	10
Ranges—electric	15
Ranges—gas	18
Refrigerators	15
Washers	13
Vacuum cleaners	10
Floor polishers	12
Water heaters—electric	10
Water heaters—gas	9

Source: *Appliance* (September 1992), pp. 46–47; (September 1995), p. 73.

refrigerators, ranges, washers, dryers, and dishwashers. Even though production costs were believed to be 10%–40% percent higher in smaller sized plants, the use of robots suggested that the optimal plant could be even smaller than previously believed.[4]

During the 1990s, the trend continued toward dedicated manufacturing facilities combining product line production in fewer larger plants to gain economies of scale. Although a dedicated production line for washing machines could be adjusted to make many different models, it could still only be used to make washing machines. Each product category required its own specialized manufacturing equipment.

All of the major home appliance manufacturers were engaged in renovating and building production facilities to gain economies of scale, improve quality, and reduce labor and materials costs. Frigidaire had just finished spending over $600 million upgrading its current factories and building new refrigerator and dishwasher plants. General Electric was investing some $1 billion over a four-year period in appliance product development and capital equipment—a 50% increase over previous spending levels. Whirlpool had completely renovated the manufacturing processes and its labor management system in its aging tooling and plating factory in Benton Harbor—thus increasing productivity more than 19%.

As the major home appliance industry had consolidated, so too had their suppliers. The purchasing function and relationship with suppliers changed considerably in the 1980s as more companies used fewer suppliers and more long-term contracts to improve quality and ensure just-in-time (JIT) delivery. Along with its global orientation, Whirlpool was also putting emphasis on working with global suppliers. Appliance companies used certification programs to ensure that their smaller supplier bases were able to supply both the needed quantity and quality of materials, parts, and subassemblies when they were needed. Full-line, full-service suppliers had an advantage over one-dimensional suppliers. Appliance makers continued to put pressure on their suppliers to institute cost-saving productivity improvements. On the other hand, they were much more willing to involve suppliers earlier in the design stage of a product or process improvement. Joe Thomson, Vice-President of Purchasing at Maytag's Galesburg Refrigeration Products unit, provides one example:

Exhibit 4   The Major Home Appliance Value Chain

Sales		100%
Manufacturing costs		65–75
Fully integrated		
raw materials	30–40%	
labor	6–10	
plant and equipment	12–20	
general administration	12–20	
Not integrated		
components	35–45	
labor and overhead	30–40	
Transportation and warehousing		5–7
Advertising		1–2
Sales and marketing		4–8
Service		2–5
Product research and development		2–5
Overhead		2–10

Source: C. R. Christensen, K. R. Andrews, J. L. Bower, R. G. Hamermesh, and M. E. Porter, "Note on the Major Home Appliance Industry in 1984 (Condensed)," *Business Policy,* 6th ed. (Homewood, Ill., Irwin, 1987), p. 339.

We made an arrangement with a large steel supplier that led to a team effort to establish hardness specifications on our cabinet and door steel to improve fabrication. This team was very successful and the quality improvement and reduction in cost reached all our expectations. The company is now supplying all of our steel requirement.[5]

These alliances between appliance makers and their suppliers were one way to speed up the application of new technology to new products and processes. For example, Maytag Company was approached by one of its suppliers who offered its expertise in fuzzy logic technology—a technology Maytag did not have at that time. The resulting partnership in product development resulted in Maytag's new IntelliSense™ dishwasher. Unlike previous dishwashers, which had to be set by the user, Maytag's fuzzy logic dishwasher automatically selected the proper cycle to get the dishes clean based on a series of factors, including the amount of dirt and presence of detergent.

Some of the key materials purchased by the U.S. appliance industry were steel (primarily in sheets and coils from domestic suppliers), plastics, coatings (paint and porcelain), motors, glass, insulation, wiring, and fasteners. By weight, major appliances consisted of about 75% steel. Sales to the major home appliance industry of steel and aluminum together accounted for 10% of total industry sales.[6]

Marketing and Distribution Channels

Due to relatively high levels of saturation in the United States, the market for major home appliances was driven primarily by the demand for replacements. Washers, ranges, refrigerators, and even microwave ovens were in more than 70% of U.S. households. (See Exhibit 5.) Generally speaking, replacements accounted for 75% of sales, new housing for 20%, and new household formation for about 5% of sales of major home appliances. Replacement demand was usually driven by existing housing turnover, remodeling, changes in living arrangement trends, introduction of new features, and price levels in the economy. Although each new house had the potential to add four to six new appliances, the

Exhibit 5 **Major Home Appliance Saturation in the United States, Western Europe, and Japan**
(Households with at least one of a particular appliance)

Appliance	United States	Western Europe[1]	Japan
Dishwashers	52%	29%	NA
Freezers	40	47	NA
Microwave ovens	89	43	87%
Ranges/ovens	99	95	NA
Refrigerators	99	97	98
Dryers	70	21	19
Washers	75	90	99
Vacuums	97	86	98
Water heaters	99	NA	30
Floor polishers	7	NA	NA
Floor shampooers	9	NA	NA

Note:

1. Composite of Austria, Belgium/Luxembourg, Switzerland, Germany, Denmark, Spain, France, Great Britain (U.K.), Greece, Italy, Ireland, Norway, the Netherlands, Portugal, Sweden, and Finland.

Source: *Appliance* (September 1995), pp. 74–75; (June 1995), p. 46; (February 1996), p. 73.

sale of an existing house also had an impact. According to J. Richard Stonesifer, President and CEO of GE Appliances, "About 4 million existing homes are sold each year, and approximately one new appliance is sold for every existing home that changes hands."[7] The National Kitchen and Bath Association estimated that about $4 billion of the total $25 billion spent annually on kitchen remodeling was for home appliances. Both the new housing and remodeling markets in the 1990s tended to emphasize more upscale appliances in contrast to the previous tendency for builders to economize by buying the cheapest national brand appliances.[8] A study by Simmons Market Research Bureau for New Home magazine revealed that more than $13 billion was spent annually by new-home owners on household goods, especially appliances. In order of importance, the appliances typically bought within the first three months of owning a new home were the refrigerator, washer, dryer, microwave oven, vacuum cleaner, dishwasher, coffeemaker, and range.[9] This phenomenon provided sales opportunities for well-positioned appliance makers because brand loyalty in the appliance industry was only 35%.[10]

Changes in U.S. demographics in the 1990s favored the highly profitable, high-end, high-profile segment of the business. This trend was detrimental to the mass market business, which emphasized cost over features. The aging of the baby boomers and the increase of two-income families had increased the upscale market, which demanded more style and costly features. Appliance manufacturers were responding by expanding product lines that emphasized quality and features. Those brands most identified in customers' minds with high product quality were most likely to do well. (See Exhibit 6.)

Exporting was reasonably strong for high-quality U.S.-made refrigerators, vacuum cleaners, and laundry appliances, but was much less than the importing of microwave ovens from Asia. For a number of reasons, exporting was not a significant factor for the U.S. major home appliance industry. The weight of most of these appliances meant high transportation costs, which translated into higher prices to the consumer. In addition, U.S.-made major appliances tended to be fairly large, whereas European and Asian markets preferred smaller appliances. As a result, most people around the world tended to buy appliances made locally, if they were available. Thus, appliance companies wanting a significant presence in other parts of the world were either acquiring local companies,

Exhibit 6   **Rating of Brands by Retailers in Terms of Customer Perception of Quality[1]**

Brand	Excellent	Very Good
Maytag	90%	9%
KitchenAid	84	14
Jenn-Air	61	35
Amana	54	40
Monogram	44	26
Whirlpool	39	56
GE	28	59
Speed Queen	8	52
Frigidaire	6	56
RCA	6	41
Tappan	2	42
Magic Chef	2	41
Hotpoint	2	39
Caloric	1	31
White–Westinghouse	1	28
Roper	1	25
Gibson	1	20
Kelvinator	0	11
Admiral	0	11

Note:
1. Responses were by 536 appliance dealers that were members of the North American Retail Dealers Association. Each brand was evaluated as excellent, very good, good, and poor. Only the percentages of excellent and very good responses are shown here.

Source: J. Jancsurak, "In Their Opinion," *Appliance Manufacturer* (April 1995), p. 45.

engaging in joint ventures, or building new manufacturing facilities in those regions in order to have a local presence.

There were two major distribution channels for major home appliances in the United States: contract and retail. A third, but less important, distribution channel was the commercial market, comprising laundromats and institutions.

Contract sales were made to large home builders and to other appliance manufacturers. Direct sales accounted for about 80% of contract sales. Firms sold appliances to the contract segment both directly to the large builders and indirectly through local builder suppliers. Since builders were very cost conscious, they liked to buy at the middle to low end of a well-known appliance brand. Consequently, appliance manufacturers with strong offerings in this range, such as Whirlpool and General Electric, tended to do very well in this market. In contrast, companies such as Maytag, which traditionally emphasized high-end products, sold little (except for the lower priced Magic Chef brand) to home builders. Whirlpool and GE designed whole kitchen concepts and sold the entire package—including their appliances—to builders. To further its advantage, Whirlpool opened a 35,000-square-foot customer center at its Benton Harbor headquarters in 1993 to demonstrate its offerings to retailers and contractors—the first such customer center in the industry.

Retail sales in the United States were made to three major kinds of outlets: (1) national chain stores and mass merchandisers; (2) department, furniture, and discount stores; and (3) appliance dealers. Sales to national chain stores and mass merchandisers were usually private brands promoted by the retailers. For example, Whirlpool had traditionally been a heavy supplier of Sears and Kenmore brand appliances to Sears,

Roebuck. Magic Chef sold similar private brand appliances to Montgomery Ward. Some 30%–40% of white goods were traditionally sold through this channel. Sears, Roebuck had been so strong in major home appliance sales that it alone sold one of four major appliances sold in the United States.

Department stores, furniture stores, and discount stores were another important channel for major appliances—selling some 20% of white goods sold in the United States. These stores usually purchased well-known brands to offer their customers. As department stores tended to alter their product offerings to more soft goods (clothing items) and less hard goods (furniture and appliances) during the 1980s, discount stores became more important in major home appliance sales. Their concern with price, however, put even more pressure on manufacturers to sell in large quantity at low price.

Appliance dealers had traditionally been an important retail outlet for white goods. About 30%–40% of major home appliances were sold through this channel. In the late 1980s and early 1990s, many locally owned stores were being replaced by national chains. Richard Haines, Executive Vice-President of Maytag Corporation, explained the impact of changes in distribution channels on his firm:

> When we [Maytag Company] decided to expand our offerings beyond laundry and dishwashers, one of the reasons we did so was the changing marketplace. What we saw happening was a significant decrease in the number of independent Mom and Pop dealerships that used to be the mainstay of the retail appliance business. The field was becoming increasingly dominated by national power retailers and by regional super stores.
>
> These new age marketers make their livings on high volume sales with relatively low unit margins. To maintain profitability, they must seek out the lowest wholesale prices possible from manufacturers on large volume buys. By purchasing only a few full lines of major appliances, today's retailers develop the clout they need with individual appliance producers to get the best pricing at wholesale and, therefore, the best margins at retail.
>
> Manufacturers who wish to compete in this new arena need a full line of products plus the capacity and manufacturing efficiency to make the volume sales mass merchants require.[11]

By the 1990s, the so-called "power retailers"—Sears, Montgomery Wards, and regional appliance chains, such as Circuit City—were selling over 60% of all retail appliances in the United States.

The *commercial market* was an additional distribution channel. Never as important to manufacturers as the contract and retail channels, this market nevertheless was an important set of customers for sales of washing machines and dryers. Laundromats and institutions, such as colleges for their dormitories, typically bought the most durable appliances made for the home market. Manufacturers simply added coin meters to the top of the washers and dryers destined for use in these commercial or public establishments. Although these home laundry appliances adapted for the commercial market comprised over 50% of sales to this channel, there were some indications that this market might be moving to commercial washers built to last 2–3 times longer than would a home washer used commercially. With regard to the makers of freezers, refrigerators, and ranges for use in business establishments such as restaurants, these were usually a different group of U.S. manufacturers (for example, Traulsen, Hobart, and Glenco) from those manufacturing home appliances.

Appliance manufacturing in 1996 was shifting from a primary emphasis on quality and reliability to speed and agility as well. This meant that manufacturers were working to improve their use of logistics in order to provide better service to their distributors. The JIT concept had been introduced during the 1980s in order to improve manufacturing efficiency. Similar concepts were now being applied in the 1990s to distribution and marketing. For example, Whirlpool introduced "Quality Express" in 1992 as part of its revamped distribution system. Quality Express used dedicated trucks, personnel, and warehousing to deliver Whirlpool, KitchenAid, Roper, and Estate brand appliances to 90% of all dealer and builder customers within 24 hours and to 100% within 48 hours. As part of the service, drivers delivering product unloaded units from the truck and put them where the customer wanted them. This service even included uncrating, customizing, and installation if desired. Other appliance companies were following Whirlpool's lead. A 1995 survey of 2,000 North American appliance dealers reported the following ranking of appliance manufacturers in terms of how well they serviced retailers:

1. Whirlpool Corporation

2. Maytag Corporation

3. General Electric Appliances

4. Amana Refrigeration Company (Raytheon's appliance unit)

5. Frigidaire Group (AB Electrolux's U.S. appliance unit) [12]

Environmental Issues and Government Regulation

The major home appliance industry had rarely been a key target for criticism regarding safety or pollution as had the U.S. steel and automobile industries, among others. By the 1980s, however, this situation had changed. Chlorofluorocarbons (CFCs) used in refrigerator and freezer insulation and in refrigerant had been linked by the early 1980s to the depletion of the earth's ozone layer. A 1987 meeting of the developed nations in Montreal resulted in a Montreal Protocol signed by 46 countries. In November 1992, the members of the Montreal Protocol and others met to firm up the agreements concerning the elimination of the use of chlorine-containing, ozone-depleting CFCs and to create a schedule for the elimination of hydrochlorofluorocarbons (HCFCs), which had substantially lower ozone-depleting potential. By 1996, CFCs had been effectively eliminated from use in appliances. Although the schedule for the phaseout of HCFCs called for similar elimination by January 1, 2030, the European Union wanted a halt by 2015. [13]

Thus, U.S. refrigerator and freezer manufacturers faced a serious dilemma. On the one hand, governments were requiring less use of chemicals crucial to cooling. On the other hand, the U.S. Department of Energy (DOE) was requiring energy conservation improvements for refrigerators and freezers. These appliances had traditionally been notorious energy hogs, consuming about 20% of the electricity used in the American home. The appliance industry had worked significantly to make products more energy efficient over the decades. For example, from 1972 to 1990, for a typical top-mount, automatic defrost refrigerator (the most popular U.S. refrigerator), the amount of energy consumed dropped from 1,986 kilowatt hours per year to 950 kilowatt hours per year (kwh/yr). Chest freezer energy consumption dropped during the same period from 1,268 kwh/yr to 575 kwh/yr. Nevertheless, the DOE mandated further energy reductions for all refrigerators and freezers. Its standards required that the average residential refrigerator/freezer manufactured after 1998 use no more energy that that used by a 60-watt light bulb. Units imported into the United States were also required to meet the regulations. The dilemma being faced by the industry in the 1990s was that a reduction in the use of CFCs and HCFCs for cooling tended to reduce the efficiency of the appliance—thus increasing energy consumption.

Another issue facing appliance manufacturers was the presence of widely different standards for major appliances in countries around the world. These standards for quality and safety were drafted by such bodies as the British Standards Institute (BSI) in the United Kingdom, Japanese Industrial Standards Committee (JISC), AFNOR in France,

DIN in Germany, CSA in Canada, and UL in the United States. These standards had traditionally created entry barriers that served to fragment the major home appliance industry by country. In 1986, the Canadian Standards Association (CSA) signed a memorandum with UL, Inc. (Underwriters Laboratories) to harmonize the Canadian and U.S. standards. The UL also signed an agreement in 1993 with Mexico's ANCE to accredit electrical products in Mexico. The International Electotechnical Commission (IEC) standards were created to harmonize standards in the European Union and eventually to serve as worldwide standards with some national deviations to satisfy specific needs. The emergence of a true global market in major home appliances required the development of common world standards. By 1996, such standards were beginning to emerge.

PRODUCTS

Major home appliances, or white goods, as they were commonly called, were generally classified as laundry (washers and dryers), refrigeration (refrigerators and freezers), cooking (ranges and ovens), and other (dishwashers, disposals, and trash compactors) appliances. In addition to making white goods, a number of appliance manufacturers also made and sold floor care appliances, such as vacuum cleaners, carpet shampooers, and floor polishers. (See Exhibits 7–10 for detailed information by appliance category on market share, average retail price, and reliability.)

COMPETITORS

In 1996, five appliance manufacturers controlled over 98% of the U.S. major home appliance market, led by Whirlpool with 35% and General Electric with 29%. (See Exhibits 10 and 11.) Of these five, only A.B. Electrolux, Whirlpool, and GE appeared to be in good position to similarly dominate other world markets. Whirlpool was gaining share in both the United States and Europe. Although A.B. Electrolux was rapidly gaining market share in Europe, its Frigidaire unit was just as rapidly losing share in the United States. General Electric's joint venture with GEC of the United Kingdom (General Domestic Appliances) was successful in Great Britain, but so far had only minimal sales to the European continent. Its U.S. market share was increasing by about the same percentage that its European share was slipping. Nevertheless, GE had a significant presence in Mexico and in other world markets. Maytag's acquisition of Hoover in 1989 failed to provide Maytag Corporation with the desired international presence in major home appliances. Its sale of Hoover's major appliance units in 1995 left Maytag with no foothold in markets outside North America. Nevertheless, Maytag was successful in slightly raising its share of the U.S. market. Thanks to Frigidaire's declining market share, Maytag moved into third place in U.S. shipments and market share for 1995. Raytheon continued to improve its U.S. market share by emphasizing its Amana division, but—like Maytag—was only active in North America.

As the major home appliance industry increasingly became more global, industry analysts wondered if purely domestic companies like Maytag and Raytheon would continue to be successful in the future. The January 1996 announcement by the powerful German-based Bosch-Siemens Hausgerate GmbH that it was planning to build a 200,000-unit-capacity dishwasher plant in North Carolina with production to commence in 1997 to serve the North American market signalled that the U.S. major home

Exhibit 7   U.S. Market Shares in Percentage by Category

Category	1983	1992	1995
A. White Goods			
Compactors			
Whirlpool	48	70[1]	92[1]
GE	26	14	—
Broan	NA	14	8
Emerson Contract	NA	—	—
Thermador/Waste King	4	1	—
Others	22[2]	1	—
Disposers			
In-Sink-Erator	61	65	64
Electrolux (Anaheim)	—	17	17
Thermador/Waste King	8	10	10
Watertown Metal Products	—	2	6
Maytag	—	2	1
KitchenAid	—	2	2
Others	31[3]	2	—
Dishwashers			
GE	22	40	36
Whirlpool	13	31[4]	36[4]
Electrolux (Frigidaire)	7	20[5]	12[5]
Maytag	7	8	14
Thermador	—	1	1
Design & Manufacturing	36	—	—
Emerson Contract	13	—	—
Others	2	—	1
Dryers, electric			
Whirlpool	47	52	52
GE	17	18	19
Maytag	15	15	15
Electrolux (Frigidaire)	15	12	10
Raytheon (Speed Queen)	5	3	4
Others	1	—	—
Dryers, gas			
Whirlpool	47	53	53
Maytag	12	17[6]	14[6]
GE	16	14	15
Electrolux (Frigidaire)	15	10	12
Raytheon (Speed Queen)	5	4	6
Norge	4	—	—
Others	1	2	—
Freezers			
Electrolux (Frigidaire)	30	76	70
W.C. Wood	NA	14	29
Whirlpool	34	5	1
Raytheon (Amana)	6	5	—
Maytag (Admiral)	22	—[8]	—[8]
Others	8[7]	—	—
Microwave ovens			
Sharp	11	20	24
Samsung	7	18	13

(continued)

Exhibit 7   **U.S. Market Shares in Percentage by Category** *(continued)*

Category	1983	1992	1995
Matsushita (Panasonic, Quasar)	5	17	14
Electrolux (Frigidaire)	9	10	7
Goldstar	1	10	9
Sanyo	13	7	6
MCD (previously Maytag)	4	6	6
Raytheon (Amana)	11	4	3
Whirlpool	4	3	5
Toshiba	3	1	—
Others	20[9]	4	13
Range hoods			
Broan	30	51[10]	52[10]
Nutone	20	14	9
Rangaire	18	12	19
Watertown Metal Products	NA	12	11
Fasco	NA	4	—
Aubrey	12	—	—
Others	20[11]	7	9
Ranges, electric			
GE	32	30	41
Whirlpool	12	30[12]	22[12]
Maytag	—	17	14
Electrolux (Frigidaire)	16	15[13]	14[13]
Raytheon (Caloric)	8	7	7
Thermador/Waste King	—	1	—
Roper	10	—	—
Tappan	6	—	—
Others	1	—	2
Ranges, gas			
Maytag	—	27	22
Electrolux (Frigidaire)	6	25[14]	22[14]
Raytheon (Caloric)	18	22	20
GE	—	19[15]	26[15]
Brown	7	3	3
Peerless-Premier	—	3	3
Tappan	NA	—	—
Roper	14	—	—
Others	7	1	4
Refrigerators, full-size, stand-alone			
GE	31	35	38
Whirlpool	30	25	27
Electrolux (Frigidaire)	23	17	15
Maytag (Admiral)	12	13	10
Raytheon (Amana)	7	8	9
Others	—	2	1
Refrigerators, compact			
Sanyo	NA	62[16]	63[17]
GE/MABE	NA	16	21
Wanbao	NA	8	10
Whirlpool/Consul	NA	2	2
Others	NA	12	4
Refrigerators, built-in			
U-Line	NA	54[18]	58[19]
Marvel Industries	NA	27	27

(continued)

Exhibit 7   **U.S. Market Shares in Percentage by Category** *(continued)*

Category	1983	1992	1995
Sub-Zero Freezer	NA	10	12
Others	NA	9	3
Washers			
Whirlpool	48	52	53
GE	18	16	17
Maytag	15	17	17
Electrolux (Frigidaire)	15	11	11
Raytheon (Speed Queen)	4	4	2
Others	—	—	—
B. Floor Care: Vacuum Cleaners			
Upright, Cannister, Stick			
Hoover	40	34	35
Eureka	21	16	37
Royal	—	13	7
Regina	—	9	1
Whirlpool	4	9	—
Electrolux	10	6	2
Ryobi (Singer)	16	5	2
Kirby	8	4	3
Matsushita (Panasonic)	—	2	9[20]
Others	1	2	4[21]
Hand-held			
Royal	NA	43[22]	43
Black & Decker	NA	40	31
Hoover	NA	6	10
Eureka	NA	3	4
Bissel	NA	—	3
Ryobi (Singer)	NA	—	3
Douglas	NA	2	3
Regina	NA	4	1
Others	NA	2	2

Notes: 1. Includes Emerson Contract, a Whirlpool unit.
2. Includes 12 for Hobart's KitchenAid, 6 for Tappan, and 4 for Amana.
3. Includes 12 for Tappan, 11 for GE, and 7 for Hobart's KitchenAid.
4. Includes Emerson Contract, a Whirlpool unit.
5. Includes Design and Manufacturing, an Electrolux unit.
6. Includes Norge, a Maytag unit.
7. Includes 5 for GE.
8. No longer makes freezers.
9. Includes 16 for GE.
10. Includes Aubrey, now part of Broan.
11. Includes 10 for GE.
12. Includes Roper, a Whirlpool unit.
13. Includes Tappan, an Electrolux unit.
14. Includes Tappan, an Electrolux unit.
15. Includes Roper, a GE unit.
16. Second column of data is 1991 data.
17. Third column of data is 1994 data.
18. Second column of data is 1991 data.
19. Third column of data is 1994 data.
20. Produces for Whirlpool.
21. Includes 1 for Bissel and 1 for Rexaire (Rainbow).
22. Second column of data is 1991 data.

Source: *Appliance Manufacturer* (February 1989), pp. 32–34; (September 1995), pp. 70–71; (April 1996), pp. 29–31.

Exhibit 8   **Average Price of Selected U.S. Major Home Appliances**
(In U.S. dollars)

Type of Product	Average Price	Highest Price	Lowest Price
Washer	$422	$496 (Maytag)	>$400 (GE, Hotpoint, Roper, Speed Queen)
Dryer	365	440 (Maytag)	NA
Refrigerator	840	NA	NA
Dishwasher	396	519 (KitchenAid)	284 (Caloric)
Microwave Oven	201	283 (Whirlpool)	120 (Emerson)
Disposer	99	NA	NA

Source: K. Edlin, "Demand Performance," *Appliance* (July 1995), p. 90.

appliance industry was about to change significantly. As the European market leader in dishwashers, Bosch-Siemens intended to expand sales of its high-end dishwashers from the 40,000 units it was exporting to North America in 1995 to a projected 100,000 units in 1998 and a 5% dishwasher market share.[14] Until now, the only foreign appliance manufacturing presence had been in floor care. Whirlpool Corporation had arranged a joint venture in 1990 with Matsushita Electric Industrial Company, Ltd., to own and operate Whirlpool's current manufacturing plant in Danville, Kentucky, to provide vacuum cleaners for Sears. Matsushita was expected to use the Kentucky facilities to expand its manufacturing and marketing base in North America.

Whirlpool

Whirlpool and General Electric had traditionally dominated the U.S. major home appliance industry. Whirlpool owed its leadership position to its 50-plus years' relationship with Sears, which historically accounted for some 40% of the company's North American sales. Sears stocked Whirlpool's own brand and Whirlpool's Kenmore and Sears brands. Sears' movement away from a heavy reliance on its private Sears and Kenmore brands toward its new Brand Central concept in the late 1980s had serious implications for Whirlpool. Nevertheless, even though it no longer dominated Whirlpool's sales, Sears continued to be Whirlpool's largest single customer in 1996 and accounted for about 20% of Whirlpool's sales. Like Maytag, major home appliances was Whirlpool's primary business.

Whirlpool revealed its excellence in product development when it successfully built a prototype to win the Super Efficient Refrigerator Program (SERP) award. The competition was sponsored by 24 utilities and offered a $30 million award (in the form of a $100 rebate to the manufacturer for each unit sold) to the manufacturer that successfully developed a CFC-free refrigerator with at least 25% more energy efficiency than current DOE standards. To win the award, Whirlpool had to produce a prototype in five months—half the usual time. The first model was introduced to the public during Earth Week in April 1994 and was 30% more efficient than DOE standards.[15]

With the completion of its purchase of Dutch-based Philips Electronics' appliance operations in 1991, Whirlpool became a serious global competitor in the emerging worldwide major home appliance industry. Sales and market share consistently increased annually in every geographic section of the company—North America, Europe,

Exhibit 9   Ratings of Major U.S. Home Appliance Reliability
(Listed in order from most to least reliable in terms of repairs)

Washers	Dryers (electric)	Dryers (gas)
KitchenAid	KitchenAid—tied 1st	Whirlpool
Whirlpool—tied 2nd	Whirlpool—tied 1st	Sears
Hotpoint—tied 2nd	Maytag—tied 3rd	Hotpoint—tied 3rd
Sears—tied 4th	Sears—tied 3rd	Maytag—tied 3rd
Maytag—tied 4th	Amana—tied 4th	GE
Amana	Hotpoint—tied 4th	
GE—tied 7th	GE—tied 4th	
Speed Queen—tied 7th	Speed Queen—tied 4th	
White-Westinghouse—tied 7th	White-Westinghouse	
Frigidaire—tied 10th	Frigidaire	
Magic Chef—tied 10th	Magic Chef	

Top-Freezer Refrigerators (no icemakers)	Top-Freezer Refrigerators (w/icemakers)	Microwave Ovens
Magic Chef	Hotpoint—tied 1st	Panasonic—tied 1st
Sears—tied 2nd	Sears—tied 1st	Goldstar—tied 1st
Whirlpool—tied 2nd	Whirlpool—tied 1st	Sanyo—tied 3rd
White-Westinghouse	GE	Sharp—tied 3rd
Frigidaire—tied 5th	Frigidaire	Emerson—tied 3rd
Hotpoint—tied 5th	Amana	Magic Chef—tied 6th
GE		Quasar—tied 6th
Amana		Sears—tied 6th
		Tappan—tied 6th
		Samsung—tied 6th
		GE—tied 11th
		Amana—tied 11th
		Whirlpool

Ranges (electric)	Ranges (gas)	Dishwashers
Whirlpool	Whirlpool	Magic Chef—tied 1st
GE—tied 2nd	Sears—tied 2nd	Whirlpool—tied 1st
Hotpoint—tied 2nd	GE—tied 2nd	Hotpoint—tied 1st
Frigidaire—tied 4th	Tappan	GE—tied 4th
Sears—tied 4th	Magic Chef	In-Sink-Erator—tied 4th
	Caloric	Amana
		KitchenAid—tied 7th
		Jenn-Air—tied 7th
		Maytag—tied 9th
		Sears—tied 9th
		Caloric
		Tappan
		White-Westinghouse
		Frigidaire

Note: Ratings based on repair history from 20,000 to 130,000 (number varies by appliance category) responses to 1994 Consumers Union Annual Questionnaire regarding appliances purchased between 1986 and 1994.

Source: "1996 Buying Guide," *Consumer Reports* (December 15, 1995), pp. 20–23.

Exhibit 10   Shares of U.S. and Western European Markets in White Goods
(Refrigerators, washing machines, dryers, ranges, and dishwashers)

Company	United States Market Share		Brands
	1991	1995	
Whirlpool	33.8%	35.0%	Whirlpool, KitchenAid, Roper
General Electric	28.2	29.3	GE, Hotpoint, RCA, Monogram
Maytag	14.2	14.4	Maytag, Hardwick, Jenn-Air, Magic Chef, Admiral, Norge
A.B. Electrolux (Frigidaire)	15.9	13.5	Frigidaire, Gibson, Kelvinator, Tappan, White-Westinghouse
Raytheon	5.6	6.2	Amana, Speed Queen, Caloric
Others	2.3	1.6	In-Sink-Erator, Brown, Peerless-Premier, Sub-Zero, W.C. Wood, etc.

Company	Western Europe Market Share		Brands
	1990	1994	
A.B. Electrolux (Sweden)	19%	23.9%	Electrolux, AEG, Buderus, Zanker, Zanussi, Thorn-EMI, Cobero
Bosch-Siemens (Germany)	13	16.0	Bosch, Siemens, Neff, Constructa, Balay, Pitsos
Whirlpool (U.S.)	10	10.7	Philips, Whirlpool, Bauknecht, Ignis
Miele (Germany)	7	6.2	Miele, Imperial
Group Brandt (France/Spain)	1	6.1	Ocean, Thomson
Liebherr (Austria/Germany)	NA	3.6	Liebherr
Temfa (France/Spain)	6	1	Thomson, Fagor, DeDetriech, Ocean
AEG (Germany)	5	2	AEG
Merloni (Italy)	4	3.1	Merloni, Ariston, Indesit, Scholtes
General Domestic App. (U.S./U.K.)	4	3.0	Hotpoint, Creda, General Electric
Candy (Italy)	4	3.1	Candy, Rosieres, Kelvinator, Gasfire
Others	28	24.0	Hoover, Crosslee, Vestfrost, etc.

Notes:

1. Group Brandt in 1994 included both the Ocean and Thomson groups (and thus Temfa).
2. AEG acquired by AB Electrolux.

Source: *Appliance* (September 1995), p. 71; (June 1995), p. 48. *Appliance Manufacturer* (April 1996), p. 29.

Latin America, and Asia. Whirlpool usually competed with General Electric to be the most profitable U.S. major home appliance company (in terms of appliance operating profit). It was first in North America and third in Western Europe in terms of market share. The company's marketing strategy was to focus on making the Whirlpool name a global brand. (Even though the company ranked only third in Europe in terms of overall market share of its Philips, Whirlpool, Bauknecht, and Ignis brands, management liked to point out that the Whirlpool brand by itself had the highest share of any brand in Europe.) It had developed a series of joint ventures and equity arrangements with appliance manufacturers throughout Asia and South America. Although its share of the Asian

Exhibit 11   Major Home Appliance Operating Results for Primary U.S. Competitors
(Dollar and Swedish kronor amounts in millions)

Company	Category	1993	1994	1995
General Electric	Revenue	$5,555	$5,965	$5,933
	Operating income	372	683	697
	Assets	2,193	2,309	2,304
Whirlpool	Revenue	$7,368	$7,949	$8,163
	Operating income	504	370	366
	Assets	4,654	5,240	6,168
Electrolux[1]	Revenue	SEK58,888	SEK66,272	SEK75,209
	Operating income	SEK869	SEK2,555	SEK2,581
	Assets	NA	NA	NA
Maytag	Revenue	$2,830	$3,181	$2,845
	Operating income	163	334	296
	Assets	2,147	2,053	1,594
Raytheon	Revenue	$1,285	$1,454	$1,473
	Operating income	45	87	81
	Assets	806	998	992

Note: Figures for Electrolux given in Swedish kronor (SEK). One U.S. dollar equals approximately 7 Swedish krona.
Source: Annual reports of respective companies.

market was still fairly small, Whirlpool together with its affiliates in Argentina and Brazil had the largest manufacturing base and market share in South America. Whirlpool in cooperation with its affiliates in Brazil and joint venture partners in India and Mexico built facilities in those countries to produce what the company called the "world washer." Debuting in 1992 in Mexico, production of the new compact washing machine was intended to meet the increasing consumer demand in developing countries.

General Electric

General Electric, with a U.S. major home appliance market share of 29%, was a strong and profitable competitor in many industries. As a business unit, GE Appliances accounted for 14% of the corporation's total sales. General Electric had a powerful name and brand image and was the most vertically integrated of the major home appliance manufacturers. Like others, it manufactured some of its components, but it was the only appliance producer to own its entire distribution and service facilities. Realizing that GE's manufacturing facilities at its 40-year-old Appliance Park near Louisville, Kentucky, were slowly losing their competitiveness, management modernized the washing machine plant at a cost of $100 million. This resulted in the 1995 introduction of GE's new Maxus washer containing a floating suspension system to reduce vibration and 40% fewer parts to reduce cost and increase reliability. The Park's refrigerator plant was next in line for a $70 million makeover. Overall the company was investing some $1 billion over a four-year period in appliance product development and capital equipment, a 50% increase over previous spending levels.

With relatively slow growth in the North American market, GE Appliances planned to continue moving into faster growing international locations. In 1989, GE paid $580 million for a joint appliance venture and other ventures with the U.K.'s General Electric Corporation (GEC). GEC was known for its mass market appliances in Europe, whereas GE was known in Europe for its high-end appliances. Named General Domestic Appliances (GDA), the joint venture was a leading (and profitable) competitor in the U.K. market with its GE, Hotpoint, and Creda brands, but was only a minor competitor on the continent. General Electric was interested in gaining a stronger position in Europe, particularly in Eastern Europe. The company was also involved with international partners in Mexico (MABE), Venezuela (Madosa), India (Godrej & Boyce Mfg. Co.), the Phillipines (Philacor), and Japan (Toshiba). Appliances manufactured by the joint ventures were primarily sold in the country of origin, with small amounts going into contiguous markets.

A.B. Electrolux

A.B. Electrolux of Sweden, with its purchase of White Consolidated Industries in 1986, became part of the U.S. major home appliance industry. Electrolux sold approximately 17 million appliances with over 40 brand names in countries around the world. After acquiring Zanussi in Italy, Tricity and Thorn EMI in the United Kingdom, WCI in the United States, and AEG in Germany, Electrolux passed Whirlpool to become the world's largest major home appliance manufacturer. Electrolux had a strong presence in every European country from Finland to Portugal and extended eastward with production facilities in Hungary, Estonia, and Russia. Leif Johansson, President and CEO, explained the corporation's growth strategy:

> We always make acquisitions to gain synergy, never just to hold the share. We normally go for short-term synergies like purchasing, speed, productivity, cost efficiency—things we can accomplish with the industrial structure that is already there, and by bringing in our expertise on how to run factories and our ability to do a great deal of internal benchmarking because of our size. Then we enter the restructuring phase, where we are investing capital and giving factories specific assignments in a Group context. . . . The entire strategy is based on turning these units into something that is worth more as part of an integrated, global group than they were as standalone units, and it has meant increased market shares for us.[16]

The household appliance area (including white goods and floor care, air conditioners, and sewing machines) accounted for slightly over 60% of total corporation sales. As of 1996, Electrolux was first in market share in Western Europe and fourth in North America. Europe accounted for about 65% of its major home appliance sales. North America accounted for approximately 30%. The rest was scattered throughout Asia, Latin America, Oceania, and Africa. Careful planning was needed by Electrolux to properly take advantage of a proliferation of brands worldwide without getting bogged down with competing internal demands for attention to each brand. After noticing Whirlpool's success with one brand across all of Europe, the company began the introduction of its own pan-European brand using the Electrolux name. The company was in the process of spending about SEK600 million over a five-year period to market the Electrolux products throughout Europe. It was also investing $50 million in Southeast Asia with an objective of becoming one of the top three suppliers of white goods in the ASEAN region by the year 2000. Leif Johansson, Electrolux President and CEO, stated how well global integration had progressed at the company:

> The integration, after 10 years, has gone so far that it's difficult to assess what is really Italian, what is really Swedish, and what is really American. We are working in multinational teams. On a team going to China, for example, very often you will find Italians, Spaniards, Swedes, and Americans working together.[17]

In 1991, the WCI Major Appliance Group was renamed Frigidaire Company in order to provide A.B. Electrolux's U.S. subsidiary the recognition earned by its pioneering namesake brand. Previously the company's brands had competed against one another and had not been designed for automated manufacturing. Consequently the quality of many of its well-known branded products had deteriorated over time. To reverse this situation, the company had invested more than $600 million to upgrade its existing plants and build new refrigerator and dishwasher plants. Top management also introduced its Vision 2000 program, using benchmarking and total quality management to boost production quality and efficiency. It was aggressively advertising its products. Nevertheless, its share of the U.S. market dropped significantly from 16.9% in 1994 to 13.5% in 1995 and had caused the company to drop from its traditional third place in the U.S. market to fourth place behind Maytag.

Maytag

Maytag Corporation, with a U.S. market share of 14%, was in a position in 1996 of having to work hard to keep from being outdistanced globally by the three powerhouses of Whirlpool, Electrolux, and GE. Realizing that the company could not successfully compete in the major home appliance industry as just a manufacturer of high-quality laundry products, the company embarked during the 1980s in the acquisition of Hardwick Stoves, Magic Chef, and Jenn-Air. These acquisitions provided Maytag the full line of appliances it needed to compete effectively in the U.S. market. Realizing that the industry was going global as well, Maytag purchased Hoover Company, a successful floor-care company in the United States and a strong white goods producer in the United Kingdom and Australia. In acquiring Hoover, Maytag unfortunately also acquired a significant amount of debt. This debt, coupled with the heavy amount of investment needed to upgrade and integrate its newly acquired facilities and operations, put a big strain on Maytag's profitability. Like Whirlpool, Maytag operated primarily in major household appliances. Not until 1994 did Hoover's European appliance business become profitable. Nevertheless, Maytag sold Hoover Australia in 1994 to Southcorp Holdings, Ltd., of Australia and Hoover Europe in 1995 to Candy S.p.A., an Italian-based appliance maker. Even though Maytag accepted losses of $16.4 million and $130 million, respectively, on the sales, the corporation was able to use the proceeds to reduce its debt. According to Chairman and CEO Leonard Hadley, "This is a strategic decision to focus on growing our core North American appliance and floor-care businesses, which include Hoover North America." [18] It was somewhat ironic that just one month after the sale, a survey in the United Kingdom revealed that of 173 household names Hoover ranked at the top of major appliance producers! [19]

In 1995, Maytag invested $13.7 million to expand its recently completed state-of-the-art dishwasher plant in Tennessee. According to Joseph Fogliano, Executive Vice-President and President of Maytag's North American Appliance Group, dishwashers were the fastest growing major appliance in the United States. He added that the growth of the corporation's dishwashers was approximately twice that of the industry. [20] This investment plus the corporation's decisions to spend $160 million upgrading its Admiral refrigerator plant and $50 million to build a new horizontal-axis washer plant indicated that Maytag had no intention of being outmanuevered by others on its own territory. Now that Maytag had shed its European Hoover "money pit" and had greatly improved its financial situation, industry analysts worried that the corporation would soon be a takeover target by another international appliance company. Other analysts wondered what kind of future faced a purely domestic Maytag Corporation, given the globalization of the industry.

Raytheon

Raytheon Company, an electronics as well as an appliances firm, was the fifth important player in the U.S. major home appliance industry. Raytheon's Appliances Group constituted 14% of the total corporation's sales and was composed of Amana Home Appliance division (including Caloric brands) and Speed Queen Company. Operating under the belief that its technological leadership in the electronics and defense industries could drive innovations in the appliance industry, Raytheon acquired enough appliance companies to assemble the full line of products necessary to compete effectively in the U.S. market. Because it was interested in broadening its offerings in home and commercial appliances, in 1995 the company purchased Unimac Company, a global leader in the front-load washer and dryer coin laundry markets. This supplemented its commercially oriented Huebsch, Menumaster, and Speed Queen lines. Given the actual and threatened cutbacks in the U.S. defense budget during the 1990s, Raytheon might need a strong appliance business to make up for any reduction in its defense-related electronics and aircraft divisions. Unfortunately Raytheon's major home appliance sales and operating profits declined every year from 1989 through 1991. Of its three home appliance brands, only Amana continued to show increasing sales and income from strong refrigerator sales.

To reverse its declining appliance fortunes, Raytheon invested $173 million into new appliance plants and equipment. All operations of the Caloric division were then combined under Amana. Speed Queen now focused on serving the commercial laundry market and on producing home laundry products for Amana to market. To support its home appliance business further, in 1994 Raytheon moved its New Product Center from Burlington, Massachusetts, to its new home appliance headquarters in Amana, Iowa, and renamed it the Appliance Technology Center. The Center was no longer to serve other Raytheon business units but to expand Amana's existing R&D by focusing exclusively on the Raytheon Appliance Group. As a result of Raytheon's investments in and restructuring of its appliance business, both sales and profits showed positive growth from 1992 forward. Nevertheless, the trend toward global acquisitions and consolidation in the appliance industry left analysts wondering if Raytheon's domestic-only home appliance division would be able to compete successfully in the coming world appliance market.

THE FUTURE: A GLOBAL APPLIANCE MARKET?

The U.S. major home appliance industry was composed of five major manufacturers with 35–40 factories and 19 major brands. Volume in the 1990s was at an all-time high. Although product quality was judged to be good, but not excellent, the products provided excellent consumer value.[21] In the short run, the outlook for major home appliance sales was conservatively positive. In North America, sales for 1996 were expected to be slightly above those for 1995 but not quite as high as the exceptionally good sales in 1994. Analysts expected a slight upturn in new U.S. single-family home construction and a 2.4% increase in home and commercial remodeling activity. Economists predicted a "rather tranquil" U.S. economy through 1997 with a 2%–2.5% increase in real gross domestic product (GDP). Consumer prices were expected to rise 2%–3% annually through 1997. Although Canadian home appliance sales dropped 8% in 1995 (coinciding with a 42% drop in home sales), the Canadian Appliance Manufacturers Association predicted a steady growth of approximately 2.3% per year, reaching an annual volume of 3.9 million units in sales by the year 2000. With a weak peso continuing to dampen economic prospects in Mexico, economists were predicting a meager 2% economic improvement in 1996.

Mexico and NAFTA

The two full-line major home appliance makers in Mexico, Vitromatic and MABE, were involved in joint ventures with U.S. firms. Whirlpool had a joint venture with Vitromatic S.A., which included three facilities in Mexico. General Electric had a joint venture with MABE, a consortium of Mexican appliance producers. This was beginning to affect the competitiveness of those U.S. firms without Mexican white goods operations: Maytag, Raytheon, and Frigidaire. Appliances exported to Mexico from the United States were subject to a 20% tariff, whereas Mexican appliances going to the United States were assessed no tariffs. The original North American Free Trade Agreement (NAFTA) allowed the Mexican tariff to continue for a 10-year period (ending in 2003) to keep Mexican businesses from being immediately overwhelmed by larger U.S. companies. One result was escalating imports into the United States of low-priced gas ranges from a MABE plant, forcing Maytag to lay off workers at its Magic Chef plant in Cleveland, Tennessee. Under NAFTA, tariffs were being phased out for various items over 5-year and 10-year periods but only for products that satisfied Rules of Origin. For example, if the Rules of Origin call for 50% regional value content (RVC), but 51% of a company's product is sourced from Asia or Europe, the company would be forced to pay the full tariff. According to Serge Ratmiroff, senior manager of international services for Deloitte & Touche in Chicago, "Mexico is not only a market just beginning to boom, but it is the front door to a potential Latin American free trade bloc."[22]

Europe

The economic climate of Western Europe was similar to that of the United States. Analysts were predicting a 2%–3% unit volume sales growth in appliances during 1996. Although no countries of the former Eastern Bloc had yet returned to 1989 levels of prosperity, continued improvement was likely. For example, the economy of the Commonwealth of Independent States was expected to grow by 1% in 1996. Because Western Europe was going through a demographic shift similar to that of the United States—toward a more middle-aged society coupled with lower overall saturation levels (see Exhibit 5) of major home appliances—sales over the long run were predicted to grow faster annually than the 1%–2% growth rate predicted for the United States. Europeans as a whole were much more concerned that their appliances be "environmentally friendly" than were consumers in North America. The continuing economic integration of the 15-member countries of the European Union—Austria, Belgium, Denmark, Finland, France, Germany, Greece, Ireland, Italy, Luxembourg, the Netherlands, Portugal, Spain, Sweden, and the United Kingdom—was providing the impetus for a series of mergers, acquisitions, and joint ventures among major household appliance manufacturers. The barriers to free trade among Western European countries were steadily being eliminated. The requirement of at least 60% local content to avoid tariffs made a European manufacturing presence imperative for any U.S. or Japanese major home appliance manufacturer.

The European appliance industry was in the final stages of consolidation. It was home to approximately 30 appliance producers, down from over 150 in the 1960s. The big three of Electrolux, Bosch-Siemens, and Whirlpool controlled over half of the market in Western Europe and were making strong inroads into Eastern Europe via joint ventures and acquisitions. Small- and medium-sized manufacturers, such as Gaggenau,

Kuppersbusch, and Seppelfricke in Germany, have managed to maintain their independence by specializing in built-in appliances. Overall, product quality was good, but not excellent.[23] As distribution shifted from being solely through furniture and kitchen studios to specialty chains and discount stores (especially in Germany), price competition was becoming increasingly important. The primary markets in Europe were Germany with 37%, Italy with 22%, and France and the United Kingdom with 10% each. Spain was the next largest market.

With its acquisitions of the powerful Italian Zanussi company, the U.K.'s Thorn-EMI, the U.S.'s White Consolidated Industries (Frigidaire), and Germany's AEG, along with three Spanish companies, Electrolux was in a good position to control the coming global market. Germany's largest domestic appliance maker, Bosch-Siemens Hausgerate GmbH, was forging a course to overtake Electrolux in Europe as well as elsewhere. It acquired a washing machine factory in Poland, the third largest domestic appliance producer in Brazil, a minority stake in the second largest appliance maker in Turkey, and majority control of a leading Chinese laundry appliance manufacturer. The company had formed an alliance with Maytag in 1993 to exchange information on new product technologies and design, but it was discontinued when Maytag sold Hoover Europe. According to CEO Hans-Peter Haase, "Today it is certainly conceivable that worldwide operating companies such as BSHG can convert a washing machine based on European technology to U.S. dimensions and sell it in America." Explaining the rationale for building a dishwasher plant in the United States in 1996, Haase said, "Once Americans accept stainless-steel interiors and we offer our product at an acceptable price, we will be able to achieve sales volumes comparable to European levels."[24] Upon acquiring Philips, the second largest European producer of white goods, Whirlpool became a key player throughout Europe and the world. It was actively involved in strategic alliances with appliance companies in Slovakia and Hungary, among other countries. It was the first company to market a pan-European brand. According to company sources, Whirlpool was the number one recognized brand name throughout Western and Central Europe by 1995. General Domestic Appliances (GDA), a joint venture by the British General Electric Corporation (GEC) and General Electric (GE) of the United States, was performing well in Britain but was only a minor player on the continent. The purchase of Hoover Europe from Maytag by the Italian-based Candy gave it immediate access to the United Kingdom to complement its presence on the continent and was a signal that it did not intend to be left behind by the "big three."

Unlike the U.S. appliance market, the European market was heavily segmented into a series of national markets. In cooking appliances, for example, over 90% of the ranges purchased in Germany were electric, whereas gas prevailed through the rest of Europe. Also, 65% of German ranges were built-in, while the percentage of built-ins outside Germany was considerably less. Top loading washers, long dominant in the United States, commanded 80% of the market in France, but front loaders dominated the rest of Europe, where washers and dryers must fit into a kitchen under a work surface or in a bathroom. Although built-in refrigerators formed only a small part of refrigerator sales in most of Europe, they constituted over 50% of the German market. The large, free-standing home appliances preferred by Americans were much less popular in Europe where smaller, energy efficient units were generally preferred. Hans G. Backman, President of Frigidaire Company and Vice-President of AB Electrolux, commented on this situation:

> Globalization of the product and globalization of the company are two different things. The appliance industry is becoming global, but the products and the consumers are still local. The more the world comes together, the more that national differences get emphasized.[25]

South America

Regional trade agreements and the lowering of tariffs made it easier to sell products such as home appliances in South America in the 1990s. The establishment of the Mercosur free-trade area among Argentina, Brazil, Uruguay, and Paraguay meant that a manufacturing presence within these countries was becoming essential to avoid tariffs. Whirlpool, with its Brazilian and Argentine affiliates, had a very strong presence in the area. AB Electrolux formed an alliance with Refrigeracao Parana S.A., the second-largest white goods company in Brazil. It also established a wholly-owned subsidiary in Argentina to market its Electrolux, Zanussi, and Frigidaire brands. Through its purchase of Continental 2001, Brazil's third-largest domestic appliance manufacturer, Bosch-Siemens was also a force in the region. General Electric held part ownership of Madosa, a leading appliance maker in Venezuela. According to the consulting firm Datamonitor, the predicted primary markets in 1998 for washers, dryers, vacuum cleaners, and dishwashers would be Argentina at $344 million (compared to $457 million for Mexico), Brazil at $250 million, Chile at $167 million, Venezuela at $150 million, Columbia at $73 million, and Peru at $50 million. Washers should constitute the largest segment for these figures as the markets for dryers, dishwashers, and vacuum cleaners were still small.[26] In Brazil, for example, the percentage of saturation was about 80% for ranges and refrigerators, 20% for washing machines, 15% for freezers and dryers, and 10% for dishwashers and microwave ovens.

Asia

In 1996, Asia was already the world's second largest home appliance market, and opportunities were still emerging. According to Roger Merriam, Vice-President of Sales and Marketing for Whirlpool Overseas Corporation, "In the U.S., we talk of households equipped with between seven and nine major appliance products. In Asia, which already accounts for 40% of the world market, it's more like four appliances per home." The saturation level of clothes washers in India and China, for example, was about 10%, compared to 54% in Mexico. About 27% of the roughly 190 million units sold worldwide were sold in Asia—more than in North America and fewer only than in Europe. The combined economies of the Asian region were expected to grow by about 6%–8% annually through the 1990s, with industry shipments of appliances likely to grow at a more rapid pace.

Although Japanese and Korean manufacturers dominated the Asian home appliance market in the 1990s, the industry was still fragmented with no single dominant company in terms of market share. The top Asian players included Hitachi, Matsushita, Mitsubishi, Sharp, and Toshiba of Japan plus Goldstar, Samsung, and Daewoo of Korea. Matsushita was the overall market leader in Asia, but had a market share of less than 10% outside Japan. Asian distribution was rapidly moving away from small retailers to power retailer organizations. AB Electrolux was establishing a full line of appliance facilities in China and India, among other Asian locations. One of the company's objectives was to be one of the top three white goods suppliers in Southeast Asia by the year 2000.[27] In purchasing Philips, Whirlpool obtained key distributors in Australia, Malaysia, Japan, Singapore, Thailand, and Taiwan. In addition, Whirlpool established joint ventures in China and India. General Electric held part ownership of Philcor in the Philippines and had a joint venture with Godrej & Boyce, India's largest appliance maker. According to Jeff Immelt, Vice-President of Worldwide Marketing and Product Management at GE Appliances, the Asian market was still young enough to justify building one's own brand instead of acquiring someone else's established brands as was done in Europe.[28]

Nevertheless, much of Asia, Africa, and significant parts of South America were not yet sufficiently developed economically to be significant markets for major home appliances. For one thing, electricity and natural gas service were not yet widely available in most developing countries. Even in those locations where electricity was available, it was not always provided consistently—power outages were a common occurrence in some countries.

The Future

Hans G. Backman, President of Frigidaire Company, predicted that domestic appliance brands would continue to dominate the U.S. market, but that both domestic and multinational brands would dominate Europe. Asia would continue to be a market share battleground dominated by multinational appliance companies from the United States, Europe, Japan, and Korea. In Asia, according to Backman, "The products will be smaller and simpler than in the U.S. or Europe, but the technologies and components will be the same. Manufacturing will be local, but may serve as a low-cost base for exporting basic low-end products to the U.S. and Europe."[29]

Robert L. Holding, President of the Association of Home Appliance Manufacturers, predicted that even though the American industry had a strong base from which to operate, it would face continuing pressures on profits. He predicted that in 25 years the number of global appliance makers would be in the 5–10 range. In terms of important considerations, Holding predicted that environmental issues and product quality would be crucial. "Creating a basic design that can be manufactured into a 'family' of brands or models will be important."[30] Because retailers had been gaining increasing leverage over manufacturers, "speed to market" and flexible low-cost manufacturing would be key to future success. In addition to energy use and air pollution laws, governments would probably enact recycled-content legislation and disposal fees for appliances. Led by the trend to locate more appliances in main living areas of the house instead of in the basement, consumers would demand quieter appliances. According to Holding, the future of individual major home appliance manufacturers would depend on their ability to provide value to the consumer.

Notes

1. David Hoyte, Executive Vice-President of Operations, Frigidaire, as quoted by M. Sanders, "ISO 9000: The Inside Story," *Appliance* (August 1994), p. 43. ("White goods" is the traditional term used for major home appliances. The contrasting term "brown goods" refers to home electronics products such as radios and televisions.)
2. J. Jancsurak, "Global Trends for 1995–2005," *Appliance Manufacturer* (June 1995), p. A-6.
3. S. Stevens, "Finessing the Future," *Appliance* (April 1990), pp. 42–43.
4. C. R. Christensen, K. R. Andrews, J. L. Bower, R. G. Hammermesh, and M. E. Porter, "Note on the Major Home Appliance Industry in 1984 (Condensed)," *Business Policy,* 6th ed. (Homewood, Ill.: Irwin, 1987), p. 340.
5. M. Sanders, "Purchasing Power," *Appliance* (June 1993), pp. 45–46.
6. "For Appliances, Coated Coil Grows by 14.6%," *Appliance Manufacturer* (June 1993), p. 10.
7. D. Davis, "1996: A Soft Landing," *Appliance* (January 1996), p. 52.
8. R. Holding, "1990 Shipment Outlook," p. 64.
9. "Buying Power—Home Purchase Triggers Sales of Appliances," *Appliance Manufacturer* (February 1989), p. 31.
10. Chuck Miller, Vice-President of Marketing, North American Appliance Group, Whirlpool Corporation, as quoted by R. J. Babyak and J. Jancsurak in "Product Design & Manufacturing Process for the 21st Century," *Appliance Manufacturer* (November 1994), p. 59.

11. R. J. Haines, "Appliance Newsquotes," *Appliance* (June 1989), p. 21.

12. J. Jancsurak, "In Their Opinion," *Appliance Manufacturer* (April 1995), p. 48.

13. M. Sanders, "The Next Generation," *Appliance* (September 1995), p. 59.

14. "BSCH to Build U.S. Plant," *Appliance* (January 1996), p. 17; "Bosch Targets U.S. Niche," *Appliance Manufacturer* (April 1996), p. 26.

15. "Designing a Winner," *Appliance Manufacturer* (May 1994), pp. W-20–W-23.

16. S. Stevens, "An Appliance Arsenal," *Appliance* (February 1995), p. E-25.

17. "Zanussi Celebrates 10 Years With Electrolux," *Appliance* (November 1994), p. 9.

18. R. Brack, "Hoover Europe Sold at Loss," *Des Moines Register* (May 31, 1995), p. 10S.

19. "Hoover Tops Quality Charts," *Appliance* (August 1995), p. 10.

20. "Maytag to Expand Dishwsher Plant," *Appliance* (December 1994), p. 29.

21. Jancsurak, "Global Trend for 1995–2005," p. A-6.

22. J. R. Stevens, "Exporting to Mexico? Take Another Look," (August 1994), p. 6.

23. Jancsurak, "Global Trend for 1995–2005," p. A-6.

24. J. Jancsurak, "Big Plans for Europe's Big Three," (April 1995), p. 28.

25. Jancsurak, "Global Trends for 1995–2005," p. A-3.

26. J. R. Stevens, "Appliance Market Grows in South America," (September 1994), p. 8.

27. Stevens, "An Appliance Arsenal," p. E-28.

28. "Global Growth Strategies," *Appliance Manufacturer* (January 1992), p. GEA-13.

29. Jancsurak, "Global Trends for 1995–2005," pp. A-3–A-6.

30. N. C. Remich, Jr., "AHAM: The Next 25 Years," *Appliance Manufacturer* (March 1993), p. 71.

Maytag Corporation (1996): Back to Basics

J. David Hunger

Leonard Hadley, CEO and Chairman of the Board of Maytag Corporation, looked up and smiled briefly as his secretary handed him the completed 1995 financial statements along with his morning cup of coffee. Warm in his office, Hadley took a moment to gaze from his second floor window at the thick blanket of snow surrounding the building. He used the steaming cup of coffee to warm his still-numb hands. Even though he lived less than a mile from the office, it had been cold driving into work today. Only 30 miles east of Des Moines, Newton shared the sub-zero temperatures of the upper Midwest in early February 1996. Hadley wasn't sure which he dreaded most: the blustery winter weather or having to explain less than expected financial results to the media and shareholders.

Hadley thought back to April 27, 1993, when he chaired his very first shareholders' meeting. He had looked forward to his promotion to Chairman of the Board that January. Accepting the gavel from his mentor, the much-respected Daniel Krumm, had been a great honor. It should have been a great year because 1993 marked Maytag's 100th birthday. Unfortunately it was overshadowed by the fact that in 1992 the company suffered its first loss since the early 1920s! As the new Chairman, Hadley's first key task had been to explain this loss to increasingly antagonistic shareholders and cynical investment bankers. The reverence that people had shown Krumm as Chairman seemed to evaporate when Hadley stood at the podium to open the floor to questions. Hadley still winced when he remembered some of those questions from that day in 1993. One person—a very angry man standing in the back right of the auditorium—still stood out in his mind. Speaking into the microphone held by an usher, but looking straight at Hadley, he asked:"How long will it be before earnings get back to the 1988 level of $1.77 per share from continuing operations? And along with that," he added, "why should we have any confidence in your answer, given the performance of the past five years?" The hush in the auditorium had been unbearable. The bittersweet nature of Maytag's 100th birthday year had not been helped by Daniel Krumm's death from cancer on November 22, 1993.

The financial reports for 1993 and 1994 had shown significant improvement. Although net income still had not reached the 1988 figure of $158 million, 1994 had been a very good year for everyone in the home appliance industry, including Maytag. As he skimmed through the financial reports for 1995, Hadley couldn't help but wonder how the shareholders and financial analysts would respond to another net loss. Maytag's management had worked hard to boost the stock price from its low of about $13 in 1993 to the current $19, but the price was still below the $29 value estimated by one financial analyst.[1]

The decisions to sell Hoover Australia and Hoover Europe had not been easy ones. Hadley had supported Daniel Krumm and the rest of the Executive Committee in their 1988 decision to acquire Chicago Pacific in order to obtain Hoover with its Australian and European operations. In retrospect, it was clear that they had paid far too much for a very marginal European business. The movie"The Money Pit" seemed to be an appropriate title for Hoover Europe. Selling off the overseas operations had meant big after-

This case was prepared by Professor J. David Hunger of Iowa State University. This case was edited for SMBP–7th Edition. All rights reserved to the author. Copyright © 1996 by J. David Hunger. Reprinted by permission. The author thanks Susan J. Martin, Director of Internal Communications of Maytag Corporation, for helpful comments on an earlier draft of this case.

tax book losses, but they had provided the corporation cash to reduce its heavy debt load. After all, if you excluded the $9.9 million after-tax settlement of the Dixie-Narco workers' lawsuit, the $5.5 million extraordinary item for early debt retirement, and the $135.4 million after-tax loss on the sale of Hoover Europe, Maytag Corporation would have shown a healthy profit in 1995.

HISTORY OF THE COMPANY

The history of Maytag Corporation falls into four distinct phases. The first phase included the entrepreneurial days at the turn of the century when the company was founded by F. L. Maytag and the company became the U.S. market leader in washing machines. The second phase was the company's retreat from market leadership in the 1950s to focus on a high-quality niche in laundry products. During the third phase, the company was revitalized under Daniel Krumm in the 1980s to become a full-line globally oriented major home appliance manufacturer through acquisitions. The fourth phase included the attempts to stabilize and refocus the corporation during the 1990s.

Entrepreneurial Energy Creates Market Leader

Fred L. Maytag (or F. L., as he was commonly called), who came to Newton, Iowa, as a farm boy in a covered wagon, joined three other men in 1893 to found the Parsons Band Cutter and Self Feeder Company. The firm produced attachments invented by one of the founders to improve the performance of threshing machines. The company built its first washing machine, the "Pastime," in 1907 as a sideline to its farm equipment. The founders hoped that this product would fill the seasonal slumps in the farm equipment business and enable the company to have year-round production.

In 1909, F. L. Maytag became sole owner of the firm and changed its name to The Maytag Company. Farm machinery was soon phased out as the company began to focus its efforts on washing machines. With the aid of Howard Snyder, a former mechanic whose inventive genius had led him to head Maytag's development department, the company generated a series of product and process improvements. Its gasoline powered washer (pioneered by Maytag), for example, became so popular with rural customers without electricity that Maytag soon dominated the small-town and farm markets in the United States.

Under the leadership of Lewis B. Maytag, a son of the founder, the company expanded from 1920 to 1926 into a national company. Using a radically new gyrator to move clothes within its tub, the Model 80 was introduced in 1922. F. L. Maytag, then serving as Chairman of the Board, was so impressed with the new product that he personally took one of the first four washers on a western sales trip. Sales of the Model 80 jumped from 16,000 units in 1922 to more than 258,000 units in 1926! The company went from a $280,000 loss in 1921 to profits exceeding $6.8 million in 1926. Throughout the 1920s and 1930s, Maytag Company had an average U.S. market share of 40%–45% in washing machines. During the Great Depression of the 1930s, Maytag never suffered a loss.

From Market Leader to Niche Manager

Unfortunately the innovative genius and entrepreneurial drive of the company's early years seemed to fade after the death of its founder. Top management became less interested in innovation and marketing than with quality and cost control practices. Bendix, a newcomer to the industry, introduced an automatic washing machine at the end of World War II that used a spin cycle instead of a wringer to squeeze excess rinse water out of clothes. Maytag, however, was slow to convert to automatic washers. Management felt that the automatic washer needed more research before it could meet Maytag quality standards. The company still had a backlog of orders for its wringer washer, and management was reluctant to go into debt to finance new manufacturing facilities. This reluctance cost the company its leadership of the industry. Even with automatics, Maytag's share of the U.S. washer market fell to only 8% in 1954. Nevertheless, the company continued to be a profitable manufacturer of high-quality, high-priced home laundry appliances.

During the 1960s and 1970s, Maytag reaped the benefits of its heavy orientation on quality products and cost control. *Consumer Reports* annually ranked Maytag washers and dryers as the most dependable on the market. Maytag washers lasted longer, needed fewer repairs, and had lower service costs when they did require service. The Leo Burnett advertising agency dramatized the concept of Maytag brand dependability by showing that Maytag products were so good that repairmen had nothing to do and were thus "lonely." The company's "Ol' Lonely" ads, which first aired in 1967 and featured the lonely Maytag repairman, were consistently ranked among the most effective on television. Profit margins were the highest in the industry. The company invested in building capacity, improved its dishwasher line, and changed the design of its clothes dryers. Maytag's plants were perceived at that time to be the most efficient in the industry. By the end of the 1970s, Maytag's share of the market had increased to approximately 15% in both washers and dryers.

Revitalization: Growth Through Acquisitions

In 1978, top management, under the leadership of CEO Daniel Krumm, decided that the company could no longer continue as a specialty manufacturer operating only in the higher priced end of the laundry market. Consequently Maytag adopted a strategy to become a full-line manufacturer and develop a stronger position in the U.S. appliance industry. Up to this point, the company had been able to finance its growth internally. The strategic decision was made to grow by acquisition within the appliance industry through debt and the sale of stock.

In 1981, Maytag purchased Hardwick Stove Company, a low-priced manufacturer of gas and electric ranges with an estimated 5% share of the range market. In 1982, the company acquired Jenn-Air, a niche manufacturer of high-quality built-in electric grill ranges. In 1986, Maytag acquired Magic Chef, Inc., a successful manufacturer of mass marketed appliances in the mid-price segment of the market. The acquisition included not only Magic Chef's best-selling ranges and other products, but also appliances sold under the Admiral, Norge, and Warwick labels, and Dixie-Narco, a leading manufacturer of soft drink vending equipment. Maytag Company and the Magic Chef family of companies were then merged under a parent Maytag Corporation on May 30, 1986, headed by Chairman and CEO Daniel Krumm.

In 1988, realizing that the U.S. home appliance market had reached maturity, top management of the new Maytag Corporation decided to extend the corporation's growth strategy to the international arena. Maytag offered close to $1 billion in cash and Maytag stock for Chicago Pacific Corporation (CP), the owner of Hoover Company. In this one step Maytag Corporation moved into the international home appliance marketplace with nine manufacturing operations in the United Kingdom, France, Australia, Mexico, Colombia, and Portugal. Hoover was known worldwide for its floor care products and throughout Europe and Australia for its washers, dryers, dishwashers, microwave ovens, and refrigerators. Prior to the acquisition, Maytag's international revenues had been too small to even report.

Reluctant Retrenchment

By 1995, Maytag Corporation had achieved its goal of becoming an internationally oriented, full-line major home appliance manufacturer. However, its profits had deteriorated significantly. Although Hoover's North American operations had always been very profitable, Hoover Europe had not shown a profit since being acquired by Maytag until 1994 when it earned a modest one. Hoover Australia had also incurred significant losses during this time. Unknown to Maytag Corporation's top management before the acquisition, Hoover's U.K. facilities were in desperate need of renovation and the product line needed to be upgraded. Some weaknesses at the South Wales facility were apparent before the purchase, but the corporation was too preoccupied with learning about the vacuum cleaner business to investigate further. Once it realized the need to modernize the U.K. facilities, Maytag's top management committed millions of dollars to renovate the laundry and dishwasher plant in South Wales and its floor care plant in Scotland.

Although some former executives talked of a culture clash between the collegial Hoover and the more rigid Maytag executives, CEO Leonard Hadley blamed Hoover's woes purely on the poor U.K. business environment. However, industry analysts concluded that the Hoover acquisition had been a strategic error. To pay for the acquisition, management not only increased long-term debt to its highest level in the company's history, but it also had to sell more stock. These actions combined with a high level of investment in the unprofitable overseas facilities to lower corporate profits and decrease earnings per share. Since other major home appliance companies continued to operate profitably, some analysts were beginning to question management's ability to run an international corporation.

After concluding that there was no way the corporation could recoup its overseas investments, Maytag sold its Hoover operations in Australia and New Zealand in December 1994 and Hoover Europe in May 1995. The sale of the Australian/New Zealand operations for $82 million resulted in a 1994 after-tax loss of $16.4 million. The sale of Hoover Europe to Candy S.p.A. of Monza, Italy, for $180 million resulted in a more significant 1995 after-tax loss of $135.4 million. In evaluating the strength of both Hoover Europe and Hoover Australia, Chairman Hadley commented, "Each lacked the critical mass alone to be strong players in their respective global theaters. As a result, we sold both businesses to focus on growth from our North American–based businesses." The sales enabled the corporation to reduce the long-term debt it had acquired in the Chicago Pacific purchase. Hadley further commented in a July 1995 letter to the shareowners that Maytag was now a much more focused corporation than it had been for the past few years.

> After the sale of Hoover Europe and Hoover Australia, we are focused clearly on our core North American–based businesses: major appliances, floor care, and vending—all businesses that we know well, have managed well, and have grown successfully into strong brand positions. We also have regained much needed financial strength and flexibility over the past two years, reducing our debt by more than $300 million.[2]

MAJOR HOME APPLIANCE INDUSTRY: WHITE GOODS

In 1996, the U.S. major home appliance industry was a very successful industry. Unlike other industries (such as automobiles and consumer electronics) that had been unable to compete against aggressive Japanese competition, U.S. major home appliance manufacturers dominated the North American market. For "white goods"—refrigerators, freezers, washing machines, dryers, ranges, microwave ovens, and dishwashers—over 84% of those sold in the United States were made domestically.[3] The industry had been very successful in keeping prices low and in improving the value of its products. Compared to 1982, major home appliance prices had increased more slowly than the increase in U.S. earnings and the consumer price index. Thus the average American consumer in 1996 could earn a new appliance in 80% fewer hours on the job than a half-century ago. For example, although the price of a Maytag automatic washing machine had risen from $280 in 1949 to $440 in 1995, it had actually declined when inflation was considered.[4] In addition, the energy efficiency of the most common major appliances had increased every year since 1972.[5] Sales had also been increasing. More appliances were made and sold in the United States in 1994 than in any preceding year. Although shipments for 1995 were slightly down, most industry analysts predicted that 1996 would be another good year for appliance makers.

Nevertheless, the major home appliance industry was facing some significant threats as well as opportunities as it moved through the last decade of the twentieth century. The North American market had reached maturity. Future unit sales were expected to grow only 1%–2% annually on average for the foreseeable future. Operating margins had been dropping as appliance manufacturers were forced to keep prices low to be competitive, even though costs kept increasing. In Western Europe, however, a market already 25% larger than the mature North American appliance market, unit sales were expected to grow 2%–3% annually on average. This figure was expected to increase significantly as Eastern European countries opened their economies to world trade. Appliance markets in Asia and Latin America were expected to grow at a rate of 5%–6% annually.[6] The industry was under pressure from governments around the world to make environmentally safe products and significantly improve appliance energy efficiency.

In 1945, there were approximately 300 major appliance manufacturers in the United States. By 1996, however, the "big five" of Whirlpool (35.0%—up from 33.8% in 1991), General Electric (29.3%—up from 28.2% in 1991), Maytag (14.4%—up from 14.2% in 1991), Frigidaire, owned by A.B. Electrolux (*no* relation to Electrolux Corporation, a U.S. company selling Electrolux brand vacuum cleaners) (13.5%—down from 15.9% in 1991), and Raytheon (6.2%—up from 5.6% in 1991) controlled over 98% of the U.S. market. The consolidation of the industry over the period was a result of fierce domestic competition. Emphasis on quality and durability coupled with strong price competition drove the surviving firms to increased efficiencies and a strong concern for customer satisfaction. The European appliance industry was in the final stages of consolidation. It was home to approximately 30 appliance producers, down from over 150 in the 1960s.[7] The big three of Electrolux (24%), Bosch-Siemens (16%), and Whirlpool (11%) controlled over half of the market in Western Europe and were making strong inroads into Eastern Europe via joint ventures and acquisitions. These three giants plus General Electric were also building a dominant presence in Latin America via acquisitions and joint ventures. Although Japanese and Korean manufacturers were important competitors in the Asian home appliance market in the 1990s, the Asian market was still fragmented with no single dominant company in terms of market share. The top Asian players included Hitachi, Matsushita, Mitsubishi, Sharp, and Toshiba of Japan and Goldstar, Samsung, and Daewoo of Korea. Matsushita was the overall market leader in Asia, but had a market share of less than 10% outside Japan.

(For additional industry information, see Case 17, "The U.S. Major Home Appliance Industry (1996): Domestic versus Global Strategies.")

MAYTAG CORPORATION BUSINESS SEGMENTS AND PRODUCTS

In early 1996, Maytag Corporation was organized into three business units: North American Appliance Group (all major home appliances), Hoover North America (all floor care appliances), and Dixie-Narco (vending machines). Previous to their sale, Hoover Europe and Hoover Australia had been managed as separate business units.

North American Major Appliances

North American major appliances contained the original Maytag Company plus the plants of Admiral, Magic Chef, and Jenn-Air, in addition to the Jackson Dishwasher plant, Maytag Customer Service, Maytag International, Inc., and Maytag Financial Services Corporation. Maytag and Admiral appliances were administered through the Maytag and Admiral Products Unit in Newton, Iowa. Jenn-Air and Magic Chef appliances were administered through the Jenn-Air and Magic Chef Products Unit in Indianapolis, Indiana. Given the corporation's interest in obtaining synergy in production and marketing among the various products, there was no attempt to identify or isolate Admiral, Jenn-Air, or Magic Chef as separate profit centers. Admiral made refrigerators for all the brands, Magic Chef made cooking products for Maytag, and so on.

Compared to its competition, Maytag's North American Major Appliance group generally ranked third or fourth in U.S. market share in each major home appliance category—usually far behind either Whirlpool or General Electric—except in washers, dryers, and gas ranges. Washers and dryers were Maytag's traditional strength. Market surveys consistently found Maytag brand laundry appliances to be not only the brand most desired by consumers (when price was not considered), but also the most reliable. Refrigeration was a traditional strength of Admiral. Although Admiral quality had been allowed to decline under previous management, it was reemphasized after the Maytag acquisition. Gas ranges had always been a particular strength of Magic Chef and were perceived as very reliable in surveys.

Exhibit 1 compares Maytag's 1995 share of the U.S. market, by home appliance category, to that of the market leader. Contrasted with 1992, a number of changes occurred to Maytag's market share. Its share of disposers dropped from 2% to 1% and to sixth place. Its share in dishwashers increased dramatically from 8% to 14%, thanks to new product designs and the Jackson plant. Its share in electric dryers was stable at 15%. Its share in gas dryers dropped from 17% to 14% and out of second place. Its share in electric ranges dropped from 17% to 14% but remained in third place. Its share in gas ranges dropped significantly from 27% to 22% and out of first place to second place. Competition from GE's joint venture with MABE in Mexico contributed to GE's taking over market leadership in gas ranges from Maytag. Maytag's share in full-sized refrigerators dropped from 13% to 10% but remained in fourth place. Hoover increased its market share in upright, cannister, and stick vacuum cleaners (from 34% in 1991 to 35% in 1995), but lost its first-place position in vacuum cleaners to Eureka, whose share grew more rapidly. Hoover's share in hand-held vacuums increased from 6% in 1991 to 10% in 1995.

Maytag and Admiral Products

Headquartered in Newton, Iowa, the original Maytag Company was the flagship of the corporation and manufactured Maytag brand washing machines and dryers in its Newton plant. It also marketed Maytag and Admiral brand cooking products made by Magic Chef and Jenn-Air, a refrigerator line manufactured by Admiral, and dishwashers

Exhibit 1   Maytag Corporation's Share of U.S. Market Compared to Market Leaders' Share by Home Appliance Category in 1995

Appliance Category	Market Leader	Leader Share	Maytag Share	Maytag Rank
Disposers	In-Sink-Erator	64%	1%	6
Dishwashers	GE and Whirlpool	36	14	3
Dryers, electric	Whirlpool	52	15	3
Dryers, gas	Whirlpool	53	14	3
Freezers	Electrolux	70	—[1]	—
Microwave ovens	Sharp	24	—[1]	—
Ranges, electric	GE	41	14	3 (tie w/Electrolux)
Ranges, gas	GE	26	22	2 (tie w/Electrolux)
Refrigerators	GE	38	10	4
Washers	Whirlpool	53	17	2 (tie w/GE)
Vacuums, regular	Eureka	37	35	2
Vacuums, hand-held	Royal	43	10	3

Note:
1. Maytag no longer makes freezers or microwave ovens.
Source: *Appliance Manufacturer* (April 1996), pp. 29–31.

manufactured at the Jackson facility. Market emphasis was on the premium-price segment and the upscale builder market. A survey of Americans found the Maytag brand to be fifteenth in a list of the strongest brand names, based on consumer recognition and perception of quality.

Located in Galesburg, Illinois, the Admiral plant manufactured refrigerators for Maytag, Jenn-Air, Admiral, and Magic Chef brands. Admiral products were marketed to the mid-price segment in conjunction with Maytag brand products. Admiral marketed private-label products, predominantly the Signature 2000 line to Montgomery Ward.

The Maytag and Admiral products unit sold Maytag and Admiral brand appliances through over 9,000 retail dealers in the United States and Canada. A relatively small number of appliances were sold overseas through Maytag Corporation's international sales arm, Maytag International. Maytag appliances were also sold through Montgomery Ward, but not through Sears. According to Leonard Hadley, Maytag/Admiral refused to join the Sears Brand Central concept because it did not want to antagonize its carefully nurtured dealers. Maytag/Admiral dealers accepted distribution through Montgomery Ward because Ward had not traditionally been as dominant a force in appliance retailing as had Sears with its strong Kenmore brand. Maytag/Admiral dealers, in turn, were very loyal and appreciated the company's emphasis on quality.

Prior to Maytag's purchase of Magic Chef (and thus Admiral) in 1986, Admiral had been owned by three different corporations. Very little had been invested into the operation by these previous owners and production quality had dropped significantly. The corporation had invested $60 million in Admiral to improve production efficiencies, enhance product quality, and increase capacity and another $160 in 1995 to further upgrade the facility.

Jenn-Air and Magic Chef Products

The Magic Chef facilities manufactured gas and electric ranges for the Admiral, Magic Chef, and Maytag brands in Cleveland, Tennessee. As part of the Jenn-Air and Magic Chef Products unit, Magic Chef also marketed refrigerators, dishwashers, laundry equipment, and microwave ovens under the Magic Chef brand to the mid-price segment and to certain private label businesses (primarily Montgomery Ward). Prior to its purchase by Maytag, Magic Chef had been a small, family run business. Its product development strategy had been to be a very fast follower. Maytag Corporation had invested $50 million in the Cleveland facilities. From this investment came new lines of Magic Chef and Maytag brand ranges.

In conjunction with Jenn-Air, the company sold Magic Chef and Norge brands directly to dealers. The two additional lower price brands of Hardwick and Crosley were sold through distributors. Like Maytag and Admiral, Magic Chef worked with Jenn-Air to use selected dealers for its Magic Chef and Norge brands. The company's medium to low price orientation had enabled it to sell successfully to builders.

The North American Free Trade Agreement (NAFTA) had created some problems for Magic Chef's range business. Under NAFTA, U.S. tariffs on Mexican imports were eliminated immediately while Mexican tariffs of 20% on U.S. imports were scheduled to be slowly phased out over a 10-year period. Escalating imports of low-priced gas ranges from a Mexican MABE plant (part of a joint venture between GE and MABE) had forced Magic Chef to lay off workers. It was estimated that imports from this and other U.S. and Mexican joint venture plants were some 500,000 units annually—close to one-third of the U.S. market. In a statement addressed to the U.S. government, Leonard Hadley urged that negotiators eliminate the tariffs on U.S.-built appliances:

> This is causing appliance manufacturers who are heavily invested in U.S. facilities to be faced with a rising volume of duty-free imports from Mexico. The high Mexican appliance tariffs make it extremely difficult for Maytag to sell its high-quality, large capacity U.S. products to consumers in Mexico.[8]

Located in Indianapolis, Indiana, as part of the Jenn-Air and Magic Chef Products Unit, Jenn-Air specialized in the manufacture of electric and gas downdraft grill-ranges and cooktops. The unit marketed Jenn-Air brand refrigerators, freezers, dishwashers, and disposers manufactured by Admiral, the corporation's Jackson plant, and other non-Maytag appliance manufacturers, such as Emerson Electric. Jenn-Air billed itself as "The Kitchen Equipment Expert" and believed that its high-quality cooking expertise complemented Maytag Company's high-quality image in laundry appliances. In 1992, Jenn-Air canceled its marketing agreements with its distributors and combined its marketing with that of Magic Chef. Magic Chef dealers were now able to sell the high-quality Jenn-Air brand in conjunction with the medium-quality Magic Chef brand, combining both brands' solid connections with home builders. Interestingly, Jenn-Air was the only Maytag Corporation brand distributed through Sears' Brand Central. This was an important consideration because Sears typically sold one of every four major home appliances sold in the United States.

Jackson Dishwashing Products

Located in Jackson, Tennessee, this was a $43 million, 400,000-square-foot, state-of-the-art manufacturing facility dedicated to producing dishwashers for the Maytag, Admiral, Jenn-Air, and Magic Chef brands. It was designed as a "team plant," with little distinction made between hierarchical levels. Upon the completion of this plant in 1992, dishwasher production was phased out at Maytag's Newton plant and the company no longer had to purchase dishwashers from GE for Magic Chef or Jenn-Air.

The dishwasher had become the fastest growing major home appliance category in North America. Maytag's U.S. market share had jumped significantly from 8% in 1992 to 14% in 1995. This growth was approximately double that of the industry. After only two years of operation, the corporation invested $13.7 million to add two more assembly lines at the Jackson plant.

Unfortunately, half the Maytag brand dishwashers produced during 1994 were later discovered to have a potentially defective component, which in some cases started fires. After receiving 140 complaints, Maytag informed the U.S. Consumer Product Safety Commission of the problem and started a program in October 1995 to notify, inspect, and repair the 231,000 potentially defective dishwashers (out of 553,000) made during that time. The defective component had been made by a long-term Maytag supplier. According to Dick Haines, President of Maytag Company, "Although the likelihood of a component failure is small, we believe the inspection program being undertaken by Maytag is another expression of our commitment to dependability." [9] With the Jackson expansion coming on line in early 1996, management hoped that publicity about the defective component would not affect 1996 dishwasher sales.

Maytag Customer Service

Headquartered in Cleveland, Tennessee, Maycor handled all parts and service for Maytag Corporation appliance brands. A consolidated and automated warehouse facility in Milan, Tennessee, replaced the four separate parts distribution operations of Maytag, Admiral, Jenn-Air, and Magic Chef.

Hoover North America

Headquartered in North Canton, Ohio, Hoover North America manufactured and marketed to all price segments upright and canister vacuum cleaners, stick and hand-held vacuum cleaners, disposable vacuum cleaner bags, floor polishers and shampooers, central cleaning systems, and commercial vacuum cleaners—and washing machines in Mexico under the Hoover brand name. It heavily advertised to the consumer. The company was almost totally integrated. In addition to the North Canton headquarters and three Stark County, Ohio, manufacturing plants, Hoover North America controlled four other facilities in El Paso, Texas, Ciudad Juarez, Mexico (a maquiladora assembly plant), Burlington, Ontario (Hoover Canada), and Industrial Vallejo, Mexico (Hoover Mexicana). Praised by industry experts as one of the best manufacturing facilities in the United States, the new North Canton "factory within a factory" was designed by an interdisciplinary team to reduce costs and improve quality.

In the United States, Hoover held 35% share of the very competitive market for residential full-sized vacuum cleaners and over half of the floor polisher market. Nevertheless, its share of the market for full-sized vacuum cleaners had dropped from 40% in 1983 when it led the industry. It only had 10% of the hand-held vacuum cleaner market compared to Royal's 43% and Black & Decker's 31%. Eureka (now part of A.B. Electrolux of Sweden) was first in 1995 full-sized cleaner sales, with a U.S. market share of 37% (up dramatically from only 16% in 1992). Royal was third in full-sized cleaner sales in 1995, with a declining market share of 7%. Growth in the U.S. floor care market exceeded that of many other appliance segments. Over 22 million vacuum cleaners were sold in the United States in 1995. Continued growth was predicted. Although over 97% of U.S.

households had at least one vacuum cleaner, many homes had two or three full-sized vacuums plus hand-held vacuums. Like major home appliances, the average life expectancies of full-sized vacuum cleaners were over 10 years.

Dixie-Narco

Dixie-Narco, Inc., was a subsidiary of Maytag Corporation that made canned and bottled soft drink and juice vending machines sold to soft drink syrup bottlers and distributors, canteen owners, and others. Headquartered in Williston, South Carolina, the group manufactured vending machines in its factory there. It also had an Electronics Division (previously called Ardac, Inc.) outside Cleveland in Eastlake, Ohio. The Eastlake facility made dollar-bill acceptors, changers, and foreign banknote acceptors for soft drink vending machines. Dixie-Narco had spent $31 million in 1990 to convert the Admiral freezer and refrigerator factory in Williston into the largest and most highly automated vending machine producing facility of its type in the country. Maytag Corporation had decided in 1989 to stop manufacturing home freezers and compact refrigerators because of decreasing profit margins and low sales and to buy whatever it needed from others. This conversion enabled Dixie-Narco to move all of its vending machine production from its old plant in Ranson, West Virginia, to the new Williston plant.

The company sold vending equipment directly to independent bottlers and full-service operators who installed banks of vending machines in offices and factories. It also marketed through bottlers directly to syrup company–owned bottlers. In 1994, Dixie-Narco introduced a new glass-front merchandiser for use by convenience stores. Instead of inserting coins into the machine to buy a product, the customer opened the machine's glass door to select a product—then paid a clerk. According to Maytag Corporation management, sales of vending machines continued to be relatively flat in the United States, but due to strong demand for Dixie-Narco products, the company was able to hold its solid share of the U.S. market. International sales had been increasing thanks to the introduction of the glass-front merchandiser. Traditional coin-fed vending machines have not been well accepted outside North America.

On November 2, 1995, Maytag Corporation announced that management had entered into a letter of intent to sell Dixie-Narco's Eastlake, Ohio, Electronics Division for a noncash book loss in the $6–$7 million range. According to Dixie-Narco President Robert Downing, "Going forward, Dixie-Narco's management resources and capital investments will be focused on our core business of designing, manufacturing, and marketing vending machines and glass front merchandisers." [10]

When asked why Dixie-Narco remained a part of Maytag Corporation, Leonard Hadley responded:

> Mechanically, a vending machine is a refrigerator, and we build thousands of refrigerators per day at our plant in Galesburg, Illinois. . . . As a marketing assignment, our Dixie-Narco customers have the same needs as our Maytag commercial laundry customers. . . . Dixie-Narco's great value to us is that it has a different set of competitors than the major home appliance business or the floor care industry. It allows us an important earnings stream from a business that our largest two major appliance competitors don't have. . . . It provides us with an important supplement to our U.S. business by allowing us an international export opportunity. [11]

Hoover Europe

Overseas, where close to 70% of its total revenues had been generated prior to joining Maytag, Hoover had become successful, not only in manufacturing and marketing upright and canister vacuum cleaners, but also (especially in Great Britain and Australia) in washing machines, dryers, refrigerators, dishwashers, and microwave ovens. Headquartered in Merthyr Tydfil, South Wales, Hoover Europe manufactured washers, dryers, and dishwashers in a nearby factory. Upright vacuum cleaners, motors for washers and dryers, and disposable vacuum cleaner bags were produced in a facility in Cambuslang (near Glasgow), Scotland. A plant in Portugal manufactured canister-type vacuums, most of which were sold on the continent. Hoover Europe marketed its products to the mid-priced segment of European markets.

British consumers accounted for 75% of Hoover's $600 million European sales. Its market position in the United Kingdom was 34% in washers (second place), 5% in dryers (third place), and 19% in dishwashers (second place). Although Hoover vacuum cleaners were big sellers in continental Europe, its major appliances were not. This concentration in Great Britain became a serious problem for Hoover in the late 1980s and early 1990s when a combination of a recession and high interest rates acted to reduce sharply Hoover's European sales.

To boost sales, Hoover Europe initiated a promotion during late 1992 and early 1993, offering customers free international airline tickets when they bought appliances for as little as $150. The overly generous offer resulted in such an overwhelming response that Maytag Corporation was forced to pay a total of more than $72 million over the three-year period 1992–1994 for sales and administrative expenses related to the promotion. The promotion also became a public relations nightmare because people complained about having trouble getting their free flights. Three British representatives from the "Hoover Holiday Pressure Group" attended Maytag's 1994 annual shareholders' meeting in Newton. They labeled the fiasco "Hoovergate" and threatened to go to Ralph Nader's group if the problem was not settled to their satisfaction. The corporation fired three top Hoover Europe executives and established a task force to examine the situation and to deal with the issue of control versus autonomy.[12]

With only $400 million in revenues, Hoover Europe was at a significant disadvantage against established European competitors such as Electrolux, Whirlpool, and GE–GEC who counted their revenues in billions. This was a big reason why Maytag Corporation decided to sell Hoover Europe to Italian-based Candy, S.p.A. in May 1995. Included in the sale were Hoover Europe's headquarters, two manufacturing sites in Britain, a plant in Portugal, and the rights to the Hoover trademark in Europe, parts of the Middle East, and North Africa. Hoover North America continued selling floor care products to the rest of the world.

Hoover Australia

Hoover Pty, Ltd., located near Sydney, manufactured vacuum cleaners, washers, and dryers. Hoover Appliances, Ltd. produced refrigerators and freezers near Melbourne. The Melbourne plant had earlier been purchased from Philips and was producing Admiral and Norge refrigerators in addition to the Hoover brand. Prior to the decision to sell Hoover Australia at the end of 1994, Maytag Corporation had been considering the possibility of manufacturing Admiral and/or Norge laundry equipment at the Sydney plant. Hoover Australia marketed its products to the mid-priced segment of the Australian and New Zealand markets.

MARKETING

Of the three brands—Maytag, Magic Chef, and Jenn-Air—only the Maytag brand had been heavily advertised to consumers. The Magic Chef and Jenn-Air brands received only cooperative advertising and promotions through dealers. Since Maytag Corporation had used Admiral primarily as a manufacturing facility to make refrigerators for other brands and for private labels (for example, Montgomery Ward's Signature line), it did little advertising of Admiral as a brand. Corporate advertising expenses had risen from $113.4 million in 1992 and $136.5 million in 1993 to $153.2 million in 1994 but fell to $134 million in 1995.

Until 1993, Maytag, Magic Chef, and Jenn-Air brands had been sold through separate dealer networks. The decision was made in late 1992 to reorganize the corporation's marketing into two major channels. The Admiral brand was positioned as a mid-priced product to be sold through Maytag dealers. This gave Maytag dealers a lower priced product to complement the relatively high-priced Maytag brand. Jenn-Air, known for its high quality, merged its dealer network into that of Magic Chef in order to make available to Magic Chef Jenn-Air's historically strong relationship with small, quality builders. The goal was to increase sales to builders—something Maytag brand appliances had traditionally been unable to do. As a result, the newly combined Magic Chef/Jenn-Air sales organization had four brands to market and could cover all quality and price levels: Norge and Hardwick as the low-end brands for special opportunities; Jenn-Air as the mid-range to high-end brand with unique styling and innovative features; and Magic Chef as the mid-range to low-end brand with less innovative but more value-oriented features.

Both Jenn-Air and Magic Chef moved their advertising business to Leo Burnett USA, the same agency responsible for Maytag's "lonely repairman" ads. No longer would the two brands focus only on dealer ads and promotions to market their products. Magic Chef planned to take some of the money it had been spending on dealer ads to spend on consumer ads to build market awareness.

In 1995, Maytag and the Leo Burnett USA advertising agency were honored by the New York chapter of the American Marketing Association with a gold "EFFIE" award for the Maytag brand's "Growing the Legend" advertising campaign. The campaign featured the Maytag repairman, "Ol' Lonely," and included TV commercials, print advertising, and point-of-purchase materials.[13] (See Exhibit 2 for The Maytag Repairman.)

Hoover floor care products had traditionally received strong advertising in all the media. The company continued its successful "Nobody does it like Hoover" consumer-oriented advertising. After noting that 70 dealers accounted for approximately 80% of Hoover's North American floor care sales, management restructured the sales organization in 1992 to serve these "power retailers" better.

STRATEGIC MANAGERS

Board of Directors

One-third of the 14-member Board of Directors was elected every year for a three-year term. From 1989 to 1994, the same members had served on the Board continuously. Three had come from the Chicago Pacific (and thus Hoover) acquisition. Of these, Lester Crown and Neele Stearns still served in early 1996. New to the board in 1994 were Wayland Hicks, a former Executive Vice-President of Xerox Corporation and CEO of Nextel Communications (a satellite cellular company), and Bernard Rethore, President of Phelps Dodge Industries (a manufacturer of truck wheels and specialty chemicals). New to the board in 1995 were Barbara Allen, Executive Vice-President at Quaker Oats Company, and Carole Uhrich, Group Vice-President at Polaroid Corporation. Leonard Hadley, CEO, served as Chairman of the Board. (See Exhibit 3 for a complete list of the board of directors.)

Exhibit 2 **The Real Maytag Repairman**

The "Ol' Lonely" Maytag repairman created for television ads in 1967 had little to do with the actual daily life of a real Maytag repairman. Michael Headlee of Michael's Maytag Home Appliance Center in Des Moines, Iowa, repairs approximately 40 malfunctioning machines per week. On average, only three of them are Maytags. Although Headlee sells only Maytag, he services all brands. No one exclusively repairs Maytag brand appliances. "You won't find one because he would starve," explained Headlee. Headlee had been working as an independent service contractor until 1991, when Maytag Company asked him to open a Maytag store.

Headlee enjoys doing stunts to show off the quality built into Maytag brand appliances. In 1992, he started a Maytag and a Kenmore washer after rigging both to run continuously. Although Maytag officials weren't too excited about his project, Headlee went ahead to see for himself which product would last longer. The Kenmore died in six months; the Maytag continued for two years.

When a customer walked into Headlee's store one day to look at refrigerators, Headlee showed him the fine points of a floor model. According to Headlee, Maytag builds for the "what ifs." For example, what if a neighbor boy uses the door as a step ladder and knocks out one of the storage bins? No problem, says Headlee. The bins are removable and adjustable. No need to replace the $180 liner or the $35 bin—only a $2 breakaway clip. "The hinges are heavier than any other in the industry. . . . Rollers? We've got the fattest rollers in the industry." To demonstrate, Headlee took out the meat–cheese drawer, turned it over on the floor, and jumped on it. According to Headlee, a person could do aerobics on the meat–cheese drawer!

Competition from "super stores" keeps profit margins low, so Headlee depends on repair work to stay in business. "We got a deck of cards. We got a cribbage board. And that keeps us pretty well occupied when we're not working on . . . a Kenmore or a Whirlpool," joked Headlee.

Source: M. A. Lickteig, "A Real Repairman Juggles Calls and Sales," *Des Moines Register* (November 1, 1994), p. M1.

Counting only personally owned shares, the executive officers and directors owned only 4.8% of Maytag's outstanding shares. (Lester Crown was the largest holder of stock with 4.27% plus 0.79% in trusts or owned by family members.) More than 60% of Maytag's stock was owned by individual shareholders. The only significant blocks of stock owned by institutional investors were the 11% owned by FMR Corporation and the 6% owned by Delaware Management Holdings, Inc.

Top Management

Many of the Maytag Corporation Executive Officers had worked their way up through the corporation and had spent most their careers immersed in the Maytag Company culture. This was certainly the case for Leonard Hadley, Chairman and CEO, who had served the company continuously since joining the company 34 years ago as a cost accountant. (See Exhibit 4 for a listing of corporate executives.)

In a move to diversify top management backgrounds, the corporation in mid 1993 hired John Cunningham to serve as Corporate Executive Vice-President and Chief Financial Officer and Joseph Fogliano to serve as Corporate Executive Vice-President and President of North American Operations. These were the second and third, respectively, most powerful corporate executive officers after Hadley. Cunningham had previously been Vice-President and Assistant General Manager of IBM's Main Frame Division. Fogliano previously had served as President and CEO of Thomson Electronics. In addition, David D. Urbani was hired in 1994 to serve as Corporate Vice-President and Treasurer. Previously, he had been Assistant Treasurer at Air Products and Chemicals.

In a surprise move, North American President Fogliano resigned from the corporation in August 1995. In an interview, Fogliano (age 55) stated that he had joined the corporation with the understanding that he would be a leading candidate to replace

Exhibit 3 **Board of Directors: Maytag Corporation**

Director	Joined Board	Position	Term Expires	Shares Owned
Barbara R. Allen (43)[1]	1995	Executive Vice-President Quaker Oats	1996[2]	100
Edward Cazier, Jr. (71)[1]	1987	Counsel to law firm of Morgan, Lewis, & Bockius	1997	11,900
Howard L. Clark, Jr. (52)[1]	1986	Vice-Chairman Shearson,Lehman, Hutton Holdings, Inc.	1996[2]	13,836
Lester Crown (70)[3]	1989	Chairman Material Service Corporation	1997	4,503,565
Leonard A. Hadley (61)	1985	Chairman and CEO Maytag Corporation	1996[2]	211,920
Wayland R. Hicks (53)	1994	CEO and Vice-Chair Nextel Corporation	1998	6,000
Robert D. Ray (67)[3]	1983	CEO IASD Health Services Corporation	1996[2]	15,600
Bernard G. Rethore (54)	1994	President Phelps Dodge Industries	1997	4,000
Dr. W. Ann Reynolds (58)[3, 4]	1988	Chancellor City University of N.Y.	1998	12,300
John A. Sivright (67)[3, 4]	1976	Senior Relationship Executive Harris Bankcorp, Inc.	1998	23,712
Neele Stearns, Jr. [1,4] (60)	1989	CEO CC Industries	1997	14,090
Fred G. Steingraber (57)	1989	Chair and CEO A.T. Kearney, Inc.	1998	15,000
Peter S. Willmott (58)	1985	Chair and CEO Willmott Services	1996[2]	35,000
Carole J. Uhrich (52)	1995	Group Vice-President Polaroid Corporation	1997	—

Notes:
1. Member of audit committee.
2. Up for reelection at April, 1996 annual meeting.
3. Member of nominating committee.
4. Member of compensation committee.
Source: Maytag Corporation, *Notice of Annual Meeting & Proxy Statement* (1996), pp. 3–8.

Leonard Hadley. As time went by, according to Fogliano, it became apparent that this was not to be. His decision to leave Maytag developed in discussions with Leonard Hadley. "These things are a matter of fit, and Len has to make a decision on that," commented Fogliano. He further explained that there may have been a lack of fit between himself and the Maytag culture.[14] Donald Lorton, President of the corporation's diversified operations, was then named acting President of the North American Appliance Group until a national search could find a replacement for Fogliano.

Four months later, John Cunningham announced that he was leaving the corporation to take a similar position with Whirlpool Corporation. Hadley commented that

Exhibit 4   Executive Officers: Maytag Corporation

Officer	Office	Became an Officer
Leonard A. Hadley (61)	Chairman and CEO	1979
Donald M. Lorton (65)	Executive VP and President of Maytag Appliances (acting)	1995
Gerald J. Pribanic (52)	Executive VP and Chief Financial Officer	1996
Brian A. Girdlestone (62)	President, Hoover Company	1996
Robert W. Downing (59)	President, Dixie-Narco	1996
Edward H. Graham (60)	Senior VP, General Counsel, and Asst. Secretary	1990
Jon O. Nicholas (56)	VP, Human Resources, Maytag Appliances	1993
Carleton F. Zacheis (62)	Senior VP, Administrative	1988
John M. Dupuy (39)	VP, Strategic Planning	1996
David D. Urbani	VP and Treasurer	1994
Steven H. Wood (38)	VP, Financial Reporting and Audit	1996

Source: Maytag Corporation, *Form 10-K* (December 31, 1995), p. 7.

Cunningham had "implemented the strategy to restructure our balance sheet that I outlined to him when he arrived here two years ago, and he did an excellent job."[15] Gerald Pribanic, Vice-President of Finance and Controller for Hoover North America, took over Cunningham's position in January 1996 as acting Corporate Vice-President and Chief Financial Officer.

In January 1996, John Dupuy joined Maytag as Corporate Vice-President of Strategic Planning. Previously, he had been a consultant with Booz, Allen & Hamilton and with A. T. Kearney.

CORPORATE CULTURE

Much of Maytag Corporation's corporate culture derived from F. L. Maytag's personal philosophy and from lessons the founder had learned when starting the Maytag Company at the turn of the century. His greatest impact was still felt in Maytag's (1) commitment to quality, (2) concern for employees, (3) concern for the community, (4) concern for innovation, (5) promotion from within, (6) dedication to hard work, and (7) emphasis on performance.

- **Commitment to quality.** Concerned when almost half the farm implements sold were defective in some way, F. L. Maytag vowed to eliminate all defects. Maytag's employees over the years had taken great pride in the company's reputation for high-quality products and being a part of "the dependability company."

- **Concern for employees.** Long before it was required to do so by law, Maytag Company established safety standards in the workplace and offered its employees accident and life insurance policies. Wages have traditionally been some of the highest in the industry.

- **Concern for the community.** Following F. L. Maytag's example, Maytag management had been active in community affairs and concerned about pollution. The decision to build its new automatic washer plant in Newton after World War II indicated the company's loyalty to the town.

- **Concern for innovation.** From its earliest years, the company was not interested in cosmetic changes for the sake of sales, but in internal improvements related to quality, durability, and safety.

- **Promotion from within.** F. L. Maytag was very concerned about building company loyalty and trust. The corporation's policy of promoting from within was an extension of that concern.

- **Dedication to hard work.** In tune with the strong work ethic permeating the midwestern United States, F. L. Maytag put in huge amounts of time to establish and maintain the company. His fabled trip West, while Chairman of the Board, to sell personally a train carload of washers set an example to his salesforce and became a permanent part of company lore.

- **Emphasis on performance.** Preferring to be judged by his work rather than by his words, F. L. Maytag was widely regarded as a good example of the Midwest work ethic.

In 1996, the Maytag Corporation still reflected its strong roots in the Maytag Company culture. Corporate headquarters were housed on the second floor of a relatively small building (compared to Maytag Company's Plant 1 and the Research and Development building surrounding it). Built in 1961, the Newton, Iowa, building still housed Maytag Company administrative offices on its first floor. Responding to a question in 1990 regarding a comment from outside observers that the corporation had "spartan" offices, Leonard Hadley, then–Chief Operating Officer, looked around at his rather small office with no windows and said, "See for yourself. We want to keep corporate staff to a minimum." Hadley felt that the headquarters location and the fact that most of the corporate officers had come from Maytag Company resulted in an overall top management concern for quality and financially conservative management. This supported then–CEO Daniel Krum's position that the corporation's competitive edge was its *dedication to quality*. According to Krum: "We believe quality and reliability are, ultimately, what the consumer wants." This devotion to quality was exemplified by a corporate policy that no cost reduction proposal would be approved if it reduced product quality in any way.

R&D AND PURCHASING

Research and Development (R&D) at Maytag had always been interested in internal improvements related to quality, durability, and safety. This orientation traditionally dominated the company's view of product development. One example was the careful way the company chose to replace in 1989 the venerable Helical Drive transmission with a new Dependable Drive™ transmission for its automatic washers. The new drive was delivered in 1975, patented in 1983, and put into test market in 1985, after it had been demonstrated that the drive would contribute to a 20-year product life. The Dependable Drive contained only 40 parts, compared to the previous drive's 65, and allowed the agitator to move 153 strokes a minute, compared to only 64 previously.

However, this methodical approach to R&D meant that Maytag Corporation might miss out on potential innovations. Realizing this dilemma, the corporation began to emphasize closer relationships with its key suppliers in both product development and process engineering. Joe Thomson, Vice-President of Purchasing at Galesburg Refrigeration Products (Admiral plant), provided one example:

> We made an arrangement with a large steel supplier that led to a team effort to establish hardness specifications on our cabinet and door steel to improve fabrication. This team was very successful and the quality improvement and reduction in cost reached all our expectations. The company is now supplying all of our steel requirements.[16]

These strategic alliances between appliance makers and their suppliers were one way to speed up the application of new technology to new products and processes. For example, Maytag Company was approached by one of its suppliers, Honeywell's Microswitch Division, offering its expertise in fuzzy logic technology—a technology Maytag did not have at that time. The resulting partnership in product development resulted in Maytag's new IntelliSense™ dishwasher. Unlike previous dishwashers, which had to be set by the user, Maytag's fuzzy logic dishwasher automatically selected the proper cycle to get the dishes clean, based on a series of factors, such as the amount of dirt, presence of detergent, and other factors.[17] According to Paul Ludwig, Business Development Manager for Honeywell's Microswitch Division, "Had Maytag not included us on the design team, we don't believe the two companies would have achieved the same innovative solution, nor would we have completed the project in such a short amount of time."[18] Terry Carlson, Vice-President of Purchasing for Maytag Corporation, stressed the importance of close relationships with suppliers:

> Strategic partnerships are a developing reality in our organization. . . . By paring our supplier base down by more than 50% in the past three years, we are encouraging greater supplier participation in our product design and production-planning processes. We're making choices to establish preferred supplier directions for our technical groups. These groups interact with their supplier counterparts. We are assigning joint task teams to specific projects, be they new-product-design oriented or continuous improvement of current products or processes.[19]

The corporation's R&D expenses were $44 million in 1992, $42.7 million in 1993, $45.9 million in 1994, and $47 million in 1995. According to Doug Ringger, Director of Product Planning for Maytag and Admiral products, the use of cross-functional teams had helped cut development time in half from what it used to be. He stated, "By having input from all areas early in the development cycle, issues are resolved before becoming problems."[20]

MANUFACTURING

Like other major home appliance manufacturers, Maytag Corporation was in the midst of investing millions of dollars in upgrading its plants and other facilities. Once considered to be the most efficient in the nation, Maytag's Newton, Iowa, plant was beginning to show its age by the late 1980s. Consequently, top management made a controversial decision to move dishwasher production from its Newton plant to a new plant in Jackson, Tennessee. This new plant was dedicated to the manufacturing of dishwashers for all the corporation's brands. This was in line with the industry trend to build "dedicated," highly efficient plants to produce only one product line with variations for multiple brands and price levels. Previously, only Maytag brand dishwashers had been made in Newton. Dishwashers had been purchased from General Electric for the Jenn-Air and Magic Chef brands.

Community leaders and union officials who had been discouraged by the corporation's dishwasher decision were jubilant in January 1994 when top management announced that it had chosen Newton as the production site for its new line of "horizontal axis" clothes washing machines. (The Iowa Department of Economic Development had offered Maytag a $1 million forgivable loan if it built the plant in Newton.[21]) A front-loader, the new washer would be similar to those currently popular in most of Europe. This type of washer was expected to use some 40% less water than comparable top loaders (vertical axis) and significantly less electricity. Like Frigidaire, Maytag concluded that only a horizontal-axis washer would meet future U.S. Department of Energy standards. In contrast, GE and Whirlpool were still unsure about the superiority of this design and were attempting to design a more efficient vertical-axis washer.

The corporation was also investing $160 million in the old Admiral refrigeration plant in Galesburg, Illinois, during the three-year period beginning 1995. As mentioned earlier, after only two years of operation, Maytag was spending $13.7 million to add two more assembly lines to its successful Jackson dishwasher plant.

HUMAN RESOURCES AND LABOR RELATIONS

Throughout the corporation, employees were organized into various labor unions. The bargaining unit representing Maytag and Admiral Products unionized employees in Newton, Iowa, was the United Auto Workers. The unions representing employees at other U.S. Maytag Corporation companies were the Sheet Metal Workers International Association (Jenn-Air facilities), the International Brotherhood of Electrical Workers (Hoover North America), and the International Association of Machinists and Aerospace Workers (Admiral and Magic Chef facilities). All the presidents of union locals belonged to a Maytag Council, which met once a year to discuss union issues.

Traditionally, the Maytag Company had had cordial relations with its local unions, but the change to a large corporation seemed to alter that union relationship. Nevertheless, the corporation had not had any strikes by any of its unions since a one-day walkout at Maytag Company in 1974. This was worthy of note, considering that during the three-year period 1990–1992 the corporation reduced employment by 4,500 people. Newton's UAW Local 997 supported a six-year contract extension in December 1993 to help entice the corporation to locate its planned horizontal-axis washing machine facility in Newton rather than at the washer plant in Herrin, Illinois, originally owned by Magic Chef. Members of the International Association of Machinists and Aerospace Workers at the Galesburg (Admiral) refrigeration plant overwhelmingly approved a five-year agreement in November 1994 that would allow the company to expand production during the peak summer months instead of closing down for two weeks for vacations. This was done partially to encourage the corporation to invest further in the plant. Mike Norville, President of Local 2063 in Galesburg, said that, although automation could result in short-term job losses, in the long-run "there will be more jobs. We're going to make a lot more (refrigerators) because we want a bigger piece of the market."[22]

In August 1995 Maytag Corporation agreed to a $16.5 million (pre-tax) settlement with 800 workers who had lost their jobs when the corporation closed Dixie-Narco's plant in Ranson, West Virginia. Although the workers had been non-union and not subject to a written contract, they claimed that Maytag officials had repeatedly told them that the new Williston factory would supplement, not replace, production at the Ranson plant. Although agreeing to the settlement, Maytag officials did not admit any wrongdoing. "The original plant closing was not what we desired, but it's what was required by economic and business realities," explained Edward Graham, Vice-President and General Counsel of Maytag. "We reluctantly agreed to settle this case even though we believe our actions in closing the plant were lawful, prudent, and reasonable."[23]

STRATEGIC PLANNING

Strategic planning had led to many of the recent changes in Maytag Corporation. In 1978, when Leonard Hadley was working as Maytag Company's Assistant Controller, CEO Daniel Krumm asked him and two others from manufacturing and marketing to serve as a strategic planning task force. Krumm asked the three people the question: *"If we keep doing what we're now doing, what will the Maytag Company look like in five years?"* The question posed a challenge—considering that the company had never done financial modeling and none of the three knew much of strategic planning. Hadley worked with a programmer in his MIS section to develop "what if" scenarios. The task force presented its conclusion to the Board of Directors: A large part of Maytag's profits (the company had the best profit margin in the industry) was coming from products and services with no future: repair parts, portable washers and dryers, and wringer washing machines.

Looking back to 1978, Hadley felt that this was yet another crucial time for the company. The Board of Directors was becoming less conservative as more outside directors came from companies that were growing through acquisitions. With the support of the Board, Krumm promoted Hadley to the new position of Vice-President of Corporate Planning. Hadley was given the task of analyzing the industry to search for acquisition candidates. Until that time, most planning had been oriented internally with little external analysis.

In 1990, then-Chairman Daniel Krumm had presented Maytag Corporation's strategic plan at the annual shareholders meeting. In addition to stressing quality, synergy, and globalization as keys, Krumm had said:

> Increasing *Profitability* is essential. . . . Our objective is to be the profitability leader in the industry for each product line we manufacture. We intend to out-perform the competition in the next five years striving for a 6.5 percent return on sales, a 10 percent return on assets, and a 20 percent return on equity. . . . However, . . . we must not emphasize market share at the expense of profitability.

It was clear by the end of 1992 that these objectives were not going to be met anytime soon. In his speech to the 1993 annual meeting, newly promoted Chairman Hadley updated the strategic plan by presenting the corporation's three current goals:

- Increased profitability

- Become number one in total customer satisfaction

- Become the third largest appliance manufacturer (in unit sales) in North America.

Profitability would be increased by growing market share in the "core" North American major appliance and floor care businesses. Hadley pointed out that "Maytag Corporation wants all its brands to beat the competition in satisfying the customer, be that customer a dealer, builder, or end user of the product."

FINANCIAL SITUATION

Return on equity (ROE) has been a weak spot of the corporation since it first embarked on the strategy of growth through acquisitions. The ROE was over 25% before the Magic Chef merger in 1986, peaked at over 30% in 1988, was nearly cut in half to 18.3% in 1989 after the Chicago Pacific acquisition, and fell to 8% in 1991. In 1992, the annual report showed a net loss for the first time since the 1920s. In 1993 and 1994, net income showed real improvement, but in 1995 it dropped again. (See Exhibits 5–7 for the com-

Exhibit 5 **Statements of Consolidated Income (Loss): Maytag Corporation**
(Dollar amounts in thousands, except per-share data)

Year Ending December 31	1995	1994	1993	1992	1991	1990
Net sales	$3,039,524	$3,372,515	$2,987,054	$3,041,223	$2,970,626	$3,056,833
Cost of sales	2,250,616	2,496,065	2,262,942	2,339,406	2,254,221	2,309,138
Gross profit	788,908	876,450	724,112	701,817	716,405	747,695
Selling, general, and administrative expenses	500,674	553,682	515,234	528,250	524,898	517,088
Reorganization expenses	—	—	—	95,000	—	—
Special charge	—	—	50,000	—	—	—
Operating income	288,234	322,768	158,878	78,567	191,507	230,607
Interest expense	(52,087)	(74,077)	(75,364)	(75,004)	(75,159)	(81,966)
Loss on business dispositions	(146,785)	(13,088)	—	—	—	—
Settlement of lawsuit	(16,500)	—	—	—	—	—
Loss of guarantee of indebtedness	(18,000)	—	—	—	—	—
Other—net	4,942	5,734	6,356	3,983	7,069	10,764
Income before income taxes, extraordinary item, and accounting changes	59,804	241,337	89,870	7,546	123,417	159,405
Income taxes	74,800	90,200	38,600	15,900	44,400	60,500
Income before extraordinary item and effect of accounting changes	(14,996)	151,137	51,270	(8,354)	79,017	98,905
Extraordinary item—loss on early retirement of debt	(5,480)	—	—	—	—	—
Effect of accounting changes for postretirement benefits other than pensions and income taxes	—	—	—	(307,000)	—	—
Cumulative effect of accounting change	—	(3,190)	—	—	—	—
Net income (loss)	$ (20,476)	$ 147,947	$ 51,270	$ (315,354)	$ 79,017	$ 98,905
Average number of shares of common stock	107,062,000	106,795,000	106,252,000	106,077,000	105,761,000	105,617,000
Per share data						
Income (loss) before extraordinary item and effect of accounting changes	$(0.14)	$1.42	$0.48	$(0.08)	$0.75	$0.94
Extraordinary item	(0.05)					
Cumulative effect of accounting change	—	0.03	—	(2.89)	—	—
Net income (loss) per share	$ (.19)	$ 1.39	$ 0.48	$ (2.97)	$ 0.75	$ 0.94

Source: Maytag Corporation, *Annual Reports.*

pany's financial statements.) Profits declined from $147.6 million in 1994 to a $20.5 million loss in 1995. If special charges were ignored, however, net income for 1995 would have been $144.7 million—down only 2% from 1994. Sales had actually increased 0.9% from 1994. In analyzing the figures, Hadley noted that each of the product lines—major appliances, floor care, and vending—had performed well, even with increasing materials costs and lower industrywide sales.

At its October 1995 meeting, the Board of Directors had authorized the repurchase of up to 10.8 million shares of the corporation's common stock, which represented 10% of the outstanding shares. The directors had also approved an increase of 12% in the

Exhibit 6   Statements of Consolidated Financial Condition: Maytag Corporation
(Dollar amounts in thousands)

Year Ending December 31	1995	1994	1993	1992	1991	1990
Assets						
Current assets						
Cash and cash equivalents	$ 141,214	$ 110,403	$ 31,730	$ 57,032	$ 48,752	$ 69,587
Accounts receivable, less allowance (1995, $12,540; 1994, $20,037; 1993, $15,629; 1992, $16,380; 1991, $14,119; 1990, $17,600)	417,457	567,531	532,353	476,850	457,773	487,726
Inventories—finished goods	163,968	254,345	282,841	249,289	314,493	335,417
Inventories—raw materials and supplies	101,151	132,924	146,313	151,794	174,589	200,370
Deferred income taxes	42,785	45,589	46,695	52,261	24,858	22,937
Other current assets	43,559	19,345	16,919	28,309	56,168	52,484
Total current assets	910,134	1,130,137	1,056,851	1,015,535	1,076,633	1,168,521
Noncurrent assets						
Deferred income taxes	91,610	72,394	68,559	71,442	—	—
Pension investments	1,489	112,522	163,175	215,433	232,231	235,264
Intangible pension asset	91,291	84,653	4,928	—	—	—
Other intangibles less amortization allowance (1995, $65,039; 1994, $56,250; 1993, $46,936; 1992, $37,614; 1991, $28,295; 1990, $18,980)	300,086	310,343	319,657	328,980	338,275	347,090
Miscellaneous	29,321	44,979	35,266	35,989	52,436	45,209
Total noncurrent assets	513,797	624,891	591,585	651,844	622,942	627,563
Property, plant, and equipment						
Land	24,246	32,600	46,149	47,370	51,147	50,613
Buildings and improvements	260,394	284,439	288,590	286,368	296,684	282,828
Machinery and equipment	1,030,233	1,109,411	1,068,199	962,006	895,025	828,464
Construction in progress	97,053	30,305	44,753	90,847	92,954	61,775
	1,411,926	1,456,755	1,447,691	1,386,591	1,335,810	1,223,680
Less allowances for depreciation	710,791	707,456	626,629	552,480	500,317	433,223
Total property, plant, and equipment	701,135	749,299	821,062	834,111	835,493	790,457
Total assets	$2,125,066	$2,504,327	$2,469,498	$2,501,490	$2,535,068	$2,586,541
Liabilities and Shareholders' Equity						
Current liabilities						
Notes payable	$ —	$ 45,148	$ 157,571	$ 19,886	$ 23,504	$ 56,601
Accounts payable	142,676	212,441	195,981	$218,142	273,731	266,190
Compensation to employees	61,644	61,311	84,405	89,245	63,845	53,753
Accrued liabilities	156,041	146,086	178,015	180,894	165,384	154,369
Income taxes payable	3,141	26,037	16,193	11,323	17,574	13,736
Current maturities of long-term debt	3,201	43,411	18,505	43,419	23,570	11,070
Total current liabilities	366,703	534,434	650,670	562,909	567,608	555,719
Noncurrent liabilities						
Deferred income taxes	14,367	38,375	44,882	89,011	75,210	71,548
Long-term debt	536,579	663,205	724,695	789,232	809,480	857,941
Postretirement benefits—not pensions	428,478	412,832	391,635	380,376	—	—
Pension liability	88,883	59,363	17,383	—	—	—
Other noncurrent liabilities	52,705	64,406	53,452	80,737	72,185	86,602
Total noncurrent liabilities	1,121,012	1,238,181	1,232,047	1,339,356	956,875	1,016,091

(continued)

Exhibit 6 **Statements of Consolidated Financial Condition: Maytag Corporation** (continued)

Year Ending December 31	1995	1994	1993	1992	1991	1990
Shareholders' equity						
Common stock						
Authorized: 200,000,000 shares (par = $1.25)						
Issued:117,150,593 shares in treasury	146,438	146,438	146,438	146,438	146,438	146,438
Additional paid-in capital	472,602	477,153	480,067	478,463	479,833	487,034
Retained earnings	344,346	420,174	325,823	328,122	696,745	670,878
Cost of common stock in treasury						
(1995, 11,745,395 shares; 1994, 9,813,893 shares;						
1993, 10,430,833 shares; 1992, 10,545,915 shares;						
1991, 10,808,116 shares; 1990, 11,424,154 shares)	(255,663)	(218,745)	(232,510)	(234,993)	(240,848)	(254,576)
Employee stock plans	(57,319)	(60,816)	(62,342)	(65,638)	(66,711)	(63,590)
Minimum pension liability adjustment	(5,656)	—	—	—	—	—
Foreign currency translation	(7,397)	(32,492)	(70,695)	(53,167)	(4,872)	28,547
Total shareholders' equity	637,351	731,712	586,781	599,225	1,010,585	1,014,731
Total liabilities and shareholders' equity	$ 2,125,066	$ 2,504,327	$ 2,469,498	$2,501,490	$2,535,068	$2,586,541
Number of employees	16,595	19,772	20,951	21,407	22,533	24,273
Stock price/share (high–low)	$21.5–$14.5	$20.125–$14	$18.625–$13	$ 21–$13	$ 17–$10	$21–$10

Source: Maytag Corporation, *Annual Reports.*

December dividend, raising the quarterly dividend from 12.5¢ to 14¢ per share. Hadley explained the decisions:

> Our balance sheet is significantly stronger than it has been at any time since 1989, and we've reduced debt by some $400 million in the past 18 months. We've shed underperforming assets, operating performance has improved, and our capital investment remains strong. As a result, we are well-positioned to increase shareholder value as we go forward. The share repurchase and dividend increase are two important steps we are able to take now. Both signal our confidence in Maytag's future and our commitment to improve the value shareowners receive from their continued investment in Maytag.[24]

Alex Silverman of *Value Line* agreed with Hadley that Maytag seemed to be turning its operations around at last. Even though he predicted that, due to the divestitures of Hoover Europe and part of Dixie-Narco, Maytag's 1996 sales would probably drop 10% from 1995, lower labor expenses, greater plant efficiencies, and reduced interest costs would more than offset rising raw materials costs and lower sales volume, resulting in increased profits. Silverman projected the stock price for the time period 1998–2000 to have a high of $35 and a low of $25 per share.[25]

In early February 1996, Maytag Corporation stock was selling at a little over $19. Nicholas Heymann, an analyst with NatWest Securities in New York, had earlier concluded that the corporation was worth up to $29 per share (when it still owned Hoover Europe).[26] Some analysts were wondering if the corporation might have no choice but to sell to a competitor by the end of the decade. The major players in the U.S. industry, such as AB Electrolux, Whirlpool, and General Electric, were moving forward through successful acquisitions to become successful global competitors. Even Bosch-Siemens, the number two appliance maker in Europe, had begun making the transition to global operations with its decision to build a dishwasher plant in North Carolina. Could a purely domestic appliance manufacturer such as Maytag survive in the coming global

Exhibit 7   Principal Business Groups: Maytag Corporation
(Dollar amounts in thousands)

Performance	North American Appliances	Vending Equipment	European Appliances
1995			
Sales	$2,663,611	$194,713	$181,200
Operating income	295,400	23,466	406
1994			
Sales	2,639,834	191,749	398,966
Operating income	321,021	21,866	420
1993			
Sales	2,311,777	156,597	390,761
Operating income	233,384	17,944	(73,581)
1992			
Sales	2,242,270	165,321	501,857
Operating income	129,680	16,311	(67,061)
1991			
Sales	2,182,567	149,798	495,517
Operating income	186,322	4,498	(865)
1990			
Sales	2,212,335	191,444	496,672
Operating income	221,164	25,018	(22,863)

Source: Maytag Corporation, *Annual Reports.*

industry? It had been widely rumored that Maytag's purchase of Chicago Pacific in 1988 had not just been to acquire Hoover but to become a less tempting takeover target. Although there was currently no talk on Wall Street about any interest in acquiring the corporation, the sale of Maytag's overseas operations and improved cash position could make the firm a tempting takeover target.

MAYTAG'S NEW STRATEGIC POSTURE

As Leonard Hadley began outlining his letter to the shareholders for the upcoming *1995 Annual Report,* he wondered how the past year's developments would be received. Cynics might point out that Hadley's big accomplishment since becoming CEO was to return the company to 1988, when Maytag had no foreign operations. Some might be very pleased, especially the current workforce. He hoped that the impact of the corporation's second net loss since the 1920s would be softened by the sale of Hoover Europe. Net income should increase significantly in the coming years. Retired shareholders would probably applaud the recent increase in dividends. Financial analysts would probably agree that the decision to buy back stock would help raise the stock price and perhaps reduce any interest in a hostile takeover. Industry analysts would probably wonder how Maytag would be able to compete in the future against globally integrated competitors in a fiercely competitive, mature U.S. industry. Now that Maytag Corporation was back on solid footing, the financial community would want some sort of strategic plan to justify any rosy predictions.

Maytag Corporation's mission statement was clearly stated on the inside front cover of the *1994 Annual Report:*

To improve the quality of home life by designing, building, marketing, and servicing the best appliances in the world.

Hadley thought back to Daniel Krumm's list of objectives at the 1990 shareholders' meeting and his own listing of three primary goals at the 1993 meeting. Although net income was negative in 1995, the sales of Hoover Europe and Hoover Australia should pave the way for solid profits, beginning in 1996. Although it could be argued that consumer surveys consistently placed the Maytag brand in the most desired category (when price was not considered), the same could not always be said of the corporation's other brands. Could a company be number one in consumer satisfaction if none of its products were first in market share? Nevertheless, Maytag Corporation did pass Frigidaire during 1995 in overall U.S. shipments and market share to move into third place in North America—a real accomplishment. Unfortunately, it was more a case of Frigidaire losing market share rather than Maytag gaining it. (Frigidaire's market share had plummeted from 16.9% in 1994 to 13.5%, whereas Maytag's market share remained at 14.4%.) The real question now seemed to be: What objectives and strategies were now appropriate? Before Hadley and the Executive Committee could propose a revised set of objectives to the Board, he needed to develop a new strategic vision for the corporation to take it through the turn of the century.

Notes

1. R. Brack, "Is Maytag Preparing for a Sale?" *Des Moines Register* (June 1, 1995), p. 8S.
2. L. Hadley, "To Our Shareowners," *Maytag Corporation Second Quarter Report* (1995), p. 2.
3. David Hoyte, Executive Vice-President of Operations, Frigidaire, as quoted by M. Sanders, "ISO 9000: The Inside Story," *Appliance* (August 1994), p. 43. ("White goods" is the traditional term used for major home appliances. The contrasting term "brown goods" refers to home electronics products such as radios and televisions.)
4. Kevin Lanning, Director of Market Research, Maytag Company, in "A Real Bargain," *Appliance Manufacturer* (November, 1993), p. M-21; K. Edlin, "Demand Performance," *Appliance* (July 1995), p. 90.
5. T. Somheil, "The Incredible Value Story—Part 3," *Appliance* (June 1992), pp. 25–32.
6. J. Jancsurak, "Global Trends for 1995–2005," *Appliance Manufacturer* (June 1995), p. A-6.
7. D. Davis, "The Value of World Leadership," *Appliance* (December 1994), p. E-6.
8. N. C. Remich, Jr., "Mexico, Drop Tariffs," *Appliance Manufacturer* (December 1994), p. 7.
9. "Maytag Announces In-Home Inspection: Will Voluntarily Replace Component," Press Release, *Maytag Corporation* (October 17, 1995).
10. "Maytag Corp. to Exit Currency Validator Business," *Maytag Corporation News Release* (November 1, 1995).
11. Interview with Leonard Hadley, Maytag Corporation, *1994 Annual Report,* p. 10.
12. W. Ryberg, "Cost of Maytag Ad Fiasco Climbs," *Des Moines Register* (April 21, 1995), p. 10S; W. Ryberg, "'Hoovergate' Winding Down," *Des Moines Register* (April 27, 1994), p. 10S.
13. Maytag Corporation News Release, 1995.
14. W. Ryberg, "Maytag's No. 2 Officer Resigns," *Des Moines Register* (August 12, 1995), p. 10S.
15. W. Ryberg, "Maytag Executive Resigns," *Des Moines Register* (December 14, 1995), p. 8S.
16. M. Sanders, "Purchasing Power," *Appliance* (June 1993), pp. 45–46.
17. A. Baker, "Intelligent Dishwasher Outsmarts Dirt," *Design News* (April 10, 1995), pp. 69–73.
18. S. Stevens, "Speeding the Signals of Change," *Appliance* (February 1995), p. 7.
19. N. C. Remich, Jr., "The Power of Partnering," *Appliance Manufacturer* (August 1994), p. A-1.
20. R. Dzierwa, "The Permanent Press," *Appliance* (September 1995), p. 48.
21. "Maytag, Fawn, Lennox, Parsons Get State Aid," (Ames, Iowa) *Daily Tribune* (June 23, 1995), p. 1A.
22. "Maytag Keeps Jobs in Galesburg," (Ames, Iowa) *Daily Tribune* (November 12, 1994), p. A4.
23. "Maytag Announces Out-of-Court Settlement in Class-Action Suit," Maytag Corporation News Release (August 3, 1995); K. Pins, "Maytag Settles Plant-Closing Case," *Des Moines Register* (August 4, 1995), p. 8S.
24. "Maytag Will Repurchase Shares; Increase Dividend," Maytag Corporation News Release (October 19, 1995).
25. A. Silverman, "Maytag Corporation," *Value Line* (December 15, 1995).
26. Brack, "Is Maytag Preparing for a Sale?" p. 8S.

Whirlpool's Quest for Global Leadership

Arieh A. Ullmann

In the Chairman's Letter of Whirlpool Corporation's *1995 Annual Report,* David R. Whit-wam, Chairman of the Board and Chief Executive Officer, stated his disappointment with the Company's recent performance:

> On a relative basis, 1995 was a good year for Whirlpool Corporation and we continued to strengthen our position as the global leader in the major home appliance industry. That said, we should have done better. On an operating basis, and compared to our own very high performance expectations, the year was disappointing—for me, our global team and you, our shareholders.[1]

He attributed this disappointing performance partly to manufacturing inefficiencies and start-up costs of a new refrigerator in the United States, partly to restructuring difficulties in Europe, as well as raw materials cost increases combined with minimal growth or even declining demand in North America and Europe. This statement was quite a change in tone compared to his pronouncement a year earlier, when he had boldly stated that the company had achieved both primary objectives—to produce "strong, short-term results" and to "building competitive advantage by continuing our expanding worldwide enterprise at all levels, and to leverage its best practices and Whirlpool's cumulative size."[2] (For key performance data see Exhibit 1.)

THE U.S. APPLIANCE INDUSTRY

Home appliances were generally classified as laundry (washers and dryers), refrigeration (refrigerators and freezers), cooking (ranges and ovens), and other appliances (dishwashers, disposals, and trash compactors). Many appliance manufacturers also made floor care goods such as floor polishers and vacuum cleaners.

Manufacturing operations consisted mainly of preparation of a metal frame to which the appropriate components were attached in automated assembly lines and by manual assembly. Manufacturing costs comprised about 65% to 75% of total operating cost, with labor representing less than 10% of total cost. Optimal sized assembly plants had an annual capacity of about 500,000 units for most appliances except microwave ovens. Unlike other industries such as textiles, variable costs played an important role in the cost structure; changes in raw materials and component costs were also significant. Component production was fairly scale-sensitive. Doubling compressor output for refrigerators, for instance, reduced unit costs by 10%–15%. There were also some scale economies in assembly but the introduction of robotics tended to reduce them while improving quality and performance consistency and enhancing flexibility.

Distribution of major appliances occurred either directly through contract sales to home builders and to other appliance manufacturers predominantly or indirectly through local builder suppliers. Traditionally, these customers were very cost conscious and thus preferred less expensive appliance brands. Retail sales represented the second distribution channel, with national chain stores and mass merchandisers such as department,

This case was prepared by Professor Arieh A. Ullmann of Binghamton University. This case was edited for SMBP–7th Edition. Copyright © 1995 by Arieh A. Ullmann. Reprinted by permission.

Exhibit 1 **Key Performance Measures: Whirlpool Corporation**

Year	Earnings per Share[1]	Return on Equity[2]	Total Return to Shareholders[3]	P/E Ratio
1990	$1.04	5.1%	2.8%	22.6
1991	2.45	11.6	6.7	15.9
1992	2.90	13.1	17.0	15.4
1993	3.19	14.2	25.8	20.8
1994	2.10	9.4	12.0	23.9
1995	2.80	11.6	20.8	19.0

Notes:
1. Earnings from continuing operations before accounting change.
2. Earnings from continuing operations before accounting change divided by average shareholders' equity.
3. Five-year annualized.

furniture, discount, and appliance stores acting as intermediaries. The consolidation of appliance distributors during the past 10 years led to the current situation where about 45% of the total appliance volume was being sold through 10 powerful mega-retailers with Sears leading with a market share of about 29%. A third, less visible channel was the commercial market such as laundromats, hospitals, hotels, and other institutions.

Industry Structure

Since World War II, when over 250 firms manufactured appliances, several merger waves had consolidated the industry while sales grew and prices held. The most recent consolidation occurred in 1986 when, within less than 1 year Electrolux purchased White Consolidated, Whirlpool acquired KitchenAid and Roper, and Maytag bought Jenn-Air and Magic Chef. Maytag's acquisition of Jenn-Air and Magic Chef increased its overall revenues by giving it brand name appliances at various price points. Likewise, Whirlpool's acquisition of KitchenAid and Roper, respectively, broadened Whirlpool's presence at the high end and low end of the market. By the end of 1995, the number of domestic manufacturers varied by type of product between 4 for dishwashers and 15 for home refrigeration and room air-conditioning equipment.

In the 1980s, the market continued to grow, primarily because of booming sales of microwave ovens, which tripled from 1980 to 1989, while washers and dryers increased in sales 34% and 52%, respectively. Appliance manufacturers realized that they must offer a complete line of appliances even if they did not manufacture all of them themselves, which was one reason for the merger activity and practice of interfirm sourcing. For example, Whirlpool made trash compactors for Frigidaire (Electrolux/White Consolidated); General Electric manufactured microwave ovens for Caloric (Raytheon) and Jenn-Air and Magic Chef (Maytag).

By 1995, five major competitors controlled 98% of the core appliance market, each of which offered a broad range of product categories and brands targeted to different customer segments. With 35% domestic market share, Whirlpool was ahead of GE (29.3%), a reversal of the leadership position compared to 5 years earlier. Whirlpool was especially strong in washers and dryers (1995: 53% share), whereas GE was ahead in refrigerators and ranges. In terms of overall market share, Maytag followed (14.4%), then Electrolux (13.5%), and Raytheon (6.2%), respectively.

Exhibit 2 Global Home Appliance Industry: Saturation Levels by Region, Demand, and Market Growth, 1994–2004

	North America	Europe[1]	Latin America	Asia
Home Appliances				
Refrigerators	100%	100%	70%	30%
Cooking equipment	100	96	90	—
Clothes washers	74	82	40	20
Clothes dryers	70	18	—	—
Dishwashers	51	30	—	—
Microwave ovens	80	40	5	8
Room air conditioners	41	—	10	8
Compactors	5	—	—	—
Freezers	40	40	—	—
Population (million)	380	1,100	380	2,900
Annual demand (million units)	46	75	17	56
Estimated annual growth rate	3%	3%	6%–8%	8%–9%

Note:
1. Includes Eastern Europe, Africa, and the Middle East.

Source: Whirlpool Corporation, *1994 Annual Report.*

Throughout the 1980s and into the 1990s competition in the United States was fierce. Industry demand depended on the state of the economy, disposable income levels, interest rates, housing starts, and consumers' ability to defer purchases. Saturation levels remained high and steady; over 70% of households had washers and over 65% had dryers (see Exhibit 2). Refrigerator demand stagnated while sales of electric ranges slowed as sales of the microwave oven boomed. Microwave sales, which had jumped from 3.5 million units in 1980 to over 10 million by 1989, started leveling out while sales of ranges dropped off drastically due to market maturation.

Factors of Competition

In this environment all rivals worked hard at keeping costs down. Had the appliance manufacturers been making automobiles, the price of a Chevrolet Caprice would have risen from $7,209 in 1980 to $9,500 in 1990, not $17,370. Over four years, Electrolux spent over $500 million to upgrade old plants and build new ones for its acquisition, White Consolidated Industries. General Electric automated its Louisville, Kentucky, plant which, over 10 years, halved the work force and raised output by 30%.

Toward the end of the 1980s, it became even more important to lower costs, monitor margins, and achieve economies of scale. The Big Five were renovating and enlarging existing facilities. Maytag built a new facility in the South to take advantage of lower cost, non-union labor. Others built twin plants on the Mexican border to profit from cheap labor. A third trend was toward focus factories where each plant produced one product category only, covering all price points.

Also, all competitors started to push into the high-end segment of the market, which was more stable and profitable. Once the domain of Maytag, it became increasingly crowded with the appearance of GE's Monogram line, Whirlpool's acquisition of

KitchenAid, and White's Euroflair models. Quality became an important feature in the competitive game. Maytag used it effectively in its famous ad of the lonely repairman. Defect rates dropped from 20 per 100 appliances made in 1980 to 10 twelve years later. Relationships with suppliers changed as companies used fewer of them than in years past. Contracts were set up over longer terms to improve quality and keep costs low with just-in-time deliveries.

A recent development was the demand by the powerful distributors for faster delivery. Distributors sought to curtail inventory costs, their biggest expense. As a consequence, manufacturers started to improve delivery systems. For instance, General Electric created its Premier Plus Program, which guaranteed three-day delivery. Sales departments were reorganized so that one sales representative would cover all of a manufacturer's brands of a given product category. Customer information services via 800-telephone numbers were also strengthened.

Innovation

Two developments—government regulation and advances in computer software—combined with intense competition accelerated product innovation. New energy standards to be enforced under the 1987 National Appliance Energy Conservation Act limited energy consumption of new appliances with the objective of reducing energy usage in appliances by 25% every five years. At the same time, the ban on ozone-depleting chlorofluorocarbons (CFCs) in refrigerators by 1995 was forcing the industry to redesign its refrigerators. Pressures were also exerted to change washer and dishwasher designs to reduce water consumption and noise levels. In 1989, the Super Efficient Refrigerator Program, Inc. (SERP) offered a $30 million award for a refrigerator prototype free of CFCs and at least 25% more energy efficient than the 1993 federal standards. The winner had to manufacture and sell over 250,000 refrigerators between January 1994 and July 1997.

As the industry globalized, more stringent government regulations outside the United States became a issue. For example, there was a concern that the more stringent environmental standards prevailing in the European Community would become law in the United States as well. Although Whirlpool supported the more stringent standards, its competitors, notably GE, opposed them.

Regarding advances in computer technology, new programs using fuzzy logic or neural networks that mimicked the human brain's ability to detect patterns were being introduced in many industries, including white goods. In Asia the use of elevators, washers, and refrigerators using fuzzy logic to recognize usage patterns was already widespread. In late 1992, AEG Hausgeräte AG, then a subsidiary of Daimler Benz's AEG unit, introduced a washer that used fuzzy logic to control water consumption automatically, depending on the size of the load, and to sense how much dirt remained in clothes.

There were also other innovations. In the late 1980s, new technologies in cooking surfaces were introduced: ceramic glass units, solid elements, and modular grill configurations. Other new customer-oriented features included the self-cleaning oven, automatic ice cube makers, self-defrosting refrigerators, pilotless gas ranges, and appliances that could be preset. Also, manufacturers worked hard to reduce the noise level of dishwashers and washing machines. Consumers became more concerned with the way appliances looked. Sleek European styling, with its smooth lines, rounded corners, and a built-in look with electronic controls, became fashionable. Another trend was the white-on-white look, which suggested superior cleanability and made the kitchen look larger.

Outlook

For the future, demand in the United States continued to look unattractive, with growth rates estimated at 3% based on a 1994 demand of 46 million units (Exhibit 2). At the prevailing saturation levels, demand was restricted mostly to replacement purchases (79%) with the remainder going to new housing and new household formation. The industry was so competitive that no single manufacturer could keep an innovation to itself for more than a year without a patent. One of the competitors summarized the situation in the North American appliance industry as follows:

> In the 1980s, four manufacturers accounted for almost all major home appliance sales in the United States, a market where approximately 40 million appliances are sold annually. Each was a tough, seasoned competitor fighting for greater sales in a market predicted to grow little in the decade ahead.[3]

THE GLOBALIZATION OF THE APPLIANCE INDUSTRY

Foreign Competition

The white goods industry was as American as baseball and apple pie. In 1992, 98% of the dishwashers, washing machines, dryers, refrigerators, freezers, and ranges sold in the United States were made domestically. Exports represented about 5% of shipments. The manufacturing plants of the industry's leaders were located in places such as Newton, Iowa (Maytag), Benton Harbor, Michigan (Whirlpool), and Columbus, Ohio (White Consolidated Industries). Each of the Big Four was nearer a corn stalk than a parking meter. Combined, these companies practically owned the market for each major appliance, with one exception—microwave ovens. These represented the lion's share of imports, which made up about 17% of total appliance sales.

The acquisition of White Consolidated Industries by A.B. Electrolux of Sweden in 1986 marked a major change in the industry. Until then, foreign competition in the United States was largely restricted to imports of microwave ovens, a segment controlled by Far East competitors from Korea (Goldstar, Samsung) and Japan (Sharp, Matsushita). Aware of the fate of other industries, many expected that it was only a matter of time before these companies would expand from their beachhead in microwave ovens and compact appliances into other segments.

Europe

Of prime attractiveness to the U.S. manufacturers was Europe. Since 1985, Western Europe had rapidly moved toward a unified market of some 320 million consumers, which was not nearly as saturated as Canada and the United States (Exhibit 2). Appliance demand was expected to grow at 5% annually. Political changes in Eastern Europe integrated these countries into the world trade system and thus added to Europe's long-term attractiveness.

During the 1970s and 1980s, the European white goods industry had experienced a consolidation similar to that in the United States. According to Whirlpool, in 1995 the number of manufacturers in Western Europe was 35, most of whom produced a limited range of products for specific geographic regions.[4] However, since the late 1980s, six companies—Electrolux Zanussi, Philips Bauknecht, Bosch-Siemens, Merloni-Indesit, Thompson, and AEG—had controlled 70% of market (excluding microwave ovens and room air conditioners). Until the mid 1980s, most companies were either producing and selling in only one national market or exporting to a limited extent to many European markets from one country. Observed Whirlpool's CEO Whitwam: "What strikes me most is how similar the U.S. and European industries are."[5] Research by Whirlpool also indicated that washers were basically alike in working components around the globe.[6]

The European market was very segmented and consumer preferences differed greatly from country to country with regard to almost every type of appliance. The French preferred to cook their food at high temperatures, splattering grease on oven walls. Thus oven ranges manufactured for France should have self-cleaning ability. However, this feature was not a requirement in Germany where lower cooking temperatures were the norm. Unlike Americans who preferred to stuff as many clothes into the washer as possible, Europeans overwhelmingly preferred smaller built-in models. Northern Europeans liked large refrigerators because they preferred to shop only once a week; consumers in southern Europe preferred small ones because they visited open-air markets daily. Northerners liked their freezers at the bottom of the refrigerators, southerners at the top. In France, 80% of washing machines were top-loaders; elsewhere in Western Europe, 90% were front-loaders. Also, European washers frequently contained heating elements, and the typical European homemaker preferred to wash towels at 95° Celsius. Gas ranges were common throughout Europe, except for Germany where 90% of all ranges sold were electric.

Given this situation, some observers were skeptical about the possibility of establishing pan-European models that would yield a sustainable competitive advantage through manufacturing, procurement, and marketing efficiencies. They claimed that the European market was actually made up of many smaller individual markets corresponding to the respective countries. Furthermore, they reasoned, many of these national markets featured strong competitors.

Distribution of white goods in Europe was different from that in North America. The larger channel, known as the retail trade, comprised independent retailers, many of whom were organized through buying groups or as multiple-store chains. The second channel, the kitchen trade, primarily comprised kitchen specialists that sold consumers entire kitchen packages. The kitchen trade was focused mainly on built-in units and not involved in laundry appliances.

A.B. Electrolux was a force in practically all of Europe with an overall 25% market share. Over 20 years, this $14-billion multinational from Sweden had undertaken more than 200 acquisitions in 40 countries spanning five businesses: household appliances, forestry and garden products, industrial products, metal and mining, and commercial services. Its expertise in managing acquisitions and integrating the newly acquired units into the organization was unequaled. For example, in 1983, Electrolux took over a money-losing Italian white goods manufacturer with 30,000 employees, 50 factories, and a dozen foreign sales companies. Within four years the Swedes had turned a company which in 1983 lost L120 billion into an efficient organization netting L60 billion. The acquisitions of Zanussi of Italy, Tricity in Britain, and three Spanish companies in anticipation of the changes in Western Europe marked the beginning of a new era in this mature industry as Electrolux sought to establish a pan-European approach to the appliance market, followed by exploring trans-Atlantic opportunities. However, in 1993 Electrolux's pan-European strategy ran into trouble. The recession, combined with Europe's market fragmentation, reduced profits far below the targeted 5% margin.

In Germany Bauknecht (Philips), Siemens-Bosch, and AEG-Telefunken were dominant; in Britain GEC's Hotpoint, and in France Thomson-Brandt were forces to be reckoned with. Merloni from Italy pursued a different approach by flooding Europe with machines produced in Italy with lower-cost labor. In 1987, Merloni gobbled up Indesit, an Italian producer in financial trouble, in order to enlarge its manufacturing base and take advantage of Indesit's marketing position in many European countries. In the late 1980s, no brand had more than 5% of the overall market, even though the top 10 producers generated 80% of the volume.

In 1989, the Americans landed in Europe. General Electric formed an appliance joint venture with Britain's General Electric Corporation (GEC), which had a strong presence in the low-priced segment of the European market, especially in the United Kingdom, and thus complemented GE's high-end European products. In the same year, Maytag acquired the Hoover Division through the purchase of Chicago Pacific. In the United Kingdom, Hoover, best known for its vacuum cleaners, also produced washers, dryers, and dishwashers, which, however, encountered acceptance problems in other European markets. Hoover was also present in Australia and, through a trading company, serviced other parts of the world. In 1989, also, Whirlpool and N.V. Philips of the Netherlands formed a joint venture that included all of Philips's European appliance division. Thus, within a short time, the Americans closed the gap relative to the geographic scope of Electrolux. In spite of concerns about differing consumer preferences in Europe, the largest U.S. appliance manufacturers established themselves before the 1992 EU Program became a reality. European Community rules required 60% local content to avoid tariffs, which, combined with the fear of a "Fortress Europe" protected by Community-wide tariffs after 1992, excluded exports as a viable strategy.

Within a very short time further agreements followed, greatly reducing the number of independent competitors in Europe. AEG started cooperating with Electrolux in washer and dishwasher production and development and, in 1994, became part of Electrolux; Bosch-Siemens formed an alliance with Maytag; the European Economic Interest Group combined several manufacturers with France's Thompson-Brandt as the leader. In spite of this trend toward consolidation in the early 1990s, Whirlpool estimated the number of European manufacturers of home appliances to be about 100.[7]

Asia

Asia, the world's second largest home appliance market, was likely to experience rapid economic growth in the near future primarily thanks to the booming economies of the Pacific Rim countries. Home appliance shipments were expected to grow at least 6% per annum through the 1990s (Exhibit 2). The biggest promise, of course, were the huge markets of the world's most populous states—China and India. However, income levels in these two markets were only approaching levels at which people could afford appliances. The Asian market was dominated by some 50 widely diversified Asian manufacturers, primarily from Japan, Korea, and Taiwan, with no clear leader emerging yet. Matsushita, the market leader, held less than a 10% market share outside Japan.

Consumer preferences in Asia were quite different from those in North America and Europe and varied widely from country to country. For example, typical Asian refrigerators ranged from 6 cu. ft to 10 cu. ft due to the lack of space. Since owning a refrigerator represented a status symbol, refrigerators were often placed in the living room. Such a prominent display created a demand for stylish colors and finishes. In India, for example, refrigerators in bright red or blue were popular. In terms of technology, both direct-cool and forced-air models were common in Asia, whereas in Europe direct-cool prevailed and in North America the forced-air version was preferred. Clothes washers had to be portable because living quarters tended to be small and because usually there was no basement to keep washers permanently hooked up to a water supply and drain.

Often they were stored in an outside hallway and moved into the bathroom and kitchen for use. Also, they had to be delivered to large apartment blocks with no elevators and thus had to be carried up many flights of stairs. Therefore washers tended to be designed as lightweight products on wheels equipped with handles for easy relocation. Technological designs varied, even though vertical-axis machines dominated. The clothes themselves also represented a challenge because they ranged from the yards of fabric used in Indian saris to simple cotton dress and Western-style clothing. Clothes dryers were virtually unknown. Washing habits were different, too. For instance, Japanese usually washed with cold water. But to get clothes clean, Japanese machines have soak cycles that can range from 30 minutes to several hours. Two-burner, tabletop cooking units were used in contrast to the ranges used in North America and Europe, reflecting the differences in cooking styles. In addition, kitchens were much smaller and baking was virtually unknown, as were dishwashers. In air conditioning, split-system units were the dominant version in Asia. In regions where air conditioners were used the better part of the year, consumers didn't want to block limited window space. Split-system units were installed high on the wall, often out of reach, making remote controls an important feature.

Latin America

Another market promising attractive growth in appliances was Latin America, once these countries could emerge from decades of political instability, economic mismanagement, and hyperinflation (Exhibit 2). Indeed, much of this was happening in the 1990s, accompanied by efforts to lower tariffs, which would stimulate trade. In 1994, the white goods industry in Latin America comprised about 65 competitors. Whirlpool expected appliance shipments to expand at a faster pace than in North America and Europe.[8]

WHIRLPOOL CORPORATION

Company Background

In early 1996, Whirlpool Corporation, headquartered in Benton Harbor, Michigan, was one of the world's leading manufacturers and marketers of major home appliances. The company's plants were located in 12 countries, and it distributed its products in over 140 countries under 28 brand names (see Exhibits 3–9). Fifteen years earlier Whirlpool executives had perceived the world primarily as consisting of the U.S. and Canadian markets, with some marginal sales in Latin America and limited export opportunities. However, the company had transformed itself and now recognized that the world encompassed four major regions: North America with 46 million units sold annually (1994) consisting of Canada, Mexico, and the United States; Europe with 50 million units (Western, Central and Eastern Europe, Africa, and the Middle East); Asia with 56 million units; and Latin America with 17 million units (the Caribbean, and Central and South America).

Located two hours by car from Chicago, Whirlpool was founded in St. Joseph, Michigan, in 1911 as the Nineteen Hundred Corporation. At the time, it was producing motor-driven wringer washers under the name Upton Machine, with the hope of selling them in quantities to large distributors. In 1916, the first order from Sears, Roebuck and Co. marked the beginning of an enduring relationship with Sears, which became its old-

Exhibit 3   Milestones of Whirlpool's Globalization

1957 • Whirlpool invested in Brazilian appliance market through purchase of equity interest in Multibras S.A., renamed Brastemp S.A. in 1972.

1969 • Entered the Canadian appliance market through an 52% equity interest in Inglis, Ltd. Sole ownership established in 1990.

1976 • Increased investment in Brazil through purchase of equity interests in Consul S.A., an appliance manufacturer, and Embraco S.A., a maker of compressors.

1986 • Purchased majority interest in Aspera S.r.l. of Fiat S.p.A., a manufacturer of compressors, located in Turin and Riva, Italy.

1987 • Entered the Indian appliance market through TVS Whirlpool Limited, a 33% each joint venture company formed with Sundaram-Clayton Limited of Madras.
     • Ownership in Inglis, Ltd., increased to 72%.

1988 • Vitromatic, S.A. de C.V., formed with Vitro, S.A., of Monterrey, Nuevo Leon, to manufacture and market major home appliances for Mexican and export markets. Whirlpool had a 49% interest.
     • Operated a maquiladora, Componentes de Reynosa, in Reynosa, Tamaulipas, to manufacture components for final assembly in the United States.

1989 • Whirlpool and N.V. Philips of the Netherlands consummated an agreement under which Whirlpool acquired a 53% interest in a joint venture company made up of Philips's former major domestic appliance division. The new company, Whirlpool International B.V. (WIBV), was to manufacture and market appliances in Western Europe. The joint venture brand names were Bauknecht, Philips, Ignis, and Laden.
     • North American Appliance Group (NAAG) formed from streamlined U.S., Canadian, and Mexican operations.
     • Affiliates in Brazil, India, and Mexico completed construction of facilities and started producing the "World Washer."

1990 • Program launched to market appliances in Europe under the dual brands Philips and Whirlpool.
     • Formed a joint venture company with Matsushita Electric Industrial Co. of Japan to produce vacuum cleaners for the North American market.
     • Created Whirlpool Overseas Corporation as a wholly-owned subsidiary to conduct industrial and marketing activities outside North America and Western Europe.

• Inglis, Ltd., became a wholly-owned subsidiary.

1991 • Acquired remaining interest in WIBV from Philips Electronics N.V.
     • Created two new global business units: Whirlpool Compressor Operations and Whirlpool Microwave Cooking Business.

1992 • Created Whirlpool Tatramat in the Slovak Republic. Whirlpool Tatramat a.s. would manufacture clothes washers for Slovakia and neighboring countries and import other WIBV major appliances for sale.
     • Began gradual phaseout of dual-branded advertising to sole Whirlpool brand by removing the Philips name in Europe.
     • Assumed control of SAGAD S.A. of Argentina from Philips.
     • Reorganized Whirlpool Europe and changed its name from WIBV to WEBV.
     • Created a global small-appliance business unit.

1993 • Reorganized NAAG.
     • Replaced WOC with two separate regional organizations in Latin America and Asia.
     • Started implementation of a new Asian strategy with Tokyo as headquarters and regional offices in Singapore, Hong Kong, and Tokyo.
     • Opened sales subsidiaries in Greece, Poland, and the Czech Republic.
     • Inglis, Ltd., became Canada's leading home appliance manufacturer.
     • Streamlined European operations with WEBV selling its Spanish refrigerator plant to IAR/Sital of Italy.

1994 • In May Whirlpool announced joint venture with Teco Electric & Machinery Co., Ltd., of Taiwan to market and distribute home appliances in Taiwan.
     • Whirlpool became a stand-alone brand in Europe.
     • Brazilian affiliates Consul and Brastemp merged to form Multibras.
     • Acquired controlling interest in Kelvinator of India, Ltd., and assumed controlling interest in TVS Whirlpool, Ltd.
     • Asian headquarters moved to Singapore; number of regions increased from three to four.
     • Exited vacuum cleaner business by selling its minority interest in the joint venture with Matsushita.
     • Acquired majority ownership in SMC Microwave Products Co., Ltd., and Beijing Whirlpool Snowflake Electric Appliance Company, Ltd.

(continued)

Exhibit 3   **Milestones of Whirlpool's Globalization** (continued)

• Created the Microwave Oven Business Unit as a global business unit.	• Obtained approval for a joint venture with Sehnzhen Petrochemical Holdings Co. to produce air conditioners.
1995 • Formed South American sales company.	• Created the Global Air Treatment Unit as a global business unit.
• New joint venture formed to produce washers called The Whirlpool Narcissus (Shanghai) Co., Ltd.	
• Acquired majority interest in Raybo Air Conditioner Manufacturing Company.	

est and largest customer, representing 20% of Whirlpool's 1995 sales. In 1948, the Whirlpool brand automatic washer was introduced. This established the dual distribution system—one product line for Sears, the other for Nineteen Hundred. The Nineteen Hundred Corporation was renamed Whirlpool in 1950, and automatic dryers were added to the company's product line. In 1955, Whirlpool merged with Seeger Refrigerator Co. of St. Paul, Minnesota, and the Estate range and air conditioning divisions of R.C.A. In 1957, Whirlpool entered the foreign market through the purchase of equity interest in Multibras S.A. of Sao Paulo, Brazil, later renamed Brastemp S.A. In 1967, Whirlpool was the first competitor in the industry to take advantage of AT&T's new 800-number service and created the Cool-Line Telephone Service, which provided customers a toll-free number to call for answers to questions and help with service.

In the mid 1980s, the limited growth potential of its established markets motivated Whirlpool to undertake a major examination of the industry. Top management decided "to remain focused on major home appliances but to expand into markets not already served by Whirlpool."[9] In 1986, the KitchenAid division of Hobart Corporation was purchased from Dart & Kraft, which marked Whirlpool's entry into the upscale segment of the appliance market as well as into small appliances. In the same year, Whirlpool sold its central heating and cooling business to Inter-City Gas Corp. of Canada. In 1985 Whirlpool purchased the assets of Mastercraft Industries Corp., a Denver-based manufacturer of kitchen cabinets. A year later a second cabinet maker, St. Charles Manufacturing Co., was acquired through the newly formed Whirlpool Kitchens, Inc. However, in March 1989, Whirlpool Kitchens was sold due to lack of fit.

North American Appliance Group

The North American Appliance Group (NAAG) was formed in 1989 from operations in the United States, Canada, and Mexico (see Exhibit 4). After several plant closings and a reshuffling of product lines between plants, a streamlined organization with a unified strategy was formed, originally around four brands. In 1992, Whirlpool reorganized its North American operations behind a strategy to create a "dominant consumer franchise" (DCF). For Whirlpool, a DCF existed "when consumers insist on our brands for reasons other than price, when they view our products as clearly superior to other appliances, [and] when they demonstrate strong loyalty in their future purchase decisions."[10] Such a strategy required, above all, a better understanding of consumer needs; merely improving product quality and keeping costs low was deemed necessary but not sufficient. The objective was to become more customer focused, which entailed a functional organization dealing with four core processes: product management, brand management, trade partner management, and logistics. Unlike the traditional functional

Exhibit 4 **North American Appliance Group in Early 1996: Whirlpool Corporation**

Principal Products	Major Brand Names	Principal Locations	Sales Offices
Automatic dryers	Acros[1]	**Corporate, Regional,**	**United States**
Automatic washers	Admiral (Canada)	**and Research and**	Atlanta
Built-in ovens	Chambers	**Engineering Center**	Boston
Dehumidifiers	Crolls[1]	Benton Harbor, Michigan	Charlotte
Dishwashers	Coolerator	**Subsidiaries**	Chicago
Freezers	Estate	Inglis, Ltd.,	Dallas
Ice makers	Inglis	Mississauga, Ontario	Dayton
Microwave ovens	KitchenAid	Whirlpool Financial Corp.,	Denver
Ranges	Roper	Benton Harbor, Michigan	Kansas City
Refrigerators	Speed Queen (Canada)	**Affiliate**	Knoxville
Room air conditioners	Supermatic[1]	Vitromatic S.A. de C.V.,	Little Rock
Trash compactors	Whirlpool	Monterrey, Mexico	Los Angeles
		Manufacturing	Miami
		Facilities	Minneapolis
		Benton Harbor, Michigan	New York City
		Celaya, Mexico	Orlando
		Clyde, Ohio	Philadelphia
		Evansville, Indiana	Pittsburgh
		Findlay, Ohio	Santurce (Puerto Rico)
		Fort Smith, Arkansas	San Francisco
		Greenville, Ohio	Seattle
		Lavergne, Tennessee	**Canada**
		Marion, Ohio	Laval, Quebec
		Mexico City, Mexico	Mississauga, Ontario
		Montmagny, Quebec	Vancouver, British Columbia
		Monterrey, Mexico	**Mexico**
		Oxford, Mississippi	Guadalajara, Jalisco
		Puebla, Mexico	Mexico City, Distrito Federal
		Reynosa, Mexico	Monterrey, Nuevo León
		Tulsa, Oklahoma	

Note:
1. Affiliate owned.

organization, the new approach employed cross-functional teams within each function with product business teams at the center.

To support its DCF strategy, Whirlpool announced a multitude of new products aimed at six discrete appliance consumer segments labeled: (1) the traditionalist, (2) the housework rebel, (3) the achiever, (4) the self-assured, (5) the proven conservative, and (6) the homebound survivor.[11] KitchenAid brand appliances were marketed to upscale consumers who looked for style and substance, typically found among achievers; Whirlpool was positioned as the brand that helped consumers manage their homes better—for instance housework rebels. Roper brand appliances were value-priced and offered basic styling and features and were a good match for the self-assured. The Estate brand line was limited to a few high-volume models and distributed through warehouse club outlets. The Kenmore Appliance Group was dedicated to serve Whirlpool's single largest customer—Sears, Roebuck and Co.

In June 1993, Whirlpool was named the winner in the $30 million Super Efficient Refrigerator Program, a success that CEO Whitwam attributed to the multidisciplinary team that had been assembled from all over the world. The SERP models eliminated CFCs completely by using a different refrigerant. Also, a different, environmentally safe blowing agent was used to expand foam insulation between the walls of the refrigerator liner and cabinet. Energy efficiency gains were achieved through better insulation, a high-efficiency compressor, and an improved condenser fan motor in conjunction with a microchip-controlled adaptive defrost control that incorporated fuzzy logic. Whirlpool had entered the SERP contest because it was consistent with the company's strategy to exceed customer expectations. Jeff Fettig, Vice-President, Group Marketing and Sales for NAAG, commented, "The SERP program allowed us to accelerate the development process and bring these products to the market sooner. Future products will be designed with these consumer expectations [regarding environmental friendliness] in mind, giving people even more reason to ask for a Whirlpool-built product next time they are in the market for a major home appliance."[12]

After an energy-efficient refrigerator with a CFC-free sealed system was launched in March 1994, the Company announced that it would introduce a new clothes washer in 1996 that would use a third of the water and energy of a conventional washer. Management hoped that consumers would be willing "to pay a premium price for the new washer."[13] In its *1993 Annual Report,* Whirlpool announced that, since 1988, NAAG had increased its regional market share by nearly a third with help from Inglis, Ltd., the Canadian subsidiary, and Vitromatic S.A., the Mexican affiliate.

In late 1994, Whirlpool initiated a major restructuring initiative, closing plants and reducing headcount in an effort to reduce costs. In 1995, Montgomery Ward, the second largest home appliance retailer in the United States, became a Whirlpool customer.

Whirlpool's Globalization

In 1995, Whirlpool's efforts to establish a global presence were more than ten years old. Already, in its *1984 Annual Report,* Whirlpool had announced that it had concluded a two-year study and adopted a plan for the next five years. Among the steps mentioned were developing new international strategies and adding sound new businesses that would complement existing strengths. The strategy was based on the assumption that, in spite of the differences in consumer habits and preferences, it was possible to gain competitive advantage by leveraging a global presence in the various regional markets. In the *1987 Annual Report,* CEO Whitwam had elaborated on the company's rationale for globalization:

> The U.S. appliance market has limited growth opportunities, a high concentration of domestic competitors and increasing foreign competition. Further, the U.S. represents only about 25% of the worldwide potential for major appliance sales.
>
> Most importantly, our vision can no longer be limited to our domestic borders because national borders no longer define market boundaries. The marketplace for products and services is more global than ever before and growing more so every day.
>
> Consumers in major industrialized countries are living increasingly similar lifestyles and have increasingly similar expectations of what consumer products must do for them. As purchasing patterns become more alike, we think that companies that operate on a broad global scale can leverage their strengths better than those which only serve an individual national market. Very likely, appliance manufacturing will always have to be done regionally. Yet the ability to leverage many of the strengths of a company on an international basis is possible only if that company operates globally."[14]

Whirlpool Trading Corporation was formed to consolidate existing international activities and explore new ventures. In January 1985, the company increased its equity interest in Inglis, which dated back to 1969, from 48% to more than 50%. In the following year, Aspera S.r.l. in Torino, Italy, a large compressor maker, was purchased from Fiat.

In the late 1950s, Whirlpool had undertaken its first expansion beyond the U.S. borders when it entered Brazil, followed by Canada in 1969 (see Exhibit 3). In 1976, Whirlpool strengthened its position in Brazil. However, globalization truly took shape in the 1980s when Whirlpool added Mexico, India, and Europe through a series of joint ventures. The moves in South America and Asia were motivated by the expectation that climbing disposable incomes in these continents would result in a growing demand for appliances that would "at least partially mirror the American consumer boom of the 1950s and 1960s." [15]

Among Whirlpool's top management, David R. Whitwam was known as a champion of Whirlpool's globalization. Whitwam had succeeded Jack Sparks who had retired in 1987 after 47 years of service, including 5 as CEO. Sparks had given Whirlpool the focus it had lacked. It was not an easy task to follow in the footsteps of such a distinguished leader.

Born in Madison, Wisconsin, Whitwam graduated from the University of Wisconsin with a B.S. in economics with honors. After eight years in the U.S. Army and the Wisconsin National Guard, he joined Whirlpool as a marketing management trainee in July 1968. One year later he was named territory sales manager for the South California sales division, and from there job descriptions did not change, only the locations. Whitwam spent time in New York and then in southern California.

Whitwam moved to corporate headquarters in 1977 when he was named Merchandising Manager for Range Products. From that post came a promotion to Director of Builder Marketing and then Vice-President, Whirlpool Sales, in 1983. In 1985, he was elected to the company's Board of Directors. On December 1, 1987, he assumed his current position as President, CEO, and Chairman of the Board of Whirlpool Corporation. Since then, he has transformed a domestically oriented $4 billion company into an $8 billion global force. Whirlpool's Corporate Vision, which was displayed in many of its publications and throughout its facilities, clearly communicated this orientation:

> Whirlpool, in its chosen lines of business, will grow with new opportunities and be the leader in an ever-changing global market. We will be driven by our commitment to continuous quality improvement and to exceeding all of our customers' expectations. We will gain competitive advantage through this, and by building on our existing strengths and developing new competencies. We will be market driven, efficient and profitable. Our success will make Whirlpool a company that worldwide customers, employees, and other stakeholders can depend on.

Whirlpool Europe B.V.

Among those most strongly convinced of the promise of the European market was David Whitwam: "The only people who say you can't have a pan-European brand are the people who don't have one themselves." [16] On August 18, 1988, Whirlpool announced a joint venture with N.V. Philips, the second largest appliance manufacturer in Europe behind Electrolux with a broad presence in many markets throughout Europe and Latin America. The deal was for a 53% interest in Philips's worldwide Major Domestic Appliance Division for $361 million in cash; the new company was called Whirlpool International B.V. (WIBV). In July 1991, Whirlpool exercised its option to purchase from Philips the remaining interest in WIBV and changed the name to Whirlpool Europe B.V. (WEBV) (see Exhibit 5). By 1994, with 13% market share, WEBV occupied the third position in Europe behind Electrolux (25%) and Bosch Siemens (15%). For financial information see Exhibits 6 and 7.

Soon after the formation of WIBV, Philips's decentralized organization was phased

Exhibit 5 Europe B.V. in 1996: Whirlpool Corporation

Principal Products	Major Brand Names	Principal Locations
Automatic dryers	Bauknecht	**European Operations Center**
Automatic washers	Ignis	Comerio, Italy
Dishwashers	Laden	
Freezers	Whirlpool	**Subsidiaries**
Microwave ovens		Whirlpool Europe B.V., Eindhoven, Netherlands
Ranges		Whirlpool Tatramat a.s., Poprad, Slovakia
Refrigerators		
		Manufacturing Facilities
		Amiens, France
		Calw, Germany
		Cassinetta, Italy
		Naples, Italy
		Neunkirchen, Germany
		Norrköping, Sweden
		Poprad, Slovakia
		Schorndorf, Germany
		Siena, Italy
		Trento, Italy
		Sales Offices
		Athens, Greece
		Barcelona, Spain
		Brussels, Belgium
		Budapest, Hungary
		Comerio, Italy
		Dublin, Ireland
		Eindhoven, Netherlands
		Espoo, Finland
		Herlev, Denmark
		Lenzburg, Switzerland
		Lisbon, Portugal
		London, United Kingdom
		Moscow, Russia
		Oslo, Norway
		Paris, France
		Poprad, Slovak Republic
		Prague, Czech Republic
		Stockholm, Sweden
		Stuttgart, Germany
		Vienna, Austria
		Warsaw, Poland

out and WIBV was split into customer-focused business units. Brands were positioned to fit the niches and conditions in Europe, an approach employed earlier in the United States. Bauknecht—Philips's most profitable brand—was aimed at the high end of the market, the dual-branded Philips/Whirlpool at the middle, and Ignis at the lower end. Later, in 1995, Whirlpool terminated its successful brand-transfer effort that had cost $110 million and dropped the Philips brand name. The Bauknecht and Philips/Whirlpool Appliance Groups received the centralized sales and marketing functions, respectively,

Exhibit 6   **Business Unit Revenues and Operating Profit: Whirlpool Corporation**
(Dollar amounts in millions)

Year Ending December 31	1995	1994	1993
Revenues			
North America	$5,093	$5,048	$4,559
Europe	2,502	2,373	2,225
Latin America	271	329	303
Asia	302	205	151
Other	(5)	(6)	130
Total appliance business	$8,163	$7,949	$7,368
Operating Profit			
North America	$ 445	$ 522	$ 474
Europe	92	163	139
Latin America	26	49	43
Asia	(50)	(22)	(5)
Restructuring[1]	—	(248)	(23)
Business dispositions[2]	—	60	(8)
Other	(147)	(154)	(116)
Total appliance business	$ 366	$ 370	$ 504

Notes:
1. Consolidation and reorganization of European and North American operations in 1993 and 1994 and closure of two North American manufacturing facilities in 1994.
2. In 1994, the minority interest in Matsushita Floor Care Company was sold, as were the European compressor operations (to its Brazilian affiliate Embraco) and its refrigerator plant in Barcelona.

which supported all of Whirlpool's European brands. National sales subsidiaries were consolidated into three sales regions to take advantage of the growing European cross-border trade. The marketing function included separate, brand-oriented components to strengthen brand identity while at the same time ensuring coordination internally. Manufacturing and technology activities were reorganized around product groups and development centers, with Germany focusing on laundry and dishwashing products and Italy on refrigeration and cooking. Key support functions (consumer services, information technology, logistics, and planning) were maintained as separate, centrally managed entities. Distribution was reconfigured toward a pan-European approach, and 10 of 28 finished goods warehouses were closed. Explained WEBV president Hank Bowman, "The idea is to put systems support in place so we can deliver products more accurately and in a more timely manner."[17] WEBV also assumed responsibility for the Middle East and Africa, which accounted for $100 million in sales, mainly in the form of kits in an attempt to boost local content and thus preempt the emergence of domestic-content rules. In late 1994, yet another reorganization was started to streamline operations on a pan-European basis in conjunction with similar efforts in North America in the hope of achieving annual cost savings of about $150 million, starting in 1997.

In 1992, WIBV started a four-year effort to redesign its products to increase manufacturing efficiency, improve product quality, and increase customer satisfaction. The goal was to renew the entire product line by 1996. Whirlpool had identified what it called a "value gap" in Europe. When benchmarking the European industry's performance against best-in-class North American and Asian players, managers found that European

Exhibit 7 **Business Segment Information: Whirlpool Corporation**
(Dollar amounts in millions)

Segment	North America	Europe	Other and (Eliminations)
Net Sales			
1995	$5,093	$2,502	$ 586
1994	5,048	2,451	450
1993	4,547	2,410	411
1992	4,471	2,645	185
1991	4,224	2,479	54
1990	4,157	2,405	43
Operating Profit			
1995	$ 314	$ 90	$ (38)
1994	311	43	16
1993	341	129	34
1992	359	101	19
1991	314	82	(3)
1990	269	86	(6)
Identifiable Assets			
1995	$2,031	$2,104	$2,033
1994	2,046	1,824	1,410
1993	1,742	1,758	1,154
1992	3,511	1,917	690
1991	3,672	2,284	489
1990	3,216	1,905	493
Depreciation Expense			
1995	$ 140	$ 105	$ 8
1994	141	98	4
1993	137	101	1
1992	142	132	1
1991	129	104	—
1990	140	107	—
Net Capital Expenditures			
1995	$ 262	$ 186	$ 29
1994	269	135	12
1993	188	116	3
1992	174	111	3
1991	183	104	—
1990	158	106	1

producers delivered significantly lower levels of customer satisfaction. Also, Europeans paid more for their appliances than did their U.S. counterparts. Explained Ivan Menezes, Vice-President, Group Marketing, WEBV, "When Whirlpool first came to Europe, the typical appliance cost 50% to 100% more in terms of daily income. In the U.S., for example, a typical consumer could, in 1991, earn the necessary dollars for a dishwasher in 3.8 days, whereas in Europe, it would have taken 7.5 days. Today that gap has closed by 15% to 20% for all appliances."[18]

A global outlook was forged in the management team. Managers were rotated between Europe and the United States to foster global thinking. The first time this move paid off was in 1991 when the VIP Crisp microwave oven, developed by a new "advanced global technology unit" in Norrköping, Sweden, was introduced and quickly became Europe's best-selling model. The VIP Crisp had a heated base plate that allows Italians to bake crisp pizza crusts and the British to fry eggs. Subsequently, the company started to import the VIP Crisp to the United States.

WEBV also made a series of moves to establish itself in the emerging markets of Central and Eastern Europe, which in 1991 represented about 11% of the world appliance market and promised attractive growth opportunities over the long term. Bauknecht was the first to set up a distribution system in East Germany after the opening of the border. In early 1992, WEBV developed distribution networks in the entire region and established a wholly-owned sales subsidiary in Hungary. In May 1992, Whirlpool took a 43.8% minority investment in Whirlpool/Tatramat a.s., a joint venture in the Slovak Republic, which manufactured and sold automatic washers and marketed products assembled at other WEBV locations. In 1994, WEBV took a controlling interest in this joint venture. A year earlier, sales subsidiaries had been opened in Poland and the Czech Republic, adding to WEBV's position in Eastern Europe, and Greece in Southeastern Europe, followed by Russia in 1995. Expansions into Romania and Bulgaria were planned for 1996.

Latin American Appliance Group

Whirlpool's foray overseas started in Latin America when, in 1958, the company purchased equity interest in Multibras S.A. of Brazil, a manufacturer of major appliances. Whirlpool's strategy in Latin America called for taking full advantage of this large emerging market by optimally positioning its brands across the entire spectrum, based on in-depth consumer research in an attempt to cultivate "customers for life."

In the crucial Brazilian market, which accounted for about half of all appliances sold in Latin America in 1994, Whirlpool held equity positions in three Brazilian companies: (1) Multibras, which in 1994 merged three sister appliance makers into one organization and with annual sales of $800 million held the market leader position in Brazil; (2) Embraco, which was one of the world's largest manufacturers of compressors and exported to 50 countries on four continents; and (3) Brasmotor S.A., which was a holding company with a majority interest in Multibras and a minority interest in Embraco. Whirlpool claimed that, based on its own research, it had the second highest brand recognition after Coca-Cola.

In January 1992, Whirlpool strengthened its position in South America by taking over control of SAGAD, Philips's white goods operation in Argentina. Except for Brazil and Argentina, the South American Sales Company, a subsidiary of LAAG, was responsible for sales throughout the region.

Originally, Whirlpool's Latin American operations were part of the Whirlpool Overseas Corporation (WOC), formed in Spring 1990 as a wholly-owned subsidiary to conduct marketing and industrial activities outside North America and Europe. It included U.S. Export Sales, the Overseas Business Group acquired from Philips in the WIBV transaction, and three wholly-owned sales companies in Hong Kong, Thailand, and Australia. Industrial activities encompassed technology sale and transfer, kit and component sales, joint venture manufacturing, and project management for affiliates.

Key responsibilities of WOC also included feeding new technologies from Whirlpool's bases in North America and Europe to its other units; ensuring optimal brand

Exhibit 8   **Latin American Appliance Group in 1996: Whirlpool Corporation**

Principal Products	Major Brand Names	Principal Locations
Automatic washers	Brastemp[1]	**Regional Headquarters**
Dishwashers	Consul[1]	Sao Paulo, Brazil
Dryers	Eslabon de Lujo	
Freezers	Semer[1]	**Subsidiaries**
Microwave ovens	Whirlpool	Latin American Sales and
Ranges		Service Company, Miami
Refrigerators		South American Sales Company,
Room air conditioners		Grand Cayman
		Whirlpool Argentina S.A.,
		Buenos Aires, Argentina

Note:
1. Affiliate owned.

positioning in each country and analyzing specific appliance design for their suitability to various markets. Conditions could vary greatly from country to country. For instance, the company sold so-called giant ovens in Africa and the Middle East. These ovens were 39 in. and 42 in. wide compared to the standard 30 in. size in the United States and were large enough to roast a sheep or goat.

In 1993, after exhaustive and detailed analysis of world markets, the company decided that its global business interests would be better served by establishing two stand-alone business units, one for Latin America called LAAG, and the other the Whirlpool Asian Appliance Group for Whirlpool's Asian operations. (See Exhibits 8 and 9.)

Whirlpool Asian Appliance Group

When Whirlpool began to pursue perceived business opportunities in Asia, it was not new to the market. It had exported home appliances to the region for over 30 years from the United States. Thanks to the acquisition of Philips's appliance business, it gained broadened access to Asian markets. However, Whirlpool realized that a viable position in Asia implied more than selling imports from NAAG and WEBV, having kits assembled by licensees, or by having appliances built to specification by local manufacturers.

Whirlpool's Asian strategy rested on the "Five Ps"—*partnerships, products, processes, people,* and a *pan-Asian approach.* The strategy was broken into three phases: start-up, building, and market leadership. Based on extensive market research, Whirlpool decided to base its foray into Asia on four specific appliance products—the so-called "T-4" of refrigerators, clothes washers, microwave ovens, and air conditioners. For a household with no appliances, a refrigerator was usually the first appliance purchased when incomes rose. A clothes washer came next. Air conditioners were important because of the prevailing heat and humidity in much of the region. Microwave ovens had become a truly global appliance with essentially standardized features and design. Whirlpool focused its efforts on China and India, the most populous countries. Market entry was supposed to occur through joint ventures, to be followed later by "greenfield" plants. Based on commonalties identified in the region, Whirlpool planned to use a pan-Asian platform, modified for specific areas to meet regional preferences. In contrast to other regions, only one brand name—Whirlpool—would be used since the market was not considered mature enough to allow for a multibrand approach.

Exhibit 9   Asian Appliance Group in 1996: Whirlpool Corporation

Principal Products	Major Brand Names	Principal Locations
Automatic washers Microwave ovens Refrigerators Room air conditioners	Bauknecht Ignis KitchenAid Raybo Roper Whirlpool **Under license** Kelvinator (India) Narcissus SMC Snowflake TVS	**Regional Headquarters and Technology Center** Singapore **Regional Offices** Hong Kong New Delhi, India Singapore **Subsidiaries** Beijing Whirlpool Snowflake Electric Appliance Co., Ltd., Beijing Kelvinator of India, New Delhi, India Whirlpool Narcissus (Shanghai) Co., Ltd., Shanghai, China Whirlpool Washing Machines, Ltd., Madras, India **Affiliates** Great Teco Whirlpool, Ltd., Taipei, Taiwan Beijing Embraco Snowflake Compressor Co., Ltd., Beijing, China **Manufacturing Facilities** Beijing, China Faridabad, India Pondicherry, India Shanghai, China Shenzhen, China Shunde, China **Sales Offices** Auckland, New Zealand Bangkok, Thailand Guanzhow, China Ho Chi Minh City, Vietnam Hong Kong New Delhi, India Noble Park, Australia Petaling Jaya, Malaysia Shanghai, China Seoul, South Korea Singapore Tokyo, Japan

In 1987, Whirlpool created a joint venture in India with Sundaram-Clayton, Ltd., called TVS Whirlpool, Ltd., which began producing semiautomatic clothes washers, the so-called "World Washer," and twin-tub washers for the Indian market.

Whirlpool's Asian expansion gained momentum in 1993 with the creation of the Whirlpool Asian Appliance Group (WAAG) (Exhibit 9) supported by a $10-million investment. A regional headquarters was established in Tokyo and later moved to Singapore, which also became the home of a pan-Asian marketing, product development, and technology center. The Asian market was further subdivided first into three, then four, operating regions: Greater China, based in Hong Kong (Peoples Republic and Hong Kong); South Asia, based in Delhi (India, Pakistan, and surrounding markets); North Asia, based in Tokyo (Japan, Korea, the Philippines, and Taiwan), and Southeast Asia, based in Singapore (Australia and New Zealand).

In 1994, Whirlpool's investment in Asia jumped to over $200 million. The company announced a joint venture with Teco Electric & Machinery Co., Ltd., to market and distribute home appliances in Taiwan as an insider. In February 1995, Whirlpool acquired a controlling interest in Kelvinator of India, Ltd., one of the largest manufacturers and marketers of refrigerators in that country. Also, Whirlpool obtained a controlling interest and day-to-day management of its existing Indian-based venture, TVS Whirlpool, Ltd. In its *1995 Annual Report,* the company announced that in the forthcoming year it would create an efficient, customer-responsive "Whirlpool of India" organization.

Also, China became the center of a series of joint ventures combined with plant expansions and upgrades. These moves marked an important milestone in that they completed Whirlpool's T-4 strategy in China.

Essential for the long-term strategy was the creation of a technology center in Singapore where a new generation of products would be designed for the Asian market and which could tap into Whirlpool's global expertise. As in Latin America, the Worldwide Excellence System was adapted to regional circumstances and provided a strong integrating mechanism. To accelerate the process, Whirlpool assembled global product teams, offered foreign assignments within the global organization to key personnel, and started hiring aggressively within the region.

ORCHESTRATING THE STRATEGY GLOBALLY

Even though Whirlpool by the end of 1995 was a global force, its U.S. exports were less than 10% of gross revenues. As Whirlpool expanded its geographic reach (see Exhibit 10), it became crucial for the company to lay the groundwork for utilizing effectively its experience worldwide in product technology and manufacturing processes and transfering it quickly to wherever it was needed and thereby leverage its global presence to gain sustainable competitive advantage. For this purpose, a number of projects and organizational functions and arrangements were put in place.

Global Business Units

Two product groups were managed and organized on a global platform. The Microwave Oven Business Unit managed microwave oven production and development activities globally with manufacturing and product development facilities in Norrköping, Sweden, and a second, low-cost source in development in Shunde, China. Whirlpool claimed that once the Shunde facility started operating, it would be one of the world's top five microwave oven manufacturers.

In late 1995, Whirlpool created the Global Air Treatment Unit, which relied on the LaVergne Division in Tennessee and Shenzhen Whirlpool Raybo Air-Conditioner Industrial Co., Ltd., which had become part of the company a few months before. An aggres-

Exhibit 10 **Changes in Global Presence, 1988–1995: Whirlpool Corporation**

	1988	1995
Revenues	$4.41 billion	$8.35 billion
Market position	Leader in North America; affiliates in Brazil, Canada, India, and Mexico	No.1 in North America, No.1 in Latin America, No.3 in Europe, Largest Western appliance company in Asia
Manufacturing locations (including affiliates)	4	12
Brands (including affiliates)	14	28
Market presence	—	>140 (in more than 140 countries)
Employees	29,110	45,435

sive growth strategy had been formulated that anticipated quadrupling volume in the first half of 1996 relative to the same period a year earlier.

In addition, Whirlpool Financial Corporation, established in 1957, served manufacturers, retailers, and consumers in the United States, Canada, and Europe. With assets exceeding $1.9 billion in 1995, it provided inventory and consumer financing to support product sales from the point of manufacture through the market channel to the consumer.

The World Washer

The "World Washer" represented an effort to create a lightweight compact washer with few parts that could be produced in developing countries where manufacturing technology was not advanced and could be sold at a price that put it within reach of many more households than the designs marketed in the industrialized world. The goal of the World Washer effort was to develop a complete product, process, and facility design package versatile enough to satisfy conditions and market requirements in various countries but with low initial investment requirements. At the same time, the World Washer was to establish a beachhead especially against the Far Eastern rivals. Not everybody in the industry shared Whirlpool's vision of global products. Commented Lawrence A. Johnson, a corporate officer of General Electric's Appliance Division, "We're not in an industry where global products work well. . . . There is also no such thing as a global brand, and it's unlikely that there will be. It's hard to change decades of brand commitment."[19]

As the name indicated, a common design was envisaged for India, Brazil, and Mexico where the washer was to be produced and marketed. Originally the plan was to replicate the project design in each of the three countries. It eventually proved necessary to develop three slightly different variations. Costs also varied widely, further affecting both product and process decisions. "In India, for example, material costs may run as much as 200 to 800 percent higher than elsewhere, while labor and overhead costs are comparatively minimal," added Lawrence J. Kremer, Senior Vice-President, Global Technology and Operations.[20]

The plants also varied subtly from each other, although the goals were identical—minimizing facility investment and avoiding big finish systems and welding stations that required extensive machinery for materials cleanup and environmental safety. In Brazil the plant was designed as a creative convection cooling system to address the high humidity and constructed of precast concrete. In India, the new facility was built in Pondicherry, just 12° north of the equator. Although the plant looked similar to the one in Brazil—except for the overhead fans—the method of construction was different. Concrete was hand mixed on location, then carried in wicker baskets to forms constructed next to the building site. The Indian construction crew cast the concrete, allowed it to cure, and then five or six men raised each 3-ton slab into place using chain, block, and tackle.

Worldwide Excellence System

Established in 1991, the Worldwide Excellence System (WES) was the company's blueprint for how it approached quality, customers, and continuous improvement worldwide. WES combined elements of other well-known quality systems: ISO 9000, the Deming approach used in Asia, and the Baldrige system used in the United States. Like the Baldrige system, WES used a point system to measure success of implementing the program. WES had seven categories (see Exhibit 11). The Whirlpool People and Leadership categories described the involvement of people at all levels in moving the corporation to excellence. Fact-Based Management, Strategic Planning, and Quality of Process and Products outlined the major internal processes for achieving excellence. Measurement and Results explained the methods used to determine what customers expected and to assess how well they were being satisfied. The continuous monitoring of Customer Satisfaction was used for unending improvement of activities and processes.

Technology Organization

Several of Whirlpool's functions were organized to take advantage of the company's technical know-how scattered around the globe. The goal was to develop advanced, innovative products and move them to market quickly and competitively. As mentioned previously, an early success in this area occurred in late 1991 when the VIP Crisp microwave oven, developed in Norrköping, Sweden, was introduced and quickly became Europe's best-selling model.

A Global Procurement organization bought all materials and components needed by the company's appliance production facilities. From procurement centers in the United States, Italy, and Singapore, it bought finished products, commodities sourced on a regional or global basis, and standardized parts and components. Most other parts and materials were sourced from suppliers located near the production facilities where they were used. In developing countries, this often implied educating and assisting local suppliers in attaining Whirlpool standards.

The Corporate Technology Development group developed product and process technology capabilities and provided technical services to Whirlpool businesses. Although centrally managed from the corporation's technology center in Benton Harbor, technology development activities were geographically dispersed in Europe, Asia, and North America.

An Advanced Product Concepts unit looked beyond current product needs for appliances Whirlpool was making. It was responsible for developing new product concepts that were identified through market research.

The Advanced Manufacturing Concepts team was responsible for bringing new manufacturing processes into the corporation and identifying and developing simulation tools and best practices to be used on a global basis.

Exhibit 11   Worldwide Excellence System: Whirlpool Corporation

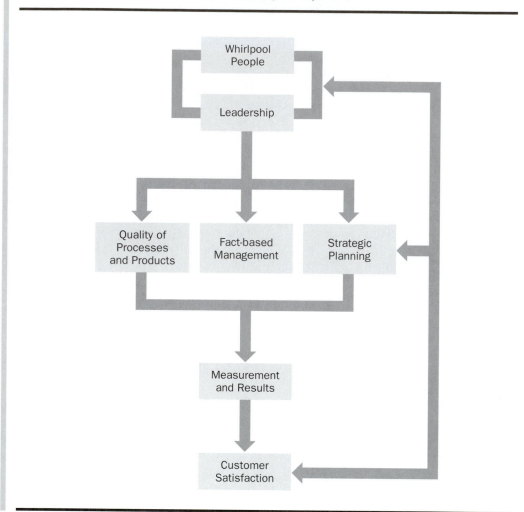

A Strategic Assessment and Support organization identified and evaluated non-traditional new product opportunities in cooperation with other units of Whirlpool. It also established corporate policy regarding product safety and computer-aided design and manufacturing; it addressed environmental and regulatory issues and intellectual property rights.

THE RACE FOR GLOBAL DOMINANCE

Whirlpool was by no means alone in its efforts to establish a global position of strength. Everybody in the industry was pursuing similar strategies. Electrolux, the leader in Europe, continued to expand aggressively, using its strong pan-European and local brands. Plans included establishing market share leadership in Central and Eastern Europe by the year 2000. A $100 million investment in China included a joint venture to manufacture water purifiers, another for compressors, and a vacuum-cleaner plant. Vacuum-cleaner manufacturing capacity was also increased in South Africa. In India, Electrolux established itself through acquisitions of majority holdings in production facilities for refrigerators and washing machines. In Thailand, Indonesia, Malaysia, and Singapore, the Swedish giant rapidly developed a strong position through a network of retailers. In Latin America, the company recently had acquired a minority interest in Brazil's second-largest white goods manufacturer, Refripar.

Besides trying to strengthen its position in North America through its alliance with Maytag where it hoped to sell its distinctively European designs beyond the export of 40,000 dishwashers, Bosch-Siemens Hausgeräte GmbH (BSHG) also vied for a larger share in other regions. In China, BSHG had acquired a majority interest in Wuxi Little Swan Co., a leading manufacturer of laundry appliances. In Brazil, BSHG had purchased Continental 2001, a large appliance producer with sales of $294 million. In Eastern Europe, it had recently completed the construction of a washing machine factory in Lodz, Poland. General Electric Appliances, a $6 billion giant in 1994, was also working hard to establish itself as a global player: "We're focusing our efforts on the world's fastest growing markets, including India, China, Southeast Asia, and South America. . . . We're also strengthening our alliances in Mexico and India, and we developed a number of new products specifically for global markets," explained J. Richard Stonesifer, GEA's President and CEO.[21]

EPILOGUE

For fiscal year 1995, Whirlpool reported per share earnings of $2.80, up from a year earlier but still below the 1993 high. For a summary of financial results see Exhibits 12, 13, and 14. A combination of events and trends had contributed to these results. First, in North America, product shipments had declined by 1.4% and operating profits had dropped by 16%. In Europe, rising raw material costs, fierce competition, and a shift by consumers to cheaper brands and models reduced Whirlpool's shipments by 2% while the industry grew by 1%. Volume in Latin America was up thanks to robust growth in Brazil in contrast to Argentina where industry shipments plummeted by as much as 50% because of the Mexican collapse. Whirlpool Asia reported an operating loss due to continuing expansion while shipments increased by 193% and revenues by 83%, respectively. David Whitwam said that the company was ahead of schedule in its restructuring effort in Europe and North America and that he anticipated significant improvements in operating efficiency for 1996. Evidently, Whirlpool felt good about its position in the industry, as indicated by the quote in his 1995 Letter to Shareholders, in spite of the lackluster short-term results.

Exhibit 12 Eleven-Year Consolidated Financial Review: Whirlpool Corporation
(Dollar amounts in millions, except per-share data)

Year Ending December 31	1995	1994	1993	1992	1991	1990	1989	1988	1987	1986	1985	1984
Consolidated Operations												
Net sales	$8,163	$7,949	$7,368	$7,097	$6,550	$6,424	$6,138	$4,306	$4,104	$3,928	$3,465	$3,128
Financial services	184	155	165	204	207	181	136	107	94	76	67	63
Total revenues	$8,347	$8,104	$7,533	$7,301	$6,757	$6,605	$6,274	$4,413	$4,198	$4,004	$3,532	$3,191
Operating profit	$ 396	$ 397	$ 482	$ 479	$ 393	$ 349	$ 411	$ 261	$296	$326	$295	$288
Earnings from continuing operations before income taxes and other items	242	292	375	372	304	220	308	233	280	329	321	326
Earnings from continuing operations before accounting change	209	158	231	205	170	72	187	161	187	202	182	190
Net earnings	209	158	51	205	170	72	187	94	192	200	182	190
Net capital expenditures	480	418	309	288	287	265	208	166	223	217	178	135
Depreciation	282	246	241	275	233	247	222	143	133	120	89	72
Dividends paid	100	90	85	77	76	76	76	76	79	76	73	73
Consolidated Financial Position												
Current assets	$3,541	$3,078	$2,708	$2,740	$2,920	$2,900	$2,889	$1,827	$1,690	$1,654	$1,410	$1,302
Current liabilities	3,829	2,988	2,763	2,887	2,931	2,651	2,251	1,374	1,246	1,006	781	671
Working capital	(288)	90	(55)	(147)	(11)	249	638	453	444	648	629	632
Property, plant and equipment—net	1,779	1,440	1,319	1,325	1,400	1,349	1,288	820	779	677	514	398
Total assets	7,800	6,655	6,047	6,118	6,445	5,614	5,354	3,410	3,137	2,856	2,207	1,901
Long-term debt	983	885	840	1,215	1,528	874	982	474	367	298	125	91
Total debt—appliance business	1,635	965	850	1,198	1,330	1,026	1,125	441	383	194	64	53
Shareholders' equity	1,877	1,723	1,648	1,600	1,515	1,424	1,421	1,321	1,304	1,350	1,207	1,096
Per-Share Data												
Earnings from continuing operations before accounting change	$2.80	$2.10	$3.19	$2.90	$2.45	$1.04	$2.70	$2.33	$2.61	$2.72	$2.49	$2.59
Net earnings	2.80	2.10	0.67	2.90	2.45	1.04	2.70	1.36	2.68	2.70	2.49	2.59
Dividends	1.36	1.22	1.19	1.10	1.10	1.10	1.10	1.10	1.10	1.03	1.00	1.00
Book value	25.08	22.83	22.80	22.67	21.78	20.51	20.49	19.06	18.83	18.21	16.46	14.97
Closing stock price—NYSE	53¼	50¼	66½	44⅝	38⅞	23½	33	24¾	24⅜	33⅞	24 11/16	23¼

Exhibit 13   Income Statement: Whirlpool Corporation (Dollar amounts in millions, except per-share data)

Year Ending December 31	Whirlpool Corporation (Consolidated)			Supplemental Consolidating Data Whirlpool with WFC on an Equity Basis			Whirlpool Financial Corporation (WFC)		
	1995	1994	1993	1995	1994	1993	1995	1994	1993
Revenues									
Net sales	$8,163	$7,949	$7,368	$8,163	$7,949	$7,368	$—	$—	$—
Financial services	184	155	165	—	—	—	219	184	193
	8,347	8,104	7,533	8,163	7,949	7,368	219	184	193
Expenses									
Cost of products sold	6,245	5,952	5,503	6,245	5,952	5,503	—	—	—
Selling and administrative	1,609	1,490	1,433	1,521	1,415	1,305	123	104	155
Financial services interest	66	51	59	—	—	—	79	63	72
Intangible amortization	31	24	25	31	24	25	—	—	—
Gain on dispositions	—	(60)	—	—	(60)	—	—	—	—
Restructuring costs	—	250	31	—	248	31	—	2	—
	7,951	7,707	7,051	7,797	7,579	6,864	202	169	227
Operating profit (Loss)	396	397	482	366	370	504	17	15	(34)
Other income (expense)									
Interest and sundry	(13)	9	6	(23)	3	19	11	8	(9)
Interest expense	(141)	(114)	(113)	(129)	(104)	(105)	—	—	—
Earnings (loss) before income taxes, other items, and accounting change	242	292	375	214	269	418	28	23	(43)
Income taxes	100	176	148	90	169	167	10	7	(19)
Earnings (loss) before equity earnings, minority interests, and accounting change	142	116	227	124	100	251	18	16	(24)
Equity in WFC	—	—	—	14	11	(28)	—	—	—
Equity in affiliated companies	72	59	16	72	59	16	—	—	—
Minority interests	(5)	(17)	(12)	(1)	(12)	(10)	(4)	(5)	(2)
Net earnings (loss) before cumulative effect of accounting change	209	158	231	209	158	229	14	11	(26)
Cumulative effect of accounting change for postretirement benefits	—	—	(180)	—	—	(178)	—	—	(2)
Net earnings (loss)	$209	$158	$51	$209	$158	$51	$14	$11	$(28)
Per share of common stock									
Primary earnings before accounting change	2.80	2.10	3.19						
Primary earnings	2.80	2.10	0.67						
Fully diluted earnings before accounting change	2.76	2.09	3.11						
Fully diluted earnings	2.76	2.09	0.67						
Cash dividends	1.36	1.22	1.19						
Average number of common shares outstanding (millions)	74.8	75.5	72.3						

Source: Whirlpool Corporation, *1995 Annual Report*, p. 37.

Exhibit 14   **Balance Sheet: Whirlpool Corporation**
(Dollar amounts in millions)

| | | | Supplemental Consolidating Data | | | |
| | Whirlpool Corporation (Consolidated) | | Whirlpool with WFC on an Equity Basis | | Whirlpool Financial Corporation (WFC) | |
Year Ending December 31	1995	1994	1995	1994	1995	1994
Assets						
Current assets						
Cash and equivalents	$ 149	$ 72	$ 125	$ 51	$ 24	$ 21
Trade receivables, less allowances of $39 in 1995 and $38 in 1994	1,031	1,001	1,031	1,001	—	—
Financing receivables and leases, less allowances	1,086	866	—	—	1,086	866
Inventories	1,029	838	1,029	838	—	—
Prepaid expenses and other	152	197	141	183	11	14
Deferred income taxes	94	104	94	104	—	—
Total current assets	3,541	3,078	2,420	2,177	1,121	901
Other assets						
Investment in affiliated companies	425	370	425	370	—	—
Investment in WFC	—	—	269	253	—	—
Financing receivables and leases, less allowances	772	717	—	—	772	717
Intangibles, net	931	730	931	730	—	—
Deferred income taxes	153	171	153	171	—	—
Other	199	149	199	149	—	—
	2,480	2,137	1,977	1,673	772	717
Property, plant, and equipment						
Land	97	73	97	73	—	—
Buildings	710	610	710	610	—	—
Machinery and equipment	2,855	2,418	2,831	2,392	24	26
Accumulated depreciation	(1,883)	(1,661)	(1,867)	(1,645)	(16)	(16)
	1,779	1,440	1,771	1,430	8	10
Total assets	$7,800	$6,655	$6,168	$5,280	$1,901	$1,628
Liabilities and Shareholders' Equity						
Current liabilities						
Notes payable	$ 1,939	$ 1,162	$ 709	$ 226	$ 1,230	$ 936
Accounts payable	977	843	896	795	81	48
Employee compensation	232	201	222	192	10	9
Accrued expenses	552	629	552	620	—	9
Restructuring costs	70	114	70	112	—	2
Current maturities of long-term debt	59	39	56	36	3	3
Total current liabilities	3,829	2,988	2,505	1,981	1,324	1,007
Other liabilities						
Deferred income taxes	234	221	114	110	120	111
Postemployment benefits	517	481	517	481	—	—
Other liabilities	181	262	181	262	—	—
Long-term debt	983	885	870	703	113	182
	1,915	1,849	1,682	1,556	233	293
Minority interests	179	95	104	20	75	75
Shareholders' equity						
Common stock, $1 par value: 250 million shares authorized, 81 million and 80 million shares issued in 1995 and 1994	81	80	81	80	8	8
Paid-in capital	229	214	229	214	26	26
Retained earnings	1,863	1,754	1,863	1,754	234	220
Unearned restricted stock	(8)	(8)	(8)	(8)	—	—
Cumulative translation adjustments	(53)	(93)	(53)	(93)	1	(1)
Treasury stock - 6 million shares at cost in 1995 and 1994	(235)	(224)	(235)	(224)	—	—
Total shareholders' equity	1,877	1,723	1,877	1,723	269	253
Total liabilities and shareholders' equity	$7,800	$6,655	$6,168	$5,280	$1,901	$1,628

Source: Whirlpool Corporation, *1995 Annual Report*, pp. 38–39.

Selected Sources

A. M. "Fleet of Foot." *Appliance Manufacturer* (May 1994), pp. 35–38.

"A Portrait of the U.S. Appliance Industry 1992." *Appliance* (September 1992).

Appliance (June 1991).

Appliance Manufacturer (February 1990), pp. 36–37.

Babyak, R. J. "Strategic Imperative." *Appliance Manufacturer,* Special section (February 1995), pp. 19–24.

Botskor, I., M. Chaouli, and B. Müller. "Boom mit Grauwerten," *Wirtschaftswoche* (May 28, 1993), pp. 64–75.

Bower, J. L., and N. Dossabhoy. "Note on the Major Home Appliance Industry in 1984 (Condensed)." Case #385-211, Harvard Business School (mimeo).

Bray, H. "Plugging into the World." *Detroit Free Press* (May 17, 1993), pp. 10F–11F.

Bylinsky, G. "Computers That Learn by Doing." *Fortune* (September 6, 1993), pp. 96–102.

DuPont, T. "The Appliance Giant Has a New President and a Global Vision." *The Weekly Home Furnishings Newspaper* (July 2, 1987), p. 1.

DuPont, T. "Whirlpool's New Brand Name." *The Weekly Home Furnishings Newspaper* (April 11, 1988).

Echikson, W. "The Trick to Selling in Europe." *Fortune* (September 20, 1993), p. 82.

Fisher, J. D. "Home Appliance Industry." *Value Line* (December 22, 1989), p. 132.

Ghoshal, S., and P. Haspeslagh. "The Acquisition and Integration of Zanussi by Electrolux: A Case Study." *European Management Journal* (December 1990), pp. 414–433.

Hunger, D. J. "The Major Home Appliance Industry in 1990: From U.S. to Global." (mimeo, 1990).

Jackson, T. "European Competition Hurts Whirlpool." *Financial Times* (October 14–15), p. 6.

Jancsurak, J. "Holistic Strategy Pays Off." *Appliance Manufacturer,* Special section (February 1995), pp. 3–6.

Jancsurak, J. "Big Plans for Europe's Big Three." *Appliance Manufacturer* (April 1995), pp. 26–30.

Jancsurak, J. "Wanted: Customers for Life." *Appliance Manufacturer,* Special section (February 1995), pp. 36–37.

Maruca, R. F. "The Right Way to Go Global. An Interview with Whirlpool CEO David Whitwam." *Harvard Business Review* (March–April 1994), pp. 135–145.

Naj, A. K. "Air Conditioners Learn to Sense if You're Cool." *Wall Street Journal* (August 31, 1993), p. B1.

R. J. B. "Demystifying the Asian Consumer," *Appliance Manufacturer,* Special section (February 1995), pp. 25–27.

R. J. B. "Multifaceted Strategy." *Appliance Manufacturer,* Special section (February 1995), pp. 28–29.

Schiller, Z. "The Great Refrigerator Race." *Business Week* (July 5, 1993), pp. 78–81.

Schiller, Z. "GE Has a Lean, Mean Washing Machine." *Business Week* (November 20, 1995), pp. 97–98.

Standard & Poor's. "Waiting for the Next Replacement Cycle." *Industry Surveys* (November 1991), pp. T102–T105.

Standard & Poor's. "Poised for a Moderate Recovery." *Industry Surveys* (November 1992), pp. T96–T101.

Treece, J. B. "The Great Refrigerator Race." *Business Week* (July 15, 1993), pp. 78–81.

Weiner, S. "Growing Pains," *Forbes* (October 29, 1990), p. 40–41.

Whirlpool Corporation. *1987–1995 Annual Reports.*

Whirlpool Corporation. *Form 10-K* (1992, 1994, and 1995).

Whirlpool Corporation. *1992 Proxy Statement.*

Whirlpool Corporation. *Profile* (1994 and 1995).

Whirlpool Corporation. "Whirlpool 'World Washer' Being Marketed in Three Emerging Countries." News Release (undated).

Whirlpool Corporation. "Whirlpool Corporation Named Winner in $30 Million Super-Efficient Refrigerator Competition." (undated).

Zeller, W. "A Tough Market Has Whirlpool in a Spin." *Business Week* (May 2, 1988), pp. 121–122.

Notes

1. Whirlpool Corporation, *1995 Annual Report,* p. 4.
2. Whirlpool Corporation, *1994 Annual Report,* p. 2.
3. Whirlpool Corporation, *Profile* (1995).
4. Whirlpool Corporation, *Form 10-K,* (1994).
5. T. A. Stewart, "A Heartland Industry Takes on the World," *Fortune* (March 2, 1990), pp. 110–112.
6. S. Kindel, "World Washer: Why Whirlpool Leads in Appliance: Not Some Japanese Outfit," *Financial World* (March 20, 1990), pp. 42–46.
7. Whirlpool Corporation, *Form 10-K* (1992).
8. Whirlpool Corporation, *1992 Annual Report.*
9. Whirlpool Corporation, *Profile* (1994).
10. Whirlpool Corporation, *1994 Annual Report,* p. 9.
11. A. M., "Fleet of Foot," *Appliance Manufacturer* (May 1991), pp. 35–38.
12. Whirlpool Corporation, *World Washer News Release.*
13. Whirlpool Corporation, *1994 Annual Report,* p. 10.
14. Whirlpool Corporation, *1987 Annual Report,* p. 5.
15. Whirlpool Corporation, *1989 Annual Report,* p. 9.
16. T. A. Stewart, "A Heartland Industry Takes on the World."
17. R. Tierney, "Whirlpool Magic," *World Trade* (May 1993).
18. J. Jancsurak, "Marketing: Phase 2," *Appliance Manufacturer* (February 1995), pp. 8–10.
19. N. C. Remich, Jr., "Speed Saves the Day," *Appliance Manufacturer,* Special section (July 1995), p. 129.
20. Whirlpool Corporation, *World Washer News Release.*
21. N. C. Remich, Jr., "A Kentucky Thoroughbred That Is Running Strong," *Appliance Manufacturer,* Special section (July 1995), pp. 3–6.

Whirlpool: The First Venture into India

Philippe Lasserre and Jocelyn Probert

In April 1994, Whirlpool Corporation became the majority shareholder in TVS-Whirlpool, a joint venture based in Pondicherry, southern India, in which it had held a 33% stake since 1987. The company, which was established to manufacture fully automatic washing machines for the Indian market, had struggled to make headway under the management of the Indian partner and by 1994 was on the verge of collapse. The intention of Whirlpool was to turn around the company's fortunes by the end of 1995 and create a firm base for its operations in India.

BACKGROUND: THE HOME APPLIANCE INDUSTRY

The market for home appliances had matured in the United States and Europe by the mid 1980s. The United States was the largest market, accounting for 26% of worldwide demand. Growth rates were of the order of 1–2% per year for the major appliances (refrigerators, washing machines, microwave ovens, conventional ovens, dishwashers, and air conditioners). By the end of the decade, the European market overtook the United States owing to rising income levels and lower overall saturation rates, with 44 million units sold out of a world total of 180 million units.

In Asia the picture was fragmented. The Japanese market, which represented around 40% of regional demand, had already reached the saturation point by the late 1980s, and Hong Kong and Singapore also had high diffusion rates for the major appliances. Several other countries, including South Korea, Taiwan, Malaysia, and Thailand, were emerging as important new markets. However, in other countries in the region with very large populations, the home appliance industry was still at an early stage of development. Significant future growth could be envisaged in such countries as India, China, Indonesia, the Philippines, and Vietnam as rapid economic growth of 6–8% per annum spurred per capita income levels. The potential scale of these markets led to industry projections that Asia would represent 40% of world demand for home appliances, or 120 million units per annum, by the year 2004.

Significant consolidation had taken place among industry players, particularly in the United States and later in Europe. From more than 50 significant players worldwide at the beginning of the 1970s, fewer than 20 remained only a couple of decades later. Of these, Whirlpool Corporation of the U.S. and Electrolux of Sweden fiercely contested the number one position. Japanese companies were much stronger in Asia than their American or European competitors. Matsushita held a significant lead both within Japan and elsewhere in the region. Other regional players, particularly the Koreans, were also much in evidence by the early 1990s.

This case was written by Philippe Lasserre, Professor of Strategy and Management at INSEAD, and Jocelyn Probert, Research Analyst at INSEAD Euro-Asia Centre. It is intended to be used as a basis for class discussion rather than to illustrate either effective or ineffective handling of administrative situations. Copyright © 1997 INSEAD-EAC, Fontainebleau, France. Reprinted by permission.

Exhibit 1　**Whirlpool Corporation's Financial Performance**
(Dollar amounts in US$ millions)

	1995	1994	1993	1992	1991
Total revenues	$8,347	$8,104	$7,533	$7,301	$6,757
Operating profit	396	397	482	479	393
Earnings from continuing operations before tax and others	242	292	375	372	304
Net earnings	209	158	51	205	170
Net capital expenditure	480	418	309	288	287
Net earnings per share	2.80	2.1	0.67	2.9	2.45
Key ratios (%)					
Operating profit margin	4.7%	4.9%	6.4%	6.6%	5.8%
Pre-tax margin	2.9	3.6	5.0	5.1	4.5
Net margin	2.5	2.0	3.1	2.8	2.5
ROE	11.6	9.4	14.2	13.1	11.6
ROA	3.0	2.8	4.0	3.3	2.9
PER	19.0	23.9	20.8	15.4	15.9
No. of employees at year end	45,435	39,016	39,590	38,520	37,886

THE GLOBALIZATION OF WHIRLPOOL

Until the mid 1980s Benton Harbor–based Whirlpool Corporation concentrated almost exclusively on the rapidly maturing North American market. The appointment of David R. Whitwam as Chief Executive Officer in 1987 opened the way to an appraisal of the global marketplace and of the opportunities for Whirlpool to expand its presence in other regions. Although the home appliance industry thus far had remained regionalized, analysts believed that over time it would become more global in nature. Whirlpool determined to lead that process.

In 1989 Whirlpool was ready for its first major step overseas. It acquired a stake in the European appliance business of the Dutch company Philips and assumed full ownership in 1991. This turned Whirlpool into a US$6 billion company (see Exhibits 1 and 2 for recent financial results, geographical revenue, and operating profits breakdown). In 1990, Whirlpool Overseas Corporation (WOC) was established at Benton Harbor to handle exports of finished goods and components, and the sale and transfer of technology to Whirlpool licensees in existing and emerging international markets. Later, in 1992, WOC would be disbanded and separate business units established to focus on the most promising regions: Latin America and Asia. In Asia, China and India were identified as the potentially most interesting markets. In 1993, Whirlpool Asian Appliances Group (WAAG) opened its regional headquarters in Singapore.

By 1995, Whirlpool was marketing major home appliances in 140 countries worldwide under 12 brand names. It was the market leader in North and Latin America, and claimed third place behind Electrolux and Bosch-Siemens in Europe. In Asia, it was the only western home appliances company even to have a market share of 1%, but there was still substantial ground to make up against Japanese white goods producers. Whirlpool's

Exhibit 2 **Whirlpool Corporation Regional Sales Breakdown**
(Dollar amounts in US$ millions)

A. Net Sales by Business Unit

	1994	1995	Change (%)
North America	5,048	5,093	1
Europe	2,373	2,428	2
Asia	205	376	83
Latin America	329	271	−18
Other	(6)	(5)	—
Total appliance business	7,949	8,163	3

B. Operating Profit by Business Unit

	1994	1995	Change (%)
North America	522	445	−15
Europe	163	92	−44
Asia	(22)	(50)	−127
Latin America	49	26	−47
Other	(342)	(147)	57
Total appliance business	370	366	−1

goals were to be in the top 25% of all publicly traded companies in terms of creation of shareholder value, and to be the brand of choice in the top four (T-4) home appliances: refrigerators, washing machines, room air conditioners, and microwave ovens.

The first step toward a presence in Asia had actually taken place at a very early stage in Whirlpool's globalization plans. During a briefing session held at Benton Harbor by external consultants in 1987, Whirlpool became convinced that rising incomes and aspirations among India's middle class would generate substantial demand for home appliances over the next decades. Specifically it seemed that the nascent domestic washing machine market was poised for rapid growth from a low base.

That same year, Whirlpool met and signed a joint venture agreement with Sundaram Clayton, a member of India's TVS group, which wanted to enter the consumer market in anticipation of a consumer boom. The venture would manufacture automatic washing machines and produce other items such as refrigerators and microwave ovens once the washer business was on a stable footing. Each partner was to hold a 33% share in TVS-Whirlpool Ltd (TWL) and the remaining 34% of shares were to be offered to the public. Initial public offerings were at that time—and remain—a common practice in India, where well developed stock markets can offer useful risk-spreading opportunities. Under the terms of the agreement, TVS was to provide TWL's day-to-day operational management and Whirlpool would supply the technology to manufacture fully automatic washing machines. Products would be sold under the TVS-Whirlpool brand name.

TVS-SUNDARAM CLAYTON

In the early years of the twentieth century, at about the same time that the founder of Whirlpool was establishing his manual washing machine business by Lake Michigan, T. V. Sundaram Iyengar began a bus service in Madurai in the southern Indian state of Tamil Nadu. Progressive and forward-looking, his mission was to offer his customers trust, value, and service. From these three attributes, and from his own initials, came the name of his company, TVS.

Under his four sons, the company expanded from the transportation business into auto component manufacturing and then into coach-building. Even through diversification the primary focus remained on engineering and OEM manufacturing for the automotive industry. By the early 1990s, when the third generation of the family had moved into managerial positions, the TVS group comprised more than 100, companies, employed 45,000 people, and was one of the 20 largest groups in India with annual revenues of Rs.2,000 crores.[1] TVS had become a household name, particularly in the south of India, for automotive components, but it had also diversified in the 1980s into other businesses such as electronics and consumer durables. TVS was a paternalistic group, believing strongly in employee development and welfare. At the same time, the family was keen on trying out the latest management ideas from Japan, the United States, and Europe.

Diversification was aided by technical collaborations and joint ventures, but the family always retained managerial control. Important joint ventures by the Sundaram Clayton branch of TVS included Lucas-TVS Brakes and TVS-Suzuki. The latter was formed in 1984 when the government lifted a ban on new entrants to the motorcycle industry. TVS-Suzuki produced India's first 100cc motorbikes and had gained a market share of 20% by 1986, but it lost both share and money when competitors moved into the same industry segment. Accumulated losses of Rs.13 crores were wiped out only in 1993–1994.

The effect of the Indian government's generally more liberal industrial licensing policy during the 1980s encouraged the TVS group (and many other Indian groups) to expand outside core business areas through foreign collaboration. In 1985, TVS Electronics was established in Bangalore by Gopal Srinivasan, a grandson of the TVS group founder (and future founder of TVS-Whirlpool), to produce computer peripherals. This was the group's first move into non-automotive consumer goods, and the early years revealed its inexperience in this field. Severe quality problems were finally overcome by 1990, but it was not until 1994 that TVS Electronics finally wiped out its accumulated losses.

THE MARKET FOR WASHING MACHINES IN INDIA

The concept of a middle class with significant purchasing power began to develop in India only in the second half of the 1980s. Even ten years later, the size and scope of the middle class remained a subject of debate. A recent survey by India's National Council of Applied Economic Research classified households—which have an average of 5.6 people each—into five bands (Exhibit 3). The same survey highlighted the lower living costs for rural families, giving them greater purchasing power than their urban counterparts, and the importance of the black market in raising household income among the poorer segments of the population.

Exhibit 3 **Distribution of Households, by Income, 1993–1994**
(Households, in thousands)

Income Category	Urban	Rural	Total
Up to Rs.20,000	15,804	74,736	90,540
Rs.20,001–40,000	14,228	26,456	40,684
Rs.40,001–62,000	7,344	8,619	15,963
Rs.62,001–86,000	3,377	2,862	6,239
Above Rs.86,001	2,273	1,621	3,894
Total	43,026	114,294	157,320

Note: US$1 = Rs.31 in 1993/4

Source: Indian Marketing Demographics, National Council for Applied Economic Research.

As recently as 1980, the washing machine market in India was nonexistent (even televisions sold in tiny numbers—just 150,000 units a year in a country with a population of 670 million people). By 1983, annual production of washers was still a mere 10,000 units. It was not until 1988–1989 that the market for semi-automatic (twin-tub) washing machines began to develop. By 1990, total installed production capacity had grown to 800,000 units per year and the market was worth US$200 million. Consumers' purchasing priorities lay with appliances other than washing machines: refrigerators, TVs, and motorbikes came first. The 1990s was expected to be the consumers' decade and a boom in washing machine sales was forecast, similar to the one in 1984–1990 that had turned refrigerators from a luxury product to a necessity in the perception of the consumer.

The washing machine market was divided into three segments in the late 1980s:

- **Manual washers** were the biggest sellers. They had neither timer controls nor programming capabilities and had no spin-dry function. Such machines were produced by India's small-scale industry and retailed at around Rs.3,000.

- **Semi-automatic machines** constituted the fastest growing segment. They could be programmed but required a physical transfer of the clothes from the washing tub to the spin-dry basket. Most machines on the market were designed to wash 2.5 kg of clothes at any one time. The technology involved in producing twin-tub washers was relatively simple. Machines were priced at Rs.5,000–6,000, and market size in 1990 was approximately 200,000 units. Videocon, with the technical collaboration of Matsushita, introduced the product to India in 1988–1989 and dominated the segment. It was joined in the market by a BPL-Sanyo joint venture in 1993. Both of these Japanese-influenced companies mounted impressive marketing campaigns.

- **Fully automatic machines,** which cost Rs.9,000 in 1990, were affordable to only a tiny segment of the population. Their production initially depended on imported kits on which high import duties were levied. A joint venture between IFB and Bosch of Germany began marketing fully automatic front-loading washers at approximately the same time that TVS-Whirlpool launched its product.

As with other home appliances, sales were seasonal. The period March–May was the most quiet for washing machine sales, whereas the festival season, which lasted from September to December, was very busy. Retail channels in India were undeveloped and presented a major challenge to manufacturers seeking to distribute their product. Product and brand awareness among consumers was very limited. It was not until the mid 1990s that customers began to pay more attention to the idea of purchasing a branded good from a reputable shop. Advertising also was becoming more important.

India presented several problems to appliance manufacturers from industrialized nations. Many homes lacked running water or were subject to cuts in the supply: top-loading washing machines could be filled with buckets of water, but overflows would affect electrical parts; the quality of the water supply was poor, often containing salt or soil, which would damage the motor; the electricity supply was erratic, and although the specified voltage in India was 240 volts, the actual range was 170–270 volts; rats got inside the appliance cabinet and gnawed through the electrical wiring; machines risked damage from transportation for long distances over bad roads and from manual loading and unloading of trucks; machines had to be lightweight and easily maneuverable because customers tended to keep them in the bedroom or corridor and move them to the water supply as necessary; and finally, the controls needed to be foolproof because customers often failed to operate their machines properly.

Project managers at TVS-Whirlpool expected fast growth in the overall washer market, to the extent that India would catch up with other international markets within a couple of years. They also forecast a rapid shift from semi-automatic to fully automatic machines.

THE EARLY YEARS OF TWL: A SHAKY START

Under the leadership of Gopal Srinivasan, the TWL joint venture in 1988 became TVS's second sortie into the consumer goods industry. A site was chosen near Pondicherry (see Exhibit 4) rather than in Madras or Bangalore where other TVS manufacturing units were located because both these cities were crowded and suffered water and electricity supply problems. Pondicherry, however, had ample water and power, and the authorities promised rapid completion of the licensing formalities in order to encourage industrialization of the region. The initial capital investment by TWL in land and the installation of a factory to produce automatic washing machines was Rs.40 crores (US$26.7 million).

The Product

Whirlpool introduced to the joint venture technology for a fully automatic machine, dubbed the World Washer. The World Washer was a totally new product developed by Whirlpool engineers to meet the demands of developing markets worldwide, notably Brazil and Mexico as well as India. Capable of washing 5kg loads, compared with the 2.5kg washers generally sold in India, the machine boasted electro-mechanical controls and had a sturdy design to help it cope with the rigors of the environment in which it would operate. TWL engineers traveled to the United States for training.

In India, Whirlpool's partners wanted to incorporate style changes specifically for the local market. Srinivasan, for example, wanted the machine to evoke the image of the traditional Indian washing stone (against which clothes were beaten to get them clean) and therefore requested a sloping lid instead of the originally planned flat lid. Such design alterations delayed the start of production from 1989 to August 1990, by which time the washing machine market had already begun to boom. Given the scale of TWL's investment costs, the project's break-even point was a very high 5,000 units per month.

Exhibit 4 The Indian Subcontinent

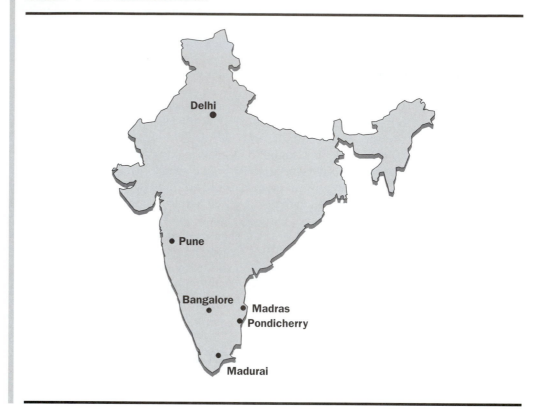

Even before they were ready to begin manufacturing washing machines, the managers of TWL were looking ahead to development of the next product. The R&D department employed 32 people in 1990 (compared with only eight in 1995) out of a total staff of 270, and time and resources were devoted to investigating the market for refrigerators, microwave ovens, and other home appliances. People went on research trips to Italy.

By December 1990, after five months of operation, only 1,800 World Washers had been produced; even fewer were sold, reflecting the traditional weakness of the TVS group in consumer distribution. The price, Rs.9,000, was high relative to prevailing monthly disposable incomes among the middle class. Unanticipated problems emerged. The greatest concern was damage during the washing process to the delicate fabric of saris, the traditional dress of Indian women: these 6–8 meter-long pieces of material would catch and tear in the small gap between the agitator and the drum that allowed for the agitator's movement. This issue was much greater in the south—the TVS group's home base and therefore TWL's main market—because women there wore saris more frequently than their northern counterparts. The machines also suffered greater damage in transit than the joint venture had anticipated, and many arrived at dealer showrooms in poor condition.

Low output and low sales continued during 1991 and 1992. A recession in India in 1992 coincided with the arrival of new market entrants, while the fall of the rupee (from Rs.18 to Rs.25) played havoc with costs. TWL was the market leader in the tiny fully automatic segment in 1991, but it was overtaken in 1992 by IFB, which had made a low-cost tie-up with the German company Bosch. Only 2,000–2,500 units per month were coming off TWL's line, significantly below break-even level. The capital investment was way out of proportion for the sales being achieved. According to V.A. Raghu, who became managing director in mid 1994, the problem was "strategically poor timing. One year later would have been all right, but the market wasn't ready for automatic washing machines and we were never able to cater to the mass market. Our market assessment was poor and we introduced the wrong product."

Meanwhile the semi-automatic segment of the washer market had become too big and was growing too fast for TWL to ignore. Thanks to the clever advertising of the twin-tub manufacturers, semi-automatics had even begun to take share from the fully automatic machines. By 1992, TWL's financial situation was so poor that the company decided to introduce its own semi-automatic machine in an attempt to boost sales and cash flow. "We lost one and a half years through not introducing a twin tub," acknowledges Raghu.

Whirlpool did not have twin-tub technology, the market for such products having disappeared from North America and Europe. Technology was bought from Daewoo of Korea. There was no external technical support, but the leadership of A. Karunakaran, who was chosen to head the twin-tub project team, "revealed the worth of the company and the people," according to one of the managers involved. Another Rs.4 crores were invested in tooling for the new product.

TWL launched its twin-tub machine in June 1992 at a price of nearly Rs.7,000. It was more expensive than the models dominating the market, but it could wash 5kg of clothes against their 2.5kg. Inflation meanwhile had pushed the price of TWL's automatic washer to Rs.13,000. Monthly twin-tub output quickly climbed to meet automatic washer production levels and from January 1993 consistently outstripped them. A second shift was introduced to handle the new line. In 1993, TWL's average monthly production of twin tubs was approximately 2,000 units, compared with barely 1,300 automatics.

Supplier Issues

TWL was set up as an assembly operation, dependent on components that were 80–90% sourced externally. The joint venture ran quickly into supplier base problems. Several potential suppliers were based in the Pondicherry region, but their business when the TWL plant was built was still exclusively geared toward the agricultural community. Nor had the TVS group's substantial network of suppliers in the automotive component business any experience in the washing machine industry.

Many different companies made components for TWL, but little attention was paid to their ability to deliver what was required or to the quality of the parts they produced. Competitors in the washing machine business like Videocon overcame supplier problems by importing the critical components. As a major consumer goods company, Videocon also had the advantage of in-house facilities such as injection moulding, which could be used to make washing machines and reduce its dependence on external sources. Even when components reached the TWL factory, it routinely took 15 days for them to be checked and ready for use on the line.

TWL had no leverage to persuade suppliers either to raise the quality of their components or to respect delivery deadlines because its own limited output meant it could only purchase in small volumes. Supplier schedules changed at short notice depending on the TWL marketing department's assessment of volume sales and the consequent impact this would have on production plans. Suppliers could not produce at consistent levels and suffered their own cash flow problems. As TWL's cash flow situation deteriorated, they became less willing to deliver goods on credit. "Normally the supplier base should stabilize after 1–2 years," commented the process engineering manager, Narayana Reddy, "but even after three years it did not because of our inability to commit to volumes."

Financial Issues

The failure of the forecast take-off in automatic washing machine sales seriously affected TWL's cash flow position. Not only was the company's product ahead of its time, but macroeconomic issues including a severe consumer credit squeeze in 1991–1992 also hurt sales. The lack of financing possibilities strangled the nascent consumer market.

TWL was operating in a high-margin, low-volume business, which made it very sensitive to changes in volume. Low sales deprived the company of the financial resources to make necessary investments in dealer development, further hindering its market penetration. Dealers were less interested in working with single-product firms like TWL than with companies like Videocon, which made a range of consumer durables. Competitors gave dealers 30–45 days' credit, whereas TWL required immediate payment.

TWL could not afford to invest in advertising and brand-building to stimulate customer interest in the TVS-Whirlpool name. Because manpower additions were regarded as extra costs, the sales force never reached critical mass. TVS was known for its engineering prowess, American technology was generally little known in India and therefore poorly evaluated, and the Whirlpool name was unfamiliar. TWL's marketing activity was limited to the top income segment only, even though twin-tub machines needed wider distribution to reach potential purchasers in a broader range of household income groups. Fortunately market growth from 1993 pushed the company along.

Suppliers became reluctant to deliver components unless TWL could guarantee payment, forcing the company to finance its operating costs through bank loans from 1992. The interest burden rose to 12% of sales. A debilitating debt spiral had begun.

Human Resources

Because Gopal Srinivasan was also the managing director of TVS Electronics, he was able to transfer managers to TWL in Pondicherry. Within the entire TVS group there were plenty of opportunities for executives to circulate to new projects or to existing ventures whose management team needed strengthening. Several managers came to join the new company from other parts of the TVS group between 1988 and 1993. Srinivasan was not afraid to seek people with external experience. A. Karunakaran, who played a key role heading TWL's twin-tub project in 1992 and would later become the plant manager, was hired in 1990 from his position as works general manager at Hero Motors, the moped manufacturer.

The TVS group enjoyed an excellent reputation as an employer. Welfare benefits were much more generous than the norm and labor relations were harmonious, in contrast to the situation in many Indian factories. From the day of its inception, TWL had never suffered a single day of stoppages by its in-house union. All employees were carefully selected and instilled with the core values of the group—a sense of business ethics and customer orientation. Workers were required to have at least 10 years of schooling, even for semi-skilled tasks such as assembly. Many blue-collar employees were recruited from the surrounding villages. New graduate engineers were taken on as junior managers. Staff turnover among the 250 employees and managers was minimal.

Srinivasan was a typical Indian manager-owner in the sense that decision-making powers were entirely vested in him. Nothing was delegated to his managers, even though they were trained in problem-solving techniques: he required from them an analysis of the problems on which to base his decisions. Also, he was based in Madras and visited the plant only 1–2 times per week. He was positively viewed by his employees, however, thanks to his good communication skills, and information flowed relatively well for an Indian company despite multiple layers of management.

He was described by one of his staff as "a true grandson of the founder, with an MBA from the United States, very progressive and open to new ideas but lacking in experience. And that experience was not provided by his business managers either." As a team they lacked the constancy of purpose needed to put the factory on the right track. Srinivasan always wanted to try out new management theories. He would send staff for training and introduce the techniques on-site, only to change again a few weeks later when a new management system was brought to his attention. "The TVS management was very systems-oriented, but its weakness was in integrating those systems," remembers one manager. Tasks were functionally organized, and the root causes of production problems were hard to identify. "We spent a lot of time firefighting, but everyone was reluctant to accept responsibility for a problem, particularly as business conditions worsened."

The lack of organizational focus was mirrored in the lack of market focus: TWL paid little attention to market development yet sought to introduce products for which demand barely existed. Design changes also affected sales. "Most Indian companies were totally inward-looking, they didn't understand the marketplace. The restyled world washer incorporated the ideas of the Indian management but they didn't appeal to the consumers," explained one engineer. Despite its shortcomings in marketing, TWL tried hard to be a customer-oriented company.

The combination of managerial, product, and financial weaknesses left TWL on the brink of sick industry status,[2] "despite the good people employed and the effort put in." Many companies declared to be "sick" remained in a state of limbo for years.

WHIRLPOOL TAKES OVER

By late 1993, TWL's equity was reduced to zero, cash flow was weak, and accumulated losses had risen to Rs.35 crores (US$10 million). Production was running at only 3,000 washing machines per month against a break-even point of 5,000 units. Without a new injection of cash, the factory would be declared "sick." Morale at the factory was low.

Other TVS family members were unwilling to pump new funds into the venture. Whirlpool faced the choice of increasing its stake by investing more cash or letting the joint venture die. It conducted a new study of the market, which suggested that the macroeconomic environment (a more favorable personal tax structure, economic liberalization, reform of the banking sector) supported further gains in middle-class income and strong growth in the washing machine market from 1995 onwards.

The American company agreed to support TWL, on the condition that it gained full managerial control. In the opinion of Whirlpool managers, it would be more expensive for them to start anew in India than to try to turn around the existing venture. Despite the financial difficulties, TVS-Whirlpool had become a recognized brand name, particularly in the south, and the joint venture had an established distribution network. In the fully automatic washing machine segment, it had the second highest market share in value terms, behind IFB, with 25%, and was in joint third place alongside IFB for twin tubs behind Videocon and BPL-Sanyo (see Exhibit 5). Although the scale of manufacturing was small, the basic set-up was good. On the negative side, TWL was deeply in the

Exhibit 5   Share of Washer Market (value) Trends

A. Total Market

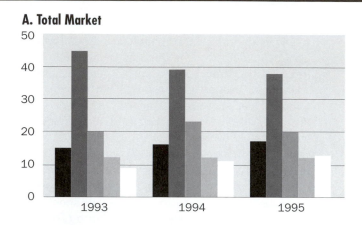

B. Fully Automatic

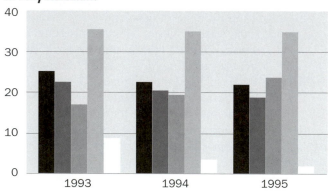

C. Twin Tub

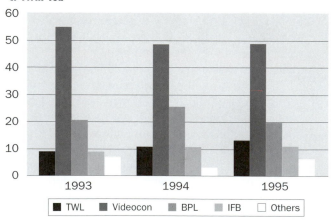

Source: Whirlpool.

red, the volume was inadequate, market share was not improving, promotion of the product was insufficient, and the internal image of quality production was low.

In April 1994, Whirlpool took majority control. Through a capital increase from Rs.19 crores to Rs.30 crores, Whirlpool's stake in TWL rose to 51%, while TVS's fell from 33% to 27.5%. The publicly held stake declined to 21.5%. The new capital was used to pay off part of TWL's debts and to finance investment plans. In March 1996, Whirlpool would buy out TVS completely, to hold 78.5% of the outstanding shares. This was the first time managerial control of a TVS group company had passed into another's hands.

Gopal Srinivasan left the company with most of the senior management team. V. A. Raghu, lately the export director, became the new managing director and A. Karna-karan was promoted to plant manager. Garrick D'Silva, a Sri Lankan with years of experience working for multinationals in Australia, Thailand, and India but a newcomer to Whirlpool, joined the managerial team. Reactions by the staff at Pondicherry to the change of management and ownership were mixed. Those familiar with Whirlpool were convinced that the Americans would give them access to new technology and funding; the workers were uncertain over Whirlpool's degree of commitment to the Pondicherry operation and to India as a whole.

The challenge was great. TWL had to turn around in 1995, mobilize its resources, and cut costs. It had to demonstrate to Whirlpool regional headquarters in Singapore and to corporate headquarters in Benton Harbor that it was a viable prospect. Whirlpool was embarking on a series of major investments in China, which were demanding significant managerial attention as well as funds, and it also wanted a bigger presence in India.

THE TURNAROUND

The period April–October 1994 was one of transition. The change of ownership meant redundancies, a feeling of discomfort among those remaining, and a general sentiment that TVS should not have sold out. A SWAT team comprising Whirlpool retirees who knew the company, though not the Pondicherry operation, arrived from Benton Harbor that summer to work with groups of the local staff. A steady stream of Whirlpool visitors from Benton Harbor and Singapore followed over the next months. The aim was to develop a comprehensive strategy to turn around the business in 1995. "During 1994 we planned and conceptualized; in 1995 we had to execute," said one of the new management team.

The goals laid out for 1995 included 100% growth in output and sales and a focus on both cost and quality consciousness. Suppliers and dealers had to be convinced that under Whirlpool the future for TWL would be different. Employees had to feel implicated in the drive for quality production and customer satisfaction. Market share goals, volume targets, and quality standards were laid out. TWL also had to attain a cost structure more acceptable to Whirlpool, and strict cost reduction programs were accordingly put into place. More refined targets for each of these issues would be set in subsequent years.

Monthly question-and-answer sessions between the workers and the managing director were established, and the senior managers met daily to discuss the implementation of the change program. An important tool in this process was policy deployment, a "software system" that set out in structured fashion how to capture business priorities and issues. Each year every manager would have a set of policy objectives to attain that would dovetail with the objectives of fellow managers. Because each element was

Exhibit 6   **Annual Production at TWL, 1990–1995**

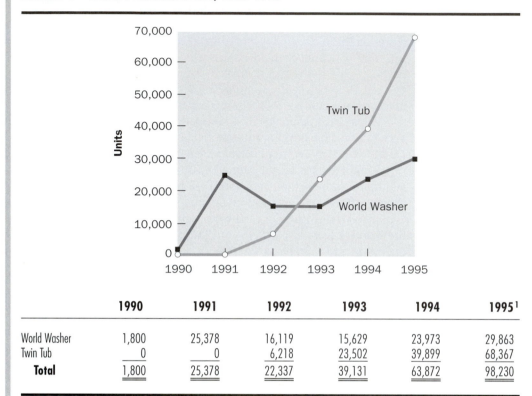

	1990	**1991**	**1992**	**1993**	**1994**	**1995**[1]
World Washer	1,800	25,378	16,119	15,629	23,973	29,863
Twin Tub	0	0	6,218	23,502	39,899	68,367
Total	1,800	25,378	22,337	39,131	63,872	98,230

Note:
1. 11 months. Actual production for the whole of 1995 was 121,511 units.

Source: Whirlpool.

measurable, progress could be tracked on a monthly basis and decisions on corrective action taken rapidly. Effort was made on a continual basis to use competitive intelligence—what competitors were doing, pricing movements, new product launches—to measure the company's position and to understand customers' concerns.

Whirlpool also introduced its Worldwide Excellence System (WES) to Pondicherry. WES was the blueprint for the Whirlpool approach to quality, customers, and continuous improvement worldwide. Compromising on product quality by using defective parts was no longer acceptable. The factory had to produce machines that were world class, not simply "good enough" for the Indian market.

Using WES and policy deployment, the job responsibilities and goals for each employee were clearly defined. Special skills were applied to address design weaknesses that affected both costs and quality (e.g., the motor control board). Factory layout was improved and non–value added or duplicated work eliminated. Efforts focused on getting the job right the first time, dramatically reducing the number of machines requiring rectification of faults at the end of the line. Whirlpool believed in constant production, whatever the state of the market, and for the first time the factory—and its suppliers—began working to the stability of an annual plan. Output doubled to 64,000 units in 1994 and again to 120,000 units in 1995 (Exhibit 6). Meanwhile, the number of production line workers rose only from 70 to 73. The turnaround plan underlined the importance of concentration on core competencies. Non-core activities—component production, infor-

mation technology, security, housekeeping, maintenance, canteen management, etc.—
were all farmed out to external operators.

Whirlpool was shocked by the low standard and irregular supply of externally
sourced components. A team set up in 1994 began working with individual suppliers to
improve their performance, and for the first time some of TWL's process engineers were
involved in the relationship. This developed into a full-fledged strategy for supplier development. Gradually a feeling of partnership between TWL and its suppliers emerged,
replacing the "them and us" attitude that had prevailed earlier. At the same time, TWL
began to streamline its supplier network, seeking a single source for each major component rather than the 3–4 suppliers the TVS group traditionally used. It also sought to
persuade its key suppliers to move closer to the Pondicherry site.

Reaching the Customer

To understand better its customers' needs, TWL had to focus its marketing approach.
Also, the marketplace had become more competitive than when TWL first began operations. Marketing had to become more professionalized, and greater attention paid to
brand building.

Whirlpool's Singapore regional headquarters had been working during 1994 to
build a profile of the "Asian consumer" and had collected a substantial amount of data
from India in the process. In 1995, the newly established Whirlpool South Asia office in
Delhi began profiling TWL's target group in significantly greater detail. The customer target emerged as some 15 million households in urban areas. They were to be the exclusive focus of the company's product and communication strategies.

Analysis of the available data suggested that TWL's immediate potential lay in towns
with a population of one million or more, but that even towns of fewer than 500,000
people offered medium and long-term potential (Exhibit 7). Only 0.2% of rural households had washing machines, compared with 6.1% of urban households. However,
two-fifths of urban households in the highest income bracket already owned washing
machines. It seemed to Whirlpool that the best window of opportunity for their fully
automatic machines lay among people earning Rs.36,000–78,000 per annum, whereas
twin tubs could be sold to households in the Rs.18,000–56,000 income brackets who
might eventually trade up to fully automatics. Exhibit 8 shows data on ownership of a
variety of consumer durables in 1994.

Market data also showed that fully automatic machines accounted for 23% of
washer sales by volume but 38% by value. Companies like Videocon, which mostly sold
twin tubs, had a greater share of the market by volume than by value. Even though 60%
of TWL sales were also twin tubs, the share of its automatic washer sales was sufficiently
great for it to have a higher share of the overall market by value than by volume. Exhibit 9
shows Whirlpool's estimates of washing machine market size and growth.

Under the old management team, TWL distributed through approximately 700 outlets in the major cities of India, with an emphasis in the south. The northern region remained relatively undeveloped despite good market growth there. From the second half
of 1995, the marketing effort was handled entirely by Whirlpool's South Asia office in
Delhi, under whose guidance distribution was concentrated on urban areas, particularly
the key cities in the consumer belt of north and west India. An increase in TWL's direct
sales force from 22 to 45 people (although manpower in all other functions was reduced)
and a clearer advertising focus led to an almost doubling of sales in the final quarter of
1995. Meanwhile the market as a whole grew by 28%. TWL's market share rose from

Exhibit 7 Washing Machine Ownership Class, Urban India

A. By Town Size

Town Size	Total No. Households (million)	Washing Owners (million)	Dispersion (%)	Penetration (%)
<100,000	14.3	0.3	9.8	1.7
100,000–500,000	9.5	0.4	16.4	4.4
500,001–1,000,000	4.3	0.3	9.6	6.0
1,000,001–5,000,000	6.4	0.6	24.1	9.7
>5,000,000	7.7	1.0	40.1	13.4
Total	42.2	2.6	100.0	6.1

B. By Income Group

Income Group (Rs. per annum)	Total No. Households (million)	Washing Owners (million)	Current Dispersion (%)	Penetration (%)
Up to Rs.18,000	16.2	0.2	6.0	1.0
Rs.18,001–36,000	13.9	0.4	16.3	3.0
Rs.36,001–56,000	6.8	0.5	19.6	7.4
Rs.56,001–78,000	3.2	0.7	25.7	20.6
Above Rs.78,000	2.1	0.8	32.4	40.4
Total	42.2	2.6	100.0	6.1

Source: Whirlpool (derived from NCAER 1993).

Exhibit 8 Household Ownership of Consumer Durables (%)

Product	Urban	Rural	Total
Bicycles	49.23	49.57	49.48
Mopeds	6.96	1.53	3.02
Scooters	14.15	1.72	5.12
Motorcycles	5.03	1.62	2.55
B&W TVs	41.40	10.32	18.82
Color TVs	17.81	1.93	6.27
Cassette recorders	40.24	12.99	20.44
Radios (portables)	46.57	38.08	40.40
VCRs	4.59	0.11	1.34
Pressure cookers	54.98	10.84	22.91
Mixer/grinders	28.42	2.58	9.64
Refrigerators	21.67	1.41	6.95
Washing machines	7.64	0.28	2.30
Electric irons	34.41	7.02	14.51
Ceiling fans	75.54	14.96	31.53
Table fans	27.79	10.77	15.42
Sewing machines	18.53	6.19	9.56
Wristwatches (mechanical)	101.69	73.21	81.00
Wristwatches (quartz, etc.)	56.06	19.43	29.45
Water heaters (storage)	2.62	0.04	0.75
Water heaters (instant)	3.21	0.03	0.90

Source: National Council for Applied Economic Research, 1996.

Exhibit 9   Washing Machine Market Size and Growth

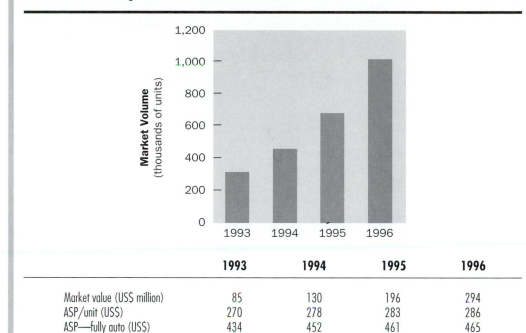

	1993	**1994**	**1995**	**1996**
Market value (US$ million)	85	130	196	294
ASP/unit (US$)	270	278	283	286
ASP—fully auto (US$)	434	452	461	465
ASP—twin tub (US$)	227	232	230	232

Note: ASP: average selling price.

Source: Whirlpool South Asia.

12.9% in 1994 to an average of 14.2% in 1995 (but 17% at the end of the year). This left it in third place overall, behind Videocon and BPL Sanyo.

A market share target of 20.6% was set for 1996. To achieve this, sales skills had to be addressed. Recruitment and training of sales staff required greater attention, and more discipline had to be brought into the sales process. For the first time, the sales force was put onto an incentive system.

TWL also began to make greater efforts to educate consumers about the product and get proper customer feedback that could be passed to the production side. Value re-engineering for the customer became the priority of the R&D department, in contrast to the pure engineering focus of the past. Customer satisfaction was a key issue under Whirlpool management, and service incidence ratios (SIR)—the number of times a service engineer had to intervene—began to be tracked more methodically and problems solved. "We were looking at it before, but there were too many other things going on," said one engineer. Between mid 1994 and the end of 1995, the SIR ratio for automatic machines was cut from 60% after six months of life (MOL) to below 25%.

Human Resources

Personnel changes were an early part of the 1994 reorganization process. A big advantage for TWL during this period was its short history. There had been no time in its six years of existence (four of operation) to create a heavy burden of corporate memory, and the staff was young and open to change.

Whirlpool gave managers the choice of remaining at TWL under its leadership or moving to other parts of the TVS group, but it also had to streamline the hierarchy. In common Indian company fashion, the number of management levels under the old leadership had multiplied, and 12 grades of manager supervised the work of fewer than 200 employees. Between April and October 1994, 53 nonunionized managers were asked to leave. The blue-collar staff (which had always been kept lean) was left untouched. Only six of the remaining managers were more than 30 years old. No expatriates were permanently based in Pondicherry.

Whirlpool was favorably impressed by the similarity of its core values with those of TWL: integrity, loyalty, the need to do well, the desire to be very professional. A senior manager who had experienced both regimes pointed out, "Because of the similar values, we were quickly in a position to adapt to a professional environment." Still, there were culture gaps between the two companies: one was a Midwest American company with a fact-based, low-risk orientation; the other was a southern Indian company with conservative, traditional attitudes. Differences of style emerged, as one person explained: "In India there is a lot of intellectual, general talk before action. This can be very frustrating for expatriates." And again, "Indians never say no, they can't handle something—and they may only achieve 80%. They are not inefficient, but there's no follow-up." Staff at TWL felt that their South Indian conservatism and intellectualism had helped the factory to continue functioning during the difficult transition phase while redundancies were taking place: "Even though people felt bad, there was no impact on functional results."

After the highly centralized management system under Srinivasan, the remaining managers had to learn to take responsibility and accept accountability. It was difficult at first to make decisions. Whirlpool introduced a performance-based compensation scheme for the entire management team and inaugurated cross-functional teamworking for problem solving. The teams took time to work well together. Everyone had to learn to operate in a spirit of openness and trust with colleagues. TWL operated a leaner organization under Whirlpool, creating a greater work load for individuals. "Even if it is practically possible, it is a big psychological issue when the jobs of three or four managers are being done by one person," said one manager. It took time for confidence to grow back after the redundancies.

LOOKING TO THE FUTURE

Whirlpool in India

In October 1994, Whirlpool established a new entity, Whirlpool South Asia, in Delhi as a subregional headquarters under the umbrella of the Singapore regional headquarters. Garrick D'Silva became head of this operation, which would oversee the multinational's development in India and Pakistan. He was regarded as a good "people" person, and his experience in the fast moving consumer goods industry had given him strong marketing skills. Gradually he gathered a team of people around him, some from Pondicherry, others hired from other companies, to rationalize, coordinate, and create synergies between the various businesses that Whirlpool was developing in India.

In February 1995, Whirlpool announced it would take a 51% stake in one of India's leading refrigerator manufacturers, Delhi-based Kelvinator of India (KOI), at a cost of Rs.300 crores (US$97 million). KOI was significantly larger than TWL, with five times the turnover, a workforce of 8,000, and a leading 30% market share. It was also unprofitable and its range of direct cool refrigerators was outdated. After 30 years of activity, KOI's management system was well entrenched. Whirlpool's challenge was to pull KOI out of a "slow death" syndrome, while at the same time replacing the well-known Kelvinator brand name with the Whirlpool name.

Another project was the construction of a US$119 million plant to produce refrigerators in Pune, on the west side of India. This was a global manufacturing platform making 750,000 units per year of a state-of-the-art, CFC-free, no-frost refrigerator designed by Whirlpool in Evansville, with research input from India, China, and Mexico. Whirlpool South Asia was scheduled to take over the project as a turnkey operation when construction was completed in September 1997.

Whirlpool's consumer finance arm was also preparing to establish operations in India to facilitate dealer financing and, later, consumer business. Several competitors already had financing activities.

Finally, research was going on into the feasibility of manufacturing and selling air conditioners in India from late 1997. Already the marketplace was becoming crowded, but air conditioners were one of Whirlpool's key T-4 products.

Whirlpool Washers Manufacturing Limited

Back in Pondicherry, meanwhile, TWL was renamed Whirlpool Washers Manufacturing Limited (WWML) in October 1995 to reflect the changed ownership and a rebranding exercise. Henceforth all products would bear only the Whirlpool name and logo. The TVS-Whirlpool name would gradually disappear. The marketing effort would be steadily integrated with the refrigerator business, dealer networks merged, and salesmen trained to handle both products.

Under Whirlpool guidance, WWML also began new product development. The Twist, a twin-tub machine capable of washing 3.5 kg of clothing, entered the test-marketing phase in November 1995. This was the first product to bear only the Whirlpool brand name, but it was again based on bought-in technology, this time from Goldstar of Korea. It was also only the third washing machine model produced in Pondicherry since the company began in 1990. The Taj Mahal, a fully automatic machine replacing the original World Washer, would also carry only the Whirlpool name when it reached the market in July 1996. The Taj Mahal was jointly developed in Benton Harbor, Singapore, and Pondicherry and incorporated some elements of a design used earlier in Brazil. Other new products were in the pipeline too: a low-cost fully automatic machine and a semi-automatic single tub washer, with tentative launch dates in October 1996.

In early 1996, WWML began to import a top-of-the-line, top-loading tumble washer from France to extend its product line and to compete with European style front-load tumble washers. Import duties, however, made the French machines very expensive.

The production target at WWML for 1997 would be 380,000 units per year, rising to over 400,000 in 1998. Videocon was already making more than 400,000 washers in 1995. WWML's ambition was to consolidate the Whirlpool brand in 1996–1997 and to compete for first place in the market by the end of the century.

A Signal from Wall Street

Whirlpool had poured a lot of money into India since 1994—US$120 million on the Pondicherry operation and KOI combined—and it was in the process of investing a similar sum in the Pune plant. Pepsi and Coca-Cola together had spent less than that in five years in India, or Procter & Gamble in eight years. At the same time, Whirlpool had

Exhibit 10 **Stockmarket Trends**

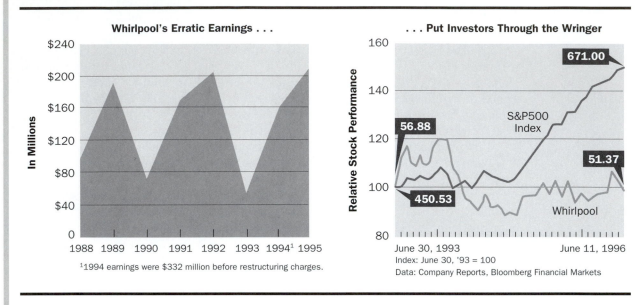

Whirlpool's Erratic Earnings . . .

[1] 1994 earnings were $332 million before restructuring charges.

. . . Put Investors Through the Wringer

Index: June 30, '93 = 100

Data: Company Reports, Bloomberg Financial Markets

Source: *Business Week* (June 24, 1996).

ambitious plans in China that were also expensive. Wall Street, meanwhile, was becoming concerned by the combined effects of weak demand in Europe, heavy start-up costs in Asia, and increased competition (Exhibit 10). Although Whirlpool expected to turn a US$50 million loss in Asia into a profit by 1997, analysts predicted a longer timescale.[3]

According to Raghu, "Pondicherry is our benchmark for how to do it in India." The plant still had progress to make with Whirlpool's Worldwide Excellence System, raising quality while attaining a more desirable cost structure. The challenge was to make the product the best in its class in India and on a par with world levels. It had to be the brand of choice for the consumer, although "people don't even know yet what is Whirlpool." WWML made a book profit in 1995 but still had to clear its accumulated losses. Meanwhile, Whirlpool had taken on significantly more costly projects. Could the Indian operations make a tangible contribution to Whirlpool's business in the near future?

Competition in the Indian home appliance industry had intensified significantly by 1995, and price wars had begun, based on short-term promotions and purchase incentives such as free gifts. Would Whirlpool's washing machines become more popular than their Japanese and European competitors' models?

Notes

1. The value of the rupee against the U.S. dollar has moved as follows: 1998—Rs.15; 1989—Rs.17; 1990—Rs.18; 1991—Rs.25; 1992—Rs.26; 1993—Rs.31; 1994—Rs.31; 1995—Rs.33. In early 1996, US$1 = Rs.33.85. The Indian counting system uses the terms "crore" and "lakh" to signify ten million and one hundred thousand, respectively.
2. Companies that had exhausted their entire net worth (shareholders' capital plus reserves) would be referred to a special board that would attempt to find an alternative solution to closure, whether through restructuring, a change of management, or a merger with a suitable existing company.
3. "Did Whirlpool Spin Too Far Too Fast?" *Business Week* (June 24, 1996).

Kmart Corporation (1998):
Still Searching for a Successful Strategy

James W. Camerius

Floyd Hall, Chairman, President, and Chief Executive Officer of Kmart Corporation since June 1995, was pleased with Kmart's financial results reported in the fiscal first quarter of 1998. Earnings had more than tripled from year-earlier levels. Net income for the quarter ending April 29 rose to $47 million from $14 million a year earlier. He was very optimistic about the company's future. The financial information convinced him that a new corporate strategy that he introduced recently would revitalize Kmart's core business, its 2,136 discount stores, and put the company on the road to recovery. Industry analysts had noted that Kmart, once an industry leader, had posted 11 straight quarters of disappointing earnings and had been dogged by persistent bankruptcy rumors. Analysts cautioned that much of Kmart's growth reflected the strength of the consumer economy and that uncertainty continued to exist about the company's future in a period of slower economic growth.

Kmart Corporation was one of the world's largest mass merchandise retailers. After several years of restructuring, it was composed largely of general merchandise businesses in the form of traditional Kmart discount department stores and Big Kmart (consumables and convenience) stores as well as Super Kmart Centers (food and general merchandise). It operated in all 50 of the United States and in Puerto Rico, Guam, and the U.S. Virgin Islands. It also had equity interests in Meldisco subsidiaries of Melville Corporation that operated Kmart footwear departments. Measured in sales volume, it was the third largest retailer and the second largest discount department store chain in the United States.

The discount department store industry was perceived to have reached maturity. Kmart, as part of that industry, had a retail management strategy that was developed in the late 1950s and revised in the early 1990s. The firm was in a dilemma in terms of corporate strategy. The problem was how to lay a foundation for a bottoming out of Kmart's financial decline and provide a new direction that would reposition the firm in a fiercely competitive environment.

THE EARLY YEARS

Kmart was the outgrowth of an organization founded in 1899 in Detroit by Sebastian S. Kresge. The first S.S. Kresge store represented a new type of retailing that featured low-priced merchandise for cash in low-budget, relatively small (4,000 to 6,000 square feet) buildings with sparse furnishings. The adoption of the "5¢ and 10¢" or "variety store" concept, pioneered by F.W. Woolworth Company in 1879, led to rapid and profitable development of what was then the S.S. Kresge Company.

Kresge believed it could substantially increase its retail business through centralized buying and control, developing standardized store operating procedures, and expanding with new stores in heavy traffic areas. In 1912, the firm was incorporated in Delaware. It

---

had 85 stores with sales of $10,325,000, and, next to Woolworth's, was the largest variety chain in the world. In 1916, it was reincorporated in Michigan. Over the next 40 years, the firm experimented with mail order catalogues, full-line department stores, self-service, a number of price lines, and the opening of stores in planned shopping centers. It continued its emphasis, however, on variety stores.

By 1957, corporate management became aware that the development of supermarkets and the expansion of drug store chains into general merchandise lines had made inroads into market categories previously dominated by variety stores. It also became clear that a new form of store with a discount merchandising strategy was emerging.

The Cunningham Connection

In an effort to regain its competitiveness in 1957 and possibly save the company, Frank Williams, then President of Kresge, nominated Harry B. Cunningham as General Vice-President. This maneuver was undertaken to free Cunningham, who had worked his way up the ranks in the organization, from operating responsibility. He was being groomed for the presidency and was given the assignment to study existing retailing businesses and recommend marketing changes.

In his visits to Kresge stores, and those of the competition, Cunningham became interested in discounting—particularly a new operation in Garden City, Long Island. Eugene Ferkauf had recently opened large discount department stores called E.J. Korvette. The stores had a discount mass-merchandising emphasis that featured low prices and margins, high turnover, large free-standing departmentalized units, ample parking space, and a location typically in the suburbs.

Cunningham was impressed with the discount concept, but he knew he had to first convince the Kresge Board of Directors, whose support would be necessary for any new strategy to succeed. He studied the company for two years and presented it with the following recommendation:

> We can't beat the discounters operating under the physical constraints and the self-imposed merchandise limitations of variety stores. We can join them—and not only join them, but with our people, procedures, and organization, we can become a leader in the discount industry.

In a speech delivered at the University of Michigan, Cunningham made his management approach clear by concluding with an admonition from the British author Sir Hugh Walpole: "Don't play for safety, it's the most dangerous game in the world."

The Board of Directors had a difficult job. Change is never easy, especially when the company has established procedures in place and a proud heritage. Before the first presentation to the Board could be made, rumors were circulating that one shocked senior executive had said:

> We have been in the variety business for 60 years—we know everything there is to know about it, and we're not doing very well in that, and you want to get us into a business we don't know anything about.

The Board of Directors accepted H. B. Cunningham's recommendations. When President Frank Williams retired, Cunningham became the new President and Chief Executive Officer and was directed to proceed with his recommendations.

The Birth of Kmart

Management conceived the original Kmart as a conveniently located one-stop-shopping unit where customers could buy a wide variety of quality merchandise at discount prices. The typical Kmart had 75,000 square feet, all on one floor. It generally stood by itself in a high-traffic, suburban area, with plenty of parking space. All stores had a similar floor plan.

The firm made an $80 million commitment in leases and merchandise for 33 stores before the first Kmart opened in 1962 in Garden City, Michigan. As part of this strategy, management decided to rely on the strengths and abilities of its own people to make decisions rather than employing outside experts for advice.

The original Kresge 5 & 10 variety store operation was characterized by low gross margins, high turnover, and concentration on return on investment. The main difference in the Kmart strategy would be the offering of a much wider merchandise mix.

The company had the knowledge and ability to merchandise 50% of the departments in the planned Kmart merchandise mix and contracted for operation of the remaining departments. In the following years, Kmart took over most of those departments originally contracted to licensees. Eventually all departments, except shoes, were operated by Kmart.

By 1987, the 25th anniversary year of the opening of the first Kmart store in America, sales and earnings of Kmart Corporation were at all-time highs. The company was the world's largest discount retailer with sales of $25,627 million, and it operated 3,934 general merchandise and specialty stores.

On April 6, 1987, Kmart Corporation announced that it agreed to sell most of its remaining Kresge variety stores in the United States to McCrory Corporation, a unit of the closely held Rapid American Corporation of New York.

CORPORATE GOVERNANCE

Exhibit 1 shows the 15 members of the Board of Directors of Kmart. The two internal members were Floyd Hall, Chairman and CEO of Kmart, and Warren Flick, President and Chief Operating Officer (COO) of U.S. Kmart Stores. Seven board members joined the Board since 1995: (1) Stephen F. Bollenbach, (2) Richard G. Cline, (3) Floyd Hall, (4) Robert D. Kennedy, (5) Robin B. Smith, (6) William P. Weber, and (7) James O. Welch, Jr. Exhibit 2 lists the corporate officers.

THE NATURE OF THE COMPETITIVE ENVIRONMENT
A Changing Marketplace

The retail sector of the United States economy went through a number of dramatic and turbulent changes during the 1980s and 1990s. Retail analysts concluded that many retail firms were negatively affected by increased competitive pressures, sluggish consumer spending, slower-than-anticipated economic growth in North America, and recessions abroad. As one retail consultant noted:

> The structure of distribution in advanced economies is currently undergoing a series of changes that are as profound in their impact and as pervasive in their influence as those that occurred in manufacturing during the 19th century.

This changing environment affected the discount department store industry. Nearly a dozen firms like E.J. Korvette, W.T. Grant, Arlans, Atlantic Mills, and Ames passed into bankruptcy or reorganization. Some firms like Woolworth (Woolco Division) had withdrawn from the field entirely after years of disappointment. St. Louis–based May

Exhibit 1   Board of Directors: Kmart Corporation

James B. Adamson[4]
Chairman and Chief Executive Officer
Flagstar Companies, Inc.

Lilyan H. Affinito[1,3,5]
Former Vice Chairman of the Board
Maxxam Group, Inc.

Stephen F. Bollenbach[4]
President and Chief Executive Officer
Hilton Hotels Corporation

Joseph A. Califano, Jr.[4]
Chairman and President
The National Center on Addiction and
Substance Abuse at Columbia University

Richard G. Cline[2,3,5]
Chairman, Hawthorne Investors, Inc.
Former Chairman and Chief Executive Officer
NICOR, Inc.

Willie D. Davis[2]
President
All Pro Broadcasting, Inc.

Enrique C. Falla[1]
Senior Vice-President
The Dow Chemical Company

Joseph P. Flannery[3,4,5]
Chairman of the Board, President
and Chief Executive Officer
Uniroyal Holding, Inc.

Warren Flick[2]
President and Chief
Operating Officer,
U.S. Kmart Stores
Kmart Corporation

Floyd Hall[3]
Chairman of the Board, President
and Chief Executive Officer
Kmart Corporation

Robert D. Kennedy[4]
Former Chairman and Chief
Executive Officer
Union Carbide Corporation

J. Richard Munro[2,3,5]
Chairman of the Board
Genentech, Inc.

Robin B. Smith
Chairman and Chief
Executive Officer
Publishers Clearing House

William P. Weber[1]
Vice Chairman
Texas Instruments Incorporated

James O. Welch, Jr.[2]
Former Vice Chairman
RJR Nabisco and Chairman
Nabisco Brands, Inc.

Notes:
1. Audit Committee
2. Compensation and Incentives Committee
3. Executive Committee
4. Finance Committee
5. Nominating Committee

Source: Kmart Corporation, *1997 Annual Report.*

Department Stores sold its Caldor and Venture discount divisions, each with annual sales of more than $1 billion. Venture announced liquidation in early 1998.

Senior management at Kmart felt that most of the firms that had difficulty in the industry faced the same situation. First, they were very successful five or ten years ago but had not changed and, therefore, had become somewhat dated. Management that had a historically successful formula, particularly in retailing, was perceived as having difficulty adapting to change, especially at the peak of success. Management would wait too long when faced with a threat in the environment and then would have to scramble to regain competitiveness.

Exhibit 2   **Executive Officers: Kmart Corporation**

A. Officers

Floyd Hall (58)
Chairman of the Board, President and Chief Executive Officer since June 1995. Previously he served concurrently as Chairman and Chief Executive Officer of the Museum Company, Alva Reproductions, Inc., and Glass Masters, Inc., from 1989 to 1995.

Warren Flick (53)
Director, President and Chief Operating Officer, U.S. Kmart Stores since November 1996. Mr. Flick joined the company as Executive Vice-President, President and General Merchandise Manager, U.S. Kmart stores in December 1995. Prior to joining Kmart Corporation, he was the Chairman and Chief Executive Officer of Sears de Mexico, Sears, Roebuck & Co. from 1994 to 1995; Group Vice-President, Men's, Kids, Footwear and Home Fashions, Sears, Roebuck & Co. from 1993 to 1994; and Group Vice-President, Men's, Kids and Footwear, Sears, Roebuck & Co. from 1992 to 1993.

B. Executive Vice-Presidents

Laurence L. Anderson (55)
Executive Vice-President and President, Super Kmart since August 1997. Prior to joining the company, Mr. Anderson was President and Chief Operating Officer—Retail Food Companies, SuperValu, Inc., from 1995 to 1997; and Executive Vice-President, SuperValu, Inc./Vice-Chairman, Wetterau, Inc., from 1992 to 1995.

Warren Cooper (52)
Executive Vice-President, Human Resources & Administration since March 1996. Previously, he was the Senior Vice-President, Human Resources, General Cable from 1995 to 1996; Vice-President, Human Resources, the Sears Merchandise Group, Sears, Roebuck & Co. from 1993 to 1995; and Vice-President, Corporate Human Resources, Sears, Roebuck & Co. from 1987 to 1993.

Donald W. Keeble (48)
Executive Vice-President, Store Operations since February 1995. Mr. Keeble has served as an executive officer of the company since 1989. Prior to his current position, he held the following positions at Kmart Corporation: Executive Vice-President, Merchandising and Operations from 1994 to 1995; and Senior Vice-President, General Merchandise Manager, Fashions from 1991 to 1994.

Anthony N. Palizzi (54)
Executive Vice-President, General Counsel since 1992. Mr. Palizzi has served as an executive officer of the company since 1985.

Marvin P. Rich (52)
Executive Vice-President, Strategic Planning, Finance and Administration since 1994. Previously, he was Executive Vice-President, Specialty Companies, Wellpoint Health Networks/Blue Cross of California from 1992 to 1994.

C. Senior Vice-Presidents

William N. Anderson (50)
Senior Vice-President and General Merchandise Manager—Hardlines since September 1996. Prior to joining Kmart Corporation, he served as President and Chief Operating Officer, Oshman's Sporting Goods, Inc., from 1994 to 1996; and Senior Vice-President and General Manager, Ames Department Stores, Inc. from 1992 to 1994.

Andrew A. Giancamilli (47)
Senior Vice-President, General Merchandise Manager—Home and Consumables since June 1997. Mr. Giancamilli has served as an executive officer of the company since 1996. Prior to his current position, he was Senior Vice-President and General Merchandise Manager, Consumables and Commodities from 1996 to 1997. Mr. Giancamilli joined the company in 1995 as Vice-President, Pharmacy Merchandising and Operations. Prior to joining the company, he was President, Chief Operating Officer, Director, Perry Drug Stores, Inc. from 1993 to 1995; and Executive Vice-President, Chief Operating Officer, Perry Drug Stores, Inc. from 1992 to 1993.

Ernest L. Heether (51)
Senior Vice-President, Merchandise Operations Planning and Replenishment since April 1996. Prior to joining the company, he served as Senior Vice-President, Merchandise Operations, Bradlees, Inc., from 1993 to 1996; and Vice-President, Merchandise Planning and Control, Caldor from 1990 to 1993.

Paul J. Hueber (49)
Senior Vice-President, Store Operations since 1994. Mr. Hueber has served as an executive officer of the company since 1991. Prior to his current position, he was Vice-President, West/Central Region from 1991 to 1994.

Donald E. Norman (60)
Senior Vice-President, Chief Information Officer since December 1995. Mr. Norman joined the company in 1995 as Divisional Vice-President, Business Process Reengineering, Merchandise Inventory Controls. Previously he was President, DNA, Inc., from 1994 to 1995; and Senior Vice-President, Logistics, Ames Department Stores from 1990 to 1994.

William D. Underwood (56)
Senior Vice-President, Global Sourcing since 1994. Mr. Underwood has served as an executive officer of the company since 1998. Prior to his current position, he was Senior Vice-President, General Merchandise Manager—Hardlines from 1991 to 1994.

Martin E. Welch III (49)
Senior Vice-President and Chief Financial Officer since 1995. Previously, he was Senior Vice-President, Chief Financial Officer, Federal-Mogul Corporation from 1991 to 1995.

(continued)

Exhibit 2   **Executive Officers: Kmart Corporation** *(continued)*

Jerome J. Kuske (45)

Senior Vice-President, General Merchandise Manager—Health and Beauty Care/Pharmacy since June 1997. Previously Mr. Kuske served as Vice-President, General Merchandise Manager—Health and Beauty Care/Pharmacy from 1996 to 1997 and Divisional Vice-President, Consumables and Commodities from 1995 to 1996. Prior to joining the company, he was Senior Vice-President, Merchandising and Marketing, Perry Drug Stores, Inc., from 1994 to 1995; and Senior Vice-President, Operations, Payless Drug Stores, Inc. from 1992 to 1994.

James P. Mixon (53)

Senior Vice-President, Logistics since June 1997. Prior to joining Kmart, Mr. Mixon was Senior Vice-President, Logistics/Service, Best Buy Stores, Inc., from 1994 to 1997; and Senior Vice-President, Distribution/Transportation, Marshalls Stores, Inc., from 1987 to 1994.

E. Jackson Smailes (54)

Senior Vice-President, General Merchandise Manager—Apparel since August 1997. Previously Mr. Smailes was President and Chief Executive Officer, Hills Department Stores from 1995 to 1997; and Executive Vice-President, Merchandise and Marketing, Hills Department Stores from 1992 to 1995.

Note:

1. The name, age, position, and a description of the business experience for each of the executive officers of the company is listed above as of August 31, 1997. The business experience for each of the executive officers described above includes the principal positions held by them since 1992.

Source: Kmart Corporation, *1998 Annual Report.*

Wal-Mart Stores, Inc., based in Bentonville, Arkansas, was an exception. It was especially growth oriented and had emerged in 1991 and continued in that position through 1997 as the nation's largest retailer as well as largest discount department store chain in sales volume. Operating under a variety of names and formats, nationally and internationally, it included Wal-Mart stores, Wal-Mart Supercenters, and SAM'S Warehouse Clubs. The firm found early strength in cultivating rural markets, merchandise restocking programs, "everyday low-pricing," and the control of operations through company-wide computer programs that linked cash registers to corporate headquarters.

Sears, Roebuck, & Co., in a state of stagnated growth for several years, completed a return to its retailing roots by spinning off to shareholders its $9 billion controlling stake in its Allstate Corporation insurance unit and the divestment of financial services. After unsuccessfully experimenting with an "everyday low-price" strategy, management chose to refine its merchandising program to meet the needs of middle market customers, who were primarily women, by focusing on product lines in apparel, home, and automotive.

Many retailers such as Target (Dayton Hudson), which adopted the discount concept, attempted to go generally after an upscale customer. The upscale customer tended to have a household income of $25,000 to $44,000 annually. Other "pockets" of population were served by firms like Zayre, which had served consumers in the inner city before being acquired by Ames Department Stores, and Wal-Mart, which initially served the needs of the more rural consumer in secondary markets.

Kmart executives found that discount department stores were being challenged by several retail formats. Some retailers were assortment-oriented, with a much greater depth of assortment within a given product category. To illustrate, Toys-R-Us was an example of a firm that operated 20,000-square-foot toy supermarkets. Toys-R-Us prices were very competitive within an industry that was very competitive. When the consumers entered a Toys-R-Us facility, there was usually no doubt in their minds that if the product wasn't there, no one else had it. In 1997, however, Toys-R-Us was challenged by industry leader Wal-Mart and other firms that offered higher service levels and more aggressive pricing practices.

Some retailers were experimenting with the "off price" apparel concept in which name brands and designer goods were sold at 20% to 70% discounts. Others, such as

Home Depot and Menards, operated home improvement centers that were warehouse-style stores with a wide range of hard-line merchandise for both do-it-yourselfers and professionals. Still others opened drug supermarkets that offered a wide variety of high turnover merchandise in a convenient location. In these cases, competition was becoming more risk oriented by putting three or four million dollars in merchandise at retail value in an 80,000 square-foot facility and offering genuinely low prices. Jewel-Osco stores in the Midwest, Rite Aid, and a series of independents were examples of organizations employing the entirely new concept of the drug supermarket.

Competition was offering something that was new and different in terms of depth of assortment, competitive price image, and format. Kmart management perceived this as a threat because these were viable businesses and hindered the firm in its ability to improve and maintain share of market in specific merchandise categories. An industry competitive analysis is shown in Exhibit 3.

EXPANSION AND CONTRACTION

When Joseph E. Antonini was appointed Chairman of Kmart Corporation in October 1987, he was charged with the responsibility of maintaining and eventually accelerating the chain's record of growth, despite a mature retail marketplace. He moved to string experimental formats into profitable chains. As he noted:

> Our vision calls for the constant and never-ceasing exploration of new modes of retailing, so that our core business of U.S. Kmart stores can be constantly renewed and reinvigorated by what we learn from our other businesses.

In the mid 1970s and throughout the 1980s, Kmart became involved in the acquisition or development of several smaller new operations. Kmart Insurance Services, Inc., acquired as Planned Marketing Associates in 1974, offered a full line of life, health, and accident insurance centers located in 27 Kmart stores primarily in the South and Southwest.

In 1982, Kmart initiated its own off-price specialty apparel concept called Designer Depot. A total of 28 Designer Depot stores were opened in 1982 to appeal to customers who wanted quality upscale clothing at a budget price. A variation of this concept, called Garment Rack, was opened to sell apparel that normally would not be sold in Designer Depot. A distribution center was added in 1983 to supplement them. Neither venture was successful.

Kmart also attempted an unsuccessful joint venture with the Hechinger Company of Washington, D.C., a warehouse home center retailer. However, after much deliberation, Kmart chose instead to acquire, in 1984, Home Centers of America of San Antonio, Texas, which operated 80,000-square-foot warehouse home centers. The new division, renamed Builders Square, had grown to 167 units by 1996. It capitalized on Kmart's real estate, construction, and management expertise and Home Centers of America's merchandising expertise. Builders Square was sold in 1997.

Waldenbooks, a chain of 877 book stores, was acquired from Carter, Hawley Hale, Inc., in 1984. It was part of a strategy to capture a greater share of the market with a product category that Kmart already had in its stores. Kmart had been interested in the book business for some time and took advantage of an opportunity in the marketplace to build on its common knowledge base. Borders Books and Music, an operator of 50 large format superstores, became part of Kmart in 1992 to form the "Borders Group," a division that would include Waldenbooks. The Borders Group, Inc., was sold during 1995.

Exhibit 3 An Industry Competitive Analysis, 1997

	Kmart	Wal-Mart	Sears	Dayton Hudson
Sales (000)	$32,183	$117,958	$41,296	$27,757
Net income (000)	249	3,526	1,188	751
Sales growth	2.4%	12%	8%	9%
Profit margin	.8%	2.9%	2.9%	2.7%
Sales/sq. ft.	211	N/A	318	226
Return/equity	5%	19.8%	20%	16.8%

Number of stores:

Kmart Corporation
Kmart Traditional Discount Stores—2,037
Super Kmart Centers—99

Wal-Mart Stores, Inc. (includes international)
Wal-Mart Discount Stores—2,421
Supercenters—502
SAM'S Clubs—483

Sears, Roebuck, & Company
Full-Line Stores—833
Hardware Stores—255
HomeLife Furniture Stores—129
Sears Dealer Stores—576
Sears Tire Group:
    Sears Auto Centers—780
    National Tire & Battery stores—326
Sears Parts Group:
    Parts America stores—576
    Western Auto stores—39
    Western Auto (locally owned)—800

Dayton Hudson Corporation
Target—796
Mervyn's—269
Department Store Division—65

Source: Companies' annual reports.

The Bruno's Inc. joint venture in 1987 formed a partnership to develop large combination grocery and general merchandise stores or "hypermarkets" called American Fare. The giant, one-stop-shopping facilities of 225,000 square feet traded on the grocery expertise of Bruno's and the general merchandise of Kmart to offer a wide selection of products and services at discount prices. A similar venture, called Super Kmart Center, represented later thinking on combination stores with a smaller size and format. In 1998, Kmart operated 99 Super Kmart Centers, all in the United States.

In 1988, the company acquired a controlling interest in Makro Inc., a Cincinnati-based operator of warehouse "club" stores. Makro, with annual sales of about $300 million, operated "member only" stores that were stocked with low-priced fresh and frozen groceries, apparel, and durable goods in suburbs of Atlanta, Cincinnati, Washington, and Philadelphia. PACE Membership Warehouse, Inc., a similar operation, was acquired in 1989. The "club" stores were sold in 1994.

PayLess Drug Stores, which operated super drug stores in a number of western states, was sold in 1994 to Thrifty PayLess Holdings, Inc., an entity in which Kmart maintained a significant investment. Interests in The Sports Authority, an operator of large-format sporting goods stores, which Kmart acquired in 1990, were disposed of during 1995.

On the international level, an interest in Coles Myer, Ltd., Australia's largest retailer, was sold in November 1994. Interests in 13 Kmart general merchandise stores in the Czech and Slovak Republics were sold to Tesco PLC at the beginning of 1996, one of the United Kingdom's largest retailers. In February 1998, Kmart stores in Canada were sold to Hudson's Bay Co., a Canadian chain of historic full-service department stores. The interest in Kmart Mexico, S.A.de C.V. was disposed of in FY 1997.

Founded in 1988, OfficeMax with 328 stores was one of the largest operators of high-volume, deep-discount office products superstores in the United States. It became a greater than 90% owned Kmart unit in 1991. Kmart's interest in Office Max was sold during 1995.

In 1998, Kmart maintained an equity interest in Meldisco subsidiaries of Melville Corporation, operators of Kmart footwear departments.

THE MATURATION OF KMART

Early corporate research revealed that on the basis of convenience, Kmart served 80% of the population. One study concluded that one out of every two adults in the United States shopped at a Kmart at least once a month. Despite this popular appeal, strategies that had allowed the firm to have something for everybody were no longer felt to be appropriate for the 1990s. Kmart found that it had a broad customer base because it operated on a national basis. Its strategies had assumed the firm was serving everyone in the markets where it was established.

Kmart was often perceived as aiming at the low-income consumer. The financial community believed the Kmart customer was blue collar, low income, and upper lower class. The market served, however, was more professional and middle class because Kmart stores were initially in suburban communities where that population lived.

Although Kmart had made a major commitment in more recent years to secondary or rural markets, these were areas that had previously not been cultivated. The firm, in its initial strategies, perceived the rural consumer as different from the urban or suburban customer. In re-addressing the situation, it discovered that its assortments in rural areas were too limited, and there were too many preconceived notions regarding what the Nebraska farmer really wanted. The firm discovered that the rural consumer didn't always shop for bib overalls and shovels but shopped for microwave ovens and the same things everyone else did.

The goal was not to attract more customers but to get the customer coming in the door to spend more. Once in the store, the customer was thought to demonstrate more divergent tastes. The upper income consumer would buy more health and beauty aids, cameras, and sporting goods. The lower income consumer would buy toys and clothing.

In the process of trying to capture a larger share of the market and get people to spend more, the firm began to recognize a market that was more upscale. When consumer research was conducted and management examined the profile of the trade area and the profile of the person who shopped at Kmart in the past month, they were found to be identical. Kmart was predominately serving the suburban consumer in suburban locations. In 1997, Kmart's primary target customers were women between the ages of 25 and 45 years old, with children at home and with household incomes between

$20,000 and $50,000 per year. The core Kmart shopper averaged 4.3 visits to a Kmart store per month. The purchase amount per visit was $40. The purchase rate was 95% during a store visit. The firm estimated that 180 million people shopped at Kmart in an average year.

In "lifestyle" research in markets served by the firm, Kmart determined there were more two-income families, families were having fewer children, there were more working wives, and customers tended to be homeowners. Customers were very careful how they spent their money and were perceived as wanting quality. This was a distinct contrast to the 1960s and early 1970s, which tended to have the orientation of a "throw away" society. The customer had said, "What we want is products that will last longer. We'll have to pay more for them but will still want them and at the lowest price possible." Customers wanted better quality products but still demanded competitive prices. According to a Kmart *Annual Report,* "Consumers today are well educated and informed. They want good value and they know it when they see it. Price remains a key consideration, but the consumers' new definition of value includes quality as well as price."

Corporate management at Kmart considered the discount department store to be a mature idea. Although maturity was sometimes looked on with disfavor, Kmart executives felt that this did not mean a lack of profitability or lack of opportunity to increase sales. The industry was perceived as being "reborn." It was in this context, in 1990, that a series of new retailing strategies designed to upgrade the Kmart image were developed.

THE RENEWAL PROGRAM

The strategies that emerged in the 1990s to confront a changing environment were the result of an overall reexamination of existing corporate strategies. This program included accelerated store expansion and refurbishing, capitalizing on dominant lifestyle departments, centralized merchandising, more capital investment in retail automation, an aggressive and focused advertising program, and continued growth through new specialty retail formats.

This five-year, $2.3 billion program involved virtually all 2,300 Kmart discount stores. There would be approximately 250 new full-size Kmart stores, 620 enlargements, 280 relocations, and 30 closings. In addition, 1,260 stores would be refurbished to bring their layout and fixtures up to new store standards.

One area receiving initial attention was improvement in the way products were displayed. The traditional Kmart layout was by product category. Often these locations for departments were holdovers from the variety store. Many departments would not give up prime locations. As part of the new marketing strategy, the shop concept was introduced. Management recognized that it had a sizable "do-it-yourself" store. As planning management discussed the issue, "nobody was aware of the opportunity. The hardware department was right smack in the center of the store because it was always there. The paint department was over here and the electrical department was over there." "All we had to do," management contended, "was put them all in one spot and everyone could see that we had a very respectable 'do-it-yourself' department." The concept resulted in a variety of new departments such as "Soft Goods for the Home," "Kitchen Korners," and "Home Electronic Centers." The goal behind each department was to sell an entire lifestyle-oriented concept to consumers, making goods complementary so shoppers would want to buy several interrelated products rather than just one item.

The program also involved using and revitalizing the space Kmart already had under its control. This took the form of remodeling and updating existing stores. The program would involve virtually all U.S. Kmart discount stores. The new look featured a broad "poppy red" and gold band around interior walls as a "horizon"; new round, square, and honeycombed racks that displayed the full garment; relocation of jewelry and women's apparel to areas closer to the entrance, and redesigning of counters to make them look more upscale and hold more merchandise.

Name brands were added in soft and hard goods as management recognized that the customer transferred the product quality of branded goods to perceptions of private label merchandise. In the eyes of Kmart management, "If you sell Wrangler, there is good quality. Then the private label must be good quality." The company increased its emphasis on trusted national brands such as Rubbermaid, Procter & Gamble, and Kodak, and put emphasis on major strategic vendor relationships. In addition it began to enhance its private label brands such as Kathy Ireland, Jaclyn Smith, Route 66, and Sesame Street in Apparel. Additional private label merchandise included K Gro in home gardening, American Fare in Grocery and Consumables, White-Westinghouse in appliances, and Penske Auto Centers in automotive services. Some private labels were discontinued following review.

Additional programs emphasized the quality image. Pro golfer Fuzzy Zoeller was engaged to promote golf equipment and other associated products. Mario Andretti, who raced in the Championship Auto Racing Teams' Indy car series, agreed to co-sponsorship of his car with associated promotion.

Kmart hired Martha Stewart, an upscale Connecticut author of lavish best-selling books on cooking and home entertaining, as its "life-style spokesperson and consultant." Martha Stewart was featured as a corporate symbol for housewares and associated products in advertising and in-store displays. Management visualized her as the next Betty Crocker, a fictional character created some years ago by General Mills, Inc., and a representative of its interest in "life-style" trends. The "Martha Stewart Everyday" home fashion product line was introduced successfully in 1995 and expanded in 1996 and 1997. A separate division was established to manage strategy for all Martha Stewart label goods and programs. Merchandise was featured in the redesigned once-a-week Kmart newspaper circular that carried the advertising theme: "The quality you need, the price you want."

Several thousand prices were reduced to maintain "price leadership across America." As management noted, "It is absolutely essential that we provide our customers with good value—quality products at low prices." Although lowering of prices hurt margins and contributed importantly to an earnings decline, management felt that unit turnover of items with lowered prices increased significantly to "enable Kmart to maintain its pricing leadership that will have a most positive impact on our business in the years ahead."

A "centralized merchandising system" was introduced to improve communication. A computerized, highly automated replenishment system tracked how quickly merchandise sold and just as quickly put fast-moving items back on the shelves. Satellite capability and a point-of-sale (POS) scanning system were introduced as part of the program. Regular, live satellite communication from Kmart headquarters to the stores would allow senior management to communicate with store managers and allow for questions and answers. The POS scanning system allowed a record of every sale and transmission of the data to headquarters. This enabled Kmart to respond quickly to what's new, what's in demand, and what would keep customers coming back.

A new corporate logo was introduced as part of the new program. The logo featured a big red "K" with the word "mart" written in smaller white script inside the "K." It was designed to signify the changes taking place inside the store.

The company opened its first Super Kmart Center in 1992. The format combined general merchandise and food with an emphasis on customer service and convenience and ranged in size from 135,000 to 190,000 square feet. The typical Super Kmart operated 7 days a week, 24-hours a day, and generated high traffic and sales volume. The centers also featured wider shopping aisles, appealing displays, and pleasant lighting to enrich the shopping experience. Super Kmarts featured in-house bakeries, USDA fresh meats, fresh seafood, delicatessens, cookie kiosks, cappuccino bars, in-store eateries and food courts, and fresh carry-out salad bars. In many locations, the center provided customer services like video rental, dry cleaning, shoe repair, beauty salons, optical shops, express shipping services, and a full line of traditional Kmart merchandise. To enhance the appeal of the merchandise assortment, emphasis was placed on "cross merchandising." For example, toasters were featured above the fresh baked breads, kitchen gadgets were positioned across the aisle from produce, and baby centers featured everything from baby food to toys. At the beginning of 1998, the company operated 99 Super Kmart Centers and served 21 states with this regionally based combination store format.

THE PLANNING FUNCTION

Corporate planning at Kmart was the result of executives', primarily the senior executive, recognizing change. The role played by the senior executive was to get others to recognize that nothing is good forever. "Good planning" was perceived as the result of those who recognized that at some point they would have to get involved. "Poor Planning" was done by those who didn't recognize the need for it. When they did, it was too late to survive. Good planning, if done on a regular and timely basis, was assumed to result in improved performance. Kmart's Michael Wellman, then Director of Planning and Research, contended, "planning, as we like to stress, is making decisions now to improve performance tomorrow. Everyone looks at what may happen tomorrow, but the planners are the ones who make decisions today. That's where I think too many firms go wrong. They think they are planning because they are writing reports and are aware of changes. They don't say, 'because of this, we must decide today to spend this money to do this to accomplish this goal in the future.'"

Kmart management believed that the firm had been very successful in the area of strategic planning. "When it became necessary to make significant changes in the way we were doing business," Michael Wellman suggested, "that was accomplished on a fairly timely basis." When the organization made the change in the 1960s, it recognized there was a very powerful investment opportunity and capitalized on it—far beyond what anyone else would have done. "We just opened stores," he continued, "at a great, great pace. Management, when confronted with a crisis, would state, 'It's the economy, or it's this, or that, but it's not the essential way we are doing business.'" He noted, "Suddenly management would recognize that the economy may stay like this forever. We need to improve the situation and then do it." Strategic planning was thought to arise out of some difficult times for the organization.

Kmart had a reasonably formal planning organization that involved a constant evaluation of what was happening in the marketplace, what competition was doing, and what kinds of opportunities were available. Management felt a need to diversify because it would not be a viable company unless it was growing. Management felt it was not going to grow with the Kmart format forever. It needed growth and opportunity, particularly for a company that was able to open 200 stores on a regular basis. Michael Wellman, Director of Planning and Research, felt that, "Given a 'corporate culture' that was accustomed to challenges, management would have to find ways to expend that energy. A corporation that is successful," he argued, "has to continue to be successful. It has to have a basic understanding of corporate needs and be augmented by a much more rigorous effort to be aware of what's going on in the external environment."

A planning group at Kmart represented a number of functional areas of the organization. Management described it as an "in-house consulting group" with some independence. It was made up of (1) financial planning, (2) economic and consumer analysis, and (3) operations research. The chief executive officer (CEO) was identified as the primary planner of the organization.

REORGANIZATION AND RESTRUCTURING

Kmart financial performance for 1993 was clearly disappointing. The company announced a loss of $974 million on sales of $34,156,000 for the fiscal year ended January 26, 1994. Chairman Antonini, noting the deficit, felt it occurred primarily because of lower margins in the U.S. Kmart stores division. "Margin erosion," he said, "stemmed in part from intense industry-wide pricing pressure throughout 1993." He was confident, however, that Kmart was on track with its renewal program to make the more than 2,350 U.S. Kmart stores more "competitive, on-trend, and cutting merchandisers." Tactical Retail Solutions, Inc., estimated that during Antonini's seven-year tenure with the company, Kmart's market share in the discount arena fell to 23% from 35%. Other retail experts suggested that because the company had struggled for so long to have the right merchandise in the stores at the right time, it had lost customers to competitors. An aging customer base was also cited.

In early 1995, following the posting of its eighth consecutive quarter of disappointing earnings, Kmart's Board of Directors announced that Joseph Antonini would be replaced as chairman. It named Donald S. Perkins, former chairman of Jewel Companies, Inc., and a Kmart director, to the position. Antonini relinquished his position as President and Chief Executive Officer in March. After a nationwide search, Floyd Hall, 57, and former Chairman and CEO of the Target discount store division of Dayton-Hudson Corporation, was appointed Chairman, President, and Chief Executive Officer of Kmart in June 1995.

Kmart announced a restructuring of its merchandising organization in 1996 aimed at improving product assortments, category management, customer focus, sales, and profitability. The company had also concluded the disposition of many non-core assets, including the sale of the Borders group, OfficeMax, The Sports Authority, and Coles Myer. It had closed 214 underperforming stores in the United States and cleared out $700 million in aged and discontinued inventory in the remaining Kmart stores.

The corporate mission was "to become the discount store of choice for middle-income families with children by satisfying their routine and seasonal shopping needs as well as or better than the competition." Management believed that the actions taken by the new president would have a dramatic impact on how customers perceived Kmart, how frequently they shopped in the stores, and how much they would buy on each visit. Increasing customer's frequency and the amount they purchased on each visit were seen as having a dramatic impact on the company's efforts to increase its profitability.

In 1996, Kmart converted 152 of its traditional stores to feature a new design that was referred to as the high-frequency format. These stores were named Big Kmart. The stores emphasized those departments that were deemed the most important to core customers and offered an increased mix of high frequency, everyday basics, and consumables in the pantry area located at the front of each store. These items were typically priced at a one to three percentage differential from the leading competitors in each market and served to increase inventory turnover and gross margin dollars. In an addition to the pantry area, Big Kmart stores featured improved lighting, new signage that was easier to see and read, and adjacencies that created a smoother traffic flow.

Floyd Hall felt Kmart's financial results for 1997 and early 1998 reflected the major financial restructuring that was underway at the company. Since joining the company, his top priority had been to build a management team with "a 'can-do' attitude that would permeate all of our interaction with customers, vendors, shareholders, and one another." Major changes were made to the management team. In total, 23 of the company's 37 corporate officers were new to the company's team since 1995. The most dramatic restructuring had taken place in the merchandising organization where all four of the general merchandise managers responsible for buying organizations joined Kmart since 1995. In addition, 15 new divisional vice-presidents joined Kmart during 1997. Significant changes also were made to the Board of Directors with nine of 15 directors new to the company since 1995. Hall argued that the company had turned a corner and that it was "finally and firmly on the road to recovery."

FINANCIAL SITUATION—KMART VERSUS WAL-MART

Kmart's financial position is shown in Exhibits 4, 5, and 6. A 10-year (1988–1997) record of financial performance of Kmart and Wal-Mart is shown in Exhibit 7. In FY 1990, Kmart's sales were $32,070,000,000, and Wal-Mart's sales were $32,601,594,000. In FY 1997, Kmart's sales were up slightly to $32,183,000,000 (an increase of $113,000,000, or 0.035%), while Wal-Mart's sales increased to $117,958,000,000 (an increase of $85,356,406,000, or 261.8%). Wal-Mart's sales increase over the years was 755.3 times that of Kmart's sales increase (see Exhibit 6). Wal-Mart's FY 1997 net income was $3,526,000,000 compared with Kmart's net income of $1,336,000,000 for the past seven fiscal years (FY 1990–FY 1997). Kmart had 2,136 stores. Wal-Mart had 2,421 Wal-Mart stores, 483 SAM's Clubs, and 502 Supercenters, for a total of 3,406 stores.

Exhibit 4   Consolidated Statement of Operations: Kmart Corporation
(Dollar amounts in millions, except per-share data)

Fiscal Year Ending	January 28, 1998[1]	January 29, 1997[1]	January 31, 1996[1]
Sales	$32,183	$31,437	$31,713
Cost of sales, buying, and occupancy	25,152	24,390	24,675
Gross margin	7,031	7,047	7,038
Selling, general, and administrative expenses	6,136	6,274	6,876
Voluntary early retirement program	114	—	—
Other (gains) losses	—	(10)	41
Continuing income before interest, income taxes, and dividends on convertible preferred securities of subsidiary	781	783	121
Interest expense, net	363	453	434
Income tax provision (credit)	120	68	(83)
Dividends on convertible preferred securities of subsidiary, net of income taxes of $26 and $16	49	31	—
Net income (loss) from continuing operations before extraordinary item	249	231	(230)
Loss from discontinued operations, net of income taxes of $(3) and $(139)	—	(5)	(260)
Loss on disposal of discontinued operations, net of income taxes of $(240) and $88	—	(446)	(30)
Extraordinary loss, net of income taxes of $(27)	—	—	(51)
Net income (loss)	$ 249	$ (220)	$ (571)
Basic/diluted income (loss) per common share			
Continuing operations	$ .51	$ .48	$ (.51)
Discontinued operations	—	(.01)	(.57)
Loss on disposal of discontinued operations	—	(.92)	(.06)
Extraordinary item	—	—	(.11)
Net income (loss)	$ .51	$ (.45)	$ (1.25)
Basic weighted average shares (millions)	487.1	483.6	459.8
Diluted weighted average shares (millions)	491.7	486.1	459.9

Note:
1. The company's fiscal year is February through January.

Source: Kmart Corporation, *1998 Annual Report.*

Exhibit 5   **Consolidated Balance Sheets: Kmart Corporation**
(Dollar amounts in millions, except per-share data)

Fiscal Year Ending	January 28, 1998	January 29, 1997
Assets		
Current assets		
Cash and cash equivalents	$ 498	$ 406
Merchandise inventories	6,367	6,354
Other current assets	611	973
Total current assets	7,476	7,733
Property and equipment, net	5,472	5,740
Property held for sale or financing	271	200
Other assets and deferred charges	339	613
Total assets	$13,558	$14,286
Liabilities and Shareholders' Equity		
Current liabilities		
Long-term debt due within one year	$ 78	$ 156
Trade accounts payable	1,923	2,009
Accrued payroll and other liabilities	1,064	1,298
Taxes other than income taxes	209	139
Total current liabilities	3,274	3,602
Long-term debt and notes payable	1,725	2,121
Capital lease obligations	1,179	1,478
Other long-term liabilities	965	1,013
Company obligated mandatorily redeemable convertible preferred securities of a subsidiary trust holding solely 7-3/4% convertible junior subordinated debentures of Kmart (redemption value of $1,000)	981	980
Common stock, $1 par value, 1,500,000,000 shares authorized; 488,811,271 and 486,996,145 shares issued, respectively	489	486
Capital in excess of par value	1,620	1,608
Retained earnings	3,343	3,105
Treasury shares and restricted stock	(15)	(37)
Foreign currency translation adjustment	(3)	(70)
Total liabilities and shareholders' equity	$13,558	$14,286

Source: Kmart Corporation, *1998 Annual Report.*

Exhibit 6   **Consolidated Selected Financial Data: Kmart Corporation**
(Dollar amounts in millions, except per-share data)

	Fiscal Year[1]				
	1997	**1996**	**1995**	**1994**	**1993**
Summary of Operations[2]					
Sales	$32,183	$31,437	$31,713	$29,563	$28,039
Cost of sales, buying, and occupancy	25,152	24,390	24,675	22,331	20,732
Selling, general, and administrative expenses	6,136	6,274	6,876	6,651	6,241
Interest expense, net	363	453	434	479	467
Continuing income (loss) before income taxes	418	330	(313)	102	(306)
Net income (loss) from continuing operations[3]	249	231	(230)	96	(179)
Net income (loss)	249	(220)	(571)	296	(974)
Per Share of Common					
Basic continuing income (loss)	$ 0.51	$ 0.48	$ (0.51)	$ 0.20	$ (0.46)
Diluted continuing income (loss)[4]	0.51	0.48	(0.51)	0.19	(0.46)
Dividends declared	—	—	0.36	0.96	0.96
Book value	11.15	10.51	10.99	13.15	13.39
Financial Data					
Working capital	$ 4,202	$ 4,131	$ 5,558	$ 3,562	$ 3,793
Total assets	13,558	14,286	15,033	16,085	15,875
Long-term debt	1,725	2,121	3,922	1,989	2,209
Long-term capital lease obligations	1,179	1,478	1,586	1,666	1,609
Trust convertible preferred securities	981	980	—	—	—
Capital expenditures	678	343	540	1,021	793
Depreciation and amortization	660	654	685	639	650
Ending market capitalization—common stock	5,469	5,418	2,858	6,345	9,333
Inventory turnover	3.5	3.5	3.4	3.2	2.9
Current ratio	2.3	2.1	2.9	1.7	1.9
Long-term debt to capitalization	32.4%	37.2%	51.1%	37.7%	38.5%
Ratio of income from continuing operations to fixed charges[5]	1.5	1.4	—	1.1	—
Basic weighted average shares outstanding (millions)	487	484	460	427	408
Diluted weighted average shares outstanding (millions)[4]	492	486	460	456	408
Number of Stores					
United States	2,136	2,134	2,161	2,316	2,323
International and other	—	127	149	165	163
Total stores	2,136	2,261	2,310	2,481	2,486
U.S. Kmart store sales per comparable selling square foot	$ 211	$ 201	$ 195	$ 181	$ 182
U.S. Kmart selling square footage (millions)	151	156	160	166	160

Notes:

1. **The company's fiscal year is January through February (January 31, 1997 to February 1, 1998).**
2. Kmart Corporation and subsidiaries ("the Company" or "Kmart") fiscal year ends on the last Wednesday in January. Fiscal 1995 consisted of 53 weeks.
3. Net income from continuing operations in 1997 includes a $114 million ($81 million net of tax) non-recurring charge related to the Voluntary Early Retirement Program. The net loss from continuing operations in 1993 included a pretax provision of $904 million ($579 million net of tax) for store restructuring and other charges.
4. Consistent with the requirements of Financial Accounting Standards No. 128, preferred securities were not included in the calculation of diluted earnings per share for 1997, 1996, and 1994 due to their anti-dilutive effect. Due to the company's loss from continuing operations in 1995 and 1993, diluted earnings per share is equivalent to basic earnings per share.
5. Fixed charges represent total interest charges, a portion of operating rentals representative of the interest factor, amortization of debt discount and expense, and preferred dividends of majority owned subsidiaries. The deficiency of income from continuing retail operations versus fixed charges was $305 and $315 million for 1995 and 1993, respectively.

Source: Kmart Corporation, *1997 Annual Report*, p. 17.

Exhibit 7   **Comparison of Financial Performance:**
Kmart Corporation and Wal-Mart Stores, Inc., 1980–1997
(Dollar amounts in thousands)

A. Kmart Financial Performance

Fiscal Years (February 1–January 31)

Fiscal Year	Sales	Assets	Net Income	Net Worth
1997	32,183,000	13,558,000	249,000	6,445,000
1996	31,437,000	14,286,000	(220,000)	6,146,000
1995	34,389,000	15,397,000	(571,000)	5,280,000
1994	34,025,000	17,029,000	296,000	6,032,000
1993	34,156,000	17,504,000	(974,000)	6,093,000
1992	37,724,000	18,931,000	941,000	7,536,000
1991	34,580,000	15,999,000	859,000	6,891,000
1990	32,070,000	13,899,000	756,000	5,384,000
1989	29,533,000	13,145,000	323,000	4,972,000
1988	27,301,000	12,126,000	803,000	5,009,000
1987	25,627,000	11,106,000	692,000	4,409,000
1986	23,035,000	10,578,000	570,000	3,939,000
1985	22,035,000	9,991,000	472,000	3,273,000
1984	20,762,000	9,262,000	503,000	3,234,000
1983	18,597,900	8,183,100	492,300	2,940,100
1982	16,772,166	7,343,665	261,821	2,601,272
1981	16,527,012	6,673,004	220,251	2,455,594
1980	14,204,381	6,102,462	260,527	2,343,172

B. Wal-Mart Financial Performance

Fiscal Years (February 1–January 31)

Fiscal Year[1]	Sales	Assets	Net Income	Net Worth
1997	117,958,000	45,384,000	3,526,000	18,503,000
1996	104,859,000	39,604,000	3,056,000	17,143,000
1995	93,627,000	37,541,000	2,740,000	14,756,000
1994	82,494,000	32,819,000	2,681,000	12,726,000
1993	67,344,000	26,441,000	2,333,000	10,753,000
1992	55,484,000	20,565,000	1,995,000	8,759,000
1991	43,886,900	15,443,400	1,608,500	6,989,700
1990	32,601,594	11,388,915	1,291,024	5,365,524
1989	25,810,656	8,198,484	1,075,900	3,965,561
1988	20,649,001	6,359,668	837,221	3,007,909
1987	15,959,255	5,131,809	627,643	2,257,267
1986	11,909,076	4,049,092	450,086	1,690,493
1985	8,451,489	3,103,645	327,473	1,277,659
1984	6,400,861	2,205,229	270,767	984,672
1983	4,666,909	1,652,254	196,244	737,503
1982	3,376,252	1,187,448	124,140	488,109
1981	2,444,997	937,513	82,794	323,942
1980	1,643,199	592,345	55,682	248,309

Note:

1. The company's fiscal year is January through December, and its accounting year is February through January.

Source: *Fortune,* financial analyses; Kmart Corporation, annual reports; and Wal-Mart stores, Inc., annual reports.

References

Robert Berner, "Kmart's Earnings More Than Tripled in First Quarter," *Wall Street Journal* (May 14, 1998), p. A13.

Molly Brauer, "Kmart in Black 'in 6 Months,' " *Detroit Free Press* (January 26, 1996), p. E1.

"Where Kmart Goes Next Now That It's No. 2," *Business Week* (June 2, 1980), pp. 109–110, 114.

John Bussey, "Kmart Is Set to Sell Many of Its Roots to Rapid-American Corp's McCrory," *Wall Street Journal* (April 6, 1987), p. 24.

Eleanore Carruth, "Kmart Has to Open Some New Doors on The Future," *Fortune* (July 1977), pp. 143–150, 153–154.

"Why Chains Enter New Areas," *Chain Store Executive* (December 1976), pp. 22, 24.

"It's Kresge . . . Again," *Chain Store Executive* (November 1975), p. 16.

Subrata N. Chakravarty, "A Tale of Two Companies," *Forbes* (May 27, 1991), pp. 86–96.

Robert E. Dewar, "The Kresge Company and the Retail Revolution," *University of Michigan Business Review* (July 2, 1975), p. 2.

Christina Duff and Joann S. Lubin, "Kmart Board Ousts Antonini as Chairman," *Wall Street Journal* (January 18, 1995), p. A3.

Vickie Elmer and Joann Muller, "Retailer Needs Leader, Vision," *Detroit Free Press* (March 22, 1995), pp. 1A, 9A.

Melinda G. Guiles, "Attention, Shoppers: Stop That Browsing and Get Aggressive," *Wall Street Journal* (June 16, 1987), pp. 1, 21.

Melinda G. Guiles, "Kmart, Bruno's Join to Develop 'Hypermarkets,' " *Wall Street Journal* (September 8, 1987), p. 17.

Paul Ingrassia, "Attention Non Kmart Shoppers: A Blue-Light Special Just for You," *Wall Street Journal* (October 6, 1987), p. 42.

"Kmart Looks to New Logo to Signify Changes," *Wall Street Journal* (September 13, 1990), p. 10.

"Kmart Will Expand Line With Purchase of Warehouse Club," *Wall Street Journal* (December 14, 1990), p. 4.

Janet Key, "Kmart Plan: Diversify, Conquer: Second Largest Retailer Out to Woo Big Spenders," *Chicago Tribune* (November 11, 1984), pp. 1–2.

Kmart Corporation, *1990 Annual Report,* Troy, Michigan.

Kmart Corporation, *1995 Annual Report,* Troy, Michigan.

Kmart Corporation, *1996 Annual Report,* Troy, Michigan.

Kmart Corporation, *1997 Annual Report,* Troy, Michigan.

Kmart Corporation, *Kmart Fact Book,* Troy, Michigan, 1997.

Jerry Main, "Kmart's Plan to Be Born Again," *Fortune* (September 21, 1981), pp. 74–77, 84–85.

Russell Mitchell, "How They're Knocking the Rust Off Two Old Chains," *Business Week* (September 8, 1986), pp. 44–48.

Faye Rice, "Why Kmart has Stalled," *Fortune* (October 9, 1989), p. 79.

Bill Saporito, "Is Wal-Mart Unstoppable?" *Fortune* (May 6, 1991), pp. 50–59.

Francine Schwadel, "Attention Kmart Shoppers: Style Coming to This Isle," *Wall Street Journal* (August 9, 1988), p. 6.

Francine Schwadel, "Kmart to Speed Store Openings, Renovations," *Wall Street Journal* (February 27, 1990), p. 3.

Patricia Sellers, "Attention, Kmart Shoppers," *Fortune* (January 2, 1989), p. 41.

Barry Stavro, "Mass Appeal," *Forbes* (May 5, 1986), p. 128, 130.

Patricia Sternad, "Kmart's Antonini Moves Far Beyond Retail 'Junk' Image," *Advertising Age* (July 25, 1988), pp. 1, 67.

Michael Wellman, Interview with Director of Planning and Research, Kmart Corporation (August 6, 1984).

David Woodruff, "Will Kmart Ever Be a Silk Purse?" *Business Week* (January 22, 1990), p. 46.

Wal-Mart Stores, Inc. (1998): Rapid Growth in the 1990s

James A. Camerius

David Glass assumed the role of President and Chief Executive Officer at Wal-Mart, the position previously held by Wal-Mart's founder Sam Walton. Known for his hard-driving managerial style, Glass gained his experience in retailing at a small supermarket chain in Springfield, Missouri. He joined Wal-Mart as Executive Vice-President for Finance in 1976. He was named President and Chief Operating Officer in 1984. In 1998, as he reflected on growth strategies of the firm, he suggested: "Seldom can you count on everything coming together as well as it did this year. We believe we could always do better, but we improved more this year than I can ever remember in the past. If Wal-Mart had been content to be just an Arkansas retailer in the early days, we probably would not be where we are today."

A MATURING ORGANIZATION

In 1998, Wal-Mart Stores, Inc., of Bentonville, Arkansas, operated mass merchandising retail stores under a variety of names and retail formats, including Wal-Mart discount department stores; SAM's Wholesale Clubs, wholesale/retail membership warehouses; and Wal-Mart Supercenters, large combination grocery and general merchandise stores in all 50 states. In the International Division, it operated in Canada, Mexico, Argentina, Brazil, Germany, and Puerto Rico, and through joint ventures in China. It was not only the nation's largest discount department store chain, but it had surpassed the retail division of Sears, Roebuck & Co. in sales volume as the largest retail firm in the United States. The McLane Company, a support division with over 36,000 customers, was the nation's largest distributor of food and merchandise to convenience stores and served selected Wal-Marts, SAM's Clubs, and Supercenters. Wal-Mart also continued to operate a small number of discount department stores called Bud's Discount City. A financial summary of Wal-Mart Stores, Inc., for the fiscal years ending January 31, 1997 and 1998, is shown in Exhibit 1.

THE SAM WALTON SPIRIT

Much of the success of Wal-Mart was attributed to the entrepreneurial spirit of its founder and Chairman of the Board, Samuel Moore Walton (1918–1992). Many considered him one of the most influential retailers of the century.

Sam Walton or "Mr. Sam" as some referred to him, traced his down-to-earth, old-fashioned, home-spun, evangelical ways to growing up in rural Oklahoma, Missouri, and Arkansas. Although he was remarkably blasé about his roots, some suggested that it

---

This case prepared by Professor James W. Camerius of Northern Michigan University. This case was edited for SMBP–7th Edition. All rights reserved to the author. Copyright © 1998 by James W. Camerius. Reprinted by permission.

Exhibit 1 **Consolidated Statements of Income: Wal-Mart Stores, Inc.**
(Dollar amounts in millions, except per-share data)

Year Ending January 31 [1,2]	1998	1997	1996	1995	1994
Revenues					
Net sales	$117,958	$104,859	$93,627	$82,494	$67,344
Other income—net	1,341	1,319	1,146	918	641
Total revenues	119,299	106,178	94,773	83,412	67,985
Costs and expenses					
Cost of sales	93,438	83,510	74,505	65,586	53,444
Operating, selling, and general and administrative expenses	19,358	16,946	15,021	12,858	10,333
Interest costs					
Debt	555	629	692	520	331
Capital leases	229	216	196	186	186
Total expenses	113,580	101,301	90,414	79,150	64,294
Income before income taxes	5,719	4,877	4,359	4,262	3,691
Provision for income taxes					
Current	2,095	1,974	1,530	1,572	1,325
Deferred	20	(180)	76	9	33
Total	2,115	1,794	1,606	1,581	1,358
Income before minority interest and equity in unconsolidated subsidiaries	3,604	3,083	2,753		
Minority interest and equity in unconsolidated subsidiaries	(78)	(27)	(13)		
Net income	$ 3,526	$ 3,056	$ 2,740	$ 2,681	$ 2,333
Net income per share	$ 1.56	$ 1.33	$ 1.19	$ 1.17	$ 1.02

Note:
1. Financial information is for the previous (1998–1997, 1997–1996, 1996–1995, 1995–1994, and 1994–1993) calendar year.
2. Fiscal year is February 1, 1997, through January 31, 1998, for fiscal year 1997.

Source: Wal-Mart Stores, Inc., *1998 Annual Report.*

was the simple belief in hard work and ambition that had "unlocked countless doors and showered upon him, his customers, and his employees . . . , the fruits of . . . years of labor in building [this] highly successful company."

"Our goal has always been in our business to be the very best," Sam Walton said in an interview, "and, along with that, we believe that in order to do that, you've got to make a good situation and put the interests of your associates first. If we really do that consistently, they in turn will cause . . . our business to be successful, which is what we've talked about and espoused and practiced." "The reason for our success," he said, "is our people and the way that they're treated and the way they feel about their company." Many have suggested it is this "people first" philosophy that guided the company through the challenges and setbacks of its early years and allowed the company to maintain its consistent record of growth and expansion in later years.

There was little about Sam Walton's background that reflected his amazing success. He was born in Kingfisher, Oklahoma, on March 29, 1918, to Thomas and Nancy Walton. Thomas Walton was a banker at the time and later entered the farm mortgage business and moved to Missouri. Sam Walton, growing up in rural Missouri in the depths of the Great Depression, discovered early that he "had a fair amount of ambition and enjoyed working." He completed high school at Columbia, Missouri, and received a Bachelor of Arts Degree in Economics from the University of Missouri in 1940. "I really had no idea what I would be," he said, adding as an afterthought, "at one point in time, I thought I wanted to become President of the United States."

A unique, enthusiastic, and positive individual, Sam Walton was "just your basic home-spun billionaire," a columnist once suggested. "Mr. Sam is a life-long small-town resident who didn't change much as he got richer than his neighbors," he noted. Walton had tremendous energy, enjoyed bird hunting with his dogs, and flew a corporate plane. When the company was much smaller, he could boast that he personally visited every Wal-Mart store at least once a year. A store visit usually included Walton leading Wal-Mart cheers that began, "Give me a W, give me an A, . . ." To many employees he had the air of a fiery Baptist preacher. Paul R. Carter, a Wal-Mart Executive Vice-President, was quoted as saying, "Mr. Walton has a calling." He became the richest man in America and by 1991 had created a personal fortune for his family in excess of $21 billion.

Sam Walton's success was widely chronicled. He was selected by the investment publication *Financial World* in 1989 as the "CEO of the Decade." He had honorary degrees from the University of the Ozarks, the University of Arkansas, and the University of Missouri. He also received many of the most distinguished professional awards of the industry like "Man of the Year," "Discounter of the Year," "Chief Executive Officer of the Year," and was the second retailer to be inducted into the Discounting Hall of Fame. He was recipient of the Horatio Alger Award in 1984 and acknowledged by *Discount Stores News* as "Retailer of the Decade" in December 1989. "Walton does a remarkable job of instilling near-religious fervor in his people," said analyst Robert Buchanan of A.G. Edwards. "I think that speaks to the heart of his success." In late 1989, Sam Walton was diagnosed to have multiple myeloma, or cancer of the bone marrow. He continued serving as Chairman of the Board of Directors until his death in early 1992.

CORPORATE GOVERNANCE

Exhibit 2 provides the 14 members of Wal-Mart's Board of Directors. Four are internal members: (1) S. Robson Walton, Chairman, (2) David D. Glass, CEO and President, (3) Donald G. Soderquist, Vice-Chairman and Chief Operating Officer (COO), and (4) Paul R. Carter, Executive Vice-President—Wal-Mart Realty.

THE MARKETING CONCEPT

Genesis of an Idea

Sam Walton started his retail career in 1940 as a management trainee with the J.C. Penney Co. in Des Moines, Iowa. He was impressed with the Penney method of doing business and later modeled the Wal-Mart chain on "The Penney Idea" as reviewed in Exhibit 3. The Penney Company found strength in calling employees "associates" rather than clerks. Penney's, founded in Kemerer, Wyoming, in 1902, located stores on the main streets of small towns and cities throughout the United States.

Following service in the U.S. Army during World War II, Sam Walton acquired a Ben Franklin variety store franchise in Newport, Arkansas. He operated this store successfully with his brother, James L. "Bud" Walton (1921–1995), until losing the lease in 1950. When Wal-Mart was incorporated in 1962, the firm was operating a chain of 15 stores. Bud Walton became a Senior Vice-President of the firm and concentrated on finding suitable store locations, acquiring real estate, and directing store construction.

Exhibit 2 Board of Directors and Corporate Officers: Wal-Mart Stores, Inc., 1998

A. Directors

Jeronimo Arango	E. Stanley Kroenke
Paul R. Carter	Elizabeth A. Sanders
John A. Cooper, Jr.	Jack C. Shewmaker
Stephen Friedman	Donald G. Soderquist
Stanley C. Gault	Dr. Paula Stern
David D. Glass	John T. Walton
Frederick S. Humphries	S. Robson Walton

B. Corporate Officers

Chairman of the Board	S. Robson Walton
CEO, President	David D. Glass
Vice-Chairman, COO	Donald G. Soderquist
Executive VP, President—Wal-Mart Realty	Paul R. Carter
Executive VP—Merchandising	Bob Connolly
Executive VP, COO—Operations, Wal-Mart Stores Division	Thomas M. Coughlin
Executive VP—Specialty Division	David Dible
Executive VP, President—SAM's Club Division	Mark Hansen
Executive VP, President—International Division	Bob L. Martin
Executive VP, CFO	John B. Menzer
Executive VP, President—Wal-Mart Stores Division	H. Lee Scott
Executive VP—Supercenter	Nick White
Senior VP, Secretary—General Counsel	Robert K. Rhoads
Senior VP, Finance—Treasurer	J. J. Fitzsimmons

Source: Wal-Mart Stores, Inc., *1997 Annual Report.*

Exhibit 3 The Penney Idea, 1913

1. To serve the public, as nearly as we can, to its complete satisfaction.
2. To expect for the service we render a fair remuneration and not all the profit the traffic will bear.
3. To do all in our power to pack the customer's dollar full of value, quality, and satisfaction.
4. To continue to train ourselves and our associates so that the service we give will be more and more intelligently performed.
5. To improve constantly the human factor in our business.
6. To reward men and women in our organization through participation in what the business produces.
7. To test our every policy, method, and act in this way: "Does it square with what is right and just?" Vance H.

Source: Vance H. Trimble, *Sam Walton: The Inside Story of America's Richest Man* (New York: Dutton), 1990.

The early retail stores owned by Sam Walton in Newport and Bentonville, Arkansas, and later in other small towns in adjoining southern states, were variety store operations. They were relatively small operations of 6,000 square feet, were located on "main street," and displayed merchandise on plain wooden tables and counters. Operated under the Ben Franklin name and supplied by Butler Brothers of Chicago and St. Louis, they were characterized by a limited price line, low gross margins, high merchandise turnover, and concentration on return on investment. The firm, operating under the Walton

5 & 10 name, was the largest Ben Franklin franchisee in the country in 1962. The variety stores were phased out by 1976 to allow the company to concentrate on the growth of Wal-Mart discount department stores.

Foundations of Growth

The original Wal-Mart discount concept was not a unique idea. Sam Walton became convinced in the late 1950s that discounting would transform retailing. He traveled extensively in New England, the cradle of "off-pricing." After he had visited just about every discounter in the United States, he tried to interest Butler Brothers executives in Chicago in the discount store concept. The first Kmart, as a "conveniently located one-stop-shopping unit where customers could buy a wide variety of quality merchandise at discount prices," had just opened in Garden City, Michigan. Walton's theory was to operate a similar discount store in a small community, and in that setting, he would offer name brand merchandise at low prices and would add friendly service. Although Butler Brothers executives rejected the idea, Walton implemented the concept on his own. The first "Wal-Mart Discount City" opened in late 1962 in Rogers, Arkansas.

Wal-Mart stores would sell nationally advertised, well-known brand merchandise at low prices in austere surroundings. As corporate policy, they would cheerfully give refunds, credits, and rain checks. Management conceived the firm as a "discount department store chain offering a wide variety of general merchandise to the customer." Early emphasis was placed on opportunistic purchases of merchandise from whatever sources were available. Heavy emphasis was placed on health and beauty aids (H&BA) in the product line and "stacking it high" in a manner of merchandise presentation. By the end of 1979, there were 276 Wal-Mart stores located in 11 states.

The firm developed an aggressive expansion strategy. New stores were located primarily in towns of 5,000 to 25,000 population. The stores' sizes ranged from 30,000 to 60,000 square feet with 45,000 being the average. The firm also expanded by locating stores in contiguous areas, town by town, state by state. When its discount operations came to dominate a market area, it moved to an adjoining area. Whereas other retailers built warehouses to serve existing outlets, Wal-Mart built the distribution center first and then spotted stores all around it, pooling advertising and distribution overhead. Most stores were less than a six-hour drive from one of the company's warehouses. The first major distribution center, a 390,000-square-foot facility opened in Searcy, Arkansas, outside Bentonville in 1978.

National Perspectives

By 1991, the firm had 1,573 Wal-Mart stores in 35 states with expansion planned for adjacent states. Wal-Mart had become the largest retailer and the largest discount department store in the United States.

As a national discount department store chain, Wal-Mart Stores, Inc., offered a wide variety of general merchandise to the customer. The stores were designed to offer one-stop shopping in 36 departments, which included family apparel, health and beauty aids, household needs, electronics, toys, fabric and crafts, automotive supplies, lawn and patio, jewelry, and shoes. In addition, at certain store locations, a pharmacy, automotive supply and service center, garden center, or snack bar were also operated. The firm operated its stores with an "everyday low price" as opposed to putting heavy emphasis on special promotions, which would call for multiple newspaper advertising circulars.

Stores were expected to "provide the customer with a clean, pleasant, and friendly shopping experience."

Although Wal-Mart carried much the same merchandise, offered similar prices, and operated stores that looked much like the competition, there were many differences. In the typical Wal-Mart store, employees wore blue vests to identify themselves, aisles were wide, apparel departments were carpeted in warm colors, a store employee followed customers to their cars to pick up their shopping carts, and the customer was welcomed at the door by a "people greeter" who gave directions and struck up conversations. In some cases, merchandise was bagged in brown paper sacks rather than plastic bags because customers seemed to prefer them. A simple Wal-Mart logo in white letters on a brown background on the front of the store served to identify the firm. Consumer studies determined that the chain was particularly adept at striking the delicate balance needed to convince customers its prices were low without making people feel that its stores were too cheap. In many ways, competitors like Kmart sought to emulate Wal-Mart by introducing people greeters, by upgrading interiors, by developing new logos and signage, and by introducing new inventory response systems.

A "Satisfaction Guaranteed" refund and exchange policy was introduced to allow customers to be confident of Wal-Mart's merchandise and quality. Technological advancements like scanner cash registers, hand-held computers for ordering of merchandise, and computer linkages of stores with the general office and distribution centers improved communications and merchandise replenishment. Each store was encouraged to initiate programs that would make it an integral part of the community in which it operated. Associates were encouraged to "maintain the highest standards of honesty, morality, and business ethics in dealing with the public."

THE EXTERNAL ENVIRONMENT

Industry analysts labeled the 1980s and early 1990s as eras of economic uncertainty for retailers. Many retailers were negatively affected by increased competitive pressures, sluggish consumer spending, slower-than-anticipated economic growth in North America, and recessions abroad. In 1995, Wal-Mart management felt the high consumer debt level caused many shoppers to reduce or defer spending on anything other than essentials. Management also felt that the lack of exciting new products or apparel trends reduced discretionary spending. Fierce competition resulted in lower margins, and the lack of inflation stalled productivity increases. By 1998, the country had returned to prosperity. Unemployment was low, total income was relatively high, and interest rates were stable. Combined with a low inflation rate, buying power was perceived to be high and consumers were generally willing to buy.

Many retail enterprises confronted heavy competitive pressure by restructuring. Sears, Roebuck & Co., based in Chicago, became a more focused retailer by divesting itself of Allstate Insurance Company and its real estate subsidiaries. In 1993, the company announced it would close 118 unprofitable stores and discontinue the unprofitable Sears general merchandise catalog. It eliminated 50,000 jobs and began a $4 billion, five-year remodeling plan for its remaining multi-line department stores. After unsuccessfully experimenting with an "everyday low-price strategy," management chose to realign its merchandise strategy to meet the needs of middle market customers, who were primarily women, by focusing on product lines in apparel, home, and automotive. The new focus on apparel was supported with the advertising campaign, "The Softer Side of Sears."

A later company-wide campaign broadened the appeal: "The many sides of Sears fit the many sides of your life." Sears completed its return to its retailing roots by selling off its ownership in Dean Witter Financial Services, Discover Card, Coldwell Banker Real Estate, and Sears mortgage banking operations.

The discount department store industry by the early 1990s had changed in a number of ways and was thought to have reached maturity by many analysts. Several formerly successful firms like E.J. Korvette, W.T. Grant, Atlantic Mills, Arlans, Federals, Zayre, Hecht's, and Ames had declared bankruptcy and as a result either liquidated or reorganized. Venture announced liquidation in early 1998. Regional firms like Target Stores and Shopko Stores began carrying more fashionable merchandise in more attractive facilities and shifted their emphasis to more national markets. Specialty retailers such as Toys R Us, Pier 1 Imports, and Oshman's were making big inroads in toys, home furnishing, and sporting goods. The "superstores" of drug and food chains were rapidly discounting increasing amounts of general merchandise. Some firms like May Department Stores Company with Caldor and Venture and Woolworth Corporation with Woolco had withdrawn from the field by either selling their discount divisions or closing them down entirely. The firm's remaining 122 Woolco stores in Canada were sold to Wal-Mart in 1994. All remaining Woolworth variety stores in the United States were closed in 1997.

Several new retail formats had emerged in the marketplace to challenge the traditional discount department store format. The superstore, a 100,000–300,000-square-foot operation, combined a large supermarket with a discount general-merchandise store. Originally a European retailing concept, these outlets were known as "malls without walls." Kmart's Super Kmart Centers, American Fare, and Wal-Mart's Supercenter Store were examples of this trend toward large operations. Warehouse retailing, which involved some combination of warehouse and showroom facilities, used warehouse principles to reduce operating expenses and thereby offer discount prices as a primary customer appeal. Home Depot combined the traditional hardware store and lumberyard with a self-service home improvement center to become the largest home center operator in the nation.

Some retailers responded to changes in the marketplace by selling goods at price levels (20% to 60%) below regular retail prices. These off-price operations appeared as two general types: (1) factory outlet stores like Burlington Coat Factory Warehouse, Bass Shoes, and Manhattan's Brand Name Fashion Outlet, and (2) independents like Loehmann's, T.J. Maxx, Marshall's, and Clothestime, which bought seconds, overages, closeouts, or leftover goods from manufacturers and other retailers. Other retailers chose to dominate a product classification. Some super specialists like Sock Appeal, Little Piggie, Ltd., and Sock Market offered a single, narrowly defined classification of merchandise with an extensive assortment of brands, colors, and sizes. Others, as niche specialists, like Kids Mart, a division of Woolworth Corporation, and McKids, a division of Sears, targeted an identified market with carefully selected merchandise and appropriately designed stores. Some retailers like Silk Greenhouse (silk plants and flowers), Office Max (office supplies and equipment), and Toys 'R' Us (toys) were called "category killers" because they had achieved merchandise dominance in their respective product categories. Stores like The Limited, Limited Express, Victoria's Secret, and The Banana Republic became mini-department specialists by showcasing new lines and accessories alongside traditional merchandise lines.

Kmart Corporation, headquartered in Troy, Michigan, became the industry's third largest retailer after Sears, Roebuck & Co. and the second largest discount department store chain in the United States in the 1990s. Kmart had 2,136 stores and $32,183 million in sales at the beginning of 1998. The firm was perceived by many industry analysts and

Exhibit 4   **Competitive Sales and Store Comparison 1987–1997**

Year	Kmart		Wal-Mart	
	Sales (thousands)	Stores[1]	Sales (thousands)	Stores[1]
1997	$32,183,000	2,136	$117,958,000	3,406
1996	31,437,000	2,261	104,859,000	3,054
1995	34,389,000	2,161	93,627,000	2,943
1994	34,025,000	2,481	82,494,000	2,684
1993	34,156,000	2,486	67,344,000	2,400
1992	37,724,000	2,435	55,484,000	2,136
1991	34,580,000	2,391	43,886,900	1,928
1990	32,070,000	2,350	32,601,594	1,721
1989	29,533,000	2,361	25,810,656	1,525
1988	27,301,000	2,307	20,649,001	1,364
1987	25,627,000	2,273	15,959,255	1,198

Note:
1. Number of general merchandise stores.

consumers in several independent studies as a laggard. It had been the industry sales leader for a number of years and had recently announced a turnaround in profitability. In the same studies, Wal-Mart was perceived as the industry leader even though according to the *Wall Street Journal* "they carry much the same merchandise, offer prices that are pennies apart and operate stores that look almost exactly alike." "Even their names are similar," noted the newspaper. The original Kmart concept of a "conveniently located, one-stop-shopping unit where customers could buy a wide variety of quality merchandise at discount prices," had lost its competitive edge in a changing market. As one analyst noted in an industry newsletter, "They had done so well for the past 20 years without paying attention to market changes, now they have to." Kmart acquired a new Chairman, President, and Chief Executive Officer in 1995. Wal-Mart and Kmart sales growth over the period 1987–1997 is reviewed in Exhibit 4. A competitive analysis is shown of four major retail firms in Exhibit 5.

Some retailers like Kmart had initially focused on appealing to professional, middle-class consumers who lived in suburban areas and who were likely to be price sensitive. Other firms like Target (Dayton Hudson), which had adopted the discount concept early, attempted to go generally after an upscale consumer who had an annual household income of $25,000 to $44,000. Some firms such as Fleet Farm and Menard's served the rural consumer, while firms like Chicago's Goldblatt's Department Stores and Ames Discount Department Stores chose to serve blacks and Hispanics in the inner city.

In rural communities, Wal-Mart success often came at the expense of established local merchants and units of regional discount store chains. Hardware stores, family department stores, building supply outlets, and stores featuring fabrics, sporting goods, and shoes were among the first to either close or relocate elsewhere. Regional discount retailers in the Sunbelt states like Roses, Howard's, T.G. & Y., and Duckwall-ALCO, who once enjoyed solid sales and earnings, were forced to reposition themselves by renovating stores, opening bigger and more modern units, remerchandising assortments, and offering lower prices. In many cases, stores like Coast-to-Coast, Pamida, and Ben Franklin closed at an announcement that Wal-Mart was planning to build in a specific community.

Exhibit 5   An Industry Comparative Analysis, 1997

	Wal-Mart	**Sears**	**Kmart**	**Target**
Sales (millions)	$117,958	$36,370	$32,183	$20,368
Net income (thousands)	3,526	1,188	249	1,287
Net income per share	1.56	3.03	.51	N/A
Dividends per share	.27	N/A	N/A	N/A
Percent sales change	12.0%	8.0%	2.4%	14%

Number of stores:

Wal-Mart and subsidiaries
Wal-Mart stores—2,421
SAM's Clubs—483
Supercenters—502

Sears Roebuck & Co. (all divisions)
Sears Merchandise Group
Department stores—833
Hardware stores—255
Furniture stores—129
Sears dealer stores—576
Auto/tire stores—780
Auto parts stores
Western Auto—39
Parts America—576
Western Auto Dealer stores—800

Kmart Corporation
General Merchandise—2,136

Dayton Hudson Corporation
Target—796
Mervyn's—269
Department stores—65

Source: Corporate annual reports.

"Just the word that Wal-Mart was coming made some stores close up," indicated a local newspaper editor.

CORPORATE STRATEGIES

The corporate and marketing strategies that emerged at Wal-Mart were based on a set of two main objectives that had guided the firm through its growth years. In the first objective, the customer was featured, "Customers would be provided what they want, when they want it, all at a value." In the second objective, the team spirit was emphasized, "Treating each other as we would hope to be treated, acknowledging our total dependency on our Associate-partners to sustain our success." The approach included aggressive plans for new store openings; expansion to additional states; upgrading, relocation, refurbishing, and remodeling existing stores; and opening new distribution centers. The plan was to not have a single operating unit that had not been updated in the past seven years. For Wal-Mart management, the 1990s were considered: "A new era for Wal-Mart; an era in which we plan to grow to a truly nationwide retailer, and should we continue to perform, our sales and earnings will also grow beyond where most could have envisioned at the dawn of the 1980s."

In the decade of the 1980s, Wal-Mart developed a number of new retail formats. The first SAM's Club opened in Oklahoma City, Oklahoma, in 1983. The wholesale club was an idea that had been developed by other firms earlier but which found its greatest success and growth in acceptability at Wal-Mart. SAM's Clubs featured a vast array of product categories with limited selection of brand and model, cash-and carry business with limited hours, large (100,000 square foot), bare-bone facilities, rock bottom wholesale prices, and minimal promotion. The limited membership plan permitted wholesale members who bought membership and others who usually paid a percentage above the ticket price of the merchandise. At the beginning of 1998, there were 483 SAM's Clubs in operation. A revision in merchandising strategy resulted in fewer items in the inventory mix with more emphasis on lower prices.

Wal-Mart Supercenters were large combination stores. They were first opened in 1988 as Hypermarket*USA, a 222,000-square-foot superstore that combined a discount store with a large grocery store, a food court of restaurants, and other service businesses such as banks or video tape rental stores. A scaled-down version of Hypermarket*USA was called the Wal-Mart SuperCenter, similar in merchandise offerings, but with about half the square footage of hypermarkets. These expanded store concepts also included convenience stores and gasoline distribution outlets to "enhance shopping convenience." The company proceeded slowly with these plans and later suspended its plans for building any more hypermarkets in favor of the smaller SuperCenter. In 1998, Wal-Mart operated 502 SuperCenters. It also announced plans to build several full-fledged supermarkets called "Wal-Mart Food and Drug Express" with a drive-through option as "laboratories" to test how the concept would work and what changes would need to be made before a decision were made to proceed with additional units. The McLane Company, Inc., a provider of retail and grocery distribution services for retail stores, was acquired in 1991. It was not considered a major segment of the total Wal-Mart operation.

On the international level, Wal-Mart management had a goal to be the dominant retailer in each country it entered. With the acquisition of 122 former Woolco stores in Canada, the company exceeded expectations in sales growth, market share, and profitability. With a tender offer for shares and mergers of joint ventures in Mexico, the company had a controlling interest in Cifra, Mexico's largest retailer. Cifra operated stores with a variety of concepts in every region of Mexico, ranging from the nation's largest chain of sit-down restaurants to a softline department store. Plans were also proceeding with start-up operations in Argentina and Brazil as well as China. The acquisition of 21 "hypermarkets" in Germany at the end of 1997 marked the company's first entry into Europe, which management considered "one of the best consumer markets in the world." These large stores offered one-stop-shopping facilities similar to Wal-Mart Supercenters. The international expansion accelerated management's plans for the development of Wal-Mart as a global brand along the lines of Coca-Cola, Disney, and McDonald's. "We are a global brand name," said Bobby Martin, President of the International Division of Wal-Mart, "To customers everywhere it means low cost, best value, greatest selection of quality merchandise and highest standards of customer service." Some changes were mandated in Wal-Mart's international operations to meet local tastes and intense competitive conditions. "We're building companies out there," said Martin.

"That's like starting Wal-Mart all over again in South America or Indonesia or China." Although stores in different international markets would coordinate purchasing to gain leverage with suppliers, developing new technology and planning overall strategy would be done from Wal-Mart headquarters in Bentonville, Arkansas. At the beginning of 1998, the International Division of Wal-Mart operated 500 discount stores, 61 SuperCenters, and 40 SAM's Clubs.

Several programs were launched to "highlight" popular social causes. The "Buy American" program was a Wal-Mart retail program initiated in 1985. The theme was "Bring It Home to The USA," and its purpose was to communicate Wal-Mart's support for American manufacturing. In the program, the firm directed substantial influence to encourage manufacturers to produce goods in the United States rather than import them from other countries. Vendors were attracted into the program by encouraging manufacturers to initiate the process by contacting the company directly with proposals to sell goods that were made in the United States. Buyers also targeted specific import items in their assortments on a state-by-state basis to encourage domestic manufacturing. According to Haim Dabah, president of Gitano Group, Inc., a maker of fashion discount clothing that imported 95% of its clothing and now makes about 20% of its products here, "Wal-Mart let it be known loud and clear that if you're going to grow with them, you sure better have some products made in the U.S.A." Farris Fashion, Inc. (flannel shirts); Roadmaster Corporation (exercise bicycles); Flanders Industries, Inc. (lawn chairs); and Magic Chef (microwave ovens) were examples of vendors that chose to participate in the program.

From the Wal-Mart standpoint, the "Buy American" program centered around value—producing and selling quality merchandise at a competitive price. The promotion included television advertisements featuring factory workers, a soaring American eagle, and the slogan: "We buy American whenever we can, so you can too." Prominent in-store signage and store circulars were also included. One store poster read: "Success Stories—These items formerly imported, are now being purchased by Wal-Mart in the U.S.A."

Wal-Mart was one of the first retailers to embrace the concept of "green" marketing. The program offered shoppers the option of purchasing products that were better for the environment in three respects: manufacturing, use, and disposal. It was introduced through full-page advertisements in the *Wall Street Journal* and *USA Today.* In-store signage identified environmentally safe products. As Wal-Mart executives saw it, "customers are concerned about the quality of land, air, and water, and would like the opportunity to do something positive." To initiate the program, 7,000 vendors were notified that Wal-Mart had a corporate concern for the environment and to ask for their support in a variety of ways. Wal-Mart television advertising showed children on swings, fields of grain blowing in the wind, and roses. Green and white store signs, printed on recycled paper, marked products or packaging that had been developed or redesigned to be more environmentally sound.

Wal-Mart had become the channel commander in the distribution of many brand name items. As the nation's largest retailer and in many geographic areas the dominant distributor, it exerted considerable influence in negotiation for the best price, delivery terms, promotion allowances, and continuity of supply. Many of these benefits could be passed on to consumers in the form of quality name brand items available at lower than competitive prices. As a matter of corporate policy, management often insisted on doing business only with producer's top sales executives rather than going through a manufacturer's representative. Wal-Mart had been accused of threatening to buy from other producers if firms refused to sell directly to it. In the ensuing power struggle, Wal-Mart executives refused to talk about the controversial policy or admit that it existed. As a representative of an industry association representing a group of sales agencies representatives suggested, "In the Southwest, Wal-Mart's the only show in town." An industry analyst added, "They're extremely aggressive. Their approach has always been to give the customer the benefit of a corporate saving. That builds up customer loyalty and market share."

Another key factor in the mix was an inventory control system that was recognized as the most sophisticated in retailing. A high-speed computer system linked virtually all the stores to headquarters and the company's distribution centers. It electronically logged every item sold at the checkout counter, automatically kept the warehouses informed of merchandise to be ordered, and directed the flow of goods to the stores and even to the proper shelves. Most important for management, it helped detect sales trends quickly and speeded up market reaction time substantially. According to Bob Connolly, Executive Vice-President of Merchandising, "Wal-Mart has used the data gathered by technology to make more inventory available in the key items that customers want most, while reducing inventories overall."

DECISION MAKING IN A MARKET-ORIENTED FIRM

One principle that distinguished Wal-Mart was the unusual depth of employee involvement in company affairs. Corporate strategies put emphasis on human resource management. Employees of Wal-Mart became "associates," a name borrowed from Sam Walton's early association with the J.C. Penney Co. Input was encouraged at meetings at the store and corporate level. The firm hired employees locally, provided training programs, and through a "Letter to the President" program, management encouraged employees to ask questions, and made words like "we," "us," and "our" a part of the corporate language. A number of special award programs recognized individual, department, and division achievement. Stock ownership and profit-sharing programs were introduced as part of a "partnership concept."

The corporate culture was recognized by the editors of the trade publication *Mass Market Retailers* when it recognized all 275,000 associates collectively as the "Mass Market Retailers of the Year." "The Wal-Mart associate," the editors noted, "in this decade that term has come to symbolize all that is right with the American worker, particularly in the retailing environment and most particularly at Wal-Mart." The "store within a store" concept, as a Wal-Mart corporate policy, trained individuals to be merchants by being responsible for the performance of their own departments as if they were running their own businesses. Seminars and training programs afforded them opportunities to grow within the company. "People development, not just a good program for any growing company but a must to secure our future," is how Suzanne Allford, Vice-President of the Wal-Mart People Division, explained the firm's decentralized approach to retail management development.

"The Wal-Mart Way" was a phrase that management used to summarize the firm's unconventional approach to business and the development of the corporate culture. As noted in an report referring to a recent development program: "We stepped outside our retailing world to examine the best managed companies in the United States in an effort to determine the fundamentals of their success and to 'benchmark' our own performances. The name 'Total Quality Management' (TQM) was used to identify this vehicle for proliferating the very best things we do while incorporating the new ideas our people have that will assure our future."

THE GROWTH CHALLENGE

And what of Wal-Mart without Mr. Sam? "There's no transition to make," said Glass, "because the principles and the basic values he used in founding this company were so sound and so universally accepted." "As for the future," he suggested. "There's more opportunity ahead of us than behind us. We're good students of retailing and we've studied the mistakes that others have made. We'll make our own mistakes, but we won't repeat theirs. The only thing constant at Wal-Mart is change. We'll be fine as long as we never lose our responsiveness to the customer." Management identified four key legacies of Sam Walton to guide the company's "quest for value" in the future: (1) Every Day Low Prices, (2) Customer Service, (3) Leadership, and (4) Change.

Wal-Mart Stores, Inc., had for over 25 years experienced tremendous growth and, as one analyst suggested, "been consistently on the cutting edge of low-markup mass merchandising." Much of the forward momentum had come from the entrepreneurial spirit of Samuel Moore Walton. The company announced on Monday, April 6, 1992, following Walton's death, that his son, S. Robson Walton, Vice-Chairman of Wal-Mart, would succeed his father as Chairman of the Board. David Glass would remain President and CEO.

A new management team was in place. Management felt it had positioned the firm as an industry leader. A number of new challenges, however, had to be met. It had predicted as early as 1993 that Wal-Mart's same-store growth would likely slip into the 7%–to–8% range in the near future. Analysts were also concerned about the increased competition in the warehouse club business and the company's move from its roots in Southern and Midwestern small towns to the more competitive and costly markets of the Northeast. Wal-Mart "supercenters" faced more resilient rivals in the grocery field. Unions representing supermarket workers delayed and in some cases killed expansion opportunities. Some analysts said that "the company is simply suffering from the high expectations its stellar performance over the years has created." In early 1996, management acknowledged that 1995 had not been a "Wal-Mart year." After 99 consecutive quarters of earnings growth, Wal-Mart management said profit for the fiscal fourth quarter ending January 31 would decline as much as 11% from the year before. Much of the company sales growth in 1996 and 1997 was attributed to the opening of new stores in an expansion program. Same-store sales growth in 1996 and 1997 was 5% and 6%, respectively, when compared with the previous year's sales performance.

FINANCE

The financial position of the company is presented in Exhibits 6 and 7.

The real growth of Wal-Mart can be measured against Kmart, which was the number one discount retailer in FY 1989 (see Exhibit 4). In FY 1990, Kmart's sales were $32,070,000 and Wal-Mart's sales were $32,601,594, so Wal-Mart became the number one discount store. In 1995, Kmart sales were $34,389,000 (up $2,319,000 or 7.2% over FY 1990) and Wal-Mart's sales were $93,627,000 (up $61,025,406 or 187.2% over FY 1990). During FY 1997, Kmart sales were $32,183,000,000 (up $113,000,000 or .035% over FY 1990) and Wal-Mart's sales were $117,958,000,000 (up $85,356,406,000 or 261.8% over FY 1990).

Exhibit 6   **Consolidated Balance Sheets: Wal-Mart Stores, Inc.**
(Dollar amounts in millions)

Fiscal Year Ending January 31	1998	1997
Assets		
Current assets		
Cash and cash equivalents	$ 1,447	$ 883
Receivables	976	845
Inventories		
At replacement cost	16,845	16,193
Less LIFO reserve	348	296
Inventories at LIFO cost	16,497	15,897
Prepaid expenses and other	432	368
Total current assets	19,352	17,993
Property, plant, and equipment, at cost		
Land	4,691	3,689
Buildings and improvements	14,646	12,724
Fixtures and equipment	7,636	6,390
Transportation equipment	403	379
	27,376	23,182
Less accumulated depreciation	5,907	4,849
Net property, plant, and equipment	21,469	18,333
Property under capital lease		
Property under capital lease	3,040	2,782
Less accumulated amortization	903	791
Net property under capital leases	2,137	1,991
Other assets and deferred charges	2,426	1,287
Total assets	$45,384	$39,604
Liabilities and Shareholders' Equity		
Current liabilities		
Accounts payable	$ 9,126	$ 7,628
Accrued liabilities	3,628	2,413
Accrued income taxes	565	298
Long-term debt due within one year	1,039	523
Obligations under capital leases due within one year	102	95
Total current liabilities	14,460	10,957
Long-term debt	7,191	7,709
Long-term obligations uder capital leases	2,483	2,307
Deferred income taxes and other	809	463
Minority interest	1,938	1,025
Shareholders' equity		
Preferred stock ($.10 par value; 100 shares authorized, none issued)		
Common stock ($.10 par value; 5,500 shares authorized, 2,241		
and 2,285 issued and outstanding in 1996 and 1995, respectively)	224	228
Capital in excess of par value	585	547
Retained earnings	18,167	16,768
Foreign currency translation adjustment	(473)	(400)
Total shareholders' equity	18,503	17,143
Total liabilities and shareholders' equity	$45,384	$39,604

Source: Wal-Mart Stores, Inc., *1998 Annual Report.*

Exhibit 7 11-Year Financial Summary: Wal-Mart Stores, Inc.
(Dollar amounts in millions, except per-share data)

	1998	1997	1996	1995	1994	1993	1992	1991	1990	1989	1988
Net sales	$117,958	$104,859	$93,627	$82,494	$67,344	$55,484	$43,887	$32,602	$25,811	$20,649	$15,959
Net sales increase	12%	12%	13%	22%	21%	26%	35%	26%	25%	29%	34%
Comparative store sales increase	6%	5%	4%	7%	6%	11%	10%	10%	11%	12%	11%
Other income—net	1,341	1,319	1,146	914	645	497	404	262	175	137	105
Cost of sales	93,438	83,510	74,505	65,586	53,444	44,175	34,786	25,500	20,070	16,057	12,282
Operating, selling, and general and administrative expenses	19,358	16,946	15,021	12,858	10,333	8,321	6,684	5,152	4,070	3,268	2,599
Interest costs											
Debt	555	629	692	520	331	143	113	43	20	36	25
Capital leases	229	216	196	186	186	180	153	126	118	99	89
Provision for income taxes	2,115	1,794	1,606	1,581	1,358	1,171	945	752	632	488	441
Minority interest and equity in unconsolidated subsidiaries	(78)	(27)	(13)	4	(4)	4	(1)	—	—	—	—
Net income	3,526	3,056	2,740	2,681	2,333	1,995	1,609	1,291	1,076	838	628
Per share of common stock											
Net income—basic and diluted	$1.56	1.33	1.19	1.17	1.02	.87	.70	.57	.48	.37	.28
Dividends	0.27	0.21	.20	.17	.13	.11	.09	.07	.06	.04	.03
Financial Position											
Current assets	$19,352	$17,993	$17,331	$15,338	$12,114	$10,198	$8,575	$6,415	$4,713	$3,631	$2,905
Inventories at replacement cost	16,845	16,193	16,300	14,415	11,483	9,780	7,857	6,207	4,751	3,642	2,855
Less LIFO reserve	348	296	311	351	469	512	473	399	323	291	203
Inventories at LIFO cost	16,497	15,897	15,989	14,064	11,014	9,268	7,384	5,808	4,428	3,351	2,652

Net property, plant, and equipment and capital leases	23,606	20,324	18,894	15,874	13,176	9,793	6,434	4,712	3,430	2,662	2,145
Total assets	45,384	39,604	37,541	32,819	26,441	20,565	15,443	11,389	8,198	6,360	5,132
Current liabilities	14,460	10,957	11,454	9,973	7,406	6,754	5,004	3,990	2,845	2,066	1,744
Long-term debt	7,191	7,709	8,508	7,871	6,156	3,073	1,722	740	185	184	186
Long-term obligations under capital leases	2,483	2,307	2,092	1,838	1,804	1,772	1,556	1,159	1,087	1,009	867
Shareholders' equity	18,503	17,143	14,756	12,726	10,753	8,759	6,990	5,366	3,966	3,008	2,257
Financial Ratios											
Current ratio	1.3	1.6	1.5	1.5	1.6	1.5	1.7	1.6	1.7	1.8	1.7
Inventories/working capital	3.4	2.3	2.7	2.6	2.3	2.7	2.1	2.4	2.4	2.1	2.3
Return on assets [1]	8.5%	7.9%	7.8%	9.0%	9.9%	11.1%	12.0%	13.2%	14.8%	14.6%	13.7%
Return on shareholders' equity [2]	19.8%	19.2%	19.9%	22.8%	23.9%	25.3%	26.0%	27.7%	30.9%	31.8%	31.8%
Other Year-End Data											
Number of domestic Wal-Mart stores	1,921	1,960	1,995	1,985	1,950	1,848	1,714	1,568	1,399	1,259	1,114
Number of domestic Supercenters	441	344	239	147	72	34	10	9	6	3	2
Number of domestic SAM's Club units	443	436	433	426	417	256	208	148	123	105	84
International units	601	314	276	226	24	10	—	—	—	—	—
Number of associates	825,000	728,000	675,000	622,000	528,000	434,000	371,000	328,000	271,000	223,000	183,000
Number of shareholders	245,884	257,215	244,483	259,286	257,946	180,584	150,242	122,414	79,929	80,270	79,777

Notes:
1. Net income before minority interest and equity in unconsolidated subsidiaries/average assets.
2. Net income/average shareholders' equity.

Source: Wal-Mart Stores, Inc., *1998 Annual Report.*

Wal-Mart's sales increases over seven years were 755.3 times that of Kmart. Wal-Mart had 1,721 stores in FY 1990, while Kmart had 2,350 stores. In FY 1997, Wal-Mart had 3,406 stores, while Kmart had 2,136 stores.

References

"A Supercenter Comes to Town," *Chain Store Age Executive* (December 1989), pp. 23–30+.

Michael Barrier, "Walton's Mountain," *Nation's Business* (April 1988), pp. 18–20+.

Joan Bergman, "Saga of Sam Walton," *Stores* (January 1988), pp. 129–130+.

Karen Blumenthal, "Marketing with Emotion: Wal-Mart Shows the Way," *Wall Street Journal* (November 20, 1989), p. B3.

Arthur Bragg, "Wal-Mart's War on Reps," *Sales & Marketing Management* (March 1987), pp. 41–43.

Molly Brauer, "Sam's: Setting a Fast Pace," *Chain Store Age Executive* (August 1983), pp. 20–21.

Pat Corwin, Jay L. Johnson, and Renee M. Rouland, "Made in U.S.A.," *Discount Merchandiser* (November 1989), pp. 48–52.

"David Glass's Biggest Job Is Filling Sam's Shoes," *Business Month* (December 1988), p. 42.

Christy Fisher and Patricia Sternad, "Wal-Mart Pulls Back on Hypermart Plans," *Advertising Age* (February 19, 1990), p. 49.

Christy Fisher and Judith Graham, "Wal-Mart Throws 'Green' Gauntlet," *Advertising Age* (August 21, 1989), pp. 1+.

Johnathan Friedland and Louise Lee, "The Wal-Mart Way Sometimes Gets Lost in Translation Overseas," *Wall Street Journal* (October 8, 1997), pp. A1, A12.

"Glass Is CEO at Wal-Mart," *Discount Merchandiser* (March 1988), pp. 6+.

Kevin Helliker, "Wal-Mart's Store of the Future Blends Discount Prices, Department-Store Feel," *Wall Street Journal* (May 17, 1991), pp. B1, B8.

Kevin Helliker and Bob Ortega, "Falling Profit Marks End of Era at Wal-Mart," *Wall Street Journal* (January 18, 1996), p. B1.

John Huey, "America's Most Successful Merchant," *Fortune* (September 23, 1991), pp. 46–48+.

Jay L. Johnson, "Are We Ready for Big Changes?" *Discount Merchandiser* (August 1989), pp. 48, 53–54.

Jay L. Johnson, "Hypermarts and Supercenters—Where Are They Heading?" *Discount Merchandiser* (November 1989), pp. 60+.

Jay L. Johnson, "Internal Communication: A Key to Wal-Mart's Success," *Discount Merchandiser* (November 1989), pp. 68+.

Jay L. Johnson, "The Supercenter Challenge," *Discount Merchandiser* (August 1989), pp. 70+.

Kevin Kelly, "Sam Walton Chooses a Chip Off the Old CEO," *Business Week* (February 15, 1988), p. 29.

Dick Kerr, "Wal-Mart Steps Up 'Buy American,'" *Housewares* (March 7–13, 1986), pp. 1+.

Louise Lee, "Discounter Wal-Mart Is Catering to Affluent to Maintain Growth," *Wall Street Journal* (February 7, 1996), p. A1.

Louise Lee and Joel Millman, "Wal-Mart to Buy Majority Stake in Cifra," *Wall Street Journal* (June 4, 1997), pp. A3+.

"Management Style: Sam Moore Walton," *Business Month* (May 1989), p. 38.

Barbara Marsch, "The Challenge: Merchants Mobilize to Battle Wal-Mart in a Small Community," *Wall Street Journal* (June 5, 1991), pp. A1, A4.

Todd Mason, "Sam Walton of Wal-Mart: Just Your Basic Homespun Billionaire," *Business Week* (October 14, 1985), pp. 142–143+.

Emily Nelson, "Wal-Mart to Build a Test Supermarket in Bid to Boost Grocery-Industry Share," *Wall Street Journal* (June 19, 1998), p. A4.

"Our People Make the Difference: The History of Wal-Mart," Video Cassette (Bentonville, AR: Wal-Mart Video Productions, 1991).

Tom J. Peters and Nancy Austin, *A Passion for Excellence* (New York: Random House), pp. 266–267.

Cynthia Dunn Rawn, "Wal-Mart vs. Main Street," *American Demographics* (June 1990), pp. 58–59.

Sharon Reier, "CEO of the Decade: Sam M. Walton," *Financial World* (April 4, 1989), pp. 56–57+.

"Retailer Completes Purchase of Wertkauf of Germany," *Wall Street Journal* (December 31, 1997), p. B3.

Howard Rudnitsky, "How Sam Walton Does It," *Forbes* (August 16, 1982), pp. 42–44.

Howard Rudnitsky, "Play It Again, Sam," *Forbes* (August 10, 1987), p. 48.

"Sam Moore Walton," *Business Month* (May 1989), p. 38.

Francine Schwadel, "Little Touches Spur Wal-Mart's Rise," *Wall Street Journal* (September 22, 1989), p. B1.

Kenneth R. Sheets, "How Wal-Mart Hits Main St.," *U.S. News & World Report* (March 13, 1989), pp. 53–55.

Sarah Smith, "America's Most Admired Corporations," *Fortune* (January 29, 1990), pp. 56+.

Alison L. Sprout, "America's Most Admired Corporations," *Fortune* (February 11, 1991), pp. 52+.

"The Early Days: Walton Kept Adding 'a Few More' Stores," *Discount Store News* (December 9, 1985), p. 61.

Shannon Thurmond, "Sam Speaks Volumes About New Formats," *Advertising Age* (May 9, 1988), p. S-26.

Vance H. Trimble, *Sam Walton: The Inside Story of America's Richest Man* (New York: Dutton, 1990).

"Wal-Mart Spoken Here," *Business Week* (June 23, 1997), pp. 138+.

Wal-Mart Stores, Inc., *1996 Annual Report,* Bentonville, AR.

Wal-Mart Stores, Inc., *1997 Annual Report,* Bentonville, AR.

Wal-Mart Stores, Inc., *1998 Annual Report,* Bentonville, AR.

"Wal-Mart's 'Green' Campaign To Emphasize Recycling Next," *Adweek's Marketing Week* (February 12, 1990), pp. 60–61.

"Wal-Mart Rolls Out Its Supercenters," *Chain Store Age Executive* (December 1988), pp. 18–19.

"Wal-Mart: The Model Discounter," *Dun's Business Month* (December 1982), pp. 60–61.

"Wal-Mart to Acquire McLane, Distributor to Retail Industry," *Wall Street Journal* (October 2, 1990), p. A8.

"Wholesale Clubs," *Discount Merchandiser* (November 1987), pp. 26+.

"Work, Ambition—Sam Walton," Press Release, Corporate and Public Affairs, Wal-Mart Stores, Inc.

Jason Zweig, "Expand It Again, Sam," *Forbes* (July 9, 1990), p. 106.

Nordstrom Inc., 1998

Stephen E. Barndt

INTRODUCTION

Nordstrom, a Seattle-based fashion specialty retail chain, operated 67 apparel, accessory, and shoe department stores; 24 clearance and discount clothing stores; and five small specialty stores in Alaska, Arizona, California, Colorado, Connecticut, Georgia, Hawaii, Illinois, Indiana, Maryland, Michigan, Minnesota, New Jersey, New York, Ohio, Oregon, Pennsylvania, Texas, Utah, Virginia, and Washington.

The company attained a position of leadership and an outstanding reputation for service. Salesperson attention to the customer, selection of goods, product return policy, and amenities to make shopping an enjoyable experience were acknowledged to be extraordinary in the industry. Capitalizing on this trend-setting customer service to differentiate itself from competition, Nordstrom grew aggressively while major competing chains did not.

After many years as a regional retail chain servicing the Northwest states, in the late 1970s Nordstrom started a major expansion into California and Utah. Growth in the Northern and Southern California areas was steady through the 1980s, and in 1988 the company started a move from Western regional focus to that of a national retailer with the opening of a store in Virginia. With expansion of stores, net sales grew 1,209% from fiscal year 1980 through 1997. Sales in fiscal year 1997 approximated $4.85 billion.

COMPANY HISTORY [1]

John W. Nordstrom immigrated to the United States from Sweden in 1887 at the age of 16 and worked for a number of years as a logger, miner, and laborer. After earning $13,000 gold mining in the Klondike, he settled in Seattle where, in 1901, he opened a shoe store in partnership with shoemaker Carl Wallin. In 1923 Wallin and Nordstrom opened a second store in Seattle. John Nordstrom's three sons bought his interest in the store in 1928 and Carl Wallin's in 1929, establishing a tradition of "family" ownership and management.

In the early years under John Nordstrom, two basic philosophies were developed that guided business practice. The first was a customer orientation in which the company emphasized offering outstanding service, selection, quality, and value. The second was a policy of selecting managers from among employees who had experience on the sales floor. All of the Nordstrom family members who attained management positions started their careers as salesmen.

Rapid growth did not begin until after World War II. Starting an expansion in 1950

This case was prepared by Professor Stephen E. Barndt of Pacific Lutheran University, with the assistance of Pinda Ratanachan. This case was edited for SMBP–7th Edition. Copyright © 1998 by Stephen E. Barndt. Reprinted by permission.

Exhibit 1 Growth, 1977–1998: Nordstrom, Inc.

Year Ending January 31	Number of Company-Operated Stores	Total Square Footage
1978	24	1,446,000
1979	26	1,625,000
1980	29	1,964,000
1981	31	2,166,000
1982	34	2,640,000
1983	36	2,977,000
1984	39	3,213,000
1985	44	3,924,000
1986	52	4,727,000
1987	53	5,098,000
1988	56	5,527,000
1989	58	6,374,000
1990	59	6,898,000
1991	63	7,655,000
1992	68	8,590,000
1993	72	9,224,000
1994	74	9,282,000
1995	76	9,998,000
1996	78	10,713,000
1997	83	11,754,000
1998	92	12,614,000

Source: Nordstrom, Inc., *1985, 1986, 1987, 1989, 1992, 1993, 1994, 1995, 1996,* and *1997 Annual Reports.*

with the opening of two new stores, growth continued so that by 1961 there were eight shoe stores and 13 leased shoe departments in Washington, Oregon, and California.

In 1963, Nordstrom diversified into women's fashion apparel with the acquisition of Best's Apparel and its stores in Seattle and Portland. Before the 1960s ended, five new Nordstrom Best stores offering clothes, shoes, and accessories had been opened.

The 1970s saw additional changes and rapid, steady growth. Management was passed to the third generation of Nordstroms in 1970, and the company went public in 1971, accompanied by a change in name to Nordstrom, Inc. Continued growth in the Northwest provided the company with 24 stores by 1978. Geographical expansion to California began in 1978. By 1987, Nordstrom's Southern California presence was reflected in its position of first or second in market share for women's suits, women's blazers, men's tailored pants, women's dresses, women's coats, women's shoes, and men's shoes in the Los Angeles market.[2] By 1998, Nordstrom operated 25 large specialty department stores and six Nordstrom Rack discount stores in California. National expansion had begun in 1988 with the opening of a store in Virginia and by 1997 another 29 had been opened in the East and Midwest. The Rack line of stores was started in 1983 and had grown to 22 stores in 1997. Exhibit 1 shows the growth in Nordstrom stores during the 20 years ended January 31, 1998. During 1997, Nordstrom opened three main stores, two Racks, two Faconnable boutiques, two shoe stores, and expanded two Racks. In early 1998, another two main stores and two new Racks were opened.

THE FASHION SPECIALITY RETAIL INDUSTRY

Fashion specialty goods include apparel, shoes, and accessories. The market for apparel, shoes, and accessories was relatively mature, with a 1987 through 1996 ten-year growth rate approximating 4.4%. Through most of the 1980s, sales growth averaged 7% per year but recession and changes in consumer spending resulted in an overall growth in apparel sales of less than 3% in four of the five years between 1990 and 1995. In 1996, total U.S. sales of apparel, shoes, and accessories were $113.7 billion. Women's apparel and accessories accounted for 29.3% of the total, and shoes another 16.9%. Men's and boy's wear sales amounted to 9%.[3]

The fashion goods market was segmented into several imprecise levels of perceived quality and price. The custom-made goods market was at the high end, followed by designer/style-setting goods, then popular mid-priced goods, and finally the low-priced utility goods market.

Through the 1980s, the aging of the population into higher income categories, economic prosperity in general, and increased representation of women in the workforce and in higher salaried positions resulted in greater appeal of the higher quality, style-setting fashions. Retailers that catered to market segments, such as fashion-conscious women who desired upscale goods, did well.

In the 1990s, three conditions combined to reduce the nature and growth of the fashion apparel retail segment. First, consumers had become more value (quality and price) conscious and were less willing to pay high prices for clothes. Second, an aging population, although it had more to spend, tended to spend a lower proportion of its income on clothing. Third, a trend had developed toward more casual dress, requiring less be spent to maintain a useful wardrobe of clothing.[4]

The 1990s also saw change in consumer preference among distribution channels. The heightened interest in value for the money coupled with a lower level of interest in shopping around for bargains had increased the popularity of everyday low-priced stores such as factory outlets and warehouse clubs. In addition, many consumers became less interested in store shopping, switching to more convenient at-home shopping via catalogs and interactive media.

COMPETITION

Fashion retailing had traditionally been a very competitive field with stores relying heavily on differentiation through an emphasis on quality, service, or other means of adding value. Competitors included traditional department stores, e.g. Lazarus, Macy's, Bloomingdale's, May, and Jordan Marsh; general merchandise chain stores, e.g., Sears, K-Mart; specialty retailer chains, e.g., The Gap, The Limited, Brooks Brothers, and Nordstrom; cut-price outlets, e.g., Filene's Basement; and independent boutiques.

Most retailers positioned themselves to serve a single segment of the market. Many department stores were exceptions, offering stylish fashions "upstairs" and discounted standard or clearance goods in their bargain basement departments. Exhibit 2 provides a general view of the kinds of retailers that tended to serve the various market segments and what they offered.

Competition was often intense with rivals in close proximity to one another. This was especially true for firms located in shopping malls. Nordstrom, which catered to the upscale, fashion-conscious market, was located in malls and downtown shopping dis-

Exhibit 2   Competitor Specialization by Segment

Market Segment	Types of Stores Serving the Segment	Emphasis in Marketing
Custom	Independent specialty shops	One of a kind, quality
Style-setting/fashion conscious	Upscale fashion specialty chains, boutiques	Name, quality, service
Popular, mid-priced	Department stores, independent and chain specialty stores	Availability, variety, price, service
Low-priced	Discount department stores, general merchandisers	Price, accessibility, convenience

tricts. As a consequence, Nordstrom was typically in face-to-face competition with a number of strong, major competitors. For example, in its California markets, a Nordstrom store was likely to face several of the following competitors: Macy's, Broadway, Neiman Marcus, and Saks Fifth Avenue. The Tysons Corner, Virginia, store competed directly with Macy's, Bloomingdale's, and Saks Fifth Avenue. The Fashion Valley, California, store competed with Neiman Marcus, Saks, Macy's, and Robinson-May. All of these competitors were major chain department stores or chain specialty stores. Of course, Nordstrom also faced competing independent boutiques and specialty stores in all of its locations.

The Federated and May Department Store chains, as well as Nordstrom, were commited to growth. Federated and May planned to build new stores and remodel or close others. Federated budgeted $525 million for capital improvements in and expansion of its Macy's and Bloomingdale's stores prior to 2000, and May Department Stores planned to spend $2 billion to add 125 new stores within five years.

Prior to 1990, when the economy was strong, discount clothing retailers did not present a direct competitive threat as they served a distinctly different market segment. Under conditions of economic recession, customers who suffer loss or uncertainty of income tend to become more price sensitive. When this happens, fashion clothing customers may become more cautious in their spending and more price-value (rather than quality-value) conscious. As a result, fashion retailers lose sales because of both nonspending and switching to cut-price retailers. This is what happened starting in 1990. Nordstrom was particularly hard hit because 42% of its square footage was in California (in 1995), a state with severe economic woes that continued through the mid 1990s. In the post-1990 period, as the recession receded, it appeared that the foothold the price-value retailers had established in the apparel market was not going to go away. Many consumers continued to shop the off-price stores for quality, branded apparel at low prices.

COMMON INDUSTRY PRACTICES

Generally the apparel retailing market was saturated with numerous competitors vying for customers. Low profits, low growth, consolidation, and restructuring were common outcomes.

Although fashion retailers did not all follow the same strategies, several popular strategic moves had been widely followed to varying degrees. These included market segmentation, selective location, growth through acquisition, cost containment, and price discounting.

In the 1980s, most fashion retailers focused on a single market segment. The higher priced, higher quality stylish market was particularly attractive because of the greater growth in this segment and the higher margins available on such goods. This attractiveness led some firms to establish new lines of focused stores and others to refocus current stores. Each of these alternatives presented disadvantages. Developing new retail lines can require considerable capital for new business startup or acquisition of existing businesses. Refocusing had been difficult for many because an identity, once established, is difficult to change. For example, Sears, long a retailer of low-priced and popular fashions, initially clouded its image and confused potential customers when it tried to upgrade its product offerings.

In contrast to focusing on single market segments, many department stores sought further market diversification in order to serve higher income customers without losing others. This diversification involved creating stores within a store with departments divided into mini boutiques each aimed at a specific fashion niche.

Another market diversification move aimed at competing for the value-conscious customer. Outlet malls began taking business away from traditional shopping malls. As a consequence, some large mid to high-end retailers opened clearance stores to compete. Macy's, Saks Fifth Avenue, Bloomingdale's, Neiman Marcus, and Nordstrom were among those operating cut-price outlets.[5]

A shift in shopping from neighborhood and downtown locations to suburban and urban shopping malls made locating stores in malls or close proximity thereto essential. Picking the malls and other locations that were attractive with respect to customer demographics and then gaining access to needed square footage were key factors for success. Firms that gained the new prime locations in growing areas tended to have significant advantages over competitors with older stores in declining shopping areas.

In the mature fashion market with low market growth, companies that desired growth had to capture the business of competitors. This often involved attempting to entice competitors' customers through superior marketing. Or, alternatively, it involved acquiring going-concern competitors to gain market share or broader segment coverage. The latter, a growth through acquisition strategy, had been widely followed in the industry. Federated Department Stores, The Limited, May Department Stores, and Carter Hawley Hale Stores, among others, engaged in significant use of acquisition for growth.

Rapid expansion through acquisition left many chains in debt and strapped for cash. For example, Campeau Corporation, which owned Allied Stores and Federated Department Stores, entered bankruptcy in late 1989 and subsequently sold its Bullocks and I. Magnin chains to Macy's and its Filene's chain to May Department Stores. Later, as the recession reduced cash flow, the Carter Hawley Hale and Macy's department store chains were also forced into Chapter 11 bankruptcy. The Campeau Corporation's former department store chains emerged from bankruptcy in 1992, as an independent Federated Department Stores, Inc. Then, late in 1994, Federated acquired Macy's and, in 1996, acquired Broadway's chain of 82 stores.

Aside from such drastic measures as divestiture, debt-laden firms were commonly in a perpetual search for ways to reduce operating costs. They also tended to be conservative, not investing in innovation or taking major risks. Many such firms were followers, only attempting to duplicate the moves of a competitor after those moves have been proven successful.

Price competition was common, especially among department stores. This included constant rounds of sale prices, in place of stocking top-of-the-line goods, to lure customers. Such heavy reliance on price discounting to increase sales rather than on enhanced merchandising and marketing was reflected in price-oriented advertising.

Lower prices (with lower margins), in general, and heavy debt burdens, in particular, drove many of the larger corporations toward cost reduction. Because labor and inventory were major cost categories, they became the target of cutbacks. Among many stores, inventories were maintained at low to moderate levels and emphasized a limited breadth of fast turnover styles. Labor cost reduction affected direct selling and support. Sales cost reductions were achieved by replacing commission pay with straight hourly wages, increased use of relatively inexperienced, lower paid salespeople, and a reduction of work hours and, therefore, the size of the on-duty sales force. At the same time, some competitors such as Federated and May had consolidated, standardized, and centralized buying and warehousing functions to further reduce costs.

The 1990s saw increased emphasis on private-label merchandise that could be sold at lower prices without sacrificing profit margins. However, by the late 1990s, shoppers were demanding more nationally branded products.

NORDSTROM STRATEGIC POSTURE

Although Nordstrom's greatest appeal had been to college-educated women aged 50 to 64 with household incomes in excess of $50,000, it was focusing on attracting 25 to 30 year olds.[6]

The Nordstrom strategy emphasized merchandise and service tailored to appeal to the affluent and fashion-conscious shopper without losing its middle-class customers. The large Nordstrom specialty department stores catered to their target market with an unparalleled attention to the customers, guaranteed service, and a wide and deep line of merchandise. The success of this strategy made the company one that competitors feared and attempted to follow. Its competitive strength was implied in the statement that "Nordstrom is sometimes known as the 'Black Hole' into which shoppers disappear, never to enter nearby stores."[7]

Store architecture and merchandise differed from store to store. Each was custom-designed to fit lifestyles prevailing in the local geographic and economic environment. In every location, merchandise selection, local tastes, and customer preferences helped shape the store looks on the inside. For example, the downtown San Francisco and Seattle stores provided their mainstay clientele, the upscale professionals, with large men's clothing and accessories selections.

In addition to its mainline stores, Nordstrom also operated 23 Nordstrom Rack stores, one Last Chance cut-price clearance store, three Faconnable boutiques, and two small shoe stores.

The Racks served as discount outlets offering clearance merchandise from the main stores plus some merchandise purchased directly from manufacturers. They catered to bargain shoppers who valued Nordstrom quality.

Starting in 1994, Nordstrom diversified into the shop-at-home market through catalog and e-mail sales. Both catalog and e-mail sales featured Nordstrom quality goods and personal service as well as convenience.

The company had tried and abandoned two business ventures. After many years of operation, Nordstrom closed its small Place Two youth fashion chain. Three of the four Place Two stores were closed in 1994 and the last one in 1995. In addition, Nordstrom Factory Direct, a discount store featuring close-out merchandise and Nordstrom label products, was converted to a Rack.

Product Lines

Nordstrom's specialty department stores carried focused lines of classically styled, relatively conservative merchandise. A *New York Times* writer described the merchandise as "primarily classic and not trendy, the selection limited to styles with broad appeal."[8]

Approximately 70% of the merchandise featured was available at all Nordstrom stores, while the other 30% was unique to each store or region.[9] Women's fashions accounted for the largest share of the Nordstrom product line. However, men's wear appeared to be gaining in emphasis in some locations. For example, men's wear made up 18% of the inventory and 21% to 22% of total sales in the downtown San Francisco store.[10] This contrasted with a 17% share of sales from men's wear company-wide. Exhibit 3 shows the company-wide sales breakdown by merchandise category.

Nordstrom carried both designer and private label merchandise. As stated by one analyst, Jennifer Black Groves, "they really have focused on finding a balance in the business between novelty and basics, private label versus brands."[11] Private and exclusive labels were carried on 25% of the merchandise. Men's apparel and men's and women's shoes were the largest private label lines where approximately 50% of men's clothes and 25% of shoes carried the Nordstrom name. Beginning in the early 1990s, the company began placing more emphasis on developing exclusive brands of quality clothing. In addition to the Nordstrom brand, company stores offered Classiques, Callaway Golf, Entier, Evergreen, Faconnable, Hickey Freeman, and Greta Garbo company-exclusive brands.

Designer lines made up the bulk of the merchandise. Nordstrom featured apparel lines by Gianfranco Ferre, Carolina Herrera, Donna Karan, Calvin Klein, Anne Klein, Christian Lacroix, Claude Montana, Thierry Mugler, Carolyne Roehm, Gianni Versace, and Vera Wang among others in its various stores. The Faconnable line of men's wear was sold throughout the chain. Selection of lines and styles was largely based on wants indicated in direct customer feedback.

The company kept alert to changes in both taste for and profitability of its product offerings. It had a history of change. If a new line of merchandise appeared to better serve customers than an existing one, Nordstrom did not hesitate to make the switch. For example, the company closed out its fur salons and converted the space into departments carrying more profitable merchandise such as large-size women's apparel. Subsequently three of the new stores in the Midwest region opened fur salons to cater to customer demand.

The volume of its orders allowed Nordstrom to develop a broad base of 12,000 to 15,000 suppliers. No one supplier had significant bargaining power.

In mid 1996, Nordstrom changed the merchandise mix in most of its women's apparel departments in response to changing customer profiles and vendor product offerings. Although management believed these changes would better position women's apparel departments for future growth, they resulted in sales decreases in many of the departments. These decreases offset increases in other areas of business. In addition, portions of Nordstrom's holiday merchandising strategy were not executed as well as planned. Nordstrom was continuing to evaluate its merchandise mix to meet customers' changing needs and increase sales.[12]

The major 1996 merchandise reconfiguration that involved shifting familiar lines of women's apparel to different departments confused customers. In addition, the company was slow in bringing in hot-selling brands such as Lauren by Ralph Lauren. It also changed some of its private label designs, appealing to some customers but turning off others.[13]

Exhibit 3   Merchandise Sales by Category: Nordstrom, Inc.

Merchandise Category	Share of 1997 Sales (%)
Women's Apparel	36
Women's Accessories	20
Shoes	20
Men's Apparel and Furnishings	18
Children's Apparel and Accessories	4
Other	2

Source: Nordstrom, Inc., *1995 Annual Report.*

In 1997, most of Nordstrom's merchandising problems were corrected. Merchandise relayout was complete and more major brand apparel was being stocked.

Merchandising

Nordstrom's merchandising was noted for its extensive inventories and dedicated, help-ful salesforce. However, Nordstrom also differed from rivals in several other ways.

The typical store had 50% more salespeople on the floor than similar sized competi-tors. The salesforce used its product knowledge to show appropriate merchandise to customers, assist them in their selections, and suggest accessories. Salespeople kept track of their regular customers' fashion tastes and sizes and then called them or sent notes about new merchandise in which they might have an interest.

The company carried a very large inventory, providing an unusually wide selection of colors and sizes. Average inventory cost of $65 per square foot at Nordstrom com-pared to $40 and less than $30 per square foot at May and Federated, respectively.[14] With an inventory almost twice as large per square foot as its department store competitors, Nordstrom had a depth of inventory almost comparable to smaller specialty stores while offering a more complete line. As an indication of the inventory intensity, the San Fran-cisco Center (downtown) store had $100 million invested in opening day inventory, in-cluding 100,000 pairs of shoes, 10,000 men's suits, and 20,000 neckties.

Nordstrom was one of the industry leaders in dividing its stores into small bou-tiques featuring targeted merchandise mixes. Rather than featuring a single type of merchandise, departments offered a variety of items, e.g., coats, suits, or dresses, all keyed to a particular lifestyle. Departments were added or changed to serve evolving customer needs. For instance, in response to growth in the number of women in higher level management positions, women's tailored clothing departments were added. Al-though designer fashions were generally not given special treatment in display, the company introduced special departments to display some of its higher priced designer apparel.

Luxurious settings that used polished wood and marble were used in place of the chrome and bright colors common in competing stores. Merchandise was arranged in departments according to lifestyles. Stores featured clusters of antiques and open dis-plays of merchandise usually arranged at right angles to each other. Mannequins were used sparingly. A piece of antique furniture was a more commonly used display prop. Merchandise was displayed without bulky anti-theft tags. In addition, there was no closed-circuit television, presenting a less intimidating atmosphere to customers. In-stead, Nordstrom relied on the presence of its large salesforce to discourage theft.

Nordstrom spent less on advertising than was commonly spent by its competitors. The company relied heavily on word of mouth to attract customers. The advertising that was used emphasized styles and breadth of merchandise selection rather than price.

Pricing

Prices were competitive with comparable merchandise. Nordstrom followed the same mark-up practices common to retail fashion stores, but prices tended to be high, reflecting the company's selectivity in providing high-quality merchandise. However, they were committed to providing value and not being undersold on their merchandise. If a customer found an item carried by Nordstrom for sale cheaper at another store, Nordstrom matched that lower price.

Consumer caution in spending during the recession that started at the end of the 1980s placed downward pressure on prices in the industry. Nordstrom responded with a shift to a greater share of value-priced merchandise. A major means of providing lower priced, quality merchandise was the substitution of Nordstrom private and exclusive-label goods for branded goods. This value-pricing strategy continued through the 1990s.

Customer Service

High inflation in the 1970s and significant increases in the cost of goods and labor caused most department stores and specialty retailers to cut services to prevent prices from skyrocketing and to remain competitive with the discount retailers that had become popular. This period of rising costs forced consumers to accept the decrease in service in exchange for affordable prices.

Under recent conditions of lower inflation and higher incomes, the public raised its expectations of service. Many Americans became tired of self-service or inattentive sales help. Two-income households and busy professionals became hooked on convenience and were willing to pay for it. At the same time, retailers who shifted to lower levels of customer service had difficulty in upgrading service. Understaffing in sales positions and overwork coupled with low pay and lack of a career path did not provide the conditions necessary to motivate employees to improve service.

Nordstrom never cut service and therefore did not have to overcome structural, motivational, or cultural barriers to provide satisfying service. The company was already there—it was the undisputed leader in customer service. Nordstrom's excellent service was anchored on the salesforce and supported by company policy and investment in facilities and personnel.

At Nordstrom, a customer could expect to be in a department no longer than two minutes before a salesperson appeared to answer questions, explain merchandise, and make suggestions. This salesperson was prepared to escort the customer to merchandise in other departments to help find what he or she wanted and then process the sale all at once. As an example of this kind of service, a sales representative showed up at a Nordstrom store as it opened at 9:30 A.M. The sales representative, who was dressed in jeans and complementary casual attire, explained that she needed to be completely outfitted so that she could make a sales presentation at a college over an hour away in two hours. She had arrived in town with only her briefcase. An airline had misdirected her luggage. A sales clerk helped her select a suit and then brought merchandise to fill out the outfit from other departments including such items as shoes, hose, a slip, blouse, and scarf. The sales clerk also facilitated opening a charge account to make the purchase possible. The sales representative left Nordstrom 45 minutes later attired for her presentation.

Sales clerks routinely attended customers in dressing rooms, bringing them alternative items of apparel or sizes to try on. They also routinely sent thank you notes and announcements of sales and arrival of merchandise they thought would be of interest to the customer. Other examples of the extraordinary out-of-the-way types of service that had been noted of Nordstrom sales personnel included warming up customer's cars on cold days, paying parking tickets for customers who couldn't find legal parking, personal delivery of items to the customer's home, and ironing a newly bought item of apparel so the customer could wear it back to work.

Nordstrom also offered a personal shopper service. This service freed the customer from the time and effort to travel through various departments and select items. The personal shopper, working from the customer's shopping list, visited departments, selected candidate items of merchandise, accumulated them, and held them for the customer's review and purchase at a convenient time.

Extraordinary service stemmed from several mutually supportive factors. First, the number of salespeople on the floor was high—50% higher than was common. This meant the sales clerks were not so rushed and had the time to wait on customers. Second, the salesforce was carefully recruited. Third, pay was higher than in comparable positions elsewhere and, in addition, was partly based on performance (volume of sales). This meant that the sales clerk who satisfied customers earned more. In addition, there was a kind of peer pressure to sell more (satisfy more customers) because those who earned more were seen as role models. Last, Nordstrom had a powerful corporate culture that stressed attentiveness to the customer. This culture was well established, having been instituted under John W. Nordstrom and reinforced ever since.

The company had been successful in transferring this culture to its new stores at their start up. A key practice in establishing the Nordstrom culture in new stores was to open them under the leadership of a cadre of experienced Nordstrom managers and salespeople who provided guidance and training to the locally hired personnel. For example, when Nordstrom opened a new store in Indianapolis, about 50 of 500 employees were moved from other Nordstrom stores.

In keeping with the feeling that the customer was "queen or king" and was always right, Nordstrom had a no-questions-asked merchandise return policy. The company willingly replaced or refunded the price of any item of merchandise whether new or used, with or without a sales receipt. Probably the best known of many refund folklore tales was the case where an individual, who had bought a pair of tires from the same store when it was under other ownership, returned them to Nordstrom for a refund. The purchase price of the pair of tires was refunded even though Nordstrom did not and never had sold tires.

Luxurious settings and furnishings made the shopper feel special. Standard extras in many of the stores included a musician playing enjoyable music on a baby grand piano, free coat and package checking, play areas for children, extra large dressing rooms, free gift wrap at the cash register, and tea for weary customers as they tried on apparel in the dressing rooms. Newer, larger stores featured even more extras. For example, the San Francisco Center store had a beauty treatment spa, four restaurants, a pub in the men's department, and valet parking to help it differentiate itself from competition. The remodeled and enlarged Bellevue Square store featured a mother's room, where a mother could nurse a child in private. The store's new English style restaurant provided customers waiting for a table a pager to beep them back from shopping when their table was ready.[15] All new stores routinely featured family restrooms where a parent could take a child of the opposite sex.

The company also had its own Nordstrom charge card and a Nordstrom VISA card to make buying more convenient for its customers and, at the same time, generate additional revenue. The Nordstrom VISA offered rebates on total annual store purchases of $1,000 or more, starting at 1% and reaching 5% for $5,000 or more in sales.

Location

Nordstrom targeted growing affluent communities with long-term economic growth prospects and strong shopping environments for its stores. Although the majority of its stores were located in suburban shopping centers, others were located in large and small city central business districts. In either type of location, Nordstrom chose to locate close to other retailers because of the drawing power of a concentration of shopping facilities. Exhibit 4 shows the locations and size of the company's stores in May 1998.

As a late entrant in many regions, e.g., the East, Midwest, and Southern and Northern California, Nordstrom had an advantage in its selection of store sites in growing high-income areas. Early entrant chains often found themselves doing business in outdated stores in older, less economically attractive areas. However, the industry was mature with most attractive shopping districts saturated with retailers. Finding locations attractive for growth with adequate available square footage required buying out competitors or a geographically extended search. Following its coverage of virtually all major Pacific Northwest markets in the 1970s and very early 1980s, Nordstrom channeled its growth to California. By the late 1980s, Nordstrom had covered most of the attractive California markets, limiting its further growth there. This forced the company to search for expansion opportunities in several other geographical regions. Nordstrom began opening stores in a number of selected locations spread across the East, Northeast, South-central, Midwest, Southeast, and Intermountain West regions. Such growth was opportunistic involving new shopping mall space in growth areas or occupancy of vacated space in older shopping centers. An example of the latter was Nordstrom's entry into the Paramus, New Jersey, market in a store vacated when May Department Stores closed its Hahne's chain.

Seven distribution centers were located in regions to serve stores. These included distribution centers opened in Maryland and Iowa to serve the growing number of stores in surrounding states.

Shopping at Home

In 1993, Nordstrom established an independent Direct Sales Division to provide its quality products and services to a growing shop-at-home segment.

The company launched a 68-page catalog featuring a broad spectrum of Nordstrom private label and designer styles in January 1994. Catalog personal shoppers were used to handle customers' questions and orders via a toll-free 24-hour-a-day telephone number. Orders were shipped from a Cedar Rapids, Iowa, warehouse by Federal Express or the U.S. Postal Service and included free gift boxes. All packages were packed with a return label for no-cost return should the customer be dissatisfied. The company planned to issue new catalogs about six times a year. Nordstrom claimed the catalog venture was successful in its first year with 300,000 customers from across the United States.[16] Later, in 1995, Nordstrom added another catalog targeted to men. In 1997, the direct sales catalog division grew 51% to sales of $156 million.[17]

In 1997, the company instituted e-mail sales. Customers could communicate through e-mail to their personal shopper who, as the single point of contact, provided information on available merchandise, took orders, and kept them advised of newly arrived items that might be of interest.

Exhibit 4 Nordstrom Stores

Type	Store Location	State	Square Feet	Year Started
Nordstrom	Seattle/downtown	WA	245,000	1963
Nordstrom	Portland/Lloyd	OR	150,000	1963
Nordstrom	Seattle/Northgate	WA	122,000	1965
Nordstrom	Portland/downtown	OR	174,000	1966
Nordstrom	Tacoma	WA	134,000	1966
Nordstrom	Bellevue	WA	285,000	1967
Nordstrom	Seattle/Southcenter	WA	170,000	1968
Nordstrom	Yakima	WA	44,000	1972
Nordstrom	Spokane	WA	121,000	1974
Nordstrom	Tigard	OR	189,000	1974
Nordstrom	Anchorage	AK	97,000	1975
Nordstrom	Vancouver	WA	71,000	1977
Nordstrom	Costa Mesa	CA	235,000	1978
Nordstrom	Lynnwood	WA	127,000	1979
Nordstrom	Brea	CA	195,000	1979
Nordstrom	Salt Lake City	UT	140,000	1980
Nordstrom	Salem	OR	71,000	1980
Nordstrom	Clackamas	OR	121,000	1981
Nordstrom	Murray	UT	110,000	1981
Nordstrom	San Diego	CA	156,000	1981
Nordstrom	Cerritos	CA	122,000	1981
Nordstrom	San Matro	CA	149,000	1982
Nordstrom	Ogden	UT	76,000	1982
Rack	Costa Mesa	CA	50,000	1983
Rack	Clackamas	OR	28,000	1983
Nordstrom	Glendale	CA	147,000	1983
Nordstrom	Walnut Creek	CA	193,000	1984
Nordstrom	Palo Alto	CA	187,000	1984
Nordstrom	Canoga Park	CA	154,000	1984
Nordstrom	San Diego	CA	130,000	1984
Rack	Woodland Hills	CA	48,000	1984
Rack	San Diego	CA	57,000	1985
Rack	Lynwood	WA	25,000	1985
Nordstrom	Redondo Beach	CA	161,000	1985
Nordstrom	San Diego	CA	151,000	1985
Nordstrom	Corte Madera	CA	116,000	1985
Nordstrom	Los Angeles	CA	150,000	1985
Nordstrom	Montclair	CA	133,000	1986
Nordstrom	Escondido	CA	156,000	1986
Rack	Portland	OR	19,000	1986
Rack	Chino	CA	30,000	1987
Nordstrom	Santa Ana	CA	169,000	1987
Rack	Colma	CA	31,000	1987
Rack	Seattle	WA	42,000	1987
Nordstrom	Santa Clara	CA	165,000	1987
Nordstrom	San Francisco Center	CA	350,000	1988
Nordstrom	San Francisco	CA	174,000	1988
Nordstrom	McLean	VA	253,000	1988
Nordstrom	Sacramento	CA	190,000	1989
Nordstrom	Arlington	VA	241,000	1989

(continued)

Exhibit 4   Nordstrom Stores (continued)

Type	Store Location	State	Square Feet	Year Started
Rack	Bellingham	WA	20,000	1990
Nordstrom	Paramus	NJ	272,000	1990
Rack	San Leandro	CA	44,000	1990
Nordstrom	Santa Barbara	CA	186,000	1990
Rack	Prince William	VA	46,000	1990
Nordstrom	Pleasanton	CA	173,000	1990
Nordstrom	Riverside	CA	164,000	1991
Nordstrom	Edison	NJ	266,000	1991
Nordstrom	Bethesda	MD	225,000	1991
Nordstrom	Oak Brook	IL	249,000	1991
Rack	Salt Lake City	UT	31,000	1991
Rack	Silver Spring	MD	37,000	1992
Nordstrom	Freehold	NJ	174,000	1992
Nordstrom	Bloomington	MN	240,000	1992
Rack	Towson	MD	31,000	1992
Nordstrom	Towson	MD	205,000	1992
Last Chance	Phoenix	AZ	26,000	1992
Faconnable	New York	NY	10,000	1993
Rack	Philadelphia	PA	43,000	1993
Nordstrom	Annapolis Mall	MD	162,000	1994
Nordstrom	Skokie	IL	209,000	1994
Nordstrom	Arcadia	CA	151,000	1994
Rack	Schaumburg	IL	45,000	1994
Rack	Auburn	WA	48,000	1995
Nordstrom	Indianapolis	IN	216,000	1995
Nordstrom	Millburn	NJ	188,000	1995
Nordstrom	White Plains	NY	219,000	1995
Nordstrom	Schaumburg	IL	215,000	1995
Nordstrom	Dallas	TX	249,000	1996
Nordstrom	Littleton	CO	245,000	1996
Nordstrom	King of Prussia	PA	238,000	1996
Nordstrom	Troy	MI	258,000	1996
Rack	Northbrook	IL	40,000	1996
Rack	Factoria	WA	46,000	1997
Faconnable	Beverly Hills	CA	17,000	1997
Nordstrom	Beachwood	OH	231,000	1997
Faconnable	Costa Mesa	CA	8,000	1997
Rack	Hempstead	NY	48,000	1997
Nordstrom	Garden City	NY	241,000	1997
Nordstrom	Farmington	CT	189,000	1997
Shoe Store	Ala Moana	HI	8,000	1997
Shoe Store	Ala Moana	HI	14,000	1997
Nordstrom	Atlanta	GA	243,000	1998
Nordstrom	Overland Park	KS	219,000	1998
Rack	Hillsboro	OR	51,000	1998
Rack	Bloomington	MN	41,000	1998

Source: Nordstrom, Inc., *1997 Annual Report*

Nordstrom was interested in gaining an early entry in interactive electronic media that allowed it to provide personalized selling including a single point of contact personal shopper who developed knowledge of the customer's size, color, and style preferences. To further this end, Nordstrom Personal Touch America, an electronic mail shopping service, was introduced in 1994. Media tests included offering merchandise sales via Internet and interactive TV systems. Shopping via two-way television was tested on systems from US West in Omaha, Nebraska, and Bell Atlantic in Fairfax County, Virginia.[18] Such systems let the customer talk with a salesperson, asking questions and specifying wants or needs, be shown appropriate merchandise on the TV screen, and place an order using a menu on the screen.[19]

MANAGEMENT AND ORGANIZATION

Nordstrom reflected the importance it placed on serving the customer with an inverted pyramid of role importance. Sales and sales-support people had the most important roles and were at the top of the pyramid. Department managers were next with the role of supporting the salespeople. Merchandise managers, buyers, and store managers followed in importance as they carried out functions helping the department managers. The senior executives and the board of directors who were furthest removed from the customer were at the bottom. Nordstrom operationalized its inverted pyramid concept with selective centralized and decentralized decision making. Strategic and significant financial decisions were made at the top level in the organization, and operational decisions were made at the region, store, and department level. The managers in each region, store, and department had responsibility and accountability for profit or costs. They were given the autonomy and authority to make decisions regarding their area. This decentralized management allowed managers to be entrepreneurially creative in tailoring each store's merchandise and layout to its customers. Free of decision making for regional and store operations, top management was able to concentrate on growth issues.

The management hierarchy, shown in Exhibit 5, could be described in terms of three levels of responsibility: top or executive level, mid level, and store level. The top level consisted of the chairman of the board, 45-year-old John J. Whitacre, and six co-presidents, who were the fourth generation of Nordstroms. The chairman had strategic management responsibility, concentrating on setting the strategic direction and major expansion decisions. The co-presidents, Blake W. Nordstrom, 37, Erik B. Nordstrom, 34, J. Daniel Nordstrom, 35, James A. Nordstrom, 36, Peter E. Nordstrom, 35, and William E. Nordstrom, 34, each oversaw one or more of nine business operating units. In addition, John Nordstrom, 60, Bruce Nordstrom, 64, and brother-in-law John A. McMillan, 66, who had earlier served as co-chairmen, remained on the board and served as its executive committee.

The mid-management level comprised the general managers in charge of the nine autonomous business operating units, divisional merchandise managers, regional managers, and various corporate staff officers in charge of merchandise categories, store planning, operations, information services, human resources, legal, and other functions. Structuring the corporation into nine operating units was implemented in early 1998. The nine operating units consisted of:

- Northwest Stores
- California Stores
- East Coast Stores

Exhibit 5   Management Structure: Nordstrom, Inc.

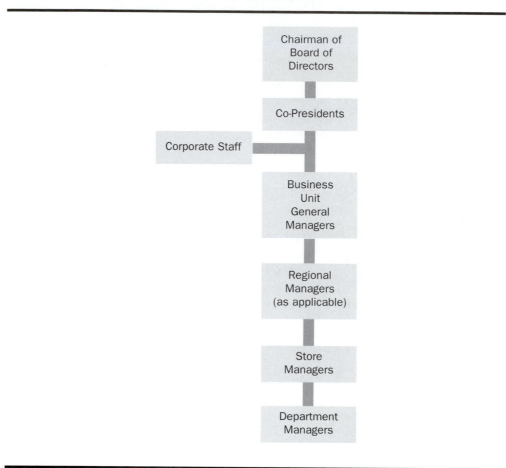

- Midwest Stores

- Rack Clearance and Off-Price Stores

- Direct (Catalog) Sales

- Faconnable Boutiques

- Nordstrom Product Group (that developed and oversaw manufacture of company private-brand products)

- Nordstrom National Credit Bank

Each business unit developed its own planning strategy and, when applicable, had its own group of buyers.

Operational management of the stores was the responsibility of store managers with the assistance of their staff and department managers. Stores and departments had their own buyers, although buyers at the business unit level took over some buying to gain purchasing economies.

Throughout the company, idea generation and operational decision making were encouraged, expected, and supported at the lowest levels where the individual had the appropriate information. Managers in the sales departments routinely made decisions on what inventory to carry and whether to accept checks, lower prices to stay competitive, and accept returned merchandise, without consulting higher level managers or staff specialists.

Units and the individuals in them were goal-driven. As stated by Richard Stevenson in a *New York Times Magazine* article, "the life of a Nordstrom salesperson is defined by goals. Departmental, storewide, and company goals. Qualitative and quantitative goals."[20] Store goals were set for the year and both reflected and influenced departmental goals. Department goals influenced salesperson goals. Yearly goals were translated into monthly goals. Daily goals were more changeable and reflected pro rata accomplishment of monthly goals as well as historical performance. On a daily basis, departments aimed to surpass sales of the same day last year by a set level and individual goals were adjusted accordingly. If the department was behind in reaching its monthly goal, the daily goals of the department and each sales clerk were likely to be pegged higher to get back on track.

Salespeople and sales departments were kept aware of the level of their goal accomplishment and were provided rewards for goal achievement. Salespeople were reminded of the day's goal and could be asked during the day how they were doing. Reaching goals was praised and when longer term goals, e.g., annual personal goals, were achieved, recognition was public, often in the form of an announcement or letter from an executive. Top performing salespeople were admitted to the Pacesetters' Club. Pacesetters received a certificate, a new "Pacesetter" business card, a 33% discount on Nordstrom merchandise (rather than the standard 20%), and a night on the town.

The company also promoted performance and conformity to its standards of customer service through the widespread use of heroics. The exploits of employees who made unusual or extraordinary efforts to please customers or who had specially noteworthy levels of sales were communicated through the organization, formally and informally, so that they might serve as role models. This technique, along with the use of goals, served as a powerful indicator of the kinds of behavior the company wanted and rewarded.

HUMAN RESOURCES

Nordstrom had approximately 41,000 year-long full- or part-time employees in addition to seasonal hires. The company liked to hire young people who had not learned behaviors inconsistent with the Nordstrom customer service values and then start them in sales positions. The actual decision of who to hire was left to the sales department managers rather than to a staff personnel department. The company's hiring practice, in conjunction with its major expansion, had left the company with a workforce that was relatively young and often college educated. Even its mid- and top-level managers were young. Top managers were in their mid 30s to mid 40s. Mid-level vice-presidents ranged in age from mid 30s to mid 50s.

The company followed a promote-from-within policy. Because the company was growing fast, this served as a motivator to those who aspired to rapid advancement. Promotions to line management positions were made from among employees with sales and customer contact experience. Those who were promoted to higher level positions were encouraged and expected to keep in contact with customers. For example, the company's buyers, who all started in sales positions, spent a large amount of their time on the sales floor to learn what the customers wanted.

Acceptable behavior was not narrowly specified. For the most part, the culture took care of that. Employees were given basic guidance in a short, one page 5" × 8" employee handbook on card stock that said:

> Our number one goal is to provide
> **outstanding customer service.**
> Set both your personal and
> professional goals high.
> We have great confidence in your
> ability to achieve them.
> Nordstrom Rules:
> Rule #1: **Use your good
> judgment in all situations.**
> There will be no additional rules.[21]

Initial training was brief, taking about one and a half days, and stressed product knowledge and how to work cash registers and attend the customer. Formal indoctrination took the form of reading a handbook and either viewing a videotape or listening to a lecture on the company's history.

Other expectations were transmitted in various ways and would bring on corrective actions if violated. One of these was dress. Employees were expected to wear neat business attire. Further, it was understood that the attire *should* be acquired from Nordstrom. Personal business, including telephone calls, was not to be conducted in a customer area. Abuse of employee discount privileges, violation of criminal law, rudeness to a customer, and unacceptable personal conduct were grounds for immediate dismissal. In addition, sales personnel were under constant pressure to achieve the high sales levels expected of them. An article in *Planning Review* highlighted the use of pressure for sales performance: "Twice each month all employees' sales per hour are publicly posted by department, with their names ranked in order from worst to best. If employees miss their quota three months in a row they are dismissed."[22] Underperforming employees usually left on their own as did those who were uncomfortable with constant pressure to meet goals and be nice to the customer no matter what the customer did or how he or she behaved. The remaining employees were loyal to the company and accepting of its cultural values.

To motivate its salesforce, Nordstrom used goals, heroics, recognition, and promotion from within as already discussed. Additional major motivational forces were monetary compensation and morale boosting and attitude shaping programs.

High pay was a very important factor in attracting, retaining, and motivating employees. Base pay ranged from about $5 to $11 per hour plus commissions of 6.75% to 13%. Above average salespeople could earn $75,000 to $80,000 per year.[23] With these kind of earnings, Nordstrom's sales employees' compensation was high relative to the rest of the industry.

Commission pay tied rewards directly to sales and customer service performance. The higher the sales to satisfied customers, the greater the reward. Since returned merchandise was subtracted from the sales clerk's sales and therefore decreased commission income, selling for the sake of a sale alone was discouraged.

Monetary rewards and public recognition were supplemented with motivational speeches and skits, along with pep-talk meetings. The objectives of these techniques were to build employees' confidence in their ability to perform to higher limits, in general, and to get them worked up to capitalize on the selling opportunities associated with one of the major annual sales, in particular.

With its high level of compensation and culture that emphasized the employee and her or his contributions, Nordstrom was ranked among the better employers. The company attempted to make union representation unnecessary and unattractive. The only locations where employees had been represented by a union was the western part of Washington State. From mid 1989, Nordstrom was engaged in an open dispute with locals 1001 and 367 of the United Food & Commercial Workers Union. The union, through these locals, represented approximately 2,000 Nordstrom employees. After a long and bitter contest, Nordstrom employees elected to decertify local 1001 in 1991. A year later, in 1992, local 367 withdrew its representation on the eve of a decertification election when it was clear the union would lose.

Most of Nordstrom's customers were female and, as might be expected, so were most of its employees. Female employees made up 70% of the workforce, and the company was moving toward more female and minority representation in managerial positions. Although the co-chairman and the co-presidents were men, 43% of the other officers of vice-president or higher level and 61% of store managers were women. Minority persons represented 31% of total employment and 20% of management in 1995 as contrasted with 27% and 16% in 1992.[24] In 1997, 34% of the employees and 22% of the managers were minorities. Five of the nine business unit managers were women.[25]

THE NORDSTROM IMAGE

Nordstrom was well known as a premium service retailer. Its reputation for service and selection of merchandise provided the company with a mystique. As a result, Nordstrom received a great deal of favorable free publicity. New store openings were preceded with numerous articles in the local press that helped create perceptions that Nordstrom offered a superior shopping experience. Continuing favorable reports in the media reinforced that perception. The company was consistently rated high and usually highest in customer satisfaction in surveys such as the Retail Satisfaction Index and Consumer Reports. For example, in a *Women's Wear Daily* survey, Nordstrom was rated highest in customer service, ambience, and exchange and third in variety, selection, quality, and fit.[26] The press had published these ratings, reinforcing the idea that Nordstrom provided superior service.

Although much publicity had been favorable, several unfavorable charges and accusations surfaced. These included labor union allegations of wrongdoing and black-interest charges of discrimination.

In late 1989, the United Food & Commercial Workers Union charged that Nordstrom encouraged its salespeople to work "off the clock," taking inventory, writing thank you notes, making home deliveries, or tracking down hard-to-find garments over the phone. Thus the union was claiming that salespeople spent time working for the company for which they were not compensated. The Washington State Department of Labor and Industries subsequently found Nordstrom in violation of state wage laws and directed the company to reimburse workers for work performed without pay. The union followed up with a class action lawsuit on behalf of 50,000 past and present Nordstrom employees in Washington, Oregon, California, Utah, Alaska, and Virginia seeking compensatory damages and penalties. Without admitting guilt, the company agreed to pay back wages and legal fees to qualifying present and former employees.[27]

The union also engaged in an attempt to discredit Nordstrom's image with customers. The union alleged the company required its employees to wear garments it was promoting during work hours, then allowed putting the merchandise back on the rack, sometimes without cleaning. Subsequently Oregon sued Nordstrom for selling used lipstick, shoes, and other merchandise at its Oregon stores. Without admitting any wrongdoing, Nordstrom settled the suit with Oregon, paying the state $25,000.[28] The company claimed its employees were encouraged but not required to wear Nordstrom clothing. The Nordstrom clothing they wore must have been purchased. Employees could buy their clothing at a discount.

In an unrelated incident, a sales clerk in a California Nordstrom store filed a lawsuit alleging that Nordstrom invaded her privacy through use of a hidden video camera placed in a small room used by some employees to change clothes and relieve themselves. Nordstrom contended that the room was not an employee lounge and the camera was there to monitor a safe containing high-value merchandise.[29]

In 1992, the company was targeted by African American interests. First, seven blacks filed a class action lawsuit claiming discrimination against blacks in recruitment, hiring, and promotion. Subsequently a group calling itself People Against Racism at Nordstrom (PARAN) targeted Nordstrom for a national boycott based on the allegations of discrimination.[30] Later, another six plaintiffs entered the lawsuit. However, by late 1992, twelve had withdrawn. Another lawsuit was filed in 1995 by ten African Americans alleging racial discrimination at the Arden Fair store in Northern California.[31] Nordstrom denied the allegations of discrimination.

In spite of union and black interest charges, Nordstrom was generally considered to be a good community citizen. It had a record of supporting social program fund raising in its communities. For example, in its hometown, it provided the Seattle Housing Group with $4.7 million, more than half the cost to build a 100-unit low-income housing project.

Nordstrom started a "Healthy Beginnings" free program to help expectant mothers avoid risks to themselves and their pregnancies. Under the program, they received educational materials, pregnancy risk screenings, a toll-free hot line, and a Nordstrom gift certificate.[32] Within the company, Nordstrom introduced a family leave program in 1991, allowing up to 12 weeks of unpaid leave to care for newborn or newly adopted children or seriously ill family members.

Nordstrom was a leader in catering to people with disabilities. In 1992, the company was awarded an "Excellence in Access Award" for making its stores accessible to disabled customers and providing special services to them. Also in 1992, Nordstrom received an EDI (Equality/Dignity/Independence) award from the National Easter Seal Society for featuring models with disabilities in its catalogs.[33] Then, in 1993, Nordstrom won a state award for trying to eliminate barriers in its stores and for using models with disabilities in advertising.[34]

Support for minorities and women included a vendor program that, since its inception, had spent $ 1.4 billion for products and services from minority and women-owned businesses. The company also sponsored more than 50 charity events per year that promoted diversity and benefited minority organizations.[35] Nordstrom received recognition for outstanding efforts to recruit and promote employees of color, as a top company in policies toward women in the workplace, and as one of the 100 best companies offering employment opportunities for Hispanic people. Further, Nordstrom claimed it employed a greater percentage of African Americans in every region where it did business than that minority's share of the population.[36] Many special and minority interest groups supported and praised Nordstrom for its efforts.

The company established business practice guidelines for its vendors and monitored their compliance. The guidelines covered adherence to laws, health and safety standards, environmental protection, and employment practices including use of child and forced labor.[37]

FINANCIAL POSITION

Over the 10-year period from February 1988 through January 1998, Nordstrom experienced continuous growth in sales. Net earnings were less consistent, trending upward in fiscal years 1988, 1991 through 1994, and in 1997 but dropping in the other years (see Exhibit 6). Fiscal year 1988, ending January 31, 1989, was the best year of the 10 in terms of return on sales and equity, and was second to fiscal year 1994 in return on assets.

While the company had been profitable every year, it suffered reduced profitability in relative and absolute terms starting in its fiscal year 1989. A continuing recession in California, where Nordstrom had 38% of its square footage (on January 31, 1991), was one major factor explaining the reduced profitability. Profits suffered in two ways. Growth in sales was less than in the years prior to the recession and competition for customers forced price markdowns. As a consequence, overall sales per store continued to climb but at a reduced rate, and net earnings per store declined relative to FY 1988 and 1994, the best of the 10 years from 1988 through 1997. As shown in Exhibit 7, earnings per store in FY 1989 through 1993 failed to continue the upward climb started in 1986. Although 1994 showed a substantial improvement, as sales and company efficiency improved, performance deteriorated again in 1995. The company attributed the poorer profitability in FY 1995 to slowing demand and a decrease in sales in stores open at least 14 months, reduced sales at several stores as a result of new store openings in the same markets, high operating costs associated with the direct mail catalog business, and higher interest expenses from borrowing to finance customer accounts receivable associated with its Nordstrom VISA card.[38]

Net earnings and earnings per store declined further in 1996 for several reasons. First, the company's changes in its merchandise were not well received and shifting various lines of clothing among departments confused customers. As a consequence, sales of women's apparel was weak. Second, higher markdowns resulting from the need to reduce the inventory of low-demand merchandise reduced profit margins. Third, the company was slow to bring in high-demand, designer-brand products, again losing sales. Fourth, new stores in the Chicago and New Jersey markets cannibalized sales in earlier stores in those markets. Fifth, the company experienced higher expenses associated with developing company-branded products and higher bad debt charge-offs as the VISA card grew in acceptance.[39]

The company was one of the leaders in sales per square foot, a key measure of efficiency in the industry. In 1994, the department store industry averaged $179 in sales per square foot. Although Nordstrom was not directly comparable to general department stores because it sold only apparel, shoes, and accessories that can be densely stocked, it could be compared to specialty stores. In 1994, specialty stores averaged $233 in sales per square foot.[40] Ann Taylor Stores sold $576 per square foot in fiscal year 1993, while The Gap sold $463 and the Limited sold $278.[41] As shown in Exhibit 8, Nordstrom stores averaged $381 in its fiscal year 1992, $383 in 1993, $395 in 1994, $382 in 1995, $377 in 1996, and $384 in 1997. Many of the company's new stores exceeded $400 per square foot in their first year. The company's best sales of $600 per square foot was reached at the South Coast Plaza store in 1987. Nordstrom stores also got off to a quicker start than was common. "On the average, it takes a Nordstrom store between one and two years before it reaches chainwide sales per square foot performance. This compares to an industry average of about five years."[42] Although Nordstrom's per-foot sales increased on both real and constant dollar bases through January 31, 1990, the following years did not show a continuation of the trend.

In 1996, net earnings per store decreased, while the number of stores increased.

Exhibit 6   **Average Per-Store Performance: Nordstrom, Inc.**
(Dollar amounts in thousands)

Fiscal Year	Number of Stores	Net Sales per Store	Net Earnings per Store
1983	39	$19,710	$1,032
1984	44	21,788	925
1985	52	25,036	963
1986	53	30,753	1,376
1987	56	34,290	1,656
1988	58	40,137	2,126
1989	59	45,273	1,948
1990	63	45,935	1,838
1991	68	46,762	1,997
1992	72	47,527	1,897
1993	74	48,513	1,898
1994	76	51,243	2,671
1995	78	52,737	2,117
1996	84	53,651	1,777
1997	92	52,735	2,024

Source: Nordstrom, Inc., *Annual Reports,* 1987 through 1997.

These new stores were generally not as productive as Nordstrom's average store because the customer base and traffic patterns are developed over time.[43]

Efforts to improve profitability included both cost cutting and revenue enhancement. The company undertook a systematic attack on inventory costs through information transfer. It instituted management information systems to improve its inventory ordering and vendor service. Its inventory management system and electronic data interchange let suppliers and Nordstrom buyers communicate and obtain updated information about inventories, status of orders, and payments. Buyers could initiate reorders through the system. Sales demand was tracked by item by store, identifying the level and location of inventories, and initiating transfer of inventory between locations. As a result of the various improved inventory control practices, fiscal year 1994 gross margins were up two percentage points over fiscal year 1993.[44] However, coincident with sales that were lower than expected in 1995, inventories became excessive and selling, general, and administrative expenses became underabsorbed, eroding the gross margin.

Merchandise margins decreased again in 1996 due to higher markdowns, which resulted from the merchandise changes in the company's apparel departments, a lower markup, and sales that were below expectations.[45]

Nordstrom spent considerably less on advertising than was common among competitors. As compared to an industry average of 4% of sales, Nordstrom spent only a little more than 2% (2.4% in 1997) on advertising. The low level of advertising expenditures allowed the company to pay more in salesperson compensation without eroding profit margins. One reason that Nordstrom got by with less advertising is that it was able to capitalize on the mystique created by the many feature articles that were written about the company and its services.

To increase sales in an otherwise depressed market in the 1990s, the company shifted to more lower priced merchandise. This was largely carried out by replacing

Exhibit 7 Statement of Profit and Earnings, FY 1987–97: Nordstrom, Inc.
(Dollar amounts in thousands, except per-share data)

Fiscal Year Ending January 31	1998	1997	1996	1995	1994	1993	1992	1991	1990	1989	1988
Net sales	$4,851,624	$4,453,063	$4,113,517	$3,894,478	$3,589,938	$3,421,979	$3,179,820	$2,893,904	$2,671,114	$2,327,946	$1,920,231
Costs and expenses											
Cost of sales and related buying and occupancy	3,295,813	3,082,037	2,806,250	2,599,553	2,469,304	2,339,107	2,169,437	2,000,250	1,829,383	1,564,056	1,300,883
Selling, general, and administrative	1,322,929	1,217,590	1,120,790	1,025,347	940,579	902,083	831,505	747,770	669,159	582,973	477,488
Net interest	34,250	39,400	39,295	30,664	37,646	44,810	49,106	52,228	49,121	39,977	32,952
Service charge income	(108,581)	(129,469)	(125,130)	(96,644)	(88,509)	(86,140)	(87,443)	(84,660)	(55,958)	(57,492)	(53,825)
Total costs and expenses	4,544,411	4,209,558	3,841,205	3,558,920	3,359,020	3,199,860	2,962,605	2,715,588	2,491,705	2,129,514	1,757,498
Earnings before taxes	307,213	243,505	272,312	335,558	230,918	222,119	217,215	178,316	179,409	198,432	162,733
Income taxes	121,000	96,000	107,200	132,600	90,500	85,500	81,400	62,500	64,500	75,100	70,000
Net earnings	$ 186,213	$ 147,505	$ 165,112	$ 202,958	$ 140,418	$ 136,619	$ 135,815	$ 115,816	$ 114,909	$ 123,332	$ 92,733
Earnings per share ($)	2.40	1.82	2.02	2.47	1.71	1.67	1.66	1.42	1.41	1.51	1.13
Dividends per share ($)	.53	.50	.50	.385	.34	.32	.31	.30	.28	.22	.18
After tax return on sales	.038	.033	.040	.052	.039	.040	.043	.040	.043	.053	.048
Asset turnover	1.69	1.68	1.51	1.62	1.65	1.67	1.56	1.52	1.56	1.54	1.56
Return on assets	.065	.055	.060	.085	.064	.067	.067	.061	.067	.082	.075
Return on equity	.13	.10	.12	.15	.12	.13	.14	.14	.16	.19	.17

Source: Nordstrom, Inc., *Annual Reports*, 1991, 1992, 1994, 1995, 1996, 1997, and 1998.

Exhibit 8   Sales per Square Foot: Nordstrom, Inc.

Year Ending January 31	Sales per Square Foot ($)	Consumer Price Index of Retail Apparel and Upkeep (1982–1984=100)		Sales per Square Foot Corrected for Price Rises ($)
		Year	Index	
1981	$184	1980	90.9	$202
1982	200	1981	95.3	210
1983	205	1982	97.8	210
1984	243	1983	100.2	243
1985	267	1984	102.1	262
1986	293	1985	105.0	279
1987	322	1986	105.9	304
1988	349	1987	110.6	316
1989	380	1988	115.4	329
1990	398	1989	118.6	336
1991	391	1990	124.1	315
1992	388	1991	128.7	301
1993	381	1992	131.9	289
1994	383	1993	133.7	286
1995	395	1994	133.4	296
1996	382	1995	131.9	290
1997	377	1996	131.7	286
1998	384	1997	132.9	289

Notes: Retail apparel price index is a composite including men's and boy's apparel, women's and girl's apparel, infant's and toddler's apparel, footwear, other apparel, and apparel services.

Sources: Nordstrom Inc., *Annual Reports, 1988, 1991, 1995, 1996, 1997,* and *1998;* and U.S. Department of Commerce, *Statistical Abstract of the United States 1996,* p. 483; *Economic Indicators,* February 1998, p. 23; and U.S. Labor Department, *Monthly Labor Review,* June 1995, p. 100, and December 1995, p. 92.

nationally branded merchandise with Nordstrom exclusive brand and private label goods. This allowed selling at lower prices without major reductions in margins.

Another move to boost revenues involved establishing the Nordstrom National Credit Bank in Colorado to issue and service its credit card operations. With a federally chartered national bank, Nordstrom was allowed to charge its cardholders in any state the maximum interest allowed in the state where chartered. The bank did not engage in any checking or saving and loan operations—it only handled credit card operations. In response to customers shifting from use of Nordstrom charge cards to general-purpose cards, e.g., Visa and Mastercard, the company had issued its own co-branded Nordstrom Visa card, starting in 1994.

During 1996, the company's proprietary credit card balances did not increase because of continuing competition from third-party cards. The company also reduced its efforts to promote its VISA credit card because of concerns about rising charge-offs.

The company expected to spend about $650 million on new stores and $200 million on refurbishing existing stores over three years. They used internally generated operating earnings, debt, and proceeds from the sale of common stock to finance such growth. Debt was preferred over equity as a source of capital. However, Nordstrom avoided the high level of debt that plagued many of its competitors. Incremental, store-by-store growth was managed so that only relatively modest increases in debt were needed to supplement operating earnings in financing growth. In fact, Exhibit 9 shows a general decline in use of debt since 1993.

Nordstrom's current ratio hovered near 2.0 from FY 1992 through 1997. Over the 10 years ending January 31, 1998, the current ratio ranged from a low of 1.69 to a high of 2.39. Except for 1997, the quick ratio was in excess of one. In addition, Nordstrom had available a $500 million line of credit to use as liquidity support for short-term debt.

Book value per share of common stock increased steadily from $7.86 in FY 1988 to $19.34 in FY 1997. At the end of FY 1997, 250,000,000 shares of common stock were authorized and 76,259,052 shares were issued. The company repurchased shares in 1995, 1996, and 1997. Exhibit 10 shows total shareholders' equity and other elements of the company's financial structure for the 10 years ending January 31, 1998.

CURRENT INDUSTRY TRENDS

The general trend followed by chain specialty and department stores was to become more like Nordstrom. Nordstrom's success had awakened many of its competitors. They now saw customers' satisfaction with salesforce efficiency, competence, and attitudes as a key success factor in market segments other than the low-price end. This realization prompted competing chains to start switching from an emphasis on rock-bottom costs to one of serving the customers.

Actually improving services was easier said than done. Years of understaffing and lack of attention to the customer resulted in salesforces that were not accustomed to providing excellent service. Efforts to upgrade customer service could clash with the corporate culture that developed in chain stores under these conditions. Changing customer service values was slow and required consistent communication and reinforcement of desired attitudes and behaviors.

The first and most pronounced change introduced in major chains to boost sales and upgrade customer service was the conversion of salespeople's compensation from hourly pay to commissions. The general intent of this change to commissions was to foster greater concern for satisfying the customer and therefore making the immediate and future sales. The following examples illustrate the scale of the trend toward commission pay. Macy's converted stores located in competition with Nordstrom's to commission sales compensation. Carter Hawley Hale Stores had its chains and their stores' salesforce on 100% commission. Prior to entering bankruptcy, Campeau Corporation made plans to have 90% of the salespeople in its Jordan Marsh, Maas Brothers-Jordan Marsh, Stern's, The Bon Marche, Abraham & Straus, Bloomingdale's, Burdines, Lazarus, and Rich-Goldsmith's chains on commission by the end of 1990. Bloomingdale's already had 13 of its salesforces on 100% commission by mid 1989.

Conversion to commission pay was costly initially and payoffs came slowly. However, the payoffs could be significant. For example, one chain reduced its selling costs as a percent of sales by one percentage point, while at the same time increasing sales staff hours by 10%.[46]

Several other trends were less pronounced than the movement to commission pay but had a potential impact on service competitiveness. One was the addition of sales staff. Macy's increased both its salesforce and their training. Macy's also eliminated departments such as home furnishings, linens, housewares, and electronics and replaced them with expanded apparel, shoes, and accessories departments. This is indicative of the movement toward focusing on higher margin and higher priced merchandise,

Exhibit 9 **Liquidity and Debt Ratios, FY 1992–1997: Nordstrom, Inc.**

Year Ending January 31	1998	1997	1996	1995	1994	1993
Current ratio	1.69	1.99	1.94	2.02	2.10	2.39
Quick ratio	.82	1.03	1.19	1.11	1.16	1.34
Long-term debt/equity	.29	.22	.26	.28	.38	.46
Long-term debt/total assets	.15	.12	.13	.16	.20	.23
Total debt/total assets	.48	.45	.48	.44	.46	.49

Note: Total debt is calculated as total liabilities and equity less equity.

Source: Nordstrom, Inc., *Annual Reports,* 1993, 1994, 1995, 1996, 1997, and 1998.

including designer labels. In addition, the consolidation of operations and centralization of selected functions had continued and building medium-sized stores was favored.

As mentioned earlier, fashion retailers had lost sales to outlet stores that offered branded clothing at low prices. Many large department stores and fashion specialty chains had or were opening cut-price outlets to capture the growing price-value segment.

COMPANY PLANS

Growth was expected to continue at the rate of about three to five new large specialty department stores per year (see Exhibit 11). These large stores would range in size from about 150,000 to 250,000 square feet. In addition, approximately 15 more Nordstrom Racks would be opened by 2001. Distribution centers were to be established to serve the stores in geographical areas new to Nordstrom.

Nordstrom had no plans to expand its operations to foreign nations. National expansion was to be targeted at the Mid-Atlantic, Northeast, Southeast, Southcentral, Midwest, and Intermountain West regions.

The company planned to enter a new area and open several stores within a very few years to make more efficient use of the required supporting distribution center and the regional staff. The company also planned to open its new stores under the leadership of experienced employees relocated or promoted from other Nordstrom stores. As in the past, this cadre would be relied on to anchor and communicate the Nordstrom culture.

Within the mainline Nordstrom stores, service, quality, and selection were expected to remain as the major bases of differentiation. Likewise, merchandising was to remain the same except that the company was placing greater emphasis on value merchandise and popular brand names. In early 1998, the company was moving toward increasing its advertising. It started a search for an advertising agency to take on a national branding campaign.

The growth of off-price clothing sales prompted Nordstrom to test that market. Nordstrom tried two different cut-price discount store concepts to specifically cater to the low priced, branded goods market. One was a discount store that carried the Nordstrom name and offered quality Nordstrom private-label merchandise. The Nordstrom Factory Direct store opened in Philadelphia in 1993 but was later closed and converted to a Rack. The second discount-type store carried non-Nordstrom goods and carried a different name. This Last Chance outlet store opened in Arizona in 1993 and continued in operation through 1997.

Exhibit 10 Selected Indicators of Financial Position, FY 1987–97: Nordstrom, Inc.
(Dollar amounts in thousands of dollars)

Year Ending January 31	1998	1997	1996	1995	1994	1993	1992	1991	1990	1989	1988
Cash, prepaid expenses, and miscellaneous current assets	104,504	97,891	92,546	93,892	164,161	98,726	85,516	83,462	71,516	44,262	26,099
Accounts receivable, net	664,448	714,589	893,927	675,891	565,151	584,379	585,490	558,573	519,656	465,929	391,387
Merchandise inventories	826,045	719,919	626,303	627,930	585,602	536,739	506,632	448,344	419,976	403,795	312,696
Total current assets	1,594,997	1,532,399	1,612,776	1,397,713	1,314,914	1,219,844	1,177,638	1,090,379	1,011,148	913,986	730,182
Property, plant, and equipment, net	1,252,513	1,152,454	1,103,298	984,195	845,596	824,141	856,404	806,191	691,937	594,038	502,661
Other assets	17,653	17,654	16,545	14,875	16,971	9,184	7,833	6,019	4,335	3,679	1,424
Total assets	2,865,163	2,702,507	2,732,619	2,396,783	2,177,481	2,053,170	2,041,875	1,902,589	1,707,420	1,511,703	1,234,267
Current liabilities	942,606	769,387	832,313	690,454	627,485	511,196	553,903	551,835	489,888	448,165	394,699
Total long-term debt	420,865	380,632	439,943	373,910	438,574	481,945	—	—	—	—	—
less current portion	(101,129)	(51,302)	(74,210)	(75,967)	(102,164)	(41,316)	—	—	—	—	—
equals LTD due beyond one year	319,736	329,330	365,733	297,943	336,410	440,629	502,199	478,742	440,613	369,520	260,343
Other liabilities	127,763	112,608	111,601	64,586	47,082	49,314	46,542	45,602	43,669	54,077	46,016
Shareholders' equity	1,475,058	1,473,192	1,422,972	1,343,800	1,166,504	1,052,031	939,231	826,410	733,250	639,941	533,209

Source: Nordstrom, Inc., *Annual Reports,* 1988 through 1998.

Exhibit 11   **Planned Additions to Large Specialty Store Chain**

	Location	Open Date	Square Footage (000)
1998			
Downtown Seattle (expand)	Seattle, WA	Aug.	145
Scottsdale Fashion Square	Scottsdale, AZ	Sept.	239
1999			
MacArthur Center	Norfolk, VA	March	160
Fashion Valley (expand)	San Diego, CA	Summer	68
River Park Square	Spokane, WA	Aug.	128
Providence Place	Providence, RI	Sept.	190
Mission Viejo Mall	Mission Viejo, CA	Sept.	180
Columbia Mall	Columbia, MD	Fall	170
2000			
Hurst, TX			
Boca Raton, FL			
Atlanta, GA			
Honolulu, Hawaii			
Columbia, MD			
2001			
St. Louis, MO			
Coral Gables, FL			
Pittsburgh, PA			
Other Possible Future Sites			
Boston			
Cincinnati			
Houston			
Las Vegas			

Nordstrom was committed to its entry in the shop-at-home segment. Catalog sales was well established as a separate organizational unit to provide personalized service. In addition, the company was poised to position itself as a first mover in interactive video. Nordstrom believed that when this medium was perfected and reached more homes, it would have an advantage because of its commitment to exceptional service. As discussed earlier, the company had launched e-mail sales in 1997.

Notes

1. This brief history of Nordstrom draws heavily on Nordstrom's *1987 Annual Report,* pp. 5–12.
2. "Nordstrom's Expansion Blitz," *Chain Store Age Executive* (December 1988), pp. 49–50, 53.
3. "Retailing: General," *Standard & Poor's Industry Surveys* (July 24, 1997), p. 10.
4. "Retailing: General," *Standard & Poor's Industry Surveys* (July 24, 1997), p. 12.
5. Adrienne Ward, "Department Stores Play the Outlet Game," *Advertising Age* (January 27, 1992), p. 56 and Faye Rice, "Haute Discount," *Fortune* (September 20, 1993), p. 16.
6. "Nordstrom, Inc. Opening 16 New Stores Over Next Three Years; Will Target Generation X," *Women's Wear Daily* (October 7, 1996), p. 10.
7. Jan Shaw, "Executives Catch Nordstrom Fever in Opening Week," *San Francisco Business Times* (October 10, 1988), p. 10.

8. Richard W. Stevenson, "Watch Out Macy's, Here Comes Nordstrom," *New York Times Magazine* (August 27, 1989), p. 35.

9. Nordstrom, *1987 Annual Report,* p. 12.

10. Robert Sharoff, "Chicago Seen as Good Move for Nordstrom," *Daily News Record* (January 6, 1989), pp. 2, 11.

11. "The Major Chains: Dominance Through More Doors: Nordstrom," *WWD infotracs Supplement to Women's Wear Daily,* (June 1997), pp. 19+.

12. Nordstrom, *1996 Annual Report,* p. 10.

13. Lee Moriwaki, "Minding Store After Disappointing Financial News, Nordstrom Sets Out to Prove It Hasn't Lost Its Luster," *The Seattle Times* (April 13, 1997), p. E1.

14. Seth Lubove, "Don't Listen to the Boss, Listen to the Customer," *Forbes* (December 4, 1995), pp. 45–46.

15. "Beep Me Up, Nordy," *The Seattle Times* (November 7, 1994), p. E1.

16. Nordstrom, *1994 Annual Report,* p. 8.

17. "Nordstrom to Plant Seeds of Fusion Throughout US," *The Seattle Times* (May 21, 1997), p. D1.

18. "Nordstrom Part of US West Two-Way TV Shopping Test," *The Seattle Times* (July 27, 1994), p. D2; and Michael Krantz, "Trial by Wire," *Mediaweek* (March 20, 1995), pp. 25–28.

19. Sylvia Wieland Nogaki, "Nordstrom Heads Home-Department Store Plans Catalog, TV Shopping Services," *The Seattle Times* (May 18, 1993), p. D1.

20. Stevenson, "Watch Out Macy's," p. 39.

21. *Nordstrom Employee Handbook,* undated.

22. "Nordstrom: Respond to Unreasonable Customer Requests!" *Planning Review* (May/June 1994), p. 18.

23. Seth Lubove, "Don't Listen to the Boss," pp. 45–46.

24. Mary Ann Gwinn, "Nordstrom Succession: Glass Ceiling in Place," *The Seattle Times* (June 25, 1995), p. F1.

25. "Nordstrom Diversity Program Delivers," *Minority Market Alert* (November 1996), p. 8.

26. "Nordstrom chain top-ranked for customer service, ex-change, and ambience," *Women's Wear Daily* (November 25, 1996), p. S-4.

27. "Nordstrom Labor Suit Settled," *Los Angeles Times* (January 12, 1993), pp. D1 and 2.

28. "Nordstrom Settles Merchandise Resale Complaint in Oregon," *Seattle Post Intelligencer* (March 27, 1991), p. B6.

29. "Nordstrom Clerk Sues, Says Store Invaded Her Privacy," *The Seattle Times* (July 8, 1990), p. A7.

30. Debra Prinzing, "Nordstrom and Minorities," *Puget Sound Business Journal* (May 29, 1992), p. 12.

31. "Nordstrom: Discrimination Suit Without Merit," *The Seattle Times* (July 15, 1995), p. C1.

32. "Healthy Beginnings," *The Seattle Times* (December 2, 1991), p. D9.

33. "Nordstrom Receives Easter Seal Award for Innovative Catalogs," *PR Newswire* (September 23, 1992).

34. "Nordstrom Wins State Award for Eliminating Barriers," *The Seattle Times* (November 11, 1993), p. D1.

35. "Nordstrom Diversity Program Delivers," *Minority Markets Alert* (November 1996), p. 8.

36. Debra Prinzing, "Nordstrom and Minorities," p. 12.

37. "Business Digest," *The Seattle Times* (May 12, 1994), p. E2.

38. Nordstrom, *1995 Annual Report.*

39. Nordstrom, *1996 Annual Report.*

40. *Standard & Poor's Industry Surveys* (May 9, 1996), p. R83.

41. Ester Wachs Book, "The Treachery of Success," *Forbes* (September 12, 1994), pp. 88–90.

42. "Nordstrom's Expansion Blitz," *Chain Store Age Executive* (December 1988), p. 50.

43. Nordstrom, *1996 Annual Report,* p. 10.

44. Sylvia Wieland Nogaki, "Inventory, Higher Sales Boost Nordstrom Profits," *The Seattle Times* (February 22, 1995), p. D1.

45. Nordstrom, *1996 Annual Report,* p. 11.

46. "Now Salespeople Really Must Sell for Their Supper," *Business Week* (July 31, 1989), pp. 50, 52.

The Home Depot, Inc. (1998):
Growing the Professional Market

Thomas L. Wheelen, Jay Knippen, Edward S. Mortellaro Jr,. and Paul M. Swiercz

On April 23, 1998, Arthur M. Blank, President and Chief Executive Officer (CEO) was presiding over a strategic planning session for new strategies for each of Home Depot's six regional divisions (see "Organizational Structure") for the professional contractor market. Home Depot's management estimated this market to be $215 billion in 1997. Home Depot has been concentrating on the Do-It-Yourself/Buy-It-Yourself market sector, which Home Depot management had estimated to be $100 billion in 1997. Home Depot sales were $24.1 billion in 1997. Exhibit 1 shows the combined sales for the Do-It-Yourself/Buy-It-Yourself sector and the professional sector to be $365 billion. The heavy industry sector was treated as a separate market sector. In 1998, Home Depot had less than 4% of the $215 billion professional sector.

In early April 1998, the company's management announced a new store format. In 1998, the company planned to build four new smaller stores with about 25% (25,000 square feet) of the existing store size. These stores would be similar to local hardware stores or Ace Hardware stores.

THE HOME DEPOT, INC.

Founded in Atlanta, Georgia, in 1978, Home Depot was the world's largest home improvement retailer and ranked among the 10 largest retailers in the United States. At the close of fiscal year 1997, the company was operating 624 full-service, warehouse-styled stores—555 stores in 44 states and five EXPO Design Center stores in the United States, plus 32 in four Canadian provinces (see Exhibit 2).

The average Home Depot store had approximately 106,300 square feet of indoor selling space and an additional 16,000–28,000 square feet of outside garden center, including houseplant enclosures. The stores stocked approximately 40,000–50,000 different kinds of building materials, home improvement products, and lawn and garden supplies. In addition, Home Depot stores offered installation services for many products. The company employed approximately 125,000 associates, of whom approximately 7,900 were salaried and the remainder of the employees were paid on an hourly basis.

Retail industry analysts had credited Home Depot with being a leading innovator in retailing by combining the economies of warehouse-format stores with a high level of customer service. The company augmented that concept with a corporate culture that valued decentralized management and decision making, entrepreneurial innovation and risk taking, and high levels of employee commitment and enthusiasm.

The stores served primarily the Do-It-Yourself (DIY) repair person, although home

This case was prepared by Professors Thomas L. Wheelen and Jay Knippen of the University of South Florida, Edward S. Mortellaro Jr., DMD, private practice in Periodontics, Brandon, FL., and Professor Paul M. Swiercz of the George Washington University. The authors would like to thank the research assistants, Carla N. Mortellaro and Vincent E. Mortellaro, for their support. This case may not be reproduced in any form without written permission of the copyright holder, Thomas L. Wheelen. This case was edited for SMBP–7th Edition. Copyright © 1999 by Thomas L. Wheelen. Reprinted by permission.

Exhibit 1   **Total Market for Do-It-Yourself/Buy-It-Yourself Sector, Professional Sector, and Heavy Industry Sector**

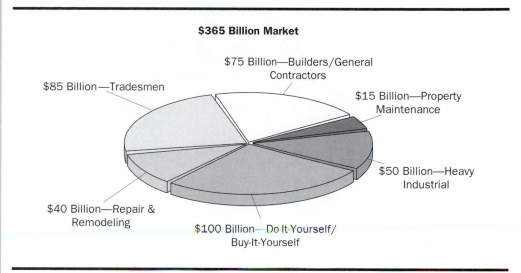

$365 Billion Market

$75 Billion—Builders/General Contractors

$15 Billion—Property Maintenance

$85 Billion—Tradesmen

$50 Billion—Heavy Industrial

$40 Billion—Repair & Remodeling

$100 Billion—Do-It-Yourself/ Buy-It-Yourself

Note: Home Improvement Research Institute, 1997 Product Sales Estimates; U.S. Census Bureau Product Sales Estimates.

Source: The Home Depot, Inc., *1997 Annual Report,* p. 3.

improvement contractors, building maintenance professionals, interior designers, and other professionals have become increasingly important customers.

Home Depot also owned two wholly-owned subsidiaries, Maintenance Warehouse and National Blind & Wallpaper Factory. The company also owned Load 'n Go, an exclusive rental truck service for their customers.

HISTORY [1]

Home Depot's Chairman, Bernard Marcus, began his career in the retail industry in a small pharmacy in Milburn, New Jersey. He later joined the Two Guys Discount Chain to manage its drug and cosmetics departments and eventually became the Vice-President of Merchandising and Advertising for the parent company, Vornado, Inc. In 1972 he moved into the Do-It-Yourself home improvement sector as President and Chairman of the Board at Handy Dan/Handy City. The parent company, Daylin, Inc., was chaired by Sanford Sigoloff. He and Marcus had a strong difference of opinion over control, and one Friday at 5:00 P.M. in 1978, Marcus and two other Handy Dan top executives were discharged.

That weekend, Home Depot was born when the three men—Bernard Marcus, Arthur Blank (who became President of Home Depot), and Ronald Brill (who became Chief Financial Officer)—laid out plans for the Do-It-Yourself chain. Venture capital was provided by investment firms that included Inverned of New York as well as private investors. Two key investors were Joseph Flom, a takeover lawyer, and Frank Borman, then Chairman of Eastern Airlines.

When the first stores opened in Atlanta in 1979, the company leased space in three former Treasury Discount Stores with 60,000 square feet each. All three were suburban

Exhibit 2   Store Locations: Home Depot, Inc.

The Home Depot Canada
32 stores

Western Division
153 stores

Midwest Division
63 stores

Northeast Division
137 stores

Southwest Division
86 stores

Southeast Division
148 stores

Western Division	153
Location	Number of Stores
Arizona	**18**
Phoenix	14
Prescott	1
Tucson	3
California	**96**
Bakersfield	1
Fresno	3
Los Angeles	51
Modesto	1
Sacramento	5
San Diego	11
San Francisco	23
Stockton	1
Colorado	**10**
Colorado Springs	2
Denver	7
Pueblo	1
Idaho	**1**
Boise	1
Nevada	**5**
Las Vegas	3
Reno	2
Oregon	**7**
Eugene	1
Portland	6
Utah	**4**
Salt Lake City	4
Washington	**12**
Seattle/Tacoma	11
Spokane	1

Southeast Division	148
Location	Number of Stores
Alabama	**6**
Birmingham	3
Huntsville	1
Mobile	1
Montgomery	1
Florida	**63**
Daytona Beach/ Melbourne/ Orlando	10
Ft. Lauderdale/Miami/ West Palm Beach	25
Ft. Myers/Naples	6

Ft. Walton	1
Gainesville/Ocala	3
Jacksonville	4
Pensacola	1
Tallahassee	1
Tampa/ St. Petersburg	12
Georgia	**32**
Athens	1
Atlanta	24
Augusta	1
Columbus	1
Dalton	1
Macon	1
Rome	1
Savannah	1
Valdosta	1
Indiana	**1**
Clarksville	1
Kentucky	**3**
Lexington	1
Louisville	2
Mississippi	**1**
Horn Lake	1
North Carolina	**18**
Asheville	1
Charlotte	6
Fayetteville	1
Greensboro/ Winston-Salem	3
Hickory	1
Raleigh	5
Wilmington	1
South Carolina	**7**
Charleston	1
Columbia	2
Greenville/ Spartanburg	4
Tennessee	**17**
Chattanooga	2
Johnson City/ Kingsport	2
Knoxville	3
Memphis	3
Nashville	7

Northeast Division	137
Location	Number of Stores
Connecticut	**13**
Hartford	6

New Haven	3
Danbury/Fairfield/ Norwalk	4
Delaware	**1**
Christana	1
Maine	**2**
Bangor	1
Portland	1
Maryland	**14**
Baltimore	8
Washington, DC area	**6**
Massachusetts	**17**
Boston	13
Southern Mass.	3
Springfield	1
New Hampshire	**4**
Manchester	1
Nashua	1
Portsmouth	1
Salem	1
New Jersey	**25**
Northern New Jersey	19
Southern New Jersey	6
New York	**32**
Albany	2
Buffalo	4
Hudson Valley	4
Johnson City	1
New York City/ Long Island	16
Rochester	3
Syracuse	2
Pennsylvania	**20**
Allentown/ Bethlehem	2
Harrisburg/Reading	3
Philadelphia	10
Pittsburgh	3
Scranton/ Wilkes-Barre	2
Rhode Island	**1**
Warwick	1
Vermont	**1**
Williston	1
Virginia	**7**
Washington, DC area	7

Southwest Division	86
Location	Number of Stores
Arkansas	**2**
Little Rock	2
Illinois	**1**
O'Fallon	1
Kansas	**1**
Kansas City	1
Louisiana	**9**
Baton Rouge	1
Lafayette	1
Lake Charles	1
New Orleans	5
Shreveport	1
Mississippi	**3**
Gulfport	1
Jackson	2
Missouri	**7**
Columbia	1
Kansas City	2
St. Louis	4
New Mexico	**3**
Albuquerque	3
Oklahoma	**6**
Oklahoma City	4
Tulsa	2
Texas	**54**
Austin	5
Beaumont	1
Corpus Christi	1
Dallas/Ft. Worth	21
El Paso	2
Houston	16
Lubbock	1
Midland	1
San Antonio	6

Midwest Division	63
Location	Number of Stores
Illinois	**24**
Chicago	23
Quincy	1
Indiana	**2**
Evansville	1
Hobart	1
Iowa	**1**
Waterloo	1

Michigan	**22**
Detroit	14
Flint/Saginaw	3
Grand Rapids	2
Kalamazoo	1
Lansing	1
Traverse City	1
Minnesota	**10**
Minneapolis/ St. Paul	10
Ohio	**4**
Boardman	1
Cleveland	2
Toledo	1

Home Depot Canada	32
Location	Number of Stores
Alberta	**4**
Calgary	2
Edmonton	2
British Columbia	**8**
Vancouver	8
Manitoba	**1**
Winnipeg	1
Ontario	**19**
Kitchener	1
London	1
Ottawa	2
Toronto	14
Windsor	1

EXPO Design Center	5
Location	Number of Stores
Atlanta	1
Dallas	1
Long Island	1
Miami	1
San Diego	1
TOTAL STORES	**624**

Source: Home Depot, Inc., *1994 Annual Report*, p. 32, and *1997 Annual Report*, p. 36.

locations in the northern half of the city. Industry experts gave Home Depot 10-to-1 odds it would fail.

In 1980, a fourth Atlanta store opened, and the company had annual sales of $22.3 million. The following year, Home Depot ventured beyond Atlanta to open four stores in South Florida and also had its first public offering at $12 a share. By early 1990, its stock had soared by 7,019% and split eight times. In May 1995, an original share was worth $26,300.

In the early 1980s, inflation rose over 13%, and unemployment was as high as 9.5%. These were rough times for most start-up companies, but Home Depot prospered as hard-pressed shoppers sought out the best buy. The company was voted the Retailer of the Year in the home center industry in 1982 and had its first stock splits.

By 1983, Marcus was a nationally recognized leader in the Do-It-Yourself industry. New Orleans was a strong market with many homeowners and young people, so Home Depot moved in with three stores. Other additions were in Arizona and Florida. Two stores opened in Orlando, in the backyard of the Winter Haven–based Scotty's, and one more opened in South Florida. Home Depot's strong drawing power became evident as customers passively waited in long checkout lines.

In 1984, Home Depot's common stock was listed on the New York Stock Exchange. It was traded under the symbol "HD" and was included in the Standard & Poor's 500 Index. Marcus believed about the only restraint Home Depot faced that year was its ability to recruit and train new staff fast enough. However, Home Depot was soon to face other problems. In December, things briefly turned sour when Home Depot bought the nine-store Bowater Warehouse chain with stores in Texas, Louisiana, and Alabama. Bowater had a dismal reputation. Its merchandise didn't match Home Depot's, and nearly all its employees had to be dismissed because they were unable to fit into the company's strong customer service orientation.

Of the 22 stores opened in 1985, most were in eight new markets. Going into Houston and Detroit were moves into less hospitable terrain. The company lost money with promotional pricing and advertising costs. This rapid expansion into unknown territories also took management's attention away from the other stores. The media quickly noted that Home Depot was having problems and suggested that its troubles could be related to rapid expansion into the already crowded home center business. Home Depot's earnings dropped 40% in 1985.

Marcus had to regroup in 1986. He slowed Home Depot's growth to 10 stores in existing markets, including the first super-sized store with 140,000 square feet. Home Depot withdrew from the Detroit market, selling its five new stores. By 1987, six California stores and two Tennessee stores had opened, and the company had sales of $1 billion. In that same year, Home Depot introduced an advanced inventory management system; as a result, inventory was turned 5.4 times a year instead of the 4.5 times for 1986. The company also paid its first quarterly dividend.

In 1988, 21 stores opened, with heavy emphasis in California. For the second time, Home Depot was voted the Retailer of the Year in the home center industry.

Home Depot expanded its market beyond the Sunbelt in early 1989 by opening two stores in the northeast—East Hanover, New Jersey, and North Haven, Connecticut. By the end of the year, there were five stores in the Northeast.

The year 1989 was also a benchmark year for technological developments. All stores began using Universal Product Code (UPC) scanning systems to speed checkout time.

The company's satellite data communications network installation improved management communication and training. Sales for the year totaled $2.76 billion, and plans were made to open its initial contribution of $6 million to the Employee Stock Ownership

Plan (ESOP). On its tenth anniversary, Home Depot opened its 100th store (in Atlanta) and by the year's end had become the nation's largest home center chain.

Thirty stores opened in 1990, bringing the total to 147, with sales of $3.8 billion. The largest store—140,000 square feet—was in San Diego. To handle more volume per store, Home Depot developed and tested a new store productivity improvement (SPI) program designed to make more effective use of existing and new store space and to allow for more rapid replenishment of merchandise on the sales floor. The SPI program involved the renovation of portions of certain existing stores and an improved design for new stores with the goal of enhanced customer access, reducing customer shopping time, and streamlining merchandise stocking and delivery. As part of SPI, the company also experimented with modified store layouts, materials handling techniques, and operations.

Home Depot continued its expansion by opening an additional 29 stores to bring the total number of stores to 174 in 1991, which generated total sales of $5.1 billion. In addition, the company's SPI program proved successful and was implemented in substantially all new stores and in selected existing stores. Home Depot also continued to introduce or refine a number of merchandising programs during fiscal 1991. Included among such programs were the introduction of full-service, in-store interior decorating centers staffed by designers and an expanded assortment in its lighting department. In 1991, management created a new division, EXPO Design Centers. The first store was opened in San Diego. EXPO Design Centers' niche was the extensive use of computer-aided design technology that the store's creative coordination used. It was targeted to upscale homeowners. These features were of assistance to customers remodeling their bathrooms and kitchens. To assist this strategy further, Home Depot offered a selection of major kitchen appliances. The product line offered was the top of the line. This allowed Home Depot to remain a leading-edge merchandiser.

From 1991 through 1995, many of the new merchandising techniques developed for the Home Depot EXPO were transferred to the entire chain. In 1994, the second EXPO store opened in Atlanta and was mostly dedicated to offering design services. The Atlanta store was 117,000 square feet, and the San Diego store was 105,000 square feet. In 1995 these stores were expanded in California, New York, and Texas. This division was expected to grow to 200 to 400 stores.

By the end of fiscal year 1992 Home Depot had increased its total number of stores to 214, with annual sales of $7.1 billion. Earlier that year, the company had begun a company-wide rollout of an enlarged garden center prototype, which had been successfully tested in 1991. These centers, which were as large as 28,000 square feet, featured 6,000- to 8,000-square-foot greenhouses or covered selling areas, providing year-round selling opportunities and significantly expanded product assortment. Also during 1992, the company's "installed sales program," which it began testing in three selected markets in 1990, became available in 122 stores in 10 markets. This program targeted the buy-it-yourself customer (BIY), who would purchase an item but either did not have the desire or the ability to install the item. Finally, the company announced its national sponsorship of the 1994 and 1996 U.S. teams at the Winter and Summer Olympics.

During 1993, Home Depot introduced Depot Diners on a test basis in Atlanta, Seattle, and various locations in South Florida. Depot Diners were an extension of the company's commitment to total customer satisfaction and were designed to provide customers and employees with a convenient place to eat. The company continued to develop innovative merchandising programs that helped to grow the business further. The installed sales program became available in 251 stores in 26 markets, with approximately 2,370 installed sales vendors who, as independent, licensed contractors, were authorized to provide service to customers. By the end of fiscal year 1993, Home Depot had opened an additional 50 stores and sales were $9.2 billion, up by 30% from 1992.

From the end of fiscal year 1989 to the end of fiscal year 1994, the company increased its store count by an average of 24% per year (from 118 to 340) and increased the total store square footage by 28% per year (from 10,424,000 to 35,133,000). Home Depot entered the Canadian market on February 28, 1994. The company entered into a partnership with and, as a result, acquired 75% of Aikenhead's Home Improvement Warehouse. At any time after the sixth anniversary of the purchase, the company had the option to purchase, or the other partner had the right to cause the company to purchase, the remaining 25% of the Canadian company. Home Depot Canada commenced operations with seven stores previously operated by Aikenhead's. Five additional stores were built during fiscal 1994, for a total of 12 stores at fiscal year end. Approximately nine additional new Canadian stores were planned for a total of 21 by the end of fiscal year 1995.

The company also made its initial entry into the Midwest by opening 11 stores in the region's two largest markets: Chicago, Illinois, and Detroit, Michigan. Approximately 16 new stores were scheduled for 1995, and by the end of 1998, the company expected approximately 112 stores to open.

During fiscal year 1994, Home Depot began developing plans to open stores in Mexico. The first store was scheduled to open in 1998. Although the company was already building relationships with key suppliers in Mexico, entry into the market was to be cautious and slow, paying special attention to Mexico's volatile economy. On a long-term basis, however, the company anticipated that success in Mexico could lead to more opportunities throughout Central and South America. Home Depot planned to expand its total domestic stores by about 25% per year, on average, over the foreseeable future. The international openings were to be above and beyond this figure. Management felt that its growth was optimal, given its financial and management resources.

In 1995, the company offered more private-label products. The company used the "Homer" character on all its private products and its advertisements. The first 24-hour store was opened in Flushing, New York. Ben Sharon of *Value Line* said, "[Home Depot's] ability to adopt different characteristics among regions and markets should keep Home Depot ahead of the industry in the years ahead."[2] By the end of 1995, the company had a total of 423 stores, of which 400 were Home Depot stores, 19 were Canadian stores in three provinces, and four EXPO stores.

In March 1995, *Fortune* announced that Home Depot had made its list of America's Most Admired Corporations. Home Depot ranked 8.24, or fifth overall in the competition. In 1996, Home Depot ranked second. The company ranked first for rate of return (39.0%) for the past 10 years. The top four companies were Rubbermaid (8.65), Microsoft (8.42), Coca-Cola (8.39), and Motorola (8.38). *Fortune* stated, "The winners chart a course of constant renewal and work to sustain culture that produces the very best products and people."[3] Over 1,000 senior executives, outside directors, and financial analysts were surveyed. Each corporation was rated in 10 separate areas.

Home Depot had encountered local opposition to locating one of its stores in a small community in Pequannock Township, New Jersey. A group called "Concerned Citizens for Community Preservation" mobilized to prevent Home Depot from opening a store in the town. Members of the group posted flyers and signs throughout the township. These flyers documented Home Depot's alleged "legacy of crime, traffic, and safety violations." The flyers stated, "Our kids will be crossing through this death trap," referring to Home Depot's proposed parking lot. Another flyer asked, "How will we be protected?"[4]

In July 1995, Home Depot filed a lawsuit against Rickel Home Centers, a closely-held competitor based in South Plainfield, New Jersey, claiming that "[Rickel] used smear tactics in a concerted effort to block Home Depot from opening stores in Pequannock and Bloomfield, about 25 miles to the south."[5] The suit stated that Rickel had published false statements "impugning Home Depot's name, reputation, products, and services." The suit named Rickel and Bloomfield citizens' groups as defendants.

This was not the first time that citizens' groups had tried to stop a new store or development. Wal-Mart had a severe challenge when it was trying to open a new store in Bennington, Vermont. In 1997, the company opened its first store in Williston, Vermont.

On July 20, 1995, Dennis Ryan, President of CrossRoads, announced the opening of the first of Home Depot's new rural chain, CrossRoads, in Quincy, Illinois. A second store was planned to be opened in Columbus, Missouri, in January or February 1996. The target market for this chain was farmers and ranchers who shopped in smaller, rural towns across America. At that time, there were about 100 farm and home retailers, with about 850 stores and annual sales of $6 billion. A typical CrossRoads store would have about 117,000 square feet of inside retail space, plus a 100,000-square-foot lumberyard. In contrast, the average size of a Tractor Supply Company (a competitor) store was about one-tenth the size of a CrossRoads store and did not have a lumberyard. Dennis Ryan said, "This really is a Home Depot just tailored to this [Quincy] community."[6]

The store carried the typical products of Home Depot. In addition, CrossRoads carried pet supplies, truck and tractor tires and parts, work clothing, farm animal medicines, feed, and storage tanks, barbed wire, books (such as *Raising Sheep the Modern Way*), and other items. Employees would install engines and tires and go to the farm to fix a flat tractor tire.[7] The company soon terminated this strategy because the stores did not generate sales and profits that Home Depot expected. The existing CrossRoads stores were renamed Home Depot stores.

By year-end 1996, the company acquired Maintenance Warehouse/America Corporation, which was the leading direct mail marketer of maintenance, repair, and operating products to the United States building and facilities in management market. The company's 1996 sales were approximately $130 million in an estimated $10 billion market. Home Depot management felt this was "an important step towards strengthening our position with professional business customers."[8] The company's long-term goal was to capture 10% of this market.

At the end of 1996, the company had 512 stores, including 483 Home Depot stores and five EXPO Design Centers in 38 states, and 24 stores in Canada.

In 1997, the company added 112 new stores for a total of 624 stores in 41 states. Stores in the United States were 587 Home Depot stores and five EXPO Design Center stores plus 32 stores in four Canadian provinces. This was a 22% increase in stores over 1996. Two-thirds of the new stores in fiscal 1997 were in existing markets. The company "continues to add stores to even its most mature markets to further penetrate and increase its presence in the market."[9]

The company planned to add new stores at a 21–22% annual growth rate, which would increase stores from 624 at the end of 1997 to 1,300 stores at the end of fiscal 2001. This meant the company would have to increase its associates from approximately 125,000 at the end of 1997 to 315,000 in four years (2001).

During 1998, Home Depot planned to open approximately 137 new stores, which would be a 22% increase in stores. The company planned to enter new markets— Anchorage, Alaska; Cincinnati and Columbus, Ohio; Milwaukee, Wisconsin; Norfolk and Richmond, Virginia; San Juan, Puerto Rico; Regina, Saskatchewan, and Kingston, Ontario in Canada; and Santiago, Chile. The company intended to open two stores in Santiago during fiscal 1998. To facilitate its entry into Chile, Home Depot entered into a joint venture agreement, in fiscal 1997, with S.A.C.I. Falabella, which was the largest department store retailer in Chile. The company's position on the joint venture was that it "was proving to be beneficial in expediting The Home Depot's startup in areas such as systems, logistics, real estate, and credit programs."[10]

This global expansion fit the company's stated vision to be one of the most successful retailers in the next millennium. According to management, "the most successful retailers . . . will be those who, among other things, can effectively profitably extend their reach to global markets."[11] Home Depot management "plans to employ a focused, regional strategy, establishing platform markets for growth into other markets."[12]

CORPORATE CULTURE

The culture at Home Depot was characterized by the phrase, "Guess what happened to me at Home Depot?" This phrase showed Home Depot's bond with its customers and the communities in which it had stores and was a recognition of superb service. Home Depot called this its "orange-blooded culture."

The orange-blooded culture emphasized individuality, informality, nonconformity, growth, and pride. These traits reflected those of the founders of the company, who, within hours of being fired from Handy Dan, were busily planning the Home Depot stores to go into competition with the company from which they had just been summarily dismissed. The culture was "really a reflection of Bernie and I [sic]," said Blank. "We're not formal, stuffy folks. We hang pretty loose. We've got a lot of young people. We want them to feel comfortable."[13]

The importance of the individual to the success of the whole venture was consistently emphasized at Home Depot. Marcus's statements bear this out: "We know that one person can make a difference, and that is what is so unique about The Home Depot. It doesn't matter where our associates work in our company, they can all make a difference."[14] While emphasizing the opportunities for advancement at Home Depot, Marcus decried the kind of "cradle to grave" job that used to be the ideal in America and is the norm in Japan. To him, this was "a kind of serfdom."[15] Home Depot attempted to provide excellent wages and benefits, and superior training and advancement opportunities, while encouraging independent thinking and initiative.

Informality was always in order at Home Depot—"spitballs fly at board meetings"—and there was always someone around to make sure that ties got properly trimmed. When executives visited stores, they went alone, not with an entourage. Most worked on the floors in the beginning and knew the business from the ground up. They were approachable and employees frequently came forward with ideas and suggestions.

Nonconformity was evident in many different areas of the company—from the initial warehouse concept to the size and variety of merchandise to human resource practices. Both Marcus and Blank "flout conventional corporate rules that foil innovation." Training employees at all levels was one of the most powerful means of transmitting corporate culture, and Home Depot used it extensively. One analyst noted that Home Depot (in a reverse of the "top-to-bottom" training sequence in most organizations) trained the carryout people first: "The logic is that the guy who helps you to your car is the last employee you come in contact with, and they want that contact to be positive."[16]

Company management perception of what the customer finds on a visit to a Home Depot store is a "feel good" store. The company defined a feel good store as "a place where they *feel good* about walking in our doors, *feel good* about consulting our knowledgeable associates, *feel good* about paying a low price, and *feel good* about returning time after time."[17]

The Home Depot was built on a set of values that fostered strong relationships with its key constituencies. The company's management embraced the values of taking care of its people, encouraging an entrepreneurial spirit, treating each other with respect, and being committed to the highest standards. For the customers, management believed that excellent customer service was the key to company success, and that giving back to the communities it served was part of its commitment to the customer. Importantly, management believed that if all employees lived all of these values, they would also create shareholder value.

The Home Depot's long-term growth planning was taking place with full recognition of the importance of the company's culture to its future success. Its goal was for each associate to not only be able to explain the company's culture of respect, trust, ownership, and entrepreneurial spirit, but most importantly, to believe it and live it.

The management of Home Depot was often asked how the company had managed to grow so fast for as long as it had and still be successful, both financially and with its customers. They responded that aggressive growth required adapting to change, but continued success required holding fast to the culture and values of the company as the company grew.[18]

In addition, Home Depot recognized its role in the community, and strove to be known as a good "corporate citizen." In one community, a woman lost her uninsured home and teen-aged son to a fire. Home Depot's management responded, along with other residents, by providing thousands of dollars of free materials and supplies to assist in the rebuilding effort. In another incident, a community organization sponsored a graffiti cleanup, and the Home Depot store in the area donated paint and supplies to assist in the project. These were just a few of the stories that communities told about Home Depot, which also participated in Habitat for Humanity and Christmas in April, and had provided over $10 million to help fund many community projects in the United States and Canada. The company also was active in environmental activities and promoted environmentally healthy building and home improvement practices.

Merrill Lynch stated about Home Depot's culture that its "entrepreneurial culture and heavy dedication toward customer service, combined with its large merchandise selection, has resulted in a retailer that leads its industry by almost every performance measure."[19]

CORPORATE GOVERNANCE

Board of Directors

The Board of Directors of Home Depot were as follows.[20]

Bernard Marcus (68) had been Co-Founder, Chairman, and Chief Executive Officer since the inception of the company in 1978 until 1997, when he passed the title of CEO to Arthur M. Blank, and remained as Chairman. He had served on many other boards. He owned 21,842,890 shares (2.98%) of the company's stock.

Arthur M. Blank (55) had been Co-Founder, President, Chief Operating Officer, and Director since the company's inception, and was named Chief Executive Officer in 1997. He had served on many other boards. He owned 12,182,614 shares (1.66%).

Ronald M. Brill (54) had been Executive Vice-President and Chief Financial Officer since March 1993. He joined the company in 1978 and was elected Treasurer in 1980. He owned 872,392 shares of the company's stock.

Frank Borman (70) had been a Director since 1983. He had been a NASA astronaut and retired U.S. Air Force colonel. He was the retired Chairman and Chief Operating Officer of Eastern Airlines and presently was the Chairman of Patlex Corporation. He was a major investor in 1983 and owned 265,782 shares of the company's stock. He served on many other boards.

Barry R. Cox (44) had been a Director since 1978. For the past 20 years, he had been a private investor. He owned 1,650,243 shares of stock.

Milledge A. Hart, III (64) had been a Director since 1978. He served as Chairman of the Hart Group, Chairman of Rmax Inc., and Chairman of Axon, Inc. He served on many other boards. He owned 1,733,185 shares of the company's stock.

Donald R. Keough (71) had been a Director since April 1993. He was President and Chief Operating Officer and Director of Coca-Cola Company until his retirement in April 1993. He owned 20,304 shares of the company's stock. He served on many other boards.

John I. Clendenin (63) had been a Director since 1996. He had been Chairman and Chief Executive Officer of BellSouth Corporation for the last five years until his retirement in 1996 and remained Chairman until 1997. He owned 5,477 shares of the company's stock.

Johnnetta B. Cole (61) had been a Director since 1995. Dr. Cole served as President of Spelman College in Atlanta, Georgia, from 1987 until July 1997. She served on many other boards and foundations. She owned 4,803 shares of the company's stock.

Kenneth G. Langone (62) had been a Co-Founder and Director since the company's inception. He had served as Chairman, President, Chief Executive Officer, and Managing Director of Invened Associates, Inc., an investment banking and brokerage firm. He served on many other boards. He owned 6,850,243 shares of the company's stock.

M. Faye Wilson (60) had been a Director since 1992. She had been Executive Vice-President of Bank of America NT&SA since 1992. She owned 16,743 shares of the company's stock.

The Directors were paid $40,000 per annum, of which $10,000 was in the form of restricted shares of common stock, and an additional $1,000 fee and expenses for each meeting. The Executive Committee included Messrs. Marcus, Blank, and Langone. The Audit Committee included Messrs. Borman, Cox, Hart, and Keough. The Compensation Committee included Messrs. Borman, Clendenin, Cox, and Keough. The Human Resource Committee included Dr. Cole, Mr. Langone, and Ms. Wilson.

FRM (Fidelity) Corporation owned 55,991,937 (7.65%) shares of common stock.

Top Management

Key executive officers of Home Depot, besides Bernard Marcus, Arthur M. Blank, and Ronald M. Brill, who served on the Board, were as follows:[21]

Mark R. Baker (40) has been President of the Midwest Division since December 1997. Mr. Baker first joined the company in 1996 as Vice-President—Merchandising for the Midwest Division. Prior to joining Home Depot, from 1992 until 1996, Mr. Baker was an Executive Vice-President for HomeBase in Fullerton, California.

Bruce W. Berg (49) has been President—Southeast Division since 1991. Mr. Berg joined the company in 1984 as Vice-President—Merchandising (East Coast) and was promoted to Senior Vice-President (East Coast) in 1988.

Marshall L. Day (54) has been Senior Vice-President—Chief Financial Officer since 1995. Mr. Day previously served as Senior Vice-President—Finance from 1993 until his promotion to his current position.

Bill Hamlin (45) was recently named Group President and continues to serve as Executive Vice-President—Merchandising. Prior to being named Executive Vice-President—Merchandising, Mr. Hamlin served as President—Western Division from 1990 until 1994.

Vernon Joslyn (46) has been President—Northeast Division since 1996. Mr. Joslyn previously served as Vice-President—Operations for the Northeast Division from 1993 until his promotion to his current position.

W. Andrew McKenna (52) was named Senior Vice-President—Strategic Business Development in December 1997. Mr. McKenna joined Home Depot as Senior Vice-President—Corporate Information Systems in 1990. In 1994 he was named President of the Midwest Division and served in that capacity until he assumed the duties of his current position.

Lynn Martineau (41) has been President—Western Division since 1996. Mr. Martineau most recently served as Vice-President—Merchandising for the company's Southeast Division from 1989 until his promotion to his current position.

Larry M. Mercer (51) was recently named Group President and has been Executive Vice-President—Operations since 1996. Mr. Mercer previously served as President—Northeast Division from 1991 until his promotion to his current position.

Barry L. Silverman (39) has been President of the Southwest Division since July 1997. Mr. Silverman previously served as Vice-President—Merchandising of the Northeast Division from 1991 until his promotion to his current position.

Bryant W. Scott (42) has been President of the EXPO Design Center Division since 1995. Since 1980, Mr. Scott has served in a variety of positions, including Vice-President—Merchandising for the Southeast Division.

David Suliteanu (45) was named Group President—Diversified Businesses in April 1998. Mr. Suliteanu previously served as Vice-Chairman and Director of Stores for Macy's East, a position he held from 1993 until he joined Home Depot in April 1998.

Annette M. Verschuren (41) has been President of The Home Depot Canada since 1996. In 1992, Ms. Verschuren formed Verschuren Ventures Inc. and remained there until joining Michaels of Canada Inc. in 1993 where she served as President until joining the company.

In 1997, Bernard Marcus, who had been CEO since the company's inception in 1978, passed the title to Arthur M. Blank. Mr. Blank now served as President and CEO. Exhibit 3 shows all the officers of Home Depot.

ORGANIZATIONAL STRUCTURE

The official organizational structure of Home Depot (see Exhibit 4) was much like that of other retail organizations, but according to a human resources spokesperson, the environment was so relaxed and casual people felt like they could report to anyone. Marcus and Blank presided at the top of Home Depot's organizational chart and were supported by Executive Vice-Presidents: Executive Vice-President and Chief Administrative Officer; Executive Vice-President of Merchandising and Group President; and Executive Vice-President of Operations and Group President.

Exhibit 3   Officers: Home Depot, Inc.

Corporate

Bernard Marcus
Chairman of the Board

Arthur M. Blank
President and Chief Executive Officer

Ronald M. Brill
Executive Vice-President and
Chief Administrative Officer

Bill Hamlin
Executive Vice-President
Merchandising and Group President

Larry M. Mercer
Executive Vice-President
Operations and Group President

David Suliteanu
Group President, Diversified Services

Alan Barnaby
Senior Vice-President, Store Operations

Marshall L. Day
Senior Vice-President,
Chief Financial Officer

Pat Farrah
Senior Vice-President, Merchandising

Bryan J. Fields
Senior Vice-President, Real Estate

Ronald B. Griffin
Senior Vice-President
Information Services

Richard A. Hammill
Senior Vice-President, Marketing

W. Andrew McKenna
Senior Vice-President
Strategic Business Development

Stephen R. Messana
Senior Vice-President, Human Resources

Dennis Ryan
Senior Vice-President, Merchandising

Lawrence A. Smith
Senior Vice-President, Legal and Secretary

Terence L. Smith
Senior Vice-President, Imports/Logistics

Richard L. Sullivan
Senior Vice-President, Advertising

Robert J. Wittman
Senior Vice-President, Merchandising

Mike Anderson
Vice-President, Information Services

Ben A. Barone
Vice-President, Credit Marketing

Dave Bogage
Vice-President, Management and
Organization Development

Patrick Cataldo
Vice-President, Training

Gary C. Cochran
Vice-President, Information Services

Charles D. Crowell
Vice-President, Distribution Services

Kerrie R. Flanagan
Vice-President, Merchandise Accounting

Mike Folio
Vice-President, Real Estate

Frank Gennaccaro
Vice-President, Merchandising

Paul Hoedeman
Vice-President, Information Services

Ted Kaczmarowski
Vice-President
Construction/Store Planning

Bill Peña
Vice-President/General Manager
International Development

William K. Schlegal
Vice-President, Imports

Kim Shreckengost
Vice-President, Investor Relations

Don Singletary
Vice-President, Human Resources—
North American Stores

Grady Stewart
Vice-President, Operations

Carol B. Tomé
Vice-President, Treasurer

DeWayne Truitt
Vice-President
Compensation and Benefits

Gregg Vickery
Vice-President, Controller

Edward A. Wolfe
Vice-President, Loss Prevention

Ken Young
Vice-President, Internal Audit

Midwest Division

Mark Baker
President

H. George Collins
Vice-President, Store Operations

Robert Gilbreth
Vice-President, Store Operations

Steven L. Mahurin
Vice-President, Merchandising

Michael J. Williams
Vice-President, Human Resources

Northeast Division

Vern Joslyn
President

Jeff Birren
Vice-President, Store Operations

Carol A. Freitag
Vice-President, Human Resources

William G. Lennie
Vice-President, Merchandising

Michael McCabe
Vice-President, Store Operations

Pedro Mendiguren
Vice-President, Store Operations

Southeast Division

Bruce Berg
President

(continued)

Exhibit 3   Officers: Home Depot, Inc. *(continued)*

Tony Brown
Vice-President, Store Operations

Dennis Johnson
Vice-President, Merchandising

Eric Johnson
Vice-President, Store Operations

H. Gregory Turner
Vice-President, Store Operations

John Wicks
Vice-President, Merchandising

Southwest Division

Barry L. Silverman
President

Jerry Edwards
Vice-President, Merchandising

Frank Rosi
Vice-President, Human Resources

Tom Taylor
Vice-President, Store Operations

Western Division

Lynn Martineau
President

Terry Hopper
Vice-President, Store Operations

Ethan Klausner
Vice-President, Merchandising

Bruce Merino
Vice-President, Merchandising

Timothy J. Pfeiffer
Vice-President, Store Operations

Thomas "Buz" Smith
Vice-President, Store Operations

Greg Lewis
Division Controller

The Home Depot Canada

Annette M. Verschuren
President

John Hayes
Vice-President, Merchandising

Dennis Kennedy
Vice-President, Store Operations

EXPO Design Center Division

Bryant Scott
President

Christopher A. McLoughlin
Vice-President, Division Controller

Steve Smith
Vice-President, Merchandising

Maintenance Warehouse

Jonathan Neeley
President

Jim Ardell
Vice-President, Merchandising

Mike Brown
Vice-President, Information Systems

Bill Luth
Vice-President, Marketing

Steven L. Neeley
Vice-President, Sales

Kevin Peters
Vice-President, Logistics

Ron Turk
Vice-President
Chief Financial Officer

Jeffrey R. Wenham
Vice-President, Human Resources

National Blind & Wallpaper Factory

David Katzman
President

Rick Kovacs
Senior Vice-President, Merchandising

David Littleson
Chief Financial Officer

Steve Kaip
Vice-President, Information Systems

Debra Russell
Vice-President, Operations

Bob Shepard
Vice-President
Installation/Retail Development

Source: The Home Depot, Inc., *1997 Annual Report,* p. 36.

There were three Group Presidents, of which two were also Executive Vice-Presidents. The other was the Group President of Diversified Businesses. These executives were supported by 13 Senior Vice-Presidents (see Exhibit 4). The company had 21 Vice-Presidents at the corporate level.

The organization was divided into seven divisions:

1. Southeast Division,

2. Western Division,

3. Northeast Division,

4. Midwest Division,

5. Home Depot Canada Division,

6. Southwest Division, and

7. EXPO Design Centers.

Each division was headed by a President, who was supported by Vice-Presidents of Merchandising and Store Operations. Under each Vice-President in a division was a group of regional managers responsible for a number of stores. There were a number of Vice-Presidents at the division level, some of which included Legal, Information Services, Logistics, Advertising, the Controller, and Human Resources.

At the store level, Home Depot was set up much as would be expected—with a manager, assistant managers, and department managers. The average Home Depot store had one manager whose primary responsibility was to be the master delegator. Four to six assistants usually presided over the store's 10 departments. Each assistant manager was responsible for one to three departments. One assistant manager was responsible for receiving and the "back end" (stock storage area), in addition to his or her departments. The assistant managers were supported by department managers who were each responsible for one department. The department managers reported directly to the assistant managers and had no firing/hiring capabilities. Assistant managers normally handled ordering and work schedules, and so on. Department managers handled employees' questions and job assignments. In a recent change, human resource officers were made responsible for recruiting, staffing, employee relations, and management development for each division.[22]

Home Depot Canada (Aikenhead's)

On February 28, 1994, Home Depot acquired a 75% interest in Aikenhead's Home Improvements Warehouse chain of seven warehouses in Canada for approximately $161,584,000. It was a joint venture with Molson Companies, Ltd.; Home Depot served as the general partner. Stephen Bebis, a former Home Depot officer, developed the chain along the Home Depot concept. He initially served as President of this unit and was replaced by Annette M. Verschuren in 1995.

OPERATIONS[23]

The stores and their merchandise were set up so that all of the stores were very similar. The company's corporate headquarters was responsible for the "look," but individual managers could change a display or order more or less of a product if they could justify the change. The managers within individual stores made decisions regarding their employees, such as firing and hiring, but they looked to headquarters in areas such as training. One manager of a store in Georgia said that if he did not like a particular display or promotion, it was at his discretion to change it or drop it. The manager went on to say that he and other store managers work hand in hand with corporate headquarters and that if he wanted to make "major" changes or had a significant store or personnel problem, he would deal with headquarters.

During 1994, Home Depot introduced a prototype store format, which offered about 32,000 more square feet of selling space and a significantly broader and deeper selection of products and services, as well as a more convenient layout than the traditional stores. These "Type V" stores were designed around a design center, which grouped complementary product categories.

Exhibit 4   Organizational Chart: Home Depot, Inc.

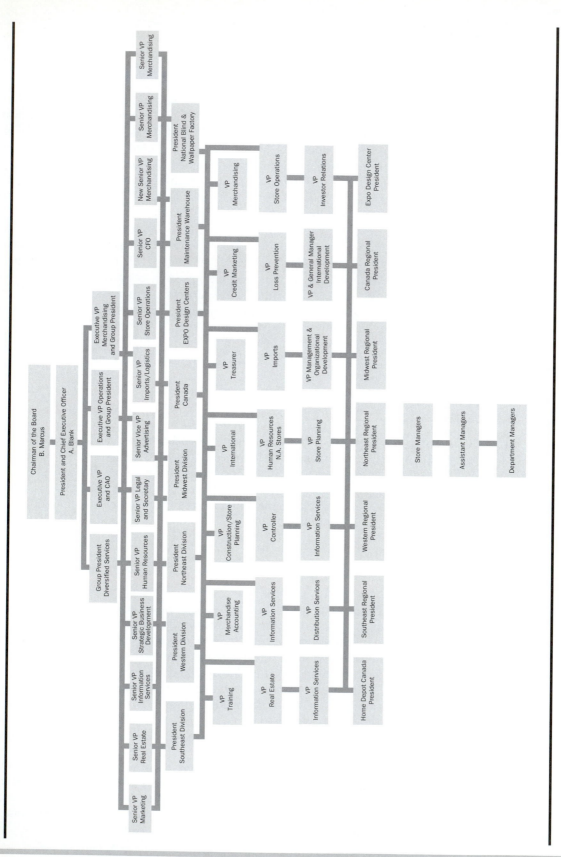

Note: This does not include the company's wholly-owned subsidiaries: (1) National Blind & Wallpaper Factory and (2) Maintenance Warehouse.

Source: Company records.

Operational efficiency had been a crucial part of achieving low prices while still offering a high level of customer service. The company was constantly assessing and upgrading its information to support its growth, reduce and control costs, and enable better decision making. From the installation of computerized checkout systems to the implementation of satellite communications systems in most of the stores, the company had shown that it had been and would continue to be innovative in its operating strategy.

By fiscal year 1994, each store was equipped with a computerized point-of-sale system (POS), electronic bar code scanning systems, and a minicomputer. These systems provided efficient customer checkout with approximately 90% scannable products, store-based inventory management, rapid order replenishment, labor planning support, and item movement information. In fiscal year 1994, faster registers were introduced along with new check approval systems and a new receipt format to expedite credit card transactions.

Home Depot's attitude of complete customer satisfaction has led the company to constantly seek ways to improve customer service. When the company was faced with clogged aisles, endless checkout lines, and too few salespeople, it sought creative ways to improve customer service. Workers were added to the sales floor. Shelfstocking and price tagging were shifted to nighttime, when the aisles are empty. The changes were worth the expense because now employees were free to sell during the day. In an effort to ease customer crowding, Home Depot used a "clustering" strategy to locate new stores closer to existing ones.

The company also operated its own television network (HDTV). This money-saving device allowed Home Depot's top executives to get instant feedback from local managers and also allowed training and communications programs to be viewed in the stores. Management's operating philosophies and policies were more effectively communicated because information presented by top management could be targeted at a large audience. This addition had increased employee motivation and saved many dollars by making information available in a timely manner.

Home Depot was firmly committed to energy conservation and had installed reflectors to lower the amount of lighting required in a store. The reflectors darkened the ceiling but saved thousands of dollars a year in energy bills. Further, the company had pursued a computerized system to maintain comfortable temperatures, a challenge due to the stores' concrete floors, exposed ceilings, and open oversized doors for forklift deliveries. The system also had an automated feedback capability that could be used for equipment maintenance.

The adoption of the Point-of-Sale (POS) technology had improved each store's ability to identify and adapt to trends quickly. The information provided by this technology was transferred to computer centers in Atlanta and Fullerton, California, where consumer buying trends were traced. This allowed Home Depot to adjust its merchandising mix and track both buyer trends and inventory.

In 1987, the company had introduced an advanced inventory management system that allowed it to increase inventory turnover significantly, from 4.1 in 1985 to 5.7 in 1994. This let Home Depot carry $40 million less in inventory, tying up less working capital to finance it. This efficiency allowed a cost structure that was significantly lower than the competition's.

In 1994, the company introduced phone centers to serve its customers who called to inquire about pricing and availability of merchandise. Adding experienced salespeople to a phone bank to answer calls quickly and efficiently had increased weekly phone sales. Without having to respond to phone calls, the sales staff could better concentrate on serving in-store customers.

The company continued to see greater efficiency as a result of its Electronic Data

Interchange (EDI) program. Currently over 400 of the company's highest volume vendors were participating in the EDI program. A paperless system, EDI electronically processed orders from stores to vendors, alerted the store when the merchandise was to arrive, and transmitted vendor invoice data.

In fiscal year 1994, stores were outfitted with Electronic Article Surveillance (EAS) detectors, which triggered an alarm if a person exited the store with merchandise that had been affixed with an EAS label that had not been desensitized at the cash register. The system was proving to be a deterrent to theft, with many stores reporting reductions in shoplifting offenses.

Home Depot continuously experimented with new operating concepts, such as CrossRoads and EXPO Design Centers. Its investment in new retail technology and its willingness to streamline operations for the benefit of the customer and employees had paid off in areas such as inventory turnover, in-stock turnover, in-stock inventory positions, queuing problems, employee motivation, and information flow from the company's buyers to its store-level managers and employees.

Merchandising[24]

If Home Depot's advertising strategy of creating awareness of the company's stores and encouraging do-it-yourselfers (DIYs) to tackle more at-home projects was getting people into the stores, the merchandising mix was aimed at getting people to buy. According to Marcus, "We could sell them anything . . . but we don't. We don't want the customer to think we're a discounter, food store, a toy store, or anything else, because it would confuse [them]."[25] Home Depot wanted to be thought of as the DIY warehouse, nothing less.

Advertising

The company maintained an aggressive campaign, using various media for both price and institutional policy. Print advertising, usually emphasizing price, was prepared by an in-house staff to control context, layout, media placement, and cost. Broadcast media advertisements were generally institutional and promoted Home Depot "the company," not just pricing strategy. These advertisements focused on the "You'll feel right at home" and "Everyday Low Pricing" ad slogans, name recognition, and the value of Home Depot's customer service. Although the company had grown over the years, the goal of its advertising was still to project a local flavor. The Western Division maintained its own creative department because of its different time zone and unique product mix. The company attempted to use information from the field in the various markets and put together an effective advertising campaign. The company still relied heavily on print media.

Home Depot sponsored the 1996 U.S. Summer Olympic Games in Atlanta. Through the sponsorship, Home Depot had hoped to further its ties with the home improvement customer, create sales opportunities, further differentiate itself from competitors, maintain its corporate culture, and support key businesses in the community. Home Depot began 1994 by unveiling a program to help pave the Olympic Park in Atlanta with engraved bricks, hiring athletes to work in the stores and office while they trained for the Games, and continuing a cooperative partnership with vendors in the Home Depot Olympic Family. This partnership had grown to include 29 key suppliers in the United States and 26 in Canada. Each member of the "Family" represented a specific home improvement product category and could participate in many of Home Depot's Olympic Games promotions.

The company participated in the Olympic Job Opportunities Program, in which Home Depot provided part-time jobs for 100 hopeful Olympic athletes as they trained for the Olympics. Twenty-six of the American and Canadian athletes participated in the Olympic Games and six earned medals. The company planned to remain a sponsor for at least the next six years for the Olympic Games in 2000, 2002, and 2004. The company also acted as a sponsor for the 1998 Winter Olympic Games.

Customer Target Market

Home Depot stores served primarily do-it-yourselfers, although home improvement contractors, building maintenance professionals, interior designers, and other professionals had become increasingly important customers. DIY customers continued to be the core business and made up approximately two-thirds of the total home improvement segment. DIY customers bought materials for the home and installed them personally.

Due to the increasing home improvement activity, buy-it-yourself (BYI) customers began to emerge. BIY customers chose products, made the purchase, and contracted with others to complete the project or install the furnishings. Home Depot was catering to this segment by expanding its installed sales program company-wide.

Home Depot also continued to target the professional business customer. It had set up a commercial credit program, provided commercial checkout lines in the stores, and had hired additional associates with experience in various professional fields.

The typical DIY customer was a married male homeowner, aged 25–34, with a high school diploma or some college, and had an annual income of $20,000 to $40,000. Projections through 1999 indicated that households headed by 25–35-year-olds with earnings over $30,000 would increase 34%–38% by 1999. The 45–54 age group was earning over $30,000 and was expected to increase by 40%.

Economics

The DIY industry exhibited a demand pattern that was largely recession-proof. Because a mere 15% of Home Depot's business came from contractors, a downturn in home construction had only a modest impact on Home Depot sales. In addition, analysts pointed out that, during hard times, consumers could not afford to buy new or bigger homes; instead they maintained or upgraded their existing homes. Home improvement spending had declined in only one recession during the past 20 years. The new strategy to penetrate the professional market might affect the company's sales more in future recessions.

Merchandising Strategy

The company's *1994 Annual Report* stated that Home Depot's goal was to be "The Do-It-Yourself Retailer." Merchandising included all activities involved in the buying and selling of goods for a profit. It involved long-range planning to ensure that the right merchandise was available at the right place, at the right time, in the right quantity, and at the right price. Success depended on the firm's ability to act and react with speed, spot changes, and catch trends early.

During 1994, Home Depot refined its merchandising function to be more efficient and responsive to customers. The new structure gave Division Managers responsibility for specific product categories, and specialists in each of these categories made sure the business lines were kept current. There were also field merchants who worked with the stores to ensure proper implementation of new programs as well as the maintenance of any ongoing programs. This approach strengthened product lines, got the right merchandise to the customers, reduced administration costs, and prepared Home Depot to expand into additional product lines.

The merchandising strategy of Home Depot followed a three-pronged approach: (1) excellent customer service, (2) everyday low pricing, and (3) wide breadth of products.

Each Home Depot store served 100,000 households with a median income of $45,000. Of those households, 75% were owner-occupied. In 1997, Home Depot responded to the demographics of certain markets by expanding its service hours to 24 hours a day in 15 store locations.

Home Depot continued to introduce or refine several merchandising programs during fiscal 1997. Key among them was the company's ongoing commitment to becoming the supplier of choice to a variety of professional customers, including remodelers, carpenters, plumbers, electricians, building maintenance professionals, and designers. According to management, the company had reacted to the needs of this group by enhancing and increasing quantities of key products for professional customers. In addition, the company was testing additional products and service-related programs designed to increase sales to professional customers, including expanded commercial credit programs, delivery services, and incremental dedicated staff.

The company's installed sales program was available, with varying services offered, in all of the company's stores. The company authorized approximately 3,500 installed sales vendors who, as independent licensed contractors, provide services to customers. This program targeted the BIY customer, who would purchase a product but did not have the desire or ability to install it.

Construction on the company's new Import Distribution Center (IDC), located in Savannah, Georgia, was completed in fiscal 1997. Built with the intention of servicing the company's stores located east of the Rocky Mountains, the IDC began shipments in April 1997, and by the end of fiscal 1997 was servicing all targeted stores. The 1.4-million-square-foot facility was staffed with approximately 600 associates. The IDC enabled the company to directly import products not currently available to customers or offer products currently sourced domestically from third-party importers. Other benefits included quicker turnaround deliveries to stores, lower costs, and improved quality control than would be possible if the products were purchased through third-party importers.

The company sponsored the "1997 National Home and Garden Show Series." Bringing together 16 of the nation's most successful consumer shows under one national sponsorship provided maximum exposure and support to the shows. Through this sponsorship, the company played a key role in bringing the most innovative lawn and garden, interior design, and home improvement products and services to the attention of the general public.

Home TLC, Inc., an indirect, wholly-owned subsidiary of The Home Depot, Inc., owned the trademarks, "The Home Depot," and "EXPO," as well as the "Homer" advertising symbol and various private label brand names that the company uses. The company's operating subsidiaries licensed from Homer TLC, Inc., the right to use this intellectual property. Management believed that the company's rights in this intellectual property were an important asset of the company.

Home Depot was the only big-box retailer to offer a number of other exclusive, high-quality products such as Pergo® laminate flooring, Ralph Lauren® paints, and Vigoro® fertilizer. Each of these products made The Home Depot unique from its competitors and provided its customers with a better selection of products. Home Depot's proprietary products included Behr Premium Plus paints, Hampton Bay ceiling fans and lighting products, Husky tools, and Scott's lawnmowers. These proprietary products provided Home Depot customers with a quality product at a value price and often filled a needed void in the product offerings.

Following the success of Home Depot's best-selling *Home Improvement 1-2-3*™ book, the company recently released *Outdoor Projects 1-2-3*™, the company's latest how-to book sold in Home Depot stores and bookstores. For the past three years, Home Depot has sponsored *HouseSmart with Lynette Jennings*™, one of the highest-rated shows on The Discovery Channel®. The company planned to extend its reach to tomorrow's homeowners in 1998 through *Homer's Workshop*™, the first how-to, project-oriented television program for children.

Clustering Strategy

The clustering strategy had been employed to allow Home Depot's aggressive expansion program. Home Depot had intentionally cannibalized sales of existing stores by opening other stores in a single market area. The short-run effect was to lower same-store sales, but a strategic advantage was created by raising the barrier of entry to competitors. It reduced overcrowding in the existing stores. It also allowed the company to spread its advertising and distribution costs over a larger store base, thereby lowering selling, general, and administrative costs. The company's 1997 gross margin was 28.1%.

Customer Service

The availability of sales personnel to attend to customer needs was one clear objective of the Home Depot customer service strategy.

Customer service differentiated Home Depot from its competitors. The provision of highly qualified and helpful employees, professional clinics, and in-store displays had developed into a customer service approach referred to as "customer cultivation." It gave DIY customers the support and confidence that no home project was beyond their capabilities with Home Depot personnel close at hand.

Home Depot employees went beyond simply recommending appropriate products, tools, and materials. Sales personnel cultivated the customer by demonstrating methods and techniques of performing a job safely and efficiently. This unique aspect of the company's service also served as a feedback mechanism—employees helping the next customer learn from the problems and successes of the last one.

All of the stores offered hands-on workshops on projects such as kitchen remodeling, basic plumbing, ceramic tile installation, and other activities in which customers in a particular locality had expressed interest. Offered mainly on weekends, the workshops varied in length, depending on complexity. Only the most experienced staff members, many of them former skilled craftsmen, taught at these workshops. Promotion of the workshops was done through direct mail advertising and in-store promotion.

At many Home Depot stores, customers could rent trucks by the hour through Load 'N Go™, Home Depot's exclusive truck rental service. The company also expanded a tool rental service to more stores during fiscal 1998. In addition, the company's special order capabilities should improve, due in part to the acquisition in November 1997 of National Blind & Wallpaper Factory and Habitat Wallpaper & Blinds stores, which became wholly-owned subsidiaries of Home Depot. When integrated with the stores beginning in fiscal 1998, the innovative ordering systems of these companies should give Home Depot the capability to handle wallpaper and window covering special orders in a more efficient, cost-effective, and convenient manner for customers.

Pricing Strategy

Home Depot stressed its commitment to "Everyday Low Pricing." This concept meant across-the-board lower prices and fewer deep-cutting sales. To ensure this, Home Depot employed professional shoppers to check competitors' prices regularly.

One of the major reasons that Home Depot was able to undercut the competition by as much as 25% was a dependable relationship with its suppliers. The company conducted business with approximately 5,700 vendors, the majority of which were manufacturers. A confidential survey of manufacturers conducted by Shapiro and Associates found that Home Depot was "far and away the most demanding of customers." Home Depot was most vocal about holding to shipping dates. Manufacturers agreed that increased sales volume had offset concessions made to Home Depot.

Products

A typical Home Depot store stocked approximately 40,000–50,000 products, including variations in color and size. The products included different kinds of building materials, home improvement products, and lawn and garden supplies. In addition, Home Depot stores offered installation services for many products. Each store carried a wide selection of quality and nationally advertised brand name merchandise. The contribution of each product group was as follows.[26]

	Percentage of Sales		
Product Group	**Year Ending February 1, 1998**	**Year Ending February 2, 1997**	**Year Ending January 28, 1996**
Plumbing, heating, lighting, and electrical supplies	27.1%	27.4%	27.7%
Building materials, lumber, floor, and wall coverings	34.2	34.0	33.9
Hardware and tools	13.5	13.4	13.2
Season and specialty items	14.8	14.7	14.8
Paint and others	10.4	10.5	10.4
	100.0%	100.0%	100.0%

The company sourced its store merchandise from approximately 5,700 vendors worldwide, and no single vendor accounted for more than 5% of total purchases.

Average Store Profile

According to Bob Evans in the Store Planning Division of Home Depot, all of the stores were company-owned, not franchised, and most were freestanding, built to Home Depot's standards.

Home Depot owned 74% of its buildings in 1997, leasing the remainder. Marcus planned to increase that percentage. In 1989, the company had owned only about 40% of its stores. Although the company preferred locations surrounded by shopping centers, Marcus insisted that the company was not interested in being attached to a shopping center or mall. Stores were placed in suburban areas populated by members of the Home Depot target market. Ownership provided Home Depot with greater operational control and flexibility, generally lower occupancy loss, and certain other economic advantages. Construction time depended on site conditions, special local requirements, and related factors. According to Evans, depending on "if we have to move a mountain, fill a canyon, level a forest, or how many gopher turtles are in the ground that we have to relocate," building a store can take up to a year.

Current building standards were 108,000 square feet for each store itself and 16,000 to 28,000 square feet of outside selling space for the garden department. Stores did vary, however, because the company "will make the store fit the land," and many of the original stores were located in leased strip-center space. Home Depot had increased its average store size from about 97,000 to 108,000 square feet, with an additional 20,000–28,000 square feet of outside (garden) selling space. The average weighted sales per square foot was $406, $398, $390, $404, and $398 for 1997, 1996, 1995, 1994, and 1993, respectively. The weighted average weekly sales per operational store was $829,000; $803,000; $787,000; $802,000; and $764,000 for 1997, 1996, 1995, 1994, and 1993, respectively. Although Marcus would like to see stores averaging 120,000 square feet, Evans said that "the hundred [thousand square-foot size] is what we're building most of [sic]." Some stores had thousands of customers a week and "just get too crowded," according to Evans. Marcus had estimated that "in some cases, we have 25,000–30,000 people walking through a store per week."

Because of the large number of customers, older stores were being gradually remodeled or replaced with new ones to add room for new merchandise, to increase selling space for what is already there, and sometimes even to add more walking room on the inside—and more parking space.

Because merchandising and inventory were centrally organized, product mix varied slightly from store to store. Each, however, sported the Home Depot look: warehouse style shelves, wide concrete-floored aisles, end-displays pushing sale items, and the ever-present orange banners indicating the store's departments. Most stores had banners on each aisle to help customers locate what they're looking for. Regional purchasing departments were used to keep the stores well stocked and were preferred to a single, strong corporate department "since home improvement materials needed in the Southwest would differ somewhat from those needed in the Northeast."

Information Systems

Each store was equipped with a computerized point-of-sale system, electronic bar code scanning system, and a UNIX server. Management believed these systems provided efficient customer check-out (with an approximately 90% rate of scannable products), store-based inventory management, rapid order replenishment, labor planning support, and item movement information. Faster registers as well as a new check approval system and a new receipt format had expedited transactions. To better serve the increasing number of customers applying for credit, the charge card approval process time had been reduced to less than 30 seconds. Store information was communicated to the Store Support Center's computers via a land-based frame relay network. These computers provided corporate, financial, merchandising, and other back-office function support.

The company was continuously assessing and upgrading its information systems to support its growth, reduce and control costs, and enable better decision making. The company continued to realize greater efficiency as a result of its electronic data interchange (EDI) program. Most of the company's highest volume vendors were participating in the EDI program. A paperless system, EDI electronically processed orders from buying offices to vendors, alerted the stores when the merchandise was to arrive, and transmitted invoice data from the vendors and motor carriers to the Store Support Center. In addition, during fiscal 1997 the company continued to develop new computer systems to facilitate and improve product order replenishment in Home Depot stores.[27]

The Year 2000 Problem

The company was currently addressing a universal situation commonly referred to as the "Year 2000 Problem." The Year 2000 Problem related to the inability of certain computer software programs to properly recognize and process date-sensitive information relative to the year 2000 and beyond. During fiscal 1997, the company developed a plan to devote the necessary resources to identify and modify systems impacted by the Year 2000 Problem, or implement new systems to become year 2000 compliant in a timely manner. The cost of executing this plan was not expected to have a material impact on the company's results of operations or financial condition. In addition, the company had contacted its major suppliers and vendors to ensure their awareness of the Year 2000 Problem. If the company, its suppliers, or vendors were unable to resolve issues related to the year 2000 on a timely basis, it could result in a material financial risk.[28]

Human Resources[29]

Home Depot was noted for its progressive human resources policies, which emphasized the importance of the individual to the success of the company's operations.

Recruitment/Selection

Throughout its entire recruiting process, Home Depot looked for people who shared a commitment to excellence. Also, management recognized that having the right number of people, in the right jobs, at the right time was critical. Employee population varied greatly among stores, depending on store size, sales volume, and the season of the year. In the winter, a store could have had fewer than 75 employees and in the spring would add another 25–40 employees. Some of the larger northeastern stores had as many as 280 employees. Full-time employees filled approximately 90% of the positions.

When a store first opened, it attracted applications through advertisements in local newspapers and trade journals such as *Home Center News.* A new store would usually receive several thousand applications. When seasonal workers and replacements were needed, help-wanted signs were displayed at store entrances. Walk-in candidates were another source, and applications were available at the customer service desk at all times. There was no formal program to encourage employees to refer their friends for employment. At the management level, the company preferred to hire people at the assistant manager level, requiring them to work their way up to store manager and beyond. Historically the company often hired outside talent for senior positions. Now that the company had grown, Home Depot believed that, whenever possible, executives should come up through the ranks, although management from the outside was occasionally brought in. To support its growing infrastructure, Steve Messana served as Senior Vice-President for Human Resources.

Interviews were scheduled one day per week; however, if someone with trade experience applied, an on-the-spot interview might be conducted. "Trade" experience included retail, construction, do-it-yourself, or hardware. The company tended to look for older people who brought a high level of knowledge and maturity to the position. In addition to related experience, Home Depot looked for people with a stable work history who had a positive attitude, were excited, outgoing, and hard workers.

The selection process included preemployment tests (honesty, math, and drugs). The stores displayed signs in the windows that said that anyone who used drugs need not apply. Interviews were conducted with three or four people—an initial qualifier, the administrative assistant in operations, an assistant manager, and the store manager. Reference checks were completed prior to a job offer. More in-depth background checks (financial, criminal) were conducted on management-level candidates.

To help ensure that Home Depot selected the best qualified people, during fiscal 1997 the company designed a proprietary automated system for identifying the best candidates for store sales associate positions. This system, which had been through extensive validation testing, screened candidates for competencies and characteristics inherent to Home Depot's best sales associates. The company planned to use this system to evaluate additional positions in the future.

Retention

Employee turnover varied from store to store. In the first year of operations, turnover could run 60%–70% but would fall below 30% in future years. The company's goal was to reduce turnover to below 20%. The major causes of turnover were students who returned to school, employees who were terminated for poor performance, and tradespeople who considered Home Depot an interim position (often returning to their trade for a position paying as much as $50,000 per year). Very few people left the organization looking for "greener pastures" in the retail industry.

Career development was formally addressed during semiannual performance reviews, with goals and development plans mutually set by employees and managers. The company was committed to promotions from within and had a formal job-posting program. Vacancy lists were prepared at the regional level and distributed to the stores. Store managers were promoted from within. Affirmative action plans were used to increase female and minority representation.

Compensation

Employees were paid a straight salary. Bernard Marcus said, "The day I'm laid out dead with an apple in my mouth is the day we'll pay commissions. If you pay commissions, you imply that the small customer isn't worth anything." Most management-level employees were eligible for bonuses that were based on such factors as a store's return on assets and sales versus budget. Assistant managers could receive up to 25% of their base salary in bonuses, and store managers could earn up to 50% if their stores' performance warranted. Store managers could earn $50,000 to $120,000. The typical employee earned $10 to $14 per hour.

During fiscal year 1988, the company established a leveraged Employee Stock Ownership Plan (ESOP), covering substantially all full-time employees. In 1989, the company made its initial contribution to the ESOP of $6 million, which represented about $0.05 per share. Fully funded by the company, the ESOP was established to provide additional retirement security for the employees, while simultaneously reducing taxable income and discouraging hostile takeover attempts. At February 1, 1998, the ESOP held a total of 10,161,272 shares of the company's common stock in trust for plan participants. The company made annual contributions to the ESOP at the discretion of the Board of Directors. All employees eligible for the ESOP were entitled to receive a substantial portion of their annual salary in profit sharing. Tim Sparks, 31, who started out loading customers' cars in the lot at the age of 19 and managed a store in Jacksonville, Florida, said, "My father was a peanut farmer in Alabama. Dirt poor. Where else could a son go from that to being a millionaire?"

Recognition programs emphasized good customer service, increased sales, safety, cost savings, and length of service. Badges, cash awards, and other prizes were distributed in monthly group meetings.

Communication was the key by which Home Depot perpetuated its culture and retained its people. That culture included an environment in which employees were happy and where they felt productive and secure. The company sold employees on their role in Home Depot's success—they were giving the company a return on its assets. The environment avoided bureaucracy, was informal and intense, and encouraged honesty and risk taking. Each store maintained a strong open-door policy, and a manager would spend two or three hours discussing a concern with an employee.

Top management was equally accessible to employees through frequent visits to the stores. An in-house TV broadcast, "Breakfast with Bernie and Arthur," was held quarterly. Impromptu questions were solicited from the employees. Department managers met with employees weekly to provide new information and solicit feedback. Worker opinions also mattered at the top. When the company planned to open on New Year's Day, the employees voted to close and prevailed. When the company wrote a checkout training manual, a store cashier from Jacksonville helped write it. Internal sales charts were posted on bulletin boards so that employees would know how their store compared with others in the area.

Training

Home Depot believed that knowledgeable salespeople were one of the keys to the company's success and spent a great deal of time training them to "bleed orange." Callers to the home office found that corporate executives spent most of their time in the stores training employees. "We teach from the top down, and those who can't teach don't become executives," said one top executive. Training costs to open a new store were about $400,000 to $500,000.

Regular employees went through both formal and on-the-job training. Classes were held on product knowledge (giving the employee "total product knowledge . . . including all the skills a trade person might have"); merchandising concepts, and salesmanship (so that they could be sure that a customer has available, and would purchase, everything needed to complete a project); time management; personnel matters; safety and security; and how to interpret the company's various internally generated reports.

Each new employee was required to go through a rigorous week-long orientation, which introduced new hires to Home Depot's culture. To ensure that employees were convinced of the company's commitment, Bernard Marcus, Arthur Blank, and Ron Brill conducted many of the management training sessions. New employees were then paired with experienced associates in the stores to gain first-hand knowledge of customer service and general store operations. They trained an average of four weeks before working on their own. Even then, when there were no other customers in the department, newer employees would watch more experienced employees interact with customers to learn more about products, sales, and customer service. Employees were cross-trained to work in various departments, and even the cashiers learned how to work the sales floor.

The Home Depot Television Network allowed the company to disseminate policies and philosophies, product upgrades, and so on. With the ability to target special or mass audiences, the training possibilities were endless. The fact that the programs were broadcast live, with telephone call-ins, enhanced their immediacy and made interaction possible.

According to management, Home Depot's training programs were key to arming associates with the knowledge they needed to serve customers. During fiscal 1997, the company made several changes to its human resources and training programs to prepare for and support Home Depot's future growth plans. To address the unique growth needs of its divisions, new human resources officers were responsible for areas such as recruiting, staffing, employee relations, and management development in their divisions. They were also responsible for areas such as recruiting, staffing, employee relations and management development in their divisions. They were also responsible for implementing the store training programs that take entry-level sales associates from the basics to becoming project experts and, ultimately, masters in their respective departments.

Employees

As of the end of January 1998, the company employed approximately 125,000 people, of whom approximately 7,900 were salaried and the remainder were on an hourly basis. Approximately 76% of the company's employees were employed on a full-time basis. There were no unions. The company has never suffered a work stoppage.

INDUSTRY AND COMPETITORS

Retail Building and Supply Industry

The retail building supply industry was moving rapidly from one characterized by small, independently run establishments to one dominated by regional and national chains of vast superstores. Home Depot developed the concept of the all-in-one discount warehouse home improvement superstore, designed to be all things to all people. The main rival to Home Depot was Lowe's, which had been replacing its older, smaller stores with new superstores. Other companies in the industry were facing the challenge by reconfiguring their stores and by targeting niche segments, but some were being forced to close stores in the face of increased competition.

In 1997, the retail building supply industry showed mixed results. The stronger companies (Home Depot and Lowe's) got stronger, and the weak struggled. The largest two operators, Lowe's and Home Depot, extended their dominance, especially in the Do-It-Yourself (DIY) segment of the market (see Exhibit 5). Small regional operators such as Grossman in the Northeast were liquidated.

In 1997, Leonard Green & Partners bought out both Hechinger and Builders Square, formerly owned and started by Kmart, in an effort to turn the two struggling chains into one profitable chain.[30]

The retail building supply industry served two distinct clients—the professional building contractor and the DIY homeowner. The DIY customer had grown in importance over the past few years. Home Depot's main competitors were:

- *Hechinger,* located in the mid-Atlantic states and recently acquired by Leonard Green & Partners. Hechinger had financial problems for several years before it was acquired.

- *Lowe's* was located in 22 states with 442 stores and had recently moved into large metropolitan areas—Dallas and Atlanta. The company had developed regional distribution centers to better serve its growing markets. Lowe's 1997 sales were estimated to be $10,190,000,000 and second to Home Depot with sales of $24,156,000,000 for 1997 (see Exhibit 5).

- *BMC* was renamed Building Materials Holding Corporation. The company had over 50 stores in 10 western states and was focusing on the professional/contractor market segment.

- *Hughes Supply* had 310 stores, principally in Florida, Georgia, and other southeastern states. The 1997 sales were estimated to be $1,810,000,000. The company made 13 acquisitions in 1996, which added about $340 million to its sales base. After these acquisitions, Hughes was in new territories—upper New York and California. The company focused on the professional/contractor market segment (see Exhibit 5).

- *Wolohan Lumber* had 58 stores located in Illinois, Indiana, Kentucky, Ohio, and Wisconsin. The company strategy was to focus on the professional/contractor market segment. The 1997 sales were estimated to be $425,000,000 (see Exhibit 5).

Exhibit 5 provides a summary of the key information on these companies.

The industry did not have barriers to entry in the form of patents or special technology. There was a major learning curve on efficiently managing a 100,000-square-foot store. The superstore warehouses tried to serve all market segments, but they had become increasingly consumer-orientated. Because of this, smaller competitors were focusing their strategies on the professional constructor segment of the market.[31]

Eagle Hardware & Garden of Seattle, Washington, operated 24 home improvement stores. Its founder, David Heerensperger, viewed Home Depot's entry into Seattle as a "war." He said, "They are aiming for us, but we're a thorn in their side. Eagle is the first home center they haven't completely run over."[32]

Eagle's stores averaged 128,000 square feet, compared to Home Depot's 103,000 square feet. Eagle offered other services, namely, a custom-design section, free chain-cutting station, fences, and an idea center where customers could watch videotapes and live demonstrations of home improvement techniques. Heerensperger began preparing for Home Depot's onslaught six years ago. He came up with a design for new stores that were brighter and more elegant than Home Depot's stores. He took into consideration women customers by reducing rack-type displays.[33] Eagle was building the largest stores in the industry in the West Coast and Northwest markets. Eagle planned to maintain a managed-growth strategy.

According to Ronald Pastore, real estate expert, "Between 1992 and 1994, 55% of all new retail square footage was built by big-box retailers (like Wal-Mart and Home Depot)."[34] In 1994, these retailers accounted for 80% of all new stores.

There had been a rampant construction of new retail space over the past 20 years. The supply of retail space nationally was 19 square feet for each person, and this was more than double the level of 20 years ago. The supply had far exceeded the population in growth for the same period. Christopher Niehaus, real estate investment banker, said, "That number is too high. It needs to come down."[35] He predicts that the discount sector is heading for the " 'biggest shake-out' in retailing because of overbuilding."[36] Don McCrory, real estate expert, said, "Our question is, if the big-box tenants go out of business, what do you do with the enormous box?"[37]

The Professional Business Segment[38]

Early in fiscal 1997, Home Depot began a formal study of the professional business customer market. The findings of this study clearly indicated that there were many opportunities to grow its presence in the pro market that fit within the company's core business. The study also indicated that many of these opportunities could be captured inside its stores.

Estimated professional business customer sales across all channels in the United States were approximately $265 billion in 1997, substantially higher than the $100 billion Do-It-Yourself market. Excluding the heavy industrial sector, the majority of which

Exhibit 5   **Retail Building Supply Industry**

A. Competitors

Company	Number of Stores		Sales in Millions ($)			
	2000–2002	1997	2000–2002	1998	1997	1996
Homebase, Inc.	105	84	$ 1,900.0	$ 1,500.0	$ 1,465.0	$ 1,448.8
Home Depot	**1,050**	**624**	**54,000.0**	**30,100.0**	**24,600.0**	**19,535.0**
Hughes Supply	362	310	2,500.0	1,960.0	1,810.0	1,516.1
Lowe's Companies	620	442	17,500.0	11,900.0	10,190.0	8,600.2
Woloham Lumber	75	58	620.0	410.0	425.0	430.4
Industry totals and averages			$66,000.0	$42,000.0	$38,050.0	$33,287.0

Company	Net Profit in Millions ($)				Net Profit Margins %			
	2000–2002	1998	1997	1996	2000–2002	1998	1997	1996
Homebase, Inc.	$ 38.0	$ 24.0	$ 21.0	$ 21.4	2.0%	1.6%	1.4%	1.5%
Home Depot	**2,790.0**	**1,455.0**	**1,145.0**	**937.7**	**5.2**	**4.8**	**4.7**	**4.8**
Hughes Supply	70.0	50.0	40.0	32.5	—	2.6	2.2	2.1
Lowe's Companies	645.0	405.0	345.0	292.2	3.7	3.4	3.4	3.4
Woloham Lumber	12.5	6.0	5.0	6.7	—	1.5	1.2	1.6
Industry totals and averages	$2,310.0	$1,510.0	$1,330.0	$1,287.2	3.6%	3.6%	3.5%	3.5%

B. Industry Indicators

	2000–2002	1998	1997	1996
Sales in millions ($)	$66,000.0	$38,050.0	$33,287.0	$27,152.0
Number of stores	2,350	1,980	1,860	1,922
Net profits in millions ($)	$ 2,310.0	$ 1,510.0	$ 1,330.0	$ 1,287.0
Net profit margin (%)	3.6%	3.6%	3.5%	3.6%

Note: Shaded areas are projections.

Source: *Value Line,* January 16, 1998, pp. 884, 888–892.

was outside Home Depot's core business, the pro market opportunities for the company totaled approximately $215 billion. Home Depot's share of this market was less than 4% in 1998.

The initial focus for growing sales in the professional market was on the professional business customer who already shopped in Home Depot stores, but also made purchases at other retail and wholesale outlets. By listening and responding to his or her needs, the company intended to make Home Depot this customer's supplier of choice.

Late in fiscal 1997, Home Depot began a test in its stores in the Austin, Texas, market designed to increase professional customer sales while continuing to serve the strong and growing Do-It-Yourself customer market.

The test in Austin included incremental associates primarily responsible for serving and building relationships with the professional business customer. Professional business customers in these stores were assisted at a Pro Service Desk to more quickly meet their product and service needs. In addition, customized services, such as enhanced ordering and credit programs and a menu of product delivery options were available to the pro customer. The test, which was to be expanded to additional stores in fiscal 1998, was helping the company to successfully develop and refine its formula for serving the professional business customer inside its stores.

There were other ways to reach the professional customer, too. During fiscal 1997, Home Depot distributed its ProBook™ professional equipment and supply catalog to professional customers across North America. The ProBook contained over 15,000 products from its stores chosen especially for facility maintenance managers and the building trades. In addition, the company's longer term growth initiatives included exploring opportunities for serving professional customers with more specialized needs through distribution channels outside Home Depot stores.

The total professional business customer market was estimated to be $265 billion in 1997 (see Exhibit 6). The heavy industry with an estimated $50 billion in sales was treated as a separate sector. The professional business market ($215 billion) consisted of four subsectors: (1) tradesmen ($85 billion), (2) builders/general contractors ($75 billion), (3) repair and remodeling ($40 billion), and (4) property maintenance ($15 billion).

The $215 billion professional business customer target market can be further separated by volume of expenditures. The typical Home Depot pro customer was a repair and remodel professional who purchased up to $200,000 of products annually, but tended to buy less than 10% of this amount from the company. The Home Depot planned to capture more of this customer's sales by responding to the distinct product and service needs of this professional. (See Exhibit 7.)

The company purchased Maintenance Warehouse as part of Home Depot's strategy to penetrate the professional market.

Do-It-Yourself (DIY) Industry

The Home Depot occupied the number one position in the DIY industry with sales of $24.1 billion, more than twice its nearest competitor, Lowe's Companies. Home Depot had approximately 24% market share. Clearly the $100 billion industry was extremely fragmented. The industry remained dominated by small- to mid-sized stores, with only a handful of the top retailers operating stores about 100,000 square feet in size. The trend was clearly moving in the direction of bigger stores, however, as companies such as Lowe's and Home Depot enjoyed success with their large-store formats. As these companies continued to roll out their superstores at an aggressive rate, industry analysts expected the industry to consolidate over time, with the major retailers gaining their share at the expense of the smaller, less efficient DIY chains.

Home Depot was regarded as the premier operator in the DIY industry. The following list shows the six top competitors in 1996. However, based on competitors' announced expansion plans, Home Depot believed that the level of direct competition would increase to 22% of its total store base. The largest and most formidable foe facing Home Depot was the North Carolina chain, Lowe's. Since 1995, Lowe's had gone into more direct competition with Home Depot in more cities as both companies expanded. As Home Depot added more stores in Lowe's market, analysts believed that Lowe's could face increased margin pressure. Lowe's had been able to maintain its profit margin at 3.4% since 1996. Because Home Depot was more geographically dispersed than Lowe's and had a more balanced portfolio of stores, Home Depot was better able to be

Exhibit 6 **Professional Business Customer Market**

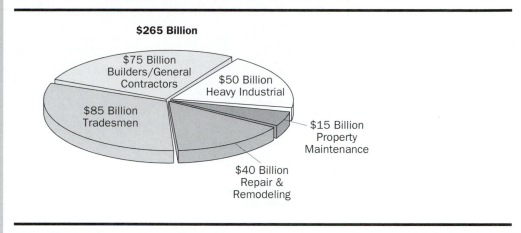

$265 Billion

- $75 Billion Builders/General Contractors
- $50 Billion Heavy Industrial
- $85 Billion Tradesmen
- $15 Billion Property Maintenance
- $40 Billion Repair & Remodeling

Source: The Home Depot, *1997 Annual Report*, p. 4.

price competitive in these markets. The top six retail building supply companies in 1996 were as follows:

1. Home Depot
2. Lowe's Companies
3. Payless Cashways
4. Builders Square
5. Menard's
6. Hechinger's

Other competitors were Sutherland Lumber, Wickes Lumber, and Scotty's.

America's do-it-yourselfers spent approximately $100 billion in home improvement products in 1997, up more than 6% from the previous year. This all-important customer group was getting larger in number and more confident and capable to take on home improvement projects every year. In addition, demographic changes were taking place within the Do-It-Yourself customer group that had important implications for the future of the home improvement industry. Home Depot was positioning itself to continue to grow its share of this industry segment as these changes took place.

The rate of home ownership in the United States continued to grow as first-time buyers entered the housing market at a rapid pace and baby-boomers moved in force to more expensive homes and second homes. During 1997, existing single-family home sales reached their highest point on record, and new single-family home sales showed strong increases from the previous year. In addition, studies showed that the average age of existing homes continued to increase, and people were staying in their homes later in life. All of these trends enhanced Home Depot's opportunities to add new stores across North America as well as to increase sales in its existing stores.[39]

The $100 billion DIY market breaks into five market segments: (1) lumber and building materials, (2) lawn and garden, (3) plumbing and electrical, (4) hardware and tools, (5) paint and supplies, and (6) hard surface flooring. Exhibit 8 shows their market segment shares.

Exhibit 7 U.S. Professional Business Customer Profile—$215 Billion Total Target Market

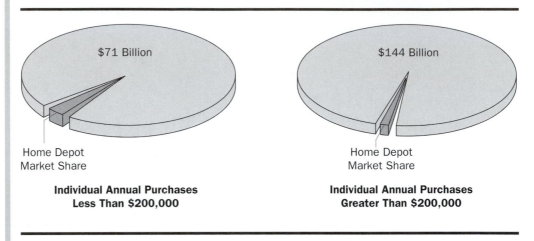

Source: The Home Depot, Inc., *1997 Annual Report,* p. 7.

HomeBase, formerly HomeClub, was acquired by Zayre Corporation, a discount retail chain, in 1986. It was consolidated with BJ's Wholesale Club and renamed Waban, Inc. Zayre spun the company off to shareholders on June 14, 1989. In July 1997, Waban spun off the company to shareholders and was renamed HomeBase. In 1997, the company had to write off $27 million to cover store closings. The company was changing its strategy from being defensive to a more aggressive stance, such as accelerating store remodeling program. Analysts said, "This is an extremely competitive industry, and profit margins are small, so only the well-managed companies prosper and survive." He went on to say, "Look at Kmart; the company could not effectively manage Builders Square. They had to sell it off." [40]

FINANCE

The 10-year performance of Home Depot in selected key growth financial indicators is as follows.

	Compound Growth Rate	
Financial Indicator	**5-year Annual**	**10-year Annual**
Net sales	27.6%	32.5%
Earnings before taxes	28.3	35.6
Net earnings	27.5	36.6
Total assets	23.4	35.8
Working capital	19.9	33.6
Merchandise inventory	30.8	32.8
Net property and equipment	32.3	38.8
Long-term debt	9.1	37.9
Shareholders' equity	25.2	36.3
Capital expenditures	28.4	32.8
Number of stores	23.9	23.6
Average total company weekly sales	27.6	32.5
Number of customer transactions	23.8	27.6
Average sale per transaction	$3.00	$3.70
Weighted average sales per square foot	$1.00	$4.40

Exhibit 8 $100 Billion Do-It-Yourself Market

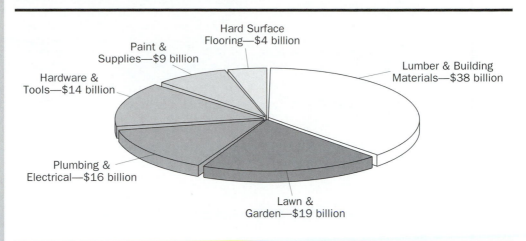

Source: The Home Depot, Inc., *1997 Annual Report*, p. 8.

These compound growth rates had provided Home Depot shareholders with 48 consecutive quarters of growth in sales and earnings. Fiscal year (FY) 1997 was from February 3, 1997, to February 1, 1998. Fiscal year (FY) is the company's financial year.

Exhibit 9 shows that the average sale per transaction had increased from $33.92 in 1990 to $43.63 in 1997, or 28.7%. During the same period, average total company weekly sales had increased from $72,000 to $465,000, or 545.8%. The weighted average weekly sales per operating store had increased from $566,000 in 1990 to $829,000 in 1997, or 464%. The weighted average sale per square foot had increased from $322 in 1990 to $406 in 1997, or 25.5%.

If someone had invested $1,000 on June 30, 1982, in Home Depot, on June 28, 1997, the investment would have been worth $152,479. Only two stocks surpassed Home Depot's performance: Keane ($321,022) and Mark IV Industries ($269,265).

Exhibits 9, 10, and 11 provide the company's ten-year selected financial and operating income highlights, consolidated statement of earnings, and balance sheet.

Exhibit 9   Ten-Year Selected Financial and Operating Highlights: Home Depot, Inc.
(Dollar amounts in thousands, except where noted)

	5-Year Annual Compound Growth Rate	10-Year Annual Compound Growth Rate	Fiscal Years[3]									
			1997	1996[1]	1995	1994	1993	1992	1991	1990[1]	1989	1988
Statement of Earnings Data												
Net sales	27.6%	32.5%	$24,156	$19,535	$15,470	$12,477	$9,239	$7,148	$5,137	$3,815	$2,759	$2,000
Net sales increase—%	—	—	23.7	26.3	24.0	35.0	29.2	39.2	34.6	38.3	38.0	37.6
Earnings before taxes[2]	28.3	35.6	2,002	1,535	1,195	980	737	576	396	260	182	126
Net earnings[2]	27.5	38.6	1,224	938	732	605	457	363	249	163	112	77
Net earnings increase—%[2]	—	—	30.5	28.2	21.0	32.2	26.1	45.6	52.5	46.0	45.9	41.9
Diluted earnings per share ($)[2,3,4,5]	24.4	31.0	1.64	1.29	1.02	0.88	0.67	0.55	0.39	0.30	0.21	0.15
Diluted earnings per share increase—%[2]	—	—	27.1	26.5	15.9	31.3	21.8	41.0	30.0	42.9	40.0	36.4
Weighted average number of common shares outstanding assuming dilution[3,4]	1.7	4.6	762	732	717	714	711	699	662	608	574	519
Gross margin—% of sales	—	—	28.1	27.8	27.7	27.9	27.7	27.6	28.1	27.9	27.8	27.0
Store selling and operating—% of sales	—	—	17.8	18.0	18.0	17.8	17.6	17.4	18.1	18.2	18.3	17.8
Pre-opening expense—% of sales	—	—	0.3	0.3	0.4	0.4	0.4	0.4	0.3	0.4	0.3	0.4
General and administrative expense—% of sales	—	—	1.7	1.7	1.7	1.8	2.0	2.1	2.3	2.4	2.5	2.4
Net interest income (expense)—% of sales	—	—	—	0.1	0.1	(0.1)	0.3	0.4	0.3	(0.1)	(0.1)	(0.1)
Earnings before taxes—% of sales[2]	—	—	8.3	7.9	7.7	7.8	8.0	8.1	7.7	6.8	6.6	6.3
Net earnings—% of sales[2]	—	—	5.1	4.8	4.7	4.8	5.0	5.1	4.8	4.3	4.1	3.8
Balance Sheet Data and Financial Ratios												
Total assets	23.4%	35.8%	$11,229	$9,342	$7,354	$5,778	$4,701	$3,932	$2,510	$1,640	$1,118	$699
Working capital	19.9	33.6	2,004	1,867	1,255	919	994	807	624	301	274	143
Merchandise inventories	30.8	32.8	3,602	2,708	2,180	1,749	1,293	940	662	509	381	294
Net property and equipment	32.3	38.8	6,509	5,437	4,461	3,397	2,371	1,608	1,255	879	514	332
Long-term debt	9.1	37.9	1,303	1,247	720	983	874	844	271	531	303	108
Shareholders' equity	25.2	36.3	7,098	5,955	4,988	3,442	2,814	2,304	1,691	683	512	383
Book value per share ($)[3]	22.9	31.2	9.70	8.26	6.97	5.06	4.17	3.46	2.67	1.29	0.99	0.75
Long-term debt to equity—%	—	—	18.4	20.9	14.4	28.6	31.1	36.6	16.0	77.7	59.1	28.1
Current ratio	—	—	1.82:1	2.01:1	1.89:1	1.76:1	2.02:1	2.07:1	2.17:1	1.73:1	1.94:1	1.74:1
Inventory turnover	—	—	5.4x	5.6x	5.5x	5.7x	5.9x	6.3x	6.1x	6.0x	5.9x	5.8x
Return on beginning equity—%	—	—	19.5	18.8	21.3	21.5	19.9	21.5	36.5	31.9	29.2	23.9

Exhibit 9 **Ten-Year Selected Financial and Operating Highlights: Home Depot, Inc.** *(continued)*
(Dollar amounts in thousands, except where noted)

	5-Year Annual Compound Growth Rate	10-Year Annual Compound Growth Rate	Fiscal Years[3]									
			1997	1996[1]	1995	1994	1993	1992	1991	1990[1]	1989	1988
Statement of Cash Flows Data												
Depreciation and amortization	32.4%	38.8%	$283	$232	$181	$130	$90	$70	$52	$34	$21	$15
Capital expenditures	28.4	32.8	1,525	1,248	1,308	1,220	900	437	432	400	205	105
Cash dividends per share ($)[3]	28.6	43.5	0.19	0.15	0.13	0.10	0.07	0.05	0.04	0.02	0.02	0.01
Store Data[6]												
Number of stores	23.9%	23.6%	624	512	423	340	264	214	174	145	118	96
Number of states	16.6	17.8	41	38	31	28	23	19	15	12	12	10
Number of Canadian provinces	—	—	4	3	3	3	—	—	—	—	—	—
Square footage at year-end	26.0	26.8	66	54	44	35	26	21	16	13	10	8
Increase in square footage (%)	—	—	23.1	21.6	26.3	33.2	26.3	26.8	24.1	27.4	26.9	33.4
Average square footage per store (in thousands)	1.6	2.6	106	105	105	103	100	98	95	92	88	86
Store Sales and Other Data[6]												
Comparable stores sales increase—%[7]	—	—	7	7	3	8	7	15	11	10	13	13
Average total company weekly sales	27.6%	32.5%	$465	$369	$298	$240	$178	$137	$99	$72	$53	$38
Weighted average weekly sales per operating store (in thousands)	2.7	7.1	829	803	787	802	764	724	633	566	515	464
Weighted average sales per square foot ($)[7]	1.0	4.4	406	398	390	404	398	387	348	322	303	282
Number of customer transactions	23.8	27.6	550	464	370	302	236	189	146	112	84	64
Average sale per transaction ($)	3.0	3.7	43.63	42.09	41.78	41.29	39.13	37.72	35.13	33.92	32.65	31.13
Number of associates at year-end (actual)	26.2	29.9	124,400	98,100	80,800	67,300	50,600	38,900	28,000	21,500	17,500	13,000

Notes:
1. Fiscal years 1996 and 1990 consisted of 53 weeks; all other years reported consisted of 52 weeks.
2. Excludes the effect of the $104 million non-recurring charge in fiscal 1997.
3. All share and per-share data have been adjusted for a three-for-two stock split on July 3, 1997.
4. Share and per-share data have been restated for the adoption of SFAS 128 "Earnings per Share."
5. Diluted earnings per share for fiscal 1997, including the $104 million non-recurring charge, were $1.55 (see note 9 of the Notes to Consolidated Financial Statements).
6. Excludes Maintenance Warehouse and National Blind and Wallpaper Factory.
7. Adjusted to reflect the first 52 weeks of the 53-week fiscal years in 1996 and 1990.

Source: Home Depot, Inc., *1997 Annual Report*, first page fold-out.

Exhibit 10   Consolidated Statement of Earnings: Home Depot, Inc.
(Dollar amounts in millions, except per-share data)

Fiscal Year Ending[1]	February 1, 1998	February 2, 1997	January 28, 1996
Net sales	$24,156	$19,535	$15,470
Cost of merchandise sold	17,375	14,101	11,184
Gross profit	6,781	5,434	4,286
Operating expenses			
Selling and store operating	4,287	3,521	2,784
Pre-opening	65	55	52
General and administrative	413	324	270
Non-recurring charge	104	—	—
Total operating expenses	4,869	3,900	3,106
Operating income	1,912	1,534	1,180
Interest income (expense)			
Interest and investment income	44	25	19
Interest expense	(42)	(16)	(4)
Interest, net	2	9	15
Minority interest	(16)	(8)	—
Earnings before income taxes	1,898	1,535	1,195
Income taxes	738	597	463
Net earnings	$ 1,160	$ 938	$ 732
Basic earnings per share	$1.59	$1.30	$1.03
Weighted average number of common shares outstanding	729	719	709
Diluted earnings per share	$1.55	$1.29	$1.02
Weighted average number of common shares outstanding assuming dilution	762	732	717

Notes:
1. Fiscal year (FY) 1997 was February 3, 1997 to February 1, 1998.
2. Notes were deleted.

Source: Home Depot, Inc., *1997 Annual Report*, p. 21.

Exhibit 11 **Consolidated Balance Sheet: Home Depot, Inc.**
(Dollar amounts in millions, except per-share data)

Fiscal Year Ending[1]	February 1, 1998	February 2, 1997
Assets		
Current assets		
Cash and cash equivalents	$ 172	$ 146
Short-term investments, including current maturities		
of long-term investments	2	413
Receivables, net	556	388
Merchandise inventories	3,602	2,708
Other current assets	128	54
Total current assets	4,460	3,709
Property and equipment, at cost		
Land	2,194	1,855
Buildings	3,041	2,470
Furniture, fixtures, and equipment	1,370	1,084
Leasehold improvements	383	340
Construction in progress	336	284
Capital leases	163	117
	7,487	6,150
Less accumulated depreciation and amortization	978	713
Net property and equipment	6,509	5,437
Long-term investments	15	8
Notes receivable	27	40
Cost in excess of the fair value of net assets acquired, net of accumulated amortization of $18 at February 1, 1998 and $15 at February 2, 1997	140	87
Other	78	61
Total assets	$11,229	$9,342
Liabilities and Shareholders' Equity		
Current liabilities		
Accounts payable	$ 1,358	$1,090
Accrued salaries and related expenses	312	249
Sales taxes payable	143	129
Other accrued expenses	530	323
Income taxes payable	105	49
Current installments of long-term debt	8	2
Total current liabilities	2,456	1,842
Long-term debt, excluding current installments	1,303	1,247
Other long-term liabilities	178	134
Deferred income taxes	78	66
Minority interest	116	98
Shareholders' Equity		
Common stock, par value $0.05. Authorized: 1,000,000,000 shares; issued and oustanding—732,108,000 shares at February 1, 1998 and 720,773,000 shares at February 2, 1997	37	36
Paid-in capital	2,662	2,511
Retained earnings	4,430	3,407
Cumulative translation adjustments	(28)	2
Total shareholders' equity	7,101	5,956
Less: shares purchased for compensation plans	3	1
	7,098	5,955
Total liabilities and shareholders' equity	$11,229	$9,342

Notes:
1. Fiscal year (FY) 1997 was February 3, 1997 to February 1, 1998.
2. Company consolidated balance sheet showed **Commitments and contingencies** instead of **Total liabilities and shareholders' equity**.

Source: Home Depot, Inc., *1997 Annual Report,* p. 22.

Notes

1. This section is based on Paul M. Swiercz's case "The Home Depot, Inc.," as it appears in *Cases in Strategic Management,* 4th ed., Thomas L. Wheelen and J. David Hunger (Reading, Mass.: Addison-Wesley, 1993), pp. 367–397. It is referred to as Swiercz in further citations. Any information beyond 1989 is new to this case.
2. Ben Sharav, "Home Depot," *Value Line* (July 21, 1995), p. 888.
3. Rahul Jacob, "Corporate Reputation," *Fortune* (March 6, 1995) pp. 54–55.
4. Eleena Lesser and Anita Sharpe, "Home Depot Charges a Rival Drummed Up Opposition to Stores," *Wall Street Journal* (August 18, 1995), p. A-1.
5. *Ibid.*
6. Chris Roush, "Home Depot Reaches a Cross Roads," *The Atlanta Journal* (July 16, 1996), p. P6.
7. *Ibid.*
8. The Home Depot, Inc., *1996 Annual Report,* p. 5.
9. The Home Depot, Inc., *1997 Annual Report,* p. 16.
10. *Ibid.*
11. *Ibid.*
12. *Ibid.*
13. *St. Petersburg Times* (December 24, 1990), p. 11.
14. *Business Atlanta* (November 11, 1988).
15. *Ibid.*
16. *Chain Store Executive* (April 1983), pp. 9–11.
17. The Home Depot, Inc., *1995 Annual Report,* p. 3.
18. The Home Depot, Inc., *1997 Annual Report,* p. 13. This was directly quoted with minor editing.
19. *Ibid.,* p. 5.
20. The Home Depot, Inc., *Form 10-K* (February 1, 1998), pp. 8–9. The material was abstracted, *1997 Annual Meeting of Shareholders Notice,* pp. 3–6.
21. The Home Depot, Inc., *1997 Form 10-K,* pp. 8–9.
22. The Home Depot, Inc., *1997 Annual Report,* p. 35.
23. Swiercz, "The Home Depot, Inc."
24. *Ibid.,* The Home Depot, Inc., *1996 Annual Report,* p. 13, and The Home Depot, Inc., *1997 Form 10-K,* pp. 4, 10–11. Some paragraphs in this section are directly quoted with minor editing.
25. Susan Caminiti, "The New Champs of Retailing," *Fortune* (September 1990), p. 2.
26. The Home Depot, Inc., *1997 Form 10-K,* p. 3. The table is directly quoted.
27. *Ibid.,* The Home Depot, Inc., *1997 Form 10-K,* pp. 6–7. This section was directly quoted with minor editing.
28. The Home Depot, Inc., *1997 Annual Report,* p. 20. This section was directly quoted with minor editing.
29. Swiercz, "The Home Depot, Inc.," and The Home Depot, Inc. *1997 Annual Report,* pp. 12–13.
30. Ben Sharav, "Retail Building Supply Industry," *Value Line* (January 16, 1998), p. 884.
31. Ben Sharav, "Home Depot," *Value Line* (July 21, 1995), p. 884.
32. Robert LaFranco, "Comeuppance," *Forbes* (December 4, 1995), p. 74.
33. *Ibid.,* pp. 74–75.
34. Mitchell Pacelle, "Retail Building Surge Despite Store Glut," *Wall Street Journal* (January 17, 1996), p. A-2.
35. *Ibid.*
36. *Ibid.*
37. *Ibid.*
38. The Home Depot, Inc., *1997 Annual Report,* pp. 6–7. The first five paragraphs were directly quoted with minor editing.
39. *Ibid.,* p. 80.
40. Robert Berne and William M. Bulkeley, "Kmart and Waban Consider Combining Home Improvement Chains in New Firm," *Wall Street Journal* (February 4, 1997), p. A-3.

Seven-Eleven Japan: Managing a Networked Organization

Ben M. Bensaou

Toshifumi Suzuki had been a radical since his university days when he was a frequent student protester. Now, despite his unorthodox approach, the 64-year-old executive has become one of Japan's most esteemed company presidents. When, in the early 1970s, he proposed to bring from the United States the concept of the convenience store, he faced strong skepticism within Ito-Yokado, Seven-Eleven Japan's parent company, and within the industry. Despite the opposition, he persevered and adapted the innovative concept to the Japanese context, starting a "revolution" in the Japanese distribution system. To explain the continual success of his company, Suzuki likes to explain that "we are not in the retail business but rather in the *information* business." For him, the bottle of shampoo sitting on the shelf at a Shizuoka store is a "bundle of information." This vision of the retail industry has led Seven-Eleven Japan to be the first retailer to install, in 1991, an ISDN network (Integrated Service Digital Network). Indeed, ever since the creation of the company in 1973, Suzuki has heavily invested in information technology (IT) applications to link his business processes to those of his business partners, the franchisees' stores, the wholesalers, and the manufacturers.

Critics in the industry, however, are now questioning whether the new and costly investments in networking technology are really necessary. Seven-Eleven Japan indeed might have benefited from a first mover advantage, consistently improving its financial position, but it is now under the threat of competitors who have been implementing similar information systems. How can Suzuki sustain 7-Eleven's competitive advantage in a rapidly saturating domestic retail market? What does it take to stay number one in Japan? Is it time to expand internationally and export the CVS (convenience store) concept back to the United States and to new markets in Europe and Asia? How can Suzuki transfer to a Western context the unique capabilities he has created and nurtured in the domestic market over the last 20 years?

THE JAPANESE DISTRIBUTION SYSTEM

Some Western experts view the Japanese distribution system as a major barrier to trade. They describe it as highly inefficient and hold it responsible for the high prices Japanese consumers pay. Traditional retailing in Japan consists of a conservative, multi-tiered, and outmoded system that brings together a large number of small wholesalers and retailers into a complex and exclusive network of tight relationships, based on not only economic efficiency but also human considerations (Exhibit 1). Japanese manufacturers generally control the distribution of their wares, and retailers have to select goods from wholesalers' limited offerings. In exchange, shops are able to return unsold goods to wholesalers. Stores then tend to be full of high-priced goods that consumers don't necessarily want. Today most Japanese small retailers are independent, yet belong to such informal but tight and cooperative vertical networks. These are held together by mutual interest

This case was written by Ben M. Bensaou, Associate Professor of Information Technology and Management at INSEAD with the participation of H. Uchino, K. Mitani, and M. Noishiki, INSEAD MBA, on the basis of published documents. It is intended to be used as a basis for class discussion rather than to illustrate either effective or ineffective handling of an administrative situation. Copyright © 1997 INSEAD-EAC, Fontainebleau, France. Reprinted by permission.

and long-term personal as well as business relationships. These develop over time between well-known partners and are maintained and nurtured by personal contacts, frequent visits, gifts, mutual services, financing, and support in difficult times. Newcomers can only enter through introductions.

Already in feudal Japan, manufacturers were the ones controlling large, multi-tiered channels through which they marketed their products. At the time, the manufacturing class enjoyed much higher prestige than the merchant class. Their prestige and stature further increased later as they were credited with Japan's post–World War II economic success. In the Tokugawa era, Japan consisted of many small, largely self-contained provinces that developed their own local distribution system independently of each other. Mobility of goods and people across the four main islands was then extremely limited. To gain access to any area, producers had to rely on intermediaries who knew and could deal with customers in sometimes remote villages. Over time, this practice led to the building of close relationships between the different players in this intricate distribution system.

Even today, products typically pass through three or more levels of wholesalers—the national or primary wholesalers, the secondary wholesalers, and the local ones. The manufacturer designates the primary wholesaler who would coordinate the regional level and perform the handling, financing, physical distribution, warehousing, inventory, promotion, and payment collection functions for him. In addition, since the 1950s, wholesalers are asked to accept on the manufacturers' behalf all the unsold products returned by the retailers. Before ending up in Mr. Nishida's store in Shibuya, Tokyo, an eyeglasses frame would travel from Horikawa Seisakusho's production site in Sabae, Fukui prefecture (500 km from Tokyo), to the manufacturer's exclusive national wholesaler in Sabae. The large wholesaler then distributes its products through a close network of selected regional wholesalers all over Japan. The regional wholesaler in Fuchu (an eastern suburb of Tokyo) should carry the total inventory for the East Tokyo area. From his warehouse, the eyeglasses would be dispatched to one of the multiple local wholesalers and finally to retailers in the Shibuya-ku district.

Manufacturers still maintain a tight control over the relationships. They set the price at which the product needs to be sold and dictate the criteria on which are based the rebates they attribute to wholesalers and retailers. These rebates are based not only on quantity purchased, but also on loyalty and service, criteria that favor the small retailers and wholesalers. A large number and variety of rebates are offered in Japan. They include rebates for quantity, early payment, achieving sales targets, service performance, keeping inventory, sales promotion, loyalty to supplier, following manufacturers' pricing policies, cooperation with the manufacturer, and contributing to its success. The system was historically established by manufacturers to ensure total support for their products and their marketing strategies, and to exclude rival manufacturers from the channel. The negotiated and long-term nature of the rebates and the fact that they are secret increases manufacturers' power and strengthens their control over channel activities.

The Japanese retail sector in Japan is still dominated by small retailers (Exhibit 2). These local, small, "mom-and-pop" stores carry wide assortments in a narrow product line. They typically lack managerial and planning skills and thus have to rely on the wholesalers for inventory and distribution performance. In addition, given their limited size, they are often unable to bear the risks associated with carrying a wide range of products, and with financing and managing their own retail outlet. To support them, manufacturers and large wholesalers have implemented the product return system and various financing programs. Small shops, however, have been facing new threats first coming from newly developed retail structures, such as department stores and supermarkets. In 1956, they lobbied the government for the introduction of the Department

Exhibit 1   International Comparisons of Distribution Systems

A. A Comparison of Distribution Structures

	Japan (1988)	US (1982)	UK (1984)	France (1987)	West Germany (1985)
Number of retail stores (000)	1,628	1,731	343	565	320
Population (millions)	121	231	56	55	61
Number of retail stores per 10,000 people	134	75	61	103	52
Number of wholesalers per 10,000 people	36	18	17	14	19
Number of retail stores per wholesaler	3.7	4.2	3.6	7.3	2.7
Number of employees per store	4.2	1.9	2.0	1.6	1.8
Number of retail stores per 10km	43.1	1.8	14.0	10.0	12.8

B. US and Japan's Retail Systems: Food and Non-Food Sectors

Number of Employees	US (1982) Food		Non-Food		Japan (1985) Food		Non-Food	
	Stores	Sales	Stores	Sales	Stores	Sales	Stores	Sales
0–2	23.7	2.5	50.6	7.9	60.1	17.0	56.0	10.6
3–9	46.1	13.7	31.0	25.0	35.0	50.5	38.1	39.8
10–19	12.6	9.2	10.2	17.0	3.1	4.0	4.0	13.5
20–49	11.2	29.0	6.0	20.9	1.5	18.6	1.5	10.7
50–99	5.0	29.7	1.6	13.1	0.3	8.2	0.3	5.1
100+	1.4	15.9	0.6	16.1	0.0	2.1	0.1	20.3
Total percentages	100.0	100.0	100.0	100.0	100.0	100.0	100.0	100.0
Percentage of total	9.5	22.6	90.5	77.4	41.2	31.3	58.8	68.7

Source: A. Goldman, 1992.

Stores Law, regulating the opening and business hours of larger outlets. Later, when the first superstores and supermarkets were met with wide customer acceptance, the government introduced more restrictive regulations, i.e., the Large Retail Stores (LRS) Law. Initially applied to stores with an area greater than 1,500 m², it was later extended in 1979 to stores 500 m² and over. New guidelines were issued in 1982, giving more power to the local governments in these regulatory matters. Applications were now reviewed by special councils. The views of the local chamber of commerce and of the Council for Coordination of Commercial Activity (CCCA) regarding the impact of the proposed retail store on the local economy and on the small stores in the surrounding area weighed heavily in decisions. At present, no time limits existed on these negotiations and the process that originally took a year or so now took between seven and eight years, and in some instances even 15, to complete. Regulations have therefore effectively protected the small retailers and have helped the traditional sector to maintain its position. Under heavy pressure from abroad, changes to the LRS law have recently been proposed.

Despite these rigidities in the system, the intricacies of the multi-tiered channels and the high price of goods, consumer surveys indicate that Japanese consumers are generally content with their distribution system. Living in small houses or apartments with little storage space, Japanese housewives cherish shopping in specialty stores in their neighborhood and usually display a strong loyalty to the small, local stores. Relationships

Exhibit 2 The Key Players in the Japanese Retail Industry

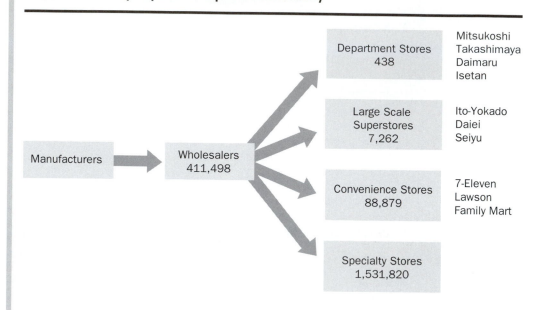

A. Supermarkets: 18% of the total retail market in 1991 (14,848,900 million ¥)

	Market Share	Operating Revenue (100 million ¥)	Income before Income Taxes (100 million ¥)	Employees
Daiei	10.1	20,259	275	46,045
Ito Yokado	8.9	14,596	972	32,076
Seiyu	6.9	10,950	160	23,657
Jusco	5.0	10,413	296	24,993
Nichii	4.9	7,671	291	20,025
Uny	3.6	5,558	174	12,461
Nagasakiya	2.8	4,374	41	11,009
Izumiya	2.6	4,002	151	n/a
Tsujitsuya	2.0	3,283	51	n/a
Maruetsu	2.2	3,213	82	10,722
Others	51.2	n/a	n/a	n/a

B. Department Stores: 8% of the total retail market in 1991

	Market Share	Operating Revenue (100 million ¥)	Income before Income Taxes (100 million ¥)	Employees
Mitsukoshi	9.0	8,766	110	11,867
Takashimaya	8.6	8,430	134	9,782
Daimaru	6.2	6,083	61	7,312
Matsuzakaya	5.1	5,020	100	7,246
Isetan	4.8	4,682	141	5,683
Tokyu	4.2	4,106	92	4,945
Hankyu	3.6	3,552	114	5,440
Sogo	3.2	3,106	73	3,651
Hanshin	1.3	1,221	22	n/a
Matsuya	1.2	1,116	16	n/a
Others	52.8	n/a	n/a	n/a

between customers and the store owner tend to be long lasting. Some of these small stores are not necessarily run on a profit-making basis. Typically the store is part of the owner's residence, and in most instances, the wife and her retired husband work together. Overall the productivity of the distribution system has been low. Small retailers are unable to keep pace with rapidly changing consumer needs and invest in improving their operations. In a 1982 survey, annual sales per retailer in Japan amounted to $219,000 versus $600,000 in the United States (Exhibit 1).

THE FORCES FOR CHANGE

In the 1950s, with rising income, rapid urbanization, and increased mobility, consumer preferences gradually changed. The concept of the *supermarket* was introduced to Japanese consumers around this time. These new stores, such as Daiei, Ito-Yokado, Seiyu, and Jusco, carried everyday items and sold them at low prices. They could offer competitive prices due to the large volume rebates they secured from large wholesalers. The 1970s and 1980s brought prosperity and affluence. Consumers did not just look for the cheapest product any more, but were now sensitive to the quality of the product and the service. At the same time, the social fabric of Japanese society was evolving. More women entered the labor force, the traditional, extended family structure started to disintegrate, and people wanted more leisure time. This period, in fact, represented a turning point in the evolution of the Japanese distribution system, as it moved from a manufacturer-centered system to a customer-oriented system. Listening to consumer needs became the critical success factor.

The Japanese retail industry flourished and grew to provide customers with a wide range of retail formats fiercely competing against each other. First, there was the large number of small traditional mom-and-pop stores that carried a narrow range of items but provided the convenience of neighborhood proximity. Large department stores, such as Mitsukoshi or Takashimaya (Exhibit 2), carried a wide range of items and catered to the high end of the market. Historically, these *hyakka-ten* were rich cloth merchants of the Edo or Tokugawa period (1600–1868) who later expanded their business to become large retailers. The supermarkets, on the other hand, carried a large range of items at discount prices that would appeal to the middle and low end of the market. Other players in the retail business included convenience stores, discount stores, and direct mail businesses, each of them focusing on a different factor for success—convenience, discounts, and market targeting, respectively.

THE CONVENIENCE STORE CONCEPT

Ito-Yokado was founded by Masatoshi Ito in 1946 as a 66-square-foot family clothing store in Tokyo. By 1960, Ito had expanded his business into a ¥384 million company. The same year, he visited the United States and saw multi-item superstores for the first time. Upon his return to Japan, he started a new chain of superstores offering a range of food and clothing products. He further expanded his business into other distribution areas, such as restaurants, department stores offering a full range of products, discount stores, and convenience stores. By 1988, the Ito-Yokado group had grown into the second largest retailer group in Japan and one of the most profitable ones, with 32 companies, 4,000 stores, and 60,000 employees (Exhibits 3, 4, and 5). It was at a business seminar in Tokyo in 1968 that Toshifumi Suzuki, Executive Manager of Ito-Yokado's New

Business Development division, first heard of the concept of convenience stores, at the time very popular in the United States. He came to realize that bringing small retailers into a new franchise of convenience stores would, on the one hand, provide the small shop owners with the management and merchandising skills they were lacking to survive, and on the other hand, provide customers with the benefits of the traditional, small neighborhood retailer. The restrictive LSR regulation did not encourage further development of the supermarket chain concept and provided the right context for an innovative solution that leveraged the pre-existence of a large number of protected small "neighborhood" stores.

Without his president's direct approval, Toshifumi Suzuki flew to the United States and directly negotiated with Southland, owner of 7-Eleven, to bring the convenience store concept to Japan. President Ito and others at Ito-Yokado were convinced that it was too early to introduce the concept into the Japanese distribution system, which was already saturated with a very large number of small retailers. Despite the commonly held skepticism and sometimes outright opposition within the mother company, Suzuki proceeded with his plans and in 1974 opened the first 7-Eleven convenience store in Japan in Kohtoh-ku, an eastern suburb of Tokyo. He later explained: "At the time, I was young and very eager to find a way we could prosper together with small retailers. I was convinced that a convenience store franchise was the best solution." After the contract had been signed, Suzuki realized that the Southland concept of convenience store had to be *adapted* to the Japanese market and was convinced that the American operational know-how could not be directly transferred to the Japanese distribution system context. The challenge for Seven-Eleven Japan was to develop new business systems all on its own. In particular, the differences in consumer behavior between the United States and Japan translated into large differences in the strategy and implementation Suzuki pursued for Seven-Eleven Japan. Japanese consumers were generally more sensitive to product and service quality, more fickle, and less price sensitive. To meet such customer requirements within the constraints of limited shelf space and storage capacity, it was necessary to offer a wide range of well-targeted products and to provide additional services 24 hours a day, 7 days a week.

STRATEGY

After graduating in economics from Chuo University, Suzuki worked for Tokyo Shuppan Hanbai, one of Japan's largest book wholesalers. At 31, he was noticed by one of his clients, Ito-Yokado, and was later asked to join the company. At the time, Ito-Yokado owned only four stores in the Tokyo area but was one of the fastest growing companies in Japan. At first Suzuki was in charge of personnel and advertisement. In 1970, years later, he became Executive Director for the New Business Development division. His most influential success was the creation of alliances with large regional retailers and with the Denny's chain of restaurants. His fundamental belief in the importance of customer satisfaction was repeatedly reinforced in all of his policies throughout his career. In particular, his obsession with customer satisfaction was at the origin of the Seven-Eleven Japan practice of continuous item control, frequent delivery, and the heavy use of information technology (IT) applications. To get an objective assessment of customer needs, he preferred to rely on inexperienced people. In his view, "merchandising consists in identifying customer needs . . . and experience or expertise might contaminate a manager's judgment." Unlike many retail managers, he rarely visited stores. His approach was more analytical—hence his faith in a high-tech computer system to keep in touch with cus-

Exhibit 3   **7-Eleven Japan and the Competition**

A. Outlook of CVS Industry and Main Franchise Chains (1988)

CVS Chains	Sales (billion ¥)	No. of Stores	Parent Company
7-Eleven	780	3,940	Ito-Yokado
Lawsons	430	3,570	Daiei
Family Mart	264	1,725	Seibu Saisons
Sun-Every Yamazaki	223	2,061	Yamazaki Bread
Kmart	90	778	UNY

B. Outlook of CVS Industry and Main Franchise Chains (1988)

CVS Chains	Sales per day (1$ = ¥125)	Store Space (m^2)	Gross Margin (%)	Full-Time Clerks
7-Eleven	$4,048	98	27.4	4
Lawsons	3,156	100	28.8	8
Family Mart	3,200	90	26.5	6
Sun-Every Yamazaki	3,200	96	27.0	4
Kmart	2,794	132	22.0	4

C. Royalties

CVS Chains	Royalties (% of gross profit)	Contract Length (years)
7-Eleven	45	15
Lawsons	32	10
Family Mart	35	10

tomer tastes. Suzuki's hunger for information gave birth to weekly meetings involving some 160 managers to discuss the tiniest matters affecting the company, from curtain sales in northern Japan to the reasons peach sales flopped.

Seven-Eleven Japan had been changing its concept of "convenience store," constantly adjusting to changing consumer behavior. Suzuki described 7-Eleven stores as "stores where you can find a solution for any of your daily life problems. We always try to plan and design a store in such a way that young people, in particular, can get whatever they need at any time they want." Suzuki agreed that the productivity level of traditional small retailers was extremely low, mainly because most of these mom-and-pop stores had grown out of touch with consumer needs and thus were losing business to large retailers. He subsequently built a strategy for his franchise business to address what he believed were the two main reasons for the failure of small, and even large, retailers: they ignored (1) the importance of convenience to the customer and (2) the quality of the products and the service. In surveys, customers typically complained about:

- The products they were looking for being sold out

- The long waiting lines at cashiers

- The stores being closed when they needed the service

Exhibit 4 **Seven-Eleven Japan and Competition**

A. Japan's Top Five Retailers by Total Store Sales (1996)

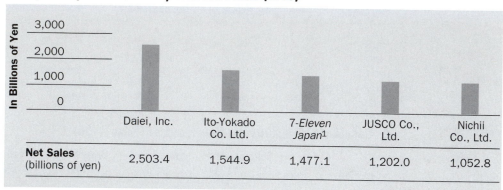

	Daiei, Inc.	Ito-Yokado Co. Ltd.	7-Eleven Japan[1]	JUSCO Co., Ltd.	Nichii Co., Ltd.
Net Sales (billions of yen)	2,503.4	1,544.9	1,477.1	1,202.0	1,052.8

Note: 1. Sales of all Seven-Eleven Japan stores

B. Japan's Top Five Retailers by Ordinary Profit (1996)

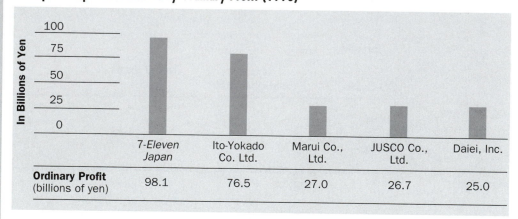

	7-Eleven Japan	Ito-Yokado Co. Ltd.	Marui Co., Ltd.	JUSCO Co., Ltd.	Daiei, Inc.
Ordinary Profit (billions of yen)	98.1	76.5	27.0	26.7	25.0

C. Sales by Japanese Convenience Stores

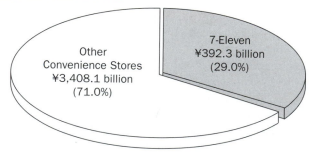

Other Convenience Stores
¥3,408.1 billion
(71.0%)

7-Eleven
¥392.3 billion
(29.0%)

☐ Convenience store sales are for fiscal 1994 and are taken from the *Nikkei Ryutsu Shinbun*.

▨ The 7-Eleven sales figure is for the period ended February 28, 1995.

Exhibit 5   **Seven-Eleven Japan Performance**

A. Total Number of Retail Stores and of 7-Eleven Stores in Japan

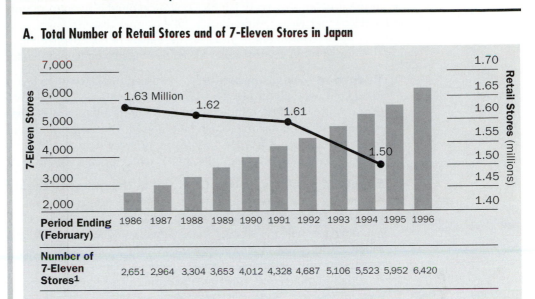

Period Ending (February)	1986	1987	1988	1989	1990	1991	1992	1993	1994	1995	1996
Number of 7-Eleven Stores[1]	2,651	2,964	3,304	3,653	4,012	4,328	4,687	5,106	5,523	5,952	6,420

Note: Number of 7-Eleven stores includes stores in Hawaii.

B. Average Daily Sales at New Stores in Their First Fiscal Year of Operation

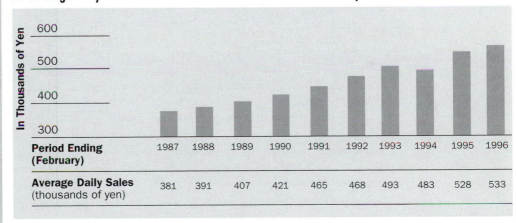

Period Ending (February)	1987	1988	1989	1990	1991	1992	1993	1994	1995	1996
Average Daily Sales (thousands of yen)	381	391	407	421	465	468	493	483	528	533

Source: 7-Eleven Japan, *An Introduction to Investors* (1996).

- Product freshness

- The contact with store personnel

For Seven-Eleven Japan, the first complaint was considered as the most critical problem to be dealt with. "If you cannot get me the fresh tofu I need for dinner tonight, I won't come back to your store," complained a housewife to her usual store. In essence, small retail stores were losing not only profit opportunity, but also customer loyalty. In response to this issue, 7-Eleven made it clear in its franchisee guidelines that "for them, 30 items sold out from a portfolio of 3,000 should represent a 'stock-out rate' of 100%

and not 1%." The basic mission of a Seven-Eleven Japan store was to provide solutions for all the problems of everyday life. A store offered a variety of high-quality products and services that were required on a daily or on a distress basis, or that just made life easier or more "convenient." Under Suzuki's leadership, Seven-Eleven Japan had therefore developed three key principles to define a quality convenience store:

1. **Reduction of lost opportunity.** A missed opportunity to sell an item because it is sold out was believed to represent up to three times the value of the actually realized profit. Suzuki therefore encouraged the development of operational processes to reduce this opportunity cost: "We need to not simply identify what particular products customers like, but more importantly, we should accurately determine when, where, in which quantities and at which price these products are needed."

2. **Supply of products just-in-time and in the quantity required.** The simplest way of reducing opportunity cost is to keep large inventories of a wide range of products. Unfortunately this solution could not be applied in convenience stores in Japan where shelf and storage space were limited and running large stocks was prohibitive. Moreover, planning customers' future needs presented major challenges. Seven-Eleven Japan pursued a strategy of supplying products that were in demand on a just-in-time basis, thereby eliminating dead items and slow selling items and replacing them by the faster selling ones.

3. **Franchise strategy.** To support his fundamental concept of co-prosperity between large supermarkets and the traditional small retailers system, Suzuki adopted a franchise system. From the beginning, he did not invest in American-style "greenfield" stores, where it is the franchiser who buys the "walls," or builds the store from the ground up. On the contrary, 70% of Seven-Eleven Japan stores were modified from old family-owned stores (e.g., rice, meat, or liquor stores). In other words, the store owner provided part of the financing, between US$ 200,000 and 300,000, in addition to saving on the cost of land and the building. It was also the expression of the long-term commitment to store profitability by the owner. The relationship between franchiser and franchisee was also distinctly one of reciprocal obligations. The franchisee was an independent business that gave Seven-Eleven Japan large royalties and a long-term commitment, and concentrated on the tasks of selling and effectively managing his inventory. In exchange, the franchiser provided the information back-up (i.e., data and analysis capabilities), implemented efficient operational systems to support planning and delivery of products, negotiated with the suppliers, advertised on a national scale, and developed new products that satisfied customers.

OUTSOURCING POLICY

Seven-Eleven Japan was also known for its outsourcing policy and superior ability to manage supplier relationships. Suzuki explained that retailing is a "quick response business," and that his company should therefore concentrate only on what they do better and outsource the rest. Since its creation, the company had never directly owned any manufacturing and logistics operations. Although its competitors tried to develop their own capabilities to circumvent the inefficiency and complexity of the existing Japanese distribution system, Seven-Eleven Japan identified an exclusive wholesaler for each region, assuring them of a long-term business relationship and large purchase volumes. In return for this exclusivity, these regional wholesalers were required to improve their operations and increase their performance standards. For instance, strict quality requirements in terms of freshness and taste were imposed. Seven-Eleven Japan had even outsourced its critical information technology. Although it had been spending about $80 million per year on IT, it had about 20 people running its electronic data system department. Their role was to develop a systems vision that fit with the business strategy, while the rest of the software and hardware design was subcontracted to the Nomura Research Institute (NRI), a subsidiary of Nomura Securities and the second largest systems integrator in Japan. In 1990, the company invested $200 million to replace its third-generation information systems. The multiple vendors involved, such as NTT and NRI, viewed the development of an IT infrastructure for 7-Eleven as a way of taking the lead over their own direct competitors.

"Selecting and negotiating with the various subcontractors, wholesalers, and small retailers was not easy," confides Suzuki. The long opening hours and the frequent deliveries did not attract many candidates at first. Also, the rationalized distribution system crafted by 7-Eleven—for instance, adopting a single exclusive regional wholesaler policy for each product category—created conflict within the traditional wholesale system. Over time, however, the Seven-Eleven Japan system proved highly reliable and efficient, gradually drawing more and more proponents. In the early 1980s, while competitors were diversifying and opening more stores, Seven-Eleven Japan concentrated on cost cutting and efficiency improvements. In its push for profitability, Ito-Yokado dropped inefficient wholesalers and forced the ones it retained to raise their standards. "It was tough for us because we had to make a huge investment to upgrade our information system for [them]" said a manager at a Tokyo-based wholesaler. "But if we'd refused, we'd have been cut off and gone out of business." Once those standards were met, wholesalers appreciated the feedback they were getting from the quick and precise sales data. Manufacturers also benefited, improving their sense of what customers wanted. "[Their] information system is so good that we can instantly find out which goods of ours are selling and how much," said a salesman at Tokyo Style, a large garment maker that makes an exclusive line for Ito-Yokado. By 1992, the company had built a network of 123 common distribution centers all over Japan, each of them created and operated by wholesalers and suppliers.

IMPLEMENTATION PROCESSES

Item Selection

First of all, a store needs to display at least 3,000 distinct items in order to be perceived by the customer as a convenience store. However, the store space available for a 7-Eleven franchisee is on average about 100 m^2. It thus becomes critical to carry the proper range of products. For example, to recommend to franchisees items from the 3,000 different soft drink products available on the market (of which 1,200 are regularly replaced every year), Seven-Eleven Japan used data analysis techniques to narrow down the list to 100 items. In one experiment, it was found that, under similar conditions, stores carrying a well-targeted range of only 70 items could sell 30% more than the regular stores with 100 items. Seven-Eleven Japan also used point of sale (POS) systems to identify customer trends and enhance its product differentiation. It can test new products and new brands in days rather than weeks or months. Year to year, 70% of merchandise in a given store will be new.

This meant that Seven-Eleven Japan was constantly monitoring and analyzing customer needs and tastes. It recently introduced a new innovation: weather forecasting and "human temperature studies." Weather terminals were used in stores to forecast orders for ice cream, bento boxes, sandwiches, oden (Japanese winter meal), and other items for which it had been observed that sales varied with weather conditions. Also, umbrellas kept in storage could be displayed if rain was forecast. Sandwiches do not sell well on rainy days, and on a sunny weekend, bentos sell extremely well. The weather also influenced the ingredients within a lunch box, and with three deliveries a day and orders for the next day accepted until 6:00 P.M., stores could precisely adjust their product mix to customer needs. The outlook of a store will typically be different in the morning or in the evening, whether the main customers are students on their way to school or "salarymen" on their way back.

Seven-Eleven Japan targeted all individuals living or working in the vicinity (i.e., within 300 m walking distance) of the store. A new store opened only if there were enough population density within this area and no direct competition. The primary segmentation was therefore by geography. Then customers could be classified according to their shopping habits.

1. **Immediate consumption.** These are mainly younger people, often singles, who do not have much time to cook for themselves. They want to buy typically foods/drinks for instant consumption. The main competition for this segment is fast food chains, take-out food stores and restaurants, or easy home cooking.

2. **Distress and daily.** These are customers who make "distress" purchases or buy daily supplies, e.g., fresh bread, vegetables, or dairy products, while they may have done their weekly shopping at a discount store or supermarket. This is typically the local neighborhood population.

3. **One-stop shopping.** These are customers who typically like to do all their food shopping in their neighborhood stores. This can include older people attached to their local community, people without a car, or working men and women who have little time to go shopping (especially during working hours).

The distinction between these three categories of customers reflected their different requirements for products, time, and habits of purchase. The key value proposition to achieve for Seven-Eleven Japan was therefore to deliver customer satisfaction for all three types of customers.

Item-by-Item Control

The items kept in stock and on the shelf were precisely selected for the targeted customers and product quality was kept high. 7-Eleven discovered that customer loyalty was driven more by specific items than by item categories. The implication was that the franchiser needed to plan demand and delivery on an item-by-item basis and could not rely on aggregate estimates per category of item, due to the observed high variance within product categories. In other words, Seven-Eleven Japan stores held just the right amount of stock for those selling items. Product turnover was high, and goods were always new and food extremely fresh. For instance, the shelf life of a "bento" lunchbox was 3 to 4 hours. Sales were registered on the POS system and slow or nonselling items were discontinued immediately. The product life cycle of branded drinks was short and tightly followed fashion. Stores could quickly switch from low-selling brands to the more fashionable ones according to sales data and the "top selling ranking" analysis. One could find all product types found at regular supermarkets, yet, Seven-Eleven Japan stores carried only a limited number of brands for each category. Sales by brands were also closely monitored and the portfolio of brands continually adjusted. Non-performing brands were ruthlessly deleted. To achieve such a tight item-by-item control, the Electronic Data

Systems department proposed a POS (point of sale) system solution, whereby data could be gathered online about which product was selling and where. Using these statistics, store owners could adjust their product mixes and supply requests quickly enough to respond to movements in customer demand. The same data, aggregated over time, allowed franchiser and franchisees to forecast long-term demand and plan new product launches.

New Product Development

Early on, 7-Eleven Japan identified the fast-food business as a high growth niche where it could leverage its efficient planning and delivery systems (Exhibit 6). For instance, fast foods now represented 40% of the total items on shelves and 30.6% of total sales. The chain differentiated itself from the competition by focusing on quality control of ingredients, cooperation with producers at the development and preparation stages, and strict control of freshness during delivery. The commitment to fast-food products' quality reached all the way to top management. Board directors themselves met to taste the new "bento" lunch boxes as they were developed.

Freshness/Quality of Products

Price in Japanese convenience stores was typically at a 10% premium over the average price at a large supermarket. Customers were therefore ready to pay a premium for freshness, quality of products, and convenience. To meet customer requirements for quality, Seven-Eleven Japan implemented a system of frequent and small lot deliveries (Exhibit 7). It had recently invested in temperature-controlled vans to preserve food quality and freshness.

Value-Added Services

To provide further convenience for its customers, Seven-Eleven Japan decided to offer value-added services. It started a home delivery parcel service in cooperation with a large transportation company, first with Nittsu Corporation and afterwards with Yamato. Leveraging its extensive electronic network with manufacturers, suppliers, wholesalers, and retail stores, Seven-Eleven Japan now provided online bill payment services for utilities (e.g., electricity and gas), insurance (e.g., life and car insurance), and telephone (e.g., NTT and KDD) (Exhibit 8). In 1992, it initiated a new mail order service business. In addition, beyond their direct retailing role, convenience stores had also become in urban areas a social center for younger crowds (Exhibit 8). They came and read magazines or bought concert tickets, music, or computer games.

Market Dominance Strategy

In its quietly aggressive way, Suzuki had been shaking up the conservative Japanese retail industry. His expansion strategy had been to penetrate new territory by building a critical mass of at least 50 to 60 franchisees (Exhibit 9). The resulting market presence contributed to:

- Distribution and logistics efficiency
- Operations and information systems effectiveness
- Franchisee support efficiency (i.e., field consultants)

Exhibit 6   Seven-Eleven Japan Performance

A. Sales of Fast Food

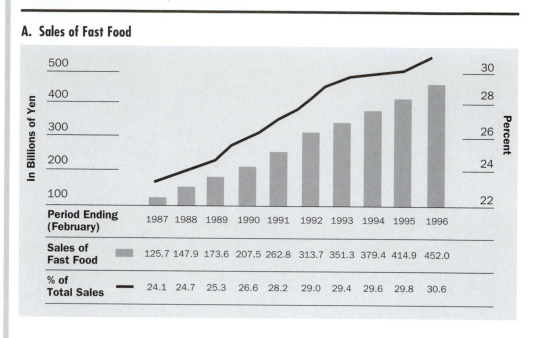

Period Ending (February)	1987	1988	1989	1990	1991	1992	1993	1994	1995	1996
Sales of Fast Food	125.7	147.9	173.6	207.5	262.8	313.7	351.3	379.4	414.9	452.0
% of Total Sales	24.1	24.7	25.3	26.6	28.2	29.0	29.4	29.6	29.8	30.6

B. Percentage of 7-Eleven Stores That Sell Liquor

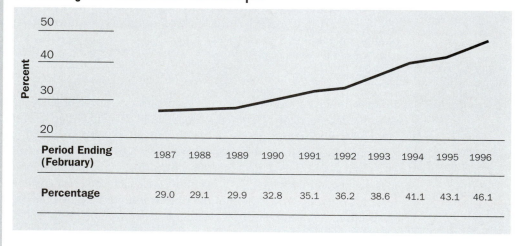

Period Ending (February)	1987	1988	1989	1990	1991	1992	1993	1994	1995	1996
Percentage	29.0	29.1	29.9	32.8	35.1	36.2	38.6	41.1	43.1	46.1

- 7-Eleven corporate image
- Higher entry barriers for competitors

Service Quality

First, accessibility was important. Stores were located in dense neighborhoods and stayed open all day. The intuitive store layout made it easy to find items even for the first time. In a country where space is at a premium, stores must create a warm, friendly atmosphere that not only attracts customers but also gives them a much valued sense of space and freedom. Shopping at Seven-Eleven Japan did not only provide tangible/

Exhibit 7 Seven-Eleven Japan Performance

A. Return on Equity and Revenue

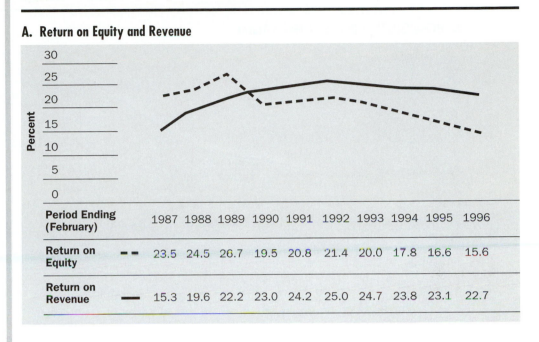

Period Ending (February)		1987	1988	1989	1990	1991	1992	1993	1994	1995	1996
Return on Equity	--	23.5	24.5	26.7	19.5	20.8	21.4	20.0	17.8	16.6	15.6
Return on Revenue	—	15.3	19.6	22.2	23.0	24.2	25.0	24.7	23.8	23.1	22.7

B. Number of Deliveries per Store per Day

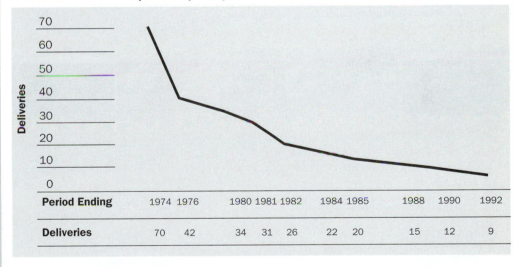

Period Ending	1974	1976	1980	1981	1982	1984	1985	1988	1990	1992
Deliveries	70	42	34	31	26	22	20	15	12	9

Source: 7-Eleven Japan, *An Introduction to Investors* (1996).

material satisfaction (e.g., goods and foods to consume) but also intangible satisfaction, such as good service, safety, a sense of relaxation, and a feeling of belonging to a community. The design of the store was very important, and nothing at Seven-Eleven Japan was left to chance. All parameters of store layout and design were analyzed and carefully chosen to deliver the value proposition to the customer. From the outside, the large 7-Eleven red and green logo flanked with red and green stripes around the store helped

Exhibit 8   Seven-Eleven Japan Performance

A. Utility Bills Paid Through 7-Eleven Stores

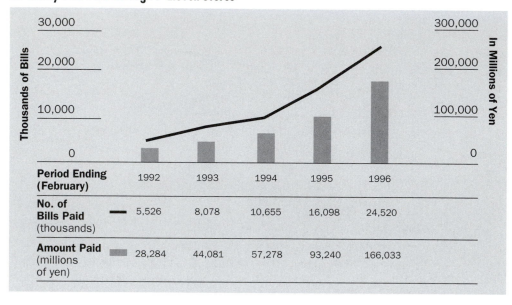

Period Ending (February)	1992	1993	1994	1995	1996
No. of Bills Paid (thousands)	5,526	8,078	10,655	16,098	24,520
Amount Paid (millions of yen)	28,284	44,081	57,278	93,240	166,033

B. Customer Profile

Gender and Marital Status

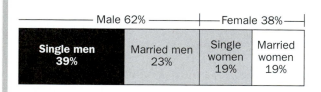

62% of customers are men

Age

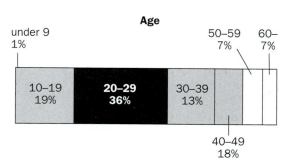

55% of customers are between the ages of 10 and 29

Frequency of Store Visits

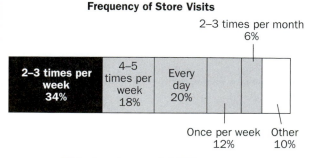

72% of customers visit 7-Eleven
at least twice per week

Time It Takes Customers to Reach a 7-Eleven Store

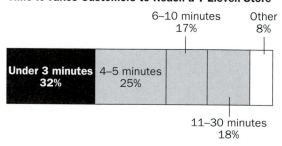

57% of customers come to 7-Eleven
from less than five minutes away

Exhibit 9   **7-Eleven Japan's Expansion Strategy**

Map of Japan showing store counts by prefecture:

- Hokkaido 501
- Niigata 166
- Gunma 222
- Miyagi 247
- Yamanashi 112
- Fukushima 287
- Tochigi 237
- Shiga 61
- Kyoto 52
- Ibaraki 282
- Hiroshima 201
- Chiba 538
- Yamaguchi 109
- Saitama 596
- Fukuoka 418
- Kanagawa 673
- Tokyo 952
- Nagano 258
- Shizuoka 269
- Saga 82
- Kumanoto 72

Global Expansion (15,490 stores in 22 countries)

Sweden	31	Malaysia	93
Norway	39	Singapore	77
Denmark	11	Philippines	83
UK	53	Guam	10
Spain	89	Canada	451
Turkey	9	USA	5,552
China	22	Mexico	221
Taiwan	1,158	Puerto Rico	12
Korea	110	Brazil	14
Hong Kong	328	Australia	153
Thailand	554	*Japan*	*6,420*

customers identify the store from the distance. The front side was a see-through window revealing the activity inside, in particular the crowd standing behind the window browsing through their favorite magazines and newspapers. Inside the store, the lighting was kept very bright (twice the brightness level at other stores). The store was always spotless, regularly cleaned, and safe, providing a comfortable, relaxing, and refreshing feeling to the visitor. Customers were reassured when they saw others in the store shopping or browsing and found that the store carried most of the branded products they knew. A visit to a Seven-Eleven Japan store had become for many a daily experience, "you get used to it, it becomes part of your daily routine."

The typical layout, the result of thorough research and experimentation, guides customers through various product categories, facilitating customer purchase decisions, increasing their purchase desire, and therefore maximizing sales. Response time is dictated by customers. They may want to quickly choose a product/service and leave the store immediately or alternatively, they may want to spend a long time in the store just browsing, relaxing, reading magazines, and enjoying the ambiance. After attracting the customer from outside, the store layout guides her from the magazine section, to the drinks section, the snacks, food, and finally dessert section before she faces the cashier surrounded by attractive items for impulse purchases and various added services. Also, the layout of the store, its product mix, and the items allocation to shelf space may change during the day, during the week (week days different from week ends), and seasonally as customer needs shift. If an item was doing well, it got its own section to make it more accessible to customers. Recently, when its regular partner, Sapporo Beer, failed to catch onto the "Ice" beer fever that came from the United States, Seven-Eleven Japan successfully introduced a special section for Miller Ice beer, an American beer selling at ¥178 for 355 ml, when the domestic brand was priced at ¥225 for 350 ml.

OPERATIONS

Just-in-Time Delivery System

Seven-Eleven Japan developed the Combined Delivery System, whereby the same kind of products coming from different suppliers could be *centralized* in a CDC (Combined Delivery Center). This represented a revolution for the suppliers whose products were traditionally delivered separately through exclusive channels. The benefit for 7-Eleven Japan was that it involved fewer deliveries from the producers to the wholesalers. Instead of ordering and then storing crates of a given product, a store operator may simply order the few items he judged were needed. Overall, in 18 years, it managed to reduce the average number of vehicles visiting each store from 70 to 9 a day (Exhibit 7). It also introduced the Temperature-Controlled Combined Delivery System, whereby items were grouped not by type, but on the basis of their required storage temperature: frozen foods were put together in a −20°C container, chilled products in a 5°C container, and rice balls and bentos in the 20°C compartment, while processed foods would stay in a room temperature area. By 10:00 A.M., all stores in the Seven-Eleven Japan chain verified their data and placed orders needed that evening, as well as those needed the next morning and afternoon. Orders were transited by the host computer and were dispatched to the producers throughout the country by 10:30 A.M. Newly produced lunch boxes, for instance, arrived at CDCs (Combined Delivery Centers) by 2:00 P.M. and would be delivered to the individual stores by 6:00 P.M. the same day.

Information Systems

Suzuki used to say: "Don't rely on the POS system. Information technology is merely a tool to achieve business strategy. We shouldn't use the technology unless we can understand what the information means on paper." However, after its first introduction of a high-capacity online network in 1989, Seven-Eleven Japan began to explore new services that could take advantage of this new capability. In other words, while he was true to his original principle, Suzuki started to be influenced by technology when formulating his business strategy. When he opened his first store in 1974, order and sales data were orally exchanged back and forth between headquarters and the retail stores over regular telephone lines. However, as the number of stores increased, it became physically more difficult to do business this way. In 1975, for the first time, data was sent over phone lines directly to the mainframe computer at headquarters. Four years later, in collaboration with the computer vendor, NEC, 7-Eleven first developed and installed in each retail store a standalone order entry management system to support franchisees' activities. The next step, in 1979, was to put all these terminals online and to connect them to other business partners. This was the first example of a value-added network (VAN) in the industry (Exhibit 10).

The next challenge was to design and implement an electronic order booking system (EOB) and a point of sale system (POS). An EOB is a small, hand-held machine with a floppy disk drive that store managers use to key in the next orders as they walk around their store. The data on the diskette is then loaded onto the Terminal Controller (TC, i.e., the minicomputer within each store) and sent to the host system. On the other hand, a POS is a system with which a store operator can read bar codes on packages and automatically enter a sale into the system (Exhibit 11). Originally introduced in the United States, this type of system was used to increase the productivity and reliability of cashier operators because it reduced entry errors and triggered automatic replenishment. However, Seven-Eleven Japan introduced its POS systems rather to collect sales data and to use the information for merchandising and item-by-item control processes. For instance, the cash register would not open until the operator entered the data about the gender and estimated age of the customer. This data was also first loaded onto the TC in the back office and was later sent electronically to the host computer. In 1991, 7-Eleven installed, in collaboration with NTT and NRI, the first ISDN network in Japan, integrating all these separate information systems into a common network platform (Exhibit 11). This network linked all the franchise stores to corporate offices in Tokyo and all around Japan via optical fiber. ISDN allowed ten times more data to be exchanged 30 times faster and at one-fourth the cost of previous technologies. For example, headquarters had access to daily sales data on every single item for each of its 6,420 stores (in 22 of Japan's 47 prefectures, Exhibit 9) the afternoon of the next day. Before ISDN, it used to take more than a week. As a result, Seven-Eleven Japan could capture and analyze consumer purchasing patterns virtually on a real-time basis. (See Exhibit 9.)

Operation Field Counselors (OFC)

In exchange for high royalties (Exhibit 3) and their long-term commitment, Seven-Eleven Japan provided franchisees with constant service from field representatives. Japan was divided into 66 districts, serviced by a total of 1,000 Operation Field Counselors (OFCs). Reporting to a district manager, these OFCs provided the human backup to the 7-Eleven franchise system. Each of them supervised between six and seven stores, providing

Exhibit 10 **7-Eleven Japan's Systems Structure**

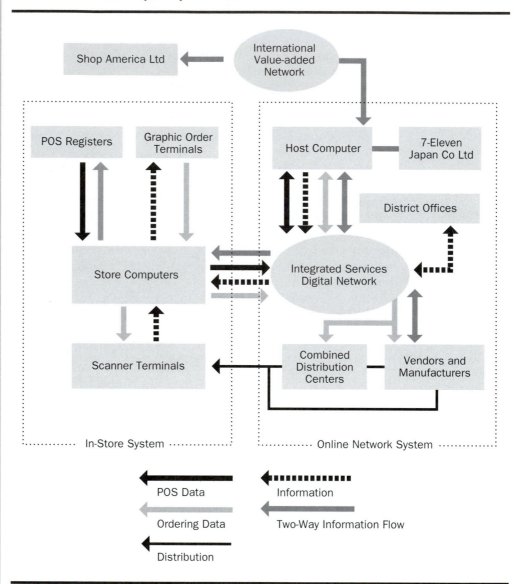

(i) advice on ordering and on the use of information systems and (ii) information on the portfolio of available items. The person-to-person contact with store managers was also a key element of the 7-Eleven franchise system. The counselors conveyed information, criticisms, and suggestions for improvements from and between store operators, all the way back to headquarters. Their frequent visits, two or three times a week, also had the effect of motivating the owners and staff of small remote stores. Once, a customer was put on a waiting list for a game CD and asked to come back on a specified date. The item was not in the store on the promised day. The OFC personally hand-delivered the CD to the customer that same evening.

Suzuki spends more than $1 million per year holding weekly meetings that bring

Exhibit 11   **Information System: 7-Eleven Japan's Store**

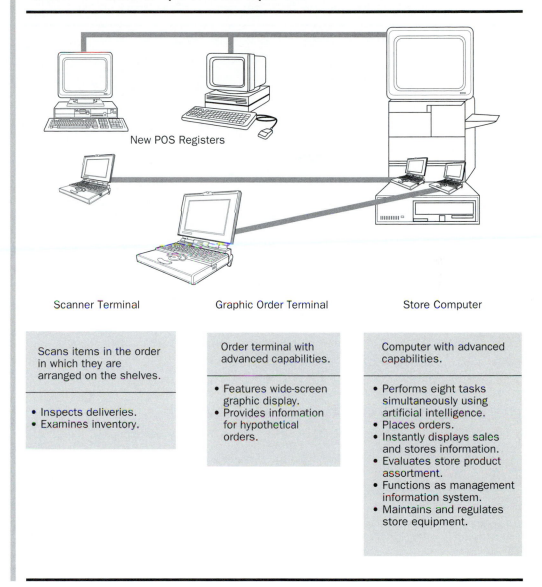

New POS Registers

Scanner Terminal

Graphic Order Terminal

Store Computer

Scans items in the order in which they are arranged on the shelves.	Order terminal with advanced capabilities.	Computer with advanced capabilities.
• Inspects deliveries. • Examines inventory.	• Features wide-screen graphic display. • Provides information for hypothetical orders.	• Performs eight tasks simultaneously using artificial intelligence. • Places orders. • Instantly displays sales and stores information. • Evaluates store product assortment. • Functions as management information system. • Maintains and regulates store equipment.

together all the OFCs from all over Japan to headquarters in Tokyo. "It is not enough to exchange information. The information has no value unless it is understood and properly integrated by the franchisees and makes them work better," Suzuki repeats at each meeting. Before starting a new store, the new franchisees and their wives are first brought to the central training center for a month and then go through a two-month, on-the-job training in one of the regular stores. Training helps diffuse corporate policy and explain the need for high quality of data input and the importance of daily operation and service quality. Suzuki explains: "We became successful because we've concentrated on retailing, shared information with staff, and encouraged them constantly to respond to changes."

Exhibit 12 **Information Systems and Distribution System Improvements and Performance**
(Average Stock Turnover Time, Daily Sales, and Gross Profit Margin per Store)

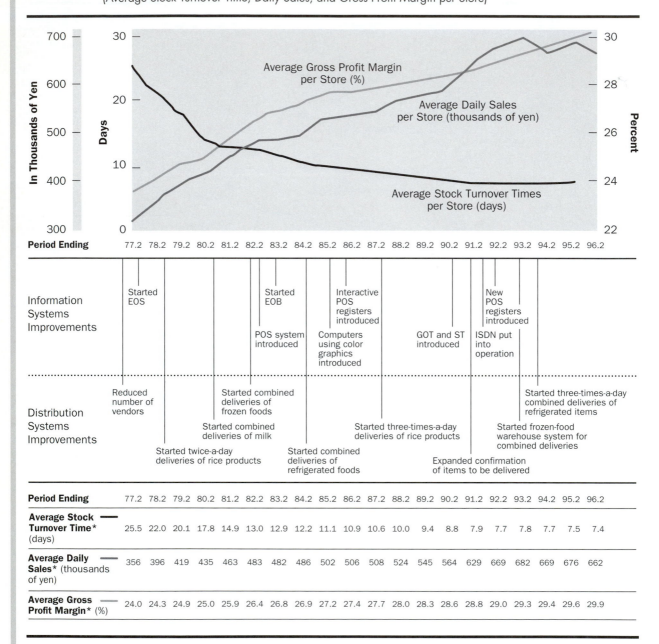

Period Ending	77.2	78.2	79.2	80.2	81.2	82.2	83.2	84.2	85.2	86.2	87.2	88.2	89.2	90.2	91.2	92.2	93.2	94.2	95.2	96.2
Average Stock Turnover Time* (days)	25.5	22.0	20.1	17.8	14.9	13.0	12.9	12.2	11.1	10.9	10.6	10.0	9.4	8.8	7.9	7.7	7.8	7.7	7.5	7.4
Average Daily Sales* (thousands of yen)	356	396	419	435	463	483	482	486	502	506	508	524	545	564	629	669	682	669	676	662
Average Gross Profit Margin* (%)	24.0	24.3	24.9	25.0	25.9	26.4	26.8	26.9	27.2	27.4	27.7	28.0	28.3	28.6	28.8	29.0	29.3	29.4	29.6	29.9

*Per-store figures.

BUSINESS PERFORMANCE

A look at average store sales at Seven-Eleven Japan and its direct competitors shows average daily sales of $7,000 compared to $4,430 of the industry average. (See Exhibit 12.) In 1991, after 17 years of sustained growth in sales and profits, Seven-Eleven Japan showed no intention of slowing its expansion. Since its creation, the company had achieved one of the highest returns on equity in the industry, testifying to the performance of its outsourcing principle. Since 1993, sales for Seven-Eleven Japan have been exceeding those of its parent company, the Ito-Yokado supermarket chain. The same year, Seven-Eleven Japan's net income became the largest in the retail industry and remained number one.

However, the Japanese market was rapidly saturating as competition intensified. Since the 1970s, the number of CVS stores in Japan had multiplied 20-fold to number some 50,000 stores, with one store for approximately 2,000 people. Total sales in Japanese convenience stores were in excess of the sales of all Japanese department stores. More Coca-cola, batteries, and panty hose were sold in convenience stores than anywhere else in Japan. Lunch box (bento) sales in CVS stores were larger than the overall sales of McDonald's in Japan. Some competitors were preparing expansion strategies for countries outside Japan. At the same time, European retailers and distributors, for instance, were trying to develop convenience formats of their own. Ito-Yokado recently teamed up with the world's largest and second-largest retailers—Wal-Mart of the United States in 1993 and Germany's Metro in 1994. In 1990, Southland filed for bankruptcy after an attempt to win new customers with heavily discounted goods backfired. No other United States retailer was interested in trying to rescue the chain, so Southland turned to Seven-Eleven Japan. Suzuki has been able to bail out the U.S. company—without yet introducing the information technology.

Mr. Nakauchi, CEO of Daiei, the number one supermarket chain in Japan and parent company of Lawson, a key competitor to Seven-Eleven Japan, was recently quoted saying "In the twenty-first century, supermarkets will not be able to survive in Japanese retailing. Only discount stores and convenience stores will. Lifestyles will gradually change because of more women working, more single people, and the 24-hour society. Mothers will cook less at home and family members will not have as many meals at home. Therefore, supermarkets will be less necessary. Lunch boxes will become more popular, and this will increase demand at convenience stores for food and other items to be available at any time." This is a signal for even greater competition in the domestic convenience store industry, but also may be opening the doors to competition beyond the borders of Japan.

The Body Shop International PLC (1998): Anita Roddick, OBE

Ellie A. Fogarty, Joyce P. Vincelette, and Thomas L. Wheelen

I am not taking a back seat. I have no intention of marginalizing myself from this business as a non-working director. I just can't see myself retiring. I will still do what I do best—that's marketing, styling, image, store design and so on.

—Comment from Anita Roddick on the prospect of handing over the reins at the company she founded.[1]

Asked what her new role as co-chairman would actually mean, she said: "I have no bloody idea."[2]

On May 12, 1998, Anita Roddick announced that she would cede her post of Chief Executive Officer of The Body Shop International PLC to Patrick Gournay. She admitted she was bored with basic retail disciplines such as distribution. Anita would rather spend time with the Dalai Lama, whom she met the day before stepping down. Anita moved alongside her husband Gordon as executive co-chairman. She said titles are meaningless and "tomorrow's job is exactly the same as yesterday's."[3]

Patrick Gournay, an experienced international business manager, had worked 26 years with Groupe Danone, the multi-product food group headquartered in Paris with sales of £8 billion. He was the Executive Vice-President of Danone's North and South American division, with strategic responsibilities for eight companies in five countries.[4] Gournay had never heard of The Body Shop until he was approached by headhunters (executive recruiters). He met Anita and Gordon to ask them if they really wanted to change. "It was important to me to establish that Anita in particular was ready for a change, for someone to come in and take responsibility for the business. We spent a lot of time talking about that and the conclusion is clear."[5] Although he admitted he was not an activist, he realized that The Body Shop "is not just an average cosmetics company, it is something unique."[6]

Gournay was granted options of over 2.5 million shares that may be exercised at 123½ (pounds). Half the performance-related options were exercisable between May 2001 and May 2008. The other half were exercisable between May 2003 and May 2008. These options may be exercised only if normalized earnings per share over any three consecutive years exceed growth in the retail prices index for the same period by at least 4%.[7]

On July 14, 1998 (Bastille Day), Gournay began his work at The Body Shop. He planned to focus on defining the roles and processes within the company. He felt the operations needed to be made more flexible and more innovative. Gournay thought the expansion program should continue with South America as an obvious starting point, based on his previous experience. His long-term targets included India and China. He and Anita agreed that due to high store rents, more emphasis should be placed on direct selling operations, perhaps even replacing some stores with this effective new method. Gournay's future plans included tackling the issue of extending the Body Shop brand. Anita was interested in directing that expansion to include leisure services such as weekend retreats.

Also in 1998, The Body Shop shareholders approved a joint venture with Bellamy Retail Group LLC to manage the operations of The Body Shop, Inc., in the United States, giving the owner up to 51% of the company at a future date.

Anita admitted that several previous senior appointments from outside failed to work. But she promised this time would be different. "It will have to work. There is no option." [8]

ANITA RODDICK: THE ENTREPRENEUR

> I certainly had no ambition to start a big international company. I did not want to change the world; I just wanted to survive and be able to feed my children.
>
> —Anita Roddick, OBE

In 1942, Anita Perellas was born to Italian immigrant parents and grew up working in the family-owned cafe, the Clifton Cafe, in Littlehampton, West Sussex, England. She wanted to be an actress, but her mother, Gilda, wanted her to be a teacher. Her mother told her to "be special" [and] "be anything but mediocre." [9] She received a degree in education from Newton Park College of Education at Bath. In 1963, her senior year, she received a three-month scholarship to Israel, which enabled her to do research for her thesis, "The British Mandate in Palestine."

After graduation, she taught for a brief time at a local junior school. She then accepted a position in Paris with the *International Herald Tribune* in its library. Her next position was with the United Nations International Labour Organization in Geneva. She worked on women's rights in Third World countries. She said of her United Nations experience that she learned "the extraordinary power of networking, but I was appalled by the money that was squandered on red tape and all the wining and dining that was going on with no apparent check on expenses. I found it offensive to see all of those fat cats discussing problems in the Third World over four-course lunches at the United Nations Club." [10]

With the money saved from her United Nations position, she decided to satisfy her quest to travel. She boarded a boat bound for Tahiti via the Panama Canal. She went on to visit Africa. During her travels, she developed a deep interest in and curiosity of the beauty practices of women that she encountered. She focused on the effectiveness and simplicity of these beauty practices.

After returning to England, she met Gordon Roddick at El Cubana, her family-owned club. He was an adventurer who loved to travel and write poetry. They got married in Reno, Nevada, on a trip to San Francisco to visit friends in 1970. After the birth of their two daughters, Justine in 1969 and Samantha in 1971, they decided to settle down. They purchased a Victorian hotel, St. Winifred Hotel, in Littlehampton, which required substantial renovations. They resided in part of the hotel while renovating the guest quarters. The next Roddick enterprise was the Paddington's restaurant in the center of Littlehampton. They borrowed £10,000 from the bank to lease and renovate the restaurant. [11] This was a time-consuming enterprise for the couple. They had no social or family life while running the Paddington and residing in and staffing the hotel, St. Winifred. Anita said, "We did not have time for each other and our marriage was beginning to suffer as a result, exacerbated by the fact we had no privacy; being at St. Winifred's was like living in a commune with a lot of elderly people. And despite all the leisure time we had sacrificed, we were not making much money. All we were doing was surviving." [12] Paddington became the most popular place in the town, especially on a Saturday night. Gordon crawling into bed one night said, "This is killing us," . . . [and] "I can't cope with it any more. Let's pack it in." [13]

In 1976, Gordon and Anita agreed that Gordon should fulfill his dream of riding horseback across the Americas from Buenos Aires to New York City. The 5,300-mile horseback trek would take about two years to complete. Anita said, "I have admired people who want to be remarkable, who follow their beliefs and passions, who make grand gestures." [14] Anita wanted a real home life, which as entrepreneurs they had never had, and she wanted to spend some time with her children, who were four and six. She needed a business to survive and feed the children, so they decided she needed to open a shop.

THE BODY SHOP

Anita decided to sell naturally based cosmetics in five sizes so that her customers had a choice. She felt that "people tend not to trust their gut instincts enough, especially about those things that irritate them, but the fact is that if something irritates you it is a pretty good indication that there are other people who feel the same. Irritation was a great source of energy and creativity." [15] She had been dissatisfied with the purchase of body lotion because most stores sold only one size. [16] Her dissatisfaction led her to question why she could not buy cosmetics by weight or bulk, like groceries or vegetables, and why a customer could not buy a small size of a cream or lotion to try it out before buying a big bottle. These were simple enough questions, but at the time there were no sensible answers. [17] She and Gordon discussed her concept for a shop where she could sell cosmetic products in a cheap container and in different sizes. He liked the concept. Anita decided to sell products made from "natural ingredients." The environmental green movement had not yet started.

She obtained a £4,000 bank loan (approximately $6,000) to open the first Body Shop at 22 Kensington Gardens, Brighton. The shop opened Saturday, March 26, 1976, at nine o'clock. By noon, Anita had to call Gordon and ask him to come to the shop and work. At six o'clock, they closed the shop and counted the daily receipts of exactly £130. She had a goal of £300 of weekly receipts to cover her living costs. [18]

Just before she opened the shop, she had encountered opposition over the shop name, The Body Shop. The name came from the generic name for auto repair shops in the United States. Two nearby funeral homes threatened to sue her over the shop's name. She contacted the local newspaper about the pending lawsuits. The article on her plight helped draw attention to her new shop. Based on this experience, she developed a company policy of never spending a cent on advertising. [19] It has been estimated that The Body Shop receives £2,000,000 of free publicity each year based on the company's and Anita's position on key social problems. The shop's logo was designed by a local art student at a cost of £25.

In developing the design of The Body Shop, Anita based it on "a Second World War mentality (shortages, utility goods, and rationing) imposed by sheer necessity and the fact that I had no money. But I had a very clear image in my mind of the kind of style I wanted to create: I wanted it to look a bit like a country store in a spaghetti western." [20]

The first products—all 25 of them—were composed of natural ingredients that Anita could gather and mix together herself rather inexpensively. The cheapest bottles she could find were those used by hospitals to collect urine samples and she offered to fill any bottle the customer would bring in. The labels were plain and simple, as they still are today, and handwritten. The store also carried knick-knacks to fill space, including cards, books, and jewelry; sometimes this merchandise accounted for 60% of the turnover. She developed loyal clients.

Perhaps because Anita sprayed Strawberry Essence on the sidewalks in the hopes that potential customers would follow it, the first store did well. After a successful summer, Anita decided to open a second store in Chichester and approached the bank for a £4,000 loan. She was turned down because she had no track record. So, she turned to a friend, Ian McGlinn, who owned a local garage. Ian received a 50% interest in the company for his investment.[21] In 1998, he owned 45,666,768 (23.5%) of the ordinary shares. The Roddicks owed 48,237,136 shares. Ian played no role in the management of the company. Anita felt, "To succeed you have to believe in something with such a passion that it becomes a reality."[22] This was one of the two principal reasons for the company's initial success. The other was that Anita had to survive while Gordon was away. Exhibit 1 shows a timeline of the key highlights of the company.

FRANCHISING AS A GROWTH STRATEGY

A friend's daughter, Chris Green, wanted to open her own shop in Hove. The Roddicks agreed and thought it was a great idea. Their only interest was selling her products. There were no fees or contracts. Another friend, Aidre, wanted to open a shop with her parents in Bognor Regis. They gave her the same deal.

Gordon had returned home before the two shops were opened. He could see the potential of the business to grow, but no bank wanted to lend them money.

Gordon hired a lawyer to develop a franchising contract. The formula was based on a license to use The Body Shop name and to sell its products, and the franchisee would put up the money. In 1978, the first franchise outside the United Kingdom was opened in Brussels. The franchise fee was 300 pounds.[23] Women owned all the initial franchises. Anita felt that "men were good at the science and vocabulary of business, at talking about economic theory and profits and loss figures (some women are, too, of course). But I could also see that women were better at dealing with people, caring, and being passionate about what they are doing."[24]

During this time, the company was developing its own style of "respond[ing] to needs rather than creating them."[25] The company was run in an informal way as an extended big family. Anita understood the concept of developing a niche around a competitive advantage. She said, "A true key to success is knowing what features set you apart from the competitor."[26] And also, "We had stuck closely to a policy of being open and honest about our products, and it was paying dividends among our customers who were increasingly irritated by the patently dishonest advertising of the cosmetics industry. Women in the 1980s were less and less inclined to fall for the 'buy this mixture of oil and water and you will be a movie star' pitch dreamed up in the expensive offices of advertising agencies."[27]

By 1982, the Roddicks were exercising much stricter control over what could and could not be done in the shop. They had learned, from experience, that it was absolutely essential to maintain a strong identity.[28] The company opened shops at the rate of two a month. They had shops in Iceland, Denmark, Finland, Holland, and Ireland.

During these early franchising years, the biggest mistake management made was offering three choices of shop styles to franchisees—dark green, dark mahogany stain, or stripped pine. Anita quickly recognized that the shops looked different, and as such the shops lost their distinctiveness. So she persuaded all the shops to return to the dark green.[29]

Anita kept strict control over the franchising process. At times, 5,000 franchise applications were in process. The franchise process included a home visit, a personality

Exhibit 1   A Timeline: The Body Shop

1976	Anita Roddick opens the first branch of The Body Shop in Brighton on England's south coast.
1977	The first franchise of The Body Shop opens in Bognor Regis, England.
1978	The first branch opens outside the United Kingdom in Brussels, Belgium.
1984	The Body Shop goes public. With a placing of 95p ($1.38), shares close at £1.65 ($2.39) on the first day of dealing.
1985	The Body Shop runs its first in-shop campaign, "Save the Whale" with Greenpeace.
1986	The Body Shop launches its cosmetic range, called Colourings, and Mostly Men, a skin care line for men.
1987	The Body Shop establishes its first Trade Not Aid initiative in Nepal.
1988	The first U.S. branch of The Body Shop opens in New York.
	Soapworks, a soap-making plant for The Body Shop, opens in Easterhouse, Scotland.
	Queen awards Anita Roddick the Order of the British Empire (OBE).
1989	One million people sign The Body Shop's petition to "Stop the Burning" in the Amazon Rainforest.
	Anita receives the United Nations' Global 500 Environment Award.
1990	2.6 million people sign The Body Shop's "Against Animal Testing" petition.
	The Body Shop launches its Eastern European Drive of volunteers to renovate three orphanages in Halaucesti, Romania.
	The Body Shop opens in Tokyo, Japan.
1991	*The Big Issue,* a paper sold by and for the homeless, is launched by The Body Shop in London.
	Anita is awarded the World Vision Award by the Centre for World Development Education in recognition of Trade Not Aid initiative.
	The Body Shop marks Amnesty International's 30th anniversary with a campaign to increase membership.
1992	The Body Shop's voter registration drive in the United States signs up more than 33,000 voters.
	The Company publishes the results of the first environmental audit, *The Green Book,* in the United Kingdom.
	The Body Shop opens its first American community-based shop on 125th Street, Harlem.
1993	The Body Shop opens its 1,000th shop.
	The American "Reuse/Refill/Recycle" campaign increases awareness of the refill and recycling services available at The Body Shop.
	The Body Shop USA joins with other corporations in signing the CERES Principles, an environmental code of conduct.
	The Body Shop USA joined forces with the Ms. Foundation to support the first annual Take Our Daughters to Work Day.
	The Body Shop USA is honored by the NAACP for excellence in minority economic development.
	"Protect & Respect" project, on AIDS education and awareness, is launched.
1994	The Body Shop launches its biggest ever international campaign in 30 markets and more than 900 shops to gain public support influencing the U.N. Convention on International Trade in Endangered Species to enforce regulations governing trade in endangered species.
1995	The Body Shop introduces The Body Shop Direct home selling operation.
1996	The first shop in the Philippines opens.
	First social audit published.
	The Body Shop is recognized in the 1996 PR Week award categories for Best International Campaign and Best Overall PR Campaign in the United Kingdom for the Ogoni people of Nigeria campaign.
	Largest ever petition on animal testing—over 4 million signatures from 16 countries—was presented to the European Parliament and Commission in Brussels in November.
1997	Created an international Franchisee Advisory Board.
	Won the Retail Week Store Design of the Year Award for its new format stores.
1998	With Amnesty International, launched Make Your Mark on May 11 in Atlanta, Georgia, with the Dalai Lama.
	Published *Naked Body,* a 50-page magazine featuring articles on hemp, beauty tips, a photo of a woman's naked lower body, and an interview with a London prostitute.

Source: The Body Shop, "This Is the Body Shop" (November 1994), pp. 3–4, and author's additions.

test, and an assessment of the applicant's attitude toward people and the environment. The process could take three years to complete. In the final interview with Anita, she was known to ask unexpected questions ("How would you like to die?" "Who is your favorite heroine in literature?") This type of applicant process could ensure that the franchisee would adhere to the principles and image of The Body Shop. After being selected to own a franchise, owners underwent extensive training on products, store operations, and merchandising techniques.

In 1985, The Body Shop Training School opened. The curriculum focused on human development and consciousness-raising. Anita said, "Conventional retailers trained for a sale; we trained for knowledge. They trained with an eye on the balance sheet; we trained with an eye on the soul."[30] The courses centered on "educating" the participant, not training. In the customer care course, the teacher "encouraged the staff to treat customers as potential friends, to say hello, smile, make eye contact and to offer advice if it was wanted, to thank them and always to invite them back."[31] She viewed money spent on staff training as an investment and not as an expense.

Franchisees had mixed feelings over developments at The Body Shop to pursue direct selling at home parties through Body Shop Direct and sales of products over the Internet. Some felt threatened and wanted to sell back their stores. They felt customers would bypass their shops and order on the Web. Others felt these new distribution channels would help them rather than take sales away.

In 1998, The Body Shop had over 1594 shops in 47 countries (see Exhibit 2) and traded in 24 languages worldwide. The Body Shop expected to open 70 new stores in 1999, almost all of which would be franchised.[32]

ANITA RODDICK'S PHILOSOPHY AND PERSONAL VALUES TRANSLATE INTO CORPORATE CULTURE AND CITIZENSHIP

Below are some of Anita's most salient quotes on the issues of our time:

It is immoral to trade on fear. It is immoral to make women feel dissatisfied with their bodies. It is immoral to deceive a customer by making miracle claims for a product. It is immoral to use a photograph of a glowing 16-year-old to sell a (beauty) cream aimed at preventing wrinkles in a 40-year-old.[33]

I think all business practices would improve immeasurably if they were guided by "feminine" principles—qualities like love and care and intuition.[34]

I honestly believe I would not have succeeded if I had been taught about business.[35]

We communicate with passion and passion persuades.[36]

I learned there was nothing more important to life than love and work.[37]

Passion persuades and by God I was passionate about what I was selling.[38]

In a society in which politicians no longer lead by example, ethical conduct is unfashionable, and the media does not give people real information on what is happening in the world, what fascinates me is the concept of turning our shops into centers of education.[39]

You can be proud to work for the Body Shop and boy, does that have an effect on morale and motivation.[40]

I have never been able to separate Body Shop values from my personal values.[41]

I think the leadership of a company should encourage the next generation not just to follow, but to overtake.[42]

When you take the high moral road, it is difficult for anyone to object without sounding like a fool.[43]

Whenever we wanted to persuade our staff to support a particular project we always tried to break their hearts.[44]

Exhibit 2   **Shop Locations by Regions: The Body Shop** [1]

	Number of Shops			First Shop Opening
	February 1998	**February 1997**	**February 1996**	
Europe				
Austria	17	17	15	1979
Belgium	18	18	18	1978
Cyprus	3	3	3	1983
Denmark	19	20	19	1981
Eire	11	11	10	1981
Finland	24	23	21	1981
France	23	32	34	1982
Germany	72	67	60	1983
Gibraltar	1	1	1	1988
Greece	51	46	44	1979
Holland	50	51	50	1982
Iceland	3	2	2	1980
Italy	53	50	46	1984
Luxembourg	2	2	2	1991
Malta	3	1	1	1987
Norway	24	24	21	1985
Portugal	12	11	9	1986
Spain	65	63	59	1986
Sweden	48	44	42	1979
Switzerland	28	28	27	1983
Total Shops	**527**	**514**	**484**	
United Kingdom				
Total Shops	**263**	**256**	**252**	1976
Asia				
Bahrain	2	2	2	1985
Brunei	3	3	3	1993
Hong Kong	16	13	11	1984
Indonesia	17	13	8	1990
Japan	116	87	58	1990
Korea	5	0	0	1997
Kuwait	9	8	3	1986
Macau	3	2	2	1993
Malaysia	25	22	21	1984
Oman	4	4	2	1986
Phillipines	7	3	0	1996
Qatar	1	1	1	1987
Saudi Arabia	33	25	21	1987
Singapore	16	15	12	1983
Taiwan	34	21	14	1988
Thailand	12	9	8	1993
UAE	5	5	4	1983
Total Shops	**308**	**233**	**170**	

(continued)

Exhibit 2 **Shop Locations by Regions: The Body Shop** (continued)

	Number of Shops			First Shop Opening
	February 1998	February 1997	February 1996	
Australia and New Zealand				
Australia	62	59	57	1983
New Zealand	14	12	11	1989
Total Shops	**76**	**71**	**68**	
America Excluding USA				
Antigua	1	1	1	1987
Bahamas	3	3	3	1985
Bermuda	1	2	2	1987
Canada	119	119	115	1980
Cayman Islands	1	1	1	1989
Mexico	5	4	4	1993
Total Shops	**130**	**130**	**126**	
USA				
Total Shops	**290**	**287**	**273**	1988
Grand Total Shops	**1,594**	**1,491**	**1,373**	

Note:
1. The company shops (1998) are located as follows:
   - USA 210, UK 67, Singapore 16, France 15.
   - Number of countries: 47.
   - Number of languages company traded in: 24.

Source: The Body Shop, *1998* and *1997 Annual Reports,* pp. 68 and 48.

You have to look at leadership through the eyes of the followers and you have to live the message. What I have learned is that people become motivated when you guide them to the source of their own power and when you make heroes out of employees who personify what you want to see in the organization.[45]

I do not believe women have a chance in hell of achieving their desired status and power in business within the foreseeable future. My daughters might see it, but I won't.[46]

If you have a company with itsy-bitsy vision, you have an itsy-bitsy company.[47]

The thought that every day might be my last, and the desire to make the most of every moment, drives me on.[48]

These were the statements of a unique woman who had a strong personal value system that she clearly articulated. She saw herself as a concerned citizen of the world, who continuously searched and developed solutions for its problems; a leader in the green political movement; a very successful business leader; a spokesperson for those without a voice in the world arena; a wife; a mother; and a daughter. She served the needs of the underprivileged and the environment. Anita was a trader. She said, "I am not rushing around the world as some kind of loony do-gooder; first and foremost I am a trader looking for a trade."[49]

In 1988, Anita was knighted by Queen Elizabeth into the Order of the British Empire (OBE).

UNITED STATES MARKET

History

By 1987, the company received about 10,000 letters from the United States inquiring about franchising opportunities and asking when stores would be opened so they could purchase products.

Before opening the first U.S. store, the Roddicks negotiated for the trademark to The Body Shop. Two companies, owned by the Saunders and Short families, held the rights between them to "The Body Shop" name. Their trademark covered the United States and Japan, which represented 40% of the world's consumers. Gordon negotiated to buy the rights in both countries for $3,500,000.

The first shop was opened in New York on Broadway and 8th Street on July 1, 1988. A few weeks before opening, there was much questioning whether The Body Shop could succeed in the United States without advertising. A Harvard Business School professor was quoted in the *Wall Street Journal* saying that the company needed, "at minimum," a major launch advertising campaign. Anita had the quote reprinted on a postcard with her response: "I'll never hire anyone from the Harvard Business School." [50]

The first shop was an instant success, and over the next two years, 13 more company-owned shops were opened. Initially the company had a hard time trying to locate in malls because it was an unknown. Management asked their mail-order customers, who lived within a 110-mile radius of a proposed shop, for a letter-writing campaign. It was very successful. The first franchised store in the United States was opened in Washington, DC, in 1990.

After this successful start in the United States, The Body Shop began to run into trouble. Unsuccessful managers, too many product lines, copycat rivals who discount, and too few products created specifically for the U.S. consumer were some of the biggest problems. Many U.S. stores were located in expensive major cities that led to high real estate costs. By 1995, critics were saying that U.S. consumers no longer bought into the company's political message. Price-driven consumers did not rate The Body Shop as a premium brand. Instead, they enjoyed the aggressive discounting by Body Shop rivals Garden Botanica and Bath & Body Works. Turnover in Body Shop U.S. leadership and low brand recognition due to lack of advertising contributed to the problem.

Joint Venture

In January 1997, Adrian Bellamy was appointed to the position of non-executive director of The Body Shop. From 1983 until he retired in 1995, Bellamy had served as Chairman and CEO of DFS Group Limited—the U.S.-based global duty-free and luxury goods retailer. He also served as a non-executive director of GAP Inc., Gucci Group NV, and Williams-Sonoma. He approached The Body Shop board with the idea for a joint venture. The terms of the deal were as follows:

- Bellamy Retail Group (BRG) LLC would pay The Body Shop a non-refundable $1 million to acquire options over the U.S. business.

- BRG would immediately take over management responsibility of The Body Shop in the United States with options to buy 49% of the company at its net asset value between 2000 and 2002, provided it met performance targets.

Bellamy had a further option to acquire another 2% of the company at a later date. The targets were to reach breakeven by 2000, a profit of $1 million in 2001, and $4 million for 2002. The option lapsed if aggregate losses of $4 million or more occurred in the United States in 2000 and 2001.[51]

At the June 19, 1998, shareholders' meeting, only a handful of shareholders voted against the management.[52] Bellamy planned to focus the new U.S. regime on boosting sales per square foot by improving retail operations and marketing and also by cutting operating costs. He planned to focus on better customer service, improved promotions, and a balanced product range.[53]

As of February 1998, there were 290 shops in the U.S. Retail sales were £98.5 million ($161.6 million) and £100.6 million ($165.0 million) for 1998 and 1997, respectively. As of June 1998, The Body Shop U.S. was not taking applications for new franchises.

MISSION STATEMENT

The company's mission statement dedicated its business to the pursuit of social and environmental change:

To creatively balance the financial and human needs of our stakeholders: employees, customers, franchisees, suppliers, and shareholders.

To courageously ensure that our business is ecologically sustainable, meeting the needs of the present without compromising the future.

To meaningfully contribute to local, national, and international communities in which we trade, by adopting a code of conduct which ensures care, honesty, fairness, and respect.

To passionately campaign for the protection of the environment and human and civil rights, and against animal testing within the cosmetics and toiletries industry.

To tirelessly work to narrow the gap between principle and practice, while making fun, passion, and care part of our daily lives.[54]

CORPORATE GOVERNANCE

Board of Directors

The *Annual Report* stated the Directors' responsibilities. The Directors were required by company law to prepare financial statements for each financial year that give a true and fair view of the state of affairs of the company and the group and of the profit or loss of the group for that period.

In preparing those financial statements, the Directors were required to:

- Select suitable accounting policies and then apply them consistently.

- Make judgments and estimates that are reasonable and prudent.

- State whether applicable accounting standards have been followed, subject to any material departures disclosed and explained in the financial statements.

- Prepare the financial statements on the going concern basis unless it is inappropriate to presume that the company will continue in business.

The Directors were responsible for maintaining proper accounting records that disclose with reasonable accuracy at any time the financial position of the company and to enable them to ensure that the financial statements comply with the Companies

Act. They were also responsible for safeguarding the assets of the company and hence for taking reasonable steps for the prevention and detection of fraud and other irregularities.[55]

There were ten board members, of which seven were Executive and three Non-Executive Directors. The first non-executive directors had been appointed in 1995.

The board members were as follows:[56]

Anita L. Roddick, OBE	Chief Executive
T. Gordon Roddick	Chairman
Stuart A. Rose	Managing Director
Eric G. Helyer	Executive
Ivan C. Levy	Executive
Jane Reid	Executive
Jeremy A. Kett	Executive
Terry G. Hartin	Executive
Penny Hughes	Non-Executive
Aldo Papone	Non-Executive
Adrian D. Bellamy	Non-Executive

Remuneration for the Executive Directors in 1998 was as follows:[57]

(British pound amounts in thousands)			
Name	**Salary**	**Benefits**	**Total**
A. L. Roddick	140	22	162
T. G. Roddick	140	22	162
S. A. Rose	250		250
E. G. Helyer	161		161
J. Reid	220		220
J. A. Kett	155		155
T. G. Hartin	286	7	293
I. C. Levy	198	56	254

The Remuneration Committee recommended that the salaries of both Anita and Gordon Roddick be at a rate of £300,000 per annum, but the Roddicks have chosen to be remunerated at the level set out in the preceding table (an increase of £5000 each).

Directors' share holdings in 1998 were as follows:[58]

A. L. Roddick	24,010,456
T. G. Roddick	24,226,680
E. G. Helyer	10,000
I. C. Levy	300
T. G. Hartin	15,785
A. Papone	3,000

Ian McGlinn, who had loaned £6,000 to Anita to open her second shop, owned 45,666,768 (23.5%) ordinary shares. The Prudential Corporation owned 6,911,146 (3.6%) ordinary shares, and the Aeon Group had an interest in 6,700,000 (3.5%).

Top Management

Anita said about Gordon and her roles that "Gordon rarely accompanies me on shop visits because we are each more comfortable in our chosen roles of high profile and low profile. Outsiders often think of Gordon as a shadowy figure, but that is certainly not how he is viewed within The Body Shop. He is well known to everyone, much loved, and deeply respected as the real strength of the company. Our relationship bequeathed a very distinct management style to the company—loosely structured, collaborative, imaginative, and improvisatory, rather than by the book—which matured as the company expanded. I think Gordon provides a sense of constancy and continuity, while I bounce around breaking the rules, pushing back the boundaries of possibility, and shooting off my mouth. We rarely argue . . . it is never about values. His calm presence and enormous influence are rarely taken into account by critics who see The Body Shop as a flaky organization led by a madwoman with fuzzy hair."[59]

GROUP STRUCTURE AND ORGANIZATION

The Body Shop International PLC had stakes in six principal subsidiaries as of February 28, 1998 (see Exhibit 3). The operating structure is shown in Exhibit 4.

MARKETING AND ADVERTISING

The company had no marketing or advertising department. In 1979, Janis Raven was hired to handle public relations. She helped to publicize the company for its image and stances on public social issues. An analyst felt that the lack of an advertising and marketing budget contributed to low repeat customer sales. Customers came in looking for a gift for a friend or out of curiosity. Once the customer satisfied his or her need, there seemed to be little incentive for the customer to come back. Product Information Manuals (PIMs) were available to all customers and staff to increase their knowledge or answer questions about every Body Shop product. These manuals contained information about how the products were made, a listing of product ingredients, and the uses for each product. Many potential customers were not sure what products the company offered.

Anita Roddick used regular visits by regional managers to keep tight control over shop layout, window displays, PIM handouts, and operating style. Anita viewed marketing as hype; instead she wanted to establish credibility by educating the customer. She viewed the shop as the company's primary marketing tool. In 1990, The Body Shop was nominated to the United Kingdom Marketing Hall of Fame.

By 1997, Body Shop products were regularly accused of being "tired" and "lacking innovation."[60] One critic went so far as to say that the product mix would not be out of place in Woolworth's.[61] Recognizing this, The Body Shop placed a high priority on rationalizing the product range. The goal was to refocus on core lines and values, communicate effectively with consumers, and create new products that were young, funky, energizing, and marketed efficiently.[62]

Packaging also received a new look in 1997. Instead of continuing with dark green labels, clear labels were phased in to create a more sophisticated look. Colorings of makeup cases went from gun metal gray to metallic green.[63]

Complaints of cluttered, dark, uninviting shops led The Body Shop to design a new store format. The new store format performed well in the United Kingdom during the

Exhibit 3   **Principal Subsidiaries: The Body Shop International PLC**

The Body Shop Inc. (90% owned, USA)[1]
Responsible for U.S. retail activities.
The Body Shop (Singapore) Pte Limited (100% owned, Singapore)[1]
Responsible for The Body Shop retail outlets in Singapore.
Soapworks Limited (100% owned, Great Britain)[1]
Manufactures soap and related products.
Skin & Hair Care Preparations Inc. (100% owned, USA)[1]
U.S. holding company. Does not trade.
The Body Shop Direct Limited (100% owned, Great Britain)[1]
Makes direct sales through a home-selling program.
The Body Shop (France) SARL (100% owned, France)[1]
Operates The Body Shop retail outlets in France.

Note: 1. Shows % holding ordinary shares and country of incorporation and operation.

Source: The Body Shop, *1998 Annual Report*, p. 52.

first year, 1997. The Body Shop planned to open up to 150 new format stores within two years.[64] Five U.S. stores scheduled to undergo face lifts in 1998 were straying from the signature green look of old stores. Brighter lighting, hardwood floors, a bolder storefront logo, and light green, bright orange, and yellow colors were intended to help consumers locate products more easily.[65]

In 1997, The Body Shop launched a self-esteem campaign featuring Ruby Ruben-esque, a plus-sized doll, as the spokeswoman. A strategic alliance formed with British Airways provided amenity kits from The Body Shop to over two million passengers who flew Club World each year.

PRODUCT DEVELOPMENT AND PRODUCTION

In 1998, the company introduced three major new lines of products: Hemp, Aromatherapy, and Bergamot. In May 1998, The Body Shop unveiled a five-product body care line for dry skin formulated with hemp. It featured hand protector, lip conditioner, soap, elbow grease, and three-in-one oil for dry skin sold in metal tins with hemp leaf designs on the packaging. The Body Shop developed educational pamphlets to distribute in-store describing the essential fatty acids and amino acids found in the herb. Support of hemp farmers at the local level was begun immediately. In the United States, the 1970 Controlled Substance Act made it illegal to grow marijuana. The difference between drug-grade marijuana and industrial hemp is the level of Tetrahydrocannabinol (THC). Marijuana contains high levels of THC, which is psychoactive, whereas hemp has so little THC that it's virtually drug-free.[66]

Anita handed out packets of hemp seeds that carried the message: "Do not attempt to use this plant as a narcotic. You would need to smoke a joint the size of a telegraph pole to get high." Within a week of going on sale, the Hemp range accounted for 5% of total sales.[67]

Aromatherapy—the use of essential oils to enhance physical and mental well-being—fit in well with the values of The Body Shop. Products in this range included

Exhibit 4   Operating Structure

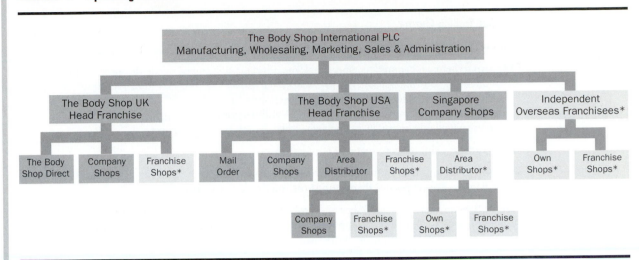

*Group-owned.

Source: The Body Shop, *1996 Annual Report.*

shower gel, massage oils, foaming milk bath, and bath oils organized into four collections: Energizing, Balancing, Relaxing, and Sensual.

Products made with Bergamot oil were a key component of the Aromatherapy range. A Bergamot is a small bitter, yellow-green citrus fruit grown in Calabria, Italy. Bergamot oil was reputed to have a stimulating effect that reinvigorated the mind and imparted a feeling of well-being. Because its oil could be produced synthetically at very low cost, the Bergamot orchards in Italy had been cleared, destroying the local economy. Anita was trying to reverse the decline in the region by increasing the demand for the fruit and thereby bringing jobs and income to the area. This Community Trade relationship had been developed from the collaboration between Simone Mizzi, the Italian Head Franchisee of The Body Shop, The Body Shop International, and the Calabrian authorities. The Body Shop's Trading Charter and Mission are included in Exhibit 5.

In-house manufacturing facilities at Littlehampton, Glasgow, and Wake Forest in the United States produced approximately 60% of The Body Shop products, excluding accessories. Bulk production of toiletries rose 13% to 9,427 tonnes from 1997 at the Watersmead plant. The U.S. facility filled 11.8 million units, up 4% from 1997.

Soapworks, a wholly-owned subsidiary of The Body Shop, manufactured soap and essential oil filling for the Aromatherapy range. Anita opened the facility in Easterhouse, Scotland, an area with historically high unemployment. When Soapworks was founded, the company made a commitment to donate 25% of its cumulative after-tax profits to local community projects. Between 1989 and 1998, the group had made or provided for donations of £274,810. Soapworks manufactured 30 million units in 1998, which was an increase of 4% over 1997.

Anita spent up to five months a year traveling the world looking for new product ideas and ingredients. Her samples were brought back to Watersmead where they were analyzed for their potential and durability. The department was backed up by anthropological and ethnobotanical research in traditional uses of plants, herbs, fruits, flowers, seeds, and nuts.

Exhibit 5   **Trading Charter and Mission: The Body Shop**

A. Our Trading Charter

The way we trade creates profits with principles.

We aim to achieve commercial success by meeting our customers' needs through the provision of high quality, good value products with exceptional service and relevant information which enables customers to make informed and responsible choices.

Our trading relationships of every kind—with customers, franchisees, and suppliers—will be commercially viable, mutually beneficial, and based on trust and respect.

Our trading principles reflect our core values.

We aim to ensure that human and civil rights, as set out in the Universal Declaration of Human Rights, are respected throughout our business activities.

We will establish a framework based on this declaration to include criteria for workers' rights embracing a safe, healthy working environment, fair wages, no discrimination on the basis of race, creed, sex or sexual orientation, or physical coercion of any kind.

We will support long-term, sustainable relationships with communities in need.

We will pay special attention to those minority groups, women, and disadvantaged peoples who are socially and economically marginalized.

We will use environmentally sustainable resources wherever technically and economically viable. Our purchasing will be based on a system of screening and investigation of the ecological credentials of our finished products, ingredients, packaging, and suppliers.

We will promote animal protection throughout our business activities. We are against animal testing in the cosmetics and toiletries industry. We will not test ingredients or products on animals, nor will we commission others to do so on our behalf. We will use our purchasing power to stop suppliers' animal testing.

We will institute appropriate monitoring, auditing, and disclosure mechanisms to ensure our accountability and demonstrate our compliance with these principles.

B. Direct Trading: Our Mission

The Body Shop believes that all trading should be viewed as an exercise in ethics. This is the attitude we seek to apply to all goods and services within the company and its retail shops.

Our ethical trading program helps create livelihoods for economically stressed communities, mostly in the majority world. Although trading with such communities is currently just a small percentage of all our trade, we intend to increase this practice wherever possible.

Fair Prices. The Body Shop will pay for the products it purchases. While our program aims to benefit the primary producers directly, we also recognize the value of commercial intermediaries. Where world market prices are applicable, we commit ourselves to pay these prices or more.

Partnership. Both sides must benefit commercially. We aim to develop long-term relationships if possible, and plan to work in partnership to solve potential problems. We aim to help our trade partners achieve self reliance.

Community Benefits. The company will work with a variety of trading partners—cooperatives, family businesses, tribal councils—with the intention of benefiting the individual worker as much as possible. We can't control the dispersal of community benefits that we provide. That process is determined by local needs, which may mean anything from funds managed by consensus to direct payments to individual producers.

(continued)

Exhibit 5   Trading Charter and Mission: The Body Shop (continued)

Respect. Our trading relationships are based on respect. The guidelines we are developing for sustainable development ensure that we respect all environments and cultures that may be affected by our trade. Wherever possible, we use renewable natural materials and skills that are appropriate to local cultures.

Cooperation. The Body Shop is committed to an open relationship with other fair trade organizations and places great emphasis on maintaining dialogue with organizations that are helping to define the path to sustainable development.

Accountability. We believe it is essential that our trading policy be measurable, audited, and open to scrutiny, and we are energetically seeking the mechanisms to achieve that goal. We already use an open approach to assess our impact on the environment and to promote our opposition to animal testing in the cosmetics industry by monitoring our suppliers.

Our trading practices are not the solution to everyone's needs. We simply see them as one component of the help we feel qualified to give. We will also help trading partners to broadly assess the likely social and environmental impact of developing trade.

In committing itself to the above aims, The Body Shop believes it is creating a trading policy that will satisfy the needs of our business, our trading partners, and our customers. Letting consumers know that neither places nor peoples have been exploited in getting our products to market helps The Body Shop customer make informed, responsible choices.

Source: The Body Shop, handouts.

HUMAN RESOURCES MANAGEMENT

Most of the employees in the company were women under 30. Anita constantly worked at communications within the company. Each shop had a bulletin board, a fax machine, and a video player with which she provided the staff a continuous stream of information concerning new products, causes that she supported, or status reports on her latest trip. The in-house video production company produced "Talking Shop," which was a monthly multilingual video magazine. It also produced training tapes and documentaries on social campaigns.

Anita encouraged upward communication through a suggestion system, DODGI (The Department of Damned Good Ideas), and through regularly scheduled meetings of a cross-section of staff, often at her home. She set up the "Red Letter" system so an employee could directly communicate with a director and bypass the normal chain of communications.

She believed in educating her employees and customers. In 1985, The Body Shop Training Center was opened in London and began offering courses on the company's products and philosophy, customer services, and hair and skin care problems. Sessions were held on key social issues such as AIDs, aging, management by humor, drug and alcohol abuse, and urban survival. She discussed the idea of opening a business college. She said, "You can train dogs and you can train horses, but we wanted to educate and help the people realize their potential."[68]

The Body Shop empowered its staff. It encouraged debate, encouraged employees to speak out and state their views. Anita wanted her staff to be personally involved in social campaigns. She said, "One of the risks of corporate campaigning is that the staff start to fall in love with doing good and forget about trading."[69]

Anita had problems recruiting staff for the U.S. headquarters, located in New Jersey, because employees were not willing or able to embrace the company's culture. She went on to say, "Most of them came from conventional, moribund jobs and seemed confused by the idea of a company being quirky or zany or contemptuous of mediocrity. I could never seem to get their adrenaline surging. We are a company in which image, design, style, and creativity are of paramount importance, but we were unable to find employees who appreciate these qualities."[70] Headquarters for the United States were moved to Wake Forest (Winston-Salem), North Carolina in 1993. Although in 1998, in the face of the troubled U.S. market, Anita admitted that it had been a mistake to move the U.S. Headquarters to North Carolina instead of a big city like New York or San Francisco.

The company created "the Company Care Team, a five-person group that is taking responsibility for The Body Shop's performance as a caring employer. The team coordinated childcare through the company's Family Centre and through the launch in April 1994 of programs offering financial help with childcare for all company staff. A counselor service provided 24-hours confidential counseling services for employees and their families."[71]

GLOBAL CORPORATE CITIZENSHIP

The company clearly stated its position on the key global issue of corporate citizenship in its publication, *This Is the Body Shop:*[72]

Human and Civil Rights

The Body Shop is committed to supporting and promoting social and environmental change for the better. We recognize that human and civil rights are at the very heart of such change.

We're All in This Together

Working with organizations like Amnesty International, Human Rights Watch, the Unrepresented Nations and Peoples Organization, and the Foundation for Ethnobiology, The Body Shop has tried to promote awareness of our responsibility as human beings. What happens to one of us affects us all. We can no longer pretend it is none of our business if people suffer, whether they're on the other side of the world or in our own backyards. Here are a few successful examples of work by The Body Shop in both those areas:

- In 1990, The Body Shop started a relief drive to fund volunteers to renovate orphanages in Romania, where thousands of children had been abandoned under the regime of dictator Nicolae Ceacescu. The Project has been so successful that we've now extended it to Albania.

- In 1993, the Body Shop Foundation donated £162,000 ($234,900) to "Rights and Wrongs," a weekly human rights television series created by Globalvision Inc. on a non-profit basis. By focusing on the human rights revolution around the world, the series explained how interrelated many of our problems are.

- In 1993, our biggest campaign in the U.S. focused attention on people living with HIV and AIDS. Working with groups like the American Red Cross, the San Francisco AIDS Foundation, the Gay Men's Health Crisis, and the National Leadership Coalition on AIDS, we developed a multi-faceted campaign, focusing particularly on women and teenagers who are the fastest growing risk groups for HIV infection. Using the theme "Protest & Respect," our campaign included a new corporate policy on life threatening illness; training for all our employees; educational materials on safer sex and living with HIV and AIDS for distribution in our shops; outreach to local community groups; and funding support for organizations which assist people with HIV and AIDS.

- The Body Shop Foundation was founded in 1989. The company donated £0.9 million to the foundation in 1997/98, up from £0.75 million in 1996/97.[73]

Against Animal Testing

The Body Shop is against animal testing of ingredients and products in the cosmetics industry. We do not test our products or ingredients on animals. Nor do we commission others to test on our behalf. We never have and we never will.

We will never endorse the use of animal tests in the cosmetics or toiletries industry. However, no cosmetics company can claim that its manufactured ingredients have never been tested on animals by somebody at some stage for someone. We support a complete ban on the testing of both finished cosmetic products and individual ingredients used in cosmetic products.

We work with leading animal welfare organizations to lobby for a complete ban on animal testing of cosmetic ingredients and products. We also encourage our ingredient suppliers and those who want to become our suppliers to stop animal testing by making our position on animal testing clear to them. We require our suppliers of raw materials to provide written confirmation every six months that any material they supply to us has not been tested by them for the cosmetics industry for the last five years.

The "5-year rolling rule" is the most effective mechanism for change. Every six months, our technical information specialists send out hundreds of declarations requiring all our suppliers to certify the last date of any animal testing they have conducted on behalf of the cosmetics industry on any ingredient which they supply to us.

If a supplier fails to complete the form, the company is pursued until we get the information we need. If no declaration is forth coming, or if the company reports conducting an animal test for any part of the cosmetics industry within the last five years, we immediately stop buying the ingredient from that supplier and look for alternative suppliers who have not tested on animals within the previous five years. If no supplier can be found who meets the 5-year rule, we will try to reformulate the product without that ingredient. If we cannot reformulate, we will stop making the product.

Some companies who adopt an against-animal-testing policy take a "fixed cut off date" stance, declaring they will not use an ingredient which comes into existence after a specific date. This position does little to persuade ingredient suppliers, who continue to develop new ingredients, to stop animal testing. A "fixed cut off date" company provides no market for new ingredients, forcing suppliers to continue dealing with those cosmetic companies which require tests. In addition, the extent to which a company's suppliers adhere to its rule may be questionable since most "cut-off" date companies never recheck with their suppliers to see if previously untested ingredients have been re-tested.

The Body Shop polices the 5-year rule. It's not just the rule itself that provokes the changes we want. It's the policing with regard to each ingredient. As our ingredient suppliers trade with new customers and in new markets, they are confronted by additional demands for animal testing. Our twice yearly declarations ensure they continue to meet our requirements.

We rely upon a number of alternative techniques to help assess a product's safety. At The Body Shop, customer safety is paramount. We believe (as do many experts) that the reliability of animal testing is questionable. In developing products we use natural ingredients, like bananas and Brazil nut oil, as well as others with a long history of safe human usage. Our ingredients and/or finished products are subject to in-vitro testing methods such as Eytex, human patch testing, SPF testing, and analytical procedures.

Working for the World's Wildlife

All around the world animals are in danger of extinction as their food sources are threatened, their natural habitats diminish, and environmental degradation takes its toll. The Body Shop takes action on several fronts to keep this critical issue in the public eye.

The Body Shop has a long established commitment to helping endangered species. Over the years, The Body Shop and its franchisees have raised hundreds of thousands of dollars, locally, nationally, and internationally, to support a host of campaigns and projects. We also work hard to inform the public and influence governments the world over to protect the environment and stop the illegal trade in endangered species.

Care for the Environment

The Body Shop believes it just isn't possible for any business to claim to be environmentally friendly because all commerce involves some environmental impact. But at The Body Shop, we take responsibility for the waste we create. We aim to avoid excessive packaging, to refill our bottles, and to recycle our packaging and use raw ingredients from renewable sources whenever technically and economically feasible.

The most accessible aspect of our environmental practice for customers is our refill service. Customers bring back their empty, clean containers and we refill them with the same product at a discount. This conserves resources, reduces waste, and saves money. We also accept our packaging back for recycling. At the same time, we're always searching for new ways to reduce our impact on the environment. In the United Kingdom, we are investing in wind energy with the ultimate aim of putting back into the national grid as much electricity as we take out.

In the United States, we've yet to achieve the level of environmental management reached in the United Kingdom and, unsurprisingly, we've had some growing pains which we've done our best to minimize. For instance, we discovered that because of regulations in some states, our larger bottles required special labels to comply with the state's recycling program. So we used a special stick-on label while we phased out stock of that particular bottle.

A New Kind of Audit

To create a framework for our environmental commitment, we have introduced an annual environmental audit pursuant to European Community Eco-management and Audit Regulation at our U.K. headquarters. The results of the audit are publicly available. [See Exhibit 6 for results of first social audit.] By setting targets to meet on a yearly basis, the audit process is a constant challenge to our commitment, as well as a campaigning platform for us and a role model for other companies. And it's a constant reminder to staff that good environment housekeeping is everyone's business.

Having relocated our headquarters to Wake Forest, NC, from Cedar Knolls, NJ, we are now committed to publishing a comprehensive and externally verified environmental audit statement like "The Green Book," which is published annually in the United Kingdom. Our internal reviews have helped us identify problems to work on and get our staff more involved in environmental management as well.

We are beginning to execute environmental reviews at our principal subsidiaries, retail outlets, and overseas franchises. All will be subject to independent examinations which will eventually result in separately accountable environmental management procedures.[74]

In 1995, the company commissioned Professor Kirk Hanson, a leading American professor in business ethics and social responsibility at the Graduate School of Business of Stanford University, to conduct an independent evaluation of the company's social performance and make recommendations for improvements.[75]

A Brief Summary of Our Environmental Policy

1. Think Globally as a constant reminder of our responsibility to protect the environment.

2. Achieve Excellence by setting clear targets and time scales within which to meet them.

3. Search for Sustainability by using renewable resources wherever feasible and conserving natural resources where renewable options aren't available.

4. Manage Growth by letting our business decisions be guided as much by their environmental implications as by economics.

5. Manage Energy by working towards replacing what we must use with renewable resources.

Exhibit 6 Results of Social Audit—The Good News and *The Bad News:* The Body Shop

Employees	Franchisees	Customers
93% agreed or strongly agreed that The Body Shop lives up to its mission on the issues of environmental responsibility and animal testing.	94% of UK and 73% of US franchisees agreed or strongly agreed that The Body Shop campaigns effectively on human rights, environmental protection, and animal testing.	The Body Shop scored an average of 7.5 out of 10 for campaigning effectively on human rights, environmental protection, and animal protection.
79% agreed or strongly agreed that working for The Body Shop has raised their awareness of pressing global issues.	90% of UK and 80% of US franchisees felt that the company provides reliable and honest information to them on social issues.	The Body Shop scored an average of 9 out of 10 for its stance against animal testing among British customers.
23% felt the best way for them to develop their career was to change companies.	*More than one-fifth of UK and US franchisees expressed no opinion on the majority of issues related to doing business with The Body Shop.*	*Many customers in the UK and US are still confused by what is natural.*
53% disagreed or strongly disagreed that the behavior and decision making of managers was consistent throughout the company.	*43% of UK and 64% of US franchisees disagreed that The Body Shop's sales divisions communicated their long-term strategy clearly to the franchisees.*	*UK customer complaints rose from 18.3 per 100,000 transactions in 1992/93 to 20.9 per 100,000 transactions in 1994/1995.*

Suppliers	Shareholders	Community Involvement
95% agree or strongly agree that the Body Shop takes active steps to make its business more environmentally responsible.	90% agreed or strongly agreed that The Body Shop takes active steps to make its business more environmentally responsible.	In 1994/95 The Body Shop's directly employed staff gave an estimated 19,500 hours to projects in the community.
Prompt payment, clarity of delivery and purchase order requirements, and fairness of quality assurance arrangements were all recognized by 80% or more.	78% were satisfied with the information they receive on The Body Shop's financial performance.	87% of recipients of funding from The Body Shop Foundation agreed or strongly agreed that The Body Shop takes active steps to make its business more environmentally responsible.
One-fifth disagreed or strongly disagreed that The Body Shop's purchasing and logistics functions are well structured and efficient.	*29% disagreed or strongly disagreed that the company enjoys the trust of the financial community.*	*75% of The Body Shop employees do not participate actively in the community volunteering program.*
8% claimed to have experienced ethically corrupt behavior in their dealings with individual members of The Body Shop staff.	*33% had no opinion or disagreed that The Body Shop has a clear long-term business strategy.*	*Nearly half the recipients of funding disagreed or strongly disagreed that it was easy to identify the right decision makers in The Body Shop Foundation.*

Source: The Body Shop.

6. Manage Waste by adopting a four-tier approach: reduce, reuse, recycle, and as last resort, dispose by the safest and most responsible means possible.

7. Control Pollution by protecting the quality of land, air, and water on which we depend.

8. Operate Safely by minimizing risk at every level of our operations: for staff, for customers, and for the community in which the business operates.

9. Obey the Law by complying with environmental laws at all times.

10. Raise Awareness by continuously educating our staff and our customers.

Community Outreach

The Body Shop believes that businesses should give something back to the communities in which they trade. We try to do that in a number of different ways.

Harlem

We opened our 120th American shop on 125th Street in Harlem in 1992. Staffed in part by residents of the community, this shop is helping to contribute to the economic revitalization of the Harlem community. Fifty percent of the post-interest, pre-tax profits from the shop are placed in a fund which will be used to open other community-based shops around the country, while the other 50% is given to a fund (monitored by an advisory group of local community leaders) for Harlem community projects.

Community Projects

We encourage all of our employees to do volunteer work and allow them four hours each month of paid time to do it! Community projects are as diverse as our staff and the communities in which we trade. They range from Adopt-a-Highway clean-ups, to delivering meals to homebound people with AIDS, to working with children who have been physically abused, to serving meals to the homeless.

Local Events

In addition to regular community projects work, our employees frequently help out with local events. Recent projects have included a Harlem street fair, participation in AIDS walkathons, and benefit dances to raise money for the Kayapo Indians in Brazil. Many shops do makeovers, foot and hand massages, and aromatherapy massages and donate the proceeds to local organizations. And staff also frequently give talks to various community groups on a wide range of topics—from endangered species to how The Body Shop does business to the rights of indigenous people.[76]

GLOBAL OPERATIONS AND FINANCIAL RESULTS

Retail Sales

Worldwide retail sales grew by 5% to £604.4 million in 1998. This reflected growth of 14% in Asia, 9% in the Americas (excluding the United States), 6% in Europe, 4% in Australasia, 3% in the United Kingdom, and a decline of 2% in the United States. The retail sales by region are shown below, with prior year figures restated at comparable exchange rates:[77]

Retail Sales by Region
(British pound amounts in millions)

Region	1998	1997	% Change	% of Operating Profit
United Kingdom	£165.0	£161.0	3	27
Europe	148.0	139.5	6	25
United States	98.5	100.6	(2)	16
Americas (excluding USA)	50.0	45.9	9	8
Asia	108.3	95.2	14	18
Australia and New Zealand	33.8	32.6	4	6
Total	£603.6	£574.8		

Worldwide, comparable shop sales growth was unchanged year to year, reflecting a combination of 7% growth in the Americas (excluding the United States), 2% growth in the United Kingdom, 1% growth in Europe, an unchanged position in Australasia, a 5% decline in the United States, and a 6% decline in Asia. Japan was the major influence on the performance in Asia where comparable store sales declined by 19%.

Customer transactions showed a 1% decrease during 1998 to 86.5 million. The average transaction per customer increased by 5% to £6.84. Customer transactions in 1998 by geographic region were: United Kingdom—37%; Europe—24%; United States—12%; Americas (excluding the United States)—9%; Asia—13%, and Australia and New Zealand—5%.

Turnover

Turnover (a term used in the United Kingdom) was a combination of retail sales (excluding sales taxes) through company-owned shops and wholesale revenue for goods sold to franchisees.[78]

The *1998 Annual Report* stated "Group turnover for the year increased by 8% to £293.1 million, of which 60% relates to international markets. Of the total turnover, 60% represented wholesale sales to franchisees and 40% was achieved in retail sales through company-owned stores, mail order, and The Body Shop Direct. The change reflects the higher proportion of company-owned stores, with retail sales of £117.7 million being 24% higher than in the previous year. The growth in 1998 turnover also reflects higher exports, which, including sales to overseas subsidiaries, increased by 7% to £107.8 million.[79]

Operating Profits

The operating profits of the company's six geographic regions were as follows:[80]

Operating Profit (Loss) by Region
(British pound amounts in millions)

Region	1998	1997	% Change	% of Operating Profit
United Kingdom	£11.2	£13.6	−18	37
Europe	8.0	8.1	−1	20
United States	(1.7)	(3.0)	—	—
Americas (excluding USA)	3.4	3.0	13	16
Asia	15.4	14.7	5	8
Australia and New Zealand	1.8	2.0	−10	5
Total	**£38.1**	**£38.4**		

Management Analysis by Regions

This section is management analyses of operations by geographic regions as reported in the company's *1998 Annual Report*.[81]

United Kingdom

The company acted as the head franchisee in the United Kingdom, managing wholesale and retail activities. Seven new shops were opened during the 1998 financial year, giving a total of 263 stores at year's end of which 67 were company-owned. In line with the company's strategy to operate stores located in large cities, ten shops were purchased from franchisees during the year.

Region: **United Kingdom**	1998	1997	
Shops at year end	263	256	
Shop openings	7	4	

Category	**£m**	**£m**	**Change**
Retail sales	£165.8	£161.2	+3%
Turnover	116.2	103.1	+10%
Operating profit	11.2	13.6	−18%

Total retail sales grew by 3% in the year to February 1998, with comparable store sales up by 2% from the previous year. The comparable store sales excluded sales realized through The Body Shop Direct, the home selling program, which were included in the total retail sales figure. The Body Shop Direct continued to move forward, with over 1,100 registered consultants at the year's end. More than 60,000 parties were held during the year, reaching some 625,000 customers.

The testing of the new store design progressed, with seven of these stores operating by the year's end. The Body Shop anticipated that up to 15 of these new designs would be fitted in existing and new stores during 1998.

Turnover in the United Kingdom grew by 10%, ahead of the growth in retail sales due to the larger number of company-owned stores. Operating profit was 18% lower, with the profit from the additional company-owned stores being offset by an increase in marketing expenses and higher costs associated with The Body Shop Direct.

United States

The company's subsidiary, The Body Shop Inc., functioned as the head franchisee for the United States. The head office, filling facilities, and main distribution center were based in Wake Forest, North Carolina.

Store openings were minimal, with a net increase of three stores during the year. Of the 290 stores at the period's end, 210 were company-owned with 68 stores that were purchased from franchisees during the year. This number included 16 shops that were acquired with the southeastern distributorship. Once most of the lowest performing franchised stores had been bought, The Body Shop anticipated few store buy-backs in 1998.

Region: **USA**	1998	1997	
Shops at year end	290	287	
Shop openings	3	14	

Category	**$m**	**$m**	**Change**
Retail sales	161.6	165.0	−2%
Turnover	128.1	119.6	+7%

Category	**£m**	**£m**	**Change**
Retail sales	98.5	100.6	−2%
Turnover	78.0	73.1	+7%
Operating profit	(1.7)	(3.0)	

Total retail sales in the United States were 2% lower than in the previous year, reflecting the low number of new store openings together with a comparable store sales decline of 5%. Other than Manhattan, which performed slightly better than the average, sales performances were similar across the regions.

Fewer new product introductions, poor retailing, and competitive pressures continued to affect sales performance.

Turnover in the United States was 7% higher given the larger number of company-owned stores. The U.S. operating results were a combination of the margin realized in the United Kingdom on supplying goods to the United States, together with the margin arising from wholesale and retail activities within the United States. The operating loss of £1.7 million showed an improvement on the 1997 result although the result was similar year to year if the effect of currency changes were excluded.

Europe

The 13 net store openings in Europe reflected 41 openings and 28 closures, with nine closures in France. The 6% total retail sales growth achieved in Europe reflected the store openings and a 1% increase in comparable store sales.

Region: **Europe United**	1998	1997	
Shops at year end	527	514	
Shop openings	13	30	
Category	**£m**	**£m**	**Change**
Retail sales	148.0	139.5	+6%
Turnover	42.0	39.3	+7%
Operating profit	8.0	8.1[1]	−1%

Note: 1. Excluding the exceptional item relating to France. The exceptional item related to a provision of £6.5 million (£4.3 million after tax) in respect of facilities extended to the former head franchisee in France prior to the acquisition of the French business in November 1997.

Comparable store sales performance varied across the region with markets such as Holland, Sweden, Finland, and Ireland showing the strongest underlying growth. Other markets, such as France, Germany, and Spain, showed improving trends with negative comparable store sales reversing in the second six months. The improvements being achieved in France reflected a rationalization of the store base there and the successful introduction of a stronger retail agenda following the acquisition of the business during the year.

Turnover in Europe grew by 7%, with operating profit similar to the previous year.

Asia

Of the 75 new store openings in Asia, 29 were in Japan. The Body Shop anticipated fewer store openings in Asia during the current year given the economic difficulties in a number of South East Asian countries.

Region: **Asia**	1998	1997	
Shops at year end	308	233	
Shop openings	75	63	
Category	**£m**	**£m**	**Change**
Retail sales	108.3	95.2	+14%
Turnover	37.5	35.7	+5%
Operating profit	15.4	14.7	+5%

Retail stores in the Asian region showed growth of 14%, with comparable store sales declining by 6%. Excluding the impact of Japan, where comparable store sales declined by 19%, comparable store sales in the region grew by 4%. Although Taiwan, Malaysia, Indonesia, and Saudi Arabia all showed strong positive underlying growth, other markets such as Singapore and Thailand saw comparable store sales declines. The first shop opened in Korea at the end of March 1997, with five stores opening by the year's end.

Americas (excluding the United States)

Total retail sales grew by 9%, with comparable store sales growth of 7%. These results were mainly influenced by the sales performance in Canada, which continued to benefit from a focused marketing and retail program.

Region: **Americas** (excluding the United States)	1998	1997	
Shops at year end	130	130	
Shop openings	—	4	
Category	**£m**	**£m**	**Change**
Retail sales	50.0	45.9	+9%
Turnover	12.8	9.9	+29%
Operating profit	3.4	3.0	+13%

Turnover was 29% higher, with operating profit 13% up from the previous year.

Australia and New Zealand

Total retail sales in Australia and New Zealand increased by 4%, with comparable store sales unchanged from the previous year.

Region: **Australia and New Zealand**	1998	1997	
Shops at year end	76	71	
Shop openings	5	3	
Category	**£m**	**£m**	**Change**
Retail sales	33.8	32.6	+4%
Turnover	6.6	6.7	−1%
Operating profit	1.8	2.0	−10%

Turnover was down 1% and operating profit was down 10% from the previous year mainly due to the timing of product shipments.

Exhibits 7 and 8 show the company's balance sheets and consolidated profit and loss accounts.

Exhibit 7   Balance Sheets: The Body Shop[1,2]
(British pounds in millions)

Year Ending February 28	Group		Company	
	1998	**1997**	**1998**	**1997**
Fixed Assets				
Tangible assets	78.4	74.9	50.7	52.7
Investments	2.0	0.5	50.2	15.8
	80.4	75.4	101.2	68.5
Current Assets				
Stocks	47.7	34.8	28.5	21.2
Debtors	47.0	45.0	59.5	65.6
Cash at bank and in hand	29.6	47.1	21.3	39.0
	124.3	126.9	109.3	125.8
Creditors: amounts falling due within one year	70.4	59.0	59.3	44.9
Net current assets	53.9	67.9	50.0	80.9
Total assets less current liabilities	134.3	143.3	151.2	149.4
Creditors: amounts falling due after more than one year	2.9	13.0	0.0	0.1
Provisions for liabilities and charges				
Deferred tax	1.1	0.2	1.9	0.6
Total assets	£130.3	£130.1	£149.3	£148.7
Capital and Reserves				
Called up share amount	9.7	9.7	9.7	9.7
Share premium account	42.8	42.1	42.8	42.1
Profit and loss account	77.8	78.3	96.8	96.9
Shareholders' funds	£130.3	£130.1	£149.3	£148.7

Notes:
1. These financial statements were approved by the Board on May 13, 1998.
2. Notes were deleted.

Source: The Body Shop, *1998 Annual Report,* p. 39.

Exhibit 8   Consolidated Profit and Loss Account: The Body Shop
(British pounds in millions, except per ordinary share data)

Year Ending February 28	1998	1997
Turnover	£293.10	£270.80
Cost of sales	115.90	111.90
Gross Profit	177.20	158.90
Operating expenses—excluding exceptional item	139.10	120.50
Operating expenses—exceptional item	0	6.50
Operating Profit	38.10	31.90
Interest payable (net)	0.10	0.20
Profit on Ordinary Activities Before Tax	38.00	31.70
Tax on profit on ordinary activities	15.20	14.10
Profit for the Financial Year	22.80	17.60
Dividends paid and proposed	10.80	9.10
Retained profit	£ 12.00	£ 8.50
Earnings per ordinary share including exceptional item	11.8p	9.2p
Earnings per ordinary share excluding exceptional item	11.8p	11.4p

Notes:
1. Turnover represents the total amounts receivable in the ordinary course of business for goods sold and services provided and excludes sales between companies in the Group, discount given, Value Added Tax (VAT), and other sales taxes.
2. Other notes were deleted.

Source: The Body Shop, *1998 Annual Report*, p. 38.

Notes

1. Nigel Cope, "Roddick Quits Helm at Body Shop," *Independent* (May 21, 1998), p. 21.
2. *Ibid.*
3. "They Said It," *Daily Telegraph* (May 16, 1998), p. 33.
4. "Body Shop. Capitalism and Cocoa Butter," *The Economist* (May 16, 1998), p. 66.
5. Rufus Olins, "Body Shop Calls in Corporate Man," *The Sunday Times* (May 17, 1998).
6. *Ibid.*
7. Sarah Cunningham, "Body Shop Offers Golden Handcuffs," *Times* (May 15, 1998).
8. Rufus Olins, "Body Shop."
9. Anita Roddick, *The Body Shop.* (NY: Crown Publishers, Inc.), 1991, p. 43.
10. *Ibid.*, p. 52.
11. *Ibid.*, pp. 55–62.
12. *Ibid.*, p. 66.
13. *Ibid.*
14. *Ibid.*, p. 67.
15. *Ibid.*, p. 68.
16. *Ibid.*
17. *Ibid.*
18. *Ibid.*, p. 77.
19. *Ibid.*, p. 68.
20. *Ibid.*, p. 74.
21. *Ibid.*, pp. 85–86.
22. *Ibid.*, p. 86.
23. *Ibid.*, p. 92.
24. *Ibid.*, pp. 94–95.
25. *Ibid.*, pp. 96–97.
26. *Ibid.*, p. 101.
27. *Ibid.*
28. *Ibid.*, p. 100.
29. *Ibid.*
30. *Ibid.*, p. 143.
31. *Ibid.*, p. 144.
32. The Body Shop, *1998 Annual Report*, p. 25.
33. The Body Shop, *1995 Annual Report*, p. 15.
34. *Ibid.*, p.17.
35. *Ibid.*, p.20.
36. *Ibid.*, p.25.
37. *Ibid.*, p.49.
38. *Ibid.*, p.81.
39. *Ibid.*, p.108.

40. *Ibid.,* p.115.
41. *Ibid.,* p.123.
42. *Ibid.,* p.226.
43. *Ibid.,* p.158.
44. *Ibid.,* p.178.
45. *Ibid.,* p.214.
46. *Ibid.,* p.217.
47. *Ibid.,* p.223.
48. *Ibid.,* p.231.
49. *Ibid.,* p.181.
50. *Ibid.,* p. 137.
51. James Fallon. "Body Shop Shakeup Brings New CEO," *WWD* (May 13, 1998), p. 3.
52. Robert Wright. "Body Shop US Venture Approved," *Financial Times* (June 23, 1998), p. 28.
53. Ernest Beck. "Body Shop Founder Roddick Steps Aside as CEO," *Wall Street Journal* (May 13, 1998), p. B14.
54. The Body Shop. *Our Reason for Being* (handout).
55. The Body Shop. *1998 Annual Report,* p. 25.
56. *Ibid.,* p. 32.
57. *Ibid.,* p. 36.
58. *Ibid.*
59. Anita Roddick, pp. 235–236.
60. "Loosening One's Grip," *Cosmetic Insiders' Report,* no. 11, vol. 17.
61. Ruth Nicholas, "New Age Finds a New Face," *Marketing* (May 21, 1998), p. 15.

62. *Ibid.*
63. Diane Seo, "Body Shop Hopes Hemp Will Plant Seeds of Recovery," *LA Times* (February 26, 1998), p. D1.
64. Fallon, p. 3.
65. Seo, p. D1.
66. Alev Aktar, "Hemp: A Growing Controversy" *WWD* (February 13, 1998), p. 8.
67. Nicholas, p. 15.
68. *Ibid.,* p. 143.
69. *Ibid.,* p. 125.
70. *Ibid.,* p. 135.
71. The Body Shop, *1994 Annual Report,* p. 22.
72. The Body Shop, *This Is The Body Shop,* (Nov. 1994), p. 57. All 5 paragraphs below are directly taken from this source.
73. The Body Shop, *1998 Annual Report,* p. 67.
74. The Body Shop, *This Is The Body Shop* (Nov. 1994), pp. 6–8. All 15 paragraphs below are directly taken from this source.
75. The Body Shop, *1995 Annual Report,* p. 3.
76. The Body Shop, *This Is The Body Shop* (Nov. 1994), pp. 8–9.
77. The Body Shop, *1998 Annual Report,* pp. 25–29.
78. *Ibid.*
79. *Ibid.*
80. *Ibid.,* pp. 18–20.
81. *Ibid.*

Inner-City Paint Corporation (Revised)

Donald F. Kuratko and Norman J. Gierlasinski

HISTORY

Stanley Walsh began Inner-City Paint Corporation in a run-down warehouse, which he rented, on the fringe of Chicago's "downtown" business area. The company is still located at its original site.

Inner-City is a small company that manufactures wall paint. It does not compete with giants such as Glidden and DuPont. There are small paint manufacturers in Chicago that supply the immediate area. The proliferation of paint manufacturers is due to the fact that the weight of the product (52½ pounds per 5-gallon container) makes the cost of shipping great distances prohibitive. Inner-City's chief product is flat white wall paint sold in 5-gallon plastic cans. It also produces colors on request in 55-gallon containers.

The primary market of Inner-City is the small- to medium-sized decorating company. Pricing must be competitive; until recently, Inner-City had shown steady growth in this market. The slowdown in the housing market combined with a slowdown in the overall economy caused financial difficulty for Inner-City Paint Corporation. Inner-City's reputation had been built on fast service: it frequently supplied paint to contractors within 24 hours. Speedy delivery to customers became difficult when Inner-City was required to pay cash on delivery (C.O.D.) for its raw materials.

Inner-City had been operating without management controls or financial controls. It had grown from a very small two-person company with sales of $60,000 annually five years ago, to sales of $1,800,000 and 38 employees this year. Stanley Walsh realized that tighter controls within his organization would be necessary if the company was to survive.

EQUIPMENT

Five mixers are used in the manufacturing process. Three large mixers can produce a maximum of 400 gallons, per batch, per mixer. The two smaller mixers can produce a maximum of 100 gallons, per batch, per mixer.

Two lift trucks are used for moving raw materials. The materials are packed in 100-pound bags. The lift trucks also move finished goods, which are stacked on pallets.

A small testing lab ensures the quality of materials received and the consistent quality of their finished product. The equipment in the lab is sufficient to handle the current volume of product manufactured.

Transportation equipment consists of two 24-foot delivery trucks and two vans. This small fleet is more than sufficient because many customers pick up their orders to save delivery costs.

This case was prepared by Professor Donald F. Kuratko of Ball State University and Professor Norman J. Gierlasinski of Central Washington State University. This case was edited and revised for SMBP–7th Edition. Copyright © 1984 by Donald F. Kuratko and Norman J. Gierlasinski. Reprinted by permission.

FACILITIES

Inner-City performs all operations from one building consisting of 16,400 square feet. The majority of the space is devoted to manufacturing and storage; only 850 square feet is assigned as office space. The building is 45 years old and in disrepair. It is being leased in three-year increments. The current monthly rent on this lease is $2,700. The rent is low in consideration of the poor condition of the building and its undesirable location in a run-down neighborhood (south side of Chicago). These conditions are suitable to Inner-City because of the dusty, dirty nature of the manufacturing process and the small contribution of the rent to overhead costs.

PRODUCT

Flat white paint is made with pigment (titanium dioxide and silicates), vehicle (resin), and water. The water makes up 72% of the contents of the product. To produce a color, the necessary pigment is added to the flat white paint. The pigment used to produce the color has been previously tested in the lab to ensure consistent quality of texture. Essentially, the process is the mixing of powders with water, then tapping off of the result into 5- or 55-gallon containers. Color overruns are tapped off into 2-gallon containers.

Inventory records are not kept. The warehouse manager keeps a mental count of what is in stock. He documents (on a lined yellow pad) what has been shipped for the day and to whom. That list is given to the billing clerk at the end of each day.

The cost of the materials to produce flat white paint is $2.40 per gallon. The cost per gallon for colors is approximately 40%–50% higher. The 5-gallon covered plastic pails cost Inner-City $1.72 each. The 55-gallon drums (with lids) are $8.35 each. (see Exhibit 1).

Selling price varies with the quantity purchased. To the average customer, flat white sells at $27.45 for 5 gallons and $182.75 for 55 gallons. Colors vary in selling price because of the variety in pigment cost and quantity ordered. Customers purchase on credit and usually pay their invoices in 30 to 60 days. Inner-City telephones the customer after 60 days of nonpayment and inquires when payment will be made.

MANAGEMENT

The President and majority stockholder is Stanley Walsh. He began his career as a house painter and advanced to become a painter for a large decorating company. Walsh painted mostly walls in large commercial buildings and hospitals. Eventually, he came to believe that he could produce a paint that was less expensive and of higher quality than what was being used. A keen desire to open his own business resulted in the creation of Inner-City Paint Corporation.

Walsh manages the corporation today in much the same way that he did when the business began. He personally must open *all* the mail, approve *all* payments, and inspect *all* customer billings before they are mailed. He has been unable to detach himself from any detail of the operation and cannot properly delegate authority. As the company has grown, the time element alone has aggravated the situation. Frequently, these tasks are performed days after transactions occur and mail is received.

The office is managed by Mary Walsh (Walsh's mother). Two part-time clerks assist her, and all records are processed manually.

Exhibit 1   **Paint Cost Sheet: Inner-City Paint Corporation**

	5 Gallons	55 Gallons
Sales price	$ 27.45	$ 182.75
Direct material	(12.00)	(132.00)
Pail and lid	(1.72)	(8.35)
Direct labor	(2.50)	(13.75)
Manufacturing overhead ($1/gallon)	(5.00)	(5.00)
Gross margin	$ 6.23	$ 23.65
Gross profit ratio	22.7%	12.9%

The plant is managed by a man in his twenties, whom Walsh hired from one of his customers. Walsh became acquainted with him when the man picked up paint from Inner-City for his previous employer. Prior to the eight months he has been employed by Walsh as plant manager, his only other experience has been that of a painter.

EMPLOYEES

Thirty-five employees (20 workers are part-time) work in various phases of the manufacturing process. The employees are nonunion, and most are unskilled laborers. They take turns making paint and driving the delivery trucks.

Stanley Walsh does all of the sales work and public relations work. He spends approximately one-half of every day making sales calls and answering complaints about defective paint. He is the only salesman. Other salesmen had been employed in the past, but Walsh felt that they "could not be trusted."

CUSTOMER PERCEPTION

Customers view Inner-City as a company that provides fast service and negotiates on price and payment out of desperation. Walsh is seen as a disorganized man who may not be able to keep Inner-City afloat much longer. Paint contractors are reluctant to give Inner-City large orders out of fear that the paint may not be ready on a continuous, reliable basis. Larger orders usually go to larger companies that have demonstrated their reliability and solvency.

Rumors abound that Inner-City is in difficult financial straits, that it is unable to pay suppliers, and that it owes a considerable sum for payment on back taxes. All of the above contribute to the customers' serious lack of confidence in the corporation.

FINANCIAL STRUCTURE

Exhibits 2 and 3 are the most current financial statements of Inner-City Paint Corporation. They have been prepared by the company's accounting service. No audit has been performed because Walsh did not want to incur the expense it would have required.

Exhibit 2   Balance Sheet for the Current Year Ending June 30: Inner-City Paint Corporation

Current Assets

Cash	$ 1,535	
Accounts receivable (net of allowance for bad debts of $63,400)	242,320	
Inventory	18,660	
Total current assets		$262,515
Machinery and transportation equipment	47,550	
Less accumulated depreciation	15,500	
Net fixed assets		32,050
Total assets		$294,565

Current Liabilities

Accounts payable	$217,820	
Salaries payable	22,480	
Notes payable	6,220	
Taxes payable	38,510	
Total current liabilities		$285,030
Long-term notes payable		15,000

Owners' Equity

Common stock, no par, 1,824 shares outstanding		12,400
Deficit		(17,865)
Total liabilities and owners' equity		$294,565

Exhibit 3   Income Statement for the Current Year Ending June 30: Inner-City Paint Corporation

Sales		$1,784,080
Cost of goods sold		1,428,730
Gross margin		$ 355,350
Selling expenses	$ 72,460	
Administrative expenses	67,280	
President's salary	132,000	
Office manager's salary	66,000	
Total expenses		337,740
Net income		$ 17,610

FUTURE

Stanley Walsh wishes to improve the financial situation and reputation of Inner-City Paint Corporation. He is considering the purchase of a computer to organize the business and reduce needless paperwork. He has read about consultants who are able to quickly spot problems in businesses, but he will not spend more than $300 on such a consultant.

The solution that Walsh favors most is one that requires him to borrow money from the bank, which he will then use to pay his current bills. He feels that as soon as business conditions improve, he will be able to pay back the loans. He believes that the problems Inner-City is experiencing are due to the overall poor economy and are only temporary.

The Vermont Teddy Bear Co., Inc. (1998): Challenges Facing a New CEO

Joyce P. Vincelette, Ellie A. Fogarty, Thomas M. Patrick, and Thomas L. Wheelen

"A teddy bear is almost a 100-year-old product that has been made in every conceivable size, style, fabric, and price combined with a saturated market. Yet the teddy bear industry stands as a model of strength and durability. Every year, bear makers create and market hundreds of original models."[1]

Vermont Teddy Bear Company was founded in 1981 by John Sortino selling hand-sewn teddy bears out of a push-cart in the streets of Burlington, Vermont. Since this time, the company's focus has been to design, manufacture, and direct market the best teddy bears made in America using quality American materials and labor.

Until 1994, Vermont Teddy Bear experienced a great deal of success and profitability. Problems arose in 1995. Since 1995, the company has had two CEOs. It changed its name to The Great American Teddy Bear Company and then changed it back to The Vermont Teddy Bear Company when customers got confused. From its inception, Vermont Teddy had been known for its Bear-Gram delivery service. In 1996, the company decided to shift emphasis away from Bear-Grams to other distribution channels. By 1998, the company decided to renew its emphasis on Bear-Grams. Vermont Teddy has always been proud of the fact that its teddy bears were made in America with American materials and craftsmanship. In 1998, the company changed this philosophy by exploring the offshore sourcing of materials, outfits, and manufacturing in an effort to lower costs.

Elisabeth Robert assumed the titles of President and Chief Executive Officer in October 1997 and began to cut costs and position the company for future growth. According to Robert, there were many reasons to invest in The Vermont Teddy Bear Company. "I believe that there is growth potential in this company. We are going to regain our balance this year. This is a rebuilding year. We are taking key steps to reposition the company. The move offshore is going to provide this company an opportunity to become more profitable. We will gain additional flexibility with price points. There is opportunity for us to expand from a regional brand to a national brand. While we continue to emphasize the premium teddy bear gift business, we intend to expand into larger markets. There is now a whole new opportunity for us in the corporate incentives and promotions market as well as the wholesale market. We have weekly inquiries from companies who recognize our brands. These companies would love to buy and resell our product or use our product as a corporate gift. Our growth will come not only from expansion of our radio markets but in the corporate and wholesale markets as we use offshore manufacturing alternatives to move to broader price points."[2]

According to Robert, "our competitors are the people who sell chocolates, flowers, and greeting cards. We target the last minute shopper who wants almost instant delivery."[3] Gift purchases account for 90% of the Company's sales.[4] "We thought we were in the teddy bear business," said Robert. "In fact we are in the gift and personal commu-

---

This case was prepared by Professor Joyce P. Vincelette, Ellie A. Fogarty, Business Librarian, and Professor Thomas M. Patrick of the College of New Jersey, and Professor Thomas L. Wheelen of the University of South Florida. They would also like to thank Matthew Tardougno for his assistance on this project. This case was edited for SMBP–7th Edition. This case may not be reproduced in any form without written permission of the copyright holder, Thomas L. Wheelen. Copyright © 1998 by Thomas L. Wheelen. Reprinted by permission.

nications business. Our competition isn't Steiff (the German toy manufacturer): it's 1-800 Flowers.[5]

On one beautiful June day in Vermont, Elisabeth Robert reflected on the enormous tasks to be accomplished. She wondered if she could successfully reposition her company and return it to profitability. Was she making the correct strategic decisions?

HISTORY: WHY A BEAR COMPANY?

The Vermont Teddy Bear Co., Inc., was founded in 1981 by John Sortino. He got the inspiration for the teddy bear business shortly after his son Graham was born. While playing with his son, he noticed that Graham had many stuffed animals, but they were all made in other countries. Sortino "decided that there should be a bear made in the United States."[6]

He decided to design and manufacture his own premium-quality teddy bears. To turn his concept into reality, Sortino taught himself to sew and enrolled in drawing classes. In 1981, his first creation, Bearcho, was a bear whose thick black eyebrows and mustache resembled those of Groucho Marx. His first bear line included Buggy, Fuzzy, Wuzzy, and Bearazar, the bear with super powers. In 1982, Vermont Teddy Bear Company began limited production of Sortino's early designs using five Vermont homesewers. In 1983, Sortino took his operation to the streets where he sold his handmade bears from a pushcart on the Church Street Marketplace in downtown Burlington, Vermont. Four days later he sold his first bear. By the end of 1983, 200 bears were sold. He concluded from his selling experiences that customers "want bears that are machine washable and dryable. They want bears with joints. They want bears that are cuddly and safe for children. They want bears with personality."[7]

In 1984, Vermont Teddy was incorporated under the laws of the State of New York and Sortino's pushcart business had turned into a full-time job. To facilitate bear manufacturing, local homeworkers were contracted to produce an assortment of the founder's original designs. Even though the company opened a retail store in Burlington, Vermont, in 1985, the majority of the company's products were sold through department stores such as Macy's and Nieman Marcus during the 1980s. As the retail industry consolidated through mergers and store closings during the late 1980s, Sortino realized that a new market needed to be found for his bears. In search of a new customer base, Sortino turned to a local radio station and began advertising the company's products. This advertising strategy paved the way for the "Bear-Gram," where customers could send the gift of a Vermont Teddy Bear by placing an order through the company's 800 number.

The company initiated its Bear-Gram marketing strategy in 1985 in the Burlington, Vermont area. Local radio advertisements aired on WXXX in Burlington and customers called an 800 number to order the product. It was not until shortly before Valentine's Day in 1990 that the company introduced radio advertising of its Bear-Gram product on radio station WHTZ ("Z-100") in New York City, positioning the Bear-Gram as a novel gift for Valentine's Day and offering listeners a toll-free number to order from the company's facility in Vermont. The test proved to be successful, and the Bear-Gram concept was expanded to other major radio markets across the country. These radio advertisements were generally read live by popular radio personalities. John Sortino believed that the radio had been a successful medium for the Bear-Gram for several reasons. He believed that the use of popular radio personalities lent credibility to the product. In addition, because the disk jockey could give away a few bears, more air-time was spent on the product than the paid "60 seconds."[8] He also believed that radio advertising allowed for flexibility in the use of advertising copy, which could be adjusted as the company changed its marketing focus.

Due to the success of the Bear-Gram concept, Vermont Teddy's total sales of $400,000 in 1989 rose to $1.7 million in 1990 and over $5 million in 1991.[9] As sales increased, a larger manufacturing facility was needed. In 1991, the company leased and moved into a new factory space and guided factory tours began. The larger production facilities made it possible for Vermont Teddy Bear to begin producing bears in bulk and to enter into larger sales agreements with retail establishments. In 1992, *Inc.* magazine listed Vermont Teddy as the eightieth fastest growing company in the United States with sales totaling $10.6 million.[10]

Vermont Teddy Bear went public on November 23, 1993. By this time, sales totaled $17 million.[11] In 1993, the company was named the first national winner of the Dun & Bradstreet "Best of America" Small Business Award and was ranked as the fifty-eighth fastest growing company in the United States by *Inc.* magazine.[12] Also in 1993, the company was the recipient of the Heritage of New England Customer Service Award. Previous recipients of the award included L.L.Bean, Inc., Boston Beer Company, and Ben & Jerry's Homemade, Inc.[13]

In 1994, construction began on a new factory and retail store in Shelburne, Vermont, which opened for business in the summer of 1995. In 1994, *Inc.* magazine listed Vermont Teddy Bear, with sales totaling $20.5 million, as the twenty-first fastest growing small, publicly owned company in the United States and named the company "Small Business of the Year."[14]

Prior to 1994, Vermont Teddy Bear had experienced a great deal of success and profitability, with sales growth in excess of 50% for three consecutive years.[15] However, 1994 marked the beginning of the company's financial troubles. The company's expenses increased in accordance with its anticipated growth, but sales did not increase as rapidly.

Vermont Teddy Bear's rapid growth during the 1990s taxed the organizational structure and efficiency of the company's operations. Due to the company's declining financial situation, on June 20, 1995, the company's founder, President and Chief Executive Officer, John Sortino, resigned. Sortino recognized that the future success of the company "depends on the transition from an entrepreneurial company to a professionally managed organization." He further stated, "I wanted to assist the company in positioning itself for the arrival of a new CEO. I will provide guidance to the company in a consulting role, and I will retain my position on the Board of Directors."[16]

On August 2, 1995, R. Patrick Burns was appointed as President and CEO. Also in 1995 Elisabeth Robert joined the company as Chief Financial Officer. Outside observers wondered if the company could successfully make the transition to a new CEO and generate enough sales to pull itself out of debt and remain profitable.

In its attempts to turn the company around, the new management team eliminated several unprofitable marketing ventures (such as its sponsorship of a NASCAR circuit race car and driver) and reduced general and administrative costs. By 1996, the new team had generated a profit of $152,000.[17]

During the later part of 1996, Vermont Teddy Bear took on a new trademarked name, "The Great American Teddy Bear Company," in an attempt to broaden brand appeal and take advantage of national and international distribution opportunities. Even though the "Vermont" name gave good name recognition in the Northeast, the company felt that it had less impact in other parts of the country. They were wrong. Customers became confused, and Disney's entry into the personalized teddy bear gift market with their "Pooh-Grams" added to the confusion. The confusion contributed to a decrease in Bear-Gram sales. By Valentine's Day, the company returned to its established mark, The Vermont Teddy Bear Company.

Late in 1996, the new management team began to explore opportunities for growth. They believed that the emphasis of the company should shift from the Bear-Gram business to other distribution channels. Their new five-year plan included opening new retail stores and expanding the catalog.

By 1997, retail sales were the fastest growing part of Vermont Teddy's business. Sales for the factory retail store in Shelburne for the fiscal year ending June 30, 1996, were 19% ahead of 1995.[18] It appeared obvious to top management that retail was a growing profit center for the company. The company's factory store had become a major Vermont tourist destination and had averaged 130,000 visitors a year since opening in July 1995.[19] As a result, the company became interested in high tourist traffic areas for retail expansion, hoping to duplicate this success at other retail locations.[20]

The location for the company's second retail store was North Conway, New Hampshire, a major tourist destination in both winter and summer months. The store opened in July 1996. The third retail location opened at 538 Madison Avenue in New York City in February 1997. The New York City location was chosen because it had been the number one market for Bear-Grams since the company began advertising on radio in 1990. The company believed that the New York store would benefit from the millions of dollars of radio advertising that the company had invested in this market. The fourth store opened in Freeport, Maine, on August 16, 1997, two doors down from L.L. Bean.

Fiscal 1997 was a disappointing year for Vermont Teddy. After a year of controlling costs and a return to profitability in 1996, they had set out in pursuit of revenue growth in 1997. The 1997 initiatives included an expanded catalog and the new retail stores. As part of the shift away from Bear-Grams, the company down-sized their radio media buying department. The company lost money on their catalog programs, and the new retail stores were not as profitable as expected. Resources diverted to expanding secondary marketing channels, coupled with accelerating changes in the radio industry, contributed to a decline in Bear-Gram sales. The end result was a loss of $1,901,795 in fiscal 1997.[21]

Because of Vermont Teddy Bear's declining performance, R. Patrick Burns chose to step down as President and CEO in October 1997. Elisabeth Robert assumed the title of President and CEO and retained the title of Chief Financial Officer.

According to CEO Robert, "When we made the decision to expand our distribution channels in the areas of retail and catalog, our focus was on being a teddy bear category killer. We thought we were in the teddy bear business. Now what I believe is that we are in the Bear-Gram business, the gift business, and the impulse business. This is a completely different marketplace. Our competitors are the people who sell chocolates, flowers, and greeting cards. We target the last-minute shopper who wants almost instant delivery."[22] She further stated that "the primary focus of the company would return to maximizing returns in the radio Bear-Gram business which constituted the majority of the company's annual revenue."[23]

In 1998, the management team began seriously looking at the profitability of their various retail locations. They also began looking at the catalog, intending to optimize its size and product offerings to ensure its future profitability.

CORPORATE GOVERNANCE

As of June 30, 1998, The Vermont Teddy Bear Co., Inc., had a total of seven Board members and two Executive Officers, both of whom were also members of the Board of Directors.

Board of Directors and Executive Officers[24]

The Board members, Executive Officers, and their experience and qualifications were as follows.

R. Patrick Burns (53) had been President and CEO of Vermont Teddy Bear from 1995 until 1997. He had been a Director of the company since 1995. He planned to remain active as a consultant to the company focusing on developing strategic marketing partnerships for the next two years. Prior to joining the company, he was the Chief Executive Officer of Disney Direct Marketing. He had also held senior management positions at J. Crew, Inc., and at L. L. Bean, Inc.

Joan H. Martin (74) was a private investor who had been a Director of the company since 1991. Martin had no business experience during the past eight years apart from managing her private investment portfolio.

Fred Marks (70) became a Director of the company in 1987 and became its Treasurer and Chairman of the Board in 1989. He served as the company's Chief Financial Officer until January 1995 and Treasurer until 1996. Previously Marks had served as Chairman of the Board of two privately held companies: Selection, Ltd., a manufacturer of remote controls for computers and televisions; and Contaq Technologies, a manufacturer of ultrasonic instruments.

Elisabeth B. Robert (43), Director, Chief Executive Officer, President, Treasurer and Chief Financial Officer, joined the company in 1995 as the Chief Financial Officer replacing Stephen Milford. She was appointed a Director of the company in January 1996 and Treasurer of the company in April 1996. She assumed the titles of CEO and President from R. Patrick Burns who stepped down from the positions in October 1997. Before joining Vermont Teddy, Robert served as the Chief Financial Officer for a high-tech start-up company specializing in remote control devices, where she was also a founding partner.

Spencer C. Putnam (52), Director, Vice-President, and Secretary, joined the company as its Chief Operating Officer in June 1987 and continued in this role. He had been a Director of the company and Secretary of its Board since 1989. Before joining the company, Putnam was the Director of the Cooperative Education Program at the University of Vermont.

David W. Garrett (55) had been a director of the company since 1987. He was a Vice-President of First Albany Corporation, an investment banking and brokerage firm. Garrett was also President of the Garrett Hotel Group, a private hotel development and management firm and President of The Black Willow Group. Ltd., a private company which owned and operated The Point, a luxury hotel in Saranac Lake, New York.

Jason Bacon (64) became a director of the company in 1997. He was a consultant to nonprofit organizations and a private investor focusing on real estate and securities with international perspective. Prior to his involvement with Vermont Teddy Bear, he served as a Managing Director at Kidder, Peabody & Company.

Ownership

As of June 30, 1998, there were 5,183,733 shares of the company's common stock outstanding held by 1,553 shareholders.[25] Approximately 2,551,300 shares or approximately

49.2% of the stock was owned beneficially by the current directors and officers of the company. These figures did not include options or warrants held by current directors and officers, their spouses or minor children to purchase shares of the company's Common Stock or Series B Preferred Stock.[26]

In November 1993, the company made an Initial Public Offering (IPO) of 5,172,500 shares of common stock. The stock ranged from $17.19 to $11.44 from offering to December 31, 1993. Prior to the IPO, 4,000,000 shares of common stock were outstanding and held by nine shareholders. Ninety shares of non-voting Series A Preferred Stock were held by shareholder Joan H. Martin. This preferred stock had an 8% cumulative dividend and liquidation value of $10,000 per share. On July 12, 1996, the company privately placed 204,912 shares of Series B preferred stock. This stock was held by 12 shareholders and was not entitled to any dividends or voting rights. The 204,912 Series B shares were convertible into 482,441 shares of common stock.[27]

The following individuals owned more than 5% of the company's stock as of June 30, 1998.[28]

Beneficial Owner	Number of Shares	Percent Owned
Joan H. Martin	1,840,975	35.5
Fred Marks	600,500	11.6
Margaret H. Martin	267,000	5.2
Spencer C. Putnam	84,000	1.6
R. Patrick Burns	17,625	0.3
Jason Bacon	5,500	0.1
Elisabeth B. Robert	2,700	0.1

Notes were deleted.

Vermont Teddy has never paid cash dividends on any of its shares of common stock. The high and low stock prices for 1998 were:[29]

Quarter Ending	High	Low
June 30, 1998	$1.63	$1.06
March 31, 1998	$1.63	$0.75
December 31, 1997	$2.13	$0.88
September 30, 1997	$2.56	$1.06

COMPANY PHILOSOPHY

From its founding by John Sortino in the early 1980s until 1998, the company's focus had been to design and manufacture the best teddy bears made in America, using American materials and labor. The company believed that apart from its own products, most of the teddy bears sold in the United States were manufactured in foreign countries, and that the company was the largest manufacturer of teddy bears made in the United States. The company's Mission Statement can be seen in Exhibit 1.

This philosophy was modified significantly in 1998 with the company's decision to explore the offshore sourcing of materials and manufacturing alternatives in an effort to lower the company's cost of goods sold and to broaden its available sources of supply. Company customer surveys revealed that price was more important to potential customers than the "Made in America" label.[30] During 1998, the company began purchasing

Exhibit 1 **Mission Statement: The Vermont Teddy Bear Co., Inc.**

The Vermont Teddy Bear provides our customers with a tangible expression of their best feelings for their families, friends, and associates. We facilitate, communicate, and therefore participate in caring events and special occasions that celebrate and enrich our customers' life experiences.

Our products will represent unmatchable craftsmanship balanced with optimal quality and value. We will strive to wholesomely entertain our guests while consistently exceeding our external and internal customer service expectations.

The Vermont Teddy Bear brand represents the rich heritage of the "Great American Teddy Bear" begun in 1902. We are the stewards of a uniquely American tradition based on the best American virtues including compassion, generosity, friendship, and a zesty sense of whimsy and fun.

raw materials for bear production and some teddy bear outfits from offshore manufacturers. Vermont Teddy felt that plush materials from offshore were of better quality and less costly than those produced in the United States. They felt that importing these materials would enable them to produce a better, lower cost product and would provide the flexibility to meet a broader range of price points in response to customer needs.[31] The company planned to continue to handcraft the 15-inch "classic" teddy bear in Vermont for those customers interested in an American-made product. The new label read, "Made in America, of domestic and foreign materials."[32] The company also planned to explore opportunities to introduce new teddy bear products made offshore to their design specifications at significantly lower cost points for sale initially into the wholesale and corporate channels.

With this change in philosophy, the company was committed to understanding its potential offshore partners and to ensuring that its partners provided decent, lawful working conditions. It required that all offshore vendors sign a written statement to this effect prior to any business dealings.[33]

Exhibit 2 details Vermont Teddy's statement of Stakeholder Beliefs. The company believed that the quality, variety, and creativity of the company's products, and its commitment to customer service, were essential to its business. Its manufacturing practices were environmentally sound. The company sought to use the best available materials for its bears. Customer service policies rivaled those of L.L. Bean. Each bear was sold with a "Guarantee for Life," under which the company undertook to repair or replace any damaged or defective bear at any time even if eaten by the family dog or destroyed by a lawn mower.[34]

PRODUCTS AND SERVICES

Vermont Teddy Bear made old-fashioned, handmade, jointed teddy bears ranging from 11 to 72 inches tall, in six standard color selections including tan, honey, brown, and black. More than 100 different bear outfits were available for customers to outfit and individualize their bears or to emphasize certain relevant characteristics of the receiver such as policewoman, gardener, doctor, or racing car driver. Some of the more popular outfits included tutus, wedding gowns, tuxedos, business suits, and sports uniforms. Bears could also be dressed in a wide variety of outfits that personalized the bear for significant life events, such as a new baby, get well, birthdays, graduations, weddings, and "I love you." A collection of bears could also be designed for schools, sports teams, businesses, and other organizations. New "edgier" products were added in 1997 such as

Exhibit 2   Stakeholder Beliefs: The Vermont Teddy Bear Co., Inc.

Our customers are the foundation of our business. Exceeding their expectations *everyday* will form the backbone of our corporate culture. Zealous pursuit of "world class" customer service will build a self-fulfilling cycle of pride, partnership, team spirit, and personal commitment in every player in our company.

Our employees are our internal customers. The philosophy that applies to our external customers extends also to our internal associates. We will cultivate a results-oriented environment that encourages fairness, collaboration, mutual respect, and pride in our organization. Pro-active, positive, open-minded confrontation among well-intentioned colleagues will ensure innovation, reject complacency, and stimulate individual growth. Our company supports employee diversity and provides clear opportunities for each of us to reach our full personal and professional potential.

Our investors provide capital in good faith, and we are accountable for creating a realistic return while protecting the assets of our company. Our financial strength and profitability are essential to fulfilling all of our stakeholder commitments.

Our vendors provide a partnership opportunity for innovative product development, unsurpassed external customer service, and mutual prosperity. This is based on exceeding our customers' expectations for unique, innovative, high-quality communications and products delivered to our customers where and when they want them at a price that reinforces our reputation for perceived value.

Our community deserves our commitment to being ethically, legally, and environmentally responsible while remaining fiscally sound. We will support organizations and individuals with values similar to ours and participate actively in those enterprises that seek to improve local and world conditions for future generations. We will seek to maintain a dynamic balance between meeting our commitment to our community and maintaining the viability of our own enterprise.

"Shredder, the Snowboarder Bear," targeted primarily at radio customers. As of June 30, 1998, 40% of the outfits were outsourced to overseas contractors.[35] Prices for the bears in standard outfits ranged from $40 to more than $200. Custom-made clothing was available at an additional cost.

Until 1997, bear materials were mostly American made, though mohair fur used for the premium bears came from Europe. All other fur was hypoallergenic, plush polyester. Bears were stuffed with virgin Dacron 91, a fire retardant filler for safety. Vermont teddy bears had movable joints, a feature associated with traditional, high-quality teddy bears. These joints were made from recycled Ben and Jerry's ice cream containers. In keeping with the company's attempt to produce the bears with domestic materials, the bears' eyes had come from the only eye maker left in America. Noses and paw pads were ultra-suede, also 100% American made.[36] Using American-made materials had been one of the methods by which Vermont Teddy Bear differentiated its products from those of its competitors. The company's 1998 move to the offshore sourcing of raw materials represented a significant departure from the company's historical position as an American manufacturer using almost exclusively American materials.[37]

In addition to the products it manufactured, Vermont Teddy Bear sold items related to teddy bears, as well as merchandise from other manufacturers featuring the logo of Vermont Teddy Bear. It did a small amount of licensing with Tyco, Landmark, and a manufacturer of children's and women's sleepwear. Some items such as clothing, jewelry, and accessory ornaments were available primarily at the company's retail stores and through its direct mail catalog. The company also sold stuffed toys that had been manufactured by other companies, such as Gund and Steiff.[38] Vermont Teddy Bear planned to alter this strategy in 1999 to focus more attention on the sale of the company's own manufactured products, including those manufactured offshore.

In addition to manufacturing and selling bears and bear-related merchandise to individual consumers, the company's Corporate Division provided unique and original customized products for corporations. Vermont Teddy also silk-screened or embroidered bears on clothing with the customer's logo, slogan, or team name. In 1998, the company planned to offer a line of offshore-manufactured ancillary products for corporate customers and outlets such as QVC.[39] Information about products offered through the company's Corporate and Wholesale Programs could be found on the company's web site.

MARKETING STRATEGIES AND DISTRIBUTION METHODS

Vice-President of Sales was Katie Camardo. Robert D. Delsandro was appointed Vice-President of Marketing and Design in May 1998. He had been employed by the Vermont Teddy Bear Company as Creative Director since 1996 and had been responsible for developing a completely new look for the company's products, retail stores, printed promotional materials, and catalog. He was credited with creating the new "edgier" look of Vermont Teddy Bear.[40]

Although many teddy bear producers defined their product as a toy and marketed solely to children, Vermont Teddy Bear marketed its bears as an attractive gift or collectible for both children and adults. The company defined its target market as "children between the ages of 1 to 100." [41]

The company was primarily known for its Bear-Gram delivery service. Bear-Grams were personalized teddy bears that were delivered directly to recipients as gifts for holidays and special occasions. Bear-Grams were gift boxed in unique containers complete with "air-holes" for the bear. The bears were accompanied by a personal greeting from the sender.

Orders for Bear-Grams were generally placed by calling a toll-free number (1-800-829-BEAR) and speaking with company sales representatives called "Bear Counselors." Customers could also visit the company's website (**www.vtbear.com**) and place their orders online. "Bear Counselors" entered an order on a computer, which was part of the company's computer network of approximately 250 workstations that linked order entry with sales and accounting systems. The company had plans to upgrade, expand, and integrate its computer systems, including the purchase of an inventory control system. In 1994, the company installed a new telephone system, which improved its telemarketing operations and was designed to accommodate future growth in telephone call volume. The company strove to provide rapid response to customer orders. Orders placed by 4 P.M. EST (3 P.M. on the Internet) could be shipped the same day. Packages were delivered primarily by UPS and other carriers by next day air or ground delivery service.[42] The company also sought to respond promptly to customer complaints. The company believed that, as a result of the quality of its products and service, it had established a loyal customer base.

The company attributed its success to this direct-marketing strategy. Since 1990, when the Bear-Gram was introduced to prime-time and rush hour audiences in the New York City market, the company had continued to rely primarily on Bear-Gram advertising. It had also continued to focus its advertising on morning rush-hour radio spots, with well-known personalities such as Don Imus and Howard Stern, promoting the bears.

For the fiscal year ending June 30, 1998, Bear-Grams accounted for 70.2% of net revenues of $17.2 million. The percent of net revenues for the company's primary distribution methods can be seen in Exhibit 3. Included in Bear-Gram revenues were sales from the company's Internet website. Other principal avenues of distribution included company-owned retail stores, direct mail catalogs, and licensing and wholesale agree-

Exhibit 3   Primary Distribution Methods: Vermont Teddy Bear Co., Inc.

Year Ending June 30	1998	1997	1996	1995
Bear Grams [1]	72.0%	70.0%	75.8%	78.7%
Retail Operations	18.0%	17.7%	12.9%	9.2%
Direct Mail	9.2%	10.9%	7.2%	8.8%
Other	0.8%	1.4%	4.1%	3.3%

Note:
1. Excludes Bear-Gram revenues from retail operations.

Source: Vermont Teddy Bear Co., Inc., *1998 Annual Report*, p. 3.

ments. The company's sales were heavily seasonal, with Valentine's Day, Christmas, and Mother's Day as the company's largest sales seasons.[43] For Valentine's Day 1998, more than 47,000 bears were sent out by people across the country who wished to say "I love you."[44]

During the summer of 1997, Vermont Teddy Bear Company began doing business on the Internet with a new website designed to inform and entertain Internet subscribers. The website provided a low-cost visual presence and was developed for the purpose of supporting the radio advertising of Bear-Grams. Pictures of the product and other information could be accessed. A total of 396,000 hits to the website were recorded during fiscal 1998, more than double the 195,000 hits recorded during fiscal 1997.[45] By August 1998, 10–20% of Vermont Teddy's business was being handled online.[46] All radio advertisements were tagged with a reference to the website, which, in turn, provided visual support for the radio advertising and the opportunity for customers to place orders online.[47]

Since 1990, the company had extended its Bear-Gram marketing strategy beyond New York City to include other metropolitan areas and syndicated radio programs across the United States. During the fiscal year 1998, the company regularly placed advertising on a total of 44 radio stations in 12 of the 20 largest market areas in the United States.[48] Exhibit 4 shows the company's largest markets. Exhibit 5 shows the most frequent reasons given by customers for purchasing a Vermont Teddy Bear-Gram. The company was featured on Dateline NBC, Tuesday, December 17, 1996. Newsbroadcaster Stone Phillips interviewed R. Patrick Burns, President and CEO, on the subject of American companies that manufactured products in the United States.[49]

In 1998, the company was planning to expand its radio advertisements into new markets including Minneapolis, Dallas, and Milwaukee and to examine opportunities to consolidate radio advertising buys through annual contacts with major stations.[50]

The company had explored additional methods to market Bear-Grams and to publicize its toll-free telephone number. In June 1993, the company's toll-free number was listed for the first time in the AT&T toll-free telephone directory. Before then, the toll-free number was not readily available to customers, except in radio advertisements. Vermont Teddy Bear also expanded its listings in metropolitan phone book Yellow Pages and initiated the use of print advertising in magazines and newspapers, as well as advertising on billboards and mass transit panels.

Vermont Teddy Bear believed that the popularity of Bear-Grams created an opportunity for catalog sales. For the fiscal year ending June 30, 1998, direct mail accounted for 9.2% of net revenues.[51] In addition, repeat buyers represented 33% of sales, giving the company an opportunity to use its customer database in excess of 1,500,000

Exhibit 4 **Vermont Teddy Bear's Largest Markets**
(Percentage of Bear-Grams for the 12 months ending June 30)

Markets	1998	1997	1996	1995
New York City	37.8%	40.8%	35.5%	38.6%
Boston	13.4	13.2	9.5	9.5
Philadelphia	8.9	11.6	8.9	7.3
Chicago	6.5	8.9	7.3	8.5
Los Angeles	6.3	5.8	4.0	3.8

Source: Vermont Teddy Bear Company, Inc., *1998 Annual Report*, p. 4.

names.[52] The company introduced its first catalog for Christmas in 1992. By 1994, catalog sales accounted for 16.7% of sales.[53] Vermont Teddy planned to prepare three catalogs in 1995, but the management shakeup that resulted in Patrick Burns's becoming CEO caused the company to scale back its plans. Instead it mailed just 165,000 copies of an eight-page book to previous customers. The small-size book kept up the company's presence but did not have the pages nor the product range to boost holiday sales. Quarterly sales dropped 24% below December 1994 levels.[54]

In 1996, to compensate for the decline in radio advertisement effectiveness, the company increased December 1996 catalog circulation to approximately 1 million. To increase its catalog circulation, Vermont Teddy Bear acquired additional mailing lists from prominent catalog companies, including Disney, FAO Schwarz, Hammacher-Schlemmer, Saks Fifth Avenue, and Harry & David. To strengthen its retail and catalog offerings, Vermont Teddy broadened the scope of its product line. New items included lower priced teddy bears, company-designed apparel, toys, books, and jewelry, as well as plush animals from other manufacturers such as Gund and Steiff.

Its Valentine mailing in 1997 amounted to 600,000 catalogs. Direct mail revenues increased from 1996, but they did not meet expectations due to the poor performance of rented mailing lists. In addition, the company incurred higher than anticipated costs due to the outsourcing of the order fulfillment process and was left with inflated inventories due to lower than expected sales.

During fiscal 1998, more than 15 million circulated pages were mailed to prospective customers. CEO Robert believed that Vermont Teddy's in-house list, which stood at 1.4 million names, would be a profitable future source of business. The company planned to increase the number of circulated pages during 1999, primarily through renting and exchanging of additional names from other catalogs and mailing to more names on the in-house mailing list.[55] It planned to handle all catalog fulfillment at company facilities in Shelburne. It also planned to continue to develop its own internal systems to adapt to the requirements of its catalog customers as the catalog business grew.[56]

During fiscal 1998, sales from retail operations accounted for 18.0% of net revenues.[57] Due to the continued unprofitability in its retail stores, the company reversed its retail expansion strategy in fiscal 1998. Vermont Teddy Bear's New York City retail outlet was closed to the public on December 7, 1997, due to structural problems. A sales profile for the store reaffirmed the company's core market. Bear-Grams accounted for 60–70% of the store's purchases—the same product that was being sold through the radio advertisements, without the overhead of New York rents.[58]

The company planned to close its retail location in Freeport, Maine, in August 1998 and its North Conway, New Hampshire, store in October 1998. CEO Robert commented,

Exhibit 5   **Most Frequent Reasons for Purchasing Bear-Grams: Vermont Teddy Bear Co., Inc.**
(Percentage of Bear-Grams for the 12 months ending June 30)

Reasons for Purchases	1998	1997	1996	1995
Valentine's Day	27.7%	22.1%	20.8%	19.2%
Birthdays	11.8	11.6	13.4	15.9
New Births	11.6	10.3	12.8	9.9
Get Wells	11.0	9.7	12.0	10.4
Christmas	8.4	5.6	8.6	10.4

Source: Vermont Teddy Bear Company, Inc., *1998 Annual Report*, p. 4.

"After two successful holidays at Valentine's Day and Mother's Day, it is more clear than ever, that focusing on radio Bear-Grams is the right strategy. Retail apart from our highly successful factory store here in Shelburne, is not a distribution channel that fits our current business. We are in the Bear-Gram business, offering a convenient, creative and expressive gift delivery service. It makes no sense to ship out a Bear-Gram from an expensive retail store front." [59]

The Shelburne factory store had continued to be successful as the company added new merchandise. To make the store more entertaining and interactive, the company invested $100,000 in its renovation in 1996.[60] Programs such as "Make a Friend for Life," which enabled customers to stuff, dress, and personalize their own bear and "virtual" factory tours, using video and theatrical demonstrations of teddy bear making received favorable responses from customers.[61]

In November 1996, the company announced that it had joined forces with Gary Berghoff to produce a video that promoted the company's new "Make a Friend for Life" products.[62] Berghoff was known for playing the character Radar O'Reilly in the *M*A*S*H* television show and was famous for his relationship with his teddy bear.

Vermont Teddy Bear had also targeted children's literature as a way of generating name recognition. A children's book, *How Teddy Bears Are Made: A Visit to the Vermont Teddy Bear Factory,* was available for purchase and could be found at libraries. The company also began to publish other children's books in order to develop characters for their teddy bears.

Beginning September 1, 1997, the Vermont Teddy Bear Co., Inc., introduced nationally a line of officially licensed NFL Teddy Bears. The NFL Bear was offered in 14 different teams and wore NFL Properties' uniforms and gear, including officially licensed jerseys, pants, and Riddell helmets.[63] NFL Properties, Inc., was the licensing and publishing arm of the National Football League. To advertise this new product, Vermont Teddy enlisted Wayne Chrebet, wide receiver for the NY Jets, and Mark Chmura, tight end for the Green Bay Packers, to be spokespeople for the NFL Teddy Bears. Chrebet and Chmura were featured in radio and print advertisements in New York and Milwaukee, respectively. The company believed that officially licensed NFL Bears would be a popular choice for sports fans, especially during the football and Christmas seasons. The company advertised the bear on sports-talk radio in metropolitan areas around the country.[64]

Vermont Teddy Bear conducted business almost exclusively in the United States. Bears could be shipped abroad, but it was very expensive. Some bears were shipped into Canada, and some radio advertising was done in Montreal. The added shipping charges, along with unfavorable exchange rates, caused price resistance to the products in

Canada. In 1995, the company test marketed both the Bear-Gram and the use of the 800 number via radio advertising in the United Kingdom. Test results indicated that both were successful, but the program had to be eliminated because the company did not have the corporate infrastructure or the financial resources to support it.[65] The company had some trademarks registered in Great Britain and Japan and had discussions with companies in both of these countries. According to Robert, "These are the two countries that seem to have the most interest in Vermont Teddy's products."[66]

Vermont Teddy Bear's management believed that there were a number of opportunities to increase company sales. The company's strategy for future growth included increasing sales of Bear-Grams in existing markets, expanding sales of Bear-Grams in new market areas, increasing direct-mail marketing of teddy bears through mail-order catalogs and similar marketing techniques, increasing sales of premium teddy bears through wholesale channels to unaffiliated retail stores, and increasing the company's retail store sales through increased factory tours and visits.[67] Management was also interested in expanding sales through its Corporate Division.

FACILITIES AND OPERATIONS

In the summer of 1995, in an effort to consolidate locations and improve manufacturing efficiency, the company relocated its offices, retail store, and manufacturing, sales, and distribution facilities to a newly constructed 62,000-square-foot building on 57 acres in Shelburne, Vermont. The new site was approximately 10 miles south of Burlington, the state's largest city. The new buildings were designed as a small village, the Teddy Bear Common, to promote a warm and friendly atmosphere for customers as well as employees. The new facility was estimated to have cost $7,900,000.[68] The company intended to minimize lease costs by subleasing any unused space. On September 26, 1995, the company had entered into a $3.5 million commercial loan with the Vermont National Bank. Repayment of the mortgage loan was based on a 30-year fixed-principal payment schedule, with a balloon payment due on September 26, 1997.[69]

On July 18, 1997, Vermont Teddy completed a sale-leaseback transaction with W. P. Carey and Co., Inc., a New York–based investment banking firm, involving its factory headquarters and a portion of its property located in Shelburne. W. P. Carey bought the 62,000-square-foot headquarters facility and its 15-acre site, leaving the company with ownership of the additional land. W. P. Carey was not interested in acquiring the other building lots on the site due to their zoning restrictions. This financing replaced the company's mortgage and line of credit, which was about to come due on September 26, 1997.[70]

The company had a three-year lease on 10,000 square feet of inventory space at a separate location in Shelburne for $56,000 annually.[71] The company also had the following lease agreements for its retail stores:[72]

Location	Square Footage	Annual Rent	1999 Rent Obligation	End of Lease Obligation
North Conway, NH	6,000	$ 49,608	$ 28,938	1/31/1999
New York City, NY	2,600	$300,000	$300,000	10/23/2006
Freeport, ME	6,000	$240,000	$25,644	8/6/1998

For in-house manufacturers, all production occurred in the Shelburne manufacturing space, which included state-of-the-art packing and shipping equipment. The plant manager was Brad Allen. Visitors and guests were given the opportunity to take guided or self-directed tours that encompassed the entire teddy bear making process. The factory tour had become such a popular tourist attraction that approximately 129,000 visitors toured the factory and retail store in fiscal 1998. Since moving to its new location in 1995, more than 390,000 visitors had toured the facilities.[73]

In 1994, when the company was looking for a new location, it purchased only the 15-acre parcel it built on in Shelburne. Then the company bought the surrounding property because it wanted some control in the kind of neighbors it would have. As of June 30, 1998, plans to sell or lease the other lots had not been successful due to stringent zoning restrictions on the site. The zoning restrictions required that less than a quarter of the space be devoted to retail, effectively ruling out any kind of direct retail or outlet mall approach, which is the kind of business that could take advantage of the visitor traffic to the teddy bear factory. The company proposed a project for this unused space involving an attempt to bring together up to 50 Vermont manufacturers in a cooperative manufacturing, demonstration, and marketing setting—a made-in-Vermont manufacturing/exhibition park. Investors expressed concerns about the capital investment requirement.[74]

Vermont Teddy Bear began using Sealed Air Corp's Rapid Fill air-filled packaging (air bags) system to protect its teddy bears from damage during shipping in 1997. Previously it had used corrugated cardboard seat belt inserts to package the bears during shipping, but found that there were drawbacks, including minor damage to the products and the high cost of postage. Sealed Air's inflatable plastic bags were lighter than the corrugated inserts resulting in savings in postage costs and the plastic bags did not damage the bears with plush fur. Vermont Teddy Bear saved $150,000 in postage costs in 1997 and could realize $30,000–$40,000 in additional savings in 1998.[75]

Vice-President of Data Processing was Bonnie West. According to CEO Robert, Vermont Teddy Bear's desktop computers were in need of updating. However, West believed the company's call centers had state-of-the-art technologies, including PC terminals and very-high-tech telephone switching equipment that allowed the company to handle significant call volume. The company also had a high-tech shipping system, including state-of-the-art multicarrier software so that if a major carrier like UPS went on strike, it could immediately make adjustments.

HUMAN RESOURCE MANAGEMENT

Vermont Teddy Bear employees were known as the "Bear People," a term that expressed management's appreciation and respect for their dedication. Beth Peters was Vice-President of Human Resources. As of June 30, 1998, the company employed 181 individuals, of whom 94 were employed in production-related functions, 67 were employed in sales and marketing positions, and 20 were employed in administrative and management positions.[76] None of the employees belonged to a union. Overall, the company believed that favorable relations existed with all employees.[77]

The company supplemented its regular in-house workforce with homeworkers who performed production functions at their homes. The level of outsourced work fluctuated with company production targets. As of June 30, 1998, there were 21 homeworkers producing product for the company. Homeworkers were treated as independent contractors for all purposes, except for withholding of federal employment taxes. As independent contractors, homeworkers were free to reject or accept any work offered by the company.[78] Independent contractors allowed the company flexibility in meeting heavy demand at holiday periods such as Christmas, Valentine's Day, and Mother's Day. This relationship also allowed the homeworkers flexibility in scheduling their hours of work.

BEAR MARKET

The teddy bear was first created in the United States in 1902. The Steiff Company of Grengen/Brenz, Germany, displayed one at a fair in Leipzig in 1903. Thomas Michton of Brooklyn, New York, was credited with creating the name "Teddy Bear" in honor of President Theodore Roosevelt. At the time of the naming, President Roosevelt had been on a well-publicized hunting trip in Mississippi while negotiating a border dispute with Louisiana. When he came up empty-handed from his hunting, his aides rounded up a bear cub for the President to shoot. His granddaughter, Sarah Alden "Aldie" Gannett, said, "I think he felt he could never face his children again if he shot anything so small. So he let it go." [79]

The incident was popularized in cartoons by Clifford Berryman of the *Washington Post.* Michton and his wife stitched up a couple of honey-colored bears and then displayed them in their novelty store window along with a copy of Berryman's cartoon.

The bears sold in a day. Michton made another stuffed bear and sent it to President Roosevelt requesting his permission to use his name. Roosevelt replied with a handwritten note: "I doubt if my name will mean much in the bear business, but you may use it if you wish." It was simply signed "T.R." [80]

Teddy bears today fall into one of two broad categories: either to a subsegment of the toy industry, plush dolls and animals, or are part of the collectibles industry. Although no one knows exactly how many teddy bears are sold each year, it is known that teddy bears accounted for 70–80% of the $1 billion plush toy industry in 1997. [81] "Bears sell across every season, occasion, and holiday," said Del Clark, director of merchandising for Fiesta, a Verona, California, maker of stuffed animals. [82] Not only have bears historically been a steady seller, but returns of teddy bears are almost nonexistent. [83]

The U.S. toy industry (including teddy bears, dolls, puzzles, games, action figures and vehicles, and preschool activity toys) was estimated to be worth $25 billion in sales and had been growing at an annual rate of more than 3%. [84] With its combination of a large demographic base of children and a population with a high level of disposable income, the U.S. toy market was larger than those of Japan (the number 2 market) and Western Europe combined. [85] Most toys that are sold in the United States were made in foreign countries. Chinese-produced toys represented about 30% of all U.S. toy sales due to inexpensive labor and favorable duty rates on imports. [86] The big toy manufacturers were buying each other's operations and those of smaller toy makers. In 1997, the number 1 toy manufacturer, Mattel (maker of Fisher-Price toys and Barbie dolls), bought Tyco Toys, formerly ranked number 3. Hasbro (maker of G.I. Joe, Monopoly, and Milton Bradley toys) was the number 2 toy maker. Some games and toys maintained popularity over time, others were passing fads. It was difficult to predict which would remain popular over time. In the 1990s, marketing appeared to be the key to success. Toy production and marketing were regularly integrated with movies and television programs. For example, Star Wars action figures and other merchandise accounted for about one-third of number 3 toy maker Galoob Toys' 1997 sales of $360 million. [87] Small toy makers found it difficult to compete with the multimillion-dollar marketing campaigns and the in-depth market research of companies like Mattel, although there was always an exception such as Beanie Babies.

During 1997, manufacturers' shipments of plush products rose 37.5%, from $984 million to $1.4 billion, largely as a result of the Beanie Baby craze.[88] Designed by Ty Warner, the owner of Ty, Inc., Beanie Babies had been the big sales item since 1996 when they generated sales of $250 million. The $5 toys were produced in limited numbers and sold through specialty toy stores rather than through mass-market retailers. Beanie Baby characters no longer in production fetched up to $3000 among collectors. Some retailers reported a decline in the sales of other plush toys due to the demand for Beanie Babies.[89]

Competitors of Vermont Teddy Bear were of various types. Major plush doll manufacturers such as Mattel and Hasbro were considered competition in this subsegment of the toy industry. More direct competition for Vermont Teddy came from other bear manufacturers including Steiff of Germany, Dakin, Applause, Fiesta, North American Bear, and Gund, the leading maker of toy bears. Information about some of these direct competitors is presented in Exhibit 6.

In general, these competitors relied on sales through retail outlets and had much greater financial resources to drive sales and marketing efforts than did Vermont Teddy Bear. Unlike Vermont Teddy Bear, these companies depended on foreign manufacturing and sources of raw materials, enabling them to sell comparable products at retail prices below those currently offered by Vermont Teddy. In addition, small craft stores had begun to sell locally produced all-American-made teddy bears, and publications had been developed to teach people to craft their own bears.

The collectible market in bears had recently been booming with people seeking bears as financial investments. Collectible bears are those that are meant to be displayed, not drooled or spit up on by their owners. "In the past five to ten years we've seen a tremendous growth in the upscale bear, the limited editions, and the artist-designed bears," said George B. Black, Jr., director of the Teddy Bear Museum in Naples, Florida.[90] The "collectible" segment of the plush market generated $441 million in consumer sales for 1996, up from $354 million in 1995. Collectible plush sales for 1997 were expected to reach nearly $700 million. This would make plush one of the fastest growing categories in the $9.2 billion collectibles industry.[91] Collectible bears started at about $25 but could cost $1,000 or more. This number was somewhat misleading, considering that the value of a collectible bear can be in excess of $50,000. A 1904 Steiff "Teddy Girl" bear sold at a Christie's auction in 1994 for a record $171,380.[92]

Two trade magazines, *Teddy Bear and Friends* and *Teddy Bear Review,* targeted the collectibles market. These magazines tell bear collectors where they can buy and sell old bears. In 1998, major bear shows and jamborees were held in at least 25 states, as well as hundreds of bear making retreats and workshops.[93]

The concept of Bear-Grams lent itself to two distinct groups of competitors. Vermont Teddy Bear competed not only with soft plush stuffed animals, especially teddy bears, but also with a variety of other special occasion greetings such as flowers, candy, balloons, cakes, and other gift items that could be ordered by phone for special occasions and delivered the next day. Many of these competitors had greater financial, sales, and marketing resources than Vermont Teddy Bear.[94]

PATENTS, TRADEMARKS, AND LICENSES

The company's name in combination with its original logo was a registered trademark in the United States. In addition, the company owned the registered trademarks in the

Exhibit 6 **Competition: The Vermont Teddy Bear Co., Inc.**

Steiff

High-quality bears are manufactured in Germany and the Far East. The bears are not individually customized. The company's trademark is a button sewn into the ear of each bear. Prices of Steiff bears range from $50 for a 6-inch-tall bear to several thousand dollars for a life-size model. The bears are sold in a variety of outlets from discount stores and supermarkets to high-end specialty shops and antique stores.

Gund

This mass producer of a wide range of plush animals established an Internet website, allowing users to view and purchase products. Bears are manufactured overseas, primarily in Korea. Appearance of the bears is different from Vermont Teddy Bears', with shorter noses and limbs. They offer a broad range of styles and prices.

Teddy Bear Factory

This is the only other American manufacturer of teddy bears. The company is located in San Francisco and highly regional in its sales and marketing efforts. Vermont Teddy Bear advertises in the San Francisco Bay area but does not consider the Teddy Bear Factory to be strong competition because of the size and because its market is so regional.

North American Bear Company

This middle-sized company manufactures all of its bears in the Orient, primarily in Korea. Appearance of the bears is different from Vermont Teddy Bears', with shorter noses and limbs. The company advertises in trade magazines and has begun to do consumer advertising. It sells to retailers in Europe and Japan and collectors and gift shops in the United States.

Applause Enterprises, Inc.

This company focuses on manufacturing plush toy versions of Sesame Street, Looney Tunes, Star Wars, Muppets, and Disney characters as well as nonplush toys. Company was formed by the 1995 merger of plush toy maker Dakin and a company founded by Wallace Berrie.

United States for "The Vermont Teddy Bear Company," "Bear-Gram," "Teddy Bear-Gram," and "Make-A-Friend-For Life." The company also owned the registered service marks "Bear Counselor," "Vermont Bear-Gram," and "Racer Ted," and had applications pending to register the company's second and third company logos, "Bearanimal," "Coffee Cub," "Vermont Bear-Gram," "Vermont Baby Bear," "The Great American Teddy Bear," "All-American Teddy Bear," "Beau and Beebee," "Teddy-Grams," and "Vermont Teddy Wear." [95]

Vermont Teddy Bear also owned the registered trademark "Vermont Teddy Bear" in Japan and had an application pending to register "The Great American Teddy Bear" in Japan. [96]

Although the company had continuously used the "Bear-Gram" trademark since April 1985, its initial application to register the mark on June 13, 1990, was rejected by the U.S. Patent and Trademark Office due to prior registration of the mark "Bear-A-Grams," by another company on June 7, 1988. The company reapplied to register "Bear-Gram," and its application was approved on November 5, 1996.

The company also claimed copyright, service mark, or trademark protection for its teddy bear designs, its marketing slogans, and its advertising copy and promotional literature.

On May 16, 1997, Vermont Teddy Bear sued Disney Enterprises, Inc., for injunctive relief and unspecified damages claiming that Disney copied its bear-by-mail concept with Pooh-Grams based on Disney's Winnie the Pooh character. The complaint accused Disney of unfair competition and trademark infringement saying the Pooh-Gram is "confusingly similar" to Bear-Grams in name, logo, how it is personalized, how it is delivered, and even how it is marketed. [97] Disney introduced Pooh-Grams in its fall 1996 catalog and escalated its promotion of the product using the Internet, print, and radio advertising. Disney disagreed saying that the Vermont Teddy lawsuit was without merit because Winnie the Pooh has been a well-known Disney character for 25 years and there are all kinds of grams—mail-grams, candy-grams, money-grams, telegrams, flower-grams—not just Bear-Grams.

On September 9, 1997, Vermont Teddy announced that it had entered into an agreement to resolve its dispute with Walt Disney Co. Under the agreement, Disney will continue to offer its Pooh-Gram products and services but will voluntarily limit its use of the Pooh-Gram mark in certain advertising and will adequately distinguish its trademarks and service marks from those of Vermont Teddy Bear. Vermont Teddy in turn will be allowed to offer certain Winnie-the-Pooh merchandise for sale in its mail order catalogs but cannot offer the merchandise with its Bear-Gram program.[98]

FINANCE

On November 23, 1993, Vermont Teddy Bear Co., Inc., sold 1.15 million shares of stock at $10 a share through an underwriting group led by Barrington Capital Group L.P. The stock rose as high as $19 before closing the day at $16.75, an increase of 67.5% in its first day of trading. The market's reaction to the IPO signaled that investors thought the stock was undervalued at $10 and that the company had a great deal of growth potential. During fiscal 1998, the company's stock price fluctuated between $2.56 and $0.75 a share. This was an indication that investors reconsidered the growth potential of Vermont Teddy Bear.

Vice-President of Finance was Mark Sleeper. Exhibits 7 and 8 detail Vermont Teddy Bear's financial situation. Prior to 1994, Vermont Teddy Bear had experienced a great deal of success and profitability. The company's net sales increased 61% from $10,569,017 in 1992 to $17,025,856 in 1993, while the cost of goods sold decreased from 43.1% of sales to 41.8% during the same time period. Net income increased 314% from $202,601 in 1992 to $838,955 in 1993.

Sales reached a peak in 1994 at $20,560,566. This represented a 21% growth over 1993. Unfortunately profits did not experience similar growth. Had it not been for an almost $70,000 tax refund, the company would have experienced a net loss in 1994. The company's net profit fell to $17,523 after taxes in 1994 due to a substantial increase in both selling expense and general and administrative expenses. These two items combined for an increase of 35% over comparable figures for 1993.

In 1995, sales fell to $20,044,796. Although this represented only a 2.5% decline, this decline in sales painted a picture for the next two years. While sales were decreasing, selling and general and administrative expenses continued to climb. These expenses grew by 10% to $13,463,631 in 1995. These two items represented 67% of sales in 1996, whereas they were 53% of sales in 1993.

After three years of declining sales, Vermont Teddy Bear's sales grew by 4.4% in 1998 to $17,207,543. Vermont Teddy Bear experienced a loss of $2,422,477 in 1995. It returned to profitability in 1996, earning $151,953. Unfortunately that was the last profitable year for the company. Losses were $1,901,745 in 1997 and $1,683,669 in 1998. Interest expense had risen dramatically for the company from $35,002 in 1995 to $608,844 in 1998.

The company included in its quarterly report to the SEC (Filing Date: 5/14/98) that it had been operating without a working capital line of credit since July 18, 1997. On that date, the company completed a sale-leaseback transaction involving its factory headquarters and a portion of its property located in Shelburne, Vermont. This financing replaced the company's mortgage and line of credit. The company received $5.9 million

Exhibit 7   Consolidated Balance Sheets: The Vermont Teddy Bear Co., Inc.

Year Ending June 30	1998	1997	1996	1995	1994[1]	1993[1]	1992[1]
Assets							
Current assets							
Cash and marketable securities	$ 1,527,052	$ 441,573	$ 1,121,500	$ 1,070,862	$ 2,379,760	$ 8,561,525	$ —
Accounts receivable, trade	51,538	46,304	131,550	122,679	142,029	103,762	77,815
Inventories	2,396,245	3,302,313	1,974,731	3,042,484	4,024,247	2,425,233	1,135,940
Prepaid expenses	444,229	386,947	277,502	213,236	568,680	123,886	10,681
Due from officer	—	—	—	—	565,714	—	—
Deferred income taxes	233,203	259,016	240,585	126,393	322,106	194,082	—
Total current assets	4,652,267	4,436,153	3,745,868	4,575,654	8,002,536	11,408,488	1,224,436
Property and equipment	8,844,475	9,845,935	10,300,318	10,493,214	3,052,002	861,419	589,196
Construction in progress	—	—	—	—	3,275,527	—	—
Due from officer	—	—	—	—	128,008	128,008	102,480
Deposits and other assets	903,110	272,348	98,086	102,676	121,640	97,400	14,356
Notes receivable	87,500	95,000	95,000	190,000	190,000	—	—
Total assets	$14,487,352	$14,649,436	$14,239,272	$15,361,544	$14,769,713	$12,495,315	$1,930,468
Liabilities and Shareholders' Equity							
Current liabilities							
Cash overdraft	$ —	$ —	$ —	$ —	$ —	$ —	$ 148,048
Line of credit	—	550,000	—	—	—	—	—
Notes payable, bank	45,603	—	—	—	36,748	108,748	180,748
Current installments of							
Long-term debt	231,133	3,443,096	187,095	27,805	21,981	22,793	19,075
Capital lease obligations	225,738	103,759	104,146	126,306	99,901	45,604	41,795
Accounts payable	1,846,042	2,562,536	1,353,698	2,513,468	3,336,558	1,319,499	1,604,066

(continued)

Exhibit 7 Consolidated Balance Sheets: The Vermont Teddy Bear Co., Inc. *(continued)*

Year Ending June 30	1998	1997	1996	1995	1994[1]	1993[1]	1992[1]
Accrued expenses	916,191	657,347	449,048	860,440	442,467	381,146	156,777
Income taxes payable	—	—	37,365	90,889	117,810	117,810	—
Total current liabilities	3,264,707	7,316,738	2,131,352	3,618,908	4,055,465	1,995,600	2,150,509
Construction loan payable							
Long-term debt	338,317	372,999	3,505,812	3,252,379	60,408	82,411	81,401
Capital lease obligations	5,748,182	209,054	312,814	347,874	398,220	58,883	61,350
Other liabilities	—	—	84,430	204,430	—	—	—
Accrued interest payable, debentures	—	—	—	—	—	—	958,219
Deferred income taxes	233,203	259,016	240,585	126,393	105,992	47,492	—
Total liabilities	9,584,409	8,157,807	6,274,993	7,549,984	4,620,085	2,184,386	3,251,479
Shareholders' equity							
Preferred stock $.05 par value: Authorized 1,000,000 shares Series A cumulative dividends at 8%	1,044,000	900,000	900,000	900,000	900,000	900,000	—
Preferred stock $.05 par value: Authorized 375,000 shares Series B	10,245	10,245	—	—	—	—	—
Common stock, $.05 par value: Authorized 20,000,000 shares	259,787	258,638	258,638	258,625	258,625	258,625	200,000
Additional paid-in capital	10,587,316	10,565,482	10,074,595	10,073,842	10,073,842	10,073,842	185,868
Treasury stock at cost (12,000 shares)	(106,824)	(106,824)	(106,824)	(106,824)	(106,824)	—	—
Accumulated deficit	(6,891,581)	(5,135,912)	(3,162,130)	(3,314,083)	(976,015)	(921,538)	(1,706,879)
Total shareholders' equity	4,902,943	6,491,629	7,964,279	7,811,560	10,149,628	10,310,929	(1,321,011)
Total liabilities and shareholders' equity	$14,487,352	$14,649,436	$14,239,272	$15,361,544	$14,769,713	$12,495,315	$ 1,930,468

Note: 1. Fiscal year ending December 31.

Source: Vermont Teddy Bear Company, Inc., *1998 Annual Report.*

Exhibit 8   Statement of Operations: The Vermont Teddy Bear Co., Inc.

Year Ending June 30	1998	1997	1996	1995	1994[1]	1993[1]	1992[1]
Net sales	$17,207,543	$16,489,482	$17,039,618	$20,044,796	$20,560,566	$17,025,856	$10,569,017
Cost of goods sold	7,397,450	7,068,549	7,309,038	9,101,028	8,619,580	7,123,930	4,555,424
Gross margin	9,810,093	9,420,933	9,730,580	10,943,768	11,940,986	9,901,926	6,013,593
Selling expenses	7,866,843	7,961,003	6,287,208	9,121,023	8,907,440	6,862,328	4,454,891
General and administrative expenses	3,031,716	2,938,251	2,954,601	4,342,608	3,311,306	2,184,500	1,266,770
Total expenses	10,898,559	10,899,254	9,241,809	13,463,631	12,218,746	9,046,828	5,721,661
Operating income (loss)	(1,088,466)	(1,478,321)	488,771	(2,519,863)	(277,760)	855,098	291,932
Interest income	26,126	53,267	41,092	192,156	248,987	27,887	2,152
Miscellaneous income	29,243	(11,973)	63,236	1,620	1,620	25,000	—
Interest expense	(650,572)	(464,768)	(441,146)	(35,002)	(24,848)	(97,810)	(91,483)
Income (loss) before taxes	(1,683,669)	(1,901,795)	151,953	(2,361,089)	(52,001)	810,175	202,601
Income tax provision (benefit)	—	—	—	61,388	(69,524)	(28,780)	—
Net income (loss)	$(1,683,669)	$(1,901,795)	$ 151,953	$(2,422,477)	$ 17,523	$ 838,955	$ 202,601
Preferred stock dividends	(72,000)	(72,000)	—	(72,000)	(72,000)	(53,614)	—
Net earnings (loss) common shareholders	(1,611,669)	(1,829,795)	151,953	(2,350,477)	89,523	892,569	202,601
Net earnings (loss) per common share	(0.34)	(0.38)	0.03	(0.48)	(0.10)	0.19	0.05
Weighted average number of shares outstanding	5,172,475	5,160,750	5,160,583	5,160,500	5,164,057	4,210,070	4,024,140

Note: 1. Fiscal year ending December 31.

Source: Vermont Teddy Bear Company, Inc., *1998 Annual Report.*

from this transaction. Of this amount, $3.3 million was used to pay off the mortgage and $600,000 was used to pay off the line of credit. A $591,000 transactions cost was associated with the sale-leaseback. The lease obligation was repayable on a 20-year amortization schedule through July 2017.

On October 10, 1997, Vermont Teddy received a commitment from Green Mountain Capital L.P. whereby it agreed to lend the company up to $200,000 for up to five years at 12% interest. The loan was secured by security interest in the company's real and personal property. Green Mountain Capital also received warrants to purchase 100,000 shares of common stock at an exercise price of $1.00. The warrants could be exercised any time from two years from the date of the loan to seven years from the date of the loan.

To reduce costs, the company closed its retail store in New York City and planned to close the Freeport, Maine, and North Conway, New Hampshire, stores before the end of 1998 because the revenue increases necessary to support the annual lease obligations would not be achievable in the short run. The company's lease obligation of $300,000 per year on the New York City store would continue until a replacement tenant was found.

On May 22, 1998, it was announced that The Vermont Teddy Bear Co., Inc., had signed a letter of intent with the Shepherd Group, a Boston-based private equity investment firm, for a proposed $600,000 equity investment with the company. The Shepherd Group invested in venture and existing small- to middle-market companies focusing on companies with high-growth potential and unique market-ready quality products and services. In return for the $600,000 investment, the Shepherd Group received 60 shares of Series C Preferred Stock as well as warrants to purchase 495,868 shares of Common Stock at $1.21 per share. The transaction was subject to final agreements and various approvals and conditions.

The Series C Convertible Redeemable Stock carried a 6% coupon, and each share was convertible into 8,264,467 shares of the company's Common Stock. The Preferred had voting rights, and the Shepherd Group was entitled to two seats on the company's Board of Directors.

Elisabeth Robert noted, "The additional funds will provide working capital for the company to pursue growth in the Bear-Gram channel and to maximize the benefits of importing raw materials. Additionally Tom Shepherd has strong financial and operations experience and will bring a valuable perspective to the Board of Directors. Tom's strong suit has been working with companies that have not yet realized the full potential of their brand."[99]

According to some analysts, the survival of this company was going to depend on maintaining a source of working capital, cost containment, and a rebound in sales back to their 1995 level. The company had taken an aggressive approach to ensuring survival, but this was not done cheaply. High interest rates were paid and warrants to purchase stock, at what might turn out to be a bargain price, had been issued.

Notes

1. Cynthia Crossen, "Isn't It Funny How a Bear Makes Money, Year After Year?" *The Wall Street Journal* (February 17, 1998), p. B-1.
2. "Vermont Teddy President and CEO Interview," *The Wall Streeet Journal Corporate Reporter, Inc.* (January 21, 1998).
3. *Ibid.*
4. The Vermont Teddy Bear Co., Inc., *1997 Annual Report.*
5. Richard H. Levy, "Ursine of the Times: Vermont Teddy Bear Company Pulls Back from Catalog Sales," *Direct Marketing* (February 1998), p. 16.
6. Maria Lisa Calta, "Cub Scout," *Detroit News* (March 5, 1995), pp. 22-D, 23-D.
7. *Ibid.*

8. Phaedra Hise, "Making Fans on Talk Radio," *Inc.* (December 1993), p. 62.

9. The Vermont Teddy Bear Co., Inc., *1994 Annual Report,* p. 3.

10. The Vermont Teddy Bear Co., Inc., *Company Time Line,* Information Packet, p. 2.

11. *Ibid.*

12. *Ibid.*

13. The Vermont Teddy Bear Co., Inc., *Form 10-KSB* (June 30, 1995), p. 1.

14. *Company Time Line,* p. 2.

15. The Vermont Teddy Bear Co., Inc., Press Release (April 17, 1995).

16. The Vermont Teddy Bear Co., Inc. *1994 Annual Report* (Letter to Shareholders), p. 2.

17. *The Wall Street Journal Corporate Reporter, Inc.* (January 21, 1998).

18. "The Vermont Teddy Bear Company Roars into New York City," Vermont Teddy Bear Co., Inc., Press Release (October 9, 1996).

19. "The Vermont Teddy Posts Year-End Results, Closes Equity Deal," Vermont Teddy Bear Co., Inc., Press Release (September 29, 1998), p. 1.

20. "The Vermont Teddy Bear Company Expands Retail Activities," Vermont Teddy Bear Co., Inc., Press Release (June 20, 1996).

21. The Vermont Teddy Bear Co., Inc., *1997 Annual Report* (Letter to Shareholders), p. 3.

22. *Wall Street Journal Corporate Reporter, Inc.* (January 21, 1998).

23. The Vermont Teddy Bear Co., Inc., *1997 Annual Report* (Letter to Shareholders), p. 3.

24. The Vermont Teddy Bear Co., Inc., *1997 Annual Report,* p. 22, and *1997 Proxy Statement* (October 28, 1997), pp. 6, 10, 21–23.

25. The Vermont Teddy Bear Co., Inc., *Form 10-KSB* (September 28, 1998), p. 10.

26. The Vermont Teddy Bear Co., Inc., *1997 Proxy Statement* (October 28, 1997), pp. 4–5.

27. The Vermont Teddy Bear Co., Inc., *Form 10-KSB* (September 28, 1998), p. 10.

28. The Vermont Teddy Bear Co., Inc., *1998 Proxy Statement* (July 23, 1998), p. 5.

29. The Vermont Teddy Bear Co., Inc., *Form 10-KSB* (September 28, 1998), pp. 9–10.

30. The Vermont Teddy Bear Co., Inc., *1997 Annual Report,* p. 4.

31. *Ibid.*

32. *Ibid.*

33. The Vermont Teddy Bear Co., Inc., *Form 10-KSB* (September 28, 1998), p. 6.

34. Calta, p. 22-D.

35. The Vermont Teddy Bear Co., Inc., *Form 10-KSB* (September 28, 1998), p. 6.

36. The Vermont Teddy Bear *Gazette,* summer 1995 edition, p. 7.

37. The Vermont Teddy Bear Co., Inc., *Form 10-KSB* (September 28, 1998), p. 6.

38. *Ibid.*

39. Levy, p. 16.

40. "Vermont Teddy Bear Appoints Vice-President of Marketing and Design," The Vermont Teddy Bear Co., Inc., Press Release (May 5, 1998).

41. Calta, p. 22-D.

42. The Vermont Teddy Bear Co., Inc., *Form 10-KSB* (September 28, 1998), p. 3.

43. *Ibid.*

44. The Vermont Teddy Bear Co., Inc., "Vermont Teddy Bear Posts Quarterly Profit on Increased Revenues," Press Release (May 14, 1998), p. 1.

45. The Vermont Teddy Bear Co., Inc., *Form 10-KSB* (September 28, 1998), p. 4.

46. Jim Kerstetter, "Setting Up Mom and Pop," *PC Week On-Line* (August 24, 1998), p. 1.

47. The Vermont Teddy Bear Co., Inc., *Form 10-KSB* (September 28, 1998), p. 4.

48. *Ibid.*

49. "Vermont Teddy Bear Company to be Featured on Dateline NBC, December 17, 1996," The Vermont Teddy Bear Co., Inc., Press Release (December 17, 1996).

50. The Vermont Teddy Bear Co., Inc., *1997 Annual Report,* p. 10.

51. The Vermont Teddy Bear Co., Inc., *Form 10-KSB* (September 28, 1998), p. 3.

52. *Ibid.,* p. 5.

53. The Vermont Teddy Bear Co., Inc., *1994 Annual Report,* p. 3.

54. Melissa Dowling, "Vermont Teddy Bears the Pressure," *Catalog Age* (May 1996), p. 12.

55. The Vermont Teddy Bear Co., Inc., *Form 10-KSB* (September 28, 1998), p. 5.

56. The Vermont Teddy Bear Co., Inc., *1997 Annual Report* (Letter to Shareholders), p. 4.

57. The Vermont Teddy Bear Co., Inc., *Form 10-KSB* (September 28, 1998), p. 3.

58. Levy, p. 16

59. "Vermont Teddy Bear Announces Second-Quarter Results," Press Release (February 13, 1998).

60. The Vermont Teddy Bear Co., Inc., *1997 Annual Report.*

61. The Vermont Teddy Bear Co., Inc., *1997 Annual Report* (Letter to Shareholders), p. 4.

62. "The Vermont Teddy Bear Company Joins Forces with America's Most Famous Teddy Bear Person," The Vermont Teddy Bear Co., Inc., Press Release (November 5, 1996).

63. "NFL Football Soft and Cuddly? The Vermont Teddy Bear Company Introduces Officially Licensed NFL Teddy Bears," The Vermont Teddy Bear Co., Inc., Press Release (August 27, 1997).

64. "The Vermont Teddy Bear Company Kicks Off NFL Bear-Grams," The Vermont Teddy Bear Co., Inc., Press Release (September 30, 1996).

65. *The Wall Street Journal Corporate Reporter* (January 21, 1998).

66. *Ibid.*

67. *Ibid.*

68. The Vermont Teddy Bear Co., Inc., *1997 Annual Report,* p. 13.

69. The Vermont Teddy Bear Co., Inc., *Form 10-KSB* (September 28, 1998), p. 8.

70. "Vermont Teddy Bear Refinances Factory Headquarters,"

The Vermont Teddy Bear Co., Inc., Press Release (July 21, 1997).

71. The Vermont Teddy Bear Co., Inc., *Form 10-KSB* (September 28, 1998), p. 5.

72. *Ibid.*

73. *Ibid.*

74. Edna Tenney, "A Teddy Bear's Modest Proposal," *Business Digest,* webmaster@vermontguides.com (October 10, 1997), pp. 1–3.

75. Bernard Abrams, "Switch to Air Bags Bears Watching," *Packaging Digest* (March 1998), pp. 50–52.

76. The Vermont Teddy Bear Co., Inc., *Form 10-KSB* (September 28, 1998), p. 7.

77. "Bear Necessities," *Direct Marketing Magazine* (July 1998), p. 18.

78. *Ibid.*

79. Calta, p. 23-D.

80. *Ibid.*

81. Crossen, p. B-1.

82. *Ibid.*

83. "Bullish for Bears," *The Times* (Tampa) (February 18, 1998), pp. E1–2.

84. Stuart Hampton, *Hoovers Online: Toys and Games Industry Snapshot,* 1998, p. 1.

85. J. S. Krutick, et al., "Salomon Smith Barney Toy Industry Update," *Investext Report,* number: 2715626 (June 23, 1998), p. 6.

86. Hampton, p. 2.

87. Donna Leccese, "Growth at a Price," *Playthings* (June 1998), p. 30.

88. *Ibid.*

89. The Vermont Teddy Bear Co., Inc., *1997 Annual Report,* p. 11.

90. Leccese, p. 30.

91. Calta, p. 23-D.

92. Crossen, p. B-1.

93. The Vermont Teddy Bear Co., Inc., *1997 Annual Report,* p. 11.

94. The Vermont Teddy Bear Co., Inc., *Form 10-KSB* (September 28, 1998), p. 7.

95. *Ibid.*

96. Bruce Horovitz, *USA Today* (May 27, 1997), p. B-2.

97. "Vermont Teddy Bear and Disney Settle Suit," The Vermont Teddy Bear Co., Inc., Press Release (September 9, 1997).

98. The Vermont Teddy Bear Co., Inc., *1994, 1995, 1996, 1997 Annual Reports* and Form 10-KSB (September 28, 1998).

99. The Vermont Teddy Bear Co., Inc., Press Release (May 22, 1998), pp. 1–3.

Sunbeam and Albert J. Dunlap: Maximization of Shareholder Wealth ... But at What Cost?

Patricia A. Ryan

> You're not in business to be liked. Neither am I. We're here to succeed. If you want a friend, get a dog. I'm not taking any chances; I've got two dogs.
>
> —Albert J. Dunlap[1]

Albert J. Dunlap, Chairman of the Board and CEO at Sunbeam Corp., briskly paced across his lavish office. Mounted eagles and lions decorated the executive suite; aggressive, dominant survivors that had earned the admiration of Dunlap. As they were predators in the animal kingdom, he was a predator unmatched in the corporate world. Dunlap succeeded in turning Sunbeam around after years of deterioration and had quadrupled the stock price in less than two years. Now, in March 1998, new challenges awaited Dunlap. Not one troubled company, but three: Coleman, Signature Brands, and First Alert. Not a new employer for Dunlap, but purchases he announced on March 2, 1998, to the pleasure of Wall Street. Not tearing the company down, selling it, and moving on, but staying on to rebuild a brighter Sunbeam. He pondered the actions he would take over the next few months to build the best corporation and to convince shareholders of the synergistic gain afforded by the multiple acquisitions. It would mean the consolidation of management and functional staffs, a reduction in factories and workers, the elimination of unprofitable product lines, and the creation of wealth for the shareholder. It was all in a day's work for Albert J. Dunlap.

Known by millions as "Chainsaw Al," or more recently, "Rambo in Pinstripes," Dunlap was known as a premier turnaround artist for troubled corporations. Rarely staying with one company for more than two years, the West Point graduate made millions in nine previous turnarounds and was best known for his work at Scott Paper. Now, as it appeared, he had succeeded in turning around Sunbeam. In an uncharacteristic move, Dunlap remained with Sunbeam. He made it known that he desired to complete his turnaround with the acquisition of Coleman Company, Inc., Signature Brands USA, and First Alert, Inc. The stock value had risen to $52 per share, up from $12.25 when Dunlap took over 21 months ago. How far could the stock price rise? What was the value of Sunbeam? Could Dunlap build a business as effectively as he had turned companies around? This remained to be seen as the charismatic leader entered his new venture.

HISTORY OF SUNBEAM

Two machinists, John K. Stewart and Thomas J. Clark, founded Sunbeam in 1897. They first produced sheep shears under the corporate name Chicago Flexible Shaft Company.

This case was prepared by Assistant Professor Patricia A. Ryan of Colorado State University. Presented to and accepted by the referred Society for Case Research. Reprinted by permission. This case was accepted for publication by the *Business Case Journal.* All rights reserved to the author and the SCR. This case was edited for SMBP–7th Edition. Copyright © 1999 by Patricia A. Ryan. Reprinted by permission.

In 1910, the company introduced the first branded appliance, the Sunbeam "Princess" electric iron. The Sunbeam mixmaster entered the market in 1930, followed by a series of household appliances, including toasters, electric frypans, and the "Lady Sunbeam" hair dryer. Sunbeam products became a household name in the home appliance industry. In 1960, the company acquired the John Oster Manufacturing Company, which built professional hair and animal clippers as well as premium-quality consumer electric appliances.

The merged company worked to maintain its image while at the same time expand its product lines. Facing financial distress, Allegheny International, the parent company, filed for bankruptcy in 1988. In 1990, the surviving entity emerged under the Sunbeam-Oster name. Two years later, in August 1992, Sunbeam-Oster made an offering of 20 million shares of common stock. In May 1995, the company changed its name from Sunbeam-Oster to Sunbeam.[2]

Sunbeam designed, manufactured, and marketed brand-name consumer products. Product lines included barbecue grills, outdoor furniture, and outdoor gas heaters. In addition, Sunbeam manufactured small kitchen appliances, electric and conventional blankets, home and healthcare products, wall clocks, thermometers, kitchen timers, and grooming accessories.

In the mid 1990s, it became apparent that the company was slipping. Earnings were down, and the stock price dropped precipitously upon the announcement of weak quarterly earnings. At first, the decrease in sales was blamed on unusual weather patterns that hurt sales in the grills and furniture areas. However, it soon became apparent that the outdoor products business was not at the core of the problems facing Sunbeam. Investors were uneasy about the sluggish performance, and Sunbeam appeared to be sliding downhill as the home appliance industry grew stagnant.

CORE PRODUCT CATEGORIES

The company concentrated its business in five product categories:

- **Appliances** included mixers, blenders, food steamers, bread makers, rice cookers, coffee makers, toasters, irons, and garment steamers. In 1996, this division accounted for 29% of the company's domestic net sales.

- **Health Care** included vaporizers, humidifiers, air cleaners, massagers, hot and cold packs, blood pressure monitors, and scales. In 1996, the healthcare division accounted for 11% of the company's domestic net sales.

- **Personal Care and Comfort** included shower massagers, hair clippers and trimmers, electric warming blankets, and throws. Of Sunbeam's 1996 domestic net sales, 21% came from this division.

- **Outdoor Cooking** included electric, gas, and charcoal grills and accessories. Sales from this division accounted for 29% of 1995 domestic net sales.

- **Away From Home** included clippers and related products for the professional and veterinarian trade and sales of products to commercial and institutional channels. Currently the smallest contributor to revenue, the Away From Home division generated 5% of domestic net sales in 1996.

INTERNATIONAL SALES

Small appliances, personal care products, and grills accounted for the majority of international sales with the Oster brand name maintaining the leading market share position in many Latin American countries. Primary international markets included Mexico, South America, and Central America. Additionally, Sunbeam had a manufacturing facility in Venezuela and sales offices in Hong Kong and the United Kingdom. International sales accounted for $187,005,000 or approximately 19% of Sunbeam's total net sales $984,236,000 in 1996.

THE HOME APPLIANCE INDUSTRY

Although consumer confidence was high, the home appliance industry was a mature, stable industry that faced increased price pressures and reduced profit margins. The global market had increased appeal to American household and home appliance manufacturers; however, the financial crises faced by many Asian countries prohibited expansion as planned. Overseas markets remained a high priority of most appliance manufacturers such as Whirlpool, Maytag, and Black and Decker, but, in 1998, gains remained limited.

The economic slowdown in Brazil dampened the market and endangered sales. In combination with the Asian market slowdowns, appliance manufacturers faced slim profit margins for the immediate future. However, as the cycle reverses itself, there should be abundant opportunity for growth and expansion. In the meantime, however, those companies with a strong domestic market share and the most diverse markets should emerge from 1998 with the fewest scars. It was critical that Sunbeam keep its large accounts with mass market retail giants Wal-Mart and Kmart in order to keep its products in the customers' mind.

The domestic market was becoming more price sensitive for large appliances such as refrigerators and washers. However, with all the time demands facing families in the 1990s, the consumer was still likely to continue to be willing to pay a small premium for time-saving small appliances. Therefore, successful new product development was critical for future success. In January 1998, *ValueLine* suggested that continued growth in the household products industry would require "bells and whistles be added to old products." They estimated total sales to be $72.495 billion in 1997, $77.915 billion in 1998, and $99.960 billion in 2000–2002.[3] In most cases, one company's gain tends to be another's loss. Thus the strongly competitive markets should remain a driving force because the industry would likely continue to consolidate.

CHANGES IN TOP MANAGEMENT

In October 1995, leading mutual fund managers Michael Price and Michael Steinhart, who together controlled 42% of Sunbeam's stock, placed the company on the market. Unable to reach agreeable terms with any potential buyer, they sought new management. They found Albert J. Dunlap, turnaround specialist, known as "Chainsaw Al" and "Rambo in Pinstripes" for ruthlessly cutting the fat off hefty corporations and restoring a new sense of health to the company. Just months before, he walked away from an 18-month restructuring of Scott Paper. After the sale of Scott to Kimberly Clark, the new entity became the second largest consumer products company. Dunlap left Scott Paper with $100 million in his pocket.

Sunbeam was in bad shape. Although the economy had enjoyed a record long bull market, Sunbeam's stock was down over 50%. Clearly Al Dunlap did not need a new job, but could the West Point graduate resist the challenge? In his own words,

> I was called in by the board to rescue this corporation. Of the nine restructurings I've done, this was clearly the worst. I think that Sunbeam would have ceased to exist: game, set, match. And when you are dead, what are the degrees of dead? Dead is dead. Would you rather be shot? Would you rather be hanged? Would you rather be electrocuted? The end result is the same—death.[4]

Sunbeam had become stagnant with excessive product lines, a top heavy management, and a relatively risk averse management style. Costs surmounted reasonable margins, and the company appeared immobile. The company was a mammoth without a strategic plan. Michael Price was the largest shareholder with a 21% interest and was featured as a much feared fund manager in *Fortune* magazine.[5] Price was instrumental in bringing Albert J. Dunlap aboard to turn Sunbeam around. Dunlap joined Sunbeam in July 1996. Upon the announcement of his hiring, Sunbeam's stock price surged 59%. For the past three decades, Al Dunlap had worked to turn around eight companies on three continents. (See Exhibit 1.) Over the next 18 months, Dunlap and his team cut and chiseled at the old Sunbeam. The stock price quadrupled from 12½ to just over $50 per share. It appeared that Dunlap had succeeded in increasing shareholder wealth fourfold.

Although seen by shareholders as a stagnant, overmanaged company with excessive fat to trim, Sunbeam marketed its products to a variety of retailers. These retailers ranged from large drug store chains (e.g., Eckerd and Walgreen's) to home supply centers (e.g., Home Depot and Lowes). Additional retailers included discount merchandisers (e.g., Kmart and Wal-Mart) and high-end retailers (e.g., Macy's and Bloomingdale's). Wal-Mart was Sunbeam's largest single customer in 1996, accounting for 19% of sales.

Despite the difficulties, Sunbeam maintained a strong distribution network with one of the premier mass merchandise distribution networks serving domestic U.S. and Latin American retailers. Strong warehousing and distribution capabilities included the electronic data interchange (EDI) and just-in-time inventory (JIT) systems. Extensive marketing package promotions included mass retailers, catalogs, outlet stores, television shopping, and independent distributors.

THE DUNLAPPING BEGINS

Dunlap made it clear that he perceived that his job was to maximize shareholder wealth—nothing more, nothing less. To summarize his management style, he presented four steps to restructure, or in his words, rescue a firm.[6]

- **Get the best management team.** After joining Sunbeam, Dunlap kept only one executive of Sunbeam's original management, David Fannin, the general counsel. Dunlap promoted Fannin to Executive Vice-President. The rest of the senior management were Dunlap loyalists. Dunlap's relationship with Russ Kersh went back to 1983–1986 at Lily-Tulip and 1994–1995 at Scott Paper. Kersh joined the operating committee as Executive Vice-President of Finance and Administration. Jack Dailey, a former purchasing executive at Lily-Tulip, joined Sunbeam as Vice-President of Corporate Purchasing and Logistics. Finally, Lee Griffith, former CEO of Scott Paper Canada, joined Dunlap as Vice-President of Sales. Don Uzzi, former president of

Exhibit 1   Corporate Turnaround History of "Chainsaw Al" Dunlap

Company	Years	Industry	Action
Sterling Pulp and Paper	1967–77	Private label tissue paper	Turnaround; reduced debt.
American Can	1977–82	Plastic and canning giant	Managed Performance Plastics division; one of 4 divisions. Downsized division.
Lily-Tulip Company	1983–86	Disposable cup maker	Cut salaried staff by 20% and headquarters staff by 50%.
Diamond International	1986–89	Timber and forest products	Increased cash flow 500%.
Crown-Zellerbach	1986–89	Timberlands, paper products, oil and gas, industrial supplies	Cut staff by 22%, reduced distribution centers from 22 to 4.
Australian National Industries	1989	Engineering firm	Cut staff by 47%, cut headquarters staff by 88.5%.
Consolidated Press Holdings	1991–93	Australian media conglomerate	Sold 300 of 413 companies.
Scott Paper Company	1994–95	Paper producer	Laid off 11,200 employees (31%), downsized headquarters.
Sunbeam	1996–	Household consumer durables	Cut 6,000 employees (50%), closed 18 of 26 factories, 37 of 61 warehouses, sold or consolidated 39 of 53 facilities, consolidated headquarters, eliminated 87% of company's products.

Source: *Mean Business* by Albert J. Dunlap, and *Wall Street Journal* (November 13, 1996), p. B1.

Quaker Oats beverage division, joined the team as Vice-President of Marketing and Product Development. Kersh, Dailey, Griffith, and Uzzi formed the four-person operating committee. (See Exhibit 2 for top management and Board of Directors.)

- **Cut costs and eliminate waste.** Sunbeam's total workforce was approximately 12,000 when Dunlap arrived. In the first year, six headquarters facilities were consolidated to one in Delray Beach, Florida. Headquarters staff was reduced over 50%, from 308 to 123, and management and clerical staff were cut from 1,259 to 697.[7] Additionally, the total workforce saw a reduction of 50% as unprofitable divisions were divested. Approximately 3,000 of the dismissed employees found employment with the divested divisions, and the other 3,000 lost their jobs entirely. One example of improved operating efficiency involved stock keeping units, or SKUs. A SKU is assigned to every product, for every color, style, and in many instances, for each retailer. Previously the sales staff had worked with the customer and met requests such as different wire colors for an electric blanket. Each change required a new SKU, which, over time, became unwieldy. The electric blanket segment alone had over 1300 SKUs. In the first few months, Dunlap eliminated 80% of the company's stock keeping units (SKUs) to eliminate duplication, increase efficiency, and still offer a product line with some degree of consumer choice.

- **Ask "What business am I in?"** Focus on the core business. Dunlap defined the core business to be electric appliances and appliance-related business. He sold other divisions, including outdoor furniture; gas logs; the Biddeford, Maine, plant that produced the soft shells for the electric blanket; decorative bedding; and the Time and Temperature division that manufactured outdoor clocks and thermometers.

- **Have a vision for the future.** In the case of Sunbeam, this was to develop an aggressive strategy to stimulate global expansion and growth. Dunlap set out to increase the growth of the core business by product differentiation, geographic expansion, and careful examination of new interests as lifestyles change. Sunbeam

Exhibit 2   **Top Management and Board of Directors: Sunbeam Corporation**

A. Management Team

Name	Title	Date Joined	Base Salary	Prior Position and Employer
Albert J. Dunlap, 60	Chairman and Chief Executive Officer	July 18, 1996	$2,000,000	Chairman and Chief Executive Officer, Scott Paper, April 1994–December 1995.
David C. Fannin, 52	Executive Vice-President, General Counsel, & Secretary	January 1994	$ 575,000	Partner in law firm of Wyatt, Tarrant, and Combs.
Russell A. Kersh, 44	Chief Financial Officer	July 22, 1996	$ 875,000	Executive Vice-President, Finance and Administration, Scott Paper, April 1994–December 1995.
Donald R. Uzzi, 45	Executive Vice-President, Consumer Products Worldwide	September 1996		President of Beverage Division of Quaker Oats, January 1993–July 1996.

B. Board of Directors

Name	Position	No. of Shares Owned	Date of Appointment
Albert J. Dunlap, 60	Chairman and CEO, Sunbeam	5,241,564	July 1996
Charles L. Elson, 38	Law Professor, Stetson University	9,000	September 1996
Russell A. Kersh, 44	CFO, Sunbeam	1,045,400	August 1996
Howard G. Kristol, 60	Attorney	9,000	August 1996
Peter A. Langerman, 42	Senior VP and Chief Operating Officer, Franklin Resources	0[1]	1990
William T. Rutter, 67	Senior VP/Managing Director, First Union National Bank	3,500	April 1997
Faith Whittlesey, 59	CEO, American Swiss Charitable Foundation	5,390	December 1996

Note: 1. Does not include funds owned by Franklin Mutual Advisor or Franklin Resources, which total 35,083,796 shares, or 34.8% of Sunbeam's stock.

Source: Sunbeam, *1997 Form 10-K,* p. 11 and Def 14A

released 30 domestic products and 42 international products in 1997. Upon examination of Asian sales, only $5 million a year, Dunlap realized Sunbeam shipped only 110-volt products to Asia; a continent that uses 220-volt electricity! This one change could significantly increase sales in this emerging region.

The Sunbeam and Oster brand names continued to enjoy strong market share. Sunbeam spent over $75 million to market these brand names in 1997.

DUNLAP'S PHILOSOPHY ON BOARDS OF DIRECTORS (AND COMPENSATION)

On his philosophy Dunlap commented,

> I think an executive should invest very heavily in his own company and should be focused like a laser on running that company. If he sees other companies as a better investment, that tells something about what he thinks about his own company.[8]

Dunlap's views do not allow for a rubber stamp Board of Directors. He required board members to invest a significant portion of their own investment capital in Sunbeam stock. Dunlap invested a significant portion of his wealth in Sunbeam and required the same of other board members. In December 1997, Dunlap invited Stetson law professor and shareholder activist Charles M. Elson to join the board. Elson purchased $120,000 of Sunbeam stock. "It was a daunting task. I've got more in Sunbeam than I've got in my house," Elson commented. "If Al Dunlap messes up with the company, I take a substantial hit." [9]

Dunlap did not apologize for his three-year compensation contract that had been renegotiated effective February 20, 1998. The new contract required Dunlap be paid an annual base salary of $2 million, 300,000 shares of stock, and stock options for 3.75 million shares of common stock exercisable at $36.85 per share. The exercise price was determined on February 1, 1998. Very simply, as long as the price of Sunbeam was greater than $36.85, Dunlap's options were "in-the-money," which meant he could buy the stock and immediately sell it for a profit. The options were to be exercisable in equal installments on February 1, 1998, February 1, 1999, and February 1, 2000. If there was a change in control, all stock options were immediately vested and could be exercised on the date of the change in control. He also had a luxury car, six weeks of paid vacation annually, and other executive perks. In his 1997 book, *Mean Business,* Dunlap stated "I deserved the $100 million I took away when Scott merged with Kimberly-Clark," yet he argued that the "most important person in the company is the shareholder, not the CEO, chairman of the board, . . . or the board of directors." [10] Simply put, he argued that a company could not pay a good CEO enough, or a poor CEO too little.

FINANCIAL SITUATION

Although still turning a profit, Sunbeam's margins had slimmed significantly in 1994 and 1995. Earnings dropped 83% from mid 1994 to mid 1996, operating margins were as low as 2%, and perhaps most important, the stock price dropped over 50% during that time. (For consolidated balance sheets, income statements, and cash flow statements, refer to Exhibits 3, 4 and 5, respectively.)

Dunlap was hired because he was known to quickly boost the bottom line with quick and deep layoffs, consolidation of factories and administrative offices, and movement of factory work to lower wage states or countries.

Upon being hired as CEO, in July 1996, Dunlap established a three-year goal to double sales to $2 billion via new product lines and globalization. Additionally, he instituted a 20/20/25 business plan whereby the goals were as follows: increase sales and operating margins by 20% per year, and increase ROE to 25%, a tenfold improvement over the 2.5% ROE earned previously. Prior to Dunlap's arrival, sales had fallen in 1995 from $1,065 million to $1,044 million and operating margins were running around 1%.

IMAGE OF "CHAINSAW AL" AND "RAMBO IN PINSTRIPES"

The media promulgated the nicknames given to Dunlap over the years. Sir James Goldsmith gave him the nickname Rambo in Pinstripes, intended as a complement about Dunlap's ability to venture into difficult corporate positions and successfully turn the company around. Chainsaw Al emanated from Dunlap's style for chiseling away at the fat of a large, overburdened corporation to build a more efficient and effective corporation. As Dunlap put it,

Exhibit 3   Consolidated Balance Sheets: Sunbeam Corporation
(Dollar amounts in thousands)

	December 28, 1997	December 29, 1996	December 31, 1995	January 1, 1995
Assets				
Current assets				
Cash and cash equivalents	$ 52,378	$ 11,526	$ 28,273	$ 26,330
Receivables, net	295,550	213,438	216,195	214,222
Inventories	256,180	162,252	209,106	271,406
Net assets of discontinued operations and other assets held for sale	0	102,847	101,632	0
Deferred income taxes	36,706	93,689	26,333	45,705
Prepaid expenses and other current assets	17,191	40,411	19,543	6,248
Total current assets	658,005	624,163	601,082	563,911
Property, plant, and equipment, net	240,897	220,088	287,080	233,687
Trademarks and trade names, net	194,372	200,262	214,006	220,005
Other assets	27,010	28,196	56,516	95,326
Total assets	$1,120,284	$1,072,709	$1,158,684	$1,112,929
Liabilities and Shareholders' Equity				
Current liabilities				
Short-term debt and current portion of long-term debt	$ 668	$ 921	$ 1,166	$ 6,457
Accounts payable	105,580	107,319	94,191	86,819
Restructuring accrual	10,938	63,834	13,770	0
Other current liabilities	80,913	99,509	80,204	121,377
Total current liabilities	198,099	271,583	189,331	214,653
Long-term debt	194,580	201,115	161,133	123,082
Other long-term liabilities	141,109	64,376	50,088	58,602
Non-operating liabilities	0	88,075	80,167	92,534
Deferred income taxes	54,559	52,308	76,932	69,448
Shareholders' equity				
Preferred stock (2,000,000 shares authorized, none outstanding)	0	0	0	0
Common stock (issued 88,441,479 in 1996, 87,802,667 at Dec. 1995 and 93,181,130 shares)	900	884	878	932
Paid-in capital	483,384	447,948	441,786	461,876
Retained earnings	141,134	35,118	266,698	285,990
Other	(30,436)	(25,310)	(24,880)	(20,118)
Treasury stock, at cost (4,478,814 in 1996, 5,905,600 at Dec. 1995 and 12,376,395 shares)	(63,045)	(63,388)	(83,449)	(174,070)
Total shareholders' equity	531,937	395,252	601,033	554,610
Total liabilities and shareholders' equity	$1,120,284	$1,072,709	$1,158,684	$1,112,929

Source: Sunbeam, *1997 Form 10-K,* p. F-4, and *1995 Annual Report,* p. F-4.

I'm a no-nonsense person. I'm not coming in there to listen to all the excuses they've been giving. That's what got them into trouble to begin with. I'm not here to hear what can't be done. I'm here to get results. I'm here to challenge people beyond what they've ever been challenged before. So, if that's tough, then yes, I'm tough.[11]

The number of operating plants fell from 26 to 8 since many had previously operated at

Exhibit 4   Consolidated Income Statements: Sunbeam Corporation
(Dollar amounts in thousands, except per-share data)

	December 28, 1997	December 29, 1996	December 31, 1995	January 1, 1995	January 2, 1994
Net sales	$1,168,182	$ 984,236	$1,016,883	$1,044,247	$1,065,923
Cost of goods sold	837,683	900,573	809,130	764,355	777,564
Selling, general, and administrative expense	131,056	216,129	137,508	128,836	133,886
Restructuring, impairment, and other costs	0	154,869	0	0	0
Operating earnings (loss)	199,443	(287,335)	70,245	151,056	154,473
Interest expense	11,381	13,588	9,437	6,974	6,310
Other (income) expense, net	(1,218)	1,638	173	(712)	(4,493)
Earnings (loss) from continuing operations before income taxes	189,280	(302,561)	60,635	144,794	152,656
Income taxes (benefit)					
Current	8,369	(28,062)	(2,105)	33,227	41,131
Deferred	57,783	(77,828)	25,146	26,283	22,727
Total income taxes (benefit)	66,152	(105,890)	23,041	59,510	63,858
Earnings (loss) from continuing operations	123,128	(196,671)	37,594	85,284	88,798
Earnings from discontinued operations, net of taxes	0	839	12,917	21,727	0
Estimated loss on sale of discontinued operations, net of taxes	(13,713)	(32,430)	0	0	0
Net earnings (loss)	$ 109,415	$(228,262)	$ 50,511	$ 107,011	$ 88,798
Earnings (loss) per share of common stock from continuing operations	$1.45	$(2.37)	$0.45	$1.03	$1.01
Net earnings (loss) per share of common stock	$1.25	$(2.75)	$0.61	$1.30	$1.01
Weighted average common shares outstanding	87,542	82,925	82,819	82,553	87,888

Source: Sunbeam, *1997 Form 10-K,* p. F-3, and *1995 Annual Report,* p. F-3.

approximately 40% capacity. Dunlap was not enthused with the location of the Hattiesburg, Mississippi, plant because of its lack of interstate access and air service. However, to chose to keep it and consolidate other operations into the facility due to lower wage costs. He made the plant a central point of Sunbeam's turnaround.[12]

Many senior executives aspired to reach the shareholder wealth gains that Dunlap generated, but few were able to complete the task as efficiently as Dunlap appeared to do in 1996 and 1997. The fundamental goal of the financial manager is to maximize shareholder wealth, but critics have argued that the costs may be too high. Unless the shareholder exists in a box, many argue there is a fine line between shareholder wealth maximization and firm value maximization. In the strictest of financial terms, shareholder wealth was all that mattered as long as business was conducted within the constraints of the law. Dunlap said,

> I believe in the free enterprise system. I believe in creating an environment where the American worker can succeed. I believe in rescuing companies. I believe in certain executive compensation being a percentage of wealth. I believe in boards of directors being responsible to the shareholders. But these are all highly controversial subjects. When you stand up front, you will be criticized. That is the price of the leadership.[13]

Exhibit 5   **Consolidated Statements of Cash Flows: Sunbeam Corporation**
(Dollar amounts in thousands)

	December 28, 1997	December 29, 1996	December 31, 1995	January 1, 1995	January 2, 1994
Operating Activities					
Net ernings (loss)	$ 109,415	$(228,262)	$ 50,511	$ 107,011	$ 88,798
Adjustments to reconcile earnings to cash provided by operating activities:					
Depreciation and amortization	38,577	47,429	44,174	35,766	32,175
Restructuring, impairment, and other costs	0	154,869	0	0	0
Other non-cash special charges	0	128,800	0	0	0
Estimate loss on sale of discontinued operations, net of taxes	13,713	32,430	0	0	0
Deferred income taxes	57,783	(77,828)	25,146	26,283	22,727
Increase (decrease) in cash from changes in working capital:					
Receivables, net	(84,576)	(13,829)	(4,499)	(48,228)	(43,674)
Inventories	(100,810)	(11,651)	(4,874)	(36,760)	(34,078)
Prepaid expenses and other current assets	(9,004)	4,288	(2,498)	792	(10,048)
Accounts payable	(1,585)	14,735	9,245	5,567	25,199
Income taxes payable	52,844	(21,942)	(18,452)	16,818	(19,972)
Other current liabilities	0	0	(8,032)	(15,482)	(17,443)
Restructuring accrual	(43,378)	0	0	0	0
Payment of other long-term and non-operating liabilities	(14,682)	(27,089)	(21,719)	(17,310)	(28,832)
Other, net	(26,546)	12,213	12,514	6,378	14,111
Net cash provided by operating activities	$ (8,249)	$ 14,163	$ 81,516	$ 80,835	$ 28,963
Investing Activities					
Capital expenditures	(58,258)	(75,336)	(140,053)	(90,929)	(26,656)
Decrease (increase) in investments restricted for plant construction	0	0	45,755	(46,362)	0
Purchase of businesses	0	0	(13,053)	(19,284)	(20,259)
Cash surrender value of life insurance policies	0	0	0	23,549	0
Sale of marketable securities, net	0	0	0	14,708	12,185
Other, net	90,982	(860)	0	200	1,950
Net cash used in investing activities	$ 32,724	$ (76,196)	$(107,351)	$(118,118)	$ (32,780)
Financing Activities					
Net borrowings under revolving credit facility	5,000	30,000	40,000	35,000	0
Issuance of long-term debt	0	11,500	0	78,013	0
Payments of debt obligations	(12,157)	(1,794)	(5,417)	(127,446)	(163)
Proceeds from exercise of stock options and warrants	26,613	4,684	9,818	19,151	7,772
Purchase of common stock for treasury	0	0	(13,091)	0	(174,070)
Sale of treasury stock	0	4,578	0	0	0
Payments of dividends on common stock	(3,399)	(3,318)	(3,268)	(3,169)	(3,215)
Other financing activities	320	(364)	(264)	2,606	2,306
Net cash provided by (used in) financing activities	$ 16,377	$ 45,286	$ 27,778	$4,155	$(167,370)
Net increase (decrease) in cash and cash equivalents	$ 40,852	$ (16,747)	$ 1,943	$ (33,128)	$(171,187)
Cash and equivalents at beginning of year	$ 11,526	$ 28,273	$ 26,330	$ 59,458	$ 230,645
Cash and cash equivalents at end of year	$ 52,378	$ 11,526	$ 28,273	$ 26,330	$ 59,458

Source: Sunbeam, *1997 Form 10-K,* p. F-6, and *1995 Annual Report,* p. F-6.

CHANGING CORPORATE CULTURE

Dunlap argued that there were basically three types of successful business executives: the "Jack Welch," who for many years managed a very successful company; the "Bill Gates," who developed a technology and then created a corporation around that technology; and finally, the "Al Dunlap," who moved into troubled companies to save the firm from ruin.[14] Although the three types of managers were very different in both managerial and personal skills, there was demand for each type in the corporate world of the new millennium.

Dunlap was not an advocate of corporate charitable giving. He argued that the corporate entity is responsible to maximize shareholder wealth. Dunlap believed the company should work to return maximum wealth to the shareholders. The shareholders could then make decisions about charitable donations. Dunlap stated that,

> Business is not a social experiment. Business is a very serious undertaking. I believe the shareholders own the corporation. Some people mention 15–20 constituencies. If I name enough constituencies, I'm going to get something right for someone.[15]

ACT I: THE TURNAROUND

The restructuring plan Dunlap put in place in 1996 called for the closure of 18 factories and 6 office facilities. It also required the consolidation of one headquarters located in Delray Beach, Florida, and an administrative office in Hattiesburg, Mississippi. The Hattiesburg advanced manufacturing facility employed 1,250 workers and operated at full capacity. Sunbeam was easily the city's largest employer, with an estimated annual payroll of $15 million. Dunlap expressed,

> I feel sorry for anyone who lost his [sic] job. But my job is to save the corporation and to save as many jobs as I possibly can. The real story is that I've saved 6,000 jobs and I'm proud of that.[16]

Dunlap's success appeared evident when one examined Sunbeam's stock price movement from July 1996 to March 1998. Sunbeam was selling at 12½ before he agreed to come aboard. The price immediately shot to 18⅝ and, in the course of 18 months, rose to over $50. (See Exhibit 6 for stock prices fluctuations.) Sixteen months after Dunlap's arrival, Sunbeam hired investment bankers to seek both suitors or takeover targets. Black and Decker, Whirlpool, and Maytag were rumored to be among the likely candidates for either a merger or a takeover.[17] Franklin Mutual Advisors were controlled by activist investor Michael Price, who accumulated 1.6 million shares of Black and Decker by late 1996. Franklin also held a 17.4% ownership stake in Sunbeam. Nolan D. Archibald, Black and Decker's CEO, held the company together through the 1990s despite erratic earnings performance.

Dunlap appeared to have succeeded in performing his job. In his prior turnarounds, he "rescued" the company and then moved on to "save" another company. In the case of his most famous turnaround, Scott Paper Company, he left with over $100 million in total compensation, mostly in stock. Now it appeared as though the 60-year-old Dunlap might consider another strategy: Tear the company down and then stay long enough to build the "new" company up again.

Exhibit 6   **Sunbeam Market Price Performance**[1]
(per NYSE composite tape)

		High	Low
1996	First quarter	$19.75	$15.13
	Second quarter	$17.13	$13.50
	Third quarter	$24.75	$12.25
	Fourth quarter	$29.50	$22.75
1997	First quarter	$34.50	$24.63
	Second quarter	$40.75	$29.75
	Third quarter	$45.75	$35.38
	Fourth quarter	$50.44	$37.00

Interest Rate Data	Rate
Estimated industry growth rate	3 to 7%
90-day Treasury Bill rate[2]	5.35%
Sunbeam's beta[3]	0.85
Average market return[4]	14.2%

Source 1: NYSE Composite Tape and Sunbeam, *1997 Form 10-K,* p. 12.

Source 2: *Wall Street Journal* (March 1, 1998), p. C1.

Source 3: *ValueLine* (January 16, 1998), p. 971.

Source 4: *Stocks, Bonds, Bills, and Inflation 1996 Yearbook,* Ibbotson Associates, Inc., Chicago.

ENTER (AND EXIT) THE AMERICAN MEDICAL ASSOCIATION

The American Medical Association (AMA), with a membership base of 400,000 physicians, signed an agreement with Sunbeam on August 5, 1997, that provided Sunbeam with exclusive rights to place the AMA seal on healthcare related products such as thermometers, heating pads, and blood pressure monitors. This was the first time the AMA had endorsed commercial products. Under the agreement, the AMA agreed to

- Form an advisory group to assist Sunbeam in product development.

- Include Sunbeam products in AMA consumer catalogs.

- Assist Sunbeam in the development of product inserts.

- Provide information about Sunbeam products on its World Wide Web site and explore further agreements to create links from the AMA's web page to sites designated by Sunbeam.

- Make its membership lists available for mailings by Sunbeam.[18]

Sunbeam agreed to:

- Pay royalties of 0.3% of gross sales of products trademarked in its *Health at Home* line that carry the AMA seal, plus 3% of sales in excess of the previous year's sales.

- Pay additional royalties of 1.5% to 2% for three years if the AMA helped place Sunbeam products with retailers.

- Pay 0.15% royalties for non-health products such as kitchen appliances that carry the AMA seal and for sales of health-related products outside of the United States.

- Help sell the AMA's first-aid kit and other products in Sunbeam's *Health at Home* retail displays.[19]

The estimated annual royalties payments were $1 million. There was an immediate public outcry about the ethical nature of the agreement. On August 21, the AMA sought to withdraw from the agreement. Dr. Thomas Reardon, Chairman of the AMA Board of Trustees, first argued that "the AMA has moved into the public health arena with much greater force, and that takes money."[20] However, Sunbeam could use the AMA logo even if a less expensive or superior product were developed and sold by a competitor. This raised further ethical issues among AMA members and the public. Reardon then argued that the AMA board had never approved or reviewed the controversial deal.[21] The public outcry had caused Reardon and Dr. John Seward, AMA Executive Vice-President, to issue a statement that included: "Our decision to approve the Sunbeam agreement in the form adopted was an error."

Dunlap clearly was not planning to release the AMA from the agreement. He stated, "We have a contract with the American Medical Association, which we are prepared to honor, and expect them to honor it as well."[22] The AMA, on the other hand, faced pressure from the public and its membership, and Reardon quickly tried to backtrack, commenting "We have zero tolerance for our image being tarnished."[23]

On September 8, 1997, Sunbeam asked the U.S. District Court of Chicago to either force the AMA to uphold the original contractual agreement or recover damages in excess of $20 million.[24] On September 19, the AMA fired three officers allegedly responsible for the deal: Chief Operating Officer Kenneth E. Monroe, Group Vice-President for Business and Management James F. Rappel, and Vice-President of Marketing Larry Jellen. In late September, the AMA counterattacked Sunbeam in court documents alleging the agreement would have countered the AMA's long-standing policy against product endorsements. The AMA argued that the Board did not have knowledge of the contract until after it was signed and that the three officers responsible for the deal were fired from the organization.

On December 4, 1997, P. John Seward resigned as Executive Vice-President two days before the AMA's semi-annual policy-making meeting. In a departure statement, he called the contract "a serious mistake . . . and I have always accepted that responsibility."[25] On December 9, the AMA membership voted to ban the AMA endorsement of products the AMA did not produce. Additionally they voted to require that the Board be made aware of any corporate arrangement that may have an economic impact on the AMA. It was clear that the AMA wanted to safeguard against the recurrence of this type of event. Sunbeam, on the other hand, maintained its position and remained ready to fight the battle in court.

ACT II: THE SHOPPING EXPEDITION: DISCOUNT(?) ON AISLE 5

By late 1997, Sunbeam was seeking merger and/or acquisition candidates. Dunlap made it clear that the company was either available to a suitable bidder or seeking acquisition targets for internal growth. Dunlap stated,

> We're throwing off large sums of cash. The natural sequence of events would be to make a major acquisition or merger to create even more value and to further build the corporation. If we do an acquisition, we would do an acquisition of a company that adds some synergism

to us, has good products, but really needs to be rescued itself. I'd be creating my tenth rescue mission as a part of Sunbeam.[26]

Rumors spread that Dunlap was looking at Maytag, Whirlpool, and Black and Decker. In the appliance industry, these companies were, for the most part, in good financial shape. This left little room for Dunlap to slash and chisel. Black and Decker received the most attention because of the similar product lines.

On March 2, 1998, Sunbeam announced its intentions to acquire three companies: Coleman Company, Inc., Signature Brands USA, and First Alert, Inc. Management expected the acquisitions would be completed in the second quarter of 1998.[27] Coleman was the global leader in outdoor recreational and hardware products. Signature Brands USA was the North American leader in coffee makers and consumer health products. Signature was known for Mr. Coffee™ and the Health O Meter™. First Alert was a leader in residential safety equipment such as smoke detectors and carbon monoxide detectors. Total sales for the three were approximately $1.6 billion in 1997. (See Exhibit 7 for proposed financing of the three transactions, Exhibit 8 for stock price reaction, and Exhibit 9 for revenue and income comparisons for each company.)

Coleman, clearly the largest of the three acquisitions, was the global leader in recreational and hardware products with 1997 sales of approximately $1.2 billion. Recreation was the larger of the two divisions and accounted for approximately $860 million of 1997 sales. Products included camping equipment and outdoor furniture. Brand names included Coleman, Eastpak, Powermate, and Camping Gaz. Prior to the acquisition, Coleman sold its safety and security division which constituted approximately $90 million of 1997 sales. Based in Wichita, Kansas, Coleman employed 6,000 people worldwide and operated 17 manufacturing facilities in 1997.

Geographically Coleman had a similar mix to Sunbeam with 70% of its business in the United States. It was not nearly as strong as Sunbeam in Latin America, but it held a presence in Japan. Coleman's name brands were Outdoor, Powermate, Eastpak, and Spas. Coleman's Chairman and CEO, Jerry Levin, worked to restructure Coleman without significant factory consolidation. Like Dunlap, Levin had worked to reduce the number of different SKUs. In contrast to Dunlap, Levin was a more gentle leader, more of a "corporate doctor" than consolidator.

Signature Brands was the North America coffee maker leader with Mr. Coffee, as well as the leader in consumer health products marketed under the Health O Meter brand. Sales in 1997 were approximately $275 million. Based in Glenwillow, Ohio, Signature operated two plants and employed approximately 1,000 people. Consumer products represented approximately 86%, and professional products held the remaining 14% of total revenue. The professional products division mainly sold scales to the medical profession, including hospitals, doctors, and clinics. Signature's business was domestic, with 40% of its business going to Wal-Mart and Kmart.[28]

First Alert was the worldwide leader in residential safety equipment such as smoke detectors and carbon monoxide detectors. Revenues in 1997 were approximately $187 million. Based in Aurora, Illinois, First Alert operated two plants and employed approximately 2,100. First Alert had three product categories, the largest being fire safety, which accounted for approximately 66.6% of revenues in 1997. Fire safety products included smoke detectors, fire extinguishers, fire escape ladders, and fire chests and safes. Home Safety Products accounted for 26% of 1997 revenue and included carbon monoxide detectors, rechargeable lights, radon gas detectors, and child safety products. Finally, the Home Lighting Security division produced infrared motion-sensing home lighting controls, timers, and nightlights and made up the remaining 6.2% of First Alert's 1997 sales.

On the morning of March 2, 1998, Dunlap commented,

Exhibit 7 **Proposed Acquisitions: Sunbeam Corporation**
(announced March 2, 1998)

Company	Employees[1]	Total Value	Breakdown of Proposed Financing
Coleman Company, Inc.	7,000	$2 billion	$811 million stock $260 million cash Assumed debt of Coleman Company, Inc. approximately $730.5 million.[2]
Signature Brands USA	995	$250 million	Cash of $8.25 per share of Signature stock Assumption of debt of Signature Brands USA approximately $213.1 million.[3]
First Alert, Inc.	2,125	$175 million	Cash of $5.25 per share of First Alert stock Assumption of debt of First Alert, Inc. approximately $82.9 million.[4]

Source 1: *St. Petersburg Times* (March 3, 1998), p. 1E.

Source 2: Coleman, *Form 10-K* report filed with SEC, p. F-3.

Source 3: Signature Brands, *Form 10-K* report filed with SEC, p. F-2.

Source 4: First Alert, *Form 10-K* report filed with the SEC, p. F-3.

> We said we would either do a major merger or major acquisition and here we've done $2½ billion worth of acquisitions. . . . I believe this is the first time in corporate history someone has ever acquired three separate publicly traded companies at once. So we're making new news.[29]

Dunlap's critics argued that he could not effectively run a corporation in the long run. Dunlap, on the other hand, argued that his management style represented the heart of capitalism. He argued that he took companies in the worst possible shape and then rescued them. In March 1998, he embarked on his tenth rescue mission: a triple play.

Al Dunlap commented, "If I break my watch right now, it [would still be] right twice a day."[30] Using that same logic, the stock price had ranged from $39.63 on February 23, 1998, to $52.00 on March 4, 1998. This was the same company that traded at $12.25 in July 1996 before Dunlap joined Sunbeam. Could the value of the company have changed so dramatically over the 18-month period? Given the dramatic fluctuations of the stock price over the past 21 months, the true value of Sunbeam was in question by analysts and investors alike.

Exhibit 8 Stock Price Reaction to Sunbeam's Announcement to Acquire Coleman, Signature, and First Alert

Closing Price of Common Stock	Sunbeam	Coleman	Signature	First Alert
February 23, 1998	$39.63	$19.00	$5.13	$2.75
February 24, 1998	$40.63	$20.69	$5.13	$2.75
February 25, 1998	$41.75	$19.88	$4.94	$3.38
February 26, 1998	$41.88	$20.19	$5.13	$3.19
February 27, 1998	$41.75	$20.88	$5.25	$3.13
March 2, 1998	$45.63	$30.94	$8.03	$5.16
March 3, 1998	$49.88	$32.81	$8.03	$5.14
March 4, 1998	$52.00	$35.44	$8.09	$5.13
March 5, 1998	$51.63	$34.69	$8.06	$5.13
March 6, 1998	$51.50	$34.45	$8.09	$5.16
March 9, 1998	$50.88	$34.06	$8.16	$5.13
March 10, 1998	$50.31	$33.88	$8.13	$5.13
March 11, 1998	$49.38	$33.44	$8.14	$5.13
March 12, 1998	$50.00	$33.75	$8.13	$5.13
March 13, 1998	$50.50	$34.19	$8.14	$5.13

Source: *Wall Street Journal,* Section C.

Exhibit 9   Revenue and by Division for Coleman, Signature Brands, and First Alert, 1995–1997
(Dollar amounts in thousands)

A. Coleman [1]

Division	1997	1996	1995
Outdoor recreation	$ 859,696	$ 859,611	$688,881
Hardware	294,598	360,605	244,693
Total revenue	$1,154,294	$1,220,216	$933,574
Operating income (loss)	($6,377)	($50,301)	$64,546
Net income (loss)	($2,536)	($41,893)	$39,280

B. Signature Brands [2]

Division	1997	1996	1995
Consumer products	$ 236,007	$ 247,267	$230,029
Professional products	39,701	35,710	37,858
Total revenue	$ 275,708	$ 282,977	$267,887
Operating income (loss)	$ 16,760	$ 26,225	$ 22,830
Net income (loss)	($2,212)	$ 2,721	$ 984

C. First Alert [3]

Division	1997	1996	1995
Fire safety	$ 123,942	$ 119,869	$138,402
Home safety	48,605	72,990	93,827
Home lighting security	14,394	12,748	14,037
Total revenue	$ 186,941	$ 205,607	$246,266
Operating income (loss)	($8,467)	($26,519)	$ 20,433
Net income (loss)	($7,836)	($18,702)	$ 11,437

Source 1: Coleman, *Form 10-K* report filed with SEC, pp. 7, 14.

Source 2: Signature Brands, *Form 10-K* report filed with SEC, pp. 23–25.

Source 3: First Alert, *Form 10-K* report filed with the SEC, pp. 4, 13.

Notes

1. Albert J. Dunlap with Bob Andelman, *Mean Business: How I Save Bad Companies and Make Good Companies Great,* (1997), Simon and Schuster, p. xii.
2. Sunbeam, *1997 Form 10-K,* filed with SEC March 6, 1998, p. 1.
3. *ValueLine Household Industry Analysis* (January 16, 1998), p. 955.
4. In an interview with Hedrick Smith in the "Managing Corporate Changes Series: Cutting to the Core: Albert J. Dunlap," *Films for the Humanities and Sciences* (June 1997).
5. "Mr. Price Is on the Line," *Fortune* (December 6, 1996), and "Chain Saw Al to the Rescue?" *Forbes* (August 26, 1996).
6. Dunlap, *Mean Business,* pp. 13–14, Chapters 3–6.
7. *Ibid.,* p. 281.
8. Interview with Hedrick Smith (June 1997).
9. *St. Petersburg Times* (December 8, 1997), Business 10.
10. Dunlap, *Mean Business,* pp. xi–xii.
11. Interview with Hedrick Smith (June 1997).
12. "Flash! Mississippi Town Down Twice Escapes Being Dunlapped," *Management Review* (February 1997), p. 9.
13. Interview with Hedrick Smith (June 1997).
14. *Ibid.*
15. *Ibid.*
16. *Ibid.*
17. *Wall Street Journal* (June 24, 1997), pp. A3, A6.
18. Mary Chris Jaklevic, "AMA-Sunbeam Dispute Heads to Court," *Modern Healthcare* (September 15, 1997), p. 3
19. *Ibid.*
20. Christine Gorman, "Doctor's Dilemma," *Time* (August 25, 1997), p. 64.
21. Jaklevic, "AMA-Sunbeam Dispute," p. 3.
22. "AMA Backpedals on Sunbeam Alliance, But Firms May Hold Group to Accord," *Wall Street Journal* (August 22, 1997), p. A2.
23. "The AMA Isn't Feeling So Hot," *Business Week* (September 1, 1997), p. 33.
24. "Sunbeam Asks Court to Enforce AMA Deal," *St. Petersburg Times* (September 9, 1997), p. 1E.
25. Thomas M. Burton, "AMA Top Official Quits Amid Fallout Over Sunbeam Pact," *Wall Street Journal* (December 5, 1997), p. B6.
26. Interview with Hedrick Smith (June 1997).
27. Sunbeam, *1997 Form 10-K,* filed with SEC, March 6, 1998, p. 2.
28. *PaineWebber Company Opinion* (March 31, 1998), pp. 4, 5.
29. Interview with Valerie Morris, CNN Anchor on Trading Places, excerpted from Bloomberg, March 2, 1998.
30. Interview with Hedrick Smith (June 1997).

Mikromashina of Moscow:
Problems and Opportunities of Privatization

Daniel J. McCarthy and Sheila M. Puffer

In early 1995 Viktor Levintan, the acting general director of Mikromashina of Moscow, was reviewing a proposal from an American firm, Nypro, Inc., which had offered to increase its ownership of Mikromashina from 10% to a potential 45% stake. Nypro viewed this opportunity as an extension of its global strategy as a leading worldwide plastic injection molding company. However, this offer created a dilemma for Viktor. The $300,000 represented a much needed infusion of capital for the struggling enterprise. Yet, the investment came at the price of a substantial dilution of ownership and potential loss of control for Viktor and his management team.

It would not be an easy decision for a person who had devoted his entire 35-year career to the company. Still, Viktor had developed great admiration for Nypro's president during the several years their two companies had been operating a joint venture in Moscow. Viktor did not want any outsiders to gain control of Mikromashina, but the company desperately needed capital. It was becoming increasingly difficult to survive, yet still remain independent. He expressed his feelings to the case writers by saying:

> We are not happy if a 'big papa' will swallow us fully, not even a nice papa.

He was referring to "Papa Gordon," the fond term he often used for Nypro's CEO and majority shareholder.

MIKROMASHINA'S SITUATION IN EARLY 1995

Mikromashina was a manufacturer of small household and personal care appliances that it manufactured and assembled primarily for the Russian consumer market. Its products included electric shavers, hair clippers, hair dryers, coffee grinders, food blenders, and small motors.

Mikromashina had become a private joint stock company about 18 months after the Russian government's privatization program began in 1991. In 1993, majority ownership of most former state enterprises passed from the government to Russian citizens, particularly managers and workers employed by their enterprises. The process was accomplished through distribution of vouchers representing company shares. At the outset of privatization's second phase in July 1994, the government encouraged other investors to buy stock in these privatized companies. In contrast to the first phase, which simply transferred shares, this phase aimed to bring new capital into privatized enterprises.

This case was prepared by Daniel J. McCarthy and Sheila M. Puffer, College of Business Administration, Northeastern University. Management cooperated in the field research of this case, which was written solely for the purpose of student discussion. All data are based on field research and all incidents and individuals are real. The authors thank company executives of Mikromashina and Nypro Inc., and Professor Alexander Naumov of Moscow State University, for their cooperation in developing the case. Partial funding for the preparation of this case was provided by the BFET Fellowship Program, Center for Russian and East European Studies, University of Pittsburgh, and by the International Research and Exchanges Board (IREX), Washington, DC. This case was printed in *The Case Research Journal* (Fall/Winter 1997) pp. 43–49. All other rights reserved jointly to the authors and the North American Case Research Association (NACRA). Copyright © 1997 by the *Case Research Journal* and Daniel J. McCarthy and Sheila M. Puffer. Reprinted by permission.

Mikromashina's problems included a severe decline in demand for its products. This decline developed from the eroding purchasing power of its traditional customers, as well as changing consumer preferences for more expensive imported products for those who could afford them. Other problems stemmed from supply shortages, a lack of modern equipment, and extreme difficulty collecting receivables because of the chronic nonpayment of debts among enterprises. Added to these difficulties were unprecedented layoffs of long-time employees, and the loss of valuable employees to higher paying entrepreneurial firms.

The most pressing problem for the company was its desperate financial situation, which resulted from its many business challenges and Russia's difficult economic environment. Its lack of cash flow left Mikromashina unable to pay debts or employees' salaries. With few liquid assets, its debts in early 1995 totaled approximately $500,000. In addition to back payroll and supplier debt, the company was severely behind on payments to utilities, the government, and the employee pension fund. At the end of April 1995, late-payment penalties totaled $172,100. With a continuing precipitous sales decline to the present monthly level of $55,000, and able to collect only a portion of current receivables, management struggled to reduce costs and search for new opportunities (see Exhibit 1 for breakdown of debts).

RUSSIA'S TRANSITION FROM A CENTRALLY PLANNED TO A MARKET-ORIENTED ECONOMY

Such problems were unprecedented in the communist-controlled centrally planned economy that existed prior to the break-up of the Soviet Union in late 1991. For more than 70 years, the major objective for enterprise managers was to fulfill the plans dictated by centralized industrial ministries. Thus, managers of firms like Mikromashina were rewarded for meeting production plans, and made virtually no decisions about product mix, pricing, customers, suppliers, distribution, or competition. All such decisions were made by central ministry officials, and cash was not exchanged among enterprises to pay for goods and services. Such transactions were centralized in the ministries, which were also the source of financing for capital investments, wages, and other expenses. Profit was not a major objective, but improving efficiency in using resources was rewarded with bonuses and increased funds for investment. Enterprises rarely knew their exact costs, and virtually none could determine costs for individual product lines. Yet, they were required to submit reports on financial matters and other aspects of their business to their ministries.

Managers were under pressure to meet rigid production plans and many other measures of enterprise operations, and became skilled in finding ways to do so. These practices included hoarding raw materials, vertically integrating operations, employing excess workers, and networking with other enterprise managers and government officials. Managers also reported performance results which virtually always showed them fulfilling the plan and meeting other targets.

As Russia moved toward a market-based economy in 1992, the situation for enterprise managers changed dramatically. For instance, they were free to set their own production targets and prices. They were also expected to find markets for their products as well as develop their own sources of supply. They were required to be self-financing, which meant operating profitably, since few other sources of funds existed. Yet, many enterprises operated with outmoded plants and equipment and were grossly overstaffed. Bank loans were scarce, and if available, came with exorbitant interest charges. Inflation

Exhibit 1   Debts in April 1995: Mikromashina

Payable to suppliers	$ 22,300
Bank interest due	4,400
Water and sewerage payable	35,200
Electricity payable	23,400
Heating payable	21,500
Telephone payable	1,000
Radio and television advertising	800
Taxes due	212,900
Salary payable	80,700
Other	20,900
Penalties	172,100
Total	**$595,200**

during 1992 was reported to be 2,600%, a factor contributing to a near-catastrophic devaluation of the ruble. Restrictive and ever-changing government policies, coupled with onerous and unpredictable tax laws, added to the extremely difficult environment facing managers. The situation was a traumatic change from prior times when their single objective had been to fulfill a centrally mandated plan.

MIKROMASHINA'S HISTORY OF SUCCESSFUL OPERATIONS

In the centralized economy, Mikromashina had operated successfully for over 70 years from its location only a half-hour's drive from Red Square. As part of the prestigious aircraft industry sector, the enterprise had very few problems obtaining raw materials and had a reputation for producing good quality products. Between 1977 and 1982 the plant had been awarded the "Red Banner" and the "Badge of Honor," prestigious awards from the USSR Council of Ministers. The plant was also enrolled in the All-Union Board of Honor of the USSR for its economic achievements.

The company's situation was strengthened in 1982 with the construction of a new 20,000-square-meter plant that housed 40 plastic injection molding machines and various types of metalworking equipment. Operations were vertically integrated, but raw materials such as plastic and steel tapes for shaver foils were provided by suppliers. Company operations included a technical department that designed and produced molds for plastic components, an injection molding shop that produced plastic parts, a metalworking department that cut metal tapes into perforated shaver foils and produced other small metal parts, an electroplating shop, several assembly lines, and an engineering department involved in improving products, machinery, and production operations. Like most enterprises, Mikromashina also provided numerous free employee services on-site, including a medical and dental clinic, a day-care center, kindergarten, cafeteria, and recreation areas. Other employee benefits, provided free or at a nominal charge, were children's summer camps and vacation resorts in desirable locations.

The company enjoyed a favorable position in the shortage-ridden economy. Its popular products were sometimes rationed by the Ministry according to social need, with preference given to orphanages and other needy institutions. As late as 1992, when many Russian enterprises had drastically curtailed production, Mikromashina operated at virtually full capacity and shipped 70% of its output to an independent distributor in Moscow. Mikromashina's products were well accepted by Russian consumers for their quality, reliability, and affordable price.

Market and Competitive Pressures

Like virtually all Russian manufacturing enterprises, Mikromashina's business deteriorated dramatically during the transition from a centrally controlled system to a market economy. By the spring of 1994, Mikromashina saw its markets diminish substantially, with sales declining about 60% from a year earlier. Only 20% of the decreased production was shipped to the major distributor. Viktor explained that the living standard had plunged and inflation became rampant after the government freed prices in the early 1990s. This action resulted in severely reduced disposable income for most Russians. The price of bread, for example, had increased 2,400%, from 25 kopeks to 600 rubles during that time. This increase paralleled those in the company's raw material costs. Yet, the price for Mikromashina's coffee grinders had increased only 500%, to about $10. At the same time, a class of image-conscious *nouveaux-riches* had emerged who preferred brand-name imported products, such as Braun and Moulinex, selling at 3 to 4 times Mikromashina's price. Virtually all Russian companies faced similar problems during the transition to privatization (Exhibit 2).

Viktor had looked into exporting and realized this option would not be profitable. Their coffee grinders, for instance, were sold profitably for $10 in Russia, but could be sold only for $7 in England and $5 in Iran. Another option he considered was to collaborate with former "sister" companies with whom Mikromashina had shared technology and production resources in the centrally planned economy. For instance, Mikromashina had produced shaver foil for Moscow Priborstroi, now a privatized competitor like the other "sister" firms. Levintan felt that discussing pricing with such domestic competitors might help his survival chances. He was also concerned that Mikromashina had not increased its prices fast enough to keep up with inflation. Levintan explained:

> We understand that marketing is very important.

He added, however, that Mikromashina lacked the funds to hire a hard-to-find marketing expert, whose salary could range from $500 to $1,500 a month. He considered temporarily sharing marketing talent with another company, but was not convinced that this would be enough to help solve Mikromashina's serious problems.

Financial Straitjacket

Viktor's reluctance to hire a marketing professional was evidence of the firm's dire financial situation. He stated:

> How to find financing and think about the future is our biggest worry now.

He added that competitors were experiencing the same situation, or worse. Although the company's debt had reached $500,000 by early 1995, Levintan believed that Mikromashina would not become bankrupt in the immediate future. Yet, as he explained the company's financial situation, it was clear he was in a financial straightjacket regarding investments. Not only could he not collect the company's overdue receivables of $400,000, but he was also unable to pay the $500,000 owed to creditors and employees. He explained that, even if Mikromashina were to produce more products for their major distributor and other customers, the company would not receive timely payments for

Exhibit 2 **Sources of Problems for State-Owned Enterprises in 1992 and 1995**

Problem	1992 Survey Results Mean and Interpretation (7-point scale)	1995 Estimates
1. Suppliers	5.3 serious problem	still serious
2. Government regulations	5.1 serious problem	still serious
3. Financing	5.1 serious problem	more serious
4. Political situation	4.8 quite serious	more serious
5. Technology	4.6 quite serious	more serious
6. Customers	3.9 somewhat serious	very serious
7. Labor	3.8 somewhat serious	more serious
8. Marketing	3.3 slightly serious	very serious
9. Competition	3.0 slightly serious	very serious

Note: The 1992 survey reports responses of 57 managers, including 33 directors and deputy directors. Enterprises were reported as state owned by 70% of respondents, 14% were leased from state enterprises, and 16% were privatized stock companies. Enterprise activities included manufacturing of industrial products (34%) or consumer products (13%), services (19%), R&D (21%), and other (13%).

Source: Daniel J. McCarthy and Shelia M. Puffer, "Diamonds and Rust on Russia's Road to Privatizaion: The Profits and Pitfalls for Western Managers," *Columbia Journal of World Business,* 1995, 30 (3), 56–69.

shipments. This problem was symptomatic of the cashflow gridlock which had developed among Russian companies, with nonpayment of receivables having reached $10 billion by mid 1994. Many enterprises still clung to the hope that government subsidies and a mass program to forgive debts would solve the cash crisis among enterprises.

Lacking revenues, Mikromashina was unable to pay its suppliers, many of whom had long relationships with the company. Until late 1991, under the Soviet central planning system, Mikromashina did business with more than 800 suppliers because each tended to be a highly specialized monopoly. Like so many Russian enterprises which sought to gain more control over their operations during that period, Mikromashina kept very large stockpiles of raw materials, such as 40 tons of plastic. Yet, as part of the Ministry of the Aircraft Industry, the firm had experienced far fewer supply problems than enterprises that reported to less prestigious ministries.

In 1994, Mikromashina took several stopgap measures to alleviate its cash crunch. For example, it resorted to bartering with suppliers and customers. In return for raw materials and components, the company paid suppliers with coffee grinders and even grain, vegetable oil, and sugar which had been received as payment from customers. The enterprise also began offering discounts to customers who paid in advance or on time. Management even rented space in its well-located $7 million plant to four foreign firms, including a Scottish soft drink company and a computer firm.

More drastic measures included withholding tax payments, which Viktor realized would be a serious problem in the future unless the government forgave such nonpayments. Finally, the company stopped making government-required payments to the employees' pension fund, which would have amounted to approximately one-third of total salaries. As a result, Mikromashina incurred substantial government fines and created ill will among its employees.

Organizational Disorder

The financial problems caused by upheaval in the company's markets created serious stress within the organization. Nonpayment to pension funds accompanied delays in wage payments of two to three months, with wages for July and August still unpaid in September. These problems, coupled with a lack of job security, had caused many employees to leave if they were able to find jobs elsewhere. In addition to layoffs, these resignations reduced the work force from 2,700 in 1992 to 700 in early 1995.

During this troubled period, Viktor met his objective of producing goods every day, albeit at a very reduced level. He explained:

> We must keep operating to maintain a future for the company and also for the work force. I am not happy to see our equipment stopped.

He wanted to keep a skilled workforce in place to keep the plant operational. Another of his objectives was to provide work for his employees, many of whom had over 30 years' service, and had little prospect of employment elsewhere. The latter objective was not uncommon for managers of Viktor's generation who had shouldered the responsibility of providing jobs as well as social benefits for employees. Such behavior reflected the values of Russian managers like Viktor which were sometimes similar to American managers, but at other times quite different (Exhibit 3).

In hopes of maintaining employment, Viktor had talked with several Russian and foreign companies. He proposed being a subcontractor to Braun of Germany (a subsidiary of the U.S. Gillette Company), offering to produce components and products for them. He had also negotiated with one of the new plant tenants, Meri Mate of Scotland, to employ some Mikromashina workers. Another avenue Viktor was exploring involved producing bread and other products at the plant.

Despite these efforts, nonpayment of wages, coupled with the threat of job loss, created a climate of discord in the organization. Fear, uncertainty, and personal ambition led some managers to challenge Viktor's leadership. This occurred only six months after he had become acting general manager in March 1994, replacing his long-time predecessor. Some employees feared that the company would be destroyed by opportunists who would "line their own pockets."

Viktor realized that not everybody was happy, especially since he had not yet held his first shareholder meeting. As he explained:

> Some of the "young boys" push me to hold this meeting and talk about going to court. One especially wants to get near the top, on the board of directors, and argued for more marketing and even more radical change. Some people in the middle say, "Mr. Levintan, go away." They think a new *barin* will be the answer.

Viktor's term, *barin,* referred to the powerful, paternalistic landowners and serf-owners in pre-revolutionary Russia before the turn of the century. He tried to counter the threats by buying back stock from former employees, as well as current employees he felt were not contributing to the company's success. This repurchased stock was offered to the most valuable remaining workers to retain their loyalty to him and the company. He clarified:

> We try to concentrate these shares in the hands of people who want to produce new things, or old things with new quality.

Viktor realized that some employee suspicion arose because the major beneficiaries of Russia's privatization program had been enterprise managers, ministry and other

Exhibit 3   Russian and American Conceptions of Business Ethics

	United States	
	Ethical **I**	**Unethical** **III**
Ethical	• Keeping one's word • Maintaining trust • Fair competition • Rewards commensurate with performance	• Personal favoritism (*blat*) and grease payments • Price fixing • Manipulating data • Ignoring senseless laws and regulations
Russia	**IV**	**II**
Unethical	• Maximizing profits • Exorbitant salary differentials • Layoffs • Whistleblowing	• Gangsterism, racketeering, and extortion • Black market • Price gouging • Refusing to pay debts

Source: Sheila M. Puffer and Daniel J. McCarthy, "Finding the Common Ground in Russian and American Business Ethics," *California Management Review,* 1995, 37 (2), 29–46.

government officials, and individuals with a history of illegal business dealings in the black market or shadow economy. He knew such people had been successful in amassing large blocks of shares of privatized enterprises, often at little cost, and were motivated more by self-interest than by concern for employee welfare or the future of the enterprises.

OPPORTUNITIES FROM THE MIRO JOINT VENTURE

Quality and innovation were not new to Mikromashina. In 1989, while still a state-owned enterprise, they became a 60% partner of a joint venture housed in Mikromashina's plant. Their Swiss partner, Thielmann Rotel AG, manufactured electric motors and household appliances. The joint venture agreement, among the earliest to be signed under the country's new joint venture law, followed eight years of their cooperation in manufacturing shavers at Mikromashina. The shaver model was gradually modified to European standards. At the height of production during the mid 1980s, 20% was exported to Italy, Austria, Belgium, Britain, the Netherlands, Syria, West Germany, Switzerland, and Eastern Europe. Mikromashina used its share of the joint venture profits for product development and equipment modernization.

Mikromashina's objectives in entering a joint venture were to strengthen itself as a production company and take advantage of Western marketing and technical expertise. Employing 45 people in the joint venture, Mikromashina contributed plant and equipment, low labor costs, and a ready Russian market. Still, products exported at world prices for valuable hard currency under the Rotel brand name usually provided 60% of joint venture profits. Although there were some differences in export product characteristics and packaging, quality was the same as Miro-brand products for the Russian market. Many efforts were made to improve quality in response to pressure from foreign customers, who management saw as "whipping" them for higher quality. These quality efforts enhanced Mikromashina's reputation, which had been built primarily upon high productivity.

The joint venture expanded in early 1990 to include Nypro, Inc. The privately owned American plastic injection molding company had sales at that time of over $100 million. Its numerous joint ventures were located in the United States, Europe, and Asia. Nypro's involvement in the Russian joint venture resulted from a meeting of the three parties on a Volga River cruise for American business leaders exploring the Russian market. Gordon Lankton, the president and majority shareholder of Nypro, entered his firm in the joint venture as a 20% partner by purchasing one-half of Rotel's ownership. Mikromashina retained its 60% share. The ownership positions, as well as the evolving relationships among the three companies, are shown in Exhibit 4.

Nypro brought expertise in manufacturing and assembling precision plastic components, and planned to provide engineering, tooling, and injection molding technology. As the venture developed, it was expected that modern high-technology equipment, such as process-controlled plastic injection molding machines, would be added, in addition to a tooling facility with computerized machinery. The modernized operations were to be housed in a new plant adjacent to Mikromashina's facilities, and construction began in spring 1993. The venture would initially become involved in the production of custom injection molded components utilizing Mikromashina's existing molding machines.

In early 1995, the joint venture was experiencing reduced volume, but was still operating quite successfully, and had consistently produced ruble profits for the partners. Mikromashina, by this time, had begun spending its share of profits to alleviate its own severe cash crisis, rather than reinvesting in the joint venture. Lacking investment, construction of the new plant had come to a halt in December 1993, only one-third completed. Aggravating the situation was the meteoric price increase in construction materials, which had increased 2,500%. Additionally, government legislation on land ownership was still unclear. As a result, the Western partners hesitated to invest further in the new building that optimistically had a payback of around 12 years.

By 1994, Nypro had increased its ownership of the relatively successful joint venture to 33% by purchasing shares from its partners. Mikromashina's ownership decreased to 50%, and Rotel's to 17%. Viktor, in typical Russian style, described the contrasting situations of Mikromashina and the joint venture:

> The mother is ill, but the daughter is healthier.

MIKROMASHINA'S ALTERNATIVES

As he assessed the situation, Viktor pondered a number of opportunities which he believed might improve Mikromashina's future. They ranged from continuing the stopgap survival tactics to selling out completely to foreign interests, as the government's privatization program had allowed since July 1994. He couldn't help thinking how these decisions would affect the company's ability to retain majority ownership and operating control.

The company had consistently been creative in taking short-term measures toward alleviating its serious problems. However, some, including nonpayment to the pension fund, could precipitate severe long-term problems. Actions such as layoffs, renting space, cutting production, delaying wage payments and withholding taxes had at least

Exhibit 4 **Institutional Relationships Among Mikromashina, Nypro, and Rotel**

Date	Nypro (USA)	Mikromashina (Russia)	Rotel (Switzerland)
		Ownership Percentage	
1989	0%	60%	40%
1990	20%	60%	20%
1991	33%	50%	17%

Note: Nypro's offer would increase its ownership of Mikromashina from 10 to 45%, assuring its purchase of 15% from other owners and 20% from the Russian government.

forestalled bankruptcy. This scenario had become more of a threat to enterprises under the self-financing requirements of privatization.

Performing subcontracting work for other firms remained a serious possibility, and negotiations had been held with Western companies including Gillette's Braun of Germany and Kenwood of the United Kingdom. Levintan feared, however, that such foreign firms were really interested in taking full control of the enterprise. He had proposed to Braun, for instance, that they produce two product lines together. Braun's would be higher in price and quality, while Mikromashina's brand would be lower. It seemed clear, however, that Braun was interested in having only its own product produced. Mikromashina would effectively become just a subcontractor, rather than continuing as an operating enterprise.

A related alternative resulted from Viktor's frequent contacts with foreign firms. He proposed that Mikromashina could assemble components for firms from Asia, Europe, and the U.S., giving them access to low Russian labor costs. Levintan mentioned Motorola and Gillette as being prospects, but admitted that thus far Mikromashina had not succeeded in developing such relationships. He noted that a variation of this approach would be to produce small plastic parts for items such as pagers, utilizing the larger contracting companies' molds. He believed that Nypro could be one such company.

Besides reaching out to foreign collaborators, Viktor also had the option of betting on a new production technology. An individual who owned 2.5% of Mikromashina's shares, and who had expertise in the new technology, proposed to Viktor that the company adopt it. Viktor described the person as an *akula* or *shark,* a positive term referring to an aggressive, successful mover, somebody willing to do new things. In return, Viktor considered offering him more shares from those purchased from employees and former employees interested in selling their shares.

Government support, Viktor believed, also remained a potential alternative for the company. The Russian government had expressed interest in supporting experimental nontoxic production processes. Mikromashina estimated that it would cost $1.6 million to develop such a project. Rather than depending only on uncertain Russian government funds for the project, Mikromashina was working with Nypro to obtain funding from the U.S. Agency for International Development.

NYPRO IN EARLY 1995

Nypro was one of the world's largest custom injection molders of plastic materials. The company did not manufacture final products, but acted instead as a contract manufacturer of plastic parts and components for a variety of customers. Its July 1994 fiscal-year revenues of $166 million included Nypro's share of worldwide joint venture sales. When total sales of joint ventures were included, revenues reached nearly $200 million (Exhibit 5). Nineteen ninety-four marked Nypro's ninth consecutive year of record revenues and profits. Company officials attributed their success to the strategy of locating plants very close to Nypro's major customers around the world. Additionally, the company utilized the most advanced technologies and equipment, and worked closely with customers in making process and product improvements.

Gordon Lankton had joined the private Massachusetts company in 1962 as general manager and 50% owner. He had worked in plastics at Dupont for several years after graduating with an engineering degree from Cornell University. In 1969, with company sales at $4 million, he purchased the remaining company stock, becoming the sole owner. The company's mission, formulated at the 1993 managers' conference in Ireland, stated:

> To be the best in the world in precision plastics injection molding, creating value for our customers, employees, and communities.

Lankton estimated that his company had about two-tenths of 1% of the world's plastic injection molding market. During 1994, two new company-owned plants had opened. The Chicago facility served primarily health-care industry customers, and the Oregon plant produced printer cartridge components for Hewlett-Packard. Joint venture operations were added in China and Wales to better serve the Asian and European markets. More locations and acquisitions were under consideration, as well as additional joint ventures.

LANKTON'S PERSPECTIVE

In discussing his company's global strategy, Lankton explained that Nypro followed its customers around the world and located plants next to their operations. He elaborated:

> Our global customers want us to be truly global. They want us to use the same machines, the same process controls, same mold technology, same procedures, and same computer-aided design systems, regardless of where we make their products around the world. Fortunately, information technologies are now available that make this possible and practical.

As a result of some early problems in establishing overseas operations in the early 1970s, Lankton came to favor joint ventures as Nypro's vehicle for non-U.S. operations. Each joint venture had the managing director report to the JV's own board of directors. The board itself was composed of managers and functional specialists from Nypro and the other partner. Lankton viewed Nypro's Russian joint venture as an expansion of the

Exhibit 5   1989–1994 Profit-Loss Statements and Balance Sheets: Nypro, Inc.

	1994		1993		1992		1991		1990		1989	
Net sales	$165,983	100.00%	$135,829	100.00%	$119,856	100.00%	$100,201	100.00%	$96,934	100.00%	$84,150	100.00%
Cost of sales	126,512	76.22	104,189	76.71	93,347	77.88	78,215	78.06	76,127	78.53	68,002	80.81
Gross profits	39,471	23.78	31,640	23.29	26,509	22.12	21,986	21.94	20,807	21.47	16,148	19.19
Selling	7,244	4.36	6,826	5.03	5,978	4.99	5,546	5.54	5,037	5.20	4,202	4.99
General and administration	16,807	10.13	11,481	8.45	9,972	8.31	8,035	8.02	7,446	7.67	6,018	7.16
Research and development	2,705	1.63	2,415	1.78	1,793	1.50	1,005	1.00	1,131	1.17	861	1.02
Total expenses	26,756	16.12	20,722	15.26	17,743	14.80	14,586	14.56	13,614	14.04	11,081	13.17
Operating profits	12,715	7.66	10,918	8.04	8,766	7.31	7,400	7.39	7,193	7.42	5,067	6.02
Other income (expenses)	647	0.39	415	0.31	553	0.46	915	0.91	(136)	(0.14)	(1,283)	(1.52)
Eq. in net inc. of uncon. A	605	0.36	464	0.34	202	0.17	(864)	(0.86)	(79)	(0.08)	(111)	(0.13)
Min. int. in losses of con.	(77)	(0.05)	(97)	(0.07)	(13)	(0.01)	152	0.15	(42)	(0.04)	(93)	(0.11)
Income taxes	3,064	1.84	3,194	2.36	3,002	2.50	2,450	2.45	1,998	2.07	1,675	2.00
Net income	$ 10,826	6.52%	$ 8,506	6.28%	$ 6,506	5.43%	$ 5,153	5.14%	$ 4,938	5.09%	$ 1,905	2.26%

	1994	1993	1992	1991	1990	1989
Assets						
Current assets						
Cash and short-term investments	$ 7,109	$ 8,731	$ 9,389	$ 7,258	$ 6,329	$ 2,342
Accounts and notes receivable, net allowance for doubtful accounts	27,511	20,551	17,781	16,654	13,795	14,101
Inventories	9,963	6,877	6,984	7,157	7,027	5,689
Mold costs in excess of billing	1,879	3,402	1,108	N/A	N/A	N/A
Prepaid expenses and other current assets	1,057	704	336	228	153	542
Deferred tax assets	1,000	N/A	N/A	N/A	N/A	N/A
Total current assets	48,519	40,265	35,598	31,297	27,304	22,674
Noncurrent assets						
Investments in and advances to unconstructed affiliates	6,205	5,094	3,013	1,984	2,371	2,759
Restricted bond proceeds	1,976	2,979	N/A	N/A	N/A	N/A
Other noncurrent assets	4,336	2,501	1,899	1,585	1,309	1,121
Total noncurrent assets	12,517	10,574	4,912	3,569	3,680	3,880
Property, plant, and equipment						
Land	1,169	398	55	55	255	146
Building and improvements	27,968	17,360	16,012	12,139	11,520	10,172

Machinery and equipment	57,675	31,125	27,742	23,895	22,888	19,620
Furniture and fixtures	5,495	3,738	3,227	2,542	2,145	1,613
Construction in process	6,837	3,995	390	1,812	760	1,014
(Less accumulated depreciation and amortization)	(45,359)	(28,081)	(24,029)	(20,903)	(18,237)	(17,132)
Total property, plant, and equipment	53,785	28,535	23,397	19,540	19,331	15,433
Total assets	$114,821	$79,374	$63,907	$54,406	$50,315	$41,987

Liabilities and Stockholders' Equity

Current liabilities

Current portion of long-term debt	$ 5,179	$ 1,949	$ 2,223	$ 1,664	$ 2,154	$ 1,515
Notes payable	1,344	625	1,109	1,738	1,279	740
Accounts payable	15,730	9,275	6,926	6,622	5,268	5,321
Accrued liabilities	10,408	11,983	9,277	9,267	8,868	6,622
Mold billings in excess of cost	2,304	2,022	1,689	N/A	N/A	N/A
Income tax payable	682	896	545	540	268	146
Total current liabilities	35,647	26,750	21,769	19,831	17,837	14,344

Noncurrent liabilities

Long-term debt, less current portion	25,966	9,815	8,033	6,393	9,870	11,354
Deferred gain	N/A	185	303	333	350	400
Deferred taxes	1,165	1,030	1,271	1,119	1,053	508
Minority interests	1,210	1,061	941	884	841	772
Total liabilities	63,988	38,841	32,317	28,560	29,951	27,378

Stockholders' equity

Nonvoting redemption preferred stock, par value $1; authorized 150,000 shares, not all shares issued	130	130	130	115	101	89
Nonvoting convertible preferred stock, par value $1; authorized 50,000 shares, not all shares issued	N/A	N/A	20	20	20	20
Common stock, par value $1; authorized 1,000,000 shares, issued 422,342 shares	422	422	422	422	422	422
Additional paid-in capital	8,290	6,957	7,830	4,755	3,333	2,616
Retained earnings	48,708	37,882	29,626	23,120	17,967	13,029
Treasury stock, at cost	(6,543)	(4,723)	(6,803)	(2,793)	(1,886)	(1,682)
Cumulative translation adjustment	(174)	(135)	365	207	407	115
Total stockholders' equity	50,833	40,533	31,590	25,846	20,364	14,609
Total liabilities and stockholders' equity	$114,821	$79,374	$63,907	$54,406	$50,315	$41,987

Notes:
Other income (expenses) includes other income, interest expense, and interest income.
When using percentages to arrive at 100% you must subtract gross profits, total expenses, and operating profits.

company's global strategy into a country with great market potential and a reservoir of technical and engineering talent. He also enjoyed working with Russian colleagues:

> I am amazed in my dealings with the Russians to find out how much like Americans they are. I have tried to figure out why this is the case. I think it is because they come from a diverse background like we do. They are fun loving. Just good people to be with.
>
> I am very optimistic about the future of Russia and have strong hopes for our venture there. Getting money out is a problem right now, and there really is no solution to that at present. But we are there for the long term, and as a private company, that is a risk I am willing to assume. I guess it is obvious that I am an incurable optimist.

Part of Lankton's optimism stemmed from the effective working relationship he had developed with Levintan in operating the Miro joint venture. In 1991, Lankton expressed his admiration for his colleague:

> He is the driving force of the joint venture. It would not be much of an exaggeration to say that the whole thing would die if he weren't there. He's dynamic and has an ability to develop talented young people who are loyal to him. At our board meetings, which are ten-hour marathons, he keeps everyone's attention. He himself is motivated by the desire to do a good job, to make better products and to sell them abroad. Perks such as a "dacha" (country house) or foreign travel are not his main interest.

WEIGHING THE NYPRO ALTERNATIVE

As he weighed Mikromashina's options, Viktor looked again with mixed emotions at Nypro's proposal. It had only been a few days since he had discussed it with Gordon Lankton during his latest Moscow visit. Lankton had traveled numerous times to Moscow, as he regularly did to all other Nypro locations around the world.

Mikromashina desperately needed the $300,000 which Nypro was ready to invest in the Russian company's operations. In exchange for an additional small payment to the government, Nypro would receive the government's 20% ownership. The government had retained this stake in many privatized firms under the national privatization program, and earmarked it for sale to investors. After that transaction, the Russian government would no longer be a shareholder of Mikromashina. It could always, however, influence company operations through regulations, taxation, and other policies. Viktor realized further that the infusion of capital by Nypro was only one of many benefits that a stronger relationship with the firm could bring to the struggling enterprise.

Despite the apparent advantages from a closer relationship with Nypro, Viktor reflected on his vision for the company to which he had devoted 35 years. Upon becoming acting general manager, he envisioned that Mikromashina would develop during privatization into a successful Russian company known for quality products and respected for providing employment to the many loyal workers who had served the company for so long. He recognized the positive experience he had had working with Lankton in the Miro joint venture, but was reluctant to see substantial ownership of Mikromashina pass to outsiders.

Gordon's proposal to Viktor, under Phase 2 of the Russian government's privatization program, would add to Nypro's current 10% share the 20% presently owned by the Russian government. As noted earlier, this was typical of the percentage the government had retained in most former state-owned enterprises during the first phase of privatization. The transfer would occur once the government had approved Lankton's proposal. Nypro would then invest $300,000 directly in Mikromashina and pay an additional $5,000 to the Russian government. Lankton wanted Viktor's acceptance of the Nypro proposal before submitting it to the Russian government for final approval. Viktor was aware that the American company was also negotiating with other shareholders for an additional 15% ownership, and that Lankton was confident that this purchase could be completed successfully.

The proposal also discussed other objectives for Mikromashina developed during Lankton's latest visit. Lankton's plan called for installing a modern plastic injection molding plant on the first floor of the existing premises, replacing the much less efficient Russian-made machines. The new equipment would consist of modern German-built plastic injection molding machines that were available in Moscow at a very favorable price. These would become the operation's nucleus to produce attractive, quality products and components as a contract injection molder for Russian-located U.S. and European companies. Plans for completing the adjacent, partially constructed joint venture plant had been abandoned for the foreseeable future.

Lankton believed that the key to success would be the ability to produce attractive, high-quality molded products suitable for export as well as domestic Russian consumption. He also believed that Mikromashina would have to continue cutting its workforce to fewer than 100 people in order to become competitive. These combined actions, he believed, would keep Mikromashina alive, or else it was likely to die from lack of funds. In discussing the proposal with the case writers, Lankton explained:

> Viktor is the key player in Mikromashina, and although he is nervous about this, he is a dynamo.

VIKTOR'S DILEMMA

Viktor Levintan looked again at Gordon Lankton's proposal and knew that he would have to respond quickly. The proposal fell short of fulfilling his own objectives for Mikromashina. He stated:

> The company needs new orders, new ideas, and connections with a wider range of foreign companies.

While admitting that he had made some mistakes, Viktor emphasized that he had spent his career mostly as the company's chief engineer, and he had been the acting general manager for only six months. In adjusting to his new responsibilities, Viktor arrived at his office by 8:30 A.M. every day, and left at 6:30 P.M. with his briefcase filled with the evening's work. Much of his time was devoted to evaluating "opportunities" from foreign business people who regularly visited Mikromashina, and devising short-term tactics to keep the company alive.

With less than three years until his planned retirement, Viktor sometimes wondered why he had undertaken this heavy responsibility. He had hoped to be able to help Mikromashina, and especially the loyal employees who had served the company so well. His relationships with long-time suppliers and customers also weighed heavily in his decision. Yet he realized that many employees had left or been laid off, and that relationships with suppliers and customers had changed drastically over the past year.

In addition to the long-term employees, customers, and suppliers, there was the board of directors to consider, especially the "young boys" who could cause problems unless they saw benefits for themselves. And the government might respond negatively if Mikromashina did not accept Nypro's offer. Because such an action would undermine the important government objective of capital infusion into privatized companies, the government might withhold additional subsidies from Mikromashina in retaliation.

If he were to accept Nypro's offer, Viktor had to decide how to structure the terms of his acceptance to best satisfy stakeholders and others involved in the decision. As he weighed the alternatives and reflected on how various stakeholders could be affected, Viktor summed up his feelings:

> I belong to Mikromashina. For 35 years I have contributed a lot here and I don't want to see Mikromashina destroyed. I will do anything I can to help.

A First-Time Expatriate's Experience in a Joint Venture in China

John Stanbury

THE LONG TRIP HOME

James Randolf was traveling back to his home state of Illinois from his assignment in China for the last time. He and his wife were about three hours into the long flight when she fell asleep, her head propped up by the airline pillow against the cabin wall. James was exhausted, but for the first time in many days he had the luxury of reflecting on what had just happened in their lives.

He was neither angry nor bitter, but the disruption of the last few weeks was certainly unanticipated and in many ways unfortunate. He had fully expected to complete his three-year assignment as the highest ranking U.S. manager of his company's joint venture (JV) near Shanghai. Now, after only 13 months, the assignment was over and a manager from the regional office in Singapore held the post. Sure, the JV will survive, he thought, but how far had the relationship that he had been nurturing between the two partnered companies been set back? His Chinese partners were perplexed by his company's actions and visibly affected by the departure of their friend and colleague.

Was this an error in judgment resulting from the relative inexperience of his company, Controls, Inc., as a multinational company and a partner in international joint ventures, James wondered? Or, had something else caused the shift in policy that resulted in the earlier-than-planned recall of several of the corporation's expatriates from their assignments? There had always been plans to reduce the number of expatriates at any particular location over time, but recently the carefully planned timetables seemed to have been abandoned.

Next week, James had to turn in his report covering the entire work assignment. How frank should he be? What detail should he include in his report? To whom should he send copies? There had been rumors that many senior managers were being asked to take early retirement. James did not really want to retire but could hardly contain his dissatisfaction as to how things had turned out. Maybe it would be better to take the offer, if it was forthcoming, and try to find some consulting that would make the best use of his wide spectrum of technical and managerial experience, which now included an expatriate assignment in what was considered to be one of the most difficult locations in the world.

James reflected with satisfaction on his accomplishment of the initial primary objectives, which were to establish a manufacturing and marketing presence. In fact, he was quite pleased with his success at putting in place many things that would allow the operation to prosper. The various departments within the joint venture were now cooperating and coordinating, and the relationships he had established were truly the evidence

This case was prepared by Professor John Stanbury at Indiana University at Kokomo with assistance from Rina Dangarwala and John King, MBA students. The names of the organization and the industry in which it operates, and the individuals' names and events in this case have been disguised to preserve anonymity. Presented to and accepted by the Society for Case Research. All rights reserved to the author and SCR. Copyright © 1997 by John Stanbury. This case was edited for SMBP–7th Edition. Reprinted by permission.

of this achievement. He would like to have seen the operations become more efficient, however.

The worklife that awaited him on his return was a matter of considerable concern. Reports from the expatriates who preceded him in the last few months indicated that there were no established plans to use their talents, and often early retirement was strongly encouraged by management. Beyond the obligatory physical examinations and debriefings, he had been told there was little for them to do. Many of the recalled expatriates found themselves occupying desks in Personnel waiting for responses about potential job opportunities.

He gazed at his wife, Lily, now settled into comfortable slumber. At least she had had a pretty good experience. She was born in Shanghai, but left China in 1949. The country was then in the middle of a revolution but, aside from her memory of her parents appearing extremely anxious to leave, she remembered little else about the issues surrounding their emigration to the United States. Most of her perceptions about "what it was like" in China came from U.S. television coverage, some fact, some fiction.

As the plane droned on into the night, James thought back to how this experience began.

THE COMPANY

The world headquarters of Controls, Inc. were in Chicago, Illinois. It had operations in several countries in Europe, Asia, and South America but, with the exception of several maquiladoras, all of its expansion had occurred very recently. Its first involvement in joint ventures began only three years earlier. As an in-house supplier to Filtration Inc., a huge Chicago-based international manufacturing conglomerate specializing in the design and production of temperature control and filtration systems, it had been shielded from significant competition, and most of its product lines of various electronic control mechanisms had been produced in North America. Ten years earlier, when Controls had become a subsidiary of Filtration Inc., it was given a charter to pursue business beyond that transacted with its parent. At the same time, the rules for acquiring in-house business changed as well. Controls now bid for Filtration Inc.'s business against many of the world's best producers of this equipment. The need to use cheaper labor and to be located closer to key prospective customers drove the company (Controls) to expand internationally at a rate that only a few years earlier would have been completely outside its corporate comfort zone.

A JV in China would provide Controls with an opportunity to gain a foothold in this untapped market for temperature control systems. This could pave the way for a greater thrust into the expanding Chinese economy. If the JV were successful, it could also lead to the establishment of plants to manufacture various products for the entire Asia/Pacific market.

Controls' involvement in the joint venture seemed less planned than its other expansion efforts. The Freezer and Cooler Controls Business Unit (one of Controls' key business units), headquartered in Lakeland, Minnesota, sent a team of four, consisting of two engineers and two representatives from the Finance and Business Planning Departments to investigate the possibility of partnering with a yet-to-be-identified Chinese electronics assembly operation. The team was not given an adequate budget and was limited to a visit of one month. Not being experienced international negotiators, they were only able to identify one potential partner, a Chinese state-owned firm. They quickly realized that they did not have time to conclude negotiations and returned to HQ without having met their objective. After debriefing them on their return to the United States, Controls' planners decided that the Chinese JV presented a good opportunity and sent another team to continue these negotiations. Eventually an agreement was reached with the Chinese state-owned firm. Exhibit 1 shows the organizational relationships between Filtration Inc. and its subsidiaries.

HOW IT ALL BEGAN

James Randolf had always been intrigued by the idea of securing an international assignment. His interest heightened on the day that Controls Inc. announced its intentions to expand the business through establishing a more international presence worldwide. By age 51, James had worked in managerial positions in Engineering, Quality, Customer Support, and Program Management for the last 15 of his 23 years with the company, but always in positions geographically based in Pauley, Illinois. He frequently mentioned the idea of working on an international assignment to his superiors during performance reviews and in a variety of other settings. He did not mentally target any specific country, but preferred an assignment in the Pacific Rim, due to his life-long desire to gain an even deeper understanding of his wife's cultural heritage.

Finally, two years ago, he was able to discuss his interests with the corporation's International Human Resources Manager. During this interview, he was told of the hardships of functioning as an expatriate. There could be a language problem as well as difficulties caused by the remoteness from home office. James remained interested.

A year later, James was first considered for a position that required venture development in Tokyo. At one point he was even told he had been chosen for that position. With little explanation, the company instead announced the selection of a younger, more "politically" connected "fast tracker."

When, a few months later, a discussion about the position in China was first broached by personnel, it was almost in the context of it being a consolation prize. The position, however, appeared to be one for which James was even better suited and one that would be challenging enough to "test the metal" of any manager in the company. The assignment was to "manage a joint venture manufacturing facility" located on Chongming Dao Island, about 25 miles north of Shanghai. The strategic objective of the JV was market entry into China.

Soon thereafter, in mid August 1992, James was asked to go immediately to Lakeland to meet one on one with Joe Whistler, the Director of the Freezer and Cooler Controls Business Unit, to discuss the JV. The negotiating team was still in China in the process of "finalizing" the JV agreement with the Chongming Electro-Assembly Company, a state-owned electronic device assembly operation. The corporation felt that there was a dire need to put someone on site. Joe asked if he could leave next week! James indicated that he was interested in accepting the position and that he was willing to do whatever the corporation required of him to make it happen as soon as possible. It was understood that a formal offer for the position would be processed through Personnel and communicated through James's management. When this trip didn't materialize, James wondered if this was going to be a repeat of the Tokyo assignment. Finally, in late September, James's supervisor approached him and said "If you still want it, you've got the prize."

Exhibit 1   Organization Chart: Filtration Inc.

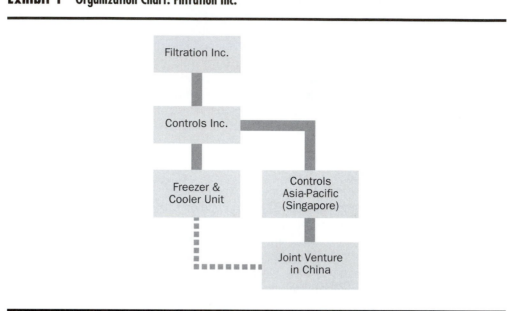

ORIENTATION

Controls' parent company, Filtration Inc., had a defined set of procedures to deal with expatriate work assignment orientation. When it was determined that James was a strong candidate to go overseas, it was arranged for James and his wife to go to Chicago for orientation training. The training began with a day-long session conducted by Filtration Inc.'s International Personnel function. James thought the training was exceptionally well done. Filtration Inc. brought in experts to discuss pay, benefits, moving arrangements, and a multitude of other issues dealing with working for the corporation in an international assignment. Part of the orientation process was a "look-see trip," the normal length of which was seven days. The trip was quickly arranged to begin two weeks later. The Randolfs were extremely excited. This would be Lily's first trip back to China. They even extended the duration of the trip to 10 days to do some investigation on their own time.

There was a considerable mix up in the planning of the "look-see" trip. Although Controls' Personnel Department in Pauley wanted to arrange the entire trip, Controls' Asia-Pacific regional office in Singapore insisted it was better for them to handle it locally. The Randolfs were supposed to have a rental car available upon arrival, but discovered that no arrangements had been made and they were forced to secure their own car. Their itinerary indicated that they had reservations at the Shanghai Inn, but they soon discovered that no reservations had been made there, either.

In Shanghai they went sightseeing on their own for three days. Afterwards, they were scheduled for seven days of official activities. They spent the following two days with an on-site consultant, who was on retainer from the JV and who showed the potential expatriates around the city. Her tour consisted of what she perceived a typical American might most like to see.

The wife of an expatriate herself, the consultant didn't speak Shanghainese or any other Chinese dialects. Travel with her was somewhat of a nightmare. As opposed to discussing the planned locations with the Chinese driver at the beginning of a day, she directed the trip one step at a time. She would show the driver a card on which was written the address of the next location and say "go here now." This approach caused considerable delays due to the inefficiencies of transversing the city numerous times and touring in a disorderly sequence. They were shown American-style shopping, American-style restaurants, and potential living accommodations. The Randolfs were told that leasing a good apartment commonly required a "kickback."

After visiting the JV's factory near Shanghai, they traveled to the regional headquarters, Controls Asia-Pacific, in Singapore to participate in an extensive orientation workshop. Again the topics included compensation policies and other matters of interest to potential expatriates, this time from the perspective of Controls Inc. James and Lily both noted a significant contrast in dealings with the regional Controls Inc. personnel staff as opposed to the "first rate" Filtration Inc. International Human Resources people. The former was by far a less polished and informed operation. Even as they departed Singapore for the United States, they were still unsure that the move was right for them. They spent the next several days reflecting on the trip and discussing their decision. They were discouraged by the lack of maintenance apparent in the factory, which was clearly inferior to U.S. standards. Things were dirty, and little effort was expended on environmental controls. The days seemed awfully gray. However, they had quickly become enamored with the Shanghai people, and this became a key factor in their ultimate decision to accept the position. As the result of their interactions with the Chinese partners and Shanghai area residents, James and Lily truly felt the promise of exciting, new, deep, long-lasting relationships.

Once they were firmly committed to the assignment, they attended a two-day orientation on living and working in China. This was provided by Prudential Relocation Services Inc. in Boulder, Colorado, and was tailored to the needs and desires of the participants. Optional curriculum tracks included the history, culture, political climate, business climate, and the people of the region. James focused his training on a business-related curriculum, which was taught by professors from a local university. Additionally, whenever an expatriate returned from China to the home office on home leave, James was given an opportunity to interface with him.

Between November (1992) and January (1993), James worked an exhausting schedule, alternating two-week periods in Pauley and at the JV in China, where lodging and meals were provided in a hotel. During this time, his wife, Lily, remained in Lakewood preparing for their permanent relocation to China. Also, Filtration Inc. held scheduled, intensive Mandarin language courses in Chicago, which James planned to attend, but due to his work schedule he was unable to take advantage of the opportunity. Finally, in January, James attended the language school for a week. Fortunately, he and Lily already spoke some Cantonese, another Chinese dialect. After James was finally on-site full time in February, he hired a language tutor to supplement this training. The orientation procedure concluded with a checklist of things that James and Controls were to accomplish after the commencement of his on-site assignment. Although all of these checklist items were eventually accomplished, priorities on the job didn't allow them to be completed in a very timely manner.

WORKPLACE ORIENTATIONS

Mandarin, China's official language, was spoken at the factory. In regions where Mandarin was not the primary language of the people, it was the language most commonly used in industry and trade and in dealing with the government. Most residents were proficient in Mandarin, although the oldest members of the population had learned it only after they had completed their formal education, if at all. Mandarin became China's official language when the alphabet was standardized in 1955. Away from the workplace, people preferred to speak Shanghainese or Chongming Dao's own similar dialect.

Chongming Dao, the actual site of the factory, was situated in the Chuang Yangtze river. At approximately 50 miles long and 18 miles wide, it is China's third largest island. Its population is approximately one million people. The residents were perceived by the Shanghainese to be poor, backward farmers.

James found that he was able to maintain residencies in Shanghai and in Chongming Dao, although all the Chinese workers, including managers, lived close to their place of work. The trip from downtown Shanghai to the plant took more than two hours. First there was an hour and a half trip to the site of the ferry departure, then came a 20-minute ferry ride, followed by another 20 minutes of travel by car. Work days at the factory were scheduled from Tuesdays through Saturdays. As is common in China, the schedules were centrally planned to alternate with those of other factories in a manner that conserved power consumption.

The Chinese partner had warehouses and a business center on the island, which, in addition to the factory, became part of the JV. The people worked under conditions that would be totally unacceptable to most American workers. There were no temperature or humidity controls. In the winter, the plant was so cold that workers wore up to six layers of clothing. In contrast, summers were very hot and humid. None of the machinery had safety guards. Tools were generally either nonexistent or inadequate. Lighting was also very poor.

The Chinese factory's workforce was primarily young women. This was in contrast to the Chinese partner's factories that James had visited, where most of the workers were men who appeared to be over the age of 40. The plant's organization and operation fostered considerable inefficiencies. There were no process controls to prevent errors and scrap. The only visible methods of quality control were extensive amounts of 100% testing and inspection performed after the product was completely assembled. The layout of the plant was awkward. There were numerous little rooms and no large expansive production areas. Operations were not laid out sequentially or even in a line. The typical mode of operation was to have numerous workers working elbow to elbow around the perimeter of a large table.

Material movement was most commonly performed by dragging large tubs of materials across the floor. Storage was disorderly and bins were generally not stacked, due to a lack of shelving. Consequently, containers of parts, partially assembled products, scrap materials, and finished assemblies could be found anywhere and everywhere. Instead of scheduling plant output, the system scheduled only the number of man-hours to be expended. This lack of direction caused a considerable amount of confusion and inefficiency. It was really more of a way of accounting for the use of the excessive labor force that existed in the factory and in the area. James often commented that he could produce as much or more output with only the number of Quality Control (QC) operators that were in the plant. By his estimates, the JV employed three times as many people as were needed. James did not think that he could change this immediately, but he felt that he could convince the Chinese management that this practice need to be changed eventually.

ADAPTING TO LIFE IN CHINA

Beyond some terrific people in Controls' Personnel Department in Pauley, who could help with specific employment-related issues, James quickly came to realize that there would be little operational support from the home office. His links back to his corporation came more from Filtration Inc. than from Controls. Filtration Inc. at least sent a monthly package of news clippings, executive briefs, and memos that had been specifically prepared for expatriates. The package allowed James to keep up somewhat on what was happening in the larger corporate setting.

Filtration Inc. had a couple dozen employees in Shanghai. It was their role to establish and implement a joint venture that the parent had negotiated with a different Chinese manufacturer than the one with which Controls had partnered. As part of this team, there were also a few representatives from Controls Inc. They were all co-located in a small office building in downtown Shanghai. It was in this corporate office environment that James found a great deal of support, a lot of helpful advice, and his unofficial mentor, a Filtration Inc. manager who had spent four years in China. At the time James wondered why he hadn't visited this office during his orientation trip.

The help that James received from Controls Inc.'s subsidiary, Controls Asia-Pacific, was often ineffective and inconsistent. Nagging policies and obligatory paperwork were typical characteristics of their assistance. There were ongoing problems finding and retaining a qualified translator for James. In the agreement, the JV was responsible for providing each expatriate with a translator. Controls-Asia/Pacific was responsible for the wage structure at the JV. The Personnel Department in Singapore established a maximum wage rate for the translator position at 2000 yuan. This rate was fair for the area, but few high-quality translators were available. When an area translator was identified, he or she would often be lost to another multinational company in the area who offered a salary of 3000 yuan. To attract translators from Shanghai would require a wage comparable to the wages one would receive in Shanghai, and 2000 yuan was significantly lower than that paid in the city.

Another aspect of employment in China that merited consideration was the movement of one's "personnel file" from a former employer to the present one. This is the rough equivalent of changing one's residency to another state in the United States. The reputation and perception of Chongming Dao was that of a rural community. This would have a negative impact on transferring a translator's file back to Shanghai in the future. Singapore didn't understand the economics and implications of this situation and refused to increase the wage rate to a level that would entice qualified translators to accept the position. James, as a result, was without a qualified translator for significant periods during his time in China. The impact on his ability to function in that setting was therefore also significant, resulting in less being accomplished than if Singapore had been more flexible.

The residence in Shanghai was available because the JV had committed to a two-year lease of an executive apartment on the twenty-second floor of the Shanghai Inn. These accommodations were quite nice and offered most of the comforts of home. The hotel complex included a supermarket, exercise facilities, a theater, and several restaurants, including Shanghai's Hard Rock Cafe. The three-bedroom apartment, which James measured to be around 1,500 square feet, was converted into a two-bedroom apartment to his specifications. Amenities included cable TV with five English-language channels. Accommodations on the island were significantly rougher. The original plan was for James to temporarily stay at the government's guest house on the factory grounds until a 12-unit housing compound was constructed in the immediate vicinity. The small rooms, intense heat, and fierce mosquitoes at the guest house proved to be unbearable, and by June, James decided to make other arrangements. These entailed staying in a hotel 17 miles away with the two other expatriates from Controls Inc. to manage the JV. Although the building was new, the quality of the construction was quite poor, which seemed to be common in China. The costs associated with constructing their compound were, by this time, estimated to be much larger than expected. Eventually a solution was reached to fix up certain aspects of the guest house and retain it as the long-term island living arrangements for them. After this, Lily always traveled with him to and from the factory.

ADAPTING TO THE WORK

In addition to James, three other Controls Inc. expatriates were assigned to the JV. The Director of Engineering and the Director of Manufacturing were on assignment from the United States. The Director of Finance was from Singapore. Each of these individuals had dual roles, that of heading up their respective departments and the assignment to bring to the JV new technology associated with their departments. The Finance Director had the particularly challenging assignment of introducing a new accounting system to the JV, one that was compatible with the Controls Inc. system. The existing system, installed by the Chinese partner, was not designed to report profits and losses, irrelevant concepts in the formerly state-owned company.

The other expatriates occasionally complained of not getting good cooperation from the Chinese workers. James never encountered this problem because he always communicated his requests directly to the workers.

One of the first problems that evolved related to differences between expatriate conditions of employment for Filtration Inc. and Controls Inc. employees. Most Filtration employees enjoyed a per diem of US$95, but Controls employees were limited to US$50 per day. Additionally, the Filtration Inc.'s visitation policies were more liberal in terms of allowing college-age children to visit their expatriate parents.

ONGOING NEGOTIATIONS

In China, a JV contract was "nice framework" from which to begin the real negotiation process. The Controls JV negotiating team viewed the contract as a conclusion to negotiations and returned to the United States in late December 1992. James soon discovered that the process of negotiations would be ongoing. On almost a daily basis, some element of the agreement was adjusted or augmented with new understanding.

A misconception held by the Controls negotiating team related to the ease of obtaining appropriate governmental approvals. Various annexes and subcontracts were yet to be finalized and approved when they departed. Some of these approvals were required from government officials with whom they had had very little interface. The impact of this miscalculation was that production in the JV didn't commence on January 1, 1993, as anticipated. Instead it took until August 1, 1993, to get the operation going.

One of the most serious issues affecting the operation of the JV that directly impacted James's effectiveness was the JV's organization structure, which was negotiated by the Controls' team. The organization chart for the JV is shown in Exhibit 2. Controls perceived the position of Chairman of the Board (COB) of Directors to be of greater importance in operating the company than that of Managing Director, thinking that they could "run the company" from that position. Consequently, when the organization chart was drawn up, Controls conceded the position of Managing Director to the Chinese partner in exchange for the right to appoint the COB for the first three of the five years. James noted that in Chinese JVs negotiated by Filtration Inc., the U.S. partner always secured the position of Managing Director.

Exhibit 2 Organization Chart: Controls-Shanghai

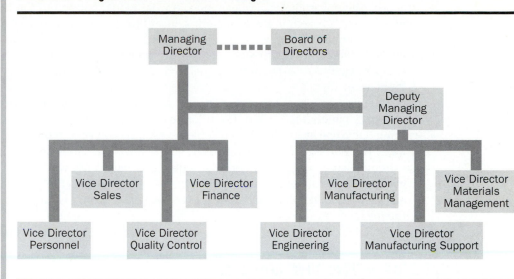

OBSERVATIONS OF CHINESE MANAGEMENT METHODS

James observed that when Chinese managers were dealing with subordinates, decision making was very top-down. Thus the Managing Director made virtually all decisions of any consequence. James was extremely fortunate that the Managing Director appointed by the Chinese partner was willing to share his power. He and the Managing Director developed an excellent relationship, which James consciously worked on in the firm belief that this was the key to business success in China. Toward the end of his time at the JV, James was frequently being left in charge of running the factory while the Managing Director was visiting outside friends of influence, customers, and potential customers. The only other manager that shared this distinction was the Director of Personnel.

The Personnel Department in this JV, as in the state-owned Chinese companies, was unusually powerful when compared to most U.S. companies with which James was familiar. It maintained the all-important employment files and was very connected to the Communist Party.

OBSERVATIONS OF CHINESE MANAGEMENT TEAM

Chinese managers at the JV were considerably more educated than the workers. They had matriculated at various universities and graduated with degrees in Engineering, Management, and the like. In one case, the manager's experience and education came from his time as a career-soldier in the Army.

INTERACTIONS WITH THE CHINESE GOVERNMENT

Prior to the formation of the JV, the Secretary for the Communist Party and the Managing Director were co-equals when it came to "running the Chongming Electro Assembly company." About 325 of the 1819 employees at the JV were Communists. After James's arrival, there was always a question as to what would happen to the Party office, which was located adjacent to the Managing Director's office. In many ways, the Party served a function similar to that of labor unions in the United States. They represented the workers and entered into discussions concerning labor relations issues. The Communist Party could be viewed as a different channel to deal with issues, and James quickly recognized them as an ally.

James's only personal experience with a government bureau was while getting his residency papers established. The rules he encountered were extremely inflexible, everything had to be just right, and no copies were allowed because the Bureau required originals. The Bureau office, which was the size of a walk-in closet in the United States, was extremely crowded, and the process required forcing one's way up through the lines to get to the table where female police officers would process the paperwork. After it was all over, he noticed that they had spelled his name wrong. He did not return to correct the mistake.

INTERACTIONS WITH THE UNION

The JV also had a labor union, but by comparison to the United States, the organization was extremely weak and superficial. James's only dealings with the union related to a request for donations for a retirees' party the union wanted to hold. Since the JV had no retirees and this was new ground for him, he referred them to the Managing Director.

GETTING IT TOGETHER

James loved to walk the floor and see what was happening in the factory. His position gave him the authority to direct actions to be taken, but often he did not have to use this authority in that way. The Chinese workers seemed to be influenced by his every action. If he would make a point to pick up trash in the parking lot, the next day he would observe that the trash had all been cleaned up. Another example was when he straightened some papers in the pigeon holes of a filing system. The next day every stack of papers was perfectly arranged. He felt that there had never been a time when he had walked the floor and it hadn't paid off in some way. He found Chinese workers to be very attentive to detail.

He was often tested by the Chinese managers and workers alike, as is not uncommon in other parts of the world. He perceived that they would test his commitment, leadership, and decision-making ability. They would determine how far this manager could be pushed. These tests provided him with the opportunity to do the right thing. A case in point was when a drunken salesperson accosted a woman in a nightclub. James took him to a private place and severely chastised him.

During his assignment, he remained cognizant of the fact that one of his jobs was to make the Managing Director look good. This required him to fire a translator on the spot when the translator remarked that anyone who wanted to stay in China was stupid.

He had great admiration for the Chinese workers at the JV. They proved to be very cooperative people. They had a great deal of pride and were very loyal to their company and the industry in which they worked. James often commented that, with informed leadership, Chinese workers would be as good as workers anywhere in the world.

What James liked best, however, was his interactions with the Chinese people. Every day brought him a new experience.

OBSERVATIONS ABOUT THE CHINESE PEOPLE

Most of the Chinese people were not Communists. They would rather ignore the political situations going on around them and get on with their lives. They were eager to learn anything they could about what Westerners could teach them. Almost without exception, they looked up to Americans and would begin to imitate them after a while. James found it very gratifying. He was also delighted with their treatment of his wife Lily, which appeared to border on reverence. James wondered about the reasons for this. Perhaps it had something to do with the fact that she, through her parents, had previously escaped Communist oppression and found a better life, which symbolized to the Chinese that there was hope for all.

James never saw a Chinese man leering at a woman, as is common in the United States. In China, sexuality was a private matter. They tended to live a simpler life than do most Westerners. Their children were treated with reverence, even doted over. Their chaotic traffic jams seemed always to be dealt with very calmly. James never observed swearing or anger, as is common in the United States. James also found that the Chinese have an attitude that they know more than Westerners do, but that this never manifested itself a boastful way. The attitude was more that at some point in time, Westerners would come around to their way of thinking. It was almost as though they played the role of a wiser urban patriarch guiding his young country cousin during the latter's first visit to the city. See Exhibit 3 for more information on Chinese culture and management.

ACTIVITIES AWAY FROM THE JOB

James and Lily had a different social life than that enjoyed in the United States. They spent hours walking and talking. Occasionally, when they were in Shanghai, they had the opportunity to see shows. They saw the acrobats, went to symphony concerts and ballet, and even joined the crowds when Foster Beer brought Australian bands to perform in a Shanghai park.

The concerns Lily had expressed prior to expatriating disappeared as she made friends and became integrated into the social fabric of the area. Because her appearance was indistinguishable from the indigenous Shanghai-area people, she was more readily accepted and learned more about local happenings than most Westerners. At one point, two months after their arrival, Lily was hospitalized with a lung infection. Even this was resolved satisfactorily. She particularly noted that the skill level of the medical practitioners seemed to be very good, from the diagnosis to the way they painlessly took blood samples. Overall she found it easy to occupy her time. She was a traditional wife, who had not worked full-time since her children were born and never had difficulty occupying the time in her life because she was a woman who was compelled to learn about everything and everybody. She spent much of her time traveling with James to and from the site. When he was working, she sought out the people and assisted at a mission nearby because she had some experience in nursing, having earned her RN before marrying James.

The Randolfs preferred to eat food with fresh ingredients, and were happy away

Exhibit 3 **Key Characteristics of Chinese Culture and Management**

Culture

One of the strong cultural beliefs among the Chinese is that their culture is the oldest and the best. It is the center of the universe, the Zhong guo—center country. They believe themselves to be totally self-sufficient. In Chinese, the character of the word "China" means "middle kingdom," thus implying that everyone other than themselves is beneath them.

Concept of Face and Time

The concept of face is of paramount importance in China. It is a person's most precious possession. Without it, one cannot function in China. It is earned by fulfilling one's duties and other obligations. Face often requires little effort, but merely an attention to courtesy in relationships with others. Face involves a high degree of self-control, social consciousness, and concern for others. In Chinese society, a display of temper, sulking, loss of self-control, or frustration creates further loss of face rather than drawing respect.

Despite having invented the clock, the Chinese never define or segment time in the way that it is approached in the West. Even today, for Chinese, time simply flows from one day to another. If a job is not completed today, they will carry it forward to the next day or the day after next. This is a manifestation of the concept of polychronic (nonlinear) time. In Western cultures, people see time as monochronic (linear).

An important cultural difference between the West and China is the Chinese custom of giving precedence to form and process in completing a task, over the task itself, an approach that is typically more time consuming.

Behavior

Chinese behavior is influenced by their brutal history. This has created a careful people. They give consideration to the repercussions of every move or decision that they make.

An important aspect of behavior involves the way the Chinese think. They think about thinking and relationships, whereas the Westerner thinks in linear patterns of cause and effects.

Another aspect that confuses the Westerner is the Chinese willingness to discuss endless possibilities even when things look hopeless.

A Chinese philosophy that relates to interacting with Westerners can be stated: Whereas a Westerner will try to tell you everything he knows in a conversation, a Chinese will listen to learn everything the Westerner knows, so that, at the end of the day, he would know both what he knew and what the Westerner knew.

Gift Giving

Chinese are conditioned to express appreciation in tangible ways, such as by giving gifts and other favors. They regard the Westerner's frequent use of "thank you" as a glib and insincere way of passing off obligations to return favors. When they do someone a favor, they expect appreciation to be expressed in some very concrete way. If all you choose to do is say "Thanks," it should be very specific and sincere, and then stop. The Chinese do not like gushy thanks. Gift giving in China is a highly developed art. Although it has greatly diminished today (there is a law forbidding government officials from accepting gifts of any kind or value), the practice remains a vital aspect of creating and nurturing relationships with people.

Living as a Foreign Guest in the People's Republic of China

Foreigners who have gone to the People's Republic of China in the last decade to help the Chinese have been given preferential treatment. Their quarters are often far more modern than those of a typical native Chinese. The expatriate is given perquisites in excess of those available to all but the top officials, fed with highest quality food, and paid salaries that are many times higher than their Chinese counterpart of the same status. They are sheltered from the harsh realities of the Chinese life and are recipients of enormous courtesy and care.

There are three main reasons for this preferential treatment. First, as a poverty stricken nation, the Chinese need to attract and retain foreigners to help them achieve a higher standard of living, by increasing their economic and technical level. Second, the Chinese believe that people from the developed nations are so used to modern comforts that they would not be able to function competently without them. Finally, there is simple pride. They want their country to be thought of favorably.

Social

Generally the sociocultural behavior of the Chinese differs greatly from that of Western societies. Family is very important to them, and obligation to them takes precedence when it conflicts with work responsibilities. Those outside the family are treated with indifference and sometimes with contempt. Decision making evolves from the opinion and support of the family. The highest respect is given to elders and ancestors. The reverence for authority and order explains why the Chinese are so careful about getting consensus from everyone. An important ideal that is fostered by the family is harmony.

The Chinese do not believe in the concept of privacy. This absence of individuality and freedom is a way of life in China.

Exhibit 3   *(continued)*

Laws Made to Be Broken

Due to their history of being encumbered by rules and taboos, the Chinese have developed a perverse and seemingly contradictory attitude toward laws and regulations. They tend to ignore them and break them to suit their purpose, as long as they think they can get away with it. A significant proportion of public Chinese behavior is based on political expediency and not on their true feelings. Since their public, official behavior is more of a survival technique than anything else, they do not feel guilty about ignoring or subverting the system. It is something they do naturally as a way of getting by.

Importance of Human Resources Management in Organizations in China

The labor environment in China is influenced by six major factors. They are National Economic Plans, the Four Modernization Programs, Political Leadership, Chinese Cultural Values, Labor Unions, and the Special Economic Zones (SEZs). The SEZs were created specially for the conduct of the joint ventures with overseas countries. The main characteristics of the SEZs that are found in a joint venture are their dominating influence on matters pertaining to the employment wage system, organizational structure, management roles, and decision making.

One of the most interesting aspects of Chinese human resource management is the unmistakable influence of some of the traditional cultural values such as guanxi (relationship), renqing (favor), mianzi (face), and bao (reciprocation) in recruitment and selection, training and development, and placement and promotion.

A definite political element is involved in the behavior of Chinese Personnel managers; those who are more party oriented base their decisions on party policies rather than on what is for the good of the company.

Maintaining Personnel Files and Their Implications

Chinese-style personnel management generally does not forgive or forget any real or imagined past transgressions by employees under their jurisdiction. Any past mistakes or offenses committed by the employee are duly recorded in the employee's file and are often used against that person.

To hire someone from another company, the other company must release the prospective employee's file. This contains the employee's work record and entitles him or her to benefits accorded to workers in the state sector. If the employer is not willing to release the file and the employee leaves, he or she loses the benefits, a risk few Chinese are willing to take. Many foreign companies have been able to complete transfers only after compensating the other company. The average payoff has been c1000 yuan (in 1992), a very modest amount in $US but one-half of one month's salary for a translator.

The Chinese can be said to be ethnocentric when it comes to their perception of people from other provinces. This can carry over into the review and acceptance of an employee's file from another province. The employee's previous place of employment can impact his future job prospects. In this case, the Shanghainese would look with disfavor on an employee file (and therefore the individual) from the poorer, less sophisticated Chongming Dao area.

A related cultural difference is that a foreign manager would examine an employee's file from the perspective of performance, whereas a Chinese manager would review the file to learn of an individual's seniority and to see if there is a history of causing dissention.

Rank

There are no official class distinctions in China, but rank among businesspeople and government bureaucrats is very important. It is very important that you know the rank of the individual you are likely to deal with and your response should be consistent with the rank. Connections and rank gain one access to the *te-quan,* or special privileges. If the top official is accompanied by the second in rank, all the discussion should be directed toward the top official and the second in rank might as well not be present.

Manufacturing and Quality Control in China

In general, the Chinese have only a rudimentary understanding of quality concepts. They almost always carry out 100% inspections to "control" quality. Because the Chinese have become accustomed to inferior quality goods, workers often do not perceive producing goods of high quality to be important. Items that do not pass quality control are offered to the employees free of charge.

The quality of technology used in China varies greatly. For the most part, the technological level resembles that of the United States in the 1950s. Computerization is scant. Materials handling is done manually. Machinery is bulky and frequently needs repair.

Scheduling of work is almost nonexistent, though work itself is assigned to groups. A typical manufacturing operation is very labor intensive, and in most cases, the workforce is excessively large. Production planning is usually based on the number of hours to be worked rather than on the number of units to be manufactured.

Infrastructure

China's economy suffers from a weak infrastructure. Electricity is unavailable at times (especially if the firm has exceeded its quota). Roads need repairs, train shipments are more often than not late, factory allocations of raw materials are (occasionally) routed to other units, and the communication systems can be considered a nightmare.

Exhibit 3 *(continued)*

Additional Note

Neither Geert Hofstede's original study (Hofstede 1980), nor his later work (Hofstede and Bond 1988) included China as a country of analysis. However, Hong Kong and Taiwan were included in both instances. The results were similar for Power Distance (Large), Individualism (Low), Uncertainty Avoidance (Low), and Confucianism (High), differing only in Masculinity (Hong Kong, high, and Taiwan, low). We would therefore expect top down decision making, centralized authority, little participative management, tolerance of uncertainty, and authority vested only in the most senior employees. This confirms the events described in the case.

from the "supermarket" society, so Lily also spent a lot of time shopping. They felt that they were able to eat quite well in China.

James and Lily learned as much of the local Shanghai dialect as they could. In spite of never becoming fully proficient, the fact that they attempted to speak it greatly pleased the local residents. They spent much of their spare time interacting with the people of the area.

Sometimes Filtration Inc. would put on a social affair for the expatriates in Shanghai. James and Lily were always invited. While on the island, however, they always ate at the restaurant in the factory. Contrary to what they were told at their orientation training, they found the Chinese to be gregarious and fun loving during meals. Meals were used as an opportunity to build relationships and share experiences.

JAMES'S RECALL AND DEPARTURE

Then one day, early in February 1994, James received the call from Singapore, which proved to be the most disappointing news he had heard during his entire China experience. Controls had chosen to recall him back to home office. He was directed to train his replacement and return home within the month.

Things had been going very well for several months now, and he was accomplishing a great many things. There was still so much he planned to do, including convince the Chinese JV partner that they needed to reduce significantly the number of workers.

Although he and Lily handled the news and the return arrangements with a great dignity, there was a great sense of disbelief and sadness associated with the recall. Jimmy Chao, his replacement, arrived two weeks later. Jimmy was a Singaporean engineer whose experience was limited to supervising production at one of Controls' factories in that country. James spent as much time getting him up to speed as was possible. Jimmy was 18 years younger than James, quite cocky, very opinionated, and aggressive. Although James provided all the coaching that he could, Jimmy was bound to do things his way.

The scene at the ferry when they departed the island for the last time was incredible. Many of the workers and all of the managers supplied by the Chinese partner were there to see them off. Many tokens of appreciation and affection were exchanged.

The plane droned inexorably on. James had, by this point in the trip, "rerun the tapes" of his whole experience over and over in his mind, and again he thought about how blessed he felt to have had the experience at all. What recommendations should I make in my report and during my debriefings? If I really think they are heading for the "ditch," it is my responsibility to steer them away from it. Oh well, these questions will have to wait until another day. It is time to get some sleep. I wonder what the temperature is in Pauley?

References

Steven R. Hendryx, "The China Trade: Making the Deal Work," *Harvard Business Review* (July–August, 1986), pp. 75–84.

————, and Michael H. Bond, "The Confucius Connection: From Cultural Roots to Economic Growth," *Organizational Dynamics* (Spring 1988), pp. 5–21.

Wenzhong Hu, and Cornelius Grove, *Encountering the Chinese: A Guide for the Americans,* Intercultural Press Inc. Yarmouth, ME, 1993.

Geert Hofstede, *Cultures' Consequences: International Differences in Work Related Values,* Sage Publications, Beverly Hills, CA, 1980.

Saha Sudhir Kumar, "Managing Human Resources in China," *Canadian Journal of Administrative Science* (Summer 1991), pp. 167–177.

Roderick Macleod, *How to Do Business with the Chinese,* Bantam Books, New York, 1988.

James J. Wall, Jr., "Managers in the People's Republic of China," *Academy of Management Executives,* (1990), pp. 19–32.

Irene Y. M. Yeung, and Rosalie L. Tung, "Achieving Business Success in Confucian Societies: The Importance of Gunaxi," *Organizational Dynamics* (Autumn 1996), pp. 54–65.

Airbus Industrie: Coping with a Giant Competitor

Richard C. Scamehorn

BAD NEWS

Volker von Tein, Managing Director of Airbus Industrie, threw his copy of the December 16, 1996, *Herald Tribune* down on his desk in disgust; not only disgust, but apprehension as well. The issue was the front page announcement by Boeing Aircraft Company's CEO Phil Condit that McDonnell-Douglas Aircraft Corporation had agreed to be purchased by Boeing for $14 billion. If this acquisition were finalized, it would make Boeing America's second largest defense supplier, but even more worrisome to Volker von Tein, it would increase Boeing's existing dominance in the world's commercial jet air transport industry. Boeing already had more than twice Airbus Industrie's market share and this new announcement might be the straw to break their back.

Von Tein gazed out the window of his Toulouse, France, office and started to consider what business strategy might give Airbus the best chance to compete.

THE HISTORY OF EUROPEAN AIRCRAFT MANUFACTURE

Airbus Industrie, a relative newcomer in the commercial air transport industry, was formed in 1970; but its formation marked a turning point. It was the first European aircraft manufacturer to enter the industry since the catastrophic failure of British Overseas Aircraft Corporation (BOAC) in the 1960s. BOAC had pioneered the development of jet passenger aircraft with its Comet Jet, but disaster struck these planes with mid-air explosions and aircraft disintegration.

The cause was finally traced to the stress-risers in the passenger windows caused by sharp, square corners rather than the rounded corners used in all aircraft today. The outward stresses caused by the pressurization of the cabin interior were transmitted to the skin of the plane's body and became acute at the window's sharp corners. At high altitudes, when the difference between the pressure inside the cabin and the outside air was maximum, the skin ruptured, causing the plane's body to explode in the sky.

Airbus learned from this and other mistakes of aircraft manufacturers and entered the industry by filling a needed niche: the world's first twin-engine, wide-body plane. This followed a tradition of European aircraft technology firsts: the first successful turbojet engine and the first successful supersonic airliner. Airbus' approach was to fill the needed niche of a short- to medium-range plane with a capacity of 250–300 passengers with the operating economies of a twin-engine transport.

This case was prepared by Richard C. Scamehorn, Executive in Residence, at Ohio University. This case was edited for SMBP–7th Edition. Copyright © 1997 by Richard C. Scamehorn. Reprinted by permission.

A PARTNERSHIP

The airline(s) of any single European country did not constitute a sufficiently large market to support the huge research and design costs to develop a new airframe. However, if several European countries banded together, their aggregate purchasing potential might justify these costs. Airbus Industrie was thus formed on December 18, 1970, as a *Groupement d'Interet Economique* (the French term for a grouping of economic interests) consisting of four private companies representing some of the world's best aircraft technology. They were Aerospatiale (of France) with 37.9% ownership, Daimler-Benz Aerospace Airbus (of Germany) also with 37.9%, British Aerospace Ltd. with 20%, and Construcciones Aeronauticas SA (CASA of Spain) with 4.2%.

With this consortium of noteworthy firms, the most industrially advanced economies of Europe became shareholders in Airbus Industrie, giving it commercial advantage within the European Common Market (later to become The European Union). Its new aircraft was labeled as the A300, which came to be known and respected around the world.

A ROUGH TAKE-OFF

The A300's first test flight was from Toulouse Blagnac Airport in France on October 28, 1972. A minor setback was experienced when it was determined that the engines for the aircraft had insufficient power, so the seating capacity was reduced to 226 passengers. Air France was the first customer with an order for six aircraft and Germany's Lufthansa soon ordered three more. Korean Air was the first non-European customer with its purchases in September 1974, followed by Indian Airlines and South African Airways. By the end of 1975, Airbus Industrie had captured a 10% market share for the year, holding firm orders for 33 planes and options for an additional 22.

Suddenly the orders dried up, and no one bought an A300 for 16 months. To make matters worse, only one option out of the total of 22 was exercised. At the assembly plant in Toulouse, the dark humor of 1976 was, "Don't miss the last train out of Toulouse." In January 1977, an important negotiation for a very large order from America's Western Airlines was lost to Boeing's new 767.

FAIR FLYING FOR AIRBUS

A sudden turn-around occurred with the important decision by Frank Borman, CEO of American's Eastern Airlines, to purchase 34 A300's. Thai Airways soon followed suit, and by the end of 1979, Airbus Industrie had booked firm orders for 133 aircraft with options for an additional 88, representing a 26% (dollar value of orders booked) market share for the year. The backlog at the end of 1979 stood at firm orders for 256 aircraft. Just as important, these orders were from 32 different airlines. Airbus already had 81 A300's operating in service with 14 different airlines. Airbus Industrie had become a world-class competitor.

THE ORGANIZATION

As a GIE, headquartered in Toulouse, France, Airbus Industrie was registered under French law. The functions performed at Toulouse were the global coordination of the design, marketing, sales, production, and support functions.

Policy control was maintained by a seven-member Supervisory Board (see Exhibit 1), consisting of one representative from each of the four owners plus the Managing Director, the Chief Operating Officer, and the Financial Controller (Chief Financial Officer).

Aerospatiale continued to be owned by the Government of France, whereas the German and British partners were privately owned. A recent change of administration in France, to a Socialist prime minister, made privatizing Aerospatiale more difficult than before.

Operating control was maintained via six Directorates (see Exhibit 2).

Direct contact with the market was maintained by the Commercial Directorate, which was responsible for all sales, contracts, and sales financing, and also established marketing strategies for all current and potential future products. Responsiveness to changing market conditions was assured by direct links with a network of regional offices and with Airbus organizations in North America and China.

The Customer Services Directorate was the largest of the six, employing 45% of the 2,850 headquarters staff personnel. This staff interfaced with more than 150 Resident Customer Support Managers located in 58 countries, which provided worldwide service on a 24-hour basis. This Customer Service Directorate supported the growing Airbus fleet in the Mideast, Asia, Africa, Latin America, Europe, and North America with a stocked inventory of more than 130,000 part numbers. This Directorate was also responsible for training customer's flight crews, cabin staff, and maintenance personnel.

The Engineering Directorate conducted research into promising new technologies and refining them into commercially viable products. As such, this Directorate was responsible for all airworthiness matters and coordinated all aspects of product safety.

The Industrial and Transport Directorate coordinated the manufacturing processes in liaison with the partner companies. The A319 and A321 airframes were assembled at Hamburg, Germany, while the other airframes were assembled at Toulouse, France. Just-in-time material flow was accomplished by the use of the A300-600 Guppie aircraft.

The Programs and Processes Directorate was responsible for improving flexibility, cutting costs, and reducing reaction time in the Airbus system.

Airbus Industrie had 2,850 personnel (this excluded personnel of the four partners' manufacturing operations), and nearly one-half of these were devoted to customer services. In addition, 92% of these personnel were located at the Toulouse headquarters and could be dispatched to any point in the world where they were needed.

MORE NEW DESIGNS

Having achieved worldwide support for their wide-body, twin engine A300, Airbus decided to enlarge its product line. In 1979, it developed a narrow-body, twin engine plane named the A320, to compete with the Boeing 757. At the same time, Airbus Industrie decided to introduce a revolutionary new concept to commercial jet aircraft: "fly-by-wire."

Exhibit 1   Supervisory Board: Airbus Industrie

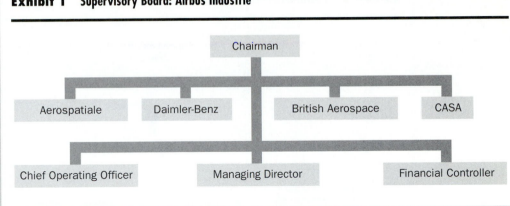

The new A320 would not have the traditional steel cables running from the flight deck to the elevators and rudder at the rear of the aircraft. Instead, instructions to the control surfaces would be sent via electronic signals along a copper wire to a servo-mechanism, which would then respond with an appropriate movement of the control surfaces. This fly-by-wire concept had been used as an advanced technology in military aircraft, but Airbus Industrie was the first to adapt it to commercial aircraft.

Customers were excited with the new technology, and by 1981 orders rolled in from Air France, British Caledonian, Adria Airways, Air Inter, and Cyprus Airways. Two variations of the A320 were then developed to meet customers' varying needs: the A319 and the A321. In 1987, following repeated successes, Airbus Industrie launched the design for a 335-seat, twin-jet, medium-range A330 along with an ultra-long range four-engine A340 with a 295-seat capacity. Both would share the same airframe and wing design and retain the already popular twin-aisle design of the A300. In addition, both would incorporate the state-of-the-art technology of fly-by-wire controls.

THE COMPLETE PRODUCT LINE-UP

By 1997, Airbus Industrie's product offerings were in three basic configurations. Within each of these configurations were several models that offered customers multiple choices in combinations of seating capacity vs. operating ranges (see Exhibit 3).

COMPETITION REMAINS STRONG

With these developments at Airbus Industrie, the competition was not idle. McDonnell Douglas, historically holding second place in global market share, had developed the MD-80, an all new aircraft to replace its earlier DC-9. This was a direct competitor of the Airbus A319. It had also launched its MD-11, a high-performance, fuel efficient version of its successful DC-10. Both aircraft garnered orders from numerous customers, particularly brand-loyal customers who had previously purchased the DC-9s and DC-10s.

Although it would seem that all these new aircraft developments would result in an industry oversupply, the airlines were quick to purchase the improved aircraft designs

Exhibit 2   Operating Directorates: Airbus Industrie

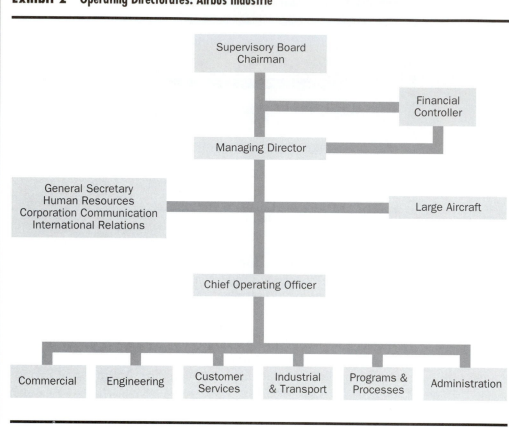

for two reasons. Airline passenger traffic was on an annual growth curve of about 6.5% per annum, which was forecast to continue. New aircraft were needed to satisfy this increased demand. The other reason was the reduction in airline ticket prices. Prices were falling at an annual rate of 1–1.5% per annum and were projected to continue. Falling ticket prices required airlines to fly the most efficient aircraft available as a cost reduction measure. In large part, this was the reason for Airbus Industrie's success with their niche A300 airframe.

Airbus Industrie had displaced Lockheed Aircraft, historically number three in market share, to a fourth place position. Although Lockheed's L-1011 Tristar was an excellent long-range plane, used by Eastern, Delta, and a number of global airlines, it was a one-of-a-kind airplane. It had neither smaller nor larger versions and thus was insufficient to support Lockheed's continued presence in the commercial jet aircraft industry. As a result, Lockheed withdrew from the industry.

Lockheed's withdrawal increased the market shares of the remaining three: Boeing with more than 50% share and Airbus Industrie and McDonnell Douglas splitting the remainder. (Market shares between McDonnell and Airbus Industrie placed one and then the other in second place, varying from one year to the next.) By the 1990s, Airbus Industrie's growing market share had pushed McDonnell to a long-term third place position.

Exhibit 3   **Aircraft Product Offering: Airbus Industrie**

	Number of Passengers	Range (in nautical miles)[1]
Single-aisle, Twin-engine		
A319	124	2,700
A320	150	2,950
A321	185	2,300
Wide-body, Twin-engine		
A300-600R	266	4,100
A310-300	220	5,150
A330	335	4,500
Wide-body, Four-engine		
A340-200	263	7,350
A340-300	295	7,150

Note: 1. Nautical miles, a distance of 2,000 yards, 13.6% longer than the statute mile of 1,760 yards.

CUSTOMER ORDERS

Following the first A300 order from Air France in 1972, Airbus Industrie had accumulated a wide array of orders from customers around the world in every configuration it offered. Through June 1997, a total of 2,274 aircraft had been ordered by 135 of the world's airlines. Exhibit 4 shows a summarization of aircraft on order.

Airbus Industrie had successfully established itself as a world-class competitor with most of the world's airlines as customers and more than 80% of its orders from outside the "home market" of Western Europe.

BOEING: THE INDUSTRY LEADER

With the advent of World War I, Bill Boeing started the Boeing Company in 1916 in response to the military's growing interest in air power. The company's first big success, during the peace between WWI and WWII, was the B-9 Bomber, called the "Death Angel."

In the mid-1930s Boeing developed Project X, later called the XB-15. Although not a success, its technology led directly to the development of the B-17. This heavy bomber, when shown to the press in 1940, had so many machine guns as protective armament that one reporter dubbed it a "Flying Fortress." The name stuck, and the B-17 was produced in larger numbers than any other large aircraft during WWII.

Boeing's further advancements came with jet-powered aircraft: the B-47 "Stratojet," the KC-135 "Tanker," and the B-52. First used by the United States Air Force during the 1950s, the B-52 remained the workhorse heavy bomber of the U.S. Air Force.

However, Boeing's greatest claim to fame was in commercial aircraft. Using the KC-135 technology, Boeing developed the world's first successful long-range commercial jet transport—the Boeing 707. This airplane created the "jet set." Passengers could now fly overnight from Europe to Asia or North America, or with a refueling stop, from Asia to North America. It cut the travel from Europe to North America from five days (by ship)

Exhibit 4   **Summarization of Aircraft Orders by Configuration: Airbus Industrie**

Model	Number of Customers	Ordered	Delivered	Backlog [1]
A. Single-aisle, Twin-engine				
A319	61	147	37	110
A320		811	577	234
A321		215	72	143
B. Wide-body, Twin-engine				
A300-600R	82	488	463	25
A310-300		259	253	6
A330		182	59	123
C. Wide-body, Four-engine				
A340	42	172	109	63
Totals	185	2274	1570	704

Note: 1. The 30 June 1997 backlog included orders for 80 aircraft and deliveries of 93 aircraft during the six months of 1997.

to eight hours, and across the Pacific from 10 days to 17 hours. It obsoleted entire fleets of steamships and made international travel so economical that it became a common event for both pleasure and business.

Boeing quickly followed this success with a mid-range Boeing 727, followed by a short-range Boeing 737. Then, in 1969, Boeing launched the area of the jumbo jets with the maiden flight of the Boeing 747 jumbo jet from New York to Los Angeles carrying 385 passengers. With this stable of safe, reliable aircraft, Boeing dominated the world's aircraft market. McDonnell Douglas developed its jumbo jet DC-10 and Lockheed had its L-1011, but neither could challenge the Boeing 747.

Boeing then increased its competitive advantage by "stretching" the 747 into a 747-SUD (Stretched-Upper-Deck) allowing 40 first-class passengers to sit in the upper level in isolated quiet. It further developed the 747-SP for ultra-long-range flights, nonstop from Sydney to Los Angeles. This was accomplished by shortening the body, removing 35 rows of seats, and using the resultant savings of weight to add fuel tanks for the increased range. The most recent design was the 747-400, a high-performance, fuel-efficient, long-range version that became the standard for long-haul, intercontinental flights.

MARKETING STRATEGIES

Throughout the 1970s and into the 1980s, Airbus Industrie suffered from industry rumors that impeded its market penetration. One rumor was that Airbus Industrie manufactured "white-tailed" airplanes: meaning that they were built on speculation of being sold. When completed, if still unsold, the vertical tail surface would remain white, awaiting the logo of an unidentified customer. In addition, the rumor suggested that European governments were financing these "white-tailed" finished goods until sold. This rumor was rigorously denied by both Airbus Industrie and the Governments of France, Britain, and Germany.

Similar rumors accused Airbus Industrie of receiving low-rate loans from these governments and leasing aircraft with "walk-away" leases that allowed customers (in effect) to default without penalty. Airbus Industrie suggested that some of these rumors emanated from the Boeing Company and were both unfair and untrue. To combat these and other rumors, Airbus Industrie published an information pamphlet. Clearing up this misinformation helped to demonstrate that Airbus Industrie was a fair competitor.

More important, Airbus Industrie developed innovative features in its aircraft that were offered by neither Boeing nor McDonnell Douglas. They included:

1. A large reduction in the number of mechanical parts

2. Comprehensive built-in diagnostic test equipment

3. Reduction of maintenance

4. Reduced airframe weight

5. Better aircraft handling

6. Easier introduction of active controls

7. Simpler auto flight system interface

8. Better optimization of control functions

9. The first inflatable passenger evacuation slide with in-fuselage storage

10. The first extended twin operations (ETOPS) with airborne auxiliary power units for high-altitude engine restarts

These features were important to airlines for both safety and operational economies. In addition, Airbus Industrie created virtually identical flight decks, handling characteristics and procedures that were shared by the A320 family and the A330/340 family. This commonality, covering aircraft from 120 seats to 400 seats, was possible only with the similar handling that could be achieved from a fly-by-wire control system. It led to Cross Crew Qualification (CCQ) and Mixed Fleet Flying (MFF) and the resultant cost benefits.

CCQ enables a pilot to train for a new aircraft type with "Difference Training" instead of a new full type rating training course because the flight decks, handling characteristics, and operational procedures of CCQ-capable aircraft are so similar. Difference Training is 70% shorter than training for a completely dissimilar aircraft. As an example, when adding four A330s to an existing fleet of 20 A320s, CCQ can reduce training costs by $500,000 per additional aircraft per year. This gets pilots out of the retraining program and back on flight duty faster, increasing crew productivity up to 20%. It results in total savings of over $1 million per additional aircraft per year.

These customer benefits were recognized by the world's airlines, and the results were reflected in the orders to Airbus Industrie and its growing market share (see Exhibit 5).

TOE-TO-TOE COMPETITION

Boeing was caught flat-footed when Airbus Industrie developed the wide-body, twin engine A300, and it took a few years for it to develop its competitive Boeing 767. Then again, when Airbus developed the narrow-body, twin engine, fly-by-wire A319/320/321 series, Boeing had to catch up with its Boeing 757. Tired of catching up, Boeing designed and was now selling its wide body, twin engine, long-range Boeing 777 (which competed with the A330).

In 1997, Boeing matched every plane of Airbus Industrie and had the 747-400, 747-SP, and the 747-SUD in addition. With this competitive advantage, Boeing took the

Exhibit 5   **Global Customer Listing: Airbus Industrie**

Customer (Airline)	Number of Aircraft[1]		
	Ordered	Delivered	Backlog
Air Canada	75	43	32
Air Inter Europe	60	45	15
Alitalia	48	25	23
All Nippon Airways	37	25	12
American Airlines	35	35	0
Federal Express	36	20	16
General Electric C	45	0	45
GPA	62	50	12
Iberia	44	32	12
Indian Airlines	41	41	0
Int'l Lease Financ	201	103	98
Korean Air	45	34	11
Lufthansa	135	120	15
Northwest Airlines	86	50	36
Philippine Airline	33	11	22
Singapore Airlines	48	39	9
Swissair	42	34	8
Thai Airways Inter	45	36	9
United Airlines	81	41	40
174 Others	1075	786	289
Total Aircraft	2274	1570	704

Notes: 1. Aircraft operating includes owned, leased, and second-hand aircraft.
2. International Lease Finance Corporation placed a $4 billion order for an additional 65 aircraft on September 1, 1997, not shown in the above data.

additional step of acquiring McDonnell Douglas. This acquisition gave Boeing the capability of selling to former McDonnell Douglas customers either a McDonnell Douglas replacement aircraft or (if the customer wanted) a Boeing aircraft.

It also allowed Boeing to shift either engineering design loads or aircraft production loads between the 200,000 employees of the combined companies. The three major facilities were located at the Puget Sound area dominated by Boeing, Southern California dominated by the original Douglas plants of McDonnell Douglas, and the St. Louis facilities of the original McDonnell plants of McDonnell Douglas.

Their combined 1996 revenues were a commanding $48 billion (roughly the economy of New Zealand), with $100 billion in backlog of firm orders.

In a unique marketing strategy, Boeing negotiated to become a "sole supplier" to its customers. In November 1996, Boeing announced an agreement with American Airlines (the world's largest) to become its sole supplier of aircraft for the next 20 years by guaranteeing it would receive the "lowest possible prices in the industry." Boeing announced a similar agreement with Delta Airlines (the world's third largest) in March 1997 and again with Continental Airlines in June 1997.

The immediate benefit to Boeing was a combined order for 244 aircraft valued at over $17 billion, with options for an even larger number. The long-term benefit ensured Boeing of a loyal customer base from some of the world's largest purchasers of aircraft.

APPROVALS OF THE MERGER

Prior to Boeing's acquisition of McDonnell Douglas, two key approvals were required:

1. The United States Federal Trade Commission

2. The European Union

Petitions to the United States' FTC might have been rejected 10–15 years ago on the rationale that the reduced competition would result in reduced research and product development leading to increased costs and prices. However, as aerospace consultant Robert Paulson says, "This is not about Boeing versus Douglas or Boeing versus Airbus. This is about the U.S. economy versus the European economy and the European economy versus the Asian economy. That's what the government should be worrying about."

As Paulson implied, the United States Federal Trade Commission subsequently approved the Boeing–McDonnell Douglas merger on July 1, 1997. However, Paulson's analysis implied a concern in Europe about the merger. This also materialized on July 4, 1997, as the Competition Committee of the European Union recommended the merger be rejected because it would be anti-competitive and thus unfair to Airbus. If this recommendation were ratified by the European Union's Commissioners, Boeing would be required to pay a fine of up to $4 billion or withdraw from the 15-country European Union market. Either of these penalties could spark a U.S.-EU trade war. The Commission allowed that if Boeing modified its position, the merger might be allowed.

Boeing and the Competition Committee of the European Union faced off and Boeing blinked first. In an attempt to mollify the European Union's concerns, Boeing told the EU that it was releasing the three major airlines (American, Delta, and Continental) from its agreement to purchase all of their aircraft from Boeing during the next 20 years. The EU's response was, "What else are you prepared to offer?" Boeing also agreed to maintain the civil-aircraft business of McDonnell Douglas as a legally separate entity for 10 years. It also agreed to license any airplane-development technology it got from the Pentagon and/or space-research contracts because McDonnell Douglas was a major defense and aerospace contractor. The EU then approved the merger.

Boeing acquired McDonnell Douglas on August 4, 1997.

FINANCIAL RESULTS

Airbus Industrie, because of its unusual partnership as a GIE, was not responsible to create either a profit or loss. Rather, the partners, pro-rata to their ownership stake, generated a profit (loss) from the manufacture and sale (to Airbus Industrie) of airframe components. However, these partners did not publicize their financial results (of Airbus Industrie component manufacture and sale). Accordingly, little information concerning the financial performance of Airbus Industrie, or its partners, has been made public.

The data in Exhibit 6 was printed in the May 7, 1997, *Wall Street Journal*, describing the announcement as "the first official statement on Airbus Industrie's bottom line." Although Airbus had never published financial results, Daimler-Benz AG, the German partner, released financial data on May 6, 1997, for the first time. Some Wall Street analysts proclaimed Airbus Industrie to be profitable during recent years, and others claimed it has never achieved profitability.

Every part (other than the engines) was supplied (manufactured or subcontracted) by an Airbus partner. Three of the four Airbus partners kept their costs to themselves

Exhibit 6   **Selected Financial Performance: Airbus Industrie**
(Dollars amounts in U.S. millions)

	1996	1995
Turnover[1]	$7,710	$9,600
Cost of sales and expenses	7,302	8,745
Net income	$ 408	$ 855

Note: 1. Turnover represents the total amounts receivable in the ordinary course of business for goods sold and services provided and excludes sales between companies in the Group, discount given, Value Added Tax (VAT), and other sales taxes.

(the exception being Daimler-Benz). Many analysts questioned whether the total GIE produced a profit, but no one knew for sure.

As the organization stood in 1997, Airbus Industrie knew for certain only the costs of its jet engines because these were purchased from manufacturers who were either U.S. based or in partnership with U.S. firms. Airbus Industrie admitted this structure was complicated and not working well. It wanted to restructure the GIE into a single command structure with profit-and-loss statements showing true costs. Such a change would require a unanimous vote of all four partners.

SEARCHING

Volker von Tein finished reading about the Boeing–McDonnell Douglas merger in the August 5, 1997, European edition of the *Herald Tribune.* He tossed the paper in his wastebasket and gazed out over the Toulouse skyline. Boeing's strategic acquisition of McDonnell Douglas posed a new and significant threat to Airbus Industrie. Von Tein would need to envision a new strategy if they were to remain a viable force in the industry by 2010.

Maintaining profitability might possibly require maintaining, or even increasing, market share. However, even European Union (EU) countries were purchasing from Boeing. British Airways had recently purchased Boeing planes, demonstrating that European Union membership alone wasn't a guarantee for sales.

Volker von Tein would need a new and bold initiative to counter Boeing's latest move because the intensity of rivalry was likely to increase. Some possible options were:

1. Airbus Industrie could increase its focus on the countries in the European Union. There was a geo-political advantage because the countries of the four partners hosted large international airlines in Lufthansa, Air France, British Airways, and Iberia Airlines. In addition to these four, other EU country airlines such as Air Inter Europe, Alitalia, SAS, and SwissAir were already customers and could be favorably courted for future business.

2. Airbus Industrie could compete on price. Because Airbus Industrie was not required by law to produce a profit, it could sell at prices below those offered by Boeing. This might cause Airbus Industrie to approach the break-even point, but the manufacturing units of the four partners could still profit from their production of major components.

3. Airbus Industrie could develop a new niche in the commercial jet aircraft market. This strategy worked well in the development of the original A300, filling a void and creating a niche that took Boeing years to replicate.

4. Airbus Industrie could venture into the European military aircraft market. The North Atlantic Treaty Organization was being expanded. Poland, the Czech Republic, and Hungary would be placing orders for their military requirements as new NATO members.

5. Airbus Industrie could diversify into related high-technology fields. The instrumentation and control technology Airbus Industrie developed for the A320's fly-by-wire could be used in other industries and might command premium prices.

Von Tein considered them all. The issue was, which one was the best? Were there other alternatives that might be even better?

Name Index

Subject Index

Case Index